A Thematic Dictionary of Contemporary Chinese

A Thematic Dictionary of Contemporary Chinese is a unique resource for intermediate to advanced students of Chinese.

The dictionary presents more than 9,000 words organized thematically in approximately 300 different subject areas. These themes cover the vocabulary necessary for daily use and for conducting meaningful conversations with native Chinese speakers on a variety of topics, from politics to business, and from hobbies to education.

Each vocabulary item is annotated with the most frequent collocations, allowing learners to improve their fluency by storing new vocabulary in larger linguistic units. Cultural and linguistic tips enable learners to grasp the vocabulary more effectively and increase their awareness of Chinese culture embedded in the language. Review exercises are provided throughout to ensure learners have ample opportunity to practice the new material.

This is a great resource for both independent study and classroom use and will be of interest to students and teachers of Chinese alike. For further understanding of Chinese expressions, students are encouraged to read *500 Common Chinese Proverbs and Colloquial Expressions* and *500 Common Chinese Idioms*.

Liwei Jiao is Lecturer of Chinese at Brown University, USA. Besides his rich experience of teaching Chinese at various levels at Renmin University of China, Durham University and University of Pennsylvania for 20 years, he publishes extensively in Chinese phraseology, language and culture, and Chinese phonetics. Among his many publications are *500 Common Chinese Idioms* (co-authored, 2010), *500 Common Chinese Proverbs and Colloquial Expressions* (co-authored, 2013), *Crossing Cultural Boundaries* (co-authored, 2009, 2015) and *A Cultural Dictionary of the Chinese Language* (forthcoming). He is a contributor to *The Routledge Encyclopedia of the Chinese Language* (edited by Sin-Wai Chan, 2016) and *Encyclopedia of China* (3rd edition, forthcoming).

Yan Yang is Associate Professor of Chinese in the College of International Students of Southeast University, China. She was a visiting scholar at Emory University, USA, from 2015 to 2017. Her publications include *Pragmatic Quantitative Research on* Shi *Structure of Modern Chinese* (2014).

Wei Liu is an Instructor in Chinese at the Hotchkiss School, USA. Prior to going to Hotchkiss, she spent seven years teaching Chinese at Harvard University, Brown University, and Wesleyan University. Wei Liu is also an AP Chinese Reader for the Educational Testing Service and a Chinese Rater for The Praxis Series assessments.

A Thematic Dictionary of Contemporary Chinese

Liwei Jiao, Yan Yang and Wei Liu

LONDON AND NEW YORK

First published 2019
by Routledge
2 Park Square, Milton Park, Abingdon, Oxon OX14 4RN

and by Routledge
52 Vanderbilt Avenue, New York, NY 10017

Routledge is an imprint of the Taylor & Francis Group, an informa business

British Library Cataloguing-in-Publication Data
A catalogue record for this book is available from the British Library

Library of Congress Cataloging-in-Publication Data
A catalog record has been requested for this book

ISBN: 978-1-138-99952-7 (hbk)
ISBN: 978-1-138-99953-4 (pbk)
ISBN: 978-1-315-65819-3 (ebk)

Typeset in Times New Roman
by Apex CoVantage, LLC

Printed and bound in Great Britain by
TJ International Ltd, Padstow, Cornwall

To my sister Jiao Lichun and brother-in-law Luo Lianyi.

– Liwei Jiao

To my family.

– Yan Yang

To my mom Wang Lanxin.

– Wei Liu

Contents

Introduction

A Thematic Dictionary of Contemporary Chinese (TDCC) is a practical dictionary consisting of 9,862 contemporary Chinese words which are grouped into 302 thematic units, typically annotated with two to three exemplary usages, and supplemented with approximately 1,000 cultural and linguistic tips as well as self-check exercises for each unit. The TDCC is customized for serious learners of Chinese with one or more years of study, either in school or by self-directed learning. Instructors of Chinese will also benefit, particularly from the cultural and linguistic tips along with the exercises in the book when they prepare for classes, create tests or develop learning materials, including the compilation of textbooks. Vocabulary plays an important role in second/foreign language teaching and learning, however, it is often neglected by educators and learners due to quantity and a lack of effective study methods. This dictionary endeavors to tackle this problem in three ways.

302 thematic units and 9,862 entries: selection and arrangement

Scientific research shows that an ordinary person's vocabulary or lexicon is composed of about 8,000 lexemes or words. This book includes approximately 9,800 entries which are sufficient for any learner of Chinese to read any printed or online Chinese book, newspaper, magazine, journal or document which is written in modern language for general readers, conduct meaningful conversations and deliver speeches of all kinds. These 9,000-plus entries may seem like a large number, however, the Chinese lexicon is intrinsically organized and intertwined according to the research and practice of two major Chinese word lists, *同义词词林* ('List of synonyms,' Mei Jiaju et al. 1983 and updated versions) and *现代汉语分类词典* (*A Thesaurus of Modern Chinese*, Su Xinchun et al. 2013,) each consisting of approximately 80,000 lexemes categorized in as many as 1,400 to 12,659 categories. Learners of Chinese do not require 80,000 lexemes and 12,000 categories, therefore the authors of this dictionary carefully selected 9,800 lexemes and distributed them into 302 categories or thematic units, with each unit consisting of about 32 lexemes on average. In this way, the numbers of both lexemes and categories are manageable. It is a pity that this book does not include Chinese modal particles and onomatopoeias, which need real sounds to be best presented.

1,000 cultural and linguistic tips

A word is not composed simply of one or more characters. It has meanings that were formed in the history of a certain culture. For example, 法 means 'law' and this could not be easier to learn. However, if you wish to know more about how the Chinese character 法(灋) came into being, you can find that the legitimacy of Chinese laws was not based on common contracts, but from heaven. There are altogether about 50,000 to 85,000 Chinese characters in the language, but if one knew the meanings of a few hundred radicals, one could reasonably guess the meaning of an unknown character. For example, 肾 is supposed to be a difficult word for most learners of Chinese, but if one knew that its lower part is 月 which usually represents a part of a human body, one could have an educated guess as below: first, it is a noun; second, it is a part of human body, but not 'face' (脸,) '肚' (belly) or '脚' (foot). In this way, the deduction is much closer to its real meaning of 'kidney.' The main types of the cultural and linguistic tips in this book are as follows:

- Radicals. For example, 艹 (grass,) 犭 (animal) and 宀 (house).
- Characters, words, idioms and other sayings. For example, 法 (law,) 托福 (TOEFL,) 雪上加霜 (go from bad to worse,) 是骡子是马, 拉出来遛遛.
- Discrimination of characters or words. For example, 法 vs. 律, 一点儿 vs. 有一点儿, and 中餐馆vs. 西餐厅.
- Neologisms: For example, 亲 (dear,) 歪果仁 (foreigner,) and 钻石王老五 (diamond bachelor).
- Grammatical functions: For example, 'suffix 子' and 'markers of professionals.'
- Synonyms and their combinations: For example, "悲, 哀, 伤" and "如, 若, 要."
- Culturally rich phrases: For example, 'One Belt One Road (Initiative)' and "水至清则无鱼."
- Others: For example, 'Typical written or colloquial words in the unit.'

Unit exercises to consolidate and check the progress of your learning

After each unit, which has 32 entries and 3 cultural and linguistic tips on average, manageable review exercises are included to consolidate and assess student learning. The key ideas behind the exercises are:

- Targeting the unit as a whole, not specific words only.
- Choosing appropriate contexts, which match the theme of the unit.
- Emphasizing pragmatic functions of entries.

- Mapping the meanings of characters and the meanings of words.
- Covering various topics, from daily life to politics.

It is the authors' best hope that users of this book, after devoting, let's say, one hour to one unit daily in study time, will significantly enlarge his or her Chinese vocabulary in six months to one year.

Background of the compilation of this dictionary and acknowledgments

TDCC is a sequel to *500 Common Chinese Idioms* and *500 Common Chinese Proverbs and Colloquial Expressions*, all of which were jointly conceived by Liwei Jiao in 2007. In compiling TDCC, Liwei Jiao is responsible for the overall design of this book, rendition of entries in traditional characters, pinyin and character to character translation, as well as the cultural and linguistic tips and appendices. Yan Yang is responsible for selection of entries to which Wei Liu and Liwei Jiao also contributed, and composing exemplary usages. Wei Liu is responsible for the English translation of entries and exemplary usages, and all exercises. Yan Yang did most of the first round proofreading, and Wei Liu and Liwei Jiao the last round.

The authors wish to express here their appreciation of the following people for their assistance in the compilation of this dictionary: Ms. Yanpei Zhang, Ms. Alison McFarland, Dr. Zhiying Lu of the University of Massachusetts, Boston, Devon Wilson from Harvard Graduate School of Education, Andrea Hartill and Rosie McEwan of Routledge. Finally, the authors want to thank our families for their continued support, without which this dictionary would not have been completed in three years.

Liwei Jiao
Yan Yang
Wei Liu

Abbreviations and grammatical terms

*:	indicates Chinese character(s)
–:	indicates that the traditional form of a Chinese character is the same as the corresponding simplified form, e.g. 人 [-] rén (man, people).
‖:	separates exemplary usages of an entry word, e.g. 两个~ two people ‖ 名~ celebrity.
~:	refers to the entry word, e.g. 人 [-] rén (man, people) <n.> man, person, people, human being: 两个~.
adj.:	adjective
adv.:	adverb
aux. v.:	auxiliary verb
bf.:	bound form, e.g. 点钟 [點鐘] diǎnzhōng (hour-clock) <bf.> o'clock: 两~ two o'clock.
conj.	conjunction
	infix
lit.:	literally
num.:	number
	particle
	plural
	prefix
pron.:	pronoun
	reduplication
	suffix
v.:	verb
vs.:	versus

302 themes

1: People, gender 人, 性别 (rén, xìngbié)
2: Age 年龄 (niánlíng)
3: Kinship terms 亲属称谓 (qīnshǔ chēngwèi)
4: Physical appearances 体格 (tǐgé)
5: Moral characters 人品 (rénpǐn)
6: Talent 才能 (cáinéng)
7: Professions 职业 (zhíyè)
8: Identification 认同 (rèntóng)
9: Social relationships 社交关系 (shèjiāo guānxi)
10: Birds, animals 鸟兽 (niǎoshòu)
11: Poultry, domestic animals 家禽, 家畜 (jiāqín, jiāchù)
12: Fish, insects, germs 鱼, 虫, 细菌 (yú, chóng, xìjūn)
13: Trees 树木 (shùmù)
14: Flowers and grass 花草 (huācǎo)
15: Grains, cash crops 粮食, 经济作物 (liángshí, jīngjì zuòwù)
16: Vegetables, fruits 蔬菜, 水果 (shūcài, shuǐguǒ)
17: Body parts, liquids and waste 身体器官 (shēntǐ qìguān)
18: Plant parts 植物部分 (zhíwù bùfēn)
19: Substances 物品 (wùpǐn)
20: Demonstrative pronouns 指示代词 (zhǐshì dàicí)
21: Shapes of objects 物体形状 (wùtǐ xíngzhuàng)
22: Parts of an object 部位 (bùwèi)
23: Astronomical objects 天体 (tiāntǐ)
24: Landforms 地貌 (dìmào)
25: Meteorology 气象 (qìxiàng)
26: Natural substances 自然物质 (zìrán wùzhì)
27: Metals 金属 (jīnshǔ)
28: Energy 能源 (néngyuán)
29: Building materials 建筑材料 (jiànzhù cáiliào)
30: Machine, tool 机器, 用具 (jīqì, yòngjù)
31: Tools for farming, fishing and hunting etc. 其他工具 (qítā gōngjù)
32: Apparatus, equipment 仪表, 器械 (yíbiǎo, qìxiè)
33: Means of transportation 交通工具 (jiāotōng gōngjù)
34: Weaponry 武器 (wǔqì)

80: Media, articles 媒体, 文章 (méitǐ, wénzhāng)
81: Shapes, forms, versions 图形, 体例 (túxíng, tǐlì)
82: Song, dance 歌舞 (gēwǔ)
83: Movie, theater 戏剧 (xìjù)
84: Fine arts 美术 (měishù)
85: Sports, games 运动, 比赛 (yùndòng, bǐsài)
86: Illness, treatment 疾病, 医疗 (jíbìng, yīliáo)
87: Numbers, amounts 数量 (shùliàng)
88: Measurements 度量 (dùliáng)
89: Units of measurement, legal and conventional 单位 (dānwèi)
90: Periods 时期 (shíqī)
91: Periods of time, points in time 时段, 时候 (shíduàn, shíhòu)
92: Calendar, year, season, month, day 历法, 年, 季节, 月, 日 (lìfǎ, nián, jìjié, yuè, rì)
93: Time within one day 一天以内的时间 (yī tiān yǐnèi de shíjiān)
94: Age 年龄 (niánlíng)
95: Space, location 空间, 方位 (kōngjiān, fāngwèi)
96: Places 地方 (dìfāng)
97: Actions with hand(s) 手部动作 (shǒubù dòngzuò)
98: Actions with feet, legs, actions (other) 腿部和脚部动作, 其他动作
99: Eye movements 眼动 (yǎn dòng)
100: Actions using mouth 嘴动 (zuǐ dòng)
101: Actions with head (others) 头部动作 (别的) (biéde tóubù dòngzuò)
102: To be born, to grow, to age 出生, 长大, 衰老 (chūshēng, zhǎngdà, shuāilǎo)
103: To be sick, to get injured, to recover 生病, 受伤, 康复 (shēngbìng, shòushāng, kāngfù)
104: Death 死 (sǐ)
105: Sexual behavior 性行为 (xìngxíngwéi)
106: Sleep 睡眠 (shuìmián)
107: Happy, sad 高兴, 悲伤 (gāoxìng, bēishāng)
108: Angry, excited 愤怒, 激动 (fènnù, jīdòng)
109: Fear, relief 害怕, 放心 (hàipà, fàngxīn)
110: To like, to dislike 喜欢, 厌恶 (xǐhuān, yànwù)
111: To indulge, to regret, to awake 沉迷, 后悔, 醒悟 (chénmí, hòuhuǐ, xǐngwù)
112: Attention, neglect 关注, 忽视 (guānzhù, hūshì)
113: To hesitate, to be determined 犹豫, 决心 (yóuyù, juéxīn)
114: To believe, to doubt, to think 相信, 怀疑, 思考 (xiāngxìn, huáiyí, sīkǎo)
115: To agree, to object, to endure 赞成, 反对, 忍受 (zànchéng, fǎnduì, rěnshòu)
116: To know, to estimate 了解, 估计 (liǎojiě, gūjì)
117: To plan, to hope, to think 计划, 希望, 主张 (jìhuà, xīwàng, zhǔzhāng)
118: Memory 记忆 (jìyì)
119: Modal verbs 能愿动词 (néngyuàn dòngcí)
120: To laugh, to cry 笑, 哭 (xiào, kū)
121: To covert emotion 传情 (chuánqíng)
122: Silence, to pretend 沉默, 假装 (chénmò, jiǎzhuāng)
123: Tired 累 (lèi)

124: Life, food and drink 生活, 饮食 (shēnghuó, yǐnshí)
125: To employ, to benefit 就业, 造福 (jiùyè, zàofú)
126: To involve 参与 (cānyǔ)
127: To use 使用 (shǐyòng)
128: To move 走动 (zǒudòng)
129: Trouble, remedy 麻烦, 补救 (máfan, bǔjiù)
130: Entertainment 娱乐 (yúlè)
131: Love, marriage 恋爱, 婚姻 (liàn'ài, hūnyīn)
132: Funerals 丧葬 (sāngzàng)
133: Lucky, successful 幸运, 成功 (xìngyùn, chénggōng)
134: Unlucky, failure 不顺, 失败 (búshùn, shībài)
135: Gain, loss 得失 (déshī)
136: Contented, frustrated 得意, 失意 (déyì, shīyì)
137: To bless, to suffer 保佑, 受灾 (bǎoyòu, shòuzāi)
138: To lose, to rescue 丢, 救 (diū, jiù)
139: To develop, to separate 发展, 分离 (fāzhǎn, fēnlí)
140: To manage, to handle 经营, 处理 (jīngyíng, chǔlǐ)
141: To control 控制 (kòngzhì)
142: To decide, to announce 决议, 宣布 (juéyì, xuānbù)
143: To arrange 安排 (ānpái)
144: To evaluate, to appoint 考评, 任用 (kǎopíng, rènyòng)
145: To approve, to establish 批准, 建立 (pīzhǔn, jiànlì)
146: To promote, to forbid 宣传, 禁止 (xuānchuán, jìnzhǐ)
147: To praise, to punish, to reform 奖励, 惩罚, 改革 (jiǎnglì, chéngfá, gǎigé)
148: Trade, deals 贸易 (màoyì)
149: Investment 投资 (tóuzī)
150: Accounting 会计 (kuàijì)
151: To accumulate 积累 (jīlěi)
152: To build, to make 建造, 加工 (jiànzào, jiāgōng)
153: To repair, to maintain 修理, 维护 (xiūlǐ, wéihù)
154: To publish 出版 (chūbǎn)
155: Traditional agricultural industries, 传统农业 (chuántǒng nóngyè)
156: To travel 出行 (chūxíng)
157: Transportation 交通 (jiāotōng)
158: To teach 教学 (jiàoxué)
159: To study, to read 学习, 阅读 (xuéxí, yuèdú)
160: Research 研究 (yánjiū)
161: To write 写作 (xiězuò)
162: Performance 演出 (yǎnchū)
163: Photography, painting 摄影, 绘画 (shèyǐng, huìhuà)
164: Sports, games 运动, 比赛 (yùndòng, bǐsài)
165: Medical treatment 医治 (yīzhì)
166: Struggle 斗争 (dòuzhēng)
167: To attack, to defend 进攻, 防守 (jìngōng, fángshǒu)
168: To capture, to surrender 攻占, 投降 (gōngzhàn, tóuxiáng)
169: Lawsuit 诉讼 (sùsòng)

170: To arrest, trial 逮捕, 审判 (dàibǔ, shěnpàn)
171: To violate (a law), 违法 (wéifǎ)
172: To punish, to pardon 惩罚, 赦免 (chéngfá, shèmiǎn)
173: Religious activities 宗教活动 (zōngjiào huódòng)
174: To socialize 交际 (jiāojì)
175: To speak 说话 (shuōhuà)
176: To express 表达 (biǎodá)
177: To criticize 批评 (pīpíng)
178: To praise, to congratulate 赞扬, 祝贺 (zànyáng, zhùhè)
179: To thank, to apologize 感谢, 道歉 (gǎnxiè, dàoqiàn), greet 问候 (wènhòu)
180: To request 请求 (qǐngqiú)
181: To give 送 (sòng)
182: To consult 协商 (xiéshāng)
183: To help, care 帮助, 照顾 (bāngzhù, zhàogù)
184: To argue 争论 (zhēnglùn)
185: To violate, to cheat, to prevent 违背, 欺骗, 阻止 (wéibèi, qīpiàn, zǔzhǐ)
186: Harm, revenge 伤害, 报复 (shānghài, bàofù)
187: Weather 天气 (tiānqì)
188: To freeze, to dissolve 冰冻, 溶解 (bīngdòng, róngjiě)
189: Verbs of natural phenomena 自然现象动词 (zìrán xiànxiàng dòngcí)
190: Verbs of motion 状态动词 (zhuàngtài dòngcí)
191: To store, to display 存放, 展示 (cúnfàng, zhǎnshì)
192: Close, separate, contact 靠近, 隔开, 接触 (kàojìn, gékāi, jiēchù)
193: To combine, to cross, to gather 结合, 通过, 集中 (jiéhé, tōngguò, jízhōng)
194: To move 移动 (yídòng)
195: To begin, to process, to end 开始, 进行, 结束 (kāishǐ, jìnxíng, jiéshù)
196: In advance, to postpone 提前, 推迟 (tíqián, tuīchí)
197: To appear, to disappear 出现, 消失 (chūxiàn, xiāoshī)
198: Verbs (yet, not yet) 已然, 未然 (yǐrán, wèirán)
199: To exceed, to spread 到期, 传播 (dàoqī, chuánbō)
200: To change 变化 (biànhuà)
201: Damage, to deteriorate 损坏, 变坏 (sǔnhuài, biànhuài)
202: To improve 好转 (hǎozhuǎn)
203: To increase, to decrease 增加, 减少 (zēngjiā, jiǎnshǎo)
204: To eliminate, need 消除, 需要 (xiāochú, xūyào)
205: Copula, connection 系词 (xìcí)
206: To originate, to belong 起源, 归属 (qǐyuán, guīshǔ)
207: Existent, non-existent 有无 (yǒuwú)
208: Same, different 相同, 不同 (xiāngtóng, bùtóng)
209: Match 匹配 (pǐpèi)
210: Relative relations 相对关系 (xiāngduì guānxì)
211: To cause 导致 (dǎozhì)
212: Good, harmful 有利, 有害 (yǒulì, yǒuhài)
213: Big, small, long, short 大, 小, 长, 短 (dà, xiǎo, cháng, duǎn)
214: High, wide 高, 宽 (gāo, kuān)
215: Deep, thick 深, 厚 (shēn, hòu)

216: Thick, thin, fat 粗, 细, 胖 (cū, xì, pàng)
217: Straight, upright 直, 正 (zhí, zhèng)
218: Round, square, surface 圆, 方, 表面 (yuán, fāng, biǎomiàn)
219: Color 颜色 (yánsè)
220: Clear, dull 清, 浊 (qīng, zhuó)
221: Fragrant, smelly, taste 香, 臭, 味道 (xiāng, chòu, wèidào)
222: Hard, soft, heavy, light, sharp, dull 硬, 软, 重, 轻, 尖锐, 钝 (yìng, ruǎn, zhòng, qīng, jiānruì, dùn)
223: Warm, cold, dry, wet, smooth 暖, 冷, 干, 湿, 滑 (nuǎn, lěng, gān, shī, huá)
224: More, less 多, 少 (duō, shǎo)
225: Adequate, exquisite 充足, 精美 (chōngzú, jīngměi)
226: Complete 完整 (wánzhěng)
227: Tight, thick, dense, cooked 密, 紧, 稠, 熟 (jǐn, mì, chóu, shú)
228: Sex, gender 性别 (xìngbié)
229: Old, young, strong, weak 老, 小, 强壮, 弱 (lǎo, xiǎo, qiángzhuàng, ruò)
230: New, old, beautiful, ugly 新, 旧, 美, 丑 (xīn, jiù, měi, chǒu)
231: Early, late, fast, slow, long, short, far, near 早, 晚, 快, 慢, 长, 短, 远, 近 (zǎo, wǎn, kuài, màn, cháng, duǎn, yuǎn, jìn)
232: Real, fake, normal 真, 假, 正常 (zhēn, jiǎ, zhèngcháng)
233: Good, bad and worse 好, 坏, 差 (hào, huài, chà)
234: Right or wrong 对, 错 (duì, cuò)
235: Advantage and disadvantage 利, 弊 (lì, bì)
236: Broad, mixed 广泛, 杂 (guǎngfàn, zá)
237: Detailed, fictional 详细, 虚拟 (xiángxì, xūnǐ)
238: Flexible 灵活 (línghuó)
239: Easy or hard 容易, 困难 (róngyì, kùnnán)
240: Primary and secondary 主要, 次要 (zhǔyào, cìyào)
241: Necessary, severeness 必要, 强烈 (bìyào, qiángliè)
242: Strong or weak 强, 弱 (qiáng, ruò)
243: Honor and humiliation 光荣, 耻辱 (guāngróng, chǐrǔ)
244: Clean, corrupted 腐败 (fǔbài)
245: Noble or lowly 贵, 贱 (guì, jiàn)
246: Intimate or distant 亲密, 疏远 (qīnmì, shūyuǎn)
247: Noticeable and unnoticeable 明显, 不明显 (míngxiǎn, bù míngxiǎn)
248: Natural or man-made 自然, 人造 (zìrán, rénzào)
249: Professional, amateur 专业, 业余 (zhuānyè, yèyú)
250: Relatives 亲戚 (qīnqi)
251: Good or evil 善, 恶 (shàn, è)
252: Honest, hypercritical 诚实, 虚伪 (chéngshí, xūwěi)
253: Strong, weak 刚强, 软弱 (gāngqiáng, ruǎnruò)
254: Solemn and humorous 庄重, 诙谐 (zhuāngzhòng, huīxié)
255: Optimistic, pessimistic 乐观 and 悲观 (lèguān, bēiguān)
256: Cautious and careless 谨慎, 疏忽 (jǐnshèn, shūhū)
257: Modest and rude 谦虚, 骄傲 (qiānxū, jiāo'ào)
258: Selfish, unselfish 公, 私 (gōng, sī)
259: Strict and tolerant 严, 宽 (yán, kuān)

260: Frugal and extravagant 简朴, 奢侈 (jiǎnpǔ shēchǐ)
261: Progressive and conservative 进步, 保守 (jìnbù, bǎoshǒu)
262: Noble, lowly 高, 下 (gāo, xià)
263: Smart, stupid 智, 愚 (zhì, yú)
264: Skillful, clumsy 巧, 拙 (qiǎo, zhuō)
265: Diligent, lazy 勤, 懒 (qín, lǎn)
266: Capable, incapable 能, 庸 (néng, yōng)
267: Safe and dangerous 安, 危 (ān, wēi)
268: Prosperous, declining 盛, 衰 (shèng, shuāi)
269: Noisy, quiet, busy, leisure 闹, 静, 忙, 闲 (nào, jìng, máng, xián)
270: Greater or lesser urgency 缓急 (huǎnjí)
271: Clean, dirty 洁, 污 (jié, wū)
272: Order and chaos 齐, 乱 (qí, luàn)
273: Joy, sorrow 悲, 喜 (bēi, xǐ)
274: Rich, poor 贫, 富 (pín, fù)
275: Fixed, flexible 定, 通 (dìng, tōng)
276: Adverbs, degree (mid-high and lower) 程度副词 (chéngdù fùcí)
277: Adverbs, degree (very high and up) 程度副词 (chéngdù fùcí)
278: Adverbs, scope 范围副词 (fànwéi fùcí)
279: Adverbs, manner 方式副词 (fāngshì fùcí)
280: Generally, normally, probably, certainly, 一般来说 (yìbānláishuō), 应该 (yīnggāi), 可能 (kěnéng), 肯定 (kěndìng)
281: Originally, contrarily, purposely, eventually 本来 (běnlái), 相反 (xiāngfǎn), 故意 (gùyì), 最终 (zuìzhōng)
282: Other modal adverbs 其他情态副词 (qítā qíngtài fùcí)
283: Adverbs, time (sequential or as planned) 时间副词 (shíjiān fùcí)
284: Adverbs, time (others) 其他时间副词 (qítā shíjiān fùcí)
285: Adverbs, frequency 频度副词 (píndù fùcí)
286: Adverbs, strong mood 强口气副词 (qiáng kǒuqì fùcí)
287: Adverbs, soft mood 弱口气副词 (ruò kǒuqì fùcí)
288: Adverbs, negation 否定副词 (fǒudìng fùcí)
289: Prepositions, space and time 时空介词 (shíkōng jiècí)
290: Prepositions, directional 方位介词 (fāngwèi jiècí)
291: Prepositions, disposal 处置介词 (chǔzhì jiècí)
292: Prepositions, introducing objects 对象 (duìxiàng)
293: Prepositions, introducing tools 工具 (gōngjù)
294: Conjunctions, coordinating 并列连词 (bìngliè liáncí)
295: Conjunctions, progressive 递进连词 (dìjìn liáncí)
296: Conjunctions, concessive 让步连词 (ràngbù liáncí)
297: Conjunctions, contrary 转折连词 (zhuǎnzhé liáncí)
298: Conjunctions, conditional 条件 (tiáojiàn)
299: Conjunctions, expressing supposition 假设连词 (jiǎshè liáncí)
300: Conjunctions, causative 因果连词 (yīnguǒ liáncí)
301: Conjunctions, sequential 顺承连词 (shùnchéng liáncí)
302: Particles 结构助词, 时态助词 (jiégòu zhùcí, shítài zhùcí)

Structure and organization of entries

Each entry is annotated with simplified Chinese, traditional Chinese, pinyin, the English translation of each compositional character of the word, part of speech, English translation of the whole word, and typically two to three examples of usage. For example:

满意 [滿-] mănyì (satisfied-intention) <adj.> satisfied: 令人~ cause satisfaction || 对他很~ very satisfied with him|| ~的答案 satisfactory answer

- '满意' is the word in simplified Chinese.
- '[滿-]' is the word '满意' in traditional Chinese and with square brackets ' [].' Since the simplified and traditional forms of 意 are the same, the character 意 is replaced by a dash '-' in this part.
    - If the simplified and traditional forms of all characters in the entry are the same, a dash '-' is used to represent the whole word.
- 'Mănyì' is the pinyin rendition of the word.
- '(Satisfied-intention)'is the character by character English rendition of the word, i. e., 满 means 'satisfied' and 意 'intention.' This part is in brackets ' ()' and a dash '-' is used between characters.
    - If an entry word has more than two characters, the way to render it depends on internal structure of the word. Simply put, only direct constituents' meanings of are rendered. For example, in the word "满意度," the direct constituents are "满意" and "度" both of which are rendered as 'satisfaction' and 'degree' respectively. "满意" is not further rendered.
    - If an entry has only one character, the way to render it depends on the closeness of the original meaning and the meaning of the character in the unit per se. For example, the word "满" is rendered as 'full,' however, for the entry word in Unit 237 on the relationship between action and time, its meaning is obviously 'fast.' But, this dictionary renders it as 'pleasant; fast' since the original meaning of "快" is 'pleasant' which is good for learners to know because the character is related to "忄" (heart) and it is widely preserved in words such as "快乐" (happy,) "不快" (unhappy) and "大快人心" (afford general satisfaction.)

  - If an entry word is grammatically complex, for example, "看得开," the grammatical part is rendered accordingly. In this case "看得开" (view-*auxiliary*-open,) "得" is rendered as 'auxiliary' and is italicized.

- '<Adj.>' is the part of speech of the word "满意" and in angle brackets '<>.'
- 'Satisfied' is the English rendition of the entry word "满意."
- '令人~ cause satisfaction || 对他很~ very satisfied with him || ~的答案 satisfactory answer' are three exemplary usages of the entry word "满意." "令人满意" and "对somebody很满意" are the two most common usages of 满意. Also, 满意 is an adjective which can modify a noun, so the third example is "满意的答案."

  - In this part, if a word used in the examples is more difficult than the entry word itself, it is annotated with pinyin. For example, in the annotation of the entry word "长途," there are two usages "长途汽车" and "长途旅行(lǚxíng)," the "汽车" is not annotated with pinyin since it is easier than 长途, but "旅行" is annotated with pinyin since it is as difficult as or more difficult than 长途.

Organization of entries within one Theme/Unit

The average of 32 entries in one Theme/Unit may be difficult to acquire all at once. This book addresses the issue by using blank line spacing to divide entries within one Theme/Unit into several subgroups. Organization of these subgroups is generally based on two criteria: closeness of meanings, and key characters; for example:

- In Theme 1 'People, gender,' there are 54 entries which are divided into four subgroups. Subgroup One includes general terms for people, such as 人 (man, person, people, human being), 人类 (human race, mankind, humanity), and 大家 (everyone). Subgroup Two includes singular and plural terms for personal pronouns of the first, second, and third persons, such as 我 (I, me, my) and 她们 (them [for females]). Subgroup Three includes terms referring to unspecified people, such as 别人 (others, other people, somebody else) and 某 (some, [a] certain [used before measure word and noun]). Subgroup Four includes gender-specified terms for people, such as 男孩 (boy) and 处女 (virgin [female]).
- In Theme 144 'to evaluate, to appoint,' there are 57 entries which are divided into 10 subgroups based roughly on the following key characters: 查 (to investigate), 审 (to check), 检 (to inspect), 验 (to test), 监 (to monitor), 点 (to count), 评 (to judge), 选 (to select), 招 (to recruit), 聘 (to employ), 任 (to appoint), and 解 (to fire).

A Thematic Dictionary of Contemporary Chinese

Theme 1: People, gender 人, 性别 (rén, xìngbié)

(See also Theme 228)

1 人 [-] rén (man, people) <n.> man, person, people, human being: 两个~ two people || 男/女~ man/woman || 名~ celebrity

2 人类 [-類] rénlèi (man-kind) <n.> human race, mankind, humanity: ~历史 mankind history || ~社会 human society || 全~ all mankind

3 人口 [-] rénkǒu (man-mouth) <n.> population: 总~ gross population || ~多/少 a large/small population || 纽约~ population of New York

4 人们 [-們] rénmen (man-*suffix*) <n.> people: ~越来越喜欢在网上买东西. People are more and more interested in shopping online.

5 老百姓 [-] lǎobǎixìng (*prefix*-100-surname) <n.> ordinary people, the 'person in the street': ~ 的生活 the lives of ordinary people

6 民众 [-眾] mínzhòng (people-mass) <n.> masses: 广大~ the mass

7 大众 [-眾] dàzhòng (huge-mass) <n.> masses, people, public: ~文化popular culture || ~情人 sweetheart, heartthrob

8 大家 [-] dàjiā (big-family) <pron.> everyone: ~别说话. Everybody please stop talking.

9 我 [-] wǒ (me) <pron.> I, me, my: 我是医生. I'm a doctor. || ~的书 my book(s) || 请给~打电话call me please.

10 我们 [-們] wǒ men (me-*suffix*) <pron.> we, us: ~的朋友 our friends || 帮助~ help us

11 自己 [-] zìjǐ (nose-I) <pron.> own, oneself: 保护~ protect yourself || ~的事请~做 do your own thing

12 自身 [-] zìshēn (nose-body) <n.> itself: 每家公司都有~的特点. Each company has its own characteristic.

13 自我 [-] zìwǒ (nose-me) <pron.> self-: ~要求self-demanding || ~价值self-worth || 这个人太~了. This person is too self-centered.

14 咱 [-] zán (we) <pron.> we (inclusive): ~俩 (liǎ) we us, both of us, the two of us || ~家人 our family

15 咱们 [-們] zán men (we-*suffix)* <pron.> we (including the person spoken to): ~国家 our country || ~自己 ourselves

16 你 [-] nǐ (you) <pron.> you: ~做吧! You do it! || ~家 your home || 他帮了~. He helped you.

17 你们 [-們] nǐ men (you-*suffix)* <pron.> you, you-all: ~什么时候回家? When will you go back home? || ~的公司your company || 我相信~. I believe in you.

18 您 [-] nín (you) <pron.> you (honorific): ~好! Hello! || ~贵姓? May I have your surname?

19 他 [-] tā (him) <pron.> he, him: ~的书 his book || ~离开了. He left. || 我在银行见到~. I saw him in the bank.

20 他们 [-們] tā men (him-*suffix)* <pron.> they, them: ~的朋友their friends || ~在看电视. They are watching TV. || 我去找~. I will go to look for them.

21 它 [-] tā (it) <pron.> it: 你知道"金门大桥"吗? 它是世界上最有名的桥. Do you know the Golden Gate Bridge? It's the most famous bridge in the world.

22 它们 [-們] tā men (it-*suffix)* <pron.> they, them (for inanimate objects): 这句话里有两个错字, 把~找出来. There are two wrong words in this sentence, please find them.

23 她 [-] tā (her) <pron.> she, her: ~的哥哥her elder brother || ~是医生. She is a doctor. || ~男朋友会去机场接~. Her boyfriend will go to the airport to pick her up.

24 她们 [-們] tā men (her-*suffix)* <pron.> them (for females): ~的房子their house || 照顾~ take care of them || ~不见了. They disappeared.

25 别人 [別-] biérén (other-people) <pron.> others, other people, somebody else: 不关心~ no regard of others, uncaring|| ~的意见 other people's opinions

26 谁 [誰] shuí (who) <pron.> who, whom: 他是~? Who's he? || ~也不知道. No one knows it.

27 大哥 [-] dàgē (older-brother) <n.> eldest brother: 我~是警察. My elder brother is a policeman. || ~, 请帮个忙? Brother, could you do me a favor?

28 大姐 [-] dàjiě (older-sister) <n.> eldest sister, old lady: 我~ my older sister || 马~ the old lady Ma

29 兄弟 [-] xiōngdì (older brother-younger brother) <n.> brothers, younger brother: 小王和小李是好~. Little Wang and Little Li are good friends. || 他们~长得很像The brothers look quite alike.

30 各位 [-] gèwèi (each-position) <bf.> everybody (a term of address): ~朋友my fellow friends/dear friends || ~先生, ~太太 ladies and gentlemen || 谢谢~ Thank you all.

31 诸位 [諸-] zhūwèi (all-position) <pron.> everyone, Sirs, ladies and gentlemen: ~早 Good morning, everyone. || ~女士, ~先生 Ladies and gentlemen!

32 同志 [-] tóngzhì (same-aspiration) <n.> comrade: 两位~ two comrades || 王~ Comrade Wang || 领导~ cadre

33 某 [-] mǒu (certain) <pron.> (used before measure word and noun) some, (a) certain: ~年/月/日 at a certain year/month/day || 张/王~ a certain person called Zhang || ~人 a certain person

34 本 [-] běn (root) <pron.> one's own, native: ~校our school || ~计划the present plan || ~公司的产品the products of our company

35 性别 [-別] xìngbié (gender-different) <n.> gender: 不同的 ~ different gender || ~歧视 (qíshì) gender discrimination

36 男女 [-] nánnǚ (male-female) <n.> male-female: ~平等 equality between men and women

37 男孩 [-] nánhái (male-child) <n.> boy: 年轻~ young boy

38 男人 [-] nánrén (male-man) <n.> a man, a male: 中年~ middle-aged men

39 男性 [-] nánxìng (male-gender) <n.> male: ~公民 male citizen || 一位~ a man || 很多人认为美国总统应该是~. Many people think that the U.S. President should be male.

40 男子 [-] nánzǐ (male-man) <n.> male, a man, a male: ~学校boys school || 年轻~ a young man || 大~主义 male chauvinism

41 先生 [-] xiānshēng (before-born) <n.> Sir, Mr., husband, teacher, title of respect: 王~ Mr. Wang || 总统~ Mr. President || 她~是医生. Her husband is a doctor.

42 女孩儿 [--兒] nǚháir (female-child) <n.> girl, daughter: 生~ give birth to a girl || 农村~ country girl || 小~ little girl

43 女人 [-] nǚrén (female-man) <n.> woman, female: 年轻~ young lady || 结了婚的~ married women

44 女士 [-] nǚshì (female-gentleman) <n.> madam, lady: 这位~ this lady || 刘~ Ms. Liu

45 女性 [-] nǚxìng (female-gender) <n.> female: 中年~ middle-aged female || 事业型~ career women || ~权利 women's rights

46 女子 [-] nǚzǐ (female-man) <n.> woman, female: ~选手female player in a competition || ~学校 girls school

47 妇女 [婦-] fùnǚ (housewife-female) <n.> woman: 农村~ country women || 老年~ old women || 保护~ protect women

48 夫人 [-] fūrén (husband-man) <n.> madam, Mrs.: 李~ Mrs. Li || 第一~ first lady || 各国大使和~ foreign ambassadors and their wives

49 太太 [-] tàitài (grande-grande) <n.> Mrs., wife, Madam, married woman, lady: 黄~ Mrs. Huang || 张老师的~ teacher Zhang's wife || 老~ the old lady

50 小姐 [-] xiǎojiě (young-sister) <n.> miss, young lady: 秘书~ young female secretary || 王~ miss Wang || 年轻~ a young lady

51 姑娘 [-] gūniang (aunt-mother) <n.> girl: (在饭馆里) ~, 请给我来一杯水. (In a restaurant) Miss, please give me a glass of water || 小~ young girl || 一位农村~ a country girl

52 阿姨 [-] āyí (*prefix*-aunt) <n.> auntie, nanny: 王~ Auntie Wang || 小王家的~是从农村来的. Little Wang's nanny is from the countryside.

53 处女 [處-] chǔnǚ (virgin-female) <n.> virgin: 她还是一个~. She is still a virgin. || ~作a maiden work || ~座 Virgo

54 熟女 [-] shúnǚ (mature-female) <n.> mature and sophisticated woman: 在台湾30多岁的女性都可以叫~. In Taiwan, a woman who is more than 30 years old can be called a mature woman.

Tips:

1 她: "她" means 'her' or 'she,' which is presumably a common word, however, this character was actually coined by the writer and professor Liu Fu (1891–1934) in 1918 during the New Culture Movement.

2 女: "女" is a character as well as a common radical, both meaning 'female.' Characters with the radical 女 include 姓 (surname), 她 (her/she), 姐 (elder sister), 妇 (housewife), 姑 (aunt, father's sister), 娘 (mom), 姨 (aunt, mother's sister) in this unit.

3 *们: 们 is a suffix to pronouns denoting plurals, e.g. 我们, 你们, 他们, 她们, 它们, 孩子们, 学生们 means 'us/we, you, them/they (males), them/they (females), them/they, children, students,' respectively. If a person's name is generalized to refer to a kind of people, it can be in plural form, for example, 爱因斯坦们 Ai in si tan men (Einstein *plural*.)

4 自: The original meaning of 自is 'nose.'

5 性: The 性 in the words 性别, 男性, 女性 in this unit means 'gender,' however, its original meaning is 'nature (of a person).'

6 Change of terms of address 称呼的变迁: In the era of Mao Zedong, 同志 (comrade) was the dominant term of address to almost everybody, old or young, male or female, cadre or ordinary worker. But after Chinese economic reform in the late 1970s, 先生 (Mr./Sir), 小姐 (Miss), and 太太 (Mrs.) were revived. Nowadays, 同志 has a strong connotation of 'gay/lesbian,' albeit the Chinese Communist Party is endeavoring to use this term of address not only in written, but also in spoken forms, between themselves.

7 LGBT+: LGBT+ stands for L (女同性恋者,) G (男同性恋者,) B (双性恋者,) T (跨性别者) and others. It is translated into Chinese as 非异性恋者 (non-heterosexual,) 彩虹族群 (literally 'rainbow group') or 性少数群体 (sexual minority.)

Exercises:

Part I: Multiple Choice (Please choose the most appropriate one.)

1 请问, _______贵姓?
A. 她 B. 他 C. 我 D. 您

2 _______姓王, 请叫我小王.
A. 我 B. 你 C. 他 D. 它

3 小王: _______, 请帮个忙, 好吗?
A. 大哥 B. 处女 C. 老百姓 D. 妇女

4 _______先生, 各位女士, 欢迎_______来到今天的音乐会.
A. 大家、本 B. 各位、你们 C. 大家、你们 D. 某、大家

5 我们今天的音乐会主要向_______展示中国的传统音乐.
A. 它们 B. 我们 C. 大家 D. 咱们

6 100多年前美国也有_______歧视、_______不平等的问题.
A. 性别、男女 B. 妇女、性别 C. 女士、男士 D. 男人、女人

7 美国100多年前的学校分为男子学校和_______学校两种.
A. 熟女 B. 处女 C. 女子 D. 姑娘

8 每个国家的历史和文化都有_______特点.
A. 咱们 B. 我们 C. 它 D. 自身

9 在台湾30多岁的女性都可以叫_______.
A. 熟女 B. 处女 C. 女孩 D. 姑娘

10 在美国现在很多事业型_______选择不生孩子或者只生一个孩子.
A. 太太 B. 女性 C. 女士 D. 女孩

Part II:

1 请写出可以称呼年轻女性的词 (Please write words that refer to young women.)

2 请写出可以称呼年轻男性的词 (Please write words that can refer to young men.)

3 请写出可以称呼中年女性的词 (Please write a word that can refer to middle-aged women.)
4 请写出可以称呼中年男性的词 (Please write words that can refer to middle-aged men)

Theme 2: Age 年龄 (niánlíng)

(See also Theme 94)

1 年龄 [-齡] niánlíng (year-age) <n.> age: 入学~ school age || 退休~ retirement age || 结婚~ marriageable age
2 年纪 [-紀] niánjì (year-record) <n.> age: ~很小 very young || ~很轻 very young age || 多大 ~? How old (is he/she)?
3 岁数 [歲數] suìshù (age-number) <n.> age, years: 多大~? How old (is he/she)?
4 虚岁 [-歲] xūsuì (empty-age) <n.> nominal age: ~73 nominal age of 73
5 周岁 [-歲] zhōusuì (complete-age) <n.> full year: 20~ 20 years old || ~不到 20 less than 20 years old

6 成年 [-] chéngnián (completed-year) <n.> adult, be of age: ~人 adult || 在中国, 年满十八岁为~. In China, a person comes of age at 18.
7 成人 [-] chéngrén (completed-man) <n.> adult: ~世界 adult world || ~礼 adult ceremony
8 未成年人 [-] wèichéngniánrén (not-completed-year-man) <n.> minor, person under legal age: ~不能进入. Underage people can not enter. || 保护 ~ protect underage people

9 老年 [-] lǎonián (old-year) <adj.> elderly, old age: ~人 the elderly || ~生活 the lives of the elderly
10 老人 [-] lǎorén (old-man) <n.> old people, the aged: 那位~ that old person || 给~让座 yield seat to the elderly || 尊敬~ respect the elderly
11 高寿 [-壽] gāoshòu (high-longevity) <n.> longevity, long life: A: 老大爷, 您今年 ~? May I ask how old you are, grandpa?
12 老头 [-頭] lǎotóuér (old-head) <n.> old person (often not polite): 这个~以前是医生. This old man used to be a doctor.
13 老太太 [-] lǎotàitài (old-lady) <n.> old lady: 那位~ that old lady
14 奶奶 [-] nǎinǎi (grandma-grandma) <n.> (informal) father's mother, paternal grandmother: 王/李~ Grandmother Wang/Grandmother Li || 老~ old grandmother

15 中年 [-] zhōngnián (middle-age) <adj.> middle-aged: ~人 middle-aged person || ~男人/女人 middle-aged man, middle-aged woman || 人到了~以后, 压力比较大. After middle age, people feel more stressed.
16 壮年 [壯-] zhuàngnián (big-age) <adj.> prime age: 他今年38岁, 正是~. This year he is 38 years old, it is the prime of life.
17 青年 [-] qīngnián (green-age) <n.> youth: 未婚~ unmarried youth || 男/女~ young men/young women
18 青年人 [-] qīngniánrén (young-age-man) <n.> young people: ~的热情 young people's enthusiasm || 英俊 (yīngjùn) 的 ~ handsome young man
19 小伙子 [-] xiǎohuǒzǐ (little-companion-*suffix*) <n.> lad, youngster, young fellow: 三位~ three youngsters || 年青的 ~ young guy || 聪明的~ smart young guy

20 姑娘 [-] gūniang (aunt-woman) <n.> girl: 那个小~ that little girl || (在饭馆儿) ~, 给我一杯水. Miss, please give me a glass of water.

21 青少年 [-] qīngshǎonián (young-younger-age) <n.> teens, teenager: 教育~ educate young people

22 青春期 [-] qīngchūnqī (youth-period) <n.> puberty, adolescence: 进入~ reach the adolescence || ~的孩子 adolescent child || ~综合症 Adolescent Syndrome

23 少年 [-] shǎonián (younger-age) <n.> juvenile: 农村~ rural youth || 三个~ three teenagers

24 小孩儿 [--兒] xiǎoháir (little-kid) <n.> child: 三个~ three children || 生~ give birth

25 儿童 [兒-] értóng (baby-boy) <n.> child, children, young one: ~ 节 Children's Day (June 1st in China) || 保护~ protect the children

26 婴儿 [嬰兒] yīng'ér (baby-kid) <n.> baby, infant: ~奶粉 infant formula || ~尿布 baby diapers

27 娃娃 [-] wáwá (baby-baby) <n.> baby, doll shaped as a baby: 布~ ragdoll || 胖~ chubby baby || 芭比~ Barbie dolls

28 宝宝 [寶寶] (treasure-*reduplication*) <n.> baby, darling: 小~ cute baby || 熊猫~ baby panda

29 宝贝 [寶貝] bǎobèi (treasure-money) <n.> baby, heart: 小~ (endearment for children) darling, dear || 她的~ 儿子her darling son

Tips:

1 年, 岁 and 龄: 年 and 岁 are both related to ripe crops, with 年 being 'year' from 'a man goes to reap ripe crops' and 岁 being 'age' from 'to use a scythe to cut ripe crops.' 龄 is related to 齿 (teeth) by which one can tell the age of a man or an animal.

2 Discrimination between 年纪, 岁数 and 年龄: All mean 'age,' but 年龄 is formal and written, whereas the other two are colloquial. 年纪 is used for old people and 岁数 is used more often for very young people.

3 周岁 and 虚岁 (xūsuì): Before the 1980s, many people in rural China tended to use 虚岁 (nominal age) when mentioning their ages. The way to count 虚岁 is, when a baby is born, he is one year old, when he passes a Chinese lunar new year (春节, spring festival,) one year should be added. If a baby happened to be born on the spring festival, he will be two years old in less than twenty-four hours. The way of 虚岁 does not conform to the laws of modern society and its usage is understandably decreasing drastically. It might be virtually extinct by the 2060s. Now the common way of counting age is 周岁 which means 'a full year of age.'

4 高寿: 高寿 is less and less frequently used. It can be heard in rural areas and for very old people.

5 姑娘(girl): 姑娘was a term of address for unmarried girls in ancient times. It has been revived since the early 2000s because the general term for 'Miss' (小姐) has carried connotations of 'prostitute.'

Exercises:

Part I: Multiple Choice (Please choose the most appropriate one.)

1 中国农村年纪比较大的人说自己年龄的时候, 常常用_______.
A. 虚岁 B. 周岁 C. 年龄 D. 年纪

2 美国人说自己年龄的时候, 常常用_______.
A. 虚岁 B. 周岁 C. 年龄 D. 年纪

3 老奶奶, 您多大_______了?
A. 虚岁 B. 几岁 C. 年纪 D. 岁

4 小王: 老奶奶, 您_______?
老奶奶: 我86岁了.
A. 年龄 B. 年纪 C. 多大 D. 高寿

5 现在很多中国学校为18周岁的学生举行_______典礼 (diǎnlǐ, ceremony).
A. 成人 B. 老年人 C. 青年人 D. 中年人

6 一般来说, 进入_______的孩子更需要家长和学校多关心.
A. 中年 B. 青春期 C. 青少年 D. 婴儿

7 一般来说_______的工作和家庭压力都很大.
A. 中年人 B. 儿童 C. 少年 D. 老头儿

8 每年的六月一号是中国的_______.
A. 婴儿节 B. 儿童节 C. 老年节 D. 壮年节

9 美国的_______奶粉在中国很受欢fl.
A. 婴儿 B. 宝贝 C. 娃娃 D. 姑娘

10 在北京公园每天晚上都有很多_______、老太太跳广场舞.
A. 少年 B. 青少年 C. 老年 D. 老头儿

Theme 3: Kinship terms 亲属称谓 (qīnshǔ chēngwèi)

(See also Theme 250)

1 亲属 [親屬] qīnshǔ (parent-category) <n.> relatives: ~关系 kinship relationship || 近~ close relatives
2 直系亲属 [--親屬] zhíxì qīnshǔ (straight-link-parent-category) <n.> immediate family members: 父母和子女都是~. Parents and children are immediate family members.
3 近亲 [-親] jìnqīn (close-relative) <n.> close relatives: ~结婚 consanguineous marriage, intermarriage || ~繁殖 (fánzhí) inbreeding
4 长辈 [長輩] zhǎngbèi (upper-generation) <n.> elders: 尊重 ~ respect for elders || 关心 ~ care for elders || 照顾~ take care of elders
5 平辈 [-輩] píngbèi (same-generation) <n.> same generation: 在中国, 跟长辈说话得很小心, 而跟~说话就可以很随便. In China, when talking to

people of an elder generation, you must be careful; whereas you can talk casually to your peers. || ~亲属 relatives of the same generation || ~关系 peer relationship

6 晚辈 [-輩] wǎnbèi (later-generation) <n.> younger generation: 关心~ care for the younger generation || 春节时候 ~给长辈拜年是中国人的传统. It is a tradition for Chinese people to pay a New Year's greeting to their elders during the Spring Festival.

7 家属 [-屬] jiāshǔ (family-category) <n.> family members: 病人~ patient's family || 军人~ soldier's family

8 亲人 [親-] qīnrén (kinship-man) <n.> family: ~ 团聚 (tuánjù) family reunion || 想念~ miss one's family

9 亲戚 [親-] qīnqī (relative by blood-relative by marriage) <n.> relative: 远房 ~ distant relatives || ~关系 kinship

10 亲- [親-] qīn (relative by blood) <adj.> by blood: ~儿子 biological son || ~爸 biological father || ~爹 biological daddy

11 后- [後-] hòu (step-) <adj.> step: ~妈 stepmother || ~爹 stepfather

12 干- [乾-] gān (foster-/god-) <adj.> of nominal kinship, (relatives) not linked by blood: ~女儿 goddaughter || ~爹 godfather || ~妈 godmother

13 祖父母 [-] zǔfùmǔ (grand-parents) <n.> paternal grandparents: 外~ maternal grandparents || 养~ support one's grandparents

14 祖父 [-] zǔfù (ancestor-father) <n.> paternal grandfather: 外~ maternal grandfather

15 祖母 [-] zǔmǔ (ancestor-mother) <n.> paternal grandmother: 外~ maternal grandfather

16 爷爷 [爺爺] yéye (grandpa-*reduplication*) <n.> paternal grandfather: 我~ my grandfather || 老~ an old grandfather || 张~ Grandfather Zhang

17 奶奶 [-] nǎinai (grandma-*reduplication*) <n.> paternal grandmother: 我~ my grandmother || 老~ an old grandmother || 李~ Grandmother Li

18 外公 [-] wàigōng (maternal-grandpa) <n.> maternal grandfather

19 外婆 [-] wàipó (maternal-grandma) <n.> maternal grandmother

20 父母 [-] fùmǔ (father-mother) <n.> parents: 亲生~ one's own parents, biological parents || 孝顺 (xiàoshùn) ~ be filial towards one's parents

21 父亲 [-親] fùqīn (father-parent) <n.> father: 亲生~ biological father || ~节 Father's Day

22 母亲 [-親] mǔqīn (mother-parent) <n.> mother: ~节 Mother's Day

23 爸爸 [-] bàba (father-*reduplication*) <n.> father: 当 ~ be a father

24 妈妈 [媽媽] māma (mother-*reduplication*) <n.> mother: 听~的话 be very obedient to one's mother

25 伯伯 [-] bóbo (elder uncle-*reduplication*) <n.> father's elder brother, uncle: 张~ Uncle Zhang || 大~ the eldest uncle

26 伯父 [-] bófù (elder-father) <n.> father's elder brother, uncle: 大~ the eldest uncle || 二~ the second uncle

27 伯母 [-] bómǔ (elder-mother) <n.> aunt (father's elder brother's wife: 大~ wife of the eldest uncle || 二~ wife of the second uncle

28 叔叔 [-] shūshu (uncle-*reduplication*) <n.> father's younger brother, uncle: 小~ the youngest uncle || 李 ~ Uncle Li

29 婶婶 [嬸嬸] shěnshen (aunt-*reduplication*) <n.> wife of father's younger brother, aunt: 大~ wife of father's first younger brother || 二~ wife of father's second younger brother

30 舅父/母 [-] jiùfù/mǔ (maternal uncle-father/mother) <n.> uncle (mother's brother) /aunt (wife of one's mother's brother) (more commonly to use舅舅, 舅妈): 大~ the eldest mother's brother/brother's wife

31 姑父/母 [-] gūfù/mǔ (paternal aunt-father/mother) <n.> husband of one's father's sister/one's father's sister, aunt: (more commonly to use 姑姑, 姑妈, 姑父) 大~ the eldest aunt/aunt's husband

32 姨父/母 [-] yífù/mǔ (maternal aunt-father/mother) <n.> aunt's husband/aunt (more commonly to use姨妈、姨父): 二~ the second aunt/aunt's husband

33 岳父 [-] yuèfù (by marriage-father) <n.> father-in-law

34 岳母 [-] yuèmǔ (by marriage-mother) <n.> mother-in-law

35 哥哥 [-] gēge (elder brother-*reduplication*) <n.> older brother, big brother

36 嫂子 [-] sǎozi (older brother's wife-*suffix*) <n.> older brother's wife: 大~ the older sister-in-law

37 姐姐 [-] jiějie (older sister-*reduplication*) <n.> older sister: 大~ big older sister || 小~ little older sister

38 姐夫 [-] jiěfu (older sister-husband) <n.> brother-in-law (older sister's husband): 他是我~. He is my brother-in-law.

39 弟弟 [-] dìdi (younger brother-*reduplication*) <n.> younger brother, littler brother: 六个 ~ six younger brothers || 大/小~ older/younger brother

40 弟媳 [-] dìxí (younger brother-wife) <n.> sister-in-law (younger brother's wife): 大~ wife of eldest younger brother

41 妹妹 [-] mèimei (younger sister-*reduplication*) <n.> one's younger sister, little sister: 大~ one's eldest younger sister || 二~ one's second younger sister

42 妹夫 [-] mèifu (younger sister-husband) <n.> brother-in-law (younger sister's husband): 大~ husband of one's eldest younger sister

43 堂兄/弟/姐/妹 [-] tángxiōng/dì/jiě/mèi (paternal-older brother/younger brother/older sister/younger sister) <n.> older paternal male cousin/paternal male cousin/older paternal female cousin/younger paternal female cousin

44 表兄/弟/姐/妹 [-] biǎo xiōng/dì/jiě/mèi (maternal cousins) <n.> cousins older than oneself (children of one's mother or father) older brother/maternal female cousins/paternal or maternal cousin who is older than oneself/paternal or maternal cousin who is younger than oneself)

45 大/小舅子 [-] dà/xiǎo jiùzǐ (older/younger-wife's brother) <n.> brother-in-law (wife's elder brother/wife's younger brother)

46 大/小姨子 [-] dà/xiǎo yízi (older/younger-wife's sister) <n.> aunt (mother's older sister/mother's younger sister)

47 夫妻 [-] fūqī (husband-wife) <n.> husband and wife: ~关系husband and wife relationship || 一对~ a couple || 结为 ~ become husband and wife

48 爱人 [愛-] àiren (love-person) <n.> wife, lover: 亲密~ intimate lover (used in Taiwan) || 老王的~在医院上班. Old Wang's wife works at the hospital.

49 丈夫 [-] zhàngfu (10 feet-husband) <n.> husband: 这是她的~. This is her husband.

50 先生 [-] xiānsheng (earlier-born) <n.> husband: 王女士的~在英国工作. Ms. Wang's husband works in England.

51 老公 [-] lǎogōng (*prefix*-old man) <n.> husband (informal): 她~是医生. Her husband is a doctor.
52 妻子 [-] qīzi (wife-*suffix*) <n.> wife: 在现代中国, 一个男人只能有一个~. One man can only have one wife in contemporary China.
53 太太 [-] tàitai (grand-madame) <n.> wife, Mrs.: 大 ~ primary wife || 二~ second wife || 王~ Mrs. Wang
54 夫人 [-] fūrén (husband's-person) <n.> wife, madam: 总统~ First Lady
55 老婆 [-] lǎopó (*prefix*-grandma) <n.> wife (informal)
56 媳妇 [-婦] xífu (son's wife-housewife) <n.> wife (informal)
57 儿媳妇 [兒-婦] érxífu (son-son's wife) <n.> daughter-in-law
58 女婿 [-] nǚxù (daughter-husband) <n.> son-in-law
59 姑爷 [-爺] gūyé (daughter-husband) <n.> son-in-law (informal)
60 前夫/妻 [-] qiánfū/qī (former-husband/wife) <n.> ex-husband/ex-wife
61 未婚夫/妻 [-] wèihūnfū/qī (not-married-husband/wife) <n.> fiancé/fiancée
62 儿女 [兒-] érnǚ (son-daughter) <n.> sons and daughters: ~都已长大成人. The children have all grown up.
63 儿子 [兒-] érzi (son-child) <n.> son: 生~ give birth to a son
64 女儿 [-兒] nǚér (female-child) <n.> daughter: 亲~ biological daughter
65 私生子/女 [-] sīshēngzǐ/nǚ (private-born-son/daughter) <n.> illegitimate son/illegitimate daughter, child born out of wedlock: 他有两个~. He has two illegitimate children.
66 侄子/女 [-] zhízi/nǚ (nephew-son/daughter) <n.> brother's son, nephew/ brother's daughter, niece
67 外甥 (女) [-] wàishēng (nǚ) (by marriage-nephew/niece) <n.> nephew/niece
68 孙子/女 [孫-] sūnzi/nǚ (grandson/daughter) <n.> grandson (son's son) / granddaughter (son's daughter)
69 外孙子/女 [-孫-] wàisūnzǐ/nǚ (by marriage-grandson/daughter) <n.> grandson (daughter's son) /granddaughter (daughter's daughter):

Tips:

1 Why is kinship terminology so important in China? In the prolonged Chinese feudal dynasties, consciousness of social hierarchy, Confucian ritual religion and the bond of extended family would be imposed upon everyone from a very early age. It would be very inappropriate to address someone incorrectly as evident from Confucius's famous saying 'If names be not correct, language is not in accordance with the truth of things. If language be not in accordance with the truth of things, affairs cannot be carried on to success' (名不正则言不顺, 言不顺则事不成, from *Zi Lu* in *The Annalects*). It is hard for most learners of Chinese to grasp the entire system of Chinese kinship terms, which is therefore not listed here. It was not until middle school age when one of the authors of this book finally learned by heart all of the kinship terms of his relatives, of whom include more than 50 first cousins. Understanding the terms in this unit is more important than using them.
2 Key kinship terms: 家属, 亲戚, 爷爷, 奶奶, 外公, 外婆, 父母, 爸爸, 妈妈, 叔叔, 舅舅, 岳父, 岳母, 哥哥, 姐姐, 弟弟, 妹妹, 表兄/弟/姐/妹, 夫妻, 丈夫, 妻子, 老公, 老婆, 儿子, 女儿, 侄子/女, 外甥/女, 孫子/女. In many areas of China, 舅舅 is more important than other same generation relatives.

3 亲-/堂-/表-/外-: These are four major indicators of how a relative is related to the speaker. 亲- indicates being from the same biological parents, for example, a 亲弟弟 is your biological/natal little brother, and a 亲叔叔 is your father's 亲弟弟. 堂- indicates second-or-more-degree relatives on your father's side, for example, you and your 堂姐 have the same grandparents or great grandparents. 表- indicates a relative on one's mother's side or of one's father's female relatives. For example, 表妹 could be a younger sister of your mother's siblings, or of your father's sisters. 外- indicates relatives on your mother/daughter's side. For example, 外公 is your mother's father, and 外孙 is your daughter's son. One exception is 外子, which is not listed above. Can you guess its meaning? It is 'son-in-law', which is uncommon in contemporary society.

Exercises:

Part I: Multiple Choice. Please choose the most appropriate one.

1 按照大陆人的说话习惯, 祖父的爱人是________.
A. 祖母 B. 外祖母 C. 外祖父 D. 父亲

2 ________不是你的长辈.
A. 大伯父 B. 叔叔 C. 舅舅 D. 侄子

3 ________不是你的晚辈.
A. 姑妈 B. 侄女 C. 外孙 D. 外甥

4 "老婆"这个词和________的意思差不多.
A. 奶奶 B. 老女人 C. 儿媳妇 D. 妻子

5 "老公"这个词和________的意思差不多.
A. 爷爷 B. 女婿 C. 姑爷 D. 丈夫

Theme 4: Physical appearances 体格 (tǐgé)

(See also Theme 17)

1 身材 [-] shēncái (body-timber) <n.> figure: ~高大 tall figure || ~矮小 short figure || ~好 good figure

2 体形 [體-] tǐxíng (body-shape) <n.> body shape: ~好 good body shape || ~匀称 (yúnchèn) body symmetry

3 外表 [-] wàibiǎo (out-appearance) <n.> appearance: 注重 ~ pay attention to appearance || ~美 beautiful appearance || ~好看 looks good

4 相貌 [-] xiàngmào (look-looking) <n.> look: ~漂亮 looks pretty || ~英俊 looks handsome || ~丑陋 (chǒulòu) looks ugly

5 举止 [舉-] jǔzhǐ (raise-stop) <n.> behavior: 言谈 ~ speech and deportment || ~优雅 (yōuyǎ) refined in manner

6 脸庞 [臉龐] liǎnpáng (face-profile) <n.> face: 可爱的~ cute face || 圆~ round face

7 眉眼 [-] méiyǎn (eyebrow-eye) <n.> facial features: ~清秀 delicate features || 小王是一个不知道~高低的人. Little Wang doesn't know how to read a person's thoughts from his/her face.

8 秃子 [禿-] tūzi (bald-*suffix*) <adj.> bald head, baldy

9 驼背 [駝-] tuóbèi (camel-back) <n.> hunchback: 他有点~. He has a slight hunchback.

10 孕妇 [-婦] yùnfù (pregnant-woman) <n.> pregnant woman: 一位~ a pregnant woman

11 病人 [-] bìngrén (ill-person) <n.> patient: 抢救 (qiǎngjiù) ~ provide emergency treatment to a patient || 耐心对待 ~ treat patients with patience

12 残疾人 [殘--] cánjírén (handicapped-man) <n.> disabled person: ~车位 handicap parking space || ~座位 accessible seating

13 盲人 [-] mángrén (blind-man) <n.> blind, visually-impaired person: ~摸象 blind person touching an elephant

14 瞎子 [-] xiāzi (blind-*suffix*) <n.> a blind person

15 聋子 [聾-] lóngzi (deaf-*suffix*) <n.> a deaf person

16 哑巴 [啞-] yǎba (dumb-*inflection*) <n.> a dumb person

17 瘸子 [-] quézi (lame-*suffix*) <n.> a lame person

18 疯子 [瘋-] fēngzi (mad-*suffix*) <n.> crazy person: 他开汽车像个~. He drives like a crazy person.

19 精神病人 [-] jīngshénbìngrén (psychosis-man) <n.> mental patient: 照顾~ take care of mental patient

20 傻子 [-] shǎzi (silly-*suffix*) <n.> idiot, fool: ~有傻福. Fortune favors fools.

Tips:

1 Suffix 子: 子 here is a suffix denoting a kind of person, for example 瞎子 (blind), 聋子 (deaf), 瘸子 (lame), 疯子 (crazy).

2 Radical 疒: The radical 疒 denotes 'illness,' for example, 病 (ill), 疾 (sick), 瘸 (lame), 疯 (crazy) in this unit and many others.

3 Suffix 巴 (bā): 巴 originally means 'big snake,' but it is commonly used in words related to parts of the body, for example 嘴巴 (mouth), 下巴 (chin), 尾巴 (wěiba, tail) and 巴掌 (bāzhǎng, palm).

Exercises:

Part I: Please put the following words in the appropriate form, respectively.

眉眼清秀、身材高大、身材矮小、体型匀称、相貌漂亮、相貌英俊、举止优雅、孕妇、驼背、秃子、病人、瞎子、聋子、哑巴、盲人、瘸子、疯子、精神病人、病人、残疾人

哪些人应该更多地得到社会的关爱	哪些词可以用来形容一个人外表美

Theme 5: Moral character 人品 (rénpǐn)

1 人品 [-] rénpǐn (man-personality) <n.> character: ~好 good character || 高尚 (gāoshàng) 的~ noble character

2 好人 [-] hǎorén (good-man) <n.> a good sort, a good man: 做~ be a good man || 相信 ~ have faith in a good man

3 老实人 [-實-] lǎoshi rén (honest-man) <n.> honest people: 他是个~. He is an honest person.

4 正派人 [-] zhèngpài rén (upright-division-man) <n.> decent people: 我们都是~. We are all decent people.

5 坏人 [壞-] huàirén (bad-man) <n.> bad guy, villain: 一帮~ a bunch of bad guys || 抓获 (zhuāhuò) ~ capture the bad guys

6 混蛋 [-] húndàn (peckerhead-ball) <n.> bastard: 老~ old bastard || ~小子 bastard kid || ~东西 assholes

7 杂种 [雜種] zázhǒng (hybrid-breed) <n.> son of bitch, bastard: 小~ little bastard || 老~ old bastard

8 王八蛋 [-] wángbādàn (tortoise-egg) <n.> son of a bitch: 这个~！ The son of a bitch!

9 小人 [-] xiǎorén (mean-man) <n.> villain: 他是个~. He is a villain.

10 两面派 [兩--] liǎngmiànpài (double-face-division) <adj.> double-faced: ~的手法 two-faced approach || 耍 ~ double-dealing

11 毒贩 [-販] dúfàn (drug-dealer) <n.> drug traffickers: 捉拿~ capture drug traffickers

12 烟鬼 [煙-] yānguǐ (tobacco-ghost) <n.> heavy smoker, opium addict: 老~ old smoker

13 酒鬼 [-] jiǔguǐ (alcohol-ghost) <n.> drunkard, alcoholic: 老~ old drunkard

14 流氓 [-] liúmáng (migrant-rascal) <n.> rogue, hoodlum, gangster: 一群~ a bunch of hooligans || 耍~ bullying

15 恐怖分子 [-] kǒngbù fènzi (terror-member) <n.> terrorist: 打击~ fight against terrorists

16 强盗 [強盜] qiángdào (by force-rob) <n.> bandit, robber: 一群~ a band of robbers || 遇到~ come across bandits

17 小偷 [-] xiǎotōu (*prefix*-steal) <n.> thief: 抓/捉~ catch a thief || 做/当~ become a thief

18 凶手 [-] xiōngshǒu (cruel-person) <n.> murderer: 杀人~ murderer || 找到~ find the murderer || 捉拿~ arrest the murderer

19 骗子 [騙-] piànzǐ (swindle-*suffix*) <n.> swindler, cheater: 大~ big cheater || 国际~ international swindlers

20 黑手党 [--黨] hēishǒudǎng (black-hand-faction) <n.> mafia: ~头目 mafia boss

21 犯人 [-] fànrén (offend-person) <n.> convict, prisoner, criminal: 成了~become a prisoner || 重要~ important criminal || 释放 (shìfàng) ~ release prisoners

22 妓女 [-] jìnǚ (prostitute-woman) <n.> prostitute: 当~ become a prostitute

23 色狼 [-] sèláng (sex-wolf) <n.> pervert, lady-killer: 在公园里你要小心~. You need to be careful of the perverts in the park.

24 色鬼 [-] sèguǐ (sex-ghost) <n.> lecher: 老~ old lecher

25 赌棍 [賭-] dǔgùn (gamble-rascal) <n.> gambler: 他是一个~. He is a gambler.

26 英雄 [-] yīngxióng (outstanding-powerful) <n.> hero: 女~ heroine || ~所见略同. Great minds think alike.

27 硬汉 [-漢] yìnghàn (tough-guy) <n.> a tough guy, a tough cookie: ~形象 a tough guy image
28 君子 [-] jūnzi (noble-man) <n.> gentleman: ~之交 friendship between gentlemen || 正人~ gentlemen
29 圣人 [聖-] shèngrén (sage-man) <n.> sage, saint: 孔~ Confucius || 完美的~ the perfect sage
30 老顽固 [-頑-] lǎo wángù (*prefix*-stubborn) <n.> old stick-in-the-mud, old diehard (for fogey): 他是个 ~. He's a stick-in-the-mud.
31 懦夫 [-] nuòfu (timid-man) <n.> coward: ~的行为 cowardly behavior
32 小气鬼 [-氣-] xiǎoqìguǐ (stingy-ghost) <n.> miser, penny-pincher: 不要跟~做生意. Don't do business with a penny-pincher.
33 粉丝 [-絲] fěnsī (*lit*. cellophane noodle-thread, *transliteration* of 'fans') <n.> fan: 女/男~ female/male fans || 铁杆~ die-hard fans
34 宅男 [-] zháinán (house-male) <n.> male otaku: 典型的~ a typical otaku or person with obsessive interests
35 宅女 [-] zháinǚ (house-female) <n.> female otaku: 她是个~. She is an otaku.
36 网红 [網紅] wǎnghóng (internet-popular) <n.> internet celebrity: ~经济 internet celebrity economy || 成为 ~ become an internet celebrity

Tips:

1 More bad guys? Generally speaking, there are more ways to describe bad guys than good guys.
2 *鬼: 鬼 itself means 'ghost,' and it is widely used for bad guys, for example, 烟鬼 (heavy smoker), 酒鬼 (alcoholic), 色鬼 (lecher) and 小气鬼 (stingy person).
3 *蛋: 蛋 itself means 'egg,' and it is often used for people with bad behavior, for example, 混蛋 (bastard), 王八蛋 (son of a bitch) and 笨蛋 (bèndàn, idiot).
4 君子 (nobleman) and 小人 (villain): They are always contrastive in Confucianism.

Exercises:

Part I: Multiple Choice. Please choose the most appropriate one.

1 "小王人品很好." 根据这句话, 小王不可能是一个________.
A. 老实人 B. 坏人 C. 好人 D. 正派人

2 下面哪种说法不是骂人的话: ________
A. 王八蛋 B. 杂种 C. 混蛋 D. 正人君子

3 Terrorist的中文意思是: ________
A. 酒鬼 B. 毒贩 C. 恐怖分子 D. 凶手

4 下面哪种人会引起警察的注意: ________
A. 黑手党头目 B. 圣人 C. 懦夫 D. 粉丝

5 如果一个人很难说服, 我们会叫他/她________
A. 老顽固 B. 小气鬼 C. 懦夫 D. 宅男

6 如果一位男士不舍得给女朋友买东西, 女朋友可能会说他是________.
A. 赌棍 B. 小气鬼 C. 酒鬼 D. 烟鬼

7 他每天都在推特 (Twitter) 上发表自己的看法, 有成千上万的粉丝, 是一个________.
A. 妓女 B. 骗子 C. 色狼 D. 网红

8 Donald Trump的________每天都会看他的Twitter.
A. 宅男 B. 宅女 C. 粉丝 D. 网红

9 很多人认为这个政治家是________. 因为他一边对老百姓说不喜欢华尔街 (Wall Street,) 一边打算重用华尔街的银行家.
A. 宅女 B. 两面派 C. 妓女 D. 犯人

10 下面哪些人物一般不会出现在美国好莱坞(Hollywood)枪战电影里.
A. 孔圣人 B. 硬汉 C. 英雄 D. 毒贩

Theme 6: Talent 才能 (cáinéng)

(See also Theme 59)

1 才子 [-] cáizi (talent-man) <n.> gifted scholar: ~佳人wit and beauty
2 才女 [-] cáinǚ (talent-woman) <n.> talented woman: 音乐~ musical talented women || 古代~ ancient talented women
3 天才 [-] tiāncái (heaven (bestow) -talent) <n.> genius: ~音乐家 talented musician || ~儿童genius children
4 高手 [-] gāoshǒu (high-hand) <n.> master: 技术~ technical expert || 业余~ amateur expert
5 大师 [-師] dàshī (grand-master) <n.> master: 建筑~ master builder || 艺术~ master artist || 音乐 ~ master musician
6 大家 [-] dàjiā (big-school) <n.> authority, great master: 书法~ great master of calligraphy || 文学 ~ literary authority
7 多面手 [-] duōmiànshǒu (multiple-facet-hand) <n.> generalist, all-rounder: 她是个~. She is an all-rounder.
8 神童 [-] shéntóng (magical-child) <n.> child prodigy: 音乐~ music prodigy || 数学~ mathematical prodigy
9 超人 [-] chāorén (top-man) <n.> superman, superhero: 女~ superwoman
10 女强人 [-] nǚ qiángrén (female-strong-man) <n.> able woman: ~越来越多了. There are more and more able women.
11 榜样 [-樣] bǎngyàng (poster-model) <n.> role model: 好~ good role model || 成为~ become a role model
12 冠军 [-軍] guànjūn (leading-general) <n.> champion: 得~ win the championship || 世界~ world champion
13 亚军 [亞軍] yàjūn (second-general) <n.> second place (in a sports contest), runner-up: 获~ win runner up
14 季军 [-軍] jìjūn (last-general) <n.> third place (in a sports contest): 夺得~ win third place
15 精英 [-] jīngyīng (elite-outstanding) <n.> elite: 社会 ~ social elite
16 知识分子 [-識--] zhīshí fènzi (knowledge-member) <n.> intellectual: 专业~ professional intellectual || 爱国~ patriotic intellectual
17 书呆子 [書--] shūdāizi (book-dull-*suffix*) <n.> nerd: 变成 ~ become a nerd

18 糊涂虫 [-塗蟲] hútú chóng (muddled-worm) <n.> blunderer, muddle-headed person: 老/小~ old/young blunderer
19 笨蛋 [-] bèndàn (dumb-egg) <n.> idiot: 你这个~！ You're an idiot!
20 白痴 [-癡] báichī (blank-idiot) <n.> idiot: 变成 ~ become an idiot
21 二百五 [-] èrbǎiwǔ (250) <n.> stupid person (lit. two hundred and fifty): 你是个~！ You are so stupid!
22 废物 [廢-] fèiwù (waste-stuff) <n.> good for nothing: 这个人什么事也不会做, 简直是个~! This person is really a good-for-nothing.
23 文盲 [-] wénmáng (literacy-blind) <n.> illiterate: 半~ semi-literate || 消灭~ eliminate illiteracy

24 *迷 [-] mí (fan) <*suffix*> fan (of): 电视~ television fans || 钱~ money fan || 财~ money grubber
25 歌迷 [-] gēmí (song-fan) <n.> song fan: 青年~ young song fans || 男/女~ male/female song fans
26 球迷 [-] qiúmí (ball-fab) <n.> ball game fan: ~会 ball game fan club
27 发烧友 [發燒-] fāshāo yǒu (fever-companion) <n.> enthusiast: 音乐~ music enthusiast || 桥牌~ bridge (cards) enthusiast
28 门外汉 [門-漢] ménwài hàn (gate-outside-man) <n.> layperson: 小王是一个电脑~. Little Wang is a computer layman. || 我在经济方面是~. I am a layman in economics.
29 新手 [-] xīnshǒu (fresh-hand) <n.> newbie: 老员工应该帮~. Old employees should help newcomers.
30 菜鸟 [-鳥] càiniǎo (rookie-bird) <n.> rookie: 职场~ workplace rookie || 电脑~ computer rookie (newbie)

Tips:

1 *手: "*手" means 'person,' for example 高手 (high (skilled) people, master), 多面手 (all-rounder) and 新手 (newbie) in this unit.
2 *迷: "*迷" means 'fan,' for example, 歌迷 (music fan), 球迷 (ball game fan) and 电视迷 (couch potato) in this unit.
3 *友: "*友" means 'companion, addict,' for example, 酒友 (boozy friend), 网友 (netizen), 棋友 (chess friend), and 发烧友 (enthusiast).
4 才 and 貌: 才 means 'talent' and 貌 'appearance.' It is great to possess both, i.e., 才貌双全, if not both, a husband with 才 and a wife with 貌 will make a good match, i.e., 郎才女貌 (lángcái nǚmào). In ancient China, a woman without talent was still considered virtuous as shown by the infamous saying: 女子无才便是德.

Exercises:

Part I: If you are a parent, think about your expectations for your child and then choose the appropriate words to fill in the following tables, based on your expectations.

天才音乐家、神通、羽毛球高手、建筑大师、艺术大师、多面手、超人、女强人、世界冠军、社会精英、书呆子、糊涂虫、笨蛋、二百五、废物、文盲、经济门外汉、电脑菜鸟

希望自己的孩子是	不希望自己的孩子是

Theme 7: Professions 职业 (zhíyè)

(See also Theme 249)

1 职业 [職業] zhíyè (duty-profession) <n.> occupation, profession: 选择~ choose an occupation || 终身~ permanent job

2 自由职业者 [--職業-] zìyóu zhíyèzhě (free-profession-person) <n.> freelancer: ~是指自己雇佣 (gùyōng) 自己的人. A freelancer is a person who works for himself or herself.

3 公务员 [-務員] gōngwùyuán (public-affair/-official) <n.> civil servant: 小~ low rank civil servant || 政府~ government civil servant

4 白领 [-領] báilǐng (white-collar) <n.> white-collar: ~工人 white-collar worker || ~阶层 white-collar social class

5 蓝领 [藍領] lánlǐng (blue-collar) <n.> blue-collar: ~工人 blue-collar worker || ~阶层 blue-collar (social class)

6 工人 [-] gōngrén (work-man) <n.> worker: 一名/个/位~ a worker || 蓝领~ blue collar worker || 普通~ ordinary worker

7 保安 [-] (to guard-safe) <n.> security: ~员 security guard || 商场 ~ security guard of shopping mall || ~公司security company

8 会计 [會計] kuàijì (computer-count) <n.> accounting: 公司~ corporate accounting

9 工程师 [--師] gōngchéngshī (construction-project/-master) <n.> engineer: 软件~ software engineer || 青年~ young engineer

10 研究员 [--員] yánjīuyuán (research-man) <n.> researcher: 高级~ senior researcher || 助理~ assistant researcher

11 警察 [-] jǐngchá (alert-examine) <n.> police: 交通~ traffic police || 有困难就找~. Ask the police for help when you have trouble.

12 演员 [-員] yǎnyuán (perform-man) <n.> actor, actress: 电影~ movie actor/actress || 著名~ famous actor/famous actress || 京剧~ Peking Opera actor/actress

13 歌手 [-] gēshǒu (sing-man) <n.> singer: 五名~ five singers || 男/女~ male singer/female singer || 当~ be a singer

14 歌星 [-] gēxīng (sing-star) <n.> singer: 红~ popular star || 摇滚乐 (yáogǔnyuè) ~ rock star

15 影星 [-] yǐngxīng (movie-star) <n.> movie star: 当~ be a movie star || 著名~ famous movie star || 男/女~ male/female movie star

16 导演 [導-] dǎoyǎn (direct-performance) <n.> director: 电影~ movie director || 总~ general director

17 模特 [-] mótè (*transliteration*) <n.> model: 服装~ clothing model || 业余~ amateur model

18 商人 [-] shāngrén (commerce-man) <n.> merchant: 大/小 ~ big merchant/ small trader

19 投资者 [-資-] tóuzīzhě (invest-capital/-man) <n.> investor: 海外~ foreign investor || 国内~ domestic investor || 中小~ small and medium investors

20 银行家 [銀--] yínhángjiā (bank-specialist) <n.> banker: 国际~ international banker

21 合伙人 [-夥-] héhuǒrén (combine-partner/-man) <n.> partner: 公司~ company partner || 全体~ all partners

22 医生 [醫-] yīshēng (medical-apprentice) <n.> doctor: 内科~ physician || 外科~ surgeon || 看~ see a doctor

23 大夫 [-] dàifū (*homonym* of 'senior official') <n.> (colloquial) doctor: 门诊~ clinic doctor

24 军人 [軍-] jūnrén (army-man) <n.> soldier: 女~ female soldier || 退伍~ veteran

25 军官 [軍-] jūnguān (army-official) <n.> officer: 男~ male officer || 海军 ~ naval officer

26 将军 [將軍] jiāngjūn (command-army) <n.> (army) general: 王~ General Wang || 不想当~的士兵不是好士兵. 'A soldier who does not want to be a general is not a good soldier.' 'Every French soldier carries a marshal's baton in his knapsack.' – Napoleon

Tips:

1 Markers of professionals: -家, -师, -者, -员, -星, -手, -人. "-家": If a person is called a –"-家," he must be very successful or at least be a professional in his field. For example, a 银行家 is a banker, not an ordinary employee in a bank. Other examples include 画家 (painter/artist), 音乐家 (musician), 小提琴家 (violinist) and 物理学家 (physicist). A "-师" is a person who is skillful at something. For example, 工程师 (engineer), 厨师 (chúshī, chef), 教师 (teacher), and 会计师 (kuàijìshī, accountant). "-者" demonstrates one's profession. For example, a 投资者 (investor) invests (投资) to live. "-员" and "-手" are like '-者.' For example, a 研究员 (researcher) does research (研究), and a 演员 (actor/actress) acts or performs. A 歌手 is a person who sings to make a living. "-星" indicates that a person is a star and is successful. For example, 歌星 is singer and 影星 is movie star. "-人" is a more general term for a profession. For example, 工人 (worker), 商人 (businessman) and 军人 (soldier).

2 三百六十行, 行行出状元: 行 (háng) means 'profession.' 出 means 'produce' and 状元 (zhuàngyuán) means 'the very best.' The whole saying means 'One may distinguish himself in any trade or profession.' Many Chinese people discriminate against some professions, however, this saying holds true.

3 蓝领 (lánlíng), 白领 (báilíng), 金领 (jīnlǐng): 蓝领 and 白领 are borrowed from the English words 'blue-collar' and 'white-collar.' 金领 is derived from 白领, meaning 'gold-collar,' which is an employee in a very high position.

4 警察 (jǐngchá): Just like 'cop' is slang for 'policeman' in English, there is slang "条子" for "警察" in Chinese.

5 Partner: It has several equivalents in Chinese: 1) 合伙人, such as 生意合伙人 business partner, 2) 伙伴, such as 语言伙伴 language partner, 3) 伴侣 (bànlǚ), such as sexual partner 性伴侣.

Exercises:

Part I: Please classify the following words into high-income, middle-income and relatively lower-income occupations (according to the actual situation in your country):

公务员、白领、蓝领、普通工人、商场保安员、会计、工程师、助理研究员、警察、著名电影演员、普通歌手、红歌星、美国著名影响、美国著名导演、业余模特、小商人、大银行家、大夫、退伍军人、外科医生、军队将军

高收入职业 high-income occupations	中等收入职业 medium-income occupations	较低收入职业 relatively low-income occupations

Theme 8: Identification 认同 (rèntóng)

1 居民 [-] jūmín (dwell-people) <n.> inhabitant, resident: 城市~ city dwellers || 当地~ local residents || 沿海~ coastal residents

2 市民 [-] shìmín (city-people) <n.> city resident: 普通~ ordinary urban residents || 小~ lower-class urban residents || 广大~ the general public

3 农民 [農-] nóngmín (farming-people) <n.> peasant: ~家庭 peasant family || 广大~ the majority of farmers

4 中产阶级 [-產階級] zhōngchǎn jiējí (middle-property-class) <n.> middle class: ~家庭 middle-class family

5 工薪阶层 [--階層] gōngxīn jiēcéng (work-salary-class) <n.> working class: 普通~ common working class

6 移民 [-] yímín (move-people) <n./v.> immigrate, emigrate, immigrant: 新~ new immigrant || 大批~ a large number of immigrants

7 外国人 [-國-] wàiguórén (outside-country-people) <n.> foreigner: ~看中国 foreigners see China || 跟~交朋友 make friends with foreigners

8 同胞 [-] tóngbāo (same-placenta) <n.> fellow citizen or countryman: 女~ female compatriots || 中国~ Chinese compatriots || 海外~ overseas compatriots

9 本地人 [-] běndìrén (this-place-people) <n.> native: 上海~ Shanghai natives || 地道的~ authentic natives

10 老乡 [-鄉] lǎoxiāng (*prefix*-hometown) <n.> fellow-townsman: 山东~ Shandong fellow-townsman || 北京~ Beijing fellow-townsman

11 邻居 [鄰-] línjū (neighbor-dwell) <n.> neighbor: 隔壁~ next-door neighbor
12 海外华人 [--華-] hǎiwàihuárén (sea-outside-Chinese-people) <n.> overseas Chinese: 全球~ global overseas Chinese
13 华裔 [華-] huáyì (Chinese-descendant) <n.> foreign citizen of Chinese origin: 第二代~ the second generation of Chinese || ~科学家 Chinese scientist || 美国~ Chinese American

Tips:

1 Importance of 'hometownship' (籍贯, jíguàn): Sharing the same hometown is important social capital for Chinese people, especially for businessmen and politicians. People who grew up in the same hometown usually share the same dialect and ideology, as well as common friends and anecdotes of local people.
2 Shanghainese and Cantonese: There is a popular joke that for Shanghainese, they are urbanites, while all other people are from rural areas, also known as "bumpkins." For Cantonese, they are southern Chinese, while all other people are northern Chinese, also known as "muddleheaded" or mentally confused.
3 ABC: It can refer to American Born Chinese, or 'Banana' (香蕉人) which have the characteristic of 'yellow on the outside, white on the inside.'
4 老外 (lǎowài): It was once an impolite term for foreigners, meaning 'ignorant foreigners,' but has now lost the sense of mocking and means 'foreigners' only.

Exercises:

Part I: Choose an answer based on your own perspectives.

1 我父母是_______. (based on your own perspectives.)
A. 中产阶级 B. 工薪阶层 C. 农民 D. 富人

2 我爷爷奶奶是_______.
A. 移民 B. 华裔 C. 本地人 D. 外国人

3 下面哪个词是"lower-class urban residents"的翻译
A. 北京当地人 B. 华裔科学家 C. 美国华裔 D. 小市民

4 我最好的朋友是_______.
A. 本地人 B. 外国人 C. 农民 D. 我老乡

5 "香蕉人"的意思是_______
A. foreigners B. American Born Chinese C. hometownship D. working class

Theme 9: Social relationships 社交关系 (shèjiāo guānxi)

(See also Themes 65, 174)

1 朋友 [-] péngyǒu (companion-friend) <n.> friend: 做~ be friends || 交~ make friends || 新~ new friend

2 同学 [-學] tóngxué (together-study) <n.> classmate: 同班~ classmates || 她是我的~. She is my classmate.
3 闺蜜 [閨-] guīmì (boudoir-honey) <n.> a woman's best friend, confidante: 我有好几个~. I have several best friends. || 男~ a woman's male friend || 她是我的好~. She is my good friend.
4 同伙 [-夥] tónghuǒ (same-group) <n.> partner, cohort, confederate: 犯罪(fànzuì) ~ criminal associates

5 敌人 [敵-] dírén (enemy-man) <n.> enemy: 战胜~ overcome enemies || 凶恶(xiōng'è) 的~ ferocious enemies
6 对手 [對-] duìshǒu (opposing-man) <n.> opponent, rival, competitor: 打败~ beat the opponent || 竞争~ opponent in a competition
7 仇人 [-] chóurén (hatred-man) <n.> personal enemy: 朋友变~ friends become enemies || 他是我的~. He is my enemy.
8 师生 [師-] shī sheng (teacher-student) <n.> teachers and students: ~关系relations between teachers and students || 全校~ all the teachers and students of the school
9 学生 [學-] xuéshēng (study-apprentice) <n.> student: 两位~ two students || 他是~. He is a student.
10 大学生 [-學-] dàxuéshēng (university-student) <n.> college student: 他是一名~. He is a college student.
11 中学生 [-學-] zhōngxuéshēng (middle school-student) <n.> middle school student: 当代~ contemporary middle school students
12 小学生 [-學-] xiǎoxuéshēng (elementary school-student) <n.> primary school student, pupil, schoolchild, beginner: 三名~ three pupils || (P.E. teacher) 在数学方面我还是个~. I am still a beginner in mathematics.
13 研究生 [-] yánjiūshēng (research-student) <n.> graduate student: 他带了五个~. He has five graduate students.
14 同事 [-] tóngshì (together-engage) <n.> colleague: 他是我的~. He is my colleague.
15 成员 [-員] chéngyuán (comprising-member) <n.> member: 家庭~ family member || 主要~ main members
16 代表 [-] dàibiǎo (substitute-manifest) <n./v.> representative: 人大~ representative of National People's Congress || 留学生~ international student representative

17 主人 [-] zhǔrén (host-man) <n.> host, owner, landlord: ~热情接待了客人. The hosts welcomed the guests enthusiastically. || 人类永远是机器的~. Human beings are always the owners of machines.
18 客人 [-] kèrén (guest-man) <n.> guest: ~来了. Guests came. || 招待~ entertain guests
19 贵宾 [貴賓] guìbīn (honorary-guest) <n.> distinguished guest, VIP: 外国~ foreign distinguished guest || 接待~ welcome distinguished guest
20 嘉宾 [-賓] jiābīn (excellent-guest) <n.> esteemed guest, honored guest,guest on a show: 女~ female guest on a show || 男~ male guest on a show
21 房东 [-東] fángdōng (house-host) <n.> landlord: 女~ female landlord
22 顾客 [顧-] gùkè (return-guest) <n.> customer: ~至上supremacy of customers || 方便~ make it convenient for customers

23 车主 [車-] chēzhǔ (vehicle-owner) <n.> vehicle owner: 三位~ three car owners || 个体~ individual car owner || 摩托车 ~ motorcycle owner

24 乘客 [-] chéngkè (ride-guest) <n.> passenger: 火车~ train passenger || 这个城市的公共汽车每天运送~一万左右. This city's buses carry about 10,000 passengers a day.

25 证人 [證-] zhèngrén (testify-man) <n.> witness: 作~ be a witness || 询问~ inquire about witness

26 猎头 [獵頭] liètóu (hunt-head) <n.> headhunter: ~公司 headhunter company

27 监护人 [監護-] jiānhùrén (supervise-protect-man) <n.> guardian: 父母是孩子的~. Parents are guardians of their children.

28 名人 [-] míngrén (famous-man) <n.> celebrity: ~签名(qiānmíng) autograph of a celebrity

29 教皇 [-] jiàohuáng (religion-king) <n.> pope: 罗马~ Roman Catholic pope

30 主教 [-] zhǔjiào (chief-priest) <n.> bishop: 大~ big bishop

31 牧师 [-師] mùshī (shepherd-master) <n.> pastor: 成为~ become a pastor

32 穆斯林 [-] Mùsīlín (*transliteration*) <n.> Muslim: ~国家Muslim country

33 喇嘛 [-] lǎma (*transliteration*) <n.> lama: 达赖 (Dálài) ~ Dalai Lama

34 情人 [-] qíngrén (affection-man) <n.> lover: ~节 Valentine's Day

35 恋人 [戀-] liànrén (love-man) <n.> lover: 新的~ new lover || 一对~ a pair of lovers

36 白马王子 [-馬--] Báimǎ wángzǐ (white-horse-prince) <n.> Prince Charming, knight in shining armor: 她希望找到一个~当男朋友. She wants to find a Prince Charming as her boyfriend.

37 灰姑娘 [-] (ash-girl) <n.> Cinderella, a sudden rags-to-riches celebrity: 几年前他还是学术界的~, 但现在非常有名. A few years ago, he was the Cinderella of the academic world, but now he is very famous.

38 对象 [對-] duìxiàng (facing-object) <n.> partner: 找~ look for a partner in marriage

Tips:

1 我有个朋友 . . . . . .: 'I have a friend. . .' has replaced 'I have a colleague/classmate. . .' when a Chinese person mentions his social connections. An old Chinese saying goes like this, "多个朋友多条路, " which means 'the more friends you have, the more options you'll have in your life.'

2 对象 (duìxiàng): It can mean 'husband or wife' and was a general term of address before the 2000s.

3 情人 vs. 情妇 (qíngfù): 情人 means 'lover' and 情妇 'mistress' which is not legally or morally accepted.

4 白马王子: It means 'Prince Charming.' It is borrowed from Western fairy tales, however, "白马" is attractive to Chinese people because they will easily associate it with 白龙马 (White Dragon Horse,) Tang Sanzang's steed, which was a handsome white dragon in the Chinese classical novel *Journey to the West*.

5 发小 (fàxiǎo) and 闺密 (guīmì): They have become very popular in recent years. 发小 (hair-young) means 'playmate of one's early age' and 闺密 (young lady's bedroom-close friend) 'confidante.' 闺密 is also written as 闺蜜.

6 研究生 (yánjiūshēng): Strictly speaking, it includes students of master degrees or Ph.D. degrees, however, the common people use it as a synonym for master's degree students.

Exercises:

Part I: Multiple Choice (Please choose the most appropriate one.)

1 下面哪个词和宗教没有关系_______
A. 教皇 B. 穆斯林 C. 牧师 D. 白马王子

2 下面哪些词没有"客人"的意思_______
A. 嘉宾 B. 贵宾 C. 顾客 D. 主人

3 下面哪个词的意思和"敌人"_______完全不同
A. 对手 B. 仇人 C. 同伙 D. 反对者

4 从小到大小王 (女) 一直是小李 (女) 最好的朋友, 小李常常说: "小王是我的_______."
A. 闺蜜 B. 灰姑娘 C. 主人 D. 名人

5 小王和小李在同一个公司工作, 她们是_______
A. 师生 B. 同事 C. 同学 D. 同伙

6 "孩子找对象对中国父母来说是件大事." 这句话里"找对象"的意思是_______
A. 找猎头 B. 找关系 C. 找男女朋友 D. 找情人

7 从法律上来说, 父母一般是未成年子女的_______
A. 代表 B. 客人 C. 证人 D. 监护人

8 'The more friends you have, the more options you'll have in your life.' 最合适的中文翻译是_______
A. 多个朋友多条路 B. 朋友多生活好 C. 朋友多是好事 D. 有朋友很好

Theme 10: Birds, animals 鸟兽 (niǎoshòu)

1 鸟 [鳥] niǎo (bird) <n.> bird: 一只~ a bird || 小~ little bird || 飞~ flying bird
2 凤凰 [鳳-] fènghuáng (male phoenix-female phoenix) <n.> phoenix: 麻雀 (máquè) 变~ A sparrow changes into a phoenix as Cinderella becomes a princess.
3 孔雀 [-] kǒngquè (very-sparrow) <n.> peacock: 白~ white peacock || ~舞 peacock dance || ~开屏 peacock fans tail feathers
4 天鹅 [-鵝] tiān'é (sky-goose) <n.> swan: 白~ white swan || ~湖 Swan Lake
5 大雁 [-] dàyàn (big-goose) <n.> big, wild goose: 一群~ a flock of wild geese || 离群的 ~ outlying geese
6 鹰 [鷹] yīng (eagle) <n.> eagle: 老~ the eagle || 白头~ bald eagle || 秃~ vulture
7 鹤 [鶴] hè (crane) <n.> crane: 仙~ crane || 丹顶~ red-crowned crane
8 鸭 [鴨] yā (duck) <n.> duck: 野~ wild duck
9 鸳鸯 [鴛鴦] yuānyāng (male mandarin duck-female mandarin duck) <n.> mandarin duck: 一对~ a pair of mandarin ducks || ~枕头 mandarin duck pillows

10 燕子 [-] yànzǐ (swallow-*suffix*) <n.> swallow: 一只 ~ a swallow

11 鸽子 [鴿-] gēzi (pigeon-*suffix*) <n.> pigeon, dove: 白~ white dove

12 麻雀 [-] máquè (home-sparrow) <n.> sparrow: 小~ little sparrow

13 鹦鹉 [鸚鵡] yīngwǔ (parrot) <n.> parrot: ~学舌 parrot (v.), imitate

14 八哥 [-] bāgē (*unknown*) <n.> crested myna (bird species of China): 两只~ two crested myna

15 啄木鸟 [--鳥] zhuómùniǎo (peck-wood-bird) <n.> woodpecker: 一只~ a woodpecker

16 乌鸦 [烏鴉] wūyā (black-crow) <n.> crow: ~嘴 crow beak, jinx

17 海鸥 [-鷗] hǎi'ōu (sea-seagull) <n.> seagull: 一群~ a flock of seagulls

18 海燕 [-] hǎiyàn (sea-swallow) <n.> sea swallow: 一只~ a sea swallow

19 企鹅 [-鵝] qǐ'é (tiptoe-goose) <n.> penguin: (皇)帝~ emperor penguin || 国王~ king penguin

20 鸵鸟 [鴕鳥] tuóniǎo (ostrich-bird) <n.> ostrich: ~政策 ostrich policy

21 兽 [獸] shòu (animal) <n.> beast: 野~ wild animal, wild beast || 猛~ beast of prey, ferocious beast

22 狮子 [獅-] shīzi (lion-*suffix*) <n.> lion: 非洲~ African lion || 石~ stone lion

23 虎 [-] hǔ (tiger) <n.> tiger: ~群 a group of tigers || 打~ fight tigers

24 老虎 [-] lǎohǔ (*prefix*-tiger) <n.> tiger: 母~ mother tiger, tigress || 她是个母~. She is a tigress.

25 豹 [-] bào (leopard) <n.> leopard: 金钱~ leopard || 猎~ cheetah

26 狼 [-] láng (wolf) <n.> wolf: 大灰~ big bad wolf || ~和小羊 the wolf and the lamb

27 大象 [-] dàxiàng (big-elephant) <n.> elephant: 一头 ~ an elephant || 一群~ a herd of elephants

28 熊 [-] xióng (bear) <n.> bear: 黑/白/灰~ black bear/polar bear/grizzly bear || 北极~ polar bear || 两只~ two bears

29 浣熊 [-] huànxióng (wash-bear) <n.> raccoon: 一头~ a raccoon

30 大熊猫 [--貓] dàxióngmāo (big-bear-cat) <n.> giant panda: 保护~ protect the giant pandas || ~是中国的国宝. The panda is a national treasure of China.

31 鼠 [-] shǔ (mouse) <n.> rat, mouse: 大~ big mouse || 死~ dead mouse/rat

32 松鼠 [-] sōngshǔ (pine-rat) <n.> squirrel: 小~ little squirrel

33 田鼠 [-] tiánshǔ (field-rat) <n.> vole

34 小白鼠 [-] xiǎobáishǔ (little-white-rat) <n.> laboratory mouse

35 黄鼠狼 [黃--] huángshǔláng (yellow-rat-wolf) <n.> weasel: ~给鸡拜年---没安好心. The weasel pays his respects to the hen – not with best intentions.

36 猴 [-] hóu (monkey) <n.> monkey: ~王 the Monkey King || 大/小~ big/little monkey || ~年 Year of the Monkey

37 金丝猴 [-絲-] jīnsīhóu (gold-silk-monkey) <n.> golden monkey

38 猩猩 [-] xīngxīng (ape) <n.> orangutan: 大~ gorilla || 黑 ~ chimpanzee

39 猎狗 [獵-] liègǒu (hunt-dog) <n.> hound: 一条~ a hound

40 导盲犬 [導--] dǎomángquǎn (guide-blind-dog) <n.> guide dog: 一条 ~ a guide dog

41 狼狗 [-] lánggǒu (wolf-dog) <n.> wolfhound: 一条~ a wolfhound

42 哈巴狗 [-] hābāgǒu (flatter-*residue*-dog) <n.> pug: 一条~ a pug
43 狼 [-] láng (wolf) <n.> wolf: 大灰~ big gray wolf || 野~ wild wolf || ~群 wolf pack

44 水牛 [-] shuǐniú (water-ox) <n.> buffalo: 一头~ a buffalo
45 黄牛 [黃-/-黃-] lǎohuángniú (yellow-ox) <n.> cattle, scalper, ox: 一头~ an ox || 老~精神 willing ox spirit
46 野牛 [-] yěniú (wild-ox) <n.> bison: 一头~ a bison
47 野兔 [-] yětù (wild-rabbit) <n.> hare: 一只~ a hare

48 鹿 [-] lù (deer) <n.> deer: ~角 antlers || ~皮 deerskin
49 长颈鹿 [長頸-] chángjǐnglù (long-neck-deer) <n.> giraffe: 一头~ a giraffe
50 梅花鹿 [-] méihuālù (plum-flower-deer) <n.> sika deer: 一头~ a sika deer
51 驯鹿 [馴-] xùnlù (tame-deer) <n.> reindeer: 一头~ a reindeer
52 骆驼 [駱駝] luòtuó (camel) <n.> camel: 一头~ a camel

53 鳄鱼 [鱷魚] èyú (crocodile-fish) <n.> crocodile: 一条~ a crocodile ||~的眼泪 crocodile tears
54 短吻鳄 [--鱷] duǎnwěn'è (short-lip-crocodile) <n.> alligator: 一只~ an alligator
55 海狮 [-獅] hǎishī (sea-lion) <n.> sea lion: ~表演 sea lion show
56 海象 [-] hǎixiàng (sea-elephant) <n.> walrus: 一只~ a walrus
57 海豹 [-] hǎibào (sea-leopard) <n.> seal: 一只 ~ a seal
58 犀牛 [-] xīniú (rhino-ox) <n.> rhino: 一头~ a rhino
59 河马 [-馬] hémǎ (river-horse) <n.> hippo: 一只 ~ a hippo
60 蛇 [-] shé (snake) <n.> snake: 一条~ a snake, one snake || 眼镜~ snake eyes || 毒~ snake venom || 响尾~ rattlesnake

61 袋鼠 [-] dàishǔ (bag-mouse) <n.> kangaroo: 一只~ a kangaroo
62 树獭 [樹獺] shùtǎ (tree-otter) <n.> otter: 一只~ an otter
63 刺猬 [-蝟] cìwèi (thorn-hedgehog) <n.> hedgehog: 一只~ a hedgehog
64 蜥蜴 [-] xīyì (lizard) <n.> lizard: 一条~ a lizard
65 变色龙 [變-龍] biànsèlóng (change-color-dragon) <n.> chameleon: 一条~ a chameleon
66 蝙蝠 [-] biānfú (bat) <n.> bat: 一只~ a bat

67 龟 [龜] guī (turtle) <n.> turtle: 乌~ turtle || 海~ sea turtle
68 王八 [-] wángbā (king-eight, or forget-eight morals) <n.> tortoise: 你这个~蛋! You bastard!

69 蛙 [-] wā (frog) <n.> frog: 青~ green frog || 牛~ bullfrog
70 蟾蜍 [-] chánchú (toad) <n.> toad: 一只~ a toad
71 蛤蟆/癞蛤蟆 [--/癩--] làiháma (leprosy-toad) <n.> toad: ~想吃天鹅肉 làiháma xiǎng chī tiān'é ròu. 'An ugly toad wants to eat swan's meat. Freely translated this is 'punch above one's weight.'
72 蝌蚪 [-] kēdǒu (tadpole) <n.> tadpole: 小~ small tadpole

73 龙 [龍] lóng (dragon) <n.> dragon: 一条~ a dragon || 神~ a magic dragon || 水~头 (water) faucet, tap || ~卷风 tornado
74 麒麟 [-] qílín (male kirin-female kirin) <n.> kirin, a mythical hooved chimerical creature. 麒 is male and 麟 female.: 一只~ a kirin || ~送子. The (auspicious) kirin delivers the child.

75 动物 [動-] dòngwù (move-thing) <n.> animal: 一种~ a kind of animal || 小~ small animal || 保护~ protect the animals

76 禽兽 [-獸] qínshòu (bird-beast) <n.> birds and beasts, inhuman: ~不如 worse than a beast, behave improperly

77 宠物 [寵-] chǒngwù (favor-animal) <n.> house pet: 养~ raise a pet || ~狗/猫 pet dog/pet cat || ~店 pet shop

Tips:

1 Radical 鸟: 鸟 is a character as well as a radical, both meaning 'bird.' When used as a radical, 鸟 is usually on the right or at the bottom of a character, for example, 鹅 (goose), 鹤 (crane), 鸭 (子) (duck), 鸽 (子) (pigeon), (乌) 鸦 (crow), (海) 鸥 (seagull), 鹦鹉 (parrot), 鹰 (eagle), and 鸳鸯 (mandarin duck), which are all listed above.

2 Radical 隹 (zhuī): Characters with the radical 隹 indicate they are birds usually with a short tail, for example, (麻) 雀 (sparrow) and 雁 (wild goose).

3 The measure word for 'bird' is 只 whose traditional form 隻 indicates 'bird' (隹).

4 Radical 犭 (quǎn): Characters with the radical 犭 indicate they are usually wild animals, for example, 狮 (lion), 猴 (monkey), 猩猩 (gorilla), 狼 (wolf). The radical 犭 itself means 犬 (quǎn, dog).

5 Radical 虫: Characters with the radical 虫indicate they are usually insects, worms or reptiles, for example, 蛇 (snake), 蜥蜴 (lizard), 蟾蜍 (toad), 蛤蟆 (toad), 蝙蝠 (bat) as listed above, and 蝉 (chán, cicada), 蜻蜓 (qīngtíng, dragonfly), 蝴蝶 (húdié, butterfly), and 蝌蚪 (kēdǒu, tadpole).

6 Binomal words: Don't be scared when you see two jaxatised and seemingly hard characters, since there is a great chance that they are binomes of animals, birds, worms or reptiles. Here are those kinds of words you have seen in this unit: 凤凰 (phoenix), 鸳鸯 (mandarin duck), 鹦鹉 (parrot), 骆驼 (camel), 蜥蜴 (lizard), 蝙蝠 (bat), 蟾蜍 (toad), 蛤蟆 (toad), and 麒麟 (kiren).

7 Juxtaposition of male and female: 鳳凰 (phoenix), 鴛鴦 (mandarin duck) and 麒麟 (kirin) are each composed of a male and female.

8 林子大了, 什么鸟都有: Literally it means 'if the woods are vast, there will be all kinds of birds,' but functions as 'there are all kinds of fish in the sea.'

Exercises:

Part I: Multiple Choice (Please choose the appropriate answer.)

1 根据字的偏旁来判断下面那种鸟可能有长尾巴? ________
A. 海燕　B. 乌鸦　C. 八哥　D. 孔雀

2 美国的国鸟是________.
A. 秃鹰　B. 凤凰　C. 大雁　D. 海鸥

3 中国的国宝动物是________.
A. 金丝猴　B. 大熊猫　C. 梅花鹿　D. 骆驼

4 哪种鸟可以形容漂亮、高雅的女孩子? ________
A. 天鹅　B. 企鹅　C. 啄木鸟　D. 喜鹊

5 你认为下面哪种动物不适合居住在大城市的人当宠物养? _______
A. 狼 B. 刺猬 C. 河马 D. 鸟

6 哪种鸟是和平的象征? _______
A. 白鸽 B. 鹰 C. 大雁 D. 仙鹤

7 _______在中国文化里是爱情的象征.
A. 麒麟 B. 老虎 C. 龙 D. 鸳鸯

8 老李工作非常努力, 任劳任怨, 像一头_______.
A. 大象 B. 豹 C. 老黄牛 D. 水牛

9 如果一个人做了很多坏事, 但是不改正, 别人可能会骂他/她_______.
A. 哈巴狗 B. 禽兽不如 C. 变色龙 D. 麻雀变凤凰

10 如果一个经常改变看法, 不坚持自己的立场, 人们可能会说他/她是_______
A. 黄鼠狼给鸡拜年 B. 禽兽不如 C. 变色龙 D. 麻雀变凤凰

***Part II:* 请用中文写出下面图中的15种动物**

Please write out 15 animals in the picture in Chinese.

Source: www.shutterstock.com/image-vector/vector-large-set-farm-theme-animals-494335144, with permission.

Theme 11: Poultry, domestic animals 家禽, 家畜 (jiāqín, jiāchù)

1 鸡 [雞] jī (chicken) <n.> chicken: 小~ chicken || ~肉 chicken meat || ~翅 (chì) chicken wings
2 母鸡 [-鷄] mǔjī (female-chicken) <n.> hen: ~下蛋 hen laying eggs || 一只~ a hen
3 公鸡 [-雞] gōngjī (male-chicken) <n.> rooster: ~打鸣 (míng) rooster crow || 铁~ stingy person (lit. iron cock)
4 火鸡 [-雞] huǒjī (fire-chicken) <n.> turkey: 一只 ~ one, a turkey || 烤~ roast turkey || 养 ~ raise turkeys
5 鸭 (子) [鴨-] yāzǐ (duck-*suffix*) <n.> duck: 烤~ roast duck || 养 ~ raise ducks
6 鹅 [鵝] é (goose) <n.> goose: 公/母/小~ male goose, gander/female goose, goose/gosling
7 兔 (子) [-] tù (rabbit-*suffix*) <n.> rabbit: 家~ domesticated rabbit, rabbit || 野~ wild rabbit, hare
8 猫 [貓] māo (cat) <n.> cat: 野~ wildcat, stray cat || 小~ kitten
9 猪 [豬] zhū (pig) <n.> pig: 养~ raise pigs || ~肉 pork ||一口/头~ a pig
10 羊 [-] yáng (sheep) <n.> sheep, goat: 三只/头~ three sheep || 养~ raise sheep || 小~ lamb
11 山羊 [-] shānyáng (mountain-goat) <n.> goat: 一头/只~ a goat
12 绵羊 [綿-] miányáng (cotton-sheep) <n.> sheep: 一头/只~ a sheep
13 马 [馬] mǎ (horse) <n.> horse: 一匹~ a horse || 赛 (sài) ~ horse race || 骑~ horseback riding || 马到成功 be victorious when the battle horses arrive, win quickly
14 牛 [-] niú (cow) <n.> cattle: 一头~ a cow || 公/母~ a bull/a cow
15 奶牛 [-] nǎiniú (milk-cow) <n.> dairy cow: 饲养 (sìyǎng) ~ breed cows || ~场 cow farm
16 黄牛 [黃-] huángniú (yellow-cow) <n.> ox, cattle: 饲养~ raise cattle || 老~ old ox, a willing ox-person who is diligent and conscientious in serving the people
17 驴子 [驢-] lǘzi (donkey-*suffix*) <n.> donkey: 一匹/头~ a donkey || 骑~ ride the donkey
18 骡子 [騾-] luózi (mule-*suffix*) <n.> mule: 一匹/头~ a mule

Tips:

1 Radical 马: Characters with the radical 马 indicate they are usually domestic animals, for example, 驴 (donkey), 骡 (luó, mule). A 骆驼 (luòtuo) looks like a horse from faraway.
2 Measure words 只 and 头: 只 (隻, zhī) is used for poultry and small sized domestic animals such as 羊 (sheep, goat,) 猫 (cat), and 兔子 (rabbit). 头 (頭) is used for larger sized domestic animals such as 牛 (cow), 驴子 (donkey) and 骡子 (mule). The measure word for pigs is interesting. If a pig is an adult, the measure word is 头, but if it is a piglet, the measure word is 只. The measure word for 马 (horse) is 匹 (pǐ.)

3 鸡 (rooster) and 狗 (dog): 鸡 (rooster, hen, or chick) and 狗 (dog) are important poultry and domestic animals, which were vital to the lives of ancient Chinese people, who in return developed a profound affection for them. However, when the two words are used together, they will usually convey a negative connotation. For example, 鸡飞狗跳 (chicken-fly-dog-jump, in turmoil) and 鸡犬升天 (chicken-dog-ascend-heaven meant that relatives and followers of a high official were promoted after him). There is even a superstition 鸡狗不到头 which means that the marriage of a couple born in the year of the rooster and the year of the dog cannot last forever.

4 是骡子是马, 拉出来溜溜 (liùliu): 溜 means 'stroll.' It literally means 'a mule or a horse, take it out for a stroll,' and functions as 'show me what you are made of.'

Exercises: Read the following words and then answer the questions in Chinese.

鸡、公鸡、母鸡、火鸡、鸭、鹅、兔、牛、奶牛、黄牛 马、羊、山羊、绵羊、驴、骡子、猫、狗

Source: Wikimedia Commons. Photography by ma luyao.

1 一般来说你们国家的人吃哪些动物的肉?
2 感恩节的时候, 美国人一般吃哪种动物的肉?
3 下面这道菜是用什么肉做的? 美国人常常吃这种肉吗?
4 "北京烤鸭"、"红烧牛肉"、"宫保鸡丁"这些菜是用什么肉做的?

5 "是骡子是马, 拉出来溜溜"这句话的意思是:

A: 骡子和马在外面才能看清楚
B: 你的能力强不强, 真正做一件事的时候就看出来了
C: 骡子和马都很喜欢出去散步

6 "这对夫妻有了孩子以后天天吵架, 家里__________的." 下面哪个词放在空白处比较合适:

A: 鸡犬升天
B: 鸡狗不到头
C: 鸡飞狗跳

Theme 12: Fish, insects, germs 鱼, 虫, 细菌 (yú, chóng, xìjūn)

1 鱼 [魚] yú (fish) <n.> fish: 一条~ a fish || 吃~ eat fish || 钓 (diào) ~ fish
2 金鱼 [-魚] jīnyú (gold-fish) <n.> goldfish: 一条~ a gold-fish
3 金枪鱼 [-槍魚] jīnqiāngyú (gold-spear-fish) <n.> tuna: 一条~ a tuna || ~罐头 (guàntou) canned tuna
4 三文鱼 [--魚] sānwényú (*transliteration*-fish) <n.> salmon: ~沙拉 salmon salad
5 沙丁鱼 [--魚] shādīngyú (*transliteration*-fish) <n.> sardine: 捕捞 (bǔlāo) ~ sardine fishing
6 鱿鱼 [魷魚] yóuyú (squid-fish) <n.> squid: ~卷 squid roll || ~丝shredded squid || 炒~ fried squid
7 章鱼 [-魚] zhāngyú (pattern-fish) <n.> octopus: 巨型~ jumbo octopus
8 鲤鱼 [鯉魚] lǐyú (carp-fish) <n.> carp: ~跳龙门 carp jumping dragon gate
9 海豚 [-] hǎitún (sea-suckling pig) <n.> dolphin: 饲养 ~ dolphin feeding || ~表演 dolphin show
10 鲸鱼 [鯨魚] jīngyú (whale-fish) <n.> whale: 一群~ a group of whales || 一条大~ a big whale || 捕捞 (bǔlāo) ~ whale fishing
11 虾 [蝦] xiā (shrimp) <n.> shrimp: ~饺 dumplings with shrimp stuffing|| 河~ river prawn || 龙~ lobster
12 龙虾 [龍蝦] lóngxiā (dragon-shrimp) <n.> lobster: 野生 ~ wild lobster || 清蒸~ steamed lobster
13 (螃) 蟹 [-] (páng) xiè (crab) <n.> crab: 第一个吃~的人the first person to eat crabs (This refers to those who dare to take risks.)
14 昆虫 [-蟲] kūnchóng (many-worm) <n.> insect: 研究~ research insects || ~学 entomology
15 虫 (子) [蟲] chóngzi (worm-*suffix*) <n.> insect, worm: 害怕~ fear of insects || 害~ pest || 益~ useful insect
16 蜻蜓 [-] qīngtíng (*bn*.dragonfly) <n.> dragonfly: 一只~ a dragonfly || 小 ~ small dragonfly
17 蝴蝶 [-] húdié (*bn.* butterfly) <n.> butterfly: 花~ a variegated butterfly || ~效应 (xiàoyìng) the butterfly effect
18 瓢虫 [-蟲] piáochóng (ladle gourd-worm) <n.> ladybug: 一只~ a ladybug
19 萤火虫 [螢-蟲] yínghuǒchón (glow worm-fire-worm) <n.> firefly: 一只~ a firefly

20 苍蝇 [蒼蠅] cāngyíng (deep green-fly) <n.> fly, housefly: 一只 (个) ~ a/one fly || 打/消灭 ~ kill flies/eliminate flies
21 蚊子 [-] wénzi (mosquito-*suffix*) <n.> mosquito: 一只 (个) ~ a mosquito || 打/消灭 ~ kill mosquitos/eliminate mosquitos || ~药 mosquito repellent
22 蚯蚓 [-] qiūyǐn (*bn.* Earthworm) <n.> Earthworm: 一条 ~ an Earthworm || 抓~ catch Earthworms || 养殖 (yǎngzhí) ~ breed Earthworms
23 蜘蛛 [-] zhīzhū (*bn.* spider) <n.> spider: ~网 spider web || ~侠 (xiá) Spiderman
24 蚂蚁 [螞蟻] mǎyǐ (*bn.* ant) <n.> ant: ~洞 anthill || ~搬家 ants moving
25 蟑螂 [-] zhāngláng (*bn.* cockroach) <n.> cockroach, roach || ~药 cockroach repellent
26 臭虫 [-蟲] chòuchóng (stinky-insect) <n.> bedbug: 预防 (yùfáng) ~ bedbug prevention || 消灭~ eliminate bedbugs
27 跳蚤 [-] tiàozǎo (jump-flea) <n.> flea: 一只~a flea || ~市场 flea market
28 虱子 [-] shīzi (louse-*suffix*) <n.> louse: 捉~ catch lice || 秃头上的~-明摆着 The lice on his bald head was evident. || 长~ lice
29 寄生虫 [--蟲] jìshēngchóng (attach-live-worm) <n.> parasite: ~病 parasitic disease || 感染 (g(arasit~ parasite infections
30 细菌 [細-] xìjūn (tiny-bacteria) <n.> bacteria: 各种~ various bacteria || ~感染bacterial infections || ~繁殖 (fánzhí) bacterial breeding
31 病毒 [-] bìngdú (disease-poisonous) <n.> virus: 三种~ three viruses || 感冒~ flu viruses || 传播~ transmission of the virus || 电脑~ computer virus
32 毛 [-] máo (mold) <n.> mildew, mold: 长了~的面包 moldy bread
33 霉 [-] méi (mildew) <n.> mold, mildew: 长~了be moldy || ~味儿the smell of mildew
34 细胞 [細-] xìbāo (tiny-cell) <n.> cell: 一个~ one cell || ~学 cytology || 人体~ human cells
35 基因 [-] jīyīn (*transliteration*) <n.> genes: ~学 genetics || 遗传 (yíchuán) ~ genetic genes || 人体~ human genes || 转~食物 genetically modified food

Tips:

1 See Unit 10 for the tip on 虫.
2 Radical 灬: The radical 灬 usually denotes 'fire or heat,' for example, 热 (hot), 照 (zhào, to shine upon), and 焦 (jiāo, scorched). However, the 灬 in 鱼 (魚) symbols a fish's tail, as it does in the bird 燕 (yàn, swallow).
3 Why do Chinese people like 鱼 (fish)? Because 鱼 and 余 (餘) are homophones of yú, and 余 (餘) has an auspicious meaning, 'surplus,' which was understandably welcomed in old times when food was scare. Therefore, many Chinese people eat fish and post pictures of fish on their walls during Chinese New Year.

Exercises:

Part I: Please answer the following questions in Chinese.

1 请写出美国人经常吃的三种鱼
2 请写出一般中国人比较喜欢吃的三种鱼

3 写出几种你比较喜欢的海鲜
4 下面哪些东西可以用来做成罐头食品 (canned food)

海豚	寄生虫	蝴蝶	金枪鱼	鱼
鲸鱼	蚊子	沙丁鱼	蚯蚓	苍蝇

5 如果一个家庭不太干净, 家里可能会出现哪些虫类

Theme 13: Trees 树木 (shùmù)

(See also Theme 18)

1 森林 [-] sēnlín (forest-woods) <n.> forest: 原始~ virgin forest || 热带~ tropical forest || 保护/破坏~ protect the forest/destruction of forests
2 树林 [樹-] shùlín (tree-woods) <n.> forest: 一片~ a piece of wood || 穿过~ through the woods
3 树 [樹] shù (tree) <n.> tree: 一棵~ a tree || 大~ a big tree || 种 (zhòng) ~ plant trees || ~种 (zhǒng) tree seeds
4 松树 [-樹] sōngshù (pine-tree) <n.> pine, pine tree: 一棵~ a pine || ~林 pine forest
5 橡树 [-樹] xiàngshù (oak-tree) <n.> oak tree: 一棵~ an oak tree
6 白桦 (树) [-樺樹] báihuàshù (white-birch-tree) <n.> birch tree: 一棵~ a birch tree
7 杨树 [楊樹] yángshù (poplar-tree) <n.> poplar (tree): 一棵~ a poplar tree
8 柳树 [-樹] liǔshù (willow-tree) <n.> willow (tree): 一棵 ~ a willow
9 果树 [-樹] guǒshù (fruit-tree) <n.> fruit tree: 一棵~ a fruit tree || ~开花/结果 flowering fruit tree/fruit tree results
10 苹果树 [蘋-樹] píngguǒshù (apple-tree) <n.> apple tree: 一棵~ an apple tree
11 梨树 [-樹] líshù (pear-tree) <n.> pear tree: 一棵 ~ a pear tree
12 杏树 [-樹] xìngshù (apricot-tree) <n.> apricot tree: 一棵~ an apricot tree
13 桃树 [-樹] táoshù (peach-tree) <n.> peach tree: 一棵~ a peach tree
14 樱桃树 [櫻-樹] yīngtáoshù (cherry-tree) <n.> cherry tree: 一棵~ a cherry tree
15 核桃树 [--樹] hétáoshù (walnut-tree) <n.> walnut tree: 一棵~ a walnut tree Note: 核桃 is sound change of 胡桃 in which the 胡 means Hun, an ancient tribe in northern China.
16 竹子 [-] zhú zǐ (bamboo-*suffix*) <n.> bamboo: 一根~ one bamboo stalk, one bamboo shoot
17 树木 [樹-] shùmù (tree-wood) <n.> trees (in general): 砍伐 (kǎnfá) ~ felling trees || ~种类 tree species || 花草 ~ flowers and trees

Tips:

1 木, 本, 末: 木 is obviously pictographic. 本 (běn) and 末 (mò) are augmented pictographs, meaning 'root' and 'branch' respectively. 本末倒置 (běnmò dàozhì) means 'upside down' literally, but functions as 'put the cart before the horse.'

2 木, 林, 森: From the number of the componental 木 we can guess that 林 (lín) means 'woods' and 森 (sēn) 'forest.' The Chairman of the National Government of the Republic of China from 1931 to 1943 was named 林森.
3 十年树木, 百年树人: This Chinese doctrine means 'it takes ten years to grow a tree, but 100 years to rear a person.' The leading figure of modern Chinese literature, 鲁迅 (Lu Xun or Lu Hsün, 1881–1936) had the real name 周树人.

Exercises: Please answer each of these questions.

1 请写出六种水果树的名称

2 请写出在美国可以经常看到的树木名称

Theme 14: Flowers and grass 花草 (huācǎo)

1 植物 [-] zhíwù (plant-thing) <n.> plant, flora: 有毒~ poisonous plants || 珍稀 (zhēnxī) ~ rare plants || ~学 botany
2 花 [-] huā (flower) <n.> flower: ~园 flower garden || 种/养~ plant/raise flowers
3 鲜花 [鮮-] xiānhuā (fresh-flower) <n.> fresh flowers: 开满~ full of flowers || ~盛开 flowers in full bloom
4 牡丹 [-] mǔdān (male-red) <n.> peony: 一朵~ a peony || ~被称为花中之王. The peony is called the king of flowers.
5 荷花 [-] héhuā (lotus-flower) <n.> lotus: 夏日~ summer lotus
6 玫瑰花 [-] méiguīhuā (red gem-round gem-flower) <n.> rose: 一束~ a bouquet of roses || 两朵 ~ two roses
7 菊花 [-] júhuā (chrysanthemum-flower) <n.> chrysanthemum: ~茶 chrysanthemum tea
8 康乃馨 [-] kāngnǎixīn (*transliteration*) <n.> carnation: 一束~ a bunch of carnations
9 茉莉花 [-] mòlìhuā (*transliteration*-flower) <n.> jasmine: ~茶 jasmine tea
10 兰花 [蘭-] lánhuā (orchid-flower) <n.> orchid: 一株 (zhū) ~ an orchid
11 梅花 [-] méihuā (plum-flower) <n.> plum blossom: ~香自苦寒来 plum blossom out of the bitter cold
12 桃花 [-] táohuā (peach-flower) <n.> peach blossom: ~运 man's luck in love
13 杏花 [-] xìnghuā (apricot-flower) <n.> apricot blossom: ~树apricot tree || ~开了apricot blossom
14 樱花 [櫻-] yīnghuā (cherry-flower) <n.> oriental cherry: 日本~ japanese flowering cherry
15 草 [-] cǎo (grass) <n.> grass: ~地 meadow || ~原 grassland || ~根 grassroots
16 三叶草 [-葉-] (three-leaf-grass) <n.> clover: 白花~ clover with white flowers || 红花~ clover with red flowers

17 幸运草 [-運-] xìngyùncǎo (lucky-grass) <n.> lucky clover, four-leaf clover: 一片~ a piece of lucky clover || 四叶草代表着幸运, 所以也叫做~. The four-leaf clover represents luck, so it's also called the lucky clover.

18 薰衣草 [-] xūnyīcǎo (*transliteration*-grass) <n.> lavender: 浪漫~ romantic lavender. Note: 薰衣is a transliteration of the Latin word 'lavare.'

Tips:

1 Radical 艹: Names of most flowers and plants have this radical 艹 which means grass, for example, 花, 草, 蘭 (兰, orchid), 茉莉 (jasmine), 菊 (chrysanthemum), and 荷 (lotus) in this unit.

2 Peony (牡丹): The peony is widely regarded as the national flower of the People's Republic of China, while plum blossom (梅花) is the official national flower of the Republic of China.

3 梅兰竹菊 (méi lán zhú jú): They are plum, orchid, bamboo and chrysanthemum, considered to be the 'four noblemen' of all flowers by ancient Chinese literati. Paintings and poetry of these plants were a major literary phenomena in ancient China. Interestingly enough, all of the four characters come with the second tone in Mandarin Chinese.

Exercises: Please read the following words and then answer the questions in Chinese.

牡丹、荷花、玫瑰花、菊花、康乃馨、茉莉花、兰花 梅花、桃花、杏花、樱花、幸运草、薰衣草

1 美国人一般会送给什么人红玫瑰?

2 在美国康乃馨一般会送给谁? 什么时候送?

3 樱花是哪个国家的国花? 美国哪个地方的樱花最有名?

4 牡丹是哪个国家的国花?

5 上面哪些花是在春天开的? 哪些花是在夏天开的? 哪些花是在秋天开的? 哪些花是在冬天开的?

6 哪种草表示幸运? 哪种草对睡眠有好处?

Theme 15: Grains, cash crops 粮食, 经济作物 (liángshí, jīngjì zuòwù)

1 粮食 [糧-] liángshí (grain-food) <n.> grain, food: 生产~ production of grain || 爱惜 (àixī) ~ cherish food || ~丰收 food harvest

2 小麦 [-麥] xiǎo mài (small-wheat) <n.> wheat: 种~ plant wheat || 收~ harvest wheat || ~粉wheat flour

3 大麦 [-麥] dàmài (big-wheat) <n.> barley: ~粥 (zhōu) barley porridge || 种植~ plant barley

4 玉米 [-] yùmǐ (jade-rice) <n.> corn: ~面 corn flour || ~粥 corn porridge || ~棒子corn cob

5 水稻 [-] shuǐdào (water-rice in a field) <n.> rice paddy: : 种植~ plant rice paddy || ~田paddy land

6 高粱 [-] gāoliáng (tall-sorghum) <n.> sorghum: 《红~》*Red Sorghum* (Chinese film) || ~酒sorghum liquor

7 小米 [-] xiǎomǐ (small-rice) <n.> millet: ~饭 cooked millet || ~粥 (稀饭) millet congee

8 红豆 [紅-] hóngdòu (read-bean) <n.> red bean: ~汤 red bean soup || ~粥 red bean porridge

9 绿豆 [綠-] lǜdòu (green-bean) <n.> green bean: ~汤 mungbean soup || ~粥 congee with mungbean

10 大豆 [-] dàdòu (big-bean) <n.> soybean: 加工~ process soybeans || ~油 soybean oil

11 花生 [-] huāshēng (flower-grow) <n.> peanut: ~酱 (jiàng) peanut jam || ~油 peanut oil || 对~过敏 be allergic to peanut

12 红薯 [紅-] hóngshǔ (red-yam) <n.> sweet potato: 烤~ roasted sweet potato

13 马铃薯 [馬鈴-] mǎlíngshǔ (horse-bell-yam) <n.> potato: 种~ plant potato

14 土豆 [-] tǔdòu (soil-bean) <n.> potato: 炒~ fried potatoes || ~片potato slices || ~丝shredded potato

15 芝麻 [-] zhīmá (reishi-hemp) <n.> sesame: ~酱 sesame paste || ~油 sesame oil Note: the original name of 芝麻 is 脂麻, which means 'grease-hemp' literally.

16 甘蔗 [-] gānzhè (sweet-sugarcane) <n.> sugarcane: 一根~ one sugarcane || 种植~ plant sugarcane || 加工~ process sugarcane

17 甜菜 [-] tiáncài (sweet-vegetable) <n.> beet: 一个~ a beet || 种植 ~ plant beets || 加工~ process beets

18 棉花 [-] miánhuā (cotton-flower) <n.> cotton: ~糖 cotton candy || 生产~ produce cotton || 种~ plant cotton

19 烟草 [煙-] yāncǎo (smoke-grass) <n.> tobacco: 种植 ~ plant tobacco || ~工业 tobacco industry || ~大王 tobacco king

20 茶 [-] chá (tea) <n.> tea: 喝~ drink tea || 凉~ cold tea

21 可可 [-] kěkě (*transliteration*) <n.> cocoa: ~豆 cocoa beans || ~粉 cocoa powder

22 咖啡豆 [-] kāfēidòu (*transliteration*-bean) <n.> coffee beans: 磨 (mò) ~ ground coffee beans || 一袋~ a bag of coffee beans

Tips:

1 Radical 米: 米 originally meant spikes of rice, and later, its meaning extended to small rice-like grains, for example, 小米 (millet), 大米 (rice), 玉米 (corn seed), 高粱米 (gāoliángmǐ, sorghum) and even 花生米 (peanut). Almost all characters with the radical 米 are related to grains or their products, for example, 粮 (liáng, grain, food), (高) 粱 (liáng, sorghum), 粒 (lì, seed), 粗 (cū, coarse (rice)), 精 (jīng, fine (rice)), 糟 (zāo, dregs, dross), 糕 (gāo, cake), and 糟糕 (terrible, bad). 米 has another meaning 'meter,' which is apparently a transliteration of '*me*ter.'

2 研究研究 (yánjiu yánjiu): At the beginning of Chinese economic reform, if a government official said he needed to 研究研究 (yánjiu yánjiu, literally it meant 'I'll think about it') when requested to do a favor. So street-smart people would know that he was probably hinting that you should give him some presents like 烟酒 (cigarettes and liquor) since 烟酒烟酒 (yānjiǔ yānjiǔ) and 研究研究 (yánjiu yánjiu) are almost homophones. Nowadays, if this were to happen in a similar scenario, cigarettes and liquor could scarcely settle the matter unless the wine is a brand enjoyed by French King Louis XV and the cigar was once cherished by British Prime Minister Winston Churchill.

3 请喝茶 (Please drink tea): In ancient China, when the host said 请喝茶 (please drink tea) to the guest, he meant that the guest needs to leave. This is called 端茶送客 (duānchá sòngkè, to raise a teacup to send the guest away.) Nowadays, people do not say 请喝茶 due to the prosody of modern Chinese, but they often say 再喝一点儿茶 (to drink a little more tea), which functions as the ancient 请喝茶 does.

4 烟酒茶糖 (yānjiǔchátáng): They are cigarettes, alcohol, tea and candy, once considered major recreational necessities beside food before the 2000s.

Exercises:

Part I: Multiple Choice (Please choose the appropriate answers.)

1 下面哪些农作物在美国农场里会大规模种植_______.
A. 咖啡豆 B. 小米 C. 水稻 D. 玉米

2 下面哪些农作物可以做成面包_______.
A. 小麦 B. 小米 C. 水稻 D. 玉米

3 "Tobacco King"的意思是_______.
A. 可可大王 B. 烟草大王 C. 甜菜大王 D. 芝麻大王

4 下面哪些是美国人很少吃的东西: _______.
A. 红豆粥 B. 绿豆粥 C. 土豆 D. 花生

5 “Whole wheat bread”的中文翻译是________

A. 红薯 B. 马铃薯 C. 芝麻 D. 全麦面包

6 下面的广告是想提倡________

Source: http://m.90sheji.com/sucai/16522213.html

A. 节约用水 B. 爱惜烟草 C. 爱惜粮食 D. 节约用电

7 100% cotton shirt可以翻译成________

A. 纯棉衬衫 B. 棉花衬衫 C. 一百分棉衬衫 D. 百分之百棉衬衫

8 下面这张照片可以叫________

Source: https://commons.wikimedia.org/wiki/File:%E4%B8%B0%E6%BB%A1%E5%B1%AF_%E7%A7%8B%E6%94%B6_-_panoramio.jpg. Photograpy by大漠1208.

A. 种植甘蔗 B. 粮食丰收 C. 烟草大王 D. 磨咖啡豆

Theme 16: Vegetables, fruits 蔬菜, 水果 (shūcài, shuǐguǒ)

1 蔬菜 [-] shūcài (vegetable-greens) <n.> vegetable: 新鲜~ fresh vegetables || 生产 ~ produce vegetables || ~水果vegetable and fruit
2 生菜 [-] shēngcài (eating raw-vegetable) <n.> lettuce: ~沙拉lettuce salad || 一棵~ a lettuce
3 西兰花 [-蘭-] xīlánhuā (western-chinese kale-flower) <n.> broccoli: 蒸 (zhēng) ~ steamed broccoli
4 芦笋 [蘆筍] lúsǔn (reed-bamboo shoot) <n.> asparagus: 一把~ a bunch of asparagus || 炒 ~ stir-fried asparagus
5 洋葱 [-蔥] yángcōng (foreign-onion) <n.> onions: 切~ cut the onions || 炒 ~ fried onions
6 大蒜 [-] dàsuàn (big-garlic) garlic<n.> garlic: 一头~ a head of garlic
7 辣椒 [-] làjiāo (spicy-pepper) <n.> pepper: 红/青~ red/green peppers || ~油chili oil
8 萝卜 [蘿蔔] luóbo (turnip-white) <n.> radish: ~汤radish soup || 白~ white radish
9 胡萝卜 [-蘿蔔] húluóbo (*Hu*-turnip) <n.> carrot: 牛肉炖 (dùn) ~ beef stew carrot || ~营养 (yíngyǎng) 丰富. Carrots are nutritious.
10 西红柿 [-紅-] xīhóngshì (western-red-persimmon) <n.> tomato: ~炒鸡蛋 scrambled eggs with tomato || ~鸡蛋汤 tomato and egg soup || 新鲜~ fresh tomatoes

11 黄瓜 [黃-] huánggua (*Hu*-melon) <n.> cucumber: 凉拌 (bàn) ~ cold cucumber salad || 一根/条~ a cucumber

12 豆角 [-] dòujiǎo (bean-horn) <n.> green bean: 干~ dried green beans || 炒~ stir-fried green beans

13 豆芽 [-] dòuyá (bean-sprout) <n.> bean sprout: 绿~ green bean sprout || 黄~ yellow bean sprout

14 白菜 [-] báicài (white-vegetable) <n.> Chinese cabbage: 洋~ cabbage || 一颗 a head of cabbage || 一棵~ a cabbage

15 茄子 [-] qiézi (eggplant-*suffix*) <n.> eggplant: 红烧 ~ braised eggplant || 圆~ round eggplant || 长~ long eggplant

16 冬瓜 [-] dōngguā (winter-melon) <n.> wax gourd: ~汤 wax gourd soup

17 水果 [-] shuǐguǒ (juicy-fruit) <n.> fruit: 热带~ tropical fruit || 进口~ imported fruit || 新鲜~ fresh fruit

18 西瓜 [-] xīguā (western-melon) <n.> watermelon: ~汁watermelon juice

19 苹果 [蘋-] píngguǒ (apple-fruit) <n.> apple: ~汁apple juice

20 梨 [-] lí (pear) <n.> pear: ~汁pear juice

21 桃 [-] táo (peach) <n.> peach: ~汁peach juice || ~干dried peach

22 桔子 [橘-] júzi (tangerine-*suffix*) <n.> orange: ~皮orange peel || ~汁orange juice

23 柚子 [-] yòuzi (grapefruit-*suffix*) <n.> grapefruit: ~茶 grapefruit tea

24 香蕉 [-] xiāngjiāo (fragrant-banana) <n.> banana: 一根 ~ a banana || ~人 American of Asian ancestry

25 葡萄 [-] pútao (*transliteration* of Greek word 'botris') <n.> grape: 一串 (chuàn) ~ a bunch of grapes || ~干raisins || ~酒wine

26 杏 [-] xìng (apricot) <n.> apricot: ~树 apricot tree || ~花apricot blossom || ~仁 (rén) almond

27 李子 [-] lǐzi (plum-*suffix*) <n.> plum: ~树 plum tree

28 草莓 [-] cǎoméi (grass-berry) <n.> strawberry: ~ 酱 strawberry jam || ~蛋糕strawberry cake

29 蓝莓 [藍-] lánméi (blue-berry) <n.> blueberry: ~汁blueberry juice

30 树莓 [樹-] shùméi (tree-berry) <n.> raspberry: 种~ plant raspberry

31 樱桃 [櫻-] yīngtáo (cherry-peach) <n.> cherry: 中国有句俗语 (súyǔ): "~好吃树难栽 (zāi). " There is a popular saying in China that the cherry is good to eat, but the tree is hard to plant.

32 枣 [棗] zǎo (jujube) <n.> jujube, dates: ~树 jujube tree || 红~ red dates || 青~ green dates

33 菠萝 [-蘿] bōluó (pineapple) <n.> pineapple: ~汁 pineapple juice

Tips:

1 Vegetables introduced to China: Throughout the history of China, many foreign vegetables were introduced to China and their names left some marks. For example, 胡 was a people who lived in Central Asia and 胡萝卜 (carrot) and 黄瓜 (see the next note for details) were introduced from there, 洋 means 'foreign,' which is how 洋葱 (onion) and 洋芹 (celery) got their names. 西

means 'Western,' which is how 西兰花 (broccoli,) 西红柿 (tomato,) 西瓜 (watermelon) and 西芹 (celery) got their names.

2 黄瓜: The original name is 胡瓜 (húguā) because it was introduced from Central Asia, which was conventionally called 胡地 (*Hu*'s territory.) Later an emperor tabooed "胡" in his time and 胡瓜 was therefore changed to 黄瓜.

3 豆角 (green bean): It is also called 豆荚 (dòujiá, bean-legume.)

4 茄子 (qiézi, eggplant): Like English-speakers say 'cheese' when taking pictures, the Chinese people say 茄子 (qiézi.) Try to say 'qiézi' and observe the shape of your mouth.

5 樱桃 (yīngtáo, cherry): There are two explanations to the origin of 樱桃. One is that 黄莺 (huáng *yīng*, orioles) like this kind of fruit, and the other is that this kind of fruit resembles small dark jades (璎珠, *yīng* zhū.)

6 菠萝 (bōluó, pineapple): It is called 鳳梨 (凤梨, fènglí) in Taiwan. 鳳梨酥 (凤梨酥, fènglísū, pineapple cake) is a famous local snack in Taiwan.

Exercises:

Part I: Answer the following questions based on your own perspectives.

西兰花、芦笋、洋葱、大蒜、辣椒、萝卜、胡萝卜、黄瓜、豆角、豆芽、白菜、茄子、冬瓜

1 读一读上面给出的词, 选出你喜欢吃的菜, 写下来

____

2 读一读上面给出的词, 选出你不喜欢吃的菜, 写下来

____

西瓜、苹果、梨、桃子、香蕉、菠萝、桔子、柚子、葡萄、杏、李子、蓝莓、樱桃、草莓、树莓、枣

3 读一读上面给出的词, 选出你喜欢吃的水果, 写下来

____

4 读一读上面给出的词, 选出你不喜欢吃的水果, 写下来

____

Theme 17: Body parts, liquids and waste 身体器官 (shēntǐ qìguān)

(See also Theme 4)

1 全身 [-] quánshēn (whole-body) <n.> whole body: ~的力气 the strength of the body/ all of one's strength || 他~上下都是名牌. He is covered in famous brands from head to toe.

2 一身 [-] yīshēn (entire-body) <n.> whole body: 流了~汗 one's whole body was covered in sweat. || 小王年纪轻轻就~病. Illness gripped Xiao Wang's whole body.

3 身体 [-體] shēntǐ (body-body) <n.> body: ~健康 body health || 检查~ physical exam

4 四肢 [-] sìzhī (four-limb) <n.> four limbs: ~着地 four limbs to touch on the ground || ~发达 physically strong || ~灵活 be quick on one's feet and arms

5 角 [-] jiǎo (horn) <n.> horn, tip: 鹿/牛~ deer antlers/ bull horns || 冰山一~ the tip of the iceberg

6 头 [頭] tóu (head) <n.> head, top: 抬~ raise one's head || 转 (zhuàn) ~ turn one's head || ~疼 one's head is hurting

7 脑 [腦] nǎo (brain) <n.> brain: 人~ human brain || 左/右~ left/right brain || ~科学 neuroscience

8 大脑 [-腦] dànǎo (large-brain) <n.> brain: ~发育 (fāyù) brain development || ~细胞 brain cell || ~功能 brain function

9 小脑 [-腦] xiǎonǎo (small-brain) <n.> cerebellum: ~发达 developed cerebellum

10 脑子 [腦-] nǎozi (brain-*suffix*) <n.> brain: 动~ use one's head || ~很笨 stupid, slow-witted

11 头发 [頭髮] tóufa (head-hair) <n.> hair: 黑~ black hair || 假~ wig

12 五官 [-] wǔguān (five-organ) <n.> facial features: ~端正 (duānzhèng) well-proportioned facial features || ~科 Ophthalmology

13 面 [-] miàn (face) <n.> face: ~子 face || 当~ face to face || ~带微笑 wear a smile on one's face

14 脸 [臉] liǎn (face) <n.> face: 一张~ a face || 洗~ wash one's face

15 耳朵 [-] ěrduo (ear-earlobe) <n.> ear: 一只~ a ear || 猪~ pig ear || 大/长~ big/ long ear

16 眼睛 [-] yǎnjīng (eye-eyeball) <n.> eye: 睁开/闭上~ open/close eyes

17 眼里 [-裏] yǎnlǐ (eye-inside) <n.> in one's eyes, perspective: 在中国人~名牌是地位的象征. In the eyes of the Chinese people, name brands are status symbols. || 看在 ~, 记在心里. See with your eyes, and remember with your heart.

18 鼻子 [-] bízi (nose-*suffix*) <n.> nose: 大~ big nose || 高~ high bridged nose || 抽 (chōu) ~ sniff

19 口 [-] kǒu (mouth) <n.> mouth: 不好意思说出~ embarrassed to say || 说一~流利的汉语 speak fluent Chinese || ~是心非. Say yes and mean no.

20 嘴 [-] zuǐ (mouth) <n.> mouth: 张/闭~ open/close your mouth || 一 (满) ~脏话 a dirty mouth

21 舌 [-] shé (tongue) <n.> tongue: 卷 (juǎn) ~ curl the tip of the tongue || 多嘴多~ gossipy and meddlesome || 白费口~ waste one's breath

22 舌头 [-頭] shétou (tongue-*suffix*) <n.> tongue: 他说话老是大~. He often lisps. || 别在背后嚼 (jiáo) ~. Don't gossip behind people's backs.

23 牙 [-] yá (molar, tooth) <n.> tooth, teeth: 一颗~ a tooth || 刷~ brush teeth || ~疼 toothache

24 胡子 [鬍-] húzi (beard-*suffix*) <n.> beard, mustache: 刮 (guā) ~ shave one's beard || 满脸~ full beard || 白~ white beard

25 脖子 [-] bózi (neck-*suffix*) <n.> neck: 长~ long neck || 歪~ crooked neck || 伸长~ extend one's neck
26 肩 [-] jiān (shoulder) <n.> shoulder: 双/两~ both/two shoulders
27 背 [-] bèi (back) <n.> the back: ~上 on one's back || ~靠大山 back against the mountain
28 胸部 [-] xiōngbù (chest-part) <n.> chest: ~丰满 voluptuous chest
29 乳房 [-] rǔfáng (milk-house) <n.> breast, boobs: 一对~ a pair of breasts || 丰满的~ plumpy breasts
30 胃 [-] wèi (stomach) <n.> stomach: ~痛 stomachache || ~不舒服 stomach is uncomfortable
31 肚子 [-] dùzi (belly-*suffix*) <n.> belly: ~疼 have a stomachache, suffer from abdominal pain || ~饿 be hungry/starving
32 肚脐 [-臍] dùqí (belly-belly button) <n.> navel, belly button: ~眼belly button
33 腰 [-] yāo (waist) <n.> lower back, waist: 弯~ bend one's lower back
34 臀部 [-] túnbù (buttock-part) <n.> buttocks: 在~打针 give an injection in the buttock
35 屁股 [-] pìgǔ (hip-thigh) <n.> butt: 打~ hit one's butt || 光~ bare butt

36 心 [-] xīn (heart) <n.> heart: ~情 emotion || 热~ warmhearted
37 心脏 [-臟] xīnzàng (heart-organ) <n.> heart: ~病 heart disease || 人造~ artificial heart
38 肝 [-] gān (liver) <n.> liver: ~炎 hepatitis || ~硬化 (yìnghuà) cirrhosis (of the liver) || ~功能 ability of the liver
39 肺 [-] fèi (lung) <n.> lung: 左/右~ left/right lung || ~病 liver disease || ~炎 (yán) pneumonia
40 胆 [膽] dǎn (gallbladder) <n.> gallbladder, courage: ~结石 gallstone || ~大/小 be brave/timid
41 肠 [腸] cháng (intestine) <n.> intestine: 大/小~ large/small intestine || 香~ sausage
42 膀胱 [-] pángguāng (bladder) <n.> bladder: ~破裂 (pòliè) bladder burst
43 肾 [-] shèn (kidney) <n.> kidney: ~功能 kidney function || 补~ tonify the kidney || ~虚 (xū) renal deficiency
44 尿道 [-] niàodào (urinary-tract) <n.> urinary tract: ~炎 urethritis
45 肛门 [-門] gāngmén (anus-door) <n.> anus

46 胳膊 [-] gēbo (armpit-arm) <n.> arm: ~粗 thick arm || 长~ long arms || 一只~ one arm
47 手 [-] shǒu (hand) <n.> hand: 双~ two hands || 举~ raise one's hand || 洗~ wash hands
48 手腕儿 [--兒] shǒuwànr (hand-wrist) <n.> wrist, trick, gimmick: 抓住~ grab one's wrist || 耍 (shuǎ) ~ play tricks || 政治~ political tactics || 他很有~. He is full of gimmicks.
49 手指 [-] shǒuzhǐ (hand-finger) <n.> finger: 五根~ five fingers || 小~ small fingers || 咬~ bite one's fingers (nails)
50 指甲 [-] zhǐjia (finger-nail) <n.> fingernail: 剪 (ji-] z~ cut fingernail || 染 (rǎn) ~ paint fingernails
51 腿 [-] tuǐ (leg) <n.> leg: 两条~ two legs || 大~ thigh || 踢 (tī) ~ kick one's leg

52 膝盖 [-蓋] xīgài (knee-cover) <n.> knee: ~受伤 hurt one's knees || 抱着~ hold one's knees
53 大腿 [-] dàtuǐ (big-leg) <n.> thigh: 两条~ two thighs || 拍~ pat one's legs
54 小腿 [-] tuǐ (small-leg) <n.> lower leg, calf: 两条~ two calfs || ~肚 calf
55 脚 [-] jiǎo (foot) <n.> foot: 一双~ a pair of feet || 两只~ two feet || 洗~ wash one's feet
56 尾巴 [-] wěibā (tail – *suffix*) <n.> tail: 牛~ cow tail || 兔子~ rabbit tail || 长~ long tail
57 骨头 [-頭] gǔtou (bone-*suffix*) <n.> bone: 一块/根~ a piece of bone || 大/硬~ big/hard bone || 猪/肉~ pig/meat bone
58 骨髓 [-] gǔsuǐ (bone-marrow) <n.> marrow: 深入~ enter into the marrow || ~细胞 marrow cell
59 神经 [-經] shénjīng (nerve-channel) <n.> nerve: 视觉~ sensory nerves || ~不正常 unnatural nerves
60 器官 [-] qìguān (organ-organ) <n.> organ: 发音~ oral organ || 各种~ every type of organ
61 关节 [關節] guānjié (join-joint) <n.> joint, key point: 手指~ finger joints || ~点 joints||~疼 joint pain
62 肌肉 [-] jīròu (muscle-meat) <n.> muscle: 背部~ back muscles || ~结实 (jiēshi) solid muscles
63 血管 [-] xuèguǎn (blood-vessel) <n.> blood vessel: 一根~ a blood-vessel || 心~ heart and blood vessels || 软化 ~ soften blood vessels
64 淋巴 [-] línbā (*transliteration of* lymph) <n.> lymph: ~细胞 lymph cells || ~癌 (ái) lymphoma
65 皮 [-] pí (peel, hide, skin) <n.> skin: 羊~ sheepskin || ~毛 fur/skin and hair || 果~ fruit peel
66 皮肤 [-] pífū (skin-skin) <n.> skin: 黄~ yellow skin || ~黑 the skin is black || ~好 the skin is good
67 痣 [-] zhì (mole) <n.> mole: 一颗~ a mole || 长~ have a mole || 红~ birthmark/potmark
68 雀斑 [-] quèbān (sparrow-speckle) <n.> freckle: 长~ have freckles || 满脸~ face covered with freckles
69 老年斑 [-] lǎoniánbān (old-age-freckle) <n.> liver spots: 去除~ remove liver spots || 防治 (fángzhì) ~ prevent and cure liver spots
70 粉刺 [-] fěncì (pink-pimple) <n.> acne: 长~ have acne || 治~ treat acne || 黑头~ blackhead
71 毛 [-] máo (hair) <n.> fur, hair: 羊~ sheep wool || ~线 knitting wool
72 眉毛 [-] méimáo (eyebrow-hair) <n.> eyebrows, brow: 细~ thin eyebrows || 皱 (zhòu) ~ frown one's eyebrows || 拔 (bá) ~ pluck one's eyebrows
73 腋毛 [-] yèmáo (armpit-hair) <n.> armpit hair: 刮~ shave armpit hair
74 生殖器 [-] shēngzhíqì (procreate-organ) <n.> genitals, genitalia: 男性~ mail genitals || 女性~ female genetalia || 外~ external genital organs
75 阴部 [陰-] yīnbù (genital-part) <n.> genitalia: 外~ outer genitalia
76 阴道 [陰-] yīndào (genital-tract) <n.> vagina: ~口vaginal opening

77 子宫 [-] zǐgōng (fetus-home) <n.> womb: 保养~ take good care of the womb
78 阴茎 [陰莖] yīnjīng (genital-stalk) <n.> penis: ~勃起 (bóqǐ) penis erect
79 睾丸 [-] gāowán (testis-ball) <n.> testicles: 两个~ two testicles
80 卵子 [-] luǎnzi (egg – *suffix*) <n.> ovum, egg: 排出~ ovulate || ~受精 fertilzed egg
81 精子 [-] jīngzi (sperm-*suffix*) <n.> sperm: 产生~ produce sperm || 成熟的~ mature sperm
82 胚胎 [-] pēitāi (embryo-fetus) <n.> embryo: ~发育 developing embryo || 早期~ early stage embryo || ~期 embryo period

83 血 [-] xuè (blood) <n.> blood: 流/出~ flowing blood || 鲜~ fresh blood || 一滴~ a drop of blood || 止~ stop the bleeding
84 血液 [-] xuèyè (blood-liquid) <n.> blood, human blood: ~循环 (xúnhuán) cycle blood
85 分泌物 [-] fēnmìwù (secrete-substance) <n.> secreta: 特殊~ special secretion || 眼~ eye secretion
86 汗 [-] hàn (sweat) <n.> sweat: 出~ sweat || 擦~ wipe sweat
87 汗水 [-] hànshuǐ (sweat-water) <n.> sweat: 辛勤 (xīnqín) 的~ sweat after hard work || 一滴~ a drop of sweat || 满身~ covered in sweat
88 泪 [淚] lèi (tear) <n.> tear: 流~ flowing tears || 一滴~ a teardrop
89 泪水 [淚-] lèishuǐ (tear-water) <n.> tears: 眼里含着~ eyes were filled with tears || 擦干~ wipe one's eyes dry
90 唾液 [-] tuòyè (saliva-liquid) <n.> saliva: 流~ salivating || 分泌 (fēnmì) ~ secrete saliva
91 痰 [-] tán (phlegm) <n.> phlegm: 一口~ a mouth full of phlegm || 吐~ spit phlegm
92 鼻涕 [-] bítì (nose-snivel) <n.> mucus: 流~ flowing mucus || 擦~ wipe mucus
93 奶 [-] nǎi (milk) <n.> milk: 喝~ drink milk || 牛~ cow's milk
94 例假 [-] lìjià (routine-holiday) <n.> menstrual period: 来~了 one's period is coming || ~不准 irregular period
95 大便 [-] dàbiàn (major-excrement) <n.> defecate, have a bowel movement, shit: ~通畅 (tōngchàng) bowels open || ~不通 (suffer from) constipation
96 小便 [-] xiǎobiàn (minor-urine) <n.> urine: ~多 pee a lot || ~失禁 (shījìn) be unable to controle one's bladder || 两次~ pee two times
97 屎 [-] shǐ (shit) <n.> shit, stool: 拉~ shit || 狗~ dog shit
98 尿 [-] niào (pee) <n.> pee: 撒 (sā) ~ take a leak, pee || ~液 urine

Tips:

1 Radical 月 (ròu): The simplified Chinese form 月 represents two radicals. One is 'moon' (yuè) and the other 'meat, flesh' (ròu.) In this unit there are many characters with this radical, for example 肢 (limb,) 脑 (brain,) 脸 (face,) 胡 (wattle,) 胳膊 (arm,) 腋 (armpit,) 腕 (wrist,) 肩 (shoulder,) 背 (back,) 胸 (chest,) 脏 (internal organ,) 肝 (liver,) 肺 (lung,) 胆 (gallbladder,) 肠 (intestine,) 胃 (stomach,) 膀胱 (bladder,) 肾 (kidney,) 肚 (belly,) 脐 (bellybutton,) 腰 (waist,) 臀 (buttlock,) 肛 (anus,) 股 (thigh,) 膝 (knee,) 腿 (leg,) 脚 (foot,) 骨 (bone,) 肌 (muscle,) 肤 (skin,) 胚胎 (fetus.)

2 Radical 尸 (shī): It resembles and means 'a dead body.' Characters with this radical include 屍 (traditional form, shī, corpse,) 屎 (shǐ, shit,) 尿 (niào, urine, pee,) 屁 (pì, fart) and 尾 (wěi, tail).

3 面 (miàn) vs. 脸 (liǎn): Both mean 'face' but 脸 became common after the Tang dynasty.
4 血: It can be pronounced as xuè and xiě. When pronouced as xuè, 血 means 'blood (from deeper inside of the human body,)' but when pronounced as xiě, 血 means 'blood (from the skin of human body or from nonhuman creatures.)' So the blood of a dog is 狗血 (xiě.) Xiě is more colloquial. 流血 has two meanings. One is to shed blood (liúxuè,) for example, 为了国家的安全而流血 (to shed blood for the safety of the nation,) the other is to bleed (liúxiě,) for example, 她的手指被纸割伤了，流血了 (she has a papercut, and her finger is bleeding.)
5 大姨妈 (dàyímā): It is a euphemism that means 'menstruation' (月经,) for example "(我) 大姨妈来了" (my period has come.)
6 脑洞大开 (nǎodòng dàkāi): It is an Internet neologism from around 2015, meaning 'indulge in unrestrained imagination.'

Exercises:

Part I: Please look at the pictures and write the Chinese names of the body parts or organs you know.

1

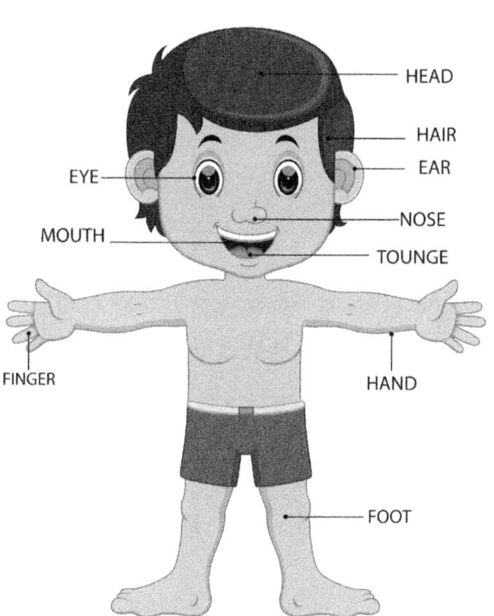

Source: www.shutterstock.com/image-vector/vector-illustration-boy-body-parts-diagram-615211463, with permission.

____

____

2

ANATOMY OF THE HUMAN BODY

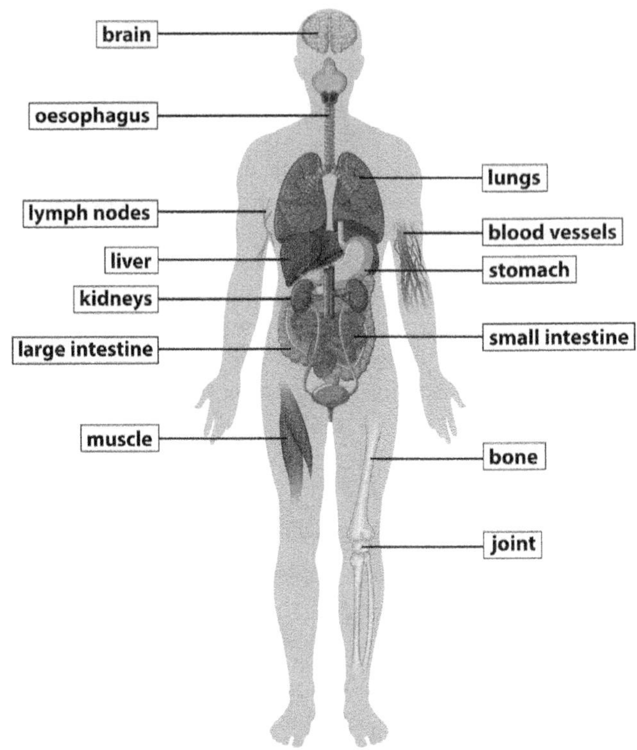

Source: www.shutterstock.com/image-vector/diagram-showing-anatomy-human-body-illustration-458358346, with permission.

Part II: Multiple Choice (Please choose appropriate one)

1 女生: "今天我大姨妈来了, 不能去运动了." 这句话里"大姨妈"的意思是 ________.

A. 妈妈的姐姐　　B. 月经　　C. 卵子

2 看了这本书以后小王脑洞大开, 决定辞掉工作, 到全世界去旅行. 这里的"脑洞大开"意思是________.

A. indulge in unrestrained imagination　　B. a hole in his brain　　C. his brain is open

3 "大便"的口语是________.

A. 拉屎　　B. 很方便　　C. 非常便宜

4 "小便"的口语是 ________.

A. 撒尿　　B. 小小的方便　　C. 便宜一点儿

Part III: Write down the characters with "月" radical.

Theme 18: Plant parts 植物部分 (zhíwù bùfēn)

(See also Theme 13)

1 种子 [種-] zhǒngzi (seed-*suffix*) <n.> seed: 一粒/颗~ a seed || 小麦~ wheat seed || ~ 选手seed players
2 根 [-] gēn (root) <n.> root: 树~ tree roots || ~源source, origin || ~基foundation, basis, groundwork
3 茎 [莖] jìng (stem) <n.> stem (of a plant), stalk: 花~ stems of a flower
4 枝 [-] zhī (branch, twig) <n.> branch, twig: 树~ tree branches
5 叶子 [葉-] yèzi (leaf-*suffix*) <n.> leaf, foliage: 一片~ a leaf
6 花瓣 [-] huābàn (flower-petal) <n.> flower petal: 美丽的~ beautiful flower petals || 一片~ a flower petal
7 花苞 [-] huābāo (flower-bud) <n.> flower bud: 玫瑰~ rose bud
8 花蕾 [-] huālěi (flower-bud) <n.> flower bud: 山茶~ the camellia bud
9 花蕊 [-] huāruǐ (flower-stamen) <n.> stamen, pistil: 娇嫩 (jiāonèn) 的~ soft stamen
10 花粉 [-] huāfěn (flower-pollen) <n.> pollen: ~ 过敏 be allergic to pollen || 传播~ carry pollen from flower to flower
11 芽 [-] yá (sprout, shoot) <n.> bud, sprout, germ, shoot: 发~ germinate, to bud, to sprout || 草~ grass sprouts || 柳~ willow sprouts
12 苗 [-] miáo (seedling) <n.> young plant, sprout, seedling: 麦~ wheat seedling || 树~ young trees || 拔~助长 pull up a young plant to help it grow (spoil things by excessive enthusiasm)
13 藤 [-] téng (vine) <n.> vine, cane, rattan: 葡萄 (pútao) ~ grapevine || 一根~ a vine
14 常春藤 [-] chángchūnténg (perennial-green-ivy) <n.> Ivy: ~名校 Ivy League universities.
15 果实 [-實] guǒshí (fruit-fruit) <n.> fruit, gains: 结出~ bear fruit || ~累累 (léiléi) fruit growing in close clusters, fruit hanging heavy on the trees || 劳动/胜利~ fruits of labor/fruits of victory
16 果皮 [-] guǒpí (fruit-skin) <n.> skin of fruit, peel, rind: 削 (xiāo) ~ peel the fruit
17 果肉 [-] guǒròu (fruit-meat) <n.> pulp, flesh of fruit, mesocarp: 水果 ~ fruit pulp
18 果汁 [-] guǒzhī (fruit-juice) <n.> juice: 纯 ~ pure juice || 喝~ drink juice
19 果核 [-] guǒhé (fruit-pit) <n.> pip, pit, stone: 水果的~ pit of fruits
20 果仁 [-] guǒrén (fruit-kernel) <n.> fruit kernel: 多种~ multiple kernels
21 树根 [樹-] shùgēn (tree-root) <n.> tree roots: 老~ old tree roots
22 树皮 [樹-] shùpí (tree-bark) <n.> tree bark: 剥 (bāo) ~ peel off tree skin
23 树干 [樹幹] shùgàn (tree-trunk) <n.> tree trunk: 笔直的~ straight tree trunk
24 树枝 [樹-] shùzhī (tree-branch) <n.> branch, twig: 干~ dry twig || 粗~ a bough || 小~ small twig
25 树叶 [樹葉] shùyè (tree-leaf) <n.> leaf, leaves: 一片~ a leaf

26 红叶 [紅葉] hóngyè (red-leaf) <n.> red leaves: 秋天的~ red autumnal leaves || 观赏~ see and enjoy red leaves

27 黄叶 [黃葉] huángyè (yellow-leaf) <n.> yellow leaves: ~飘落 (piāoluò). Yellow leaves descend slowly and lightly.

Tips:

1 常春藤 (chángchūnténg): It means 'ivy' in general as well as 'Ivy League' in education. It is called 常青藤 (chángqīngténg) in Taiwan. It is a dream of the Chinese people and Chinese Americans to see their children enter an Ivy League school (藤校.) The course of entering an Ivy League school is called 爬藤 (páténg, to climb the ivy.)

2 香山红叶 (Xiāngshān Hóngyè): Red Leaves of the Fragrant Hill in Beijing is a famous scenic site there in October each year. Red leaves are rare in China, so during the festival, there are probably more tourists than red leaves.

3 歪果仁 (wāiguǒrén): If without tones, wāiguǒrén will be 'waiguoren' which will be easily associated with 外国人 (wàiguórén, foreigner.) Actually, 歪果仁 (literally 'crooked-fruit-kernel') is a neologism meant to refer to foreigners on the Internet.

Exercises:

Part I: Translate the following English in the picture into Chinese.

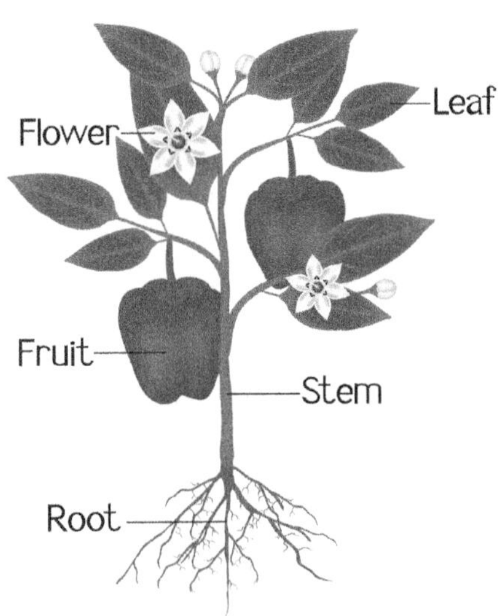

Source: www.shutterstock.com/image-vector/illustration-showing-parts-plant-red-pepper-1018043545, with permission.

____

____

Part II: Use the given bound form on the left as a guide to help you think of other words with the same character. Feel free to use your dictionary when needed. Then write down the English definition of each of the words you've written.

果 (fruit): 果实 fruit

____

____

____

____

树 (tree): 树干 tree trunk

____

____

____

____

Theme 19: Substances 物品 (wùpǐn)

1 物体 [-體] wùtǐ (object-body) <n.> body, substance: 运动的~ the object of motion || 圆形~ round body, shape || 发光~ shiny object
2 东西 [東-] dōngxi (east-west) <n.> object, stuff: 任何~ any thing || 一样的~ same object || 好~ good object, stuff
3 事物 [-] shìwù (thing-object) <n.> thing, object: 具体 (jùtǐ) ~ specific object || 新~ new object || 个别~ specific object
4 物质 [-質] wùzhì (object-substance) <n.> material, substance: ~需要 material needs || ~基础 (j(ateribasic materials || ~文化 materialistic culture
5 固体 [-體] gùtǐ (solid-body) <n.> solid body: ~食物 solid food || ~电池 solid battery
6 液体 [-體] yètǐ (liquid-body) <n.> liquid, fluid: 变成 ~ turn into liquid
7 气体 [氣體] qìtǐ (gas-body) <n.> gas: 有害~ harmful gas || 变成~ turn into gas
8 资源 [資-] zīyuán (material-resource) <n.> resources: 自然~ natural resources || 人力~ human resources || ~丰富 abundant resources
9 整体 [-體] zhěngtǐ (whole-body) <n.> whole entity, entire body: 一个~ a whole entity || ~结构 whole structure || 社会~ social entity
10 中介 [-] zhōngjiè (middle-medium) <n.> intermediary: ~ 公司 intermediary company || ~物 intermediary structure
11 原料 [-] yuánliào (raw-material) <n.> raw (or rough) material: 工业~ industrial materials || ~不足 the raw materials are insufficient
12 材料 [-] cáiliào (material-material) <n.> material: 建筑~ building materials || 化工~ chemical materials
13 燃料 [-] ránliào (flammable-material) <n.> fuel: 用~ 作燃料 use coal as fuel

14 物资 [-資] wùzī (goods-material) <n.> goods and materials: 军用~ goods and materials for military use || 废旧~ waste and old materials

15 设施 [設-] shèshī (establish-set up) <n.> equipment, facilities: 基础~ basic materials || 电气~ electrical equipment || 通讯~ telecommunication installations

16 设备 [設備] shèbèi (establishment-equipment) <n.> equipment, facilities: 更新~ new equipment || 旧~ old equipment

17 柴米油盐酱醋茶 [---鹽醬--] chái mǐ yóu yán jiàng cù chá (charcoal-rice-oil-salt-sauce-vinegar-tea) <n.> firewood, rice, oil, salt, soy sauce, vinegar and tea (chief daily necessities): 开门七件事~ Firewood, rice, oil, salt, soy sauce, vinegar and tea are the seven necessities to begin a day.

18 货 [貨] huò (property, money, goods) <n.> goods, money: 美国~ American product || 真~ authentic goods || 假~ fake goods

19 商品 [-] shāngpǐn (trade-item) <n.> commodity, goods, merchandise: 购买~ purchase goods || 进口/ 出口~ imported goods, exported goods

20 产品 [產-] chǎnpǐn (produce-item) <n.> product, produce: 新/老~ new, old product || 电子~ electronic product

21 农产品 [農產-] nóngchǎnpǐn (agricultural-product) <n.> agricultural products: 收购~ purchase agricultural products || 美国 ~价格比较低. The price of American agricultural products is low.

22 物品 [-] wùpǐn (object-item) <n.> article, good: 贵重~ valuable goods || 私人~ privately-owned goods

23 用品 [-] yòngpǐn (use-item) <n.> articles for use, products: 日常~ daily use products || 厨房~ kitchen products

24 日用品 [-] rìyòngpǐn (daily-use-item) <n.> daily use products: 买~ buy daily use products || 生活~ articles used in every day life || 家庭~ household products (used frequently)

25 成品 [-] chéngpǐn (finished-item) <n.> end product, finished product: 半~ half-finished product || ~油 refined oil

26 精品 [-] jīngpǐn (premium-item) <n.> quality good, premium product: 一件~ a premium product || 艺术~ premium art product || 国产~ goods produced by the government

27 百货 [-貨] bǎihuò (varied-goods) <n.> general merchandise: 日用~ articles of daily use || ~公司 general merchandise of a corporation

28 行李 [-] xinglǐ (go-travel) <n.> luggage: 大件~ large luggage || 收拾~ organize/pack luggage || 托运~ check luggage

29 礼物 [禮-] lǐwù (gift-thing) <n.> present: 一份~ a present || 生日~ birthday present || 送/ 收~ give/ receive a present

30 礼 [禮] lǐ (offer sacrifice to gods, respect, courtesy, gift) <n.> gift: 送~ give a gift || 收 ~ receive a gift

31 奖 [獎] jiǎng (encourage, prize) <n.> prize: 获/得~ receive/obtain a prize || 金/ 银~ gold prize/ silver prize || 一等 ~ first place

32 奖品 [獎-] jiǎngpǐn (prize-item) <n.> prize, award, trophy: 凡是参加这次篮球比赛的人都会得到一份~. Everyone participating in this basketball competition will receive an award.

33 艺术品 [藝術-] yìshùpǐn (art-item) <n.> are piece, work of art: 杰出的~ outstanding art pieces || 优秀的~ exceptional art pieces || 欣赏~ appreciate works of art
34 珠宝 [-寶] zhūbǎo (pearl-jade) <n.> jewelry, pearls and jewels, head ornaments: ~店 jewelry shop || ~商 jewelry store || ~首饰 jewelry
35 危险品 [-險-] wēixiǎnpǐn (dangerous-item) <n.> dangerous goods: 携带 (xiédài) ~ carry dangerous goods || 化学~ dangerous chemical goods
36 垃圾 [-] lājī (trash) <n.> trash: ~袋 trash bag || 扔~ throw away trash || 捡~ collect trash

Tips:

1 女人 and 货 (huò): 货 means 'goods, merchandise.' In ancient China, women were discriminated against and associated with 货, for example, 贱货 (jiànhuò, contemptible wretch,) 浪货 (lànghuò, loose woman,) 骚货 (sāohuò, lascivious woman,) 二手货 (èrshǒuhuò, divorced woman) and 赔钱货 (péiqiánhuò, girl).
2 行李 (xíngli): It means 'luggage' and is probably an erroneous form of 行旅 (literally 'go-travel,' travel, luggage.)
3 垃圾 (lājī): It means 'trash.' Most researchers think this Mandarin word was borrowed from the Wu Dialect. The standard pronunciation of 垃圾 is lājī, however, before 1949, it was called 'lèsè' which is closer to the pronunciation in the Wu Dialect and is preserved in the Taiwan National Language (國語.)

Exercises:

Part I: Use the given bound form on the left as a guide to help you think of other words with the same character. Feel free to use your dictionary when needed. Then write down the English definition of each of the words you've written.

品 (goods): 危险品 dangerous goods

____

____

____

____

____

____

____

Part II: Read the following sentences and fill in each blank with the appropriate word or phrase from the options given.

1 资源、原料、物质

a. 现代科学认为__________有三种形态: 固体、液体和气体.
b. 美国是一个自然________丰富的国家.
c. 中国生产汽油的__________大部分是进口的, 也就是说中国进口了大量石油.

2 设施、设备、材料、垃圾

a. 目前世界上很多国家都在积极研制环保_________, 以减少环境污染.
b. 中国的基础_______建设发展得非常快, 几乎大部分省市都有高速铁路.
c. 目前中国生产的工业________质量不断提高, 出口到很多国家.
d. 跟日本相比, 中国处理________的技术还有待提高.

Theme 20: Demonstrative pronouns 指示代词 (zhǐshì dàicí)

1 这 [這] zhè (this) <pron.> this: ~杯酒 this cup of wine || ~是我的房间. This is my room.
2 这个 [這個] zhège (this-MW) <pron.> this: ~人this person || ~房间 this room || ~国家this country
3 那 [-] nà (that) <pron.> that: ~是谁的书? Whose book is that? || ~一天that day
4 那个 [-個] nàge (that-MW) <pron.> that: ~人that person || ~男孩 that boy || ~夏天 that summer
5 它 [-] tā (it) <pron.> it: ~ 有四条腿. It has four legs || ~们they (for inanimate objects) || 其~ other
6 前者 [-] qiánzhě (former-*one*) <pron.> the former: 这两个候选 (hòuxuǎn) 人中, ~更适合 (shìhé) 这个职位 (zhíwèi). Of the two candidates, the former seems to be more eligible for the position.
7 后者 [後-] hòuzhě (latter-*one*) <pron.> the latter: 老王和老李是好朋友, 前者是老师, ~ 是医生. The old Wang and the old Li are good friends. The former is a teacher, the latter is a doctor.
8 某个 [-個] mǒuge (some-MW) <pron.> some, a certain: ~地方some place || ~问题 some problems || ~方面 some aspects
9 某某 [-] mǒu mǒu (some-some) <pron.> some, a certain: ~ 大学 a certain college || ~公司a certain company || ~人some person
10 另 [-] lìng (another) <pron.> another: ~一人another person || ~一面 another aspect || ~一方 another aspect
11 此 [-] cǐ (this) <pron.> this: ~时 this time || ~地 this place || ~人 this person
12 本 [-] běn (one's own, itself, this) <pron.> in the sense of this one is only used on formal occasions: ~人the person himself || ~国 the country itself || ~报 the newspaper itself
13 其 [-] qí (its) <pron.> third person pronoun (he, she, it, his, her, its): ~人some people || ~事his thing || ~价格 its price

14 这些 [這-] zhèxie (this-some) <pron.> these: ~人these people || ~水果 these fruits || ~问题 these problems
15 那些 [-] nàxie (that-some) <pron.> those: ~人those people || ~树 those trees || ~地方 those places
16 一些 [-] yīxie (some) <pron.> some: ~人some people || ~地方 some places || ~问题 some questions
17 其他 [-] qíta (its-other) <pron.> other, else: ~人 other people || ~地方other places || ~国家 other countries
18 其余 [-餘] qíyú (its-remainder) <pron.> the rest, the remainder: ~的钱 the remainder of the money || ~时间 the remaining time || ~四个人the other four people
19 别的 [-] bié de (other-*suffix*) <pron.> other: ~人other person || ~时间 other time || ~地方other places
20 某些 [-] mǒuxie (certain-some) <pron.> some, certain (things): ~人some people || ~事some things || ~学校 some schools

21 哪 [-] nǎ (which) <pron.> which: ~位which person || ~个 which one
22 哪些 [-] nǎxie (which-some) <pron.> which: ~人which people || ~地方 which places || ~书 which books
23 什么 [-麼] shénme (what-*affix*) <pron.> what: 你要~菜? Which dish do you want? || 你想写~? What do you want to write? || 你想说~? What do you want to speak?
24 什么样 [-麼樣] shénme yàng (what-like) <pron.> what kind of: ~的衣服 what kind of clothes || ~的人what kind of person || ~的情况 what kind of circumstances
25 怎么样 [-麼樣] zěnme yàng (how-like) <pron.> how: 去上海~? How about going to Shanghai? || 你看~? What do you think? || 吃得~? How is your meal?
26 怎样 [-樣] zěn yàng (how-like) <pron.> how: ~走 how to walk || ~学 how to learn || ~用 how to use
27 东西 [東-] (east-west) <n.> stuff, thing: 好~ good stuff || 很多~ many stuff || 吃的~ eating stuff

Tips:

1 Zhèi and nèi: They are fused pronunciations of 这一 and 那一 spoken in informal occasions.
2 Be cautious of 那个 (nèige): The Chinese pronunciation of 那个 sounds similar to a derogatory term, which is offensive to African Americans.
3 其他 vs. 其它: Both means 'other, others.' Their distinctions were once very clear: 其他 is on people and 其它 is on nonhuman things, but the recent trend is 其他 is replacing 其它.
4 怎么 vs. 怎样 vs. 怎么样: They function in almost the same way as 'how to. . . ,' for example, 怎么/怎样/怎么样写这个字? (How to write this character?) 怎么 can indicate a rhetorical question but the other two cannot, for example, 她今天怎么不太高兴? (How come is she not happy today?) 怎样 and 怎么样 can be used after a suggestion and make the sentence a tag question, for example, 今天晚上我们一起去看电影怎样/怎么样? (How about we go to the movies tonight?) When 怎么样 is negated, it (不怎么样) has a

particular meaning of 'not good,' for example, 这个人/这个人的想法不怎么样 (This guy/This guy's idea is not good.)

5 Things: 东西, why not 南北? There is no universally accepted answer. One explanation is that in the Eastern Han Dynasty, there were two capitals, the eastern capital in Luoyang and the western capital in Chang'an. Businessmen went to buy from either Luoyang or Chang'an (买东 or 买西,) therefore 东西 became synonymous with things. The second explanation is that in the Tang Dynasty, the capital Chang'an had two markets, 东市 and 西市, and 东西 became synonymous with things. The third explanation is related to the 'Five Elements' of which the phase of south (南) is 'fire' (火) and the north (北) 'water' (水.) 水 and 火 (water/flood and fire) are not good for one's home, but the phase of 东 (木, wood) and 西 (金, gold) are good for one's home. Therefore, 东西, not 南北 became a synonym for things.

Exercises:

Part I: Multiple Choice. Make sure to choose the most appropriate answer.

1 ___________具有130年历史, 主要生产高档女士服装.
A. 本　B. 那　C. 它

2 美国历史上有两位布什总统, 老布什总统和小布什总统. ________是父亲, _______是儿子.
A. 这个、哪个　B. 这些、哪些　C. 前者、后者

3 小张付了学费以后把________的钱都存进了银行.
A. 这个　B. 其余　C. 那个

4 小张不清楚自己到底想找_________的女朋友.
A. 什么样　B. 怎么　C. 某个

5 每次周末回家, 妈妈总是给小张准备很多好吃的_________.
A. 事情　B. 一些　C. 东西

6 在中国中年人的压力很大, 一方面要培养孩子, _________还要照顾 (zhàogù, take care of) 父母.
A. 另一方面　B. 某个方面　C. 其他

Theme 21: Shapes of objects 物体形状 (wùtǐ xíngzhuàng)

1 板 [-] bǎn (board of wood) <n.> board, plank, plate: 木~ wood board || 黑~ blackboard || 木地~ wood floor || 平~电脑 flat screen computer || 一块~ a piece of board

2 块 [塊] kuài (piece) <n.> piece, lump, chunk: 小~ small pieces || 把肉切成~儿 cut the meat into cubes

3 片 [-] piàn (slice) <n.> flat, thin piece, slice, flake: 土豆~ slices of potato || 肉~ slices of meat

4 面儿 [麵兒] miànr (powder) <n.> powder: 辣椒 (làjiāo) ~ pepper powder || 胡椒 (hújiāo) ~ black pepper powder || 药~ medicinal powder

5 末 [-] mò (powder) <n.> dust, powder: 茶叶~ tea dust || 粉~ dust, powder || 蒜 (suàn) ~ garlic powder
6 点 [點] diǎn (dot) <n.> dot, spot, drop (of liquid): 黑~ blackspot || 雨 ~ raindrop || 污 (wū) ~ stain
7 粒 [-] lì (grain) <n.> small particles, grain: 米~ rice grain || 沙~ grains of sand || ~~皆 (jiē) 辛苦. Every single grain is the fruit of hard work.
8 杆 [-] gān/gǎn (pole) <n.> shaft, pole: 笔~ penholder || 电线~ electric pole
9 丝 [絲] sī (silk) <n.> threadlike thing, silk: ~绸silk || ~带silk ribbon || 把土豆切 (qiē) 成细~. Cut the potatoes into fine shreds.
10 条 [條] tiáo (strip) <n.> strip, slip, long narrow piece: 纸~ slip of paper || 薯 (shǔ) ~ fries || 面~ noodle
11 带 [帶] dài (belt) <n.> belt, ribbon: 领~ tie || 丝~ silk ribbon || 皮~ leather belt || 安全~ safety belt
12 球 [-] qiú (ball) <n.> ball: 地~ the Earth || 雪~ snowball || 气~ balloon
13 团 [團] tuán (ball) <n.> ball, sth. shaped like a ball: 饭~ rice ball || 缩 (suō) 成一~ curl up into a ball || 把面揉 (róu) 成一个~儿 knead dough into a ball.
14 网 [網] wǎng (net) <n.> net, network, web: 渔~ fishing net || 铁路~ railway network || 互联~ internet

Tip:

1 One Belt One Road (Initiative): It is called 一带一路 in Chinese. The 'Belt' (带, dài) refers to the '21st-century Maritime Silk Road' and the 'Road' (路, lù,) 'the Silk Road' which is much more famous than the former. Linguistically, it should be called 一路一带, however, leaving aside the 一, '路带' makes no sense, but '带路' (to lead) makes a lot of sense, for a country striving for worldly glory.

Exercises:

Part I: Translate the following phrases into English.

黑板 ______________________
木块 ______________________
面包片 ______________________
薯条儿 ______________________
胡椒面 ______________________
雨点儿 ______________________
米粒 ______________________
肉丝儿 ______________________
领带 ______________________
气球 ______________________
饭团 ______________________
互联网 ______________________

Theme 22: Parts of an object 部位 (bùwèi)

1 头 [頭] tóu (head) <n.> head, top: 桥~ either end of a bridge || 烟~ cigarette end || 船~ the bow of ship
2 顶 [頂] dǐng (crown of the head, top) <n.> crown of the head, top: 头~ crown of the head || 山~ the top of the mountain || 屋~ roof || 楼~ top of a building
3 嘴 [-] zuǐ (mouth) <n.> anything shaped or functioning like a mouth: 瓶~ the mouth of a bottle || 茶壶 (hú) ~ the spout of a teapot || 闭上~ keep one's mouth shut
4 口 [-] kǒu (mouth) <n.> classifier for things with mouths (people, domestic animals, cannons, wells etc): 门~ doorway, gate || 电梯~ the exit of the elevator
5 角 [-] jiǎo (horn, corner) <n.> corner: 桌子~ corner of a table || 左上~ the upper left corner || 英语~ 'English Corner'
6 脚 [-] jiǎo (foot) <n.> foot: 山~ the foot of the mountain || 椅子~ the chair feet || 裤 (kù) ~ bottom of a trouser leg
7 侧 [側] cè (side) <n.> side: 一~ one side || 西~ the western side || 左~ the left side
8 底 [-] dǐ (bottom) <n.> bottom: 瓶~ the bottom of the bottle || 河~ the bottom of the river || 海~ the bottom of the sea
9 末 [-] mò (tip of tree, end) <n.> end, last stage: 明朝~年the end of the Ming Dynasty || 学期~ the end of a school term || 排队排在~尾stand at the end of a queue || 邮件的 ~尾at the end of the email
10 边 [邊] biān (border) <n.> side, edge, margin: 另一~ another side || 街道两~ both sides of the street || 左 ~ the left side
11 面 [-] miàn (face, surface, side) <n.> face, top, side, surface: 表~ surface || 桌~ top of a table, tabletop, desktop || 海~ sea surface
12 表面 [-] biǎomiàn (out-side) <n.> surface: 地球~ surface of the Earth || 浮 (fú) 上~ rise to the surface || ~光滑 (guānghuá) smooth surface
13 刺 [-] cì (pierce, thorn) <n.> thorn, splinter: 手上扎了个~ get a thorn in one's hand || 鱼~ fishbone

Tips:

1 Embodiment: Embodiment is an important device used to refer to parts of an object in Chinese. The most illustrious one is heart (心, xīn,) for example, 圆心 (yuánxīn, center of a circle) and 核心 (héxīn, core).
2 口 vs. 嘴 (zuǐ): Both mean 'mouth,' but 口 is more literal and 嘴 more colloquial. Therefore, words with 嘴 tend to be informal or even negative, for example, 乌鸦嘴 (wūyāzuǐ, jinx) and 尖嘴猴腮 (jiānzuǐ hóusāi, pointed-mouth-ape-chin, to have a wretched appearance).

Exercises:

Part I: Translate the following phrases into English.

门口 ______________________________

茶壶嘴 ______________________________

山顶 ______________________

山脚 ______________________

桥头 ______________________

桥尾 ______________________

海面 ______________________

海底 ______________________

地球表面 ______________________

地球内部 ______________________

Theme 23: Astronomical objects 天体 (tiāntǐ)

1 大自然 [-] dàzìrán (vast-nature) <n.> nature: 热爱~ love nature || 美丽的~ beautiful nature
2 宇宙 [-] yǔzhòu (infinite space-infinite time) <n.> universe, cosmos: ~飞船 spaceship || ~大爆炸 (bàozhà) the Big Bang || 探索 (tànsuǒ) ~ explore the universe
3 天地 [-] tiāndì (heaven-Earth) <n.> heaven and Earth, world: 广阔 (guǎngkuò) ~ vast world || 新~ new world || 艺术~ art world
4 天体 [-體] tiāntǐ (celestial-body) <n.> celestial body: ~运动 celestial movement || 自然~ natural celestial bodies
5 太空 [-] tàikōng (highest-sky) <n.> outerspace: 外~ outerspace || ~旅游 space travel || ~人 astronaut
6 银河 [銀-] yínhé (silver-river) <n.> Milky Way: ~系 the Milky Way Galaxy
7 黑洞 [-] hēidòng (black-hole) <n.> black hole: ~理论black hole theory
8 星球 [-] xīngqiú (star-planet) <n.> planet, celestial body: 外~ alien planet || 《~大战》 *Star Wars* (movie)
9 星星 [-] xīngxīng (star-*reduplication*) <n.> star: 一颗~ a star || 满天~. The sky was filled with stars.
10 星系 [-] xīngxì (star-system) <n.> galaxy: 超巨~ supergiant galaxy || 巨~ giant galaxy || 矮~ dwarf galaxy || 河外~ extragalactic system, external galaxy
11 星座 [-] xīngzuò (star-constellation) <n.> constellation: 大熊~ bear constellation || 十二~ 12 constellations
12 太阳 [-陽] tàiyáng (greatest-*yang*) <n.> sun: 红~ red sun || ~光 sunlight || 晒 (shài) ~ be in the sun
13 太阳系 [-陽-] tàiyángxì (solar-system) <n.> solar system: 太阳是~的中心. The sun is the center of the solar system.
14 水星 [-] shuǐxīng (mercury-star) <n.> Mercury
15 金星 [-] jīnxīng (gold-star) <n.> Venus
16 地球 [-] dìqiú (Earth-globe) <n.> Earth: 离开~ leave Earth || ~人 Earthling || ~上空 above the Earth
17 火星 [-] huǒxīng (fire-star) <n.> Mars
18 木星 [-] mùxīng (wool-star) <n.> Jupiter
19 土星 [-] tǔxīng (soil-star) <n.> Saturn
20 天王星 [-] tiānwángxīng (sky-king-star) <n.> Uranus
21 海王星 [-] hǎiwángxīng (ocean-king-star) <n.> Neptune

22 冥王星 [-] míngwángxīng (netherworld-king-star) <n.> Pluto

23 彗星 [-] huìxīng (comet-star) <n.> comet: 一颗~ a comet || ~尾巴 tail of a comet || 哈雷~ Halley's Comet

24 扫帚星 [掃--] sàozhǒuxīng (broom-star) <n.> comet, jinx, bearer of bad luck: 别人都叫他~ other people called him a bearer of bad luck || 碰到~ encounter a jinx || 你这~ ! You're a jinx!

25 北斗星 [-] běidǒuxīng (north-dipper-star) <n.> the Big Dipper: 在晚上人们能依靠~识别方向. In the evening, people can rely on the Big Dipper to identify what direction they are walking in.

26 寿星 [壽-] shòuxīng (longevity-star) <n.> Canopus (god of longevity): 老 ~ venerable old man (or lady) (respectful form of address to the old)

27 流星 [-] liúxīng (shooting-star) <n.> meteor, shooting star: 一道 ~ a meteor shot || 大步 ~向前走stride forward || 快若 ~ swift as a shooting star

28 卫星 [衛-] wèixīng (guard-star) <n.> satellite: 一颗~ a satellite || 人造~ man made satellite || 发射~ deploy a satellite

29 恒星 [-] héngxīng (fixed-star) <n.> fixed star: 一颗~ a fixed star || 发现~ discover a star || ~爆炸 star explosion

30 行星 [-] xíngxīng (moving-star) <n.> planet: 小~ small planet

31 月亮 [-] yuèliàng (moon-bright) <n.> moon: 半个~ half a moon || 圆圆的~ round moon || ~上升. The moon is rising.

32 月球 [-] yuèqiú (moon-globe) <n.> moon: 登上~ land on the moon || ~背面 far side of the moon

33 月 [-] yuè (moon) <n.> moon: 明~ bright moon || 圆~ round moon || ~缺 (quē). The moon is fading.

34 陨石 [隕-] yǔnshí (fall from the sky-stone) <n.> meteorite: 一块/颗~ a piece of a meteorite/ a meteorite

35 北极 [-極] běijí (north-pole) <n.> north pole: ~星 the North Star || ~熊 polar bear

36 南极 [-極] nánjí (south-pole) <n.> south pole: ~光 reflection of the south pole || ~大陆 The Antarctic Continent || ~风 Arctic wind

37 赤道 [-] chìdào (southern-line) <n.> the equator

38 经线 [經綫] jīngxiàn (longitude-line) <n.> longitudinal line

39 纬线 [緯綫] wěixiàn (latitude-line) <n.> latitudinal line

40 大气层 [-氣層] dàqìcéng (atmosphere-layer) <n.> atmosphere: 地球~ the Earth's atmosphere

41 地震带 [--帶] dìzhèndài (Earthquake-belt) <n.> Earthquake belt, seismic zone: 太平洋~ the Pacific Earthquake belt || 火山~ volcanic seismic zone

42 板块 [-塊] bǎnkuài (block-plate) <n.> plate (geology): 太平洋~ pacific plate || ~构造 plate tectonics || 非洲~ Africa plate

43 地表 [-] dìbiǎo (Earth-surface) <n.> Earth's surface: ~温度 temperature of the Earth's surface || ~水 surface water || ~河流surface run-off

44 地核 [-] dìhé (Earth-core) <n.> Earth's core

45 地幔 [-] dìmàn (Earth-mantle) <n.> Earth's mantle

46 地壳 [-殼] dìqiào (Earth-crust) <n.> Earth's crust: ~运动 crustal movement || ~下降 the crust descends || ~深处 the depths of the Earth's crust

47 地心 [-] dìxīn (Earth-nucleus) <.n> Earth's core: ~引力 gravity
48 地质 [-質] dìzhì (Earth-texture) <n.> geology: ~构造 geological structure || ~资源 (zīyuán) geological resources

Tips:

1 Taoism and nature (自然, zìrán): There is a line in *Lao Tzu*, 人法 (fǎ, make law from) 地, 地法天, 天法道 (Tao), 道法自然 (nature), which means 'Man takes his law from the Earth, the Earth takes its law from Heaven, Heaven takes its law from the Dao. The law of the Dao is its being what it is.' (translation by James Legge) This being said, 自然 (nature) is the ultimate standard for all rules.
2 太: It means 'highest, greatest, supreme,' for example, 太空 (outer space,) 太阳 (the sun) and 太和殿 (Tàihédiàn, Hall of Supreme Harmony).
3 银河 (yínhé) and 牛奶路 (niúnǎilù): 银河 means 'the Milky Way,' which was mistakenly translated as 牛奶路 (literally 'milk-way') by someone in 1922. "牛奶路," along with "常凯申" (Chiang Kai-shek, 蒋介石,) was another similar mistake in 2008 and became synonymous with 'erroneous translation' in Chinese.
4 寿星 (shòuxīng): It means 'longevity god,' which can otherwise refer to an elderly person whose birthday is being celebrated.
5 月亮: The sun is called 太阳 and the moon is called 太阴 (娘娘) by some people in rural areas. 阴 (yin) and 阳 (yang) are antonyms.
6 赤道 (chìdào): It means 'the equator,' which is south of China. The School of Yin-yang thought the color of the south (火, fire) is 赤 (red,) therefore the equator is called 赤道.

Exercises:

Part I: Answer the following questions in Chinese.

1 请写出地球的构造

2 请写出太阳系的九大行星

3 美国加州位于哪个地震带?

4 请举一个目前无法解释的宇宙奥秘 (àomì, mystique)

5 'The Milky Way Galaxy' 的中文意思是什么? 跟太阳系相比哪个大, 为什么?

Theme 24: Landforms 地貌 (dìmào)

1 大陆 [-陸] dàlù (large-land) <n.> mainland, continent: 欧洲~ The European continent || 中国~ Chinese mainland || 新 ~ new continent

2 陆地 [陸-] lùdì (land-earth) (dry) <n.> land: 一块 ~ a piece of dry land || ~生活 life on land

3 内陆 [-陸] nèilù (inner-land) <n.> inland, interior: ~国家 landlocked country || ~湖 landlocked lake || ~地区 landlocked region

4 山 [-] shān (mountain) <n.> mountain: 一座~ a mountain || 上/下~go to a mountain/ go down a mountain || 大~ large mountain

5 山峰 [-] shānfēng (mountain-peak) <n.> mountain peak: 一座~ a mountain peak || 高高的 ~ tall mountain peak || 最高~ tallest mountain peak

6 高峰 [-] gāofēng (high-peak) <n.> peak, summit: 攀登 (pāndēng) ~ climb a summit || 珠穆朗玛峰是世界最~. Mount Everest is the highest peak in the world.

7 山谷 [-] shān'gǔ (mountain-valley) <n.> mountain valley: 坠 (zhuì) 入~ fall into a valley || 宁静 (níngjìng) 的~ peaceful and tranquil mountain valley

8 山坡 [-] shānpō (mountain-slope) <n.> hillside, mountainside: 小~ small hillside || 滚 (gǔn) 下~ roll down the hillside || 爬上~ climb up the hillside

9 盆地 [-] péndì (basin-Earth) <n.> basin: 一个~ a basin || 变成~ turn into a basin

10 火山 [-] huǒshān (fire-mountain) <n.> volcano: ~爆发 (bàofā) volcano eruption || 活~ active volcano || 死~ dead volcano

11 冰山 [-] bīngshān (ice-mountain) <n.> iceberg: 一座 ~ an iceberg || ~喷发 (pēnfā) volcanic eruption || ~地震 (dìzhèn) volcanic earthquake

12 峡谷 [-] xiágǔ (gorge-valley) <n.> gorge: 大~ Grand Canyon

13 悬崖 [懸-] xuányá (hang-precipice) <n.> cliff: 掉下~ fall off a cliff || 万丈~ massive cliff

14 坡 [-] pō (slope) <n.> slope: 上/下 ~ go uphill/ downhill || 经济滑 (huá) ~ economic downturn

15 平原 [-] píngyuán (flat-plain) <n.> flat, plains: ~地区 flat land || 东部~ eastern plains || 三大~ three large plains

16 高原 [-] gāoyuán (high-plain) <n.> plateau, highland: 黄土~ loess plateau || 青藏 (qīngzàng) ~ Qinghai-Tibetan plants

17 草地 [-] cǎodì (grass-Earth) <n.> grassland, meadow: 青青的~ light green meadows || 一片~ a grassland || 不许踩踏 (cǎità) ~! Keep off the grass!

18 草原 [-] cǎoyuán (grass-plain) <n.> grassland: 一片~ a grassland || 大~ large grassland || ~地区 grassland region

19 沼泽 [-澤] zhǎozé (natural pond-marsh) <n.> marsh, swamp: 一片~ a marsh || ~地区 a marsh region || 大~ a large marsh

20 沙漠 [-] shāmò (sand-desert) <n.> desert: 大~ large dessert || 进~ enter the desert || ~地区 desert region

21 岛 [島] dǎo (island) <n.> island: 小~ small island || 海~ ocean island || ~上 on the island

22 三角洲 [-] sānjiǎozhōu (triangle-islet) <n.> delta: 长江~ Yangtze delta || ~平原 delta flatland

23 岸 [-] àn (bank) <n.> bank, shore: 河~ river bank || 海~ ocean shore || 上~ on the shore
24 滩 [灘] tān (beach) <n.> beach: 沙 ~ beach || 海 ~ ocean beach || 河~ ocean beach
25 海 [-] hǎi (sea) <n.> sea, ocean: ~水 ocean water || 公~ international ocean || 沿~ along the ocean
26 海洋 [-] hǎiyáng (sea-ocean) <n.> sea, ocean: ~资源 ocean resources || ~生物marine organisms || 无边的~ the boundless ocean
27 大海 [-] dàhǎi (big-sea) <n.> ocean: 面向~ face the ocean || 蓝色的~ blue ocean || 在~上航行 go on an ocean voyage
28 海湾 [-灣] hǎiwān (sea-gulf) <n.> bay, gulf: ~地区 bay aera || ~战争 Gulf War (1991) || 深水~ deep ocean bay
29 印度洋 [-] yìndùyáng (Indian-ocean) <n.> Indian Ocean
30 太平洋 [-] tàipíngyáng (great-peaceful-ocean) <n.> Pacific Ocean
31 大西洋 [-] dàxīyáng (big-west-ocean) <n.> Atlantic Ocean
32 北冰洋 [-] běibīngyáng (north-ice-ocean) <n.> Arctic Ocean

33 江 [-] jiāng (big river) <n.> river: ~ 水 river water || ~边 by the river || 过~ cross the river
34 河 [-] hé (river) <n.> river: 一条~ a river || 大~ a big river || 过~ cross the river
35 溪 [-] xī (brook, stream) <n.> stream: 小~ little stream || ~水 stream water
36 湖 [-] hú (lake) <n.> lake: 一个~ a lake || 大~ big lake || ~水 lake water
37 池塘 [-] chítáng (pool-pond) <n.> pond: 小~ a small pond || 大~ a big pond
38 泉 [-] quán (spring) <n.> spring: 山~ mountain spring || 温 ~ warm spring || ~水 spring water
39 喷泉 [噴-] pēnquán (spray-spring) <n.> fountain: 音乐 ~ musical fountain
40 瀑布 [-] pùbù (waterfall-cloth) <n.> waterfall: 世界上最著名的~ the most famous waterfall in the world
41 田 [-] tián (till, farmland, field) <n.> field: 农~ agricultural field || 种~ plant field
42 沟 [溝] gōu (ditch) <n.> ditch, channel: 一条~ a ditch || 水~ water ditch || 地~ drainage/sewer

43 亚洲 [亞-] yàzhōu (*transliteration of A*sia-continent) <n.> Asia
44 非洲 [-] fēizhōu (*transliteration of Afri*ca-continent) <n.> Africa
45 北美洲 [-] běiměizhōu (north-*transliteration of* A*me*rica-continent) <n.> North America
46 南美洲 [-] nánměizhōu (south-*transliteration of* A*me*rica-continent) <n.> South America
47 欧洲 [歐-] ōuzhōu (*transliteration of Eu*rope-continent) <n.> Europe
48 大洋洲 [-] dàyángzhōu (big-ocean-continent) <n.> Oceania
49 南极洲 [-極-] nánjízhōu (south-pole-continent) <n.> the Antarctic Continent

Tips:

1 大陆 (dàlù): It has two meanings. One is 'continent,' and the other is 'Mainland China.'

2 江 and 河: In archaic Chinese, 江 and 河 referred to the Yangtze (Changjiang) and the Yellow River (Huang He), respectively. Later, both were generalized as 'river.'
3 The Chinese translation of some foreign place names: Some earlier translations were influenced by Cantonese, for example, 美利坚 is from the Cantonese pronunciation of 'A*merican*.'
4 *国: Only six foreign countries are called *国 in Chinese. They are 英国 (England, UK,) 法国 (France,) 德国 (Germany,) 俄国 (Russia,) 美国 (America, U.SA.,) 泰国 (Thailand) and 韩国 (S. Korea.) The first five were very influential in China in the 19th century, and the last two names are from their original or native written forms in Chinese.
5 Choice of Chinese characters for foreign place names: To avoid confusion between names of foreign persons or places and Chinese words, Xinhua News Agency, China's state news agency, stipulated that names of foreign persons or places should be rendered with uncommon Chinese characters. For example, annotation of compositional characters of Palestine (巴勒斯坦, Bālèsītǎn) and Ethiopia (埃塞俄比亚, Áisàiébǐyà) is impossible or meaningless.

Exercises:

Part I: Answer the following questions in Chinese.

1 请写出世界上的七大洲

____

2 请写出世界上的四大洋

____

3 请写出世界水存在的形式, 例如: 海、湖 . . . .

____

4 请写出世界上陆地的形式, 例如: 平原、高山 . . . .

____

Theme 25: Meteorology 气象 (qìxiàng)

1 风 [風] fēng (wind) <n.> wind: 热/暖/凉/冷~ hot/warm/cool/cold wind || 北~ north wind || 一阵 (zhèn) ~ a gail of wind || 刮 (guā) ~ blowing wind, be windy
2 微风 [-風] wēifēng (tiny-wind) <n.> mild wind: 一阵~ a gale of mild wind || ~吹拂 (chuīfú) the mild wind has blown
3 台风 [颱風] táifēng (*transliteration of* typhoon) <n.> typhoon: 十级 ~ level 10 typhoon || 刮~ cutting typhoon || 一场~ a typhoon
4 飓风 [颶風] jùfēng (*transliteration of* hurricane) <n.> hurricane: 一阵~ a hurricane || ~天气hurricanes

5 龙卷风 [龍捲風] lóngjuǎnfēng (dragon-twist-wind) <n.> tornado: 刮~ have a tornado || 一股~ a tornado

6 云 [雲] yún (cloud) <n.> cloud: 白~ white cloud || 一朵 ~ a cloud || 多 ~ lots of clouds

7 乌云 [烏雲] wūyún (black-cloud) <n.> black cloud: 一片/块/朵~ a black cloud || ~翻滚 (f(a blacrolling black clouds || ~密布 dense black clouds

8 云层 [雲層] yúncéng (cloud-level) <n.> cloud level: 飞机在 ~上面飞行. The plane flew above the clouds.

9 晚霞 [-] wǎnxiá (evening-colorful cloud) <n.> sunset glow (or clouds): ~预示 (yùshì) 明天又是好天气. The splendid evening clouds means another fine day tomorrow.

10 彩虹 [-] cǎihóng (colorful-rainbow) <n.> rainbow: 一道~ a rainbow || 大雨过后~出现在天空中. A rainbow hung high in the sky after the heavy rain.

11 雨 [-] yǔ (rain) <n.> rain: 下~ rain || 一场~ a rain || 多~. There is lots of rain.

12 小雨 [-] xiǎoyǔ (light-rain) <n.> light rain, drizzle: 一阵~ a shower of light rain || 一场~ a light rain

13 大雨 [-] dàyǔ (heavy-rain) <n.> heavy rain: 一场~ a heavy rain || 下~ rain heavily

14 暴雨 [-] bàoyǔ (storm-rain) <n.> torrential rain, rainstorm: 一场~ a rainstorm || 连日~ torrential rain for days || 下了一阵~. There was a downpour.

15 暴风雨 [-風-] bàofēngyǔ (storm-wind-rain) <n.> rainstorm: 一场~ a rainstorm || ~的天气 rainstorm weather || 遇到~ encounter a rainstorm

16 风暴 [風-] fēngbào (wind-storm) <n.> windstorm: 一场~ a windstorm || 冰~ a wind and ice storm || 热带~ tropical windstorm

17 瓢泼大雨 [-潑--] piáopōdàyǔ (gourd ladle-pour-heavy-rain) <idiom> downpour, heavy rain: 午后下起了 ~. It rained cats and dogs in the afternoon.

18 阵雨 [陣-] zhènyǔ (periodic-rain) <n.> shower (of rain): 今天有~. There are showers today.

19 梅雨 [-] méiyǔ (plum-rain) <n.> monsoon: ~季节 monsoon season

20 雪 [-] xuě (snow) <n.> snow: 下~ falling snow || 大~ large snow || 一场~ a large snow

21 冰雪 [-] bīngxuě (ice-snow) <n.> snow and ice: ~融化 (rónghuà) thawing snow || ~覆盖 (fùgài) snow cover || 高山~ high mountain snow

22 暴风雪 [-風-] bàofēngxuě (storm-wind-snow) <n.> snow storm: 一场~ a snowstorm || 遇到~ encounter a snowstorm || 特大~ an especially large snow storm

23 冰 [-] bīng (ice) <n.> ice: 结 (jié) ~ freeze, ice up || ~块 a piece of ice || ~山 iceberg

24 冰雹 [-] bīngbáo (ice-hail) <n.> hail, hailstone: 一阵~ a hailstorm || 一场~ a hailstorm

25 霜 [-] shuāng (frost) <n.> frost: 一层~ a layer of frost || 秋天的~ autumn frost || 下~ falling frost

26 露 [-] lù (dew) <n.> dew: ~水dew

27 雾 [霧] wù (fog) <n.> fog: 晨 ~ early morning fog || 浓 ~ dense fog

28 雾霾 [霧-] wùmái (fog-haze) <n.> haze, smog: ~天 smoggy day || 严重的~ serious smog || ~ 污染 (wūrǎn) smog pollution

29 闪电 [閃電] shǎndiàn (flash-lightning) <n.> lightning: 一道~ a bolt of lightning || 蓝色的~ blue lightning || 刺目 (cìmù) 的~ dazzling lightning
30 雷 [-] léi (thunder) <n.> thunder: 打~ a thunder clap || ~声 sound of thunder
31 潮水 [-] cháoshuǐ (tide-water) <n.> tidewater, tide: ~上涨 (shàngzhǎng) rising tide
32 潮汐 [-] cháoxī (morning tide-night tide) <n.> morning and evening tide: ~力 force of the tide
33 洪水 [-] hóngshuǐ (flood-water) <n.> flood: 大~ large flood || 发~ a coming flood || 一场~ a flood area

Tips:

1 Super 风 (fēng): The wind (风) is a natural phenomenon. It is suitable to combine风 with words of other natural phenomena and 风 is always in front of other words. For example, 风云 (wind-cloud, stormy or unstable situations,) 风雨 (wind-rain, trials and hardships,) 风霜 (wind-frost, hardships of a journey or in one's life,) 风雪 (wind-snow, snowstorm,) 风雷 (wind-thunder, tempest,) 风浪 (wind-tide, storm) and 风潮 (wind-tide, unrest).
2 风, 云, 雨: They mean wind, cloud and rain, respectively, and their combinations, 风云, 风雨 and 云雨 (cloud-rain, to have sexual intercourse) are words.
3 冰 (bīng,) 霜 (shuāng,) 雪 (xuě): They mean ice, frost and snow, respectively, and their combinations, 冰霜 (to look severely,) 冰雪 (to be pure like ice and snow) and 霜雪 (adversity) are words.
4 Uncertainty of life: Life could be uncertain, so there is a saying in Chinese, 人有悲欢离合 (bēi huān lí hé, sorrow, joy, parting, reunion), 月有阴晴圆缺 (yīn qíng yuán quē, shaded, clear, wax, wane), which means 'the moon does wax, the moon does wane, and so men meet and say goodbye' (translated by Lin Yutang.)
5 梅雨 (méiyǔ): It means 'monsoon,' a rainy season when plums (梅子, méizi) are maturing in Taiwan in May and June and in the lower Yangtze River in June and July.

Exercises:

Part I: Multiple Choice. Make sure to choose the most appropriate answer.

1 下面哪些天气是自然灾害 (zāihài, disaster)
A. 雷、露　　B. 阵雨、小雨　　C. 冰雹、暴风雨
2 下面哪些自然现象只会在海边发生
A. 潮水、潮汐　　B. 梅雨、彩虹　　C. 乌云、晚霞

Part II: Fill in the blank with an appropriate measure word.

阵、道、场、朵 (片)
一________小雨　　一________彩虹　　一________暴雨
一________微风　　一________闪电　　一________云

Part III: Answer the following questions in Chinese.

1 美国东部地区夏季会有什么自然灾害?

2 美国东部地区冬季会有什么自然灾害?

3 美国南部地区会有什么自然灾害?

4 最近几十年北京地区出现过哪些自然灾害?

5 雾霾在哪些世界大城市出现过?

6 中国台湾会出现什么自然灾害?

7 你的家乡出现过什么自然灾害?

Theme 26: Natural substances 自然物质 (zìrán wùzhì)

1 声音 [聲-] shēngyīn (sound-voice) <n.> sound, noise, voice: 熟悉 (shúxī) 的~ familiar voice || 提高~ raise one's voice
2 声 [聲] shēng (sound) <n.> sound: 发~ make a sound || 歌~ sound of a song || 响~ sound
3 大声 [-聲] dàshēng (loud-sound) <bf> large sound, loudly: ~说话 speak loudly || ~唱歌 sing loudly
4 小声 [-聲] xiǎoshēng (small-sound) <n.> small sound, softly: ~聊天 (liáotiān) chat quietly
5 铃声 [鈴聲] língshēng (bell-sound) <n.> the sound of a bell, ringing bell: 电话 ~ the ringing phone || ~响了 the sound of a ringing bell || 一串 (chuàn) ~ the chorus of bells
6 笑声 [-聲] xiàoshēng (laughter-sound) <n.> the sound of laughter: 一阵/片/串~ a wave/burst of laughter || 欢快的~ joyous laughter || 听见~ hear laughter
7 哭声 [-聲] kūshēng (crying-sound) <n.> the sound of crying: 听到~ hear crying || 一阵~ a wave of weeping || ~洪亮 (hóngliàng) loud and clear laughter
8 掌声 [-聲] zhǎngshēng (applause-sound) <n.> the sound of applause: 热烈 (rèliè) 的~ the loud sound of applause || ~响起 growing sound of applause || 一阵~ a burst of applause
9 光 [-] guāng (light, ray) <n.> ray, light: 太阳~ sunlight || 红 ~ ultraviolet || 一束 (shù) ~ a ray of light
10 阳光 [陽-] yángguāng (sun-light) <n.> ray of sunlight: ~充足 abundant sunlight || 温暖的~ warm rays of sunlight || ~ 灿烂 (cànlàn) sunny

11 日光 [-] rìguāng (sun-light) <n.> sunlight: ~不足 insufficient sunlight || 强烈的~ strong sunlight

12 月光 [-] yuèguāng (moon-light) <n.> moonlight: 银色的~ silver moonlight || ~下 under the moonlight

13 灯光 [燈-] dēngguāng (lamp-light) <n.> lamplight: 在~下 under the lamplight || 白色的~ white glow of lamplight

14 光线 [-綫] guāngxiàn (light-ray) <n.> ray of light: 一束~ a ray of light || 太阳~ a ray of sunlight || ~暗 a faint ray of light

15 色 [-] sè (color of face, color) <n.> color: 彩~ colorful || 黄~ yellow || 变~ change colors

16 色彩 [-] sècǎi (color-rich colors) <n.> color: ~鲜艳 (xiānyàn) vibrant colors || ~丰富 (fēngfù) abundant colors || ~单调 (dāndiào) monotonous colors

17 颜色 [顏-] yánsè (color-color) <n.> color: 深/浅~ dark/light black || 各种~ every type of black || 不同的~ different shades of black

18 黑色 [-] hēisè (black-color) <n.> black: ~皮肤 black skin || ~头发 black hair

19 红色 [-] hóngsè (red-color) <n.> red: ~的花 red flower || ~光 red light

20 橙色 [-] chéngsè (orange-color) <n.> orange: ~的桔子 orange tangerine

21 黄色 [黃-] huángsè (yellow-color) <n.> yellow: ~的花 yellow flowers || ~电影blue film

22 绿色 [綠-] lǜsè (green-color) <n.> green: ~的树叶 green tree leaves

23 青色 [-] qīngsè (cyan-color) <n.> light green: ~的大衣light green coat

24 蓝色 [藍-] lánsè (blue-color) <n.> blue: ~星球 blue star

25 紫色 [-] zǐsè (purple-color) <n.> purple: ~的喇叭花 purple morning glory

26 灰色 [-] huīsè (grey-color) <n.> gray: ~汽车 gray car || ~的天空 gray sky

27 粉色 [-] fěnsè (pink-color) <n.> pink: ~的裙子 pink dress || ~花朵 pink flower

28 棕色 [-] zōngsè (brown-color) <n.> brown: ~的眼睛 brown eyes || ~的熊 (xióng) brown bear

29 金色 [-] jīnsè (gold-color) <n.> gold (color): ~沙滩 (shātān) gold sand beach || ~卷发 (juǎnfà) golden curls || ~的阳光 golden rays of light

30 银色 [-] yínsè (silver-color) <n.> silver (color): ~的月光 silver rays of moonlight || ~飞机 silver plane || 涂着~ silver paint

31 气 [氣] qì (cloud, air) <n.> air: 打/充~ pump/inflate with air || 天然~ natural gas

32 空气 [-氣] kōngqì (empty-air) <n.> air: 新鲜~ fresh air || ~潮湿 (cháoshī) moist air || ~污染 polluted air

33 冷气 [-氣] lěngqì (cold-air) <n.> cold air: 冒~ emit cold air || 开~ start the air conditioner || 一股 (gǔ) ~ a burst of cold air

34 暖气 [-氣] nuǎnqì (warm-air) <n.> warm air: 装 (zhuāng) ~ install heating || 有/没有~. There is/isn't heating. || 室内~ interior heating

35 气体 [氣體] qìtǐ (air-substance) <n.> gas: 有害~ harmful gas || 多种 ~ multiple forms of gas || 变成~ turn into gas

36 氧气 [-氣] yǎngqì (oxygen-air) <n.> oxygen (gas): 缺乏 (quēfá) ~ lack oxygen || 吸入~ breath in gas || 需要~ need gas

37 废气 [廢氣] fèiqì (waste-gas) <n.> exhaust, waste gas or steam: 工业~ industrial exhaust || 排出~ emit exhaust || 一股 ~ a burst of exhaust

38 尾气 [-氣] wěiqì (tailpipe-gas) <n.> tailpipe exhaust: 汽车 ~ exhaust from a car's tail pipe || ~污染 tailpipe pollution || ~处理 smog check

39 二氧化碳 [-] èryǎnghuàtàn (two-oxygen – *ized*-carbon) <n.> carbon dioxide (CO2): 产生~ produce CO2 || 呼出~ breath out CO2 || 吸收~ breath in CO2

40 水 [-] shuǐ (water) <n.> water: 冷/热~ cold/hot water || 河/海/湖~ river/ocean/lake water || 喝~ drink water

41 水分 [-] shuǐfèn (water-element) <n.> moisture content: ~充足. The moisture is ample. || ~多 a lot of moisture || 吸收~ absorb in moisture

42 泉水 [-] quánshuǐ (spring-water) <n.> spring water: 一股~ a burst of spring water || 清凉的~ cool and refreshing spring water || 喝~ drink spring water

43 雨水 [-] yǔshuǐ (rain-water) <n.> rain water: 多 ~ lots of rain water || ~充沛 (chōngpèi) plentiful spring water || 缺少~ lack rainwater

44 开水 [開-] kāishuǐ (boiled-water) <n.> boiling water, boiled water: 烧~ boil water || 一杯~ a glass of boiled water

45 污水 [-] wūshuǐ (polluted-water) <n.> polluted water, dirty water: 生活~ domestic sewage || 排出~ emit sewage || ~处理 waste management

46 自来水 [-來-] zìláishuǐ (self-come-water) <n.> tap water: 用~ use tap water || 供应~ supply of tap water || 吃 ~ drink tap water

47 水蒸气 [--氣] shuǐzhēngqì (water-vapor) <n.> vapor, water vapor: ~也是一种气体. Water vapor is also a gas.

48 泡 [-] pào (bubble, foam) <n.> bubble: 气~ air bubble || 水~ water bubble || 吐一个~ saliva bubble

49 海浪 [-] hǎilàng (sea-wave) <n.> ocean wave: 白色的~ white waves || 一个接一个的~ one wave after another

50 波浪 [-] bōlàng (wave-big wave) <n.> wave: ~起伏 rising and falling waves || ~滚滚 (gǔngǔn) rolling waves || 大~ large waves

51 土 [-] tǔ (soil, earth, land) <n.> earth, dust: 一层~ a layer of earth || 挖~ dig earth || 干/湿~ dry/moist earth

52 味道 [-] wèidào (taste-truth) <n.> taste, flavor: 羊肉的~ lamb flavor || 鲜美的~ delicious flavor

53 味儿 [-兒] wèir (taste-*suffix*) <n.> taste, flavor, smell: 有/没有~ has/doesn't have taste || 怪~ strange flavor/smell || 香~ sweet smell

54 脚印 [-] jiǎoyìn (foot-print) <n.> footprint: 一行/串~ a trail of footprints || 大~ large footprints

55 影子 [-] yǐngzǐ (shadow-*suffix*) <n.> shadow: 自己的~ one's own shadow

56 烟 [煙] yān (smoke) <n.> smoke: 冒 (mào) ~ emit smoke || 黑/轻~ black smoke/ light smoke || 一股/缕 (lǚ) ~ a billow/strand of smoke

57 火 [-] huǒ (fire) <n.> fire: 着~ catch on fire || 点/生/灭/救 ~ light/make/extinguish/fight a fire || 一把~ a fire

58 化石 [-] huàshí (fossilized-stone) <n.> fossil: 人类 ~ mankind fossil || 变成 ~ turn into a fossil || 一块~ a piece of fossil

Tips:

1 颜 (yán) and 色 (sè): 颜 is related to 页 (head) and originally meant 'glabella,' an area between the eyebrows and above the nose. The meaning of 颜 was later generalized as 'face' and then 'color.' 色 originally meant 'color of the face' and was later generalized as 'color.'

2 青色 (qīngsè): It means 'cyan' and is a kind of blue (蓝色, lánsè. There a famous Chinese saying 青出于蓝而胜于蓝 (shortened to 青出于蓝 qīngchūyúlán, which literally means '青' is out of '蓝,' to surpass one's master in learning) from *Xunzi*.

Exercises:

Part I: Answer the following questions.

声音、大声、小声、笑声、歌声、哭声、掌声、阳光、月光、灯光、光线

1 读一读上面词, 写出跟"声"有关系的词

____

2 读一读上面词, 写出跟"光"有关系的词

____

水分、泉水、雨水、污水、开水、冷水、空气、自来水、水蒸气、暖气、冷气、氧气、废气、尾气

3 读一读上面词, 写出跟"水"有关系的词

____

4 读一读上面词, 写出跟"光"有关系的词

____

5 写一写你最喜欢的四种颜色

____

Theme 27: Metals 金属 (jīnshǔ)

1 金 [-] jīn (gold) <n.> gold: ~项链 (xiàngliàn) a gold necklace || ~戒指 (jièzhi) a gold ring || ~手链a gold bracelet || ~牌the gold medal
2 黄金 [-] huángjīn (yellow-gold) <n.> gold: 一克~ one gram of gold || ~市场 the gold market
3 银 [銀] yín (silver) <n.> silver: ~牌 the silver medal || ~戒指a silver ring || ~项链a silver necklace
4 铜 [銅] tóng (copper) <n.> copper: ~钱 copper cash || ~牌a copper medal
5 铁 [鐵] tiě (iron) <n.> iron: ~门iron gate || ~饭碗iron rice bowl-secure job || 他俩的关系很~. Their relationship is very strong.
6 钢 [鋼] gāng (steel) <n.> steel: ~刀 steel knife || 不锈~ stainless steel || 炼~ make steel
7 锡 [錫] xī (tin) <n.> tin, stannum (Sn): ~纸tin foil || ~矿tin mine
8 铅 [鉛] qiān (lead) <n.> lead, plumbum (Pb): 含~ contain lead || ~笔pencil || ~粉lead oxide
9 合金 [-] héjīn (compound-metal) <n.> alloy: 铝~ aluminum alloy || 进口~ imported alloy || ~材料alloy material

10 铝 [鋁] lǚ (aluminum) <n.> aluminum (Al): ~膜 (mó) aluminum film || ~锅 (guō) aluminum pan

11 有色金属 [---屬] yǒusèjīnshǔ (color-metal) <n.> non-ferrous metal: ~基地 nonferrous metal base || ~品种Non-ferrous metal varieties

12 稀有金属 [---屬] xīyǒujīnshǔ (rare-metal) <n.> rare metal: ~材料rare metal materials || ~矿石rare metal ore || ~开采rare metal mining

Tips:

1 Radical 钅: 钅 is 金 (jīn, gold) as a radical. Actually the original meaning of 金 is 'metal,' which was narrowed to one of the metals, 'gold.'

2 金银 (jīnyín) vs. 铜铁 (tóngtiě): 金 (gold) and 银 (silver) are naturally rare metals, so this characteristic is also reflected in language. For example, 真金白银 means 'real money.' 铜 (copper) and 铁 (metal) are base metals (贱金属, literally 'cheap-metal,') and there is a word 破铜烂铁 (pòtóng làntiě) which means 'scrap metal.'

3 黄金 (huángjīn): It means '(yellow) gold' and can refer to a dog breed 'golden retriever' among dog owners.

Exercises:

Part I: Answer the following questions.

金、银、铜、铁、钢、铝、铅、合金、有色金属、稀有金属

1 读一读上面词, 写出哪些材料的价格比较贵

______

2 读一读上面词, 写出哪些材料的价格比较便宜

______

Theme 28: Energy 能源 (néngyuán)

1 电 [電] diàn (lightning, electricity) <n.> electricity: 民用~ electricity for civil use || 用~ use electricity || ~吉他electric guitar

2 电力 [電-] diànlì (electricity-power) <n.> electric power, power: ~不足lack of electricity || 需要~ electricity is needed || 节省~ save electricity

3 水电 [-電] shuǐdiàn (hydraulic-power) <n.> hydraulic power generation: ~供应water and electricity supply || ~系统 (xìtǒng) water and electricity systems || ~站hydropower station

4 火电 [-電] huǒdiàn (thermal-power) <n.> thermal power generation: ~系统 thermal power system || ~站hydropower station

5 核电 [-電] hédiàn (nuclear-power) <n.> nuclear power: 发展~ develop nuclear power || ~技术nuclear technology || ~站nuclear power plant

6 石油 [-] shíyóu (rock-oil) <n.> petroleum, oil: ~价格oil prices || ~产量oil production || ~产品petroleum products

7 原油 [-] yuányóu (crude-oil) <n.> crude oil, proto-petroleum: ~产量crude oil production || ~生产crude oil production || 加工 ~ processing crude oil

8 汽油 [-] qìyóu (vapor-oil) <n.> gasoline: 一升~ one liter of gasoline

9 煤 [-] méi (coal) <n.> coal: ~矿 (kuàng) coal mine || 产~ produce coal || 烧~取暖burn coal to keep warm

10 煤气 [-氣] méiqì (coal-gas) <n.> coal gas: 打开~ light the coal gas || ~中毒 (zhòngdú) gas poisoning || 用电取暖比用 ~取暖安全. It is safer to use an electric heater than a gas heater.

11 天然气 [--氣] tiānránqì (natural-gas) <n.> natural gas: 使用~ use natural gas || ~运输natural gas shipping

12 太阳能 [-陽-] tàiyángnéng (solar-energy) <n.> solar energy: 利用~ use solar energy || ~热水器solar water heaters || 储存 (chǔcún) ~ store solar energy

13 风能 [風-] fēngnéng (wind-power) <n.> wind power: ~产业wind energy industry || 以~为动力wind-powered, wind-driven

14 核能 [-] hénéng (nuclear-energy) <n.> nuclear energy: ~武器 (wǔqì) nuclear weapons || ~安全nuclear energy security || ~开发nuclear energy development

15 地热能 [-熱-] dìrè'néng (Earth-heat-energy) <n.> geothermal energy: 利用~ use geothermal energy || ~开发geothermal energy development || ~储量 (chǔliàng) geothermal reserves

16 沼气 [-氣] zhǎoqì (marsh-gas) <n.> marsh gas, methane: 产生~ produce marsh gas || ~池methane tank, digester || ~发电methane power prodiction

Tip:

1 电 (電, diàn): It can mean 'electricity' or 'lightning,' however, 'electricity' was introduced into the language a few thousand years later than 'lightning,' for this reason all uses of 电 in Chinese idioms (a marker of traditional and formal language) mean 'lightning.'

Exercises:

Part I: Answer the following questions.

水电、火电、风能、核能、太阳能、天然气、地热能、沼气、煤气、石油、汽油

1 读一读上面词, 写出哪些能源是绿色能源

____

2 读一读上面词, 写出哪些能源容易污染环境

____

Theme 29: Building materials 建筑材料 (jiànzhù cáiliào)

(See also Theme 35)

1 木头 [-頭] mùtóu (wood-*suffix*) <n.> wood: ~房 wooden house || 一根/块~ a wooden rod/ a piece of wood || ~架子 wooden cupboard
2 木材 [-] mùcái (wood-material) <n.> wood, timber: 上等~ first class lumber || ~加工 lumber processing
3 沙子 [-] shāzi (sand-*suffix*) <n.> sand: 一堆/粒~ a grain of sand || 挖~ dig in the sand

4 石头 [-頭] shítou (stone-*suffix*) <n.> stone, rock: 一块~ a rock || 大/小~ a large/small rock || ~桌子 rock slab
5 大理石 [-] dàlǐshí (Dali, Yunnan-stone) <n.> marble: 白色~ white marble || ~建筑 (jiànzhù) marble building || 开采~ mining marble
6 花岗岩 [-崗-] huāgāngshí (pattern-hard-rock) <n.> granite: 黑色 ~ black granite || ~圆柱 granite column || ~加工 granite processing
7 石灰石 [-] shíhuīshí (lime-stone) <n.> limestone: 天然 ~ natural limestone || 开采 ~ mining limestone

8 泥 [-] ní (mud) <n.> mud: 挖 ~ dig mud || 黄~ yellow mud
9 水泥 [-] shuǐní (hydraulic-mud) <n.> cement: ~大桥 cement bridge || 一堆~ a pile of cement
10 砖 [磚] zhuān (brick) <n.> brick: 一块~ a brick || 红 ~ red brick || 地~ ground tile
11 瓦 [-] wǎ (Earthenware, tile) <n.> tile: 一块~ a tile || ~片 a piece of tile || 琉璃 (liúlí) ~ glazed tile
12 瓷砖 [-磚] cízhuān (ceramic-brick) <n.> ceramic tile: 贴~ tile fixing || 一块~ a piece of tile
13 泡沫 [-] pàomò (bubble-foam) <n.> foam, froth: ~橡胶 (xiàngjiāo) foam rubber || ~灭火 anti-flame foam
14 胶 [膠] jiāo (glue, gum) <n.> glue, rubber: ~棒 rubber rod || 感光~ light sensitive rubber || 涂一层 ~ spread a layer of rubber
15 皮 [-] pí (hide, skin, leather) <n.> skin, leather: ~衣 leather clothes || ~箱 leather box || ~夹克 leather jacket
16 塑料 [-] sùliào (plastic-material) <n.> plastic: ~袋 plastic bag || ~盒 plastic box || ~拖鞋 plastic sandals
17 橡胶 [-膠] xiàngjiāo (oak-rubber) <n.> rubber: ~树rubber tree || ~厂rubber factory || ~手套rubber gloves
18 玻璃 [-] bōli (*derivation* of *binome* 琉璃 liúlí) <n.> glass: 几块~ a few pieces of glass || 彩色~ colored glass || ~杯 glass cup

19 玉 [-] yù (jade) <n.> jade: ~器 jade ware, jade article || ~镯 (zhuó) jade bracelet
20 珍珠 [-] zhēnzhū (treasure-pearl) <n.> pearl: 一颗/串~ a pearl/ a string of pearls || 采集~ collect pearls || ~项链 pearl necklace
21 宝石 [寶-] bǎoshí (precious-stone) <n.> precious stone, gem: 红/蓝~ ruby/ sapphire || 彩色~ colorful gems || 天然/人造~ natural/man-made gems
22 铂金 [鉑-] bójīn (platinum-gold) <n.> platinum: ~项链 platinum necklace || ~戒指 platinum ring

23 钻石 [鑽-] zuànshí (drilling-stone) <n.> diamond: 一颗~ a diamond || ~耳环 diamond earrings || 真~ real diamond

24 水晶 [-] shuǐjīng (clear-crystal) <n.> crystal: ~灯 crystal light || ~鞋 crystal shoes || ~花瓶 crystal flower vase

25 陶瓷 [-] táocí (pottery-ceramic) <n.> pottery and porcelain, ceramics: 彩色~ colored ceramics || 日用~ ceramics of everyday use || ~杯 ceramic cup

Tips:

1 Porcelain capital of China: Several cities claim this title including, Jingdezhen, Jiangxi, Chaozhou, Guangdong, Liling, Hunan and Dehua, Fujian, but most people think it is Jǐngdézhèn (景德镇.)

2 铂金 (bójīn): Chinese people often call it 白金.

3 玻璃 (bōli): It means 'glass.' Recently, it also has meant 'gay' in certain communities.

4 钻石王老五 (zuànshí Wáng Lǎowǔ): It means 'diamond bachelor' and originates from Cantonese.

5 Which is more precious, gold (黄金,) diamond (钻石,) pearl (珍珠) or jade (玉)? For Chinese people, especially those who are rich and well-educated, the answer is 玉 (yù, jade.) They think 玉 has five virtues, many of which are virtues esteemed by Confucius.

Exercises:

Part I: Answer the following questions.

木头、木材、沙子、石头、大理石、水泥、砖、瓦、瓷砖、胶、塑料、橡胶、玻璃
玉、珍珠、宝石、铂金、砖石、水晶、陶瓷、黄金、泡沫

1 读一读上面的词, 写出哪些材料可以用来做首饰 (shǒushì, Jewelry)

2 读一读上面的词, 写出哪些材料可以用来盖房子

3 读一读上面的词, 写出哪些材料可以用来做家具

Theme 30: Machine, tool 机器, 用具 (jīqì, yòngjù)

(See also Theme 32)

1 工具 [-] gōngjù (work-tool) <n.> tool: 基本~ basic tool || 交通~ means of transportation || 重要的~ an important tool

2 机器 [機-] jīqì (machine-appliance) <n.> machine: 发明~ invent machine || ~生产 manufacture machine || 一台新/旧~ a new/old machine

3 机械 [機-] jīxiè (machine-instrument) <n.> machinery: 自动~ automatic machine || 农业~ farm machine || ~设备 (shèbèi) machinery equipment
4 零件 [-] língjiàn (part-item) <n.> parts (of a machine): 飞机~ airplane parts || 自行车~ bicycle parts || 小~ small parts
5 配件 [-] pèijiàn (fitting-item) <n.> parts, replacements: 电脑~ computer parts || 零~ small parts || 汽车~ car parts

6 弹簧 [彈-] tánhuáng (spring-spring coil) <n.> spring: 装~ install a spring || 拉长~ pull a string || ~床 spring bed
7 发条 [發條] fātiáo (motion-coil) <n.> coil string: 给表上~ wind up a watch
8 螺丝刀 [-絲-] luósīdāo (screw-knife/driver) <n.> screwdriver: 一把~ one screwdriver || 电动 ~ motor screwdriver || 大号~ large screwdriver

9 发动机 [發動機] fādòngjī (start-machine) <n.> engine, motor: 新型~ new type of engine || 汽车~ car engine
10 引擎 [-] yǐnqíng (*transliteration of* engine) <n.> engine: 发动 ~ start an engine || 汽车/飞机 ~ car engine, plane engine || 蒸汽/喷气~ steam engine
11 蒸汽机 [--機] zhēngqìjī (steam-vapor-engine) <n.> steam engine: 发明~ invent steam engine || 老式~ old-styled steam engine
12 马达 [馬達] mǎdá (*transliteration of* motor) (electric) <n.> motor: 启动 ~ start a motor || 微型~ miniature motor

13 熔炉 [-爐] rónglú (smelt-furnace) <n.> smelting furnace: 一座~ a smelting furnace || 美国是个大~. The U.S. is a big melting pot.
14 挖土机 [--機] wātǔjī (dig-soil-machine) <n.> excavator: 一辆/台~ an excavator
15 推土机 [--機] tuītǔjī (push-soil-machine) <n.> bulldozer: 一辆 / 台~ a bulldozer
16 铲车 [鏟車] chǎnchē (forklift-truck) <n.> forklift truck: 一辆 / 台~ a forklift truck
17 起重机 [--機] qǐzhòngjī (lift-heavy-machine) <n.> hoist/crane: 重型~ heavy-duty crane || 电动~ electric crane || 一台~ a crane
18 升降机 [--機] shēngjiàngjī (lift-drop-machine) <n.> lift: 安全~ safety lift || 载 (zài) 人~ manned lift || 自动 ~ automatic lift
19 电梯 [電-] diàntī (electric-ladder) <n.> elevator: 三部~ three elevators || 自动~ automatic elevators || 坐/乘 (chéng) ~ take an elevator

20 滑轮 [-輪] huálún (glide-wheel) <n.> pulley, block: 装~ install pulley
21 千斤顶 [--頂] qiānjīndǐng (thousand-*jin*-jack) <n.> hoisting jack: 液压 (yèyā) ~ hydraulic pressure hoisting jack || 充气 ~ inflate hoisting jack || 一台~ one hoisting jack
22 机器人 [機--] jīqìrén (mechanical-man) <n.> robot: 一个/台~ one robot || 安装~ install/fix a robot || 家务~ household robots

Tip:

1 Importance of 工具 (tool): There is a very famous Chinese saying which emphasizes the importance of tools. It is 工欲善其事, 必先利其器 (gōng yù shàn qí shì, bì xiān lì qí qì, or 'if a worker wants to do a good job, he must first sharpen his tools. Good tools are a prerequisite to success.')

Exercises:

I: Translate the following sentences into English.

1 "美国是个大熔炉," 意思是说美国是一个多元文化国家.

2 英国是世界上第一个使用蒸汽机的国家.

3 很多重型机械, 例如挖土机、铲车、起重机等等都是中国生产的.

4 德国制造机器人的技术很先进.

5 日本的汽车发动机质量很好.

Theme 31: Tools for outdoor work or leisure activities 其他工具 (qítā gōngjù)

1 五金 [-] wǔjīn (five-metal) <n> hardware: ~工具 hardware tools || ~零件 hardware components || ~ 商店 hardware store
2 农具 [農-] nóngjù (farm-tool) <n> farm tools: 铁制 (Tiě zhì) ~ iron tools || 播种 (Bōzhòng) ~ sewing tools || 新~ new tools
3 锄 [鋤] chú (hoe) <n.> hoe: 短~ short hoe || 一把~ a hoe
4 犁 [-] lí (plow) <n.> plow: 拉~ pull plow || 一张~ a plow
5 磨 [-] mò (mill) <n.> mill, millstone: 水 ~ water mill || 推~ turn a millstone
6 拖拉机 [--機] tuōlājī (hall-drag-machine) <n.> tractor: 一辆 ~ one tractor (measure word) || 开 ~ operate tractor
7 水泵 [-] shuǐbèng (water-pump) <n.> water pump: 农用 ~ agricultural use for water pump
8 鱼竿 [魚-] yúgān (fishing-pole) <n.> fishing rod: 一根~ (*Gēn) one fishing rod (measure word) || 伸缩 ~ telescopic fishing rods
9 鱼钩 [魚鈎] yúgōu (fishing-hook) <n.> hooks (for fishing): 吞 (Tūn) ~ swallow hook || 大号 ~ big size hook
10 鱼线 [魚綫] yúxiàn (fishing-line) <n.> fishing line: 一根 ~ one fishing line (measure word)
11 渔网 [漁網] yúwǎng (fishing-net) <n.> fishing net: 一张 ~ one fishing net (measure word) || 撒 ~ (Sā) spread net
12 网 [網] wǎng (net, web) <n.> net: 蜘蛛~ (Zhīzhū) spiderweb || 渔 ~ fishing net || 一张 ~ one net (measure word)
13 蜂箱 [-] fēngxiāng (bee-box) <n.> beehive: 整理~ tidy up beehive
14 猎枪 [獵槍] lièqiāng (hunting-gun) <n.> shotgun: 举起~ lift shotgun || 背 (bēi) 着~ carrying a shotgun || 一把~ a shotgun

15 刀 [-] dāo (knife) <n.> knife: 一把 ~ one knife (measure word) || 铅笔 ~ (Qiānbǐ) pencil knife || 短/长 ~ short/long knife
16 剪刀 [-] jiǎndāo (cut-knife) <n.> scissors: 一把 ~ one scissor set (measure word) || 大/小 ~ big/small scissors
17 模型 [-] móxíng (model-mold) <n.> model: 楼房 ~ building model || 飞船 ~ spaceship model || 汽车 ~ car model
18 型 [-] xíng (mold, model, type) <n.> type, model: 球 ~ ball/sphere model || 拱 (Gǒng) ~ arch model || 环 (Huán) ~ ring/loop model

Tips:

1 五金 (wǔjīn): It originally meant five metals, i. e., 金 (jīn, gold,) 银 (yín, silver,) 铜 (tóng, copper,) 铁 (tiě, iron) and 锡 (xī, tin.) It was later generalized as 'metal.'
2 剪刀手 (jiǎndāoshǒu): It is a V-sign widely adopted by Asian girls when they take pictures.
3 鱼线 (yúxiàn) vs. 渔网 (yúwǎng): They mean 'fishing line' and 'fishing net' respectively. Both are for fishing, however, the first one is represented by 鱼 (fish) and the second one by 渔 (fishing.)

Exercises:

Part I: Answer the following questions in Chinese.

1 请写出几种以前农村使用的农具

____

2 请写出几种钓鱼使用的东西

____

3 请写出几种打猎使用的东西

____

Theme 32: Apparatus, equipment 仪表, 器械 (yíbiǎo, qìxiè)

(See also Theme 30)

1 仪表 [儀錶] yíbiǎo (apparatus-meter) <n.> meter: 电子 ~ electric meter || 精密 (jīngmì) ~ precision meter
2 水表 [-] shuǐbiǎo (water-meter) <n.> water meter: 安装 ~ install the water meter || 总 ~ general water meter
3 电表 [電-] diànbiǎo (electricity-meter) <n.> electricity meter: 万用 ~ multi-meter || 计费 ~ billing meter
4 温度计 [溫-計] wēndùjì (temperature-meter) <n.> thermometer: 华氏~ Fahrenheit thermometer || 摄氏~ Celsius thermometer || 一支 ~ a thermometer
5 里程表 [-] lǐchéngbiǎo (mileage-meter) <n.> odometer: 汽车~ car odometer

6 罗盘 [羅盤] luópán (gong-plate) <n> compass: 发明~ invent the compass || 磁 (cí) 力~ magnetic compass

7 指南针 [--針] zhǐnánzhēn (point-south-needle) <n.> compass: 航海 ~ sea voyage compass || 新型 ~ new compass

8 雷达 [-達] léidá (*transliteration of* radar) <n.> radar: 激光 (jīguāng) ~ laser radar || 地面 ~ ground radar

9 挂钟 [掛鐘] guàzhōng (hang-clock) <n.> hanging clock: 新式~ new clock || 石英~ quartz clock

10 电话 [電話] diànhuà (electric-talk) <n.> phone: 一部~ one phone || 打~ make a call || 接 ~ take a call

11 手机 [-機] shǒujī (hand-phone) <n.> cellphone: 智能 (zhìnéng) ~ smartphone || 一部~ one phone || ~号码phone number

12 投影机 [--機] tóuyǐngjī (project-shadow-machine) <n.> projector: 使用~ use a projector || 大屏幕 (píngmù) ~ a big screen projector

13 话筒 [話-] huàtǒng (phone-tube) <n.> microphone: 放下~ put the microphone down || 拿起~ get the microphone

14 充电器 [-電-] chōngdiànqì (charge-electricity-appliance) <n.> charger: 快速~ fast charger || 太阳能~ solar power charger || 手机~ cell phone charger

15 按钮 [-鈕] ànniǔ (push-button) <noun> button: 按下~ push the button || 电源 (diànyuán) ~ power button

16 插头 [-頭] chātóu (plug-head) <noun> plug: 插上~ plug in || 拔下 ~ unplug

17 插座 [-] chāzuò (plug-socket) <noun> socket: 标准 ~ standard socket || 安装~ install the socket

18 尺 [-] chǐ (⅓ m, ruler) <n.> ruler: 一把~ one ruler || 三角~ triangle ruler || 电子~ electric ruler

19 尺子 [-] chǐzi (ruler-*suffix*) <n.> ruler: 一把~ one ruler

20 秤 [-] chèng (scale) <n.> scale: 电子~ electronic scale || 弹簧 (tánhuáng) ~ spring scale

21 天平 [-] tiānpíng <n.> balance scale: 一架~ one balancing scale

22 针 [針] zhēn (needle) <n.> needle: 打~ get a shot || 指南~ compass

23 手术刀 [-術-] shǒushùdāo (operation-knife) <n.> scalpel: 一把 ~ one scalpel || 激光 ~ laser scalpel

24 听诊器 [聽診-] tīngzhěnqì (listen-diagnose-apparatus) <n.> stethoscope: 挂上~ hang the stethoscope

25 防毒面具 [-] fángdúmiànjù (prevent-poison-mask) <n.> gas mask: 戴~ wear a gas mask

26 试管 [試-] shìguǎn (test-tube) <n.> test tube: 空~ empty test tube || 洗~ wash test tube

27 血压计 [-壓計] xuèyājì (blood-pressure-meter) <n.> blood pressure meter: 电子 ~ electric blood pressure meter

28 体温计 [體溫計] tǐwēnjì (body-temperature-meter) <n.> body temperature monitor: 电子~ electric thermometer || 一支 ~ one thermometer

Tips:

1 天平 vs. 秤 (chèng): Both mean 'scale,' but 秤 is conventional and 天平 borrowed probably from Japanese. Actually the two compositional characters,

天 and 平 perfectly reflect the meaning of scales, 'equal (ity)' and 'fair,' since 天 means 'utmost' and 平 'level, equal, fair, just.'

2 Compass and 指南针 (zhǐnánzhēn): The needle of a compass should point to the north, but the Chinese word "指南针" indicates the direction is south. An earlier form and name of the Chinese compass was called 司南 (sīnán), which 司 means 'point, take charge of.'

Exercises:

Part I: Read the following words and then answer the questions in Chinese.

手术刀、听诊器、血压计、体温计、天平、尺子、称、电源按钮、插头、插座、充电器、投影机、智能手机、电话、指南针、雷达、挂钟、温度计、水表、电表、汽车里程表

1 上面这些物品哪些是你家里有的东西?

2 上面这些物品哪些是在医院里可以看到的?

3 那种东西在汽车里可以看到?

4 那些东西会在学校看到?

Theme 33: Means of transportation 交通工具 (jiāotōng gōngjù)

(See also Themes 37, 157)

1 车 [車] chē (vehicle, car) <n.> car, vehicle: 一辆新~ a new car || 上/下~ get in and out of the car || 开~ drive a car

2 车辆 [車輛] chēliàng (cart-*measure word* for carts) <n.> vehicles: 来往~ vehicles shuttling to and fro || 大批~ large number of vehicles || 各种 ~ different vehicles

3 机动车 [motor vehicle] jīdòngchē <n.> motor vehicle: 大型~ large motor vehicle || 非~ non-motor vehicle || ~车道motor lane

4 飞机 [飛機] fēijī (flying-machine) <n.> plane: 七架~ seven planes || 坐~ by plane || 上/下~ get on and off a plane

5 直升机 [-升機] zhíshēngjī (vertical-lift-plane) <n.> helicopter: 一架~ get on helicopter || 乘 (chéng) ~ take helicopter || 驾驶 (jiàshǐ) ~ drive helicopter

6 火车 [-車] huǒchē (fire-car) <n.> train: 一列~ one train || 坐/乘 ~ ride/take train || 开~ drive train

7 轻轨 [輕軌] qīngguǐ (light-rail) <n.> light rail: 乘~ take the light rail || ~线路 light rail line

8 公共汽车 [---車] gōnggòngqìchē (public-car) <n.> bus: 坐/乘~ take the bus || 三辆~ three buses

9 公交车 [--車] gōngjiāochē (public-transportation-car) <n.> public transport vehicle, town bus: 三十五路 ~ no.35 bus

10 巴士 [-] bāshì (*transliteration* of bus) <n.> bus: ~站bus stop

11 大巴 [-] dàbā (big-bus) <n.> a big bus, tourist bus: 豪华 (háohuá) ~ luxury tourist bus

12 中巴 [-] zhōngbā (medium-bus) <n.> medium- sized bus, van: 一辆~ a van,~车van

13 小巴 [-] xiǎobā (mini-bus) <n.> minibus: 一辆~ a minibus

14 出租车 [--車] chē (rent-car) <n.> taxi: 一辆~ one taxi || 叫~ call taxi || 坐~ take taxi

15 的士 [-] dīshì (*transliteration* of taxi) <n.> taxi: 坐~ take a taxi

16 电车 [電車] diànchē (electric-car) <n.> tram: 一辆~ one tram || 坐~ take a tram || 有轨/无轨 (guǐ) ~ tramcar/trolleybus

17 客车 [-車] kèchē (passenger-bus) <n.> coach bus: 一辆~ one coach bus || 长途 ~ long distance coach bus || 乘坐~ take a coach bus

18 快车 [-車] kuàichē (fast-bus/train) <n.> express train: 直达~ direct express train || 坐~ take express train || 一列~ one express train

19 慢车 [-車] mànchē (slow-bus/train) <n.> slow train: 坐~ take slow train || 搭乘 (dāchéng) ~ ride slow train || ~道 slow train lane

20 汽车 [-車] qìchē (vapor-car) <n.> automobile, car: 三辆~ three automobiles || 坐/开~ take a car/ drive a car

21 电动车 [電動車] diàndòngchē (electricity-moved-car) <n.> electric car, electric bicycle: 一辆~ one electric car || 骑~ ride an electric bike

22 轿车 [轎車] jiàochē (sedan-car) <n.> sedan car: 一辆~ one sedan car || 小~ compact sedan car

23 吉普车 [--車] jípǔchē (*transliteration* of jeep-car) <n.> jeep: 军用 ~ military jeep || 一辆 ~ one jeep || 开 / 坐~ drive a jeep/ take a jeep

24 跑车 [-車] pǎochē (run-car) <n.> sports car: 一辆~ one sports car || 红色的 ~ red sports car || 开 ~ drive sports car

25 轮子 [輪-] lúnzi (wheel-*suffix*) <n.> wheel: 车~ car wheel || 铁 (tiě) ~ steel wheel

26 摩托 [-] mótuō (*transliteration* of motor) <n.> motorcycle: 骑/坐~ drive motorcycle/ ride motorcycle || 一辆~ one motorcycle || ~车 a motorcycle

27 三轮车 [-輪車] sānlúnchē (three-wheel-cart) <n.> tricycle: 一辆~ a tricycle || 坐~ take tricycle

28 马车 [馬車] mǎchē (horse-cart) <n.> carriage: 坐~ take a carriage || 一辆~ a carriage

29 自行车 [--車] zìxíngchē (self-go-vehicle) <n.> bike: 一辆~ a bike || 骑~ ride the bike

30 单车 [單車] dānchē (single-vehicle) <n.> bicycle: 骑~ ride bicycle

31 船 [-] chuán (boat, ship) <n.> boat: 一条~ one boat || 坐~ ride boat || 大/小~ big boat /small boat

32 船只 [-隻] chuánzhī (ship-*measure word* for boats) <n.> vessels, shipping: 往来~ shipping traffic || 载货~ carrying vessels || ~失事 shipwreck
33 轮船 [輪-] lúnchuán (wheel-boat) <n.> steamship, steamboat: 坐~ take a steamer || 一艘 (sōu) ~ a steamer || 远洋~ ocean liner
34 游艇 [-] yóutǐng (tour-boat) <n.> yacht: 一艘~ a yacht || 豪华~ luxury boat
35 排 [-] pái (raft) <n.> row stick: 竹~ bamboo row stick || 木~ wood row stick
36 飞船 [飛-] fēichuán (fly-boat) <n.> spacecraft: 一艘~ a spacecraft || 载人~ manned spacecraft || 宇宙 (yǔzhòu) ~ spaceship

Tips:

1 车 (車, chē): The traditional form and especially the oracle form are vivid depictions of a vehicle.
2 舟 (zhōu) vs. 船 (chuán): Both mean 'boat,' but 船 has been more commonly used since the Han dynasty. 舟 is more archaic and preserved in idioms such as 破釜沉舟 (pòfǔ chénzhōu, 'break the pots and sink the boats, burn one's bridges,') 同舟共济 (tóngzhōu gòngjì, cross the river together in the same boat, overcome difficulties together) and 刻舟求剑 (kèzhōu qiújiàn, to inscribe boat for sword, to act foolishly without regard to changed circumstances).

Exercises:

Part I: Answer the following questions in Chinese.

1 请写出几种陆地上的公共交通工具

2 请写出几种私人交通工具 (private vehicles)

3 请写出几种空中的交通工具

4 请写出几种水中的交通工具

5 请写出几种人力交通工具 (man-powered vehicle)

Theme 34: Weaponry 武器 (wǔqì)

(See also Theme 71)

1 军备 [軍備] jūnbèi (military-equipment) <n.> arms: ~竞赛 (jìngsài) arms race || 扩充~ expand arms
2 武器 [-] wǔqì (military-hardware) <n.> weapon: 一个/件~ a weapon || 放下~ put down weapon || 新式~ new weapon

3 常规武器 [-規--] chángguīwǔqì (conventional-weapon) <n.> Conventional Weapons: 削減 (xuējiǎn) ~ lighten weapon || 现代化~ modern weapon

4 核武器 [-] héwǔqì (nuclear-weapon) <n.> nuclear weapons: 新型 ~ new nuclear weapons || 制造 ~ manufacture nuclear weapons

5 大规模杀伤性武器 [-規-殺傷---] dàguīmóshāshāngxìngwǔqì (large-scale-killing-weapon) <n.> weapon of mass destruction (WMD): 扩散 (kuòsàn) ~ defuse WMD || 销毁 (xiāohuǐ) ~ destroy WMD || 使用 ~ use WMD

6 生化武器 [-] shēnghuàwǔqì (biochemical-weapon) <n.> biochemical weapon: 研制 (yánzhì) ~ develop biochemical weapon || 反 ~ counter biochemical weapon

7 激光武器 [-] jīguāngwǔqì (laser-weapon) <n.> laser weapons: 新型 ~ new laser weapons || 发展~ development of laser weapons || 太空~ space laser weapons

8 刀 [-] dāo (knife) <n.> knife: 一把~ one knife || 尖~ sharp knife

9 匕首 [-] bǐshǒu (ladle-handle) <n.> dagger: 一把 ~ one dagger || 拔 (bá) 出~ pull out a dagger || 锋利 (fēnglì) 的 ~ a sharp dagger

10 剑 [劍] jiàn (sword) <n.> sword: 一把~ one sword || 拔 (bá) ~ pull out a sword || 舞~ sword dancing

11 枪 [槍] qiāng (spear, gun, rifle, firearms) <n.> gun: 一把/支~ one gun || 手~ handgun || 放~ fire a gun

12 火枪 [-槍] huǒqiāng (powder-firearms) <n.> firearms: 端 (duān) 着~ carrying firearms

13 步枪 [-槍] bùqiāng (infantryman-rifle) <n.> rifle: 自动~ auto rifle

14 气枪 [氣槍] qìqiāng (air-rifle) <n.> airsoft: 玩具~ toy airsoft

15 机关枪 [機關槍] jīguānqiāng (trigger-gun) <n.> machine gun: 轻 ~ light machine gun || 重 ~ heavy machine gun

16 炮 [-] pào (cannon) <n.> big gun, cannon: 大~ big cannon || 向敌人开~ fire at the enemy

17 高射炮 [-] gāoshèpào (high-shoot-artillery) <n.> anti-aircraft: 一门~ one anti-aircraft || 轻型 ~ light anti-aircraft

18 弹药 [彈藥] dànyào (bullet-gunpowder) <n.> ammo: 装~ loaded ammo || 补充 ~ supplementary ammo || 一批~ a number of ammo

19 炸弹 [-彈] zhàdàn (explosive-bomb) <n.> bomb: 扔~ throw a bomb || ~爆炸 (bàozhà) bomb explosion

20 炸药 [-藥] zhàyào (explosive-gunpowder) <n.> explosive (material): 两包~ two packs of explosives || 装~ load explosive || 新式~ new explosive

21 子弹 [-彈] zǐdàn (small-bullet) <n.> bullets: 六颗/发~ six bullets || 装满 ~ loaded with bullets || 挡 (dǎng) 住~ block bullets

22 炮弹 [-彈] pàodàn (cannon-shell) <n.> artillery shell: 一颗/发~ one shell || 发射~ fire shell

23 手榴弹 [--彈] shǒuliúdàn (hand-throw-grenade) <n.> hand grenade: 一颗/枚 (méi) ~ one hand grenade || 扔 ~ throw a grenade

24 催泪弹 [-淚彈] cūilèidàn (expel-tear-bomb) <n.> tear gas: 一颗/枚~ one tear gas || 施放 (shīfàng) ~ cast tear gas

25 毒气弹 [-氣彈] dúqìdàn (poisonous-gas-bomb) <n.> poison gas bomb: 一颗/枚~ one gas bomb || 放 ~ fire gas bombs

26 信号弹 [-號彈] xìnhàodàn (signal-bomb) <n.> signal flare: 一颗/枚~ one signal flare || 红色 ~ red signal flare || 求救 (qiújiù) ~ help signal flare
27 照明弹 [--彈] zhàomíngdàn (flash-bomb) <n.> flash bomb: 一颗/枚~ one flash bomb || 发射 (fāshè) ~ launch flash bomb
28 烟雾弹 [煙霧彈] yānwùdàn (smoke-bomb) <n.> smoke bomb: 一颗/枚~ one smoke bomb || 放 ~ drop smoke bomb
29 地雷 [-] dìléi (land-mine) <n.> landmines: 一颗~ one landmine || 埋 (mái) ~ buried landmine || 挖 (wā) ~ dig landmine
30 鱼雷 [-] yúléi (fish-mine) <n.> torpedo: 一枚~ one torpedo || 发射 ~ launch torpedo
31 燃烧弹 [-燒彈] ránshāodàn (burn-bomb) <n.> fire bomb: 一枚 ~ one fire bomb || 发射 ~ launch fire bomb

32 导弹 [導彈] dǎodàn (guided-missile) <n.> missile: 弹道 (dàndào) ~ trajectory missile || 巡航 (xúnháng) ~ cruise missile || 洲际 (zhōujì) ~ intercontinental missile
33 原子弹 [--彈] yuánzǐdàn (atomic-bomb) <n.> atomic bomb: 一颗~ one atomic bomb || 投 (tóu) ~ cast atomic bomb || 制造 ~ manufacturing atomic bomb
34 氢弹 [氫彈] qīngdàn (hydrogen-bomb) <n.> hydrogen bomb: 一枚/颗~ one hydrogen bomb || ~爆炸exploding hydrogen bomb
35 核弹 [-彈] hédàn (nuclear-bomb) <n.> nuclear bomb: 一颗/枚 ~ one nuclear bomb || ~爆炸exploding nuclear bomb

36 坦克 [-] tǎnkè (*transliteration* of tank) <n.> tank: 一辆~ one tank || 轻型 ~ light tank
37 装甲车 [裝-車] zhuāngjiǎchē (armored-car) <n.> armored car: 一辆~ one armored car
38 飞机 [飛機] fēijī (flying-machine) <n.> plane: 一架~ one plane || 私人~ private jet
39 战斗机 [戰鬥機] zhànd òujī (fight-plane) <n.> fighter jet: 一架~ one fighter jet || 现代 ~ modern fighter jet || 军用 ~ military fighter jet
40 轰炸机 [轟-機] hōngzhàjī (bomb-plane) <n.> bomber: 一架 ~ one bomber || 轻型 ~ light bomber
41 运输机 [運輸機] yùnshūjī (transport-place) <n.> transport plane: 一架~ one transport plane || 水上~ amphibious transport plane || 军用~ military transport plane
42 侦察机 [偵-機] zhēnchájī (reconnoitre-plane) <n.> reconnaissance airplane: 一架~ one reconnaissance airplane
43 舰艇 [艦-] jiàntǐng (warship-barge) <n.> warship, naval vessel: 一艘~ one warship || 水下~ underwater warship
44 军舰 [軍艦] jūnjiàn (military-warship) <n.> warship, military naval vessel
45 航空母舰 [---艦] hángkōngmǔjiàn (aviation-home-warship) <n.> aircraft carrier
46 巡洋舰 [--艦] xúnyángjiàn (cruise-ocean-warship) <n.> cruiser
47 潜艇 [潛-] qiántǐng (hidden-barge) <n.> submarine: 核~ nuclear-powered submarine

48 矛 [-] máo (spear) <n.> spear: 一支~ one spear || 长~ long spear
49 盾 [-] dùn (shield) <n.> shield: ~形shield shape || 木~ wooden shield

50 弓 [-] gōng (bow) <n.> bow: 一把~ one bow || 拉~ pull bow
51 箭 [-] jiàn (arrow) <n.> arrow: 一支~ one arrow || 放/射 ~ shoot arrow

Tips:

1 武 (wǔ): It is composed of two parts, 止 (zhǐ) and 戈 (gē, dagger-axe.) Some anti-war scholars explain the purpose of 武 is to stop (止) a war (戈,) however, the original meaning of 止 is 'foot.' Therefore, the original meaning of 武 is 'a soldier marches (止) with his weapon (戈),' in other words, he is 'valiant.'
2 弹 (dàn): It is related to 弓 (bow.) Before modern explosive bullets or cannon shells were invented, 弹 meant '(small) bullet,' so is there an idiom that says "弹丸之地" (dànwánzhīdì, a tiny area.)

Exercises:

Part I: Answer the following questions in Chinese.

1 请写出三种古代时候人们使用的武器

2 请写出五种海上使用的现代武器

3 请写出五种"枪"

4 炸弹和原子弹哪一个危害 (wēihài, harm) 更大?

5 你赞成朝鲜 (N. Korea) 的洲际导弹 (intercontinental ballistic missle)实验吗? 为什么?

6 常规武器和核武器哪一种危害大?

7 你们国家有没有生化武器? 你觉得是否应该禁止 (jìnzhǐ, prohibit) 使用这种武器? 为什么?

Theme 35: Architecture 建筑 (jiànzhù)

(See also Theme 33)

1 建筑 [-築] jiànzhù (establish-ram Earth) <n.> building, architecture: 古代~ ancient architecture || 民用~ civil architecture
2 房间 [-間] fángjiān (room-space) <n.> room: 五个~ five rooms || 小/大~ small/large room || 走进~ enter the room

3 房屋 [-] fángwū (room-house) <n.> house: 一栋 (dòng) /座/幢~ a house || 公共/私有~ public/private housing || 修建~ repairing a house

4 房子 [-] fángzi (room-*suffix*) <n.> house: 两间/栋~ two homes || 新/旧~ new/old house || 买/租~ buy/rent a house

5 住房 [-] zhùfáng (stay-house) <n.> housing: 一间/套~ a house || 临时 (línshí) ~ temporary housing || ~宽敞 (kuānchang) spacious housing

6 民居 [-] mínjū (people-dwell) <n.> local-style dwellings, folk house: 南方~ southern folk house || 传统~ traditional dwellings

7 住宅 [-] zhùzhái (stay-residence) <n.> residence, dwelling: 一座/幢/间~ a residence || 私人~ private residence || ~区 residential quarters

8 楼房 [樓-] lóufáng (building-house) <n.> a building with two or more stories: 一幢~ one building with two or more stories || 小~ a small two story building || 新 ~ a new building with two or more floors

9 写字楼 [寫-樓] xiězìlóu (write-character-building) <n.> office building: 一座/幢~ one office building || 租~ rent an office building || 高档 (gāodàng) ~ high grade office building

10 公寓 [-] gōngyù (public-residence) <n.> apartment: 一套~ one apartment || 住~ live in an apartment || 出租 ~ rent out an apartment

11 别墅 [別-] biéshù (another-villa) <n.> villa: 一栋/幢~ one villa || 私家~ a private villa

12 教室 [-] jiàoshì (teach-room) <n.> classroom: 阶梯 (jiētī) ~ terrace classroom || 走进~ enter a classroom || 大/小~ large/small classroom

13 教学楼 [-學樓] jiàoxuélóu (teach-learn-building) <n.> teaching building: 一座~ a teaching building || 新~ a new teaching building

14 剧场 [劇場] jùchǎng (play-field) <n.> theater: 一座~ a theater || 进入~ enter a theater || 露天~ open air/ outdoor theater

15 歌剧院 [-劇-] gējùyuàn (sing-play-courtyard) <n.> opera house: 悉尼~ Sydney Opera House || 中央~ center opera house

16 博物馆 [--館] bówùguǎn (plentiful-thing-house) <n.> museum: 科学~ science museum || 历史~ history museum || 航空~ aeronautics museum

17 美术馆 [-術館] měishùguǎn (art-house) <n.> art museum: 国际~ international art museum || 当代~ contemporary art museum

18 展览馆 [-覽館] zhǎnlǎnguǎn (exhibit-house) <n.> exhibition (center): 音乐~ music exhibition || 农业~ farming exhibit

19 画廊 [畫-] huàláng (painting-corridor) <n.> gallery: 开~ open gallery || 艺术~ art gallery || 一家~ a gallery

20 实验室 [實驗-] shíyànshì (experiment-room) <n.> laboratory: 一间~ a laboratory || 化学~ chemistry lab

21 室 [-] shì (room) <n.> room: 指挥~ command room || 经理~ management room

22 图书馆 [圖書館] túshūguǎn (book-house) <n.> library: 一座~ a library || 去~ go to the library || 公共~ public library

23 阅览室 [閱覽-] yuèlǎnshì (read-room) <n.> reading room: 两间/个 ~ two reading rooms || 报刊~ newspaper reading room

24 屋子 [-] wūzi (house-*suffix*) <n.> room: 三间~ three bedroom || 大/小/空~ large/small/empty room || 走进~ enter the room

25 洗手间 [--間] xǐshǒujiān (wash-hand-space) <n.> bathroom: 男/女~ men/women restroom || 上/去~ go to the bathroom

26 院 [-] yuàn (courtyard) <n.> yard, courtyard: 前/后~ front/backyard || 东/西~ east/west yard
27 院子 [-] yuànzi (courtyard-*suffix*) <n.> courtyard: 两个~ two yards || 露天~ open air yard
28 车库 [車庫] chēkù (vehicle-warehouse) <n.> garage: 地下~ underground garage || 多层~ multileveled garage
29 病房 [-] bìngfáng (ill-room) <n.> sickroom: 一间~ a sickroom || 外科~ surgery sickroom || 走进~ enter the sickroom
30 仓库 [倉庫] cāngkù (grainery-warehouse) <n.> warehouse: 一间~ a warehouse || 食品~ foodstuff warehouse || 棉花~ cotton warehouse
31 楼 [樓] lóu (building) <n.> a building with two or more stories, floor: 上/下~ go up/downstairs || 六~ sixth floor
32 大楼 [-樓] dàlóu (large-building) <n.> multi-storied building: 一栋/幢/座~ one multistoried building || 三层/整层~ three floored building/ entire floor || 办公/宿舍/教学~ office/dorm/teaching multistoried building
33 宿舍 [-] sùshè (lodge-house) <n.> hostel, living quarters, dormitory: 集体 ~ dormitory || 学生~ students' hostel (or dormitory) || 职工~ living quarters for staff and workers
34 礼堂 [禮-] lǐtáng (ritual-hall) <n.> assembly hall: 大/小~ large/small assembly hall || 学校~ school assembly hall
35 墙 [墻] qiáng (wall) <n.> wall: 一面/道~ a wall || 高~ a tall wall || 靠~ lean against a wall
36 城堡 [-] chéngbǎo (city-fort) <n.> castle: 一座 ~ a castle || 古老的 ~ an old castle
37 树屋 [樹-] shùwū (tree-house) <n.> treehouse: 搭建~ put up/ build a treehouse || 小~ a small treehouse

Tips:

1 Types of houses or rooms: Since there are so many characters which mean house or room, let's introduce them one by one, with ample examples.

1 房, 屋, 室, 厅, 间, 院, 库

a. 房 (fáng): 厨房 (kitchen,) 书房 (studyroom,) 房东 (landlord,) 房地产 (real estate)
b. 屋 (wū): 屋子 (room,) 屋顶 (roof,) 树屋 (treehouse)
c. 室 (shì): 卧室 (bedroom,) 浴室 (bathroom)
d. 厅 (tīng): 客厅 (living room,) 餐厅 (dining room,) 大厅 (hall, lobby,) 门厅 (hallway)
e. 间 (jiān): 卫生间/洗手间 (lavatory, bathroom,) 房间 (room)
f. 院 (yuàn): 院子 (yard, courtyard,) 后院 (backyard,) 歌剧院 (opera house,) 四合院 (Beijing courtyard)
g. 库 (kù): 车库 (garage,) 仓库 (warehouse)

2 楼, 堂, 馆, 舍, 寓, 所, 宅, 堡

h. 楼 (lóu): 楼房 (storied building,) 高楼 (tall building,) 写字楼 (office building,) 教学楼 (teaching building)

i. 堂 (táng): 礼堂 (auditorium,) 纪念堂 (memorial hall)
j. 馆 (guǎn): 图书馆 (library,) 博物馆 (museum,) 展览馆 (exhibition hall,) 旅馆 (hotel,) 茶馆 (tea house)
k. 舍 (shè): 宿舍 (dormitory,) 寒舍 (hánshè, cold-house, my humble home)
l. 寓 (yù): 公寓 (apartment)
m. 所 (suǒ): 住所 (living place,) 交易所 (exchange,) 公共场所 (public place,) 律师事务所 (law office,) 厕所 (restroom)
n. 宅 (zhái): 住宅区 (residential area,) 豪宅 (mansion)
o. 堡 (bǎo): 城堡 (castle)

2 公寓 (gōngyù): In the 1980s, when an overseas Chinese person returned to China and said he lived in a 公寓, the listener would show much admiration and thought that he lived in a mansion (豪宅, háozhái) of his own.

Exercises:

Part I: Use the given bound form on the left as a guide to help you think of other words with the same character. Feel free to use your dictionary when needed. Then write down the English definition of each of the words you've written.

馆 *(term for certain service establishments):* 图书馆 *library*

____

____

____

____

____

室 *(room)* 卧室 *bedroom*

____

____

____

Part II: Answer the following questions in Chinese.

1 世界上最有名的歌剧院在哪个城市?

____

2 你喜欢住公寓还是别墅? 为什么?

____

3 你经常去画廊吗? 为什么?

---

4 城堡一般在哪些地方比较多? 它是古代建筑还是现代建筑?

Theme 36: Parts of architecture 建筑组成 (jiànzhù zǔchéng)

1 大门 [-門] dàmén (large-door) <n.> gate: 学校~ school gate || 进~ enter gate || 看 (kān) ~ keep gate
2 台阶 [臺階] táijiē (platform-stair) <n.> steps: 上~ climb steps || 五级~ five steps
3 门 [門] mén (door) <n.> door: 关/开/锁 (suǒ) ~ close door/open door/lock door || 校~ school door || 房~ house door
4 大厅 [-廳] dàtīng (large-hall) <n.> hall: 接待 (jiēdài) ~ reception hall || 车站~ station hall || 展览 (zhǎnlǎn) ~ exhibition hall
5 客厅 [-廳] kètīng (guest-hall) <n.> living room: 走进~ into the living room || 一个/间 ~ a living room || 大/小~ big/small living room
6 厅 [廳] tīng (hall) <n.> hall: 客~ guest hall || 饭/餐~ dining hall || 大 ~ big hall
7 屋 [-] wū (house) <n.> house: 三间 ~ three houses || 老 ~ old house || 小木~ small treehouse
8 传达室 [傳達-] chuándáshì (pass-arrive/-room) <n.> communication hall: 一间~ a communication room || 学校 ~ school communication room
9 厕所 [廁-] cèsuǒ (lavatory-place) <n.> bathroom: 公共~ public bathroom || 男/女~ men/women bathroom || 上/去~ go bathroom
10 厨房 [廚-] chúfáng (kitchen-room) <n.> kitchen: 一间~ a kitchen || ~小 small kitchen || 大~ big kitchen
11 卫生间 [衛-間] wèishēngjiān (hygiene-room) <n.> bathroom: 两个~ two bathrooms || 公共 ~ public bathroom
12 卧室 [臥-] wòshì (lie down-room) <n.> bedroom: 一间 ~ one bedroom || 走进~ enter bedroom
13 书房 [書-] shūfáng (book-room) <n.> study: 两间~ two study rooms || 新 ~ a new study room || 小/大 ~ small/big study room
14 地下室 [-] dìxiàshì (ground-under/-room) <n.> basement: 一间~ a basement || 潮湿 (cháoshī) 的~ wet basement
15 洗衣间 [--間] xǐyījiān (wash-clothes-room) <n.> laundry room: 小~ a small laundry room
16 衣帽间 [--間] yīmàojiān (clothes-cap-room) <n.> closet: 打开~ open closet || 小 ~ a small closet
17 地板 [-] dìbǎn (ground-board) <n.> floor: 木~ wood floor || 睡~ sleep on the floor || 擦 (cā) ~ mop the floor
18 楼道 [樓-] lóudào (building-path) <n.> corridor: 打扫~ clean corridor || 在~里at the corridor
19 地毯 [-] dìtǎn (ground-rug) <n.> carpet: 厚~ thick carpet || 红 ~ red carpet

20 楼梯 [樓-] lóutī (building-ladder) <n.> stairs: 上/下~ up/down stairs || 走~ walk stairs || 三级~ three level stairs
21 墙壁 [牆-] qiángbì (wall-partition wall) <n.> wall: 一面~ one side wall || 卧室~ bedroom wall
22 天花板 [-] tiānhuābǎn (top-pattern-board) <n.> ceiling: 玻璃 (bōli) ~ glass ceiling || 职场~ job market ceiling
23 阁楼 [閣樓] gélóu (chamber-building) <n.> attic: 小~ small attic
24 瓦 [-] wǎ (roof tile) <n.> roof tile: 灰~ gray roof tiles || 一片~ a piece of tile
25 屋顶 [-頂] wūdǐng (house-top) <n.> roof: 大~ large roof || 圆~ round roof
26 窗子 [-] chuāngzi (window-*suffix*) <n.> window: 两个/扇 (shàn) ~ two windows/fan window || 玻璃~ glass window
27 窗户 [-戶] chuānghu (window-door) <n.> window: 开/关~ open/close window
28 阳台 [陽臺] yángtái (sun-platform) <n.> balcony: 在~上 on the balcony || 大/小~ big/small balcony
29 舞台 [-臺] wǔtái (dance-platform) <n.> stage: 走下~ go down stage || 戏剧 (xìjù) ~ theater stage
30 柱子 [-] zhùzǐ (pillar-*suffix*) <n.> pillar: 十根~ ten pillars || 木/石/铁 ~ wood/stone/iron pillars || 大型~ large pillars

Tips:

1 Radical 宀 (mián): Radical 宀 means 'house.' Its traditional form is like the simple cross-section of a house. All characters with this radical are related to house, for example 家 (home), 室 (room), 宫 (palace), 客 (guest), 安 (peaceful, derived from the meaning of a girl (女) in a house (宀)), 宅 (zhái, residence) and 宿 (sù, sleep overnight).

2 Radical 穴 (xué): Radical 穴 means 'cave,' for example, 空 (empty, hollow), 窗 (window), 穿 (chuān, penetrate), 窑 (yáo, kiln), 窖 (jiào, pit, cellar), 窝 (wō, nest, den), 窠 (kē, den), and 穷 (qióng, end (of a cave), poor).

3 Radicals 厂 (hǎn) and 广 (yǎn): 厂 (厰, 廠), as a simplified character, reads as chǎng and means 'factory,' however, as a radical, it reads as hǎn and means 'rock shelter.' For example, 厚 (hòu, thick (of a mountain or Earth's crust)). The following characters, 厅 (tīng), 厨 (chú), 厕 (cè), 厦 (shà), 厢 (xiāng), look like they have the same radical 厂 (hǎn), but, their traditional forms are all related to another similar radical 广 (yǎn), 厅 (廳), 厨 (廚), 厕 (廁), 厦 (廈), 厢 (廂). 广 (yǎn) means 'hall,' therefore, 厅 (廳, hall), 厨 (廚, kitchen), 厕 (廁 lavatory), 厦 (廈, big building), 厢 (廂, side room). The simplified character 广 (guǎng) is from the traditional character 廣, which means 'large room.'

4 Radicals 尸 (shī) and 户 (hù): From 屋 (wū, room) and 居 (jū, reside), one may guess the shared radical of these two characters, 户 is related to house, however, 尸 means 'corpse,' for example, 尿 (niào, urinate), 屎 (shǐ, excrement), 尾 (wěi, tail). The original meaning of 户 is a piece of door, therefore, 门 (門) means 'door' (double 户), and 房 (house).

Exercises:

Part I: Answer the following questions in Chinese.

1 写一写你理想房子的布局 (overall arrangement) 和装修 (decoration)

房子前面有

房子后面有

房子里有

Theme 37: Traffic infrastructure, agricultural infrastructure 交通建筑, 农用建筑 (jiāotōng jiànzhù, nóngyòng jiànzhù)

(See also Theme 33)

1 道路 [-] dàolù (path-road) <n.> road: 修建 (xiūjiàn) ~ build a road || 一条~ a road || 宽阔 (kuānkuò) 的~ a wide road
2 公路 [-] gōnglù (public-road) <n.> highway: 一条~ a highway || 修~ repair the highway || 高速~ expressway
3 马路 [馬-] mǎlù (horse-road) <n.> road: 穿过 ~ cross a street || 大/小/新/宽敞的/笔直的~ big/small/new/spacious/straight road || 一条~ a street
4 大街 [-] dàjiē (broad-street) <n.> street: 扫 ~ clean the street || 两条~ two streets
5 地铁 [-鐵] dìtiě (ground-rail) <n.> subway: 坐 ~ ride the subway || ~站 subway station || ~口subway entrance
6 铁路 [鐵-] tiělù (iron-road) <n.> railway: 一条~ a railway || 修建 ~ build a railway || ~线 subway lines
7 高铁 [-鐵] gāotiě (high speed-rail) <n.> high-speed rail: 修~ build a high speed train || 坐~ ride a high speed train || ~票 high speed train ticket
8 地铁站 [-鐵-] dìtiě zhàn (subway-station) <n.> subway station: 五个 ~ five subway stations || 进/出~ enter/exit subway station || 大~ a big subway station
9 机场 [機場] jīchǎng (airplane-station) <n.> airport: 国际~ international airport || 去~ go to the airport || 一个新 ~ a new airport
10 街 [-] jiē (street) <n.> street: 小吃~ snack street || 上~ go shopping || 逛~ go window-shopping
11 街道 [-] jiēdào (street-path) <n.> street: 一条~ a street || 主要 ~ the main street || 穿过~ cross a street
12 路 [-] lù (road) <n.> road: 一条~ a road || 大/小/新/老~ big/small/new/old road
13 胡同儿 [-] hútòng er (probably a transliteration of Mongolian Худг which means 'well') <n.> alley: 一条~ an alley || 小~ a small alley

14 巷子 [-] xiàngzi (alley-*suffix*) <nl> alley: 一条~ an alley || 空 ~ an empty alley
15 桥 [橋] qiáo (bridge) <n.> bridge: 一座 ~ a bridge || 过~ cross the bridge || 修/造~ repair/build the bridge
16 站 [-] zhàn (post, station) <n.> station: 汽车~ bus station || 火车~ train station
17 车站 [車-] chēzhàn (vehicle-station) <n.> rail station, bus stop: 开往~ bound for the station/headed towards || 出~ leave the station || 地下~ underground station
18 站台 [-] zhàntái (station-platform) <n.> platform (in a railway station): 火车 ~ train platform || 进入~ enter the platform || 二号~ Platform No.2

19 信号灯 [-號燈] xìnhàodēng (signal-light) <n.> signals: 航行~ navigation light || 交通~ traffic light || 红色~ red light
20 红绿灯 [紅綠燈] hónglǜdēng (red-green-light) <n.> traffic light: 等~ wait for the traffic light
21 斑马线 [-馬綫] bānmǎxiàn (zebra-line) <n.> crosswalk: 过马路要走~. Walk in the zebra crossing area when you cross the street.

22 码头 [碼頭] mǎtóu (pile-*suffix*) <n.> pier: 船靠~ moor on the pier || 停在~ stopped at the pier || 一座~ a pier
23 桥梁 [橋樑] qiáoliáng (bridge-bridge) <n.> bridge: 一座~ a bridge || 建造~ construct a bridge
24 运河 [運-] yùnhé (transport-river) <n.> canal: 一条~ a canal || 开~ open a canal || 修~ repair a canal
25 港口 [-] gǎngkǒu (port-mouth) <n.> port: ~城市port city || 在~钓鱼 fishing at the port
26 加油站 [-] jiāyóuzhàn (add-oil-station) <n.> gas station: 一个/座~ a gas station || 新~ new gas station || 中型~ medium-sized gas station
27 井 [-] jǐng (well) <n.> well: 一口~ a well || 挖 ~ dig a well || ~水 water from the well
28 通道 [-] tōngdào (through-path) <n.> aisle: 海上~ sea passage || 一条~ an aisle || 秘密 (mìmì) ~ a secret passage

29 园 [園] yuán (garden) <n.> garden: 菜~ vegetable garden || 水果~ fruit garden || 香蕉~ banana garden
30 水库 [-庫] shuǐkù (water-reservoir) <n.> reservoirs: 修 ~ repair reservoir || 大型/小型/中型 ~ large/small/medium-sized reservoir || 一座~ a reservoir
31 渠道 [-] qúdào (ditch-path) <n.> channel: 疏通 (shūtōng) ~ dig channels || 修~ repair a channel || 排水/灌溉 (guàngài) ~ drainage/irrigation channels
32 池子 [-] chízi (pool-*suffix*) <n.> pond: 两个~ two ponds || 水~ water pond || 洗澡/洗手~ bath tub/sink
33 库 [庫] kù (warehouse) <n.> storage place: 车~ garage || 油~ oil depot || 水~ water reservoirs

Tips:

1 道 vs. 路 vs. 街: They mean 'way,' 'road' and 'street' respectively. In ancient China, 道 were usually one way, so there is a saying "一条道跑到黑" ('to go down a road until its end, be single-minded, be as stubborn as a mule').

路 were usually two ways and much broader than 道, so there is a rendered saying "条条大路通罗马，" (all roads lead to Rome.) 街 are usually crossed streets.

2 地铁 vs. 捷运 (捷運, jiéyùn): Both mean 'subway' but 地铁 is used in mainland China and 捷運 in Taiwan. 地铁 (underground-rail,) as the name suggests, is railway underground, 捷運 (rapid-transit) is a rapid means of transportation.

3 渠道 (qúdào) vs. 管道 (guǎndào): Both mean 'channel.' In mainland China, 渠道 is usually abstract, meaning a means of communication, and in Taiwan, it is called 管道 in this sense. However, 管道 alway means concrete tubes in mainland China.

4 China's Four Great New Inventions (新四大发明): The Four Great Inventions are the compass (指南针, zhǐnánzhēn,) gunpowder (火药, huǒyào,) paper-making (造纸术, zàozhǐshù) and printing (印刷术, yìnshuāshù.) In 2017, the term of Four Great New Inventions spread on the Internet. The inventions are high-speed rail (高铁,) lockless shared bicycles (共享单车, gòngxiǎng dānchē,) Alipay and e-commerce (网购, wǎnggòu, online shopping.)

Exercises:

Answer the following questions.

1 写出五个你们城市的公共交通建筑

---

2 .外国媒体说的中国"新四大发明"是指哪些东西

---

3 ."条条大路通罗马"的英文意思是什么?

Theme 38: Garden, palace 园林, 宫殿 (yuánlín, gōngdiàn)

1 公园 [-園] gōngyuán (public-garden) <n.> park: 去~ go to the park || 海洋~ sea park

2 花园 [-園] huāyuán (flower-garden) <n.> garden: 一座美丽的~ a beautiful garden || 走进~. Enter the garden.

3 亭子 [-] tíngzi (pavilion-*suffix*) <n.> pavilion: 木~ wood pavilion || 竹~ bamboo pavilion || 搭 (dā) ~ build pavilion

4 牌坊 [-] páifāng (board-arch) <n.> memorial arch: 石头/木~ Stone arch/wood arch || 立（贞节）~ build a memorial arch putting up to one's chastity || 一座~ a memorial arch

5 碑 [-] bēi (tablet) <n.> monument: 一块 ~ A monument || 路~ road monument || 纪念 (jìniàn) ~ memorial monument

6 动物园 [動-園] dòngwùyuán (animal-garden) <n.> zoo: 参观~ visit the zoo || 国家~ national zoo || 大型~ big zoo

7 宫 [宮] gōng (palace) <n.> palace: 王/皇~ palace/palace || 迷~ maze || 故~ The Forbidden City

8 塔 [-] tǎ (pagoda) <n.> tower: 一座~ A tower || 灯~ lighthouse || 石~ stone tower

9 园 [園] yuán (garden) <n.> garden: 圆明~ Yuanmingyuan. The Old Summer Palace, known in Chinese as Yuanming Yuan ('Gardens of Perfect Brightness'), was originally called the Imperial Gardens (*Yù Yuán*), and is a complex of palaces and gardens in present-day Haidian District, Beijing, China. || 颐和 (Yíhé) ~ Summer palace || 公~ park

10 园林 [園-] yuánlín (garden-forest) <n.> garden: 私家~ private garden || 一座~ a garden || 苏州~ Suzhou Garden || 皇家~ royal garden

11 宫殿 [宮-] gōngdiàn (palace-hall) <n.> palace: 一座~ a palace || 艺术~ art palace || 豪华 (háohuá) 的~ luxurious palace

12 皇宫 [-宮] huánggōng (royal-palace) <n.> imperial palace: 新~ new imperial palace

13 故宫 [-宮] gùgōng (ancient-palace) <n.> The Forbidden City: 游览 (yóulǎn) ~ visit The Forbidden City || ~博物院 (bówù yuàn) The Palace Museum

14 白宫 [-宮] báigōng (white-palace) <n.> The White House: 美国总统府~ American presidential residence: The White House

15 白金汉宫 [--漢宮] báijīnhàngōng (*transliteration*-palace) <n.> Buckingham Palace: 英国的王宫是~. The royal palace in England is Buckingham Palace.

16 凡尔赛宫 [-爾賽宮] fán'ěrsàigōng (*transliteration*-palace) <n.> The Palace of Versailles: ~是巴黎著名的宫殿. The Palace of Versailles is a famous palace in Paris.

17 卢浮宫lúfú gōng<n.> the Louvre: ~是世界四大博物馆之一. The Louvre is one of the four largest museums in the world.

18 冬宫 [-宮] dōnggōng (winter-palace) <n.> Winter Palace: ~原来是俄罗斯的皇宫. The Winter Palace was formerly the imperial palace in Russia.

19 华表 [華-] huábiǎo (flower-mark) <n.> marble pillar (ornamental column in front of places, tombs): 北京天安门城楼有两对~, 城内一对, 城外一对. There are two pairs of *huabiao* at Tiananmen Square, with one pair located inside the gate, and one pair outside.

20 石狮子 [-獅-] shíshīzi (stone-lion) <n.> stone lion: 在中国, ~是守卫大门的神兽 (shòu). In China, the stone lion is the sacred animal guarding the gate.

21 四合院 [-] sìhéyuàn (four (sides) -enclosed-yard) <n.> four-walled courtyard: 北京~ beijing style four-walled courtyard || 小~ small courtyard

22 广场 [廣場] guǎngchǎng (vast-square) <n.> square: ~ 舞 square dance || 市民~ civil square

23 天安门广场 [--門廣場] tiān'ānmén guǎngchǎng (heaven-peace-gate-square) <n.> Tiananmen Square: 数万群众在北京~观看国庆升旗仪式 (yíshì). Tens of thousands of people watched the National Day flag-raising ceremony at Beijing's Tiananmen Square.

24 时代广场 [時-廣場] shídài guǎngchǎng (times-square) <n.> Times Square: ~是美国纽约曼哈顿 (mànhādùn) 的一块繁华 (fánhuá) 的街区. Times Square is a busy neighborhood in Manhattan, New York. || 越来越多的中国企业登陆纽约~. More and more Chinese companies are landing in Times Square in Manhattan.

25 庄园 [莊園] zhuāngyuán (village-plantation) <n.> manor: 一座~ a manor || 大/小~ large / small manor

Tips:

1 吕 (lǚ): Original meaning of 吕 is backbone. It is also a collective name for the even numbers of the 12 pitches of a flute. But in 宫, it resembles the windows (rooms) of cave dwellings.
2 广场舞 (guǎngchǎngwǔ): Now you can easily find that in almost any large community in China, many people, old and young, male and female, spontaneously perform广场舞 (square dances) mostly in the morning or after dinner. 广场舞 demonstrates the openness of Chinese culture.

Exercises:

Part II: Answer the following questions in Chinese.

1 写出北京和纽约最有名的广场

---

2 写出中国、美国、俄罗斯、法国最有名的宫殿

---

3 在中国跳广场舞的人一般是:
a)中老年人 b)年轻人 c)少年儿童

Theme 39: Sacred architecture 祭祀建筑 (jìsì jiànzhù)

1 坛 [壇] tán (temple) <n.> Altar: 奖~ platform for awards || 乐 ~ music altar
2 天坛 [-壇] tiāntán (heaven-altar) <n.> Temple of Heaven (in Beijing): ~是中国皇帝的祭 (jì) 天的场所. The Temple of Heaven is a Chinese imperial complex of religious buildings.
3 地坛 [-壇] dìtán (Earth-altar) <n.> Temple of Earth (in Beijing): ~的建筑都是方的. All the buildings in the Temple of Earth (in Beijing) are square.
4 日坛 [-壇] rìtán (sun-altar) <n.> Altar to the Sun (in Beijing): ~公园Beijing Altar of the Sun (Ritan Park)
5 神坛 [-壇] shéntán (god-altar) <n.> Altar for a God (shrine): 走下 ~ down altar || 设立~ the establishment of altars
6 庙 [廟] miào (temple) <n.> temple: 一座~ A temple || 龙王~ Dragon King Temple || 破~ broken temple
7 文庙 [-廟] wénmiào (literati-temple) <n.> Confucian Temple: ~是纪念 (jìniàn) 孔子的建筑. The Confucian Temple is a building to honor Confucius.
8 妈祖庙 [媽-廟] māzǔmiào (Matsu-temple) <n.> Matsu Temple: 福建省 (fújiàn shěng) 有很多~. There are many Matsu Temples in Fujian Province.

9 观 [觀] guàn (Taoist temple) <n.> Taoist temple: 道 ~ taoist temple || 白云~ Baiyun Temple
10 道观 [-觀] dàoguàn (Taoist-temple) <n.> Taoist Temple: 一所 ~ a Taoist Temple || 建 ~ build a Taoist Temple
11 教堂 [-] jiàotáng (religion-hall) <n.> church: 一座~ a church || 大/小~ cathedral (large) /small church || 基督~ Christian church
12 墓 [-] mù (tomb) <n.> tomb: 古 ~ ancient tomb || 祖~ ancestral tomb || 盗 (dào) ~ tomb raiders
13 陵 [-] líng (mound) <n.> tomb: 皇~ imperial tomb || 内~ inner tomb || 外~ outer tomb
14 陵墓 [-] língmù (tomb-mound) <n.> tomb: 一座~ a big tomb || 修建~ build a big tomb
15 坟 [墳] fén (grave) <n.> grave: 一座~ a grave || 新~ new grave || 上~ visit a grave to honor the memory of the dead
16 寺 [-] sì (temple) <n.> temple: 大/小~ small/large temple || ~门 temple door || 一座~ a temple
17 清真寺 [-] qīngzhēnsì (tranquil-pure-temple) <n.> mosque: 一座~ a mosque || 大~ large/The Great Mosque
18 长城 [長-] chángchéng (long-wall) <n.> Great Wall: 修筑 (xiūzhù) ~ build The Great Wall || 不到~非好汉. He who has never been to The Great Wall is not a true man || 古~ Ancient Great Wall

Tips:

1 Why did Chinese emperors build mausoleums? Mausoleums were built for the emperors' next lives. In the Han Dynasty, building work on a mausoleum started from the second year after an emperor ascended the throne and usually lasted until his death. One third of the state's revenue would be set aside for building the emperor's mausoleum.
2 Locations of 天坛, 地坛, 日坛 and 月坛 in Beijing: They are located in the south, the north, the east and the west respectively. Why? Ancient Chinese people believed 天 is *yang* and 地 is *yin*, so the two temples are in the south and north. The sun rises in the east, and the moon sets in the west, so 日坛 and 月坛 are in the east and west. Ancient Chinese people also believed 天圆地方 (heaven is round and the Earth is square), so the main buildings in 天坛 are round.

Exercises:

Part I: Read the following words and then answer the following questions in Chinese.

天坛、地坛、日坛、神坛、文庙、妈祖庙、道观、教堂、寺庙、清真寺、陵墓

1 哪种建筑是基督徒 (Christian) 活动的地方?

---

2 哪种建筑是道教徒 (Taoist) 活动的地方?

3 哪种建筑是佛教徒 (Buddhist) 活动的地方?

4 哪三个中国古代祭祀建筑 (sacred architecture) 现在在北京还存在?

Theme 40: Furniture, home appliances 家具, 家电 (jiājù, jiādiàn)

1 家具 [-] jiājù (home-tool) <n.> furniture: 老式/新式/西式/中式~ old furniture/new furniture/Western-style furniture/Chinese furniture || 红木~ redwood furniture
2 床 [牀] chuáng (bed) <n.> bed: 一张~ a bed || 双人/单人 ~ double bed/single bed
3 柜子 [櫃-] guìzi (box-*suffix*) <n.> cabinet: 木~ a wooden cabinet || 铁~ an iron cabinet
4 衣柜 [-櫃] yīguì (clothes-box) <n.> wardrobe: 大~ a big wardrobe || 做一个~ make a wardrobe
5 书柜 [書櫃] shūguì (book-box) <n.> bookcase, book cabinet: 打一个~ make a bookcase || 打开~ open the bookcase
6 书架 [書-] shūjià (book-frame) <n.> bookshelf: 放在~上put something on the bookshelf || 简易~ a simple bookshelf || 实木~ solid wood bookshelf
7 桌子 [-] zhuōzi (table-*suffix*) <n.> table, desk: 一张~ a table || 木头~ wooden table || 擦~ wipe a table
8 饭桌 [飯-] fànzhuō (eat-table) <n.> dining table: 把碗放在~上. Put the bowl on the dining table. || 他们喜欢在~上谈解决世界问题的办法. They like to talk about ways to solve world problems at the dinner table.
9 书桌 [書-] shūzhuō (book-table) <n.> desk: 一张~ a desk || ~上放着台灯. A lamp is arranged on the desk.
10 电脑桌 [電腦-] diànnǎozhuō (computer-table) <n.> computer desk: 一张~ a computer table
11 写字台 [寫-臺] xiězìtái (write-character-platform) <n.> writing desk: 一张~ a writing desk
12 梳妆台 [-妝臺] shūzhuāngtái (comb-dress up-platform) <n.> dressing table: 西式~ Western style dressing table || 中式~ Chinese style dressing table
13 沙发 [-發] shāfā (*transliteration*) <n.> sofa: 一套~ a sofa set || 双人~ loveseat || ~凳 ottoman
14 躺椅 [-] tǎngyǐ (recline-chair) <n.> deck chair: 一把~ a deck chair || 躺在~上lie on a deck chair
15 凳子 [-] dèngzi (stool-*suffix*) <n.> stool: 一个~ a stool || 高~ a high stool
16 椅子 [-] yǐzi (chair-*suffix*) <n.> chair: 一把~ a chair || 皮~ leather chair || 电脑~ computer chair

17 轮椅 [輪-] lúnyǐ (wheel-chair) <n.> wheelchair: 坐~ take a wheelchair || 推着 ~ pushing a wheelchair || ~服务wheelchair service

18 电器 [電-] diànqì (electricity-appliance) <n.> electrical appliance: 家用~ household appliances || 修理 (xiūlǐ) ~ fix appliances

19 家电 [-電] jiādiàn (home-electric appliance) <n.> household appliances: ~产品home appliance product || ~企业household appliances enterprise

20 空调 [-調] kōngtiáo (air-adjust) <n.> air conditioner: 开/关~ turn on/turn off air conditioner || 安装~ install air conditioner

21 吸尘器 [-塵-] xīchénqì (inhale-dust-appliance) <n.> vacuum cleaner: 一台~ a vacuum

22 冰箱 [-] bīngxiāng (ice-box) <n.> refrigerator: 一台~ a refrigerator

23 烤箱 [-] kǎoxiāng (roast-box) <n.> oven, baking box: 一台~ an oven

24 烤面包机 [-麵-機] kǎo miànbāo jī (roast-bread-machine) <n.> roaster: 一台~ a roaster

25 微波炉 [--爐] wēibōlú (micro-wave-oven) microwave <n.> microwave: 一台a microwave

26 电饭锅 [電飯鍋] diànfànguō (electricity-food-pot) <n.> rice cooker: 一个~ a rice cooker

27 榨汁机 [--機] zhàzhījī (extract-juice-machine) <n.> juicer: 一台~ a juicer

28 洗衣机 [--機] xǐyījī (wash-clothes-machine) <n.> washing machine: 一台 ~ a washing machine || 全自动~ automatic washing machine

29 烘干机 [-乾機] hōnggānjī (burn-dry-machine) <n.> dryer: 美国家庭普遍使用~ A dryer are universally used by American families.

30 热水器 [熱--] rèshuǐqì (heat-water-appliance) <n.> water heater: 节能 ~ energy saving water heater

31 吹风机 [-風機] chuīfēngjī (blow-wind-machine) <n.> hair dryer: 一个~ a hair dryer

32 加湿器 [-濕-] jiāshīqì (add-humidity-appliance) <n.> humidifier: 空气 ~ air humidifier

33 电熨斗 [電--] diànyùndǒu (electricity-pressing-flatiron) <n.> electric iron: 一个~ an electric iron

Tips:

1 电 (電, diàn): From its traditional form 電, we can easily tell that it is related to weather since its radical is 雨. The original meaning of 电 is lightning. It was not until recent centuries that 电 gained the meaning of electricity. In other words, all the 电 in Chinese idioms mean 'lightning' or its derivative meanings. FYI, a newer word related to 电 is 电子, which means 'electronic,' or 电子计算机 (diànzǐ jìsuànjī, computer) and 电子商务 (diànzǐ shāngwù, e-commerce) and other related compounds.

2 机 (jī) and 器 (qì): Words with the character 机 and listed above include 洗衣机, 烘干机, 吹风机, 榨汁机, 烤面包机 and words with 器 include 吸尘器, 热水器, 加湿器. The difference between XX机and XX器 is somewhat blurred based on the function of the noun designated. Basically a XX机 is supposed to consume energy and a XX器 has a part-like a container.

Exercises:

Part I: Answer the following questions in Chinese.

1 请写出五种做饭使用的电器

2 写出五种你家里的家具

3 美国人什么时候开始普遍使用洗衣机和烘干机的?

4 美国的大学宿舍一般有空调吗? 为什么?

5 吸尘器、热水器、加湿器这三种东西哪些你会经常使用?

Theme 41: Daily necessities 日用品 (rìyòngpǐn)

1 包 [-] bāo (fetus, bundle) <n.> bag: 皮/布~ leather bag/cloth bag || 钱~ wallet, purse || 背~ (bēibāo) backpack
2 钱包 [錢-] qiánbāo (money-bag) <n.> wallet, purse: 掏出~ take out wallet || 我~丢了. My wallet is lost.
3 书包 [書-] shūbāo (book-bag) <n.> school bag: 背着~ carrying school bag || 打开 ~ open school bag
4 电脑包 [電腦-] diànnǎobāo (computer-bag) <n.> computer bag: 手提~ portable computer bag
5 背包 [-] bēibāo (back-bag) <n.> backpack: 背着~ carry backpack
6 手提包 [-] shǒutíbāo (hand-lift-bag) <n.> handbag, carrying bag: 提着/拎着 ~ carrying handbag
7 旅行包 [-] lǚxíngbāo (travel-bag) <n.> travel bag: 背着~ carry backpack
8 盆 [-] pén (basin) <n.> basin, tub: 脸~ basin for washing hands and face || 洗澡~ bathtub
9 壶 [壺] hú (vase) <n.> kettle, pot: 茶~ teapot || 水~ kettle
10 瓶 [-] píng (jug) <n./m.w.> bottle: 酒~ wine bottle || 一 ~可乐a bottle of Cola
11 瓶子 [-] píngzi (bottle-*suffix*) <n.> bottle: 玻璃~ glass bottle || 空~ empty bottle
12 花瓶 [-] huāpíng (flower-vase) <n.> vase: 水晶~ crystal vase || 瓷 (cí) ~ porcelain vase
13 暖水瓶 [-] nuǎnshuǐpíng (warm-water-vase) <n.> thermos flask or bottle: 一个~ a thermos
14 杯 [-] bēi (cup) <n./m.w> glass, cup: 酒~ wine cup || 茶~ tea cup
15 袋 [-] dài (sack) <n./m.w.> bag: 纸~ paper bag || 塑料~ plastic bag || 一~水果a bag of fruit
16 袋子 [-] dàizi (bag-*suffix*) <n.> bag, sack: 布~ cloth bag

17 手袋 [-] shǒudài (hand-bag) <n.> handbag: 女式~ women handbag || 提着~ carrying a handbag
18 盒 [-] hé (box) <n./m.w.> case, box: 饭~ lunch-box || 鞋~ shoe case || 一 ~饼干a box of cookies
19 盒子 [-] hézi (box-*suffix*) <n.> box: 眼镜~ glasses box || 铁~ iron box || 方~ square box
20 箱子 [-] xiāngzi (chunk-*suffix*) <n.> box, case: 大/小~ big/small box || 打开~ open box
21 信箱 [-] xìnxiāng (mail-box) <n.> mailbox: 空~ empty mailbox || 打开~ open mailbox

22 锅 [鍋] guō (pot) <n.> pot: 一口/个~ a pot || 铁~ iron pot || 炒菜~ wok
23 切菜板 [-] qiēcàibǎn (cut-vegetable-board) <n.> cutting board: 一块 ~ a cutting board || 木头~ wooden cutting board || 塑料~ plastic cutting board
24 盘 [盤] pán (plate) <n./m.w.> plate: 瓷~ china plate || 烤~ roast plate || 一~菜a dish
25 盘子 [盤-] pánzi (plate-*suffix*) <n.> plate, tray: 一个~ a plate || 端 (duān) ~ carry a tray/plate
26 碗 [-] wǎn (bowl) <n./m.w.> bowl: 饭~ rice bowl || 一 ~汤a bowl of soup
27 勺 [-] sháo (spoon) <n./m.w.> spoon: 汤~ soup spoon || 饭 ~ food spoon || 一~汤one spoon soup
28 叉子 [-] chāzi (fork-*suffix*) <n.> fork: 一把~ a fork || 用~吃东西eat food with forks || 不锈钢~ stainless steel fork
29 筷子 [-] kuàizi (chopstick-*suffix*) <n.> chopstick: 一双~ a pair of chopstick || 银~ silver chopsticks

30 浴缸 [-] yùgāng (bath-jug) <n.> bathtub: 按摩 (ànmó) ~ massage bathtub
31 毛巾 [-] máojīn (cloth-towel) <n.> towel: 一条 ~ a towel || 湿/干~ wet/dry towel
32 镜子 [鏡-] jìngzi (mirror-*suffix*) <n.> mirror: 一面~ a mirror || 照~ look into the mirror
33 刷子 [-] shuāzi (brush-*suffix*) <n.> brush: 一把~ a brush || 鞋~ shoe brush
34 牙刷 [-] yáshuā (tooth-brush) <n.> toothbrush: 儿童~ kids toothbrush || 电动~ electric toothbrush
35 衣架 [-] yījià (clothes-rack) <n.> coat hanger: 把衣服挂在~上. Put your clothes on hangers. || 塑料~ plastic coat hanger
36 洗衣粉 [-] xǐyīfěn (wash-clothes-powder) <n.> detergent, washing powder: 一袋~ a bag of washing powder
37 洗衣液 [-] xǐyīyè (wash-clothes-liquid) <n.> detergent, laundry/liquid detergent: 一瓶~ a bottle of washing powder
38 漂白剂 [--劑] piǎobáijì (rinse-white-medicament) <n.> bleach: 食品~ food bleaching agent || 衣服~ laundry bleach

39 被子 [-] bèizi (quilt-*suffix*) <n.> quilt: 一床/条~ a quilt || 盖~ cover quilt || 厚/薄~ thick/thin quilt
40 毯子 [-] tǎnzi (rug-*suffix*) <n.> blanket: 一条~ a blanket || 羊毛~ wool blanket
41 床单 [-單] chuángdān (bed-sheet) <n.> bed sheet: 一条~ a bed sheet || 换~ change bed sheet || 双人~ double size bed sheet

42 枕头 [-頭] zhěntóu (pillow-*suffix*) <n.> pillow: 一个~ a pillow || 单人 ~ single size pillow || 双人~ double size pillow

43 灯 [燈] dēng (lamp) <n.> light: 开/关~ turn on/off light || 电~ electric light
44 吊灯 [-燈] diàodēng (hang-lamp) <n.> ceiling lamp: 水晶~ crystal ceiling lamps || 豪华 (háohuá) ~ luxurious ceiling lamps || 一盏~ a ceiling lamp
45 落地灯 [--燈] luòdìdēng (ground-lamp) <n.> floor lamp: 一盏 (zhǎn) ~ a floor light || 豪华 ~ luxurious floor lights
46 台灯 [臺燈] táidēng (stand-lamp) <n.> desk lamp, table desk: 一盏 ~ a desk or table lamp

47 钟 [鐘] zhōng (clock) <n.> clock, bell: 敲~ ring bell || ~声 bell tone
48 表 [錶] biǎo (watch) <n.> time watch: 一块 ~ a watch || 男/女 ~ men/women watch || 电子 ~ electronic watch
49 闹钟 [鬧鐘] nàozhōng (alarm-clock) <n.> alarm clock: 上~ set an alarm clock
50 日历 [-曆] rìlì (day-calendar) <n.> calendar: 在线~ online calendar || 工作~ work calendar || 旅游~ traveling calendar
51 相机 [-機] xiàngjī (photo-machine) <n.> camera: 一架/台~ a camera || 数码 ~ digital camera || 全自动~ automatic camera
52 相册 [-冊] xiàngcè (photo-book) <n.> album: 一本~ an album || 家庭 ~ family album || 老~ old album
53 相框 [-] xiàngkuàng (photo-frame) <n.> picture frame: 摆着~ displaying the picture frame || 挂~ hang picture frame || 水晶~ crystal picture frame

54 扇子 [-] shànzi (fan-*suffix*) <n.> fan: 一把~ a fan || 扇/摇~ use a fan
55 伞 [傘] sǎn (umbrella) <n.> umbrella: 一把~ an umbrella || 雨~ umbrella || 遮阳~ beach umbrella
56 锁 (头) [鎖頭] suǒ (lock-*suffix*) <n.> locker: 一把~ a locker || 开~ open locker
57 卡子 [-] qiǎzi (wedge-*suffix*) <n.> clip: 塑料~ plastic clip || 头发~ hair clip
58 针 [針] zhēn (needle) <n.> needle: 一根~ a needle || 毛衣~ knitting needle
59 线 [線/綫] xiàn (thread) <n.> thread, string, wire: 一根~ a thread || 毛~ knitting yarn or thread || 棉~ cotton thread – or 'cord' (for a computer or other electronics)
60 火柴 [-] huǒchái (fire-firewood) <n.> match: 一根/盒 ~ a match/a box of match || 划~ strike a match
61 眼镜儿 [-鏡兒] yǎnjìng er (eye-mirror) <n.> eyeglasses: 一副~ a pair of glasses || 戴 (dài) ~ wear eyeglasses
62 装饰 [裝飾] zhuāngshì (dress up-decorate) <n.> ornament, decoration: ~材料finishing material || 汽车~ automobile decoration
63 包装 [-裝] bāozhuāng (wrap-pack) <n.> packaging, wrapping: 外~ outside packaging || 大/小~食品larger packed food/smaller packed food || 食品~ food packaging

Tips:

1 Radicals 皿 (mǐn), 瓦 (wǎ), 缶 (fǒu): The radical 皿 means 'container,' for example, 盘 (plate), 盒 (box), 盐 (yán, salt), and 盖 (gài, lid, cover). The radical 瓦 means 'earthenware,' for example, 瓶 (bottle) and 瓷 (cí, porcelain,

china). The radical 缶 means 'jar,' for example, 缸 (gāng, jug), 缺 (quē, vessel is broken, short of), and 罐 (guàn, jar, canister).

2 锅碗瓢盆 (guō wǎn piáo pén): Literally, they are pot, bowl, ladle and basin. Put together, they mean 'pots and pans, basic cookware.' For example, 我刚搬家, 得买一些锅碗瓢盆 (I just moved and need to buy some basic cookware).

Exercises:

Part I: Answer the following questions in Chinese.

1 请写出五种厨房用品

___

2 请写出五种浴室用品

___

3 请写出四种床上用品

___

4 你家的灯有哪几种?

___

5 "小王结婚以后天天围着锅碗瓢盆转," 意思是: _______

a) 小王结婚以后卖锅碗瓢盆.
b) 小王结婚以后主要在家做饭, 做家务.
c) 小王结婚以后特别喜欢锅碗瓢盆.

Theme 42: Clothes 服装 (fúzhuāng)

1 服装 [-裝] fúzhuāng (clothes-dress) <n.> clothes, clothing: 儿童~ children's clothing || ~公司Garment company, clothing company
2 时装 [時裝] shízhuāng (fashion-dress) <n.> the latest fashion in clothes: 一套~ a suit of fashion clothes
3 布 [-] bù (linen, cloth) <n.> cloth: 一块 ~ a piece of cloth || ~鞋cloth shoes
4 衣服 [-] yīfú (upper clothes-clothes) <n.> clothes: 穿/脱/做~ wear clothes, take off clothes, make clothes
5 外衣 [-] wàiyī (outer-clothes) <n.> outerwear: 披着~ lay out ones outerwear || 脱下~ take off top layer of clothes
6 内衣 [-] nèiyī (inner-clothes) <n.> underwear: 换~ change underwear || 男士~ men's underwear || 女士~ women's underwear ('panties')
7 上衣 [-] shàngyī (upper-clothes) <n.> blouse: 穿上~ put on a blouse
8 大衣 [-] dàyī (long-clothes) <n.> coat: 冬~ winter coat || 男士~ men's coat
9 羽绒服 [-絨-] yǔróngfú (feather-fabric-clothes) <n.> down coat: 女士~ women's down coat || 长款 (kuǎn) ~ long down coat/full length down coat || 新款~ a coat in the latest style
10 风衣 [風-] fēngyī (wind-clothes) <n.> windbreaker jacket

11 雨衣 [-] yǔyī (rain-clothes) <n.> raincoat

12 西装 [-裝] xīzhuāng (western-dress) <n.> suit: 一套 ~ a suit || 男士~ men's suit || 高级~ high quality suit

13 套装 [-裝] tàozhuāng (suit-dress) <n.> suit: 职业~ business suit || 女式~ women suit

14 晚礼服 [-禮-] wǎnlǐfú (evening-ceremony-dress) <n.> formal evening wear, evening dress: 穿~ wear an evening ceremony dress

15 毛衣 [-] máoyī (fur-clothes) <n.> sweater: 一件a sweater

16 衬衣 [襯-] chènyī (inner garment-clothes) <n.> shirt

17 背心 [-] bèixīn (back-heart) <n.> vest

18 连衣裙 [連--] liányīqún (connect-clothes-skirt) <n.> dress: 一条~ a dress || 真丝~ a dress made of pure silk

19 裙子 [-] qúnzi (skirt-*suffix*) <n.> skirt: 长/短~ a long/short skirt || 穿~ wear a skirt

20 裤子 [褲-] kùzi (trousers-*suffix*) <n.> pants: 一条 ~ a pants || 休闲~ casual pants

21 牛仔裤 [--褲] niúzǎikù (cow-boy-trousers) <n.> jeans: 女士~ women's jeans

22 短裤 [-褲] duǎnkù (short-trousers) <n.> shorts: 运动~ gym shorts

23 紧身裤 [緊-褲] jǐnshēnkù (tight-body-trousers) <n.> tight pants: 穿~ wear tight pants

24 鞋 [-] xié (shoe) <n.> shoe: 一双~ a pair of shoes || 穿/脱~ wear shoes/take off shoes || 新~ new shoes

25 皮鞋 [-] píxié (leather-shoe) <n.> leather shoes: 穿~ wear leather shoes || 高跟~ leather shoes with heels || 擦~ polish (or 'clean') leather shoes

26 高跟鞋 [-] gāogēnxié (high-heel-shoe) <n.> high heels

27 运动鞋 [運動-] yùndòngxié (sport-shoe) <n.> sneaker: 男/女~ men's/women's sneaker

28 拖鞋 [-] tuōxié (drag-shoe) <n.> slipper: 塑料 ~ plastic slippers || 棉~ winter slippers

29 凉鞋 [涼-] liángxié (cool-shoe) <n.> sandal

30 帽子 [-] màozi (helmet hat-*suffix*) <n.> hat: 一顶~ a hat || 戴~ wear hat

31 围巾 [圍-] wéijīn (encircle-towel) <n.> scarf: 一条~ a scarf || 戴~ wear scarf

32 手套 [-] shǒutào (hand-cover) <n.> glove, mitten: 戴~ wear || 一副~ a pair of gloves

33 袜子 [襪-] wàzi (sock-*suffix*) <n.> socks: 一双~ a pair of socks || 丝~ silk stockings || 棉~ quilted stockings

34 胸罩 [-] xiōngzhào (breast-coop) <n.> bra: 戴~ wear bra || 解开~ unhook bra

35 睡衣 [-] shuìyī (sleep-clothes) <n.> sleepwear: 一套~ a set of sleepwear

36 袖子 [-] xiùzi (sleeve-*suffix*) <n.> sleeve: 长/短~ long/short sleeves

37 项链 [項鏈] xiàngliàn (neck-chain) <n.> necklace: 一条~ a necklace || 戴~ wear necklace || 金~ golden necklace

38 耳环 [-環] ěrhuán (ear-ring) <n.> earing: 一对~ a pair of earings || 戴~ wear earing || 钻石~ diamond earing

39 戒指 [-] jièzhǐ (warn-finger) <n.> ring: 戴~ wear ring || 金~ golden ring || 结婚~ wedding ring

Tips:

1 Radical 衤: This radical means 衣, clothes. Characters with this radical include 装 (dress,) 衬衫 (shirt,) 裙 (skirt,) 裤 (trousers/pants,) 袋 (bag, pocket,) 袜 (socks) and 袖 (sleeve), which are listed above.
2 Radicals 衤 and 礻: They look alike but are very different in meaning. As stated above, 衤 means 'clothes,' while 礻 means 'god' since its original form 示 is a symbol of ancestral tablets. Many common Chinese characters have 礻 as their radical. For example, 福 (fú, happiness, luck, fortune,) 祝 (zhù, pray, wish) and 神 (shén, god).
3 衣食住行 (yīshízhùxíng): Literally, they mean 'clothing, food, shelter and transportation' and function as 'basic necessities of life.'
4 Saying "人靠衣装, 佛靠金装" (rén kào yīzhuāng, fó kào jīn zhuāng): 靠 means 'to rely on, to depend on,' and 佛 means 'Buddha.' The whole saying means 'fine clothes make the man.' It vividly shows the importance of dress, especially in the current Chinese society.
5 件: 件 (jiàn) is a general measure word for clothes. Its original meaning was 'to distinguish' since it is related to 人 and 牛, which is a large animal and can be easily distinguished.

Exercises:

Part I: Answer the following questions in Chinese.

1 你衣柜里有什么衣服?

2 你最贵的衣服是什么衣服? 什么牌子的? 多少钱?

3 你有什么鞋? 哪种鞋最舒服? 哪种鞋最漂亮?

4 你最贵的鞋是什么鞋? 什么牌子的? 多少钱?

5 你什么时候会穿晚礼服?

Theme 43: Cultural and artistic supplies 文艺用品 (wényì yòngpǐn)

(See also Theme 130)

1 乐器 [樂-] yuèqì (music-vessel/instrument) <n.> instrument: 弹奏 (tánzòu) ~ play instrument低音~ bass instrument || 打击~ percussion instrument

2 琴 [-] qín (zither) <n.> a general name for certain musical instrument: 弹~ play lyre || 拉~ play lyre || 练~ practice lyre

3 钢琴 [鋼-] gāngqín (iron-zither) <n.> piano: 一架~ a piano || 弹~ play piano || ~曲

4 电子琴 [電--] diànzǐqín (electronic-zither) <n.> electronic keyboard: 弹~ play electronic keyboard || 多功能~ multi-function keyboard

5 提琴 [-] tíqín (hold-zither) <n.> the violin family: 大/小/中~ cello/violin/viola || 拉~ play cello/violin/viola

6 风琴 [風-] fēngqín (wind-zither) <n.> organ: 弹~ play organ || 演奏~ perform organ || 一架~ an organ

7 手风琴 [-風-] shǒufēngqín (hand-wind-zither) <n.> accordion: 拉~ play accordion || 演奏~ perform accordion

8 口琴 [-] kǒuqín (mouth-zither) <n.> mouth organ: 吹~ play mouth organ

9 古琴 [-] gǔqín (ancient-zither) <n.> guqin, a seven-stringed plucked instrument in some ways similar to the zither: 弹~ play guqin

10 号 [號] hào (horn) <n.> any brass-wind instrument: 小~ trumpet || 军~ bugle

11 萨克斯管 [薩---] sàkèsīguǎn (*transliteration*-tube) <n.> saxophone: 吹~ play saxophone

12 鼓 [-] gǔ (drum) <n.> drum: 打~ play drum || 爵士~ a jazz tomtom

13 吉他 [-] jítā (*transliteration*) <n.> guitar: 弹~ play guitar || 一把/个~ a guitar

14 二胡 [-] èrhú (2 (strings) -foreign (zither)) <n.> erhu (a two-stringed bowed instrument with a lower register): 拉~ paly erhu || 一把/个~ a erhu

15 笛子 [-] dízi (flute-*suffix*) <n.> flute: 吹~ play flute || 一支~ a flute

16 摄像机 [--機] shèxiàngjī (take in-picture-machine) <n.> video camera: 一台~ a video camera

17 照相机 [--機] zhàoxiàngjī (shoot-image-machine) <n.> camera: 数码~ digital camera || 两部/架/个~ two cameras || 水下~ underwater camera

18 屏幕 [-] píngmù (screen-curtain) <n.> screen: 电视~ TV screen || 电脑~ computer screen

19 麦克风 [麥-風] màikèfēng (*transliteration*) <n.> microphone: 无线~ wireless microphone

20 光盘 [-盤] guāngpán (laser-disc) <n.> DVD: 一张~ a DVD || 电影~ movie DVD

21 录像 [錄-] lùxiàng (record-picture) <n.> videotape: 播放~ play video || 看~ watch videotape

22 唱片 [-] chàngpiān (sing-disc) <n.> gramophone record: 一张~ a gramophone record || 录~ make a gramophone record || 听~ listen to a gramophone record

23 磁带 [-帶] cídài (magnet-tape) <n.> magnetic tape: 一盘/盒~ a magnetic tape || 放~ play a magnetic tape

24 胶卷 [膠-] jiāojuǎn (rubber-roll) <n.> roll film: 电影~ movie film roll || 彩色~ polychrome film || 黑白~ black and white film roll

Tips:

1 琴棋书画 (qínqíshūhuà): Literally, they are zither, chess, calligraphy and painting. In ancient China, a talented and civilized person must master these four skills.

2 Radical 玨: All Chinese characters with the radical 玨 are musical instruments. For example, 琴, 瑟 (sè, a 50-string plucked instrument), 琵琶 (pípa, Chinese lute).
3 Equal temperament: It is called 十二平均律 in Chinese. In 1584, A Ming Dynasty Prince Zhu Zaiyu first described the equal temperament through accurate mathematical calculations.

Exercises:

Part I: Answer the following questions in Chinese.

1 请写出几种西洋乐器

---

2 请写出几种中国乐器

---

3 你会什么乐器? 学了多长时间了?

---

4 "她子琴棋书画样样精通," 这句话的意思是:

a) 她会下棋和画画.
b) 她会弹琴和写书.
c) 她有多种才能.

Theme 44: Sports, games 体育 (tǐyù)

(See also Themes 85, 164)

1 球 [-] qiú (ball) <n.> ball: 踢/打~ play ball || 玩~ play ball || ~门the mouth of the goal
2 球拍 [-] qiúpāi (ball-racket) <n.> racket: 一对 ~ a pair of racket || 网~ tennis racket || 乒乓~ ping-pong racket
3 篮球 [籃-] lánqiú (basket-ball) <n.> basketball: 打~ play basketball || 举行 ~ 比赛hold a basketball contest
4 排球 [-] páiqiú (row-ball) <n.> volleyball: 男子 ~ men's volleyball || 女子~ women's volleyball || ~沙滩~ beach volleyball. This term was coined in 1930.
5 足球 [-] zúqiú (foot-ball) <n.> football: 踢~ play football || ~比赛football match
6 橄榄球 [-欖-] gǎnlǎnqiú (olive-ball) <n.> rugby, American football: 打 ~ play American football || 美式~ American football
7 棒球 [-] bàngqiú (bat-ball) <n.> baseball: 打~ play baseball
8 网球 [網-] wǎngqiú (net-ball) <n.> tennis: 打~ tennis
9 羽毛球 [-] yǔmáoqiú (feather-ball) <n.> badminton: 打~ play badminton
10 高尔夫球 [-爾--] gāo'ěrfū qiú (*transliteration*-ball) <n.> golf: 打~ play golf
11 冰球 [-] bīngqiú (ice-ball) <n.> ice hockey: 打~ play ice hockey

12 乒乓球 [-] pīngpāngqiú (*onomatopoetic*-ball) <n.> table tennis: 打~ play table tennis
13 壁球 [-] bìqiú (wall-ball) <n.> squash: 打~ play squash
14 板球 [-] bǎnqiú (board-ball) <n.> cricket: 打~ play cricket
15 保龄球 [-齡-] bǎolíngqiú (*transliteration*-ball) <n.> bowling: ~馆bowling alley || 打~ play bowling

16 棋 [-] qí (chess) <n.> chess: 下~ play chess || ~子chessman
17 象棋 [-] xiàngqí (analog-chess) <n.> chess: 国际~ international chess || 中国~ chinese chess || 下~ play chess
18 围棋 [圍-] wéiqí (enclose-chess) <n.> Go chess: 下~ play Go chess

19 滑板 [-] huábǎn (slide-board) <n.> skateboard: 玩~ play skateboard
20 钓鱼杆 [釣魚-] diàoyúgān (fishing-pole) <n.> fishing rod: 一根 ~ a fishing rod
21 跳绳 [-繩] tiàoshéng (jump-rope) <n.> jump rope: 一根 ~ a jump rope
22 哑铃 [啞鈴] yǎlíng (dumb-bell) <n.> dumbbell: 举~ lift dumbbell
23 跑步机 [--機] pǎobùjī (jog-machine) <n.> treadmill: 多功能~ multiple function treadmill

24 毽子 [-] jiànzi (shuttlecock-*suffix*) <n.> shuttlecock: 踢 ~ kick shuttlecock
25 玩具 [-] wánjù (play-tool) <n.> toy: 电动~ power-driven toy || 塑料~ plastic toy
26 皮球 [-] píqiú (leather-ball) <n.> ball: 拍~ play ball
27 气球 [氣-] qìqiú (air-ball) <n.> balloon: 吹~ blow balloon || 彩色 ~ colorful balloon
28 烟花 [煙-] yānhuā (smoke-flower) <n.> fireworks: 放~ shoot fireworks || 看~ watch fireworks
29 游戏机 [遊戲機] yóuxìjī (game-machine) <n.> game player: 玩/打~ play game player
30 跳舞毯 [-] tiàowǔtǎn (dance-carpet) <n.> dancing blanket: 一块~ a piece of dancing blanket
31 彩票 [-] cǎipiào (gamble-ticket) <n.> lottery ticket: 一张~ a lottery ticket || 买~ buy a lottery ticket || 中~ win the lottery
32 电影票 [電--] diànyǐngpiào (movie-ticket) <n.> movie ticket: 一张 ~ a movie ticket || 买~ buy a movie ticket
33 门票 [門-] ménpiào (gate-ticket) <n.> entrance ticket: 公园~ park entrance ticket

Tips:

1 Games using balls, big and small: In China, the three major ball games are 篮足排, namely 篮球 (basketball), 足球 (soccer), and 排球 (volleyball,) in all of which China's national teams, men's and women's, are not top competitors in the world, except for in women's volleyball. Understandably, China is extremely good at two games using small balls, 乒乓球 (ping-pong, table tennis) and 羽毛球 (badminton), both of which do not require direct physical contact. Ping-pong diplomacy in the early 1970s paved the way for U.S. President Richard Nixon to visit Beijing. The Chinese cherish this event and

call it 小球转动大球 (xiǎoqiú zhuàndòng dàqiú, small ball-rotate-large ball), a metaphor explaining that this event normalized Sino-U.S. diplomatic relations and thus greatly changed international relations.

2 下棋 and 手谈 (shǒután): An elegant name for 下围棋 (to play the game Go) is 手谈, which means 'communicate with hands,' to emphasize that it is more than a game.

3 烟花: Two other forms of 烟花 are 烟火 or 焰火 (yànhuǒ). The three forms are similar in sound. It is said China produces a large majority of the world's fireworks, including the annual July 4th fireworks in the U.S. and the fireworks for the Olympic Games' opening ceremonies.

Exercises:

Part I: Answer the following questions based on your own perspectives.

篮球、排球、足球、网球、橄榄球、棒球、冰球、羽毛球、壁球、板球、高尔夫球、保龄球

1 读一读上面给出的词, 选出你喜欢的运动, 写下来

2 读一读上面给出的词, 选出你不喜欢的运动, 写下来

3 读一读上面给出的词, 写出哪些是中国人说的"大球运动," 写下来

4 读一读上面给出的词, 写出哪些是中国人说的"小球运动," 写下来

Theme 45: Office supplies 办公用品 (bàngōng yòngpǐn)

(See also Theme 67)

1 电脑 [電腦] diànnǎo (electronic-brain) <n.> computer, laptop: 一台 ~ a computer || 开/关~ turn on/ shut down computer || 笔记本~ laptop
2 计算机 [計-機] jìsuànjī (calculate-machine) <n.> computer: ~语言computer language || 电子~ electronic computer
3 硬件 [-] yìngjiàn (hard-ware) <n.> hardware: 电脑~ computer hardware
4 软件 [軟-] ruǎnjiàn (soft-ware) <n.> software: 电脑~ computer software || 设计~ design software
5 光盘 [-盤] guāngpán (optical-disk) <n.> compact disk: 一张~ a CD || 制作~ make a CD
6 U盘 [U盤] U pán (U-disk) <n.> U disk: 一个~ a U disk || 存在~ storage in U disk
7 键盘 [鍵盤] jiànpán (key-board) <n.> keyboard: 电脑 ~ computer keyboard || 按动~ press on the keyboard || ~输入keyboard input

8 键 [鍵] jiàn (key) <n.> key: 琴~ piano key || 按 ~ key-press || 黑~ black key || 白~ white key

9 打印机 [--機] dǎyìnjī (print-machine) <n.> printer: 一台~ a printer || 数字~ digital printer || 激光~ laser printer

10 复印机 [複-機] fùyìnjī (copy-machine) <n.> copier, copy machine: 电子~ electronic copier || 高速~ high speed copier || 静电xerox copier

11 扫描仪 [掃-儀] sǎomiáoyí (scan-machine) <n.> scanner: 红外线~ infrared ray scanner || 图象~ image scanner

12 投影仪 [--儀] tóuyǐngyí (project-machine) <n.> projector: 家用~ household projector || 进口~ imported projector || 微型~ mini projector

13 传真机 [傳-機] chuánzhēnjī (fax-machine) <n.> fax: 数码~ digital fax || 无纸~ paperless fax machine

14 办公桌 [辦--] bàngōngzhuō (office-desk) <n.> office desk: 一张 ~ an office desk

15 电脑椅 [電腦-] diànnǎoyǐ (computer-chair) <n.> computer chair: 一把~ a computer chair

16 票 [-] piào (ticket) <n.> ticket: 买~ buy ticket || 火车~ train ticket || 电影~ movie ticket

17 机票 [機-] jīpiào (airplane-ticket) <n.> air ticket: 一张a plane ticket || 单程~ one-way ticket || 往返~ round trip ticket

18 车票 [車-] chēpiào (vehicle-ticket) <n.> train or bus ticket: 单程~ a single ticket/往返~ round-trip ticket

19 邮票 [郵-] yóupiào (postage-certificate) <n.> stamp: 一张~ a stamp || 贴~ stick on a stamp

20 发票 [發-] fāpiào (sale-certificate) <n.> invoice: 一张~ an invoice/bill || 开~ make out an invoice

21 证 [証] zhèng (certificate) <n.> certificate: 出生~ birth certificate || 结婚~ marriage certificate

22 证件 [證-] zhèngjiàn (prove-item) <n.> credentials: 检查~ check your credentials || 出示~ show your credentials

23 证书 [證書] zhèngshū (certificate-document) <n.> certificate: 游泳~ swimming certificate || 获得一张~ get a certificate

24 证明 [證-] zhèngmíng (prove-true) <n.> testimonial, proof: 工作~ testimonial of work || 存款 (cúnkuǎn) ~ proof of deposit

25 身份证 [--證] shēnfènzhèng (identification-proof) <n.> identification card: 办~ apply for identification card || 带~ bring your identification card

26 驾照 [駕-] jiàzhào (drive-license) <n.> driver license: 考~ take driving test

27 护照 [護-] hùzhào (protect-license) <n.> passport: ~号码passport number || 办~ apply for a passport ||持中国~ hold a Chinese passport

28 绿卡 [綠-] lǜkǎ (green-card) <n.> permanent resident card (Green Card): 美国~ American permanent resident card || 获得~ get a Green Card

29 本子 [-] běnzi (book-*suffix*) <n.> notebook: 一个~ a notebook || 买~ buy a notebook

30 日记本 [-記-] rìjìběn (daily-record-book) <n.> diary: 写在~上write on a diary

31 笔记本 [筆記-] bǐjìběn (note-book) <n.> notebook: 一个~ a notebook || 厚厚的~ a thick notebook || ~电脑laptop

32 纸 [紙] zhǐ (paper) <n.> paper: 一张~ a piece of paper

33 笔 [筆] (brush) <n.> pen, pencil: 一支~ a pen/pencil || 毛~ writing brush

34 钢笔 [鋼筆] gāngbǐ (iron-pen) <n.> pen: 一支~ a pen

35 圆珠笔 [圓-筆] yuánzhūbǐ (round-ball-pen) <n.> ballpoint pen: 一支~ a ballpoint pen || 红~ a red ballpoint pen || 蓝~ a blue ballpoint pen

36 铅笔 [鉛筆] qiānbǐ (lead-pen) <n.> pencil: 一支~ a pencil || 红色~ a red pencil || 彩色~ colored pencil

37 墨 [-] mò (ink) <n.> ink: 造~ make ink || 一块~ a piece of ink || 用~ use ink

38 砚 [硯] yàn (inkstone) <n.> ink stone: 制~ make an ink stone || 名~ a famous ink stone

39 墨水 [-] mòshuǐ (ink-water) <n.> ink: 红/蓝~ red/blue ink || 一瓶 ~ one bottle of ink || 老王肚子里有很多~. Lao Wang is very knowledgeable.

40 文件夹 [--夾] wénjiànjiā (file-folder) <n.> folder: 一个~ a folder

41 卡 [-] kǎ (card) <n.> card: 一张~ a card || 银行~ a bank card || 借书~ check out card

42 信用卡 [-] xìnyòngkǎ (credit-card) <n.> credit card: 办~ get a credit card || 用~ use a credit card

43 银行卡 [銀--] yínhángkǎ (bank-card) <n.> bank card: 办~ get a bank card || 用~ use a bank card

44 贺卡 [賀-] hèkǎ (congratulate-card) <n.> greeting card: 生日~ birthday card || 寄~ mail a greeting card || 一张~ a greeting card

45 礼品卡 [禮--] lǐpǐnkǎ (gift-card) <n.> gift card: 买一张~ buy a gift card

46 优惠券 [優--] yōuhuìquàn (preferential-ticket) <n.> coupon: 领取~ get a coupon || 食品~ food voucher

47 名片 [-] míngpiàn (name-card) <n.> business card: 一张~ a business card || 交换~ exchange business card

48 牌 [-] pái (board) <n.> brand, tag: 名~ famous brand, name tag || 车~ car plate

49 车牌 [車-] chēpái (vehicle-plate) <n.> license plate: ~号码license plate number

50 金牌 [-] jīnpái (gold-medal) <n.> gold medal: 一块/枚~ a gold medal || 获得~ win the gold medal

51 名单 [-單] míngdān (name-list) <n.> list of names, roster: 学生~ student roster||候选人~the list of candidates || 黑~ blacklist

52 菜单 [-單] càidān (dish-list) <n.> menu: 照着~点菜order dishes according from the menu || 一张~ a menu

53 铃 [鈴] líng (bell) <n.> bell: 门~ doorbell || 按 ~ ring the bell

54 国旗 [國-] guóqí (national-flag) <n.> national flag: 一面~ a national flag || 升~ raise the national flag

55 黑板hēibǎn [-] (black-board) <n.> blackboard: 一块~ a blackboard || 擦~ clean the blackboard || 看~ look at the blackboard

56 信封 [-] xìnfēng (letter-cover) <n.> envelope: 拆 (chāi) 开~ open the envelope

57 胶带 [膠-] jiāodài (sticky-band) <n.> tape: 双面~ double adhesive tape

58 胶水 [膠-] jiāoshuǐ (sticky-water) <n.> glue

59 图钉 [圖釘] túdīng (book-nail) <n.> drawing pin, thumbtack: 大/小~ large/small thumbtack

60 订书机 [訂書機] dìngshūjī (bind-book-machine) <n.> stapler

61 尺子 [-] chǐ zi (ruler-*suffix*) <n.> ruler: 一把~ a ruler
62 橡皮 [-] xiàngpí (rubber-elastic) <n.> rubber: 一块~ a rubber
63 圆规 [圓規] yuánguī (circle-compass) <n.> compasses: 一个~ a pair of compasses
64 三角板 [-] sānjiǎobǎn (triangle-board) <n.> set-square: 一块 ~ a set-square

Tips:

1 器 (qì): The four 口 indicate 'vessels' and 犬 means 'dog.' The character 器 indicates 'a dog guards many vessels,' so it means 'vessels.'
2 机器 (jīqì) vs. 仪器 (yíqì): 机器 means 'machine' and 仪器 'apparatus.'
3 卡 (qiǎ, kǎ): When it is pronounced as qiǎ, it means 'checkpoint' or 'be wedged, stuck.' 卡 (kǎ) is used to transliterate foreign words such as 卡车 (truck) and 卡路里 (calorie.) The 卡 (kǎ) 卡片 (card) and 信用卡 (credit card) is a transliteration of 'card.'

Exercises:

Part I: You are donating 20 office supplies to a remote rural primary school in China. Please write 20 things you think are the most needed in this elementary school.

	办公用品 (中文)	办公用品 (英文)	数量
1			
2			
3			
4			
5			
6			
7			
8			
9			
10			
11			
12			
13			
14			
15			

Theme 46: Food 饮食 (yǐnshí)

(See also Themes 16, 124)

1 西餐 xīcān (Western-food) <n.> Western-style food: ~厅 (tīng) Western-style food restaurant
2 中餐 zhōngcān (Chinese-food) <n.> ~馆 Chinese restaurant
3 早餐 zǎocān (morning-food) <n.> breakfast: 一份 (fèn) ~ a portion of breakfast
4 午餐 wǔcān (noon-food) <n.> lunch: 一顿 (dùn) ~ a lunch || 吃~ eat lunch
5 晚餐 wǎncān (evening-food) <n.> supper, dinner: 吃~ eat supper || 丰盛的~ a rich (generous) dinner
6 主食 zhǔshí (principal-food) <n.> staple food: 中国人/西方人的~ Chinese/ Westerners' staple food || 今晚的~ tonight's staple food
7 副食 fùshí (auxiliary-food) <n.> non-staple food: ~店 grocery

8 饭 [飯] fàn (food) <n.> meal: 一顿~ a meal || 早/午/晚~ breakfast/lunch/dinner
9 米饭 [-飯] mǐfàn (rice-food) <n.> (cooked) rice: 一碗 (wǎn) ~ a bowl of rice || 白米饭white rice || 糙米饭 (cāo –) brown rice
10 粥 zhōu (porridge) <n.> porridge, congee: 一碗 (wǎn) ~ a bowl of congee || 大米/小米/绿豆~ rice/millet/mung bean congee
11 稀饭 [稀飯] xīfàn (thin-food) <n.> gruel: 一碗~ a bowl of || 吃/喝~ Note: It could mean 喜欢 (like) in internet language since some southern Chinese dialects do not discriminate between 'f-' and 'h-,' this makes 欢 (huan) and 饭 (fan) sort of similar in sound.
12 面食 [麵-] miànshí (flour-food) (cooked) <n.> wheat food: 做~ Note: Some Chinese provinces such as Shanxi, Shaanxi, He'nan and Gansu are known for their wheat foods.
13 面包 [麵-] miànbāo (flour-bun) <n.> bread: 一片~ a slice of bread || 一块~ a piece of bread || 一袋 (dài) ~ a loaf of bread || 全麦 (mài) ~ whole wheat bread
14 面条儿 [麵條兒] miàntiáo er (flour-strip) <n.> noodle: 一碗~ a bowl of noodles
15 方便面 [--麵] fāngbiànmiàn (convenient-noodle) <n.> instant noodle: 一袋 (dài) /碗~ a bag/bowl of instant noodle || 泡/煮 (pào/zhǔ) ~ steep/boil instant noodle
16 包子 bāozi (stuffed-*suffix*) <n.> (steamed) stuffed bun: 一个~ a stuffed bun || 一笼 (lóng) ~ a tray of stuffed buns
17 馒头 [饅頭] mántou (bun-*suffix*) <n.> (steamed) bun: 一个~ a steamed bun || 蒸 (zhēng) ~ steam bun
18 饺子 [餃-] jiǎozi (dumpling-*suffix*) <n.> dumpling: 包~ make dumplings
19 汤圆 [湯圓] tāngyuán (soup-ball) <n.> glutinous pudding: 一个/碗~ a (bowl) of glutinous pudding || 煮 (zhǔ) ~ boil glutinous pudding
20 粽子 zòngzi (rice dumpling-*suffix*) <n.> traditional Chinese rice pudding eaten at the Dragon Boat Festival: 一个~ a rice pudding || 包~ make/wrap rice pudding

21 菜 cài (vegetable/dish) <n.> dish: 一道~ a course of dish || 做~ make/cook dishes
22 美食 měishí (delicious-food) <n.> fine food, delicacy: ~家epicure || ~节 food festival

23 菜单 [-單] càidān (dish-list) <n.> menu: 一份~ a menu
24 开胃菜 [開--] kāiwèicài (whet-appetite-dish) <n.> appetizer, starter: 一道~ an appetizer
25 小吃 xiǎochī (small-food) <n.> snack: 风味~ local flavors || ~店 snack bar
26 肉 ròu (meat of animals) <n.> meat: 鸡~ chicken || 牛~ beef || 猪 (zhū) ~ pork || 羊~ lamb || 鱼~ fish || 一块~ a piece/chunk of meat
27 海鲜 [-鮮] hǎixiān (sea-fresh) <n.> seafood: ~汤 ~ seafood soup
28 烤肉 kǎoròu (roast-meat) <n.> roast meat, barbecue: ~店 barbecue shop || 做~ make roast meat
29 香肠 [-腸] xiāngcháng (fragrant-intestine) <n.> sausage: 一根~ a sausage || 烤~ baked sausage || 灌 (guàn) ~ fill/make sausage
30 烤鸭 [-鴨] kǎoyā (roast-duck) <n.> roast duck: 一只~ a roast duck || 北京~ Beijing roast duck
31 鸡蛋 [鷄-] jīdàn (chicken-egg) <n.> (chicken) egg: 一盒 (hé) ~ a carton/box of eggs || 鲜 (xiān) ~ fresh egg
32 豆腐 tòufu (bean-curd) <n.> bean curd, tofu: 老~ firm tofu
33 汤 [湯] tāng (soup) <n.> soup: 鸡蛋~ egg drop soup
34 火锅 [-鍋] huǒguō (fire-pot) <n.> hot pot: ~店 hot pot restaurant || 吃~ have some hot pot
35 点心 [點-] diǎnxīn (bit-regard) <n.> light refreshments, dim sum: 吃~ eat refreshments || 做~ make refreshments || 传统~ traditional refreshments
36 茶 (chá) 点 (tea-refreshment) refreshments: 吃~ eat refreshments

37 快餐 kuàicān (fast-food) <n.> fast food: 一份~ a fast food || ~店 fast food restaurant || 西式~ Western style fast food || 中式~ Chinese style fast food
38 盒饭 [-飯] héfàn (box-food) <n.> boxed lunch: 一个~ a boxed lunch || 吃~ eat a boxed lunch
39 套餐 tàocān (set-meal) <n.> set meal: 经济 (jīngjì) ~ a value meal
40 签语饼 [簽語餅] qiānyǔbǐng (sign-word-cookie) <n.> fortune cookie: 一个~ a fortune cookie

41 酒 [-] jiǔ (liquor) <n.> alcoholic drink, wine, liquor: 一杯/瓶~~ a glass/bottle of liquor || 喝醉 (zuì) ~ get drunk || ~吧wine bar
42 白酒 [-] báijiǔ (clear-liquor) <n.> colorless spirit distilled from grains: 一瓶~ a bottle of Chinese spirits || 喝~ drink Chinese spirits
43 红酒 [-] hóngjiǔ (red-wine) <n.> wine: 一杯~ a cup of red wine || 品尝~ taste red wine || 喝~ drink red wine
44 啤酒 [-] píjiǔ (*transliteration* of beer-liquor) <n.> beer: 冰~ cold beer || 喝~ drink beer || 一杯~ a cup of beer

45 咖啡 [-] kāfēi (*transliteration* of coffee) <n.> coffee: 喝~ drink coffee || 一杯~ a cup of coffee
46 茶 [-] chá (tea) <n.> tea: 泡~ make tea || 喝~ drink tea || 一杯 ~ a cup of tea
47 绿茶 [綠-] lǜchá (green-tea) <n.> green tea: 中国 ~ chinese green tea
48 红茶 [紅-] hóngchá (red-tea) <n.> black tea: 泡一杯~ make a cup of black tea
49 奶茶 [-] nǎichá (milk-tea) <n.> milk tea: 珍珠~ bubble milk tea

50 果汁 [-] guǒzhī (fruit-juice) <n.> juice: 一瓶~ a bottle of juice || 新鲜~ fresh juice
51 酸奶 [-] suānnǎi (sour-milk) <n.> yogurt: 喝~ yogurt || 一瓶~ a bottle of yogurt
52 矿泉水 [礦--] kuàngquánshuǐ (mine-spring-water) <n.> mineral water: 一瓶~ a bottle of mineral water || 喝~ drink mineral water
53 纯净水 [純淨-] chúnjìngshuǐ (pure-clear-water) <n.> purified water: 一瓶~ a bottle of purified water || 喝~ drink purified water
54 自来水 [-來-] zìláishuǐ (self-come-water) <n.> tap water: 用~冲洗wash with tap water
55 甜点 [-點] tiándiǎn (sweet-dessert) <n.> dessert: 吃~ eat dessert || 各式~ all kinds of dessert
56 蛋糕 [-] dàngāo (egg-cake) <n.> cake: 一块 ~ a piece/slice of cake || 奶油~ cream cake || 生日~ bithday cake
57 饼干 [餅乾] bǐnggān (cake-dried) <n.> biscuit, cookie: 一块~ a cookie || 夹心~ sandwich biscuit
58 巧克力 [-] qiǎokèlì (*transliteration* of chocolate) <n.> chocolate: 一块~ a piece of chocolate
59 奶糖 [-] nǎitáng (milk-candy) <n.> toffee: 一颗 (kē) ~ a toffee
60 水果糖 [-] shuǐguǒtáng (fruit-candy) <n.> fruit drops: 一颗~ a fruit drops
61 冰激淋/冰淇淋[-] bīngjīlíng (ice-*transliteration* of cream) <n.> ice cream: 巧克力~ chocolate ice cream
62 冰棍儿 [--兒] bīnggùn er (ice-stick) <n.> popsicle: 一根 ~ a popsicle
63 冰沙 [-] bīngshā (ice-granulated) <n.> slushie: 红豆/绿豆~ red/green bean slushie

Tips:

1 Radical 饣: A key radical in the constituent characters of words about food is 饣 (食) which constitutes the semantic part of the following characters: 饭fàn, food, 饮yǐn, drink, 饱bǎo, full, 饺jiǎo, dumpling, 饼bǐng, pancake, 饿è, hungry, 馆guǎn, guesthouse, 馒mán, bun, 饥jī, famine, very hungry, 餐cān, meal etc.
2 来 . . . (food): If one dines at a small restaurant or food stand, the typical way to order food is "老板, 来+ number + MW + food name," for example, "老板, 来碗牛肉面" (Boss, a bowl of beef noodles, please.)
3 中餐馆 (zhōngcānguǎn) vs. 西餐厅 (xīcāntīng): They mean Chinese or Western restaurants, however, 西餐厅 is more common than 西餐馆, so is 中餐馆 over 中餐厅.

Exercises:

Part I: Multiple Choice

1 What are included in the Chinese一日三餐?
A. 早餐 B. 午餐 C. 晚餐 D. 下午茶 E. 开胃菜

2 An American couple wants to eat authentic Chinese fast food, please recommend what they should eat from the following selections:
A. 签语饼 B. 面条 C. 包子 D. 方便面 E. 饺子

3 What are Chinese staple foods?
A. 饺子 B. 面条 C. 包子 D. 馒头 E. 米饭

4 What are Chinese non-staple foods?
A. 粥 B. 海鲜 C. 烤肉 D. 香肠 E. 火锅

5 What are the foods special for Chinese festivals?
A. 稀饭 B. 汤圆 C. 粽子 D. 汤 E. 饺子

6 Select and form a fast food set meal according to Chinese eating habits.
A. 海鲜盒饭 B. 汤 C. 粥 D. 火锅 E. 开胃菜

7 What materials are suitable for making Chinese style soups?
A. 点心 B. 签语饼 C. 盒饭 D. 豆腐 E. 鸡蛋

Part II: Classify the following words as Chinese main foods or non-staple foods.

米饭 稀饭 馒头 饺子 菜 香肠 鸡蛋 火锅
饭 面包 包子 汤圆 肉 烤鸭 汤 豆腐
粥 面食 面条儿 粽子 海鲜 烤肉

主食	副食

Part III: The canteen in your school will hold a Chinese food festival. You are responsible for assisting to write a week's menu. Please choose the correct foods to make a Chinese diet menu.

签语饼	点心	西式快餐	开胃菜	海鲜	烤肉	盒饭	套餐
米饭	稀饭	馒头	饺子	菜	香肠	鸡蛋	火锅
开胃菜	面包	包子	汤圆	肉	烤鸭	汤	豆腐
粥	面食	面条儿	粽子	小吃			

时间	星期一	星期二	星期三	星期四	星期五
早餐	主食 副食	主食 副食	主食 副食	主食 副食	主食 副食

午餐	主食 副食	主食 副食	主食 副食	主食 副食	主食 副食
晚餐	主食 副食	主食 副食	主食 副食	主食 副食	主食 副食

Theme 47: Medicine 药品 (yàopǐn)

1 药 [藥] yào (medicine) <n.> medicine: 吃/服~ take medicine || 开~ prescribe a medicine
2 药物 [藥-] yàowù (medicine-stuff) <n.> medicine: ~治疗medication
3 医药 [醫藥] yīyào (cure-medicine) <n.> remedy and medicine: ~费medical costs || ~代表pharmaceutical sales
4 西药 [-藥] xīyào (Western-medicine) <n.> Western medicine: ~成分Western medicine ingredients || 服用~ take Western medicine || ~药丸 (yàowán) Western medicine pills
5 中药 [-藥] zhōngyào (Chinese-medicine) <n.> traditional Chinese medicine: 喝 -take Chinese medicine || 一味~ a dose of Chinese medicine || 一副~ a package of Chinese medicine || ~方子a prescription for Chinese medicine
6 处方药 [處-藥] chǔfāngyào (cure-method-medicine) <n.> prescription medicine: 非~ non-prescribed medicine
7 补药 [補藥] bǔyào (supplement-medicine) <n.> tonic, invigorator: 吃~ eat invigorator
8 退烧药 [-燒藥] tuìshāoyào (recede-fever-medicine) <n.> antipyretic, fever reducer: 吃/服~ take fever reducer
9 感冒药 [--藥] gǎnmàoyào (flu-medicine) <n.> cold medicine: 吃/服~ take cold medicine
10 止疼药 [--藥] zhǐténgyào (stop-pain-medicine) <n.> painkiller: 吃/服~ take painkiller
11 消炎药 [--藥] xiāoyányào (eliminate-inflammation-medicine) <n.> antibiotic medicine: 吃/服~ take antibiotic medicine
12 麻醉药 [--藥] mázùiyào (anesthetic-medicine) <n.> anesthetic, narcotic: 打~ inject anesthetic
13 安眠药 [--藥] ānmiányào (sound-sleep-medicine) <n.> sleeping pill: 吃/服~ take sleeping pill

14 避孕药 [--藥] bìyùnyào (avoid-pregnancy-medicine) <n.> contraceptive medicine: 吃/服~ take contraceptive medicine

15 针 [針] zhēn (needle) <n.> injection: 打~ give or have an injection || 退烧~ fever injection

16 药水 [藥-] yàoshuǐ (medicine-liquid) <n.> liquid medicine: 眼~ eyedrops || 涂~ apply liquid medicine || 杀虫~ desinsection liquid medicine

17 药膏 [藥-] yàogāo (medicine-ointment) <n.> ointment: 涂~ rub the ointment

18 药片 [藥-] yàopiàn (medicine-tablet) <n.> pill: 一片~ a piece of pill || 吃~ take pills

19 药酒 [藥-] yàojiǔ (medicine-alcohol) <n.> medicated wine: 喝~ drink medicated wine || 一杯~ a cup of medicated wine

20 膏药 [-藥] gāoyào (ointment-medicine) <n.> plaster, medicine patch: 止疼~ Analgesic plaster || 贴~ apply a plaster to || 狗皮~ dog skin plaster. Dog skin plaster was originally a traditional Chinese medicine and was used to quickly reduce swelling and pain. In a modern Chinese language environment, some do not refer to 'dog skin plaster,' as medicine, but to another rich derogatory meaning, such as selling 'dog plaster' means the seller is a fraud.

21 止咳糖浆 [---漿] zhǐkétángjiāng (stop-cough-sugar-syrup) <n.> cough sirup: 一瓶~ a bottle of cough syrup || 喝~ drink cough syrup

22 维生素 [維--] wéishēngsù (*transliteration*, also maintain-life-element) <n.> vitamin: 含~ contain vitamin || 多种~ multiple vitamins || 缺~ vitamin deficiency

23 钙片 [鈣-] gàipiàn (calcium-tablet) <n.> calcium tablet: 一块 ~ a piece of calcium tablet || 儿童~ children calcium tablet

24 蜂蜜 [-] fēngmì (bee-honey) <n.> honey: ~水 honey water

Tips:

1 Method to name medicines: It is easy, 'function'+药 (medicine). For example, 退烧药 ('recede-fever'+药), 止疼药 ('stop-pain'+药), 消炎药 ('eliminate-inflammation'+药), 避孕药 ('avoid-pregnancy'+药), 麻醉药 ('anesthetic'+药), and 安眠药 ('sound-sleep'+药) which are all listed above, and even 减肥药 ('reduce-fat'+药, weight loss pills, diet pills).

2 Forms of medicine: Common forms of Chinese medicine include 膏 (gāo, ointment), 丸 (wán, pill), 片 (piàn, tablet), 针 (zhēn, needle/injection), 粉 (fěn, powder), 水 (liquid) and 酒 (jiǔ, liquor). They are used usually after 药, for example, 药酒 (medicine-liquor, medical liquor).

3 良药苦口利于病 (liángyào kǔkǒu lìyú bìng): This proverb means 'good medicine is bitter to the taste, but beneficial for your health.'

4 吃错药 (chī cuò yào): When a person acts differently or weirdly, others say he 吃错药了, which means he 'ate the wrong medicine' literally, but functions as 'he is weird (today).'

Exercises:

Part I: Please translate the doctor's Chinese prescription into English.

姓名	张小红	性别	女	年龄	22岁
病因	感冒				
医生建议					
1. 服感冒药 (西药、药片): 一日二次, 一次二片 2. 服退烧药 (西药、药片): 一日二次, 一次二片 3. 服咳嗽糖浆 (中药、药水): 一日三次, 一次一杯 (10ml) 4. 如果头疼很严重, 可以服止疼药: 一日一次, 一次二片					

Theme 48: Toxic substances 有毒物品 (yǒudú wùpǐn)

1 毒 [-] dú (poison) <n.> poison, toxin: 贩 (fàn) ~ drug trade || 吸~ take drugs || 食物中 (zhòng) ~ food poisoning

2 毒品 [-] dúpǐn (poisonous-thing) <n.> narcotic drugs, narcotics: 制造~ make narcotic drugs || ~贩子drug dealers

3 毒气 [-氣] dúqì (poisonous-air) <n.> poison gas: 使用~ use poison gas || 排放~ discharge poison gas

4 鸦片 [鴉-] yāpiàn (*transliteration*, crow-pill) <n.> opium: 抽~ smoke opium || ~战争opium war, First Opium War (Britain's invasion of China, 1840–1842, Second Opium War, 1856–1860)

5 冰毒 [-] bīngdú (ice-drug) <n.> ice, popular name for methamphetamine hydrochloride, a deadly addictive stimulant drug: 制造~ make methamphetamine hydrochloride || 吸~ take methamphetamine hydrochloride || 贩卖~ sale methamphetamine hydrochloride

6 大麻 [-] dàmá (big-hemp) <n.> marijuana: 抽~ smoke marijuana || ~叶 marijuana leaf

7 地沟油 [-溝-] dìgōuyóu (ditch-oil) <n.> cooking oil that has been used and discarded. In China, sometimes illegally recovered from gutter and sewers, repossessed and sold back to restaurants.: 治理~ govern drainage oil

8 瘦肉精 [-] shòuròujīng (lean-meat-powder) <n.> lean meat powder: 使用~ use lean meat powder

9 染色剂 [--劑] rănsèjì (dye-color-chemical preparation) <n.> staining agent: 化学~ chemical staining agent

10 烟 [煙] yān (smoke, tobacco) <n.> smoke, tobacco, cigarette: 抽/吸~ smoke cigarette || 一支~ a cigarette || 戒 (jiè) ~ quit smoking

Tips:

1 毒 (dú): The original meaning of 毒 was 'poisonous grass' which was generalized to be 'poison, poisonous.'

2 五毒俱全 (wǔdú jùquán): It usually means five bad habits of men, e.g. 吃 (extravagant eating,) 喝 (drinking alcohol,) 嫖 (piáo, patronize prostitutes,) 赌 (dǔ, gambling) and 抽 (chōu, smoking.)

3 贩毒 (fàndú): It means 'traffick in drugs, drug trafficking,' which, if convicted, a person will receive the death penalty if found in China, no matter whether the person is Chinese or a foreigner. The severity of the punishment might be due to national psychological scars left by the two Opium Wars in the 1840s and 1850s.

4 鸦片 (yāpiàn): It was also called 阿片 (ā piàn) which is closer to 'opium' in sound.

Exercises:

Part I: answer the following questions in Chinese.

1 "瘦肉精、染色剂"这些东西在你们国家的食品中有没有出现过? 为什么?

____

2 在你们国家食品中使用"地沟油"是不是违法的?

____

3 在你们国家公共场合可以吸烟吗? 为什么?

____

4 你住的城市吸大麻是不是合法的? 你觉得大麻应该合法化吗? 为什么?

____

5 在你们国家制造毒品合法吗? 你觉得毒品生产和交易应该合法化吗? 为什么?

____

Theme 49: Thing, course 事情, 过程 (shìqíng, guòchéng)

1 事情 [-] shìqíng (thing-affair) <n.> affair, matter, thing: ~真相 the truth of the matter
2 事 [-] shì (thing, matter) <n.> affair, matter, thing: 一件~ a thing || 好/坏~ good/bad thing
3 事故 [-] shìgù (thing-accident) <n.> accident: 意外~ unexpected accident || 出~ have an accident
4 事件 [-] shìjiàn (thing-piece) <n.> event, incident: 恐怖 (kǒngbù) ~ terrorist incident || 历史~ historical event || 紧急 (jǐnjí) ~ emergency case
5 事实 [-實] shìshí (thing-fact) <n.> fact: 大量~ a large number facts || 历史~ historical facts || 客观~ objective facts
6 时事 [時-] shíshì (current-event) <n.> current events: 关心~ have interest in current affairs || ~评论commentary on current affairs || ~论坛current affairs symposium

7 环境 [環-] huánjìng (surrounding-circumstance) <n.> environment: 保护~ protect environment || 自然~ natural environment || 家庭~ home environment
8 场合 [場-] chǎnghé (circumstance-situation) <n.> occasion: 公共~ a public occasion || 外交~ a diplomatic occasion
9 气氛 [氣氛] qìfēn (air-atmosphere) <n.> atmosphere, air: 紧张的~ tense atmosphere || 节日~ festive air
10 背景 [-] bèijǐng (back-setting) <n.> background: 社会~ social background || 文化~ cultural background || 历史~ history background
11 历史 [歷-] lìshǐ (past-history) <n.> history: 人类~ human history || 中国~ china's history || ~发展history development
12 前后 [-後] qiánhòu (before-after) <n.> around, from beginning to end, altogether: 春节~ around the spring festival || 这篇小说从写作到完成, ~用了一年的时间. The novel took a year to write altogether, from start to finish || 他~去过中国四五次. He has been to China four or five times altogether.

13 现实 [現實] xiànshí (current-reality) <n.> reality: ~生活 real life || ~意义 practical or immediate significance || 面对~ face the facts, bring someone back to reality
14 现状 [現狀] xiànzhuàng (current-situation) <n.> present situation, existing circumstances: 安于 ~ be content with things as they are || 改变~ change the present status || 对~不满 be dissatisfied with one's present condition
15 现象 [現-] xiànxiàng (appearing-phenomenon) <n.> phenomena: 自然/社会~ natural/social phenomenon || 表面~ appearance || 普遍 (pǔbiàn) ~ common phenomena

16 形势 [-] xíngshì (appearance-trend) <n.> situation: 国际 ~ international situation || 国内~ domestic situation || 经济~ economic situation
17 总体 [總體] zǒngtǐ (over-body) <n.> overall, total, general: ~方案overall plan || ~收入 total income || 从~看in general
18 主流 [-] zhǔliú (main-stream) <n.> mainstream, essential or main aspect, main trend: 当代世界的~ the main trend in the world today || ~媒体 (méitǐ) mainstream media

19 情况 [-況] qíngkuàng (affair-condition) <n.> situation, circumstances: 实际~ the actual situation || 紧急~ emergency || 说明自己的~ state one's case

20 情景 [-] qíngjǐng (affair-scene) <n.> scene, sight: 可怕的~ the gruesome sight || 电影里的 ~ the scene in movie

21 情形 [-] qíngxíng (affair-circumstance) <n.> circumstances, situation, state of affairs: 照现在的~看as the case stands || 在那样的~下in such case

22 状况 [狀況] zhuàngkuàng (state-condition) <n.> condition, state: 健康 (jiànkāng) ~ state of health || 道路~ state of the roads || 天气~ weather conditions

23 状态 [狀態] zhuàngtài (state-situation) <n.> state, condition: 政府宣布进入紧急~ the government declared a state of emergency || 这两国实际上处于战争~. A virtual state of war exists between the two countries.

24 潮流 [-] cháoliú (tide-trend) <n.> tide, trend: 时代~ historical trend || 艺术~ art trend || 反~ go against the tide

25 前途 [-] qiántú (future-journey) <n.> future, prospect: 有~ have a great future || 对~很乐观be optimistic about the future || 光明的~ bright future

26 趋势 [趨勢] qūshì (tend-trend) <n.> tendency, trend: 发展~ the political trends of the time || 上升 ~ a rising swing or trend || 总的~ general trend

27 优势 [優勢] yōushì (superior-situation) <n.> advantage: 资源 (zīyuán) ~ resource advantage || 占~ be predominant, has an advantage

28 劣势 [-勢] lièshì (inferior-situation) <n.> disadvantage, inferior position: 处于~地位in inferior position

29 风险 [風險] fēngxiǎn (wind-risk) <n.> risk, hazard: 很大的~ full of hazard || ~投资venture capital || 冒 (mào) ~ take risks

30 危险 [-險] wēixiǎn (danger-risk) <n.> danger: ~品dangerous goods, hazardous article || 遇到~ be in danger || 生命~ life-threatening

31 危机 [-機] wēijī (danger-crucial point) <n.> crisis: 能源 (néngyuán) ~ energy crisis || 经济~ financial crisis

32 问题 [問題] wèntí (ask-qustion) <n.> question, issue: 问 (提) ~ ask a question || 回答~ answer a question || 解决 (jiějué) ~ solve a problem

33 疑问 [-問] yíwèn (doubt-ask) <n.> doubt: 有~ be in doubt || 毫无~ there is no doubt

34 误会 [誤會] wùhuì (mistake-understand) <.n> misunderstanding: 引起~ cause misunderstanding || 一场小~ a small misunderstanding

35 阴影 [陰-] yīnyǐng (shadow-image) <n.> shadow: 打骂孩子会给孩子留下心理~. Beating children will leave a psychological shadow on a child. || 走出~ be out of the shadows

36 秘密 [-] mìmì (mysterious-secret) <n.> secret, confidential: 揭开大自然的~ unravel the secrets of the universe || 商业~ trade secrets || 泄漏 (xièlù) ~ reveal one's secret

37 隐私 [隱-] yǐnsī (hidden-privacy) <n.> privacy: 个人~ personal privacy || ~权right of privacy || 公开~ public a privacy

38 故障 [-] gùzhàng (accident-obstacle) <n.> malfunction, fault, failure: 日本车很少出现~. Japanese cars rarely fail. || 前方出现了道路~. A road fault appeared ahead. || 机械~ mechanical failure

39 对象 [對-] duìxiàng (target-object) <n.> object: 研究~ object of study || 保护~ protected object

40 倾向 [傾-] qīngxiàng (incline-toward) <n.> tendency, inclination: 政治~ political inclination || 改变不良~ rectify the undesirable tendencies

41 目的 [-] mùdì (view-goal) <n.> purpose: 生活的~ the purpose of one's life || 她学习的~是为了当医生. Her purpose in learning is to become a doctor.

42 目标 [-標] mùbiāo (view-target) <n.> target, objective: 射击 (shèjī) ~ shooting target || 最终~ ultimate objective || 达到 ~ attain one's objective

43 指标 [-標] zhǐbiāo (point-target) <n.> index: 质量~ quality index || 经济~ economic indicators

44 路线 [-綫] lùxiàn (path-line) <n.> route, line: 旅行~ the route of a journey || 马克思主义~ marxist line || 政治~ political line

45 方针 [-針] fāngzhēn (direction-principle) <n.> guiding principle: 指导~ guidelines || 制定~ make guiding principle

46 出路 [-] chūlù (out-path) <n.> a way out (of a difficult situation): 中国农业的根本~ 在于机械化. The fundamental way out lies in reform and openness. || 找~ find a way out

47 原因 [-] yuányīn (original-reason) <n.> reason, cause: 主要~ main reason || 根本~ root cause || 几点~ a few reasons

48 缘故 [緣-] yuángù (cause-reason) <n.> reason: 由于那个~ for that reason

49 来源 [來-] láiyuán (come-source) <n.> source: 资金~ source of capital

50 理由 [-] lǐyóu (ground-justification) <n.> reason, ground: 没有~抱怨 have no grounds for complaint || 这些要求毫无~. These demands have neither rhyme nor reason.

51 根据 [-據] gēnjù (ground-according to) <n./v.> basis, grounds, on the basis of: 事实~ factual basis || ~经验based on experience

52 依据 [-據] yījù (base-according to) <n./v.> basis, grounds, on the basis of: 法律~ legal basis || 毫无~ utterly baseless || 理论~ theoretical basis

53 证据 [證據] zhèngjù (prove-evidence) <n.> proof: ~不足without adequate proof || 有力的~ strong proof || 直接~ direct evidence (of) || 掌握 (zhǎngwò) ~ understand/grasp/weigh the evidence

54 立场 [-場] lìchǎng (stand-place) <n.> standpoint: ~坚定a firm stand || 政治~ the standpoint in politics

55 程度 [-] chéngdù (measure-degree) <n.> level, degree: 文化~ degree of literacy || 在很大~上 to a high degree || 贫富~ degree of wealth

56 角度 [-] jiǎodù (angle-degree) <n.> angle, point of view: 从这个~看 seen from this angle || 不同的~ different angles

57 途径 [-徑] tújìng (way-trail) <n.> way, channel, approach: 外交~ diplomatic channels || 通过非法~ through illegal ways || 成功的唯一~是勤奋 (qínfèn) the one way to succeed is to work hard

58 渠道 [-] qúdào (channel-road) <n.> irrigation ditch, medium of communication, channel: 加州的~可以把水引进沙漠. California canals can take water to the desert. || 通过各种~ through various channels || 外交 ~ diplomatic channels

59 平台 [-臺] píngtái (flat-platform) <n.> platform: 脸书为人们提供了自由交流的~. Facebook provides a platform for people to communicate freely. || 电子商务~ e-commerce platform

60 过程 [過-] guòchéng (course-process) <n.> process, procedure, course: 生产 ~ manufacturing process || 发展~ 中in the process of development || 全部~ (the) entire process

61 阶段 [階-] jiēduàn (stage-section) <n.> stage, phase: 中国正处于发展的重要~. China is in an important stage in its development.

62 经过 [經過] jīngguò (experience-course) <n.> process, course: 事情的全部~ the whole process from beginning to end || 这件事的~是这样的. This how it happened.

63 经历 [經歷] jīnglì (experience-undergo) <n.> experience: 一段~ an experience || 工作~ work experience

64 纠纷 [糾紛] jiūfēn (knot-dispute) <n.> dispute, issue: 引起~ cause dispute || 国际~ international disputes || 家庭~ family disputes

65 官司 [-] guānsī (official-charge) <n.> lawsuit: 打~ go to court || (打) 赢~ win the lawsuit || (打) 输 ~ lose the lawsuit

66 案子 [-] ànzi (case-*suffix*) <n.> legal case: 一件~ a case || 办/破~ handle a case/clear up a case || 离婚~ a divorce case

67 例子 [-] lìzi (example-*suffix*) <n.> example: 举~ for example || 典型的~ typical example || 类似的 ~ similar example

68 变化 [變-] biànhuà (change-convert) <n./v.> change, variation: 气温的~ variations of temperature || 发生很大~ the great changes have taken place || 市场在不断~. The market is in a constant state of flux.

69 常规 [-規] chángguī (normal-regulation) <n.> convention, common practice, routine: 按照~办事follow the routine || 打破~ break with convention || ~武器conventional weapon

70 高潮 [-] gāocháo (high-tide) <n.> climax: 达到~ reach a climax || 在圣诞节期间, 广告战已经达到~. The advertising campaign reached a climax at Christmas.

71 真相 [-] zhēnxiàng (true-appearance) <n.> real situation, real facts, truth: 不明~ be ignorant of the facts || 查明~ discover the truth || ~大白. The truth has come out.

72 胜负 [勝負] shèngfù (win-lose) <n.> victory or defeat, success or failure: 不分~ come out even || 决定 ~ decide the outcome

73 作用 [-] zuòyòng (act-use) <n.> effect, role: 副~ side effect || 发挥~ play a role || 积极~ positive role

74 职能 [職-] zhínéng (duty-function) <n.> function: 政府~ government functions || 基本~ basic functions || 转变~ change the function

75 功能 [-] gōngnéng (work-function) <n.> features, function: 智能手机的~远远多于普通手机. Smartphones are far more functional than ordinary phones. || ~强大 the features are powerful || 多~ multifunctional

76 性能 [-] xìngnéng (attribute-function) <n.> function (of a machine, etc.), performance: 日本车大部分~很好most Japanese cars perform well. || ~稳定 (wěndìng) stable performance || 良好的~ good performance

77 用处 [-處] yòngchù (use-area) <n.> use: 大有~ be very useful || 一点~也没有utterly useless || 只学汉语单词~不大, 一定要把单词放在句子里学. Learning Chinese words in isolation is not very useful. You must learn words in sentences.

78 用途 [-] yòngtú (use-way) <n.> use, purpose: ~广泛 (guǎngfàn) widely used || 有多种~ have multiple purposes || 重要的~ the most important use

79 产物 [產-] chǎnwù (produce-thing) <n.> outcome, result, product: 竞争 (jìngzhēng) 是市场经济的~. Competition is a product of the market economy.

80 结果 [結-] jiéguǒ (yield-fruit) <n.> result, outcome: 调查~ survey results || 比赛 ~ the result of game

81 后果 [後-] hòuguǒ (later-result) <n.> consequence, aftermath: 严重的~ serious consequences || 不良~ bad consequences || ~不堪设想. The consequences would be too ghastly to contemplate.

82 效果 [-] xiàoguǒ (render-result) <n.> effect, result: ~不大not be very effective || 音乐~ music effect || 取得显著 (xiǎnzhù) 的~ achieve good results

83 成效 [-] chéngxiào (achieved-result) <n.> effect, result: 取得~ get results || 有/没有~ be effective/not effective || 显著的remarkable results

84 反响 [-響] fǎnxiǎng (back-sound) <n.> repercussions, echo, repercussions: ~ 很大the repercussions is great || 引起强烈的~ cause strong repercussions

Tips:

1 事 (shì): The original meaning of 事 was related to 吏 (lì, government official) and 之. It was the same as 吏 in oracle forms, thus meaning 'government post' from which evolved meanings such as 'occupation,' 'affair' and 'thing'.

2 情况 (qíngkuàng) vs. 情形 (qíngxíng) vs. 情景 (qíngjǐng): To be honest, the conception of this book started from the discrimination of these three words and a few others more than ten years ago. When Liwei Jiao was approached by his students for discrimination of these words, he thought it would be done in 15 minutes, however, five hours later he was still working on it. At last, he concluded that a learner has to know the meaning of each compositional character rather than the meaning of an entire word to really understand the exquisite difference between the words. All three words here can be translated as 'situation, condition.' However, the 况 (況, kuàng) in 情况 originally meant 'cold water,' as one dipped his hand(s) in to water to feel the coldness. This denotes an exquisite connotation of 'course of an action or a deed' or 'change.' The 景 (jǐng) in 情景 originally meant 'sunlight' from which evolved the meaning 'scene.' 情景 is more like a picture of a situation painted in your mind. The 形 (xíng) in 情形 means 'shape, form.' To know a shape or form, one has to have an overall perception of something, so 情形 has a connotation of 'a comprehensive view.' If we use a 'movie' as a simile, 情景 is like a 'close-up,' 情形 'panorama' and 情况 'motion.'

Exercises:

Part I: Use the given bound form in bold as a guide to help you think of other words with the same character. Feel free to use your dictionary when needed. Then write down the English definition of each of the words you've written.

事 *(thing, matter)*: 事情 *affair, thing*

____

____

____

____

情 *(affair)*: 情况 *situation*

____

____

____

____

Part II: Read the following sentences and fill in each blank with the appropriate word or phrase from the options given.

1 优势、理由、趋势

a) 现在中国艺术品在国际艺术品市场上出现了流行的_______, 但是西方艺术仍然处于_______地位.
b) 这位美国大学生选择学习中国京剧的_______是它是中国特有的文化艺术.

2 角度、出路、过程

a) 这个农村学生认为上好大学是他走向成功的唯一_______.
b) 李教授的这本书从各个______分析了中国农村教育的问题. 在写这本书的______中, 李教授多次到中国贫困山区进行调研.

3 经验、经历、经过

a) 李教授一生_______了很多困难, 最后获得了幸福的晚年.
b) 李教授关于农村教育的书是_______三年多的调查研究写出来的.
c) 有人认为中国教育改革可以借鉴发达国家的_______.

4 用处、作用、目的

a) 一些中国家长认为有些大学专业比如哲学、语言学等等_______不大, 学完这些专业以后几乎找不到工作.
b) 一些中国家长认为让孩子上好大学的_______就是将来能够找到好工作.
c) 有人认为中国高考有缩小贫富差距的_______, 因为贫困地区的学生能够通过高考改变命运.

5 后果、结果、效果

a) 一些教育专家认为体罚对孩子来说几乎没什么_______, 只能给他们的心理和身体健康造成不良_______.
b) 一般来说, 每年12月15号左右一些美国名校会公布他们的提前录取______.

Theme 50: Rules, methods 规律, 方法 (guīlǜ, fāngfǎ)

1 规律 [規-] guīlǜ (rule-regulation) <n.> law, regular pattern: 一般~ standard rule || 基本~ basic principle || 有~ be regular
2 原理 [-] yuánlǐ (principle-truth) <n.> principle: 基本~ a basic principle || 科学~ scientific principle
3 办法 [辦-] bànfǎ (solution – manage-rule) <n.> solution: 有~ have a solution || 新 ~ a new solution || 想 ~ think of a solution
4 点子 [點-] diǎnzi (spot, point, idea-*suffix*) <n.> idea, point: 好~ good idea || 出 ~ come up with ideas || 他~ 很多. He's full of ideas.
5 方法 [-] fāngfǎ (way-rule) <n.> method: 思想~ the way of thinking || 简单的~ simple method || 工作~ the way of working
6 方式 [-] fāngshì (way-form) <n.> way: 各种 ~ multiple ways || 说话~ a way of speaking || 生活~ way of life, lifestyle
7 用法 [-] yòngfǎ (use-way) <n.> use, usage: 两种~ two uses || ~多 lots of ways to use || ~不同 different uses
8 做法 [-] zuòfǎ (do-way) <n.> the way of doing things: 这种~ this way of doing things || 传统~ traditional way of doing things
9 措施 [-] cuòshī (carry out-measure) <n.> method: 有效 (yǒuxiào) ~ an effective method || 主要~ primary method || 采取~ use a method
10 诀窍 [訣竅] juéqiào (knack-key) <n.> secret of success, knack-key: 有/没有~ there is a/there is no key to success || 掌握~ know the trick || 记忆~ memory tricks
11 秘诀 [-訣] mìjué (secret-knack) <n.> secret: 成功的~ the secret to one's success || 长寿的 ~ the secret to longevity
12 窍门 [竅門] qiàomén (key-way) <n.> key to a problem, knack-way: 小 ~ a little trick || 找~ try to find the key to a problem

13 手续 [-續] shǒuxù (handle-procedure) <n.> procedure: 办~ go through formalities || ~费 a handling fee || 复杂的~ over-elaborate procedure, tedious formalities

14 理 [-] lǐ (reason) <n.> reason: 没~ without reason || 讲~ argue, reason with sb. || 同~ for the same reason

15 道理 [-] dàolǐ (law-truth) <n.> reason: 讲~ reason things out || 有~ reasonable, be well-founded || 大~ great truth, major principle

16 真理 [-] zhēnlǐ (true-truth) <n.> truth: 伟大的~ a great truth || 普遍 (pǔbiàn) ~ a universal truth || 追求~ seek truth

17 公道 [-] gōngdào (just-way) <n.> fair, justice: 办事~ even-handed, be impartial || 价格 ~ fair price || 买卖~ fair in business, fair deal

18 正义 [-義] zhèngyì (upright-justice) <n.> justice: 为~ 而战fight for justice || 主持~ uphold justice || ~的立场 just position

19 情理 [-] qínglǐ (reason-truth) <n.> reason: 合乎~ it stands to reason || 不近 ~ unreasonable || 在~之中 not be surprising

20 人情 [-] rénqíng (people-affection) <n.> feelings: 做个~ do sb. a favor || 重~ emphasis the importance of friendship || 欠他一份~ owe him a favor

21 逻辑 [邏輯] luójí (transliteration of logic) <n.> logic: 有~ have logic || ~ 上的错误error in logic || 合乎~ be logical

22 哲理 [-] zhélǐ (philosophical-theory) <n.> philosophical theory, philosophy: 生活~ life philosophy || 富有 ~ be philosophical

23 机制 [機-] jīzhì (machine-system) <n.> system: 民主~ the democratic system || 竞争 (jìngzhēng) ~ competitive system || 管理~ management system

24 概念 [-] gàiniàn (generalized-concept) <n.> concept: 基本~ basic concepts || 不同的~ different concepts || 新~ new concepts

25 含义 [-義] hányì (implied-meaning) <n.> meaning, implication: 基本~ essential meaning || 深刻的~ deep meaning || 特殊~ special meaning

26 意思 [-] yìsī (intention-thought) <n.> meaning, idea, intention: 表达~ express one's intention || 本来的~ original meaning || 大概~ overall meaning

27 意义 [-義] yìyì (meaning-objective) <n.> meaning, sense, significance: 在某种~上in a sense || 重大历史~ historic significance || 毫无~ there's no point

28 定义 [-義] dìngyì (define-meaning) <n.> definition: 下~ give a definition || 各种~ multiple definitions || 科学~ scientific definition

29 线索 [綫-] xiànsuǒ (thread-rope) <n.> clue: 一条~ a clue, lead || 新~ a new clue || 找到~ find a clue

30 眉目 [-] méimù (eyebrow-eye) <n.> progress, prospect of a solution: 有/没有~ have/not have a potential solution || 弄清~ make the things clear

31 条理 [條-] tiáolǐ (thread-order) <n.> orderliness, proper arrangement: 有~ well-organized || 文章~清楚. The article is well-organized. || 他工作很有 ~. He is a methodical worker.

32 思路 [-] sīlù (thought-path) <n.> train of thought: 基本~ a basic thought || 打断~ interrupt one's train of thought || 他的~很清楚. He thinks very clearly.

33 构思 [構-] gòusī (construct-thought) <n.> draw up a mental outline, plan: 艺术~ artistic thought || ~巧妙 clever thought || 总体~ overall construct

34 构想 [構-] gòuxiǎng (construct-idea) <n.> idea, conception: 总体~ overall conception || 新的~ new conception || "一国两制"的~ the concept of 'one country, two systems'

Tips:

1 意思 (yìsi): The main meaning of 意思 is 'meaning,' but the usage of 意思 is much more than that. The following is a widespread play on language: 小王给局长 (bureau director) 送红包 (red envelope). 局长: "你这是什么*意思*?" 小王: "没什么, *意思意思*." 局长: "你这就*不够意思*了." 小王: "*小意思*, 小意思." 局长: "你这人真*有意思*." 小王: "其实也*没别的意思*." 局长: "那我就*不好意思*了." 小王: "是我*不好意思*了." Xiao Wang sends a red envelope (containing money) to a bureau director. Director: What do you *mean*? Xiao Wang: Nothing, it's *a token* (of appreciation.) Director: You *make me feel embarrassed*. Xiao Wang: Just *a small token*. Director: You are *interesting*. Xiao Wang: Actually I *had no other intentions*. Director: Then I will take it *with guilty feeling*. Xiao Wang: It's me who should *feel guilty* (since the money is not much.)

2 理 (lǐ): It means 'reason' as in words such as 条理, 原理, 道理, 情理, 真理, 哲理, which are all listed above. The original meaning of 理 is 'to treat (and polish) jade.' You need to treat jade along its veins, which denote 'nature and reason.'

Exercises:

Part I: Use the given bound form as a guide to help you think of other words with the same character. Feel free to use your dictionary when needed. Then write down the English definition of each of the words you've written.

理 (truth): 真理 truth

____

____

____

____

____

____

____

____

义 (meaning): 含义 implied meaning

____

____

____

____

Part II: Multiple Choice. Make sure to choose the most appropriate answer.

1 经过几个月的讨论, 美国政府的减税 (tax cut) 计划终于有了________, 据说很快就会交到国会 (Congress) 投票.
A. 眉目 B. 线索 C. 条理

2 中国的内蒙古东部地区发现了一个大型油田, 这对当地经济发展有着重大的_______.
A. 含义 B. 定义 C. 意义

3 这栋房子里发生了盗窃 (dàoqiè, theft) 案 (àn, case), 警方为了寻找________彻底 (chèd____se),) n tw检查了整栋房子.
A. 意思 B. 线索 C. 眉目

4 《圣经》(*The Bible*) 上有很多富有________的话, 影响着基督徒 (Jīdūtú, Christian) 的生活方式.
A. 概念 B. 机制 C. 哲理

5 有人认为到一个新地方旅行最重要的是了解当地的风土________.
A. 情理 B. 人情 C. 逻辑

6 这家公司的产品价格_______, 质量优良, 受到了所有消费者的欢fl.
A. 公道 B. 真理 C. 正义

7 在美国买卖房子要办法律_______.
A. 窍门 B. 手续 C. 秘诀

8 目前中国政府正在采取_______阻止中国的资金外流.
A. 措施 B. 诀窍 C. 秘诀

9 小张的专业是经济学, 但是他对经济学的基本_______一窍不通.
A. 用法 B. 做法 C. 原理

10 科学研究一般要发现事物内部的基本________.
A. 方法 B. 办法 C. 规律

Theme 51: Life, fate 生活, 命运 (shēnghuó, mìngyùn)

(See also Theme 124)

1 生命 [-] shēngmìng (live-life) <n.> life: 新~ new life || 失去~ loss of life || ~安全 safety life (time period)
2 人生 [-] rénshēng (human-life) <n.> life: ~道路 life's road || ~目标 life's goal || 美好的~ a beautiful life
3 寿命 [壽-] shòumìng (longevity-life) <n.> lifespan: 平均 ~ every lifespan || ~长/短 long/short life || 延长 (yáncháng) ~ extend life
4 日子 [-] rìzi (day-*suffix*) <n.> days of (someone's) life: 好~ a good day || 过~ live one's days
5 生活 [-] shēnghuó (live-survive) <n.& v.> live, life: 私 ~ private life || 夜~ night life || ~方式 life method
6 柴米油盐 [---鹽] cháimǐyóuyán (fuel-rice-oil-salt) <idiom> fuel, rice, oil and salt and basic daily necessities: 一般老百姓的生活都是处理 "~"这类事情. Ordinary people's life is to deal with such trivial things as fuel and food.

|| 这对夫妻常常为了~的小事吵. The couple often quarreled over the little things.

7 家长里短 [-長--] jiāchánglǐduǎn (domestic trivialities) <idiom> domestic trivia: 两人开始谈一些~. They began to talk about domestic trivialities gradually.

8 衣食住行 [-] yīshízhùxíng (clothing-food-shelter-travel) <idiom> basic necessities of life: 有人认为中国政府应该多关心贫困地区老百姓的~问题. Some people think that the Chinese government should pay more attention to the basic living problems of ordinary people in poor areas.

9 家常便饭 [---飯] jiāchángbiànfàn (home style-family meal) <idiom> plain home cooking: 一顿~ a home cooked meal || 吃 ~ eat a common meal

10 饭局 [飯-] fànjú (meal-feast) <n.> dinner party, feast: 赶 ~ catch a dinner party || 工作 ~ work feast || 他的~多. He has a lot of dinner parties.

11 年夜饭 [--飯] niányèfàn (new year's-eve-meal) <n.> New Year's Eve family dinner: 吃 ~ have a New Year's Eve family dinner || 准备~ prepare a New Year's Eve family dinner

12 团圆饭 [團圓飯] tuányuánfàn (reunion-meal) <n.> family reunion dinner: 吃 ~ have a family reunion dinner

13 消息 [-] xiāoxī (news-message) <n.> news, information: 听到~ hear the news || 好/坏~ good/bad information || 几个~ a few bits of information

14 信息 [-] xìnxī (information-message) <n.> information: 交流, 传递 (chuándì) ~ information exchange, to transmit information || 新~ new information || 基本~ basic information

15 情报 [-報] qíngbào (situation-report) <n.> intelligence situation-report: ~可靠 reliable report || 得到 ~ obtain intelligence || 搜集 (sōují) ~ gather intelligence

16 喜讯 [-訊] xǐxùn (happy-news) <n.> happy news: 传来~ good news comes in

17 噩耗 [-] èhào (shocking-news) <n.> shocking news: 传来~ for shocking news to arrive || 接到receive shocking news

18 传言 [傳-] chuányán (spread-words) <n./v.> rumor: 听到~ hear a rumor || 散布~ spread rumors

19 传闻 [傳聞] chuánwén (spread-hearsay) <n.> rumor: 可靠的~ a reliable rumor || 分手的~ rumors of parting || 听到~ hear the rumor

20 风声 [風聲] fēngshēng (wind-sound) <n.> rumor: 听到~ get wind of something || ~很紧the situation is tense || 透露 ~ leak information

21 小道消息 [-] xiǎodàoxiāoxī (unauthoritative-source-information) <n.> gossip: 传播~ spread gossip || 各种~ all kinds of gossip

22 谣言 [謠-] yáoyán (rumor-words) <n.> rumor: 相信~ believe a rumor || 制造~ create rumors || 传播~ spread rumors

23 绯闻 [緋聞] fēiwén (pink-news) <n.> gossip about sex scandals: 明星~ sex scandal concerning a celebrity || 传 ~ spread sex scandal rumors

24 花边新闻 [-邊-聞] huābiānxīnwén (flower-laced-news) <n.> media gossip, tabloid news: 一条~ a media gossip || 制造~ make tabloid news

25 要闻 [-聞] yàowén (important-news) <n.> important news: 国际 ~ national news || 经济 ~ economic news

26 经验 [經驗] jīngyàn (experienced-verified) <n.> experience: ~丰富/不足have rich experience / lack experience || 工作~ work experience || 积累 (jīlěi) ~ accumulate experience

27 体会 [體會] tǐhuì (experience-comprehend) <n./v.> know from experience, personal experience, feel: 谈~ talk about personal experience || 深有~ have an intimate knowledge of || 有了孩子以后, 他~ 到当父母是多么不容易. After having a child, he realized how difficult it is for parents.

28 体验 [體驗] tǐyàn (experience-verified) <n./v.> learn through practice: ~生活 personally experience real life || 亲身~ personal experience

29 心得 [-] xīndé (heart-get) <n.> what one has learned from work, study etc: 交换 ~ exchange personal experience and knowledge || 谈谈学习~ talk about what one has gained from study

30 代价 [-價] dàijià (cost-price) <n.> price, cost: ~大 large cost || 作为 ~ as the cost || 付出~ pay the cost

31 教训 [-訓] jiàoxùn (instruct-sermonize) <n./v.> lesson, teach sb. a lesson: 他~了儿子一顿. He read his son a lesson. || 吸取~ draw a lesson || 失败的~ lesson written in failure

32 警钟 [-鐘] jǐngzhōng (warning-bell) <n.> warning bell, alarm: 敲~ sound a warning || ~长鸣. Alarm bells rang out.

33 记忆 [記憶] jìyì (memorize-remember) <n.> memory, remember: 短时~ temporary memory || 失去~ lose memory || 青春的~ memories of youth

34 印象 [-] yìnxiàng (impress-image) <n.> impression: 好/坏~ good impression/ bad impression || ~很深 deep impression || 难忘的~ hard to forget impression

35 身世 [-] shēnshì (life-experience) <n.> one's (unfortunate) life experience: 不幸的~ wretched fate || 悲惨 (bēicǎn) 的 ~ tragic life || ~不凡 unusual life

36 阅历 [閱歷] yuèlì (witness-experience) <n.> experiences: 生活~ life's experience || 缺乏 (quēfá) ~ lack experience || 丰富的~ rich experience

37 遭遇 [-] zāoyù (unexpectedly-meet) <n./v.> meet with, encounter: ~不幸meet with misfortune || 悲惨的~ tragic experience

38 悲欢离合 [-歡離-] bēihuānlíhé (sorrow-joy-part-reunite) <idiom> joys and sorrows: 人有~, 月有阴晴圆缺. One's life has joy and sorrow, and the moon has darkness and light.

39 酸甜苦辣 [-] suāntiánkǔlà (sour-sweet-bitter-spicy) <idiom> joys and sorrows of life: 充满~ be filled with joy and sorrow || 尝遍~ have experienced the joys and sorrows of life || ~的人生 the life with joys and sorrows

40 顺境 [順-] shùnjìng (smooth-circumstance) <n.> easy circumstances: 遇到~ encounter easy circumstances || 身处 ~ be in a place of adversity

41 逆境 [-] nìjìng (adverse-circumstance) <n.> adverse (or unfavorable) circumstances: 遇到~ encounter adversity || 处于~ be located in an adverse situation

42 走下坡路 [-] zǒuxiàpōlù (go-downhill-road) <v.> go downhill, decline: 开始~ start to go downhill/decline

43 命 [-] mìng (order, destiny, fate, life) <n.> fate, life: 他的~很好, 从小到大没吃过苦. He's had a good life, from a young age to adulthood he's never endured hardship. || 救~ save one's life

44 命运 [-運] mìngyùn (destiny-luck) <n.> destiny, fate: 共同的~ shared destiny || 把握 (bǎwò) ~ take control of one's destiny || ~的安排 destined arrangements

45 运气 [運氣] yùnqì (luck-destiny) <n.> fortune, luck: ~好 good fortune || 碰~ run into good fate

46 好运 [-運] hǎoyùn (good-luck) <n.> good luck, fortune: 交~ have good luck || 走~ have good luck || 得到~ achieve good fortune

47 幸 [-運] xìngyùn (fortunate-luck) <adj.> good fortune, good luck: ~数字 lucky number || ~儿 a lucky one || ~的孩子 a lucky child

48 苦命 [-] kǔmìng (hard-lot) <n.> cruel fate, cruel life: 她是一个~人. She has suffered a hard life.

49 福祸 [-禍] fúhuò (fortunate-unfortunate) <n.> disaster and happiness: 难测~ hard to fathom the disaster and fortune || ~相依. For disaster and happiness are reliant on one another.

50 福气 [-氣] fúqì (fortunate-destiny) <n.> good luck: 有 ~ have good luck || 好~ have good luck

51 幸福 [-] xìngfú (fortunate-lucky) <n.> happiness, wellbeing: 个人~ individual happiness || 终身~ lifelong happiness || 追求~ pursue happiness

52 耳福 [-] ěrfú (ear-fortunate) <n.> good fortune or hearing sth. rare or beautiful: 有 ~ have the good fortune of hearing something rare or beautiful || 大饱 ~ enjoy to the full listening to music || ~不浅 have a deep enjoyment

53 口福 [-] kǒufú (mouth-fortunate) <n.> tasty food, very nice to eat: 有 ~ have tasty food (the good fortune of having a good meal) || 大饱 ~ eat one's fill

54 眼福 [-] yǎnfú (eye-fortunate) <n.> good fortune to see sth. rare or beautiful: 有~ have the good fortune of seeing something rare or beautiful || 大饱 ~ feast one's eyes

55 艳福 [艶-] yànfú (beauty-fortunate) <n.> man's good fortune in love affairs: 有~ have good fortune in love affairs || ~不浅 have a lot of good fortune in love affairs || 享~ enjoy good fortune in love affairs

56 灾 [災] zāi (disastrous fire, disaster) <n.> calamity, disaster: 火~ a fire disaster || 水~ a flood

57 灾害 [災-] zāihài (disaster-harm) <n.> calamity, disaster-harm: 躲避~ avoid disasters || 地震~ an earthquake disaster || 水旱~ flood and drought disaster

58 灾难 [災難] zāinàn (disaster-calamity) <n.> suffering, disaster-catastrophe: 一场~ a disaster zone || 带来~ bring about disaster || 巨大的~ a massive disaster

59 天灾人祸 [-災-禍] tiānzāirénhuò (natural-disaster-man-made-calamity) <idiom> natural and man-made calamities: 遇到~ encounter disaster || 各种 ~ multiple forms of disaster

60 战乱 [戰亂] zhànluàn (war-chaos) <n.> chaos of war: ~不断 continuous chaos || 遭遇 (zāoyù) ~ encounter chaos || 连年~ multiple years of chaos

61 隐患 [隱-] yǐnhuàn (hidden-danger) <n.> hidden trouble, lurking danger: 安全~ potential safety hazard || 消除 ~ eliminate hidden trouble || 重大 ~ a massive lurking danger

62 洪灾 [-災] hóngzāi (flood-disaster) <n.> big flood: 特大~ an especially large flood || 遭~ create a flood

63 地震 [-] dìzhèn (earth-quake) <n./v.> earthquake: 发生~ for an earthquake to occur || 大/小~ large/small earthquake || ~波 seismic (earthquake) wave

64 火灾 [-災] huǒzāi (fire-disaster) <n.> fire (as a disaster): 发生~ for a fire to occur (large scale) || 引起~ lead to a fire || 一场~ an area with a fire

65 水灾 [-災] shuǐzāi (water-disaster) <n.> flood: 发生~ for a flood to occur || 遭~ suffer a flood || 一场 ~ a flood zone

66 饥荒 [饑-] jīhuāng (starvation-famine) <n.> famine, starvation: 闹~ suffer from famine || 遭~ suffer from famine || 一场~ a famine (area)

67 沙尘暴 [-塵-] shāchénbào (sand-dust-storm) <n.> sandstorm: 遇到~ encounter a sandstorm || 特大 ~ an especially large sandstorm || ~天气 a sandstorm weather

68 海难 [-難] hǎinàn (sea-disaster) <n.> perils of the sea: ~ 事故 a maritime issue || 一场 ~ a disaster at sea

69 海啸 [-嘯] hǎixiào (sea-howl) <n.> tsunami: 发生~ for a tsunami to occur || 引起~ lead to a tsunami

70 车祸 [車禍] chēhuò (vehicle-accident) <n.> traffic accident: 发生~ lead to a traffic accident || 一场~ the site of an accident || 重大~ a serious accident

71 股灾 [-災] gǔzāi (stock-disaster) <n.> market crash: 全球~ a worldwide market crash || 遇上 ~ for a market crash to occur

72 空难 [-難] kōngnàn (aviation-disaster) <n.> aviation accident, plane crash: 一次~ a plane crash || ~事故 an unfortunate plane crash

73 苦难 [-難] kǔnàn (suffer-misery) <n.> suffering, misery: 经历~ an experience of suffering || 遭受~ encounter suffering

74 挫折 [-] cuòzhé (frustrated-setback) <n.> setback, reverse: 遭受 ~ encounter a setback || 严重 ~ a serious setback

75 失败 [-敗] shībài (fail-defeated) <n.> be defeated, lose (a war): 遭到~ encounter defeat || 战争的 ~ war, warfare || 彻底 ~ not come to anything

76 失利 [-] shīlì (lose-advantageous) <v.> suffer a setback: 高考~ suffer a setback on the college entrance exams || 连连 ~ a continuous string of setback

77 困难 [-難] kùnnán (trouble-difficult) <n.> difficulty: 遇到~ encounter a difficulty || 克服~ surmount a difficulty || 种种~ a multitude of difficulties

78 患难 [-難] huànnàn (suffer-adversity) <n.> trials and tribulations: 共~ shared trials and tribulations || ~与共 go through thick and thin || ~夫妻husband and wife who have gone through difficult times together

79 恩怨 [-] ēnyuàn (favor-enmity) <n.> feeling of gratitude or resentment: 个人 ~ feel a mix of gratitude and resentment || ~分明 know clearly whom to show gratitude and against whom to feel resentment

80 恩情 [-] ēnqíng (kindness-affection) <n.> loving-kindness: 不忘~ unforgettable kindness || 报答~ pay back deep affection

81 实惠 [實-] shíhuì (material-benefit) <n.> material benefit: 有, 没有~ have, have no material benefit || 得到~ obtain material benefit || 很多~ lots of material benefits

82 好处 [-處] hǎochù (good-place) <n.> good, benefit: 得到~ obtain benefits || 带来~ bring about benefit || 捞~ bring about a good benefit

83 甜头 [-頭] tiántou (sweet-*suffix*) <n.> sweet taste: 尝到~ come to the good of

84 小便宜 [-] xiǎopiányí (small-advantage) <n.> small gain, petty-advantage: 贪~ always on the lookout for petty advantages || 占~ gain petty advantages

85 仇恨 [-] chóuhèn (hatred-hate) <n.> hatred-hate: 民族 ~ national hatred || 充满 ~ be filled with hatred || 产生~ lead to hatred

86 矛盾 [-] máodùn (spear-shield) <n.> problem, conflict: 有/没~ there is/is not a conflict || 家庭~ household conflict || 内部~ internal conflict
87 冲突 [衝-] chōngtū (assault-clash) <n.& v.> conflict, clash: 发生~ for a clash to occur || 戏剧 (xìjù) ~ a theatrical conflict || 地区~ a regional clash
88 代沟 [-溝] dàigōu (generation-gap) <n.> generation-gap: 有~ for there to be a generation gap || 形成~ form a generational gap || 巨大的~ a large generational gap
89 分歧 [-] fēnqí (separate-divergent) <n.> difference, divergence: 有~ be a divergence || 出现 ~ for a divergence to appear || 根本 ~ a root difference
90 隔阂 [-閡] géhé (partition-obstructed) <n.> estrangement, misunderstanding: 有~ an estrangement || 产生~ for an estrangement to occur || 消除 ~ resolve a misunderstanding

Tips:

1 This is life: This popular English saying is translated into Chinese as 这就是生活, which is close to it but not as authentic as 这就是命 (this is fate.)
2 您高寿 (gāoshòu) 了? : It means 'may I ask how old you are?', which is very pleasant for elders to hear. Longevity (长寿 or 高寿) was the most common theme in ancient Chinese auspicious culture. Below is a very popular calligraphy production, which depicts 100 ways to write the character '寿' (longevity.)

3 灾 (災, zāi): It means 'disaster.' The upper part of the traditional form '災' is '巛' which means 'river, water,' and the lower part of '災' is '火' (fire.) The Chinese has a saying '水火无情' (flood/water and fire have no mercy) because floods and fires can cause disaster (灾.)

4 八卦 (bāguà) and 八婆 (bāpó): 八卦 can mean the Eight Diagrams of I-Ching or 'gossip' which originated from Cantonese. Women who like to gossip are called 八婆. 婆 means 'granny.' 八婆 includes young women who like to gossip.

5 矛盾 (máodùn): 矛 means 'spear' and 盾 'shield,' and in combination they mean 'contradiction' or 'contradictory,' for example 自相矛盾 (zìxiāngmáodùn, self-contradictory.) One of the greatest modern Chinese writers 沈雁冰 (1896–1981) had a pen name 茅盾, which is more known than his real name. Please note the person 茅盾 is slightly different from the word 矛盾 in form.

6 突 (tū): It means 'suddenly' which derives from the two compositional parts of 突, namely 犬 (quǎn, dog) and 穴 (xué, cave, hole,) or a dog (suddenly) jumps out of a cave/hole. Words with 突 includes 突然 (tūrán, suddenly) and 突发事件 (tūfā shìjiàn, emergency).

Exercises:

Part I: Use the given bound form as a guide to help you think of other words with the same character. Feel free to use your dictionary when needed. Then write down the English definition of each of the words you've written.

难 (disaster):　　苦难　　misery, great suffering

____

____

____

____

____

灾 (disaster):　　天灾　　natural disaster

____

____

____

____

____

福 (good fortune): 福气 good luck

____

____

____

____

____

Part II: Read the following words and then answer the questions.

柴米油盐、家长里短、家常便饭、走下坡路、悲欢离合、酸甜苦辣
天灾人祸、艳福不浅、小道消息、花边新闻、个人恩怨、占小便宜

1 所谓的"天灾"有哪些?

2 所谓的"人祸"有哪些?

3 你们国家的哪些媒体喜欢报道"小道消息"?

4 你们国家的哪些媒体喜欢报道明星的"花边新闻"?

5 有人觉得美国正在"走下坡路," 你觉得呢?

6 你会不会跟喜欢占小便宜的人做朋友? 为什么?

7 __________见面后最喜欢聊的话题就是柴米油盐、家长里短.
a) 总统 b) 教授 c) 家庭主妇

8 小张工作态度非常差, 上班迟到对他来说像是__________.
a) 个人恩怨 b) 家常便饭 c) 酸甜苦辣

9 他十岁的时候父母都去世了, 自己一个人尝遍了人间的__________.
a) 酸甜苦辣 b) 艳福不浅 c) 家常便饭

10 小李的女朋友是个非常漂亮的模特, 朋友们都说小李__________.
a) 艳福不浅 b) 悲欢离合 c) 酸甜苦辣

Theme 52: Essence, rubbish 精华, 糟粕 (jīnghuá, zāopò)

1 精华 [-華] jīnghuá (essence-flower) <n.> essence: 报告的~ essence of the report || 思想的~ essence of thought || 人生的~ essence of life

2 精髓 [-] jīngsuǐ (essence-marrow) <n.> kernel, essence: 思想~ the essence of a thought || 中华文化的~ the essence of Chinese culture || 把握领导讲话的~ grasp the essence of the leader's speech

3 奇葩 [-] qīpā (rare-flower) <n.> rare flower, wonderful work: 一朵~ a rare flower || 艺术~ wonderful work of art || 这是他做过的最~的事. This is one of the rarest opportunities he has encountered.

4 遗产 [遺產] yíchǎn (left-property) <n.> inheritance, legacy: 继承 (jìchéng) ~ inherit a legacy || 文化~ a historical legacy

5 传家宝 [傳-寶] chuánjiābǎo (pass-generation-treasure) <n.> heirloom: 节俭是中国人的~. Plain living is a cherished heritage of the Chinese people. || 这块玉是他们家的~. This jade is their family heirloom.

6 世界文化遗产 [----遺產] shìjiè wénhuà yíchǎn (world-cultural-heritage) <n.> world cultural heritage: 这座小镇被列为~. This small city has been named a UNESCO World Heritage site. || 长城被评为~. The Great Wall has been named a World Heritage site.

7 百宝箱 [-寶-] bǎibǎoxiāng (treasure chest/ box of a hundred treasures) <n.> treasure case: 她这个箱子真是一个~呀, 里面有故事书、玩具还有很多漂亮的贴画. This chest is filled with a 100 treasures. Inside there are stories, toys and many pictures.

8 聚宝盆 [-寶-] jùbǎopén (bowl of treasure, place rich in natural resources) <n.> treasure bowl – place rich in natural resources, a cornucopia:这个新产品很受市场欢迎, 成了该公司的~. This new product is very popular on the market and has become the company's cornucopia.

9 摇钱树 [搖錢樹] yáoqiánshù (shake-money-tree) <n.> cash cow: 这个产品是谷歌公司的~. This product has always been a cash cow for the Google corporation.

10 残余 [殘餘] cányú (remnant-remain) <n./adj.> remains, remaining: ~力量 remaining strength || 封建~思想 remnants of feudal thought

11 残渣 [殘-] cánzhā (remnant-residue) <n.> remains: 食物~ remaining food || ~剩饭 leftover food

12 粪土 [糞-] fèntǔ (dung-dirt) <n.> muck, dung and dirt: 视金钱如~ consider money as beneath contempt, thoroughly disdain money

13 遗毒 [遺-] yídú (left-poison) <n.> evil legacy, harmful tradition: 封建思想的~ the evil legacy of feudalist thinking

14 糟粕 [-] zāopò (draff-sediment) <n.> dross: 儒家思想的~ the dross of Confucianism

15 障碍 [-礙] zhàng'ài (block-obstruct) <n.> obstacle, barrier: 扫除~ clear away obstacles || 语言~ language barrier || 制造~ create obstacles

16 阻碍 [-礙] zǔ'ài (hinder-obstruct) <n./v.> block, hinder: 受到~ be hindered || ~交通block the traffic || 减少~ reduce hinder

17 阻力 [-] zǔlì (obstruction/resistance-strength) <n.> obstruction: ~大 a large obstruction || 遇到~ encounter an obstruction

18 绊脚石 [絆--] bànjiǎoshí (stumbling block, obstacle) <n.> stumbling block, obstacle: 他是我们成功路上的~. He is but a stumbling block on our path to victory. || 轻视实践 (shíjiàn) 是科技进步的~. Looking too little at application is a stumbling block of innovation.

19 拦路虎 [攔--] lánlùhǔ (a road-blocking tiger) <n.> a lion in the way, block: 学习上的~ learning block

20 退堂鼓 [-] tuìtánggǔ (retreat-court-drum) <n.> drum-beating announcing signaling the adjournment of the court: 遇到困难就打~ retreat in the face of hardship.

21 贸易壁垒 [貿--壘] màoyì bìlěi (trade-barrier) <n.> trade barrier: 设置 (shèzhì) ~ establish a trade barrier || 打破~ break a trade barrier.

22 束缚 [-縛] shùfù (tie-bind) <n./v.> tie, bind up: 摆脱~ cast off one's ties || 思想~ bind one's thoughts || 导演不应该~演员的演出. A director should not bind up an actor's performance.

23 枷锁 [-鎖] jiāsuǒ (cangue-shackles) <n.> yoke, shackles, chains: 精神~ spiritual shackles || 戴上~ put on shackles.

24 屏障 [-] píngzhàng (wall-barrier) <n.> protective screen, defense: 一道天然的~ a natural defense || 绿色~ a green protective screen

25 遮羞布 [-] zhēxiūbù (disguise/cover up) <n.> fig leaf, gee-string, disguise: 一块~ a fig leaf (to cover an area) || 有人认为"爱国主义"其实就是政治家的一块~. Some people think that 'patriotism' is actually a cover up strategy for politicians.

26 烟雾弹 [煙霧彈] yānwùdàn (smoke bomb) <n.> smoke shell: 制造~ create a smoke screen || 降价促销 (cùxiāo) 只是公司的~, 实际目的是为了清理积压 (jīyā) 的产品. The corporation's efforts to decrease the promotion of sales is just a smokescreen. In reality, the goal is to clear out overstocked goods.

Tips:

1 精华 (jīnghuá) vs. 糟粕 (zāopò): 精华 means 'essence' and 糟粕 'dross.' The Chinese like to say 取其精华, 去其糟粕 which means 'take the cream, discard the dross.'

2 奇葩 (qīpā): It originally means 'rare flower' which has a positive connotation, however, it has recently become an irony of someone who acts very different from the ordinary people. In the later sense, the measure word for 奇葩 is usually '个,' not the usual one for flowers, '朵.'

3 Three-character colloquial sayings: There are more than the usual number of three-character colloquial sayings in this unit, for example, 传家宝, 百宝箱, 聚宝盆, 摇钱树, 绊脚石, 拦路虎, 退堂鼓, 遮羞布, 烟雾弹, which are all listed above.

Exercises: Multiple Choice. Make sure to choose the most appropriate answer.

1 这块玉是老王家的_______, 从二百多年前就一代代地传下来.
A. 传家宝 B. 百宝箱 C. 聚宝盆

2 这本中文语法书像一个语法________, 里面什么有用的语法都能找到.
A. 奇葩 B. 摇钱树 C. 百宝箱

3 “老王视金钱如粪土,” 这句话的意思是

A. 老王不喜欢钱的味道 B. 老王根本不在乎钱 C. 老王看钱的时候觉得不舒服

4 老王是这家科技公司的_______, 因为他每年为公司开发十几种新产品.

A. 遮羞布 B. 摇钱树 C. 烟雾弹

5 “学物理专业太难了, 小王想打退堂鼓,” 这句话的意思是

A. 物理专业很难, 小王想去学打鼓
B. 物理专业很难, 小王想放弃
C. 物理专业很难, 小王想用鼓打败它

6 “在追求真理的道路上会有很多绊脚石,” 这句话的意思是

A. 在追求真理的道路上会有很多障碍
B. 在追求真理的道路上会有很多封建遗毒
C. 在追求真理的道路上会有很多残渣

7 这位企业家说他会尽快偿还公司的债务, 但是很多人不相信, 认为他是在放_______.

A. 退堂鼓 B. 遮羞布 C. 烟雾弹

8 保护世界文化遗产就是在保护人类文明的_______.

A. 束缚 B. 糟粕 C. 精华

9 有人认为美国宪法可以体现美国民主精神的_______.

A. 精髓 B. 枷锁 C. 屏障

10 在中国古代, 长城是一道天然_______, 阻挡少数民族进攻汉族人地区.

A. 障碍 B. 阻碍 C. 屏障

11 小王在学习上遇到“拦路虎”的时候, 就会向老师请教. 这里的“拦路虎”意思是

A. 屏障 B. 障碍 C. 束缚

12 有人认为对待不同文化的态度应该是“去其______, 取其________.”

A. 遗毒、精髓 B. 精华、糟粕 C. 糟粕、精华

Theme 53: Image, scene 情景 (qíngjǐng)

1 外观 [-觀] wàiguān (outside-looks) <n.> exterior condition, exterior appearance: 这座大楼的~像一个球. The building was like a ball in appearance.

2 形态 [-態] xíngtài (form-posture) <n.> shape, form: 自然~ natural form || ~各异come in every shape || ~变化to change form

3 形象 [-] xíngxiàng (form-image) <n.> image: 女性~ women image || 城市~ city image || 注重 ~ pay more attention to image

4 形状 [-狀] xíngzhuàng (form-shape) <n.> shape: 星星~ star shape || 三角形~ triangle shape || 各种~ all kinds of shapes

5 样 [樣] yàng (pattern) <n.> looks, shape: 变~ out of shape || 火~的热情fire-like enthusiasm || 棉花~的白云white clouds like cotton

6 样子 [樣-] yàngzi (looks-*suffix*) <n.> looks, shape: 什么 ~ what is it like || 不成~ out of shape

7 造型 [-] zàoxíng (created-mold) <n.> make a model, modeling: ~独特unique modeling || 人物~ character modeling

8 化身 [-] huàshēn (change-body) <n.> embodiment: 正义的~ the embodiment of justice || 蛇的~ the embodiment of snakes

9 奇形怪状 [---狀] qíxíng guàizhuàng (strange-form-odd-shape) <adj.> strangely shaped: ~的石头strangely shaped rock

10 形 [-] xíng (form) <n.> shape: 圆~ circular shape || 方~ square shape || 长方~ rectangle

11 地形 [-] dìxíng (ground-form) <n.> terrain, topography: ~复杂with a varied topography || ~图topography map

12 状 [狀] zhuàng (shape) <n.> shape: 杯~ cup-shaped || 块 ~ block-shaped || 粒~ granular

13 型 [-] xíng (mold) <n.> type: 车~ vehicle models || 脸 ~ face shape || 发 ~ hairstyle

14 态 [態] tài (posture, state) <n.> state: 变~ abnormal || 病~ morbid state || 常~ ordinary state || 固 ~ solid state || 液 ~ liquid state || 气~ gaseous

15 心态 [-態] xīntài (mind-state) <n.> mind-set: ~好good mentality || 不安的~ a state of anxiety

16 动态 [動態] dòngtài (dynamic-state) <n.> dynamic state: 工作~ trend of work || ~分析dynamic analysis || 发展~ development trend

17 式 [-] shì (style) <n.> style: 西~ western style || 旧~ old style

18 样式 [樣-] yàngshì (pattern-style) <n.> style: 衬衫 ~ the style of the shirt || 最新 ~ the newest design || ~独特 a special design

19 款式 [-] kuǎnshì (model-style) <n.> style: 衣服~ clothing styles || ~多many styles || 最新~ latest styles

20 格式 [-] géshì (form-style) <n.> format: 文件~ file formats || 固定~ fixed formats || 按~填表fill the form according to the format

21 模式 [-] móshì (mold-style) <n.> mode, method: 固定 ~ fixed mode || 一套/种~ a set of mode || 消费~ consumption model

22 包装 [-裝] bāozhuāng (wrap-pack) <n.> package, wrapping: 外~ overwrap || 新~ new packing || 食品~ food packing

23 景 [-] jǐng (image, landscape) <n.> scene, view: 远~ long-range view || 美~ beautiful view || 夜~ night piece

24 风光 [風-] fēngguāng (wind-scenery) <n.> natural scenic view: 自然 ~ natural view || ~秀丽 (xiùlì) beautiful view

25 风景 [風-] fēngjǐng (wind-landscape) <n.> landscape: ~优美 beautiful landscape || 自然~ natural scenery || ~区scenic spot

26 景色 [-] jǐngsè (landscape-scenery) <n.> scene: 迷人的~ charming scene || 夏天的~ summer scenery

27 景物 [-] jǐngwù (scenery) <n.> scenery: 自然~ natural scenery || 远处的~ distant scenery || 周围的~ surrounding scenery

28 前景 [-] qiánjǐng (future-scene) <n.> prospect: 市场~ market expectation || 发展~ prospects || 美好的 ~ bright future

29 全景 [-] quánjǐng (full-scene) <n.> panoramic view: 公园~ park prospects || 城市 ~ city prospects

30 场景 [場-] chángjǐng (place-scene) <n.> scene: 生活~ life scene || 舞台~ stage scene
31 场面 [場-] chángmiàn (place-appearance) <n.> scene, spectacle: 感人的~ a moving scene || 精彩 (j(a movin的~ wonderful scene
32 景象 [-] jǐngxiàng (scene-phenomenon) <n.> sight: 热闹~ lively scene || 眼前的~ the scene before a person || 秋天 ~ autumn scene
33 面貌 [-] miànmào (face-looking) <n.> appearance: ~一新 take on a completely new look || 社会~ the look of society || 精神~ mental outlook
34 气象 [氣-] qìxiàng (air-phenomenon) <n.> atmosphere: 新~ new look || 社会新 ~ new social atmosphere

Tips:

1 景 (jǐng) and 象 (xiàng): The original meaning of 景 is sunlight, from which evolved the meaning 'scene.' The original meaning of 象 is elephant, from which evolved meanings such as ' (big) image, appearance and symbol'.
2 形 and 型: Both are pronounced as 'xíng,' but 形 is 'shape' and 型 'model, type.' Common shapes include 圆形 (circle, round,) 三角形 (triangle,) 长方形 (rectanglar) and 正方形 (square). 型 originally meant 'mold made with mud' from which evolved meanings such as 'model, type,' for example, 大型, 小型, 巨型 (jùxíng, giant, gigantic,) and 新型 (new model/type).

Exercises:

Part I: Use the given bound form as a guide to help you think of other words with the same character. Feel free to use your dictionary when needed. Then write down the English definition of each of the words you've written.

形 (form,shape): 形象 image

____

____

____

____

____

式 (type, style): 样式 style

____

____

____

____

____

景 (view, scene): 景色 scenery, view

____

____

____

____

____

Theme 54: Properties 性质 (xìngzhì)

1 性质 [-質] xìngzhì (nature-character) <n.> quality, nature: ~不同 different qualities || 根本~ basic differences || 社会~ societal differences
2 属性 [屬-] shǔxìng (category-nature) <n.> attribute, property: 生理 ~ physiology attributes || 自然~ natural attributes || 社会~ societal attributes
3 音色 [-] yīnsè (sound-color) <n.> tone of color (or quality): 小提琴的~ tones of color of violin || ~变化 change in color || 明亮的~ bright tones of color
4 磁性 [-] cíxìng (magnet-property) <n.> magnetism, magnetic: ~强/弱 strong, weak magnetism || 有~的声音 magnetic sound || 产生~ generate magnetism
5 惯性 [慣-] guànxìng (usual-property) <n.> inertia: 每一个人都有思维~. Everyone has his psychological inertia. || ~大large amount of inertia
6 弹性 [彈-] tánxìng (elastic-property) <n.> elasticity, resilience: 有~ have elasticity || ~大 large elasticity || 价格 ~ price elasticity
7 阳性 [陽-] yángxìng (positive-nature) <n.> positive, masculine: 药检~ positive drug test || 检验结果是 ~. The result of testing is positive.
8 阴性 [陰-] yīnxìng (negative-nature) <n.> negative, feminine: 血液 (xuèyè) 检查结果都是~, 没什么可担心的. The blood test was negative, so there is nothing to worry about.
9 中性 [-] zhōngxìng (neutral-nature) <n.> neutral: ~皮肤 neutral skin. || ~服装 neutral clothing
10 显性 [顯-] xiǎnxìng (apparent-nature) <n.> dominance: ~基因 dominant gene || ~表现 dominant expression || ~遗传 (yíchuán) dominant inheritance
11 隐性 [隱-] yǐnxìng (hideous-nature) <n.> recessive, hidden: ~基因 recessive gene || ~遗传 heredity || ~关系 hidden relationships
12 急性 [-] jíxìng (acute-nature) <n.> acute: ~中毒 (zhòngdú) acute poison, fast acting posing || ~病acute disease || ~发作 acute breakout
13 慢性 [-] mànxìng (slow-nature) <n.> chronic, slow: ~中毒 slow poisoning || ~病 chronic disease

14 毒性 [-] dúxìng (poisonous-property) <n.> toxicity: 无~ nonpoisonous || ~弱 low levels of poison
15 药性 [藥-] yàoxìng (medicine-property) <n.> property of a medicine: 这种药~不强. This is a mild medicine.
16 感性 [-] gǎnxìng (sense-nature) <n.> emotional, perception: ~经验 emotional experience || ~认识 know one's emotions
17 地区性 [-區-] dìqūxìng (region-property) <n.> regional, local: ~文化 regional culture || ~差异 regional differences
18 共性 [-] gòngxìng (common-property) <n.> general character, common nature: 有~ have commonality || 语言的 ~ common nature of languages
19 爆炸性 [-] bàozhàxìng (explosive-property) <adj.> explosive, sensational: ~新闻 sensational news || ~消息 sensational information
20 决定性 [決--] juédìngxìng (decide-nature) <adj.> decisive: ~作用 decisive action || ~因素decisive element
21 对称性 [對稱-] duìchènxìng (symmetric-property) <n.> symmetry: ~原理 symmetric principle
22 必要性 [-] bìyàoxìng (necessary-nature) <n.> necessity: 有~ have necessity. || 客观~ objective necessity. || 存在的~ existing necessity
23 一次性 [-] yīcìxìng (one-time-nature) <adj.> once only, disposable: ~筷子 disposable chopsticks || ~解决问题 solve a problem once and for all || ~产品 disposable product
24 主动性 [-動-] zhǔdòngxìng (initiative-nature) <n.> proactive, take the initiative: 有~ be proactive || ~强 strong initiative || 提高~ increase initiative
25 自觉性 [-覺-] zìjuéxìng (self-conscious-nature) <n.> (level of political) awareness, consciousness: 有~ have awareness || ~高 a high level of self-consciousness

26 性别 [-別] xìngbié (gender-difference) <n.> sex distinction: 不分~ not distinguish by gender || ~差异 gender difference || ~不同 different genders
27 男性 [-] nánxìng (male-gender) <非谓形容词> male: ~成员 male worker || ~公民 male citizen
28 女性 [-] nǚxìng (female-gender) <非谓形容词> female: ~成员 female worker || ~公民 female citizen
29 人性 [-] rénxìng (human-nature) <n.> normal human feelings: ~很复杂. Human nature is complicated. || 灭绝 ~的暴行 inhuman atrocities || 不通~ unfeeling and unreasonable

30 特点 [-點] tèdiǎn (distinguishing-point) <n.> characteristic: 两个~ two characteristics || 主要~ primary characteristic || 有~ have a characteristic
31 特色 [-] tèsè (distinguishing-feature) <n.> characteristic: 民族~ ethnic characteristic || 时代~ generational characteristic || 有~ have a distinguishing characteristic
32 特征 [-徵] tèzhēng (distinguishing-character) <n.> characteristic, feature: 运动~ athletic characteristic || 共同的~ shared characteristic || 重要的~ important characteristic

33 差别 [-別] chābié (difference-distinction) <n.> difference, disparity: 有/没有~ there is/isn't a difference || 年龄 (niánlíng) ~ difference in age || 男女~ male-female difference

34 差距 [-] chājù (difference-gap) <n.> gap, disparity: 收入~ income gap || 价格~ gap in price || ~大 large gap

35 差异 [-異] chāyì (difference-diversity) <n.> difference: 地区~ difference between ranges || 气候~ difference in weather || 大小~ size difference

36 区别 [區別] qūbié (differentiate-distinction) <n.> difference: 根本~ root difference || 明显的~ obvious difference || 有/没有~ there is, isn't a difference

37 距离 [-離] jùlí (from-to) <n.> distance: ~远 far distance || 有~ there is a distance || 近~ short range

38 千差万别 [--萬別] qiānchā wànbié (a thousand-differences – ten thousand-distinctions) <idiom> differ in thousands of ways: ~的情况 these matters differ in a multitude of ways || 中国学生去国外留学的原因~. There is a vast multitude of reasons why Chinese exchange students go abroad to study.

39 高下 [-] gāoxià (high-low) <n.> relative superiority or inferiority: 这两个人的技术水平不分 ~. The two of them are equally matched in their skills.

40 好坏 [-壞] hǎohuài (good-bad) <n.> good and bad: ~不分 cannot tell good from bad || 辨别 ~ tell good from bad

41 上下 [-] shàngxià (up-down) <adj.> high and low, from top to bottom: ~级 levels from high to low || ~关系relationship between high level and low level

42 优劣 [優-] yōuliè (superior-inferior) <n.> good and bad, superior and inferior: 产品 ~ superior and inferior goods || 方法 ~ superior and inferior methods

43 时差 [時-] shíchā (time-difference) <n.> time difference, jet lag: 倒~ overcome jet lag

44 温差 [溫-] wēnchā (temperature-difference) <n.> difference in temperature: ~大 large difference in temperature

45 得失 [-] déshī (gain-loss) <n.> gain and loss, success and failure: 个人~ personal gains and losses || 计较~ haggle over gains and losses

46 利弊 [-] lìbì (advantage-disadvantage) <n.> advantages and disadvantages: 各有~ each has advantages and disadvantages || 权衡 (quánhéng) ~ weigh advantages disadvantages

47 利害 [-] lìhài (benefit-harm) <n.> fierce, terrible, positive and negative: ~关系 mixed relationship || 权衡~ weigh the positives and negatives

48 长处 [長處] chángchù (merit-place) <n.> good qualities: 发挥~ display one's good qualities || 有~ have good qualities || 别人的~ other people's good qualities

49 强项 [-項] qiángxiàng (strong-item) <n.> key strength: 数学是他的 ~. Math is the subject he knows best.

50 优点 [優點] yōudiǎn (superior-point) <n.> strong (or good) point: 有/没有~ there is/isn't a superior point || 很多~ there are lots of advantages

51 公益 [-] gōngyì (public-benefit) <n.> public good, public interest: ~组织 nonprofit organization || ~事业 a cause for the public good || ~劳动 work for the public good

52 好处 [-處] hǎochu (good-place) <n.> good, benefit: 有 (三个) ~ have benefits, have three benefits || 吃水果的~ benefits of eating fruit || 对身体有~ there are benefits for one's body

53 利益 [-] lìyì (advantage-benefit) <n.> interest, benefit: 有/没有~ there is/isn't benefit || 个人~ personal benefit || 长远~ distant benefit

54 短处 [-處] duǎnchu (short-place) <n.> shortcoming, weakness: 避 (bì) 开~ avoid one's shortcomings || 有 ~ have shortcomings || 很多~ many shortcomings
55 毛病 [-] máobìng (hair-defect) <n.> trouble, mishap, defect: 挑~ find fault || 坏~ negative trouble || 克服这个~ overcome a fault
56 缺点 [-點] quēdiǎn (imperfect-point) <n.> shortcoming, defect: 有/没有~ there is/isn't a shortcoming || ~多/ 少 many/few shortcomings || 克服~ overcome a shortcoming
57 缺陷 [-] quēxiàn (imperfect-fault) <n.> defect, drawback: 有/没有~ there is/is not a defect || 大/ 严重~ large/serious defect || 生理~ physiological defect
58 弱点 [-點] ruòdiǎn (weak-point) <n.> weakness, weak point: 有~ have a weakness || 致命 (zhìmìng) 的 ~ a life threatening weakness || 人性的~ personal weakness
59 通病 [-] tōngbìng (common-fault) <n.> common failing: 成了~ be a common failing
60 瑕疵 [-] xiácī (flaw-blemish) <n.> flaw, defect: 有~ have a defect || 毫无~ without defect
61 弊病 [-] bìbìng (disadvantage-malpractice) <n.> malady, evil, drawbacks: 有~ have drawbacks || 产生~ result in disadvantages || 社会~ social evils
62 坏处 [壞處] huàichu (bad-place) <n.> harm, disadvantage: 没有 ~. There is no harm. || 从~着想, 往好处努力. Prepare for the worst; strive for the best. || 最大的~ the largest disadvantage

Tips:

1 性 (xìng): The original meaning of 性 is 'natural instinct', since it is related to 忄 (心, heart,) and from 'natural instinct' evolved meanings such as 'nature, character, sex and gender.'
2 毛病 (máobìng): It originally meant 'the color of the hair of a horse is imperfect, with defects.' Now it means 'defect, illness, fault.' If a person "有毛病," it means he is weird or freakish.
3 缺 (quē): The original meaning of 缺 is 'a pottery with a notch,' from which evolved the meaning of 'imperfect' in words such as 缺点 (shortcoming.)
4 Juxtaposed antonyms meaning 'category': If two antonyms are used in a compound word, it could mean a category which the two antonyms fall under. For example, 好坏 means 'good' and 'bad' individually but 'quality' as a compound. Other words of this kind include 上下 (above-below, about,) 得失 (gain-loss, result) and 优劣 (superior-inferior, quality, level).

Exercises:

Part I: Write an antonym for each word in the table. You can refer to the given words.

个性、阳性、好处、优点、长处、弱项、急性、显性、感性

共性v.s.	阴性v.s.	坏处v.s.
缺点v.s.	短处v.s.	强项v.s.
慢性v.s.	阴性v.s.	理性v.s.

Part II: Read the following sentences and fill in each blank with the appropriate word or phrase from the options given.

1 弊病、通病、利益、公益

a) 一有时间就低头看手机是大多数人的________.
b) 美国人自以为完美的民主制度已经暴露 (bàolù, expose) 出很多_________.
c) 有的中国电影明星很热衷 (rèzhōng, fall over oneself for) 于从事_______活动.
d) 中国政府认为国家_______最重要, 应该放在第一位.

2 缺陷、毛病、缺点、优点

a) 小王不喜欢德国车, 因为德国车在使用五年以后就会经常出_______.
b) 日本车的_______是省油, ________是车身不够耐撞.
c) 对于身体天生有_______的人, 中国政府会为他们提供一定的福利 (fúlì, welfare).

3 得失、特点、利弊

a) 坚持是所有成功者的共同_______.
b) 这位政府官员全心全意为老百姓服务, 从不计较个人_______.
c) 小王在权衡了________以后决定辞去现在的工作, 到新公司任职 (rènzhí, take office).

4 差距、温差、时差、千差万别

a) 中国北方夏季的时候早晚______很大.
b) 北京跟纽约的_______是12小时.
c) 在中国, 农村人跟城市人的生活水平_______还很大.
d) 世界各地的风俗习惯__________, 非常不一样.

Theme 55: Categories, factors 范畴, 因素 (fànchóu, yīnsù)

1 范围 [範圍] fànwéi (confine-perimeter) <n.> scope, sphere, range dimension: 在一定的~之内 within a certain scope || 活动~ scope of activities || 世界 ~ worldwide
2 规模 [規-] guīmó (compass-mold) <n.> scale, size: 大~ on a large scale || 苹果公司的生产~扩大了一倍. Apple's production doubled.
3 全场 [-場] quánchǎng (whole-site) <n.> the whole audience, all those present: ~观众the whole audience || ~起立! All rise up!
4 层面 [層-] céngmiàn (layer-facet) <n.> layer: 多~ 分析multidimensional analysis || 心理~ psychological level || 语义~ semantic level
5 圈子 [-] quānzi (circle-*suffix*) <n.> circle, community: 生活life circle. || 华人~ chinese people circle || 朋友~ a circle of friends
6 牢笼 [-籠] láolóng (trap-cage) <n.> cage, trap: 陷入~ get caught in a cage || 逃出 ~ escape from the cage
7 视野 [視-] shìyě (view-field) <n.> field of view: 开阔 ~ too widen one's (field of) vision || ~宽/狭窄wide/tunnel vision

8 官场 [-場] guānchǎng (official-circle) <n.> officialdom: ~生活 official life || ~规则official rules || ~黑暗official darkness

9 商海 [-] shānghǎi (business-sea) <n.> commercial circles: 进入~ enter commercial circles || ~沉浮 (chénfú) ups and downs in commercial circles

10 画坛 [畫壇] huàtán (world of art, painting-circle) <n.> painting circles: 中国~ china's painting circles || 登上~ climb atop the world of art || ~大师 a master in the world of art

11 歌坛 [-壇] gētán (world of music, singing-circle) <n.> circles of singers: 欧美~ European and American circles of singers || 退出~ withdraw from the world of music

12 乐坛 [樂壇] yuètán (music-circle) <n.> music circles: 流行 ~ pop music circles || 国际~ international music circles

13 体坛 [體壇] tǐtán (sports-circle) <n.> sporting world: 国际~ international cporting world || 告别~ bid farewell to the sporting world

14 文坛 [-壇] wéntán (literary-circle) <n.> literary world: 当代~ contemporary literary world

15 界 [-] jiè (boundary) <n.> world, circles: 自然~ natural world || 外~ the outside world || 教育educational circles/艺术~ art circles/体育~ sports circles

16 基地 [-] jīdì (base-place) <n.> base: 培训~ training base || 海军~ naval base || 生产~ production base

17 上下 [-] shàngxià (up-down) <n.> up and down, from top to bottom: 全国~ the whole nation from the leadership to the masses || 公司~ the whole company

18 方面 [-] fāngmiàn (direction-side) <n.> side, hand: 多/两/几~ many sides or parties/both sides or parties/several sides or parties || 这/那个 ~ this side/that side || 一 ~ . . . . . ., 另一 ~ . . . . . . on the one hand . . ., on the other hand. . . .

19 处处 [處處] chùchù (place-place) <n.> everywhere, in all aspects: 中国父母总是想 ~保护孩子, 帮助孩子. Chinese parents always want to protect their child and provide for their child in every way.

20 单方 [單-] dānfāng (single-side) <n.> one-sided, unilateral: ~行为unilateral act || ~撕毁 (sīhuǐ) 合同unilaterally tear up the contract

21 一边 [-邊] yībiān (one-side) <n.> one side: ~长, ~短. One side is long and another side is short. || 放在 ~ put aside || 躲在~ hide aside

22 两边 [兩邊] liǎngbiān (two-side) <n.> on both sides: 街道~ on the both sides of street || ~的商店 stores on both sides || 左右~ left and right sides

23 两侧 [兩側] liǎngcè (two-side) <n.> on both sides: 房子~ on the both sides of house || 东西~ east and west sides

24 甲方 [-] jiǎfāng (first-party) <n.> party A: 合同的~ party A of the contract

25 乙方 [-] yǐfāng (second-party) <n.> Party B: 合同的~ party B of the contract

26 警方 [-] xiàofāng (police-side) <n.> police: 机场~加强了检查. The airport police strengthened their inspection.

27 对方 [對-] duìfāng (opposite-side) <n.> the other side: ~的年龄 the age of the other || ~的意见 the opinions of the other side || 关心~ care about each other

28 双方 [雙-] shuāngfāng (both-side) <n.> both sides, the two parties: 男女~ both men and women || 比赛 ~ both sides of game || 买卖~ buyers and sellers

29 彼此 [-] bǐcǐ (that-this) <pron.> each other: ~ 对立be again each other || ~支持 (zhīchí) support each other || ~信任 trust each other

30 多方 [-] duōfāng (multiple-party) <n.> multi-party: 引起 ~争议 cause many disputes || 引起~调查 cause multi-party investigation
31 男方 [-] nánfāng (male-side) <n.> the bridegroom's or husband's side: ~家庭 the husband's side of the family || ~亲友 friends and relatives from the husband's side || ~的姓 the husband's last name
32 女方 [-] nǚfāng (female-side) <n.> the bride's or wife's side: ~家庭 the wife's side of the family || ~亲友 friends and relatives from the wife's side || ~的姓 the wife's last name
33 官方 [-] guānfāng (government-side) <n.> official, of or by the government: ~数字official figures || ~评论official comments || ~代表 official representative
34 民间 [-間] mínjiān (people-among) <n.> folk, nongovernmental: ~音乐 folk music || ~ 歌手folk singer || ~团体civil society

35 面 [-] miàn (side) <n.> side: 黑暗~ dark side || 事物都有两~ 性. Every coin has two sides.
36 表面 [-] biǎomiàn (out-side) <n.> surface: ~情况 surface condition || ~现象surface phenomena || 从 ~ (上) 看superficially
37 系统 [-統] xìtǒng (relation-system) <n./adj.> system: 三大~ three systems || 公交~ public transportation systems || ~分析system analysis
38 体系 [體-] tǐxì (integral-system) <n.> system: 经济~ economic system || 管理~ management system || 科学~ scientific system
39 系列 [-] xìliè (relation-row) <n.> series: ~产品series of products || ~活动 series of activities || 两个~ two series
40 网 [網] wǎng (net) <n.> net: 电~ power grid || 关系 ~ people network || 互联 ~ internet
41 网络 [網絡] wǎngluò (net-wind) <n.> net: 神经 (shénjīng) ~ neural networks || 关系~ people network || 社会~ social network
42 结构 [結構] jiégòu (connect-frame) <n.> structure: 房屋的~ house structure || 复杂的~ complex structure || 社会~ social structure
43 构造 [構-] gòuzào (frame-build) <n.> structure: 生理~ physiological structure || 身体~ body structure || 汉字的~ the structure of Chinese characters
44 环节 [環節] huánjié (link-sector) <n.> link: 两个~ two links || 主要~ main link || 中心~ central link

45 种类 [種類] zhǒnglèi (kind-category) <n.> kinds: ~多many kinds || 商品~ commodity classification
46 类型 [類-] lèixíng (category-type) <n.> types: 三种~ three types || 不同~ different type || 新的 ~ new type
47 类 [類] lèi (category) <n.> class, category, kind, type: 人/鸟~ human being/birds || 感冒~药品cold drugs || 服装~商品clothing goods
48 多种 [-種] duōzhǒng (multiple-kind) <n.> a variety of: ~ 方法 a variety of methods || ~问题 a variety of problems
49 品种 [-種] pǐnzhǒng (product-kind) <n.> breeds, varieties: 水果~ fruit breeds || 增加~ increase the variety || ~多many varieties
50 项目 [項目] xiàngmù (itemized-item) <n.> project, events: 四个~ four projects || 比赛~ events of the game || 重大~ important project
51 奖项 [獎項] jiǎngxiàng (award-item) <n.> awards: 重要~ important awards || 各种~ various awards

52 物种 [-種] wùzhǒng (organism-kind) <n.> species: 热带 ~ tropical species || 《~起源》Origin of Species

53 顶级 [頂級] dǐngjí (top-level) <n.> top: ~品牌top brands || ~餐厅top restaurant
54 程序 [-] chéngxù (process-sequence) <n.> procedure: 工作~ working procedures || 法律~ legal proceedings || 固定~ fixed procedure || 按~做 follow the procedure to do
55 次序 [-] cìxù (order-sequence) <n.> order: 先后 ~ precedence order || 按~ in order || 有~地站好stand in order
56 排名 [-] páimíng (rank-order) <n.> ranking order: ~第一 number one of the ranking list || 不分 ~ regardless of ranking
57 顺序 [順-] shùnxù (conform-sequence) <n.> order: 字母~ alphabetical order || 按~ in order
58 层次 [層-] céngcì (layer-order) <n.> level: 四个~ four levels || 高~人才high-level talents
59 名次 [-] míngcì (name-order) <n.> position in a name list: 总~ overall ranking || 排 ~ rank

60 航班 [-] hángbān (flight-schedule) t<n.> fligh: 国际/国内 ~ international flights/domestic flights || ~延误 (yánwù) flight delay || ~取消 cancel flights
61 白班 [-] báibān (day-shift) <n.> day shift: 上~ be on the day shift || 我大年初二上~. I worked the day shift during the second day of the New Lunar Year.
62 晚班 [-] wǎnbān (evening-shift) <n.> night shift: 上~ be on the night shift || ~工人 night shift worker
63 夜班 [-] yèbān (night-shift) <n.> late night shift: 上~ be on the late night shift || ~工人 night shift worker || 值~ on night shift (or duty)
64 早班 [-] zǎobān (morning-shift) <n.> early morning shift: 上~ be on the early morning shift
65 中班 [-] zhōngbān (noon-shift) <n.> noon shift: 上~ be on the noon shift
66 日程 [-] rìchéng (time-schedule) <n.> schedule: ~安排schedule || ~很紧/忙tight/busy schedule
67 流程 [-] liúchéng (flow-procedure) <n.> process: 工作~ work process || 生产 ~ production process
68 应届 [應-] yīngjiè (should-arrive) <adj.> this year's, the current year's: ~毕业生 graduating student or pupil
69 往届 [-] wǎngjiè (previously-arrive) <adj.> previous session: ~毕业生preceding-year-pupil

70 要素 [-] yàosù (essential-factor) <n.> essential factor, element: 两个~ two elements || 基本~ basic element || 生产 ~ essential production factors
71 因素 [-] yīnsù (reason-factor) <n.> factor, element: 客观~ objective factor || 重要~ important factor || 多种 ~ a variety of factors
72 元素 [-] yuánsù (primary-element) <n.> element: 多种~ a variety of elements || 中国~ chinese elements
73 部分 [-] bùfèn (part-section) <n.> part: 两个~ two parts || 重要~ important part
74 成分 (份) [-] chéngfèn (composing-element) <n.> ingredient, content: 主要 ~ the main ingredients || 药物~ drug ingredients || 营养~ nutrient content

75 养分 [養-] yǎngfèn (nutrition-element) <n.> nutrient: 吸收~ absorb nutrient || ~充足sufficient nutrient || 缺乏~ lack of nutrients

76 营养 [營養] yíngyǎng (provide-nutrition) <n.> nutrition: 缺乏~ lack of nutrition || 加强 ~ strengthen nutrition || ~不良malnutrition

77 外表 [-] wàibiǎo (out-looking) <n.> appearance, exterior, outside: 看~ judge people by appearances || ~好看 look nice

78 面目 [-] miànmù (face-eye) <n.> face: 真实~ the true face, true colors || ~全非beyond recognition

79 基本 [-] jīběn (fundamental-root) <adj.> basic, fundamental: ~情况basic situation || ~规律the basic law || ~原则 the basic principle

80 基础 [-] jīchǔ (fundamental-foundation) <n.> foundation, basis: ~知识rudimentary knowledge || 奠定 (diàndìng) /打~ lay the foundation for || 以事实为~ on the basis of facts || 牢固的~ solid foundation

81 关键 [關鍵] guānjiàn (key-bolt) <n./adj.> key, crucial: ~问题/时刻the key issue/ the crucial moment || 成功的~ the key to success || 事情的~ the key to things

82 关口 [關-] guānkǒu (pass-mouth) <n.> strategic pass, juncture, key moment: 重要~ important pass || 病人现在处于生命危险的~. The patient is at a dangerous juncture.

83 关头 [關頭] guāntóu (key-*suffix*) <n.> key moment, juncture: 在紧要~ at a critical moment || 生死~ juncture when one's life is at stake, critical juncture

84 瓶颈 [-頸] píngjǐng (bottle-neck) <n.> bottleneck: 发展~ bottleneck in development || 中国经济遇到了~. China's economic development has encountered bottlenecks.

85 枢纽 [樞紐] shū'niǔ (center-hub) <n.> junction, hub: 交通~ transportation junction || 经济~ economic hub || 国际~ international hub

86 焦点 [-點] jiāodiǎn (focus-spot) <n.> focus: 争论的~ point at issue || ~人物 central figure || 这就是问题的~. That is the heart of the matter.

87 热点 [熱點] rèdiǎn (hot-spot) <n./adj.> hot, hot spots: ~问题 hot issue || ~新闻breaking news || 新的~ new hot spots

88 卖点 [賣點] màidiǎn (selling-point) <n.> selling point: 产品 ~ product selling point || 最大~ the biggest selling point

89 机遇 [機-] jīyù (opportunity-chance) <n.> opportunity: 抓住~ seize the opportunity || 特殊~ special opportunity

90 时机 [時機] shíjī (right moment-opportunity) <n.> right moment: 好~ good time || 抓住~ embrace a good chance || ~成熟 (chéngshú) 了. The time is ripe.

91 机会jīhuì [機會] (opportunity-occasion) <n.> chance: 抓住~ seize the chance || 有/没有~ get the chance/ have no chance || ~平等equality of opportunity

92 中心 [-] zhōngxīn (middle-center) <n.> center: ~工作central task || 以发展经济/保护环境为~ take the economic development /environmental protection as the central task

93 重点 [-點] zhòngdiǎn (main-point) <n.> key point: 工作~ key emphasis in work || ~学校key school || ~问题key issue

94 核心 [-] héxīn (nucleus-center) <n.> core: 领导 ~ the core of leadership || ~思想core concept, core idea || 团队的~ the core of the team

95 本质 [-質] běnzhì (essential-nature) <n.> nature, essence: 人的~ human nature || 教育的~ the nature of education || ~问题 the nature of an issue

96 主导 [-導] zhǔdǎo (lead-guide) <n./v.> domination, dominate, lead: 起~作用play a dominant role
97 主体 [-體] zhǔtǐ (main-body) <n.> subject, main body: 市场~ market players || 以学生为~的教学student-centered teaching
98 客体 [-體] kètǐ (object-body) <n.> object: 研究的~ the object in research
99 实体 [實體] shítǐ (solid-body) <n.> entity: 经济~ economic entity || ~经济the real economy

Tips:

1 方: The original meaning of 方 was parallel boats, from which evolved meanings such as 'parallel, equal, square and side'.
2 种类 (zhǒnglèi) vs. 类型 (lèixíng): 种类 means 'kind' and 类型 'type.' Generally 类型 is a hypernym of 种类. You can say 这种类型 (this type.)
3 Taxonomic ranks: They are kingdom (界, jiè,) phylum or division (门,) class (纲, gāng,) order (目,) family (科, kē,) genus (属, shǔ) and species (种, zhǒng.)
4 Opportunities (机遇, jīyù): The Chinese saying 机不可失 (shī, lose), 时不再来 has an exact equivalent in English, 'opportunities never knock twice.'

Exercises:

Part I: Answer the following questions in Chinese.

1 请写出你所知道的带"方"的名词

2 请写出你所知道的带"界"的名词

3 请写出你所知道的带"坛"的名词

4. 请写出你所知道的带"点"的名词

5 请写出你所知道的带"关"的名词

Part II: Please translate the following Chinese sentences into English.

1 纽约是一个国际经济枢纽.

2 这位总统是全国媒体的焦点人物.

3 有人认为教育的本质应该是让人人机会平等.

______

4 目前中国经济发展遇到了瓶颈. 因此, 解决这一问题成为中国政府的工作重点.

______

5 邓小平的改革开放政策为中国经济发展打下了牢固 (solid) 的基础.

______

Theme 56: Standards 标准 (biāozhǔn)

1 标准 [標準] biāozhǔn (standard-measure) <n.> standard: 高~ high standards || 制定 (zhìdìng) ~ set standards || 发音~ speak with perfect pronunciation
2 规范 [規範] guīfàn (regulation-rule) <n.> standard, norm: 行为 ~ acting norms || 科学~ scientific standards || 基本 ~ basic standards
3 原则 [-則] yuánzé (prime-criterion) <n.> principle: 基本~ basic principles || 有, 没有~ have, not have principles || 重要~ important principles
4 前提 [-] qiántí (pre-put forward) <n.> prerequisite: ~条件 prerequisite conditions || 基本~ basic conditions || 大~ heavy prerequisites
5 条件 [條-] tiáojiàn (clause-item) <n.> condition: 生活~ life conditions || 重要~ important conditions || 符合 (fúhé) ~ meet the conditions
6 规格 [規-] guīgé (regulation-specification) <n.> specifications, requirement: 统一 (tǒngyī) ~ overall requirements || 多种 ~ multiple requirements || 产品~ product specifications
7 准则 [準則] zhǔnzé (norm-criterion) <n.> norm, standard: 做人~ norms for being a person || 行动 ~ standard actions || 最高~ highest standards
8 信条 [-條] xìntiáo (faith-clause) <n.> articles of faith, creed: 人生 ~ life creed || 基本~ basic creed
9 榜样 [-樣] bǎngyàng (advertise-model) <n.> example, model: 做~ serve as a model || 树立 ~ establish a model || 学习~ study from example
10 楷模 [-] kǎimó (pattern-model) <n.> model, paragon: 树立~ establish a model || 学习的 ~ a model of study || 时代 ~ a generational model
11 典范 [-範] diǎnfàn (typical-model) <n.> model, example: 艺术 ~ an art model || 树立 ~ establish a model
12 样板 [樣-] yàngbǎn (sample-plate) <n.> sample, plate, model: 改~ alter the sample || 标准 ~ the standard sample || ~戏model opera
13 界限 [-] jièxiàn (boundary-limit) <n.> demarcation line: 划分~ lay out a demarcation line || 打破~ remove the dividing line
14 边界 [邊-] biānjiè (border-boundary) <n.> boundary, border: 内部~ internal boundary || 两国~ boundary between two nations || ~问题 a border issue
15 境界 [-] jìngjiè (realm-boundary) <n.> boundary: 思想 ~ boundary of thought || 精神 ~ energy level || 新 ~ new boundary
16 地平线 [--綫] dìpíngxiàn (land-level-line) <n.> horizon: ~上出现了一只船. A ship became visible on the horizon.
17 贫困线 [貧-綫] pínkùnxiàn (poverty-line) <n.> poverty line, poverty level: ~以下 below the poverty line || ~标准standard of poverty line

18 分数线 [-數綫] fēnshùxiàn (grade-line) <n.> dividing line: 录取~ admission line, entry score || 降低 ~ lower the entry score || 最低 ~ the lowest entry score
19 上限 [-] shàngxiàn (upper-limit) <n.> upper limit: 年龄~ age limit || 接近~ be approaching the upper limit
20 下限 [-] xiàxiàn (lower-limit) <n.> lower limit: 速度~ the lowest speed || 接近 ~ be approaching the lower limit
21 底线 [-綫] dǐxiàn (bottom-line) <n.> endline, baseline: 道德 ~ the moral baseline || 价格 ~ the price baseline || 靠近~ rely on the baseline || 这个人没~. This guy is shameless.
22 权限 [權-] quánxiàn (power-limit) <n.> limits of authority: 管理~ the limit of management authority || ~下放 relinquish authority
23 极端 [極-] jíduān (extreme-end) <n.> extreme, extremity: 走~ walk to an extreme || 两个~ two extremes || 另一个~ the other extreme
24 极限 [極-] jíxiàn (extreme-limit) <n.> extreme: 速度~ the speed limit || 超越 (chāoyuè) ~ exceed the extreme || ~运动extreme exercise
25 顶点 [頂點] dǐngdiǎn (top-point) <n.> apex, peak, summit: 达到~ reach the summit || 高兴到~ the peak of happiness
26 尺寸 [-] chǐcùn (foot-inch) <n.> measurement, dimensions: 量~ measurement || 大小~ measurement size || 衣服~ clothing measurement
27 大小 [-] dàxiǎo (big-small) <n.> size: ~不同 different size || 鞋子 ~ shoe size || 房间 ~ size of a room
28 轻重 [輕-] qīngzhòng (light-weight) <n.> weight: 不分~ not differentiate by weight || 对违法活动, 要根据情节~, 加以处罚 (chǔfá). In regards to illegal activities, one must weigh things based upon the circumstances, before adding punishments.
29 分寸 [-] fēncùn (inch-1/10 inch) <n.> proper limits for speech, action: 没有~ no limits of speech || ~感 sense of discretion (relating to speech) || 注意~ pay attention to proper limits of speech
30 高低 [-] gāodī (high-low) <n.> height, pitch: 不分~ not separate by height || 收入 ~ salary level || 地位/分数~ place, ranking
31 质量 [質-] zhìliàng (quality-quantity) <n.> quality: 高~ high quality || 保证~ high guarantee || ~低 low quality
32 档次 [檔-] dàngcì (order-level) <n.> grade: 提高~ raise the grade || 拉开~ raise the grade || 请客的~ grade of host
33 水平 [-] shuǐpíng (water-horizontal) <n.> standard, level: 技术~ technology level || 文化~ cultural level || 高~ high standard
34 品味 [-] pǐnwèi (grade-taste) <n.> quality, taste, appreciation: 有 ~ have good taste in sth. || 文化 ~ cultural taste || ~高雅 (gāoyǎ) elegant appreciation
35 根底 [-] gēndǐ (root-bottom) <n.> grounding in basic skills: 有 ~ be well grounded in basic skills || ~扎实have a good grounding

Tips:

1 高大上: This word was coined on the Internet in 2013, meaning *高端* (gāoduān, high-end,) *大气* (of good taste) and *上档次* (shàngdàngcì, top grade.) For example, some Chinese want to have 高大上 English names.
2 八个样板戏 (yàngbǎnxì): The Eight Model Plays were the only eight Peking operas allowed to be performed in China during the Cultural

Revolution (1966–76.) Needless to say, the themes of the eight operas were all revolutionary.

3 Who is the model (楷模, kǎimó) of all Chinese? Confucius said it was 周公 (Zhōu Gōng, the Duke of Zhou, 11th century BCE,) but the people after Confucius said Confucius was the model and thus revered him as 大成至圣先师 (dàchéng zhìshèng xiānshī, most accomplished, greatest sage, first teacher.) The Duke of Zhou and Confucius were too obscure to be modeled, but there was a man who lived in the late Qing Dynasty. He is 曾国藩 (Zēng Guófān, 1811–1872,) a statesman, military general and Confucian scholar who was revered as 千古完人 (a flawless/perfect man through the ages.)

Exercises:

Part I: Multiple Choice. Make sure to choose the most appropriate answer.

1 张女士家里布置 (bùzhì, arrange) 得很有_______, 既高雅又简洁.
A. 口味 B. 品味 C. 气味

2 张女士从小就学习京剧, 所以她的京剧________很扎实, 表演______也很高.
A. 根底、水平 B. 水平、根底 C. 根据、水平

3 海底捞是一家很上______的火锅店, 不仅服务优良, 菜品_______也很好.
A. 质量、档次 B. 档次、质量 C. 重量、档次

4 这两个优秀的乒乓球运动将在世界乒乓球大赛上比试水平_______.
A. 高低 B. 高矮 C. 穷富

5 小王在领导面前说话很有_______, 受到了领导的赏识 (shǎngshí, appreciation).
A. 尺寸 B. 分寸 C. 轻重

6 有些女孩子为了自己变得更美会走_______, 一次又一次地整容.
A. 极端 B. 顶点 C. 极限

7 小王认为做人应该有______, 那就是不能做违反道德 (dàodé, morals) 和法律的事情.
A. 上限 B. 权限 C. 底线

8 小王半夜开始爬长城, 为的就是在长城上看到太阳从________上升起的那一刻.
A. 贫困线 B. 地平线 C. 分数线

9 美国政府决定在_________上建立一道高墙来阻挡非法移民的进入.
A. 界限 B. 边界 C. 境界

10 雷锋是上世纪六十年代中国人学习的_______.
A. 榜样 B. 信条 C. 规格

11 苹果公司生产手机的质量_______很高, 所以手机质量很好.
A. 标准 B. 规范 C. 原则

12 中国西部地区的自然_______不太好, 因此发展农业比较困难.
A. 准则 B. 条件 C. 前提

Theme 57: Appearance 仪表 (yíbiǎo)

1 仪表 [儀-] yíbiǎo (appearance-looking) <adj> appearance: ~ 堂堂dignified appearance || ~整洁 (zhěngjié) clean and tidy appearance

2 人品 [-] rénpǐn (man-quality) <n> character: ~好 good character || ~高尚 noble character

3 风度 [風-] fēngdù (demeanor-bearing) <n.> grace: 有/没有~ have/not have grace || 绅士 (shēnshì) ~ gentleman

4 气质 [氣質] qìzhì (temperament-disposition) <adj> temperament: 浪漫 (làngmàn) ~ romantic temperament || 东方 ~ oriental temperament || 有 ~ have a temperament

5 派头 [-頭] pàitou (style-*suffix*) <n> style: 一副学者~ academic style || 有 ~ have a style panache || 好大的 ~ have a lot of panache

6 洋相 [-] yánxiàng (foreign-looking) <n> social blunder: 出~ make a fool of yourself || ~百出make a spectacle of oneself

7 丑态 [醜態] chǒutài (disgraceful-appearance) <n> disgraceful situation: ~百出 lots of buffoonery

8 傲气 [-氣] àoqì (arrogant-air) <adj> arrogant: ~十足 pure arrogance || 杀杀他的~ quell sb.'s arrogance || 他太~了, 总是看不起人. He is very proud and always holds others in contempt.

9 朝气 [-氣] zhāoqì (youthful-spirit) <adj> vitality: ~蓬勃 (péngbó) vigorous || 富有~ energetic || 充满~ full of vitality

10 老气 [-氣] lǎoqì (old-spirit) <adj> old-fashioned, maturity: ~横秋 (héngqiū) lacking in youthful vigor || 显得 ~ appear old-fashioned

11 书生气 [書-氣] shūshēngqì (student – like) <adj> bookish: 充满~ full of bookishness || ~十足 pure bookishness

12 男子气 [--氣] nánziqì (man – like) <adj> manly: 充满~ full of manliness || 他换了新发型, 更显~. He changed up his hairstyle, which made him look more manly.

13 女人味 [-] nǚrénwèi (woman – like) <adj> feminine: 有~ have femininity || ~十足 be completely feminine

14 呆气 [-氣] dāiqì (dull-looking) <n> stupidity: ~十足 pure stupidity || 研究学问不可不有几分~. The people who do research should be a little dull.

15 傻气 [-氣] shǎqì (stupid, muddleheaded-looking) <n> muddleheaded: 冒~ speak or act foolishly || 穿上这件大衣, 他显得有点~. When putting on the overcoat, he looked a little bit stupid.

16 孩子气 [--氣] háiziqì (childish-spirit) <adj> childish: 有点 ~ be a little childish || 他身上还有~. He appeared somewhat childish.

17 态度 [態-] tàidù (attitude-bearing) <n.> bearing: 工作~ working attitude || 科学的~ scientific attitude || ~好 good attitude

18 体型 [體-] tǐxíng (body-shape) <n> body type: ~高大 big figure || ~丰满 (fēngmǎn) large body

19 个头 [個頭] gètóu (height-*suffix*) <n> size: ~矮 short size || ~大big size || 中等~ middle size

20 三围 [-圍] sānwéi (three-perimeter) <n> bust-waist-hip measurement: 标准~ standard measurements || ~尺寸size of bust-waist-hip

21 姿势 [-勢] zīshì (appearance-posture) <n> 身体~ body posture|| ~优美 graceful carriage, graceful bearing || 摆个~ 拍照 pose for a photo

22 吃相 [-] chīxiàng (eat-looking) <n> table manners: ~难看bad manners
23 舞姿 [-] wǔzī (dance-posture) <n> dancing: ~优美 beautiful dancing || 动人的 emotionally moving dance
24 手势 [-勢] shǒushì (hand-gesture) <n> 打/做~ make a gesture|| 不礼貌的~ an offensive gesture
25 步伐 [-] bùfá (march-kill) <n> 加快~ quicken one's pace || ~灵活 at a flexible pace || 跟上时代的~ keep pace with the times
26 脚步 [-] jiǎobù (foot-step) <n.> 停下~ stop one's footsteps || 加快~ quicken one's pace

27 表情 [-] biǎoqíng (expression-feeling) <n.> 脸部的~ facial expression || 丰富的/毫无~ with great expression/ have an impassive face || ~自然wear a natural expression
28 神情 [-] shénqíng (spirit-expression) <adj> look: ~严肃 (yánsù) serious look || 紧张的~ tense look || 得意的 ~ delightful look
29 眼光 [-] yǎnguāng (eye-light) <n.> eye, view, sight: 好奇的~ curious eyes || 有~ have a good sense of judgment || 用老~ 看待新事物judge new things by old standards
30 目光 [-] mùguāng (eye-light) <n.> sight, view, vision: 冷冷的~ cold eyes || 羡慕的~ an admiring look ||~ 短浅 shortsighted
31 眼神 [-] yǎnshén (eye-expression) <n> expression in one's eyes, glance, eyesight: 明亮的~ bright eyes || 痛苦(tòngkǔ) 的~ painful look|| ~不好 have poor eyesight
32 脸色 [臉-] liǎnsè (face-expression) <n.> complexion, look, facial expression: ~不好 do not look well|| ~苍白 look pale || 看人~行事 adjust one's behavior to someone else's expression
33 气色 [氣-] qìsè (morale-color) <n> complexion, color: ~很好 have a rosy complexion|| ~不好 be very pale, there isn't much color in one's face
34 笑脸 [-臉] xiàoliǎn (smiling-face) <n.> smiling face: 一张/副~ a smiling face || 露出~put on a smile on one's face
35 笑容 [-] xiàoróng (smiling-expression) <n.> smile, smiling expression: 满面~ be all smiles || 露出~ a smile playing on one's face || 甜甜的~ a sweet smile
36 愁眉苦脸 [---臉] chóuméi kǔliǎn (anxious-eyebrow-unpleasant-face) <idiom> frowned expression: 整天 ~ frowning all day long

37 面貌 [-] miànmào (face-appearance) <n.> face, features, appearance(of things), look: 精神~ mental outlook, spirit || 本来~ original face || ~一新 take on a new look, look completely new
38 模样 [-樣] múyàng (model-look) <n.> appearance, look: 这副~ this appearance || 干部~ a person who looks like a cadre
39 外貌 [-] wàimào (out-appearance) <n> appearance, exterior, looks: 英俊的~ handsome appearance || 改变~ change appearance
40 长相 [長-] zhǎngxiàng (looking-appearance) <n> looks, features, appearance: ~平常/一般 ordinary/ normal appearance || ~好 good-looking|| ~差不多 look very much alike
41 相貌 [-] xiàngmào (appearance-looking) <n> facial features, looks, appearance: ~丑陋 (chǒulòu) have ugly features || ~英俊have handsome features
42 美貌 [-] měimào (beautiful-looking) <n> good looks, attractive, beautiful: 青春~ youthful beauty || ~ 女孩儿 a beautiful girl

43 穿戴 [-] chuāndài (wear-wear) <v./n.> apparel, dress, get dressed: 讲究~ be particular about one's dress || 入时 be fashionably dressed || ~朴素 (pǔsù) be simple dressed

44 打扮 [-] dǎbàn (*prefix*-dress) <n> <n./v.> way or style of dressing, dress up: 运动员~ be dressed like a sportsman || 西式~be dressed in Western style|| 得体的~ suitable dressed

Tips:

1 穿 (chuān) and 戴 (dài): Both mean 'to wear,' but the object of 戴 is usually above one's chest, such as 帽子 (hat,) 眼镜 (eyeglasses,) 耳环 (earrings,) 项链 (necklace,) 胸罩 (bra,) 胸针 (brooch) and 手表 (watch,) 手套 (gloves,) 手铐 (handcuffs) and 脚镣 (shackles). 穿 and 戴 can be combined, meaning 'to dress,' for example, 她今天穿戴得很鲜亮 (she is very brightly dressed today.)

2 愁眉苦脸 (chóuméi kǔliǎn) vs. 笑逐颜开 (xiàozhú yánkāi): If one is worried and has a long face, he is 愁眉苦脸, whereas if one has a smiley face, he is 笑逐颜开. 笑 is good for your health, but 愁 is not. There is a common saying 笑一笑, 十年少, 愁一愁, 白了头, which literally means 'a smile can make one ten years younger, but worry makes one's hair gray.'

3 吃相难看: It originally meant ' (one) eats lousily,' however, it has an extended meaning, 'one is so greedy as not to pay any attention to morals.' For example, if a company copied the design of Apple's certain model, we can say that the company '吃相太难看.' This probably originated from the Shanghai dialect.

4 出洋相: It means 'to make an exhibition of oneself.' 洋 here means 'foreign.' When China was invaded and humiliated by foreign countries again and again in the Qing Dynasty, the Chinese invented this word to mock foreigners as a way to fight back.

5 攒人品 (zǎnrénpǐn): It is usually used to warn someone not to be arrogant since any bad deed will come back to the one who did it. 攒人品 can be translated roughly as 'to build up the fondness of the masses.'

Exercises:

Part I: Match up the following expressions to the appropriate column. Make sure your words describe the situation mentioned in the column.

a) 人品好 b) 有气质 c) 傲气十足 d) 老气横秋 e) 朝气蓬勃
f) 有女人味 g) 有男子气 h) 呆气十足 i) 十分孩子气 j) 相貌丑陋
k) 讲究穿戴

1. 上面哪些仪表特征是你喜欢的?

____

____

2. 上面哪些仪表特征是你不喜欢的?

Part II: Multiple Choice. Make sure to choose the most appropriate answer.

1 "小王整天愁眉苦脸的," 这句话的意思是
A. 小王一直不太高兴 B. 小王的眉毛和脸不太好看 C. 小王一整天脸色都不好

2 "小王这个人面对好处的时候, 吃相太难看," 从这句话可以看出小王这个人
A. 非常爱吃东西, 不注意吃东西的时候好看不好看
B. 人品不怎么样
C. 有派头, 但是没有气质

3 "攒钱不如攒人品"这句话的意思是
A. 追求金钱不如追求道德
B. 喜欢钱不如喜欢人的气质
C. 有钱人不如人品好的人

4 "他今天出洋相了"跟下面哪句意思不同
A. 他今天气色很好 B. 他今天丢面子了 C. 他今天丢脸了

5 下面哪组词跟人的动作没有关系
A. 步伐、脚步 B. 目光、眼神 C. 舞姿、手势

6 下面哪组词跟人的身材没有关系
A. 态度、气色 B. 三围、个头 C. 体型、个子

Theme 58: Strength 力量 (lìliàng)

1 力 [-] lì (power) <n.> power: 内/外~ internal/external power || 出~ exert oneself || ~大无比having matchless strength
2 力量 [-] lìliàng (power-capacity) <n.> power: 有/没有~ have no power || 军事~ military strength || 巨大的~ huge power
3 力气 [-氣] lìqì (power-air) <n.> physical strength, effort: 有/没有~ have/have no strength || 花~ make an effort || 觉得全身没 ~ feel weak all over
4 力度 [-] lìdù (power-degree) <n> strength, force, intensity, power: 加大~increase the impact and momentum of doing sth. || 加强打假~ fight more forcefully against counterfeit goods
5 体力 [體-] tǐlì (body-strength) <n.> physical strength: ~好good physical strength || 恢复 (huīfù) ~ restore physical strength || ~劳动physical labor
6 脑力 [腦-] nǎolì (brain-capacity) <n.> mental capacity: ~工作 mentally demanding job || ~活动mentally demanding activity || ~劳动 mentally demanding labor
7 人力 [-] rénlì (man-power) <n.> manual labor: 大量的~ big manual labor || 浪费 (làngfèi) ~ waste manual labor || ~不足insufficient manual labor

8 劳力 [勞-] láolì (labor-force) <n> labor force: 壮 ~ strong labor force || 缺乏~ lack of labor force || 剩余 (shèngyú) ~ surplus labor force
9 全力 [-] quánlì (all-strength) <adv.> with all one's effort: 尽 ~ make full effort || ~支持fully stand by || ~投入工作 fully devote oneself to work
10 活力 [-] huólì (vigorous-strength) <n.> vigor: 有/没有~ have/have no vigor || 充满~ be full of vigor || 增强~ enhance vigor
11 精力 [-] jīnglì (vigor-strength) <n.> energy: 有/没有~ have/ not have energy || 集中 (jízhōng) ~ concentrated energy || 主要~ primary energy

12 阳气 [陽氣] yángqì (yang-qi) <n> Yang-energy: ~虚弱 (xūruò) deficiency of Yang-energy || ~上. The Yang-energy is rising.
13 元气 [-氣] yuánqì (vitality-qi) <n> vitality: 伤~ hurt one's vitality || 恢复~ restore vitality || ~充足 adequate vitality
14 视力 [視-] shìlì (see-capacity) <n> vision: ~好 good vision || ~下降 (xiàjiàng) decreased vision || 检查 ~ vision test
15 听力 [聽-] tīnglì (hear-capacity) <n.> hearing: ~检查 hearing test || ~下降 decreased hearing || 提高~ improve hearing

16 暴力 [-] bàolì (violent-force) <n.> violence: 用~ use violence || 语言~ hurtful words || ~行为 violent behavior
17 武力 [-] wǔlì (military-force) <n> military force: 使用~ use military power || ~征服 (zhēngfú) conquest military power || ~统一unify military power
18 潜力 [潛-] qiánlì (potential-strength) <n.> potential: 巨大的 ~ powerful potential || 有/没有~ have/not have potential || 发挥~ develop potential
19 实力 [實-] shílì (real-strength) <n.> strength: 国家~ national strength || 软~ soft power || 经济~ economic strength
20 国力 [國-] guólì (national-power) <n> national power: ~雄厚 (xiónghòu) strong national power || ~增加increase national power || ~强盛 (qiángshèng) strong national power
21 财力 [財-] cáilì (financial-power) <n> financial power: ~不足insufficient financial power || ~有限limited financial ability || 节省~ save financial assets
22 魅力 [-] mèilì (charming-power) <n> charm: 个人~ individual charm || 充满 ~ full of charm || 缺乏 ~ lack of charm
23 影响力 [-響-] yǐngxiǎnglì (influence-force) <n> influential force: 产生~ produce influence || 富有~ rich influence || 提高~ more influence
24 自制力 [-] zìzhìlì (self-control-ability) <n> self-control: ~差 poor self-control || 缺乏 (quēfá) ~ lack of self-control || 失去~ lose self-control
25 吸引力 [-] xīyǐnlì (attract-power) <n> attraction: 有 ~ attractive || 充满~ full of attraction || 强大的~ powerful attraction

26 弹力 [彈-] tánlì (elastic-strength) <n> elasticity: ~ 十足full of elasticity || ~裤stretch pants || ~好good elasticity
27 引力 [-] yǐnlì (attract-force) <n.> attractive force: 地球 ~ Earth's gravitational force || ~弱weak attractive force || 万有~ gravity
28 重力 [-] zhònglì (heavy-force) <n.> gravity: 克服~ overcome gravity || ~作用gravitational effect || ~加速度gravitational acceleration
29 爆发力 [-發-] bàofālì (explode-force) <n.> explosive force: 产生~ produce explosive force || ~强strong explosive force || ~大big explosive force

30 压力 [壓-] yālì (press-force) <n.> pressure: ~很大 great pressure || 家庭~ family pressure || 就业/精神/经济~ pressure from job/spiritual pressure/economic pressure || 承受 (chéngshòu) ~ withstand pressure

31 动力 [動-] dònglì (motivate-strength) <n.> motivation/propulsion: 强大的 ~ powerful motivation || 重要的~ important motivation || 学习~ learning motivation

32 耐力 [-] nàilì (endure-strength) <n.> endurance: ~差/好 poor endurance/good endurance || ~训练 (xùnliàn) endurance training || 提高~ improve endurance

33 能量 [-] néngliàng (energy-strength) <n.> energy: 巨大的 ~ powerful energy || 产生 ~ produce energy || ~大a lot of energy

Tips:

1 力: The Bronze form of 力 is like a plow. One needs 'strength' to use a plow to plow the land, so 力 means 'physical strength, effort.'

2 人力, 物力 and 财力 (cáilì): They are often used together, meaning 'manpower, material and financial resources.'

3 压力 (yālì) vs. 动力: 压力 means 'pressure' and 动力 'motivation.' Chinese people like to say 把压力变成动力 (turn pressure into motivation.)

Exercises: Please put the given Chinese words or phrases in the appropriate column.

有潜力、自制力强、耐力好、有学习动力、有个人魅力、有暴力行为、有活力、缺乏自制力、尽全力工作、富有影响力、能承受压力

这些品质对个人发展有正面影响	这些品质对个人发展有负面影响

Theme 59: Titles, honor, talent 称号, 荣誉, 才能 (chēnghào, róngyù, cáinéng)

(See also Theme 6)

1 称号 [稱號] chēnghào (name-title) <n.> honorific title: 她获得了世界冠军 (guànjūn) ~. She has won the title of the world's champion.

2 职称 [職稱] zhíchēng (professional-title) <n.> professional ranks or titles: 高级/中级~ title of a senior/junior professional post || ~评定evaluate professional ranks and titles

3 头衔 [頭銜] tóuxián (head-title) <n.> honor titles or official ranks: 博士~ doctorate || 他有十多个~. He has more than a dozen titles. || 正式~ official title

4 名声 [-聲] míngshēng (fame-reputation) <n.> reputation: ~不好bad reputation

5 名气 [-氣] míngqì (fame-manner) <n.> reputation, name: ~大big name || 有 ~ be well-known

6 权威 [權-] quánwēi (power-prestige) <n.> authority: ~著作 (zhùzuò) the fundamental piece|| ~人物a person of authority

7 资历 [資歷] zīlì (qualification-experience) <n.> qualifications and record of service: ~浅lack of qualifications || 政治~ political qualifications

8 大腕 [-] dàwàn (top-wrist/vine) <n.> top notch: 互联网~ leading person in an Internet field || 商界~ business giant || 明星~ famous movie star (Note: The 腕 in 大腕 might be the wrong word of 万 or 蔓, which means 'name/vine' in the underworld.)

9 伟人 [偉-] wěirén (great-man) <n.> great man: 一代~ a great man of one generation

10 大人物 [-] dàrénwù (big-figure) <n.> important person, big shot: 当~ be a great man || 成为~ become a big shot

11 小人物 [-] xiǎorénwù (trivial-figure) <n.> unimportant person, nonentity: 微不足道的~ person of no consequence, nobody

12 名人 [-] míngrén (famous-person) <n.> celebrity: 文化界~ celebrities in cultural circles || 历代~ great figures through the ages

13 贵族 [貴-] guìzú (noble-clan) <n.> nobleman: 封建~ feudal nobles || 出身于~ be born into the aristocracy || 精神~ intellectual elite

14 豪门 [-門] háomén (rich and powerful-gate) <n.> rich and powerful family: ~子弟sons of the rich || ~生活the life in the rich and powerful family

15 先知 [-] xiānzhī (fore-know) <n.> prophet, a person of foresight: 默罕默德是伊斯兰教的~. Muhammed is the prophet of Islam.

16 圣人 [聖-] shèngrén (wise-man) <n.> sage: 孔子被认为是古代中国最伟大的~. Confucius is considered the greatest of the ancient Chinese sages.

17 泰斗 [-] tàidǒu (Mount Tai-The Big Dipper) <n.> a leading authority: 学界~ a leading magnate in academic field || 音乐~ a leading magnate in music

18 君子 [-] jūnzi (noble-man) <n.> a man of moral character, gentleman: 伪(wěi) ~ hypocrite || 正人~ a man of moral integrity

19 小人 [-] xiǎorén (mean-man) r<n.> a base person, villain, vile character: 卑鄙~ despicable person || 自私自利的~ selfish person

20 元老 [-] yuánlǎo (pioneer-veteran) <n.> senior statesman, founding member: 公司~ founding member of a company || 学校~ senior statesman of a college or school

21 骨干 [-幹] gǔgàn (bone-main) <n.> backbone: 公司~ key employee of a company || ~企业backbone enterprise

22 精英 [-] jīngyīng (essencial-outstanding) <n.> elite: 商界 ~ business elite || 政界~ the political elite || ~学校elite school

23 顶梁柱 [頂--] dǐngliángzhù (uphold-beam-pillar) <n.> pillar, backbone: 家里的~ the pillar person of a family

24 流氓 [-] liúmáng (stray-rogue) <n.> rogue, hoodlum, gangster: 耍~ behave like a hoodlum, sexually harass || ~习气hooliganism || ~团伙gang of hooligans

25 花花公子 [-] huāhuāgōngzi (dazzling-princeling) <n.> playboy: 她与一个~交上了朋友, 以至大学一年级两门课程不合格. She got involved with a playboy and failed two freshman courses.

26 富二代 [-] fù'èrdài (rich-second-generation) <n.> affluent second generation: 越来越多的~喜欢通过消费奢侈品来显示他们的身份和地位. The rapidly expanding affluent second generation is seeking to define their identity and quality of life via luxuries.

27 官二代 [-] guān'èrdài (official-second-generation) <n.> the second governor generation: 据说中国的~更容易在政府部门担任高级职务. It is said that China's second generation of government officials are more likely to hold senior positions in government.

28 拜金女 [-] bàijīnnǚ (worship-gold-girl) <n.> gold digger, materialistic woman: ~看重金钱而不是看重爱情. Materialistic women value money more than love.

29 泼妇 [潑婦] pōfù (shrewish-woman) <n.> shrew: ~骂街 shout abuses like a shrill housewife

30 本领 [-領] běnlǐng (root-collar) <n.> ability, capability: 有~ have the ability || 学~, 趁年轻. A tree must be bent while it is young.

31 本事 [-] běnshì (root-matter) <n.> skill, ability: 学 ~ learn some skill || 没有~ have no ability

32 标题 [標題] biāotí (sign-forehead) <n.> headline: 一个新闻~ a headline of news || 大/小~ main heading/subheading || 好~ good headline

33 才能 [-] cáinéng (talent-able) <n.> talent: 管理~ manageme talent || 埋没 (máimò) 自己的~ hide one's talents

34 个性 [個-] gèxìng (individual-personality) <n.> personality, individual character: ~很强strong character || 他是个很有~的人. He is a man of individuality.

35 功夫 [-] gōngfū (martial-skill) <n.> Kong Fu: 练~ practice Kong Fu || 中国~ Chinese Kong Fu

36 技术 [-術] jìshù (technique-skill) <n.> technology: 学~ learn technology || 新~ new technology || 科学~ science and technology

37 科技 [-] kējì (science-technology) <n.> science and technology: 先进~ sophisticated technologies || ~进步advance science and technology

38 科研 [-] kēyán (scientific-research) <n.&v.> scientific research: 搞~ engage in scientific research || ~工作the work of scientific research || ~成果the achievement of scientific research

39 名 [-] míng (name, fame) <n.> name: 出~ be famous || 书~ the name of a book

40 名称 [-稱] míngchēng (name-call) <n.> name (of a thing or organization): 学科~ subject name || 产品~ product name || 疾病 (jíbìng) ~ disease name

41 名字 [-] míngzì (name-alias) <n.> name: 你叫什么~? What's your name?

42 能力 [-] nénglì (capable-strength) <n.> ability: 他工作~强. He is a capable worker. || 生活~很差be poor in managing one's life

43 牌 [-] pái (sign, board) <n.> plate, sign, brand, trademark: 名~ famous brand || 正~ authentic product || 福特~汽车Ford car

44 牌子 [-] páizi (sign-*suffix*) <n.> plate, sign, brand, trademark: 车~ number plate || 老/新~ old/new brand name || 砸 (zá) ~ ruin the reputation of a product or company

45 题 [題] tí (exercise) <n.> exercise, question: 练习~ exercises, exercise problems || 三道~ three exercises || 做/答~ answer the questions

46 性格 [-] xìnggé (nature-character) <n.> character: ~温和mild character || 内向/外向~ introverted/extroverted character

47 姓 [-] xìng (surname) <n. / v.> surname: ~李One's surname is Li || 中国人~在前, 名在后 When Chinese people speak their name, they put the surname first and the given name last.

48 才 [-] cái (talent) <n.> talent: 有/没有~ capable/non capable || 多~多艺 be gifted in many ways

49 道德 [-] dàodé (moral-norm) <n.> morality: 传统~ traditional morality || ~败坏 (bàihuài) moral degradation

50 地名 [-] dìmíng (place-name) <n.> name of a place: 外国~ foreign place name || 两个~ two names of places

51 高科技 [-] gāokējì (high-technology) <n.> high technology: ~企业high-tech company || ~园区high-tech park || ~产品high-tech product

52 工艺 [-藝] gōngyì (craft-art) <n.> technique: 生产~ the production technique || 新~ new technique

53 技能 [-] jìnéng (skill-capability) <n.> skill: 游泳~ swimming skill || 学习~ study skill

54 技巧 [-] jìqiǎo (skill-trick) <n.> technique: 写作~ writing technique || 高超的~ a high degree of skill

55 理智 [-] lǐzhì (rational-wise) <n.> reason, intellect: 失去~ lose one's reason || 缺乏 (quēfá) ~ lack reason

56 面子 [-] miànzi (face-*suffix*) <n.> face: 有/没~ feel great/ lose one's face || 留~ save one's face || 给~ show due respect for, give sb. face

57 名牌儿 [-] míngpáir (famous-brand) <n.> famous brand: ~大学famous university

58 名义 [-義] míngyì (name-nominal) <n.> name: 各种~ all sorts of names || 个人~ individual name || 以学生~ in the name of students

59 名誉 [-譽] míngyù (fame-reputation) <n.> reputation: 学校的~ school reputation || 丢~ lose one's reputation || 恢复~ recover one's reputation

60 脾气 [-氣] píqì (spleen-energy) <n.> temper: ~好/坏 good temper/bad temper || 发~ lose temper

61 品牌 [-] pǐnpái (merchandise-brand) <n.> brand: 企业~ the corporate branding || 国际~ international brand || 注重 ~ focus on brand

62 品质 [-質] pǐnzhì (merchandise-quality) <n.> character, quality: 优良~ good qualities || ~低劣 (dīliè) be of poor quality || 道德~ moral character

63 商标 [-標] shāngbiāo (merchandise-mark) <n.> trademark: 名牌~ a well-known brand || 注册~ registered trademark

64 素质 [-質] sùzhì (real-quality) <n.> quality of a person: ~差/好 good quality/bad quality || 提高~ enhance the quality || 身体 ~ physical quality

65 题目 [題-] tímù (title-subject) t<n.> title, topic: 文章~ article title || 讨论~ discussion topic

66 天才 [-] tiāncái (gifted-talent) <n.> gifted person: 音乐~ music talent || 这位教练有眼光发现~. The coach has a keen eye for spotting talent.

67 信用 [-] xìnyòng (trustworthy-use) <n.> credit: 讲~ stress credit || 商业~ business credit || ~危机credit crisis

68 姓名 [-] xìngmíng (last name-first name) <n.> full name: 写~ write down your full name || 真实~ true full name || 留下~ leave full name

69 修养 [-養] xiūyǎng (temper-cultivate) <n.> accomplishment, self-cultivation: 提高/加强~ elevate/enhance the mind || 有艺术 ~ be artistically accomplished

70 眼光 [-] yǎnguāng (eye-sight) <n.> eye, sight, view: ~ 短浅 shortsighted || 好奇的~ curious sight

71 勇气 [-氣] yǒngqì (brave-energy) <n.> courage: 鼓起~ pluck up courage || 缺乏~ lack of courage

72 智慧 [-] zhìhuì (intelligent-wise) <n.> wisdom: 集体~ collective wisdom || 充满~ be full of wisdom

73 智力 [-] zhìlì (intelligence-strength) <n.> intelligence: 发展~ develop intelligence || ~低下/超常low intelligence/gifted || ~测验intelligence test

74 智能 [-] zhìnéng (intelligence-ability) <n.> intelligence: 人工~ artificial intelligence || ~手机smart phone (智慧型手機 in Taiwan)

Tips:

1 Chinese social hierarchy: In both ancient and modern China, people are divided into various grades and ranks, so the official titles and job titles are very important. Chinese people were divided roughly into four classes, 士 (shì, officials/scholars,) 农 (nóng, farmers/peasants,) 工 (gōng, artisans) and 商 (shāng, merchants) throughout history. In the Yuan Dynasty, they were divided into ten levels/castes, (1) 官 (guān, high officials/bureaucrats,) (2) 吏 (lì, petty officials,) (3) 僧 (sēng, Buddhist monks,) (4) 道 (dào, Taoists priests,) (5) 医 (yī, physicians,) (6) 工 (gōng, artisans,) (7) 匠 (jiàng, carpenters/workers,) (8) 娼 (chāng, prostitutes,) (9) 儒 (rú, Confucian scholars) and (10) 丐 (gài, beggars). A dysphemism 臭老九 (chòulǎojiǔ, Stinking Old Ninth) was coined thereafter to refer to educators and Confucian scholars, and was unfortunately widely used even in the 1960s and 1970s during the Cultural Revolution.

2 无知少女: Literally it means 'ignorant young lady' or 'knowledge shallow,' but now this term is also political slang for four kinds of people, 无党派人士 'non-partisan,' 知识分子 'known intellectuals,' 少数民族 'national minorities' and 女性 'females' who have greater chances of being promoted in the government.

3 白骨精 (báigǔjīng): It is known as the role of White Bone Spirit, a demon in the classic Chinese mythological novel *Journey to the West*. Now in the job market it refers to three kinds of people, 白领 (báil the job market it r骨干 (gáil the job market i精英 (jīngyīng, elite.)

4 德 (dé, integrity) vs. 才 (cái, ability): If a person owns both, 德才兼备 (décái jiānbèi, to have both integrity and ability) that is perfect, but some people are 有才无德 (to have talent without virtue.) How about a person without talent? For women this is nevertheless not a bad thing according to this 'notorious' saying 女子无才便是德 (a woman is virtuous if she lacks talent, ignorance is a woman's virtue) in the Ming and Qing dynasties.

Exercises:

Part I: Read the following words and then answer the questions.

科学界大腕儿、商界精英、豪门、贵族、科学界泰斗、正人君子、伪君子、小人、公司骨干、 精英学校、公司的顶梁柱、流氓、花花公子、富二代、官二代、拜金女、泼妇、天才

1 上面哪些词是贬义词 (negative word)?

____

2 "公司骨干、公司顶梁柱"哪个是口语?

____

3 "科学界大腕儿、科学界泰斗"哪个是口语?

____

4 哪两个词专门用来描述女的?

____

5 请写出两所精英学校的名称, 高中或者大学都可以.

____

Part II: Read the following sentences and fill in each blank with the appropriate word or phrase from the options given.

1 名气、权威、称号、资历

a) 这个城市最近荣获了"全国卫生城"的_______.
b) 老王是公司元老, 以他的_______可以提升为副总经理了.
c) 说起北京菜, ________最大的就是北京烤鸭了.
d) 白教授是研究世界气候变化问题的最_______专家.

2 牌子、地名、标题、商标

a) 为了吸引读者, 《人民日报》 (*People's Daily*) 新闻的________写得比以前生动多了.
b) 年轻人穿衣服一般会选择一些比较流行的______.
c) "春田" (Springfield, Oregon) 是一个普通的美国________, 但是因为动画连续剧"辛普森一家" (*The Simpsons*, U.S. TV series) 而闻名.
d) 在中国如果你想开一家公司来生产商品, 得先去工商局注册_______.

3 质量、智力、素质、信用

a) 手机刚刚在中国普及的时候, _______最好的手机是诺基亚 (Nokia) 手机.
b) ________教育在中国提倡 (tíchàng, advocate) 了二十几年了, 但还没有真正实行.
c) 中国的________体系还不完善, 所以大家认为"失信"不是什么大事.
d) 学校不仅要重视学生的________发展, 也要重视学生的道德水平.

4 能力、性格、工艺品、技巧

a) 杰克打算买一些中国_______带回美国送朋友当礼物.
b) 在有些体育运动中, 体能没有体育_______重要.
c) 大公司在招聘 (zhāopìn, recruit) 员工的时候看重的是应聘者的________, 而不是学历. 但是应聘者的________也很重要, 因为性格好的人更能够跟别人合作顺利.

5 才能、智能、个性

a) 小王有很强的领导_______, 大家都愿意听从他在工作上的安排.
b) 在中国学校, 有_______的学生往往不被老师喜欢.
c) 中国华为 (Huawei) 公司生产的_______手机不仅质量好, 价格也比苹果手机便宜.

Theme 60: Thought 思想 (sīxiǎng)

(See also Theme 63)

1 思想 [-] sīxiǎng (think-consider) <n.> thoughts, mind: 文化~ cultural thoughts || ~深刻 (shēnkè) deep thought || 解放~ emancipate the mind
2 思维 [-維] sīwéi (think-think) <n.> thinking, thoughts: 人的~ human being's mind || 改变~ change of thinking || ~定式 the mindset Note: 维=惟, meaning 'think.'
3 头脑 [頭腦] tóunǎo (head-brain) <n.> brain, mind: ~清醒 (qīngxǐng) the mind is clear || 有/没有~ has sense to do something/has no sense to do something
4 意识 [-識] yìshí (conscious-realize) <n.> consciousness: 自我 ~ self-awareness || 独立~ independent consciousness || 竞争 (jìngzhēng) ~ competition consciousness
5 感受 [-] gǎnshòu (feel-receive) <n./v.> feeling, feel: 真正的~ the real feeling || 谈谈~ talk about the feeling || 各种~ all sorts of feelings
6 观念 [觀-] guānniàn (observe-idea) <n.> concept: 新~ new concepts || 传统~ traditional view || 文化~ cultural concepts
7 精神 [-] jīngshén (essence-spirit) <n.> spirit: 科学~ scientific spirit || 时代~ the spirit of the age || 乐观~ optimism
8 内心 [-] nèixīn (inner-heart) <n.> heart, innermost being: ~的感情inner emotion || ~充实inner enrichment || ~世界the inner world

9 心里 [-裏] xīnlǐ (heart-inside) <n.> in the mind: ~高兴be happy in one's mind || ~明白be clear in one's mind || ~难过. One's heart is filled with pain.

10 心理 [-] xīnlǐ (heart-reason) <n.> psychological, mental: ~问题psychological problems || ~变化psychological change

11 忠心 [-] zhōngxīn (loyal-heart) <n.> loyalty: 老王一向对公司非常~. Mr. Wang is consistent in his loyalty to the company.

12 信心 [-] xìnxīn (confident-heart) <n.> faith, confidence: 对自己有信心~ be confident in oneself || 失去/缺乏~ lose one's faith/lack confidence || 充满~ be full of confidence

13 诚信 [誠-] chéngxìn (honest-trustworthy) <n.> integrity, honesty: 有/没有~ be in good faith/not be in good faith || ~是企业生存和发展的根本. Honesty is fundamental to the survival and development of an enterprise.

14 心灵 [-] xīnlíng (heart-soul) <n.> soul: 美好的~ beautiful soul || 幼小的~ young heart || 纯真的~ pure spirit

Tips:

1 Radical 心 (xīn): Ancient Chinese people thought that the heart was the organ for thinking, so verbs related to psychological activities in Chinese characters have the radical 'heart' (心/忄), for example 'thought' (思想,) miss (念,) sense (感) and so on.

2 心里 vs. 心理: Both are pronounced as 'xīnlǐ,' but 心理 is more related to mentality and psychology, whereas 心里 to the heart and the mind.

3 Chinese communist thoughts: They are 毛泽东思想 (Máo Zédōng Sīxiǎng, Mao Zedong Thought,) 邓小平理论 (Dèng Xiǎopíng Lǐlùn, Deng Xiaoping Theory,) 三个代表重要思想 (Sāngè Dàigbiǎo Zhòngyào Sīxiǎng, the Three Represents,) 科学发展观 (Kēxué Fāzhǎnguān, Scientific Outlook on Development) and 习近平新时代中国特色社会主义思想 (Xí Jìnpíng Xīnshídài Zhōngguó Tèsè Shèhuìzhǔyì Sīxiǎng, Xi Jinping Thought on Socialism with Chinese Characteristics for a New Era.)

Exercises: Read the following sentences and fill in each blank with the appropriate word or phrase from the options given.

1 诚信、心灵、自信心

a) 教育的本质应该是培养人的美好_______.
b) 如果一个社会缺乏________, 那意味着社会道德水平低下, 法律体系也不完善.
c) 中国父母一般对孩子表扬很少, 批评很多, 不利于培养 (p(于培养很少善水平低下ead t孩子的________.

2 心中、忠心、心理

a) 中国共产党要求她的党员对党要________. 在党员_______党的利益是第一位的.
b) 一味强调孩子的成绩, 给孩子太大压力, 会给孩子带来________问题, 不利于孩子的健康成长.

3 观念、头脑、内心、精神

a) 不管父母怎么骂孩子, 但在______深处他们还是觉得自己的孩子最好.
b) 在科学研究上要有乐观_______, 也就是不怕失败, 坚信只要努力坚持就一定会取得成果.
c) 一般来说中国人的家庭________都比较强.
e) 小王______灵活, 能够迅速对付工作中出现的紧急情况.

4 意识、思想、感受、思维

a) 跨过美国和墨西哥边境, 你就会________到不同文化的冲击.
b) 电视刚开始出现的时候, 很少有人________到电视的意义以及对今后社会发展的影响.
c) 中国古代哲学________跟《圣经》(*The Bible*) 中的一些看法有很多相似的地方.
e) 古希腊 (Xīlà, Greece) 文化影响了西方人的________方式.

Theme 61: Feelings 感觉 (gǎnjué)

1 感觉 [-覺] gǎnjué (sense-feel) <n./v.> feel like, feel, feeling: 你~怎么样? How do you feel now? || 我~很舒服. I am feeling well. || 天气真暖和, ~像春天一样. The weather is so warm. It feels like spring.
2 直觉 [-覺] zhíjué (direct-sense) <n.> intuition, hunch: 凭/靠~ follow one's hunch || 要相信自己的~. You should follow your hunch.
3 视觉 [視覺] shìjué (view-sense) <n.> vision: ~效果 (xiàoguǒ) visual effect || ~不好bad vision || 恢复~ restore vision
4 听觉 [聽覺] tīngjué (listen-sense) <n.> hearing: ~灵敏 (língmǐn) have a sharp ear || 凭~来辨别 (biànbié) 声音 identify the sound by hearing
5 嗅觉 [-覺] xiùjué (smell-sense) <n.> sense of smell: ~灵敏have a keen sense of smell || 失去~ lose the sense of smell
6 味觉 [-覺] wèijué (taste-sense) <n.> sense of taste: ~失灵lose one's sense of taste
7 触觉 [觸覺] chùjué (touch-sense) <n.> tactile sensation, sense of touch: ~器官 (qìguān) tactile organ

8 感情 [-] gǎnqíng (sense-feeling) <n.> affection: 真 ~ true affection || 浪费~ squander one's affection || 有/没有~ have affection/ have no affection
9 情感 [-] qínggǎn (feeling-sense) <n.> emotion, feeling: 丰富的~ rich emotion || 真实的~ the true feeling || 克制 (kèzhì) ~ control one's emotion
10 激情 [-] jīqíng (passionate-feeling) <n.> passion: 充满 ~ be full of passion || 爱国~ patriotic passion
11 心情 [-] xīnqíng (heart-feeling) <n.> mood: 轻松的~ relaxed mood || ~平静calm mood || ~紧张nervous
12 爱情 [愛-] àiqíng (love-feeling) (romantic) <n.> love: 甜蜜的~ sweet love || 享受 (xiǎngshòu) ~ enjoy love || ~故事love story
13 爱心 [愛-] àixīn (love-heart) <n.> loving heart: 充满~ be full of love || 一片~ a piece of love
14 气 [氣] qì (angry) <n./v.> make sb. angry, anger: 生~ be angry || 消~ feel relieved || ~得发抖shake with anger

15 民意 [-] mínyì (people-will) <n.> public opinion: 尊重 (zūnzhòng) ~ respect for public opinion || 违背 (wéibèi) ~ contrary to public opinion || 代表~ on behalf of the public opinion || ~测验 (cèyàn) public opinion polls

16 乐趣 [樂-] lèqù (happy-delight) <n.> fun: 没有~ there is no fun || 充满 (有) ~ there is a lot of fun

17 信念 [-] xìnniàn (believe-thought) <n.> belief, faith: 生活~ life belief || 共同的~ common belief || ~坚定 (jiāndìng) firm belief

18 意志 [-] yìzhì (will-aspiration) <n.> will: ~坚定be determined || ~消沉 (xiāochén) be in depression || 坚强的~ a strong will

19 毅力 [-] yìlì (fortitude-strength) <n.> perseverance: 惊人的~ amazing perseverance || 有/没有~ with perseverance/without perseverance

20 兴趣 [興-] xìngqù (interest-delight) t<n.> interest: 有/没~ show interest in sth. /show no interest in sth. || ~大be very interested in sth. || 个人~ personal hobby

21 理想 [-] lǐxiǎng (reasonable-idea) <n.> ideal: 远大~ broad ideal || 实现/失去~ live up to ideal/lose one's ideal

Tips:

1 觉 (覺, jué): It is related to 见 (seen) in meaning and 學 (xué) in sound. It means 'awake, wake up' from which evolved meanings such as 'feel, sense.' Human beings have five senses, 视觉, 听觉, 嗅觉, 味觉, 触觉 which are all listed above, and arguably the sixth sense, extrasensory perception (第六感觉, dì-liù gǎnjué.) Chinese monks and nuns like 觉 since it has the meaning 'arouse.' 觉 has another sound 'jiào', which means 'sleep.'

2 *觉 and 灵敏 (língmǐn): All senses can be modified by 灵敏, which means 'sharp, sensitive.'

3 先知先觉, 后知后觉 and 不知不觉: Dr. Sun Yat-sen divided the Chinese people into three groups 先知先觉 (foresighted,) 后知后觉 (slow-thinking) and 不知不觉 (unenlightenable) according to their enthusiasm for revolution.

4 The Republic: Plato's famous work *The Republic* is translated as 理想国 (Lǐxiǎng Guó) in Chinese.

Exercises:

Part I: Use the given bound form as a guide to help you think of other words with the same character. Feel free to use your dictionary when needed. Then write down the English definition of each of the words you've written.

觉 (to feel): 感觉 feel like

____

____

____

____

情 (feeling): 感情 affection

____

____

____

____

Part II: Read the following sentences and fill in each blank with the appropriate word or phrase from the options given.

1 意志、兴趣、信念、民意

a) 中国共产党一直教导自己的党员要坚持共产主义________.
b) 据说美国的共和党在最近的________调查中支持率很高.
c) 中国国家队的运动员一般_______都很坚强，受了伤还每天坚持锻炼 (duànliàn, practice).
d) 他是对社会问题很感_______, 决定在大学选社会学当专业.

2 理想、毅力、乐趣、爱心

a) 自从开了经典名著阅读课以来，孩子们从阅读经典作品中获得了极大的________.
b) 世界永远和平或许只是个________, 但是我们应该为之努力.
c) 小张特别有_______, 为了学好英文, 他每天早上五点就起床背英文单词和课文.
d) 这位老师非常有_______, 看到一些孩子因为家里穷买不起午饭, 就每天自己为这些孩子花钱买午饭.

Theme 62: Desires, ideas 愿望, 想法 (yuànwàng, xiǎngfǎ)

1 愿望 [願-] yuànwàng (desire-hope) <n.> wish, desire: 强烈的~ strong desire || 共同~ common wishes || 实现~ achieve desire
2 希望 [-] xīwàng (wish-hope) <n.> hope: 有/没有~ there is hope/there is no hope || 满怀~ be full of hope
3 志愿 [-願] zhìyuàn (aspiration-desire) <n.> will, willing: 高考~ college entrance exam will || ~者volunteers
4 心愿 [-願] xīnyuàn (heart-desire) <n.> wish: 怀着共同的~ be filled with common wish || 完成~ fulfill a wish || 满足~ satisfy one's wish
5 意愿 [-願] yìyuàn (will-desire) <n.> will: 人民的~ the will of the people || 共同~ common will || 违背 (wéibèi) ~ be against their will
6 要求 [-] yāoqiú (request-demand) <n.> requirement, demand: 达到~ meet the requirements || 合理~ reasonable requirements || 政治~ political demands
7 需要 [-] xūyào (need-want) <n.> needs: 生存~ survival needs || 发展~ development needs || 实际~ the actual needs
8 需求 [-] xūqiú (need-demand) <n.> demand, needs: 生活~ life needs || 感情~ emotional needs || 有/没有~ there is demand/there is no demand

9 食欲 [-] shíyù (eat-desire) <n.> the appetite: 有 (产生) /没有~ have an appetite/have no appetite || 满足 ~ satisfy the appetite || ~好good appetite

10 性欲 [-] xìngyù (sex-desire) <n> sexual desire: ~强 strong sexual desire || 产生 ~ have sexual desire || 有~. There is sexual desire.

11 想法 [-] xiǎngfǎ (think-way) <n.> ideas: 产生新~ a new idea come into being || 提出~ raise an idea || 谈谈你的~ talk about your opinion

12 意见 [-見] yìjiàn (thought-opinion) <n.> opinion: 提~ give some opinions || 不同~ different opinions || 保留~ reserve one's opinion

13 主意 [-] zhǔyì (definite-thought) <n.> idea, mind, plan: 打~ think of a plan || 有/没有~ have an idea/have no idea || 改变~ change one's mind

14 主张 [-張] zhǔzhāng (hold-opinion) <n.> proposition, advocate, claim: 提出~ make claims || 中国政府~和平外交. The Chinese government advocates peaceful diplomacy.

15 观点 [觀點] guāndiǎn (view-point) <n.> idea, opinion: 一种~ an opinion || 基本~ the basic opinion || 传统~ the traditional opinion

16 看法 [-] kànfǎ (view-way) <n.> view: 你对这件事的~是什么? What do you think about this? || ~一致agree with somebody.

17 共识 [-識] gòngshí (common-understanding) <n.> agreement: 达成~ make an agreement

18 动机 [動機] dòngjī (motivate-intention) <n.> motive, motivation: 心理~ psychological motivation || 学习~ learning motivation || ~不同different motives

19 策略 [-] cèlüè (stratagem-strategy) <n.> tactic, strategy: 学习~ learning strategy || 讲~ care about strategy || 改变~ change the strategy

20 战略 [戰-] zhànlüè (fight-strategy) <n.> strategy: 伟大~ great strategy || 发展~ the strategy of development

21 眼光 [-] yǎnguāng (eye-ray) <n.> sight: ~短浅short-sighted || 很有~ insightful || 科学的~ scientific sight

22 阴谋 [陰謀] yīnmóu (secretly-scheme) <n.> plot, conspiracy, intrigue: ~活动 conspiracy || 政治~ political intrigue || 揭露 (jiēlù) ~ expose the plot

23 用心 [-] yòngxīn (use-heart) <n.> motive, intention: ~良苦well-meaning || 政治~ political intention || 恶毒的~ malicious intention

24 创意 [創-] chuàngyì (creative-idea) <n.> creativity: 美术~ art creativity || 产生~ have creativity || 有/没有~ creative/uncreative

25 幻想 [-] huànxiǎng (illusory-thought) <n.> pipe dream, illusion: 抱有~ cherish illusions || 丢掉~ cast away illusions || 生活在~的世界里live in a world of fantasy

26 梦 [夢] mèng (dream) <n.> dream: 做~ have a dream || 美~ beautiful dream || 噩 (è) ~ bad dream

27 梦想 [夢-] mèngxiǎng (dream-thought) <n.> dream: 有/没有~ have dream/no dream || 满足~ satisfy his dream || 美好的~ good dream

28 蓝图 [藍圖] lántú (blue-plan) <n.> blueprint: 一张~ a blueprint || 改革的~ the blueprint of reformation || 理想的 ~ ideal blueprint

29 手段 [-] shǒuduàn (hand-means) <n.> means (of doing sth.): 非法~ illegal means || 采取~ apply a measure

30 手法 [-] shǒufǎ (hand-method) <n.> ploy, technique: 欺骗 (qīpiàn) 的~ the trick of deception || 作案~ crime tactic

31 设计 [設計] shèjì (design-plan) <n./v.> design: 舞台 (wǔtái) ~ the stage design || ~道路design (a) road || 房屋~ design (a) house

32 决心 [決-] juéxīn (resolute-heart) <n./v.> resolution: 下~ make a resolution || 他~学一门新的专业. He decided to learn a new major. || 他们有~打败对手. They are determined to defeat the opponent.

Tips:

1 策略 (cèluè): It means 'tactics, strategy.' The three most representative works on 策略 are 孙子兵法, 三十六计 and 战国策. '孙子兵法' (Sūnzi Bīngfǎ, the *Art of War*) is an ancient Chinese military treatise, which contains many classical military strategies and tactics, and was later elevated to a way of thinking in East Asian countries. "三十六计" (Sānshíliù Jì, *Thirty-Six Stratagems*) is a Chinese essay, which illustrates a series of stratagems originally used for politics and war, but were later widely applied in many social aspects including business. '战国策' (戰國策, Zhànguócè,) *Stratagems of the Warring States* is a text of histories of major states in the Warring States period (fifth to third centuries BCE) with a focus on political manipulation by politicians, strategists and lobbyists.

2 'I have a dream' by MLK, Jr.: It is translated as 我有一个梦想 (Wǒ yǒu yíge mèngxiǎng) in Chinese.

3 阳谋 (yángmóu): It is said Chairman Mao Zedong coined this word after 阴谋 (yīnmóu, plot) in 1949. 阳谋 can be translated roughly as 'open conspiracy.'

4 食色性也 (shí sè, xìng yě): It was first recorded in *Mencius* and means 'desire for food and sex is natural.' However, the concept was from Confucius. He said, "饮食男女, 人之大欲存焉." In a modern expression, it is 食欲 and 性欲 are natural.

Exercises:

Part I: Multiple Choice. Make sure to choose the most appropriate answer.

1 小王下________要学中文, 而且能十分精通 (jīngtōng, be expert at) 中文.
A. 决心 B. 梦想 C. 主意

2 有人认为实现人人平等只是人类的________罢了, 根本不可能实现.
A. 梦 B. 梦想 C. 蓝图

3 毛泽东时代给中国人画出的宏伟 (hóngwěi, magnificent, grand) ________是2000年实现四个现代化.
A. 意愿 B. 心愿 C. 蓝图

4 大多数年轻人都_______自己能够一夜间成为千万富翁, 但实际上很难实现.
A. 幻想 B. 创意 C. 梦

5 有些人认为: 只要达到目的, 可以不择_______.
A. 阴谋 B. 手段 C. 用心

6 这位篮球教练非常有_______, 总是能够发现最有潜力 (qiánlì, potential) 的运动员, 吸收到自己的篮球队里.
A. 手法 B. 战略 C. 眼光

7 中美两国就朝鲜半岛核武器实验的问题达成__________.
A. 策略 B. 动机 C. 共识

8 中国父母一般________ 孩子先工作再结婚. 孩子一般也会听从父母的_________.
A. 看法、想法 B. 战略、意见 C. 主张、意见

9 美国一直支持台湾, 是因为台湾对美国有重要的_________意义.
A. 眼光 B. 主意 C. 战略

10 近年来, 台湾民进党一直积极________独立, 在国际社会上成为一个主权国家.
A. 想法 B. 要求 C. 需要

11 台湾老百姓__________台湾跟大陆不要发生战争, 两岸和平共处.
A. 愿望 B. 希望 C. 心愿

12 这道菜做得太好了, 色香味俱全 (jùquán, all complete), 一看就有__________.
A. 需求 B. 食欲 C. 性欲

Theme 63: Religion, beliefs 宗教, 信仰 (zōngjiào, xìnyǎng)

(See also Themes 60, 173)

1 宗教 [-] zōngjiào (ancestral-religion) <n.> religion: 信仰~ have religious beliefs || 反~ anti-religion || ~节日religious holiday
2 信仰 [-] xìnyǎng (faith-worship) <n.> faith: 有/没~ have faith/ no faith || 政治~ political beliefs || 宗教~ religious beliefs
3 佛 [-] fó (Buddha) <n.> Buddha: 信~ believe in Buddha || ~学Buddhism || ~寺 (sì) Buddha temple
4 佛教 [-] fójiào (Buddha-religion) <n.> Buddhism: ~文化 Buddhist culture
5 道教 [-] dàojiào (Tao-religion) <n.> Taoism: ~盛行 (shèngxíng). Taoism is widespread.|| ~音乐Taoism music
6 基督教 [-] jīdūjiào (Christ-religion) <n.> Christianity: 信~ believe in Christianity || 传播 (chuánbō) ~ spread Christianity || ~文化Christian culture
7 天主教 [-] tiānzhǔjiào (heaven-host-religion) <n.> Catholicism
8 东正教 [東--] dōngzhèngjiào (east-orthodox-religion) <n.> Orthodox
9 伊斯兰教 [--蘭-] yīsīlánjiào (transliteration of Islam-religion) <n.> Islam
10 犹太教 [猶--] yóutàijiào (transliteration of Judah-religion) <n.> Judaism
11 印度教 [-] yìndùjiào (Indian-religion) <n.> Hinduism
12 儒家思想 [-] rújiāsīxiǎng (Confucian-thought) <n.> Confucianism: ~的影响 (yǐngxiǎng) 很大. Confucianism has great influence.
13 上帝 [-] shàngdì (heaven-king) <n.> God: 信~ believe in God || 感谢~ thank God
14 神 [-] shén (god) <n.> god: 财~ the god of money || 众~ gods || 基督教认为~创造了世界. Christians think God created the world.
15 天堂 [-] tiāntáng (heavenly-hall) <n.> heaven: 上~ go to heaven || 人间 ~ the heaven in the world || 购物~ shopping heaven
16 圣经 [聖經] shèngjīng (holy-scripture) <n.> Bible: 读~ read the Bible || ~故事Bible stories

17 佛经 [-經] fójīng (Buddhist-scripture) <n.> Buddhist scriptures: 翻译~ translate Buddhist scriptures || ~故事the Sutra story
18 古兰经 [-蘭經] gǔlánjīng (*Transliteration* of Quran-scripture) <n.> the Quran: 《~》是伊斯兰教的经典. The Quran is the classical text in Islam.
19 邪教 [-] xiéjiào (evil-religion) <n.> evil cult, heretical sect: 打击~ combat evil cult || ~组织evil cult organization || 反对~ oppose evil cults
20 龙 [龍] lóng (dragon) <n.> dragon: 望子成~ hope one's children will have a bright future || 属~ be born in the year of the dragon
21 鬼 [-] guǐ (ghost) <n.> ghost: 怕~ be afraid of ghosts

22 唯物主义 [---義] wéiwùzhǔyì (only-material – ism) <n.> materialism: 历史~ historical materialism || 辩证~ dialectical materialism
23 唯心主义 [---義] wéixīnzhǔyì (only-ideal – ism) <n.> idealism: 主观 ~ subjective idealism || 客观~ objective idealism
24 辩证法 [辯證-] biànzhèngfǎ (dialectic-method) <n.> dialectics: ~思想thought of dialectics || 主观~ subjective dialectics || 客观~ objective dialectics
25 马克思主义 [馬---義] mǎkèsīzhǔyì (Marx – ism) <n.> Marxism: 信仰~ believe in Marxism || 研究~ study Marxism || 当代~ contemporary Marxism
26 共产主义 [-產-義] gòngchǎnzhǔyì (commune – ism) <n.> communism: 国际~ international communism || ~事业the cause of communism || ~精神communist spirit
27 资本主义 [資--義] zīběnzhǔyì (capital – ism) <n.> capitalism: ~国家capitalist country || 国际~ international capitalism
28 社会主义 [-會-義] shèhuìzhǔyì (social – ism) <n.> socialism: 建设 (jiànshè) 有中国特色的~. build socialism with Chinese characteristics. || ~事业the cause of socialism || ~国家 a socialist country
29 *主义 [-義] zhǔyì (-ism) <n.> -ism: 国际~ internationalism || 法西斯 (fǎxīsī) ~ fascism || 自由 ~ liberalism

Tips:

1 龙 (龍, lóng): It means 'dragon.' The Chinese dragon has four feet, two horns, scales but no wings. It is a symbol of imperial power, strength and auspiciousness in Chinese culture. 小龙 is a folk name for the snake (蛇, shé.)
2 马恩列斯毛 (Mǎ, Ēn, Liè, Sī, Máo): They are Marx (马克思), Engels (恩格斯), Lenin (列宁), Stalin (斯大林) and Mao (毛泽东), the greatest leaders esteemed by the Communist Party of China.
3 多研究些问题, 少谈些主义: It means 'more research on issues, less talk about principles,' which is the title and core idea of an article written by Hu Shi on July 20, 1918. It was quickly accepted by Chinese liberal intellectuals.
4 天主教 (Tiānzhǔjiào): It means 'Catholicism,' whose Chinese name originated from a Confucian saying '至高莫若天, 至尊莫若主' (the highest is the *heaven*, and the most respectable is the *monarch*,) which Xú Guāngqǐ and Matteo Ricci came across around 1600.
5 道教 vs. 道家: 道教 is a religion and 道家 is a philosophy, although many common people do not have a clear idea of their differences.

6 放下屠刀, 立地成佛 (fàngxià túdāo, lìdì chéng fó): It means 'a butcher becomes a Buddha the moment he drops his cleaver,' which was meant to convince people that they can change if they believes in Buddhism. Interestingly, 鲁迅 (Lǔ Xùn, 1881–1936,) a great writer once wrote this famous quotation "放下佛经, 立地杀人" (literally menaing 'one puts down Buddhist scripture right at that place he will kill others.')

ExerciseTs:

Answer the following questions in Chinese.

1 世界上有哪些比较知名的宗教?

---

2 世界上知名宗教使用哪些宗教读本?

---

3 儒家思想一般影响了哪些国家的文化? (至少说出两个国家)

---

4 你觉得中国是资本主义社会还是社会主义社会?

---

5 你觉得共产主义会在全球实现吗? 为什么?

Theme 64: Groups 群体 (qúntǐ)

1 社会 [-會] shèhuì (society-organization) <n.> society: 人类~ human society || 国际~ international society || 全 ~ the whole society
2 世界 [-] shìjiè (30 years-boundary) <n.> world: 全~ the whole world || 内心~ the inner world || 走向~ becoming more international
3 全球 [-] quánqiú (whole-globe) <n.> whole world, the whole globe: ~力量 global force || ~闻名 world famous || 遍布 (biànbù) ~ spread all over the world
4 全世界 [-] quánshìjiè (whole-world) <n.> the whole world: ~人民 people all over the world || ~各地 all over the world || ~范围 global scope
5 天下 [-] tiānxià (heaven-under) <n.> everything under heaven: 统一 (tǒngyī) ~ unite the world || ~ 大事great undertakings || ~大乱 chaos on Earth
6 人间 [-間] rénjiān (human-world) <n.> the human world: 来到 ~ came into the human world || 离开 ~ left the human world || ~悲剧 (bēijù) human tragedy
7 中外 [-] zhōngwài (Chinese-foreign) <n.> Chinese-foreign: ~游客 Chinese and foreign tourists || ~人士 Chinese and foreign public figures || ~学生 Chinese and foreign students
8 族 [-] zú (arrowhead, clan) <n.> clan, race, ethnic group: 汉~ Han ethnic group (China's main ethnic group) || 外~ not of the same clan || 全~ the whole clan
9 种族 [種-] zhǒngzú (race-ethnicity) <n.> race, ethnicity: ~主义 racism || ~隔离 (gélí) racial segregation || ~歧视 (qíshì) racial prejudice

10 民族 [-] mínzú (nationality-ethnicity) <n.> nationality, ethnic group: 五十六个~ 56 ethnicities (the official recognized minority groups of China) || 少数~ ethnic minority || ~关系 ethnic relations

11 少数民族 [-數--] shǎoshùmínzú (minor-ethnicity) <n.> ethnic minority: 北方~ ethnic minority of the northern country

12 中华民族 [-華--] zhōnghuámínzú (Chinese-ethnicity) <n.> the Chinese Nation: ~的历史 the Chinese Nation's history || ~的子孙 descendants of the Chinese nation || ~的未来 the future of China

13 白人 [-] báirén (white-man) <n.> white-person: ~区 an area where people are predominantly white || ~总统a white president

14 黑人 [-] hēirén (black-man) <n.> black person: ~歌手black singer

15 华人 [華-] huárén (Chinese-man) <n.> Chinese person: ~圈 a close social circle of Chinese people || 海外~ Overseas Chinese citizen (born in China, Taiwan)

16 拉丁裔 [-] lādīngyì (Latin-descendent) <n.> Latino: ~歌手Latino singer || ~美国人Latino Americans

17 土著 [-] tǔzhù (original-inhabitant) <n.> aboriginal: ~部落 aboriginal tribe || ~印第安人 native Indian || ~语言 aboriginal language

18 单位 [單-] dānwèi (single-unit) <n.> unit, single-place: 工作~ employer, work unit || 有关 ~ related units || 新的~ a new unit

19 公司 [-] gōngsī (public-manage) <n.> corporation: 一家/个 ~ a corporation || 大/小~ large/small corporation || 外国~ foreign corporation

20 企业 [-業] qǐyè (expect-business) <n.> business enterprise: 私人~ private business || 重点 ~ key business, a key enterprise || 办 ~ run enterprises

21 集团 [-團] jítuán (gather-group) <n.> group, conglomerate: 领导~ leadership team || 军事~ military group

22 集体 [-體] jítǐ (assemble-body) <n.> collective, team: ~观念 collective idea || ~主义 collectivism || 爱~. Love the collective.

23 群体 [-體] qúntǐ (group-body) <n.> community, group: 弱势 (ruòshì) ~ underprivileged groups || 企业~ groups of enterprises || 人类~ the human community

24 团 [團] tuán (round, group) <n.> group, circle: 剧~ theater troupe || 旅游~ travel group || 记者~ press corps

25 团体 [團體] tuántǐ (group-body) <n.> organization, group, team: 妇女~ women's group || 演出~ performing arts group || 小~ a small group

26 代表团 [--團] dàibiǎotuán (representative-group) <n.> representative group, delegation: 画家~ artist delegation || 乒乓球 ~ ping team (top athletes represented) || 三个~ three delegations

27 组织 [組織] zǔzhī (group-organize) <n.> group, organization: 女工~ women workers organization || 党~ political organization || 地方~ local, regional organization

28 个体 [個體] gètǐ (individual-body) <n.> individual: 生命~ one's life || ~发展 individual growth

29 派 [-] pài (branch, school, faction) <n.> sect, group, school: 浪漫 (làngmàn) ~ romantics || 印象 (yìnxiàng) ~ impressionists || 古典~ (of the) classical school

30 家 [-] jiā (home) <n.> home: ~门 home door || 回~ go back home

31 家庭 [-] jiātíng (home-courtyard) <n.> household, family: 农民/工人/贵族~ a family of farmers/ a family of workers/family of aristocrats || 大, 小~ large family, small family || ~贫困, 富裕 poor, wealthy family
32 全家 [-] quánjiā (whole-family) <n.> the whole family: ~老少 the whole family – young and old || 我们~ our whole family
33 人家 [-] rénjiā (people-home) <n.> household, family (often referring to someone else's family): 四户~ four families || 普通~ average family || 附近的~ nearby families
34 家园 [-園] jiāyuán (home-garden) <n.> home, homeland: 重建~ rebuild one's homeland || 精神~ spiritual home

35 同行 [-] tóngháng (same-profession) <n.> peer, person of the same trade, occupation, industry: 国外 ~ foreign peer || 建筑界~ peer of architecture field
36 社 [-] shè (god of land, sacrificial place, society) <n.> organized body, society: 报~ newspaper press || 茶~ tea house || 村~ agricultural community
37 旅行社 [-] lǚxíngshè (travel-agency) <n.> travel agency: 中国~ Chinese travel agency || 国际~ international travel agency
38 一行 [-] yīxíng (same-group) <n.> a group traveling together: 代表团~ 五人 the five-person delegation || 总统及其~ the president and accompanying officials
39 团队 [團隊] tuánduì (group-team) <n.> group, team: 工作~ work group || 整个~ the whole group
40 学会 [學會] xuéhuì (academic-group) <n.> institute: 历史~ history institute || 布鲁金斯学会~ Brookings Institute || 成立~ establish an institute
41 协会 [協會] xiéhuì (associate-group) <n.> association: 机器人~ robotics association || 足球~ football (soccer) association || 作家~ a writers association

Tips:

1 **界 (jiè) vs. *坛 (tán): Both mean 'professor/circle of' but generally speaking, modifiers of 界 are disyllabic and those of 坛 are monosyllabic. For example, 音乐界 vs. 乐坛, 体育界 vs. 体坛, 电影界 vs. 影坛, 足球界 vs. 足坛 etc. 政界 vs. 政坛 and a few more pairs are exceptions.
2 世界 (world) vs. 天下 (under the heavens): The word "世界" appeared in Chinese after 700 but the word "天下" appeared in the earliest book Shangshu (*Book of Documents*.) Some scholars used this and argued that China had a broader view than the Western world.
3 企业 (qǐyè): It means 'enterprise' and was borrowed from the Japanese.
4 群体 (qúntǐ) vs. 团体 (tuántǐ): Both mean 'group' but 团体 is more organized, whereas 群体 is not necessarily very organized.

Exercises:

Part I: Answer the following questions in Chinese.

1 美国有哪些种族?

---

2 中国有多少个民族? 哪个民族占人口大多数?

---

3 你们国家有没有国有企业? 经营 (jīngyíng, run) 得怎么样?

---

4 你觉得你们国家更重视集体主义还是个人主义?

---

5 你们国家有没有种族歧视问题? 或者民族问题? 为什么?

Part II: Read the following sentences and fill in each blank with the appropriate word or phrase from the options given.

1 全球、天下、世界、人间

a) 在当今_______, 反对_______化的国家不多.
b) 中国古代皇帝认为_______的土地和财富 (cáifù, wealth) 都是他自己的.
c) 中国古代神话故事的"织女"是一个天上的仙女, 因为喜欢_______的生活就偷偷跑到地上来玩儿.

2 旅行社、团队、协会

a) 美国大公司招聘员工时很看重应聘者的________合作精神.
b) 如果想去中国旅行你可以找当地的_________为你代办签证.
c) 中国足球_______主要作用是开展各种关于足球的民间活动, 促进中国足球运动发展

3 全家、同行、人家、家园

a) 美国中西部地区地广人稀, 有时候开车几个小时才可以看见一处________.
b) 每一次自然灾后后, 人们面临的首要问题就是重建________.
c) 老王________最近要去欧洲旅行.
d) 老王跟老李都是医生, 他们是________, 所以聊起天来可说的特别多.

4 家庭、代表团、古今中外、组织

a) 中国体育________在2016年的奥运会上取得了第二名的成绩.
b) 这本书里收集了很多________的名人故事.
c) 目前的中国农村还有一些贫困________, 他们甚至还没有解决温饱问题. 因此, 中国政府号召这些地区的党________要集中精力做好扶贫工作.

Theme 65: Status, position 身份地位 (shēnfèn, dìwèi)

(See also Themes 9, 174)

1 等级 [-級] děngjí (grade-level) <n.> grade, rank: 最高~ highest ranking || 划分~ divide by rank || 社会~ social rank
2 地位 [-] dìwèi (place-location) <n.> position, status: 社会~ social position || ~高/低 high-level, low-level position || 有, 没有~ has, does not have status

3 上级 [-級] shàngjí (higher-level) <n.> higher level: ~领导 high level authority || ~部门superior department || ~法院superior court

4 下级 [-級] xiàjí (lower-level) <n.> lower level: ~职员 lower level worker || ~机关low level institution

5 职位 [職-] zhíwèi (post-position) <n.> position, post: 领导~ administrative position || ~高/低 high/low level position || 重要~ important position

6 岗位 [崗-] gǎngwèi (station-post) <n.> a post, a job: 工作~ employment position || 会计 (kuàijì) ~ accounting position || 不同的~ different positions

7 基层 [-層] jīcéng (bottom-level) <n.> basic or primary level: ~组织 lower level group || ~法院 lower level court || 深入~ go down to the grassroots

8 身份 [-] shēnfèn (one's-status) <n.> status, capacity: 作家~ writer (occupation) || 公开~ public identity, status || 特殊的~ special status

9 资格 [資-] zīgé (qualification-standard) <n.> qualifications, seniority: 教师~ teacher certification || 入学~ admission qualification || 有/没有~ has, does not have (the) qualification(s)

10 势力 [勢-] shìlì (influence-power) <n.> power, ability to influence: 强大的~ strong power, influence || 黑暗~ dark influence, power || 外来~ foreign power

11 关系 [關係] guānxì (connected-related) <n.> connections, relationship: 师生~ teacher-student relations || 中美~ Chinese-American relations || 友好~ friendly relations

12 友谊 [-誼] yǒuyì (friend-friendship) <n.> friendship: 深厚的~ deep, solid friendship || 增进 (zēngjìn) ~ enhance the relationship

13 学历 [學歷] xuélì (academic-experience) <n.> academic credentials: ~低/高 low-level, high-level academic credentials || 大学 ~ bachelor's (undergraduate) credential

14 学位 [學-] xuéwèi (academic-level) <n.> place in school, academic degree: 学士/硕士 (shuòshì) /博士~ undergraduate, masters, doctoral student || 获得~ obtain (a) credential

15 博士 [-] bóshì (extensive-scholar) <n.> doctor, Ph.D.: ~学位doctor's degree || ~生Ph. D. candidate || 念~ study for a doctorate

16 硕士 [碩-] shuòshì (erudite-scholar) <n.> master, graduate student: 授予~学位award a master's degree || ~研究生master graduate student || 文学~ Master of Arts

17 学士 [學-] xuéshì (learned-scholar) <n.> undergraduate student: ~学位bachelor's degree

18 老家 [-] lǎojiā (native-home) <n.> hometown: 离开~ leave one's hometown || 回~ return to your hometown (place of origin) || ~人 people from your hometown

19 国籍 [國-] guójí (national-origin) <n.> nationality, citizenship:中国~ Chinese nationality || 双重~ dual nationality

20 主人 [-] zhǔrén (host-person) <n.> host: 女~ hostess || 小~ little host || 房子的~ host of the house

21 仆人 [僕-] púrén (servant-person) <n.> servant: 做~ be a servant || 忠实 (zhōngshí) 的~ faithful servant

22 老板 [-闆] lǎobǎn (*prefix*-board) <n.> boss, manager: 大~ big boss || 王~ Boss Wang || 店~ the boss of a shop

23 领导 [領導] lǐngdǎo (lead-direct) <n.> administrator: 当~ take on a leadership role || 校~ school leaders || 主要~ main leaders
24 员工 [員-] yuángōng (staff-worker) <n.> worker, employee: 公司~ corporate employee || 全体~ all employees || 固定 (gùdìng) ~ permanent employee
25 职员 [職員] zhíyuán (post-staff) <n.> office worker: 小~ normal staff || 公司~ company staff || 普通~ common staff

26 人大代表 [-] réndàdàibiǎo (people's-congress-representative) <n.> Representative of the National People's Congress: 选~ select a representative for the National People's Congress || ~的意见opinions of Representative of the National People's Congress
27 议员 [議員] yìyuán (congress-member) <n.> member of a legislative body, UK – Member of Parliament, U.S. – Congressman or Congresswoman: 国会~ 国会~ congressman || 市~ city representative || 下议院~ Member of Parliament (MP) (UK politics)
28 大使 [-] dàshǐ (chief-ambassador) <n.> ambassador: 驻 (zhù) 外~ overseas ambassador || 文化~ cultural ambassador || 中国~ Chinese ambassador

29 董事长 [--長] dǒngshìzhǎng (supervise-affair-chairperson) <n.> Chairman of the Board: 公司~ chairman of the company || 担任~ undertake Chairman of the Board
30 总裁 [總-] zǒngcái (general-director) <n.> president (of a company): 副~ vice president || 担任~ undertake a president || 银行~ bank president
31 首席执行官 [--執--] shǒuxízhíxíngguān (chief-executive-officer) <n.> Chief Executive Officer: 谷歌公司的~ Google's CEO || 担任~ take the role of a CEO
32 高管 [-] gāoguǎn (high-executive) <n.> executive: 银行~ bank executive || 上市公司~ Executive of a top company
33 主任 [-] zhǔrèn (direct-responsible) <n.> Director: 办公室~ office director || 副~ vice director || 孙~ director Sun || 老~ the old director
34 经理 [經-] jīnglǐ (manage-administer) <n.> manager: 总~ general manager || 副~ vice manager || 当~ be a manager

Tips:

1 Social status: 'Equality' (平等, píngděng) is a concept that appeared considerably late in China, probably from the last decade of the 19th century.
2 Dream of '人上人': Because in ancient China, people were often classified into nine levels which is shown in sayings such as "人分三六九等" (people are in various grades and ranks) and "吃得苦中苦, 方为人上人" (if you can endure the worst of hardships, you will climb to the highest place on the social ladder, or 'no cross, no crown.') "人上人" (upper class, top dog) was or is the ideal societal position for a myriad of Chinese people.
3 President: It has at least three equivalents in Chinese, namely 总统 (zǒngtǒng, head of a state/country,) 总裁 (zǒngcái, the highest titled officer of a corporation) and 校长 (xiàozhǎng, the highest officer of a university.)
4 CEO: It is translated as 首席执行官 in mainland China, 行政總裁 in Hong Kong and 執行長 in Taiwan.
5 老板: It appeared in Chinese probably in the 17th century and was originally addressed to owners of stores or shops.

6 博士 (bóshì): Now it means 'doctoral degree,' but this word appeared very early in Chinese. For example, the Qin and Han dynasties had 博士 who specialized in the classics, and the Tang and Song dynasties had茶博士 who were experts at making tea.
7 关系 (guānxì): It means 'social connections.' Now a similar word 人脉 (rénmài) is becoming popular.

Exercises:

Part I: Read the following words and then answer the questions.

职员、董事长、经理、高管、首席执行官、总裁、国会议员、驻外大使、人大代表、学历、硕士、博士、学士、国籍、资格、能力、地位、等级、上级、下级、基层岗位、领导岗位、主人、仆人

1 "职员、董事长、部门经理、首席执行官," 请按照权力 (quánlì, power) 从多到少排列 (páiliè, put in order) 这些词

______

2 "硕士、学士、博士," 请按照学历从低到高排列这些词

______

3 你们国家公民可以有双重 (shuāngchóng, dual) 国籍 (guójí, nationality) 吗? 你们国家现在还有没有等级观念?

______

4 你觉得学历越高能力越大吗? 为什么?

______

5 "国会议员、驻外大使、人大代表," 哪个职位只有在中国才有? 哪个职位跟国家外交关系最大? 美国的"国会议员"是终身任职的吗?

______

6 "上级、基层岗位、领导岗位、主人、下级、仆人," 请选出合适的反义词填空.

上级 ______
基层岗位 ______
主人 ______

Theme 66: Customs 风俗 (fēngsú)

1 风俗 [風-] fēngsú (trend-custom) <n.> custom: 地方~ regional customs || ~习惯 customs and habits || 春节~ Spring Festival customs
2 习惯 [習慣] xíguàn (usual practice-habit) <n.> habit, customs: 传统~ traditional customs || 好/坏~ good/bad customs || 生活~ life habits

3 传统 [傳統] chuántǒng (passing-system) <n.> tradition: 优良~ good traditions || 文化~ cultural traditions || 音乐~ musical traditions

4 礼貌 [禮-] lǐmào (polite-looking) <n.> courtesy, politeness: 有/没有 ~ has/doesn't have manners || ~的行为 polite behavior || 注意~ mind one's manners

5 仪式 [儀-] yíshì (ceremony-form) <n.> ceremony/rite: 举行~ conduct a ceremony || 婚礼~ wedding ceremony || ~开始 to start a ceremony

6 开幕式 [開--] kāimùshì (opening-curtain-ceremony) <n.> opening ceremony: 出席 (chūxí) ~ attend the opening ceremony || 主持~ host an opening ceremony || 举行~ conduct an opening ceremony

7 闭幕式 [閉--] bìmùshì (closing-curtain-ceremony) <n.> closing ceremony: 举行~ conduct a closing ceremony || 出席~ attend a closing ceremony || 大会~ general closing ceremony

8 典礼 [-禮] diǎnlǐ (solemn-ceremony) <n.> ceremony: 毕业~ graduation ceremony || 开学~ start of school ceremony || 结婚~ wedding ceremony

9 婚礼 [-禮] hūnlǐ (wedding-ceremony) <n.> wedding: 办~ hold a wedding || 中式/西式~ Chinese style/ Western style wedding || 举行~ hold a wedding

10 节 [節] jié (bamboo joint, joint, festival) <n.> holiday: 中秋~ Mid-autumn Festival || 端午 (duānwǔ) ~ Dragon Boat Festival || 情人~ Valentine's Day

11 节日 [節-] jiérì (festival-day) <n.> holiday: 庆祝~ celebrate holidays || ~快乐happy holidays || 宗教~ feast day

12 除夕 [-] chúxī (parting-evening) <n.> New Year's Eve (Lunar Calendar): ~之夜New Year's Eve || 过~ celebrate New Year's Eve

13 春节 [-節] chūnjié (spring-festival) <n.> Spring Festival, Chinese New Year: 过~ spend the Chinese New Year || 欢度~ joyously celebrate the Spring Festival

14 元宵节 [--節] yuánxiāojié (first- (full moon) night-festival) <n.> Lantern Festival (15th day of the new year): 正月 (zhēngyuè) 十五日是~. The 15th day of the first month in the Chinese lunar calendar is the Lantern Festival.

15 清明节 [--節] qīngmíngjié (clear-bright-festival) <n.> Tomb Sweeping Festival: ~在每年的四月四日至四月六日之间. Tomb Sweeping Festival is between April 4 and April 6 on the lunar calendar every year.

16 端午节 [--節] duānwǔjié (beginning-fifth-festival) <n.> Dragon Boat Festival: 每年农历的五月初五是~. May 5th on the Chinese lunar calendar every year is Dragon Boat Festival.

17 七夕 [-] qīxī (seventh-evening) <n.> seventh evening of the seventh month (lunar calendar) (when the herd boy and the weaving girl are supposed to meet): ~就是中国的情人节. The seventh evening of the seventh month (lunar calendar) is Chinese Valentine's Day.

18 中秋节 [--節] zhōngqiūjié (mid-autumn-festival) <n.> Mid-Autumn Festival: ~是家人团聚 (tuánjù) 的日子. Mid-Autumn Festival is a day for the gathering of family members.

19 国庆节 [國慶節] guóqìngjié (national-celebration-festival) <n.> National Day: 庆祝~ celebrate National Day || 十月一日是中国的~. October 1st is the National Day of China.

20 新年 [-] xīnnián (new-year) <n.> New Year: ~好/快乐 Happy New Year 庆祝~ celebrate New Year

21 元旦 [-] yuándàn (first-day) <n.> New Year's Day: 过~ celebrate New Year's Day || ~晚会New Year's Day Evening Celebration

22 情人节 [--節] qíngrénjié (lover-day) <n.> Valentine's Day: 二月十四日是~. February 14th is Valentine's Day.

23 劳动节 [勞動節] láodòngjié (labor-day) <n.> Labor Day: 五月一日是国际~. May 1st is International Labor Day.

24 复活节 [復-節] fùhuójié (resurrection-day) <n.> Easter: ~彩蛋Easter egg || 复活节是在公元前325年建立的基督教节日. Easter is a Christian holiday established in 325 BC.

25 独立日 [獨--] dúlìrì (independence-day) <n.> Independence Day: 美国的~在七月四日. July 4th is the American Independence Day.

26 感恩节 [--節] gǎn'ēnjié (thank-kindness-day) <n.> Thanksgiving: 共度~ celebrate Thanksgiving together

27 万圣节 [萬聖節] wànshèngjié (10,000-spirit-day) <n.> Halloween: 万圣节是一天穿着服装和吃糖果. Halloween is a day to wear costumes and eat candy.

28 圣诞节 [聖誕節] shèngdànjié (saint-born-day) <n.> Christmas: 过~ spend Christmas || 庆祝~ celebrate Christmas

29 狂欢节 [-歡節] kuánghuānjié (wild-celebration-day) <n.> Mardi Gras, Carnival

30 逾越节 [--節] yúyuèjié (transgress/passover-festival) <n.> Passover (Jewish holiday): 庆祝~ celebrate Passover

Tips:

1 风俗 (fēngsú): 风俗 means 'custom.' It is understandable that different places within China have remarkably different customs due to their long and complex histories. There is a Chinese saying, which shows these remarkable differences, "十里不同风, 百里不同俗," which means 'two different places have different customs even though they are just ten or 100 miles apart.'

2 劳动节 (Láodòngjié): It means ' (International) Workers' Day' in China and 'Labor Day' in the United States. In China, it is on May 1st, and in the U.S. it is on the first Monday in September.

3 万圣节 (Wànshèngjié): It means Halloween and is also called 鬼节 (Guǐjié, literally 'ghosts' day.')

4 端午节 (Duānwǔjié): It is on the fifth day in the lunar month of May in China. 端 means 'beginning' and 午 was originally '五' which was changed due to a taboo because Emperor Xuanzong of Tang (685–762) was born on the fifth day in the lunar month of August.

Exercises:

Part I: Answer the following questions in Chinese.

1 西方有哪些重要的节日?

____

2 中国有哪些重要的节日?

3 基督教有哪些重要的节日?

4 你觉一个国家的传统和风俗是否应该全部保留? 为什么?

5 你参加过哪些重要的仪式 (yíshì, ceremony)?

Theme 67: Work, activities 工作, 活动 (gōngzuò, huódòng)

(See also Theme 45)

1 事业 [-業] shìyè (achievement-career) <n.> career, undertaking: 革命~ revolutionary achievement|| 干~ developing career || 以~为重take the career as priority
2 职业 [職業] zhíyè (occupation-career) <n.> occupation, profession: 有/没有~ have a profession || ~习惯habit related to profession || 他从事什么~? What does he do?
3 职务 [職務] zhíwù (post-duty) <n.> post, duties, jobs: 临时 (línshí) ~ temporary post || 担任厂长~ be a chief person of a factory || 解除~ relieve one's post
4 劳动 [勞動] láodòng (labor-work) <n.> physical labor, work: 家务~ housework || 农业 ~ agriculture work, farm labor || 参加 ~ take part in the work
5 产业 [產業] chǎnyè (produce-industry) <n.> industry: 基础 (jīchǔ) ~ fundamental industry || ~落后/发达undeveloped /developed industry || 现代 ~ modern industry
6 工业 [-業] gōngyè (work-industry) <n.> industry: 本国的~ country's industry || 轻~ light industry || 电子~ electric industry
7 农业 [農業] nóngyè (agriculture-industry) <n.> agriculture: ~生产agricultural produce || ~工具agriculture tools || ~劳动agriculture labor
8 商业 [-業] shāngyè (commerce-industry) <n.> commerce, business: ~企业business enterprise || ~部门business department || ~活动commerce activity
9 交通 [-] jiāotōng (cross-through) <n.> transportation, traffic: 公共~ public transportation || ~不便/发达 inconvenient transportation/good transportation || ~堵塞 (dǔsè) traffic jam
10 服务业 [-務業] fúwùyè (service-industry) <n.> service industry: ~发达developed service industry || 公共~ public service industry || 从事~ do service work
11 行业 [-業] hángyè (profession-industry) <n.> trade industry: 特殊 (tèshū) ~ special industry || 新兴 (xīnxīng) ~ new industry || 不同~ different industry
12 金融 [-] jīnróng (money-finance) <n.> finance, banking: ~政策 (zhèngcè) financial policy || ~市场financial market || ~风暴 (fēngbào) poor financial situation

13 保险 [-險] bǎoxiǎn (insure-safety) <n.> insurance: 买~ buy insurance || 房屋~ house insurance || 一份~ a piece of the insurance || ~公司insurance company

14 贸易 [貿-] màoyì (trade-exchange) <n.> trade: ~发达have a well- developed trade || 对华~ trade with China || 出口~ trade export

15 生意 [-] shēngyì (earn a living-idea) <n.> business: 做~ do business || 谈~ discuss business || 一笔~ a business

16 买卖 [買賣] mǎimài (buy-sell) <n.> trading: 做~ do trade || 谈~ discuss trade || 一笔~ a trade

17 业务 [業務] yèwù (business-affair) <n.> vocational work, professional work: 懂~ understand one's profession || 钻研/精通(zuānyán/ jīngtōng) ~ diligently study one's profession/ technically proficient|| ~水平the level of professional work

18 工商 [-] gōngshāng (industry-commerce) <n.> industry and commerce: ~业business industry || ~管理business administration

19 工程 [-] gōngchéng (construction-progression) <n.> engineering, project: 一项~ a project|| 重点的~ key project || 建筑~ construction engineering

20 活动 [-動] huódòng (move-exercise) <n.> activity: 重要~ important activity || 进行 ~ carry out activity || 参加~ attend an activity

21 会 [會] huì (assemble, meet, meeting) <n.> meeting, conference: 大~ conference || 年~ annual conference || 开~ have a meeting/conference

22 会议 [會議] huìyì (meeting-discussion) <n.> meeting, conference: 出席~ attend a meeting || 参加~ participate in meeting || 举行~ hold a meeting

23 大会 [-會] dàhuì (general-meeting) <n.> general assembly: 参加 ~ participate in general assembly || 开~ open general assembly || 代表~ congress || 召开~ convoke a general assembly

24 峰会 [-會] fēnghuì (summit-meeting) <n.> summit: 全球~ global summit || 商业~ business summit || 行业 ~ industry summit

25 娱乐 [-樂] yúlè (entertain-amuse) <n.> amusement, entertainment, recreation: ~圈entertainment circle || ~活动recreational activities, recreation || ~场所 place of recreation

26 文娱 [-] wényú (cultural-entertainment) <n.> cultural recreation, entertainment: ~活动recreational activities ||~节目entertainment, recreational program || ~演出recreational performance

27 演唱会 [--會] yǎnchànghuì (sing-concert) <n.> singing performance: 看~ watching singing performance || 开~ hold singing performance || 三场~ three rounds of singing concerts

28 音乐会 [-樂會] yīnyuèhuì (music-concert) <n.> music concert: 听~ listening to music concert || 参加/举行~ participate in music concert || 室内~ indoor music concert

29 运动会 [運動會] yùndònghuì (sports-event) <n.> sports event: 开~ open/ begin the sports event || 参加~ participate in sports event || 举行~ hold a sports event

30 亚运会 [亞運會] yàyùnhuì (Asian-games) <n.> Asian Games: 本届/上届/下届 (jiè) ~ current/last/next Asian Games || 办/举办~ hold the Asian Games || 开~ begin the Asian Games

31 展览会 [-覽會] zhǎnlǎnhuì (exhibition-event) <n.> exhibition: 举办 ~ held exhibition || 参加 ~ take part in exhibition || 图书~ books exhibition
32 博览会 [-覽會] bólǎnhuì (extensive-view-event) <n.> expo: 国际~ international expo || 大型~ large expo
33 车展 [車-] chēzhǎn (vehicle-exhibition) <n.> vehicle exhibition: 参加~ participate in auto show || 国际~ international auto show
34 奥展会 [奥運會] àoyùnhuì (Olympic-sports-games) <n.> Olympic games: 举办~ hold the Olympic Games || 参加~ participate in Olympic Games || ~冠军 (guànjūn) Olympic champion
35 游戏 [遊戲] yóuxì (amuse-play) <n./v.> game: 玩~ play (a) game || 做~ play games || 参加~ participate in game
36 宴会 [-會] yànhuì (entertain at a banquet-event) <n.> banquet: 参加~ take part in banquet || 举行~ hold (a) banquet || 生日~ birthday banquet
37 晚会 [會] wǎnhuì (evening-party) <n.> evening party, an evening of entertainment: 开~ hold a party || 音乐~ an evening of entertainment || 春节联欢 (liánhuān) ~ Spring Festival Gala
38 座谈会 [-談會] zuòtánhuì (sit-talk-event) <n.> forum: 召开~ held forum || 参加~ participate in forum || 专家~ expert forum
39 讲座 [講-] jiǎngzuò (lecture-seat) <n.> lecture: 举办~ hold (a) lecture || 学术 ~ academic lecture || 电视~ TV lecture

40 手工 [-] shǒugōng (hand-work) <n./adj.> manual, handwork: ~操作 manual operation || ~劳动 manual labor || 上 ~课handwork class
41 家务 [-務] jiāwù (household-work) <n.> housework: 做/干~ do housework || ~劳动housework labor || ~活housekeeping
42 动作 [動-] dòngzuò (move-do) <n.> movement, motion, action: 两个~ two actions || 舞蹈(wǔdǎo) ~ dance movements ||~ 缓慢 slow in action
43 行动 [-動] xíngdòng (act-move) <n.> action, operation: 爱国~ patriotic action || 军事~ military operation|| 实际~ actual action
44 行为 [-為] xíngwéi (act-do) <n.> behavior: 不良~ bad behavior || 自私的~ selfish behavior || 违法~ illegal behavior
45 举动 [舉動] jǔdòng (action-move) <n.> movement, move, act, activity: ~反常abnormal behavior || 轻率的~ rash act
46 表现 [-現] biǎoxiàn (show-appear) <n.> expression, manifestation, behavior, performance: ~很好 behave oneself well|| 多种~ many different kinds of performances || 市场~ market performance

Tips:

1 会 (會, huì): 會 is related to 亼 (jí, to gather together, to assemble) and 曾 (many, more,) therefore, it means 'to gather together' or 'to assemble.' All 会 involve more than one person, no matter whether it is 约会 (yuēhuì, dating,) 集会 (jíhuì, assembly,) 会议 (huìyì, meeting, conference,) 音乐会 (yīnyuèhuì, concert,) 音动会 (yùndònghuì, sports games) or 宴会 (yànhuì, banquet.)

2 业 (業, yè): 业 originally meant 'wooden board, slab' from which evolved meanings such as 'course of study' such as 毕业 (bìyè, graduate) and 'cause,

achievement' such as 事业 (shìyè, career.) 业 is widely used in industries, such as 工业, 农业, 商业, 服务业, which are all listed above and 金融业 (financial industry,) 保险业 (insurance industry,) 教育业 (education sector,) 旅游业 (tourism,) 娱乐业 (entertainment industry).

3 晚会 (wǎnhuì): It means 'evening party', which is transliterated as 派对 (派對, pàiduì) in places such as Taiwan and Hong Kong.

Exercises:

Part I: Read the following words and then answer the questions.

工业、农业、商业、服务业、金融业、保险业、对外贸易、奥运会、亚运会、冬运会、国际博览会、国际峰会、车展、演唱会、音乐会、春节联欢晚会

1 你们国家的经济产业有哪些？哪些产业是无污染 (wūrǎn, pollution) 的绿色产业？

---

2 哪些词是关于大型国际会议的词

---

3 哪些词是关于大型运动会的词

---

4 哪些词是关于娱乐方面的

---

5 哪些词是关于大型展览活动的词

Theme 68: Administration 行政 (xíngzhèng)

1 国 [國] guó (state, country) <n.> country: 中~ china || 大~ great power || 全~ whole country

2 国家 [國-] guójiā (country-family) <n.> nation: 落后~ underdeveloped countries || 发达~ developed countries || 东方~ eastern countries

3 中国 [-國] zhōngguó (central-country) <n.> China: ~人 Chinese person || ~话 Chinese language || ~问题 questions about China

4 中华 [華] zhōnghuá (central-China) <n.> Chinese country: ~民族 (mínzú) Chinese nation || ~儿女Chinese people || ~文化 Chinese culture

5 祖国 [-國] zǔguó (native-country) <n.> native country: 爱~ love your country || 离开~ leave your country || 保卫~ defend your country

6 全国 [-國] quánguó (whole-country) <n.> nationwide: ~人民all the people of the nation || ~人口nation's population || ~各地everywhere in the country

7 中央 [-] zhōngyāng (middle-center) <n.> center: ~政府 central government || ~的决定the decision of the central government || ~机构central agency

8 首都 [-] shǒudū (primary-capital) <n.> capital: ~北京 capital Beijing || ~人民People of the capital city || ~机场 airport of the capital

9 政府 [-] zhèngfǔ (administration-court) <n.> government: 省/市~ province/city government || 中国~ Chinese government || 中央/地方~ central/local government

10 省 [-] shěng (province) <n.> province: 东北三~ northeastern three provinces || 各~ every province || ~政府province government

11 区 [區] qū (area, district) <n.> area: 自治~ autonomous region || 特~ special zone

12 市 [-] shì (market, town, city) <n.> city: 全~ the whole city || ~医院 city hospital || ~区 urban region

13 城市 [-] chéngshì (wall-market) <n.> city: 一座大~ a big city || 一线~ first-tier cities || 沿海~ coastal cities

14 北京 [-] běijīng (north-capital city) <n.> Beijing: 首都~ the capital – Beijing || ~市 city of Beijing || ~大学 Beijing University

15 上海 [-] shànghǎi (upper-riverside) <n.> Shanghai: ~市city of Shanghai || 去~ go to Shanghai

16 香港 [-] xiānggǎng (fragrant-harbor) <n.> Hong Kong: ~人 Hong Kong people || ~地区Hong Kong area

17 澳门 [-門] àomén (bay-gate) <n.> Macao: ~地区Macao area

18 台北 [臺-] táiběi (Taiwan-north) <n.> Taipei: ~市city of Taipei || ~人民Taipei people

19 县 [縣] xiàn (county) <n.> county: 五个~ five counties || 全~ the whole county || 自治~ autonomous county

20 镇 [鎮] zhèn (press down, town) <n.> small town: 两个~ two small towns || ~政府 local government || 乡~ villages and towns

21 乡 [鄉] xiāng (township) <n.> countryside: 同~ person from the same town as you || 全~ the whole countryside || 下~ go to the countryside

22 村 [-] cūn (village) <n.> village: 进~ go to a village || 全~ whole village

23 村庄 [-莊] cūnzhuāng (village-hamlet) <n.> village or hamlet: 十几个~ around ten villages

24 外国 [-國] wàiguó (foreign-country) <n.> foreign country: ~人 foreigners || ~公司 foreign company

25 国际 [國際] guójì (country-between) <n.> international: ~关系 international relations || ~经济 international economy || ~市场 international market

26 联合国 [聯-國] liánhéguó (united-nation) <n.> United Nations: ~大会 UN general assembly || ~ 代表 UN representative || ~总部 UN headquarters

27 国会 [國會] guóhuì (nation-assembly) <n.> parliament, Congress: 美国~ American Congress || ~选举 congressional elections || 召开~ convene Congress

28 议会 [議會] yìhuì (consult-assembly) <n.> parliament: 市~ city council || 国民~ national parliament || ~政治/民主 political parliament

29 党 [黨] dǎng (500 families, clique, political party) <n.> party: 在野~ the party that is not in office || 执政 (zhízhèng) ~ ruling party || 共产~ Communist party

30 政党 [-黨] zhèngdǎng (political-party) <n.> political party: 成立~ found a political party || ~关系 political party relations

31 共和党 [--黨] gònghédǎng (republican-party) <n.> Republican Party: ~政府Republican government || ~代表Representatives of the Republican Party || ~人Republican Party members

32 民主党 [--黨] mínzhǔdǎng (democratic-party) <n.> Democratic Party: ~政府Democratic Party government || ~代表Representatives of Democratic Party || ~领袖 (l(presentleader of Democratic Party

33 保守党 [--黨] bǎoshǒudǎng (conservative-party) <n.> The Conservative Party: ~政府The Conservative Party government || ~人The Conservative Party member

34 联盟 [聯-] liánméng (allied-alliance) <n.> alliance: 结成~ form an alliance || 经济~ economic alliance || 青年~ young alliance

35 机构 [機構] jīgòu (organization-organ) <n.> group, organization: 新闻~ organization of the press || 领导~ leader's organization || 工作~ worker's organization

36 机关 [機關] jīguān (organization-office) <n.> office, group: 政府~ government body || 领导~ leader's office || 国家权力~ organs of state power

37 部门 [-門] bùmén (section-branch) <n.> department: 有关~ relevant departments || 重要~ important departments

38 *长 [*長] zhǎng (old, chief, head) <n.> head, chief: 部~ department leader || 省~ governor of a province || 市~ mayor || 县~ head of county || 州~ governor || 厅~ head of provincial government || 局~ director of the department || 处~ office head || 科~ chief of a department

39 班长 [-長] (class-head) <n.> class monitor: 当 ~ serve as class leader || 老 ~ senior class leader

40 部 [-] bù (section, department, ministry) <n.> section, department: 外交~ the Ministry of Foreign Affairs || 国防 ~ the Ministry of National Defense || 商务 ~ Commerce Department

41 厅 [廳] tīng (hall, department) <n.> department: 交通~ transportation department || 警察 (jǐngchá) ~ police agency || 财政~ General Office of Finance

42 司 [-] sī (command, a level of government) <n.> department under a ministry: 教育~ Education Department || 新闻~ Information Department || 亚洲~ Asia Department

43 局 [-] jú (constrained, bureau) <n.> bureau: 公安~ Public Security Bureau || 教育~ Bureau of Education || 卫生~ Health Bureau

44 处 [處] chù (location, division) <n.> division, department: 保卫~ Security Department || 人事~ personnel division

45 科 [-] kē (sort, section) <n.> a division or subdivision of an administrative unit: 行政~ administration department || 财务~ accounting department

46 办事处 [辦-處] bànshìchù (handle-affair-office) <n.> office agency: 设~ open office agency || 成立~ establish office agency || 街道~ sub-district office

47 组 [組] zǔ (group) <n.> group: 小~ small group

48 海关 [-關] hǎiguān (sea-customs) <n.> customs house, customs: 中国~ China's customs || 进~ entry customs || 过~ get through customs

49 大使馆 [--館] dàshǐguǎn (ambassador-house) <n.> embassy: 驻外~ embassy in foreign country || 各国~ embassies

50 邮局 [郵-] yóujú (post-office) <n.> post office: 去~寄包裹 (bāoguǒ) go to the post office to mail a package

51 政治 [-] zhèngzhì (political affairs-administrate) <n.> politics: ~力量 political power || ~工作political work || ~教育political education

52 行政 [-] xíngzhèng (implement-administration) <n.> administration: ~命令 administrative order || ~管理administrative management || ~部门administrative division || ~机关administration organ || ~工作clerical work || ~人员 administration staff

53 公务 [-務] gōngwù (public-affairs) <n.> official business: 日常~ office routine || 处理 ~ deal with official work || ~员civil servants

54 集权 [-權] jíquán (centralize-power) <n.> centralization of power: 中央~ centralization of state power || 高度~ high centralization of power || 加强~ enhance the centralization of power

55 直辖市 [-轄-] zhíxiáshì (direct-govern-city) <n.> municipality directly under the central government: 中国有四个~, 北京、天津、上海和重庆. There are four municipalities in China, Beijing, Tianjin, Shanghai and Chongqing.

Tips:

1 党 (黨, dǎng): In the Chinese context, when 党 is mentioned on its own, it refers to the Chinese Communist Party (CCP,) however, 黨 in ancient Chinese had a negative connotation. It referred to a clique or a cabal.

2 政府 (zhèngfǔ): In the Tang and Song dynasties, the place where a prime minister worked was called 政府.

3 台湾 (臺灣, Táiwān): The PRC claims that Taiwan is a part of China, albeit Taiwan has different expressions. When these two ideas collide and the mainland side has the upper hand, Taiwan becomes '中华台北' (Zhōnghuá Táiběi.) Please watch the opening ceremony of the 2008 Beijing Olympics for a more specific idea.

4 Hierarchy of Chinese administrative divisions: 省级 (shěngjí, provincial level,) 地级 (dìjí, prefectural level,) 县级 (xiànjí, county level,) 乡级 (xiāngjí, township level,) 村级 (cūnjí, village level.)

5 Chinese administrative levels: There are five levels, namely 国家级 (guójiā jí, state level,) 省部级 (shěng/bù jí, province/ministry level,) 司厅局级 (sī/tīng/jú jí, department/bureau level,) 县处级 (xiàn/chù jí, division level) and 乡镇科级 (xiāng/zhèn/kē jí, section level.)

6 官大一级压死人 (guān dà yì jí yā sǐ rén): Hierarchy was and still is highly valued by Chinese society, which is reflected in a saying "官大一级压死人" (literally 'post-higher-one-level-crush-death-people') which means 'officials one rank superior overpower the inferior.'

7 中*, 央 (yāng) *, 国*: When they are used in abbreviations, '中*' usually means 'Chinese-,' for example, 中日关系 (Sino-Japanese relations,) '央*' means 'central-,' for example, 央视 (Chinese Central Television,) 央行 (central bank,) '国*' means 'state-,' for example, '国资委' (guózīwěi, state-owned Assets Supervision and Administration Commission.)

Exercises:

Part I: Answer the following questions in Chinese.

1 请按照从大到小的顺序 (shùnxù, order) 排列中国的行政区域 (qūyù, region, area): 省 (直辖市) 、区、市、县 (区) 、村、乡 (镇)

---

2 请按照从大到小的顺序排列中国的行政机关: 科、局、部、厅

---

3 中国是民主国家还是中央集权国家? 为什么?

---

4 请写出美国的两个主要政党

---

5 "国会、议会、邮局、大使馆、海关," 哪些是美国的政治机构? 哪个是美国的外交机构? 哪个是美国的国家安全机构?

---

6 你觉得"联合国"对世界的影响力大不大? 为什么?

Theme 69: Legality 法制 (fǎzhì)

(See also Theme 169)

1 法制 [-] fǎzhì (legal-system) <n.> legal system, legality: ~教育education in legality || 加强社会主义~ strengthen the socialist legal system || ~社会 legal system society
2 法律 [-] fǎlǜ (law-law) <n.> law: 服从~ obey the law || 国家~ national law || ~责任 (zérèn) legal responsibility
3 法规 [-規] fǎguī (law-regulation) <n.> laws and regulations: 教育~ educational laws || 劳动~ labor laws || 遵守 (zūnshǒu) ~ abide by the law
4 法 [-] fǎ (law) <n.> law: 基本~ basic law || 教育~ educational law || 懂 (dǒng) ~ understand the law

5 政策 [-] zhèngcè (political-tactic) <n.> policy: 对外开放~ open foreign policy || 经济~ economic policy
6 制度 [-] zhìdù (formulate-rule) <n.> system: 工作~ working system || 民主~ democracy
7 规定 [規-] guīdìng (regulate-stipulate) <n.> rule, regulation, stipulate: 有关~ relevant rules || 法律~ legal ruling || 一条~ a rule/regulation
8 规则 [規則] guīzé (regulate-criterion) <n.> rule, law: 违反 (wéifǎn) ~ violate the law || 遵守~ abide to the law || 制定 establish law

9 纪律 [紀-] jìlǜ (discipline-law) <n.> discipline: 遵守~ keep discipline || 违反~ not maintain discipline || 课堂~ classroom discipline

10 命令 [-] mìnglìng (order-demand) <n./v.> order, command: ~部队前进 order the army to go forward || 下~ send an order || 服从~ obey the order

11 条约 [條約] tiáoyuē (item-agreed) <n.> treaty, pact: 不平等 ~ an unfair treaty || 签订 (qiāndìng) ~ sign a treaty || 国际~ international treaty

12 合约 [-約] héyuē (mutual-agreement) <n.> contract: 签订~ sign a contract || ~期满 complete a contract (time)

13 合同 [-] hétóng (mutual-consensus) <n.> (business) contract: 签~ sign a contract || 违反~ violate a contract || 解除~ abolish a contract

14 工会 [-會] gōnghuì (labor-union) <n.> trade union, labor union: 市~ city labor union || 总 ~ federal union || 加入~ enter a union

15 法院 [-] fǎyuàn (legal-courtyard) <n.> court of justice: 最高 ~ highest court || 国际 ~ international court || 地方~ regional court

16 法庭 [-] fǎtíng (legal-court) <n.> court, tribunal: 最高~ highest court || 国际 ~ international court || 上~ go to the court

17 警察局 [-] jǐngchájú (police-station) <n.> police station, headquarters: 当地~ local police station || 市~ city police station || 一所~ a police station

18 派出所 [-] pàichūsuǒ (dispatch-out-place) <n.> local police station: 当地~ local police station

19 监狱 [監獄] jiānyù (jail-prison) <n.> prison, jail: 进~ enter prison || 蹲 (dūn) ~ stay in jail || 一所~ a jail

20 戒毒所 [-] jièdúsuǒ (rehabilitate-drug-place) <n.> drug rehabilitation center: 进~ enter a drug rehabilitation center

21 罪恶 [-惡] zuì'è (crime-evil) <n.> crime, evil, sin: 各种 ~ all sorts of sins, all sorts of evils || 战胜 ~ defeat evil || ~多端 guilty of all kinds of evil

22 处罚 [處罰] chǔfá (punish-penalize) <n.> punish, penalize: 减免~ reduce or waive a crime || 作出~ penalize || 受到~ receive a penalty

23 处分 [處-] chǔfèn (punish-duty) <n.> disciplinary action, punishment: 受~ receive disciplinary action || 严重的~ serious disciplinary action || 给他~ assign him disciplinary action

24 死刑 [-] sǐxíng (death-penalty) <n.> death penalty: 判~ assign the death penalty || 处~ be on death row || 执行 (zhíxíng) ~ conduct the death penalty

25 有期徒刑 [-] yǒuqītúxíng (fixed-term-imprisonment) <n.> fixed-term imprisonment: 判处~ assign a fixed imprisonment || ~十年 a ten-year imprisonment

26 无期徒刑 [無---] wúqītúxíng (no-term-imprisonment) <n.> life imprisonment: 判~ decide to assign a life in prison

27 刑期 [-] xíngqī (penalty-term) <n.> term of imprisonment: 最高~ the highest terms of imprisonment || 满~ complete the term of imprisonment

28 轨道 [軌-] guǐdào (track-route) <n.> track, proper way of doing things, proper course: 法制~ the legal track || 发展~ expansion track || 上~ be on track

29 法治 [-] fǎzhì (law-rule) <n.> rule of law: ~社会 society governed by law || ~观念law concept

30 专制 [專-] zhuānzhì (autocratic-system) <n.> autocracy: ~国家 autocratic nation

Tips:

1 法 (fǎ): 法 was originally written as 灋, which is related to 氵 (水, water,) 廌 (zhì, a mythic celestial animal) and 去 (to go, away.) 氵 (water) is naturally inclined to be level, thus indicating 'fair, just.' 廌 was said to be able to identify the person who was wrong in court and use his horns or unicorn to hit and make him leave (去.) It is interesting that if the myth had some ground, it indicates that the legitimacy of Chinese laws was from heaven (天, tian,) but not based on a common contract.
2 法 and 律 (lǜ): As laws, 律 was more common than 法 in ancient China, from the Qin Dynasty to the Qing Dynasty. For example, the most influential law was 'Tang Code' (唐律.) By the way, laws in the Bible are called 律法, when translated into Chinese.
3 法制 vs. 法治: Both are pronounced as fǎzhì, but the former means 'legal system, legality', while the latter 'rule of law' is opposite of the 人治 (rule of man.)

Exercises:

Part I: Answer the following questions in Chinese.

1 你们国家哪些机构可以处理犯罪的问题?

____

2 你觉得你们国家是法治社会还是人治社会? 为什么?

____

3 你们国家有死刑吗? 有无期徒刑吗?

____

4 你觉得现在工会在你们国家是否具有积极作用? 为什么?

____

5 "法律、法规、规定", 请按照影响范围从小到大的顺序排列这些词

____

6 国际社会针对制止全球变暖的问题签订了_______, 目的是约束 (yuēshù, restrain) 各国减少污染, 共同解决全球变暖问题.
a)条约 b) 合同 c) 命令

Theme 70: Right, responsibility 权利, 责任 (quánlì, zérèn)

1 权 [權] quán (scale, weigh, power) <n.> power, right, authority: 人~ human rights || 特 ~ special privilege|| 有/没~ have the right to/ to not have the right to
2 权力 [權-] quánlì (power-strength) <n.> right: ~很大great power || 特殊~ special right || 有/没~ have/not have the right to
3 政权 [-權] zhèngquán (political-power) <n.> political power: 国家~ state power || 夺取~ usurp state power|| 反动~ reactionary regime

4 职责 [職責] zhízé (duty-obligation) <n.> duty, obligation: 光荣的~ honorable duty || 履行 (lǚxíng) ~ perform a duty || 完成~ fulfill a duty

5 责任 [責-] zérèn (obligation-responsibility) <n.> duty, responsibility: 有/没有~ have/not have duty || 负/尽~ take responsibility, be responsible || ~重大 large responsibility

6 义务 [義務] yìwù (justice-affair) <n.> duty, obligation: 有/没有~ have/not have duty || 尽/承担 (chéngdān) ~ bear responsibility || 公民的~ citizen's duty

7 任务 [-務] rènwù (responsibility-affair) <n.> assignment, mission: 完成~ complete an assignment || 一项/个~ an assignment

8 负担 [負擔] fùdān (carry on the back-shoulder) <n.> burden, load: 家庭~ household burden || ~重 heavy burden || 增加/减轻 ~ increase/reduce a burden

9 专利 [專-] zhuānlì (exclusive-advantage) <n.> patent right: 一项发明~ establish patent law || 获取 (huòqtab~ receive patent rights || ~技术 patented technology

10 权利 [權-] quánlì (right-advantage) <n.> right: 争取~ fight for the right || 有~说话 have the right of (free) speech || 批评的~ right to criticize

11 人权 [-權] rénquán (human-right) <n.> human right: 侵犯 (qīnfàn) ~ infringe upon human rights || 尊重 ~ respect human rights || ~问题 human rights issue

12 财产权 [財產權] cáichǎnquán (property-right) <n.> property rights: 掌握 (zhcáichǎn~ hold property rights || ~不可侵犯 property rights that cannot be infringed upon

13 知识产权 [-識產權] zhīshíchǎnquán (knowledge-property-right) <n.> intellectual property rights: 侵害~ impact intellectual property rights

14 民权 [-權] mínquán (civil-right) <n.> civil rights: ~自由 the right to freedom || 绝对~ absolute rights || ~运动 the Civil Rights Movement

15 自由 [-] zìyóu (self-decide) <n.> freedom, liberty: 言论~ free speech || 爱好~ freedom of hobbies || 有/没有~ have/don't have hobbies

16 主权 [-權] zhǔquán (sovereign-right) <n.> sovereign rights: 国家~ sovereign nation || 侵犯~ infringe on sovereign rights || ~平等 equality of sovereign rights

17 三权分立 [-權--] sānquánfēnlì (three-power-separately-establish) <n.> separation of the three powers: 西方的民主就是~, 多党竞选, 等等. Western democracy includes, among other features, the separation of the three powers and multiparty elections.

18 权力制衡 [權---] quánlìzhìhéng (power-check-balance) <n.> check and balances of power: 三权分立、~是美国民主制度的重要特点. The separation of the three powers and the checks and balances of power are important features of U.S. democracy.

19 女权 [-權] nǚquán (woman-right) <n.> women's rights: ~运动 women's rights movement || 提高~ raise women's rights

20 特权 [-權] tèquán (special-right) <n.> privilege: 行使~ exercise one's privileges || 享有~ share privilege || 地方~ regional privilege

21 专卖权 [專賣權] zhuānmàiquán (exclusive-sell-right) <n.> exclusive right to sell: 产品~ the right to sell goods || 烟草~ the right to sell tobacco

22 隐私权 [隱-權] yǐnsīquán (privacy-right) <n.> right of privacy: 个人~ individual privacy rights || 侵犯~ encroach on privacy rights || 保护~ protect one's privacy rights
23 肖像权 [--權] xiàoxiàngquán (portrait-right) <n.> portrait/photography rights: 侵犯~ encroach on photography rights || 保护~ protect one's portrait rights || 名人~ professional photography rights
24 所有权 [--權] suǒyǒuquán (ownership-right) <n.> proprietary right(s): 财产~ property rights || 土地~ property rights || 商品~ commodity proprietary rights
25 自主权 [--權] zìzhǔquán (self-decide-power) <n.> power to make one's own decisions: 婚姻~ the right to make the decision to marry || 活动~ the right to take action || 扩大~ increase one's personal rights

Tips:

1 权 (權, quán): Originally 权 was a kind of tree, and later, it meant 'scale' and from which evolved meanings such as 'power' and 'rights.'
2 权力 (權力, quánlì): 权力 means 'power.' To coin a phrase "民主是个好东西" (democracy is a good thing), which was once popular around 2006. The phrase "权力是个好东西" means (power is a good thing) in China, and that is why there is much 权钱交易 (quánqián jiāoyì, trading power for money) and 权色交易 (quánsèjiāoyì, trading power for sex.) Government officials are reluctant to lose their power, so 有权不使, 过期作废 (yǒuquán bùshǐ, guòqī zuòfèi,), which means 'if one has power but does not use it, it will expire anyway,' in other words, 'maximize the use of your power while you still have it.'
3 权力 vs. 权利: Both are pronounced as 'quánlì,' but 权力 means 'power' and 权利 'right.' Ordinary people do not have any administrative 权力 (power) but they have the 权利 (right) to be educated.

Exercises:

Part I: Answer the following questions in Chinese.

1 请写出你知道的关于"权利"的词

____

2 "三权分立"、"权利制衡"是哪些国家的政治制度？ (写出两个国家就可以)

____

3 有人认为中国的"人权"问题还需要改善, 你同意吗? 为什么?

____

4 在你们国家公民要承担哪些义务? (写出两个就可以)

____

5 你觉得你们国家的政权是掌握在人民手里吗? 为什么?

____

Theme 71: Military, war 军事, 战争 (jūnshì, zhànzhēng)

(See also Theme 34)

1 战争 [戰爭] zhànzhēng (battle-contend) <n.> war: 世界~ world war || 发动~ wage war || 结束~ end war

2 第一次世界大战 (一战) [------戰] Dì-yīcì Shìjiè Dàzhàn (Yīzhàn) (first-world-war) <n.> World War One: 英国在~以前是世界上最强大的国家. The United Kingdom was a mighty empire before World War I. || ~是1914年爆发的. World War I broke out in 1914.

3 第二次世界大战 (二战) [------戰] Dì-èrcì Shìjiè Dàzhàn (Èrzhàn) (second-world-war) <n.> World War Two: 1939年, ~爆发 (bàofā). World War II broke out in 1939.

4 星球大战 [---戰] xīngqiúdàzhàn (star-war) <n.> *Star Wars* 《~》是很有名的科幻电影. *Star Wars* is a famous science fiction movie.

5 内战 [-戰] nèizhàn (civil-war) <n.> civil war: 美国~ the United States Civil War || ~爆发 erupt in Civil War

6 冷战 [-戰] lěngzhàn (cold-war) <n.> the Cold War: ~时期 Cold War era || 东西方~ East to West Cold War

7 战斗 [戰鬥] zhàndòu (battle-fight) <n.> fight, battle: 一场 ~ a battle field || 投入 ~ throw (oneself, troops, etc.) into the battle

8 战术 [戰術] zhànshù (battle-tactic) <n.> military tactics: 题海~ exercises packed teaching method || 包围 ~ encircle the enemy (military tactic) || 整套~ complete set of military tactics

9 战略 [戰-] zhànlüè (war-strategy) <n.> strategy: ~目标 strategic goal || ~地位 strategic position

10 兵法 [-] bīngfǎ (military-tactic) <n.> military strategy and tactics/ art of war: 孙子~ Sun-tzu's *Art of War* (China's ancient classic on military strategy) || 古代~ ancient military tactics

11 战场 [戰場] zhànchǎng (battle-field) <n.> battlefield, battleground: 亚洲~ Asian battleground || 主要~ important battleground

12 国防 [國-] guófáng (national-defense) <n.> national defense: ~力量 national defense power || ~建设 establish a national defense || ~现代化 modernize national defense

13 军队 [軍隊] jūnduì (army-troop) <n.> armed forces: 自己的~ one's own armed forces || 现代化~ modern armed forces || 一支~ a military division

14 部队 [-隊] bùduì (unit-troop) <n.> army, armed forces: 守卫~ guard armed forces || 地方~ regional army || 维和~ armed forces to maintain social stability

15 总部 [總-] zǒngbù (general-headquarters) <n.> general headquarters: 军区~ military base headquarters || 武警~ armed police headquarters

16 队伍 [隊-] duìwǔ (troop-group) <n.> troops, ranks: 一支 ~ a division of troops || 消防~ firefighting battalion || 起义~ military revolt

17 陆军 [陸軍] lùjūn (land-force) <n.> ground (or land) force: ~基地 ground force base || 法国~ French ground force || ~部队 ground force armed troops

18 海军 [-軍] hǎijūn (sea-force) <n.> navy: 建设~ establish a navy || 强大的~ powerful navy || ~力量 naval force

19 海军陆战队 [-軍陸戰隊] (navy-land-battle-troop) <n.> marines, marine corps: 美国~有很强的战斗力. The United States Marine Corps has very high combat effectiveness.

20 空军 [-軍] kōngjūn (air-force) <n.> air force: 发展~ expand the Air Force || ~基地 Air Force base || 美国~ American Air Force

21 解放军 [--軍] jiěfàngjūn (liberate-army) <n.> liberation army: 人民~ The People's Liberation Army

22 特种兵 [-種-] tèzhǒngbīng (special-type-force) <n.> special forces: ~部队 special forces troops || 当~ become a special forces operative

23 武警 [-] wǔjǐng (armed-police) <n.> armed police: ~部队 armed police troops || ~战士 armed fighters/armed police

24 联邦调查局 [聯-調--] Liánbāngdiàochájú (federal-investigation-bureau) <n.> U.S. Federal Bureau of Investigation: ~ 抓住了这个罪犯 (zuìfàn).

25 中央情报局 [---報-] Zhōngyāngqíngbàojú (central-intelligence-bureau) <n.> U.S. Central Intelligence Agency (CIA): ~是美国最大的情报机构. The CIA is the largest intelligence agency in the United States.

26 国家安全局 [國----] Guójiā'ānquánjú (national-security-bureau) <n.> National Security Bureau (NSB) (TW)/NSA U.S.: 中国~ China National Security Agency

27 间谍 [間諜] jiàndié (spy-espionage) <n.> spy: ~活动 spying, espionage || 商业~ commerce spy || 抓捕~ catch a spy

28 退伍兵 [-] tuìwǔbīng (retired-army-soldier) <n.> soldiers retired or being discharged from active military service: 安置~ support retired military members

29 盟军 [-軍] méngjūn (allied-force) <n.> allied forces: 英美~ English-American Allied Forces

30 侵略军 [--軍] qīnlüèjūn (invade-army) <n.> invading army, aggressor troops: 日本~ Japanese Aggressors

31 战区 [戰區] (war-zone) <n.> theater command: 东部~ Eastern theater command

32 集团军 [-團軍] (group-corps) <n.> group army

33 军 [軍] jūn (encircle, army, corps) <n.> armed forces, army (consisting of two or more divisions): 红 ~ Red Army || 白~ White Army || 新四~ New Fourth Army || ~队 armed forces

34 师 [師] shī (division) <n.> troops, a division of army: 步兵~ infantry division || 正义之~ army fighting for a just cause

35 旅 [-] lǚ (brigade) <n.> brigade, troops, force: 加强~ reinforced brigade || 第二~ Second brigade

36 团 [團] tuán (round, regiment) <n.> regiment, group, organization: 野战兵团 ~ field army || 旅游~ tourist group || 芭蕾舞~ ballet troupe || 中国共青~ the Communist Youth League of China

37 营 [營] yíng (encamp, battalion) <n.> battalion, camp: 难民~ refugee camp || 夏令~ summer camp || 炮兵~ artillery battalion

38 连 [連] lián (man-drawn carriage, link, company) <n.> company: 一个营有三个~. A battalion has three companies.

39 排 [-] pái (push, platoon) <n.> platoon, volleyball team: ~长 platoon leader || 中国女~ the Chinese women's volleyball team || 中国男~ the Chinese's men's volleyball team

40 班 [-] bān (divide, squad) <n.> squad, class, team: 辅导~ tutorial class || 炊事 (chuīshì) ~ cookhouse squad, kitchen squad

Tips:

1 班 (bān): In the educational setting 班 (class) is very important. The original meaning of 班 is related to 王 (玉, yù, jade) and 刂 (刀, knife) which in combination denote 'to use a knife to divide a jade equally,' in other words, 'to divide, separate, part.' A 班 (class) is a division of students.
2 Civil War (美国内战): It is also called (美国) 南北战争.
3 孙子兵法 (Sūnzǐ Bīngfǎ): It is the *Art of War* which is valued by not only the Chinese but also the United States Military Academy, West Point.
4 *子: If a person in Chinese history was called 'surname + 子,' he must be outstanding in philosophy or a closely related field. The well-known "子" include 孔子 (Confucius,) 孟子 (Mencius,) 荀子 (Xúnzǐ,) 老子 (Lǎozǐ,) 庄子 (Zhuāngzǐ,) 墨子 (Mòzǐ,) 韩非子 (Hánfēizǐ,) 孙子 (Sūnzǐ) . . . The last one might be 朱子 (朱熹, Zhū Xī, 1130–1200.)

Exercises: Answer the following questions in Chinese.

1 写出人类历史上两次大的战争和时间

---

2 "冷战"发生在哪两个大国之间?

---

3 你觉得"星球大战"会不会发生? 为什么?

---

4 美国有哪些机构是用来保障 (bǎozhàng, protect) 国家安全的?

---

5 你们国家的军队有哪些种类?

---

6 请按照从小到大的顺序排列这些关于军队组织结构的词: 连、排、班、军、师、旅、团、营

---

7 "人民解放军"是哪个国家军队的称呼?

---

8 你们国家退伍军人的福利 (fúlì, welfare) 怎么样? 你认为国家应该照顾退伍军人吗? 为什么?

Theme 72: Economy, currency, price 经济, 货币, 价格 (jīngjì, huòbì, jiàgé)

1 经济 [經濟] jīngjì (manage-help) <n.> economy: ~基础 economic base || ~建设 economic development bonds || ~困难 economic difficult

2 计划经济 [計劃經濟] jìhuàjīngjì (planned-economy) <n.> planned economy: ~和市场经济都是发展经济的手段. A market economy and a planned economy are both means to develop the economy.

3 市场经济 [-場經濟] shìchǎngjīngjì (market-economy) <n.> market economy: 发展 ~ market economy expansion || ~体制 market economy system

4 虚拟经济 [-擬經濟] xūnǐjīngjì (virtual-economy) <n.> hypothetical/virtual economy: ~是虚拟世界中存在的经济体, 通常在互联网中交换虚拟商品. A virtual economy is an emergent economy existing in a virtual world, usually exchanging virtual goods in the context of an Internet game. || 有人认为~应该为实体经济服务. Some people think that the virtual economy should serve the real economy.

5 价值 [價-] jiàzhí (price-value) <n.> price: 实用~ practical value || 新闻~ news value || 自我~ personal value

6 价 [價] jià (price) <n.> price: 票~ ticket price || 菜~ price of vegetables || 肉~ price of meat

7 价格 [價-] jiàgé (price-specification) <n.> price: ~便宜/贵 cheap/expensive price || 市场~ market price || 提高~ price increase

8 价钱 [價錢] jiàqián (price-money) <n.> price: ~便宜/贵 cheap/expensive price || 好~ good price

9 物价 [-價] wùjià (goods-price) <n.> price of goods: ~高/低 high/low price of good || ~上涨 (shàngzhǎng) a rise in the price of goods || ~稳定 (wěndìng) stable price

10 代价 [-價] dàijià (cost-price) <n.> cost, price: 付出~ pay the price || ~高/低/大/小 high/low/large/small price || 不惜任何代价~ be ready to pay any price, at any cost

11 成本 [-] chéngběn (complete-cost) <n.> cost: ~高/低the cost is high/low || 降低/增加~ decrease/increase costs || 生产~ production costs

12 开销 [-銷] kāixiāo (pay-expense) <n.> spending, expense: 一笔 ~ an expense || 日常~ daily expenses || 住院的~ the expenses of hospitalization

13 支付 [-] zhīfù (pay out-tender) <v.> payment: ~方式 payment method || 网上~ online payment || 手机 ~ phone payment

14 银行转账 [銀-轉賬] yínhángzhuǎnzhàng (bank-account transfer) <n.> bank account transfer: 银行在线转账online bank transfer || ~五万元 bank transfer of 50,000 yuan || 怎么办理~? How do I handle a bank transfer?

15 货币 [貨幣] huòbì (goods-coin) <n.> currency: 新~ new currency || ~政策 new policy || 伪造 (wěizào) ~ counterfeit (or forged) money

16 纸币 [紙幣] zhǐbì (paper-currency) <n.> paper currency: 发行~ print currency || ~贬值 (biǎnzhí) devalue currency || 两张 ~ two bills (currency)

17 硬币 [-幣] yìngbì (hard-coin) <n.> coins: 一枚~ a coin

18 面值 [-] miànzhí (face-value) <n.> face value, par value: ~大 large face value || ~为一百元的纸币the face value of this bank note is 100 yuan.

19 外币 [-幣] wàibì (foreign-currency) <n.> foreign currency: 用~支付payment in foreign currency || ~价格foreign currency prices
20 外汇 [-匯] wàihuì (foreign-exchange) <n.> foreign exchange: ~收入 foreign exchange earnings (or income) || 换/花~ exchange currency || 一笔~ a large amount of foreign currency
21 现金 [現-] xiànjīn (cash-money) <n.> ready money, cash: 用~支付pay in cash || ~交易cash transactions || 提取~ withdraw cash
22 元 [圓] yuán (yuan) <c.> unit of money: 五~钱 five yuan

23 人民币 [--幣] rénmínbì (people's-currency) <n.> RMB – Chinese monetary unit: ~贬值RMB devaluation || 发行~ issue RMB
24 美元 [-] měiyuán (American-dollar) <n.> U.S. dollar: 换~ exchange U.S. dollars
25 欧元 [歐-] ōuyuán (European-dollar) <n.> euro: ~升值. The euro appreciated. || ~危机euro crisis
26 英镑 [-鎊] yīngbàng (English-pound) <n.> pound, sterling: ~区sterling area || ~贬值pound devaluation
27 加元 [-] jiāyuán (Canadian-dollar) <n.> Canadian dollar: ~大跌Canadian dollar plunged
28 日元 [-] rìyuán (Japanese-Yen) <n.> Japanese yen: ~价格Japanese yen price || ~兑美元yen to dollar
29 港币 [-幣] gǎngbì (Hong Kong-money) <n.> Hong Kong dollar: ~换人民币Hong Kong dollar to RMB
30 台币 [-幣] táibì (Taiwanese-money) <n.> Taiwan dollar: 新~ New Taiwan Dollar (NTD)

31 存折 [-摺] cúnzhé (deposit-booklet) <n.> bankbook: 活期~ current bank book || 银行~ bankbook || 开~ open the bankbook
32 账户 [賬-] zhànghù (account-head) <n.> account: 存款~ savings account || 支票~ checking account
33 支票 [-] zhīpiào (draw-certificate) <n.> check: 开~ write a check || 空白 ~ blank check || 一张~ a single check
34 股票 [-] gǔpiào (stock-certificate) <n.> stock: 买~ buy stocks || 炒~ speculate in shares || 发行~ issue stocks
35 保险 [-險] bǎoxiǎn (insure-risk) <n.> insurance: 医疗~ health insurance || 养老~ elderly insurance || 房屋~ house insurance
36 基金 [-] jījīn (reserve-money) <n.> fund: 教育~ education fund || 住房~ housing fund || 保险~ insurance fund
37 虚拟货币 [-擬貨幣] xūnǐhuòbì (virtual-money) <n.> cyber currency: ~交易virtual currency trading || 发行~ issue cyber money
38 比特币 [--幣] bǐtèbì (bit-coin) <n.> bitcoin (virtual currency): ~交易bitcoin trading || ~兑换bitcoin exchange

39 券 [-] quàn (deed, ticket, certificate) <n.> certificate, ticket: 优惠 (yōuhuì) ~ preferential/favorable ticket || 购物~ certificate of purchase
40 食品券 [-] shípǐnquàn (food-certificate) <n.> food coupon, food stamp: 美国穷人可以每月从政府领取~. Poor people in the U.S. can collect food stamps from the government every month.
41 代金券 [-] dàijīnquàn (substitute-money-certificate) <n.> cash equivalent ticket: 银行~ a bank note || 购物 ~ a note for purchase || 一张~ a cash equivalent ticket

Tips:

1 经济 (經濟, jīngjì): 经济 means 'economy.' It seems this word was borrowed from Japanese, however, the Japanese coined this term based on an original Chinese expression, 经世济民 (經世濟民, jīngshì jìmín) which means 'to manage/govern the world/society and to help/aid the people.' "济民" is the goal of "经世."
2 币 (幣, bì): When 币 is mentioned, people will think of 'coin' in their minds, however, the original meaning of 币 (幣) was silk since it is related to 巾 which means 'cloth, silk.' From 'silk,' 币 (幣) evolved meanings such as 'present,' 'property' and then the current 'coin, money.'
3 股 (gǔ) and 股票 (gǔpiào): 股 means 'thigh' which has a connotation of 'strong.' 股 is widely used in business world, such as 股东 (shareholder,) 入股 (become a shareholder,) 股票 (stock,) 股市 (stock market) and 股价 (stock price).

Exercises:

Part I: Answer the following questions in Chinese.

1 请写出你所知道的外币

---

2 在你们国家使用手机支付的人多不多?

---

3 支票和现金, 哪个你使用的比较多?

---

4 你们国家大城市的物件怎么样? 生活成本高不高?

---

5 你们国家老百姓的投资方式一般有哪些? 你觉得哪种比较安全、稳定?

---

6 在你们国家政府是否给穷人发放食品券? 为什么?

---

7 你觉得比特币是不是虚拟货币? 比特币能不能取代政府发行的货币?

Theme 73: Tax, business transactions 税, 账目 (shuì, zhàngmù)

1 资金 [資-] zījīn (fund-money) <n.> fund: 需要~ require funds || 投入~ invest in a fund || ~不足 not have enough funds
2 外资 [-資] wàizī (foreign-capital) <n.> foreign capital: 引进~ introduce foreign capital || 利用~ take advantage of foreign capital || ~银行 foreign capital bank

3 公款 [-] gōngkuǎn (public-money) <n.> government money: ~吃喝 consume using government money || 挪用 (nuóyòng) ~ misuse of government money || ~旅游 go traveling using government money
4 货款 [貨-] huòkuǎn (goods-money) <n.> payment for goods: 支付~ pay money for buying or selling goods || 收取~ charge money for selling goods || 拖欠~ fall behind to pay money for goods
5 汇款 [匯-] huìkuǎn (remit-money) <n./v.> remittance, remit: 一笔~ a remittance || 收到~ receive the remittance
6 钱 [錢] qián (copper coin, money) <n.> money: 一笔~ a sum of money || 付~ pay for it
7 收入 [-] shōurù (collect-income) <n.> income: 增加~ Increase Income || 家庭~ family income || 没有~ no income
8 巨款 [-] jùkuǎn (vast-sums) <n.> vast sums: 一笔~ a colossal sum of money || 花费~ spend immense sums of money
9 赔款 [賠-] péikuǎn (compensate-money) <n./v.> pay an indemnity, indemnity, reparations: 保险~ Insurance Claim || 巨额 (jù'é) ~ large amount of indemnity || 战争~ reparations of war
10 专款 [專-] zhuānkuǎn (special-fund) <n.> special fund: ~专用 special fund for special purpose || ~支出 special fund disbursement || 教育~ education special fund

11 财产 [財產] cáichǎn (money-property) <n.> property: 公共~ public property || 个人~ private property || 国家~ state property
12 财富 [財-] cáifù (money-wealth) <n.> wealth: 物质~ materialistic wealth || 精神~ spiritual wealth || 创造~ create wealth
13 金钱 [-錢] jīnqián (gold-money) <n.> money: 花费 ~ spend money || 崇拜 (chóngbài) ~ worship money || ~交易 monetary exchange
14 存款 [-] cúnkuǎn (deposit-money) <n.> deposit: 一笔~ a deposit || 定期~ time deposit || 活期 demand deposit
15 贷款 [貸-] dàikuǎn (loan-money) <n.> loan: 银行~ bank loan || 一笔~ a loan || 还~ pay the loan
16 捐款 [-] juānkuǎn (donate-money) <n.> donate: 一笔~ donate remittance || 很多~ donate a lot || 各项~ all types of donations
17 利 [-] lì (sharp, quick, advantage) <n.> advantage: 有~ (可图) profitable || ~大于弊the advantages far outweigh the disadvantages
18 利润 [-潤] lìrùn (profit-payment) <n.> profit: 获得 ~ gaining of profit || ~低 low profit || 纯~ pure profit
19 利息 [-] lìxī (profit-interest) <n.> interest: 存款 ~ deposit interest rates || ~高 high interest rates || 付~ pay interest
20 收益 [-] shōuyì (gain-benefit) <n.> earnings: 经济~ economical earnings || 合法 ~ legal earnings || 取得~ obtain the benefits

21 税 [-] shuì (tallage, tax) <n.> tax: 收~ collect taxes || 交~ pay taxes || 房地产 ~ real estate tax
22 遗产税 [遺產-] yíchǎnshuì (inheritance-tax) <n.> inheritance tax: 交~ pay inheritance tax || 征收 (zhēngshōu) ~ collect inheritance tax
23 财产税 [財產-] cáichǎnshuì (property-tax) <n.> property tax: 提高~ raise property taxes
24 房产税 [-產-] fángchǎnshuì (real estate-tax) <n.> real estate tax: 交~ pay property tax || 征收~ collect property tax

25 个人所得税 [個----] gèrénsuǒdéshuì (individual income-tax) <n.> individual income tax: 征收~ collect individual income tax || 交纳 (jiāonà) ~ pay individual income tax

26 消费税 [-費-] xiāofèishuì (consumption-tax) <n.> the consumption tax: 交~ pay the consumption tax

Tips:

1 款 (kuǎn): The main meanings of 款 are (1) 'money,' for example 贷款 (dàikuǎn, loan,) (2) 'form, style,' for example 款式 (kuǎnshì, style,) (3) 'signed name,' for example 落款 (luòkuǎn, sign one's name.) However, the original meaning of 款 is 'sincere,' which is still kept in words such as 款待 (kuǎndài), which means 'to treat cordially.'

2 税 (shuì): It means 'tax.' Benjamin Franklin said there were only two things certain in life: death (死, sǐ) and taxes (税, shuì.) Compared to European countries and the United States, China has a much lower tax rate, however, this situation is changing and China will inevitably raise tax rates and levy new taxes.

Exercises:

Part I: Use the given bound form as a guide to help you think of other words with the same character. Feel free to use your dictionary when needed. Then write down the English definition of each of the words you've written.

款 (sum of money, fund): 贷款 loan

____

____

____

____

____

____

税 (tax): 消费税 consumption tax

____

____

____

____

____

____

Part II: Part II: Read the following sentences and fill in each blank with the appropriate word or phrase from the options given.

财产、外资、财富、利润、利息、资金、收入

1 从上世纪80年代开始中国开始引进________, 吸引外国投资者. 他们给中国带来大量_________, 促进了经济快速发展, 但同时也产生了很多环境污染问题.
2 据报道美国90%的_________只掌握在1%的华尔街富人手里.
3 美国宪法规定保护公民的私有_________.
4 现在工业产品的_________越来越低, 但是银行贷款的_________却越来越高, 所以很多投资者不愿意投资工业.
5 美国的中产阶级近十年来________停止了增长, 这意味着他们的生活水平并没有提高.

Theme 74: Income, expense, cost 收入, 花费 (shōurù, huāfèi)

1 收入 [-] shōurù (receive-income) <n.> income: 个人~ individual income || 家庭~ family income || 国民~ national income
2 薪水 [-] xīnshuǐ (firewood-water) <n.> salary, payroll: 一份~ a salary || 领~ receive a salary || ~低/高 low/high salary
3 工资 [-資] gōngzī (work-money) <n.> salary, (monthly) payment: 高/低~ high salary/low salary || 教师~ teacher salary || 拿~ get salary
4 补贴 [補貼] bǔtiē (supplement-subsidize) <n.> subsidy: 得到~ receive subsidies || 高温~ high-temperature subsidy || 住房~ subsidized housing
5 福利 [-] fúlì (fortune-benefit) <n.> welfare: 社会~ social welfare || 职工~ employee welfare || ~好 good welfare
6 奖金 [獎-] jiǎngjīn (reward-money) <n.> bonus, prize money: 诺贝尔~ Nobel Prize money || 获得/拿到~ receive prize money/a bonus || 一笔~ a bonus
7 奖学金 [獎學-] jiǎngxuéjīn (award-study-money) <n.> scholarship: 得到~ receive a scholarship || 全额 (quán'é) ~ full scholarship || 提供~ offer a scholarship
8 费 [費] fèi (money, cost) <n.> expense: 活动~ activity expense || 广告~ advertising expense || 办公~ office expense || 水电~ utility expense || 手机~ cell phone expense || 电话~ telephone expense
9 费用 [費-] fèiyòng (cost-expense) <n.> expense, cost: 生活~ living expense || ~低/高high/low expense (or cost) || 一笔~ a fee
10 学费 [學費] xuéfèi (study-cost) <n.> tuition: 交/付~ pay tuition || 收~ collect tuition || 一笔~ tuition
11 经费 [經費] jīngfèi (routine-expense) <n.> funding: 教育~ education funding || ~不多low funding || 增加~ increase funding
12 预算 [-] yùsuàn (pre-calculation) <n.> budget: 家庭~ family budget || 超过~ exceed the budget || 全部~ the entire budget

13 开支 [開支] kāizhī (expense-payment) <n.> spending: 家庭~ family spending || 增加~ increase spending || 节省~ save spending

14 生活费 [--費] shēnghuófèi (live-expense) <n.> living expenses: 人均~ per capita living expenses || 一个月~ monthly living expenses || 提供~ provide living expenses

15 房租 [-] fángzū (house-rent) <n.> rent: 交~ pay the rent || ~收入rental income || 三个月的~ rent for three months

16 租金 [-] zūjīn (rent-money) <n.> rent: 收/交~ collect/pay the rent || ~高/低 high/low rent || 住房~ housing rent

17 罚金 [罰-] fájīn (punishment-money) <n.> fine: 交~ pay the fine || 扣 (kòu) ~ collect the fine || 处以~ impose a fine

18 手续费 [-續費] shǒuxùfèi (procedure-charge) <n.> commission charges: 收/交~ receive/pay commission charges || 收取/缴纳 (jireceiv~ receive/pay commission charges

19 小费 [-費] xiǎofèi (petty-expense) <n.> tip: 给~ give a tip || ~高high tip || 一笔~ a tip

20 红利 [紅-] hónglì (auspicious-profit) <n> dividend: 分~ pay dividends || 股份 ~ stock dividend || 拿~ receive dividends

21 股份 [-] gǔfèn (stock-share) <n> stock/share: ~公司 joint-stock company || 获得~ acquire shares/stocks || ~制度 (zhìdù) shareholding system

22 报酬 [報-] bàochóu (return-reward) <n> returns: 得到~ get returns || 劳动~ returns to labor || ~低returns are low

23 待遇 [-] dàiyù (treat-treat) <n> treatment: ~好good treatment || 同等 ~ equal treatment || 不平等的~ unequal treatment

24 外快 [-] wàikuài (outside-earning) <n> extra gains/extra money: 捞~ make extra gains/money || 赚~ earn extra gains/money || 挣~ earn extra gains/money

25 自费 [-費] zìfèi (own-expense) <n.> self-financing/at one's own expense: ~留学 study abroad at one's own expense || ~购买to buy with one's own money || ~旅游travel at one's own expense

26 公费 [-費] gōngfèi (public-expense) <n.> at public expense: ~留学study abroad at public expense || ~旅游to travel at public expense

27 收费 [-費] shōufèi (collect-fee) <n> charge: ~标准 fee standard || ~合理 reasonable charge || ~多 high charge

28 零花钱 [--錢] línghuāqián (incidental-expense-money) <n.> allowance: 给~ give allowance || ~不多low allowance

Tips:

1 费 (費, fèi): 费 is a key character in this unit. It means 'to cost, to spend, expense' since it is related to 贝 (money.)

2 Why did the Chinese once ask others about their income? In the era of the planned economy, the people's income disparity was not large at all, so people asked about others' income and would then comment for a little while. Nowadays, income disparity is sky-rocketing. A poor worker's annual income may be less than one hour's or even one minute's worth of a rich businessman's earnings. Who wants to lose face?

Exercises:

Part I: Use the given bound form as a guide to help you think of other words with the same character. Feel free to use your dictionary when needed. Then write down the English definition of each of the words you've written.

费 (expense): 学费 tuition

____

____

____

____

____

____

____

Part II: Multiple Choice. Make sure to choose the most appropriate answer.

1 小张是个热心人, 常常帮助别人, 不计任何________.
A. 外快 B. 报酬 C. 奖金

2 这家公司的________非常好, 员工的收入包括: 工资、三餐______和年底_______.
A. 待遇、补贴、红利 B. 红利、待遇、补贴 C. 补贴、待遇、红利

3 如果政府的总______超过了______, 政府就因为没有钱办公而关门.
A. 收入、开支 B. 开支、预算 C. 收入、预算

4 小李下班后常常到别的公司打工, 来挣点儿________.
A. 外快 B. 罚款 C. 福利

5 小李因为开车超速, 被警察________了.
A. 租金 B. 罚款 C. 预算

6 所谓的"大股东"就是占有公司________非常多的人.
A. 股份 B. 手续费 C. 薪水

7 美国的服务行业一般都要收取_________, 表示客人对他们服务的认可.
A. 零花钱 B. 小费 C. 收费

8 美国孩子会通过做家务或者帮邻居干活的方式赚取 (zhuànqǔ, earn) _______.
A. 生活费 B. 收入 C. 零花钱

Theme 75: Factories, stores, shops 工厂, 店铺 (gōngchǎng, diànpù)

1 厂 [廠] chǎng (plant, factory) <n.> plant/mill: 造纸~ paper mill || ~长plant/mill manager
2 工厂 [-廠] gōngchǎng (work-factory) <n.> factory: 办~ run a factory
3 厂商 [廠-] chǎngshāng (factory-businessman) <n.> manufacturer/firm: 外国~ foreign firm/manufacturer || 生产~ manufacturer/producer
4 市场 [-場] shìchǎng (market-place) <n.> market: 国内/国外~ domestic/international market || 有/没有~ there is/is not a market || 图书~ book market
5 商场 [-場] shāngchǎng (business-place) <n.> mall: 大~ big mall || 百货~ shopping mall || 一家~ a mall
6 商城 [-] shāngchéng (business-city) <n.> mall: 网上~ online mall || 家电~ appliance mall || 一座~ a mall
7 店 [-] diàn (store) <n.> store: 书~ book store || 网~ online store || 分/总~ branch/head office, branch/main store
8 商店 [-] shāngdiàn (business-store) <n.> shop/store: 大型/小型~ large/small shop/store || 食品~ food shop/store
9 酒店 [-] jiǔdiàn (liquor-hotel) <n.> hotel: 住~ stay at a hotel
10 超市 [-] chāoshì (super-market) <n.> supermarket: 逛 (guàng) ~ shop at a supermarket
11 宾馆 [賓館] bīnguǎn (guest-house) <n.> hotel: 住~ stay at a hotel || 大~ big hotel
12 旅店 [旅-] lǚdiàn (travel-hotel) <n.> inn: 住~ stay at an inn
13 旅馆 [旅館] lǚguǎn (travel-house) <n.> tavern: 住~ stay at a tavern || 小~ a small tavern

14 食堂 [-] shítáng (dine-hall) <n.> dining hall: 大/小~ large/small dining hall || 吃 ~ eat at a dining hall
15 餐厅 [-廳] cāntīng (eat-hall) <n.> restaurant: 室内~ indoor restaurant
16 餐馆 [-館] cānguǎn (eat-house) <n.> restaurant/cafeteria: 中/西~ a Chinese/Western restaurant/cafeteria
17 饭馆 [飯館] fànguǎn (food-house) <n.> restaurant: 吃~ eat at a restaurant
18 饭店 [飯-] fàndiàn (food-store) <n.> restaurant: 开~ open a restaurant

19 银行 [銀-] yínháng (silver-firm) <n.> bank
20 华尔街 [華爾-] huá'ěrjiē (transliteration-street) <n.> Wall Street

21 诊所 [診-] zhěnsuǒ (diagnose-place) <n.> clinic: 开~ open a clinic || 口腔~ dental clinic
22 药店 [藥-] yàodiàn (medicine-store) <n.> pharmacy: 开~ open a pharmacy
23 书店 [書-] shūdiàn (book-store) <n.> bookstore: 开~ open a bookstore || 逛~ shop at a bookstore
24 咖啡店 [-] kāfēidiàn (coffee-store) <n.> cafe
25 茶馆 [-館] cháguǎn (tea-house) <n.> teahouse
26 小吃店 [-] xiǎochīdiàn (snack-store) <n.> snack bar
27 甜品店 [-] tiánpǐndiàn (sweet-stuff-store) <n.> dessert shop
28 蛋糕店 [-] dàngāodiàn (cake-store) <n.> cake shop
29 花店 [-] huādiàn (flower-store) <n.> florist (shop)

30 美发厅 [-髮廳] měifàtīng (beautify-hair-hall) <n.> hairdressing salon:
31 按摩店 [-] ànmódiàn (massage-store) <n.> massage parlor
32 黑市 [-] hēishì (black-market) <n.> black market: ~ 买卖black market business
33 大卖场 [-賣場] dàmàichǎng (huge-sell-place) <n.> hypermarket, large warehouse-like self-service retail store: 手机~ phone hypermarket || 水果~ fruit hypermarket
34 小卖部 [-賣-] xiǎomàibù (small-sell-area) <n.> small shop attached to a school, factory, theater, etc. (selling cigarettes, confectionery, cold drinks, etc.): 开~ open a small shop
35 便利店 [-] biànlìdiàn (convenient-store) <n.> convenience store: (used in Taiwan) 24小时~24-hour convenience store
36 夜市 [-] yèshì (night-market) <n.> night market: 逛~ shop at a night market
37 地摊 [-攤] dìtān (ground-vendor) <n.> street vendor: 摆~ start a street vendor

Tips:

1 Measure word 家 (jiā): Generally all shops, stores, restaurants, hotels share the same measure word '家' since they need people to manage it.
2 Head of a store or a shop: Before he or she was called 经理 (jīnglǐ, manager) but now is usually called 店长 (diànzhǎng, head of the store/shop.)
3 老字号 (lǎozìhào): It is 'time-honored brand.' By 2017, there were altogether 1,128 of these 中华老字号 (Chinese time-honored brands) in China, mainly in industries such as foods, traditional medicines and restaurants, with a history of 160 years on average.

Exercises:

Part I: Answer the following questions in Chinese.

1 你家附近有没有餐馆、咖啡馆和茶馆? 有没有24小时便利店? 为什么?

---

2 你家附近有没有美发厅或者按摩店?

---

3 你家离诊所或者药店近不近?

---

4 你家附近有没有银行和书店?

---

5 在美国你逛过夜市或者早市吗?

---

6 你学校餐厅的饭菜怎么样?

Theme 76: Culture, subjects 文明, 学科 (wénmíng, xuékē)

1 文明 [-] wénmíng (culture-enlightenment) <n.> civilization: 现代~ modern civilization || 物质~ material civilization || 东方/西方~ Eastern/Western civilization

2 文化 [-] wénhuà (culture-civilize) <n.> culture: 东方/西方~ Eastern/Western culture || 传统~ traditional culture || 有/没有~ be cultured/to be uncultured

3 科学 [-學] kēxué (measurement-knowledge) <n.& adj.> science: 自然~ natural science || 社会~ social science || 现代~ modern science

4 知识 [-識] zhīshí (know-experience) <n.> knowledge: 有/没有~ have/lack knowledge || 历史/科学/地理~ historical/scientific/geographical knowledge || 学~ learn knowledge

5 常识 [-識] chángshí (common-knowledge) <n.> common sense: 基本~ basic common sense || 卫生~ common sense of hygiene || 生活~ common sense of life

6 理论 [-論] lǐlùn (treatment-argument) <n.> theory: 法学~ legal theory || 重大~ significant theory || ~基础 (jīchǔ) theoretical basis

7 学术 [學術] xuéshù (study-skill) <n.> academics: ~研究 academic research || ~自由 academic freedom || ~观点 academic viewpoint

8 学问 [學問] xuéwèn (study-ask) <n.> learning/knowledge: 一门~ a branch of knowledge/study || 古老的~ ancient wisdoms || 有/没~ be learned/unlearned

9 学科 [學-] xuékē (study-subject) <n.> subject/discipline: 专门~ specialized subject/discipline || 独立的~ independent subject/discipline || 分支~ branch

10 人文科学 [---學] rénwénkēxué (humanity-science) <n.> humanities: ~通常包括语言、文学、历史、哲学等学科. Humanities usually include languages, literature, history, philosophy and other disciplines.

11 社会科学 [-會-學] shèhuìkēxué (social-science) <n.> social sciences

12 自然科学 [---學] zìránkēxué (nature-science) <n.> natural sciences

13 生命科学 [---學] shēngmìngkēxué (life-science) <n.> life sciences

14 数学 [數學] shùxué (calculation-subject) <n.> mathematics

15 物理 [-] wùlǐ (thing-law) <n.> physics

16 化学 [-學] huàxué (change-subject) <n.> chemistry

17 生物 [-] shēngwù (live-thing) <n.> biology

18 神学 [-學] shénxué (god-subject) <n.> theology

19 哲学 [-學] zhéxué (wise-subject) <n.> philosophy

20 人类学 [-類學] rénlèixué (man-kind-subject) <n.> anthropology

21 社会学 [-會學] shèhuìxué (society-subject) <n.> sociology

22 经济学 [經濟學] jīngjìxué (economy-subject) <n.> economics: 宏观 (hóngguān) ~ macroeconomics || 微观~ microeconomics || 政治~ political economy

23 心理学 [--學] xīnlǐxué (psychology-subject) <n.> psychology

24 语言学 [語-學] yǔyánxué (language-subject) <n.> linguistics

Tips:

1 学 (學, xué): In the oracle forms 學 did not have the 子 which was added to the bronze forms. The origin of 學 is controversial, but two points are agreed.

One is that it is related to 宀 (a house,) and the other is 'two hands.' Thus, we can infer that 學 should be related to an action happening with two hands in a house. When the 子 (child) was added, the meaning of 學 became clear. It is 'to learn.'

2 What did Confucius teach his disciples? Confucius taught his disciples 六艺 (Six Arts) which includes 'Rites (禮/礼, lǐ,) Music (樂/乐, yuè,) Archery (射, shè,) Charioteering (御, yù,) Calligraphy (書/书, shū) and Mathematics (數/数, shù.)'

3 What is more important, studying or something else? At the beginning of 改革开放 (Chinese economic reform,) there was a saying, which inspired a few generations. It is"'学好数理化, 走遍天下都不怕" (xuéhǎo shùlǐhuà, zǒubiàn tiānxià dōu búpà), which means 'as long as you learned mathematics, physics and chemistry well, you can survive anywhere under the heavens.' Now this saying is extinct and replaced by "拼爹" (pīndiē, literally 'to compete daddies'), which means 'competition of family background' or 'wealth over work.'

Exercises:

Part I: Answer the following questions in Chinese.

1 一般的美国大学会开设哪些专业?

___

2 你喜欢学习自然科学还是社会科学? 为什么?

___

3 你觉得西方文明比东方文明先进吗? 为什么?

___

4 你觉得东方文化跟西方文化有没有共同点?

___

5 有人说"知识就是力量" (by Francis Bacon), 你同意这种说法吗? 为什么?

___

Theme 77: Education 教育 (jiàoyù)

(See also Theme 158)

1 教育 [-] jiàoyù (teach-educate) <n.> education: 免费~ free education || 正面~ positive education || 大学/中学/小学~ college/middle school/elementary school education

2 学科 [學-] xuékē (study-subject) <n.> discipline: 一门~ a discipline || 独立的~ independent discipline || 分支~ branch

3 专业 [專業] zhuānyè (special-profession) <n.> major: 计算机~ computer science major || 建筑 (jiànzhù) ~ architecture major

4 研究所 [-] yánjīusu (research-institute) <n.> research institute: 动物~ animal research institute

5 学校 [學-] xuéxiào (study-school) <n.> school, institution: 高等~ institution of higher learning || 公立~ public school || 私立~ private school

6 大学 [-學] dàxué (major-subject) <n.> college, university: 上~ go to college/university || 重点~ important university || ~毕业graduate from college/university

7 专科 [專-] zhuānkē (specialized-subject) <n.> college for professional training: ~学校 school or college for vocational training

8 本科 [-] běnkē (regular-subject) <n.> undergraduate: 大学~ undergraduate college || ~毕业 graduate with a bachelors degree || 读~ study as an undergraduate

9 中小学 [--學] zhōngxiǎoxu (middle-elementary-school) <n.> elementary/middle school: ~教育elementary/middle education

10 中学 [-學] zhōngxué (middle-school) <n.> middle school: 上~ go to middle school || ~毕业graduate from middle school

11 高中 [-] gāozhōng (high-middle school) <n.> high school: 考~ apply to high school || 普通~ a regular high school || ~毕业 graduate from high school

12 初中 [-] chūzhōng (junior-middle school) <n.> junior high school: 读~ study in a junior high school || ~学生junior high school student || ~二年级second grade in junior high school

13 小学 [-學] xiǎoxué (minor-subject) <n.> elementary school: 上~ go to elementary school || 读~ study in elementary school || 教~ teach in elementary school

14 幼儿园 [-兒園] yòu'éryuán (kid-garden) <n.> kindergarten: 上/去~ go to kindergarten || 私人~ private kindergarten

15 托儿所 [-兒-] tuō'érsuǒ (entrust-child-place) <n.> nursery/childcare center: 上~ go to nursery || 办~ establish a nursery

16 学院 [學-] xuéyuàn (study-institute) <n.> college: 美术~ art college || 女子~ girls' college || 成立~ found a college

17 文理学院 [--學-] wénlǐxuéyuàn (arts-science-college) <n.> liberal arts college, School of Arts and Sciences (in a university): ~一般都比较小, 但是教学质量非常高. The liberal arts colleges in the United States are generally small, but the teaching quality is very high.

18 医学院 [醫學-] yīxuéyuàn (medical-school) <n.> medical school

19 法学院 [-學-] fǎxuéyuàn (law-school) <n.> law school

20 神学院 [-學-] shénxuéyuàn (theology-school) <n.> divinity school

21 商学院 [-學-] shāngxuéyuàn (business-school) <n.> business school

22 社区大学 [-區-學] shèqūdàxué (community-college) <n.> community college

23 职业技术学院 [職業-學] zhíyèjìshùdàxué (professional-college) <n.> vocational and technical college || 中国的~一般培养学生的工作技能. China's vocational and technical colleges generally develop students' work skills.

24 系 [-] xì (department) <n.> department: 历史~ Department of History || 经济~ Department of Economics

25 年级 [-級] niánjí (school year-grade) <n.> grade: 低/高~ lower/higher grade || 一/二/三/四~ first/second/third/fourth grade

26 班级 [-級] bānjí (class-grade) <n.> class: 先进~ advanced class || ~活动class activity

27 培训班 [-訓-] péixùnbān (train-class) <n.> training class: 办~ start a training class || 职业~ professional training class

28 课 [課] kè (class, course) <n.> class: 汉语~ chinese class || 上/下~ go to/leave class || 第三~ the third class

29 课程 [課-] kèchéng (subject-course) <n.> course: 七门~ seven courses || 必修/选修~ required/elective course || 专业~ professional course

30 课堂 [課-] kètáng (class-room) <n.> classroom: 大学~ college classroom || ~学习classroom learning || 走出~ walk out of a classroom

31 练习 [練習] liànxí (practice-study) <n.> practice, exercise: 做~ do exercises || 听说~ listening and speaking practice || 动作~ practice the moves

32 作业 [-業] zuòyè (do-work) <n.> homework: 家庭~ homework || 课堂~ schoolwork || 做~ do homework

33 功课 [-課] gōngkè (work-class) <n.> homework

34 高考 [-] gāokǎo (advanced-examination) <n.> college entrance exam: 参加~ take the college entrance exam || 成人~ the college entrance exam for adults

35 试卷 [試-] shìjuàn (test-paper) <n.> test paper: 一份/张/套~ a piece of test paper || 发~ distribute the test papers || 交~ hand in the test papers

36 试题 [試題] shìtí (test-question) <n.> problem: 一道/个~ a problem || 出~ make up a problem || 做~ work on a problem

37 考题 [-題] kǎotí (examination-question) <n.> test problem: 出~ make up a test problem || 数学~ math test problem || 三道/个~ three test problems

38 答案 [-] dá'àn (answer-question) <n.> answer keys, answer: 找到~ find an answer || 正确/错误~ correct/false answer

Tips:

1 小学 and 大学: Nowadays, they mean 'elementary school' and 'college/university,' but in ancient China, 小学 was a subject area on the form, phonology and meaning of characters, while 大学 was meant to make people civilized. Poetry, history, rites and music were subjects in 大学.

2 Graduate school: It is called 研究生院 (yánjiūshēngyuàn) in mainland China and 研究所 (yánjiūsuǒ) in Taiwan.

3 考试 (kǎoshì, examination): Many Westerners criticize Chinese examinations, in both the ancient (the Chinese Imperial Examinations, 科举, kējǔ) and the contemporary (高考, the College Entrance Examinations) times. Actually all Chinese examinations were based on merit, which gave young people of lower classes an opportunity to change their own fate and those of their direct and indirect families. This was the greatest justice that lower class people could enjoy. It could be highly possible that you would not have been able to read this book if there were no 高考 in China since the initiator of this book might be hoeing the land in a rural village in China now.

4 所: 所is a general measure word for schools, institutions and colleges.

Exercises:

Part I: Translate the following phrases into English

Liberal arts college ____________________
Law school ____________________
Medical school ____________________
Teachers college ____________________
Divinity school ____________________
College entrance exam ____________________

Part II: Read the following words and then answer the questions.

托儿所、幼儿园、中学、小学、大学、研究所、社区大学、职业学校、培训班、本科、专科、博士、硕士、系、年级、课程

1 "托儿所、幼儿园、中学、小学、大学、研究所," 请按照受教育程度从低到高的顺序排列这些词

____

2 "本科、专科、博士、硕士," 请按照学历从低到高的顺序排列这些词

____

3 你们国家有没有社区大学? 如果有学费高不高?

____

4 在你们国家选择上职业学校的学生多不多?

____

5 你现在的学校大概有多少个系? 你们学校大概开设了多少门课程?

____

6 你参加过课外活动培训班吗? 是学什么的?

____

Theme 78: Language 语言 (yǔyán)

1 文字 [-] wénzì (simple character-compound character) <n.> character: 古~ ancient character || 拼音~ pinyin || 古埃及 (Āijí) ~ ancient Egyptian writing
2 字母 [-] zìmǔ (letter-origin) <n.> letter: 拉丁 ~ Latin letter || 英语~ English letter
3 汉字 [漢-] hànzì (Chinese-character) <n.> Chinese character: 写 ~ write Chinese characters || 常用~ commonly used Chinese characters
4 字 [-] zì (character) <n.> character: 汉~ Chinese character || 写~ write a character
5 词 [詞] cí (word) <n.> word: 时间~ words denoting time || 新/旧~ new/old word

6 词语 [詞語] cíyǔ (word-phrase) <n.> word: 常用~ commonly used words || 外来~ loan words

7 词汇 [詞匯] cíhuì (word-collection) <n.> vocabulary: ~表vocabulary list || 专业~ professional vocabulary || 基本~ basic vocabulary

8 语法 [語法] yǔfǎ (language-rule) <n.> grammar: 汉语~ chinese grammar || ~结构grammatical structure || ~意义grammatical significance

9 话 [話] huà (speech) <n.> words/sentence/paragraph: 一句/段 (duàn) ~ a sentence/a paragraph || 他说的~ his words || 鼓励 (gǔlì) 的~ encouraging words

10 语音 [語-] yǔyīn (language-sound) <n.> speech sound: ~变化change in speech sounds || 标准~ standard speech sound

11 语调 [語調] yǔdiào (language-melody) <n.> intonation: ~低沉 deep tones || 丰富的~ rich tones || 清晰 (qīngxī) 的~ clear tones

12 声调 [聲調] shēngdiào (sound-tone) <n.> tone: 汉语普通话有四个~. There are four tones in Mandarin. || 方言 ~ tones of a dialect || 提高~ raise one's voice

13 句子 [-] jùzi (sentence-*suffix*) <n.> sentence: 短/长~ short/long sentence

14 段落 [-] duànluò (section-stop) <n.> paragraph: 划分 (huàfēn) ~ divide into paragraphs

15 篇章 [-] piānzhāng (piece-chapter) <n.> chapter: 新~ new chapter || 感人的~ touching chapters

16 语气 [語氣] yǔqì (speak-manner) <n.> tone: 加强~ strengthen the tone || ~友好friendly tone || 激动 (jīdòng) 的~ excited tone

17 书法 [書-] shūfǎ (script-method) <n.> calligraphy: 练~ practice calligraphy || 写~ write calligraphy || 爱好 ~ love calligraphy

18 手写体 [-寫體] shǒuxiětǐ (hand-write-style) <n.> handwriting: 通用的~ common handwriting || 漂亮的~ pretty handwriting

19 草书 [-書] cǎoshū (cursive-script) <n.> cursive: 写~ write cursive

20 楷书 [-書] kǎishū (regular-script) <n.> regular script

21 印刷体 [--體] yìnshuātǐ (print-style) <n.> printed style: 书写有手写体和~两种形式. There are two written forms, the cursive and the printed.

22 书面语 [書-語] shūmiànyǔ (written-language) <n.> written language: ~色彩written language flavor || ~形式 form of written language

23 口语 [-語] kǒuyǔ (oral-language) <n.> spoken language: 日常~ words and expressions for everyday use || 练习 ~ practice oral expression || ~表达能力ability in oral expression

24 俚语 [-語] lǐyǔ (rustic-language) <n.> slang: 常用的~ common slang || 英语 ~ english slang

25 成语 [-語] chéngyǔ (fixed-language) <n.> idiom: 两条~ two idioms || 用~ use an idiom

26 俗语 [-語] súyǔ (folk-language) <n.> common saying: 咱们还是一步步来吧. ~说得好, 贪多嚼不烂. Let's take things a step at a time. You know what they say. If you run after two hares you will catch neither.

27 谚语 [諺語] yànyǔ (proverb-language) <n.> proverb: ~说: 早起的鸟儿有食吃. As the saying goes: the early bird catches the worm.

28 语言 [語-] yǔyán (language-speech) <n.> language: 口头/书面~ oral/written language || 网络~ internet language

29 母语 [-語] mǔyǔ (mother-language) <n.> mother tongue: 汉语是他的~. Chinese is his native language.

30 外语 [-語] wàiyǔ (foreign-language) <n.> foreign language: 学/说~ study foreign language || ~课 foreign language class || 懂~ know a foreign language

31 英文 [-] yīngwén (English-script) <n.> English: ~名字English name || ~字母English letter || ~报English newspaper

32 英语 [-語] yīngyǔ (English-language) <n.> English: 说/讲~ speak English || ~新闻English news || ~热English mania

33 德语 [-語] déyǔ (Germany-language) <n.> German: 说~ speak German || 用~ use German

34 法语 [-語] fǎyǔ (France-language) <n.> French: 讲~ speak French || 听~ listen to French || ~电影French movie

35 西班牙语 [---語] xībānyáyǔ (Spain-language) <n.> Spanish: 说~ speak Spanish || 学~ learn Spanish || 讲~ speak Spanish

36 日语 [-語] rìyǔ (Japan-language) <n.> Japanese: 说~ speak Japanese || 学~ study Japanese || 讲~ speak Japanese

37 俄语 [-語] é'yǔ (Russia-language) <n.> Russian

38 阿拉伯语 [---語] ālābóyǔ (Arab-language) <n.> Arabic

39 双语 [雙語] shuāngyǔ (bi-language) <adj.> bilingual: ~儿童a bilingual child || ~国家bilingual country

40 汉语 [漢語] hànyǔ (Chinese-language) <n.> Chinese: 说 ~ speak Chinese || 学~ study Chinese || 现代~ modern Chinese

41 中文 [-] zhōngwén (Chinese-script) <n.> Chinese: 说/讲~ speak Chinese || ~报纸/杂志 Chinese newspaper/magazine || ~节目Chinese TV program

42 华语 [華語] huáyǔ (Chinese-language) <n.> Chinese: 说~ speak Chinese || ~文化Chinese culture || ~电影Chinese movie

43 国语 [國語] guóyǔ (national-language) <n.> national language, putongha, common speech(of the Chinese language): ~电影Chinese movie || 说~ speak standard Chinese

44 普通话 [--話] pǔtōnghuà (common-speech) <n.> Mandarin: 说~ speak Mandarin || 学~ study Mandarin || 北方~ northern Mandarin

45 地方话 [--話] dìfānghuà (local-speech) <n.> dialect: 南京~ Nanjing dialect || 说~ speak dialect

46 方言 [-] fāngyán (local-speech) <n.> dialect: 湘~ Xiang dialect || 吴~ Wu dialect || 各地~ various dialects

47 口语 [-語] kǒuyǔ (spoken-language) <n.> spoken language

48 部首 [-] bùshǒu (part-head) <n.> radicals by which characters are arranged in traditional Chinese dictionaries: 按~排列 (páiliè) sort characters under their radicals

49 偏旁 [-] piānpáng (left part of a compound character-right part of a compound character) <n.> radical: 汉字~ elements of Chinese characters || 表示声音的~ phonetic elements of Chinese characters

50 旁 [-] páng (radical) <n.> radical: 木~ the Mu radical || 人字~ the Ren radical || 偏~ radical

51 点 [點] diǎn (dot) <n.> dot: 这个字左边有三~. This character has three dots on its left.

52 横 [橫] héng (horizontal) <n.> horizontal stroke

53 竖 [豎] shù (vertical) <n.> vertical stroke
54 撇 [-] piě (throw) <n.> leftward slanting line
55 折 [-] zhé (turn) <n.> 90-degree downward turn

56 标点 [標點] biāodiǎn (mark-punctuation) <n.> punctuation: 加~ add a punctuation || ~符号punctuation marks
57 逗号 [逗號] dòuhào (comma-mark) <n.> comma
58 分号 [-號] fēnhào (divide-mark) <n.> semicolon
59 句号 [-號] jùhào (period-mark) <n.> period
60 问号 [問號] wènhào (question-mark) <n.> question mark
61 感叹号 [-嘆號] gǎntànhào (exclamation-mark) <n.> exclamation point
62 冒号 [-號] màohào (attention-mark) <n.> colon
63 引号 [-號] yǐnhào (quote-mark) <n.> quotation marks
64 省略号 [--號] shěnglüèhào (omit-mark) <n.> ellipsis
65 括号 [-號] kuòhào (include-mark) <n.> parentheses: 加~ add parentheses || 写在~里write between parentheses || 大/小 ~ braces/parentheses
66 书名号 [書-號] shūmínghào (book-name-mark) <n.> book title marks
67 着重号 [著-號] zhuózhònghào (emphasis-mark) <n.> emphasis marks
68 符号 [-號] fúhào (symbol-mark) <n.> symbol: 标点~ punctuation marks || 数学~ math symbol || 音乐~ music symbol
69 百分点 [--點] bǎifēndiǎn (percentage-point) <n.> percentage point: 八个~ eight percentage points || 提高三个~ increase by three percentage points || 降低两个~ decrease by two percentage points
70 密码 [-碼] mìmǎ (secret-code) <n.> password: 邮箱~ email password || 设~ set a password || 遗传 (yíchuán) ~ genetic code

Tips:

1 语言 (language) vs. 方言 (dialect) vs. 文字 (writing system): The most exemplary case is the language situation in Hong Kong. It can be summarized as 三言两语双文. 三言 refers to 粤方言/粤语 (Cantonese,) 普通话 (Mandarin/Standard Chinese) and 英语 (English.) 两语 refers to 汉语 (Chinese) and 英语 (English.) 双文 refers to 英文 (English) and 中文 (traditional characters and simplified characters.)
2 部首 (bùshǒu): Ancient Chinese dictionaries catalogued characters by grouping them according to a shared part. The group is called 部 (section.) The first character of a 部 is actually the shared part, and thus called 部首 (literally 'the lead/first character of a section.') The first Chinese dictionary, 说文解字 (Shuōwén Jiězì) has 540 部首, which were later reduced to 214 from the Ming Dynasty and adopted by the Qing Dynasty but further reduced to 189 by 新华字典 (Xīnhuá Zìdiǎn), which was first published in 1953 and had sold 0.56 billion copies by July 28, 2015. Now the Chinese Ministry of Education stipulates that there are 201 Chinese radicals.
3 Punctuation marks: Ancient Chinese text did not have punctuation marks, and use of modern punctuation marks started from 1919.
4 顿号 (dùnhào): 顿号 is a slight-pause mark used to set off items in a series and is written as 、. Learners of Chinese should feel happy when they see this

mark in text since it strongly indicates that items before and after this mark are of the same category. For example, when you see "她去过日本、葡萄牙和牙买加." you can surely guess that 葡萄牙 and 牙买加 are two countries and they have nothing to do with 牙 (tooth.) 葡萄牙 (Pútáoyá) is Portugal and 牙买加 (Yámǎijiā) is Jamaica, to satisfy your curiosity.

Exercises:

Part I: Answer the following questions in Chinese.

1 西方国家语言一般有哪些?

____

2 亚洲国家的语言一般有哪些?

____

3 你会说哪些外语?

____

4 汉字的笔画有哪些说法?

____

5 你知道哪些汉语的标点符号? 请写出来

____

6 中国书法一般有哪些字体?

____

7 汉语在大陆以外还有哪些叫法?

____

8 哪种语言有"声调、部首、偏旁"这些说法?

____

9 英文有没有"口语和书面语"的说法? 请举一个例子

____

Theme 79: Literature 文学 (wénxué)

1 文艺 [-藝] wényì (literature-art) <n.> art: ~作品artwork || ~活动 artistic activity || 爱好~ be passionate about art
2 文学 [-學] wénxué (script-art) <n.> literature: 报告~ literature review || 外国~ foreign literature || 儿童~ children's literature
3 小说 [-說] xiǎoshuō (trivial-views) <n.> novel: 看/写~ read/write novels || 长篇/中篇/短篇~ long/medium length/short novel || 一部/本/篇~ a novel
4 故事 [-] gùshì (old-story) <n.> story: 民间~ folklore || 讲一个~ tell a story
5 童话 [-話] tónghuà (children-story) <n.> fairytale: 一篇~ a fairytale || ~故事fairytale

6 神话 [-話] shénhuà (god-story) <n.> myth: ~故事 myth || 古代 ~ ancient myth || 希腊 (Xīlà) ~ greek myth

7 寓言 [-] yùyán (imply-speech) <n.> allegory, fable: ~故事allegory || 民间~ folk fable || 科学~ scientific allegory

8 剧本 [劇-] jùběn (drama-script) <n.> script: 写/看 ~ write/read a script || 文学~ literary script

9 脚本 [-] jiǎoběn (foot-script) <n.> script: 文学~ literary script || 戏剧~ drama script || ~设计script design

10 诗 [詩] shī (poem) <n.> poem: 一首~ a poem || 唐 (táng) ~ Tang poetry

11 诗歌 [詩歌] shīgē (poem-ballad) <n.> poetry: 写~ write poetry || 民间~ folk poetry || 古典 (gǔdiǎn) ~ classical poetry

12 诗词 [詩詞] shīcí (poem-varied length poem) <n.> poetry: 一篇~ a poem || 古典~ classical poetry || 旧 ~ old poetry

13 古诗 [-詩] gǔshī (ancient-poem) <n.> ancient poem: 一首~ an ancient poem || 背~ recite an ancient poem

14 儿歌 [兒-] érgē (children-song) <n.> nursery rhyme: 唱~ sing a nursery rhyme || 念~ read a nursery rhyme

15 童谣 [-謠] tóngyáo (children-ballad) <n.> nursery rhyme: 一支~ a nursery rhyme || 古代~ ancient nursery rhyme

16 宋词 [-詞] sòngcí (Song Dynasty-poetry) <n.> Song Dynasty poetry: 一首~ a Song Dynasty poem

17 对联 [對聯] duìlián (antithetical-couplet) <n.> antithetical couplets: 一副~ antithetical couplets || 贴 ~ paste the antithetical couplets || 写~ write antithetical couplets

18 散文 [-] sǎnwén (free-writing) <n.> prose, essay: 当代~ contemporary prose/essay || ~集 a collection of essays || 文学~ literary essay

19 随笔 [隨筆] suíbǐ (informal-writing) <n.> essay: 文化~ cultural essay || 杂文~ essay

20 传记 [傳記] zhuànjì (biography-record) <n.> biography: ~文学biography || 人物 ~ biography || 伟人~ biographies of great people

21 自传 [-傳] zìzhuàn (self-biography) <n.> autobiography: 口述~ oral autobiography || ~色彩 autobiographical tint/tone || ~影片 autobiographical film

22 游记 [-記] yóujì (travel-note) <n.> travelogue: 山水~ landscape travelogue || 科学~ science travelogue

23 报道 [報-] bàodào (report-say) <n./v.> report: 新闻 ~ news report || 详细 ~ detailed report

24 消息 [-] xiāoxī (news-message) <n.> message: 发~ send a message || 刊登 (kāndēng) ~ post/publish a message || 一条/则~ a message

25 通讯 [-訊] tōngxùn (communicate-news) <n.> dispatch: ~报道 news dispatch/report || 新闻~ news dispatch

Tips:

1 Chinese literature and rhyming: Ancient Chinese verses are usually short and rhymed, so they are easy to memorize and recite.

2 Chinese children's literature: In ancient China, children had three primary readers, which include 三字经 (Three Character Classic,) 百家姓 (Hundred

Family Surnames) and 千字文 (Thousand Character Classic), which gave children a basic knowledge of Chinese culture and history. These three books are collectively called "三百千" (3–100–1,000.)

3 对联 (duìlián): 对联 means 'antithetical couplet' and was the basic training for ancient Chinese literature. 对联 are commonly seen at important cultural sites such as palaces, temples, tombs, funerals and on many families' gates in the spring festival. A 对联 is composed of two parts, which are usually opposite in tone patterns and meanings. For example, "黑发不知勤学早, 白首方悔读书迟," which means 'at a young age, I did not know that I should have studied diligently, and when I became old, I just regretted/found that it was too late to read books.'

黑	发	不	知	勤	学	早
hēi	fà	bù	zhī	qín	Xué	Zǎo
Black	hair	not	know	diligently	Study	Early
White	head	just	regret	read	Book	Late
bái	shǒu	fāng	huǐ	dú	shū	Chí
白	首	方	悔	读	书	迟

Many well-educated Chinese love 对联, so does the first author of this book. Here is the upper scroll or first line of a 对联 for readers of this book to complete: 林森入森林, 只见树木. Here are notes for readers' attention. (1) It includes 木 林森, all of which have the radical 木, (2) 林森 (Lín Sēn, 1868–1943) was Chairman of the National Government of the Republic of China from 1931 until his death. (3) It implies a proverb "只见树木, 不见森林," which means 'unable to see the forest for the trees.' Please do not feel frustrated if you cannot come up with a good one. This is supposedly hard for 99.99% of, if not all, native Chinese people.

4 篇 (piān): The original meaning of 篇is 'bamboo script.' 篇 is a general measure word for literary works.

Exercises:

Part I: Read the following words and then answer the questions in Chinese.

游记、自传、散文、现代诗歌、唐诗宋词、剧本、小说、童话、民间故事、神话、寓言故事、随笔、人物传记、外国文学、中国文学

1 以上这些文学作品你最喜欢读哪些?

____

2 一般来说孩子最喜欢读什么样的文学作品?

____

3 对外国人来说读唐诗宋词是否容易? 为什么?

---

4 你经常写随笔或者游记吗? 为什么?

---

5 你读过名人写的自传吗? 是谁的?

---

6 你喜欢哪个国家的文学?

---

7 你喜欢现代诗歌还是古代诗歌? 为什么?

Theme 80: Media, articles 媒体, 文章 (méitǐ, wénzhāng)

1 媒体 [-體] méitǐ (medium-body) <n.> media: 新闻~ news media || 社交~ social media || 电视~ TV media
2 传媒 [傳-] chuánméi (broadcast-medium) <n.> media: 大众~ public media || 西方~ western media || ~公司media company
3 报刊 [報-] bàokān (newspaper-journal) <n.> periodical: 四家/ 份~ four periodicals || 西方~ western periodical || 进步~ progressive periodical
4 报纸 [報紙] bàozhǐ (report-paper) <n.> newspaper: 一家~ a newspaper || 一张/份中文~ a Chinese newspaper || 看~ read the newspaper
5 报 [報] bào (judge, report, newspaper) <n.> newspaper: 看~ read the newspaper || 一份~ a newspaper || 大/小 ~ major, tabloid newspaper
6 杂志 [雜誌] zázhì (miscellaneous-record) <n.> magazine: 几本~ a few magazines || 看~ read the magazine
7 期刊 [-] qīkān (periodic-publication) <n.> periodical journals, magazines, etc., publication: 办~ start a publication
8 刊物 [-] kānwù (publish-thing) <n.> publication: 办~ start a publication || 内部~ internal publication || 文学~ literary publication
9 刊 [-] kān (cut, engrave, print, publish, publication) <n.> publication: 月~ monthly publication || 本~ our publication || 出~ issue a publication
10 报社 [報-] bàoshè (newspaper-agency) <n.> newspaper office: 一家~ a newspaper office || ~记者newspaper reporter
11 杂志社 [雜誌-] zázhìshè (magazine-agency) <n.> magazine publisher: 一家~ a magazine publisher || 某~ some magazine publisher
12 出版社 [-] chūbǎnshè (publishing-agency) <n.> publisher: 美术~ art publisher || 科学~ science publisher
13 编辑部 [編輯-] biānjíbù (editorial-department) <n.> editorial department: 报纸~ newspaper editorial department
14 电视 [電視] diànshì (tele – vision) <n.> television, TV: 看~ watch TV || 上 ~ be on TV || ~节目 TV program
15 电视台 [電視臺] diànshìtái (TV-station) <n.> TV station: 五家~ five TV stations || 中央/地方 ~ central, local TV station || 中国/美国 ~ Chinese/American TV station

16 网 [網] wǎng (net, web) <n.> internet: 上~ go on internet || ~购shop online || ~速internet speed

17 网上 [網-] wǎngshàng (net-on) <adj./adv.> online: ~聊天chat online || ~银行online bank || ~商店 online shop

18 网站 [網-] wǎngzhàn (web-site) <n.> website: 官方~ official website || 国外~ foreign website || 登陆 ~ log into a website

19 互联网 [-聯網] hùliánwǎng (inter – net) <n.> Internet: ~安全Internet security || 使用~ use the internet || 接入~ connect to the Internet

20 网页 [網頁] wǎngyè (web-page) <n.> web page, website: 设计~ design the web page || 浏览 (liúlǎn) ~ view, browse the web page || ~内容website content

21 网址 [網-] wǎngzhǐ (web-address) <n.> web page address: 网站的~ web page address || 输入 (shūrù) ~ input the web page address || 官方~ the official web page address

22 多媒体 [--體] duōméitǐ (multi – media) <adj./ n.> multimedia: ~教学multimedia education || ~技术 multimedia technique

23 排行榜 [-] páihángbǎng (ranking-list) <n.> ranking, chart: 上~ be on the chart

24 词典 [詞-] cídiǎn (word-dictionary) <n.> dictionary: 一本~ a dictionary || 汉语~ Chinese dictionary

25 字典 [-] zìdiǎn (character-dictionary) <n.> character dictionary: 一本 ~ a dictionary || 查~ consult the dictionary

26 辞典 [辭-] cídiǎn (speech-dictionary) <n.> dictionary: 两本~ two dictionaries || 动物学~ dictionary of zoology

27 电子邮件 [電-郵-] diànzǐyóujiàn (electronic-mail) <n./v.> email: 收/发~ receive/send an email || 一封~ an email

28 短信 [-] duǎnxìn (short-message) <n.> text message: 一条~ a text message || 发 ~ send a text message

29 信 [-] xìn (honest, believe, message, letter) <n.> letter: 一封 ~ a letter || 写/回~ write/respond to a letter || 寄~ send a letter

30 便条 [-條] biàntiáo (casual-slip) <n.> note: 写~ write a note || 留一张~ leave a note

31 传真 [傳-] chuánzhēn (transmit-unchanged) <n.> fax: ~电话fax || 新闻~ news fax || ~图fax chart

32 图书 [圖書] túshū (altas-book) <n.> book: 一万册 ~ 10,000 books

33 书 [書] shū (write, book) <n.> book: 五本~ five books || 电子~ electronic book || 看~ read a book

34 教材 [-] jiàocái (teaching-material) <n.> teaching material: 一套~ a set of teaching materials

35 课本 [課-] kèběn (text-book) <n.> textbook: 打开~ open a textbook || 一套 ~ a set of textbooks

36 课文 [課-] kèwén (text-script) <n.> text: 两篇 ~ two texts || 读~ read a text

37 文章 [-] wénzhāng (composition-chapter) <n.> reading, article: 一篇~ a reading, an article || 写 ~ write an article

38 论文 [論-] lùnwén (commentary-article) <n.> paper, thesis: 写~ write a paper, thesis || 一篇~ a paper, thesis || 发表 ~ publish a paper, thesis

39 稿子 [-] gǎozi (draft-*suffix*) <n.> draft: 写~ write a draft || 改~ edit a draft || 三份 ~ three drafts

40 作品 [-] zuòpǐn (work-piece) <n.> work: 一部~ a work || 文学~ literary work || 音乐~ music work

41 著作 [-] zhùzuò (write-works) <n.> acclaimed work: 一部~ an acclaimed work

42 作文 [-] zuòwén (compose-article) <n.> essay: 一篇~ an essay || 写~ write an essay || 口头~ oral essay

43 笔记 [筆記] bǐjì (pen-note) <n.> notes: 读书~ reading notes || 旅游~ travel notes || 写~ write notes

44 博客 [-] bókè (transliteration of 'blog') <n.> blog: 写~ write a blog || ~日记 journal on one's blog

45 评论 [評論] pínglùn (evaluate-comment) <n.> comment: 一篇~ a comment || 写~ write a comment || 国际~ international comment

46 启事 [啓-] qǐshì (notify-thing) <n.> notice: 一条/ 则 ~ a notice || 写~ write a notice || 招聘/ 征婚/寻车~ job postings, personals, missing car report

47 日记 [-記] rìjì (daily-record) <n.> diary: 写~ write a diary || 记~ write a diary

48 说明书 [說-書] shuōmíngshū (explain-booklet) <n.> manual: 使用~ operating manual || 一份~ a manual

49 通知书 [--書] tōngzhīshū (notify-letter) <n.> notification letter: 录取~ admission letter || 发~ send a notification letter || 病危~ notification of a patient's critical condition

50 协议书 [協議書] xiéyìshū (agreement-paper) <n.> agreement: 签订 (qiāndìng) ~ sign the agreement

51 集 [-] jí (assemble, collection) <n.> collection, anthology: 小说~ collection of novels || 散文~ collection of essays || 诗~ collection of poems

52 公告 [-] gōnggào (public-announce) <n.> announcement: 发布~ post an announcement || 大会~ conference announcement

53 专辑 [專輯] zhuānjí (special-collection) <n.> album: 六张~ six albums || 个人~ personal album || 民歌~ folk album

54 新闻 [-聞] xīnwén (new-information) <n.> news: 一条~ a piece of news || 电视~ TV news || 头条/特大~ headline news, breaking news

55 报告 [報-] bàogào (report-tell) <n.> report, lecture: 重要~ important report || 做一个~ have a lecture || 一份~ a report

56 广告 [廣-] guǎnggào (wide-statement) <n.> advertisement: 电视~ TV commercial || 做~ advertise

57 议论 [議論] yìlùn (discuss-comment) <n.> discussion: 种种~ all kinds of discussion || 发~ commenting on/gossiping about

58 说法 [說-] shuōfǎ (saying-way) <n.> statement, way of saying: 不同的~ different statements || 种种~ all kinds of sayings

59 资料 [資-] zīliào (information-material) <n.> information, data, material: 查~ look up information || 积累 (jīlěi) /搜集 (sōují) ~ collect information, data, material

60 文件 [-] wénjiàn (script-item) <n.> document, file: 一份~ a document, file || 看~ read a document, file

Tips:

1 新闻: As the two constituent characters of 新闻 implies, news should contain 'new information.' This being said, currently, if a Chinese ping pong player won a championship, it is not 新闻, but if one championship is lost, it will immediately become a piece of national news.
2 电子邮件 (diànzǐ yóujiàn): It means 'email' which was originally translated as 伊妹儿 (yīmèir, literally 'that-girl') when it came into being in Chinese. 伊妹儿, from the perspective of appreciation of literature, is much better than 电子邮件, however, it did not resonate with the majority of Internet users.
3 词典 vs. 辞典: Both are pronounced as 'cídiǎn' and mean 'dictionary.' The difference is that catalogued entries in 辞典 are increasingly longer than those in 词典, in other words, 辞典 tend to collect phrases and terms.
4 启事 vs. 启示: Both are pronounced as 'qǐshì,' but they are very different. 启事 means 'notice, announcement,' but 启示 'to enlighten, enlightenment.'\

Exercises:

Part I: Please insert the following words in the appropriate category.

(一) 报刊、报纸、杂志、学术期刊、刊物、博客、网页、网站、互联网、报社、杂志社、出版社、编辑部、电视台

传统媒体	传统媒体机构	新媒体

(二) 文学评论、作文、文章、论文、著作、字典、词典、课文、课本

个人作品	工具书	教材

Part II: Read the following sentences and fill in each blank with the appropriate word or phrase from the options given.

1 资料、广告、报告

a) 小王在电脑上写________的时候忘了保存文件，结果一晚上的工作白做了.
b) 小王做研究的时候喜欢上网查_________.
c) 康师傅方便面的________做得特别好， 在中国家喻户晓 (jiāyù hùxiǎo, widely known).

2 协议书、说明书、启事

a) 这份产品使用________里的指令使很多人感到糊涂(hútu, confused).
b) 这两家公司最近签订了________, 共同开发一种新产品.
c) 很多海外华人会在美国交友网站上刊登自己的征婚_______.

3 图书、排行榜、笔记、便条

a) 小张每周都要读一本新书, 然后写读书______.
b) 小张去找小王打球, 但小王不在宿舍, 他就给小王留了个_______.
c) 这家出版社每周都有新_______上市.
d) 《哈利波特7》 (*Harry Potter* 7) 在新书_________中名列前茅(míngliè qiánmáo, be at the top of the list).

Theme 81: Shapes, forms, versions 图形, 体例 (túxíng, tǐlì)

1 图案 [圖-] tú'àn (diagram-archive) <n.> pattern, design: 设计~ design pattern || 各种 ~ various patterns || 传统~ traditional pattern
2 图片 [圖-] túpiàn (diagram-picture) <n.> picture: 动物 ~ animal picture || 五张 ~ five pictures
3 图 [圖] tú (diagram) <n.> image, chart: 挂~ hanging picture, wall picture || 一张~ an image/a chart
4 地图 [-圖] dìtú (land-diagram) <n.> map: 一张 ~ a map || 世界 ~ world map || 城市~ city map
5 公式 [-] gōngshì (general-pattern) <n.> formula: 计算 (jìsuàn) ~ computational formula || 化学~ chemical formula || 错误的~ false formula
6 线 [綫] xiàn (thread) <n.> line: 一条~ a line || 横 (héng) ~ horizontal line || 直~ straight line
7 直线 [-綫] zhíxiàn (straight-line) <n.> straight line: 一条/根 ~ a straight line || 画~ draw a straight line || ~距离 (jùlí) linear distance
8 角 [-] jiǎo (angle) <n.> angle: 三~形triangle || 五~星 5-corner star || 多~ polygonal
9 面 [-] miàn (surface) <n.> plane: 平~ flat surface || 曲 (qū) ~ curved surface || 三个~ three planes
10 面积 [-積] miànjī (surface-accumulate) <n.> area: 土地~ land area || 森林~ forest area || 海洋~ ocean area
11 体积 [體積] tǐjī (body-accumulate) <n.> volume: ~小/大 small/large volume || 总~ total volume || ~增加 (zēngjiā) volume increase
12 圆 [圓] yuán (round) <n.> circle: 画~ draw a circle || ~形circle
13 圆柱 [圓-] yuánzhù (round-column) <n.> cylinder: ~形 cylindrical || ~体cylinder
14 三角形 [-] sānjiǎoxíng (three-angle-shape) <n.> triangle: 直角~ right triangle || 等边~ equilateral triangle || 倒 ~ inverted triangle
15 椭圆 [-圓] tuǒyuán (oval-circle) <n.> oval, ellipse: ~形ellipse || ~轨道 (guǐdào) oval track
16 圆锥 [圓錐] yuánzhuī (circle-awl) <n.> cone: ~体cone || ~形conical || ~状conical

17 饼图 [餅圖] bǐngtú (pie-diagram) <n.> pie chart: 做一个~ make a pie chart

18 柱形图 [--圖] zhùxíngtú (column-shape-diagram) <n.> bar graph: 用~表示 show with a bar graph

19 箭头 [-頭] jiàntóu (arrow-head) <n.> arrow: ~方向the direction of the arrow || ~指着正南the arrow points to the south

20 话题 [話題] huàtí (talk-subject) <n.> subject: 热门~ hot subject || 转换 (zhuǎnhuàn) ~ change subject

21 议题 [議題] yìtí (discuss-subject) <n.> topic: 中心~ central topic || 主要~ main topic

22 主题 [-題] zhǔtí (main-subject) <n.> theme: 重大~ major theme || 音乐~ music theme || 突出 ~ emphasize the theme

23 题材 [題-] tícái (subject-material) <n.> subject, theme: 农村 ~ rural subject || 故事~ story subject/theme

24 内容 [-] nèiróng (inside-content) <n.> content: 基本~ basic content || 具体~ detailed content

25 情节 [-節] qíngjié (thing-segment) <n.> plot: 故事~ story plot || ~生动 vivid plot || 戏剧 (xìjù) ~ drama plot

26 细节 [細節] xìjié (small-segment) <n.> detail: 动作~ action details || 精彩 (jīngcǎi) 的/具体~ appealing/concrete details

27 中心 [-] zhōngxīn (center-heart) <n.> center: 争论的~ center of argument || 文章的~ center of the article

28 专题 [專題] zhuāntí (special-subject) <n.> special subject: ~展览 (zhǎnlǎn) special exhibition || ~报告special report || ~节目special program

29 课题 [課題] kètí (study-subject) <n.> question for study or discussion, project, problem: 研究~ a research topic/project || 如何教育孩子, 仍然是一个热门 ~. How to educate children is still a hot topic.

30 节目 [節-] jiémù (segment-item) <n.> program: 电视~ TV program || 名牌~ famous program || 主持 (zhǔchí) ~ host a program

31 栏目 [欄-] lánmù (column-item) <n.> column: 增加 ~ add columns || 电视~ program columns

32 简介 [簡-] jiǎnjiè (brief-introduce) <n./v.> introduction: 人物~ profile || 内容~ content abstract || 作者~ introduction of the author

33 大纲 [-綱] dàgāng (main-outline) <n.> abstract, outline: 教学~ syllabus || 历史~ historical outline || 建国~ nation-building program

34 大意 [-] dàyì (main-meaning) <n.> gist: 文章 ~ gist of the article || 歌词~ gist of the lyrics

35 概要 [-] gàiyào (generalize-key) <n.> summary: 内容~ content summary || 案情 (ànqíng) ~ case summary

36 目录 [-錄] mùlù (item-order) <n.> menu, index: 图书~ book menu || 论文~ thesis index || 编~ compile a menu/index

37 风格 [風-] fēnggé (style-pattern) <n.> style: 表演~ performing style || 书写~ writing style || 独特的~ unique style

38 色彩 [-] sècǎi (color-colorful) <n.> color, flavor: 感情~ emotional coloring || 地方~ local color || 文学~ literary flavor

39 盗版 [盜-] dàobǎn (pirate-version) <n.> pirated copy: ~书 pirated edition of a book || ~碟 (dié) pirated disks || ~软件pirated software

40 电子版 [電--] diànzibǎn (electronic-version) <n.> electronic version: 做成~ make something electronic

41 正版 [-] zhèngbǎn (genuine-version) <n.> original version: ~软件original software || ~图书original book || ~音乐original music

42 旧版 [舊-] jiùbǎn (old-version) <n.> old version: ~书 old book || ~纸币old bills

43 新版 [-] xīnbǎn (new-version) <n.> new version: ~软件new software || ~教材new material

44 收藏版 [-] shōucángbǎn (collect-version) <n.> collection: 特别~ special collection || 获赠 ~ receive a collection

45 原版 [-] yuánbǎn (original-version) <adj.> original version: 英文~ original English edition || ~教材 original material || ~书 original book

46 修订版 [-訂-] xiūdìngbǎn (revised-version) <n.> revised edition: 二次~ second edition

Tips:

1 版本 (bǎnbén): 版本 means 'edition (of a book.)' 版本学 (literally 'studies of book editions') is an area of scientific study in China. Books of 宋版 (the Song edition) are extremely valuable.

2 盗版 (dàobǎn): 盗版 means 'pirated copy.' 盗版书 (pirated books,) printed or e-version, can be easily found almost everywhere in China.

Exercises:

Part I: Use the given bound form as a guide to help you think of other words with the same character. Feel free to use your dictionary when needed. Then write down the English definition of each of the words you've written.

图 *(picture):* 图案 *pattern, design*

____

____

____

____

版 *(edition):* 盗版 *pirated copy*

____

____

____

____

Part II: Read the following sentences and fill in each blank with the appropriate word or phrase from the options given.

1 议题、话题、题材

a) 小王跟同事去酒吧喝酒、聊天, ________一般都是关于球赛和网络游戏的.
b) 小王公司昨天下午召开了全体会议, 主要________是关于公司管理改革的问题.
c) 这部电影的_______很特别, 是关于九十年代中国偏远 (piānyuǎn, remote) 地区农村教育问题的.

2 情节、细节、内容

a) 这本书的________非常丰富, 值得反复阅读.
b) 这部好莱坞大片的________非常紧凑 (jǐncòu, compact), 也很刺激 (cìjī, exciting), 一下子就能吸引观众.
c) 小王的报告只写了一个概要, 还需要补充________.

3 栏目、节目、大纲

a) 《非诚勿扰》 (*If You are the One*) 是中国比较受欢fl的一个电视征婚_______.
b) 老王只看报纸上的体育________.
c) 每学期开学前, 李教授都会把课程_______放在学校的网页上.

4 风格、大意、色彩

a) 美国白宫的建筑_______非常独特.
b) 这部小说带有强烈的个人自传________.
c) 中国学校的语文课上, 学生常常需要概括 (gàikuò, summarize) 一篇的________.

Theme 82: Song, dance 歌舞 (gēwǔ)

1 艺术 [藝術] yìshù (art-way) <n.> art: 音乐~ art of music || 建筑~ art of architecture || ~美marvelous art
2 音乐 [-樂] yīnyuè (sound-music) <n.> music: 民间~ folk music || 听~ listen to music
3 民乐 [-樂] mínyuè (folk-music) <n.> folk music: ~队folk music band || ~团folk music orchestra || 中华 ~ Chinese folk music
4 交响乐 [-響樂] jiāoxiǎngyuè (simultaneously-sound-music) <n.> symphony: 古典~ classical symphony || 现代 ~ modern symphony || 听 ~ listen to a symphony
5 摇滚 [搖滾] yáogǔn (shake/rock-roll) <n.> rock and roll: 乡村~ country rock || 重金属 (jīnshǔ) ~ heavy metal rock
6 爵士乐 [--樂] juéshìyuè (transliteration-music) <n.> jazz: 西方~ Western jazz
7 乡村音乐 [鄉--樂] xiāngcūnyīnyuè (country-music) <n.> country music: 欧美~ American and European country music || 西部~ Western country music

8 电子乐 [電-樂] diànziyuè (electronic-music) <n.> electronic music: ~演奏 (yǎnzòu) electronic music performance
9 乐队 [樂隊] yuèduì (music-band) <n.> band: 一支 ~ a band || ~伴奏 (bànzòu) band accompaniment || 民族 ~ folk band
10 节奏 [節-] jiézòu (rhythm-play) <n.> rhythm: ~快fast rhythm || 有/没有~ have/not have a rhythm || 慢~ slow rhythm
11 旋律 [-] xuánlǜ (frequent-temperament) <n.> melody: 主~ theme melody || 动听的~ mellifluous melody || 音乐~ music melody
12 乐曲 [樂-] yuèqǔ (music-music of song) <n.> composition, music piece: 演奏~ perform a music piece

13 歌 [-] gē (song) <n.> song: 儿~ children's song || 唱~ sing a song
14 曲 [-] qǔ (music of song) <n.> song: 流行~ popular song || 小提琴~ violin song
15 歌声 [-聲] gēshēng (song-sound) <n.> singing: 一片/串~ singing || 欢乐的~ cheerful singing || ~响起singing begins
16 歌曲 [-] gēqǔ (song-music of song) <n.> song: 播放~ play a song || 经典~ classical song
17 国歌 [國-] guógē (national-song) <n.> national anthem: 中国~ Chinese national anthem || 唱~ sing the national anthem
18 校歌 [-] xiàogē (school-song) <n.> school song: 唱~ sing a school song
19 民歌 [-] mín'gē (folk-song) <n.> folk song: 俄罗斯~ Russian folk song || 西北~ Northwestern folk song
20 情歌 [-] qínggē (love-song) <n.> ballad: ~对唱ballad duet
21 主题曲 [-題-] zhǔtíqūqǔ (theme-music of song) <n.> theme music: 电影的~ theme music of a movie
22 主旋律 [-] zhǔxuánlǜ (main-melody) <n.> theme or subject of the music: 乐曲的~ theme or subject of the music || 肯德基把本土化作为在中国发展的~. KFC used localization as the main theme of development in China.
23 合唱 [-] héchàng (together-sing) <n.> chorus: 大~ chorus || 小~ semichorus || 男女~ mixed chorus
24 独唱 [獨-] dúchàng (single-sing) <n.> solo: 男声~ male solo || 女高音~ soprano solo
25 二（三、四）重唱 [-] èr (sān、sì) chóngchàng (double/triple/quadruple-ensemble) <n.> duo/trio/quartet: 男女~ duo/duet || 女声~ female voice duet || 男声~ male voice duet
26 卡拉OK [-] kǎlā OK (transliteration) <n.> karaoke: 唱~ sing at karaoke

27 舞 [-] wǔ (dance) <n.> dance: 跳一支~ do a dance || 孔雀 (kǒngquè) ~ pavane || 双人~ pas de deux
28 舞蹈 [-] wǔdǎo (dance-stamp) <n.> dance: 练 ~ practice dance || 民族 ~ folk dance || 现代~ modern dance
29 秧歌 [-] yāngge ((rice) seedling-song) <n.> yangko: 扭~ do the yangko Note: Young plants swing in the wind, and 秧歌 dancers imitate the swings.
30 民族舞 [-] mínzúwǔ (ethnic-dance) <n.> folk dance: 跳~ do a folk dance
31 现代舞 [現--] xiàndàiwǔ (modern-dance) <n.> modern dance: 跳~ do a modern dance

32 芭蕾舞 [-] bālěiwǔ (transliteration-dance) <n.> ballet: 跳~ dance ballet || 古典~ classical ballet || 现代~ modern ballet

33 踢踏舞 [-] tītàwǔ (transliteration of tip tap (lit. kick-step) -dance) <n.> tap dance: 跳~ do a tap dance || 爱尔兰~ irish tap dance

34 拉丁舞 [-] lādīngwǔ (transliteration-dance) <n.> Latin dance: 跳 ~ do a Latin dance

35 交谊舞 [-誼-] jiāoyìwǔ (association-dance) <n.> ballroom dance: 跳~ do a ballroom dance

36 华尔兹 [華爾茲] huá'ěrzī (transliteration) <n.> waltz: 跳~ dance a waltz || ~舞曲waltz music

37 伦巴 [倫-] lúnbā (transliteration) <n.> rumba: 跳 ~ dance a rumba

38 探戈 [-] tàn'gē (transliteration) <n.> tango: 跳~ dance a tango

39 双人舞 [雙--] shuāngrénwǔ (double-people-dance) <n.> pas de deux: 跳~ dance a pas de deux

40 独舞 [獨-] dúwǔ (single-dance) <n.> solo dance: 两段~ two solo dances || ~表演solo dance recital

41 群舞 [-] qúnwǔ (group-dance) <n.> group dance: 阿拉伯舞蹈一般是女子~. Arabian dance generally is a collective dance of women.

42 广场舞 [廣場-] guǎngchǎngwǔ (square-dance) <n.> plaza dance: 跳 ~ do a plaza dance

Tips:

1 舞 (wǔ) and 无 (無, wú): The upper part of 舞 is 无 (無), which actually means 'to (sing and) dance.' Since 无 (無, nothing, no) borrowed the form of 無 (to dance,) a part '舛' meaning 'two opposite feet' was added and thus created the new form 舞.

2 The Han Chinese and their talents to sing and dance: Generally speaking, among the 56 ethnic groups in modern China, the Han Chinese constitute 92% of the entire population but are probably the least talented in singing and dancing.

3 歌舞 (gēwǔ, sing and dance): 能歌善舞 (nénggē shànwǔ) means 'be good at singing and dancing' and is complimentary, however, 歌舞升平 (gēwǔ shēngpíng) means 'to sing and dance to extol the good times' and has negative connotations.

4 首 (shǒu): 首 means 'head.' It is also a general measure word for songs.

Exercises:

Part I: Answer the following questions in Chinese.

1 "民乐、交响乐、爵士乐、摇滚乐," 你最喜欢哪种? 为什么?

---

2 "民乐、交响乐、爵士乐、摇滚乐," 哪种音乐节奏比较快?

---

3 “乡村音乐”曾经在哪些地方比较流行?

4 请写出你知道的舞蹈种类

5 请写出你知道的歌曲种类

6 “歌舞升平”是褒义词 (bāoyìcí, commendatory term) 还是贬义词 (biǎnyìcí, derogatory term)?

7 中国老人喜欢扭秧歌和跳广场舞, 你们国家的老人也喜欢这些娱乐形式吗?

8 你喜欢唱卡拉OK吗? 你喜欢唱情歌还是摇滚歌曲?

Theme 83: Movie, theater 戏剧 (xìjù)

1 剧 [劇] jù (drama) <n.> show, play: 舞台~ stage play || 音乐~ musical play || 电视 ~ TV show, drama
2 电视剧 [電視劇] diànshìjù (TV-drama) <n.> TV show, drama: 三部 ~ three TV shows || 看 ~ watch a TV show || 室内~ indoor TV drama
3 连续剧 [連續劇] liánxùjù (successive-drama) <n.> TV series: 看~ watch a TV series || 一部~ a TV series || 长篇~ long-running TV series
4 古装剧 [-裝劇] gǔzhuāngjù (ancient-costume-drama) <n.> costume drama: 一出/部~ a costume drama
5 武侠剧 [-俠劇] wǔxiájù (martial arts-chivalry-drama) <n.> kung fu drama: 古装~ Ancient-dress kung fu drama || 拍摄 (pāishè) ~ shoot a kung fu drama || 港台~ Hong Kong and Taiwan kung fu dramas
6 电影 [電-] diànyǐng (electric-picture) <n.> movie: 一部~ a movie || 看两场 ~ see two movies || 演~ act in a movie
7 大片 [-] dàpiān (grand-movie) <n.> blockbuster movie: 好莱坞~ Hollywood blockbuster || 国际~ international blockbuster
8 影片 [-] yǐngpiān (film-movie) <n.> film: 一部~ a film || 得奖~ award-winning film || 喜剧~ comedy film
9 卡通 [-] kǎtōng (transliteration) <n.> cartoon: ~人物cartoon character || ~片animated cartoon || ~形象cartoon image
10 画面 [畫-] huàmiàn (picture-appearance) <n.> frame, scene: 一幅~ a frame || 历史~ historical scene || 生动的~ a vivid scene
11 镜头 [鏡頭] jìngtóu (lens-top) <n.> shot, lens: 长/ 短~ long, short take || 特写~ close-up shot || 拍一组~ take a group of shots
12 特写 [-寫] tèxiě (particular-describe) <n.> close-up: ~镜头 close-up shot || 脸部~ close-up of the face || 人物 ~ close-up portrait

13 蒙太奇 [-] méngtàiqí (transliteration) <n.> montage: 电影~ film montage || ~技术montage technology
14 视频 [視頻] shìpín (visual-frequency) <n.> video: 看~ watch a video || 播放~ play a video || 短~ short video
15 频道 [頻-] píndào (frequency-channel) <n.> channel: 电视~ TV channel || 新闻~ news channel || 第五~ fifth channel

16 戏 [戲] xì (play) <n.> show, opera: 三场~ three shows || 看~ watch a show || 唱~ sing an opera
17 戏剧 [戲劇] xìjù (play-drama) <n.> drama: 六部 ~ six dramas || 大型 ~ large-scaled drama
18 戏曲 [戲-] xìqǔ (play-opera) <n.> opera: 地方~ local opera || 传统~ traditional opera || 民族~ folk opera
19 话剧 [話劇] huàjù (speak-drama) <n.> play: 演~ perform a play || 现代~ modern play || ~表演 play
20 京剧 [-劇] jīngjù (Peking-drama) <n.> Peking opera: 唱~ sing a Peking opera || ~演员opera performers || 现代~ modern Peking opera
21 脸谱 [臉譜] liǎnpǔ (face-chart, book) <n.> mask: 京剧~ Peking opera mask || 黑色~ black mask || 画~ paint a mask
22 木偶戏 [--戲] mù'ǒuxì (wood-puppet-show) <n.> puppet show: 演~ perform a puppet show || 看 ~ watch a puppet show
23 皮影戏 [--戲] píyǐngxì (leather-shadow-play) <n.> shadow play: 演~ perform a shadow play || 民间 ~ folk shadow play
24 歌剧 [-劇] gējù (sing-drama) <n.> opera: 民族~ folk opera
25 喜剧 [-劇] xǐjù (hilarious-drama) <n.> comedy: 轻~ light comedy || ~色彩comic taste || ~风格comic style
26 悲剧 [-劇] bēijù (tragic-drama) <n.> tragedy: 一场~ a tragedy || ~人物tragic hero || 历史~ historical tragedy

27 魔术 [-術] móshù (magic-skill) <n.> magic: 玩~ do magic || 表演~ perform a magic show
28 相声 [-聲] xiàngshēng (mimic-sound) <n.> crosstalk: 说 ~ perform a crosstalk || 听 ~ watch a crosstalk || 单口~ monologue crosstalk
29 马戏 [馬戲] mǎxì (horse-show) <n.> circus: circus ~团 circus troupe || ~表演circus performance
30 杂技 [雜-] zájì (varied-skill) <n.> acrobatics, vaudeville: ~表演acrobatic performance
31 脱口秀 [脫--] tuōkǒuxiù (transliteration of talk-show) <n.> stand-up comedy, talk show: ~节目 stand-up comedy show || ~主持人stand-up comedy host
32 曲艺 [-藝] qǔyì (musical-art) <n.> folk art: ~节目folk art show

Tips:

1 戏 (xì) and 剧 (jù): 戏 means 'drama' and 剧 'play, opera, theater,' but their hypernym is 戏剧. 戏 is used slightly more for entertainment.

2 Facebook and 脸谱 (liǎnpǔ): When the social media platform Facebook first appeared in Chinese, the Westernized translation 脸书 (liǎnshū, lit. face-book) was despised by orthodox Chinese literati who preferred the more Chinese translation of 脸谱 (lit. face-chart, book) which, however, was not accepted by users of Facebook since it is very difficult to write after all. Language is not always scientific, but conventional sometimes.

3 Local Chinese operas: 京剧 (Jīngjù, Peking opera) is currently the most famous one, but it was known from the Qing Dynasty. To some extremely well-educated people, 昆曲 (Kūnqǔ,) a local Jiangsu opera, is elegant indeed.

Exercises:

Part I: Use the given bound form as a guide to help you think of other words with the same character. Feel free to use your dictionary when needed. Then write down the English definition of each of the words you've written.

剧 *drama* 电视剧 *TV show*

____

____

____

____

戏 *play, show* 看戏 *watch a show*

____

____

____

____

Part II: Read the following words and then answer the questions.

脱口秀、杂技、马戏、相声、魔术、电影、好莱坞大片、卡通片、视频、戏剧、话剧、京剧、木偶戏、皮影戏、歌剧、特写镜头、蒙太奇

1 上面这些艺术形式哪些是中国特有的?

____

2 你喜欢看喜剧电影还是悲剧电影? 为什么?

____

3 你常常看歌剧和话剧吗?

____

4 卡通片和好莱坞大片, 你更喜欢看哪个? 为什么?

---

5 你常常看Youtube上的视频吗? 一般是关于什么方面的?

---

6 上面这些词中哪两个词是关于电影技术的?

Theme 84: Fine arts 美术 (měishù)

1 美术 [-術] měishù (beauty-art) <n.> art: ~作品artwork || 学~ learn art
2 绘画 [繪畫] huìhuà (embroider-draw) <n.> painting: 当代~ contemporary painting
3 画 [畫] huà (draw) <n.> painting: 一幅/张~ a picture || 山水~ landscape painting || 水彩~ watercolor painting
4 图 [圖] tú (diagram) <n.> picture: 花鸟~ bird-and-flower painting || 斗牛~ bullfighting painting || 日出~ sunrise painting
5 图画 [圖畫] túhuà (diagram-draw) <n.> drawing: 一幅/张~ a drawing || 连环~ comic strips || 水彩~ watercolor drawing
6 国画 [國畫] guóhuà ([traditional] Chinese-painting) <n.> traditional Chinese painting: ~作品 traditional Chinese painting
7 西洋画 [--畫] xīyánghuà (Western-painting) <n.> Western painting: 现代~ modern Western painting
8 风景画 [風-畫] fēngjǐnghuà (landscape-painting) <n.> landscape painting: 一幅~ a landscape painting
9 山水画 [--畫] shānshuǐhuà (mountain-water-painting) <n.> Chinese landscape painting: 中国 ~ Chinese landscape painting
10 花鸟画 [-鳥畫] huāniǎohuà (flower-bird-painting) <n> bird-and-flower painting: 传统中国画有山水画、人物画和~. Traditional Chinese paintings include landscape painting, figure painting and flower and bird painting.
11 动画 [動畫] dònghuà (motion-picture) <n.> animation: ~电影 animated film || ~片animation Note: It is called "动漫" in Taiwan.
12 漫画 [-畫] mànhuà (unrestrained-drawing) <n.> comics: 一幅~ a comic || 画~ create comics
13 插画 [-畫] chāhuà (insert-drawing) <n.> illustration: ~家illustrator || 画~ draw illustrations
14 贴画 [貼畫] tiēhuà (stick-drawing) <n.> pinup: 招~ pinup poster || 剪~ cut out stickers
15 版画 [-畫] bǎnhuà (block-drawing) <n.> print: 民间~ folk print || 木~ wooden print || 石~ lithograph
16 壁画 [-畫] bìhuà (wall-painting) <n.> mural: 古代~ ancient mural || 巨幅~ large-sized mural || 石窟~ rock cave mural
17 水彩画 [--畫] shuǐcǎihuà (water-color-painting) <n.> watercolor painting: 一幅~ a watercolor painting

18 水粉画 [--畫] shuǐfěnhuà (water-powder-painting) <n.> gouache painting: 一幅~ a gouache painting
19 油画 [-畫] yóuhuà (oil-painting) <n.> oil painting: 一幅~ an oil painting || 西洋 ~ Western oil painting
20 年画 [-畫] niánhuà (new year-painting) <n.> New Year painting: 木版~ wooden new year painting || 一张~ a New Year painting
21 字画 [-畫] zìhuà (calligraphy-painting) <n.> calligraphy and paintings: 古~ ancient calligraphy and paintings || 名家~ famous calligraphy and paintings

22 雕像 [-] diāoxiàng (carve-statue) <n.> statue: 艺术~ artistic statue || 动物~ animal statue || 孔子~ Confucius' statue
23 照片 [-] zhàopiān (shoot-picture) <n.> photo: 几张~ a few photos || 洗~ develop photographs || 拍~ take photos
24 照 [-] zhào (photo) <n.> photo: 生活~ candid photo || 艺术~ artistic photo
25 彩照 [-] cǎizhào (color-photo) <n.> color photo: 一张~ a color photo
26 黑白照 [-] hēibáizhào (black-white-photo) <n.> black-and-white photo: 一张~ a black and white photo
27 遗照 [遺-] yízhào (left-over-photo) <n.> portrait of the deceased: 父亲的~ father's portrait
28 证件照 [證--] zhèngjiànzhào (ID-photo) <n.> ID photo: 拍~ take an ID photo || 一张 ~ an ID photo
29 博物馆 [--館] bówùguǎn (abundant-stuff-house) <n.> museum: 一家/座/个~ a museum || 参观~ visit a museum || 历史/艺术~ history/art museum

Tips:

1 画 (畫, huà): The upper part of the traditional form is 聿, which means 'a brush' and the middle part is 田 (field.) The original meaning of 画 (畫) is 'to draw land borders, to divide' from which evolved the meaning 'to draw, to paint.'
2 画画 (huàhuà): The first character is a verb (to draw) and the second a noun (a picture,) in combination they mean 'to paint a picture.'
3 The most famous Chinese painting: It is 清明上河图 (Qīngmíng Shànghé Tú, Along the River during the Qingming Festival) by 张择端 (Zhāng Zéduān, 1085–1145) of the Song Dynasty.
4 画鬼最容易 (huà guǐ zuì róngyì): According to a story in Han Fei Zi, the hardest thing to paint is a dog or a horse and the easiest is a ghost, since dogs and horses are known to all people, but nobody has ever seen a ghost so you can paint it as whatever you imagine.
5 画龙画虎难画骨, 知人知面不知心 (huà lóng huà hǔ nán huà gǔ, zhī rén zhī miàn bù zhī xīn): It means 'In drawing a dragon or a tiger, you show its skin, not its bones, in knowing a man, you can only know his name and face, not his heart,' or to put it simply, 'there is no way to really know a person.'

Exercises:

Part I: Read the following words and then answer the questions.

西洋画、风景画、山水画、花鸟画、动画、漫画、插画、贴画、版画、壁画、水彩画、水粉画、油画、年画、雕像、彩照、黑白照、证件照、遗照

1 哪些画算是西洋画?

____

2 哪些画算是中国画?

____

3 年画是中国哪个节日使用的?

____

4 如果想看艺术雕像, 最好去哪个国家?

____

5 哪个国家的儿童动画片很有名?

____

6 现在的证件照一般是彩照还是黑白照?

____

7 哪种照片一般是人死了以后他的家人才会使用?

____

Theme 85: Sports, games 运动, 比赛 (yùndòng, bǐsài)

(See also Themes 44, 164)

1 比赛 [-賽] bǐsài (compare-compete) <n.> game, contest: 足球~ soccer game || 看~ watch a game
2 大赛 [-賽] dàsài (major-competition) <n.> competition: 体育~ sports competition || 本次~ this competition
3 初赛 [-賽] chūsài (preliminary-competition) <n.> preliminary: 进入~ enter a preliminary
4 复赛 [複賽] fùsài (intermediary-competition) <n.> quarter-final: 进入~ reach the quarter-final
5 决赛 [決賽] juésài (final-competition) <n.> final: 进入~ reach the final || 参加~ participate in the final
6 联赛 [聯賽] liánsài (league-competition) <n.> league: 举办~ host a league || 全国 ~ national league
7 预赛 [預賽] yùsài (preliminary-competition) <n.> qualifying round: 小组~ qualifying round
8 世界杯 [--盃] shìjièbēi (World-Cup) <n.> World Cup: ~冠军World Cup champion || ~比赛World Cup competition || 参加~ participate in the World Cup

9 锦标赛 [錦標賽] jǐnbiāosài (brocade-award-competition) <n.> championship: 乒乓球 ~ ping pong championship || 世界~ world championship
10 球赛 [-賽] qiúsài (ball-game) <n.> sports game: 看~ watch a sports game

11 体育 [體-] tǐyù (physical-education) <n.> athletics: ~课athletic class || ~比赛 athletic contest || ~锻炼to exercise
12 运动 [運動] yùndòng (revolve-move) <n.> sports: ~项目sports event || 参加~ do sports
13 武术 [-術] wǔshù (martial-art) <n.> martial arts: 表演~ perform martial arts || 练~ practice martial arts || 中国~ Chinese martial arts
14 体操 [體-] tǐcāo (physical-exercise) <n.> gymnastics: 做~ do gymnastics || 自由~ floor exercises
15 健美操 [-] jiànměicāo (robust-elegant-exercise) <n.> aerobics: 做~ do aerobics
16 田径 [-徑] tiánjìng (field-track) <n.> track and field: || ~比赛 track and field || ~比赛track and field competition || ~项目track and field event
17 长跑 [長-] chángpǎo (long-run) <n.> long-distance running: ~比赛long-distance running competition
18 短跑 [-] duǎnpǎo (short-run) <n.> sprint: ~比赛sprint race

19 单打 [單-] dāndǎ (single-compete) <n.> singles: 男子/女子~ men's, women's singles || 乒乓球/ 羽毛球/网球~ ping pong, badminton, tennis singles || ~比赛singles event
20 双打 [雙-] shuāngdǎ (double-compete) <n.> doubles: 男子~ men's doubles || 羽毛球~ badminton doubles || ~冠军 doubles champion
21 举重 [舉-] jǔzhòng (lift-weight) <n.> weightlifting: ~比赛weightlifting competition || 练~ practice weightlifting
22 游泳 [-] yóuyǒng (swim-swim) <n.> swimming: 会~ can swim
23 滑冰 [-] huábīng (skate-ice) <n.> ice skating: 花样~ figure skating
24 拳击 [-擊] quánjī (fist-strike) <n.> boxing
25 柔道 [-] róudào (transliteration, lit. soft-way) <n.> judo:
26 散打 [-] sǎndǎ (fee-combat) <n.> free combat:
27 空手道 [-] kōngshǒudào (empty-hand-way) <n.> karate
28 跆拳道 [-] táiquándào (transliteration-way) <n.> taekwondo
29 太极拳 [-極-] tàijíquán (tai-chi-fist skill) <n.> shadowboxing, tai chi: 打~ do shadowboxing

30 赛车 [賽車] sàichē (race-car) <n.> car racing: ~比赛car racing competition || 超级~ super car
31 赛马 [賽馬] sàimǎ (race-horse) <n.> horse racing: ~项目horse racing event || ~活动horse racing activity || ~场horse racing course

32 体育场 [體-場] tǐyùchǎng (sport-courtyard) <n.> stadium: 露天~ outdoor stadium || 室内~ indoor stadium
33 体育馆 [體-館] tǐyùguǎn (sport-house) <n.> gymnasium: 进入~ enter a gymnasium
34 操场 [-場] cāochǎng (exercise-courtyard) <n.> playground: 在~上on the playground

35 场馆 [場館] chángguǎn (courtyard-house) <n.> venue: 比赛~ game, match, competition venue
36 游泳池 [-] yóuyǒngchí (swim-pool) <n.> swimming pool: 露天~ outdoor swimming pool || 室内 ~ indoor swimming pool || 公共~ public swimming pool
37 球场 [-場] qiúchǎng (ball-house) <n.> sports field: 露天~ outdoor field || 在~上on the field
38 俱乐部 [-樂-] jùlèbù (transliteration, lit. all-happy-place) <n.> club: 游泳 ~ swimming club || 工人~ workers' club || 音乐~ music club

Tips:

1 'Track and field' and 田径 (tiánjìng): Literally 田径 means 'field-track' in Chinese, which is the reverse order of the English 'track and field.'
2 Superlative of Chinese sports: The Chinese are extraordinarily good at the sports and games, which are played on divided courts and without bodily contact, for example, 乒乓球 (ping-pong, table tennis,) 羽毛球 (badminton) and even 女子排球 (women's volleyball.) They are currently not good at sports or games such as soccer and basketball.
3 场 (chǎng): 场 itself means 'place.' It is a general measure word for games and matches.

Exercises:

Part I: Use the given bound form as a guide to help you think of other words with the same character. Feel free to use your dictionary when needed. Then write down the English definition of each of the words you've written.

赛 *(game, competition):* 比赛 *game, contest*

____

____

____

____

____

____

____

____

Part II: Read the following words and then answer the questions.

游泳、武术、体操、健美操、田径、长跑、短跑、举重、拳击、滑冰、柔道、乒乓球单打、乒乓球双打、散打、空手道、跆拳道、太极拳、赛车、赛马

1 在上面这些体育运动中, 你擅长 (shàncháng, be good at) 哪些?

____

2 你喜欢看哪些体育比赛?

3 在奥运会比赛中, 你们国家的运动员在哪些体育项目上一般会拿金牌?

4 在奥运会比赛中, 中国运动员在哪些体育项目上一般会拿金牌?

5 "武术和太极拳"起源于哪个国家?

6 空手道和跆拳道 (táiquándào, taekwondo) 起源于哪个国家?

Theme 86: Illness, treatment 疾病, 医疗 (jíbìng, yīliáo)

(See also Themes 103, 165)

1 病 [-] bìng (illness) <n.> illness: 得~ have an illness || 生 ~ have an illness || 有很多~ have many illnesses

2 毛病 [-] máobìng ((of horse) hair-defect) <n.> defect: 肺部有~ the lung has a defect || 眼睛有~ the eye has a defect || 检查出一个小~ identify a small defect

3 疾病 [-] máobìng (sick-ill) <n.> disease: 治疗~ treat a disease || 传播 (chuánbō) ~ spread a disease || 脑部~ a brain disease

4 绝症 [絕-] juézhèng (fatal-illness) <n.> cancer: 得~ get an incurable disease || 患 (huàn) ~ have incurable disease

5 火气 [-氣] huǒqì (internal heat-qi) <n.> anger, vexation: ~大much anger || 一肚子 ~ full of anger || 忍着~ quell one's anger

6 上火 [-] shànghuǒ (emerge-internal heat) <v.> get angry: 着急 ~ get anxious and angry

7 肺炎 [-] fèiyán (lung-inflammation) <n.> pneumonia: 急性 ~ acute pneumonia || 得了~ get pneumonia || 患~ suffer from pneumonia

8 精神病 [-] jīngshénbìng (mental-illness) <n.> psychosis, mental illness: 这个人有点儿~. This person is not quite right in his head.

9 自闭症 [-閉-] zìbìzhèng (self-shut-illness) <n.> Autism: 得了~ have Autism || 患~ suffer from Autism

10 多动症 [-動-] duōdòngzhèng (excessive-move-illness) <n.> Attention Deficit and Hyperactivity Disorder (ADHD): ~儿童 hyperactive child

11 抑郁症 [-鬱-] yìyùzhèng (depression-illness) <n.> depression: 他有严重的~. He suffers from acute depression.

12 神经病 [-經-] shénjīngbìng (nerve-illness) <n.> neuropathy: 这个人有点儿~. This chap's not quite right in the head.

13 厌食症 [厭--] yànshízhèng (dislike-food-illness) <n.> Anorexia: 他得了~. He got Anorexia.

14 艾滋病 [-] àizībìng (transliteration, lit. love-overflow-illness) <n.> Acquired Immunodeficiency Syndrome (AIDS): ~患者AIDS patients || 得了 ~ got AIDS

15 性病 [-] xìngbìng (sex-illness) <n.> sexually transmitted disease (STDS): 防止~ prevent STDS || 得了~ got STDS || 治疗~ treat STDS

16 糖尿病 [-] tángniàobìng (sugar-urine-illness) <n.> Diabetes: 预防~ prevent Diabetes || 患~ got Diabetes

17 肝炎 [-] gānyán liver-inflammation) <n.> Hepatitis: 得了~ got Hepatitis || 甲型/乙型~ Hepatitis A/Hepatitis B

18 心脏病 [-臟-] xīnzàngbìng (heart-internal organ-illness) <n.> heart disease: 得了~ get heart disease || 有~ have heart disease || 严重的~ a serious heart disease

19 癌症 [-] áizhèng (cancer-illness) <n.> cancer: 得了~ got cancer || ~病人 cancer patient || ~晚期terminal cancer

20 流感 [-] liúgǎn (epidemic-flu) <n.> flu: 得了~ get the flu || 预防~ prevent the flu || 严重的~ a serious flu

21 中暑 [-] zhòngshǔ (struck-heat) <n.> heatstroke, sunstroke: 夏季要积极预防~. In summer, you should actively prevent sunstroke. || 在高温条件下工作很容易~. Working out in high temperatures makes it is easy get heatstroke.

22 近视 [-視] jìnshì (near-sight) <n./adj.> nearsightedness, nearsighted: 深度~ severely nearsighted || ~眼镜spectacles for nearsightedness || 我眼睛~. I am nearsighted.

23 红眼病 [紅--] hóngyǎnbìng (red-eye-illness) <n.> pink eye disease: 得了~ got pink eye disease || 预防~ prevent pink eye disease

24 黑死病 [-] hēisǐbìn (black-death-illness) <n.> plague: ~是1348年在欧洲爆发 (bàofā) 的一次大型瘟疫 (wēnyì). The Black Death was a major plague in Europe in 1384.

25 胃病 [-] wèibìng (stomach-illness) <n.> stomach disease: 他的~犯了. He has stomach troubles.

26 肾病 [-] shènbìng (kidney-illness) <n.> kidney disease: 慢性~ chronic kidney disease

27 骨折 [-] gǔzhé (bone-fracture) <n.> fracture: 左手~ a left hand fracture

28 皮肤病 [-] pífūbìng (skin-illness) <n.> skin disease: ~一般都很顽固. Usually, skin disease is difficult to cure.

29 帕金森症 [-] pàjīnsēnzhèng (transliteration-illness) <n.> Parkinson's disease: 患有~ have Parkinson's disease

30 伤口 [傷-] shāngkǒu (wound-cut) <n.> wound: 清洗~ clean the wound || ~痛painful wound || 包扎~ bind up a wound

31 卫生 [衛-] wèishēng (safeguard-life) <n.> hygiene: 讲 ~ care about hygiene || 注意~ pay attention to hygiene || 个人~ personal hygiene

32 医院 [醫-] yīyuàn (medical-courtyard) <n.> hospital: 五家~ five hospitals || 大~ a big hospital || 去~ go to hospital

33 手术 [-術] shǒushù (hand-operate) <n.> operation: 做/动~ do an operation/a surgery || 外科~ surgery || 大型~ a major operation

34 诊室 [診-] zhěnshì (diagnose-room) <n.> clinic: 儿科~ pediatric clinic || 外科~ surgical clinic || 回到~ return to the clinic

35 门诊 [門診] ménzhěn (counter-diagnose) <n.> outpatient service: ~时间 outpatient service time || 方便 ~ convenient outpatient service || 专科 ~ specialized outpatient service

36 疗养院 [療養-] liáoyǎngyuàn (treat-recuperate-courtyard) <n.> sanitarium: 那家旅馆将被改建成私人~. The hotel is going to be converted into a nursing home.

Tips:

1 病 (bìng) and 症 (zhèng): 病 meant 'serious illness' in ancient Chinese, but is now a very general term for 'illness,' serious or unserious. 症 means 'disease, symptom,' which can be mental illness or non-life-threatening, for example, 厌食症, 多动症 and 抑郁症, all listed above. 癌症 is serious.

2 Names of illnesses: Some got their names from the organs where the illnesses occur, for example, 肝炎 (liver-炎, Hepatitis,) 肺炎 (lung-炎, pneumonia,) 皮肤病 (skin-病, skin disease,) 心脏病 (heart-病, heart disease). Some names came from their causes, for example, 厌食症 (dislike-food-症, anorexia) and 抑郁症 (depress-症, depression).

Exercises:

Part I: Read the following words and then answer the questions.

绝症、上火、肺炎、精神病、自闭症、多动症、抑郁症、神经病、厌食症、艾滋病、性病、糖尿病、肝炎、心脏病、癌症、流感、近视、红眼病、黑死病、胃病、肾病、骨折、皮肤病、帕金森症

1 哪些病目前还是绝症, 不能被治愈 (zhìyù, be cured)?

______

2 哪些病跟心理问题或者脑部神经关系最多?

______

3 哪些病是关于内脏的疾病?

______

4 哪些病是眼睛部位的疾病?

______

5 哪些病属于流行病?

______

6 帕金森症一般出现在年轻人身上还是老年人身上?

______

7 哪些病一般会出现在小孩子身上?

______

8 "上火"是中医的说法还是西医的说法? 你相信"上火"吗? 为什么?

______

Theme 87: Numbers, amounts 数量 (shùliàng)

1 几 [幾] jǐ (several) <num.> several, a few: ~年several years || ~个人a few people || ~张照片a few pictures
2 零 [-] líng (zero) <num.> zero: 从~开始start with zero || 一百~五105 || 二~一六年2016
3 一 [-] yī (one) <num.> one: ~个one || ~杯one cup || ~天one day
4 二 [-] èr (two) <num.> two, second: ~楼 the second floor || 第~天the second day || 三分之 ~ two thirds
5 两 [兩] liǎng (two) <num.> two: ~个人two people || ~本书two books || ~杯茶two cups of tea
6 俩 [倆] liǎ (two) <num.> two: ~人two people || 兄妹~ brother and sister || 咱们~ the two of us
Note: 俩=两个
7 三 [-] sān (three) <num.> three: ~个人three people || ~天three days || ~次three times
8 四 [-] sì (four) <num.> four: ~个小时four hours || ~月April || 百分之~ four percent
9 五 [-] wǔ (five) <num.> five: ~块钱 five dollars || ~杯水five cups of water || ~位医生five doctors
10 六 [-] liù (six) <num.> six: ~个月six months || ~本杂志six magazines || ~瓶啤酒six bottles of beer
11 七 [-] qī (seven) <num.> seven: ~月July || ~天seven days || ~朵花seven flowers
12 八 [-] bā (eight) <num.> eight: 第~ the eighth || ~杯eight cups || ~月August
13 九 [-] jiǔ (nine) <num.> nine: ~月September || ~岁nine years old || ~个人nine people
14 十 [-] shí (ten) <num.> ten: ~个ten || ~年ten years || ~次ten times
15 打 [-] dá (dozen) <num.> dozen: 一~ a dozen
16 百 [-] bǎi (hundred) <num.> 100: 几~ a few hundred || 一~天100 days || ~分之五five percent
17 千 [-] qiān (thousand) <num.> thousand: 数/几~ a few thousand || 三~ 3,000 || ~家万户thousands of households
18 万 [萬] wàn (ten thousand) <num.> 10,000: 六~美元60,000 || ~人大会 a 10,000-person conference || 不远~里to travel thousands of miles
19 百万 [-萬] bǎiwàn (hundred-ten thousand) <num.> million: ~人口millions of people || ~富翁millionaires || 几~年前millions of years ago
20 亿 [億] yì (hundred-million) <num.> 100 million: 十四~人口 population of 14 hundred million || 六~人民币600 million dollars || 八十~年eight billion years
21 十亿 [-億] shíyì (ten-hundred million) <num.> billion: ~人口a billion people || ~美元 a billion dollars
22 一半 [-] yībàn (one-half) <num.> half: ~孩子half of the children || ~学校half the school || 一人~ one half per person
23 半 [-] bàn (half) <num.> half: ~ 小时half an hour || ~个香蕉half a banana || ~年half of the year

24 比例 [-] bǐlì (compare-instance) <n.> proportion, ratio: 按~ in proportion to, a ratio of || 不成~ disproportionate || 师生~ teacher-student ratio

25 比分 [-] bǐfēn (compare-score) <n.> score: ~落后 to fall behind in the score || ~领先to lead in the score || 将~追平to tie the score

26 比重 [-] bǐzhòng (compare-weight) <n.> proportion: ~大/小a large/small proportion || ~提高/下降to increase/decrease proportion || 占很大~ take up a large proportion

27 数 [數] shù (number) <n.> number: 人~ number of people || 天~ number of days || 金牌~ number of gold medals

28 数字 [數-] shùzì (number-word) <n.> number: 两个~ two numbers || 统计~ statistical figures || 天文~ an astronomical number

29 数据 [數據] shùjù (number-evidence) <n.> data: 大量~ large amount of data || ~处理data processing || 各种~ different types of data

30 数目 [數-] shùmù (number-item) <n.> amount: ~大/多big/large amount || 存款 (cúnkuǎn) ~ savings amount || ~可观a considerable amount

31 数量 [數-] shùliàng (number-amount) <n.> number: ~多 large number || ~充足/不足sufficient/deficient number

32 分数 [-數] fēnshù (score-number) <n.> score, grade: ~高/低high/low score || 考一个好~ get a good score || 考试~ test score

33 人数 [-數] rénshù (people-number) <n.> population: 职员~ staff population || ~多/少large/small population || 减少~ decrease the population

34 次数 [-數] cìshù (time-number) <n.> number of times: 练习~ number of practices || 参观~ number of visits || 唱的~ number of singing

35 指数 [-數] zhǐshù (index-number) <n.> index: 生活~ index of living || 物价~ index of price || 工资~ index of salary

36 总数 [總數] zǒngshù (total-number) <n.> total number: 人口~ total population || 金牌~ total number of medals || 女性~ total number of women

37 总量 [總-] zǒngliàng (total-amount) <n.> total amount: ~大 a large total amount || 降水~ total amount of rainfall || 商品 ~ total amount of consumer goods

38 余额 [餘額] yú'é (remain-sum) <n.> balance: 存款~ savings balance || 贷款 (dàikuǎn) ~ loan balance

39 零头 [-頭] língtóu (fraction-*suffix*) <n.> a fraction: 占~ take up a fraction || 剩下~ leave a fraction || 除去~ take away a fraction

40 金额 [-額] jīn'é (money-sum) <n.> sum of money: ~大large sum of money || 总~ total sum of money || 收费~ total charge

41 名额 [-額] míng'é (allocation-number) <n.> spot: 有/没~ have/not to have a spot || ~不多few spots || ~满了all spots are filled up

42 学分 [學-] xuéfēn (school-credit) <n.> credit: 十个~ ten credits || 修~ earn a credit || 总~ total credits

43 速度 [-] sùdù (speed-measurement) <n.> speed: 高~ high speed || 加快~ increase the speed || ~下降decrease the speed

44 效率 [-] xiàolǜ (efficient-rate) <n.> efficiency: 工作~ working efficiency || ~低low efficiency || 提高~ increase efficiency

45 产量 [產-] chǎnliàng (produce-amount) <n.> yield: 玉米~ yield of corn || 提高~ increase yield || ~高/低high/low yield

46 含量 [-] hánliàng (contain-amount) <n.> level, content: ~高 high level || 信息~ information content || 技术~ technical content

47 汇率 [匯-] huìlǜ (exchange-rate) <n.> exchange rate: 调整~ adjust the exchange rate || ~上涨exchange rate rises || ~下跌exchange rate drops

48 多少 [-] duōshǎo (more-less) <pron.> how many: ~天how many days || ~次how many times || ~人how many people

49 多数 [-數] duōshù (majority-number) <n.> majority: 大 ~ vast majority || ~孩子 majority of children || ~国家majority of countries

50 少数 [-數] shǎoshù (minority-number) <n.> few: ~人few people || ~工厂few factories || ~国家few countries

51 多半 [-] duōbàn (more-half) <num.> most: ~时间most of the time || ~部分most parts || ~座位most seats

52 分之 [-] fēnzhī (division-of) <bf> out of: 三~二two out of three/two thirds || 百 ~五十50 out of a 100/50 percent || 千 ~一one out of 1,000

53 左右 [-] zuǒyòu (left-right) <n.> around: 一百年~ around 100 years || 四十岁~ around 40 years old || 一千字~ around 1,000 characters

54 上下 [-] shàngxià (above-below) <n.> about, around: 百分之九十~ about 90 percent || 五十岁~ about 50 years old

55 单元 [單-] dānyuán (single-unit) <n.> unit: 六个~ six units || 基本~ basic unit || ~考试unit test

56 季 [-] jì (season) <n.> season: 单/双~ one/two seasons || 干/雨~ dry/rainy season || 春/夏/秋/冬~ spring/summer/autumn/winter

Tips:

1 Numbers one to ten on currency and in bank transactions: The Arabic numerals 1 to 10 and Chinese characters 一 to 十 are often written as 壹贰叁肆伍陸柒捌玖拾 on currency and in bank transactions, to make the numbers more distinct and less likely to be misread.

2 In Chinese, large numbers are counted by four digits: Traditionally, large numbers are counted by four digits, for example, 12,3456,7890. However, obviously influenced by the English custom, some recent publications may use the English custom, which requires readers to pay particular attention.

3 俩 (liǎ) and 仨 (sā): They mean "两个" (two) and "三个" (three,) therefore no more measure words are needed before nouns, for example, you cannot say "俩件衣服."

Exercises:

Part I: Use the given bound form as a guide to help you think of other words with the same character. Feel free to use your dictionary when needed. Then write down the English definition of each of the words you've written.

数 *(number):* 数据*data*

____

____

____

____

____

____

____

____

Part II: Translate the following English into Chinese.

3,000 ____________________
1,000s of households ____________________
60,000 people ____________________
5 million dollars ____________________
Population of 14 hundred million ____________________
two out of three ____________________
50 out of a 100 ____________________

Part III: Read the following sentences and fill in each blank with the appropriate word or phrase from the options given.

1 季节、上下、单元、多数

a) 中国的居民楼一般非常几个_______, 也就是几个部分, 每部分都有很多住户.
b) 加州南部一年只有两个________, 雨季和旱季.
c) 北京市的总人口在三千万_________.
d) 在北京从事服务业的人_______是外来人口.

2 产量、含量、少数、汇率

a) 清华大学的毕业生中只有_______选择回到家乡工作.
b) 2017年人民币跟美元的________是6.5: 1.
c) 美国是世界上玉米________最多的国家.
d) 德国工业的科技_______很高, 在世界上处于领先地位.

3 学分、速度、效率、名额

a) 有人认为目前世界上经济发展______最快的国家应该是印度.
b) 有人认为美国政府的工作_______远远低于中国政府.
c) 在中国读研究生至少要修完36个_________的课才能毕业.
d) 从2008年开始, 中国政府开始增加公派留学生________, 到国外留学的公派学生越来越多.

4 总量、余额、指数

a) 小张银行卡里的_______不到五百块钱.
b) 2016年中国的经济_________超过了美国.
c) 在中国一些大城市物价_______上涨很快.

Theme 88: Measurements 度量 (dùliáng)

1 高度 [-] gāodù (height-measurement) <n./ adj.> height, highly: 飞行 ~ flight height || ~重视highly emphasize

2 个子 [個-] gèzi (height-*suffix*) <n.> height: 小~ short in height || ~高tall in height || 长 (zhǎng) ~ grow in height

3 高矮 [-] gāoǎi (high-short) <n.> height: 身材~ body height || 个头~ body height || ~胖瘦height and weight

4 身高 [-] shēngāo (body-height) <n.> height: 平均~ average height || ~增长 increased height

5 深浅 [-淺] shēnqiǎn (deep-shallow) <n.> depth: ~不一various depths || 试试~ try the depth

6 深度 [-] shēndù (depth-measurement) <n.> depth: 思想~ depth of thought || 海水~ ocean depth || 缺乏~ lack depth

7 厚度 [-] hòudù (thickness-measurement) <n.> thickness: 书本~ book's thickness || 增强~ enhance thickness || 有~ have thickness

8 幅度 [-] fúdù (strip-measurement) <n.> extent: ~大 great extent || 上涨~ extent of increase || 变化 ~ extent of change

9 降幅 [-] jiàngfú (descend-range) <n.> range of decrease: ~很大great decrease

10 增幅 [-] zēngfú (increase-range) <n.> range of increase: ~大great increase

11 涨幅 [漲-] zhǎngfú (rise-range) <n.> range of rise: ~大great rise

12 升幅 [-] shēngfú (ascend-range) <n.> range of rise: ~大great rise

13 跌幅 [-] diēfú (fall-range) <n.> size of fall: ~大 great drop

14 宽度 [寬-] kuāndù (width-measurement) <n.> width: 道路~ road width || 房间 ~ bedroom width

15 宽窄 [寬-] kuānzhǎi (wide-narrow) <n.> width: ~不一 various widths || ~不等differing widths

16 粗细 [-細] cūxì (thick-thin) <n.> thickness: ~相同same thickness || ~均匀uniform thickness

17 松紧 [鬆緊] sōngjǐn (loose-tight) <n.> elasticity: ~程度degree of elasticity

18 距离 [-離] jùlí (distance to-apart from) <n.> distance: ~远long distance || 近~ short distance || 拉开/保持~ increase/maintain distance

19 长度 [長-] chángdù (length-measurement) <n.> length: 总~ total length || 量~ measure the length

20 长短 [長-] chángduǎn (long-short) <n.> length: 时间~ length of time || 衣服~ length of clothing || ~不齐various lengths

21 行程 [-] xíngchéng (walk-journey) <n.> schedule: ~紧张tight schedule || 三天的~ three-day schedule || ~顺利smooth schedule

22 双程 [雙-] shuāngchéng (double-journey) <n.> two-way trip: ~ 机票two-way plane ticket

23 往返 [-] wǎngfǎn (go-return) <n.> round trip: ~机票 round trip plane ticket

24 单程 [單-] dānchéng (single-journey) <n.> one-way trip: ~车票one-way ticket

25 难度 [難-] nándù (difficult-degree) <n.> degree of difficulty: 高~ high degree of difficulty || ~大great difficulty || 动作~ great difficulty of movement

26 音量 [-] yīnliàng (sound-volume) <n.> sound volume: 正常~ normal volume || 增大 ~ increase volume || 调节 ~ adjust volume

27 高低 [-] gāodī (high-low) <n.> level: 声音~ sound level || 收入~ salary level || 价格~ price level

28 温度 [溫-] wēndù (temperature-measurement) <n.> temperature: 最高~ highest temperature || ~降低temperature drops || 室内~ indoor temperature
29 低温 [-溫] dīwēn (low-temperature) <n.> low temperature: ~冷冻to deep freeze/to freeze at a low temperature || ~地区low temperature area
30 高温 [-溫] gāowēn (high-temperature) <n.> high temperature: ~消毒high temperature disinfection || ~天气high temperature weather
31 零上 [-] língshàng (zero-above) <n.> above zero: ~十度10 degrees
32 零下 [-] língxià (zero-below) <n.> below zero: ~十度negative 10 degrees
33 摄氏度 [攝--] shèshìdù (transliteration-measurement) <n.> Celsius: 十~ degrees Celsius
34 华氏度 [華--] huáshìdù (transliteration-measurement) <n.> Fahrenheit: 五十~50 degrees Fahrenheit
35 热度 [熱-] rèdù (hot-degree) <n.> degree of heat, heat: ~退了 the heat has abated || ~降低to reduce the degree of heat || ~过高the heat is too high
36 气温 [氣溫] qìwēn (air-temperature) <n.> temperature: ~低low temperature || 平均~ average temperature || ~升高temperature increases
37 体温 [體溫] tǐwēn (body-temperature) <n.> body temperature: 调节~ adjust the body temperature || 量~ measure the body temperature || ~下降body temperature decreases

38 坡度 [-] pōdù (slope-degree) <n.> slope: ~小small slope || ~大big slope
39 经度 [經-] jīngdù (longitude-degree) <n.> longitude: 在地球上, ~不同, 时间就不同. On Earth, time is different if the longitude is different.
40 纬度 [緯-] wěidù (latitude-degree) <n.> latitude: ~低的地方, 天气会暖和一些. Where the latitude is low, the weather will be warmer. || 低/高~ low/high latitudes || ~相同the same latitude
41 重量 [-] zhòngliàng (weight-quantity) <n.> weight: 称~ measure weight || ~轻/重heavy/light weight
42 轻重 [輕-] qīngzhòng (light-heavy) <n.> weight, severity: 不知~ not know the severity (of a situation) || 情节~ severity of a situation
43 分量 [-] fènliàng (portion-measurement) <n.> weight: ~重carry great weight || ~不足carry light weight
44 体重 [體-] tǐzhòng (body-weight) <n.> body weight: ~变化 body weight difference || 保持 ~ maintain body weight || 减轻 ~ lose body weight

45 速度 [-] sùdù (speed-measurement) <n.> speed: ~快high speed || 加快~ increase speed
46 进度 [進-] jìndù (progress-measurement) <n.> progress: ~慢 slow progress || 工作~ work progress || ~下降to reduce progress
47 可信度 [-] kěxìndù (can-trust-degree) <n.> credibility: ~高 high credibility
48 满意度 [滿--] mǎnyìdù (satisfaction-degree) <n.> satisfaction level: 客户~高high customer satisfaction || 提高~ improve one's satisfaction || 老百姓对政府工作的~不高. People's satisfaction with government work is not high.
49 浓度 [濃-] nóngdù (dense-measurement) <n.> concentration: ~高high concentration || ~小low concentration

50 浓淡 [濃-] nóngdàn (dense-thin) <n.> concentration: ~不同different concentrations

51 频率 [頻-] pínlǜ (frequency-rate) <n.> frequency: ~高 high frequency || ~快high frequency

Tips:

1 度 (dù), 量 (liàng), 幅 (fú), 率 (lǜ): 度 is related to 庶 (shù) and 又 (手, hand.) Ancient people used 'hand(s)' to measure length, therefore 度 means 'linear measure.' Common words with 度 include 长度, 宽度, 高度, 厚度, 深度, 幅度, 难度, 温度, 热度, 经度, 纬度, 坡度, 速度, 进度, 浓度, 可信度, 满意度, all listed above and 湿度 (shīdù, validity,) 效度 (xiàodù, efficiency) etc. 量 originally meant 'to weigh' and is pronounced as 'liáng.' It is related to "重" (heavy,) not "里." Later the meanings 'measuring instrument' and 'quality,' both pronounced as 'liàng,' were derived. Common words with 量 include 重量 and 音量 which are listed above, and 分量 (fènliàng, weight,) 容量 (róngliàng, volume, capacity,) 产量 (chǎnliàng, output, yield,) 含量 (hánliàng, content) etc. 幅 originally means 'width of cloth' since it is related to 巾 (cloth) and 畐 (fú.) Now it mainly means 'width,' for example, 增幅, 降幅, 涨幅, 升幅, 跌幅, all listed above. 率 means 'rate, ratio, proportion.' Words with 率 include 频率 (pínlǜ, frequency,) 效率 (xiàolǜ, efficiency,) 概率 (gàilǜ, probability,) 汇率 (huìlǜ, exchange rate,) 利率 (lìlǜ, interest rate,) 税率 (shuìlǜ, tax rate,) 圆周率 (yuánzhōulǜ, Pi,) 支持率 (zhīchílǜ, approval rating,) and 失业率 (shīyèlǜ, unemployment rate).

2 Qin's unification of measurement units: The Qin State unified China and units of currency, weight and measurement, which laid the solid foundation of a great empire.

3 Scopes composed of two antonymous words: In Chinese, there are many hypernyms, which are composed of two antonymous words, for example 长短 (long-short, length, distance,) 深浅 (deep-shallow, dark-light, depth, shade,) 轻重 (light-heavy, weight,) 高低 (high-low, height,) 宽窄 (broad-narrow, width, breadth,) 粗细 (thick-thin, size,) and 难易 (hard-easy, difficulty).

Exercises:

Part I: Use the given bound form as a guide to help you think of other words with the same character. Feel free to use your dictionary when needed. Then write down the English definition of each of the words you've written.

幅 *(range):* 降幅 *range of decrease*

____

____

____

____

____

度 *(degree)*: 深度 *depth*

____

____

____

____

____

Part II: Read the following words and then answer the questions.

长短、深浅、轻重、高低、宽窄、粗细、往返、高矮、可信度、满意度、行程、单程、双程、体重、气温、距离、幅度

1 "长短"是两个相反的形容放在一起组成了一个名词，英文意思是 "length, duration," 请在上面词中找出构词方式上跟它一样的词.

____

2 你觉得你们国家媒体的可信度高不高? 为什么?

____

3 你们国家老百姓对政府的满意度高不高? 为什么?

____

4 买机票单程票便宜还是往返票便宜?

____

5 想减轻体重有哪些好办法?

____

6 你住的地方冬天气温高还是低? 你住的地方离机场远还是近?

____

7 近十年来, 你们国家老百姓收入增加的幅度大不大? 为什么?

____

Theme 89: Units of measurement, legal and conventional 单位 (dānwèi)

Part I: Length, 长度 (chángdù):

1 公里 [-] gōnglǐ (common-mile) <c.> kilometers: 一百 ~ 100 kilometers
2 米 [-] mǐ (meter) <c.> meters: 四~高 four meters tall || 两~长 two meters long
3 厘米 [-] límǐ (hundredth-meter) <c.> centimeters: 十~ ten centimeters || 平方~ centimeters square || 立方~ centimeters cube
4 毫米 [-] háomǐ (thousandth-meter) <c.> millimeters: 几~ a couple of millimeters
5 纳米 [納-] nàmǐ (nano-meter) <c.> nanometers: ~技术 nanotechnology || ~材料 (cáiliào) nanomaterial

6 光年 [-] guāngnián (light-year) <c.> light-year: 一~就是光在一年的时间里移动的距离. One light year is the distance that light travels in a year.
7 尺 [-] chǐ (Chinese foot) <c.> chi (a unit of scale 3 chi= 1 meter): 一百~长 103 chi long || 四~布 a four-chi long cloth
8 寸 [-] cùn (Chinese inch) <c.> inches: 五~长 five inches long
9 英里 [-] yīnglǐ (British-mile) <n.> mile: 五~ five miles
10 英尺 [-] yīngchǐ (British-foot) <n.> foot: 她六~高. She is six feet tall.
11 海里 [-哩] hǎilǐ (nautical-mile) <n.> nautical mile: 三十~ 30 miles

Part II: Weight, 重量 (zhòngliàng):

12 吨 [噸] dūn (transliteration ton) <c.> ton: 一~面粉 a ton of flours
13 公斤 [-] gōngjīn (common-catty) <c.> kilograms: 五~大米 five kilograms of rice
14 千克 [-] qiānkè (1000-gram) <c.> kilograms: 四~水 four kilograms of water
15 克 [-] kè (gram) <c.> gram: 一百~黄金 100 grams of gold
16 斤 [-] jīn (catty) <c.> jin (a traditional unit of weight, each containing 10 liang and equivalent to 0.5 kilogram or 1.102 pounds): 一~苹果 a gram of apple
17 两 [兩] liǎng (tael) <c.> Liang, a unit of weight, equal to 50 grams: 五~ 250 g
18 磅 [-] bàng (transliteration pound) <c.> pound: 两~牛肉 two pounds of beef

Part III: Area, 面积 (miànjī):

19 平方 [-] píngfāng (square) <c.> square: ~米 square meters || ~公里 square kilometers || ~英里 square miles
20 亩 [畝] mǔ (mu) <c.> mu, a unit of area= 0.0667 hectares: 一~地 an area of one mu

Part IV: Volume, 容积, 容量 (róngjī, róngliàng)

21 升 [-] shēng (liter) <c.> liter: 一~水 a liter of water
22 毫升 [-] háoshēng (thousandth-liter) <c.> milliliter: 五~ five milliliters
23 立方 [-] lìfāng (cubic) <c.> cubic: ~米 cubic meter || ~体cube
24 加仑 [-侖] jiālún (transliteration gallon) <c.> gallon: 一~油 one gallon of gas

Part V: Units of currency

25 元 [-] yuán (yuan) <c.> a Chinese currency unit, yuan: 八~ eight yuan
26 角 [-] jiǎo (jiao) <c.> a Chinese currency unit, jiao= 0.1 yuan: 汽车票一元五~. A bus ticket costs one yuan and five jiao || 一~硬币 a coin worth one jiao
27 毛 [-] máo (Mao) <c.> Mao=1 jiao: 五~钱 five Mao || 一~硬币 a coin worth of one Mao || 两~纸币 a bill worth two Mao
28 分 [-] fēn (fen) <c.> a Chinese currency unit, 1 fen=0.1 jiao: 一~钱 one fen

Part VI: Units of time

29 刻 [-] kè (quarter hour) <c.> quarter of an hour: 一~钟 a quarter of an hour || 三点差一~ 2: 45 || 五点过一~ 5: 15
30 秒 [-] miǎo (second) <c.> seconds: 三~钟 three seconds

Part VII: Of people:

31 户 [戶] hù (door) <c.> household: 一~人家 one household || 六十~农民 60 households of farmers
32 伙 [夥] huǒ (group) <c.> group: 一~人 one group of people || 一~小偷 one group of thieves || 一~强盗 (qiángdào) a group of robbers
33 家 [-] jiā (home) <c.> measure word for families or business: 一~公司 a company || 三~电视台 three channels || 一~银行 one bank
34 名 [-] míng (name) <c.> measure word for people, especially those with a specific position or occupation: 六~青年 six youths || 八~画家 eight artists || 第三~ third place
35 位 [-] wèi (person) <c.> measure word for people (polite): 三~老师 three teachers || 五~医生 five doctors || 七~老人 seven senior citizens

Part VIII: Of animals:

36 匹 [-] pǐ (match) <c.> measure word for horses and cloth: 两~马 two horses || 一~布 one cloth
37 群 [-] qún (flock) <c.> a crowd of, a group of: 一~人 a crowd of people || 一~鸽子 a flock of pigeons || 一~猴子 a group of monkeys
38 条 [條] tiáo (twig) <c.> measure word for things with a long, narrow shape: 八~鱼 eight fish || 三~路 three roads || 四~河 four rivers
39 头 [頭] tóu (head) <c.> measure word for cattle or sheep: 两~牛 two cows || 三~大象 three elephants || 四~黑熊 four bears

Part IX: Of solid matter:

40 把 [-] bǎ (hold) <c.> measure word for objects with handles: 一~椅子 a chair || 一~吉他 a guitar || 一~刀 a knife || 一~糖 a handful of candy || 一~伞an umbrella
41 包 [-] bāo (bundle) <c.> a pack of: 一~点心 a dessert pack || 一~饼干 a pack of crackers || 一~烟 a pack of cigarettes
42 本 [-] běn (root) <c.> measure word for books, magazines, etc.: 一~书 a book || 两~杂志 two magazines || 三~词典 three dictionaries
43 串 [-] chuàn (string) <c.> a bunch of: 一~葡萄/香蕉 a bunch of grapes/ bananas || 一~泪珠/ 脚印 a chain of tears, a bunch of footsteps || ~项链 a necklace
44 袋 [-] dài (bag) <c.> a bag of: 五~面粉 five bags of flour || 一~土豆 a bag of potatoes || 两~桔子 two oranges
45 顶 [頂] dǐng (top) <c.> a measure word (used with 'hat,' crown and tent): 一~帽子 a hat || ~王冠 a crown || ~帐篷 (zhàngpeng) a tent
46 堆 [-] duī (pile) <c.> a pile of: 一~书 a pile of books || 一~垃圾 (lājī) a pile of trash || 一~沙子 a pile of sand
47 朵 [-] duǒ (flower) <c.> a measure word for flower or cloud: 一~花 a flower || 一~白云 a cloud || 一~玫瑰 a rose
48 份 [-] fèn (portion) <c.> portion: 一~晚饭 a dinner || 两~报纸 two newspapers || 一~礼物 a gift
49 封 [-] fēng (seal) <c.> measure word for letters: 一~信 a letter || 一~电报 a telegraph

50 幅 [-] fú (strip) <c.> measure word for pictures, posters, maps. etc.: 一~画 a painting

51 副 [-] fù (split) <c.> a pair of: 一~耳机 a pair of headphones || 一~手套 a pair of gloves || ~眼镜 a pair of glasses

52 个 [個] gè (unit) <c.> the most common measure word. If you do not know the correct measure word to go with a noun, you can use this one.: 一~苹果 one apple || 两~学生 two students || 三 ~杯子 three glasses

53 根 [-] gēn (root) <c.> measure word for long things: 一~筷子 a chopstick || 两~项链 (xiàngliàn) two necklaces || ~绳子 (shéngzi) two ropes

54 行 [-] háng (line) <c.> line: 四~字 four lines of words || 单/ 双~ single line, double line

55 号 [號] hào (number) <c.> size: 三~楼 building number three || 五~公寓 (gōngyù) apartment number five

56 盒 [-] hé (box) <c.> case, container: 一~香烟 a pack of cigarette || 一~饭 a container full of rice || ~糖 a container full of candy

57 架 [-] jià (frame) <c.> measure word for machines, aircraft etc.: 十~飞机 ten airplanes || 一~钢琴 one piano || 一~望远镜 (wàngyuǎnjìng) a pair of binoculars

58 间 [間] jiān (space) <c.> measure word for rooms: 一~房 a room || 三~宿舍 three dorms || 八~教室 eight classrooms

59 件 [-] jiàn (unit) <c.> measure word for things, affairs, clothes or furniture: 一~事情 a thing, issue, case || 三~衬衣 three shirts || 两~礼物 two gifts

60 颗 [顆] kē (head) <c.> measure word for beans, pearls and more: 十~花生 ten peanuts || 一~星星 one star || 一~牙齿 one tooth

61 块 [塊] kuài (lump) <c.> piece, lump, for gold or silver dollars, renminbi and certain types of paper money: 四~钱 four yuan || 三~饼干 three pieces of a cracker || 一~肉 three pieces of meat

62 类 [類] lèi (type) <c.> type: 二~保护动物 two types of protected animals || 这~词 this type of word || 各~水果 various type of fruits

63 辆 [輛] liàng (measure word for vehicles, carts) <c.> measure word for vehicles: 三~卡车 three trucks || 四~出租车 four taxis || 五~公交车 five buses

64 列 [-] liè (arrange) <c.> measure word for trains: 四~火车 four trains

65 门 [門] mén (door) <c.> measure word for school subjects, languages, etc.: 三~课 three classes || 一~学问/ 科学/ 艺术 one subject, science course, art course || 五~大炮 five cannons

66 面 [-] miàn (face) <c.> measure word for flat objects: 一~镜子 a mirror || 一~墙 a wall || 一~旗子 a flag

67 排 [-] pái (row) <c.> a row of: 一~窗子 a window || 一~房屋 a row of houses || 一~牙齿 a row of teeth

68 盘 [盤] pán (plate) <c.> a plate of: 一~菜 a plate of vegetables || 一~蛋糕 a plate of cake || 一~水果 a plate of fruit

69 批 [-] pī (batch) <c.> measure word for a batch of goods, and for things, people arriving at the same time: 一~新书 a batch of new books (published at about the same time) || 一~药 some medicines || 两~客人 two groups of visitors/guests

70 篇 [-] piān (bamboo script) <c.> measure word for a piece of writing: 一~短文 a short article || 一~作文 an essay || 两~报告 two reports

71 片 [-] piàn (slice) <c.> measure word for thin, flat pieces: 一~药 a pill, tablet || 一~叶子 a leaf || 一~西瓜 a slice of watermelon

72 瓶 [-] píng (jug) <c.> a bottle of: 三~酒 three bottles of beer, wine || 一~香水 a bottle of perfume || 两~油 two bottles of oil

73 扇 [-] shàn (fan) <c.> measure word for doors and windows: 一~门 a door || 一~窗 a window

74 束 [-] shù (bundle) <c.> a bundle of: 一~花 a flower bouquet || 一~阳光 a ray of sunlight

75 双 [雙] shuāng (couple) <c.> a pair of (shoes, chopsticks, etc.): 一~手 pair of hands || 一~眼睛 a pair of eyes || 一~袜子 a pair of socks

76 所 [-] suǒ (place) <c.> measure word for houses or institutions housed in a building: 一~学校 a school || 一~医院 a hospital || 一~房子 a house

77 台 [臺] tái (platform) <c.> measure word for machines, big instruments: 一~电视机a TV || 三~电脑three computers || 五~机器five machines

78 套 [-] tào (set) <c.> a set of: 两~房子 two houses || 一~衣服 an outfit, a set of clothes || 一~书 a set of books

79 团 [團] tuán (ball) <c.> a ball of: 一~棉花 a ball of cotton || 一~白云 a cloud

80 箱 [-] xiāng (box) <c.> a box of: 一~珠宝 a box of jewelry || 一~苹果 a box of apples || 两~衣服 two boxes of clothes

81 笔 [筆] bǐ (brush) <c.> measure word for sums of money, financial accounts, debts: 这~钱 this sum of money || 一~学费 this tuition sum || 两 ~收入 two sources of income

82 册 [冊] cè (book) <c.> pamphlet, booklet: 第一~ the first booklet, pamphlet || 一~材料 a book of materials || 几~书 a couple of books

83 层 [層] céng (storey) <c.> level, floor: 三~楼 three-floor building || 一~黄色a layer of yellow || 一~落叶a layer of shed leaves

84 页 [頁] yè (head) <c.> page: 第八~ the eighth page || 三百~ 300 pages

85 张 [張] zhāng (draw a bow) <c.> measure word for paper, bed, table: 三~纸 three pieces of paper || 一~床 three beds || 四~票 four tickets || 一~桌子a table

86 章 [-] zhāng (chapter) <c.> Chapter: 第五~ chapter five || 二十~ 20 chapters

87 只 [隻] zhī (a bird) <c.> measure word for animal or shoe: 两~狗 two dogs || 三~猫 three cats || 一~鞋子 one single shoe || 一~蝴蝶a butterfly

88 枝 [-] zhī (branch) <c.> measure word for flowers with stems intact: 一~花 a flower || 一~笔 a pen || 一~烟 a cigarette

89 种 [種] zhǒng (seed) <c.> type, breed: 几百~鸟 a couple hundred breeds of birds || 一~乐器 one type of instrument || 一~看法 one type of view, outlook

90 棵 [-] kē (mw. for plants) <c.> measure word for plants: 八~树 eight trees || 几~竹子 a couple of bamboo stalks|| 四~松树 four pine trees

91 座 [-] zuò (seat) <c.> measure word for mountains, buildings and similar immovable objects: 一~山 a mountain || 一~楼房 a building

Part X: Of liquid:

92 杯 [-] bēi (cup) <c.> a cup of: 一~水/酒 a cup of water, beer || 两 ~茶 two cups of tea || 三 ~咖啡 three cups of coffee

93 滴 [-] dī (drop) <c.> a drop of: 一~水 a drop of water || 一~眼泪 a drop of tears || 一~油 a drop of oil

94 壶 [壺] hú (vase) <c.> a kettle of: 一~水 a kettle of water || 一~茶 a kettle of tea || 一~酒a container of wine

Part XI: Of events:

95 班 [-] bān (divide) <c.> a trip by bus, boat, flight etc.: 上/下一~飞机 last, next flight || 第一~车 first bus || 末~船 last ship

96 遍 [-] biàn (allover, time) <c.> for actions once through, one time: 听了一~ listen for one time || 看了几~ read several times || 写了三四~ write for three or four times

97 步 [-] bù step (walk) <c.> step, stage: 走三~ walk three steps || 第二 ~ the second step || 一~一~地提高 improve sth. step by step

98 部 [-] bù (part) <c.> measure word for books, films, etc.: 一~电影 a movie || 两~小说 two novels || 第三~书 the third book

99 场 [場] chǎng (times) <c.> measure word for recreational, sports or other activities: 两~音乐会 two concerts || 三~比赛 three matches

100 次 [-] cì (stop, times) <c.> occurrence, times: 多~去美国 been to the U.S. on various occasions || 第六~见面 meeting for the sixth time || 参观了四~ visited four times

101 道 [-] dào (path) <c.> measure word for doors, walls, orders, questions and also courses in a meal: 五~题 five questions || 三~菜 three courses || 两~门 two successive doors

102 段 [-] duàn (section) <c.> section (for something long): 一~话some words || 一 ~故事 a story || 大~单人舞 a solo dance

103 顿 [頓] dùn (stop, times) <c.> measure word indicating frequency: 一~午餐 a lunch || 一天三~饭 three meals a day || 说了他一~ give him a dressing down

104 番 [-] fān (take turns) <c.> measure word for actions, deeds etc.: 下一~功夫 have put in a lots of time and effort || 观察 (guānchá) 一~ observe for a bit || 一~介绍 to introduce a little bit

105 股 [-] gǔ (thigh) <c.> measure word for sth. long and narrow, measure word for strength, smell, etc.: 一~潮流 (cháoliú) a wave of heat || 一~力量 a stream of energy || 一~香味儿 a whiff of fragrance

106 回 [-] huí (chapter, times) <c.> time, occasion, chapter: 这部小说一共一百~. This novel has 100 chapters. || 来一~这个地方 come to this place at least once || 试一~ try once

107 级 [級] jí (grade) <c.> level, rank, grade, class: 七~风 force 7 wind || 一~产品 first-class products || 一年~学生 first grade students

108 集 [-] jí (collection) <c.> episode: 二十~ 20 episodes || 前六~ first six episodes

109 节 [節] jié (joint) <c.> part, section, period: 第一~ first section, period || 三~课three classes

110 届 [屆] jiè (session) <c.> class, year: 上/往~ last/ previous year (class) || 本~ this year, class || 第五~ the fifth class, year

111 局 [-] jú (part) <c.> round, set: 一~棋 a game of chess || 第二~ second round, set || 最后一~比赛 last round, set of matches

112 句 [-] jù (sentence) <c.> sentence: 一~话 a sentence || 两~歌词 two lines of lyrics || 一~名言 a famous saying

113 卷 [-] juǎn (volume) <c.> roll: 上/下~ part one and part two of a book || 五~ five parts || 第六~ part six

114 口 [-] kǒu (mouth) <c.> mouth: 四~人 a four-person family || 一~水 some water || 几~饭 some rice

115 轮 [輪] lún (turn) <c.> round: 第三~比赛 the third round of matches || 一~波纹 a wave || 一~圆月 a full moon

116 期 [-] qī (period) <c./ n.> stage, term, issue: 第五~ the fifth stage/issue || 定~ periodic || 学~ semester

117 圈 [-] quān (circle) <c.> circle: 走一~ walk around || 跳两~ jump around twice || 绕半~ go half a circle

118 声 [聲] shēng (sound) <c.> sound: 叫一~ make a noise || 按了几~喇叭 (lǎba) press the horn a couple of times || 长叹一~ a long sigh

119 首 [-] shǒu (piece) <c.> measure word for songs and poems: 一~歌 a song || 一~诗 a poem || ~钢琴曲a piano piece

120 岁 [歲] suì (age) <c.> age: 几~ how old? || 十五~ fifteen of age

121 趟 [-] tàng (journey) <c.> measure word for a round trip: 去一~ go one time || 回家一~ a trip home || 三~车 three trips in a car

122 下 [-] xià (times) a (for verbs of action) <c.> stroke, times: 按三~ press three times || 擦 (cā) 两~ wipe, clean and smooth once or twice || 摸六~ touch something six times

123 项 [項] xiàng (neck, item) <c.> measure word for itemized things: 八~比赛 eight types of race || 一~工作 one type of work || 四~活动 four types of activities

124 阵 [陣] zhèn (period) <c.> a gust of: 一~风 a gust of wind || 一~脚步声 a burst of footsteps || 一~欢笑 a gust of laughter

125 倍 [-] bèi (times) <c.> times: 四~ four times of something || 好几~ several times

126 成 [-] céng (tenth) <c.> one tenth: 增长三~ increased 30 percent || 收入的五~ 50 percent of income || 农民占八九~. The farmers make up about 80-90 percent.

127 些 [-] xiē (some) <c.> some: 一~人 some people || 这~书 these books || 那~地方 those places

128 样 [樣] yàng (pattern) <c.> type: 一~东西 one item || 每~功课 every homework assignment || 两~菜 two dishes

129 支 [-] zhī (stick) <c.> measure word for long, thin, inflexible objects: 一~烟 a cigarette || 一~香蕉 a banana || 一~笔 a pen

130 度 [-] dù (degree) <c.> degree: 三百~电 300 degrees electricity || 气温三十~ 30 degrees in temperature || 九十~角 90 degree angle

Tips:

1 Chinese traditional units of measurement: Chinese traditional units of measurement have changed just as constantly as the dynasties did throughout the whole of pre-imperial and imperial history. Those changes adversely affected the progress of the sciences. For example, 尺 (chǐ) was one of the key units of measurement, however, the length of 尺 varied between 19.91 cm in the Zhou Dynasty to 32 cm in the Qing Dynasty. Rarely did two consecutive dynasties use the same length. Roughly speaking, one 尺 was about 24 cm before the year 500 and 30 cm between the year 500 and the year 1912.

2 Chinese traditional units of measurement in culture: They are extensively used in idioms. Here are some of them. 半斤八两 (bànjīn bāliǎng) means 'half a pound of one and eight ounces of the other' because one 斤 equalled 16 两 in the ancient times. 得寸进尺 (décùn jìnchǐ) means 'give him an inch and he'll take a mile' because one 尺 equals ten 寸. 差之毫厘, 谬以千里 (chāzhīháolí, miùyǐqiānlǐ) means the 'least difference makes poles apart' because 厘 means 'centimeter' and 毫 'milimeter.'
3 Major Imperial Units and United States Customary Units: They are: inch (英寸,) foot (英尺,) yard (码 mǎ,) mile (英里,) ounce (盎司, àngsī,) gallon (加仑, jiālún,) pound (磅, bàng).
4 双 and 单: Generally, Chinese people like things to be in pairs, so much so that they call it 好事成双 (good things come in pairs.) If you gift presents such as fine English bone china teacups, never give them in odd numbers such as five or seven. Also Chinese do not like the number 'four' since the pronunciation of it (sì) is close to that of 'to die, dead' (sǐ.) When you have to give this number, call it '两对儿' or '两双' (two pairs.)

Exercises:

Part I: Fill in each blank with the appropriate word from the options given.

1 匹、条、头

a) 一________马
b) 一________牛
c) 一________鱼

2 包、颗、把

a) 一________星星
b) 一________茶叶
c) 一________雨伞

3 串、袋、本

a) 一________书
b) 一________葡萄
c) 一________水果

4 份、幅、封

a) 一________文件
b) 一________信
c) 一________山水画

5 根、块、盒

a) 十________钱
b) 一________香蕉
c) 一________饼干

6 辆、件、架

a) 一________飞机
b) 一________汽车
c) 一________衣服

7 篇、门、片

a) 五________课
b) 一________文章
c) 一________药

8 双、套、杯、瓶

a) 一________鞋
b) 十________可乐
c) 一________西装
d) 一________热茶

9 顿、阵、趟

a) 老王跟老李在中国饭馆吃了一________饭.
b) 老王上星期去了一________纽约的中国城.
c) 昨天下午突然下了一________大雨.

10 遍、次、班、轮

a) 海南航空公司每两天有一________飞机飞往美国波士顿.
b) 小张非常喜欢这部电影, 看了三________, 还没看够.
c) 一般美国人每年都要检查 (jiǎnchá, examine) 一________身体.
d) 美国高中生的篮球比赛一般有两________.

Part II: Please sort the following words in ascending order.

1 英里、公里、米、毫米、纳米、英尺、尺、厘米

____

2 斤、两、吨、磅、公斤、克

____

3 升、毫升、加仑

____

4 元、角、分

____

5 分、秒、刻

____

Theme 90: Periods 时期 (shíqī)

1 时间 [時間] shíjiān (time-moment) <n.> time: 休息~ time for break || 比赛~ time for game/match/race || ~不多 not a lot of time

2 古代 [-] gǔdài (ancient-age) <n.> antiquity: ~国家 ancient civilization || ~汉语 ancient Mandarin || ~文化 ancient culture

3 中世纪 [--紀] zhōngshìjì (middle-century) <n.> The Middle Ages, Medieval period: ~文学 literature during the Middle Ages

4 近代 [-] jìndài (near-age) <n.> contemporary, modernity: ~史 modern history || ~社会 modern society || ~工业 modern industry

5 现代 [現-] xiàndài (current-age) <n.> modern times: ~科学 modern science || ~青年 modern teenagers || ~国家 modern nation

6 当代 [當-] dāngdài (present-age) <n.> contemporary age, modern times: ~青年 contemporary teenager || ~文学 contemporary literature || ~社会 contemporary society

7 朝代 [-] cháodài (dynasty-dynasty) <n.> dynasty: 唐宋元明四个~. The Tang, Song, Yuan and Ming are four dynasties.

8 代 [-] dài (dynasty) <n.> dynasty/era, time period: 元~ Yuan || 清 ~ Qing || 宋 ~ Song

9 王朝 [-] wángcháo (king-dynasty) <n.> dynasty: 新兴的 ~ new dynasty|| (大)清 ~ the Qing Dynasty

10 时代 [時-] shídài (time-age) <n.> time period, age, era: 新/旧~ new/old ages || 青年~ teenage era, period || 石器~ Stone Age

11 年代 [-] niándài (year-age) <n.> age, epoch: 九十~ the 90s || 战争~ war times || ~久远 distant age

12 一代 [-] yīdài (one-generation) <n.> generation: ~新人 new generation || ~青年 new generation of youth || 这/那~ this, that generation

13 岁月 [歲-] suìyuè (age-month) <n.> life time, age, life: 漫长 (màncháng) 的~ long life time || 难忘的~ unforgettable time || 青春~ adolescence, teenage years

14 日子 [-] rìzi (time-*suffix*) <n.> life time, days: 过~ live one day at a time || 难忘的~ unforgettable days || 特别的~ special, precious years/times in life

15 时期 [時-] shíqī (time-period) <n.> period: 上升~ period of improvement, ascension || 转变~ Period of change || 两个~ two periods of time

16 长期 [長-] chángqī (long-period) <n.> long-term, long period of time: ~住在国外 living abroad for a long time || ~没有工作 long-term unemployment || ~戴眼镜 to wear glasses for a long period of time

17 短期 [-] duǎnqī (short-period) <n.> short time, short-term: ~工作 temporary, short-term job || ~职员 short-term employee || ~课程 short-term college programs, courses

18 一时 [-時] yīshí (short-time) <n.> a moment: ~的强大a moment of strength || ~说不出话 a moment of inability to speak || ~慌乱 (huāngluàn) a moment of panic

19 工夫 [-] gōngfū (work-time) <n.> period of time (may be months, or mere seconds): 几天~ a couple of days || 一会儿~ a few moments || 花了很多~ spend some solid time

20 一眨眼 [-] yīzhǎyǎn (one-blink-eye) <n.> a split second: ~不见了 gone in a split second

21 周期 [-] zhōuqī (cycle-period) <n.> cycle, interval: 生产~ production cycle || ~长/短 long, short cycle || ~运动 period of motion, movement

22 日期 [-] rìqī (day-date) <n.> date: 结婚~ marriage date || 具体 (jùtǐ) ~ actual date || 确定 (quèdìng) ~ confirmed date

23 学期 [] xuéqī (study-period) <n.> semester: 上/下~ last, next semester || 三个~ trimester || 本/每~ this, every semester

24 同期 [-] tóngqī (same-period) <n.> same period: 去年~ same period last year || ~发生 happen in the same period of time || ~上学 attend school in the same class, year

25 保质期 [-質-] bǎozhìqī (guarantee-quality-period) <n.> shelf life, quality guarantee period, expiration date: ~三个月 three month shelf life || 过了~ past the expiration date

26 实习期 [實習-] shíxíqī (intern-period) <n.> internship period: 毕业~ finish the internship || ~满 complete the internship || ~一个月 a month of internship

27 青春期 [-] qīngchūnqī (youth-period) <n.> puberty: 度过~ go through puberty || 进入~ enter puberty

28 更年期 [-] gēngniánqī (change-life stage-period) <n.> menopause, climacterium: 进入~ entering menopause || 男性/女性~ male, female climacterium || ~综合症 (zōnghé zhèng) climacteric syndrome

29 经期 [經-] jīngqī (menstruation-period) <n.> menstrual cycle, menstruation: ~推迟 delayed menstrual cycle || ~不准 irregular menstruation || ~延长 menorrhagia, prolonged menstruation

30 孕期 [-] yùnqī (pregnant-period) <n.> pregnancy: ~保健 (bǎojiàn) pregnancy care || ~营养 (yíngyǎng) pregnancy nutrition

Tips:

1 Chinese historical periods: 古代 (ancient) is from antiquity to the First Opium War in 1840. 近代 is from 1840 to 1949 when the People's Republic of China was founded. 现代 (modern) is from 1949 to present. 当代 (contemporary) is basically synonymous with 现代.

2 *期 (qī): *期 usually refers to a period of time, for example 青春期 (puberty) and 保质期 (shelf life.)

Exercises:

Part I: Read the following words and then answer the questions.

古代、中世纪、近代、现代、当代、长期、短期、一眨眼的功夫、年代、时代、朝代、更年期、保质期、实习期、岁月、过平常人的日子

1 "近代、现代、古代、中世纪、当代," 请按照从以前到现在的时间顺序排列这些词

____

2 "长期"的反义词是什么?

____

3 "一眨眼的功夫"形容时间长还是时间短?

---

4 这位国家领导人退休以后"过着平常人的日子," 意思是

a) 这位国家领导人退休以后过着普通人的生活
b) 这位国家领导人退休以后跟平常人一起生活
c) 这位国家领导人退休以后跟平常人用一样的时间

5 你们国家的大学毕业时有没有实习期, 一般多长时间?

---

6 这种蛋糕的__________是三天.
a) 更年期 b) 保质期 c) 实习期

7 中国历史上文化最繁荣 (fánróng) 的________是唐朝.
a) 年代 b) 朝代 c) 岁月

8 纽约的"Times Square"的正确翻译是
a) 岁月广场 b) 时代广场 c) 时间正方

Theme 91: Periods of time, points in time 时段, 时候 (shíduàn, shíhòu)

1 期间 [-間] qījiān (period-between) <n.> period of time: 大会~ during the conference || 旅游 (lǚyóu) ~ during the tour || 新年~ during the new year
2 期限 [-] qīxiàn (period-limit) <n.> time limit: 一定~ strict deadline || 缩短 (suōduǎn) ~ shorten the time limit || ~已满 allotted time has run out
3 时候 [時-] shíhòu (time-season) <n.> time: 任何~ anytime || 进来的~ time to come in || 这个~ this time
4 时刻 [時-] shíkè (time-point) <n.> point in time: 关键 (guānjiàn) ~ the crucial moment || 困难 (kùnnan) ~ difficult time || 最后~ the final moment
5 时光 [時-] shíguāng (time-time) <n.> time: 两年~ two days' time || 好~ a good time || 一段~ a while
6 早期 [-] zǎoqī (early-period) <n.> early period: ~教育 (jiàoyù) early stage of education || ~发现 discovery from an earlier time || ~文字 text from an earlier time
7 中期 [-] zhōngqī (middle-period) <n.> middle period: 三十年代~ mid-30s || ~规划 (guīhuà) medium-term plan
8 近期 [-] jìnqī (near-period) <n.> near future, recent: ~的情况 short time situation || ~目标 aims for the near future || ~结婚 recently married
9 晚期 [-] wǎnqī (late-period) <n.> late period: 唐朝~ late Tang Dynasty || 十九世纪 ~ late 19th century || 三十年代~ late 30s
10 从前 [從-] cóngqián (from-before) <n.> past, in the past: 我~不认识他. I didn't know him. || 中国跟 ~不一样了. China is very different from what it was before.
11 过去 [過-] guòqù (pass-gone) <n.> past: ~的事 things in the past || ~的衣服 old clothing
12 最近 [-] zuìjìn (most-recent) <n.> recent: ~两个月 the last two months || ~收到 recently received || ~工作忙. Work has been busy recently.

13 现在 [現-] xiànzài (current-exist) <n.> right now: 从~起 from now on || ~的孩子 the children of today || ~不想去 don't want to go right now

14 今后 [-後] jīnhòu (today-after) <n.> in the future: ~五年内 in the next five years || ~的打算 (dǎsuàn) future plans || ~再学开车learn driving in the future

15 将来 [將來] jiānglái (will-come) <n.> future: ~的事 future things || 儿子的~ son's future || ~这个地方会有更多的工厂. There will be more factories in the future here.

16 未来 [-來] wèilái (not yet-come) <n.> future: 面向~ face the future

17 前后 [-後] qiánhòu (before-after) <n.> around, about: ~三个小时 about three hours || ~五次 about five times || ~时间 around a certain time

18 此前 [-] cǐqián (this-before) <n.> previously: ~一天 one day ago || 我 ~听说过这件事. I have heard of this thing previously.

19 当前 [當-] dāngqián (here-now) <n.> current: ~的工作 current job || ~的问题 current question || ~的任务 task at hand

20 目前 [-] mùqián (eye-before) <n.> present: ~的情况 the present situation || ~的问题 the present question

21 此后 [-後] cǐhòu (this-after) <n.> after this: ~十年 after ten years || ~不久 not long after || ~的日子 the days afterwards

22 后来 [後-] hòulái (after – ward) <n.> later: 他~教了几年书. Later, he taught for a few years. || ~的发展 later development

23 以前 [-] yǐqián (from-before) <n.> before: 上课~ before class || 十八岁~ before the age of 18 || 说话~ before speaking

24 以来 [-來] yǐlái (from – ward) <n.> since: 长期~ for a long time || 八十年代~ since the 80s || 建国~ since the founding of the country

25 近来 [-來] jìnlái (recent – ward) <n.> recent: ~很忙 be busy recently || ~天气很冷 weather has been cold recently || ~很流行 lately popular

26 至今 [-] zhìjīn (to-now) <adv.> up to now: ~已两年了. It's been two years so far. || 二零零零年~ from 2000 to now || ~还在海外 still overseas to this day

27 以后 [-後] yǐhòu (from-later) <n.> after: 毕业~ after graduating || 看了~ after seeing || 六十岁~ after being 60 years old

28 之后 [-後] zhīhòu ('s-later) <n.> later: 六天~ six days later || 回去~ after returning || 演出~ after the performance

29 之间 [-間] zhījiān ('s-between) <n.> between: 两年~ in these two years || 两次大战~ between the two wars || 两栋楼房~ between these two buildings

30 之前 [-] zhīqián ('s-before) <n.> before: 一个星期~ one week ago || 同意~ before agreeing || 下班~ before getting off work

31 平常 [-] píngcháng (common-normal) <n.> generally, usually, at ordinary times: 他~八点上班. He usually goes to work at 8 a.m. || 他 ~不逛街. He doesn't usually go shopping.

32 平时 [-時] píngshí (ordinary-time) <n.> at ordinary times: ~很忙very busy in normal times || ~很认真 very serious in normal times || ~成绩 (chéngjì) usual performance

33 从小 [從-] cóngxiǎo (from-little) <adv.> childhood: ~聪明 be intelligent from a young age|| ~爱唱歌 loved singing since childhood || ~没读过书 hasn't read a book since childhood

34 一会儿 [-會兒] yīhuìr (a-moment) <n.> a moment, a while: 等~ wait a moment || 过~ after a moment || 休息~ rest a minute

35 不久 [-] bùjiǔ (not-long) <adj.> not long, soon: 她~就要回中国了. She is returning to China soon. || ~以前 not long ago || ~以后 not long afterwards

36 半天 [-] bàntiān (half-day) <n.> half day, long time: 上~班 work for half the day || 两个 ~ two half-days || 等了 ~ wait for long time

37 半年 [-] bànnián (half-year) <n.> half a year: 上/下~ first/second half of the year || 住了 ~ live for half a year

38 上次 [-] shàngcì (last-time) <n.> last time: ~来的时候 last time something came || ~的考试 last test || ~借的书 last time somebody borrowed a book

39 下次 [-] xiàcì (next-time) <n.> next time: ~小心 be careful next time || ~注意 be cautious next time || ~活动 next activity

40 眼前 [-] yǎnqián (eye-before) <n.> present: ~利益 (lìyì) present interest || ~的事 things before us || 只顾~ only care about immediate issues

41 中间 [-間] zhōngjiān (middle-between) <n.> among: 五个月~ in these five months || 四点到九点~ between 4 and 9 || 在工人~ among workers

42 同时 [-時] tóngshí (same-time) <n.> at the same time: ~进来 come in at the same time || ~出现 appear simultaneously || ~生病 get sick at the same time

43 定期 [-] dìngqī (fixed-period) <v./adj.> at regular intervals: ~开会 meet regularly || ~换密码 regularly change a password || ~体检 regular physical check-ups

44 空儿 [-兒] kòng er (free time) <n.> free time: 有/没~ have/not have free time || 抽~ take some time || 得~ be free

45 整天 [-] zhěngtiān (whole-day) <n.> all day long: ~呆在家 stay at home all day || 走了一~ walk all day || ~想着玩 think and play all day

46 近日 [-] jìnrì (recent-day) <n.> recent: ~出版 (chūbǎn) publish recently || ~决定decide recently || ~上演 perform recently

47 明日 [-] míngrì (tomorrow-day) <n.> tomorrow: ~正午 tomorrow at noon || ~再来 come back tomorrow || ~开学 start school tomorrow

48 周 [週] zhōu (week) <n.> week: 上/下~ last/next week || 三~ three weeks || ~五 Friday

49 月底 [-] yuèdǐ (month-end) <n.> end of the month: 二 ~ end of February || 到~为止 until the end of the month || 本~ the end of this month

50 年初 [-] niánchū (year-beginning) <n.> beginning of the year: 去年/今年/明年/每年~ the beginning of last year/this year/next year/every year || ~成立 established at the beginning of the year

51 年底 [-] niándǐ (year-end) <n.> end of the year: 去年/今年/明年/每年~ the end of last year/this year/next year/every year || 到~ at the end of the year || ~前 before the end of the year

52 往年 [-] wǎngnián (former-year) <n.> in former years: ~的情况 the situation in former years || 超过 (chāoguò) ~ exceed previous years || 与 ~相比 compared with former years

53 多年 [-] duōnián (many-year) <n.> many years: 工作~ work for many years || 坚持 (jiānchí) ~ stick to for many years || ~研究 many years of research

54 原先 [-] yuánxiān (original-earlier) <n.> originally: ~的房间 original room || ~的地方 original place || ~的想法 original thought

55 以往 [-] yǐwǎng (from-past) <n.> in the past: ~几年 the past few years || ~的历史 old history || ~的经验 past experience
56 先前 [-] xiānqián (earlier-before) <n.> before, previously: ~看过 seen before || ~的习惯 previous habits || ~的速度 previous speed
57 此次 [-] cǐcì (this-time) <n.> this time: ~大会 this convention || ~地震 (dìzhèn) this earthquake || ~比赛 this game
58 如今 [-] rújīn (to-now) <n.> now: ~退休在家 currently retired at home || ~成为现实 has become a reality || 直到~ until now
59 往后 [-後] wǎnghòu (toward-future) <n.> in the future: ~的活动 future activities || ~的日子 coming days || ~推 push back the future
60 过后 [過後] guòhòu (pass-after) <n.> afterwards: 冬天~ after the winter || 春节~ after the Spring Festival || 寒假~ after winter vacation
61 事后 [-後] shìhòu (event-after) <n.> after the event: ~回忆 recall after the event || ~讨论 discussing afterwards
62 以内 [-] yǐnèi (from-within) <n.> within: 五年~ within five years || 三天~ within three days || 两小时~ less than two hours

Tips:

1 Last and next: Last time and next time are 上次 and 下次. Last year and next year are 去年和明年. Last summer and next summer are 去年夏天 and 明年夏天.
2 Temporal sequence: Researchers found that Chinese sentence structure usually follows temporal sequence, for example, 星期日/早上/八点/我开车/去机场/接朋友/来我家/住三天 (literally 'Sunday morning 8 o'clock I drive a car to the airport to pick up a friend who comes to my home to live for three days,) with each event after another by strict temporal sequence.

Exercises:

Part I: Answer the following questions in Chinese.

1 请按照从小到大的顺序排列下面三组词

a) 早期、中期、晚期、近期

____

b) 过去、现在、将来、最近

____

c) 年初、年前、年底、年中

____

2 "目前、以前、以后、以内、平时、近日、时刻," 请在下面每一个空格里填写一个意思相近的词

当前: ________
之前: ________
之后: ________
之内: ________

平常: _________
最近: _________
时候: _________

Theme 92: Calendar, year, season, month, day 历法, 年, 季节, 月, 日 (lìfǎ, nián, jìjié, yuè, rì)

1 公历 [-曆] gōnglì (common-calendar) <n.> solar calendar: 中国现在也使用~. Currently, China also uses the solar calendar.
2 农历 [農曆] nónglì (agriculture-calendar) <n.> lunar calendar: ~八月十五日是中秋节 On the Lunar Calendar, August 15th is the Chinese Moon Festival.
3 阴历 [陰曆] yīnlì (lunar-calendar) <n.> lunar calendar: ~ 年 the lunar year || 端午节是~五月五日. May 5th is the Dragon Boat Festival
4 夏令时 [--時] xiàlìngshí (summer-season-time) <n.> daylight saving time: 实行~ implement daylight savings time
5 阳历 [陽曆] yánglì (solar-calendar) <n.> solar calendar: 中国的清明节一般在~四月. The Chinese Qing Ming Festival is usually in April in the solar calendar.

6 公元 [-] gōngyuán (common-era) <n.> A.D.: ~前 B.C. || ~后A.D. || ~二零一六年 2016 A.D.
7 天干 [-] tiāngān (heavenly-stem) <n.> the heavenly stems: 十~ the ten heavenly stems
8 地支 [-] dìzhī (Earthly-branch) <n.> the Earthly branches: 十二~ the 12 Earthly branches
9 世纪 [-紀] shìjì (30 years-12 years) <n.> century: 三个~ three centuries || 二十一~ 21st century || 中~ middle ages

10 年 [-] nián (year) <n.> year: 两千~ 2000 years || 去/今/明~ last year, this year, next year || 多~ many years
11 大前年 [-] dàqiánnián (far-before-year) <n.> three years ago: ~十八岁 was 18 years old three years ago || ~毕业 了 graduated three years ago
12 前年 [-] qiánnián (before-year) <n.> two years ago: ~夏天 the summer two years ago || ~毕业 graduated two years ago || ~八月two years ago in August
13 去年 [-] qùnián (last-year) <n.> last year ago: ~四月on April last year || ~一年 the whole last year || ~初 the beginning of last year
14 今年 [-] jīnnián (now-year) <n.> this year: ~五月 this year in May || 她~六十岁. She is 60 years old this year. || ~的国庆节 this year's national day
15 明年 [-] míngnián (next-year) <n.> next year: ~再来 come back next year || ~三月 March next year || ~上半年 the first half of next year
16 后年 [後-] hòunián (behind-year) <n.> two years later: 大~ three years latter || ~完成 will finish in two years || ~毕业 will graduate in two years
17 大后年 [-後-] dàhòunián (far-behind-year) <n.> three years later: ~毕业 will graduate in three years
18 周年 [週-] zhōunián (cycle-year) <n.> anniversary: 五~ five-year anniversary || 结婚~ wedding anniversary || ~庆祝 anniversary celebration
19 全年 [-] quánnián (whole-year) <n.> annual: ~奖金 (jiǎngjīn) annual bonus || ~计划 annual plan || ~寒冷 cold all year

20 当年 [當-] dāngnián (that-year) <n.> that year: ~的老朋友 old friend back then || ~睡帐篷 slept in the tent back then || ~吃野菜 having wild vegetables back then
21 年度 [-] niándù (year-measurement) <n.> year (a period of 12 months fixed for a certain purpose): 本~ current year || 上一~ last year || ~计划 annual plan
22 学年 [學-] xuénián (school-year) <n.> school year: 四 ~ four school years || ~末 the end of the school year || 缩短~ shorten school year

23 季节 [-節] jìjié (season-joint) <n.> season: 播种 (bōzhǒng) ~ sowing season || 多雨~ rainy season || 收获 (shōuhuò) ~ harvesting season
24 四季 [-] sìjì (four-season) <n.> four seasons: 一年~ all year round || ~分明 four distinct seasons || ~如春 four seasons like spring
25 春天 [-] chūntiān (spring-weather) <n.> spring: 明年~ spring of next year || ~来了. Spring is coming.
26 春季 [-] chūnjì (spring-season) <n.> spring season: 明年~ next spring season || ~运动会 spring season sport || ~播种 spring sowing
27 夏天 [-] xiàtiān (summer-weather) <n.> summer: 明年~ next summer || 炎热的~ hot summer || ~傍晚 summer night
28 夏季 [-] xiàjì (summer-season) <n.> summer season: 去年~ summer season last year || ~的草原 grassland during summer season || ~旅游 summer season travel
29 秋天 [-] qiūtiān (fall-weather) <n.> fall: 去年~ last fall || ~来了. Fall is coming. || ~的果实 the fruit of autumn
30 秋季 [-] qiūjì (fall-season) <n.> fall season: 每年~ every year during fall season || 进入~ entering fall || ~成熟 (chéngshú) fall ripening
31 冬天 [-] dōngtiān (winter-weather) <n.> winter: ~到了 winter begins || 去年~ last winter || 寒冷的~ cold winter
32 冬季 [-] dōngjì (winter-season) <n.> winter season: ~训练 (xùnliàn) winter season conditioning || 漫长的~ long winter season || 去年~ last winter season
33 季度 [-] jìdù (season-measurement) <n.> quarter of a year: 三~ third quarter || 两个~ two quarters || 第四~ the fourth quarter
34 淡季 [-] dànjì (dull-season) <n.> off-season: 销售 (xiāoshòu) ~ sales off-season || 旅游 (lǚyóu) ~ travel off-season || 生产~ productivity off- season
35 旺季 [-] wàngjì (flourishing-season) <n.> peak season: 楼市~ property market peak season || 市场~ marketing peak season || 需求~ demand peak season
36 时节 [時節] shíjié (time-season) <n.> season: 金秋 ~ autumn season || 黄金~ golden season || 清明~ Qing Ming Festival

37 月 [-] yuè (moon/month) <n.> month: 五个~ five months || 十一~ November || 半/几个~ half/several months
38 月份 [-] yuèfèn (month-unit) <n.> month: 一二月份是北京最冷的~. January and February are the coldest months in Beijing.
39 一月 [-] yīyuè (first-month) <n.> January
40 正月 [-] zhēngyuè (definitive-month) <n.> lunar January
41 二月 [-] èr'yuè (second-month) <n.> February
42 三月 [-] sānyuè (third-month) <n.> March
43 四月 [-] sìyuè (fourth-month) <n.> April: 每年~五日左右是中国的传统节日清明节. About April 5th is the traditional Chinese Qing Ming Festival.

44 五月 [-] wǔyuè (fifth-month) <n.> May: 农历~五日是中国的传统节日端午节. The fifth day of the fifth lunar month is the traditional Chinese Dragon Boat Festival.

45 六月 [-] liùyuè (sixth-month) <n.> June: ~一日是中国的儿童节. June 1st is China's Children's Day festival.

46 七月 [-] qīyuè (seventh-month) <n.> July: 农历~七日是中国的情人节. The seventh day of the the seventh lunar month is the Chinese Valentine's Day.

47 八月 [-] bāyuè (eighth-month) <n.> August: 农历 ~十五是中国的传统节日中秋节. The 15th day of the eighth lunar month is the traditional Chinese Mid-Autumn Festival.

48 九月 [-] jiǔyuè (ninth-month) <n.> September: 农历~九日是中国的传统节日重阳节 (chóngyáng jié). The ninth day of the ninth lunar month is the traditional Chinese Double Ninth Festival.

49 十月 [-] shíyuè (tenth-month) <n.> October: 公历 ~一日是中国的国庆节. October 1st is the National Day of China.

50 十一月 [-] shíyīyuè (eleventh-month) <n.> November: ~的第四个星期四是美国的感恩节. The fourth Thursday in November is America's Thanksgiving Day.

51 十二月 [-] shí'èryuè (twelfth-month) <n.> December: ~二十五日是西方人的圣诞节. December 25th is Christmas in the West.

52 腊月 [臘-] làyuè (winter sacrifice-month) <n.> twelfth lunar month: 寒冬~ winter on the 12th lunar month

53 旬 [-] xún (10 days) <n.> a period of ten days in a month: 上~ the first ten days in a month || 中~ the second ten days in a month || 下~ the last ten days in a month

54 日 [-] rì (sun/day) <n.> day: 三月五~ March 5th || 地球~ Earth Day || 每/整/早~ Every/whole/early day

55 天 [-] tiān (heaven/day) <n.> day: 昨/今/明/~ yesterday/today/tomorrow || 第二~ the second day || 三~ the third day

56 大前天 [-] dàqiántiān (far-before-day) <n.> two days before yesterday

57 前天 [-] qiántiān (before-day) <n.> the day before yesterday: 大~ two days before yesterday

58 昨天 [-] zuótiān (yesterday-day) <n.> yesterday: ~早上 yesterday morning || ~八点 eight o'clock yesterday

59 今天 [-] jīntiān (now-day) <n.> today: ~早晨 this morning || ~十二点 12 o'clock today || 直到~ until today

60 今日 [-] jīnrì (now-day) <n.> nowaday: ~下午 this afternoon || ~的报纸 today's newspaper || 《今日美国》USA Today

61 明天 [-] míngtiān (tomorrow-day) <n.> tomorrow: ~晚上 tomorrow night || ~考试 Test tomorrow. || 美好的~ beautiful tomorrow

62 后天 [後-] hòutiān (after-day) <n.> the day after tomorrow: ~开会 have the meeting the day after tomorrow

63 大后天 [-後-] dàhòutiān (far-after-day) <n.> two days before yesterday

64 生日 [-] shēngrì (birth-day) <n.> birthday: 过~ spend the birthday || ~礼物 birthday gift

65 上周 [-] shàngzhōu (last-week) <n.> last week: ~五 last Friday || ~买的 bought it last week || ~去过 went there last week

66 下周 [-] xiàzhōu (next-week) <n.> next week: ~开会 have the meeting next week || ~放假 go on break next week
67 星期 [-] xīngqī (star-cycle) <n.> week: 三个~ three weeks || 上/下个~ the previous/following week
68 礼拜 [禮-] lǐbài (ritual-worship) <n.> week: 三个~ three weeks || ~五 Friday || ~日 Sunday
69 星期一 [-] xīngqīyī (week-first) <n.> Monday
70 星期二 [-] xīngqī'èr (week-second) <n.> Tuesday
71 星期三 [-] xīngqīsān (week-third) <n.> Wednesday
72 星期四 [-] xīngqīsì (week-fourth) <n.> Thursday
73 星期五 [-] xīngqīwǔ (week-fifth) <n.> Friday
74 星期六 [-] xīngqīliù (week-sixth) <n.> Saturday
75 星期日 [-] xīngqīrì (week-seventh) <n.> Sunday
76 星期天 [-] xīngqītiān (week/worship-day) <n.> Sunday: 下~ next Sunday || 这个~ this Sunday || ~晚上 Sunday evening
77 双休日 [雙--] shuāngxiūrì (double-rest-day) <n.> two-day weekend: 中国是1995年开始实行~的. China started the two-day weekend in 1995.
78 周末 [-] zhōumò (week-end) <n.> weekend: 过~ spend the weekend || 本/上/下~ this/last/next weekend || 长~ long weekend

79 假日 [-] jiàrì (vacation-day) <n.> holiday: 周末~ weekend holiday || 法定~ holiday by law || 春节~ lunar holiday
80 假期 [-] jiàqī (vacation-period) <n.> break: 春节~ Spring Festival break || 一个月的~ one month break || ~结束 end of break
81 暑假 [-] shǔjià (summer-vacation) <n.> summer vacation: 放~ having summer vacation || ~三个月three months of summer vacation || ~期间 during summer vacation
82 寒假 [-] hánjià (winter-vacation) <n.> winter break: 放~ have winter break || 过~ spend winter break || ~作业 homework for winter break
83 病假 [-] bìngjià (sick-vacation) <n.> sick leave: 请~ ask for sick leave
84 产假 [產-] chǎnjià (birth-vacation) <n.> maternity leave: 休~ take maternity leave || 请~ ask for maternity leave
85 婚假 [-] hūnjià (marriage-vacation) <n.> marital leave: 休 ~ take marital leave || 请~ ask for marital leave
86 长假 [-] chángjià (long-vacation) <n.> long holiday, long leave of absence: 请~ ask for a long leave of absence || 放~ having a long holiday || 休/度过~ spend a long holiday
87 黄金周 [黃--] huángjīnzhōu (gold-week) <n.> Golden Week: 国庆~ National Day Golden Week || 旅游~ traveling on Golden Week || 五一~ Labor Day Golden Week
88 纪念日 [紀--] jìniànrì (memorize-day) <n.> anniversary: 结婚~ marriage anniversary || 阵亡将士~ Memorial Day

Tips:

1 Heavenly Stems and Earthly Branches to compute time: The ten Heavenly/Celestial Stems are 甲, 乙, 丙, 丁, 戊, 己, 庚, 辛, 壬, 癸 (jiǎ, yǐ, bǐng, dīng, wù, jǐ, gēng, xīn, rén, guǐ) and the 12 Earthly Branches are 子, 丑, 寅, 卯, 辰,

巳, 午, 未, 申, 酉, 戌, 亥 (zǐ, chǒu, yín, mǎo, chén, sì, wǔ, wèi, shēn, yǒu, xū, hài.) In combination, they can form a sexagenary cycle to record years, months, days and hours. This was the main way to reckon time in ancient China until the establishment of the Republic of China in 1912, and remains in use in some fields. For example, January 1st, 2018 can be estimated as 丁酉年壬子月癸巳日.

2 礼拜 (lǐbài) vs. 星期 (xīngqī) vs. 周 (zhōu): They all mean 'week' and were borrowed from English or Japanese around the turn of the 19th century. 礼拜 (ritual-worship) is related to church services in Christianity or Islam, 星期 was derived from the astrological system, 周 was borrowed from Japanese. Monday through Saturday can be called 礼拜/星期/周'一 . . . 六,' however, Sunday can only be called as 礼拜/星期/周'日,' not '七.'

3 Four seasons: It is usually 春夏秋冬, but could be 春秋冬夏 in literary settings. 春秋 means 'a year.'

Exercises:

Part I: Answer the following questions in Chinese.

1 请写出一年中的四个季节

---

2 "去年、今年、前年、大前年、后年、大后年、明年," 请按照从前到后的时间顺序来排列这些词

---

3 "去天、今天、前天、大前天、后天、大后天、明天," 请按照从前到后的时间顺序来排列这些词

---

4 请写出五个带"假"的词

---

5 十月的第一个星期是中国的"旅游黄金周"意思是

a) 十月的第一个星期是中国人旅游最多的时候
b) 十月的第一个星期是中国的秋天
c) 十月的第一个星期是去中国旅游最贵的一周

6 "今天是老张跟太太结婚30周年纪念日," 从这句话可以看出

a) 老张跟太太已经结婚30多年了
b) 老张跟太太纪念30年前结婚的时候办了一个纪念日
c) 老张跟太太是30年前的今天结婚的

7 请写出中国几个重要传统节日的名称和时间

Theme 93: Time within one day 一天以内的时间 (yī tiān yǐnèi de shíjiān)

1 白天 [-] báitiān (bright-day) <n.> day: 四个~ four days || 春天来了, ~越来越长了. Spring has come. Days become longer and longer.

2 凌晨 [淩-] língchén (close to-morning) <n.> early morning: ~三点 three o'clock in the morning

3 黎明 [-] límíng (dark-bright) <n.> dawn, daybreak: ~前的黑暗. The darkest hour is just before the dawn.

4 清晨 [-] qīngchén (clear-morning) <n.> early morning: 每天~ every morning || ~五点钟 five o'clock in the early morning

5 早晨 [-] zǎochén (early-morning) <n.> morning: 明天~ tomorrow morning || ~五点 five o'clock in the morning

6 早上 [-] zǎoshàng (morning-*suffix*) <n.> morning: 今天~ this morning || ~六点 six o'clock in the morning

7 上午 [-] shàngwǔ (before-noon) <n.> morning: 今天~ this morning || ~九点 nine o'clock in the morning || 三个~ three mornings

8 中午 [-] zhōngwǔ (middle-noon) <n.> noon: 有一天~ one day at noon || ~十二点 at noon || 将近~ almost noon

9 下午 [-] xiàwǔ (after-noon) <n.> afternoon: 昨天~ yesterday afternoon || 三个~ three afternoons || 我~去图书馆. I will go to the library in the afternoon.

10 日夜 [-] rìyè (day-night) <n.> day and night: ~忙碌 (mánglù) busy day and night || ~不停 non stop day and night || ~工作 work day and night

11 傍晚 [-] bàngwǎn (close to-evening) <n.> towards evening, at dusk: ~散步take an evening walk || ~的时候at dusk

12 黄昏 [黃-] huánghūn (yellow-dusk) <n.> dusk: ~时候at dusk

13 晚上 [-] wǎnshàng (evening-*suffix*) <n.> evening: 今天~ this evening || 整个~ the whole evening || ~看电视 watch TV in the evening

14 夜 [-] yè (night) <n.> night: 深~ late in the night || 黑~ dark night || 过~ spend the night

15 夜里 [-裏] yèlǐ (night-in) <n.> night: 昨天~ last night || ~十二点 midnight || ~冷 cold at night

16 夜间 [-間] yèjiān (night-within) <n.> during the night: ~工作 work during the night || ~开放 open during the night || ~劳动 working during the night

17 黑夜 [-] hēiyè (dark-night) <n.> dark night: 漫长 (màncháng) 的~ long dark night || 宁静的~ quiet dark night || 两个~ two dark nights

18 半夜 [-] bànyè (half-night) <n.> midnight: 躺了~ lie down at midnight || 忙到~ busy until midnight || ~下雨了. It rained at midnight.

19 早晚 [-] zǎowǎn (morning-evening, early-late) <n.> morning and evening: ~刷牙 brush teeth morning and evening

20 时 [時] shí (time) <n.> hour, o'clock, time of day: 晚上九~ nine o'clock in the evening

21 小时 [-時] xiǎoshí (small- period of two hours) <n.> hour: 五个~ five hours || 半~ half an hour

22 钟头 [鐘頭] zhōngtóu (clock-*suffix*) <n.> hour: 十个~ ten hours || 半个多~ more than half an hour

23 点钟 [點鐘] diǎnzhōng (hour-clock) <bf.> o'clock: 两~ two o'clock || 几~ what time || 八九~ around eight or nine o'clock

24 分 [-] fēn (minute) <c.> minute: 十二点三十~ twelve thirty || 差五~四点 five to four || 九点过十~ ten past nine

25 分钟 [-鐘] fēnzhōng (minute-clock) <n.> minute: 十五~ 15 minutes || 几~ how many minutes || 半~ half a minute

26 时辰 [時-] shíchén (period of two hours) <n.> double-hour, the time for sth.: 十二个~ 24 hours || 出生的~ the time for birth || 半个~ an hour

27 北京时间 [--時間] běijīngshíjiān (Beijing-time) <n.> Beijing time: ~早晨八点 eight o'clock in the morning Beijing Time

28 当地时间 [當-時間] dāngdìshíjiān (local-time) <n.> local time: ~下午五点 five o'clock at local

29 当初 [當-] dāngchū (at-beginning) <n.> at that time: ~她就不应该离开. She shouldn't have left at the time. || ~是谁帮了你? Who helped you at that time? || ~她不过是一个普通教师. She was just an ordinary teacher at that time.

30 当时 [當時] dāngshí (that-time) <n.> at that time: 我~十六岁. I was 16 years old at that time. || ~的心情 the mood at that time

31 这时 (候) [這時-] zhèshí (hòu) (this-time) <n.> this time: ~她已结婚. She was already married at this time. || ~已经八点了. It's already eight o'clock at this time. || ~我想起来了. I remembered this time.

32 那时 (候) [-時-] nàshí (hòu) (that-time) <n.> that time: ~我还很小. I was little at that time. || ~的人 people at that time || 到~ until that time

33 那会儿 [-會兒] nàhuìr (that-moment) <pron.> at that time: 我~才十岁. I was ten years old at that time. || 我~不明白. I don't understand at that time. || 他读大学~ that time when he is in college

34 此刻 [-] cǐkè (this-moment) <n.> this moment: ~的心情 mood at this moment || 此时~ this moment || 她~睡得很香. She is sleeping really deeply at this moment.

35 此时 [-時] cǐshí (this-time) <n.> this time: 就在~ at this time || 由~起 from this time

36 多久 [-] duōjiǔ (how-long) <n.> how long: 没走 ~ haven't walked for too long || 没有~ not so long || 不知道看了~ don't know how long one has watched

37 猴年马月 [--馬-] hóuniánmǎyuè (monkey-year-horse-month) <idiom> When on Earth!: 不知道~才能住上自己的房子. I don't know when on Earth I'll be able to live in my own house. || 不知要等到~. I don't know how long I'll be waiting.

Tips:

1 时 and 小时: The ancient Chinese divided a whole day into twelve 时 (辰), which equals two hours. After the Western concept of hour was widely accepted in China in the late Qing Dynasty, 时 (辰) was further divided into two 小时 (hours.)

2 Nouns of time within a day: There are 43 nouns of time, which are shorter than one day, according to a paper by Liwei Jiao in 2002. The main time nouns and their relations are shown in the diagram below:

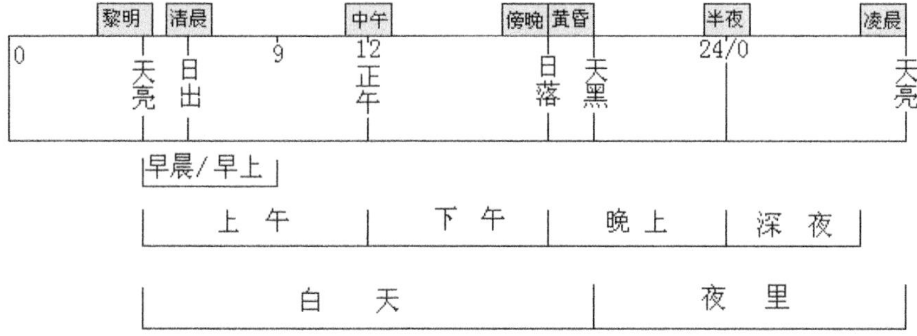

Based on a survey also in that paper, Chinese people's mental time and their boundaries are: 6 AM – 早上 (early morning) – 8 AM – 上午 (morning) – 11: 30 AM – 中午 (noon) – 1: 30 PM – 下午 (afternoon) – 5: 30 PM – 黄昏 (dusk) – 6: 00 PM – 晚上 (evening) – 10: 30 PM. We have to admit that due to substantial changes to the Chinese lifestyle after the year 2000, the boundaries of time could have changed slightly.

Exercises:

Part I: Read the following words and then answer the questions.

秒、分、小时、早上、晚上、中午、夜里、天、月、年、黄昏、黑夜、早晨、傍晚、清晨、凌晨、星期、半夜、此时此刻、猴年马月、当地时间、北京时间

1 "秒、分钟、天、小时、上午、月、年、星期," 请按照时间从短到长来排列这些词

____

2 "半夜"跟哪些词意思差不多?

____

3 早上跟哪些词意思差不多?

____

4 "傍晚"跟哪个词的意思差不多?

____

5 他常常在"凌晨"的时候醒来, 然后就无法入睡. 这里的"凌晨"大概是

a) 8:00 am.-10:00 am. b) 3:00 am.-5:00 am. c) 7:00am.-9:00 am.

6 "此时此刻"最合适的翻译是

a) this time b) at this very moment c) this moment

7 "等我生孩子还不知道猴年马月呢," 从这句话可以看出说话人

a) 知道自己什么时候生孩子 b) 知道自己是猴年马月要生孩子
c) 不打算要孩子

8 北京时间跟你们当地时间一样吗? 差多少小时?

Theme 94: Age 年龄 (niánlíng)

(See also Theme 2)

1 一生 [-] yīshēng (whole-life) <n.> life: 人的~ a person's life || 度过~ spend one's life || 短短的~ a short life
2 一辈子 [-輩-] yībèizi (one-generation) <n.> lifetime: 等~ wait for a lifetime || ~忘不了 can't forget for a lifetime
3 幼年 [-] yòunián (young-year) <n.> infancy, early childhood: 在 ~时in early childhood
4 童年 [-] tóngnián (child-year) <n.> childhood: 度过~ spend childhood || ~时代 childhood
5 小时候 [-時-] xiǎoshíhòu (young-time) <n.> youth, childhood, at young age: ~很聪明 brilliant at young age || ~的事情 things that happened at young age || ~的朋友 friends from younger age
6 青春 [-] qīngchūn (young-spring/age) <n.> youth: 浪费 (làngfèi) ~ wasted youth || 贡献 (gòngxiàn) ~ distributed youth || 美好的~ beautiful youth
7 英年 [-] yīngnián (splendid-year) <n.> prime of life: ~早逝 die at a young age
8 而立之年 [-] érlìzhīnián (hence-independent-'s-year) <n.> (formal) 30 years of age: 他已经到了~, 可是还是依靠父母. He is over 30 years old but still relies on his parents.
9 不惑之年 [-] búhuòzhīnián (not-bewildered-'s-year) <n.> (formal) 40 years of age: 我们都进入~了, 不再年轻了. We are all in our 40s, not young any more.
10 晚年 [-] wǎnnián (late-year) <n.> old age: ~生活 later life
11 有生之年 [-] yǒushēngzhīnián (have-life-'s-year) <n.> for the rest of one's life: 邓小平早年去过香港, 可是晚年以后, 他希望在~再去一次香港, 可惜他在香港回归中国之前就去世了. Deng Xiaoping visited Hong Kong at an early age, but later in his life, he hoped to visit Hong Kong again. Unfortunately, he died before Hong Kong returned to China.
12 终身 [終-] zhōngshēn (end-life) <n.> lifelong: ~大事 great event in one's life (usu. referring to marriage) || ~辛苦 (xīnkǔ) lifelong hard work || ~的追求 lifelong pursuit
13 平生 [-]píngshēng (complete-life) <n.> all one's life: 他对别人很客气, ~没有一个敌人. He has been nice to others in all his life, so he does not have any foe.
14 百年 [-] bǎinián (100-year) <n.> euphemism for 'die': 我~之后, 不要搞任何纪念活动. After I die, do not hold any commemorative activity.

15 生平 [-]shēngpíng (life-complete) <n.> (usually of the dead) all one's life: 邓小平同志~ Comrade Deng Xiaoping's life

16 年龄段 [-齡-] niánlíngduàn (age-period) <n.> age group: 那个~的孩子很多. There are many kids in that age group.

17 工龄 [-齡] gōnglíng (work-year) <n.> length of service, working year: 她有五十年的~. She has 50 years of service.

18 党龄 [黨齡] dǎnglíng (party-year) <n.> (Chinese Communist) party standing: 中华人民共和国名誉主席宋庆龄的~只有十五天. Honorary President of the People's Republic of China, Soong Ching-ling (Madame Sun Yat-sen) had a 15-day party standing.

Tips:

1 年 (nián) and 龄 (líng): 年龄 means 'age.' According to the oracle form, the upper part of 年 is 禾 (hé, crop) and the lower part 人 (man,) therefore, 年 means 'crop is ripe,' in other words, 'a year,' since people only reaped the harvest once a year. The left part of 龄 is 齿 (chǐ, teeth) by which one can know the age of a man. The right part of 龄 is 令 (lìng), which is similar in sound to 龄 (líng.) It is interesting that this compound word 年龄 was formed from the observation of two aspects, nature and human beings.

2 Age groups or life stages in Chinese: 婴儿 (yīng'ér, infant,) 幼儿 (yòu'ér, toddler,) 少儿 (child,) 少年 (early youth,) 青少年 (early youth and youth,) 青年 (youth,) 中青年 (youth and middle-aged,) 中年 (middle-aged,) 壮年 (zhuàngnián, the prime of life,) 中老年 (middle-aged and old,) 老年 (old) and 晚年 (late-year, remaining years.)

3 而立之年 and 不惑之年: Both words are excerpts from Confucius' famous saying '三十而立, 四十而不惑, 五十而知天命' (At 30, I stood firm. At 40, I had no doubts. At 50, I knew the decrees of the heaven.) Since then, 而立之年 refers to 30 years of age and 不惑之年 40.

Exercises:

Part I: Read the following words and then answer the questions.

晚年、老年、中年、壮年、中年、中青年、青年、青少年、少年、儿童、幼儿、婴儿、百年、平生、生平、一生、终身、一辈子、小时候

1 "一生"跟哪两个词的意思差不多?

---

2 "英年"跟哪两个词的意思差不多?

---

3 "他百年之后, 公司由大儿子继承(inherit)." 这句话的英文是什么?

---

4 中国人一般都希望自己"安度晚年," 这句话的意思是:

a) 中国人一般都希望自己很晚的时候幸福
b) 中国人一般都希望自己是老年人的时候生活很幸福
c) 中国人一般都希望自己是老年人的时候生活在安全的环境里

5 威廉 (William)已经进入而立之年了, 哈里 (Harry)已经进入不惑之年. 威廉和哈里, 谁大? __________ _

6 "老年、青年、中年、少年、儿童、幼儿、婴儿," 请按照时间从小到大的顺序排列这些词

Theme 95: Space, location 空间, 方位 (kōngjiān, fāngwèi)

1 空间 [-間] kōngjiān (space-among) <n.> space: 有/没有~ there is/is not space || 生活~ space, freedom in one's life || 建筑 (jiànzhù) ~ building space

2 方位 [-] fāngwèi (direction-location) <n.> directions: 全~ all around, complete || 上下~ high and low direction || 不同的~ different direction

3 方 [-] fāng (parallel, square, orientation) <n.> direction, side, square: 东~ the east/the orient || 四~ in all directions (north, south, east, west) || 上~ above/over

4 方向 [-] fāngxiàng (orientation-direction) <n.> direction, situation, circumstances: 西北~ in the direction of the north west || 火车站~ direction of the train station || 同一个~ same direction

5 位置 [-] wèizhì (location-place) <n.> location, spot: 固定~ set location || 靠窗的~ spot next to the window || 找~ find a spot

6 正* [-] zhèng (central, due) <adj.> due: ~东 due east || ~南方 due south

7 偏* [-] piān (inclined) <adj.> inclined to one side: ~左 inclined to the left || ~北 inclined north || ~西 inclined to the west

8 东 [東] dōng (east) <n.> east: ~院 eastern building, suite || 往 ~ move east || 向~ eastern direction

9 东北 [東-] dōngběi (east-north) <n.> northeast corner: ~角 northeast corner || ~地区 northeast region || ~话 northeastern dialect

10 东边 [東邊] dōngbiān (east-side) <n.> east, east side, the east of: 从~出来 emerge from the east

11 东部 [東-] dōngbù (east-part) <n.> east (geographic region – often within a country/specified region): ~地区 the east (of a country) || ~城市 eastern city || 非洲~ East Africa

12 东方 [東-] dōngfāng (east-direction) <n./adj.> the orient, the east, eastern: ~人 eastern people || ~文化 Eastern culture || ~国家 Eastern culture

13 东南 [東-] dōngnán (east-south) <n.> southeast: ~亚 southeast Asia || ~方向 southeast direction || ~风 southeast wind

14 西 [-] xī (west) <n.> west: 向/朝/往~ western direction/facing/moving towards the west || ~门/城 western gate/western city || 河~ west of the river

15 西北 [-] xīběi (west-north) <n.> northwest: 向~ northwest direction || 我国~ northwest of my country || ~风 northwest wind

16 西边 [-邊] xībiān (west-side) <n.> west, westside, the west of: 村~ the west of the village

17 西部 [-] xībù (west-part) <n.> west (geographic region – often within a country/specific region): 亚洲~ West Asia || ~地区 west region

18 西方 [-] xīfāng (west-direction) <n./adj.the west, western: ~文化 Western culture || ~国家 the Western countries || ~人 Westerners

19 西南 [-] xīnán (west-south) <n.> southwest: ~地区 southwest region || 美国~ southwest America || ~方向 southwest direction

20 南 [-] nán (south) <n.> south: 向/朝/往~ southern direction/facing/moving towards the south || ~门 south gate || ~院 southern building

21 南边 [-邊] nánbiān (south-side) <n.> south/south side/to the south of: 银行~ south of the bank || ~的窗户 southern window || 走到~ walk to the south

22 南部 [-] nánbù (south-part) <n.> south (geographic region – often within a country/specific region): 非洲~ South Africa (general region) || 江苏~ South Jiangsu (Province) || ~地区 southern region

23 南方 [-] nánfāng (south-direction) <n./adj.> the South, southern: ~人 Southern person || ~口音 Southern voice || 来自~ from the south

24 北 [-] běi (north) <n.> north: ~门 north gate || 向~ northward, facing north || 以~ the north of (suffix)

25 北边 [-邊] běibiān (north-side) <n.> north, the northern side: ~客厅 north of the living room || 超市~ north of the market || 靠 ~ border the north (side)

26 北部 [-] běibù (north-part) <n.> north (geographic region – often within a country/specific region): 欧洲~ North Europe || ~地区 north region || 最 ~ the farthest north.

27 北方 [-] běifāng (north-direction) <n.> the North, northern: ~人Northerner || ~话northern dialect || 住在~ live in the northern part of a country

28 东西 [東-] dōngxī (east-west) <n.> from east to west, east and west: ~方文化 Eastern and Western cultures

29 南北 [-] nánběi (south-north) (of territory) <n.> north and south, north to south: 大江~ all over China (north and south of the Yangtze) || ~两头 both north and south || ~距离 north/south distance

30 东西南北 [東---] dōngxīnánběi (east-west-south-north) <idiom> east, west, north and south: 分不清~ cannot differentiate the direction

31 前 [-] qián (go forward, ahead, front) <n.> front, ahead, forward: 教学楼~ in front of the classroom building || 往~走 move forward

32 前边 [-邊] qiánbiān (front-side) <n.> front, the front side: 走在~ walk in front of || ~的树林 in front of the forest || 超市~ in front of the market

33 前后 [-後] qiánhòu (front-behind) <n.> from beginning to end, around: 房屋~ all around the house || 马车的~ in front and behind the cart || ~车轮 (chēlún) around the wheel

34 前面 [-] qiánmiàn (front-area) <n.> front: 走在~ walk in front || ~的广场 in front of the square || 车~ in front of the car

35 前方 [-] qiánfāng (front-side) <n.> ahead, the front: 车~ ahead of the car || 舞台 (wǔtái) ~ the front of the stage || 送到~ send to the front

36 前头 [-頭] qiántóu (front-*suffix*) <n.> in front, at the head: 走在~ walk in the front || 教室~ the front of the classroom || ~的人 person in the lead
37 后 [後] hòu (be late, behind, back) <n.> behind, after: 大楼~ behind the building || 教室~ behind the classroom || 三天~ three days after
38 后边 [後邊] hòubiān (back-side) <n.> back, back side: ~的办公楼 behind the office building || 大树~ behind the tree || 看~ look behind
39 后面 [後-] hòumiàn (back-area) <n.> back, behind: 树林~ behind the forest || 躲在~ hide behind || 跟在~ follow behind
40 左 [-] zuǒ (left hand, left) <n.> left: ~转 turn left || ~手/眼/脑 left hand/eye/brain || 向~ left direction
41 左边 [-邊] zuǒbiān (left-side) <n.> left, left side: 坐在~ sit to the left of || ~的房间 to the left of the room || 往~走 walk in the direction of the left
42 右 [-] yòu (right hand, right) <n.> right: ~手 right hand || ~脚 right foot || ~脑 right brain
43 右边 [-邊] yòubiān (right-side) <n.> right, right side: ~窗户 right window || 走到~ walk to the right || 大门的~ the right of the door
44 左右 [-] zuǒyòu (left-right) <n.> left and right, approximately: ~两半球 approximately two half spheres || ~摇晃 (yáohuang) sway left and right || 楼房~ the left and right of the building

45 上 [-] shàng (high, top) <n.> on top, above, previous: 桌子~ on top of the desk || 墙~ on top of the wall || 楼~ the floor above
46 上边 [-邊] shàngbiān (top-side) <n.> the top, above: 眼睛~ above the eyes || ~的字 above the characters || 挂在~ hang above
47 上面 [-] shàngmiàn (top-area) <n.> above: 住在~ live above || 石头~ above the rock || ~的字 the above characters
48 下 [-] xià (below) <n.> below: 桌子~ below the desk || 山~ below the mountain || 楼~ below the building
49 下边 [-邊] xiàbiān (below-side) <n.> below: 脖子~ below the neck || 地图~ below the map || 小树~ below the tree
50 下面 [-] xiàmiàn (below-area) <n.> below, below part: 衣服~ below the clothes || 阳光~ under the radiance || 水~ under the water
51 上下 [-] shàngxià (high-low) <adv.> high and low, top and bottom: ~三层 three floors from top to bottom || ~关系 relations from important to unimportant || 全国~ the whole nation from bottom to top

52 里 [裏] lǐ (lining, inside) <n.> in: 房间~ in the room || 院子~ in the courtyard || 森林 ~ in the forest
53 里边 [裏邊] lǐbiān (in-side) <n.> inside: 汽车~ inside the car || 门~ inside the door || 坐在~ sit inside
54 里面 [裏-] lǐmiàn (inside-area) <n.> inside, interior: 脑子~ in one's brain || 书~ in a book || 住在~ move inside
55 里头 [裏頭] lǐtóu (inside-*suffix*) <n.> inside, interior: 山~ in the mountain || 心~ in one's heart || 新闻 ~ in the news
56 外 [-] wài (outside) <n.> outside: 向/对/往~ facing the outside, towards the outside, moving towards the outside || 国/城~ out of the country, out of the city || ~衣 outer clothes
57 外边 [-邊] wàibiān (out-side) <n.> outside: 站在~ stand outside || 剧场 (jùchǎng) ~ outside of the theater || 窗子~ outside of the window

58 外部 [-] wàibù (outside-part) <n.> outside, external: ~世界 outside world || ~关系 outer relationships || ~环境 outer region
59 外界 [-] wàijiè (outside-field) <n.> external (or outside) world: ~力量 external power || ~压力outside pressure || ~帮助outside help
60 外头 [-頭] wàitou (outside-*suffix*) <n.> outside, outdoor: 在~吃饭 eat outside || ~风大. The wind outside is huge. || 车站~. The car is outside.

61 内 [-] nèi (enter, inside) <n.> in, interior, inside (part, section): 市~ in the city || 门~ inside the door || 十分钟~ in ten minutes
62 内部 [-] nèibù (inside-part) <n.> interior, inside: 学校~ inside the school || ~环境 inner region || ~关系 inner relationship
63 深处 [-處] shēnchù (deep-place) <n.> abyss, depths: 树林~ deep in the forest || 内心 ~ deep in one's heart || 海底~ the ocean abyss
64 内外 [-] nèiwài (inside-outside) <n.> inside and outside, domestic and foreign: 会场 ~ inside and outside of the meeting hall || ~因素 (yīnsù) internal and external factors || ~交流 internal and external exchange

65 中 [-] zhōng (center) <n.> center, middle: 水~ in the water || 湖~ in the lake || 社会~ within society
66 中间 [-] zhōngjiān (middle-room) <n.> in, between: 房子~ in between rooms || 坐在~ sit between || 广场~ between/within the plaza
67 中心 [-] zhōngxīn (middle-center) <n.> center, heart: 市~ city center || 新闻 ~ heart of the news || 指挥~ command center
68 中央 [-] zhōngyāng (middle-center) <n.> central: 大厅~ central hall || 马路~ central road || 办公室~ central office
69 中部 [-] zhōngbù (middle-part) <n.> central section: ~地区 central region || 非洲~ Central Africa
70 当中 [當-] dāngzhōng (in-middle) <n.> in the middle, in the center: 坐在教室~ be seated in the center of the classroom || 他在热恋~. He is head over heels in love. || 在老朋友~, 杰克最有钱. Among my old friends, Jack is the richest.

71 旁 [-] páng (side, nearby) <n.> next to: 身~ next to one's body || 车站~ next to the station || 飞机~ next to the plane
72 旁边 [-邊] pángbiān (side-side) <n.> next to: 电话~ next to the phone || ~的人 the person next to || 坐在~ sit next to
73 边缘 [邊緣] biānyuán (side-edge) <n.> edge, fringe: ~地带 outer region || 森林~ outer forest || 洞口~ outer entrance (to a cave or a tunel)

74 对面 [對-] duìmiàn (opposite-side/face) <n.> opposite, right in front of: 学校~ opposite the school || ~的楼the opposite building || 坐在~ sit opposite
75 一带 [-帶] yīdài (one-belt) <n.> region, district: 长江~ Yangtze region || 华东~ East China region || 这~ this region
76 附近 [-] fùjìn (near-close) <n.> nearby: 机场~ near the airport || 公园~ near the park || ~居民 nearby neighbor
77 周围 [-圍] zhōuwéi (around-periphery) <n.> surrounding area: 办公室~ around our office || 眼睛~ around our eyes
78 隔壁 [-] gébì (partition-wall) <n.> next door: ~邻居 next door neighbor || 住在~ live next door || ~的房间 the room next door
79 四周 [-] sìzhōu (four-around) <n.> in all directions: 看看~ look in all directions || 院子~ in all directions of the courtyard || ~的一切 everything around

80 四处 [-處] sìchù (four-place) <n.> all over the place: ~求医 seek medical advice all around || ~活动 activities in all directions || ~寻找 to search everywhere

81 处处 [處處] chùchù (place-place) <adv.> everywhere, in all respects: ~有鲜花. Fresh flowers are everywhere. || ~是歌声. The sound of music is everywhere. || ~可见 can be seen everywhere

82 远处 [遠處] yuǎnchù (distant-place) <n.> distant place: ~的山 distant mountain || 看着~ look in the distance || 坐在~ sit in the distance

83 远方 [遠-] yuǎnfāng (distant-area) <n.> distant place: ~的游子 distant traveler || 飞向~ fly off into the distance || ~的天空 the distant sky

84 以上 [-] yǐshàng (from-above) <n.> above: 中等~ above average || 两个~ more than two

85 以下 [-] yǐxià (from-below) <n.> below: ~安排 the plans below || ~内容 the content below || 四年级~ below 4th grade

86 以外 [-] yǐwài (from-beyond) (of scope or range) <n.> beyond: 学校~ beyond the school || 工作~ outside of work || 欧洲~ outside of Europe

87 以内 [-] yǐnèi (from-within) <n.> within, less than: 八百米~ less than 800 meters || 边界~ within the borders || 长城~ within the grade wall

88 之间 [-間] zhījiān (its-between) <n.> between: 男女~ between a man and a woman || 同学~ between classmates || 两地~ between two regions

89 之下 [-] zhīxià (its-below) <bf.> under, beneath, less than: 高温~ below temperature || 海面~ beneath the sea || 车轮~ beneath the wheel

90 哪里 [-裏] nǎlǐ (which-place) <pron.> where: 放在~? Where should I put this? || 你从~来? Where are you from? || 老家在~? Where is your home?

91 哪儿 [-兒] nǎr (where) <pron.> where: 去~? Where are you going? || ~不舒服? Where are you uncomfortable? || 在~? Where?

92 这边 [這邊] zhèbiān (this-side) <pron.> here, this way: 坐~ sit here || 看~ look here || 山~ this part of the mountain

93 这里 [這裡] zhèlǐ (this-place) <pron.> here: 在~ here (it) is || 住~ live here || ~的房子 this room

94 这儿 [這兒] zhèr (here) <pron.> here: 停~ stop here || 放~ place here || 我~ my place

95 那边 [-邊] nàbiān (that-side) <pron.> there, that: 桥/山/河~ that bridge/mountain/river || ~的房间 that room || 到/向/朝~ made it/towards/facing there

96 那里 [-裡] nàlǐ (that-place) <pron.> there: 放在~ place there || 他哥哥~ his brother's place || 住~ live there

97 那儿 [-兒] nàr (there) <pron.> there: 你~ your place || 在~ there || 坐~ sit there

98 国内 [國-] guónèi (country-inside) <bf> domestic: ~问题 domestic issue || ~市场 domestic market || 在~ domestic

99 国外 [國-] guówài (country-outside) <bf> abroad: 在 ~工作 work abroad || ~网站 foreign website || 去~ go abroad

100 海外 [-] hǎiwài (sea-outside) <n.> overseas: ~观众 overseas views || ~市场 overseas market || 住在~ live overseas

101 境内 [-] jìngnèi (border-within) <n.> area inside the borders: 本国~ in this nation || ~生产 produced domestically/within the borders || ~企业 domestic business

102 境外 [-] jìngwài (border-outside) <n.> outer: ~机构 outer agency || 移居~ move outside || ~上市 outside of the city

103 背后 [-後] bèihòu (body back-back) <n.> behind: 门~ behind the door || 放在~ place in the back || 从~出来 enter in the back

104 到处 [-處] dàochù (arrive-place) <adv.> at all places: ~是袜子. There are socks everywhere. || ~都有饭吃. There is food to eat everywhere. || ~乱跑 run about everywhere

105 底下 [-] dǐxià (bottom-below) <n.> under, below: 床~ under the bed || 桌子~ under the desk || 地~ underground

106 太空 [-] tàikōng (highest-sky) <n.> outer space: ~飞行 fly in outer space || 飞到~ fly into outer space || ~旅行 outer space travel

107 天空 [-] tiānkōng (heaven-sky) <n.> sky: 蓝色的~ blue sky || 远处的~ distant sky || 飞上~ fly in the sky

108 天上 [-] tiānshàng (heaven-on) <n.> sky, heaven: ~的月亮 moonlight in the sky || 从~掉下来 fall from the sky || 在~ in the sky

109 空中 [-] kōngzhōng (sky-in) <n.> in the sky (of air), aerial: ~花园 garden in the sky || ~的鸟儿 bird in the sky || 飞到 ~ fly into the sky

110 山上 [-] shānshàng (mountain-on) <n.> on the mountain: 前面的~ mountain ahead || ~树木 tree on the mountain || 站在~ stand on the mountain

111 海边 [-邊] hǎibiān (sea-side) <n.> seaside, next to the ocean: 站在~ stand next to the ocean || 到~游泳swim in the ocean || 生活在~ live in the ocean

112 海底 [-] hǎidǐ (sea-bottom) <n.> ocean floor: 沉入~ sink to the bottom of the ocean || ~火山 underwater volcano || ~世界 underwater world

113 海上 [-] hǎishàng (sea-on) <n.> maritime, on the sea: ~交通 maritime communications || ~运输 (yùnshū) marine transportation || ~航行 (hángxíng) ocean shipping rout

114 沿海 [-] yánhǎi (border-sea) <n.> following/bordering the ocean: ~地区 region following the ocean || ~城市 city following the ocean || 东部~ eastern ocean border

115 岸边 [-邊] ànbiān (river bank-side) <n.> shore: 停在~ stop on the shore || 走到~ walk to the shore || 靠近~ next to the shore

116 岸上 [-] ànshàng (river bank-on) <n.> on the shore: 回到~ return to the shore || 站在~ stand on the shore || 对着~ face the shore

117 两岸 [兩-] liǎng'àn (two-river bank) <n.> two shores: 海峡/长江~ two sides of the straight/river || ~的景色 both shores scenery || 沿河~ both sides following the river

118 城里 [-裏] chénglǐ (city-inside) <n.> city, in the city: ~人 city dweller || 回到~ return to the city || ~的房屋 house in the city

119 路边 [-邊] lùbiān (road-side) <n.> roadside: ~的咖啡馆a roadside cafe || ~停车curb parking

120 楼上 [樓-] lóushàng (storied building-up) <n.> upstairs: 住~ live upstairs || ~房间 room upstairs || 在~ upstairs

121 楼下 [樓-] lóuxià (storied building-down) <n.> downstairs: ~的客厅 downstairs living room || 往~跑 run downstairs || 住~ live downstairs

122 地下 [-] dìxià (ground-under) <n.> underground: ~商场 underground market || ~车库 underground garage || ~水 underground water

123 部位 [-] bùwèi (part-location) <n.> position, place (usu. referring to the human body position or place): 受伤~ location of an injury || 发音~ position in pronunciation || 特殊 (tèshū) ~ special body place

124 面前 [-] miàqián (face-front) <n.> in the face of, facing: 在朋友~ in the face of friends || 公众~ in front of a crowd

125 眼前 [-] yǎnqián (eye-front) <n.> in front of one's eyes: 走到~ walk in front of one's eyes || 近在~ near one's eyes || ~一亮 flashed in front of one's eyes

126 跟前 [-] gēnqián (heel-front) <n.> in front (of): 车子~ in front of a car || 来到~ go to the front || 跑到~ run to the front

127 身边 [-邊] shēnbiān (body-side) <n.> at or by one's side: 在他妈妈~ at his mother's side || 把女朋友的照片放在~ keep his girlfriend's picture close at hand || 坐在~ sit by one's side

128 手里 [-裏] shǒulǐ (hand-in) <n.> in one's hand: ~有钱 money in hand || ~的书 a book in hand

129 各地 [-] gèdì (each-place) <bf> in all parts of the country: ~运动员 athletes from all over the country || ~代表 representatives from all parts of the country || 全国 ~ all over the world

130 遍地 [-] biàndì (all over-place) <adv./v.> all over the place, everywhere: ~开放 open all over the place || ~都是 everywhere || 野花~ wild flowers everywhere

131 此处 [-處] cǐchù (this-place) <n.> this place, here: 离开~ leave this place || 住在~ live in this place || 说到~ talk to this place

132 首席 [-] shǒuxí (prime-seat) <n.> seat of honor: ~地位 place of honor || ~座位 seat of honor || ~钢琴家 top piano player

Tips:

1 South-up oriented map: Ancient China had north-up oriented maps, but south-up maps were mainstream until the 13th century. One explanation is that the ancient Chinese believed 天 (heaven) to be in the south and 地 (Earth) in the north. Heaven (天) is above Earth (地) and therefore south should be up on maps. The English word compass is 指南针 (zhǐnánzhēn, pointing-south-needle) in Chinese.

2 Cardinal and intermediate directions: Chinese ways of expressing cardinal and intermediate directions are different from English ways. In English, north and south are primary, while east and west are primary in Chinese. For example, the English cardinal directions are normally listed as north, south, east and west, but in Chinese they are 东 (E,) 南 (S,) 西 (W) and 北 (N,) or 东, 西, 南 and 北. The English intermediate directions, Northeast (NE,) SE, SW, NW are 东北 (Literally east-north,) 东南 (lit. east-south,) 西南 (lit. west-south,) 西北 (lit. west-north) in Chinese.

3 正/偏+direction: '正+direction' means 'due (+) direction,' for example, 正南 means 'due south.' 偏 (piān) means 'leaning, inclined, slanting' and '偏+direction' means 'to/by (+) the direction,' for example, 偏西 (to the west) and 东北偏东 (NE by the east.)

4 这儿 vs. 这里: One of the origins of 儿 was 里, therefore, 这儿 means 这里 (here.)

5 Chinese location words: 15 location words and their combinations with 边/面/头 are in the below chart.

	东 east	西 west	南 south	北 north	前 front	后 behind	左 left	右 right	上 above/ up	下 below	里 in	外 out	内 inside	中 middle	旁 side
+边 (side)	Y	Y	Y	Y	Y	Y	Y	Y	Y	Y	Y	Y	N	N	Y
+面 (part)	Y	Y	Y	Y	Y	Y	Y	Y	Y	Y	Y	Y	N	N	N
+头 (side)	N	N	N	N	Y	Y	N	N	Y	Y	Y	Y	N	N	N

Exercises:

Part I: Use the given bound form as a guide to help you think of other words with the same character. Feel free to use your dictionary when needed. Then write down the English definition of each of the words you've written.

上 *(up)*: 上面 *on the top of, in the surface of*

____

____

____

____

下 *(down)*: 楼下 *downstairs*

____

____

____

____

左 *(left)*: 左边 *left side*

____

____

____

____

右 *(right)*: 右边 *right side*

____

____

____

____

前 *(front)*: 前头 *in front, at the head*

____

____

____

____

后 *(back)*: 后头 *back, rear*

____

____

____

____

里 *(in)*: 里面 *inside*

____

____

____

____

外 *(out)*: 外面 *outside*

____

____

____

____

Part II: Read the following sentences and fill in each blank with the appropriate word or phrase from the options given.

1 到处、首席、此处

a) "CEO"的中文意思是: ________执行官 (zhíxíngguān).
b) 飓风 (jùfēng, hurricane) 过后, 这个地方_______都是倒塌 (dǎotā, collapse) 的房屋.
c) 在中国公园你会看到这样的牌子: ________禁止吸烟, 意思是这个地方不能吸烟.

2 遍地、各地、部位

a) 尽管中国90%的人口是汉族, 但是_______老百姓的文化和生活方式都不同.

b) 17世纪的时候西方人以为中国是一个非常神秘、富有的国家，________都是黄金.
c) 现代医疗设备可以准确检测身体的各个_______的病情.

3 台上、空中、地下

a) 这座新建筑下面的________停车场非常大, 可以容纳几千辆车.
b) 京剧演员一般都知道一句话: _______三分钟, 台下十年功. 意思是每个京剧表演动作都要花很长时间练习才能学会.
c) 中国飞机航班上的女服务员一般被称为"________小姐."

4 太空、空间、海底

a) 人类探索 (tànsuǒ, explore) _______的道路还很遥远 (yáoyuǎn, far), 目前只要少数国家在其他其他星球上建立了_______站.
b) 地球上的大部分面积是被海水覆盖 (fùgài, cover) 的, 人类还没有完全弄清楚________世界的秘密.

Theme 96: Places 地方 (dìfāng)

1 地方 [-] dìfāng (place-square) <n.> place: 老~ old place || 没有~ no place || 住的~ a place to live
2 地带 [-帶] dìdài (place-belt) <n.> zone: 安全~ safety zone || 森林~ forest area || 中心~ central area
3 地区 [-區] dìqū (place-district) <n.> area: 农村~ rural area || 东部~ eastern area || 大片~ large area
4 区域 [區-] qūyù (district-territory) <n.> region: 不同~ different regions || 分布 ~ distributed areas || 小~ small area
5 地点 [-點] dìdiǎn (place-spot) <n.> location: 见面~ meeting location || 工作 ~ working location || 考试 ~ testing location
6 地址 [-] dìzhǐ (place-site) <n.> address: 联系 (liánxì) ~ contact address || 通讯 (tōngxùn) ~ contact address || 详细~ detailed address
7 出生地 [-] chūshēngdì (birth-place) <n.> birthplace: 回到~ go back to birthplace || 寻访 ~ visit birthplace
8 小区 [-區] xiǎoqū (small-district) <n.> neighborhood: 居民~ community || 住宅 (zhùzhái) ~ residential area || 工业 ~ industrial area
9 学区 [學區] xuéqū (school-district) <n.> school district: 小学~ elementary school district || 本~ this school district || 跨 (kuà) ~ cross school district
10 厂区 [廠區] chǎngqū (factory-area) <n.> factory region: ~绿化 greening factory region || 进入~ enter factory area
11 灾区 [災區] zāiqū (disaster-area) <n.> disaster area: 地震 (dìzhèn) ~ Earthquake area || 重~ heavily devastated area || ~人民 people at disaster area
12 山区 [-區] shānqū (mountain-area) <n.> mountain area: 西部 ~ western mountain area || 偏远 (piānyuǎn) ~ rural mountain area || 开发~ develop mountain area
13 社区 [-區] shèqū (commune-district) <n.> community: 华人~ Chinese community || 工业~ industrial community || 城乡 ~ urban and rural area
14 校园 [-園] xiàoyuán (school-enclosure) <n.> campus: 中学/大学~ middle school/college campus || 新/老~ new/old campus

15 景点 [-點] jǐngdiǎn (scenery-spot) <n.> scenic spot: 旅游 (lǚyóu) ~ traveling scenic spot || 新~ new scenic spot || 参观~ visit scenic spot

16 试点 [試點] shìdiǎn (trial-spot) <n.> pilot: 四个~ four pilots || 作为~ as a pilot || 搞~ organize a pilot

17 场地 [場-] chǎngdì (field-place) <n.> field: 比赛~ competition field || 活动~ activity field || 露天~ outdoor field

18 场所 [場-] chǎngsuǒ (field-location) <n.> place: 活动~ activity place || 主要~ main place || 工作~ working place

19 广场 [廣場] guǎngchǎng (wide-field) <n.> square: 天安门~ Tian'an'men Square || 时代~ Times Square || 购物~ shopping plaza

20 现场 [現場] xiànchǎng (current-place) <n.> on site: 比赛~ competition site || 赶到~ arrive at the scene || ~直播 live

21 战场 [戰場] zhànchǎng (war-field) <n.> battlefield: 上~ go on battlefield || 亚洲~ Asian battlefield || 古~ ancient battlefield

22 火葬场 [-髒場] huǒzàngchǎng (fire-bury-place) <n.> crematorium: 年轻人一般不喜欢在~工作. Young people generally do not like working in a crematorium.

23 公墓 [-] gōngmù (public-cemetery) <n.> cemetery: 革命~ revolution cemetery || 修建~ build a cemetery

24 考场 [-場] kǎochǎng (exam-place) <n.> testing center: 上~ go into the testing center || 进~ go into the testing center || 招生~ admissions testing center

25 停车场 [-車場] tíngchēchǎng (park-vehicle-field) <n.> parking lot: 大型~ large parking lot || 地下~ underground parking lot || 公共~ public parking lot

26 当场 [當場] dāngchǎng (that-spot) <adv.> on the spot: ~宣布 announce on the spot || ~表演 perform on the spot || ~道歉 (dàoqiàn) apologize on the spot

27 本地 [-] běndì (local-place) <n.> local: ~市场 local market || ~人 native people || ~情况 local condition

28 当地 [當-] dāngdì (that-place) <n.> local: ~中学 local middle school || ~儿童 local children || ~人 local people

29 外地 [-] wàidì (away-place) <n.> parts of the country other than where one is, not a native: ~人 non-local people || ~游客outside tourists

30 故乡 [-鄉] gùxiāng (old-native place) <n.> home: 回到~ come back home || 离开~ leave home

31 家乡 [-鄉] jiāxiāng (home-native place) <n.> hometown: 离开~ leave one's hometown || 回到~ back to hometown

32 本土 [-] běntǔ (native-land) <n.> native: 中国~ native Chinese || ~人 native people || ~文化 native culture

33 边境 [邊-] biānjìng (border-boundary) <n.> border: ~地区 boundary || 靠近~ close to border || 离~不远 not far away from border

34 内地 [-] nèidì (inner-land) <n.> mainland: ~城市 mainland city || 住在~ live in mainland || ~市场 mainland market

35 城区 [-區] chéngqū (city-district) <n.> district: 西/东~ west/east district || 老/新~ old/new district || 中心~ central district

36 城乡 [-鄉] chéngxiāng (city-rural) <n.> rural-urban: ~差别 rural-urban distinction || rural-urban fringe~结合 || rural-urban residents~居民

37 都会 [-會] dūhuì (capital-metropolis) <n.> metropolis: 大~ metropolis || 国际~ international metropolis

38 都市 [-] dūshì (capital-city) <n.> city: 现代~ modern city || 大~ big city || 国际~ international city

39 市区 [-區] shìqū (city-district) <n.> downtown: 靠近 ~ near downtown || 老/新~ old/new downtown || 离~不远 close to downtown

40 郊区 [-區] jiāoqū (suburb-district) <n.> suburban: 城市~ city suburban || ~中学 suburban middle school || ~农村 suburban village

41 城镇 [-鎮] chéngzhèn (city-town) <n.> town: 小~ small town || 新~ new town || 一座~ a town

42 乡村 [鄉-] xiāngcūn (rural-village) <n.> country: ~学校 country school || ~生活 country life || 各地~ rural areas

43 农村 [農-] nóngcūn (agriculture-village) <n.> village: ~市场 village market || ~人 villagers || 东北~ northeastern village

44 家里 [-裏] jiālǐ (home-inside) <n.> at home: 住在~ live at home || 从~跑出来 go out from home || 到~玩 go home to hang out

45 大道 [-] dàdào (broad-path) <n.> avenue: 一条~ an avenue || 江边~ lakeside avenue || 沿着~ along the avenue

46 十字路口 [-] shízìlùkǒu ('ten'-character-road-passage) <n.> crossroad: 走到 ~ walk to the crossroad || 下一个~ next crossroad

47 拐弯 [-彎] guǎiwān (turn-curve) <n.> turn: 大~ big turn || 楼梯~ turn at the stairs

48 街上 [-] jiēshàng (street-on) <n.> on the street: 站在~ standing on the street || 华尔~ On Wall Street || ~有很多人. There are many people on the street.

49 街头 [-頭] jiētóu (street-*suffix*) <n.> street: 走上~ walk on the street || 十字~ crisscross streets || ~小店corner store

50 路口 [-] lùkǒu (road-passage) <n.> intersection: 十字/交叉~ crossroad || 前方~ intersection ahead || 走到~ walk to the intersection

51 路上 [-] lùshàng (road-on) <n.> on the way: 在~ on the way || 回来的~ on the way back || ~的行人 pedestrians on the way

52 路线 [-綫] lùxiàn (road-line) <n.> route: 旅行~ traveling route || 飞行~ flying route || 航空~ flight route

53 管道 [-] guǎndào (tube-path) <n.> tube: 地下~ underground tube || 供水/排污~ waste pipe || 疏通 (shūtōng) ~ dredge pipe Note: In Taiwan, this word also means 渠道 (qúdào, channel).

54 轨道 [軌-] guǐdào (rut-path) <n.> orbit: 运行~ orbit || 卫星~ satellite orbit || 圆形~ circular orbit

55 航线 [-綫] hángxiàn (navigate-route) <n.> route: 新~ new route || 一条~ a route || 国际~ international route

56 线路 [綫-] xiànlù (path-road) <n.> line: 电话~ telephone line || 十条~ ten lines || ~不通 not able to get through

57 起点 [-點] qǐdiǎn (start-point) <n.> starting point: 作为~ as the starting point || ~高/低 high/low starting point || 新~ new starting point

58 途中 [-] túzhōng (route-middle) <n.> on the way: 上班~ on the way to work || 回来~ on the way back || 旅游 ~ during the trip

59 终点 [終點] zhōngdiǎn (end-point) <n.> destination: 到达~ arrive at destination || 跑到~ run to the destination || 冲过~ run through destination

60 入口 [-] rùkǒu (enter-passage) <n.> entrance: 飞机~ plane entrance || 大楼~ building entrance || 三个~ three entrances
61 出口 [-] chūkǒu (exit-passage) <n.> exit: 商场~ mall exit || 找到~ find the exit || ~在右边. The exit is on the right.
62 进口 [進-] jìnkǒu (enter-passage) <n.> entrance: 在~等你 wait for you at the entrance || 两个~ two entrances || 东边的~ east entrance
63 门口 [門-] ménkǒu (gate-passage) <n.> gate: 家/校/厂~ home/school/factory gate || 走到~ walk to the gate || 站在~ stand at the gate
64 窗口 [-] chuāngkǒu (window-passage) <n.> window: 飞机~ flight window || 小~ small window || 靠在~ by the window
65 角落 [-] jiǎoluò (corner-place) <n.> corner: 坐在~里sit in the corner || 教室的一个~ a corner of the classroom
66 地面 [-] dìmiàn (Earth-surface) <n.> ground: 离开~ leave the ground || 钻出~ come out of the ground || ~不平 uneven ground
67 空儿 [-] kòngr (space) <n.> space: 车上没~了. There is no space in the car. || 让点~给她坐. Leave some space for her to sit.

68 洞 [-] dòng (grotto) <n.> cave: 山~ mountain cave || 树~ hole in a tree || 挖~ dig a hole
69 隧道 [-] suìdào (tunnel-path) <n.> tunnel: 地下~ underground tunnels || 海底~ the undersea tunnel || 两条~ two tunnels

70 所 [-] suǒ (place) <n.> 住~ dwelling place || 处~ place, location|| 研究~ research institute
71 所在 [-] suǒzài (place-locate) <n.> where: 关键~ where the key is || 差异~ where the difference is || 问题的~ where the problem is

Tips:

1 Settlement hierarchy in China: From small to large, they are: 村/庄 (cūn/zhuāng, village,) 乡 (xiāng, township,) 镇 (zhèn, town,) 市 (shì, city) and 省 (shěng, province) /自治区 (zìzhìqū, autonomous region.) In large cities, 区 (qū, district) and 小区 (neighborhood) are subareas even though some 小区 (neighborhood) in China are larger than a medium-sized city such as Boston in terms of population. 都 (dū) means 'capital,' for example, 首都. 会 (會, huì) means 'metropolis,' for example, (大) 都会 (metropolis, such as 大都会艺术博物馆, The Met, The Metropolitan Museum of Arts) and 省会 (provincial capital.)

2 *州 (zhōu): 州 (prefecture) was an important settlement level in ancient China, and 九州 and 神州 were synonymous with China sometimes. Now 州 is still well kept in the names of some cities such as 广州, 温州, 杭州, 苏州, 扬州, 徐州, 郑州, 沧州, 兰州 and 惠州. In the U.S., 州 means 'state,' for example, Texas is 德州 (Dézhōu) which happens to be a city in Shandong, China. 洲 (zhōu) originally means 'islet in a river,' but is now mainly used in the names of continents, for example, 亚洲 (Yàzhōu, Asia,) 欧洲 (Ōuzhōu, Europe,) 非洲 (Africa,) 北美洲 (North America) and 大洋洲 (Oceania.) 澳洲 (Àozhōu) refers to Australia.

3 *各庄: If you travel in the rural areas of Northern China, you will probably see many villages named '*各庄,' for example, 王各庄. The 各 (gè) actually keeps the ancient pronunciation of 家, in other words, 王各庄 means 王家庄, which is supposed to have had a large family with the surname 王.

Exercises:

Part I: Use the given bound form on as a guide to help you think of other words with the same character. Feel free to use your dictionary when needed. Then write down the English definition of each of the words you've written.

地 *(place)*: 地方 *place*

____

____

____

____

____

区 *(area)*: 山区 *mountain area*

____

____

____

____

____

场 *(a large place used for a particular purpose)*: 飞机场 *airport*

____

____

____

____

____

口 *(mouth, entrance)*: *doorway*

____

____

____

____

Part II: Read the following sentences and fill in each blank with the appropriate word or phrase from the options given.

1 所在、研究所、隧道

a) 中国有很多家军工________研究军事武器.
b) 这家饭馆________的地段非常繁华 (fánhuá, bustling), 因此生意很好.
c) 中国和韩国正在合作开发一项海底________工程.

2 轨道、航线、边境

a) 北京到波士顿的直飞________是2015年开通的.
b) 那位政治家认为在美国和墨西哥(Mexico)________修建一堵高墙就可以阻挡 (zǔdǎng, block) 非法移民.
c) 2011年中国的高速列车行驶时脱离 (tuōlí, off) 了________, 造成巨大的人员伤亡.

3 当场、考场、角落

a) 目前中国大陆还没有设置 (shèzhì, establish) SAT考试的________, 大陆考生常常要到香港去考SAT.
b) 这个小偷在地铁上偷别人钱包, 被警察________抓住.
c) 这个办公室的________里堆放着很多旧杂志.

4 外地、学区、本土

a) 在北京、上海等大城市, ________房的价格都非常高.
b) 很多外国大公司进入中国以后都有不同程度的________化.
c) 在教育、医疗等方面有本地户口的人跟有________户口的人待遇 (dàiyù, benefit) 是不同的.

5 区域、地址、地带

a) 中国的________经济发展是不平衡 (pínghéng, balanced) 的, 东部发达, 西部相对落后.
b) 目前中国的法律还不是很完善, 有一些法律的灰色________.
c) 这家公司搬迁 (bānqiān, move) 了, 但网页上的公司________还没有更新 (gēngxīn, update).

Theme 97: Actions with hand(s) 手部动作 (shǒubù dòngzuò)

1 按 [-] àn (press down, push) <v.> push: ~门铃 push the doorbell || ~一下鼠标 click the mouse || ~下开关 push the button
2 拔 [-] bá (pull out, pull up) <v.> pluck, pull: ~萝卜 pull the carrots || ~草 pluck the weeds || ~牙 pull out a tooth
3 摆 [擺] bǎi (arrange, place, wave) <v.> wave, place: ~手 wave one's hand || ~好桌子, 准备吃饭 set the table for the meal.
4 搬 [-] bān (move, remove) <v.> move: ~椅子 move chairs || ~家具 move furniture || ~东西 move stuff
5 包 [-] bāo (wrap up) <v.> wrap: ~饺子 wrap dumplings || ~起来 wrap something up || ~礼物 wrap a gift

6 包装 [-] bāozhuāng (wrap-put into) <v.> wrap: 真空~ vacuumized wrap || 重新~ re-wrap || ~食品 wrap the food

7 抱 [-] bào (hold in the arms, embrace) <v.> embrace: ~着吉他 embracing the guitar || ~起来embrace || ~在手中 embrace in hand

8 擦 [-] cā (rub, wipe) <v.> wipe: ~口红 wipe off the lip gloss || ~眼泪 wipe the tears || ~玻璃 wipe the glass

9 插 [-] chā (insert) <v.> insert, plug: ~电源 (diànyuán) plug in power || ~花 flower arranging

10 撑 [撐] chēng (support, maintain) <v.> prop up, support: 把伞~开 put up an umbrella || 一家人的生活靠他~着. He has to support his whole family.

11 冲 [沖] chōng (rinse, flush, pour water) <v.> flush, pour water: ~澡 take a shower || ~奶粉 pour water into milk powder || ~一杯热茶 make a hot tea

12 穿 [-] chuān (put on, wear) <v.> put on: ~大衣 put on a coat || ~裤子 (kùzi) put on pants || ~袜子 (wàzi) put on socks

13 打 [-] dǎ (hit) <v.> hit: ~了一拳 give a punch || ~屁股 hit the butt || ~耳光 slap someone

14 打包 [-] dǎbāo (*prefix*-wrap) <separable word> wrap up: ~回家 wrap up and go home || ~装车 wrap up and put in car

15 打开 [-開] dǎkāi (make-open) <v.> turn on, open: ~大门 to open the door || ~电脑 to turn on the computer || ~窗子 to open the window

16 打破 [-] dǎpò (make-broken) <v.> break: ~杯子 break the cup || ~记录 (jìlù) break the record || ~常规 break the convention

17 打扫 [-掃] dǎsǎo (*prefix*-clean) <v.> clean: ~房间clean the room || ~卫生 cleaning up || ~垃圾 clean up garbage

18 戴 [-] dài (wear, put on) <v.> wear: 帽子~ wear a hat || ~眼镜 wear glasses || ~面具wear a mask

19 倒 [-] dào (pour) <v.> pour: ~咖啡 pour coffee || ~了一点水pour some water || ~一杯茶 pour a cup of tea

20 递 [遞] dì (take turns, pass) <v.> deliver, hand: ~给他一个本子 hand him a notebook || 把杯子~给我 hand me the cup

21 点 [點] diǎn (click) <v.> click: ~开文件 click on the document

22 动手 [動-] dòngshǒu (use-hand) <separable word> do it yourself: 自己~ do it yourself || 亲自~ do it yourself || ~打人 hit somebody

23 堵 [-] dǔ (stop up, block up) <v.> block: ~住出口 block the exit || ~在门外 block the door

24 翻 [-] fān (fly, turn over) <v.> search for: ~东西search for something || 乱~ search without a purpose

25 放 [-] fàng (put) <v.> put: ~在这里 put sth. here || ~在一起 put something together || 桌上~了一本书 put a book on the table

26 扶 [-] fú (support with the hand) <v.> help: ~老人 help the elderly || ~他一下 help him || ~上楼help somebody go upstairs

27 盖 [蓋] gài (hide, cover) <v.> cover: ~盖子 cover the cap || ~上盒子 cover the box || ~杯子 cover the cup

28 割 [-] gē (cut) <v.> cut: ~稻子cut rice stalks || ~麦子 cut wheat || ~肉cut meat

29 鼓掌 [-] gǔzhǎng (applaud-hand) <separable word> applaud: 很多观众起立~. Many people in the audience stood up to applaud. || 热烈~ warmly applaud || ~欢迎 give somebody a big hand
30 刮 [-] guā (scrape) <v.> shave, blow: ~胡子shave the beard || ~脸 shave the face || ~风harshly blowing wind
31 挂 [-] guà (hang) <v.> hang: ~在树上 hang on the tree || ~着一张地图 hang a map || ~窗帘 hang the curtains
32 关 [關] guān (shut, close, turn off) <v.> close, turn off: ~门 close the door || ~窗户 close the window || ~电脑 turn off the computer
33 划 [-] huá (row) <v.> row: ~船row the boat || ~水 row in the water || ~龙舟 row the dragon boat
34 挤 [擠] jǐ (push against, expel, press, squeeze) <v.> squeeze, scooch: ~时间squeeze some time || ~牙膏 squeeze some toothpaste || ~一张床scooch in one bed
35 夹 [夾] jiā (press from both sides) <v.> hold, pick: ~菜pick from some dish || ~东西hold sth. || 腋下~一本书hold a book between his, her arms
36 捡 [撿] jiǎn (pick up, collect) <v.> pick: ~东西pick something up || ~石头 pick a rock || ~垃圾pick up trash
37 剪 [-] jiǎn (cut) <v.> cut: ~头发cut hair || ~羊毛 cut wool || ~指甲 cut fingernails
38 接 [-] jiē (join, converge, meet) <v.> catch, take, receive: ~球 catch the ball || ~电话take the phone call || ~报告 receive a report
39 接到 [-] jiēdào (receive-*suffix*) <v.> recieve: ~信, 电话, 报告 receive a letter, call, report || ~消息, 通知, 任务, 命令 receive a notice, information, command
40 揭 [-] jiē (raise, take off, uncover) <v.> uncover, tear off: ~开秘密uncover the secrets || ~发expose, unmask
41 解开 [-開] jiěkāi (untie-open) <v.> untie, loosen: ~鞋带untie shoelaces || ~衣服 loosen clothes || ~绳子untie the string
42 举 [舉] jǔ (raise, lift up) <v.> raise: ~杯 raise the cup || ~例子 give an example
43 举手 [舉] jǔshǒu (raise-hand) <v.> raise hand: ~赞成 (zànchéng) raise hand for approval || ~发言 raise hand to speak
44 卷 [-] juǎn (roll up) <v.> roll: ~毛线 roll woolen || ~手帕 (shǒupà) roll a handkerchief || ~地图 roll a map
45 开 [開] kāi (open, turn on) <v.> open, turn on: ~门 open the door || ~窗 open the window || ~灯 turn on the lights
46 拉 [-] lā (pull, drag, tug) <v.> pull, draw: ~上拉链zip up || ~紧draw it tight
47 拉开 [-開] lākāi (pull-open) <separable word> pull open, draw bck: 拉得开 / 拉不开 be able, unable to be pulled || ~窗帘 draw back the curtain || ~门 pull the door open

Exercises:

Part I: Read the following sentences and fill in each blank with the appropriate word or phrase from the options given.

1 挂、摆、按、拔、搬

a) 老王告诉我到他家的时候_______门铃, 他会下楼给我开门.
b) 老王今天早上要到牙诊所去_______两颗牙, 他心里感到有些害怕.

c) 这位牙医的办公室墙上__________着他的毕业证书和牙医执照 (zhízhào, license), 办公桌上_______着家人的照片.
d) 这位牙医正打算把他的办公室_______到纽约去.

2 倒、打、擦、冲、穿

a) 日本小学生每天都要在学校_______地板, 因为这是他们学校教育的一部分.
b) 很多中国年轻人喜欢_______速溶咖啡喝.
c) 一些年轻人特别喜欢_______名牌衣服.
d) 中国人觉得给客人_______茶是表示对客人尊敬.
e) 在美国人们开车的时候_______电话是很常见的事情.

3 递、端、点、戴、堵

a) 小王看书的时候喜欢_______上耳机听音乐.
b) 开会的时候, 小王_______给我一个纸条, 上面写着: 中午一起去饭馆吃饭吧? 你来_______菜.
c) 中国的大学毕业生宁可失业也不会去饭馆当服务员, 因为他们觉得堂堂大学生怎么能_______盘子, 干体力活呢.
d) 世界上所有的大城市都存在_______车的问题, 这就是人们所说的"大城市病."

4 抱、翻、挤、扶、划

a) 北京上班族每天早上最头疼的事情就是_______地铁.
b) 一般来说, 北京的交通警察会_______老年人过马路.
c) 小王周末约朋友去公园_______船.
d) 小王手里_______着很多书, 没办法开门, 只好请同事帮忙.
e) _______开这本书的第一页, 你会看到作者的序言 (xùyán).

5 接、揭开、拉、开捡、打开

a) 明天我得去飞机场_______我父母, 他们从北京飞到纽约来看我.
b) 在机场我_______到一个钱包, ________钱包一看里面有很多美金.
c) 这本经济学著作会帮你_______经济学的秘密.
d) 早上起来, _______窗帘, 我看到很多鸟落在我窗前的树上.

48 理 [-] lǐ (treat, tidy up) <v.> tidy up: ~发 get a haircut || ~胡子 tidy up the beard
49 埋 [-] mái (bury) <v.> bury: ~炸弹 bury a bomb || ~宝藏 (bǎozàng) bury treasure || ~在地里 bury sth underground
50 摸 [-] mō (feel, touch) <v.> touch: ~脸 touch (a) face || ~头 touch (a) head
51 磨 [-] mò (grind) <v.> grind: ~面 grind flour || ~咖啡豆grind coffee beans
52 拿 [-] ná (hold, take) <v.> get: ~书包 get the backpack || ~帽子 get the hat || ~照片 get the photo
53 拿出 [-] náchū (take-out) <separable word> take out: 拿得出 be able to take out sth. || 拿不出 be unable to take out sth. || ~书 take out a book
54 拿起 [-] náqǐ (pick-up) <separable word> pick up: 拿得起 can manage to do || 拿不起 cannot manage to do || ~东西 pick sth. up
55 拿走 [-] názǒu (take-away) <separable word> carry away, be carried away: 拿得走be able to be carried away || 拿不走 be unable to be carried away || ~一本书 carry away a book

56 泡 [-] pào (steep, soak) <v.> make, soak: ~茶 make tea || ~咖啡 make coffee

57 泼 [潑] pō (splash, spill) <v.> splash: ~水 splash water || ~冷水pour cold water on, dampen the enthusiasm of

58 铺 [鋪] pū (spread) <v.> make, spread: ~床 make the bed || ~被子 spread the quilt || ~地毯 (dìtǎn) spread the rug

59 敲门 [-門] qiāomén (knock-door) <separable word> knock on the door: 敲了一下门 knocked on the door once || 轻轻~ slightly knock on the door

60 切 [-] qiē (cut, slice) <v.> cut: ~菜 cut vegetables || ~肉 cut meat || ~蛋糕 cut cake

61 取 [-] qǔ (cut off left ear, take) <v.> take: ~东西 take sth. || ~药 take medicine || ~钥匙 (yàoshi) take keys

62 扔 [-] rēng (roll, throw, cast) <v.> throw away: ~东西 throw away sth. || ~硬币 throw a coin

63 洒 [灑] sǎ (splash, spill) <v.> spill, sprinkle, spray: ~农药 spray pesticide || 把汤~了spilled the soup

64 塞 [-] sāi (stop up, block up, stuff) <v.> fill in, squeeze, stuff: 箱子不太满, 还可以~点东西. There is still room in the suitcase to squeeze a few more things in || ~进stuff in || 水管 ~住了 the waterpipe is clogged up

65 扫 [掃] sǎo (sweep) <v.> sweep: ~地sweep the floor || ~院子sweep the yard || ~落叶sweep the fallen leaves

66 扇 [搧] shān (slap, flap) <v.> slap, flap: ~耳光 slap || ~风make wind by flapping || ~翅膀 (chìbǎng) flap the wings

67 拾 [-] shí (pick up) <v.> pick: ~贝壳 pick shells || ~东西 pick sth. || ~球 pick up balls

68 刷 [-] shuā (brush) <v.> brush: ~牙 brush teeth || ~墙brush the wall || ~鞋子 brush the shoes

69 刷牙 [-] shuāyá (brush-tooth) <v.> brush teeth: 早晚~ brush teeth morning and night || 刷两次牙 brush teeth twice || 认真~ brush teeth carefully

70 摔 [-] shuāi (cast, throw) <v.> throw down: ~东西 throw down sth. || ~瓶子throw down a bottle || ~筷子throw down chopsticks

71 锁 [鎖] suǒ (lock) <v.> lock: ~门 lock the door || ~车 lock the car || ~在箱子里 lock sth. into the box

72 抬 [擡] tái (carry, raise, lift) <v.> carry, lift: ~头 lift head || ~家具carry the furniture || ~病人carry patients

73 掏 [-] tāo (dig, pull out) <v.> pull out, take out: ~钥匙 pull out keys || ~香烟 take out cigarettes || ~钱 take out money

74 提 [-] tí (lift) <v.> lift: ~水 lift water || ~袋子 lift a bag || ~东西 lift sth.

75 填 [-] tián (fill, stuff) <v.> fill: ~土 fill with dirt || ~海 fill the sea || ~坑 fill the pit

76 贴 [貼] tiē (glue, paste) <v.> glue: ~邮票glue stamps || ~广告glue advertisement || ~照片glue a picture

77 投 [-] tóu (throw) <v.> pitch: ~球pitch a ball || ~票vote

78 推 [-] tuī (push) <v.> push: ~自行车 push the bike || ~门 push the door || ~行李 push luggage

79 推开 [-開] tuīkāi (push-open/away) <v.> push open, away: ~房门 push open the door || ~窗户 push open the windows || ~医生push away the doctor

80 托 [-] tuō (hold in the palm) <v.> palm: ~盘子palm the plate || 用手~着 palm it || 往上~ palm upwards

81 拖 [-] tuō (drag, haul, pull) <v.> drag: ~着一个箱子 drag a piece of luggage

82 脱 [-] tuō (take off) <v.> take off: ~衣服take off clothes || ~鞋take off子shoes || ~袜子 take off socks

83 挖 [-] wā (dig) <v.> dig: ~洞 dig a hole || ~土dig mud || ~野菜 dig wild vegetables

84 握 [-] wò (grasp, grip, hold) <v.> shake, hold on: ~手 shake hands || ~着瓶子 hold on to bottles || ~着方向盘 hold on to the wheel

85 握手 [-] wò shǒu (shake-hand) s<separable word> shake hand: 握两次手 shake hands twice || 握我的手 shake my hand || 跟他~ shake hands with him

86 洗 [-] xǐzǎo (wash) <v.> wash: ~手 wash hands || ~衣服 wash clothes || ~脸 wash (one's) face

87 洗澡 [-] xǐzǎo (wash-bathe) <separable word> take a shower: 洗一个澡 take a shower || 洗热水澡 take a hot shower || 洗洗澡 take a shower

88 系 [繫] jì (tie) <v.> tie: ~鞋带 tie shoelaces || ~围巾 put on a scarf || ~绳子 tie a string

89 压 [壓] yā (press) <v.> press: ~在头上press onto the head || ~在玻璃板下 press underneath the glass board || ~得很低 press sth very low

90 摇 [搖] yáo (swing, shake) <v.> wag, wave: ~尾巴 wag the tail || ~ 扇子wave a fan || ~旗子wave a flag

91 拥抱 [擁-] yōngbào (embrace-hug) <v.> hug: 紧紧~ hug tightly || ~在一起 hug together

92 扎 [紮] zhā (tie, bind) <v.> tie, put up: ~领带 tie a tie || ~辫子 put up sb's hair || ~蝴蝶结 tie a bowtie

93 摘 [-] zhāi (pick, take off) <v.> pick: ~苹果pick apples || ~花pick flowers || ~下来 pick it down

94 招手 [-] zhāoshǒu (wave-hand) <v.> wave hand: 向他~ wave hand at him || 连连~ wave hand continously || ~告别wave hands to bid goodbye

95 折 [-] zhé (fold, break) <v.> fold, break: ~飞机 fold a plane || ~树枝 break a branch || ~断 break, snap sth off

96 指 [-] zhǐ (point) <v.> point at: ~着鼻子 point at the nose || ~着窗外 point at the window

97 抓 [-] zhuā (scratch, grasp, catch) <v.> catch: ~老鼠 catch mice || ~一把糖 take a handful of sweets || ~不起来 cannot manage sth.

98 抓住 [-] zhuāzhù (hold-tight) <v.> grab, capture: ~窗户 hold on to the window || ~小偷 arrest a thief || ~机会seize the opportunity

99 捉 [-] zhuō (grasp, catch) <v.> catch: ~鱼 catch fish || ~蝴蝶catch butterflies || ~虫子catch bugs

Tips:

1 Radicals meaning 'hand(s)': There are many hundred Chinese characters related with 'hand(s),' therefore, radicals meaning 'hand(s)' are probably entry-level ones for learners of Chinese to explore the etymology of Chinese characters.

2 Radical 扌: 扌 is commonly called 'tíshǒu (r)' and means 'hand.' 扌 is a strong indicator of 'hand,' for example, 打, 扫, 把, 握, 提, 携 (xié, carry in hand) etc.

3 Radical 手: 手 means 'hand' or 'fist.' Characters with this radical include 拿, 掌 (zhǎng, palm,) 摩 (mó, rub) and 擎 (qíng, lift up) etc.
4 Radical 又: 又 means 'hand.' Characters with this radical include 取 (cut off the left ear, take,) 叔 (shū, pick up) and 奴 (nú, servant, slave). The following characters got their meanings from 又 (hand,) however, analysis of their original forms is necessary in order to comprehend their meanings. We will list some characters but analyze only a few. Characters include 左 (left, assist,) 右 (right, help,) 父, 及, 反 (turn over,) 友, 有, 史 (histographer, history,) 支 (branchless bamboo, branch,) 寸 (a person's pulse on the wrist, inch,) 皮 (peel, skin) and 聿 (yù, brush) etc. 父 (fù) depicts 'a hand (又) holding a stick (丨),' meaning 'father' since in Chinese culture 'father' is a symbol of 'strictness' who instructs his children with a stick. 及 (jí) depicts 'a hand (又) catching a man (人) from behind,' therefore means 'catch, catch up with.' 友 (yǒu) depicts 'one hand (又) and another hand (又),' therefore means 'hand-in-hand, friend.' 有 depicts 'a hand (又) holding a piece of meat (月/肉),' therefore means 'rich' since in antiquity, if you had meat to eat, you were absolutely rich.
5 Radical 爪 (zhǎo, zhuǎ): 爪 depicts nails or the claw of an animal or a bird, therefore means 'to claw, hand.' For example, 采, 印 and 为 (爲) etc. 采 (cǎi) indicates 'a hand (爪) picking a tree's fruits (木),' therefore means 'to pick.' 印 (yìn) indicates 'a hand (the left part of 印) makes a man kneel down (the right part of 印),' therefore means 'official seal' since an official has the power to subdue a person. 为 (爲, wéi) depicts 'a female monkey' with the upper (爪) part being a claw, therefore means 'to do, to make, achievement.'
6 Radical 廾 (gǒng): 廾 depicts 'two hands.' Characters with this radical include 共 (same, together,) 弄, 异 (yì, strange) and 兵 etc. 弄 (nòng) is comprised of two parts. The upper part is 玉 (jade) and the lower part 廾 (two hands,) therefore 弄 means 'to play around with.' 兵 is comprised of two parts too. The upper part is 斤 (axe) and the lower part 廾 (two hands,) therefore 兵 means 'weapon, soldier.'
7 受 and 争: 受 (shòu) depicts 'a boat (舟) between one hand of a person (爪) and one hand of another person (又),' therefore means 'to receive.' 争 (zhēng) depicts 'a hand of a person (爪) and a hand of another person (又), grabbing something (like a stick),' therefore means 'to contend, to compete.'
8 与 (與, yǔ) and 兴 (興, xīng): Both characters have the same radical '舁' (yú) which depicts 'four (helping) hands.' 与 (與) means 'to offer (help,) and, with'. 兴 (興) means 'to rise, to thrive.'

Exercises:

Part I: Read the following sentences and fill in each blank with the appropriate word or phrase from the options given.

1 埋、泼、泡、拿、铺

a) 他的狗老死了, 他把狗_______在了树下.
b) 小王每个月_________三千块钱的工资.

c) 小王家里最近________了新地毯.
d) 小王想申请哈佛法学院, 他女朋友给他________冷水, 说他肯定不会被录取 (lùqǔ, admit).
e) 小王对喝茶很讲究, 一定得用矿泉水________茶.

2 扫、取、仍、敲、切

a) 他正在家看电视, 突然听见有人________门. 打开门一看原来是朋友小张, 小张拿着一个蛋糕, 进门就说: 今天是我生日, 来我们一起________蛋糕, 吃蛋糕.
b) 住在美国东北部, 冬天最冷人头疼的事情就是________雪.
c) 由于快递行业的发展, 目前在中国几乎很少有人到邮局________包裹 (bāoguǒ).
d) 一些游客非常不文明, 在风景区乱________垃圾, 污染环境.

3 贴、锁、刷、摔、抬

a) 牙医一般会建议孩子每天________两次牙.
b) 这个孩子不小心把妈妈的手机掉在地上________坏了.
c) 以前过年的时候中国人家里都要________年画.
d) 一般的高档宾馆房间里都会有一个保险箱, 客人可以把自己的贵重物品________在里面.
e) 这张床太重了, 需要三四个人才能________上楼去.

4 抓到、握手、摘、挖

a) 中国人见面的时候喜欢________问好.
b) 秋天的时候, 很多游客喜欢到苹果园________苹果.
c) 这个地区的村民常年到山上________草药, 然后卖到城里的中药店.
d) 邓小平对于中国经济发展道路有一句名言: 不管黑猫白猫, ________老鼠的就是好猫.

Theme 98: Actions with feet, legs, actions (other) 腿部和脚部动作, 其他动作

1 走 [-] zǒu (run, walk) <v.> walk: ~过去 walk over || ~小路 walk the narrow path || 向北~ walk northward
2 走路 [-] zǒulù (walk-road) <v.> walk: ~快 walk fast || ~去 go on foot || 低头~ walk with one's head down
3 走过 [-過] zǒuguò (walk-pass) <v.> walk pass: ~广场 walk pass the piazza || ~马路 walk past the street || ~木桥 walk past the wooden bridge
4 走进 [-進] zǒujìn (walk-into) <v.> walk in: ~商店 walk in the store || ~教室 walk in the classroom
5 走开 [-開] zǒukāi (walk-away) <v.> walk away: 转身~ turn around and walk away || 匆匆/急急~ walk away in a hurry || 赶紧~ walk hurriedly
6 步行 [-] bùxíng (step-travel) <v.> travel on foot: ~回家 go home on foot || ~八英里路 travel eight miles on foot || ~三天 travel on foot for three days
7 散步 [-] sànbù (stroll-step) <separable word> take a walk: 散散步take a walk || 散半小时步 take half an hour stroll || 到公园~ go for a walk in the park
8 跑 [-] pǎo (run) <v.> run, jog: 快~ run fast || ~出门 run outside || ~下楼 run downstairs

9 跑步 [-] pǎobù (run-step) <separable word> run, jog: 跑几步 jog for a ways || 练习~ practice running || ~运动 run for exercise

10 奔跑 [-] bēnpǎo (run quickly-run) <v.> run: 到处~ run about || 拼命~ run as fast as one can || 向前~ run ahead

11 行动 [-動] xíngdòng (travel-move) <v.> take actions: ~不便 be crippled || 盲目~ act recklessly || 外出~ be out on a task

12 跳 [-] tiào (jump, leap) <v.> jump, bounce: ~ 起来 jump one's feet || ~过去 jump over || ~得很高 jump high

13 蹦 [-] bèng (bounce, hop) <v.> jump, bounce: ~起来 jump one's feet || 乱~乱跳 jump energetically || 一~一跳 jump upward then forward || 又~又跳 jump upward and upward

14 踢 [-] tī (kick) <v.> kick: ~球 kick a ball || ~腿 kick a leg || ~一脚 take a kick

15 踏 [-] tà (step on, tread) <v.> step: ~地板 step on the floor || ~着台阶 step on the stairs || ~着白雪step on the snow

16 登 [-] dēng (get on a cart, ascend) <v.> ascend, mount: ~山 hike || ~上顶峰 reach the summit || ~上讲台mount the platform

17 踹 [-] chuài (stamp) <v.> kick, stomp: ~一脚 take a kick || ~门 kick the door

18 踩 [-] cǎi (step on, trample) <v.> step: ~刹 (shā) 车 step on the brake || ~油门 step on the gas || ~草坪 step on the grass

19 踮 [-] diǎn (tiptoe) <v.> tiptoe: ~着脚 tiptoe

20 跨 [-] kuà (stride) <v.> stride: ~一大步 stride || ~左腿 stride left foot first || ~上马 mount a horse

21 坐 [-] zuò (sit) <v.> sit: ~在办公室 sit in the office || ~在一起 sit together || ~在地上 sit on the ground

22 骑 [-] qí (ride) <v.> ride: ~自行车 ride a bike || ~摩托 (mótuō) 车 ride a motorcycle || ~马 ride a horse

23 蹲 [-] dūn (crouch, squat) <v.> crouch: ~在地上 crouch on the ground || ~着吃 eat while crouching || ~一小时crouch for an hour

24 立 [-] lì (stand, erect) <v.> erect, stand: ~起来 stand it up || ~在一旁 erect on the side || ~在门口 be in a upright position next the door

25 移 [-] yí (move) <v.> move: ~树 move the tree || 向前~ move forward

26 移动 [-動] yídòng (move-move) <v.> move: ~脚步 move one's feet || ~位置 (wèizhi) move a location || ~家具 move the furniture

27 转动 [轉動] zhuàndòng (spin-move) <v.> spin: ~胳膊 (gēbo) spin one's arms || ~身体 spin one's body || ~机器 spin a machine

28 站 [-] zhàn (stand) <v.> stand: ~在山上 stand on the mountain || ~在一边 stand on the side || ~在一起 stand together

29 扭 [-] niǔ (wring, swing, sprain, twist) <v.> twist: ~秧歌 (yāngge) dance || ~腰 twist one's waist || ~屁股 swing one's hips

30 背 [-] bēi (carry on one's back) <v.> carry on one's back: ~东西 carry sth on one's back || ~着包 put on a backpack || 把孩子 ~回去. Put a kid on your back and take him/her back.

31 翻 [-] fān (flip) <v.> flip: ~跟头 do a flip || ~身 flip one's body

32 倒 [-] dǎo (fall) <v.> fall: ~在地上 fall on the ground || 往床上一 ~ fall on the bed || ~了下去 fall down
33 碰 [-] pèng (collide, bump, touch) <v.> touch, bump: 头~在门上 bump one's head against the door || 别~我东西don't touch my stuff
34 闭 [閉] bì (shut, close) <v.> shut: ~着眼睛 shut one's eyes || ~着嘴 mouth shut || ~灯turn off the light
35 封闭 [-閉] fēngbì (seal-shut) <v./ adj.> seal off, close: ~火区 lockdown the fire zone || 自我~ shut down oneself || ~的地方 a closed area
36 合 [-] hé (close) <v.> close: ~上眼睛 close one's eyes || ~不上嘴 be unable close one's mouth || ~上笔记本 close the notebook
37 刻 [-] kè (engrave, carve) <v.> carve: ~名字 carve a name || ~字carve a character || ~在树上 carve on a tree

Tips:

1 Radical 走: 走 originally means 'to run' which evolved into 'to walk,' the current main meaning of 走. The upper part '土' here depicts 'a man swinging his arms and running,' and the lower part depicts a foot. Characters with this radical include 赶 (gǎn, catch up with,) 超 (chāo, surpass,) 趋 (qū, run) and 赴 (fù, go to).
2 Radical 辶: 辶 is commonly called '走之儿' (zǒuzhīr) and means 'walk, run.' Characters with this radical include 进 (move forward, enter,) 近 (close,) 迈 (mài, stride) and 逐 (zhú, chase).
3 Radical 彳 (chì): 彳 means 'to walk slowly.' Characters with this radical include 行 (xíng, to travel,) 往 (to go,) 待 (to wait) and 微 (wēi, originally 'to walk quietly').
4 Radical 足 (zú): 足 means 'foot.' There are many characters with this radical, for example, 跑 (to run,) 跳 (to jump,) 路 (road) and many others, which are annotated above.
5 步 (bù): It depicts two 'feet,' one in front and the other behind, therefore, meaning 'step.'
6 奔 (bēn): The upper part 大 depicts 'a man swinging both hands/arms' and the lower part 卉 here depicts 'three feet' which in combination means 'to run quickly.'

Exercises:

Part I: Read the following words and then answer the questions.

跑、跳、蹦、踢、踏、踩、跺、合、蹲、骑、闭、碰、站、刻

1 请写出跟"脚的动作"有关系的字

---

2 哪几个字有"关上"的意思

---

3 "父母的话牢牢刻在我心里"的意思是

a) 父母在我心里写字
b) 父母的话我写了很多遍
c) 我永远记住了父母的话

4 "今天下午我恰巧碰到了我的小学老师, 他竟然还记得我," 这句话是意思是

a) 今天下午我把小学老师撞到了
b) 今天下午我碰巧遇见了我小学老师
c) 今天下午我正好遇见了我小学老师

Part II: Read the following sentences and fill in each blank with the appropriate word or phrase from the options given.

行动、散步、步行、封闭、移动、转动

1 从1949年到1979年中国一直在_______的环境 (huánjìng, environment) 中发展经济.
2 "中国_______"是中国最大的手机通讯 (tōngxùn, communication) 公司.
3 中国正在采取_______, 减少空气污染问题.
4 现在越来越多的老年人喜欢在饭后到公园_______, 因为他们觉得走路有助于消化.
5 从地铁站_______到我家需要20分钟.
6 目前人类还不知道是什么让地球自己_______.

Theme 99: Eye movements 眼动 (yǎn dòng)

1 看 [-] kàn (look in the distance, look at, see) <v.> look, watch, see: ~电影 watch the movie || ~瀑布 (pùbù) see the waterfall
2 观看 [觀-] guānkàn (view-look) <v.> view, watch: ~演出 watch the show, performance, concert || ~风景 enjoy the view || 仔细地~ watch/view vigilantly
3 收看 [-] shōukàn (receive-watch) <v.> watch: ~电视 watch T.V. || 禁止 (jìnzhǐ) ~ be banned from watching || ~节目 watch a show
4 见 [見] jiàn (see, meet) <v.> see, meet: 十分钟后~ meet in 10 minutes || ~一次 meet for one time || ~领导 (lǐngdǎo) meet the leaders, heads, principal men
5 瞧 [-] qiáo (steal a glance, look) <v.> look, peep, glance: ~着她 look at her || ~一眼 take swift look, glance || 往里 ~ look inside
6 盯 [-] dīng (stare) <v.> stare, inspect intently: ~了一眼 stare for a quick flash || ~着电脑 stare at the computer
7 顾 [顧] gù (turn around and look at, take care of, consider) <v.> consider, take care of: 照~ take care of || 只~自己 think only of oneself || 不屑一~ not even consider smth. or someone worthy of consideration
8 注视 [-視] zhùshì (concentrate-look at) <v.> watch attentively, stare at: 我生气地~ 他. I fixed him with an angry stare. || 老板用怀疑的目光 ~着这名员工. The boss stared at this employee with unbelieving eyes.
9 凝视 [-視] níngshì (fix one's eyes on-look) <v.> gaze, stare fixedly: ~ 窗外gazing out of the window || 静静地~ gaze silently
10 环视 [環視] huánshì (around-look) <v.> circumspect: ~左右 look from left right || ~四周 look at the surroundings || ~一圈 take a look around

11 望 [-] wàng (gaze in the distance) <v.> look at, gaze in the distance: 往下 ~ look down upon

12 眺望 [-] tiàowàng (gaze at afar-look) <v.> look in the distance from a high vantage: ~远方 lookout over the distance || 举目~ lookout by raise one's eyes || ~大海 look over the oceans

13 仰望 [-] yǎngwàng (up-look) <v.> look up: ~天空 look up the sky

14 张望 [張-] zhāngwàng (look-look) <v.> peep, look around, in the distance: 向里~ peep inside || 四处~ look around everywhere

15 东张西望 [東張--] dōngzhāngxīwàng (east-look-west-look) <idiom> look here and there: 警察一般会留心那些~的陌生人. Policemen usually keep an eye open for strangers who are looking back and forth all the time.

16 眨眼 [-] zhǎyǎn (wink-eye) <v.> wink: 眨了一下眼 wink a little

17 瞪 [-] dèng (stare, glare) <v.> glare, glower: ~他一眼 glare at him

18 眯 [-] mī (narrow one's eyes) <v.> close one's eyes halfway: ~着眼 close one's eyes halfway

19 皱眉 [皺-] zhòuméi (knit one's eyebrows) <v./n.> frown: ~常常表示不高兴. A frown often denotes displeasure.

20 眉开眼笑 [-開--] méikāiyǎnxiào (eye-unfrowned-eye-smile) <idiom> exhibit a happy look: 看到女朋友, 小王马上~. Little Wang beamed with pleasure at seeing his girlfriend.

21 瞎 [-] xiā (blind) <adj.> blind: ~眼 blind, oblivious

Tips:

1 Radical 目: 目 (mù) depicts 'eye' and is a radical. Believe it or not, each of the 21 entries in this unit has at least one 目. Leaving aside the easy ones, let's analyze the hard ones. #4 '见': The traditional form is 見 on which you can find a big eye (目) and/on a man (儿/人.) #7 '顾': The traditional form is 顧 on which you can once again find an eye (目) in the right part 頁 (head.) #11 '望': One traditional form of 望 is 朢 where the upper-left part is 臣 (chén, slave, submit oneself the rule of), which is believed by scholars be a vertical eye since the person dares not look at others boldly, only daring to peek (with vertical eyes 臣) at others. This being said, 望 (朢) indicates a man 'standing on a high place' (壬) and looking (臣) at the moon (月.)

2 瞧 (qiáo): 瞧 means 看 (to look at) but is very colloquial.

Exercises:

Part I: Use the given bound form as a guide help you think of other words with the same character. Feel free use your dictionary when needed. Then write down the English definition of each of the words you've written.

看 (watch, see): 观看 watch

____

____

____

视 *(look ar)*: 注视 *look attentively at, gaze at*

____

____

____

望 *(look at, gaze inthe distance)*: 看望 *pay a visit to*

____

____

____

Part II: Read the following sentences and fill in each blank with the appropriate word or phrase from the options given.

1 眨、瞪、盯

a) 小王上地铁的时候不小心踩了别人一脚, 那个人狠狠地________了小王一眼.
b) 小孩的想象力很有意思, 他们觉得天上的星星可以_________眼睛, 所以就一闪一闪的.
c) 在美国即使你看到一个穿着很奇怪的人, 也不要________着他看, 因为这非常不礼貌.

2 环视、仰望、眺望

a) 站在长城上________四周, ______远方, 长城的雄伟壮丽 (xióngwěi zhuànglì, majestic) 尽在你眼底.
b) 夜晚当你_______星空, 你会感觉到星星离我们是那样遥远 (yáoyuǎn, faraway).

3 收看、回顾、观看

a) 一般来说, 研究性论文的开始部分都是在________某个问题的研究历史.
b) 在中国有些偏远农村还不能_________电视.
c) 今天晚上我跟父母要去_________一场话剧演出.

4 眉开眼笑、东张西望

a) 这个小孩不太喜欢学习, 上课的时候经常_________, 注意力不集中.
b) 听到自己被升职的好消息, 小张马上_________.

Theme 100: Actions using mouth 嘴动 (zuǐ dòng)

1 张嘴 [張-] zhāngzuǐ (open-mouth) <v.> open the mouth: ~大笑 laugh loudly with a gaping mouth
2 闭嘴 [閉-] bìzuǐ (shut-mouth) <v.> close one's mouth, shut up: 学生们很吵, 老师让他们~. The teacher told students to shut up since they were too noisy. || 她生气地对先生喊: ~! She shouted to her husband angrily, 'shut up!'

3 微笑 [-] wēixiào (gentle-smile) <v.> smile: 面露~ smiling face || 她脸上带着幸福的~. A happy smile appeared on her face.

4 笑 [-] xiào (smile, laugh) <v.> laugh: 微微一~ smile faintly || 哈哈大 ~ laugh heartily || 傻~ laugh foolishly

5 哭 [-] kū (cry) <v.> cry: ~鼻子 crying || 伤心地~ sadly cried

6 吃 [-] chī (eat) <v.> eat: ~饭 eat food || ~饱了 full (done eating) || ~不下 can't eat

7 喝 [-] hē (drink) <v.> drink: ~水 drink water || ~茶 drink tea || ~酒 drink alcohol

8 吸 [-] xī (inhale) <v.> inhale: ~毒 take drugs || ~烟 smoke || ~气 inhale air

9 抽 [-] chōu (take out, draw out, suck) <v.> draw out: ~烟 smoke || ~鼻子 sniffle

10 咬 [-] yǎo (bite) <v.> bite: ~人 bite someone || ~一口 take a bite || 被蚊子~了 bitten by a mosquito

11 含 [-] hán (keep in the mouth) <v.> hold in: ~着眼泪 hold in tears || 嘴里~着东西 keep something in your mouth

12 吞 [-] tūn (swallow) <v.> swallow: ~口水 swallow spit || ~一粒药 take medicine

13 吐 [-] tǔ (spit) <v.> spit: ~气 spew hot air || ~舌头 stick out your tongue || ~唾沫 (tuòmo) spit out saliva

14 喷 [噴] pēn (spurt, gush, puff) <v.> spout, spray: ~水spout water || 给蔬菜~农药spray vegetables with insecticide

15 吹 [-] chuī (blow) <v.> blow: ~一口气 heave a sigh || ~气球 blow up a balloon

16 说 [說] shuō (speak) <v.> speak: ~话 say something || 坦白地~ speak frankly

17 谈 [談] tán (talk) <v.> discuss: ~话 discuss something || ~心 heart to heart chat

18 讲 [講] jiǎng (lecture, speak, present) <v.> speak, present: ~话 make a speech || ~道理 speak reason || ~故事 tell a story

19 喊 [-] hǎn (shout, call out, yell) <v.> yell: ~ 口号 shout slogans || ~医生 call for a doctor || 大声~ yell loudly

20 叫 [-] jiào (shout) <v.> shout: 高声~ shout loudly || ~了一声 shouted something

21 唱 [-] chàng (sing) <v.> sing: ~一首歌 sing a song

22 哼 [-] hēng (hum) <v.> hum: ~着歌 humming a tune

23 招呼 [-] zhāohū (wave-call) <v.> call out: ~服务员 call out a waiter || 打~ greeting || ~几声 say a few greetings

24 吹口哨 [-] chuīkǒushào (blow-whistle) <v.> whistle: 朝她~ whistle at her

25 演讲 [-講] yǎnjiǎng (show-lecture) <v.> make a speech: 用英语~ make a speech in English

26 讨论 [討論] tǎolùn (probe-discuss) <v.> discuss: ~问题 discuss a question || 热烈地~ hotly discuss

27 争辩 [爭辯] zhēngbiàn (contend-debate) <v.> dispute, debate: 无可~ indisputable || 无休止的~ an endless debate

28 唠叨 [嘮-] láodāo (garrulous) <v.> chatter, be garrulous: 不停地~ chatter incessantly || 爱~ love chatter

29 念叨 [-] niàndāo (miss-talk) <v.> reminisce about: 反复~ reminisce over and over again

30 念念不忘 [-] niànniànbùwàng (moment-*reduplication*-not-forget) <idiom> keep in mind constantly: ~这件事 can't forget this thing

31 娓娓道来 [---來] wěiwěidàolái (tirelessly-speak out) <idiom> say in a kindly and informal fashion: 他喜欢对别人听他~, 但却不擅长倾听. While he loves hearing himself talk, he is often not very good at listening.

32 据说 [據説] jùshuō (according to-said) <v.> allegedly, it is said: ~在银行工作的人工资很高. It is said that people who work in the bank will have a high salary.

Tips:

1 演讲 (yǎnjiǎng, public speaking), 辩论 (biànlùn, debate), 讲话 (to address, speech), 汇报 (huìbào, to report to): From a very early age, people in Europe and America practiced public speaking (演讲) and debate (辩论), which were rarely seen in China until the most recent decade. In a highly stratified society like China, people of higher classes would 讲话 (to address) and people of lower classes would 汇报 (to report to) their seniors.

2 吸烟 vs. 抽烟: Both mean 'smoke,' but 吸烟 is more formal. For example, 禁止吸烟 (no smoking) and 吸烟有害健康 (smoking is harmful to health.)

Exercises:

Part I: Answer the following questions in Chinese.

1 请写出五个带"讠"旁的字

____

2 请写出十个带"口"旁的字

____

Part II: Read the following sentences and fill in each blank with the appropriate word or phrase from the options given.

1 吹口、哨招呼

a) 他没跟我打________就把我自行车骑走了, 简直跟偷车一样.
b) 他的狗训练得很好, 只要他一_______, 狗马上就跑过来.

2 演讲、争辩、辩论

a) 一般来说美国总统候选人都有很善于_______和________.
b) 小张跟同事发生冲突时, 一般不会跟同事_________对错, 只是把情况向上级 (shàngjí, superior) 领导说明.

3 念叨、娓娓道来、唠叨

a) 有的老人比较喜欢_______, 反反复复说一件事情.
b) 我上大学的时候爷爷奶奶非常想念我, 常常________我.
c) 这个新闻节目为观众带来当事人 (dāngshìrén, party to an affair) _________的亲身经历, 让观众感受到了事件的真实性.

4 据说、念念不忘

______冰岛是世界上最冷的国家. 冰岛的美丽景色我直到现在还______.

Theme 101: Actions with head (others) 头部动作 (别的) (biéde tóubù dòngzuò)

1 听 [聽] tīng (listen, hear) <v.> listen: ~音乐 listen to music || ~广播 listen a broadcast || ~录音 listen to a recording
2 听说 [聽説] tīngshuō (hear-said) <v.> hear about: ~这件事 hear about this thing || ~他的故事 hear his story || ~情况不好 hear that the situation is not good
3 听取 [聽-] tīngqǔ (listen-get) <v.> listen: ~意见 listen to an opinion || ~情况 heed the situation || ~报告 listen to a report
4 收听 [-聽] shōutīng (receive-listen) <v.> listen: ~音乐 listen to music || ~广播 listen to the radio || ~节目 listen to a program
5 偷听 [-聽] tōutīng (secretly-listen) <v.> eavesdrop: ~谈话 eavesdrop on a conversation

6 闻 [聞] wén (hear, smell) <v.> smell: ~气味 smell an odor || ~到香气 smell an aroma || 用鼻子~ use your nose to smell
7 嗅 [-] xiù (smell, sniff) <v.> sniff: ~气味 sniff an odor || 用鼻子~ sniff with one's nose
8 呼吸 [-] hūxī (breathe out-breathe in) <v.> breathe: 人工~ artificial respiration || ~困难 breathe with difficulty || 大口~. Breathe with your mouth wide open.
9 喘 [-] chuǎn (pant) <v.> breathe with difficulty: ~不过气来 gasp for breath, be out of breath || 气~ (病) asthma
10 中毒 [-] zhòngdú (got-poison) <separable word> poisoned: 中剧毒 highly toxic || 慢性~ slow poisoning

11 喝彩 [-] hècǎi (shout loudly-'Bravo!') <separable word> cheer: 连声~ repeatedly cheer || 音乐大厅里响起 ~声. Cheering burst out in the music hall.
12 欢呼 [歡-] huānhū (cheerful-cry out) <v.> hail, cheer: 阵阵~ bursts of cheers || ~胜利hail the victory
13 惊叫 [驚-] jīngjiào (frightened-shout) <v.> cry out in fear: 大声~ loudly scream || 失声 ~ an exclamation bursts out || ~一声 screamed
14 尖叫 [-] jiānjiào (sharp-shout) <v.> shriek: 大声~ loudly shriek

15 面对 [-對] miànduì (face-face) <v.> face, confront: ~现实 face reality || ~死亡 face death || ~一个复杂的问题 be faced with a complicated problem
16 点头 [點頭] diǎntóu (nod-head) <v-o> nod: 点了点头 nod your head || 连连~ nod repeatedly || ~同意 nod in agreement
17 低头 [-頭] dītóu (bow-head) <separable word> bow your head: 低一下头 bow your head a bit || ~写字 bow down and write
18 抬头 [-頭] táitóu (raise-head) <separable word> raise your head: 抬一下头 raise your head a bit || 抬起头 look up || 把头抬起来 begin raise one's head
19 摇头 [搖頭] yáotóu (shake-head) <separable word> shake your head: 摇一下头 shake your head a bit || 摇摇头 shook his/her head || 连连~ repeatedly shake one's head
20 回头 [-頭] huítóu (turn around-head) <separable word> turn one's head: ~看 turn one's head and look || 回一下头 turn one's head a bit || 回两次头 turn one's head twice

21 扭头 [-頭] niǔtóu (turn-head) <v.> turn one's head: ~看 turn one's head to look || 她没说什么, ~就走. She swung around and walked off without a word.
22 探头 [-頭] tàntóu (stretch-head) <v.> crane one's neck: ~张望 crane one's neck to look around || ~探脑stick one's head out and look around
23 转头 [轉頭] zhuǎntóu (turn-head) <v.> turn one's head,: ~看 turn one's head and look || ~说 turn around and speak

Tips:

1 听 (聽, tīng): The traditional character has three components, 耳, 德 and 壬. 壬 (tìng) is the sound part. 耳 means 'ear' and 德 (dé) 'to get,' in combination they mean 'ears got/received something,' i.e., 'to listen' or 'to hear.' The simplified form 听 was borrowed as you can see it was originally related to the 'appearance of a smile' since it was related to 'mouth' (口) not 'ear' (耳.)
2 闻 (聞, wén): The original meaning of 闻 is 'to hear' since it is related to 耳 (ear.) In this unit the meaning of 闻 is 'to smell,' however, the original meaning of 'to hear' is still predominantly kept in words such as 新闻 (news,) 不闻不问 (do not listen or ask, to be indifferent) and 举世闻名 (world-renowned).
3 扭头 vs. 转头 vs. 回头: All mean 'to turn one's head' and they function the same in this sense. If you have to differentiate between them, they might focus on the three different phases of turning, namely the beginning, the middle and the end, albeit without consensus from native speakers of Chinese. However, their differences lie in the extended meanings. 回头 has two extended meanings. One is 'to repent,' for example, 你这样下去可不行, 你得回头了 (you cannot continue like this anymore, it is time to repent.) The other is 'later,' for example, 再见, 回头聊 (bye and see you later.) 转头 has one major extended meaning 'after a short time,' for example, 这么重要的事他转头就忘了 (he forgot such an important thing in no time.)
4 呼, 叫, 喊: All mean 'to cry, to shout' and their combinations, 呼叫, 呼喊, 叫喊 have almost the same meaning.

Exercises:

Part I: Read the following words and then answer the questions.

喝彩、欢呼、惊叫、尖叫、低头、抬头、回头、扭头、探头、转头、 喘气、呼吸、偷听、点头、听说

1 上面哪些词表示"嘴"的动作?

___

2 上面哪些词表示"头"的动作?

___

3 上面哪些词表示"耳朵"的动作?

___

Part II: Read the following sentences and fill in each blank with the appropriate word or phrase from the options given.

听说、偷听、欢呼、听取、面对、中毒

1 这家公司最近召开全体股东大会, _______股东对公司管理的意见.
2 _________中国华为公司的员工餐厅非常好, 员工可以在那里吃到世界各地的美食.
3 为了防止食物_______, 这家餐厅对每种食品都进行了严格检查.
4 _______私人谈话不仅不礼貌, 其实也是一种犯罪.
5 这家公司的总经理宣布给所有员工涨20%的工资, 听到这个消息以后大家一片______.
6 经济危机到来的时候, 每家公司都要________利润 (lìrùn, profit) 急剧下降以及裁减 (cáijiǎn, cut down) 员工的问题.

Theme 102: To be born, to grow, to age 出生, 长大, 衰老 (chūshēng, zhǎngdà, shuāilǎo)

1 出生 [-] chūshēng (out-born) <v.> be born: ~在中国 be born in China || ~不久 be born not long ago || 九月~ be born in September
2 活 [-] huó (live, alive) <v.> live: ~下去 continue living || ~着 be alive || ~了一百岁 live to be 100 years old
3 开 [開] kāi (open) <v.> bloom: 花~了 the flowers are blooming || 这种花秋天~. This plant will flower in the fall.
4 开放 [開-] kāifàng (open-relieve) <v.> come in bloom: ~的桃花 blossoming peach flowers || 百花~ the flowers are in bloom || 四季~ in bloom all four seasons
5 生 [-] shēng (bear, give birth to) <v.> give birth to, have: ~孩子 give birth to a child || ~儿子 have a son || ~病 have an illness
6 生存 [-] shēngcún (live-exist) <v./n.> survive, living: 求~ trying survive || ~下去 continue living || ~能力 the ability of survival || ~权the rights of survival
7 诞生 [誕-] dànshēng (born-give birth to) <v.> be born: ~在中国 be born in China || ~于二十一世纪 be born in the 21st century
8 生长 [-長] shēngzhǎng (born-grow) <v.> grow: ~快/慢 grow quickly/slowly || 自然~ grow naturally || ~在水里 grow in water
9 开花 [開-] kāihuā (bloom-flower) <separable word> bloom: 开一朵花 a flower blooms || 冬天~ bloom in winter || 铁树~ sago palm (iron tree) bursting into blossom (It's a metaphor for very rare phenomena)
10 结果 [結-] jiéguǒ (bear-fruit) <v.> bear fruit: 中国北方的大多数果树春天开花, 夏天~. Most of the fruit trees in northern China blossom in the spring and bear fruit in summer.
11 长 [長] zhǎng (grow) <v.> grow: ~高 grow tall || ~身体 (for one's body) to grow || ~得好 grow well
12 长大 [長-] zhǎngdà (grow-big/up) <v.> grow up: ~一点 grow up a little || 慢慢/快快~ slowly/quickly grow up || 一起~ grow up together
13 成长 [-長] chéngzhǎng (mature-grow) <v.> grow up, grow to maturity: 健康~ grow healthy || 逐渐~ gradually grow || ~很快/慢 grow quickly/slowly
14 成熟 [-] chéngshú (mature-ripe) <adj.> ripe, mature: 发育~ reach maturity || 时机~ the time is ripe || 不~的意见immature opinion

15 生育 [-] shēngyù (bear-raise) <v.> bear: ~子女 bear children || ~三个孩子 bear three children

16 优生 [優-] yōushēng (better-bear-better-rise) <v.>give birth to healthy babies: ~优育 bear and rear better children || 为了提高人口质量, 中国政府提倡 ~. The Chinese government promotes Eugenics in its belief that the practice will improve the genetic quality of its population.

17 传宗接代 [傳---] chuánzōngjiēdài (carry on-ancestral line-continue-generation) <idiom> carry on the family line: 中国的传统观念认为儿子比女儿重要, 因为儿子可以~. China's traditional view is that sons are more important than daughters because sons can carry on the family line.

18 生儿育女 [-兒--] shēng'éryùnǚ (bear-son-raise-daughter) <idiom> bear and raise children: 中国的传统观念认为女人的作用是~. The traditional Chinese concept of a woman's role is to bear and raise children.

19 产 [產] chǎn (give birth to) <v.> give birth to, produce: ~了一只小羊 give birth to a little lamb || ~油produce oil

20 流产 [-產] liúchǎn (outflow-birth/fetus) <v.> miscarry: ~多次 miscarry many times || 他们的计划~了. Their project was mishandled.

21 堕胎 [墮-] duòtāi (abort-fetus) <v.> have an abortion: 非法~ illegal abortion || 反对 ~ anti-abortion

22 早产 [-產] zǎochǎn (early-birth) <v.> premature birth: ~的孩子 a child born prematurely

23 顺产 [順產] shùnchǎn (easy-birth) <v.> easy birth: ~一个男孩 easily give birth a boy

24 难产 [難產] nánchǎn (difficult-labor) <v.> difficult labor: 现在很少有女人死于~. Few women now die of difficult child labor now.

25 下 [-] xià (below, down, lay) <v.> lay (eggs), (of animals) give birth to: ~蛋 lay an egg || ~小猫 give birth to a kitten

26 养 [養] yǎng (raise) <v.> raise: ~孩子 raise a child || ~一条狗 raise a dog || ~动物 raise a pet

27 饲养 [飼養] sìyǎng (feed-raise) <v.> raise: 科学~ scientifically raise || ~家禽 raise poultry || 人工~ artificially raise

28 繁殖 [-] fánzhí (propagate-multiply) <v.> breed, reproduce: 人口~ population reproduction || 近亲~ inbreeding || ~后代 produce offspring

29 败 [敗] bài (ruin, spoil, damage) <v.> wither, spoil: 花~了 the flowers withered || 枯枝 ~叶dead twigs and withered leaves

30 凋零 [-] diāolíng (wither-fallen) <v.> wilt: 百花~ the flowers wilted

31 干枯 [乾-] gānkū (dry-wither) <v.> dry up, wither, shrivel: 小河 ~了 The stream has dried up. || ~的皮肤 wrinkled/shriveled skin

32 瘦 [-] shòu (thin, skinny) <v.> thin: ~下去 slim down || 越来越 ~ get more and more thin

33 消瘦 [-] xiāoshòu (decrease-thin) <v.> become thin: 身体~ body thins down

34 出汗 [-] chūhàn (shed-sweat) <separable word> sweat: 全身~ sweat from head to toe || 出一身汗 sweat all over

35 消化 [-] xiāohuà (consume-digest) <v.> digest: ~食物 digest food || ~不良 indigestion || 容易~ easily digestible

36 打嗝 [-] dǎgé (*prefix*-belch) <separable word> burp: 打了一个嗝 burped once

37 打喷嚏 [-噴-] dǎpēntì (*prefix*-sneeze) <separable word> sneeze: 打了一个喷嚏 sneezed once
38 打哈欠 [-] dǎhāqiàn (*prefix*-yawn) <separable word> yawn: 打了一个哈欠 yawned once
39 打呼噜 [--嚕] dǎhūlū (*prefix*-snore) <separable word> snore: 睡觉 ~ snore in one's sleep

40 方便 [-] fāngbiàn (convenience) <v.> convenience, go the lavatory: ~ 一下 go the bathroom
41 小便 [-] xiǎobiàn (small-excrement) <v.> urinate: 不要随处~ Don't urinate everywhere.
42 大便 [-] dàbiàn (large-excrement) <v.> defecate, shit
43 放屁 [-] fàngpì (pass-gas) <separable word> fart, break wind: 放了一个屁 fart once || 公共场合不能~. Be careful not to fart in public.
44 衰老 [-] shuāilǎo (deteriorate-age) <v.> deteriorate with age: 开始~ begin age poorly || 延缓~ delay old age || 皮肤~ skin aging
45 脱发 [-髮] tuōfà (lose-hair) <v.> lose hair: 引起~ cause hair loss || 防止~ prevent hair loss || 治疗~ treat hair loss

Tips:

1 优生 (yōushēng): 优 means 'excellent' and 生 'to bear, birth.' 优生 means 'Eugenics.' It happens that the pronunciation of 'Eugenics' is very close to the Chinese pronunciation of '优' (you.)
2 Euphemisms for 'to go the lavatory': The main expressions include (1) 方便一下, e.g. 不好意思, 我 (得) 去方便一下, (2) 解手 (儿) (jiěshǒu,) e.g. 我去解个手 (儿), (3) 去洗手间. 洗手间 sounds better than 卫生间 or 厕所.
3 打喷嚏 (dǎpēntì, sneeze): Some argue that most Chinese do not know how write 嚏 and therefore, Chinese characters are not necessary for learners to grasp as long as they know pinyin. But, in this vein, how many native speakers of English can spell 'onomatopoetic' correctly? If one day most Chinese did not know how write 打, it might be the right time to discuss whether to end the life of Chinese characters.

Exercises:

Part I: Read the following words and then answer the following questions in Chinese.

出生、长大、成长、成熟、生儿育女、传宗接代、衰老、死亡、生长、开花、凋零、结果、干枯、饲养、繁殖、生存、打嗝、打喷嚏、打哈欠、打呼噜

1 请写出植物的生长过程.

____

2 请写出人的成长过程.

____

3 上面哪两个词可以来描写"花死了"?

____

4 上面哪些词可以用来描写"动物"?

___

5 上面哪个词跟"吃饱了"关系最大?

___

6 上面哪个词跟"过敏或者感冒"关系最大?

___

7 上面哪些词跟"睡觉"关系很大?

___

Part II: Read the following sentences and fill in each blank with the appropriate word or phrase from the options given.

1 出汗、方便、消化、消瘦

a) 有的中国医生认为老年人不适合吃像肉类这样不容易________的食物.
b) 小张最近________了很多, 医生说他的消化系统有问题.
c) 据说中国武汉的夏天非常热, 人们从早到晚一直在_______, 如果没有空调很难度过 (dùguò, survive) 夏天.
d) 这个城市的公共厕所非常少, 想_______的外地游客常常找不到厕所.

2 早产、难产、堕胎、流产

a) 美国一些共和党的州________是违法的, 但是在一些民主党的州是合法的.
b) 小张妈妈在怀孕8个月的时候就生了他, 所以他是个_______的孩子.
c) 一百多年前孕妇 (yùnfù, pregnant woman) 死于______比例要远远大于今天.
d) 中医认为孕妇在怀孕期间不能多运动, 否则会_______.

3 传宗接代、诞生、饲养、繁殖

a) 现代人吃的肉类, 基本上都来自人工_______的动物.
b) 病菌 (bìngjūn, bacteria) 的_______速度非常快, 所以流行病一般都传播迅速.
c) 中国父母一般希望孩子工作以后赶快结婚生子, _______.
d) 西方基督教 (Jīdūjiào, Christianity) 认为耶稣 (Yēsū, Jesus) _______在大约二千年前的以色利 (Israel).

Theme 103: To be sick, to get injured, to recover 生病, 受伤, 康复 (shēngbìng, shòushāng, kāngfù)

(See also Themes 86, 165)

1 伤 [傷] shāng (wound, injure) <n./v.> wound: 严重的~ serious injury || ~身体be harmful to one's health || ~了手hurt one's hand

2 受伤 [-傷] shòushāng (get-injured) <v.> be injured: 他在这次交通事故中~了. He was wounded in this traffic accident.
3 伤亡 [傷-] shāngwáng (injury-death) <v./n.> casualties: 意外~ accidental casualties || ~事故 casualties from an accident || ~很大 casualties are large
4 流血 [-] liúxiě (shed-blood) <v.> bleed, shed blood: ~不止cannot stop bleeding || ~过多bled too much || 她的手指~了. Her finger bled.

5 病 [-] bìng (ill, sick) <v./n.> ill, injure: ~得很重 be seriously ill || ~了一场 got sick once || 一点儿小~ a mild illness
6 生病 [-] shēngbìng (fall-ill) <v.> fall ill: 生了一场病 get a sickness || 生大病 get very sick || 没生过病 have never been sick
7 发病 [發-] fābìng (outbreak-ill) <v.> onset, outbreak (disease): ~早/急 early/acute onset || 多次~ many outbreaks of a disease || 预防~ prevent a disease outbreak
8 感冒 [-] gǎnmào (infect-emerge) <v./n.> get a cold: ~十多天 have a cold for more than ten days || 重/小~ serious/light cold || 流行性~ influenza
9 过敏 [過-] guòmǐn (excessive-sensitive) <v./adj.> allergy: 对花生~ allergic to peanuts || 皮肤~ skin allergy || 容易~ sensitive allergy

10 疼 [-] téng (ache, painful) <v.> ache: 牙~ toothache || 肚子~ stomachache || 头~ headache
11 痛 [-] tòng (painful, agonizing) <adj.> pain: 伤口~ pain from a wound || 腿~ leg pain || 腰~ back pain
12 疼痛 [-] téngtòng (painful-agonizing) <v.> pain: 感到~ feel pain || ~减轻 pain reducer || 剧烈~ severe pain
13 恶心 [噁-] ě'xīn (nausea-heart) <v.> feel nausea: 引起~ induce nausea || 感到~ feel nauseous || 轻度~ feel mildly nauseous
14 烧 [燒] shāo (burn, fever) <v.> fever: ~到三十九度 have a 39°C fever || ~得迷迷糊糊 be in a fever daze || ~退了 the fever returns
15 发烧 [發燒] fāshāo (outbreak-fever) <separable word> have a fever: 发高/低烧 have a high/low fever || 感冒~ cold and fever || 容易~ easily gets a fever
16 发炎 [發-] fāyán (outbreak-inflammation) <v./n.> become inflamed from infection or injury, inflammation: 眼睛~ eye inflammation || 伤口~了. The wound has become inflamed.

17 咳 [-] ké (cough) <v.> cough: ~了两声 cough twice || ~了一晚 cough for a night || ~个不停 cough incessantly
18 肿 [腫] zhǒng (swell, swollen) <v.> swell: 冻~了 freeze swollen || 眼睛哭~了 cry and make your eyes swell || 眼睛~ eyes swell
19 晕 [暈] yūn (halo, dizzy, pass out) <v.> faint, dizzy: 头~ dizzy || ~船/车 seasick/carsick || ~过去 pass out
20 晕车 [暈車] yūnchē (dizzy-car) <v.> carsickness: ~严重 severely carsick
21 吐 [-] tù (spit, vomit) <vomit: ~血 vomit blood || 想~ feel like vomiting
22 呕吐 [嘔-] ǒutù (vomit-vomit) <v.> throw up: ~不止keep vomiting || 令人~ make one sick
23 拉肚子 [-] lādùzǐ (empty-belly) <v.> have diarrhea
24 便秘 [-祕] biànmì (excrement-constipate) <v.> constipation

25 昏 [-] hūn (dusk, evening, dark, faint) <v.> faint: 头~ dizziness || ~倒 pass out || 打~ fainted

26 疯 [瘋] fēng (mad, insane, crazy) <adj.> insane, crazy: 发~ go crazy || 急~了 gone mad || ~女人 crazy woman
27 疯狂 [瘋-] fēngkuáng (mad-crazy) <adj.> frenzied: ~购物 frenzied shopping || ~工作 frenzied work || ~的人 a frenzied person
28 拐 [-] guǎi (crane, staff, lame, limp) <v.> limp: 一~一瘸 limp along || ~着腿 limp on one leg
29 扭 [-] niǔ (wring, sprain) <v.> sprain: ~伤 sprain painfully || ~了脚 twist a foot
30 康复 [-復] kāngfù (recuperate-recover) <v.> recuperate: 早日~ get well soon || 身体~ physical rehab || 逐渐 (zhújiàn) ~ gradually recover
31 出院 [-] chūyuàn (leave-hospital) <v-o> leave the hospital, get discharged: 平安~ safely discharged || 提前 ~ early discharge || ~以后 after leaving the hospital

Tips:

1 Radical 疒: It means 'sick, ill' and its pronunciation is 'nè' although it is commonly called as 'bìngzìpáng' (the radical of 病.) All characters with this radical are related 'to be sick, illness,' for example, 病 (bìng, to be sick, illness,) 疼 (téng, to ache,) 痛 (tòng, painful,) 痒 (yǎng, itchy,) 疤 (bā, scar,) 疯 (fēng, mad,) 疗 (liáo, cure,) 症 (zhèng, symptom,) 癌 (ái, cancer,) 瘫痪 (tānhuàn, paralysis) and 癫痫 (diānxián, epilepsy).
2 发*: 发 is the main verb for illness and symptoms, and means 'outbreak, to show, to feel' in this subject area, for example, 发病 (to become sick,) 发烧 (to have a fever,) 发炎 (to inflame,) 发冷 (to feel a bit chilly,) 发热 (to have a fever,) 发痒 (to be itchy,) 发抖 (fādǒu, to tremble,) 发颤 (fāchàn, to shiver,) 发慌 (fāhuāng, to feel nervous,) 发麻 (fāmá, to be numb, to tingle,) 发黑 (to become black/dark, 发also works with other colors,) 发昏 (fāhūn, to feel dizzy,) 发傻 (fāshǎ, to show stupidity,) 发呆 (fādāi, to stare blankly,) 发愣 (fālèng, to be in a daze.)
3 Diarrhea and 拉肚子: Native speakers of English will feel a little bit disgusted upon hearing the word 'diarrhea,' so they may judge this word's Chinese equivalent, '拉肚子.' However, it is a beautiful misconception of culture. The real Chinese equivalent of the English word 'diarrhea' should be '拉稀.' Since early Chinese translators disliked 拉稀, they used 拉肚子 to translate 'diarrhea.'

Exercises:

Part I: Read the following words and then answer the questions.

发烧、恶心、疼痛、呕吐、发炎、拉肚子、便秘、流血、受伤、过敏、晕车、咳嗽、发疯、扭伤、康复、出院、发病、生病

1 "小王病好了以后, 不再住院了," 正式的说法是:

______

2 如果一个人的脑子出现了问题, 行为和正常人不同, 口语表达会说:

______

3 一个人感冒以后会有哪些症状 (zhèngzhuàng, symptom)?

---

4 一个人生病后出现哪些症状要立刻去医院急诊 (jízhěn, emergency department)?

---

5 下面这两幅图中药物是治疗 (zhìliáo, treat) 什么症状的?

---

6 下面这两幅图里的药物是治疗什么症状的?

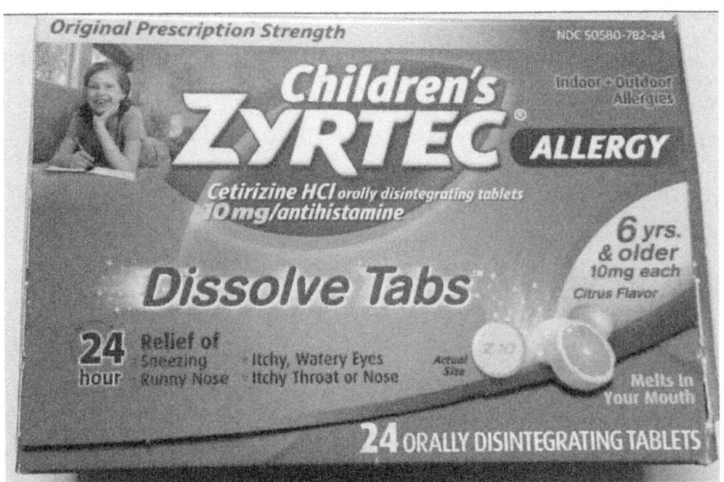

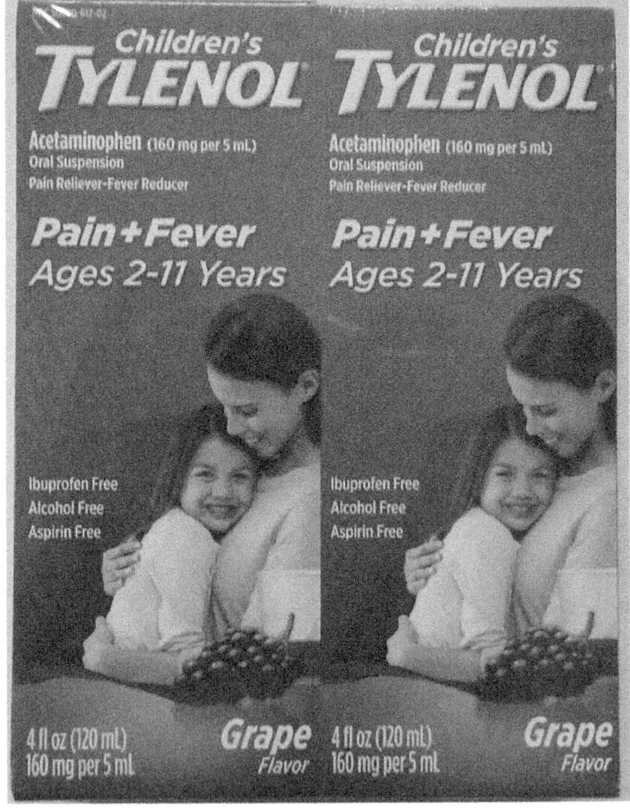

Theme 104: Death 死 (sǐ)

(See also Theme 132)

1 死 [-] sǐ (die, dead) <v./ adj.> die: 打~ kill || 病~ die of an illness || ~老鼠 dead mouse
2 死亡 [-] sǐwáng (die-decease) <v.> death: 自然~ natural death || 不幸~ unfortunate death || 中毒~ death by poison
3 去世 [-] qùshì (leave-world) <v.> pass away: 不幸~ unfortunately pass away || ~不久 pass away recently || ~三年 pass away three years ago
4 逝世 [-] shìshì (pass away-world) <v.> pass away: 有人认为毛主席的~对中国共产党来说是巨大对损失. Some people think that the death of Chairman Mao was a tremendous loss to the Chinese Communist Party.

5 牺牲 [犧-] xīshēng (sacrifice) <v./n.> sacrifice: ~生命 sacrifice a life || 巨大的~ huge sacrifice || ~时间 sacrifice time
6 丧生 [喪-] sàngshēng (lose-life) <v.> lose your life: 在暴雨中~ lost one's life in a rainstorm || 在事故中~ die in an accident || 全部~. They all lost their lives.

7 自杀 [-殺] zìshā (self-kill) <v.> commit suicide: 服药~ suicide by overdose || 慢性~ chronically suicidal || ~三次 attempt suicide three times
8 轻生 [輕-] qīngshēng (devalue-life) <v.> commit suicide: 有些年轻人因为忧郁而~. Some young people commit suicide because of their depression.
9 寻短见 [尋-見] xúnduǎnjiàn (seek-short-sighted) <v.> commit suicide: 在中国古代一些妇女在丈夫死后会~. In ancient China, some women killed themselves after their husbands died.

Tips:

1 牺牲 (xīshēng): 牺 and 牲 are both 'domestic animals for sacrifice,' but 牺 is of a uniform color while 牲 is of an entire body. Now 牺牲 means 'to die' for a good deed for a soldier or a public servant, or 'to sacrifice' something valuable, such as your time or life.
2 Euphemisms for 'to die': Generally the Chinese people lack calmness when facing death at an old age, so 'longevity' (寿 shòu, or 长寿) was the most important theme in auspicious wishes and folk arts in ancient China. Euphemisms are vital for learners of Chinese to grasp in order to communicate with the Chinese in their way. Here are some major euphemisms for 'to die,' 'dead' or 'death': (1) 走了 (left) or 没了 (gone,) for example, 他昨天走了, 她是哪天没的? (2) 永别了 (forever-parted,) for example, 他跟我们永别了, (3) 百年 (100-years) or 千古 (1, 000-ages,) for example, '我百年之后, 你 . . . . . .' '千古' is usually seen on the memorial ceremony, (4) 断气了 (stop-breathing), 出事了 (something happened), (5) 见阎王爷 (jiàn Yánwángyé, see King of Hell,) 上西天 (go to the Western Paradise) and 见马克思 ((of a CCP member) goes see Karl Marx). There are still several dozen expressions, which are rather difficult or unnecessary for learners of Chinese to know.

Exercises:

Part II: Multiple Choice. Make sure to choose the most appropriate answer.

1 (From the perspective of an ordinary Chinese person) 1976年中国华人民共和国国家主席 (zhǔxí, chairman) 毛泽东__________了.

A. 死亡 B. 死 C. 逝世

2 小王的爷爷奶奶十年前就__________了, 小王和父母都非常想念他们.

A. 去世 B. 丧失 C. 牺牲

3 据美国媒体报道在休斯顿 (Houston) 飓风 (jùfēng, hurricane) 中共有二百多人__________.

A. 丧生 B. 死 C. 轻生

4 小李失恋了, 他十分想不开, 想"寻短见." 这句话里"寻短见"的意思不是__________.

A. 自杀 B. 轻生 C. 牺牲

5 在这场反对恐怖分子 (kǒngbù fènzǐ, terrorist) 的战争中, 有几十个美国士兵________了自己年轻的生命.

A. 自杀 B. 死亡 C. 牺牲

Theme 105: Sexual behavior 性行为 (xìngxíngwéi)

1 做爱 [-愛] zuò'ài (make-love) <v.> make love
2 性交 [-] xìngjiāo (sexual-intercourse) <v.> sexual intercourse, copulation: 安全~ safe sex || ~技巧 sex skills
3 同房 [-] tóngfáng (same-room) <v.> sleep together: 总统不再和妻子~. The president banished his wife from his bed.
4 发生关系 [發-關係] fāshēngguānxì (occur-relation) <v.> have sexual relations with someone: 她和这个男的认识没几天就~了. She had sexual relations with this guy after they knew each other only a couple of days.
5 交配 [-] jiāopèi (copulate-mate) <v.> mating (animals): 驴 (lǘ) 是马和骡 (luó) ~而生的. A donkey is born from intercourse between a horse and a mule.
6 杂交 [雜-] zájiāo (mix-mate) <v.> hybridize: ~水稻hybrid rice || 他用金鱼和热带鱼~出一种金鱼的新品种. He hybridized a new goldfish from a regular goldfish and a tropical fish.
7 群交 [-] qúnjiāo (group-sex) <v.> do group sex: 在一些国家~是违法的. Group-sex is illegal in some countries.
8 手淫 [-] shǒuyín (hand-masturbate) <v./n.> masturbate, masturbation: 现代医学认为~在各个年龄段的男性女性中都很常见. Modern medicine believes masturbation is common in males and females of all ages.

9 自慰 [-] zìwèi (self-masturbate) <v./n.> masturbate, masturbation: 中国古代医学认为 ~是有害身体健康的事情. Chinese ancient medicine thinks masturbation is harmful to people's health.

10 怀孕 [懷-] huáiyùn (get-pregnant) <v.> get pregnant: ~三个月了be five months pregnant || 他的妻子~了. His wife became pregnant.

11 避孕 [-] bìyùn (avoid-pregnant) <v.> contraception: ~药contraceptive pill || ~套condom

12 不孕 [-] bùyùn (not able to-pregnant) <v.> infertility: 多年~ have not conceived for many years

Tips:

1 做爱 (zuò'ài): It was borrowed from the English term 'to make love.'

2 Euphemisms for 'sexual intercourse' in Chinese: Generally the Chinese people are very roundabout when mentioning 'sexual intercourse' in public. Some main euphemisms include: (1) 上床 (go to bed), (2) 睡觉 (sleep), (3) 那种事 (that kind of thing), (4) 房事 (room-thing), (5) 嘿咻 (hēixiu, originated from Taiwan), (6) 造人 (make-baby), (7) 交公粮 (surrender-state-tax grain, used in mainland China for a man's reluctance to make love with his wife) and (8) 啪啪啪 (onomatopoeic). Recently a previously vulgar word '打炮' (to fire-a gun, cannon) has become less or not vulgar for young adults.

3 Euphemisms for 'masturbate' in Chinese: For men, it is 打飞机 (shoot-airplane,) for women, 自摸 (self-touch.)

Exercises:

Part II: Multiple Choice. Make sure to choose the most appropriate answer.

1 中国农业科学家研究出来的_________水稻，使水稻的产量增加了两到三倍.

A. 交配 B. 杂交 C. 自慰

2 过去几十年中国的计划生育部门一直在免费为中国妇女提供_________药物, 以减少人口出生.

A. 不孕 B. 避孕 C. 怀孕

3 上世纪九十年代, 美国总统克林顿 (Clinton) 跟实习生_________的丑闻被美国媒体揭露 (jiēlù) 了出来.

A. 发生关系 B. 同房 C. 交配

4 下面哪组词可以用来描述动物的"性"

A. 行房事、做爱 B. 手淫、"打飞机" C. 交配、杂交

Theme 106: Sleep 睡眠 (shuìmián)

1 累 [-] lèi (tired) <adj.> tired: 玩~了 play until you are tired || ~极了 extremely tired
2 睡 [-] shuì (sleep) <v.> sleep: ~三个小时 sleep for three hours || ~在床上 sleep in a bed || ~得香 sleep soundly
3 睡觉 [-覺] shuìjiào (to sleep-a sleep) <v.> go to sleep: 睡一觉 sleep || 睡不着觉 cannot sleep || 睡三小时觉 go to sleep for three hours
4 睡眠 [-] shuìmián (sleep-deep sleep) <n.> sleep: 缺少~ lack of sleep || ~ 充足getting enough sleep|| 八小时~ eight hours of sleep
5 睡着 [-著] shuìzháo (sleep-*suffix*) <v.> fall asleep: 睡得着 falls asleep || 睡不着 can't fall asleep || 她~了. She fell asleep.
6 打盹儿 [--兒] dǎdǔnr (*prefix*-take nap) <v.> take a nap: 打了一个盹儿 took a nap
7 打瞌睡 [-] dǎkēshuì (*prefix*-doze off) <v.> doze off: 好~ easily dozes off || 从不~ never dozes off
8 困 [睏] kùn (sleepy) <adj.> sleepy: 小姑娘~了. The little girl was sleepy. || 很~ very sleepy || ~极了 extremely sleepy
9 犯困 [-睏] fànkùn (incur-sleepy) <v.> feel sleepy: 吃完午饭以后人最容易~. People are most vulnerable to feel sleepy after lunch.

10 梦 [夢] mèng (dream) <v./n.> dream: 白日 ~ daydream || 美国/中国~ American Dream/Chinese Dream
11 梦见 [夢見] mèngjiàn (dream-about) <separable word> dream about: 梦得见 can dream about || 梦不见 couldn't dream about || ~他 dreamed about him
12 做梦 [-夢] zuòmèng (to dream-a dream) <separable word> have a dream: 做了一个梦 had a dream || 做美梦 have a beautiful dream || 做噩 (è) 梦 have a nightmare
13 醉 [-] zuì (drunk) <v.> drunk: 喝~了 drink too much
14 醒 [-] xǐng (wake up) <v.> wake up: 叫~他 wake him up
15 清醒 [-] qīngxǐng (clear-waken) <v./adj.> clear-headed, sober: 保持 ~ keep a clear mind || 头脑~ clear-headed, sober-minded
16 苏醒 [蘇-] sūxǐng (resurrect-wake up) <v.> come to: ~过来 regain consciousness
17 失眠 [-] shīmián (fail-sleep) <v./n.> insomnia: 引起~ cause insomnia || 常常 ~ often suffer from insomnia

Tips:

1 梦 (mèng): Everyone dreams, either sweet dreams (美梦,) nightmare (噩梦, èmèng) or otherwise. Some daydream (做白日梦.) Chinese say 人生像一场梦 (life is like a dream) and the greatest Chinese novel is called *Dream of the Red Chamber* (红楼梦.)
2 睡觉 vs. 睡着: 睡觉 means 'to sleep a sleep' and is a verb-object structure, while 睡着 means 'to fall asleep' and is a verb-complement structure. For example, 昨天晚上十点我就去睡觉了, 可是睡不着 (Last night, I went to sleep at 10, however I could not fall asleep.)

Exercises:

Part II: Multiple Choice. Make sure to choose the most appropriate answer.

1 小李下午喝了很多茶, 结果晚上睡不着觉, ________了.

A. 失眠　B. 清醒　C. 苏醒

2 小李喝醉以后就睡着了, 直到第二天中午才________过来.

A. 失眠　B. 清醒　C. 苏醒

3 他出车祸 (chēhuò) 以后一直躺在医院里昏迷 (hūnmí) 不醒, 医生用尽了所有办法, 还是不能让他________过来.

A. 失眠　B. 清醒　C. 苏醒

4 他的________质量不太好, 常常________, 早上起来感觉非常累.

A. 睡眠、做梦　B. 睡觉、梦见　C. 睡眠、梦

5 他上课的时候"打瞌睡," 这里的"打瞌睡"跟下面哪个词的意思差不多

A. 醉了　B. 犯困　C. 睡着

6 有些人老年人喜欢在白天的时候________, 小睡一会儿.

A. 做个噩梦　B. 做个美梦　C. 打个盹儿

7 上世纪八九十年代很多有才华的中国年轻人来到美国留学,　追求他们的________, 因为在他们眼里美国就是自由和民主.

A. 美国梦　B. 中国梦　C. 白日梦

Theme 107: Happy, sad 高兴, 悲伤 (gāoxìng, bēishāng)

(See also Themes 120, 255)

1 乐 [樂] lè (happy) <adj.> happy: ~坏了 the happiest || 心里~开了花 heart fills with joy
2 高兴 [-興] gāoxìng (high-mood) <adj.> glad, happy: 非常~ very glad || 感到~ feel happy || ~地说 gladly say
3 快乐 [-樂] kuàilè (pleasant-happy) <adj.> happy: 生日/节日~ happy birthday/holiday || ~的事 a happy story || 觉得~ feel happy
4 欢乐 [歡樂] huānlè (joyous-happy) <adj.> joyous: 缺少~ lack joy || 充满~ filled with joy || ~的心情 a joyous mood
5 快活 [-] kuàihuó (pleasant-lively) <adj.> happy: ~地大笑 happily laugh || ~日子 a happy day
6 愉快 [-] yúkuài (cheerful-pleasant) <adj.> cheerful: 生活~ live cheerfully || ~的事 a happy thing || 心情~ be in a cheerful mood

7 开心 [開-] kāixīn (open-heart) <adj./v.> happy, feel happy, make fun of sb.: ~的事 a happy thing || 玩得很~ enjoyed oneself very much || 拿他 ~ make fun of him

8 惊喜 [驚-] jīngxǐ (surprise-pleased) <adj./n.> happy surprise: ~地发现 happily discover || ~地叫起来 give an astonished shout

9 得意 [-] déyì (satisfied-intention) <adj.> be proud of oneself: ~地笑着 smile proudly || 有点~ a little bit of self-pride || 很~ be very proud of oneself

10 乐呵呵 [樂--] lèhēhē (happy-*onomatopoeia*) <adj.> cheerful: ~地说 cheerfully say || 她整天~的. She is always cheerful and gay.

11 美滋滋 [-] měizīzī (pleased-*onomatopoeia*) <adj.> pleased with yourself: 这个学生被当选为班长, 心里~的. This student was very pleased to be elected class monitor.

12 喜洋洋 [-] xǐyángyáng (joy-*suffix*) <adj.> radiant: ~的气氛 a radiant atmosphere

13 欢天喜地 [歡---] huāntiānxǐdì (happy-heaven-joy-Earth) <idiom> with boundless joy: ~地搬进新房子 move into a new house with boundless joy

14 喜出望外 [-] xǐchūwàngwài (happy-exceed-expectation-outside) <idiom> be pleased beyond expectations: 我们队得了冠军, 大家~. We were enjoyed to hear that our team had won the championship.

15 心花怒放 [-] xīnhuānùfàng (heart-flower-full-bloom) <idiom> burst with joy: 高兴得~ happily burst with joy

16 大快人心 [-] dàkuàirénxīn (greatly-delight-people-heart) <idiom> (usu. of the punishment of an evil-doer) to the satisfaction of everyone: 盗版光碟被禁止了, 真是~! The pirated discs were banned to the great satisfaction of the people!

17 满意 [滿-] mǎnyì (satisfied-intention) <adj.> satisfied: 令人~ cause satisfaction || 对他很~ very satisfied with him || ~的答案 satisfactory answer

18 满足 [滿-] mǎnzú (satisfied-sufficient) <adj./v.> satisfy: ~需要 satisfy needs || ~好奇心 satisfy curiosity || 感到 ~ be content

19 称心 [稱-] chènxīn (suit-heart) <adj.> be gratified: ~如意 very satisfactory || ~的东西 a gratifying thing || 感到~ feel gratified

20 顺心 [順-] shùnxīn (agreeable-heart) <adj.> be satisfactory: 过得~ live one's life in happiness || 工作~ be satisfactory at work

21 骄傲 [驕-] jiāo'ào (proud-arrogant) <v./adj.> arrogant, prideful: 感到~ feel pride || 值得~ deserving of pride || ~自大 be arrogant

22 沾沾自喜 [-] zhānzhānzìxǐ (think highly of-*reduplication*-self-pleased) <idiom> be self-satisfied: 他工作上取得了一点儿成绩就~. He will be very self-satisfied once he gets a little bit of achievement in his work.

23 爽 [-] shuǎng (bright, clear, pleasant) <adj.> feel good: 人逢喜事精神~ joy puts heart into a man || 身体不~ not feel well

24 舒服 [-] shūfú (wide-clothes) <adj.> comfortable: 觉得~ feel comfortable || 心里~ comfortable at heart || 身体不~ physical discomfort

25 舒适 [-適] shūshì (comfortable-suitable) <adj.> comfortable, snug, cozy: 穿着~ cozy to wear || ~的床 a snug bed

26 轻松 [輕鬆] qīngsōng (light-relax) <adj.> relaxed: ~的心情 a relaxed mood

27 赏心悦目 [賞---] shǎngxīnyuèmù (enjoyable-heart-pleasant-eye) <idiom> find the scenery pleasing to both the eye and the mind: 令人~ please the eye and mind || 感到~ feel completely delighted

28 愁 [-] chóu (worry) <v.> worry about: ~吃 worry about having food || ~穿 worry about clothing || ~工作 worry about work

29 担心 [擔-] dānxīn (shoulder-heart) <separable word> worry, be anxious: 担什么心 worry about what? || ~找不到工作 be anxious about not finding a job

30 烦 [煩] fán (annoyed, vexed) <v.> be bothered, vexed: 心~ upset || 感到~ feel bothered || ~死了 bothered to death

31 痛苦 [-] tòngkǔ (agony-painful) <adj.> painful: ~的生活 a painful life || 精神~ mental pain || 觉得~ feel pain

32 难过 [難過] nánguò (hard-pass) <adj.> sad: 心里~ sad at heart || 有些~ have some hard times || ~地低着头 sadly bow your head

33 难受 [難-] nánshòu (hard-endure) <adj.> unwell, uncomfortable: 听了~ listened uncomfortably || 闲得~ idle uncomfortably || ~的样子 uncomfortable look

34 伤心 [傷-] shāngxīn (hurt-heart) <adj.> broken-hearted: ~地哭 broken-heartedly cry || 哭得~ cry heart-brokenly || ~事 a sad thing

35 悲伤 [-傷] bēishāng (grieved-sad) <adj.> sorrowful: ~的女孩 a sad little girl || ~的日子 a sorrowful day || 十分~ utterly sorrowful

36 灰心 [-] huīxīn (ash-heart) <adj.> lose heart: ~丧气 become discouraged || 他一遇到困难就~. He's easily disheartened by difficulties.

37 沮丧 [-喪] jǔsàng (dispirited-dejected) <adj.> dispirited, dejected: 感到~ feel dejected

38 泄气 [洩氣] xièqì (leak-ambition) <v.> feel discouraged: 他碰到困难就容易~. He easily keeps his end up in the face of difficulties.

39 失望 [-] shīwàng (lose-hope) <adj.> disappointed: 感到~ be disappointed || ~地走了 disappointedly leave || ~的心情 a disappointed mood

40 绝望 [絕-] juéwàng (exhaust-hope) <adj.> despair, desperate: 感到~ feel desperate || ~的心情 a desperate mood || ~地大叫 shout desperately

41 死心 [-] sǐxīn (die-heart) <v.> give up, admit failure: 经历了很多失败, 她还是不~. Even though she has had many failures, she still isn't giving up.

42 寒心 [-] hánxīn (cold-heart) <adj.> disappointed: 让人~ make people disappointed

43 不满 [-滿] bùmǎn (not-contented) <adj.> dissatisfied, resentful: 对工作~ dissatisfied with work || 十分~ completely dissatisfied || ~地看着她 look at her resentfully

44 遗憾 [遺-] yíhàn (leave-regret) <v./n.> regret: 感到~ feel regret || 永远~ regret forever || ~地说 regretfully say

45 叹气 [嘆氣] tànqì (sigh-breath) <separable word> sigh: 叹了一口气 had a sigh || 摇头 ~ shake your head and sigh

46 没法儿 [--兒] méifǎr (no-method) <v.> impossible: ~说 impossible to say || ~理解 impossible to understand || ~不生气 no way not to be angry

47 无法 [無-] wúfǎ (not-capable) <v.> incapable: ~离开 incapable of leaving || ~完成 incapable of completing || ~进去 unable to go in

48 无奈 [無-] wúnài (no-how) <v.> helpless, with no alternatives: 出于~ there being no alternative || ~地说 grudgingly say || 让人~ make people helpless

49 无可奈何 [無---] wúkě'nàihé (no-able to-how) <idiom> have no alternative: ~地叹气 sigh helplessly || ~地摇了摇头 shake your head helplessly

Tips:

1 *心: In the following words, the characters before '心' are to describe '心' and therefore are supposed to be used after '心,' for example, 伤心 (sad,) 灰心 (lose heart,) 死心 (give up,) 寒心 (disappointed,) 开心 (happy) and 顺心 (satisfactory.)

2 欢, 快, 乐: All mean 'happy' and their combinations, 欢快, 欢乐, 快乐 have almost the same meaning.

3 悲, 哀, 伤: All mean 'sad, hurt' and their combinations, 悲哀, 悲伤, 哀伤 have almost the same meaning.

Exercises:

Part I: Read the following words and put the words with similar meanings in the same table.

无法、无可奈何、绝望、失望、泄气、伤心、悲伤、难过、难受、烦、愁、大快人心、心花怒放、欢天喜地、开心、愉快、高兴

没法儿:
无奈:
死心:
寒心:
灰心:
痛苦:
担心:
喜出望外:
快乐:

Part II: Read the following sentences and fill in each blank with the appropriate word or phrase from the options given.

1 舒适、舒服、轻松

a) 新西兰的天气很______, 尤其是夏天.
b) 老王跟太太退休以后到了中国南方一个小城市居住, 过着平静而_______的生活.
c) 一般来说大城市的工作生活节奏 (jiézòu) 比较紧张, 中小城市则比较________.

2 赏心悦目、爽、惊喜

a) 小张昨晚开夜车写论文, 今天上课的时候觉得身体特别不________.
b) 一向学习不用功的小张这次论文写得特别好, 让教授十分________.
c) 秋天时候这个地方到处都是金黄或者火红的枫叶, 让人__________.

3 沾沾自喜、得意、骄傲

a) 这对夫妻为自己孩子在学习上取得的成绩感到__________. 但是他们不希望自己的孩子为此_________, 得意忘形, 因此一再告诉孩子要谦虚 (qiānxū).
b) 有的年轻女孩子很喜欢炫富 (xuànfù), 总是在网上__________地晒自己的新房子、新车什么的.

4 顺心、称心、满足、满意

a) 小张最近工作上非常不__________, 因为总有同事故意在工作上刁难 (diāonàn, nitpick) 他.
b) 小张打算辞职后, 慢慢找工作, 直到找到一份__________如意的.
c) 亚马逊网规定, 如果顾客对商品不________, 三个月内可以退货. 亚马逊网的服务宗旨 (zōngzhǐ, mission) 是尽量_______顾客的要求.

Theme 108: Angry, excited 愤怒, 激动 (fènnù, jīdòng)

1 气 [氣] qì (cloud, air, angry) <v.> get angry: ~得直哭 angry to tears || ~得发抖 tremble with anger || ~人 anger people
2 生气 [-氣] shēngqì (get-annoyed) <v.> take offense: 生他的气 angry with him || 对他~ get angry at him || 让人~ make people angry
3 发火 [發-] fāhuǒ (lose-anger) <v.> flare up (get angry): 别~ don't get angry || 他很有教养, 从不~. He has self-control and never loses his temper.
4 发脾气 [發-氣] fāpíqì (lose-temper) <v.> lose your temper: 向别人~ lose your temper at somebody
5 赌气 [賭氣] dǔqì (bet-anger) <v.> feel wronged and act rashly: ~辞掉工作 resign from one's job in a fit of pique || 他~走了. He left in a fit of anger.
6 气愤 [氣憤] qìfèn (angry-disgruntled) <adj.> furious: ~地说 furiously say || 感到~ feel furious
7 怒 [-] nù (anger, fury, furious) <v.> anger: ~不可言 inexpressibly angry || 大~ very angry || ~吼roar angrily
8 发怒 [發-] fānù (lose-angry) <v.> get angry: ~的时候 when angry || 容易~ easily get angry
9 愤怒 [憤-] fènnù (disgruntled-furious) <adj.> anger: 感到~ feel angry || 表达~ express anger || ~的顾客 an angry customer
10 勃然大怒 [-] bórándànù (agitated-*suffix*-greatly-angry) <idiom> fly into a rage: 这个女高中生凌晨三点才回家, 他爸爸 ~. When this high school girl came home at three in the morning, her father was enraged. || 看到这个结果, 总经理~, 把水杯摔在了地上. Seeing this result, the general manager flew into a rage and threw the water cup onto the ground.
11 怒气冲冲 [-氣衝衝, 沖沖] nùqìchōngchōng (anger-surging-*reduplication*) <idiom> in a rage: 他~地出去了. He stormed out in a rage.
12 火冒三丈 [-] huǒmàosānzhàng (anger-rise-three-*zhang*) <idiom> get really angry: Note: *zhang* is a unit of measurement, roughly 3.3 meters. 有人批评他, 他就会~. He becomes infuriated if anyone criticizes him! || 小王看到自己的新车被撞, 立刻~. When little Wang saw the damage to his new car, he went right up in the air.
13 气急败坏 [氣-敗壞] qìjíbàihuài (breath-short-discomposed) <idiom> flustered and exasperated: 在会上很多人反对总经理的计划, 于是他~地离开

了会场. At the meeting, a lot of people objected to the general manager's plan, so he left the meeting in a rage.

14 出气 [-氣] chūqì (vent-anger) <v.> give vent to one's anger: 别拿孩子~ Don't take your anger out on the kids. || 拿猫~ take one's anger out on the cat
15 发泄 [發-, 洩] fāxiè (lose-divulge) <v.> vent: ~不满 vent dissatisfaction || ~怒气 vent anger
16 闹情绪 [鬧-緒] nàoqíngxù (indulge-mood) <v.> be in a bad mood: 常常~ often be in a bad mood || 这个孩子因为父母让他做家务, 而跟父母 ~. This child was in a mood because her parents made her do housework.
17 愤愤不平 [憤憤--] fènfènbùpíng (disgruntled-*reduplication*-not-easy) <idiom> be indignant: ~地喊 shout indignantly || 很多人对新税法 ~. There has been much indignation over the new tax law.
18 打抱不平 [-] dǎbàobùpíng (fight-defend against-injustice) <idiom> defend against injustice: 他遇到不公平的事总爱~. He likes to fight for justice when he encounters inequality.

19 兴奋 [興奮] xīngfèn (rise-excited) <adj.> excited: ~ 地说 excitedly say || 感到~ feel excited || ~得跳起来 jump up excitedly
20 激动 [-動] jīdòng (stir-move) <v./adj.> excite: 内心~ inner excitement || ~地哭了 cry emotionally (stir up emotions) || ~的心情 excited mood
21 冲动 [衝動] chōngdòng (surge-move) <v./adj.> get excited: 容易~ easily excitable || 感情~ emotional impulse || 一时~ an impulse
22 兴致勃勃 [興---] xìngzhìbóbó (spirit-vigorous-*reduplication*) <idiom> in high spirits: ~地说 speak in high spirits || 很多人~地学书法, 但是遇到困难后就不学了. A lot of people start to learn calligraphy in high spirits and give up when the going gets tough.

23 感动 [-動] gǎndòng (touch-move) <v./adj.> move (emotionally), moved: ~大家 move everyone || 让人~ make people feel touched || 十分~ extremely moved
24 感人 [-] gǎnrén (move-people) <adj.> touching, moving (emotion): ~的故事 a touching story || 写得~ writing that moves people || 场面~ a touching scene
25 感慨 [-] gǎnkǎi (touch-indignant) <v.> sigh with emotion: ~万千 filled with many emotions || 说起自己的过去, 他觉得有很多~. When he spoke of his past, he sighed with emotion.
26 百感交集 [-] bǎigǎnjiāojí (hundred-feeling-cross-gather) <idiom> experience many different feelings at once: 回想起她的童年, 她~, 那时候她家非常贫穷. Recalling her childhood, she has mixed feelings. At that time, her family was very poor and she suffered a lot.

Tips:

1 Moods and vital organs: Traditional Chinese Medicine believed that human moods were associated with and could harm vital organs, for example, 怒伤肝 (anger harms the liver,) 喜伤心 (happiness/joy harms the heart,) 忧伤肺 (worry harms the lungs,) 思伤脾 (yearning harms the spleen) and 恐伤肾 (horror harms the kidneys.)
2 感人 and 感动: Because a thing or an event is touching (感人,) you are moved (感动.)

Exercises:

Part I: Use the given bound form as a guide to help you think of other words with the same character. Feel free to use your dictionary when needed. Then write down the English definition of each of the words you've written.

怒 *(anger)*: 发怒 *get anger*

____

____

____

____

气 *(enrage)*: 生气 *get angry*

____

____

____

____

Part II: Read the following words and then answer the questions.

感人、百感交集、发泄怒气、兴致勃勃、激动、兴奋、闹情绪、愤愤不平、打抱不平、发脾气、赌气、气愤、火冒三丈、怒气冲冲、勃然大怒、气急败坏、冲动

1 上面哪些词可以用来形容"感动"?

2 上面哪些词可以用来"兴奋"?

3 上面哪个词是"出气"的书面语?

4 上面哪些词可以用来形容"觉得不公平"?

5 上面哪些词有"生气"的意思?

6 你小时候跟父母"闹过情绪"吗?为什么?你有没有过赌气离家的经历?

7 你觉得一个人很冲动的情况下会不会作出正确的决定?为什么?

Theme 109: Fear, relief 害怕, 放心 (hàipà, fàngxīn)

1 怕 [-] pà (fear, be afraid) <v.> fear: ~黑 fear the dark || ~老鼠 be afraid of mice || ~脏 can't stand being dirty

2 害怕 [-] hàipà (be afraid-fear) <v.> be afraid: 很~ very afraid || ~哭声 cry out in fear || ~见到她 be afraid of seeing her

3 恐惧 [-懼] kǒngjù (dread-dread) <v./n.> fear, dread: 对死亡的~ the fear of death || ~战争fear the war || 克服~ conquer a fear

4 好奇 [-] hàoqí (fond of-curious) <adj.> curious: ~的小孩 a curious child || ~的眼光 inquisitive eyes || ~地问 ask inquisitively

5 吃惊 [-驚] chījīng (suffer-surprise) <separable word> be startled: 大吃一惊 be very shocked || 吃一大惊 a big shock || ~地问 ask in a startled tone

6 惊讶 [驚訝] jīngyà (surprised-astonished) <adj.> astonishing: 感到~ feel astonished || ~地问 ask amazedly || 令人~ induce astonishment

7 震惊 [-驚] zhènjīng (shock-surprised) <v. /adj.> shock: ~世界 shock the world || 感到~ feel shocked || 令人~ cause shock

8 大惊小怪 [-驚--] dàjīngxiǎoguài (big-surprised-small-weird) <idiom> make a fuss about nothing: 别~ don't get so excited over nothing || 一说到敏感(mǐngǎn) 话题, 他就~. When it comes to sensitive subjects, she makes a fuss. || 加州地区小地震不断, 人们早就不 ~了. Small earthquakes are so common in the California area that people never make a fuss about it.

9 大惊失色 [-驚--] dàjīngshīsè (greatly-shocked-lose-expression) <idiom> turn pale with fright: 房东在收房租的时候看到房客死了, 她~. The landlord saw the tenant die when she was collecting the rent, and she quickly turned pale. || 听到纽约双子塔被恐怖分子袭击的消息, 这位总统~. The president was greatly shocked by the news of the terrorist attack on the Twin Towers in New York.

10 慌 [-] huāng (flurried, nervous) <adj.> flurried: 心~ get nervous || ~了神 get agitated || ~了手脚 in a rush

11 惊慌 [驚-] jīnghuāng (surprised-flurried) <adj.> panic: ~地叫喊 shout in panic || ~地逃走了run away in panic

12 慌忙 [-] huāngmáng (flurried-hurriedly) <adj.> hurriedly: ~开门 hurriedly open the doors || ~走开 dash off in a rush || ~穿好衣服 throw on clothes in a rush

13 心慌意乱 [---亂] xīnhuāngyìluàn (heart-flurried-mind-confused) <idiom> be alarmed and confused: 吓得~ scared to the point of alarm and confusion

14 紧张 [緊張] jǐnzhāng (tight-draw, open) <adj.> nervous, intense: 别~ don't be nervous || ~局势tense situation || 这场比赛真~! What an exciting game!

15 不安 [-] bù'ān (not-easy) <adj.> not peaceful, unstable: 感到~ feel unstable || 烦躁~ be disturbed from hunger || 世界局势动荡 ~. The world situation is characterized by turbulence and instability.

16 忐忑不安 [-] tǎntèbù'ān (timorous-not-easy) <idiom> uneasy, apprehensive: 心情 ~ feel apprehensive || 老板让我去他办公室, 我~. I was in a funk when my employer called me into his office.

17 坐立不安 [-] zuòlìbù'ān (sit-stand-not-easy) <idiom> restless (uneasy standing and sitting): 小王在考试前总是~. Little Wang always gets antsy before a test. || 这个工作面试让我整天都~. This job interview has had me on pins and needles all day.
18 心神不定 [-] xīnshénbùdìng (heart-mind-not-settled) <idiom> be distracted, restless: ~地坐下来 distractedly sit down
19 六神无主 [--無-] liùshénwúzhǔ (six-vital organs-no-master) <idiom> at a loss, stunned: 心里~ mind is at a loss || 这位老人的妻子突然去世, 他感到~. This old man's wife's sudden death upset the balance of his mind.
20 心乱如麻 [-亂--] xīnluànrúmá (heart-chaos-like-hemp) <idiom> be utterly upset: 听到这个坏消息后, 他~, 不知该怎么办. When he heard the bad news, he was a mess and didn't know what to do.
21 着急 [著-] zháojí (burning-anxious) <separable word> worry: 着什么急 worry about what? || 心里~ worried at heart || ~买房子 worry about buying a house
22 急忙 [-] jímáng (anxious-hurry) <adj.> with haste: ~跑过来 run over hastily || ~说 speak hastily
23 焦急 [-] jiāojí (worry-anxious) <adj.> anxious: ~地等待 wait anxiously || 她行李箱丢了, 十分 ~. She is super uneasy over her lost suitcase.
24 急切 [-] jíqiè (anxious-urgent) <adj.> impatient: ~地问 impatiently ask || 小王在递交了大学申请以后, 一直在~地等待大学的录取通知. Little Wang has been waiting for the admission notice to the university after submitting his college application.
25 迫不及待 [-] pòbùjídài (pressing-not-until-wait) <idiom> too impatient to wait: ~地想知道结果 cannot wait to know the result. || 小王~地要告诉父母他被哈佛大学录取的消息. Little Wang can't wait to tell his parents that he was admitted to Harvard University.

26 不好意思 [-] bùhǎoyìsī (not-feel at ease) <v.> feel embarrassed, find it embarrassing (to do sth): 把孩子吓哭了, 他有点~. He feels embarrassed for making the child cry with fear. || 她~地说是她儿子打碎了花瓶. She was embarrassed to say that her son broke the vase. || 他 ~告诉父母他又有了新女朋友. He was embarrassed to report to his parents that he had a new girlfriend yet again.
27 放心 [-] fàngxīn (rest-heart) <v.> rest assured, be at ease: 请~ please be at ease || ~吃 relax while eating || ~地睡 rest at ease
28 安心 [-] ānxīn (settle, calm-heart) <adj.> feel relieved: ~休息 rest with relief || ~等候 wait at ease || ~读书 read contentedly

29 沉着 [-著] chénzhuó (calm-steady) <adj.> calm, steady: ~地说 calmly say || ~回答 calmly answer || 动作~ move steadily
30 镇静 [鎮靜] zhènjìng (composed-calm) <adj.> calm: 保持~ maintain calmness || ~下来 calm down || 恢复~ restore calm
31 不动声色 [-動聲-] bùdòngshēngsè (not-change-sound-expression) <idiom> stay calm and collected: ~地问 ask in a calm manner

32 从容 [從-] cóngróng (calm-unhurried) <adj.> calm, unhurried: 表情~ express calm || ~地打开盒子 leisurely open the box
33 平静 [-靜] píngjìng (tranquil-quiet) <adj.> tranquil, calm: 难以~ difficult to calm || 情绪~ calm mood || 语气 ~ calm tone
34 踏实 [-實] tāshí (step-steady) <adj.> steady: 睡得~ sleep deeply || 心里~ peace of mind
35 心安理得 [-] xīn'ānlǐdé (heart-easy-mind-justified) <idiom> with clear conscience and mind at rest: 吃得~ achieve peace of mind || ~地收下礼物 have no qualms about accepting gifts || ~地走进饭店 walk into the restaurant at ease
36 心平气和 [--氣-] xīnpíngqìhé (heart-peaceful-tone-harmonious) <idiom> even-tempered: ~地商量 discuss with an even temper || ~地交谈 converse calmly
37 当之无愧 [當-無-] dāngzhīwúkuì (deserve-it-not-ashamed) <idiom> fully deserve (a title, honor, etc.), be worthy of: 她获得冠军~! She was entirely deserving of her championship win!
38 问心无愧 [問-無-] wènxīnwúkuì (ask-heart-not-ashamed) <idiom> have a clear conscience (look into your heart without shame): 好好干才能~. Doing a good job will give you a clear conscience.

Tips:

1 忐忑 (tǎntè): From the form of 忐忑, namely 上心下心 or 心上心下 (heart up and heart down) one can easily guess it indicates 'the heart is not calm since it is up and down,' in another word, 'timorous.'
2 惊 (jīng), 恐 (kǒng), 惧 (jù): All mean 'surprised' or 'dread,' and their combinations, 惊恐, 惊惧, 恐惧 have almost the same meaning. 恐 and 惧 are synonyms from 2,000 years ago.
3 惊 (jīng), 慌 (huāng), 忙 (máng), 乱 (luàn): The formation of some Chinese compound words is logical. Take this group as an example, the four words denote four stages of chaos. After you have been surprised (惊) you would be flurried (慌) and hurry (忙) to do something, only to cause chaos (乱) in this fashion. Combinations of these four characters, 惊慌, 惊忙 (*archaic*), 惊乱, 慌忙, 慌乱, 忙乱 have more or less the same meaning.
4 急 (jí), 迫 (pò), 切 (qiè): All means 'anxious' or 'urgent,' and their combinations, 急迫, 急切, 迫切 have almost the same meaning.
5 不动声色 and 喜形于色: Some can 不动声色 (to stay calm and collected) under any circumstance, but some could 喜形于色 (happy-shown-on-face, to light up with pleasure.) The opposite of 喜形于色 is 喜怒不形于色 (one's expression is unreadable.) The difference between 不动声色 and 喜怒不形于色 is that the former describes an action, but the latter describes the disposition of a person.
6 14 idioms: It is rare to have 14 idioms out of 38 entries in a group. It seems that the ancient Chinese were very concerned with 安 (peaceful, safe, easy.)

Exercises:

Part I: Read the following words or phrases and put the words with similar meanings in the same table.

大惊失色、不用大惊小怪、紧张不安、六神无主、忐忑不安、坐立不安、心乱如麻、不动声色、从容、问心无愧、迫不及待、心慌意乱、迫不及待

很震惊:
不用吃惊:
不安:
沉着:
当之无愧:
踏实:
急切:
惊慌:
急切:

Part II: Multiple Choice. Make sure to choose the most appropriate answer.

1 有些中国孩子即使大学毕业了还是__________地享受父母所提供的一切, 认为是父母应该这样做.

A. 心乱如麻 B. 心安理得 C. 心平气和

2 小学教育应该培养孩子追求知识和真理的_________, 而不是对学习的________.

A. 恐惧、好奇 B. 好奇心、恐惧 C. 惊讶、恐惧

3 考完GRE考试以后, 他__________地想要知道考试结果.

A. 迫不及待 B. 大惊失色 C. 安心

4 现在很多年轻人对自己对未来忧虑 (yōulǜ, worried) ________, 因为社会为年轻人提供上升的空间越来越少了.

A. 着急 B. 镇静 C. 不安

5 中国有句老话说: 做人要_________, 意思就是要对得起自己的良心.

A. 紧张不安 B. 忐忑不安 C. 问心无愧

6 在人工智能方面, 谷歌公司___________处于世界领先地位.

A. 紧张不安 B. 心平气和 C. 当之无愧

Theme 110: To like, to dislike 喜欢, 厌恶 (xǐhuān, yànwù)

1 爱 [愛] ài (love) <v.> love: ~打篮球 love playing basketball || ~上同事 fall in love with a colleague || 相 ~ love each other
2 好 [-] hào (keen on) <v.> love, be fond of: ~读小说 love to read novels || ~看电视 love to watch TV || ~画画 love to draw
3 喜欢 [-歡] xǐhuān (like-happy) <v.> like: ~他 like him || ~跳舞 like dancing || ~看电影 like watching movies
4 感兴趣 [-興-] gǎnxìngqù (touch-interest) <v.> have interest in: 对科学~ have interest in science || 特别~ very interesting || 使人~ cause people to be interested
5 爱好 [愛-] àihào (love-keen on) <v/n..> interest, hobby, take great pleasure in: ~运动 like sports || ~广泛 wide-ranging hobbies || 业余~ hobby
6 喜爱 [-愛] xǐ'ài (like-love) <v.> be fond of: ~大自然 enjoy nature || ~音乐 like music || ~食物 enjoy food
7 热爱 [熱愛] rè'ài (ardent-love) <v.> love, adore: ~生活 deeply enjoy life || ~和平 love peace || ~音乐 love music
8 爱不释手 [愛-釋-] àibùshìshǒu (love-not-release-hand) <idiom> be too fond of to part with: 令人~ cause such affection that you can't give it up || 莎士比亚的书让人~. Shakespeare's works have gained the admiration of many people.
9 爱屋及乌 [愛--烏] àiwūjíwū (love-house-reach to-crow) <idiom> love all parts of someone (even love the crows on someone's roof): 西部牛仔成了人们心目中的英雄, 人们~, 牛仔服也成为流行服装了. Western cowboys have become heroes in people's minds. People have come to love everything about cowboys, and cowboy jeans have become popular clothes.

10 疼 [-] téng (ache, pain, painful) <v.> love dearly, dote on: ~孩子 dote on a child || 奶奶最~爱孙子. Granny dotes on her little grandsons.
11 心疼 [-] xīnténg (heart-ache) <v.> love dearly: ~孩子 dearly love a child || ~自己 dearly love yourself
12 惯 [慣] guàn (spoil) <v.> spoil: ~着孩子 spoiling a kid
13 宠爱 [寵愛] chǒng'ài (dote-love) <v.> dote on: 受人~ be doted on by someone || 爸爸特别~这个孩子. Dad dotes on this kid especially.
14 溺爱 [-愛] nì'ài (indulge-love) <v.> dote on: ~孩子 spoil a child
15 娇惯 [嬌慣] jiāoguàn (capricious-spoil) <v.> pamper, spoil: ~ 孩子 pamper a child
16 偏爱 [-愛] piān'ài (partial-love) <v.> favor: ~大儿子 favor the eldest son

17 爱恋 [愛戀] ài'liàn (love-feel attached) <v.> be in love with, feel attached to: ~故土 attachment to your homeland || ~之情 feelings of love || 她~着那个男人. She is head over heels in love with that man.
18 暗恋 [-戀] àn'liàn (secretly-love) <v.> secretly in love with: ~一个女孩 secretly love a girl
19 留恋 [-戀] liúliàn (stay-feel attached) <v.> nostalgic: ~过去 yearn for the past || ~故乡 nostalgic for home

20 心动 [-動] xīndòng (heart-move) <v.> emotionally affected: 为她~ be emotional for her

21 一往情深 [-] yīwǎngqíngshēn (all the way-affection-deep) <idiom> deeply attached: 对她~ be devoted to her

22 情人眼里出西施 [---裏---] qíngrényǎnlǐchūxīshī (lover-eye-in-appear-Xi Shi) <proverb> Beauty is in the eye of the beholder: 她在一般人眼里并不漂亮, 但在男朋友眼里却漂亮极了, 这就是"~." She is not beautiful in the eyes of ordinary people, but she is beautiful in the eyes of her boyfriend. Truly, 'beauty is in the eye of the beholder.'

23 相爱 [-愛] xiāng'ài (mutual-love) <v.> love each other: 彼此~ love each other || 与好朋友 ~ love your good friend || 终身~ lifelong mutual love

24 羡慕 [羨慕] xiànmù (envy-admire) <v.> envy, admire: ~高薪工作 admire high-paying jobs || ~不已 admire endlessly

25 眼红 [-紅] yǎnhóng (eye-red) <v.> covet: ~别人的钱财 covet someone else's wealth || 他对别人的成功非常~. He is envious of other people's success.

26 吃醋 [-] chīcù (eat-vinegar) <v.> be jealous (relating to love): 她喜欢~. She likes jealousy. || 她男朋友跟女同学跳了两次舞, 她觉得很~. She felt so jealous because his boyfriend danced a couple of times with his female classmates.

27 嫉妒 [-] jídù (envy-jealousy) <v.> envy: ~同事 envy a colleague

28 争风吃醋 [爭風--] zhēngfēngchīcù (fight-limelight-eat-vinegar) <idiom> fight for someone's love: 这两个女孩子为了一个男的而~. Two young girls fought with each other over a man.

29 习惯 [習慣] xíguàn (practice-custom) <v.> be used to, habit: ~早起 used to getting up early || ~下午跑步 habitually run in the afternoon || ~吃面条 habitually eat noodles

30 习以为常 [習-爲-] xíyǐwéicháng (custom-take-as-routine) <idiom> get accustomed to: 他早就对此~了. He got accustomed to this a long time ago.

31 约定俗成 [約---] yuēdìngsúchéng (agreement-settle-custom-made) <idiom> conventional, customary: ~的说法 customary way of speaking || ~的社会习惯 conventional social habits

32 上瘾 [-癮] shàngyǐn (become-addicted) <v.> become addicted: 对啤酒~ become alcoholic || 抽烟~ smoking addiction || 玩~ in the habit of playing

33 恶心 [噁, 惡-] ěxīn (disgusting-feeling) <adj.> nausea, disgust: 令人~ induce nausea || ~人 disgusting people || 觉得~ feel nauseated

34 讨厌 [討厭] tǎoyàn (incur-despise) <v.> hate: 令人~ annoying || ~广告 hate advertisement || ~说假话 hate lying

35 恨 [-] hèn (hate) <v.> hate: ~自己 hate oneself || ~战争 hate war || ~她 hate her

36 怨 [-] yuàn (grudge, blame, reproach, complain) <v.> blame, complain: ~自己 blame yourself || ~命 complain about your fate || ~父亲 complain about your father

37 抱怨 [-] bàoyuàn (complain-blame) <v.> complain: ~别人 complain about others || ~东西贵 complain that things are too expensive || ~天气不好 grumble about bad weather

38 嫌 [-] xián (suspicion, dislike) <v.> dislike, complain of: ~脏 think sth.is very dirty || ~孩子太吵feel the children are too noisy || ~声音小 complain the volume is too low

Tips:

1. 爱 (愛): Some people harshly criticize the simplified 爱 as omitting an important thing, the 心 (heart) from the traditional 愛. It should actually not be criticized since the traditional form has 夊, which means 'to linger,' but the simplified form changed it to a similar radical 友 (friend), which can indicate one aspect of love, i. e., friendship.
2. 讨厌 (討厭, tǎoyàn): It means 'to hate, disgusting,' literally. However, sometimes women can say it in a soft tone and make it mean '(you are) naughty' which carries an obvious hint of affection.
3. 西施 (Xī Shī): Xi Shi (506 BC to ?) was the first of the renowned Four Beauties of ancient China. The legend goes that when Xi Shi was washing clothes by a river, the fish saw her and all sank to the bottom of the river because Xi Shi was so beautiful and the fish felt ashamed. Xi Shi is a symbol of beauty in Chinese, so emerged the proverb 情人眼里出西施 (beauty is in the eye of the beholder.)

Exercises:

Part I: Use the given bound form here as a guide to help you think of other words with the same character. Feel free to use your dictionary when needed. Then write down the English definition of each of the words you've written.

爱 (love): 爱好 hobby, take great pleasure in

____

____

____

____

____

____

恋 (feel attached to): love, feel attached to

____

____

____

____

____

____

Part II: Matching words. There are two groups of word below. In each group, match the words in the left column with those in the right column. (Each word can be used only once.)

Formal	Informal
1.习以为常 2.讨厌 3.嫉妒 4.争风吃醋 5.溺爱子女	a.嫌 b.习惯 c.眼红 d.吃醋 e.惯

Part III: Read the following sentences and fill in each blank with the appropriate word or phrase from the options given.

1 抱怨、上瘾、羡慕

a) 水煮鱼是一道很受中国年轻人欢fl的菜, 据说经常吃会__________.
b) 在中国一些派出所 (pàichūsuǒ, police station) 警察常常___________工作太辛苦, 也得不到老百姓的理解.
c) 在毛泽东时代当兵是一份非常令人_________的工作.

2 爱屋及乌、约定俗成、爱不释手

a) 小张买了一部新手机, 他对新手机___________ _.
b) 小张虽然不喜欢狗, 但是因为女友喜欢, 所以他__________, 也开始对养狗感兴趣了.
c) 结婚前要先订婚, 这在很多国家都是___________ _的事情.

3 宠爱、情人眼里出西施、一往情深

a) 小张对女友_________, 即使女友得了癌症, 也对她不离不弃.
b) 小张是父母最__________的孩子, 为了培养他父母花了很多心血.
c) 小张的女友是个很普通的女孩子, 但是小张觉得她非常美丽、聪明, 真是____________________.

4 心动、心疼、暗恋

a) 小张偷偷___________ _那个英文系的女孩子很久了, 但是不敢去表白. 那个女孩子又漂亮又聪明, 让小张非常__________.
b) 小张父母非常__________儿子, 不仅给儿子付大学学费和生活费, 还常常给小张零花钱.

Theme 111: To indulge, to regret, to awake 沉迷, 后悔, 醒悟 (chénmí, hòuhuǐ, xǐngwù)

1 迷 [-] mí (lost, confused, addicted to) <v.> be crazy about: ~京剧 love the Peking Opera || ~上打牌 be fascinated by playing cards || ~上一位明星 be fascinated by a celebrity

2 沉迷 [-] chénmí (indulge-addicted) <v.> be absorbed in: ~于电子游戏 be absorbed in computer games || ~于网上聊天be engrossed in online chatting || ~于幻想 lost in a fantasy

3 痴迷 [癡-] chīmí (crazy about-addicted) <v.> be obsessed with: ~计算机 be obsessed with computers || 对武术 (wǔshù) ~ be obsessed with martial arts || 爱得~ love obsessively

4 迷恋 [-戀] míliàn (addicted to-feel attached to) <v.> infatuated with, indulge in: ~技术 infatuated with technology || ~画画 infatuated with painting || ~西方文化 intoxicated by Western culture

5 热衷 [熱-] rèzhōng (enthusiastic-absorbed) <v.> be fond of: ~搞关系 be fond of establishing relationships || ~于发明 obsessed with inventing || ~于工作 fond of work

6 入迷 [-] rùmí (into-addiction) <adj.> be fascinated or enchanted: 看书~了 be engrossed in a book || 学生们听这位老教授讲课听~了. The students were fascinated by the old professor's lecture. || 他玩游戏很~. He is crazy about playing video games.

7 着迷 [著-] zháomí (got-addicted) <v.> captivate, fascinate: 对电脑游戏很~ be very captivated by computer games || 令人 ~ fascinating || ~于电影 fascinated by movies

8 乐此不疲 [樂---] lècǐbùpí (enjoy-this-never-tired) <idiom> never tire of something: ~地游来游去 swim enthusiastically (never tire of it) || 对玩游戏~ never tire of playing video games

9 沉溺 [-] chénnì (sink-drown) <v.> be absorbed in: ~于痛苦之中 wallow in pain || ~于享受 partake in enjoyment || ~于喝酒 be addicted to alcohol

10 鬼迷心窍 [---竅] guǐmíxīnqiào (ghost-confuse-heart-opening) <idiom> be obsessed: 很多年轻女孩儿~, 嫁给有钱的老头儿. Many young girls seem to be bewitched by ghosts, and they are determined to marry rich old men.

11 走火入魔 [-] zǒuhuǒrùmó (go-far-enter-infatuation) <idiom> be obsessed with: 他玩电脑游戏 ~了. He became addicted to computer games

12 沉醉 [-] chénzuì (heavily-drunk) <v.> become intoxicated: ~于爱河 get drunk on love || ~于赌博 (dǔbó) intoxicated with gambling || ~在迷人的乐声中 intoxicated with enchanting music

13 纳闷 [納悶] nàmèn (soaked-depressed) <adj.> puzzled: 感到~ feel puzzled || 心里~ puzzled at heart

14 疑惑 [-] yíhuò (doubt-puzzled) <adj.> unconvinced, uncertain: 感到~ feel uncertain || ~不解 be undecided, have doubts || ~地说say uncertainly

15 百思不解 [-] bǎisībùjiě (hundred-think-not-solved) <idiom> puzzled despite deep thought: 令人~ deeply perplexing

16 后悔 [後-] hòuhuǐ (later-regret) <v.> regret: ~一辈子 regret your whole life || 深深~ deeply regret || ~发脾气 regret getting angry

17 忏悔 [懺-] chànhuǐ (repent-regret) <v.> repent, confess: 向上帝~ confess to God

18 悔改 [-] huǐgǎi (regret-change) <v.> mend your ways: 不思~ never think to mend your ways || 死不~ never repent

19 反悔 [-] fǎnhuǐ (reverse-regret) <v.> go back on your word: 永不~ never go back on your word

20 变卦 [變-] biànguà (change-diagram) <v.> break an agreement: 临时~ break an agreement at the last minute

21 觉悟 [覺-] juéwù (conscious-awake) <v./n.> understand, aware of: ~高 highly aware of || 有/没有~ have/lack understanding || 提高~ raise awareness
22 醒悟 [-] xǐngwù (wake-awake) <v.> come to realize: 猛然 (měngrán) ~ abruptly see the truth || 突然~ naturally come to realize || 彻底~ make a complete realization
23 反省 [-] fǎnxǐng (back-aware) <v.> look inwards, reflect: 深刻~ deep introspection || 自我~ self-reflection || 仔细~ careful reflection
24 反思 [-] fǎnsī (back-think) <v.> rethink, reconsider: ~失败原因 re-assess the cause of failure || 进行~ be rethinking

Tips:

1 Forms of obsession, *鬼 (guǐ), *迷 (mí), *痴 (chī), *狂 (kuáng): (1) *鬼: 鬼 itself means 'ghost' and understandably '*鬼' has a negative connotation, for example, 烟鬼 (heavy smoker,) 酒鬼 (drunkard) and 色鬼 (satyr.) (2) *迷: 迷 means 'addict, fan,' for example, 球迷 (ball game fan,) 歌迷 (music fan,) 戏迷 (theater fan,) 棋迷 (chess fan) and 财迷 (money grubber.) (3) *痴: 痴 means 'to be crazy about,' for example, 花痴 (anthomaniac, love-struck fool, obsessive love) and 情痴 (a person infatuated in love.) (4) *狂: 狂 means 'mad,' for example, 杀人狂 (homicidal maniac,) 色情狂 (sex maniac) and 暴露狂 (bàolùkuáng.) Memorize the following two idioms 鬼迷心窍 (guǐmí xīnqiào, to be possessed by a ghost, to be obsessed) and 如痴如狂 (with an air almost of idiocy), in which the four suffixes are imbedded.
2 后悔: People often 后悔 (regret), so many people say they hope there is 后悔药 (spilt milk, to undo.) If you are very regretful, you '悔得肠子 (chángzi, intestines) 都青 (green) 了.'
3 悟 (wù): 悟 means 'awake' and the Buddhist enlightenment is '觉悟' (juéwù.) In the most famous Chinese mythological novel 西游记 (*Journey to the West*) the three disciples are 孙悟空 (Sūn Wùkōng, the Monkey King,) 猪悟能 (Zhū Wùnéng, and more commonly known as Zhū Bājiè, 猪八戒, Pigsy) and 沙悟净 (Shā Wùjìng, Sand,) with a 悟 in each name.

Exercises:

Part I: Use the given bound form here as a guide to help you think of other words with the same character. Feel free to use your dictionary when needed. Then write down the English definition of each of the words you've written.

迷 *(be crazy about):* 迷人 *charming*	悔 *(regret)* 后悔*: regret*
________________	________________
________________	________________
________________	________________
________________	________________

Part II: Read the following words and then answer the following questions in Chinese.

百思不解、感到疑惑、纳闷、对......走火入魔、对......鬼迷心窍、沉迷于、乐此不疲、反悔、变卦、反省、反思、入迷、着迷

1 "老王对儿子的事情很纳闷," 这里的"纳闷"跟上面那两个词或短语的意思差不多?

---

2 "小王沉迷于电脑游戏"这里的"沉迷于"跟上面那两个词或短语的意思差不多?

---

3 "变卦"的书面语是上面哪个词?

---

4 "反省"跟上面哪个词的意思差不多?

---

5 请把这句话翻译成中文: Everbody listened to his story with rapt attention.

---

6 请把这句话翻译成中文: Little Wang is very captivated by computer games.

Theme 112: Attention, neglect 关注, 忽视 (guānzhù, hūshì)

1 关心 [關-] guānxīn (concern-heart) <v.> care for, have interest in: ~家人 care for family || ~我们 care for us || ~这个问题 be interested in this issue
2 关注 [關-] guānzhù (concern-focus) <v.> pay attention to, follow with interest: ~这个女孩 pay attention to this girl || 引起~ cause interest || 特别~ special attention
3 留心 [-] liúxīn (careful-heart) <v.> take care: ~细节 take care with details || ~观察 (guānchá) observe carefully || 处处~ always be careful
4 留意 [-] liúyì (careful-mind) <v.> take note of: ~车号 take note of the car's license plate || ~来往车辆 take note of the coming and going cars
5 在乎 [-] zàihū (attend-*suffix*) <v.> care about: ~工作 care about work || ~大小 care about size || ~输赢 (shūyíng) care about winning or losing
6 在意 [-] zàiyì (attend-mind) <v.> mind, care about: 毫不~ not mind at all || ~穿着 care about clothing || ~听 listen and take to heart
7 小心 [-] xiǎoxīn (cautious-heart) <v.> be careful: ~钱包 be careful with one's wallet || 千万~ take the utmost care || 处处~ always careful
8 重视 [-視] zhòngshì (stress-attention) <v.> attach importance to: ~家庭 value family || 高度~ think very highly of || 引起~ cause attention
9 看重 [-] kànzhòng (see-high) <v.> value, see as important: ~经验 value experience || ~学历 value education || ~年龄 value age

10 器重 [-] qìzhòng (value-high) <v.> regard highly: 受到~ be regarded highly

11 讲究 [講-] jiǎngjīu (attend-be particular) <v.> pay particular attention to: ~吃穿 pay much attention to one's food and clothing || ~卫生 pay much attention to hygiene || ~方法 pay much attention to a method

12 赏识 [賞識] shǎngshí (appreciate-know) <v.> appreciate: 得到~ receive appreciation || ~才华 appreciate talent

13 注意 [-] zhùyì (concentrate-attention) <v.> pay attention to: ~身体 pay attention to your body || ~卫生 pay attention to hygiene || ~方法 take note of a method

14 注重 [-] zhùzhòng (concentrate-value) <v.> emphasize, attach importance to: ~家庭 attach importance to family || ~实用 value function || ~自由 emphasize freedom

15 当心 [當-] dāngxīn (middle-heart) <v.> take care: ~摩托车. Look out for motorcycles. || ~身体 be careful with your body || ~感冒. Beware of catching a cold.

16 警惕 [-] jǐngtì (alert-cautious) <v.> be vigilant: 提高~ increase vigilance || 高度~ highly vigilant || ~黑熊. Watch out for black bears.

17 珍惜 [-] zhēnxī (treasure-cherish) <v.> treasure, value: ~时间 value your time || ~机会 treasure opportunity || ~生命. Treasure life.

18 爱护 [愛護] àihù (love-protect) <v.> love and protect: ~孩子 cherish children || ~家庭 cherish family || ~身体. Take care of your health.

19 不顾 [-顧] bùgù (not-regard) <v.> regardless of: ~别人 regardless of others || ~疲劳 (píláo) in spite of fatigue || ~大局, 安危 regardless of the situation, safety

20 满不在乎 [滿---] mǎnbùzàihū (fully-not-care) <v.> not at all concerned: ~地说 speak recklessly || ~的态度 an unperturbed attitude || 对一切 ~ unconcerned about everything

21 不在乎 [-] bùzàihū (not-care) <v.> not to care: ~钱 don't care about money || ~地笑 laugh without caring || 一点~ don't care at all

22 忽略 [-] hūlüè (overlook-neglect) <v.> overlook, ignore: ~行动 neglect action || ~外表 overlook appearances || ~年龄差距 ignore an age gap

23 忽视 [-視] hūshì (neglect-regard) <v.> neglect: ~教育 neglect education || ~年龄 ignore age || ~劳动 ignore labor

24 大意 [-] dàyì (light-minded) <v.> be careless: 不可~ cannot be careless

25 轻视 [輕視] qīngshì (light-regard) <v.> look down on, belittle: ~妇女 look down on women || ~知识 belittle knowledge || ~教师 look down on teachers

26 冷淡 [-] lěngdàn (cold-indifferent) <v.> treat coldly: 态度~ a cold attitude || 性~ frigid, frigidity || 脸色~ a cold expression || 对他~ give him the cold shoulder

27 无所谓 [無--] wúsuǒwèi (cannot say) <v.> be indifferent: ~地说 indifferently say || ~好坏 not care about good or bad || ~的态度 an indifferent attitude

28 无视 [無視] wúshì (not-regard) <v.> disregard, ignore: ~观众 ignore the audience || ~事实 disregard reality || ~法律 ignore the law

29 顾不上 [顧--] gùbùshàng (regard-not-able) <v.> cannot manage: ~吃饭 unable to eat food || ~家 can't take care of the house || ~回答 unable to answer

30 看不起 [-] kànbùqǐ (look-not-up) <v.> scorn: ~自己 scorn yourself || ~别人 look down on others

31 鄙视 [-視] bǐshì (despise-look) <v.> disdain, look down on: ~ 劳动 look down on physical labor || ~乡下 disdain the countryside

32 蔑视 [-視] mièshì (disdain-look) <v.> scorn, despise: ~法律 (fǎlǜ) scorn the law || ~经典 despise the classics || ~女人 despise women

33 看得起 [-] kàndéqǐ (look-*auxiliary*-up) <v.> think highly of: ~自己 think highly of yourself || ~别人 think highly of others || ~你们 think highly of you guys

34 可怜 [-] kělián (worth-pity) <v.> pity: ~这个老人 pity this old person || ~那个小家伙 pity that naughty little kid

35 可惜 [-] kěxī (worth-cherish) <v.> what a pity: ~你没看到. What a pity you didn't see it. || ~没有机会 it is a pity to not have an opportunity || ~晚了 a pity that something is late

36 理 [-] lǐ (carve jade, administer, pay attention to) <v.> pay attention to: ~人 pay attention to people || 不~他 ignore him || 别~她. Don't pay attention to her.

37 舍不得 [捨--] shèbùdé (abandon-not-able) <v.> be unwilling to: ~走 unwilling to leave || ~花钱 unwilling to pay money

38 同情 [-] tóngqíng (same-feeling) <v.> sympathize with: ~她的遭遇 show sympathy for her misfortune || 令人~ induce sympathy

39 原谅 [-諒] yuánliàng (pardon-excuse) <v.> excuse: ~这个护士 excuse this nurse || 请 ~ please excuse me || 多多~ excuse greatly

40 专心 [專-] zhuānxīn (concentrate-heart) <adj.> concentrate: ~画画 concentrate on painting || 工作 ~ work with great concentration || ~吃饭 concentrate on eating

Tips:

1 *视: In this unit the '视' in the following words means 'to regard, to look upon,' for example: 重视 (to attach importance to,) 轻视 (to look down upon,) 忽视 (to neglect,) 无视 (to disregard,) 鄙视 (to despise) and 蔑视 (to disdain.)

2 可*: 可 means 'worth' in '可*' structure, for example, 可怜 (pitiful) and 可惜 (what a pity!)

3 鄙视链 (chain of contempt): In an old country like China where social hierarchy was (or is) apparent, people and things were often ranked. The people of a higher rank would usually look down upon those of a lower rank, and this is called 鄙视链 (the chain of contempt). For example, people who play the cello (大提琴, dàtíqín) would despise those who play the violin, and so on. Here is a long chain: 大提琴 (cello) > 小提琴 (violin) > 钢琴 (piano) > 古琴 (seven-stringed Chinese zither) > 古筝 (Chinese zither) > 吉他 (guitar) > 笛子 (flute) > 口琴 (harmonica).

4 珍惜: It means 'to cherish.' A long monologue on 珍惜 in a 1995 movie *A Chinese Odyssey Part Two: Cinderella* (大话西游2) touched hundreds of millions of people's heartstrings: 曾经有一段真挚的爱情摆在我眼前, 我没有去珍惜, 等到失去了才后悔莫及, 尘世间最痛苦的事莫过于此, 如果上天能给我一个再来一次的机会, 我希望能对那个女孩说我爱你, 如果非要给这爱加一个期限的话, 我希望是一万年 (There was once a true love

in front of me, but I did not cherish it and cannot be more regretful after having lost it. Nothing in the world can be more painful than this. If the heavens could give me only one more chance, I want to say 'I love you' to that girl. If a time limit had to be imposed on this love, I hope it is 10,000 years.)

Exercises:

Part I: Write an antonym for each word in the table. You can refer to the given words.

忽视、轻视、冷淡、看不起、舍不得、尊重

关心vs.	重视vs.	热情vs.
看得起vs.	舍得vs.	鄙视vs.

Part II: Put the words with similar meanings in the same table.

看不起、蔑视、不在乎、在乎、留心、留意、同情别人、大意

鄙视:
满不在乎:
在意:
可怜别人:
粗心:

Part III: Read the following sentences and fill in each blank with the appropriate word or phrase from the options given.

1 爱护、讲究、赏识

a) 广东人对早餐很_______, 广东早茶在全国都非常有名.
b) 现在的学生一般都不太_______自己的眼睛, 只要一有时间就看手机、看电脑.
c) 小张工作特别努力认真, 因此得到了老板的_______, 被提升为部门经理.

2 顾不上、珍惜、无所谓

a) 我父母常常告诉我要_______时间, 多做有意义的事情.
b) 我父母常常对我说上不上名牌大学________, 重要的是要自强、自立、热爱生活.
c) 有些父母因为工作忙, _________关注孩子的心理问题.

3 关注、关心、器重、看重

a) 最近美国媒体特别_______黑人跟警察的冲突问题.
b) 大公司一般很________员工的能力, 而不是学历.
c) 他工作能力强, 领导非常________他, 给他安排了很多重要的工作.
d) 这家公司的领导很________员工的生活问题, 经常帮准员工解决生活上的困难.

Theme 113: To hesitate, to be determined 犹豫, 决心 (yóuyù, juéxīn)

1 决心 [決-] juéxīn (decide-mind) <v.> make up your mind: ~帮助他. Make up your mind to help him. || ~弄明白 determined to gain understanding || ~改变. Make up your mind to change.
2 决定 [決-] juédìng (decide-determine) <v.> decide: ~改学小提琴 decide to study the violin || ~先找个地方休息 decide to first look for a place to rest
3 奋斗 [奮鬥] fèndòu (strive-fight) <v.> struggle, strive: 努力~ work hard || 长期~ long-term struggle || 共同~ jointly struggle
4 认定 [認-] rèndìng (believe-firm) <v.> firmly believe: ~这块青石是宝石 decide that this piece of limestone is a gem || ~是他写的 believe that he wrote it || ~一个方向 set your mind in a direction
5 发誓 [發-] fāshì (make-swear) <v.> vow: 对天~ vow to heaven || ~戒烟 (jièyān) vow to quit smoking || ~不来了 swear not to come
6 立志 [-] lìzhì (set-aspiration) <v.> be determined: ~当画家 be determined to become a painter || ~学医 be determined to study medicine
7 下狠心 [-] xiàhěnxīn (make-cruel-hearted) <v.> decide with determination: ~让孩子住校 decide to make the child live at school || ~治理污染 (wūrǎn) decide to control pollution || ~戒酒 decide to quit alcohol

8 犹豫 [猶-] yóuyù (shilly-shally) <v./adj.> hesitate, be irresolute: ~很久 hesitate for a long time || 态度~ a hesitant attitude || 心情~ feel hesitant
9 迟疑 [遲-] chíyí (hesitate-dubious) <v./adj.> hesitate: ~了一会 hesitate for a moment || ~地说 hesitantly say || 有点 ~ a little bit hesitant
10 动摇 [動搖] dòngyáo (move-shake) <v.> waver, shake: ~信仰 waver in your faith || ~信心 shake your confidence || 地位~ shake in one's position
11 花心 [-] huāxīn (unfaithful-heart) <adj.> fickle in love affairs, unfaithful: ~男人 man who falls in love easily, unfaithful man
12 三心二意 [-] sānxīn'èryì (three-heart-two-mind) <idiom> undecided, half-hearted: 他做练习的时候~的. He is half-hearted when he practices.

Tips:

1 花: Its original and the main contemporary meaning is 'flower', which is usually positive, however, in the following words, especially when duplicated, 花 has a negative connotation: 花心, 花花世界 (world of sensual pleasures,) 花花公子 (playboy,) 花花太岁 (ancient Chinese playboy) and 花花肠子 (flower-flower-intestine, scheme.) We can say '在这个花花世界, 中国的花花太岁和外国的花花公子都是花心, 对女人都有花花肠子,' which requires no further explanation as long as you add up the individual meanings.
2 立志: It means 'to be determined to' or 'to set one's aspiration.' The ancient Chinese said '君子立长志, 小人常立志, ' which means 'noblemen set long term goals, whereas petty persons often set goals,' and 立长志 and 常立志 therefore contrast.
3 发誓 (fāshì): It means 'to swear, to vow.' We all swear, but the most heart-breaking vows in the whole of Chinese history were made by 窦娥 (竇娥,

Dòu É,) a character in Guan Hanqing's famous drama *Dou E Yuan* (*Injustice to Dou E*, 1291): 血溅白练 (xuě jiàn bái liàn, blood will fly onto her white clothes but not drip onto the ground after she was beheaded), 六月飞雪 (there comes a heavy snow to cover her dead body in Chuzhou of southern China in the lunar month of June) and 大旱 (hàn) 三年 (there will be a drought in Chouzhou, a city next to the fourth largest freshwater lake in China.) All three events happened after Dou E's death.

Exercises:

Part II: Multiple Choice. Make sure to choose the most appropriate answer.

1 这个孩子做什么事情都______, 非常不专心.

A. 动摇 B. 花心 C. 三心二意

2 这个孩子最近不仅学习不努力, 还常常跟同学打架, 因此他父母______要好好管教他.

A. 迟疑 B. 犹豫 C. 下狠心

3 这个孩子从小就_______要当科学家.

A. 立志 B. 发誓 C. 动摇

4 这部中国电视剧讲的是几个外地大学生毕业后在北京_______, 最后事业有成的故事.

A. 奋斗 B. 决定 C. 决心

5 他博士毕业以后_________留在美国工作, 但是因为父母非常反对, 现在他有些_______了.

A. 认定、动摇 B. 决定、动摇 C. 决心、花心

6 下面哪组词里面的"花"意思不同

A. 花心、花花公子 B. 花花肠子、花花太岁 C. 鲜花、花花公子

7 "Noblemen set a long term goal whereas the petty persons often set goals." 这句话的中文意思是

A. 君子立志: 六月飞雪, 三年大旱

B. 君子立长志, 小人常立志

C. 小人立志: 血溅白练

Theme 114: To believe, to doubt, to think 相信, 怀疑, 思考 (xiāngxìn, huáiyí, sīkǎo)

1 相信 [-] xiāngxìn (mutual-trust) <v.> trust: ~自己 trust yourself || ~科学 trust science || 很难~ difficult to trust

2 信 [-] xìn (honest, believe, trust) <v.> believe: ~自己 believe in yourself || ~上帝 believe in god || ~佛教 (Fójiào) believe in Buddhism

3 信任 [-] xìnrèn (trust-believe) <v.> have confidence in: 互相~ have confidence in each other || ~群众trust the masses || 失去~ lose trust

4 自信 [-] zìxìn (self-confident) <v./n.> self-confidence: 充满~ full of self-confidence || ~地说 self-confidently say || 有~ have self-confidence

5 坚信 [堅-] jiānxìn (firmly-believe) <v.> firmly believe: ~不疑 be convinced || ~科学真理 firmly believe in scientific truth

6 当真 [當-] dàngzhēn (take-true) <v.> take seriously: 把这事~ take this thing seriously || 说话~ speak seriously

7 认真 [認-] rènzhēn (believe-true) <v.> serious: 他太~了！ He is too serious!

8 信以为真 [--為-] xìnyǐwéizhēn (believe-with-be-true) <idiom> take as true: 大家都~. Everybody took it as the truth.

9 信仰 [-] xìnyǎng (believe-admire) <v.> believe in: ~上帝 believe in god || ~伟人 have faith in great people || ~佛教 believe in Buddhism

10 迷信 [-] míxìn (superstitious-faith) <v./n.> blind faith, superstition: ~书本 blind faith in books || ~权威, 经验 (quánwēi, jīngyàn) blind faith in authority, experience || 宗教 (zōngjiào) ~ religious superstition

11 信奉 [-] xìnfèng (believe-worship) <v.> believe in: ~新教 be a Protestant || ~共产主义follow communism || ~个人主义prescribe to individualism

12 怀疑 [懷-] huáiyí (heart-doubt) <v.> doubt: ~自己的耳朵 doubt your own ears || ~事实 doubt the truth || 产生~ produce doubt

13 猜疑 [-] cāiyí (suspicious-doubt) <v.> have misgivings: 彼此~ be suspicious of each other || 互相~ mutually suspicious

14 疑心 [-] yíxīn (dubious-heart) <n/v..> suspect, suspicion: 起 ~ become suspicious || ~他根本没看 suspect he hadn't seen it at all

15 多心 [-] duōxīn (more-mind) <v.> sensitive, paranoid: 你太~了！ You are too sensitive! || 别~！ Don't be so paranoid!

16 多疑 [-] duōyí (more-dubious) <v.> skeptical: 别~！ Don't be so skeptical!

17 疑神疑鬼 [-] yíshényíguǐ (suspicious-god-suspicious-ghost) <idiom> suspect everyone (even doubt your own shadow): 老是~ always suspicious of everything

18 半信半疑 [-] bànxìnbànyí (half-trust-half-dubious) <idiom> not quite convinced (half believe, half doubt): ~地问 ask skeptically

19 想 [-] xiǎng (think, miss) <v.> think: ~问题 think about an issue || ~办法 think of a solution || 你在~什么? What are you thinking about?

20 考虑 [-慮] kǎolǜ (consider-think over) <v.> consider: ~问题 consider an issue || ~别人 consider other people || 反复~ repeatedly consider

21 设想 [設-] shèxiǎng (assume-think) <v./n.> conceive, envision: ~两个方案 have consideration for two plans || 不堪~ inconceivable || 初步~ tentative idea

22 思考 [-] sīkǎo (think-consider) <v.> ponder: ~问题 ponder an issue || 自由~ freely ponder || ~历史 reflect on history

23 动脑子 [動腦-] dòngnǎozi (use-mind) <v.> move your mind, consider: 肯~ willing to think

24 沉思 [-] chénsī (deeply-think) <v.> be lost in thought: ~片刻 be lost in thought for a moment || 低头~ bow your head in meditation

25 设法 [設-] shèfǎ (plot-way) <v.> try to find a way: ~找到他 try to find him || ~借钱 try to borrow money
26 着想 [著-] zhuóxiǎng (adhere to-think) <v.> consider other people's needs, give thought to others: 为职工~ consider the workers' needs || 从一方面~ consider in one respect
27 假设 [-設] jiǎshè (suppose-assume) <v.> suppose, assume: ~明天天气忽然变冷, 我也有足够的衣服. Even if tomorrow's weather is abruptly cold, I still have adequate clothing. || ~我没时间去, 你就帮我将礼物送给她. Supposing I have no time to go, you can help me send her a present.
28 幻想 [-] huànxiǎng (fantasy-think) <v./n.> delusion, imagine, dream: 不切实际的 ~ fanciful ideas || 抱有~ cherish illusions || ~登上火星 dream of reaching Mars
29 想象 [-] xiǎngxiàng (think-imagine) <v./n.> imagine: 难以~ difficult to imagine || ~当时的情景 imagine the scene at that time || 浪漫 (làngmàn) 的, 丰富的~ romantic, rich imagination
30 做梦 [-夢] zuòmèng (to dream-dream) <separable word> dream, fantasy: 别~了 don't entertain such fantasies || ~也没想到 never even dreamed of || ~娶媳妇 dream of marrying a younger woman
31 联想 [聯-] liánxiǎng (associate-think) <v.> associate with: 引起~ cause association || 令人~ associated || 说起医生, 小孩就会联想到 ~打针. Children always associate the doctor with injections.

Tips:

1 心 and 'to think': Ancient Chinese believed that the organ for 'thinking' and other psychological activities was the heart (心,) therefore all characters in this theme are with the same radical '心, 忄,' for example, 思 (to ponder,) 想 (to think,) 感 (to feel,) 情 (emotion,) 爱 (愛, love,) and 恨 (hate).
2 假, 设, 想: All mean 'to suppose,' 'to assume' or 'to think,' and their combinations, 假设, 假想, 设想 have almost the same meaning.
3 思, 考, 虑: All mean 'to consider' or 'to think over,' and their combinations, 思考, 思虑, 考虑 have almost the same meaning.
4 大胆假设, 小心求证 (dàdǎn jiǎshè, xiǎoxīn qiúzhèng): It means 'to bring up a hypothesis boldly but to prove it carefully,' a research method which was put forward by a great modern scholar 胡适 (胡適, Hú Shì, 1891–1962) in 1950s.
5 联想 and Lenovo: It is hard for many people to associate the Chinese computer brand '联想' with the English computer brand 'Lenovo.' They are the same brand.
6 Suspicious (多疑, duōyí): Foxes (狐狸, húli) are cunning and suspicious, therefore there is a word 狐疑 (húyí, suspicious.) 曹操 (Cáo Cāo, 155–220,) a Chinese warlord and politician, is considered to be the most suspicious person in the history of China.

Exercises:

Part I: Use the given bound form here as a guide to help you think of other words with the same character. Feel free to use your dictionary when needed. Then write down the English definition of each of the words you've written.

信 *(believe, trust):* 相信 *believe*

____

____

____

____

疑 *(doubt):* 怀疑 *doubt*

____

____

____

____

想 *(think):* 想问题 *think about an issue*

____

____

____

____

Part II: Multiple Choice. Make sure to choose the most appropriate answer.

1 他_______也没有想到自己会买彩票中大奖.

A. 幻想 B. 想象 C. 做梦

2 小王总喜欢做白日梦, 他常常_______自己买彩票中了一千万, 然后大把大把地花钱.

A. 设想 B. 着想 C. 设法

3 "他喜欢动脑子想问题," 这句话的意思是

A. 他喜欢思考 B. 他喜欢运动头部 C. 他喜欢脑子动来动去

4 她是一个自私的人, 不管做什么事情总是先_______自己的得失.

A. 假设 B. 考虑 C. 沉思

5 她很怕担任总经理的丈夫跟公司其他女同事谈恋爱, 因此对丈夫总是_______的.

A. 怀疑 B. 疑神疑鬼 C. 信以为真

6 据说中国大陆_______基督教的人越来越多.

A. 自信 B. 信仰 C. 相信

7 一百多年前德国的马克思_______资本主义一定会灭亡，但实际上这个预言还没有实现.

A. 迷信 B. 信奉 C. 坚信

8 这个卖车的推销员说丰田车是世界上质量最好的车，听他说得头头是道, 所以我_______.

A. 信以为真 B. 多心 C. 多疑

Theme 115: To agree, to object, to endure 赞成, 反对, 忍受 (zànchéng, fǎnduì, rěnshòu)

1 认可 [認-] rènkě (admit-approve) <v.> approve: ~他的观点approve his view || 公开~ approve in public || 获得/得到~ abstain/get someone's acceptance or approval

2 同意 [-] tóngyì (agree-opinion) <v.> agree: ~她的意见agree with her opinion || ~他的请求agree her request || ~这个办法agree for this way

3 服 [-] fú (obey, convince) <v.> be convinced, convince: 我~了 I am convinced || ~管教follow someone's discipline || 以理 ~人convince the public

4 公认 [-認] gōngrèn (generally-recognized) <v.> generally acknowledge, be recognized: 这是~最好的学校. This is the best school recognized by all. || ~的看法 recognized view || 一致~ consistent recognition

5 认 [認] rèn (recognize, admit) <v.> know, admit, recognize: ~输 admit defeat || ~错 admit a fault, make an apology || ~帐 acknowledge a debt, admit what one has said or done

6 认同 [認-] rèntóng (recognize-agree) <v.> agree with: 自我~ agree with yourself || 身份~ agree with identity || 获得/得到~ get agreement

7 拥护 [擁護] yōnghù (support-defend) <v.> support: 热烈 ~ warmly support || ~和平support peace || 受到/得到 ~ receive support

8 赞成 [贊-] zànchéng (praise-help to achieve) <v.> be in favor of: ~这种说法 in favor of this view || ~他的看法in favor of his opinion || 一致 ~ consistently in favor of

9 倾向 [傾-] qīngxiàng (incline-toward) <v.> tend, tendency: ~于这种看法 tend to his opinion || ~于第三种意见tend to the third opinion || 政治~ political inclination

10 尊敬 [-] zūnjìng (honor-respect) <v.> respect: ~老人 respect the aged || 受人~ be respected || 令人/使人~ cause sb. to respect

11 尊重 [-] zūnzhòng (respect-value) <v.> respect, value, esteem: 互相~ respect each other || ~知识产权 respect intellectual property rights || ~少数民族的风俗习惯 respect the habits and customs of ethnic groups

12 钦佩 [欽-] qīnpèi (admire-express admiration) <v.> admire, respect sb. greatly: ~他的记忆力 admire his memory || ~你的勇气 admire his bravery || 值得~ worth the admiration

13 敬仰 [-] jìngyǎng (respect-admire) <v.> highly esteemed: 对他十分~ extremely respect him || 受到~ be highly esteemed by sb.

14 仰慕 [-] yǎngmù (admire-yearn) <v.> admire, look up to: ~自然admire nature || ~他的才华admire his talent

15 崇拜 [-] chóngbài (revere-worship) <v./n.> worship, adore, adoration: 他很~父亲. He worships his father. || ~电影明星 adore movie stars

16 崇尚 [-] chóngshàng (advocate-pay attention to) <v.> advocate: ~自然 advocate for nature || ~古典芭蕾advocate for classical ballet || ~节约 advocate for saving

17 敬佩 [-] jìngpèi (respect-express admiration) <v.> admire: ~老人的性格 admire old people personalities' || ~他的为人 admire himself

18 佩服 [-] pèifú (admire-convinced) <v.> admire: ~他的勇气admire his courage || ~这位作家admire this family || ~她的医术admire her medical practice

19 服气 [-氣] fúqì (convinced-heart) <v.> be convinced: 心里不大~ not too convinced || 大家听了对他更加~ everyone convinced him more

20 不服 [-] bùfú (not-convinced) <v.> disagree: ~ 管理disagree management || ~指挥 disagree command || ~判决 (pànjué) disagree with a judgment

21 信服 [-] xìnfú (believe-convinced) <v.> convince: 使观众~ convince the audience || ~这位演讲者convince the speaker

22 服输 [-輸] fúshū (admit-defeat) <v.> admit (or acknowledge) defeat: 不肯~ refuse to admit defeat || 心里不~ not admit defeat in the heart

23 服软 [-軟] fúruǎn (admit-mistake) <v.> admit defeat, acknowledge a mistake: 不服软~ stubbornly refused to admit defeat

24 反对 [-對] fǎnduì (oppose-to) <v.> oppose: ~他们结婚 oppose their marriage || 强烈~ strong opposition || ~意见 strong opinion

25 不以为然 [--為-] bùyǐwéirán (not-take-as-right) <idiom> disagree: ~地说 disagree with what was said

26 反腐 [-] fǎnfǔ (anti – corruption) <v.> combat corruption: ~工作 anti-corruption work || ~倡廉combat corruption and maintain a clean government

27 反贪 [-貪] fǎntān (anti – embezzle) <v.> anti-corruption, fight corruption: 开展 ~ 斗争 launch a struggle against corruption

28 反战 [-戰] fǎnzhàn (anti – war) <v.> anti-war: ~力量 forces against war || ~情绪 emotion against war || ~抗议 anti-war protest

29 忍 [-] rěn (endure, tolerate) <v.> endure: ~着痛 bearing pain || ~下这口气 endure under the tone || ~着眼泪 endure tears

30 忍受 [-] rěnshòu (endure-bear) <v.> endure: ~痛苦 endure pain || ~寒冷 endure cold || ~饥饿 endure hunger

31 忍不住 [-] rěnbùzhù (endure-not-able) <v.> could not help: ~笑了 could not help laughing || ~泪水 could not help crying || ~问 could not help but ask

32 受不了 [-] shòubùliǎo (bear-not-able) <v.> cannot stand: 热得~ can't stand the heat || ~污染can't stand the pollution || ~她的小姐脾气 (píqi) cannot stand her self-willed temper

33 不禁 [-] bùjīn (not able to-restrain) <adv.> cannot help: ~大笑起来 cannot help laughing || ~大吃一惊 can't help but be surprised

34 舍得 [捨-] shědé (abandon-able to) <v.> be willing to: ~下功夫be willing to work hard || ~放弃 be willing to give up || ~花钱willing to spend money

35 克服 [-] kèfú (conquer-overcome) <v.> get over: ~弱点 get over weakness || ~困难 get over difficulties || ~缺点 to get over disadvantages

Tips:

1 尊敬 vs. 尊重: Both mean 'to respect,' but the object of 尊敬 must be a person who is senior to the speaker or of higher social status. As for the object of 尊重, it could be a person who is senior to the speaker or of higher social status, an opinion, a view or a decision of a person, either senior or junior to the speaker. For example, in Chinese mindset, a teacher should not 尊敬 or 尊重 his students, however, he may 尊重 his students' decision.
2 尊, 敬, 重: All mean 'to respect' and their combinations, 尊敬, 尊重, 敬重 have almost the same meaning.
3 敬, 仰, 慕: All mean 'to respect, to admire' and their combinations, 敬仰, 敬慕, 仰慕 have almost the same meaning.

Exercises:

Part I: Use the given bound form here as a guide to help you think of other words with the same character. Feel free to use your dictionary when needed. Then write down the English definition of each of the words you've written.

忍 (bear, endure): 忍受 endure

____

____

____

____

服 (admit, obey, be convinced): 服输 admit defeat

____

____

____

____

____

反 (oppose, combat): 反对 oppose

____

____

____

____

Part II: Read the following sentences and fill in each blank with the appropriate word or phrase from the options given.

1 赞成、同意、拥护

a) 一般来说, 中国的年轻人想要结婚都得先问问父母是否________.
b) 美国的基督徒一般都不__________计划生育和堕胎 (duòtāi, abortion).
c) 这位总统得到了大多数老百姓的尊敬和__________.

2 尊敬、倾向、尊重

a) 白女士的丈夫有家庭暴力__________, 经常对她喊叫, 并向她扔东西, 因此白女士决定跟丈夫离婚.
b) 美国是一个非常________知识产权的国家.
c) 这个学校的学生都非常__________老师.

3 崇拜、崇尚、敬佩

a) 有人批评毛泽东搞个人________, 把自己当成神让老百姓来信仰.
b) 中国人在历史上非常________读书, 这主要是因为科举考试制度可以让读书人做官.
c) 我上大学时候的历史教授是我最_________的人, 因为他学识丰富, 为人正直, 甘于清贫做学术.

4 信服、服输、服气

a) 小时候我父母批评我的时候我总是觉得不________.
b) 我订购的电脑晚到了十天, 但是那家公司的客服人员给我作出了令人________的解释.
c) 一个想要成功就得有坚强的决心和不________的精神, 无论失败多少次也会有勇气重新开始.

5 舍得、不禁、克服

a) 小白特别喜欢上淘宝网购物, 看到喜欢的东西就_______想买下来.
b) 小白父母很________在我学习上花钱, 例如给我买书, 请家教什么的一花就是几千块钱.
c) 在中国农村孩子想上名牌大学, 需要__________很多人无法想象的困难.

Theme 116: To know, to estimate 了解, 估计 (liǎojiě, gūjì)

1 看来 [-來] kànlái (look-like) <v.> seem, appear, look as if (or though): 在我~ in my opinion, as I see it || 由此~ judging from this, in view of this || ~有道理. It seems justified.
2 揣测 [-測] chuǎicè (estimate-infer) <v.> speculate: ~她的来意 guess why she comes here || ~她的心理guess her feelings
3 推断 [-斷] tuīduàn (infer-judge) <v./n.> speculate: ~准确 presumably accurate || ~可能性speculate on the possibility

4 推理 [-] tuīlǐ (infer-reason) <v./n.> infer, reasoning: 用~方法 by inference || ~小说reasoning novels || 培养~能力 develop one's reasoning capacity
5 看起来 [--來] kànqǐlái (seem-like) <v.> It seems like: ~很好 it seems good || ~瘦小it seems small || ~不同. It does seem the same.
6 估计 [-計] gūjì (evaluate-calculate) <v.> estimate: 据他~ according to his estimates || 难以~ be difficult to estimate || ~时间estimated time
7 猜 [-] cāi (guess) <v.> guess: ~谜语 (míyǔ) riddles || ~不透 cannot guess || ~得不错guess very well
8 猜测 [-測] cāicè (guess-infer) <v.> guess: 难以~. It is difficult to guess. || ~她们的关系guess their relationship
9 猜想 [-] cāixiǎng (guess-think) <v.> guess: 我~他不会来了. I guess he will not come.

10 预测 [預測] yùcè (in advance-infer) <v./n.> prediction, predict: ~未来fortune telling || 难以~ Unpredictable || ~天气prediction of weather
11 预计 [預計] yùjì (in advance-calculate) <v.> expected: ~明年完成Is expected to be completed next year || ~价格estimated price || ~收入expected income
12 预料 [預-] yùliào (in advance-predict) <v.> expected: 无法~ unpredictable || 难以~ hard to predict || ~不到not expected
13 预期 [預-] yùqī (in advance-expect) <v.> expected: ~效果 expected result || ~目的expected purpose || ~结果expected outcome
14 预言 [預-] yùyán (in advance-speak) <v.> predict, prophecy: ~世界末日predict the end of the world || ~股市大跌predict the stock market crash

15 懂 [-] dǒng (understand) <v.> understand: ~英语understand English || ~足球understand soccer || 难~ hard to understand
16 理解 [-] lǐjiě (reason-understood) <v.> understanding: 互相~ understand each other || 难以/无法/容易~ difficult/impossible/easy to understand
17 了解 [瞭-] liǎojiě (understand-understood) <v.> understand: 深入~ understand deeper || ~情况 understand the situation
18 明白 [-] míngbái (plain-know) <v.> understand: ~他的意思 understand what he meant || 心里~ understand in one's heart || ~道理understand the truth
19 认识 [認識] rènshí (recognize-know) <v./n.> know, recognize: ~那个人know that person || ~汉字know Chinese characters || 肤浅的~ superficial understanding
20 掌握 [-] zhǎngwò (in charge-grasp) <v.> grasp: ~三门外语master three foreign languages || ~新技术master new technology
21 知道 [-] zhīdào (know-reason) <v.> know: ~这件事 know that event || ~出发的时间know the time to leave || ~原因know the reason
22 认得 [認-] rèndé (recognize-able to) <v.> recognize: ~路recognize the way || ~几个字recognize a few words || 你还~我吗? Can you still recognize me?
23 认定 [認-] rèndìng (believe-firm) <v.> firmly believe, set one's mind on: 法官~这个人有罪. The judge firmly believed that the man was guilty. || ~目标 set one's mind on the goal
24 识 [識] shí (know, realize, be aware) <v.> knowledge, know: ~字 learn to read, become literate || 见多 ~ 广 experienced and knowledgeable
25 熟悉 [-] shúxī (familiar-know) <v.> be familiar with: ~城市生活be familiar with city life || 对北京很 ~ be very familiar with Beijing

26 晓得 [曉-] xiǎodé (know-*suffix*) <v.> know (same as知道. only used in colloquial Chinese and in southern dialects): ~他的目的 know his purpose || ~这件事know this || ~她的脾气know her temper

27 意识到 [-識-] yìshí (realize-*suffix*) <v.> be conscious of: ~有危险 be aware of danger || 没有~问题的重要性the lack of awareness of the importance of the problem

28 发现 [發現] fāxiàn (dig-appear) <v./n.> find, discover: ~问题 discover problems|| 重要的~ important discovery || 新~ new discovery

Tips:

1 猜: It means 'to guess.' A happy song 女孩的心事你别猜 (girl-'s-mind-you-shouldn't-guess) became popular in the mid-1990s. The first two lines are 女孩的心事男孩你别猜, 你猜来猜去也猜不明白 (boys, you should never guess girls' mind, no matter how hard you try to guess, you will never understand.) A more discriminatory expression is 女人心, 海底针 (women's hearts are like a needle on the seabed, and it is impossible to be found,) in other words, you can never guess a woman's mind.

2 发现 (to discover, discovery): 发现 is fascinating, so there is a TV channel called the Discovery Channel ("发现"频道) and a space shuttle called Discovery (发现号航天飞机.)

Exercises:

Part I: Read the following sentences and fill in each blank with the appropriate word or phrase from the options given.

1 晓得、熟悉、意识到

a) 虽然我跟王教授在一个大学教书, 但是我对他其实不太________.
b) 王教授在十年前就已经_________人工智能研究将很快成为热点.
c) 小王告诉我: "你明天要早点来我家." 我回答说: "我_______了."

2 认得、了解、认定

a) _______一个国家的文化可以先从学习他们的语言开始.
b) 我不_______这个外国人是谁, 但是他竟然要请我吃饭, 太奇怪了.
c) 不管律师怎么辩解 (biànjiě, explain), 法官还是________这个人有罪.

3 掌握、理解、明白

a) _________一门外语对一个人的职业 (zhíyè, profession) 发展很有好处.
b) 这个老师教数学教得非常好, 不管多难的题他一讲学生就_______了.
c) 中美两国应该加深彼此的相互_________.

4 预期、预测、推理

a) 有人________这一届美国总统只能做四年, 因为反对他的人太多了.
b) 公司给我的奖金超出了我的________, 让我十分惊喜.
c) 一般来说, 私家侦探 (zhēntàn, detective) 的_______能力都很强.

5 识、看来、看起来、猜、懂

a) 这个人不________字, 我________他可能连小学也没上过.
b) 我给这些小学生讲了很多关于人工智能 (réngōng zhìnéng, artificial intelligence) 的事情, 但是他们都没听__________. __________我得换一下内容或者改变一下方法.
c) 这些孩子__________大概八九岁的样子.

Theme 117: To plan, to hope, to think 计划, 希望, 主张 (jìhuà, xīwàng, zhǔzhāng)

1 打算 [-] dǎsuàn (*prefix*-plan) <v./n.> plan: ~去逛街 plan to go shopping || 不~去公园not planning to go to the park || 长远的 ~ long-term plan
2 准备 [準備] zhǔnbèi (expect-prepare) <v.> prepare: ~考试prepare for a test || 为出国留学做~ prepare to go study abroad
3 规划 [規劃] guīhuà (plan-plan) <v.> plan: 进行~ the plan is in progress || ~自己的未来 plan out your future
4 策划 [-劃] cèhuà (plot-plan) <v.> plot, scheme: 市场~ market plan || 广告~ advertisement scheme || 精心~ carefully plot
5 计划 [計劃] jìhuà (scheme-plan) <v./n.> plan: ~开公司plan to open a business || 工作~ plan of study
6 设计 [設計] shèjì (design-scheme) <v.> design: ~产品 design a product || ~时装 design a fashion
7 算计 [-計] suànjì (plot-scheme) <v.> plot, reckon: ~别人 plot against other people || ~消费者 (xiāofèi zhě) reckon with consumers
8 谋划 [謀劃] móuhuà (conspire-plan) <v.> scheme: 精心~ carefully scheme
9 筹划 [籌劃] chóuhuà (plan and prepare-plan) <v.> prepare together: ~婚礼 plan out a wedding || 四处~ prepare everywhere

10 盼 [-] pàn (look, expect) <v.> hope for: ~放假 hope for vacation
11 希望 [-] xīwàng (hope-expect) <v.> hope: ~到中国旅游 hoping to go travel in China
12 想 [-] xiǎng (think, miss, want) <v.> want: 小王 ~去北京. Xiao Wang wants to go to Beijing.
13 渴望 [-] kěwàng (thirsty-hope) <v.> long for: ~改变long for change || ~爱情yearn for love
14 梦想 [夢-] mèngxiǎng (dream-want) <v./n.> dream: 人人都有~. Everyone has dreams. || ~过好日子 dream of having a good life || ~长生不老 dream of living forever and never growing old
15 盼望 [-] pànwàng (expect-hope) <v.> look forward to: 小时候我非常 ~过新年. When I was little, I looked forward to the New Year. || 父母~孩子能有出息. Parents look forward to their children's bright future.
16 期待 [-] qīdài (hope-wait) <v.> await, expect, look forward to: ~成功 expect success || 孩子们非常~圣诞节. Children are looking forward to Christmas.
17 期望 [-] qīwàng (hope-hope) <v./n.> expect: ~他的到来 expect his arrival || ~得到好消息 expect to receive good news || 充满~ be full of expectations
18 指望 [-] zhǐwàng (count- hope) <v.> count on: 不要~别人的帮助 cannot count on other people's help || 中国父母常常~儿女养老. Chinese parents often count on their children looking after them when they grow old.

19 企图 [-圖] qǐtú (anxiously expect-seek) <v.> attempt, try: ~抢银行 try to rob a bank || ~骗老人钱财 try to take old people's' money

20 试图 [試圖] shìtú (try-seek) <v.> attempt: 总统~解决美国贫富不均的问题. The President is attempting to solve America's income inequality problem.

21 求 [-] qiú (beg, request, pursue) <v.> ask for, seek: ~她帮忙ask for her help || ~稳定 seek stability || ~发展 strive to develop

22 要求 [-] yāoqiú (seek-request) <v./n.> demand: ~加工资 demand of increasing salary || 向学校提~ make demands to school

23 寻求 [尋-] xúnqiú (look-seek) <v.> seek, look for: ~帮助 seek help || ~出路 look for a way out

24 追求 [-] zhuīqiú (chase-pursue) <v.> pursue: ~幸福 pursue happiness || ~自由 seek freedom

25 追逐 [-] zhuīzhú (chase-go after) <v.> chase: ~名利 chase money and fame || ~金钱 chase after money

26 力求 [-] lìqiú (strive-seek) <v.> strive to, make every effort to: ~安全 strive for safety || ~平稳 try to be smooth

27 谋求 [謀-] móuqiú (conspire-seek) <v.> seek, strive for: ~利益 seek interest || ~生存 strive to survive

28 贪图 [貪圖] tāntú (greedy-seek) <v.> covet: ~享受covet enjoyment || ~名利covet fame and money

29 祈求 [-] qǐqiú (pray-seek) <v.> pray for: 向上帝~ pray to God || ~丰收pray for the harvest || ~太平 pray for peace

30 感到 [-] gǎndào (feel-*suffix*) <v.> feel: ~ 很高兴 feel happy || ~非常满意 feel very satisfied || ~害怕 feel scared

31 觉得 [覺-] juédé (sense-*suffix*) <v.> feel: ~好feel good || ~奇怪 feel weird || ~有趣feel interested

32 认为 [認爲] rènwéi (think-be) <v.> think: ~对/正确 think right || 美国~自己是世界警察 America thinks it's the world's policeman.

33 以为 [-為] yǐwéi (take-be) <v.> assume incorrectly: 美国~中国是发达国家. America wrongly assumes that China is a developed country.

34 主张 [-張] zhǔzhāng (advocate-proposal) <v.> view, proposition, advocate, stand for: ~改革advocate reform || 极力~全球化strongly advocate globalization

35 坚持 [堅-] jiānchí (firm-hold) <v.> persevere, stick to: ~练习 continue with practicing || ~学中文persevere in studying Chinese || ~自己的意见stick to your opinion

36 衡量 [-] héngliáng (weigh-measure) <v.> weigh, examine, consider: ~得失weigh the gains and losses || 拿美国的标准来 ~ judge by the American standard

37 计较 [計較] jìjiào (calculate-compare) <v.> argue, bicker: ~得失argue over gains and losses || ~名利 bicker about fame and money || 斤斤~ be preoccupied with personal gains and losses

38 权衡 [權-] quánhéng (steelyard scale arm-scale weight) <v.> consider, weigh: ~利弊 (lìbì) weigh the pros and cons || ~轻重consider the severity || 再三~ repeated consideration

Tips:

1 划 (劃, huà): It has two main meanings. One is 'to plan,' such as 计划, 规划, 策划, 筹划, 谋划 which are listed above and happen to be at the end of a word. The other is 'to divide,' such as 划分 (to divide), 划界 (to delimit), 划线 (to draw a line), 区划 (zoning.)

2 期, 盼, 望: All mean 'to hope, to expect' and their combinations, 期盼, 期望, 盼望 have almost the same meaning.

3 Bad desire: In this unit, 算计 (to scheme,) 企图 (to attempt,) 追逐 (to chase) and 贪图 (to covet) all have negative connotations.

Exercises:

Part I: Use the given bound form here as a guide to help you think of other words with the same character. Feel free to use your dictionary when needed. Then write down the English definition of each of the words you've written.

望 *(hope, expect):* 希望 *hope*

____

____

____

____

划 *(plan):* 计划 *map out, plan*

____

____

____

____

求 *(seek, try):* 追求 *pursue*

____

____

____

____

Part II: Read the following sentences and fill in each blank with the appropriate word or phrase from the options given.

1 计较、衡量、权衡

a) 有人说爱情是不能用金钱________的，人们不会因为一个人有钱而爱他.

b) 小白的室友特别爱________一些生活上的小事情，结果两个人相处得不是很愉快.

c) 经过_______利弊, 中国政府最终决定开始实行"一带一路"的计划.

2 坚持、主张、以为

a) 中国政府________世界上所有国家都应该互相尊重, 和平共处.
b) 小张________锻炼 (duànliàn, exercise) 了三个月, 体重减轻了20磅.
c) 这家公司_______这个新产品会很受欢迎, 没想到卖得特别不好.

3 追求、贪图、追逐

a) 草地上, 一群孩子在互相_______, 互相打闹.
b) 因为_______名利和金钱, 一些年轻女孩子愿意嫁给年纪很大的名人或者富翁.
c) 过去三十年, 中国的一些地方政府盲目 (mángmù, blindly) ______ GDP, 结果浪费了资源, 污染了环境.

4 计划、期待、设计

a) 小张_________明年去日本旅行.
b) 小张_______的服装非常美观适用, 在市场上销路 (xiāolù, sales) 很好.
c) 小张父母_______小张在事业上获得更大的成功.

Theme 118: Memory 记忆 (jìyì)

1 记得 [記-] jìdé (remember-can) <v.> remember: ~很清楚 remember something very clearly || ~她的生日remember her birthday || ~这件事remember this thing
2 记住 [記-] jìzhù (remember-firm) <v.> keep in mind: 牢牢地 ~ keep in mind firmly || ~爸爸的话. Keep Dad's words in mind. || 记得/不住can keep it in mind/ cannot keep it in mind
3 想 [-] xiǎng (think, miss) <v.> miss: ~爸爸miss dad || ~家miss home || ~亲人miss closed relatives
4 想到 [-] xiǎngdào (think-about) <separable word> think about: 每当春节的时候小王就会 ~在中国的家人. Xiao Wang thinks about his family in China every Spring Festival.
5 想起 [-] xiǎngqǐ (think-of) <v.> think of: ~小时候的事情 think of one's childhood
6 怀念 [懷-] huáiniàn (cherish-miss) <v.> miss: ~父母miss one's parents || ~故乡miss one's hometown
7 回顾 [-顧] huígù (retrospective-look) <v.> review: ~历史 review history
8 回忆 [-憶] huíyì (retrospective-think of) <v./n.> recall, memory: ~过去recall the past || 美好的~ good memories
9 回首 [-] huíshǒu (back-look) <v.> look back: ~往事look back the past
10 惦记 [-記] diànjì (miss-think) <v.> be concerned about, think about: ~家里的事情think about family || 母亲最~自己的孩子. A mother is always most concerned about her children.
11 相思 [-] xiāngsī (mutual-yearn) <n.> love knot: ~病lovesickness
12 记忆 [記憶] jìyì (memorize-recall) <v./n> memorize, memory: ~力memory power

13 想念 [-] xiǎngniàn (think-miss) <v.> miss: ~父母miss their parents || ~家乡 miss their hometown || ~朋友miss their friends
14 纪念 [紀-] jìniàn (record-memory) <v./n.> commemorate: 周年~ anniversary || ~一位音乐家commemorate a musician || 留个~ keep as a souvenir
15 留念 [-] liú'niàn (keep-memory) <v.> keep as a souvenir: 拍照~ take a photo as a souvenir || 合影~ take a group photo as a souvenir
16 怀旧 [懷舊] huáijiù (cherish-old) <v.> nostalgia: 我是一个喜欢~的人. I was like a nostalgic person.
17 悼念 [-] dàoniàn (mourn-miss) <v.> mourn for: ~亲人mourn for their relatives || 沉痛~ grieve
18 追悼 [-] zhuīdào (recall-mourn) <v.> mourn for: ~会memorial service || ~死难者 mourn for the dead
19 牵挂 [牽-] qiānguà (pull-caught) <v.> be concerned about, worry about: ~家人worry about one's family
20 忘 [-] wàng (forget) <v.> forget: ~了他forgot him || ~了带钱forgot to take money || ~了这件事 forgot this thing
21 忘记 [-記] wàngjì (forget-remember) <v.> forget: ~自己的生日forgot his own birthday || ~过去forget the past

Tips:

1 相思: It means 'lovesickness' or 'yearning between lovers,' which was a beloved topic for literati in ancient China, due to the fact that Chinese people did not have many channels to express their affections for true lovers.
2 追悼会 (memorial service): The Chinese memorial service is not completely like Western ones, which could have some happy anecdotes. Chinese ones must be solemn and grieved in dress and in voice, from the beginning to the end.
3 记得 vs. 记住: 记得 means 'to remember' and 记住 'to keep in mind.' Negation of 记得 is 不记得 (cannot remember/recall,) but for 记住, there are two negations. One is 没记住 (could not recall, tried to memorize something but forgot eventually,) and the other is 记不住 (beyond one's capacity to memorize something.) 记住 can be used in imperative sentences but 记得 cannot.

Exercises:

Part I: Use the given bound form here as a guide to help you think of other words with the same character. Feel free to use your dictionary when needed. Then write down the English definition of each of the words you've written.

念 *(miss): 想念 miss, long to see again*

____

____

____

回 *(back)*: 回家 *be back home*

____

____

____

Part II: Read the following sentences and fill in each blank with the appropriate word or phrase from the options given.

1 纪念、牵挂、怀旧

a) 小王父母今晚出去吃饭, _______结婚二十周年.
b) 小王的父母都非常喜欢______, 他们保留了所有小王小时候用过的东西.
c) 小王上大学了, 父母非常______他, 经常给他打电话.

2 记忆、想念、相思

a) 到美国以后我很少见到在中国的爷爷奶奶, 我很________他们. 在我的_________中, 我爷爷奶奶家前面有一条小河.
b) 中国古代诗歌有很多是描写青年男女________、相恋的.

3 回忆、回顾、惦记

a) 暑假过后, 她开始________今年夏天所有在海边度过的每一天.
b) 她去度假的时候非常________她的猫和狗, 常常给父母打电话问问它们怎么样了.
c) _________美国历史, 我们发现其实种族矛盾一直存在.

4 想到、记得、记住

a) 小时候的事情, 我多半都不_______了.
b) 一说到童年, 很多人都会________动画片和迪斯尼乐园 (Disneyland).
c) 这个美国学生很有语言天赋 (tiānfù, gift), 他能_______所有学过的汉字.

Theme 119: Modal verbs 能愿动词 (néngyuàn dòngcí)

1 必须 [-須] bìxū (certainly-need) <adv.> must: ~去must go || ~学 must study || ~记住 must remember
2 得 [-] děi (have to) <v.> have to: ~走了 have to go || ~睡了 have to sleep || ~吃了have to eat
3 该 [該] gāi (should) <aux. v.> should: ~工作了should work || ~吃饭了 should eat || ~睡觉了should sleep
4 不必 [-] bùbì (not-necessary) <adv.> don't have to: ~多说 do not have to say much || ~着急 need not worry || ~客气. You are welcome.
5 应该 [應該] yīnggāi (should-ought) <aux. v.> must: ~改变 must fix || ~解决 must decide || ~看到 must look at

6 应 [應] yīng (should) <aux. v.> should: ~注意should be careful || ~在礼堂举行 should be held in the auditorium || ~做的事task that must be done

7 不能不 [-] bùnéngbù (cannot-not) <aux. v.> cannot but, have to: ~考虑(kǎolǜ) have to consider || ~选择 have to select || ~关心have to care about that

8 敢 [-] gǎn (dare) <aux. v.> dare: ~说 dare to say || ~看 dare to look || ~来dare to come

9 敢于 [-於] gǎnyú (dare-to) <v.> dare to: ~去做 dare to do || ~吃螃蟹. (pángxiè) Dare to eat crabs. Dare to be the first to take a risk.

10 肯 [-] kěn (consent, be willing to) <aux. v.> be willing to: ~去be willing to go || ~说 be willing to say || ~帮忙 be willing to help

11 甘心 [-] gānxīn (willing-heart) <v.> willingly: ~接受be willing to accept || ~当医生be willing to be a doctor || 不~失败Not willing to fail

12 心甘情愿 [-] xīngānqíngyuàn (heart-willing-mind-wishing) <idiom> willingly: ~留在家里be willing to stay at home || ~同意这个办法be willing to agree with this approach

13 会 [會] huì (get together, meet, certainly, will) <aux. v.> will: ~来will come || 不 ~失败will not fail || ~拉小提琴will play the violin

14 可以 [-] kěyǐ (can-use) <aux. v.> can: ~看出来can be seen || ~解决 can resolve || ~知道can know

15 能 [-] néng (bear, capable, can) <aux. v.> can: ~跑Can run || ~找到can find || ~办到can do it

16 能够 [-] nénggòu (capable-enough) <aux. v.> be able to: ~完成be able to finish || ~记住be able to remember || ~做好be able to do well

17 得以 [-] déyǐ (so that-can) <v.> be able to: ~改变 be able to change || ~完成be able to finish || ~发展be able to develop

18 愿意 [-] yuànyì (wish-intend) <aux. v.> willing: ~做be willing to do || ~去 be willing to go || ~学习be willing to study

19 自愿 [-] zìyuàn (self-willing) <aux. v.> volunteer: ~接送孩子voluntarily pick up the child || ~结婚married on own's will || ~离职voluntarily leave

20 乐意 [樂-] lèyì (happy-willing) <aux. v.> willing: ~跟她合作be willing to cooperate with her || ~当公务员willing to be a civil servant || ~接受willing to accept

21 情愿 [-] qíngyuàn (mind-willing) <aux. v.> willingly, be willing to, would rather: ~当他的弟子willingly become his student || 两相~ by mutual consent, both parties agree of free will || ~少拿两个月工资be willing to take less than two months of salary

22 自觉 [-覺] zìjué (self-conscious) <adv.> consciously: ~交费consciously pay || ~参加consciously participate

23 值得 [-] zhídé (worth-equal) <v.> worth, merit: ~买be worth buying || ~注意merit attention

24 不值 [-] bùzhí (not-worth) <v.> not worth: ~一提not worth mentioning || ~钱not worth the money || 一文~ not worth a cent

25 足以 [-] zúyǐ (enough-can) <v.> be sufficient to: ~说明问题be enough to explain the problem || ~解释这个问题be enough to explain the problem || ~保暖be enough to keep warm

Tips:

1 甘心 and 心甘: Both mean 'willing,' but there are several differences between these two words. 1) 甘心 appeared much earlier than 心甘 in ancient texts, 2) 甘心 is more like an adverb but 心甘 an adjective, 3) Negation of 甘心 is 不甘心, whereas that of 心甘 is 心不甘, 4) 甘心情愿 and 心甘情愿 occurred with almost the same overall frequency in ancient texts, but 心甘情愿 overwhelmingly prevails in modern texts because Chinese idioms prefer parallel structures to which 心甘情愿 belongs, but 甘心情愿 does not.

2 I do: The 'I do' in the wedding vows is 我愿意 (wǒ yuànyì, I want) in Chinese.

Exercises:

Part I: Use the given bound form here as a guide to help you think of other words with the same character. Feel free to use your dictionary when needed. Then write down the English definition of each of the words you've written.

愿 *(willing):* 愿意 *willing*

____

____

____

甘 *(willing):* 不甘 *not willing*

____

____

____

Part II: Read the following sentences and fill in each blank with the appropriate word or phrase from the options given

1 值得、足以、不值

a) 这件衣服_______一万美金, 我不会买.
b) 英国是一个_______去旅游的国家, 有丰富的历史和文化.
c) 中国的高铁速度快, 质量好, ________让全世界称赞.

2 敢于、得以、心甘情愿

a) 在最近的领土争端 (zhēngduān, dispute) 问题上, 因为中国和印度双方都作了让步, 问题才最后______解决.
b) 有人认为要想创新就要_______向传统或者权威 (quánwēi, authority) 思想质疑 (zhìyí, question) 和挑战 (tiǎozhàn, challenge).
c) 中国父母常常________为子女付出所有.

3 必须、肯、不必

a) 不管父母怎么劝说, 这个孩子就是不______学钢琴.
b) 每个公民都______遵守法律.
c) 小王租的公寓______付水电费, 因为已经包括在租金里面了.

4 可以、应该、能够

a) 美国大学规定学生都______购买健康保险. 如果一个学生参加了父母公司的健康保险计划他______不在学校买健康保险.
b) 小李有健康保险, 所以保险公司______报销 (bàoxiāo, reimburse) 他这次住院的费用.

Theme 120: To laugh, to cry 笑, 哭 (xiào, kū)

(See also Theme 107)

1 笑 [-] xiào (smile, laugh) <v.> smile, laugh: ~着说 talk while smiling || 别~我 don't laugh at me || 大~ laugh heartily
2 微笑 [-] wēixiào (slight-smile) <v.> smile: 向她~ smile to her || 脸上 露出~ a smile appeared in one's face || ~地说speak with smiling
3 欢笑 [歡-] huānxiào (happy-laugh) <v.> laugh happily: 孩子们~着做游戏. The children played games while laughing happily.
4 含笑 [-] hánxiào (wear-smile) <v.> with a smile: ~不语remain silent with a smile || ~点头nod with a smile
5 干笑 [乾-] gānxiào (hollow-laugh) <v.> hollow laugh: ~ 一声have a hollow laugh
6 苦笑 [-] kǔxiào (bitter-smile) <v.> forced smile: ~一下have a forced smile || ~着摇了摇头shake a head with the forced smile
7 假笑 [-] jiǎxiào (fake-smile) <v.> smirk, make a fake smile: 很多人拍照的时候喜欢~, 让自己看起来好看一些. When taking pictures, many people like to make a fake smile, so they look good.
8 傻笑 [-] shǎxiào (foolish-laugh) <v.> simper: 这些大一的男生在晚会上就坐在那儿~. Those freshman boys were just sitting there smirking during the evening party.
9 冷笑 [-] lěngxiào (grim-laugh) <v.> sneer: ~一声have a sneer || 朝他~ sneer at him

10 哭 [-] kū (cry) <v.> cry: ~鼻子snivel || ~了一场cried a lot
11 哭哭啼啼 [-] kūkūtítí (weep-*reduplication*-wail-*reduplication*) <idiom> weep and sob:
12 痛哭 [-] tòngkū (bitterly-cry) <v.> cry one's eyes out: 失声~ cry aloud || ~流泪burst into tears
13 流泪 [-淚] liúlèi (shed-tear) <v.> tear, pipe one's eyes: 感动得~ move to tears
14 哭鼻子 [-] kūbízi (weep-nose) <v.> snivel: 偷偷地~ snivel secretly
15 号啕大哭 [號---] háotáodàkū (cry loudly-greatly-cry) <idiom> cry: 放声~ cry aloud

16 哽咽 [-] gěngyè (choke-sob) <v.> choke with sobs: 这首歌很感人, 她感到一阵~. The song was touching, and she felt a lump in her throat.
17 含泪 [-淚] hánlèi (wear-tear) <v.> in tears: ~离开leave with tears || ~送走爸爸see off my dad with tears

Tip:

1 哭笑不得: It means 'to be at a loss whether to cry or laugh,' for example '听了他的故事, 我~' (After hearing his story, I do not know whether to laugh or to cry.)

Exercises:

Part I: Read the following words and then answer the questions.

微笑、欢笑、含笑点头、干笑、苦笑、假笑、冷笑、傻笑、哭哭啼啼、痛哭、流泪、哭鼻子、嚎啕大哭、哽咽、含泪

1 上面哪些"笑"表示很高兴?

---

2 上面哪些"笑"表示带有悲伤?

---

3 上面哪些"笑"不表示一个人非常高兴?

---

4 上面哪些"哭"声音不大?

---

5 上面哪些"哭"声音很大?

Theme 121: To covert emotion 传情 (chuánqíng)

1 眉飞色舞 [-飛--] méifēi sèwǔ (eyebrow-fly-cheek-dance) <idiom> with dancing eyebrows and radiant face-enraptured, exultant: 说得~ talk with dancing eyebrows and radiant faces || 说起美国音乐, 他就~. His face lights up whenever he speaks of American music.
2 消气 [-氣] xiāoqì (vanish-anger) <v.> cool down: 消消气 cool down
3 眉来眼去 [-來--] méilái yǎnqù (eyebrow-come-eye-go) <idiom> trade flirting looks: 两个人~ two people flirted with each other
4 撒娇 [-嬌] sājiāo (let go-capricious) <v.> pout, act like a spoiled child: 向妈妈~ pout to mom || 告诉那个孩子别~. Tell that child to stop pouting.
5 发嗲 [發-] fādiǎ (act-clinger) <v.> speak in a spoiled/ privileged manner: 喜欢~ like to act coquettishly || 有人觉得~的女生很性感. Some people feel spoiled women are very sexy.
6 羞 [-] xiū (shame, shy) <adj.> shy: ~死了embarrassed to death || ~得藏起来so embarrassed to hide

7 羞答答 [-] xiūdādā (shy-*reduplication*) <adj.> shy: ~地答应了shyly agree || ~地抬头看shyly glance up
8 不好意思 [-] bùhǎoyìsī (not-feel at ease) <adj.> feel awkward: ~让别人帮忙feel awkward to ask for help || ~, 我又迟到了. I'm sorry I'm late again.
9 难为情 [難爲-] nánwéiqíng (embarrass-affection) <adj.> embarrassed: ~地摇摇头shake your head embarrassedly || 感到~ feel embarrassed
10 害臊 [-] hàisào (feel-bashful) <v.> ashamed: 感到 ~ feel ashamed || 你撒谎就不感到 ~吗? Are you ashamed for having lied?
11 带劲 [帶勁] dàijìn (with-energy) <adj.> energetic, exciting: 干得~ feel excited to do || 越说越~. The more one speaks the more energetic they get.
12 饱满 [飽滿] bǎomǎn (plump-full) <adj.> be full of: 精神~ be full of vigor || 情绪 ~ an energetic mood
13 神气 [-氣] shénqì (spirit-vigor) <adj.> vigorous, cocky: 他觉得开好车看起来很~. He thinks driving a fancy car will make him very impressive.

Tips:

1 羞 (xiū): Etymologically, it is related to 羊 (sheep) and 丑 (chǒu, actually a variant of 手) and means 'to offer' since 羊 (sheep) is an auspicious animal. This being said, it is not hard to guess that 馐 (xiū) means 'delicacy.' 羞 was later borrowed mainly as 丑 (ugly) from which evolved meanings such as 'shame' and 'shy.'
2 难为情: Parsing of this word should be 难为 and 情. 难为 means 'to embarrass' and 情 'affection.' The whole word means 'embarrassed.'
3 撒娇 (sājiāo) and 发嗲 (fādiǎ): They mean 'to act like a spoiled child, to pout' and 'to be a clinger' respectively. Young Chinese ladies are not as independent in finances and in mentality as their counterparts in the Western world, so they often 撒娇 and 发嗲.

Exercises: Multiple Choice

Make sure to choose the most appropriate answer.

1 "他觉得跟女孩子说话很害羞."意思是

A. 他不好意思跟女孩子说话.
B. 他跟女孩子说话时候很神气.
C. 他为女孩子感到害臊.

2 王教授上课的时候精神非常_______.

A. 消气 B. 饱满 C. 撒娇

3 王教授讲课的时候常常_______的, 非常投入.

A. .装模作样 B. 眉来眼去 C. 眉飞色舞

4 王经理跟新来的女秘书_______的, 让大家觉得很不舒服.

A. 眉来眼去 B. 眉清目秀 C. 带劲

Theme 122: Silence, to pretend 沉默, 假装 (chénmò, jiǎzhuāng)

1 沉默 [-] chénmò (quiet-silent) <adj./n.> silent, silence: 保持~ keep silence || ~片刻silent moment || 性格~ quiet character

2 发呆 [發-] fādāi (display-daze) <v.> be in a daze: 看着~ watch without focus || 两眼~ in a daze

3 出神 [-] chūshén (leave-soul) <v.> be spellbound, be lost in thought: 他坐在那里 ~. He sat there, lost in thought.

4 发愣 [發-] fālèng (display-distracted) <v.> be in a daze: 吓得~ too frightened and too distracted|| 有点~ a little bit absent-minded

5 装 [裝] zhuāng (baggage, dress up, pretend) <v.> pretend: 不懂~懂 pretend to understand what you don't|| ~样子pretend to be like something || ~穷pretend to be poor

6 假装 [] jiǎzhuāng (false-pretend) <v.> pretend: ~睡着了 pretend to fall asleep || ~没看见pretend not to see || ~生气pretending to be angry

7 伪装 [僞裝] wěizhuāng (feign-pretend) <v.> camouflage: ~自己disguise oneself || ~和平disguise peace

8 装腔作势 [裝--勢] zhuāngqiāngzuòshì (pretend-accent-make-posture) <idiom> put on airs: 她虽然有时候有点儿~, 但是大体还可以 ~. She is basically a nice girl, although she does put on a bit sometimes.

9 装模做样 [裝--樣] zhuāngmózuòyàng (pretend-appearance-make-manner) <idiom> act with affected manners, put on an act: ~地看报纸put on the act of reading the newspaper || ~地工作work with affected manners

10 装傻 [裝-] zhuāngshǎ (pretend-silly) <v.> pretend to be ignorant: 故意~ deliberately pretend to be foolish

11 装蒜 [裝-] zhuāngsuàn (pretend-garlic) <v.> act like they don't know, feign ignorance, play dumb: 故意~ pretend not to know on purpose || 别~了!大家都知道这件坏事是你做的. Stop pretending (ignorance) ! Everyone knows that you did the bad thing.

12 装糊涂 [裝-塗] zhuānghútú (pretend-confused) <v.> pretend to be confused: 故意~ deliberately play the fool || 少~. Stop acting stupid.

Tips:

1 装 (裝, zhuāng): The original meaning of 装 is baggage, from which evolved 'to dress up' and 'to pretend.' Now a vulgar word '装逼 (bī),' '装B (bī,) or '装13' which is used to mock someone who is 'showing off pompously and stupidly, while in fact he isn't cool at all.' The 逼, B and 13 (which resembles B if written more closely) all insinuate the English word 'p***y.'

2 装蒜 (zhuāngsuàn): It is derived from a two-part allegorical saying 猪鼻子插大葱 – 装象 (insert leeks into pig's noses – pretend to be an elephant, i.e., to pretend.) Since 大葱 (leek) and 蒜 (garlic) are similar, 装蒜 is coined later.

3 沉默是金: It is translated from the English proverb 'speech is silver and silence is golden.'

Exercises:

Part I: Multiple Choice. Make sure to choose the most appropriate answer.

1 张女士最近好像有什么心事, 在公司里非常_____, 很少跟大家说话.

A. 出神 B. 发呆 C. 沉默

2 "这个学生上课的时候呆呆地出神," 意思是

A. 这个学生上课发呆 B. 这个学生上课伪装 C. 这个学生上课假装

3 "装腔作势"跟下面哪个词意思相同

A. 装模作样 B. 装傻 C. 发愣

4 小王知道老板背地里偷税 (tōushuì, tax cheater) 漏税 (lòushuì, tax evasion), 但是他_____, 假装不知道这些事情.

A. 伪装 B. 装糊涂 C. 装假

5 这位中文系主任, 专业水平不高, 但是特别喜欢______, 假装精通 (jīngtōng, be master of) 中文教学与研究.

A. 装傻 B. 装蒜 C. 装糊涂

Theme 123: Tired 累 (lèi)

1 乏 [-] fá (wry, tired) <adj.> tired: 觉得很~ feel very tired || 走~了tired of walking || 浑身都~了. The whole body is tired.
2 乏力 [-] fálì (lack-strength) <adj.> tired, fatigue: 四肢~ weakness in arms and legs || 走路~ walking tiredly
3 没劲 [-勁] méijìn (no-strength) <adj.> tired, boring: 全身~. The body is tired. || 活着~ feel life is boring
4 疲倦 [-] píjuàn (tired-weary) <adj.> tired: 感到~ feel tired || 身体 ~ tired body || 不知~ tirelessly
5 疲劳 [-勞] píláo (tired-fatigue) <adj.> fatigue: 产生~ produce fatigue || 恢复~ restore fatigue || 过度~ excessive fatigue
6 疲惫 [-憊] píbèi (tired-exhausted) <adj.> exhausted: 脸色~ looks tired || ~的身体tired body || ~地笑笑sarcastic smile when one is tired
7 无精打采 [無---] wújīngdǎcǎi (no-spirit-throw-monetary present) <idiom> listless, in low spirits: ~地回答drawl to a reply || 他显得~. He seems in low spirits.
8 有气无力 [-氣無-] yǒuqìwúlì (have-breath-no-strength) <idiom> weakly and without strength, dispirited: 说话~ speak in a faint voice || 天气太热会让人~. A hot day makes a person listless.
9 随便 [隨-] suíbiàn (as-please) <adj.> casual: ~玩玩play casually || ~乱放casually put away || ~抓人casually arrest people
10 散漫 [-] sǎnmàn (unfettered-unrestrained) <adj.> undisciplined: 自由~ unconstrained, unruly || 生活~ loose life

11 松松垮垮 [鬆鬆--] sōngsōngkuǎkuǎ (slack-*reduplication*-perfunctory-*reduplication*) <idiom> loose: 穿得~ dressed loosely || 比赛打得~ the game played loose || 裤子~ pants loose

Tips:

1 乏 (fá): The original meaning of 乏 is 'incorrect' (the opposite of 正.) Now the main meanings of 乏 are 'lack' as in 缺乏 (quēfá, to lack) and 'tired' as in 疲乏 (pífá, tired.)
2 无精打采: It means 'lack of energy or spirit, listless.' 打采 was an old Chinese custom. If customers of a prostitute like a prostitute, they present the prostitute with monetary items.

Exercises:

Part I: Multiple Choice. Make sure to choose the most appropriate answer.

1 "中国男子排球队对美国男子排球队的比赛打得松松垮垮的." 意思是

A. 中国男子排球队打得很好
B. 中国男子排球队打得不好
C. 中国男子排球队打得不好不坏

2 自由________, 纪律性差的军队一定不是好军队.

A. 浪漫　B. 没劲儿　C. 散漫

3 父母应该从小教育孩子整洁 (zhěngjié, neat) 有序, 不能______乱放东西.

A. 乏力　B. 散漫　C. 随便

4 这个球队比赛输了, 队员们看起来都________的.

A. 无精打采　B. 疲劳　C. 疲惫

5 "小张太累了, 感到有气无力的."这句话跟下面哪句话意思不同

A. 小张很疲惫　B. 小张很疲劳　C. 小张很有精力

Theme 124: Life, food and drink 生活, 饮食 (shēnghuó, yǐnshí)

(See also Themes 46, 51)

1 住 [-] zhù (stay, reside, live) <v.> live: ~在家里live at home || ~在宿舍live in a dorm || 在船上~ living on a boat
2 居住 [-] jūzhù (dwell-reside) <v.> live: ~在岛上 living on an island || 在国外~ living oversea || 共同~ living together
3 同居 [-] tóngjū (together-live) <v.> live together: 跟女朋友~ live together with your girlfriend || 秘密~ living privately; living together unmarried

4 做客 [-] zuòkè (be-guest) <v.> be a guest: 到叔叔家~ being a guest at my uncle's house || 请朋友来~ inviting friends to come to your home

5 寄宿 [-] jìsù (away-stay) <v.> lodge, (of students) board: ~在美国人家里lodging at an American's house || ~学校boarding school
6 住宿 [-] zhùsù (live-stay) <v.> accommodation, lodging, stay at: 短期~ short-term accommodation || ~一晚one night accommodation
7 住校 [-] zhùxiào (live-school) <v.> live in school: ~学习living at school for studying purposes
8 定居 [-] dìngjū (settle-dwell) <v.> settle down, reside: 在北京~ settling down in Beijing || 回农村~ settling down in the village
9 安家 [-] ānjiā (settle-home) <v.> settle down, reside: 在郊区~ settle in the suburb
10 露营 [-營] lùyíng (outside-camp) <v.> camp: 在山上~ camping in the mountains

11 待 [-] dāi (stay) <v.> stay: ~三天stay three days || ~家里stay at home || ~得/不住can stay/can't stay
12 留 [-] liú (stay) <v.> stay: ~在农村stay in a village || ~在大学stay in a university || ~在那儿stay there
13 停留 [-] tíngliú (stop-stay) <v.> stay: ~在脑海中stay in your mind || 在这里~ stay here || ~三十分钟stay for 30 minutes
14 搬 [-] bān (move) <v.> move: ~家 move || ~出宿舍move out of dorm
15 搬家 [-] bānjiā (move-home) <separable word> move: 搬一次家move once || 经常~ move often
16 过 [過] guò (live) <v.> live, celebrate: ~日子live a life || ~春节 celebrate New Year || ~生日 celebrate birthday
17 度过 [-過] dùguò (pass-spend) <v.> live, pass (time), go through: ~童年spend one's childhood || ~危险go through the risk

18 打发 [-發] dǎfā (*prefix*-pass) <v.> pass the time: ~日子pass the days || ~时间pass the time of day || ~寂寞pass loneliness
19 过节 [過節] guòjié (celebrate-festival) <separable word> celebrate festivals: 过中秋节celebrate the Mid-Autumn Festival || 过春节celebrate the Spring Festival || 过情人节celebrate Valentine's Day
20 过年 [過-] guònián (celebrate-New Year) <bf> celebrate New Year: 回家~ go back home for New Year

21 独立 [獨-] dúlì (independent-survive) <v.> be independent: ~思考 think independently || ~生活live independently || 国家~ national independence
22 自主 [-] zìzhǔ (self-decide) <adv.> independently: 婚姻~ marital autonomy || 经济~ economic independence
23 当家 [當-] dāngjiā (manage-household affairs) <v.> take charge of family: 川普总统希望人民~做主President Trump hopes the American people can be the masters of their country. || 大儿子~. The eldest son is the master of whole family.
24 奔波 [-] bēnbō (dash-rush) <v.> be busy running about: 到处~ be busy running everywhere || 日夜~ be busy running day and night
25 操劳 [-勞] cāoláo (do-work) <v.> doing arduous or unpleasant work: 日夜~ work day and night || ~过度overwork || ~家务work hard for the housework

26 劳累 [勞-] láolèi (labor-tired) <v.> tired: 旅途~ be tired for the journey || 过度~ overwork

27 打拼 [-] dǎpīn (*prefix*-go all out) <v.> work hard: 为自己~ work hard for yourself || ~美好的生活work hard for a perfect life || 努力~ work with all efforts

28 拼 [-] pīn (go all out) <v.> go all out, fight: 因为政治观点不同, 希拉里打算和川普~到底. Because of political differences, Mrs. Clinton intends to fight Mr. Trump to the bitter end.

29 使劲 [-] shǐjìn (exert-strength) <separable word> exert all one's strength: ~喊shout at the top of one's voice || 有使不完的劲have inexhaustible energy

30 加油 [-] jiāyóu (add-oil) <v.> make an extra effort: ~干work with added vigor || 观众为运动员~. 他们喊~！~！ The spectators cheered the players on, and said, 'Come on! Come on!'

31 拼命 [-] pīnmìng (risk-life) <v.> use all one's might: ~工作break one's back to work || ~鼓掌have a good round of applause || ~学习. Try very hard to study.

32 尽力 [盡-] jìnlì (exhaust-strength) separable word> try one's best<: ~完成try one's best to complete || 每个人都要尽自己的力. Everybody should try their best.

33 开夜车 [開-車] kāiyèchē (drive-night-vehicle) <v.> work late into midnight: 明天要交论文, 今晚我得~. I must hand in my paper tomorrow. I'll have to burn the midnight oil tonight.

34 抽空 [-] chōukòng (squeeze-time) <v.> manage to find time: ~运动 find time to exercise || ~打个电话find time to make a call || ~回家find to go back home

35 偷懒 [-懶] tōulǎn (stealthy-lazy) <separable word> goof off, be lazy: 偷一会儿懒be lazy for a while

36 要饭 [-飯] yàofàn (beg-food) <v.> beg for food or money: 出来~ come out to beg food or money || 一路~ beg for food or money on his trip || 在大街上~ beg food or money on the street

37 有空儿 [--兒] yǒukòngr (have-free time) <v.> free: 晚上~ be free tonight || ~来玩儿. Please drop in when you have time. || ~看电影have time to watch movie

38 睡觉 [-覺] shuìjiào (to sleep-a sleep) <separable word> sleep: 睡一觉have a sleep || 十点~ sleep at 10: 00 || 我喜欢睡懒觉. I like to get up late.

39 上床 [-牀] shàngchuáng (go to-bed) <v.> go to bed: 九点~ go to bed at 9: 00

40 起 [-] qǐ (get up) <v.> get up: ~床get up || ~得早get up very early || ~得晚get up very late

41 起床 [-牀] qǐchuáng (get up-bed) <v.> get up: 七点~ get up at seven o'clock

42 起来 [-來] qǐlái (get up-*suffix*) <v.> get up: 早上~ get up in the morning

43 休息 [-] xiūxī (stop-rest) <v.> take a rest: ~十分钟rest 10 minutes || 好好地~ have a good rest || 得 (不) 到~ no rest

44 歇 [-] xiē (rest) <v.> rest: 歇一歇have a rest || ~一天 rest a day

45 养 [養] yǎng (support, raise, convalesce) <v.> heal, raise: ~病 rest and regain one's health || ~宠物 raise pets || ~家support family

46 疗养 [療養] liáoyǎng (remedy-convalesce) <v.> recuperate: ~两个月recuperate for two months

47 保养 [-養] bǎoyǎng (care-maintain) <v.> take good care of, maintain: ~身体take good care of our health || 车辆~ car maintenance

48 保健 [-] bǎojiàn (care-health) <v.> health protection: 卫生~ health care || ~食品health foods

49 休养 [-養] xiūyǎng (rest-convalesce) <v.> rest and recuperate: 在家~ rest and recuperate at home

50 打扮 [-] dǎbàn (*prefix*-dress up) <v./n.> dress up: 喜欢~ like to dress up || ~得漂亮dress beautifully || ~成一个公主be dressed as a princess

51 理发 [-髮] lǐfà (treat-hair) <separable word> cut hair: 理短发 cut hair short || 理一个发have a haircut

52 美容 [-] měiróng (beautify-face) <v./n.> facial beauty: 做~ have a facial beauty service || 面部~服务facial beauty service || ~产品beauty products

53 减肥 [減-] jiǎnféi (lose-weight) <separable word> lose weight: ~药/茶diet pills/tea

54 整理 [-] zhěnglǐ (tidy-treat) <v.> sort, clean up: ~房间 sort your room

55 收拾 [-] shōushí (gather-collect) <v.> tidy up: ~房间 tidy up your room || ~书桌tidy up your desk

56 晒 [曬] shài (sun-dry) <v.> sun: ~衣服dry clothes in the sun || 他们坐着~太阳they sat in the sun roasting themselves

57 点燃 [點-] diǎnrán (light-flame) <v.> light: ~香烟light a cigarette || ~蜡烛light a candle

58 点 [點] diǎn (to light) <v.> light: ~灯light a lamp || ~烟light a cigarette || ~亮lighten

59 烧 [燒] shāo (burn, cook) <v.> cook, boil: ~菜 cook dish || ~水boil water

60 热 [熱] rè (hot, heat) <v.> heat: ~饭菜heat food || ~过一次heat once

61 加热 [-熱] jiārè (increase-heat) <separable word> heat: 加一下热heat a little bit || ~五分钟heat for 5 minutes || 慢慢~ hear slowly

62 做饭 [-飯] zuòfàn (make-food) <separable word> cook: 做一顿饭 cook a meal || 做早饭cook breakfast

63 下厨 [-] xiàchú (go to-kitchen) <v.> go to the kitchen to cook or prepare a meal: 亲自~ cook by yourself

64 烹调 [-調] pēngtiáo (cook-to season) <v.> cook: ~食物 cook food || ~方法the way of cooking || 善于~ be good at cooking

65 煎 [-] jiān (pan-fry) <v.> pan-fry: ~鸡蛋pan-fry eggs || ~鱼pan-fry fish

66 烤 [-] kǎo (roast) <v.> roast: ~排骨roast ribs || ~鸡腿roast chicken legs

67 煮 [-] zhǔ (boil) <v.> boil: ~鸡蛋面 boil egg noodle || ~饺子boil dumplings

68 炖 [燉] dùn (stew) <v.> stew: ~牛肉stew beef || 清~ stew without sauce

69 熬 [-] áo (simmer) <v.> cook into porridge or thick soup: ~粥cook porridge || ~中药concoct Chinese traditional medicine

70 炒 [-] chǎo (stir-fry) <v.> saute: 把洋葱~五分钟. Saute the onions for five minutes.

71 炸 [-] zhá (fry) <v.> fry: ~面包圈 fry donuts || ~鸡fried chicken

72 蒸 [-] zhēng (steam) <v.> steam: 清~鱼steamed fish

73 红烧 [-燒] hóngshāo (brown-braise) <v.> braise in brown sauce: ~肉 pork braised in brown sauce || ~茄子eggplant braised in brown sauce

74 吃饭 [-飯] chīfàn (eat-food) <v-o> eat: 一起~ eat together

75 品 [-] pǐn (numerous, judge, savor) <v.> taste sth. with discrimination, savor: ~茶 taste tea || ~酒 taste wine

76 尝 [嘗] cháng (taste) <v.> try the flavor of: ~味道/滋味 taste the flavor || ~一口taste a bite of
77 品尝 [-嘗] pǐncháng (savor-taste) <v.> taste: ~美味taste delicious food
78 喂 [餵] wèi (feed) <v.> feed: ~饭feed food || ~病人feed the patience || ~药feed pills
79 聚餐 [-] jùcān (together-dine) <v.> have a dinner party: 在饭店~ have dinner party in the restaurant
80 请客 [請-] qǐngkè (invite-guest) <separable word> treat: 请一次客 have a treat || 我~ my treat
81 宴请 [-請] yànqǐng (banquet-treat) <v.> entertain: ~宾客entertain guests
82 招待 [-] zhāodài (invite-treat) <v.> entertain: ~客人entertain the guests
83 干杯 [乾-] gānbēi (empty-cup) <v.> cheers: 一起~ cheers together || 为我们的成功~ cheers for our success || 为他们的友谊~ cheers for their friendship
84 敬酒 [-] jìngjiǔ (toast-wine) <v.> toast: 向新娘~ toast to bride
85 猜拳 [-] cāiquán (guess-fist) <v> play the finger-guessing game (played at a dinner party by two people): ~喝酒 play a finger-guessing game while drinking|| ~取乐play a finger-guessing game for fun

Tips:

1 Chinese cooking methods: Because the Chinese like to eat hot foods, most of their cooking methods are related to fire, for example (红) 烧, 烤, 炖, 炒, 炸, 烹, 煎, 煮, 熬, 蒸, 热, all listed above and having 'fire' (火) on the left part of the characters or in the lower part (灬).
2 Banquet: A banquet is the best place to observe how Chinese people behave according to their social status, unless they are drunk. If you want to learn about Chinese culture, banquets are perhaps the best starting place.

Exercises:

Part I: Use the given bound form here as a guide to help you think of other words with the same character. Feel free to use your dictionary when needed. Then write down the English definition of each of the words you've written.

养 *(rest, heal, recuperate one's health):* 养伤 *heal the wound*

____

____

____

____

住 *(live):* 住院 *be in hospital, to be hospitalized*

____

____

____

____

居 *(live)*: 居住 *live*

____

____

____

Part II: Read the following words and then answer the questions.

煎、烤、煮、炖、熬、炒、蒸、红烧、炸

1 上面哪些烹饪方法是美国家庭最常用的?

2 上面哪些烹饪方法是中国北方家庭最常用的?

3 上面哪些烹饪方法表示做的时候要放油或者酱油?

4 上面哪些烹饪方法做的食物很健康? 为什么?

住宿、露营、安家、搬家、疗养、保养、保健、打扮、美容、减肥、开夜车

5 上面哪些词跟"住"有关系?

6 上面哪些词跟"保持健康"有关系?

7 上面哪些词跟"让自己更漂亮"有关系?

8 你会经常开夜车吗? 为什么?

Theme 125: To employ, to benefit 就业, 造福 (jiùyè, zàofú)

1 就业 [-業] jiùyè (obtain-employment) <v.> employment: 重新~ re-employment || ~机会 employment opportunity || ~困难 employment difficulties

2 工作 [-] gōngzuò (work-do) <v./n.> job, work: 在银行~ work in the bank || ~了五年 work for five years || 参加~ participate in jobs

3 干活儿 [幹-兒] gànhuór (do-work) <v.> work: 帮他 ~ help him work || 干半天活儿 work for a while || 干累活儿do the hard work

4 打工 [-] dǎgōng (*prefix*-work) <v-o> work a temporary or casual job, (of students) have a job outside of class time, or during vacation.: 他在餐馆~. He worked in a restaurant || 为了付学费, 一些大学生会在暑假~. Some college students work in the summer vacation to pay for their tuition fees.

5 求职 [-職] qiúzhí (apply for-job) <v.> apply for a job: 毕业~ look for job after the graduation || 多次 ~ apply for a job many times || ~失败 fail to get job

6 招聘 [-] zhāopìn (recruit-invite) <v.> recruitment, recruit: 公开~ the open recruitment || ~营业员recruit salesperson || ~人才recruiting talents

7 应聘 [應-] yìngpìn (accept-recruitment) <v.> apply for: ~当服务员apply for a job as a waiter || ~到高校工作 apply to work in college

8 劳动 [勞動] láodòng (labor-work) <v.> work, labor: 辛勤~ work hard || 体力~ manual labor || 脑力~ mental work

9 当 [當] dāng (equal, work as, become) <v.> become, be: ~医生be a doctor || ~老师 be a teacher

10 做 [-] zuò (do, act as) <v.> to be: ~老板being a boss || ~会计be an accountant || ~律师 be a lawyer

11 担任 [擔-] dānrèn (take upon-assign sb. to a post) <v.> assume the office of, hold the post of: ~经理work as a manager|| 谁将~下一任美国总统? Who will be the next U.S. president?

12 任 [-] rèn (assign sb. a post) <v.> take up a job, assume a post: ~总经理 hold office as a general manager || ~院长be a dean

13 加班 [-] jiābān (add-work time) <separable word> work overtime: 这个周末我需要~. I need to work overtime this weekend

14 跳槽 [-] tiàocáo (jump-manger) <v.> job hopping, leave one's work and go to another: 在大城市, ~很平常. Job-hopping is common in big cities. || 频繁~ frequent job hopping || 小王不在这儿工作了, 他上个星期~了. Little Wang doesn't work here any longer. He left to go to another job.

15 经商 [經-] jīngshāng (manage-business) <v.> do business: ~赚钱make money in business

16 做生意 [-] zuòshēngyì (do-business) <v.> do business: 会~ be good at doing business || 跟中国人~ do business with the Chinese

17 做买卖 [-買賣] zuòmǎimài (do-trade) <v.> trade: 喜欢~ like to do trade

18 从政 [從-] cóngzhèng (engage in-politics) <v.> go into politics, the career in politics: 他毕业以后打算从政~. He plans to go into politics after his graduation.

19 创业 [創業] chuàngyè (start-business) <v.> start one's own business: ~公司start-up company

20 参军 [參軍] cānjūn (join-army) <v.> join the army: 自愿~ join the army voluntarily

21 务农 [務農] wùnóng (engage in-agriculture) <v.> farming: 他在非洲 ~. He is farming in Africa. || 他家世代~. His family has been farming for generations.

22 兼 [-] jiān (and) <v.> be part of, holding two or more (official) posts at the same time: ~职part-time/secondary job || 工程师~经理 engineer and manager || 导演~翻译 (fānyì) director and translator

23 辞职 [辭職] (resign-position) <separable word> resign: 正式~ formal resignation

24 辞退 [辭-] cítuì (dismiss-leave) <v.> dismiss: ~工人dismiss workers

25 炒鱿鱼 [-魷魚] chǎoyóuyú (fry-squid) <v.> be fired: 被老板~ got fired by the boss

26 退休 [-] tuìxiū (retire-rest) <v.> retire: 提早~ early retirement || 不愿~ do not want to retire || ~工人retired workers

27 失业 [-業] shīyè (lose-employment) <v.> unemployment: 大量~ a lot of unemployment || 工人~ unemployed workers || ~人数 the number of unemployment

28 下岗 [-崗] xiàgǎng (off-post) <v.> lay off: 暂时 (zànshí) ~ temporarily lay off || ~工人 laid-off workers

29 造福 [-] zàofú (create-fortune) <v.> benefit: ~人类benefit to mankind || ~后代benefit future generatuons

30 争光 [爭-] zhēngguāng (win-honor) <v.> win an honor: 为国~ win an honor for one's country

31 争气 [爭氣] zhēngqì (win-spirit) <v.> make a good showing, win credit for : 为父母~ work hard to win honor for one's parents|| 为中国~bring credit to China|| 怪自己不~ blame oneself for the failure

32 发扬 [發揚] fāyáng (develop-enhance) <v.> carry forward: ~民主carry forward the democracy || ~优良传统carry forward the fine tradition || ~改革精神carry forward the spirit of reform

33 行善 [-] xíngshàn (do-good) <v.> do good: 劝人~ persuade people to do good

Tips:

1 跳槽 (tiàocáo): It originally means 'livestock moves to another's manger to eat,' which became 'job hopping' in the mid-1980s.

2 炒鱿鱼 (chǎo yóuyú): In ancient China, employees had to take their own bedding to the workplace, and when one was fired, he had to roll up his bedding (卷铺盖, juǎn pūgài) to leave. When you fry a squid, the meat will shrink and curl like a roll (bedroll.) 炒鱿鱼 is a Cantonese expression and means 'to lay off,' which was borrowed into Mandarin in the 1980s.

3 下岗: The term 下岗 was coined in the late 1990s and means '(temporarily) laid off' which was meant to avoid using "失业" (unemployment), for the sake of the government tauting the superiority of Communism over Capitalism.

4 兼 (jiān): The ancient form of 兼 depicts 'a hand holding two crops,' which later evolved into 'to hold two or more concurrently.' If one holds more than one position, the non-primary positions are called "兼***," for example, Chinese politician Zhou Enlai (1898–1976) was Premier (总理, 1949–1976) 兼 Foreign Minister (外交部长, 1949–1958.)

Exercises:

Read the following sentences and fill in each blank with the appropriate word or phrase from the options given.

1 下岗、炒鱿鱼、退休、打工

a) 他工作态度非常差, 经常迟到, 完不成分配 (fēnpèi, distribute) 的任务, 因此老板把他________了.
b) 在中国一般男性60岁就可以________了, 而美国需要65岁以上.
c) 这家工厂关闭了, 因此有大批工人________.
d) 美国有些高中生会在课余时间________, 增加自己的社会经验.

2 就业、劳动、创业

a) 中国政府鼓励 (gǔlì, encourage) 大学毕业生自己________, 开公司.
b) 经济危机到来的时候, 大学毕业生的________率特别低.
c) 马克思主义认为________在从猿到人的转变过程中起了重要作用.

3 经商、务农、从政

a) 在中国古代________的人虽然有钱, 但是社会地位并不高.
b) 文革时期, 大批中学生被政府派到农村________.
c) 小张从北京大学毕业以后开始________, 第一份工作是县长助理 (zhùlǐ, assistant).

4 兼职、应聘、招聘

a) 这个公司今年要__________十名大学毕业生, 但是来_________的人有一百多人.
b) 小张上大学的时候在一家公司做__________工作, 积累 (jīlěi, accumulate) 了一些工作经验.

5 跳槽、炒鱿鱼、干活、加班

a) 这个年轻人________非常勤快 (qínkuài, hardworking), 老板很喜欢他.
b) 小张公司常常让他周末的时候_________工作, 他很不喜欢. 小张决定工作一年以后就_________到别的公司.
c) 在中国八九十年代的时候, 职场上特别流行一个词是"_________," 意思是辞职或者被老板开除了.

Theme 126: To involve 参与 (cānyǔ)

1 做 [-] zuò (do) <v.> do: ~实验 (shíyàn) do an experiment || ~事 do a thing
2 从事 [從-] cóngshì (join-engage) <v.> go after, engage in: ~音乐工作 audition for music work || ~教学工作engage in teaching || ~的职业 (zhíyè) the occupation you engage in
3 搞 [-] gǎo (do, make) <v.> do: ~教学 be in teaching || ~企业 (qǐyè) be in a company || ~经济 be engaged in the economy
4 干 [幹] gàn (do, work) <v.> do: ~坏事 do a bad thing || 你~什么工作? what do you do? || ~事情 doing things
5 试 [試] shì (try) <v.> try: ~一下 a quick try || ~衣服 try on clothes || ~着开车 try to drive a car
6 试验 [試驗] shìyàn (try-test) <v.> test: 做~ do a test || 三次~ three tests || ~成功 test successfully
7 摸索 [-] mōsuǒ (feel out-seek) <v.> try to discover: ~规律 explore the law || ~经验 find out experience || ~方法 try to find a way
8 实验 [實驗] shíyàn (real-test) <v./n.> experiment: 做~ do an experiment || 两次~ two experiments || 科学~ science experiment
9 考察 [-] kǎochá (investigate-inspect) <v.> inspect: 实地~ field inspection || 出国~ exiting-the-country inspection || 仔细~ careful observation
10 分工 [-] fēngōng (divide-work) <separable word> divide up the work, division of labor: 分一下工 divide up some work || 社会~ social division of labor|| ~负责 division of labor with individual responsibility
11 合作 [-] hézuò (together-do) <v.> collaborate: 长期~ long term collaboration || 跟他~ work together with him || 共同~ cooperate with each other
12 搭档 [-檔] dādàng (connect-partnership) <v./n.> work together, partner: 跟她~ team up with her || 我的~ my partner

13 配合 [-] pèihé (coordinate-together) <v.> coordinate: ~得很好 coordinate very well || 相互~ work in coordination || 密切~ work closely with

14 服务 [-務] fúwù (serve-work) <v./n.> serve, service: 为大家 ~ serve for everyone || ~行业 seivce industry || 热心为顾客~ warm-heartedly serve the customers

15 负责 [負責] fùzé (shoulder-responsibility) <v.> be responsible for, in charge of: ~做饭 be responsible for making food || 对病人~ be responsible for patients || 由她~拍照 she is in charge of taking pictures

16 承担 [-擔] chéngdān (undertake-take up) <v.> take on: ~责任 (zérèn) take on responsibility || ~任务 take on the task || 无力~ be unable to afford college tuition.

17 替罪羊 [-] tìzuìyáng (take the place of-guilt-goat) <v.> scapegoat: 当~ serve as scapegoat || 找~ look for a scapegoat

18 保证 [-證] bǎozhèng (assure-guarantee) <v./n.> guard, certify: ~质量 quality assurance || ~帮你 pledge to help you || 安全~ safety pledge

19 担保 [擔-] dānbǎo (take up-guarantee) <v./n.> guarantee: ~完全正确 guarantee complete correctness || 以房子为~ housing guarantee || 提供~ provide assurance

20 加入 [-] jiārù (join-into) <v.> join, add: ~戏剧社 join a drama club || ~这家公司 join this company || ~一点糖 add some sugar

21 入党 [-黨] rùdǎng (join-party) <v.> join the CCP: 早日~ early joiner of the CCP || 要求~ required to join the CCP

22 参赛 [參賽] cānsài (participate-competition) <v.> participate in a match: ~选手 contestant

23 参与 [參與] cānyù (participate-take part in) <v.> participate: ~工作 be involved with a job || ~竞争 participate in a contest || 积极~ active participation

24 参展 [參-] cānzhǎn (participate-exhibition) <v.> take part in a trade show: 到各地~ go everywhere to be in a trade show || 多次~ repeatedly be in a trade show || ~作品 display products

25 排队 [-隊] páiduì (line up-line) <v.> line up: 到那边~ line up over there || ~买票 ticket line

26 参加 [參-] cānjiā (participate-join) <v.> participate, join: ~考试 take a test || ~比赛 play in a game || ~工作 start a job

27 采访 [採訪] cǎifǎng (gather-interview) <v.> interview: 现场~ on-site interview || ~了一位普通人 interview with an ordinary people || 新闻~ news interview

28 出席 [-] chūxí (appear-occasion) <v.> attend: ~会议 attend a meeting || ~活动 attend an event || ~法庭/开幕式 go to a court/ceremony

29 跟随 [-隨] gēnsuí (after-follow) <v.> follow: ~父母 follow parents || ~家人 follow family || ~多年 follow for a long time

30 共享 [-] gòngxiǎng (together-share) <v.> share: 资源 (zīyuán) ~ share resources || 与别人~ share with other people || ~单车bike-sharing

31 加盟 [-] jiāméng (join-alliance) <v.> join: ~一家公司 join a company || 正式~ officially join || 企业~ join a business

32 联手 [聯-] liánshǒu (join-hand) <v.> act together: ~做生意 do business together || 跟他 ~ work with him || 夫妻~ act together as husband and wife

33 投入 [-] tóurù (throw-into) <v./n.> put into, invest in, throw into: ~人力 thrown into labor force || ~精力put effort into || ~市场 put into the market

34 作 [-] zuò (do) <v.> do: ~工作 do a job || ~研究 do graduate studies || ~对比 make a comparison
35 在场 [-場] zàichǎng (present-occasion) <v.> be present, on the scene: 当时我没~ i wasn't there at the tim || ~观众the present audience in a theater, on TV etc || ~帮忙 be there to help
36 分享 [-] fēnxiǎng (divide-share) <v.> share: ~经验 share experiences || ~成功 share success || ~信息 share news
37 轮 [輪] lún (wheel, take turns) <v.> take turns: ~ 到他 come to his turn || ~不上 cannot be one's turn|| 一周一~ take turns once a week

38 缺席 [-] quēxí (absent-occasion) <v.> be absent: ~三次 be absent three times || ~审判 be absent from the trial
39 缺勤 [-] quēqín (absent-attendance) <v.> not be at work/school: 无故~ be absent for no reason || 连续~ continuous absence || 随意~ random absence
40 逃课 [-課] táokè (escape-class) <v.> skip class: ~ 三天 skip class for three days

Tips:

1 逃课 (táokè): It means 'to skip class,' which is a phenomenon not uncommon in college. 逃 means 'to run away, to flee, to escape,' which does not sound very positive, so students like to use other words such as 翘课 or 跷课/蹺課 (both 'qiàokè') to make this kind of behavior less culpable or sound 'cool.'
2 共享 (gòngxiǎng): It means 'to share, shared.' 共享经济 (sharing economy) is booming worldwide, including in China. It is really a breakthrough in the Chinese mindset since markets for second-hand or used items were not popular in China until the last decade.
3 实验 (shíyàn) vs. 试验 (shìyàn): 实验 means 'to experiment' and 试验 'to test, to try.' The former is more scientific and the latter refers more to 'not in the final stage.'

Exercises: Read the following sentences and fill in each blank with the appropriate word or phrase from the options given.

1 做、搞、试

a) 不管______什么工作, 兴趣都很重要.
b) 小王没当过老师, 但是他想________一试老师这种工作.
c) 有人认为工作能力不重要, 跟同事或者领导________好关系很重要.

2 实验、摸索、考察

a) 小王在一所大学的化学_________室工作, 周末的时候常常加班.
b) 小王最近要到美国大学的化学实验室进行_________.
c) 据说朝鲜的核武器经过很多年的_________, 已经发展到了最后阶段, 用不了多久就可以真正使用.

3 联手、共享、加盟

a) 最近几年, 美国的"________经济"发展很快, 例如爱彼fl (Airbnb) 、优步 (Uber) 等等.

b) 据说优步 (Uber) 公司在2016年就已经_________了中国的滴滴打车公司, 共同发展中国市场.
c) 美国政府希望与中国________解决朝鲜的核武器问题.

4 投入、在场、跟随

a) 中国政府在西亚国家_______了大量资金, 帮助它们修建高铁.
b) 小王下个月会________公司领导带西亚国家进行商务考察.
c) 小王的公司今天要召开一个重要会议, 但是因为个人原因小王不能_______.

5 缺席、逃课、出席

a) 这所大学规定, 如果学生在一门课上________ 超过五次, 就不能参加这门课的期末考试.
b) 每年五月这所大学都会召开毕业典礼,学校领导会全部_________毕业典礼, 没有人_________.

6 参与、参加、参赛

a) 在昨天的中国大学生智能机器人大赛上, 共有三十个大学代表队_________. 所有_________比赛的选手都是各个大学制作智能机器人的"高手."
b) 美国联邦调查局 (FBI) 认为来自西亚国家的恐怖分子__________了昨天的这起爆炸案 (case of explosions).

7 负责、加入、担任

a) 美国大学校长一般_________为学校筹款 (fundraising), 制定发展方向等方面的工作.
b) 小王的父亲在一所中国大学_________校长二十多年了. 他父亲是一名老党员, 1949年就_______中国共产党了.

8 保证、承担

a) 为了__________学生的身体健康, 中国教育部 (Ministry of Education) 决定为经济落后地区的农村学生提供免费的营养午餐.
b) 中国教育部规定, 如果学生在校期间出现了人身安全 (personnel safety) 问题, 学校要_________全部责任.

Theme 127: To use 使用 (shǐyòng)

1 利用 [-] lìyòng (beneficial-use) <v.> use, take advantage of: 好好~时间 make good use of one's time || ~机会 use an opportunity || 充分~ full of uses
2 弄 [-] nòng (play, make, do) <v.> make: ~两个菜 make two dishes || ~清楚/明白 make it clear
3 使 [-] shǐ (order, let, make) <v.> cause, make: ~我们懂得 make us understand || ~情况更复杂 make the situation more complex || ~你听得见 make yourself hear it
4 使用 [-] shǐyòng (make-use) <v.> use, make use of, employ: 大量~ 新技术 use a lot of new technologies || ~工具 use a tool || ~毒品 use drugs

5 选 [選] xuǎn (choose) <v.> choose: ~水果 choose fruit || ~题目 choose a topic || ~日子 choose a day

6 应用 [應-] yìngyòng (accordingly-use) <v.> apply: ~在工业上 be applied in industry || 把理论~在实践上 apply theory to practice || 实际~ real applications

7 用 [-] yòng (use) <v.> use: ~右手 use your right hand || ~烤箱 use an oven || ~车 use a car

8 采纳 [採納] cǎinà (choose-accept) <v.> accept: ~意见 accept an opinion || ~建议 accept advice || ~方法 adopt a way of doing something

9 操作 [-] cāozuò (operate-do) <v.> operate: 反复~ repeatedly operate || 手工~ manual operation || ~机器 operate a machine

10 运用 [運-] yùnyòng (wield-use) <v.> use: ~新方法 use a new method || ~科学技术 use scientific technologies || 灵活~ apply in a flexible way

11 运作 [運-] yùnzuò (wield-do) <v.> operate, work: ~ 程序 operating procedures|| ~体系 operating system|| 资本~ capital operations

12 专用 [專-] zhuānyòng (special-use) <v.> use for special purpose: ~ 停车位 parking lot for special use || ~公路 accommodation (or private) road|| ~基金fund for special use

13 实施 [實-] shíshī (really-apply) <v.> carry out: ~计划 carry out a plan || ~法律 implement a law || ~健康教育 carry out health education

14 收藏 [-] shōucáng (collect-store up) <v.> collect and store up: ~古画 collect antique paintings || ~瓷器 collect porcelain || 精心~ collect carefully

15 收集 [-] shōují (collect-gather) <v.> gather, collect: ~意见 gather ideas || ~数据 collect data || ~信息 gather information

16 搜 [-] sōu (search) <v.> look for, search: 警察正在~ 逃犯. The police officer is searching a escaped criminal. || ~身 body search

17 搜索 [-] sōusuǒ (search-seek) <v.> search, hunt for: ~ 现场 search on site || ~逃犯 hunt for a fugitive || ~信息 search for information

18 挑 [-] tiāo (pick, choose) <v.> choose: ~人 choose a person || ~学校 pick a school

19 挑选 [-選] tiāoxuǎn (pick-choose) <v.> choose, pick: ~商品 choose merchandise || ~女主角 pick out an actress || ~合作伙伴 pick a partner

20 动手 [動-] dòngshǒu (move-hand) <v.> set about (a task), start work: 自己~ do the job oneself|| 准备好以后再~ plan it out before you start the work || ~做饭 start cooking food

21 通用 [-] tōngyòng (common-use) <v.> common use, interchangeable: 国际会议~ 语言 languages used at international conferences || 全国~教材 national textbooks

22 用来 [-來] yònglái (use-for) <v.> use for: ~飞行 use for flying || ~走路 use for walking || ~当雨伞 use as an umbrella

23 用于 [用於] yòngyú (use-in) <v.> use in: ~教育 use in education || ~农村 use in the countryside || ~研究 use in studies

Tips:

1 用 (yòng): It means 'to use, use.' The oracle form of 用 resembles the shape of a 'barrel' from which the meaning of 'use' evolved.

2 弄 (nòng): It functions as the English colloquial word 'to make' or 'to do.' For example, 中午我弄俩菜, 你弄瓶白酒, 咱俩好好聊聊 (At noon I'll make two dishes, you get a bottle of alcohol, and the two of us will have a good chat.) Another example, 我的电脑让我弄坏了, 然后我就修, 结果我弄來弄去也弄不明白到底哪儿出了问题 (My computer is down, and I tried to repair it. I tried again and again and am still unable to figure out what's the problem.)

Exercises:

Part I: Use the given bound form as a guide help you think of other words with the same character. Feel free use your dictionary when needed. Then write down the English definition of each of the words you've written.

用 *(use):* 利用 *use, take advantage of*

____

____

____

____

____

____

Part II: Multiple Choice. Make sure to choose the most appropriate one

1 在小学教育中, 培养孩子的________能力非常重要.

A. 用于 B. 动手 C. 通用

2 这所小学每年都会_________有运动特长的孩子组成一个足球队.

A. 挑选 B. 搜索 C. 收集

3 这家博物馆_________了很多中国明清时期的瓷器 (chinaware) 和字画.

A. 运作 B. 专用 C. 收藏

4 最近几年人工智能 (Aritificial Intelligence) 在各个行业都________得非常广泛.

A. 实施 B. 操作 C. 应用

5 最近美国市场上有很多家用机器人, 使用这种机器人_________简单, 使用方便.

A. 操作 B. 实施 C. 采纳

Theme 128: To move 走动 (zǒudòng)

1 进 [進] jìn (move forward, enter) <v.> enter: ~门 go through a door || ~城 enter a city || ~商店 go into a shop
2 进来 [進來] jìnlái (enter-*Complement*) <v.> come in: 走~ walk in || ~一个人 one person came in || 他~了. He came in.
3 进去 [進-] jìnqù (enter-*Complement*) <v.> go in: 跑~ run inside || ~两个人 two people went in || 她~了. She went in.
4 进入 [進-] jìnrù (enter-into) <v.> enter: ~房间 enter a room || ~大公司 join a big company || ~秋天 begin the fall

5 出 [-] chū (grow up, go out) <v.> go out: 走~ walk out || ~大门 go out a big door || ~学校 exit school
6 出来 [-來] chūlái (go out-*Complement*) <v.> come out: 说~ speak out || 走~ come out || 看 ~ figure it out
7 出去 [-] chūqù (go out-*Complement*) <v.> go out: 说~ speak out || 走~ walk out || 卖~ sell out
8 外出 [-] wàichū (out-go) <v.> go out: ~办事 go away from work || ~劳动 leave physical work || ~旅游 go on tour
9 出门 [-門] chūmén (go out of-door) <v-o> leave: 已经~ already gone || 很少 ~ infrequently leave || ~旅游 leave on a tour

10 带 [帶] dàilái (belt, wear, bring) <v.> bring: ~书 bring a book || ~午饭bring lunch || ~衣服 bring clothing
11 带来 [帶來] dài (bring-*Complement*) <bf> bring, cause: ~ 方便bring convenience|| ~很大影响have a large influence || ~很多问题 cause lots of social problems
12 入 [-] rù (enter) <v.> enter, join: ~场 enter the venue for a meeting || ~党 join the CCP || ~大学 enter college
13 上 [-] shàng (high, go up) <v.> come (or go) up: ~车 get in a car || ~山 go (or climb) up a mountain || ~楼 go upstairs
14 上来 [-來] shànglái (come up-*Complement*) <v.> come up: 送~ send it up || 走~ walk up || 爬~ climb up
15 上去 [-] shàngqù (come up-*Complement*) <v.> go up: 送~ send it up || 走~ walk up there || 放~ put it there
16 下 [-] xià (below, descend, go down) <v.> go down: ~楼 go downstairs || ~山 go down the mountain || ~车 get off the car
17 下来 [-來] xiàlái (come down-*Complement*) <separable word> come down: 下得/不来 can/can't come down || 下楼来 come downstairs || 走~ walk down here
18 下去 [-] xiàqù (go down-*Complement*) <separable word> go down: 下得/不去 can/can't go down || 下楼去 go downstairs || 走~ walk down there

19 来 [來] lái (come) <v.> come: 客人~了 the guests came || 有人~了. Some people have come.
20 过来 [過來] guòlái (go over-*Complement*) <bf> come over: 跑~ run over here || 送~ bring it over || 借~ borrow
21 来到 [來-] láidào (come-arrive) <v.> arrive: ~办公室 get to the office || ~法国 arrive in France || ~一个酒吧 get to a bar

22 到来 [-來] dàolái (arrive-come) <v./n.> arrival: ~之前 before the arrival || 即将~ coming soon || 他的~ his arrival
23 去 [-] qù (go) <v.> go: ~图书馆 go to the library || ~外地 go to foreign lands || ~国外 leave the country
24 过去 [過-] guòqù (go over-*Complement*) <bf> go over: 走~ walk over there || 跳 ~ run over there || 飞 ~ fly over there

25 向前 [-] xiàngqián (toward-front) <v.> advance, forge ahead, ahead: ~看look ahead || ~走walk forward, move forward || ~发展 the forward development of
26 前进 [-進] qiánjìn (front-advance) <v.> advance: ~一大步 take one big step || 不断~ keep on advancing || 高速~ high speed forward
27 前来 [-來] qiánlái (over-come) <v.> come: ~考察 (kǎochá) come inspect || ~治病 come to cure || ~办事 come to work
28 前往 [-] qiánwǎng (go-to) <v.> go to: ~机场 go to the airport || ~采访 go to the interview || 一同~ go together
29 推进 [-進] tuījìn (push-forward) <v.> push forward: 向南~ push on southwards || ~房间 carry on with the room || ~改革 push on with reform
30 退 [-] tuì (retrait, move back) <v.> move back: ~休 retire || ~出 drop out || 后~ go backwards
31 退出 [-] tuìchū (retrait-out of) <v.> leave: ~房间 leave the room || ~会场 leave the conference room || ~历史舞台 exit a stage of history
32 倒车 [-車] dàochē (back-vehicle) <separable word> drive backwards: 倒一下车 drive backwards a bit || 开~ start reversing || 在这儿~ reverse over here
33 跟 [-] gēn (heel, follow) <v.> follow: ~进去 follow in || ~不上他 cannot follow him || ~在后头 follow in the back

34 逃 [-] táo (run away, escape, flee) <v.> flee: ~往海外 flee overseas || ~命/课 skip class || ~到乡下 flee to the countryside
35 逃跑 [-] táopǎo (flee-run) <v.> run away: 拼命~ desperately flee || 转身~ retreat || 从海上~ run away from the sea
36 逃走 [-] táozǒu (flee-away) <v.> run away: ~五个人 five people ran away || 向南~ flee southwards || 坐飞机~ flee on an airplane
37 跑 [-] pǎo (run) <v.> run: ~一千米 run 1,000 meters || ~过去 run over there
38 抓 [-] zhuā (grasp, pay special attention to) <v.> stress: ~生产 stress production || ~大事 focus on big issues || ~学习 stress studies
39 追 [-] zhuī (chase) <v.> chase: ~火车 chase a train || ~小兔子 chase a little rabbit || ~蝴蝶 chase a butterfly
40 摆脱 [擺-] bǎituō (break away from-separate from) <v.> break away from: ~小偷break away from the thief || ~贫穷 escape poverty || ~家务 (劳动) escape house chores
41 躲 [-] duǒ (hide) <v.> hide, avoid: ~债 avoid a creditor || ~在家里 hide in the house || ~起来 start hiding
42 躲避 [-] duǒbì (hide-avoid) <v.> hide: ~劳动avoid labor || ~债务 (zhàiwù) avoid debt
43 藏 [-] cáng (store, hide) <v.> hide: ~东西 hide stuff || ~在卧室 hide in the bedroom || ~在心里 hide in the heart

44 隐藏 [隱-] yǐncáng (conceal-hide) <v.> conceal, hide: ~实力 conceal strength || ~痛苦 hide pain || ~秘密 hide a secret

45 找 [-] zhǎo (look for, seek) <v.> look: ~东西 look for something || ~人 look for a person || ~老师 look for a teacher

46 寻找 [尋-] xúnzhǎo (search-look for) <v.> look for: ~原因 seek a reason || ~机会 look for an opportunity || ~道路 seek the way

47 上班 [-] shàngbān (go to-work) <v.> go to work: 准时~ go to work on time || 打车~ drive to work || 在公司~ go to work at the company

48 上街 [-] shàngjiē (go to-street) <v.> go to the street: ~买东西 go to the street to go shopping || ~溜达 (liūda) go take a walk on the street || 骑车~ bike on the streets

49 来往 [來-] láiwǎng (come-go) <v.> dealings: ~频繁 (pínfán) frequent dealings || 行人~ pedestrian dealings || ~多次 many dealings

50 脱离 [-離] tuōlí (separate-from) <v.> separate from: ~群众 separate from the crowd || ~时代 break away from the times || ~生活 break away from a lifestyle

51 往来 [來] wǎnglái (go-come) <v.> come and go: ~于两地 travel between two places || ~客车 come and go from the bus || ~车辆 get in and out of the car

Tips:

1 入 (rù) vs. 人 (rén): To beginners in Chinese, these two characters look alike, however, their meanings are poles apart. The oracle form of 入 resembles a tool with a pointy head, which can easily enter other stuff, therefore the extended meaning 'to enter' evolved. 人 resembles the left profile of a standing man with an arm and a leg.

2 来 (來, lái, come) vs. 麦 (麥, mài, wheat): Interestingly enough, 来 (來) should be the original form of 麦 (麥) and vice versa.

3 来往 (láiwǎng): 来 means 'to come' and 往 'to go.' 'Come' and 'go' make 'contact' and 'socialize.' The Chinese value 来往 so there are two sayings, "礼尚往来" (lǐshàngwǎnglái, courtesy demands reciprocity) and "来而不往非礼也" (it is impolite not to reciprocate.)

4 去 (qù): It is related to大 (人, a man) and 凵 (ground hole,) thus meaning 'to leave (danger.)'

Exercises: Please translate the following phrases into English.

中文	英文
上街买东西	
带来一些水果	
进来一个人	
进入大公司工作	
来到美国大学学习	
政府将要继续推进改革	
推出海外市场	

帮助这个地区摆脱贫困	
寻找新的机会	
理论脱离实际	
高速公路上车辆来来往往	

Theme 129: Trouble, remedy 麻烦, 补救 (máfan, bǔjiù)

1 闹事 [鬧-] nàoshì (make-trouble) <v-o> make trouble: 带头~ be the head troublemaker || 到处 ~ make trouble everywhere
2 惹是生非 [-] rěshìshēngfēi (stir-trouble-cause-dispute) <idiom> start a dispute: 从不~ never started trouble
3 胡闹 [-鬧] húnào (recklessly-play) <v.> be up to mischief: 我小时候喜欢和很多孩子~、惹事. ~ I liked to be up to mischief and make trouble with other kids when I was young.
4 撒野 [-] sāyě (let oneself go-wild) <v.> act wildly: 不许~ troublemaking not allowed
5 逞强 [-] chěngqiáng (flaunt-superiority) <v.> flaunt one's superiority: 她好(hào) 在朋友和同学面前~. She is fond of flaunting her superiority before her friends and schoolmates. || ~好 (hào) 胜 seek to prevail over others
6 逞能 [-] chěngnéng (show off-skill) <v.> show off your skills: 爱~ love to show off your skills
7 摆 [擺] bǎi (break away, arrange, show off) <v.> take on: ~架子 put on airs (act superior) || ~阔act wealthy || ~老资格to act like you have experience
8 炫耀 [-] xuànyào (dazzle-shine) <v.> flaunt: ~ 武力have a show of force || 到处~ showing off everywhere || ~自己 show off yourself
9 作秀 [-] zuòxiù (make-*transliteration* of show) <v.> make a show: 政治~ put on a political display || 善于~ be good at making a show
10 表现 [-現] biǎoxiàn (outer side-appear) <v.> show off: 好~ like to show off himself || 爱~自己love to show off || 善于~ good at showing off
11 倚老卖老 [--賣-] yǐlǎomàilǎo (rely-seniority-sell-seniority) <idiom> use your seniority: 我爷爷总是~, 把他的想法强加给我. Presuming his seniority, my grandfather always imposes his ideas upon me.
12 出风头 [-風頭] chūfēngtóu (forstall-lime light) <v.> show off, look for fame: 个人~ personal search for fame || 爱~ love the spotlight || 好~ be fond of the limelight
13 炫富 [-] xuànfù (flaunt-wealth) <v.> flaunt wealth: 很多年轻人喜欢~. Many young people like to flaunt their wealth.
14 晒* [曬] shài (sun-dry, publicize) <v.> publicize, show off, flaunt: ~孩子flaunt one's kid || ~工资单 publicize the payroll
15 编 [編] biān (put in order, weave, compile, make up) <v.> write: ~理由compile reasons || ~借口 come up with excuses || ~谎言make up a lie
16 杜撰 [-] dùzhuàn (Dù-fabricate) <v.> make up: ~事实 make up a story
17 冒充 [-] màochōng (sham-pretend) <v.> pretend to be something, feign: ~好人pretend to be a good person || ~记者 pass oneself off as a reporter
18 污辱 [汙-] wūrǔ (defile-insult) <v.> insult: ~别人 insult other people

19 犯错 [-錯] fàncuò (make-mistake) <separable word> make a mistake: 犯了个大错make a big mistake || 犯了个小错to make a little error
20 违规 [違規] wéiguī (violate-regulation) <separable word> break rules: 违了规broke the rules || ~行为illegal behavior || ~广告 illegal advertising
21 失误 [-誤] shīwù (lose-mistake) <v.> mess up: 发球~ serving fault || 工作~ work error || 判断~ error of judgment
22 误会 [誤會] wùhuì (mistake-comprehend) <v.> misunderstand: ~别人misunderstand someone || 别/不要~ don't misunderstand || ~他的意思misunderstand his meaning
23 误解 [誤-] wùjiě (mistake-understand) <v./n.> misunderstanding: 引起~ lead to misunderstanding || 产生~ cause misunderstanding || ~她的意思misunderstood her meaning

24 冒险 [-險] màoxiǎn (take-risk) <v./n.> take a risk, adventure: 喜欢~ like to take the risks|| 一些公司 ~逃税. Some companies risk evading tax payments.
25 玩火 [-] wánhuǒ (play-fire) <v.> play with fire (figuratively): ~自焚set yourself on fire || 故意 ~ deliberately play with fire (take a risk)

26 改 [-] gǎi (change, correct) <v.> correct an error: ~错 fix a mistake || ~掉坏习惯 get rid of bad habits
27 改正 [-] gǎizhèng (to correct-correct) <v.> amend: ~错误correct a mistake || ~不良习惯 correct one's bad habit || ~缺点 overcome one's shortcomings
28 纠正 [糾-] jiūzhèng (rectify-correct) <v.> correct, make right: ~姿势correct sb.'s posture || ~错字 fix a typo|| ~行业不正之风 correct malpractices in all trades and professions
29 弥补 [彌補] míbǔ (fill-make up) <v.> make up for: ~错误remedy a mistake|| ~不足 make up for shortcomings|| ~损失 make up for a loss
30 补救 [補-] bǔjiù (make up-remedy) <v.> remedy: ~办法corrective measure || ~措施remedial measure
31 澄清 [-] chéngqīng (clarify-clear) <v.> clarify: ~事实 clarify a fact || ~是非clarify rights and wrongs || ~疑点to clear up doubts
32 亡羊补牢 [--補-] wángyángbǔláo (lose-sheep-mend-pen) <idiom> lock the barn door after the sheep has been stolen: 有人认为中国在环境被污染了以后才开始保护环境, 这是 ~. Some people think China has only begun to protect the environment after environmental pollution, but is it too late to mend the damage?

Tips:

1 杜撰 (dùzhuàn): It was said that in the Song Dynasty, a poet named Dù Mò (c. 1021-c. 1089) did not follow poetic rules and forms when he wrote poems, therefore people call 'fabricated, to make up' 杜撰. 撰 itself means 'to write.'
2 污辱 (wūrǔ) vs. 侮辱 (wǔrǔ): Their pronunciations are similar and their meanings are the same, 'to insult.' They are different as the object of 侮辱 is more like 'dignity,' and that of 污辱 'virginity, divinity.' If someone was slapped in the face in public, it is 侮辱, but if a woman was raped, it is 污辱.

3 晒* (shài *): After social media was developed and became very accessible to ordinary people, many people began to show off (晒) their glorious side, such as wealth, happiness and individuality.

Exercises:

Part I: Put similar meaning words in the same table.

惹事生非、补救、纠正错误、改正错误、误解、杜撰、逞能

闹事:
弥补:
误会:
编:
逞强:

Part II: Read the following sentences and fill in each blank with the appropriate word or phrase from the options given.

1 弥补、亡羊补牢、澄清

a) 这场地震给这个地区的老百姓造成了无法_______的损失.
b) 关于这件事情我需要_________一下, 不是我做的.
c) 小偷进入室内偷走了小张的苹果电脑以后, 他才意识到应该安装一个防盗门, 真是________.

2 冒险、失误、玩火自焚

a) 年轻人吸毒等于是_________, 自己毁了自己的一生.
b) 炒股是一件很_______的投资方式, 风险很大.
c) 年轻人因为经验不足, 在工作中难免会有________.

3 污辱、犯错、违规

a) 在美国_______别人是一种违法行为.
b) 去年他在工作中多次______, 差点儿丢了饭碗.
c) 小王因为_______停车被开了一张罚单.

4 编、炫富、晒

a) 小王很喜欢_____理由, 找借口, 来说明自己没错.
b) 有些年轻人很喜欢在网上_______自己的名车、豪宅什么的, 这就是大家所说的______.

5 出风头、倚老卖老、作秀

a) 有人认为美国前总统奥巴马 (Obama) 只不过是一个会_______的政客.
b) 他很喜欢________, 不管什么事情都喜欢抢在别人前面去做.
c) 有些中国老人在公共场合训斥 (xùnchì, rebuke) 年轻人不尊重他们, 但是年轻人认为这些老人是_________.

Theme 130: Entertainment 娱乐 (yúlè)

(See also Theme 43)

1 娱乐 [-樂] yúlè (amuse-happy) <v./n.> entertain, entertainment, recreation: ~节目 an entertainment program || ~场所 place of recreation || ~大众 entertain the masses || ~圈 showbiz
2 休闲 [-閒] xiūxián (rest-leisure) <v.> leisure: ~活动 leisurely activities || ~方式 a leisurely method || ~食品 comfort food
3 玩儿 [-兒] wánr (play) <v.> play: ~游戏 play games || ~牌 play a card game || ~麻将 (májiàng) play mahjong
4 游 [遊] yóu (travel, stroll) <v.> tour: 七日~ a seven day tour || ~故宫 tour the imperial palace || ~山玩水 a sightseeing tour
5 观光 [觀-] guānguāng (see-scenery) <v.> go sightseeing: 旅游~ go sightseeing when traveling || 回国~ return from sightseeing || 去日本~ go sightseeing in Japan || ~客tourist
6 打牌 [-] dǎpái (play-cards) <separable word> play cards: 打一个小时牌 play cards for one hour
7 赌 [賭] dǔ (gamble, bet) <v.> bet: ~钱 bet money || 我~他赢. I bet he will win.
8 赌博 [賭-] dǔbó (gamble-gamble/risk) <v.> gamble: 参加~ gamble (with others) || 聚众 (jùzhòng) ~ gather to gamble || ~游戏 a gambling game
9 抽奖 [-獎] chōujiǎng (draw-prize) <separable word> lottery: 抽一等奖 win first prize in the lottery || 公开~ public lottery || 购物~ shopping lottery
10 打赌 [-賭] dǎdǔ (do-bet) <v> bet on: 跟经理~ make a bet with one's manager || 咱们打个赌. Let's make a bet.
11 抽签 [-簽] chōuqiān (draw-lot) <v> draw lots: 分组~ draw lots in a group || 抽了一个好签 draw a good sign
12 上网 [-網] shàngwǎng (go on-internet) <v.> go online: ~看新闻read news articles online || 手机~ online cellphone || 无线~ wireless Internet
13 泡吧 [-] pàobā (dillydally-club) <v> go clubbing: 泡酒吧spend time in a bar || 一起~ go clubbing together
14 捉迷藏 [-] zhuōmícáng (seek-bewilder-hide) <v.> play hide and seek: 玩~ play hide and seek || 我找他有事, 可是他跟我 (玩) ~. I was trying to find him, but he was hiding from me.
15 拔河 [-] báhé (tug-river) <v> tug-of-war: 比赛~ have a tug-of-war
16 逛 [-] guàng (stroll, visit) <v.> stroll, take a random walk: ~街 go shopping || ~商场stroll around the shopping mall || 去上海~~ go sightseeing in Shanghai
17 兜风 [-風] dōufēng (catch-wind) <n> catch the wind, go for a spin in the fresh air: 在河边骑车~, 很有意思. It's fun to take a spin on your bicycle along the river bank.
18 赶集 [趕-] gǎnjí (go-fair/market) <v> go to the farm market: 定期 ~ regularly go to the farm market
19 展览 [-覽] zhǎnlǎn (exhibit-view) <v./n.> exhibit, exhibition: 美术~ art exhibition || 图书~ books book exhibition || 小型~ a small exhibition || ~馆 museum || 摄影展 ~ a photography exhibition

20 观赏 [觀賞] guānshǎng (view-appreciate) <v> view and admire, enjoy the sight of, watch (sth marvelous): ~雕塑 (diāosù) ornamental sculpture || ~风景observe the scenery || ~自然风光observe the natural scenery
21 欣赏 [-賞] xīnshǎng (joyous-appreciate) <v.> enjoy: ~风景 enjoy the scenery || ~音乐enjoy music || ~艺术作品 enjoy works of art
22 鉴赏 [鑑賞] jiànshǎng (authenticate-appreciate) <n./v.> appreciation, appreciate: ~音乐 music appreciation || ~艺术 art appreciation

Tips:

1 好赌 (hàodǔ): It means 'to love gambling.' There is no need to prove that the Chinese are a people who loves gambling dearly. Go to any casino worldwide and you will find that Mandarin or Cantonese is the second most widely-used language, if not the first. Although every Chinese person knows proverbs such as 十赌九输 (ten-gamble-nine-lose,) 赌近盗 (dǔ jìn dào, gamble-close to-steal, if you gamble, you will definitely lose all your money, and you will have to steal to make your life or continue to gamble) and 赌场无父子 (gamblers know neither fathers nor sons), however, the Chinese cannot resist the temptation of getting rich through gambling. This is one reason why casinos aren't legal in Mainland China.
2 文物鉴赏 (wénwù jiànshǎng): It means 'appreciation of antiques.' Appraisal and trade of antiques is a popular industry because China has countless antiques from her long history. Bear in mind that there are thousands of times more fake antiques than real ones.

Exercises:

Part I: Use the given bound form as a guide help you think of other words with the same character. Feel free use your dictionary when needed. Then write down the English definition of each of the words you've written.

赏 *(view and admire):* 赏月 *enjoy a beatiful snow scene*

____

____

____

Part II: Read the following words and then answer the questions in Chinese.

打牌、赌博、上网、泡吧、逛夜市、看美术展览、看摄影展览、开车兜风、旅游观光、赶集、玩麻将、捉迷藏、拔河、看娱乐节目、欣赏音乐、欣赏艺术作品

1 上面哪些活动适合在室内进行 (indoor activities)?

____

2 上面哪些活动是在室外进行 (outdoor activities)?

---

3 上面哪些活动是你经常做的?

---

4 很多中国人喜欢玩麻将, 美国人呢?

---

5 你喜欢不喜欢逛夜市? 为什么?

Theme 131: Love, marriage 恋爱, 婚姻 (liàn'ài, hūnyīn)

1 恋爱 [戀愛] liàn'ài (feel attached to-love) <v./n.> be in love: 跟他/她~ be in love with him/her || 谈~ fall in love || 三角~ love triangle
2 约会 [約會] yuēhuì (appoint-meet) <v./n.> date: 和女朋友~ go on a date with your girlfriend || 第一次~ go on a date for the first time || 有 (一个) ~ have a date
3 拍拖 [-] pāituō (Cantonese 'attached-tow') <v> date: 跟外国人~ dating foreigners || ~四年了 dating for four years
4 追求 [-] zhuīqiú (pursue-seek) <v.> pursue: ~一个姑娘/女生 pursue a girl || ~自由pursue freedom || ~幸福 pursue happiness || ~享受pursue enjoyment
5 早恋 [-戀] zǎoliàn (early-date) <n> puppy love: 陷入~ fall in puppy love || 禁止~ prohibit puppy love
6 网恋 [網戀] wǎngliàn (online-date) <n.> online dating: 成功~ success in online dating
7 热恋 [熱戀] rèliàn (hot-date) <n> be head over heels in love, be passionately in love: 她~着她的朋友的哥哥 She is head over heels in love with her friend's older brother.
8 追 [-] zhuī (chase after, pursue) <v.> court: ~女朋友court a girlfriend
9 一见钟情 [-見鍾-] yījiànzhōngqíng (first-sight-sustain-affection) <idiom> love at first sight: 我跟他~ I fell in love with her at first sight. || 两个人~. The couple fell in love at first sight.
10 脚踩两只船 [腳-兩隻-] jiǎocǎiliǎngzhīchuán (foot-step-two-MW-boat) <proverb> (lit.) a person stepping on two boats, keeping options open: 他~, 跟两个女孩子谈恋爱. He is stepping on two boats as he fell in love with two girls.
11 劈腿 [-] pītuǐ (widely open-leg) <v> cheat: 因为男朋友~而分手 break up because of a cheating boyfriend
12 偷情 [-] tōuqíng (stealthily-affection) <n> affair, betrayal: 男女~ An affair between a man and a woman || 婚外~ have an extramarital affair || 英国王子也~. The prince of England also had an affair.
13 婚外恋 [--戀] hūnwàiliàn (marriage-outside-love) <n> an extramarital affair: 他 (有) 了~. He also had an extramarital affair.
14 失恋 [-戀] shīliàn (lose-love) <adj> be lovelorn, lose one's love: 他刚刚~了. He just lost his love.
15 求婚 [-] qiúhūn (propose-marriage) <v> propose marriage: 向女朋友~ get married to one's girlfriend || 接受他的~ accepted his proposal

16 订婚 [訂-] dìnghūn (engage-marriage) <n> engagement: 跟某人~ be engaged with someone || ~戒指engagement ring

17 聘礼 [-禮] pìnlǐ (betrothal-gift) <n> betrothal gift (from the family of the groom to family of the bride), bride-price: 下~ below the bride price || 中国古代的~可能是一头牛. In ancient China, a cow could serve as a betrothal gift.

18 结合 [結-] jiéhé (knot-combine) <v.> united in marriage, wedlock: 男女~ a man and woman bound together by marriage || 同性~ a same-sex couple bound by marriage

19 结婚 [結-] jiéhūn (knot-marriage) <v.> marry, get married: 跟他~ get married to him || ~两年 married for two years || 结了三次婚 have been married three times

20 办喜事 [辦--] bànxǐshì (hold-'happy-event') <v.> manage a wedding: 给儿子~ manage a wedding for one's son

21 离婚 [離-] líhūn (part-marriage) <v.> divorce, get divorced: 提出~ propose a divorce || 跟她~ divorce from her || 闹~ go through a divorce || 离过两次婚 have divorced twice

22 再婚 [-] zàihūn (again-marry) <n./v.> remarriage, remarry

23 改嫁 [-] gǎijià (alter-marry) <adj./v.> remarried, remarry: ~多次 remarry many times || 在以前的中国~被人看不起. In old China, remarriage was despised.

24 重婚 [-] chónghūn (double-marriage) <v.> bigamy: ~罪 the crime of bigamy || ~是违法的. Bigamy is against the law.

25 包养 [-養] bāoyǎng (chater-support) <v> have or support mistress: ~情人 (二奶) have mistresses || 求~ seeking a sugar daddy

26 早婚 [-] zǎohūn (early-marriage) <n.> early marriage: 禁止~ prohibit early marriage

27 晚婚 [-] wǎnhūn (late-marriage) <n.> late marriage: 提倡~ promote late marriage

28 已婚 [-] yǐhūn (already-married) <adj.> be married: ~妇女 a married woman

Tips:

1 婚姻 (hūnyīn): It means 'marriage.' The etymology of 婚姻 is not clear now. One explanation is that in ancient times, 婚姻 ceremonies were held in the evening (昏) since 婚姻 was also written as 昏姻 or 昏因. Another explanation is the bride's father is called 婚, and the bridegroom's father is called 姻.

2 晚婚: It means 'late marriage.' According to the latest Law of Marriage of the PRC (2017), when married for the first time, men over the age of 25 or women above the age of 23 are considered 晚婚, since the ages are three years older than the minimum age of marriage. The government had encouraged people to 晚婚, but since adjustments to end China's one-child policy in 2016, no incentive will be given to 晚婚 couples any more.

3 喜事: 喜事 means 'a happy event' and is often marriage. In a marriage ceremony, all the 喜 are written as 囍 (double of 喜) since the Chinese people strongly hold the opinion that marriage is about two people and two families.

Exercises:

Part I: Use the given bound form as a guide help you think of other words with the same character. Feel free use your dictionary when needed. Then write down the English definition of each of the words you've written.

恋 *(feel attached to)*: 恋爱 *be in love, love affair*

____
____
____
____
____
____

婚 *(marry)*: 结婚 *get married*

____
____
____
____
____

Part II: Multiple Choice. Make sure to choose the most appropriate answer.

1 小张不知道该选那个女孩儿当女友，所以就"脚踩两只船." 这句话的意思是:

A. 小张同时跟两个女孩儿谈恋爱
B. 小张不知道跟那个女孩儿去划船
C. 小张不知道自己的脚应该在那个船上

2 小李跟小王一见钟情, 这句话的意思是:

A. 小李跟小王都喜欢钟
B. 小李跟小王都喜欢见面
C. 小李跟小王第一次见面就相爱了

3 "办喜事"跟下面哪个词都意思相同:

A. 拍拖　　B. 结婚　　C. 办好事

4 "拍拖"跟下面哪个词都意思相同:

A. 约会　　B. 订婚　　C. 求婚

5 "丈夫死了以后, 她改嫁了." 这就话里"改嫁"的意思是:

A. 再婚　　B. 离婚　　C. 包养

6 “他们俩终于结合在一起了.” 这句话的意思是:

A. 他们俩终于结婚了
B. 他们俩最后同居了
C. 他们俩终于变成了一个人

7 “小李的女朋友劈腿了, 小李难过得想自杀.” 这句话的意思是:

A. 小李的女朋友把腿砍了, 小李难过得想自杀.
B. 小李的女朋友跟其他人恋爱了, 小李非常难过.
C. 小李的女朋友喜欢锻炼腿, 小李想自杀.

Theme 132: Funerals 丧葬 (sāngzàng)

(See also Theme 104)

1 吊唁 [-] diàoyàn (condole-extend condolence) <v./n.> express condolences: 参加~ participate in the condolences || ~老朋友 mourn old friends
2 悼念 [-] dàoniàn (mourn-miss) <v.> mourn: ~亲人mourn for families || ~活动memorial services
3 送葬 [-] sòngzàng (see-funeral) <v-o> attend a funeral: 为她~ attend her funeral || ~的队伍a funeral procession
4 安葬 [-] ānzàng (settle-bury) <v.> bury the dead: ~死者 bury the dead || ~在山上bury the dead on the hill
5 火化 [-] huǒhuà (fire-cremate) <v.> cremate: 尸体被~ The body was committed to the flames. || ~死者 cremate the dead || 在火葬场~ cremate the body in the crematorium
6 埋葬 [-] máizàng (bury-bury) <v.> bury: 他的遗体~在教堂的墓地. His mortal remains are buried in the churchyard. || ~穷人to bury the poor
7 戴孝 [-] dàixiào (wear-mourning dress) <v-o> wear the willow, be in mourning: 为父母~ wear the willow for parents
8 扫墓 [掃-] sǎomù (sweep-tomb) <v.> sweep the tomb: 清明~ sweep the tomb on Tomb Sweeping Day
9 上坟 [-] shàngfén (visit-grave) <v.> visit a grave to cherish the memory of the dead: 给父母~ do the sweeping graves ceremony for parents
10 祭奠 [-] jìdiàn (offer sacrifice-libate) <v.> hold a memorial ceremony for: ~死者 hold a memorial ceremony for the dead
11 祭祀 [-] jìsì (worship heaven-worship Earth) <v.> hold sacrificial ceremonies, sacrifice: ~山神sacrifice to the mountain god || ~祖先 sacrifice for an ancestor
12 祭祖 [-] jìzǔ (offer sacrifice-ancestor) <v.> worship an ancestor: 回乡~ return to your hometown to worship an ancestor

Tips:

1 葬 (zàng): The oracle form of 葬 depicts ‘a sheet in the grass on which lies a dead man,’ therefore it means ‘to bury.’ The modern form 葬 is composed of 茻 (mǎng, wild grass) and 死, omitting the part ‘一’ which symbolizes the sheet in the oracle form.

2 祭天 (jìtiān): 祭天 means 'to worship the heaven, heaven worship,' which was the holiest ceremony in the entire feudal history of China. Since the emperors of China were called 天子 (the sons of heaven,) sacrifices to the heaven were offered by the emperors (天子.) The last ceremony of 祭天 by the state of China was held in 1913.

Exercises: Multiple Choice. Make sure to choose the most appropriate answer.

1 中国人一般会在清明节的时候________, 悼念死去的亲人.

A. 祭祖　　B. 埋葬　　C. 扫墓

2 中国人一般会在过年的时候__________, 祈求祖先保佑自己的生活.

A. 安葬　　B. 祭祖　　C. 戴孝

3 中国人一般会用_________的方式来悼念死者.

A. 上坟　　B. 火化　　C. 埋葬

4 中国人过年的时候也会_______山神、财神、土地神什么的.

A. 戴孝　　B. 吊唁　　C. 祭祀

5 以前中国人在父母死去的第一年要在衣服袖子中间围一块黑布, 这就是"________."

A. 戴孝　　B. 吊唁　　C. 祭天

6 美国的教堂或者校园附近会有一些_________. 但在中国这种情况几乎没有, 因为中国人一般会在无人居住的地方_________死去的人.

A. 埋葬、墓地　　B. 墓地、埋葬　　C. 祭祀、埋了

Theme 133: Lucky, successful 幸运, 成功 (xìngyùn, chénggōng)

1 走运 [-運] zǒuyùn (be with-luck) <v-o> have luck: 他总是挺~的. He is always quite lucky. || 走好运good luck || 走大运 a lot of luck

2 幸运 [-運] xìngyùn (fortune-luck) <adj.> lucky: lucky event~事 || ~地没有受伤 luckily not got injured

3 吉利 [-] jílì (auspicious-lucky) <adj.> auspicious: ~话 auspicious words || 名字~ lucky name || "四"这个词要少说, 不~. One should say the word "four" less, since it's not auspicious.

4 吉祥 [-] jíxiáng (auspicious-propitious) <adj.> lucky, auspicious: ~物mascot || ~的图案 lucky pattern || ~如意. Everything went well.

5 顺 [順] shùn (along, obey, smooth) <adj.> lucky, smooth: 她一直很~. She has been very lucky. || 他今年不太~. He has been unlucky this year.

6 顺利 [順-] shùnlì (smooth-lucky) <adj.> successful: ~进行 proceed successfully|| ~完成successfully complete || 事情不~. Things aren't successful.

7 万事如意 [萬---] wànshìrúyì (all-thing-as-wish) <idiom> all the best: 祝你~ wish you all the best

8 趁机 [-機] chènjī (take-opportunity) <v-o> take the opportunity: ~问他一个问题take the opportunity to ask him a question

9 顺水推舟 [順---] shùnshuǐtuīzhōu (along-current-push-boat) <idiom> push the boat with the current, take advantage of situation: ~地同意了agree with taking advantage

10 成功 [-] chénggōng (accomplish-work) <n./adj.> success, successful: 取得/获得~ get success || 他的人生和事业都很~. His life and career are very successful. || ~地演出了四百多场successfully play more than 400 games

11 马到成功 [馬---] mǎdàochénggōng (horse-arrive-succeed) <idiom> instant victory: 祝你~ wish you instant victory！ || 只要您出面, 一定会~! As long as you go forward, you will certainly earn instant success!

12 胜 [勝] shèng (can bear, defeat, win) <v.> win: 三~三负 3 wins and 3 losses || 转败为~ victory over || 西班牙队~了法国队. The Spanish team beat the French team.

13 胜利 [勝-] shēnglì (victory-advantageous) <v./n.> victory: 取得~ earn victory || 伟大的~ great victory || ~的果实the fruit of victory

14 反败为胜 [-敗-勝] fǎnbàiwéishèng (turn-defeat-into-victory) <idiom> turn defeat into victory: 中国队~, 赢了韩国队. The Chinese team turned defeat into victory to beat the South Korean team.

15 凯旋 [凱-] kǎixuán (triumphant-return) <v.> triumph: ~而归 triumph and return || ~门triumphal arch, The Arc de Triomphe, Paris

16 一路顺风 [--順風] yīlùshùnfēng (all-way-favorable-wind) <idiom> bon voyage: 祝你~ wish you a good trip || 工作~ wish good luck with work

17 当选 [當選] dāngxuǎn (get-elected) <v.> be elected: ~为美国总统be elected as American president

18 赢 [贏] yíng (have a surplus, earn, win) <v.> win: ~钱win money || ~巴西队win against Brazil team || ~两场win two games

19 战胜 [戰勝] zhànshèng (fight-victory) <v.> defeat, triumph over, overcome: ~敌人defeat enemies || ~困难 overcome difficulties || ~对手defeat opponents

20 一帆风顺 [--風順] yīfānfēngshùn (full-sail-wind-favorable) <idiom> smooth sailing, go smoothly: 祝你~ wish everything goes smoothly || 她的事业~ her career goes smoothly without obstacles

Tips:

1 Auspicious words: By fair estimation, the ratio of time in which Chinese people enjoyed their lives to the time in which they struggled to live their lives before the 20th century was 1:2. In other words, the Chinese people did not live a happy life in history, therefore, 'auspice' was much cherished and reflected abundantly in the language. For example, 吉祥, 吉利, 幸运, 走运, 万事如意, 一帆风顺 (above-listed) and 大吉大利 (usually lucky), 吉祥如意 (good luck).

2 一路顺风: It had been a common auspicious wish for people traveling on land, however, air transportation is becoming more and more important. Air travelers hate turbulent air, so one should not say 一帆风顺 to them because there is a 风 in the phrase. So do fishermen and sea travelers. Now you can say '一路保重' (Take care!) in almost any scenario.

Exercises:

Part I: Multiple Choice. Make sure to choose the most appropriate answer.

1 你在机场送朋友, 上飞机前你会对她说: 祝你________.

A. 一路顺风　　B. 凯旋　　C. 一路保重

2 朋友要去参加比赛, 比赛前你会对她说: 祝你________.

A. 反败为胜　　B. 马到成功　　C. 一路顺风

3 中国足球队跟韩国足球队比赛, 看起来韩国对会赢, 可是没想到在最后五分钟中国队________打败了韩国队.

A. 顺水推舟　　B. 反败为胜　　C. 万事如意

4 过去中国人过春节的时候喜欢在家里贴上象征______的年画.

A. 吉祥　　B. 胜利　　C. 战胜

5 小张最近很_____, 买了两次彩票都中奖了.

A. 吉利　　B. 胜利　　C. 走运

6 小张看大部分同事们都同意公司的这个计划, 就________也同意了.

A. 趁机　　B. 反败为胜　　C. 顺水推舟

Theme 134: Unlucky, failure 不顺, 失败 (búshùn, shībài)

1 倒霉 [-] dǎoméi (invert-wood lintel/mildew) <v.> have bad luck: ~事 unfortunate matters || 真~ truly unfortunate || 他~透了, 刚被公司解雇 (jiěgù), 家里又着了火. He was so unlucky that after having just been fired from the corporation, his house also caught fire.

2 祸不单行 [禍-單-] huòbùdānxíng (misfortune-not-singly-come) <idiom> misfortune does not come singly: 真是~, 妻子生病在家, 他自己又被车撞了. Misfortune does not come just once. His wife was ill at home, and he was also hit by a car.

3 雪上加霜 [-] xuěshàngjiāshuāng (snow-top-add-frost) <idiom> one disaster after another: 中国经济因外资撤退 (chètuì, withdraw) 而~. China's economy has been made worse by the retreat of foreign investment.

4 不幸 [-] bùxìng (not-fortunate) <adj./adv.> unfortunately, unlucky: 生活~ unlucky life || ~失败unfortunately, it failed || ~的人unlucky person

5 出事 [-] (happen-accident) <separable word> have a accident: 他~了! He had an accident! || 出大事 have a big problem || 出了一点儿事. Something has happened. || ~地点the scene of the accident

6 好事多磨 [-] hǎoshìduōmó (good-thing-much-tribulation) <idiom> The road to success is strewn with setbacks.: 你不要太难过, ~, 这件事过去以后肯定顺顺利利的. Don't be too upset. As the saying goes, nothing good comes easily. After this incident, you will definitely be smoother for everything.

7 拔苗助长 [---長] bámiáozhùzhǎng (pull-sprout-assist-grow) <idiom> Pull the sprouts to help them grow – spoil things by excessive force: 家长不能

对孩子~, 否则只会害了孩子. Parents cannot push their children to achieve, otherwise they will only harm the children.

8 尴尬 [尷-] gān'gà (awkward) <v.> be awkward, be embarrassed: 让人~ make sb. very awkward || 造成~的局面create an an awkward situation || 他的表情很~. He looks very embarrassed.

9 进退两难 [進-兩難] jìntuìliǎngnán (advance-retreat-both-hard) <idiom> find it hard to advance or to retreat, be in a dliemna: 处在~的境地 be in a tough circumstance || 小王~, 不知道是留在学校学习还是找工作. Little Wang had a dilemma because he didn't know whether to stay at school and study or find a job and work.

10 骑虎难下 [騎-難-] qíhǔnánxià (ride-tiger-hard-get off) <idiom> unable to back down or quit: 使她~ make her feel unable to quit || 从你同意完成那项大工程开始, 我们就~了. You've had the bear by the tail ever since you agreed to finish that huge project.

11 折磨 [-] zhémó (bend-pester) <v.> cause physical or mental suffering/torment: 遭受~ suffer torment || 感情的~ emotional torment || 心理~ psychological torment || 他很变态, 总是喜欢~别人. He is very perverted and always likes to torture others.

12 煎熬 [-] jiān'áo (fry-stew) <v.> suffer, be tormented: 心理受~ suffer psychological torment || 失业的~ the torment of losing one's job.

13 闯祸 [闖禍] chuǎnghuò (act rashly-calamity) <separable word> get into trouble, bring disaster: 到处~ bring disaster everywhere || 这个富二代闯了一个大祸. This 'affluent second generation' has caused a huge mishap.

14 失败 [-敗] shībài (fail-defeated) <v./n.> be defeated: 一再~ be defeated again || ~两次 be defeated twice || ~是成功之母. Defeat is the mother of success.

15 打败 [-敗] dǎbài (beat-defeated) <v.> defeat, beat: ~敌人defeat one's enemies. || 彻底 (chèdǐ) ~对手 thoroughly defeat one's enemies.

16 输 [輸] shū (convey, contribute, defeated) <n.> lose: ~钱 lose money || ~球 lose points in a game || ~了两场 lose two matches.

17 挣扎 [掙-] zhēngzhá (struggle-pull out) <v.> struggle, attempt: 苦苦~ struggle bitterly || 内心~ have a struggle in one's heart || 垂死 (chuísǐ) ~ struggle on the edge of death

18 灭亡 [滅-] mièwáng (perish-die) <v.> be destroyed, die out: 必然~ inevitably be destoryed || 相继~ mutually be destoryed || 汉朝~以后, 中国陷入了分裂. The fall of the Han Dynasty split China apart.

19 倒闭 [-閉] dǎobì (fall-close) <v.> close down, go bankrupt: 银行~ the bank closed down || 纷纷~ go into bankruptcy one after another || 没想到, 那么大的公司也~了. It's unthinkable that a corporation that large could go into bankruptcy

20 破产 [-產] pòchǎn (lose-property) <separable word> go bankrupt: 破了产 go bankrupt. || ~企业 a bankrupt entity.

21 泡汤 [-湯] pàotāng (soak-boiling water) <v.> fall flat, come to nothing: 计划~了. For a plan to fall flat. || 下雨使我们的野餐计划~了. The rain messed up our plans to go on a picnic.

22 落空 [-] luòkōng (fall-empty) <v.> come to nothing, fall flat: 希望/美梦/计划~ for a hope/dream/plan to fall flat.

23 落选 [-選] luòxuǎn (fail-election) <v.> lose an election: 年轻的候选人赢了, 资深政治家反倒~了. The young candidate won, and the senior politician lost.

24 露 [-] lòu (reveal) <v.> reveal: ~丑 reveal ugliness. || ~破绽 (pòzhàn) reveal a flaw || ~痕迹 (hénji) reveal a mark || ~马脚 reveal tracks
25 泄露 [洩-] xièlòu (leak-reveal) <v.> leak: ~秘密 leak secrets || ~天机 give away a secret || ~国家机密leak state secrets
26 暴露 [-] bàolù (expose-reveal) <v.> expose, reveal: ~身份expose one's identity || ~目标give away one's goal || ~无遗thoroughly expose
27 出卖 [-賣] chūmài (betray-sell) <v.> betray, sell out: ~劳力 sell out || ~国家利益betray national interests || ~良心 betray one's conscience
28 水落石出 [-] shuǐluòshíchū (water-fall-stone-show) <idiom> gush out: 查个~ for information to gush out through examination || 真相~ for the real facts to gush out

Tips:

1 拔苗助长: This idiom has a variant 揠苗助长 (yàmiáo zhùzhǎng.)
2 祸不单行: Literally it means 'misfortunes never come singly,' with a free translation 'when it rains, it pours.' There is usually another preceding phrase/idiom 福无双至 (fúwúshuāngzhì) which means 'fortunes never come in pairs.'
3 雪上加霜: Literally it means 'to add frost on top of snow,' with a free translation of 'to go from bad to worse.' This idiom is usually accompanied by another phrase 伤口撒盐 which means 'to put/rub salt in the wound.'
4 水落石出: It means 'the water receded and the stones appeared,' with a free translation of 'doubts will clear up when facts are known.' This idiom is from a line of *Hòu Chìbì Fù* by Sū Shì (1037–1101,) one of the greatest writers in the entire history of China. This phrase, along with its preceding phrase 山高月小 (mountain-high-moon-small), constitute a beautiful picture full of scenery, color, motion, contrast and philosophy.
5 倒霉 (dǎoméi): In the late Ming Dynasty, before a student took the imperial examinations, he would usually erect a wood post called a 楣 (méi, lintel.) If he succeeded in the exams, the post would be kept, if he failed, he would pull out the post (倒楣) and take it away. Since 霉 (mold) is homophonic with 楣, and the mold (霉) is unpleasing, 倒楣 was evolved into 倒霉 (bad luck).

Exercises:

Part I: Use the given bound form as a guide to help you think of other words with the same character. Feel free use your dictionary when needed. Then write down the English definition of each of the words you've written.

败 (lose, defeat): 惨败 be totally defeated, suffer a crushing defeat

____

____

____

露 *(show, reveal):* 露丑 *make a fool of oneself in public, lose face*

____

____

____

Part II: Multiple Choice. Make sure to choose the most appropriate answer.

1 小张上午刚丢了钱包, 下午又把手机丢了, 真是________.

A. 水落石出 B. 骑虎难下 C. 祸不单行

2 "骑虎难下"跟下面哪个词的意思相近

A. 水落石出 B. 进退两难 C. 祸不单行

3 这个案件终于_______了, 大家都知道了案件的真相.

A. 水落石出 B. 雪上加霜 C. 好事多磨

4 小王本打算到上海旅游, 但是公司有重要工作让他加班, 所以他的旅游计划_______了.

A. 泡汤 B. 折磨 C. 倒霉

5 从纽约坐经济舱飞到上海是一件_______人的事情.

A. 泡汤 B. 折磨 C. 落空

6 自2007年以来中国经济放缓, 最近又因为外资撤退而________.

A. 雪上加霜 B. 拔苗助长 C. 好事多磨

7 让一个四岁的孩子学习数学、英语、钢琴等等, 其实就是________.

A. 雪上加霜 B. 拔苗助长 C. 好事多磨

8 经济危机到来的时候, 很多工厂________, 工人失业.

A. 倒闭 B. 落选 C. 尴尬

Theme 135: Gain, loss 得失 (déshī)

1 发财 [發財] fācái (make-fortune) <v.> get rich: ~致富become rich, enrichment || 升官~ be promoted and gain wealth || 小王很会做生意, 几年时间就~了. Xiao Wang is very good at doing business and has become prosperous in just a few years.

2 发家 [發-] fājiā (make-family fortune) <v.> build up a family fortune: ~致富enrich one's family, build up the family's fortune

3 暴富 [-] bàofù (sudden-rich) <v.> suddenly become rich: 一夜~ get rich overnight

4 丰收 [豐-] fēngshōu (plenteous-harvest) <v.> a rich crop: 粮食~ be rich in grain || 大~ a large harvest || 获得~ rich gains

5 合算 [-] hésuàn (match-calculation) <adj.> worthwhile, be a good deal: 这笔生意做得不~. This business deal was not worthwhile. || 机票打折的时候, 坐飞机~. It pays to take a plane when the air ticket is on sale.

6 划算 [-] huásuàn (one's profit-calculation) <adj.> worth it, getting money's worth: 我这所房子买得很~. I got a good deal on this house.

7 一举两得 [-舉兩-] yījǔliǎngdé (one-action-two-gain) <idiom> gain two ends at once, kill two birds with one stone: 看美剧学英语是一件~的好事情. Watching American TV while studying English is like killing two birds with one stone.

8 一箭双雕 [--雙-] yījiànshuāngdiāo (one-arrow-two-vulture) <idiom> hit two vultures with one arrow: 达到~的目的 complete two goals at once

9 一石二鸟 [---鳥] yīshíèr'niǎo (one-stone-two-bird<idiom> kill two birds with one stone: 达到~的效果 The achieved result was like killing two birds with one stone.

10 损失 [損-] sǔnshī (decrease-lose) <v./n.> loss, damage: 巨大~ a huge loss || 遭受/受到~ suffer a huge loss || 经济~ an economic loss

11 流失 [-] liúshī (wash-away) <v.> run off, be washed away: 水土~ soil erosion || 人才~ outflow of talent

12 缺失 [-] quēshī (lack-lose) <v.> deficiency, drawback: 信心~ lack confidence || 资料~ lack resources || 数据~ lack data

13 赔 [賠] péi (compensate, lose) <v.> make good a loss, compensate: ~钱 sustain financial losses, lose money in business || 你借给我的书让我弄丢了, 我~你吧. I've lost the book you lent me. Let me pay for it.

14 赔本 [賠-] péiběn (lose-capital) <v.> sustain losses in business: ~买卖 sustain losses from buying and selling || ~生意 sustain business losses || ~卖车 sustain losses in selling a car

15 亏 [虧] kuī (short of, lose) <v.> loss, deficit: ~钱 lose money || ~损make a loss || ~了两万块 lose $20,000

16 吃亏 [-虧] chīkuī (suffer-loss) <v.> suffer losses: 做生意不了解市场就要~. If you don't know the market, you'll suffer losses.

17 上当 [-當] shàngdàng (caught-fooled) <separable word> be fooled, be cheated: 上他的当 be cheated by him || 上了一个当 be cheated || ~受骗be cheated

18 上钩 [-鈎] shànggōu (take-hook) <v.> take the bait: 鱼儿~ the fish took the bait || 愿者~. The believers took the bait.

19 上圈套 [-] shàngquāntào (fall into-trap) <v.> fall in sb's trap: 引人~ lured ina trap

20 受骗 [-騙] shòupiàn (receive-deceive) <v.> deceived, fooled: ~上当 be deceived

21 失算 [-] shīsuàn (miss-calculate) <v.> miscalculate, misjudge: 聪明人也有~的时候. Even wise men are not free from miscalculations. || 屡次~ repeatedly misjudge

22 得不偿失 [--償-] débùchángshī (gain-not-compensate-loss) <idiom> the loss outweighs the gain: 发展经济的同时一定要保护环境, 否则会~. When developing the economy, we must protect the environment, otherwise it will outweigh the benefits.

23 得寸进尺 [--進-] décùnjìnchǐ (get-inch-desire-yard) <idiom> reach for a yard after getting an inch: 这个人买彩票中奖得了一辆车, 但是不满足, 还

想要一栋别墅, 真是~. This person won a car by buying lottery tickets, but he is not satisfied with that and still wants a villa. He is really insatiable!

24 杀鸡取卵 [殺鷄--] shājīqǔluǎn (kill-hen-get-egg) <idiom> kill the hen to get the eggs: 为了发展经济而牺牲环境, 就是 ~的做法. Developing the economy at the expense of the environment is no less than killing the goose to get the golden egg. || 这家知名公司消减科研经费, 等于是在 ~. The famous company that cuts back on research and development is killing the goose that lays the golden egg.

25 舍本求末 [捨----] shèběnqiúmò (abandon-root-seek-trifle) <idiom> attend trifles and neglect essentials: 有人认为美国的小学教育只注重教学方法, 而不注重教学质量, 是~的做法. Some people think that the primary education in the United States only focuses on teaching methods, and doesn't pay attention to the quality of teaching. It's attending to the trifles and neglecting the essentials.

26 舍近求远 [捨--遠] shèjìnqiúyuǎn (abandon-near-seek-far) <idiom> seek from afar what lies close at hand: 在中国很多人不在当地医院看病, 而是~到北京大医院去看病. Many people in China do not see doctors at local hospitals. They are willing to travel far to see a doctor in a Beijing hospital.

27 因小失大 [-] yīnxiǎoshīdà (for-small-lose-big) <idiom> penny wise, pound foolish: 为了省钱而缩减教育经费是~, 因为公共教育是投资未来. Education budget cuts are penny wise and pound foolish, since public education is an investment in our future. || 不要~, 给宝马车加便宜的汽油, 因为会弄坏宝马车. Don't be penny wise and pound foolish. The cheap gas will ruin your BMW car's engine in the long run.

Tips:

1 恭喜发财 (gōngxǐ fācái): This phrase, meaning 'may you be happy and prosperous,' might be the second most extensively used phrase on the Chinese New Year, only after 过年好 (Happy New Year.) Children would often use this phrase along with 红包拿来 (give me the red envelope.) 红包 is a red envelope, which contains money as a gift.

2 一箭双雕 and 一石二鸟: They have the same meaning 'to kill two birds with one stone,' but 一箭双雕 is indigenous and 一石二鸟 is borrowed from English. 一石二鸟 has a variant 一石两鸟.

3 得寸进尺: It is an idiom and means 'the more one gets, the even more he wants.' Ordinary people have a colloquial saying 蹬鼻子上脸 (dēng bízi shàng liǎn, step-nose-climb-face), which means the same as 得寸进尺.

Exercises:

1 为了发展经济而用光所有资源, 其实就是____________.

A. 杀鸡取卵、舍本求末 B.一石两鸟、一箭双雕 C. 事半功倍、因小失大

2 一箭双雕跟下面哪一组的意思相同

A. 事半功倍、舍近求远
B. 一石两鸟、一举两得
C. 因小失大、杀鸡取卵

3 "划算"跟哪个词意思差不多

A. 合算　　B. 赔钱　　C. 上钩

4 "上钩"跟哪个词意思不一样

A. 暴富　　B. 上圈套　　C. 上当

5 "得不偿失"跟哪个词意思差不多

A. 不划算　　B. 不亏本　　C. 不赔本

6 下面哪种情况算是"得寸进尺"

A. 你给这个乞丐十块钱, 他不满意, 向你要二十块钱.
B. 本来可以让父母帮忙, 他却花钱请人来做.
C. 本来一个小时可以做完的事情, 他花了半小时就做完了.

7 这个地区的青壮年劳动力__________特别严重, 几乎90%的人是老年人.

A. 缺失　　B. 损失　　C. 流失

8 这场飓风 (jùfēng, hurricane) 给这个城市造成了巨大__________.

A. 缺失　　B. 损失　　C. 流失

9 为了省钱而缩减教育经费是__________, 因为公共教育关系到国家的未来发展.

A. 得寸进尺　　B. 因小失大　　C. 事倍功半

10 中国人过春节拜年的时候喜欢说: __________.

A. 事半功倍　　B. 一石两鸟　　C. 恭喜发财

Theme 136: Contented, frustrated 得意, 失意 (déyì, shīyì)

1 得志 [-] dézhì (gain-ambition) <v.> gain ambition: 少年~ a young man gains his ambition || 小人~ mean person gains ambition
2 得势 [-勢] déshì (gain-upper hand) <v.> get the upper hand, be in the ascendance: 右派~ the right party is in the ascendance || 民主党~ the democratic party gains momentum.
3 得意 [-] déyì (reach-satisfaction) <v.> proud of oneself, pleased with oneself, complacent: 感到~ feel proud of oneself || 暗自~ secretly very pleased with oneself || ~洋洋show extreme self-complacency
4 臭美 [-] chòuměi (abhorrent-show off) <adj.> show off shamelessly, presumptuous, smug (not necessarily pejorative, often used among friends): 她打扮得很过分, 真是~! How gaudily she is dressed. What a shameless display! || 别~了. Don't be so smug.
5 春风得意 [-風--] chūnfēngdéyì (spring-breeze-reach-satisfaction) <idiom> be flushed with success: 她现在真是~, 因为她爸爸刚刚当选为美国总统, 自己公司的生意也非常红火. She is riding on the crest of success because her father has just been elected President of the United States, and her company is doing very well.

6 飞黄腾达 [飛黃騰達] fēihuángténgdá (celestial horse *Fēihuáng*-jump-'reach') <idiom> make rapid advances in one's career, have a meteoric rise: 正是靠着《Apprentice》这个电视节目, 他才真地~起来. It was by means of the *Apprentice* TV show that he really made rapid advances in his career. || 她历尽艰辛最后~. He got to the top of the tree by hard work.

7 得宠 [-寵] déchǒng (gain-dote) <v.> be a favorite: 在四个孩子当中, 小儿子最~. Of the four children, the youngest is their parents' favorite.
8 受宠 [-寵] shòuchǒng (receive-dote) <v.> recieve favor (from superiou): ~若惊overwhelmed by an unexpected favor || 她是最小的孩子, 所以在家里很~. She is the youngest child, so she is the favorite child in the family.
9 成材 [-] chéngcái (become-timber) <v.> mature timber, useful person: 这棵树已经~了. The tree has grown to full size. || 自学 ~ become a success from being self-taught || 父母都希望孩子早日~. Parents always want their children to be successful soon.
10 升官 [-] shēngguān (ascend-position) <v.> be our for power, win promotion: ~发财win promotion and get rich
11 晋升 [晉-] jìnshēng (promote-ascend) <v.> promote a higher position: ~为教授be promoted professorship || 这份工作~机会很大. The job offers prospects of promotion.
12 乔迁 [喬遷] qiáoqiān (high-move) <v.> move a better place: ~新居 moving in one's new residence
13 步步高升 [-] bùbùgāoshēng (step-step-high-ascend) <idiom> climb step by step, rise steadily: 祝您~ wish you get promotion continuously || 事业上~ rise steadily in one's career

14 出名 [-] chūmíng (outside-famous) <adj.> famous: 川菜在国内外都很~. Sichuan cuisine is famous, both at home and abroad.
15 成名 [-] chéngmíng (become-famous) <v.> become famous, make a name for oneself: 她写了一本小说, 几乎一夜~. She wrote that novel and became famous almost overnight.
16 齐名 [齊-] qímíng (equal-famous) <adj.> enjoy equal popularity, be equally famous: 华盛顿与林肯~ Washington is as famous as Lincoln || 长城与金字塔~. The Great Wall is as famous as the Pyramids || 孔子与泰山~. Confucius is as famous as Mt. Tai.
17 功成名就 [-] gōngchéngmíngjiù (success-achieve-fame-win) <idiom> win success and recognition: 他在医学领域~. He made his mark on medicine. || 那次演讲使他 ~. That speech was the making of him.
18 一举成名 [-舉--] yījǔchéngmíng (one-behavior-become-famous) <idiom> become famous overnight: 她因自己的第一部小说~. She won her overnight fame with her first novel. || 她获得了游泳冠军, ~. She made her mark by winning a swimming championship.
19 一鸣惊人 [-鳴驚-] yīmíngjīngrén (one-cry-astonish-people) <idiom> amaze the world with a single brilliant feat, an overnight celebrity: 不鸣则已, ~. The quiet ones always sneak up on you. || 中国游泳队~. The Chinese swimming team became famous overnight.

20 失落 [-] shīluò (lose-down) <v.> lose, disappointed, loss: 他感到很~. He felt deeply abandoned. || ~的一代lost generation || 她放弃事业结婚, 婚后感到非常~. She experienced a loss of identity after giving up her career to get married.

21 落魄 [-] luòpò (down-spirit) <adj.> down and out, in dire straits, downtrodden: 当我~的时候, 是她鼓舞了我. Her friendship supported me when I was in distress. || ~江湖come down in the world

22 失意 [-] shīyì (lose-satisfaction) <adj.> be frustrated, be disappointed: 人生~ be frustrated in one's life || 政治上~ be frustrated in one's political career || 情场 ~ be unlucky in love

23 失宠 [-寵] shīchǒng (lose-dote) <v.> lose favor, in disfavor: 他心情不好, 因为他在老板那里~了. He was blue because he is out of favor with his boss. || 罐头食品现在已经~了. Canned foods today stand in disgrace.

24 坎坷 [-] kǎnkē (rough) <adj.> be full of frustrations: 她为自己命运~而伤心. She was crying over her misfortune. || 人生~ be full of frustrations in one's life

25 贬职 [貶職] biǎnzhí (demote-position) <v.> demote: 被~ be demoted

26 怀才不遇 [懷---] huáicáibùyù (hold-talent-not-appreciated) <idiom> have talent but no opportunity: 他一直~. He is full of talent but has no opportunity to show it.

27 穷困潦倒 [窮---] qióngkùnliáodǎo (poor-stranded-dejected) <idiom> poverty-stricken, in straitened circumstances: 陷入~的境地be reduced destitution

28 掉价 [-價] diàojià (lower-status) <adj.> not match one's position, lose face: 她觉得大学毕业以后在饭馆当服务员很~. She feels it is beneath her to be a restaurant waitress after graduating from college.

29 丢丑 [-醜] diūchǒu (lose-'grace') <v.> lose face, disgraced: 觉得~ feel disgraced

30 丢脸 [-臉] diūliǎn (lose-face) <v.> lose face, disgrace: 觉得~ feel disgraced

31 丢人 [-] diūrén (lose-name, face) <v.> lose face, disgrace: 真~! What a disgrace!

32 献丑 [獻醜] xiànchǒu (show-immature) (speaking of one's own performance) <v.> poor show, reveal one's incompetence (or inadequacy): 在专家面前~. make a poor show in facing an expert

33 出洋相 [-] chūyángxiàng (make-foreign, silly-sight) <v.> make an exhibition (or spectacle) of oneself: 他喝醉了, 在俱乐部出了很多洋相. He got drunk and made a spectacle of himself in the club. || 不要~了！Stop making a spectacle of yourself!

34 闹笑话 [鬧-話] nàoxiàohuà (make-laughing-stock) <v.> make a fool of oneself, cut a ridiculous figure: 说外语发音不准, 有时候会~ Inaccurate pronunciation when you speak a foreign language can sometimes have comical effects.

35 丢人现眼 [--現-] diūrénxiànyǎn (lose-face-appear-ambarrassed) <idiom> lose face, disgraced, embarrassed: 真~！ What a disgrace! || 中国父母认为孩子考不上好大学是~的事情. Chinese parents think it's a disgrace that their children can't get into good colleges.

36 戴绿帽子 [-綠--] dàilǜmàozi (wear-green-hat) <v.> be a cuckold, wear horns: 如果一个中国男人的妻子有了婚外情, 人们就会说这个男的~了.

If a Chinese man's wife has an affair with someone else, people will say that the man is wearing horns.

Tips:

1 乔: The traditional form of 乔 is 喬, with the upper part being 夭 (a man walking) and the lower part 高 (high,) therefore, 乔 means 'tall,' for example 乔木 (tall trees) and 乔迁 (qiáoqiān), which is used to congratulate others moving to a new home or being promoted to a higher position. Characters with 乔 as a part also have the meaning of 'tall,' for example, 桥 (bridge) and 轿 (jiào, sedan-chair.) The other major meaning of 乔 is 'disguise,' for example 乔装 (to disguise oneself as, to dress up as.)

2 飞黄腾达: 飞黄 is a celestial horse, which is also called 乘黄. 腾达 was originally 腾踏 (to jump-step on.) This idiom is usually used for one's rapid promotion in officialdom.

3 戴绿帽子: 绿 (green) was a symbol of lowly social status in ancient China. In the Yuan Dynasty, adult men of the families with prostitutes were forced to wear 青色 (cyan) hats. Because cyan is a blue green (绿), cyan hat was later changed to 绿帽子 (cuckold). Also 绿 is loosely associated with tortoise, turtle (王八, 乌龟), which is also a curse word in Chinese.

4 失意: Deeply influenced by the Taoist dialectic way of thinking and expression, the Chinese coined many phrases such as 情场失意, 赌场得意 (qíngchǎng shīyì, dǔchǎng déyì, if you are unsuccessful in love affairs, you must be very successful in gambling) and vice versa.

Exercises:

Part I: Use the given bound form as a guide help you think of other words with the same character. Feel free use your dictionary when needed. Then write down the English definition of each of the words you've written.

得 *(get, obtain)*: 得到

____

____

____

____

失 *(lose)*: 失去

____

____

____

____

丢 *(lose)*: 丢失

____

____

____

____

名 *(name)*: 出名

____

____

____

____

Part II: Read the following words and then answer the questions in Chinese.

得意、春风得意、出名、成名、功成名就、一举成名、一鸣惊人、丢丑、丢脸、丢人、献丑、出洋相、闹笑话、丢人现眼、戴绿帽子、怀才不遇、穷困潦倒、飞黄腾达、步步高升

1 他现在正是事业"得意"的时候, "得意"还可以换成那个词?

____

2 上面还有哪两个词跟"出名"的意思差不多?

____

3 "一举成名"跟哪个词意思差不多, 都形容一下子就出名了?

____

4 "丢丑"跟哪些词的意思差不多?

____

5 哪个词的意思是太太或者女朋友跟别的男人有关系, 让他很丢脸?

____

6 在你们国家有没有"怀才不遇"的情况? 为什么?

____

7 在你们国家一个"穷困潦倒"的人有可能"飞黄腾达"吗? 为什么?

____

8 小张最近被任命为"副总经理," 你给他写一张贺卡, 最可能写些什么?

____

Theme 137: To bless, to suffer 保佑, 受灾 (bǎoyòu, shòuzāi)

1 享福 [-] xiǎngfú (enjoy-fortune) <separable word> live in comfort: 享清福 enjoy the happiness of leisure

2 享乐 [-樂] xiǎnglè (enjoy-pleasure) <v./n.> indulge in creature comforts, pleasure of life: 尽情~ enjoy the pleasures of life || 追求~ pursuit of pleasure || ~主义hedonism

3 大饱眼福 [-飽--] dàbǎoyǎnfú (greatly-satisfy-eye-fortune) <idiom> feast one's eyes: 这次展览让人~！ This exhibition was a feast for the eyes!

4 获益 [獲-] huòyì (gain-profit) <v.> profit from: ~非浅 benefit greatly || 身心~ physical and mental benefits

5 受益 [-] shòuyì (receive-profit) <v.> benefit from: ~于古典音乐 benefit from classical music || ~大 large benefit

6 沾光 [-] zhānguāng (touch-honor) <v.> benefit from association with sb. or sth.: 让孩子~ allow kids benefit from association

7 占便宜 [-] zhànpiányí (take-advantage) <v.> take advantage of: 喜欢~ likes getting an extra advantage || 占别人的便宜 make up for other people taking advantages

8 得奖 [-獎] déjiǎng (receive-prize) <v.> receive a prize: 在国际上~ receive an international prize || 多次~ receive many prizes

9 获奖 [獲獎] huòjiǎng (win-prize) <separable word> win a prize: 获一等奖 win first prize || 多次~ win many prizes || 比赛~ contest winner

10 中奖 [-獎] zhòngjiǎng (get-prize) <separable word> draw a prize-winning ticket: 中大奖 win the jackpot || ~号码 winning ticket number || ~机会 winning opportunity

11 经受 [經-] jīngshòu (undergo-receive) <v.> undergo: ~批评 experience criticism || ~考验 undergo a trial || ~痛苦 withstand pain

12 受到 [-] shòudào (receive-*suffix*) <v.> receive, obtain: ~好评 receive favorable comments || ~欢迎 be welcomed || ~鼓舞 receive encouragement

13 受灾 [-災] shòuzāi (suffer-disaster) <separable word> be hit by a natural disaster: 受大灾 suffer a big disaster || 受旱灾 be in a drought || 受虫灾 suffer from pests

14 饱受 [飽-] bǎoshòu (fully-suffer) <v.> suffer enough from, have one's fill of: ~折磨 suffer enough from torture || ~磨难 suffer enough from hardships

15 遇到 [-] yùdào (encounter-*suffix*) <v.> run into, come across: ~强盗 run into a robber || ~暴风雨 be ambushed by a storm|| ~意外的问题come across unforeseen problems

16 遇难 [-難] yù'nàn (encounter-accident) <v.> die in an accident: 不幸~ unfortunately died in an accident || 海上~ die in a maritime accident || 同时~ be killed at the same time

17 遇险 [-險] yùxiǎn (encounter-danger) <v.> be in danger: 海上~ be in danger at sea

18 遇害 [-] yùhài (encounter-murder) <v.> be murdered: 不幸~ be unfortunately murdered

19 遭遇 [-] zāoyù (suffer-encounter) <v.> encounter, suffer: ~敌人 encounter the enemy || ~水灾 suffer a flood || ~不幸 encounter misfortune

20 遭到 [-] zāodào (suffer-*suffix*) <v.> meet with, encounter: ~拒绝 meet with refusal || ~反对 meet with disapproval || ~困难 encounter difficulties

21 遭受 [-] zāoshòu (suffer-receive) <v.> suffer, sustain: ~迫害 suffer persecution|| ~自然灾害 suffer natural disasters || ~重大损失 suffer heavy losses

22 遭殃 [-] zāoyāng (suffer-disaster) <v.> suffer disaster: 战争使老百姓~. The war brought people suffering. || 夫妻关系不好, ~的是孩子. If the relationship between a husband and wife is bad, the victims will be their children.

23 挨 [-] ái (suffer, endure) <v.> endure, suffer: ~骂 be scolded || ~批评 suffer criticism || ~饿 suffer hunger

24 挨打 [-] áidǎ (suffer-beat) <separable word> take a beating: 挨了一顿打 take one beating || 挨了两次打 take two beatings

25 冤枉 [-] yuānwǎng (wronged-crooked) <v.> treat unjustly: ~好人 wrong a good person || 受~ suffer unjust treatment

26 背黑锅 [--鍋] bēihēiguō (carry-black-pot) <v.> 'carry the black wok' be made a scapegoat: 给她~ make her serve as the scapegoat

27 失窃 [-竊] shīqiè (lost-stolen) <v.> have something stolen: 国宝~ have a national treasure be stolen || 文物~ stolen artifacts

28 出轨 [-軌] chūguǐ (off-trail) <v.> go off a trail, have an extramarital affair: 他婚后~了. He had an affair after marriage. || 火车~ a train went off the rails || 经济~ economic derailment

29 失事 [-] shīshì (out of control-accident) <v.> have an accident: 飞机~ airplane crash

30 面临 [-臨] miànlín (face-confront) <v.> be confronted with: ~问题 confronted with a question || ~危机 faced with a crisis || ~挑战 confronted with a challenge

Tips:

1 Passive voice and its markers: Passive voice markers in Chinese include 被, 让, 叫 and 给, with the last three being colloquial. There are also several implicit markers at the word level, for example, 受, 遭 (zāo), 遇 (yù), 挨 (ái) and 见. The passive usage of 见 is preserved mainly in archaic words such as 见怪 (be blamed) and 见笑 (be laughed at).

2 遭, 遇, 受, 到: The first three words and their combinations, 遭遇, 遭受, 遭到, 遇到, 受到 function in almost the same way.

Exercises:

Part I: Use the given bound form as a guide to help you think of other words with the same character. Feel free use your dictionary when needed. Then write down the English definition of each of the words you've written.

受 (suffer): 受伤 be injured

____

____

____

____

遇 *(met)*: 遇到 *come across*

____

____

____

____

挨 *(endure, suffer)*: 挨骂 *be scolded*

____

____

____

____

Part II: Read the following sentences and fill in each blank with the appropriate word or phrase from the options given.

1 出轨、失窃、失事

a) 昨晚这条街上的很多居民家都发生了________事件, 目前警察正在进行调查.
b) 这家航空公司的飞机在2015年多次________, 所以乘客一般不会选择坐他们的飞机.
c) 一般的中国人对婚后________的事情持批评 (pīpíng, criticize) 态度.

2 受益、享乐、面临、遭受

a) 纽约的公共交通系统_______着很多问题.
b) 这个地方每年夏天都会________洪水.
c) 网上免费教育平台使很多农村孩子________.
d) 很多人认为中国的"富二代"只知道________, 事实上很多"富二代"不仅家庭背景好, 而且非常勤奋 (qínfèn, diligent) 努力.

3 冤枉、背黑锅、花冤枉钱、遭殃

a) 小张的领导在工作中犯了错误, 但是他让小张来________.
b) 在这件小事上花那么多时间, 真______, 不值得.
d) 小张总是_________, 他买的东西价格很高, 但质量非常一般.
c) 战争只能使人民________, 对于统治阶层 (tǒngzhì jiēcéng, the ruling class) 来说无所谓.

4 大饱眼福、占便宜、沾光

a) 中国父母一般希望自己的孩子长大后成龙成凤, 他们好跟着_______.

b) 这场话剧特别精彩, 让我_________.
c) 小王是个喜欢_______的人， 去中国饭馆吃饭的时候常常要拿回家很多免费的酱油 (jiàngyóu, soy sauce) 包.

Theme 138: To lose, to rescue 丢, 救 (diū, jiù)

1 丢 [-] diū (lose, throw) <v.> lose: ~钱包 lose your wallet || ~东西lose things || ~钥匙 (yàoshi) lose your key
2 掉 [-] diào (fall, drop) <v.> fall, lose: 我钱包~在路上了. My wallet was lost on the road. || ~了两颗牙lost two teeth || ~了一只鞋a shoe fell
3 丢掉 [-] diūdiào (throw-away) <v.> lose, throw away: ~ 时机 lose time || ~香烟 throw away a cigarette
4 丢失 [-] diūshī (lose-lose) <v.> lose: ~ 机会 lose opportunity || ~邮件 lose mails || ~东西 lose things
5 遗失 [遺-] yíshī (lose articles-lose) <v.> lose: ~证书 lose certificate || 行李~ lose luggage

6 失踪 [-蹤] shīzōng (lose-trace) <v.> go missing: 今天下午一个5岁的男孩~了. A 5-year-old boy went missing this afternoon. || 飞机突然~. The plane disappeared suddenly.
7 走失 [-] zǒushī (go-lost) <v.> lose one's way: 这个老人~了. The old man lost his way.
8 下落不明 [-] xiàluòbùmíng (whereabouts-not-clear) <idiom> missing: 那个孩子已经~一个星期了. The child had been missing for a week.
9 音信全无 [---無] yīnxìnquánwú (news-completely-lost) <idiom> have never been heard of since: 他女朋友去了美国后, ~. His girlfriend went to America and he hasn't had any information from her since.

10 迷路 [-] mílù (lose-way) <v.> get lost: 在森林里~ losing in the forest
11 迷失 [-] míshī (lose-lost) <v.> get lost: ~方向 get lost without direction

12 得救 [-] déjiù (get-rescued) <v.> be saved: 灵魂~ the soul is saved || 这个病人~了. The patient was saved.
13 获救 [獲-] huòjiù (receive-rescued) <v.> get rescued: 在地震中~ be rescued in the earthquake
14 脱险 [-險] tuōxiǎn (escape from-danger) <v.> get out of danger: 经过抢救, 病人~了. The patient was out of danger after the emergency treatment.
15 生还 [-還] shēnghuán (alive-return) <v.> be survived: 无一~. No one survived. || 被绑架者还有可能~. The kidnappers may have survived.
16 死里逃生 [-裏--] sǐlǐtáoshēng (death-inside-escape-life) <idiom> have a close shave with death: 他在那次事故中~. He narrowly survived the accident.
17 九死一生 [-] jiǔsǐyīshēng (nine-death-one-survival) <idiom> have a narrow escape from death: 冒着~的危险 at the risk of life

Tips:

1 丢失 vs. 遗失: Both mean 'to lose something' but the object of 遗失 is a visible object(s) and the object of 丢失 could be abstract such as 电子邮件 (email) and 信仰 (xìnyǎng, belief.)

2 迷路 vs. 迷失: Both mean 'to get lost' but 迷路 is verb-object structure, so there is no object after this word whereas there could be a subject after 迷失, for example '迷失方向.'

Exercises:

Read the following sentences and fill in each blank with the appropriate word or phrase from the options given.

1 九死一生、死里逃生、音信全无、下落不明

a) 他们从大地震中_________, 活了下来.
b) 战争的时候参军是__________的事情, 因为打起仗来谁也无法预料(yùliào, foresee) 生死.
c) 小张在网上投了一百多份简历找工作, 但是至今__________.
d) 据报道, 上星期一个女留学生在日本与家人失去联系, 至今________, 没有人知道她去了哪里.

2 失踪、丢、迷路、得救、掉

a) 他昨天出去玩的时候把手机______了.
b) 这个牌子的手机质量非常好, 从三楼_______到地上也不会摔坏.
c) 他不太认路, 开车的时候如果不看GPS就会一定会________.
d) 这些登山者已经_________三天了, 官方的救援 (jiùyuán) 队正在积极寻找他们. 最后, 救援队找到了这些登山者, 他们终于_______了.

Theme 139: To develop, to separate 发展, 分离 (fāzhǎn, fēnlí)

1 发展 [發-] fāzhǎn (grow-expand) <v./n.> develop: 经济~ economic development || 人的~ human development || ~很快 develop quickly
2 进步 [進-] jìnbù (advance-step) <v./n.> improve, progress: ~快/慢 improve quickly/slowly || 有很大~ make great progress || 社会~ social progress
3 上进 [-進] shàngjìn (up-advance) <v.> make progress, ambitious to improve oneself: 追求~ pursue progress || ~心 desire do better || 不断~ keep moving forward
4 长进 [長進] zhǎngjìn (grow-advance) <v./n.> make progress, progress: ~很快 quick progress || 有/ 没~ have/ haven't made progress
5 循序渐进 [--漸進] xúnxù jiànjìn (follow-order-gradually-advance) <idiom> move step by step: 学习应该~. Studies should advance step by step.
6 突飞猛进 [-飛-進] tūfēiměngjìn (abrupt-fly-sudden-advance) <idiom> advance by leaps and bounds: 科技~. Technology advances by leaps and bounds.
7 勇往直前 [-] yǒngwǎngzhíqián (brave-go-direct-forward) <idiom> advance bravely: 鼓舞大家~ encourage everyone advance bravely
8 倒退 [-] dàotuì (reverse-retreat) <v.> go backwards: 向后~ fall backwards || 步步~ step by step regression || 历史~ historical regression
9 后退 [後-] hòutuì (back-retreat) <v.> fall back: 节节~ steadily retreat || ~几步 fall back a few steps || 连连~ repeatedly fall back
10 退步 [-] tuìbù (retreat-step) <v.> fall behind, retrogress: 我一年没说中文, 口语~ 了. Not having used it for a year, my spoken Chinese has deteriorated.

11 退化 [-] tuìhuà (retreat-*suffix*) <v.> degenerate, atrophy: 翅膀~ wing atrophy || 技术~ technological deterioration || 逐渐~ gradual degeneration

12 滞后 [滯後] zhìhòu (lag-behind) <v.> lag behind: 生活~ lifestyle deficits || 价格~ price lags behind || 回声~. The echo lags behind.

13 开倒车 [開-車] kāidàochē (drive-reverse-car) <v.> turn back the clock: 开历史的倒车 try turn back history || 在改革的路上 ~ try drive backwards on the road of reform

14 走下坡路 [-] zǒuxiàpōlù (go-down-slope-road) <v.> decline: 教育正在~. Education is currently declining/slumping.

15 堕落 [墮-] duòluò (sink-fall) <v.> degenerate, become depraved: ~ 成罪犯degenerate into a common criminal || 生活~ lead a degenerate life

16 腐败 [-敗] fǔbài (rotten-decay) <v.> corrupt: 政治~ political corruption || ~的政府 corrupt government || 反~ anti-corruption

17 沉浮 [-] chénfú (sink-float) <v.> ups and downs: 人生~ life's ups and downs || 商海~ ups and downs of business || 几度~ several rises and falls

18 领先 [領-] lǐngxiān (lead-ahead) <v.> be in the lead, lead: 比分~ have the leading score || ~一步 one step ahead || ~六分 lead by six points

19 优先 [優-] yōuxiān (preferential-prioritize) <v.> take precedence, have priority: 女士~ ladies first || ~生产 prioritize production || 住房~ prioritize housing

20 抢 [搶] qiǎng (seize, rush) <v.> grab, take: ~座位 grab a seat || ~时间 be in a rush || ~着说 racing to say

21 抢先 [搶-] qiǎngxiān (rush-ahead) <v.> anticipate, preempt: ~一步 think one step ahead || ~公开 anticipate the public || ~进入市场 preemptively enter the market

22 争先恐后 [爭--後] zhēngxiānkǒnghòu (strive for-ahead-fear-behind) <idiom> strive to be first: ~举手 race to raise a hand || ~地逃跑 strive to escape first || ~发言 race to speak first

23 攀比 [-] pānbǐ (compare unrealistically-compete) <v.> compare: 盲目~ blind comparisons || 相互~ mutual comparison || 跟别人~ compared with someone else

24 团结 [團結] tuánjié (unite-tie) <v.> unite: 加强~ strengthen unity || ~同学 unite students || ~群众 unite the crowd

25 齐心 [齊-] (uniform-heart) <adj.> be of one heart: ~合作 collaborate as one || ~努力coordinate one's efforts to work together efficiently

26 聚 [-] jù (assemble, accumulate, collect) <v.> get together: ~在一起 gather together || ~了很多人 assemble many people || ~餐 dinner party, gathering

27 聚会 [-會] jùhuì (gather-meet) <n.> meeting, gathering, party: 同学~ classmate reunion || 参加~ attend parties || 三次~ three meetings

28 团聚 [團-] tuánjù (unite-gather) <v.> reunite: 全家~ family reunion || 与亲人~ reunite with loved ones

29 团圆 [團圓] tuányuán (unite-complete) <v.> family reunion: 春节是中国人全家~的日子. Chinese New Year is a date when all family members reunite.

30 别 [別] bié (divide, distinguish, leave) <v.> leave, say goodbye to: 不辞而~ go without saying goodbye || ~了家人 left family members || ~了家乡 left a hometown

31 永别 [-別] yǒngbié (forever-leave) <v.> part forever: ~人间 leave the world (die) || 跟朋友们~ part with friends forever

32 分别 [-別] fēnbié (part-leave) <v./n.> part from: ~两年 be apart for two years || 跟朋友~ part with friends || 这次 ~ this parting

33 分离 [-離] fēnlí (part-separate) <v.> separate: 和亲人~ part from a lover || 夫妻, 父子, 母女~ separation between father and wife, father and son, mother and daughter || 相互~ mutual separation

34 分手 [-] fēnshǒu (part-hand) <separable word> break up: 跟他~ break up with him || 分了两次手 break up twice || 平静地~ calmly break up

35 分居 [-] fēnjū (separate-dwell) <v.> family members living apart: 夫妻~ husband and wife living separately || ~两地 family members living in two places

Tips:

1 What is power, strength? The Chinese government values 'unity, unite' (团结, tuánjié) because they believe 团结就是力量 (unity is strength), which happens be the title of a song. Sir Francis Bacon said 'knowledge is power' (知识就是力量), but George Orwell wrote 'ignorance is strength' (无知就是力量) in his famous novel, *1984,* published in 1949.

2 有上进心: It means 'to have desire to do better,' which is a popular commendation for others in China.

3 循序渐进 (xúnxùjiànjìn): It means 'to move step by step.' In a hierarchy-oriented country like China, order or sequence is never overemphasized, therefore, 循序渐进 and similar doctrines such as 按部就班 (ànbù jiùbān, follow the prescribed order) and 一步一个脚印 (step by step, one step, one footprint) are inculcated in children from a very early age. The idea of innovation (chuàngxīn, 创新) came around the turn of this century.

4 腐败 (fǔbài, corruption) and 反腐 (fǎnfǔ, anti-corruption): They seem be two major topics in Chinese political life. They appeared five times on the first page of *The People's Daily* of Tuesday, September 19, 2017.

Exercises:

Part I: Use the given bound form as a guide help to you think of other words with the same character. Feel free use your dictionary when needed. Then write down the English definition of each of the words you've written.

分 (part): 分别 part from

____

____

____

____

____

退 *(move back, retreat)*: 倒退 *go backwards*

____

____

____

Part II: Read the following sentences and fill in each blank with the appropriate word or phrase from the options given.

1 倒退、走下坡路、退化、滞后

a) 语言学家认为如果孩子从小不跟人类一起生活, 他的语言能力就会完全______.
b) 美国服务业的发展明显________于高科技行业的发展.
c) 有人认为毛泽东发动的文化大革命就是一种文明的________.
d) 有人认为美国正在________, 因为国内的各种矛盾一天比一天严重.

2 进步、发展、上进

a) 最近小王学习上_______很快.
b) 小王是一个非常_______的学生.
c) 小王毕业以后想到深圳去_______自己的事业.

3 突飞猛进、勇往直前、循序渐进、争先恐后

a) 学习是一个_________的过程, 必须一步一步来.
b) 朝鲜制造核武器的技术取得了__________ __的进步.
c) 朝鲜政府号召老百姓_________, 跟美国斗争到底.
d) 纽约上下班高峰期间, 人们都________在地铁上抢座位.

4 腐败、攀比、堕落、团结

a) 中国政府官员的______问题还很严重.
b) 年轻人一旦吸毒就会走向________.
c) 年轻人一般喜欢_______穿着打扮.
d) 这一家公司的员工很_______, 他们互相支持、互相帮助.

6 分别、分居、聚会、团聚

a) 小李跟大学同学毕业后_______整整十年了, 今天晚上大家要在这家大酒店_______.
b) 春节是中国人全家________的节日.
c) 这对夫妻因为感情不好开始______.

Theme 140: To manage, to handle 经营, 处理 (jīngyíng, chǔlǐ)

1 管 [-] guǎn (wind instrument, administer, control) <v.> control, in charge of: 警察局~抓小偷的事. The police station is in charge of catching criminals. || ~得太多 control too much
2 管理 [-] guǎnlǐ (administer-manage) <v.> manage: ~一个公司 manage a company || 严格 (yángé) ~ strict management || 加强 ~ strong management

3 接收 [-] jiēshōu (accept-receive) <v.> receive: ~病人 admit a sick person || ~信号 receive a signal || ~节目 receive a program
4 签收 [簽-] qiānshōu (sign-receive) <v.> sign for something: ~文件 sign for a file || ~日期 date of signing || 收款人~ sign for the payee
5 收发 [-發] shōufā (receive-send) <v.> receive and send: ~邮件 receive and send mail || ~材料 receive and send materials || ~消息 receive and send news

6 治理 [-] zhìlǐ (govern-manage) <v.> administer, govern, improve: ~环境 improve the environment || ~图书市场 administer a book market || ~ 国家administer a country
7 执法 [執-] zhífǎ (execute-law) <v.> enforce the law: 交通~ traffic law enforcement || 共同~ common law enforcement || 公正~ fair law enforcement

8 办 [辦] bàn (handle) <v.> do, handle, deal with: ~护照 get a passport || ~保险 (bǎoxiǎn) get insurance || 主~ host an event
9 办理 [辦-] bànlǐ (handle-manage) <v.> handle: ~手续 handle formalities || ~驾照 get a driver's license || ~签证 (qiānzhèng) get a visa
10 办公 [辦-] bàngōng (handle-official business) <v.> work (usu. in an office), handle official business: 在家里~ work from home || ~室 office || 照常~ handle official business as usual
11 办事 [辦-] bànshì (handle-affairs) <separable word> handle affairs, work: ~认真do things concientiously|| ~拖拉do things slowly and reluctantly|| 按常规~follow the routine
12 承办 [-辦] chéngbàn (undertake-handle) <v.> undertake: ~比赛undertake a game || ~会议 manage a conference
13 经手 [經-] jīngshǒu (pass-hand) <v.> handle, deal with: ~处理 deal with by hand || ~进货 deal with a purchase || ~借款 handle a loan
14 包办 [-辦] bāobàn (completely-handle) <v.> monopolize everything, undertake to do everything by oneself: ~婚姻 forced into an arranged marriage || 一手~ monopolize, keep everything in one's own hands || ~酒席 take care of everything for banquets
15 代办 [-辦] dàibàn (on behalf-handle) <v.> act on somebody's behalf: ~绿卡 get a green card for someone || ~签证get a visa for someone

16 筹建 [籌-] chóujiàn (plan and prepare-build) <v.> prepare to build sth: ~ 公司 prepare to start a company || ~工厂 prepare to build a factory
17 补办 [補辦] bǔbàn (make up-do) <v.> make up, do after the proper time: ~手续 (shǒuxù) make up the documents || ~工作证 apply for an employee's card after starting to work|| 过期不~. Late applications are not accepted.
18 操办 [-辦] cāobàn (handle-do) <v.> prepare for: ~婚事 prepare for marriage || 交给秘书~ leave the arrangements in one's secretary's hands || 一手~ single-handedly prepare
19 操心 [-] cāoxīn (consume-mind) <v.> worry about: ~孩子 worry about children || 分外~ exceptionally worried
20 代理 [-] dàilǐ (on behalf-manage) <v.> act on behalf of sb., in a responsible position: ~厂长 act as manager of a factory || 广告 ~ ad agency
21 处理 [處-] chǔlǐ (handle-manage) <v./n.> deal with: ~问题 deal with a question || ~关系 handle a relationship || ~邮件 dispose of mail

22 料理 [-] liàolǐ (arrange-manage) <v.> arrange, manage, take care of: ~家务 do housework || ~自己的生活 take care of oneself || ~丧事(sāngshì) make arrangements for a funeral
23 破格 [-] pògé (break-regulation) <v.> break a rule (good): ~提拔 (tíbá) break a rule promote someone || ~录取 (lùqǔ) make an exception admit someone || ~用人 break a rule for an employee
24 破例 [-] pòlì (break-convention) <v.> make an exception (bad): ~招收女生 make an exception recruit girls || ~喝了点酒 make an exception and drink some beer

25 清场 [-場] qīngchǎng (clear-site) <v.> clear out: 有人打电话给警察说音乐会现场有人带着枪, 警察决定立刻~. Someone called the police to tell them that there is a guy with a gun at the concert, and the police decided to clear the venue immediately.
26 清理 [-] qīnglǐ (clear-handle) <v.> put in order, check up, sort out: ~文件 put files in order || ~车库 tidy up a garage || ~垃圾 get rid of garbage
27 销毁 [銷-] xiāohuǐ (melt-destroy) <v.> destroy by melting, burning, etc.: ~证据(zhèngjù) destroy the evidence || ~核武器 destroy nuclear weapons
28 销赃 [銷贜] xiāozāng (destroy-stolen goods) <v.> dispose of stolen goods: 尽快~ dispose of stolen goods as soon as possible|| 帮助小偷~ help the thief sell the stolen goods
29 炒股 [-] chǎogǔ (hype-stock) <v.> trade stocks: ~热 intense popular interest in trading stocks || 公款~ use public funds to trade stocks

30 放假 [-] fàngjià (away-vacation) <v.> have a vacation: ~两天 two day vacation || 放三天假 have a three day vacation
31 请假 [請-] qǐngjià (ask for-vacation) <v.> ask for vacation: 请三天假 ask for three days off || 请两次假 ask for two vacations || ~回家 ask for time off go home
32 休假 [-] xiūjià (take-vacation) <v.> take holiday: ~十天 take ten days off || 休五天假 take a five day vacation || 连续~ continuous vacation
33 值班 [-] zhíbān (be on-duty) <separable word> be on duty: 值夜班 work the night shift || 值早班 work the morning shift || 正在~ currently on duty
34 出差 [-] chūchāi (go-business trip) <separable word> go on a business trip: 出公差 public business trip || 出三天差 go on a business trip for three days || 因公~ business trip

35 经营 [經營] jīngyíng (manage-run) <v.> manage, run: ~一家书店 run a bookstore || 私人/ 集体 (jítǐ) ~ private/ collective operation || ~这家工厂多年 has managed this factory for many years
36 公办 [-辦] gōngbàn (state-run) <adj.> state-run: ~学校 state-run school || ~教育 (jiàoyù) state-run education
37 公立 [-] gōnglì (state-establish) <adj.> public: ~学校 public school || ~大学 public college
38 民办 [-] mínbàn (people-run) <adj.> privately operated: ~小学 the private primary school || ~工业 private industry || ~报纸 private newspaper
39 民营 [-營] mínyíng (people-manage) <adj.> private: ~公司 private company
40 国有 [國-] guóyǒu (state-own) <adj.> state-owned: ~财产 state-owned property || ~企业 state-owned company || 收归~ rejoin with the state (nationalize)

41 私有 [-] sīyǒu (private-own) <adj.> private: ~经济 private economy || ~财产 private property || 个人 ~ personal privacy

Tips:

1 管 (guǎn): It means 'to control.' It seems most Chinese who have certain power like to control (管) others, but the ordinary people have a saying, "管天管地, 管不了拉屎放屁 (lāshǐ fàngpì)," which means 'even if you had absolute power control over everything between heaven and Earth, you do not have the power to control too personal a matter such as pooping or farting.'

2 办公室主任: It means 'director of an office,' who in China have much more power than ordinary Westerners would imagine.

3 私立大学 and 民办大学 in China: In most developed countries, most of the best universities are private (私立, sīlì) but in China, it is just the opposite. The best private college in China could not rank on the top 100 or 200 or even a longer list of China's best colleges at the time that this dictionary was compiled. Understandably, as '私' (private, selfish) does not go along well with Communist ideology '公' (public, by the people). So private colleges in China are called 民办大学 (people-run-college.)

Exercises:

Part I: Use the given bound form as a guide to help you think of other words with the same character. Feel free use your dictionary when needed. Then write down the English definition of each of the words you've written.

办 (do, handle, deal with, manage): 办护照 get a passport

____

____

____

____

____

____

____

Part II: Read the following sentences and fill in each blank with the appropriate word or phrase from the options given.

1 公立、国有

a) 中国大城市的_______学校教学质量很好. 但是美国正相反大城市的私立学校比较好.

b) 中国关于能源 (néngyuán, energy sources) 的企业都是_________企业, 但是美国差不多都是私有企业.

2 休假、值班、请假、出差

a) 在一些公司无故________是要被扣 (kòu, deduct) 工资的.
b) 很多中国公司也有带薪__________的制度，所以员工可以没有经济负担好好休息.
c) 在中国一般来说警察需要晚上__________，以保证晚上居民的安全问题.
d) 小高这份新工作要求有50%的________时间, 不能在居住地陪伴家人.

3 收发、执法、办理、治理

a) 中国学校或者政府机关门前都有一个传达室，负责________邮件和接待来访人员.
b) 中国的环境污染需要花费大量资金与时间去________.
c) 中国的________部门是公安机关, 具体的执法人是警察.
d) 中国的民政部门__________结婚或者离婚手续.

4 代办、办事、包办、办公

a) 这家银行的_______时间是早上九点到晚上五点.
b) 在美国一些旅行社 (lǚxíngshè) 会_______去中国的签证.
c) 这家美国旅行社的________效率 (xiàolǜ, efficiency) 很高, 一般一个星期就会办完去中国的签证.
d) 以前中国人的婚姻一般是由父母________的，自己没有选择的权利.

5 处理、破格、筹建、清理

a) 这家工厂从前年就开始_______了, 但是到现在还没建成.
b) 对于客户提出的意见, 这家公司都会认真________.
c) 小王因为在研究上的巨大贡献 (gòngxiàn, contribution), 被学校________提升为教授.
d) 每个星期一都会有垃圾车来这里________居民的垃圾.

6 经营、销赃、操心、销毁

a) 这家餐馆已经在纽约_________一百多年了, 生意一直非常好.
b) 开餐馆是一件非常_________的事情，每天从早到晚都非常忙碌 (mánglù, busy).
c) 这个官员收取了别人五百万人民币的贿赂 (huìlù, bribe), 为了__________，他把所有的钱都送给了在农村的一个亲属 (qīnshǔ, relatives).
d) 为了不让警察发现自己犯罪，这个人________了所有可能会引起警察怀疑 (huáiyí, doubt) 的证据.

Theme 141: To control 控制 (kòngzhì)

1 掌握 [-] zhǎngwò (in charge-grasp) <v.> have sth.in hand, take into one's hand, control: ~军队hold military || ~权力 have the power in hand || ~资源 control resources

2 把握 [-] bǎwò (hold-grasp) <v./n.> hold, grasp: ~机会 take opportunity || 有~ be sure of sth.

3 掌管 [-] zhǎngguǎn (in charge-control) <v.> in charge of: ~新闻 in charge of news || ~现金 in charge of cash || ~人的命运 in charge of human fate

4 操纵 [-縱] cāozòng (hold-free) <v.> manipulate: ~市场 manipulate market || ~飞船 manipulate spacecraft || ~机器manipulate machine

5 控制 [-] kòngzhì (control-control) <v.> control: ~人数 control number of people || ~市场 control market || ~体重 control weight

6 支配 [-] zhīpèi (dominate-apportion) <v.> dominate: ~自然dominate nature || ~金钱dominate money || ~现实dominate reality

7 独占 [獨佔] dúzhàn (oneself-occupy) <v.> have sth. all to oneself, monopolize, take over: ~市场monopolize the market || ~国际舞台monopolize the international stage

8 垄断 [壟斷] lǒngduàn (ridge-occupy) <v.> monopolize: ~世界市场monopolize the world market || ~科学技术monopolize science and technology

9 霸占 [-佔] bàzhàn (seize by force-occupy) <v.> forcibly occupy, unlawfully seize: ~土地unlawfully occupy the land || ~别国领土forcibly occupy the territory of another country

10 主办 [-辦] zhǔbàn (host-hold) <v.> host: ~晚会host a party || ~展览host exhibition || ~学校the host school

11 主管 [-] zhǔguǎn (major-in charge of) <v.> supervise, in charge of: ~农业 in charge of agriculture || ~这个项目 supervise this project || ~经济in charge of the economy

12 指挥 [-揮] zhǐhuī (direct-command) <v.> command: ~行动command action || ~交通command traffic || 直接 ~ direct command

13 指示 [-] zhǐshì (point-show) <v./n.> instruct, instruction: 听上级~pending further instructions from the higher authorities || 下达~give instructions || ~明确clear instructions

14 带领 [帶領] dàilǐng (lead-guide) <v.> lead, guide: 老师~学生参观博物馆. The teacher guided the students around the museum. || 教练~团队打赢了篮球比赛. The coach led his team to win the basketball game.

15 率领 [-領] shuàilǐng (head-guide) <v.> head: ~全军head whole army || ~队伍head the team || ~全体学生head all students

16 统治 [統-] tǒngzhì (administer-rule) <v./n.> rule: ~世界rule the world || 在清朝政府的~下 under the rule of Qing government

17 执政 [執-] zhízhèng (take charge of-administration) <v.> be in power, in office, at the helm of state: 轮流~ take turns in power || 上台~ came power || 联合~ coalition government || ~党ruling party

18 掌权 [-權] zhǎngquán (control-power) <v.> be in power, have authority, exercise control: 重新~ regain power || 单独 ~ alone in power

19 当权 [當權] dāngquán (in charge of-power) <v.> be in power, hold power: 恶人 ~. Evil people are in power. || 民主党 ~. Democracies are in power.

20 主持 [-] zhǔchí (preside-hold) <v.> take charge of, manage, preside over: ~工作 take charge of the work || ~一台晚会 host an evening party || ~会议 preside over the meeting

21 左右 [-] zuǒyòu (left-right) <v.> control, master: ~他的行为 control his behavior || ~别人的想法control other people's thinking || ~消费者 control consumer

Tip:

1 垄 (lǒng): It means 'ridge (of tillable field.)' It is not a high frequency character, except in agricultural terminology and for the word 垄断, which means 'monopoly.'

Exercises:

Part I: Translate the following phrases into English and then answer the questions.

掌握权力________________

把握机会________________

掌管谷歌公司________________

两党轮流执政________________

垄断市场________________

控制人口________________

操纵股票市场________________

左右别人的想法__________ ______

1 你觉得把握机会对一个人是否重要, 为什么?

____

2 目前谁在掌管谷歌公司?

____

3 美国是不是两党轮流执政的国家?

____

4 中国的国有企业垄断了石油市场, 美国呢?

____

5 你认为中国是否应该控制人口? 为什么?

____

6 你觉得美国的股票市场能够被华尔街操纵吗? 为什么?

____

7 美国媒体能不能左右人们的想法? 为什么?

____

Theme 142: To decide, to announce 决议, 宣布 (juéyì, xuānbù)

1 定 [-] dìng (stable, stabilize, determine, decide) <v.> set: ~工资 set a salary || ~标准 standardize
2 规定 [規-] guīdìng (regulate-stipulate) <v.> stipulate, provide, prescribe: ~上学的年龄 provide school age || ~工作时间 provide working hours || ~教师不能经商 stipulate that teachers cannot do business
3 制定 [-] zhìdìng (make-stipulate) <v.> draw up, draft, formulate: ~计划draft a plan || ~政策(zhèngcè) formulate a policy || ~ 宪法 draw up a Constitution
4 决定 [決-] juédìng (determine-decide) <v.> decide: ~去 decide leave || ~换工作 decide change professions || ~马上报名 decide quickly sign-up
5 决策 [決-] juécè (decide-plan) <v.> make decision: 迅速~ quickly make a decision || ~错误 make a wrong decision

6 发表 [發-] fābiǎo (issue-publish) <v.> publish: ~一篇文章 publish an article || ~意见 publish an opinion || ~消息 publish news
7 公布 [-佈] gōngbù (public-promulgate) <v.> announce, publish, promulgate: ~成绩 publish grades || ~结果 announce results || ~一部法规promulgate legislation
8 宣布 [-佈] xuānbù (announce-promulgate) <v.> announce: ~开始 announce the beginning (of something) || ~退休 announce retirement || ~结束 announce the end (of something)
9 发布 [發佈] fābù (issue-promulgate) <v.> release, issue: ~信息 release information || ~命令 issue a command || 新闻~ distribute news
10 颁布 [頒佈] bānbù (promulgate-promulgate) <v.> promulgate: ~一部法规 enact laws || ~法令 promulgate a decree || ~新规定 promulgate new regulations

11 刊登 [-] kāndēng (publish-publish) <v.> publish (in a newspaper or magazine): ~文章 publish an article || ~广告 publish an ad || 如期~ publish on schedule
12 发帖 [發-] fātiě (post-a post) <v.> post: 网上~ post online || 匿名~ post anonymously
13 灌水 [-] guànshuǐ (pour-water) <v.> talk nonsense, talk about irrelevant things: 网上~ post nonsense on an Internet forum

14 令 [-] lìng (order, make) <v.> order, command, cause ab. to: ~人不满 make someone dissatisfied || ~我吃惊 surprise me || ~他马上回去 command him go back soon
15 命令 [-] mìnglìng (command-order) <v.> command: ~孩子马上睡觉 command children to go bed at once || 高声~ command loudly || ~老公做饭 command her husband to cook
16 授权 [-權] shòuquán (authorize-power) <v.> authorize: ~代理 authorized agent
17 下令 [-] xiàlìng (issue-order) <v.> order, give orders: ~停止 order stop || ~打开城门. Order the city gates to open.

18 开会 [開會] kāihuì (have-meeting) <separable word> have a meeting: 今天~ have a meeting today || 开大会 have a big meeting || 开职工大会 general staff meeting

19 建议 [-議] jiànyì (propose-suggest) <v./n.> suggest, suggestion: ~搬进去 suggest one moves in || 提出~ put forward suggestion || 三点/条~ three suggestions
20 讨论 [討論] tǎolùn (discuss-comment) <v.> discuss: ~问题 discuss a problem || 自由~ discuss freely || 参加~ participate in discussion
21 制订 [-訂] zhìdìng (formulate-make) <v.> make, formulate: ~方案 (fāng'àn) make a program (for action, etc.) || ~计划 formulate a plan || ~价格 work out a price
22 肯定 [-] kěndìng (affirm-decide) <v.> affirm, approve, be sure of: ~自己 affirm oneself || ~成绩 affirm one's achievements || 加以~ give affirmation
23 确定 [確-] quèdìng (firmly-decide) <v.> define, fix, determine: ~目标 determine the target || ~期限 fix a time frame || 很难~ be hard to determine
24 确认 [確認] quèrèn (affirm-acknowledge) <v.> confirm: ~合约 confirm a contract || ~合同 confirm a contract || ~关系 confirm the relationship

Tips:

1 制定 vs. 制订: They are homophones (zhìdìng), and the differences between their meanings are very confusing, even for native speakers. Both mean 'to make' but the object of 制定 cannot be changed easily, such as laws or regulations. As for 制订, the object of it is to close a plan or a draft, which means it could be changed later. For example, 制订学习计划 (to make a study plan,) 制定法律 (to formulate a law) and 制订法律草案 (to draft a law.)
2 我宣布, . . .: It means 'I announce' which is a formulated phrase for Chinese officials announcing openings of ceremonies. There is usually a pause after these two words.
3 令 (lìng): The upper part of the oracle form of 令 is 亼 (jí, 集, to gather) and the lower part is a kneeling man, so the whole character means 'order.' Major meaning of 令 include: (1) order, to order, for example, 命令 (order, to order) and 司令 (sīlìng, in charge of-order, commander,) (2) good, your, for example, 令尊 (lìngzūn, your beloved father.)

Exercises:

Part I: Use the given bound form as a guide to help you think of other words with the same character. Feel free to use your dictionary when needed. Then write down the English definition of each of the words you've written.

定 (set): 定工资 set a salary

____

____

____

____

布 *(declare, announce, publish):* 公布 *announce*

____

____

____

____

Part II: Read the following sentences and fill in each blank with the appropriate word or phrase from the options given.

1 制定、规定、决定、发表

a) 这个学校________学生上课时不能看手机.
b) 中国政府________要在海外推广 (tuīguǎng, spread) 中国文化.
c) 这位美国教授________了很多关于中国文化的文章.
d) 中国政府打算________关于房产税的法律.

2 宣布、刊登、发布

a) 小王向同事们________下个月要结婚.
b) 这位总统________了七项关于限制 (xiànzhì, restrict) 非法移民的命令.
c) 最近报纸上________了很多关于四川地震的消息.

3 令、命令、授权

a) 警察________这个犯罪嫌疑人 (suspect) 举起手来.
b) 最近这个城市的地铁常常出故障 (gùzhàng, malfunction), ________乘客十分不满.
c) 谷歌公司________给这家小公司使用他们的软件.

4 灌水、发帖、开会、建议

a) 这家报纸有很多________的新闻, 目的是吸引读者的注意.
b) 小王特别喜欢在脸书上________, 评论别人的照片.
c) 最近小王常常________迟到, 经理批评了他.
d) 年轻人在婚姻问题上应该多听听父母的________和忠告.

Theme 143: To arrange 安排 (ānpái)

1 整 [-] zhěng (tidy, put in order) <v.> rectify: ~军 make an education movement in the army || ~党 make an education movement in the party || ~风the rectification of incorrect styles of work or thinking
2 整合 [-] zhěnghé (integrate-combine) <v.> conform, integrate: 资源~ integration of resources || ~信息integration of information || 重新~ re-establish integration
3 整顿 [-頓] zhěngdùn (rectify-arrange) <v.> rectify: ~纪律 rectification through discipline || ~秩序 (zhìxù) re-establish order || ~领导班子/军队 reform leadership/the army
4 整治 [-] zhěngzhì (rectify-manage) <v.> renovate, repair: ~坏人punish evildoers || ~河道 river realignment || 大力~ vigorously repair
5 安排 [-] ānpái (arrange-organize) <v./n.> arrange, plan: ~工作 arrange work || 合理 ~时间 plan one's time very well || 上天的~ God's plan

6 安置 [-] ānzhì (arrange-place) <v.> place, placement: ~待业青年 place unemployed young people || ~难民 (nànmín) place refugees || ~在这儿 be placed here
7 部署 [-] bùshǔ (station-arrange) <v.> deploy: ~行动 deploy action || 打乱 ~ disrupt deployment || 统一~ unified deployment
8 组织 [組織] zǔzhī (organize) <v.> organize: ~教学 organize teaching || ~参观 organize a visit || ~讨论 organize a discussion || ~部 Organization Department
9 重组 [-組] chóngzǔ (re – organize) <v.> reorganize, restructure: 基因~ gene recombination || 企业~ make the reorganization of enterprises || ~家庭family recombination

10 调 [調] diào (promote, shift) <v.> shift: ~工作 shift jobs || ~到北京工作 shift my job Beijing
11 调动 [調動] diàodòng (transfer-move) <v.> advocate, shift: ~工作 shift jobs || ~积极性 advocate people's passion
12 调节 [調節] tiáojié (adjust-regulate) <v.> regulate, adjust: 市场~ adjust the market || ~灯光 adjust the lighting || ~温度 adjust the temperature

13 派 [-] pài (branch, appoint, send) <v.> send: ~记者采访 set up an interview with reporters || ~六人参加 send six participants || ~他去 send him to go
14 派出 [-] pàichū (send-out) <v.> send out: ~留学生 send out international students || ~飞机 send off a plane || ~代表 send a representative
15 公派 [-] gōngpài (government-send) <v.> government-sponsored: ~留学government-sponsored overseas education
16 派遣 [-] pàiqiǎn (send-dispatch) <v.> send, dispatch: ~使者到中国 send messengers to China || ~代表参加 send representatives to attend

17 发放 [發-] fāfàng (send-give) <v.> give, issue: ~工资 give salary || ~问卷 issue a questionnaire || ~录取通知书 issue an acceptance letter
18 分配 [-] fēnpèi (distribute-allocate) <v.> distribute: ~工作 distribute one's work || ~到大学当老师 distributed to work as a college professor
19 出动 [-動] chūdòng (send-move) <v.> dispatch: ~军队 dispatch the army || ~飞机 dispatch a plane || 全家~ dispatch a whole family
20 分组 [-組] fēnzǔ (divide-group) <v.> group, grouping: ~活动 group activity || ~学习 group study || ~讨论 group discussion
21 打发 [-發] dǎfā (do-send) <v.> send away: ~她走开send her away || ~时间 pass the time || ~他们 send them away

22 配备 [-備] pèibèi (allocate-equip) <v.> be equipped with: ~彩电 be equipped with color TV || ~助手 be equipped with an assistant || ~工作人员 be equipped with employees
23 配置 [-] pèizhì (equip-set up) <v.> deploy, configuration: 合理~ reasonably allocate || 资源~ the distribution of resources || 农业~ configure agriculture
24 指定 [-] zhǐdìng (designate-assign) <v.> appoint, assign, designate: ~地区 designated area || ~时间 designated time || ~位置 designated location

Tips:

1 调: When pronounced as diào, it means 'promote, shift, transfer, investigate,' for example, '调动' (to shift) and '调查' (to investigate). When pronounced

as tiáo, it means 'adjust,' for example '调节' (to adjust) and '空调' (air conditioning.)

2 组织部: It means the Organization Department (of the CCP). This department, at various levels, is extremely powerful since it determines the evaluation and promotion of cadres.

Exercises:

Part I: Use the given bound form as a guide to help you think of other words with the same character. Feel free to use your dictionary when needed. Then write down the English definition of each of the words you've written.

整 *(rectify)*: 整理 *put in order*

____

____

____

____

派 *(send)*: 派人 *send people out*

____

____

____

____

调 *(shift)*: 调工作 *shift jobs*

____

____

____

____

Part II: Read the following sentences and fill in each blank with the appropriate word or phrase from the options given.

1 整合、整顿、整理

a) 小张家里太乱了， 所以他决定周六休息的时候好好收拾、_______一下.

b) 目前房地产市场非常混乱 (hùnluàn, chaos), 所以政府决定要________房地产市场.

c) 有人说在人工智能时代________各种数据资源变得特别重要.

2 组织、重组、调动

a) 这位数学老师非常善于_______学生学习数学的积极性.
b) 下个星期学校要________学生们去参观博物馆.
c) 据说中国政府打算让所有的亏损国有企业进行________，以便更好地发挥优势.

3 公派、发放、打发

a) 最近十年中国政府的________留学生增加了五倍.
b) 中国政府给公派留学生每月________一千美元的助学金.
c) 中国很多老人用到处旅游的方式来_______自己退休以后的生活.

Theme 144: To evaluate, to appoint 考评, 任用 (kǎopíng, rènyòng)

1 查 [-] chá (check, inspect) <v.> check, look into: ~出勤 check on school attendance || ~原因look into reasons || ~眼睛have an eye examination
2 调查[調-] diàochá (survey-investigate) <v./n.> survey: 人口~ population survey || ~这个人 survey the people || 进行~ carry out a survey
3 检查 [檢-] jiǎnchá (examine-investigate) <v./n.> examine: ~作业 examine homework || 再~一遍 examine one more time || 细心~ careful examination
4 审查 [審-] shěnchá (censor-inspect) <v.> examine (plans, proposals, etc.), censor (books, films, etc.): ~经费 check up on the funds || ~论文review papers|| 电影~ censor a movie
5 查询 [-詢] cháxún (investigate-inquire) <v.> inquire: ~存款 (cúnkuǎn) inquire about savings || ~邮件 inquire about mail || ~地址 inquire about an address
6 审 [審] shěn (check, try) <v.> try: ~犯人 try a criminal || 严 ~ serious trial || 二~ second trial
7 审核 [審-] shěnhé (check-double check) <v.> check: ~案件 review a case || ~价格 check the price || 认真~ serious review
8 审批 [審-] shěnpī (check-approve) <v.> examine and approve, examine and give instructions: ~项目 approve a project || 严格~ strict approval || 通过~ pass approval
9 评审 [評審] píngshěn (review-examine) <v.> examine: 严格~ strict examination || ~科技成果 examine technological achievements
10 审阅 [審閱] shěnyuè (examine-review) <v.> review: ~材料 review materials || ~新闻 review news || 仔细~ careful review
11 安检 [-檢] ānjiǎn (security-check) <v.> security check: 机场~ airport security check || 通过~ through security check || 接受~ accept a security check
12 检测 [檢測] jiǎncè (inspect-measure) <v.> inspect: 质量 ~ quality inspection || 食品~ food inspection || 定期 ~ regular inspection
13 检验 [檢驗] jiǎnyàn (inspect-test) <v.> test: ~质量 quality test || 商品~ product testing || ~血液, 智力 blood test
14 化验 [-驗] huàyàn (chemistrical-assay) <v.> laboratory test: ~血液 blood test || ~水质 water quality test || 再次~ another test

15 考验 [-驗] kǎoyàn (examine-test) <v.> test: 经受~ be tested || ~党员 test the party member || 对你的~ for your test

16 鉴定 [鑒-] jiàndìng (inspect-determine) <v./n.> identify: 指纹 ~ fingerprint identification || ~真假 identify true and false || ~宝石 identify gems

17 监督 [監-] jiāndū (supervise-superintend) <v./n.> supervise, inspect: ~员工supervise the staff || ~工作 supervise work || 互相~ mutual supervision

18 监视 [監視] jiānshì (monitor-view) <v> monitor: 密切~ closely monitor || ~敌人 monitor the enemy || ~大气变化 monitor climate change

19 监听 [監聽] jiāntīng (monitor-listen) <v> monitor: 电子~ computer monitor || ~谈话 listen a conversation || 秘密~ secretly monitoring

20 监测 [監測] jiāncè (monitor-measure) <v.> monitor: 环境~ environmental monitoring || ~温度变化monitor temperature variation || 污染~ pollution monitoring

21 督促 [-] dūcù (supervise-urge) <v.> supervise: ~孩子 supervise a kid || 互相~ mutual supervision

22 清点 [-點] qīngdiǎn (put in order-check) <v.> check, make an inventory: ~人数 check the number of people || ~财产 inventory property || ~现金 take inventory of cash

23 查点 [-點] chádiǎn (check-count) <v.> check: ~人数 count the number of people || ~账目 check accounts

24 点名 [點-] diǎnmíng (check-name) <separable word> roll call, (to call or praise or criticize sb.) by name: ~分派任务 name tasks be assigned

25 评 [評] píng (comment, judge) <v.> judge, appraise: ~奖 discuss and determine the recipients of awards || ~分grade, score

26 评判 [評-] píngpàn (comment-judge) <v.> judge: ~别人 judge other people

27 评估 [評-] pínggū (review-assess) <v./n.> assess: 市场~ market assessment || 技术~ technological assessment

28 评论 [評論] pínglùn (comment-discuss) <v.> comment: ~天下大事 comment on world events || ~这个人 comment on this person || ~政治 discuss politics

29 评选 [評選] píngxuǎn (review-select) <v.> select: ~最佳作品 select the best works || ~一等奖 choose first place || ~好新闻 select good news

30 评价 [評價] píngjià (comment-appraise) <v./n.> comment, appraise, evaluate: ~别人 evaluate another person || 做出, 进行~ do an evaluation || 公正的~ fair evaluation

31 考核 [-] kǎohé (review-check) <v.> examine, check up on, review: 定期~ routine check || ~干部 assess a cadre || 年终~ annual staff performance review

32 考勤 [-] kǎoqín (check-attendance) <v.> check work attendance: 职工~ check staff attendance || 严格~ serious attendance check

33 选 [選] xuǎn (select) <v.> choose, select: ~班长 choose a group leader || ~代表 choose a representative || ~一种你喜欢的样式 select a style that takes your fancy

34 选举 [選舉] xuǎnjǔ (select-elect) <v./n.> elect: ~市长 elect a mayor || 民主, 投票~ democratic election || 参加~ take part in an election

35 竞选 [競選] jìngxuǎn (compete-elect) <v.> run for: ~总统 run for president || ~州长 run for governor || ~辩论 campaign debate

36 大选 [-選] dàxuǎn (general-election) <n.> general election: 总统~ general presidential election || 美国~ American general election
37 普选 [-選] pǔxuǎn (universal-suffrage) <n.> universal suffrage, general election: 香港~ Hong Kong election || 民主~ democratic suffrage

38 招 [-] zhāo (beckon, recruit) <v.> recruit: ~新生 recruit new students || ~职员 recruit staff || ~人 recruit people
39 招生 [-] zhāoshēng (enroll-student) <v.> enroll new students: 提前~ early enrollment || 统一~ unified enrollment || ~工作 enrollment work
40 录取 [錄-] lùqǔ (record-choose) <v.> enroll, admit, recruit: ~学生 enroll students || ~五个 admit five people || 择优~ merit-based admission

41 聘 [-] pìn (engage, employ, recruit) <v.> engage: ~教授 engage a professor || 特~ special engagement || 返/新~ repeat/new hire
42 聘请 [-請] pìnqǐng (recruit-invite) <v.> invite, recruit: ~律师 invite a lawyer || ~专家 invite an expert || 高薪~ high salary invitation
43 聘用 [-] pìnyòng (employ-use) <v.> employ: ~保姆 employ a nanny || ~职工 employ staff
44 选拔 [選-] xuǎnbá (select-promote) <v.> select the best: ~人才 select the best talent || ~干部 select the best cadre || ~学生 select the best student
45 提拔 [-] tíbá (raise-promote) <v.> promote: ~干部 promote a cadre || ~为主任 promote director || 得到~ receive a promotion

46 任命 [-] rénmìng (appoint-order) <v.> appoint: 紧急~ emergency appointment || ~为经理 appoint a manager || 直接~ direct appointment
47 就任 [-] jiùrèn (take-post) <v.> take office: ~总统 take office as president
48 离任 [-] lírèn (leave-post) <v.> leave office: 即将~ about to leave office || 正式~ formal departure from office
49 撤换 [-換] chèhuàn (dismiss-replace) <v.> recall, replace: ~市长 replace a mayor || 立即~ immediate replacement || 随意~ random replacement
50 免职 [-職] miǎnzhí (depose-post) <v.> depose from office: 被~ was removed from office || 依法~ legally remove from office
51 上台 [-臺] shàngtái (take-stage) <v.> rise to power (in politics), go on stage (in the theater): 新总统~ the new president rose to power || 正式~ formally rise to power
52 下台 [-臺] xiàtái (leave-stage) <v.> step down from the stage or platform, fall out of power, leave office: 轰~ hoot sb. off the platform, oust sb. from office (or power) || 总统快~了. The president will leave office soon.

53 接 [-] jiē (join, meet, take over) <v.> take over, succeed to: ~班 take over a job || 你~他的工作 you take over his job
54 换届 [換屆] huànjiè (shift-term) <v.> change personnel upon completion of a term of office: ~选举 election at expiration of office terms

55 裁员 [-員] cáiyuán (cut off-employee) <v.> lay off: 大量~ many layoffs || 公司~ company layoffs
56 解雇 [-] jiěgù (dismiss-employment) <v.> fire: ~工人 fire a worker || 被公司~ fired by the company
57 解聘 [-] jiěpìn (dismiss-letter of contract) <v.> fire: ~副教授 dismiss an associate professor || ~员工 dismiss an employee

Tips:

1 选举 (xuǎnjǔ): Most Chinese elections are indirect elections (间接选举), for example, of the President of China (国家主席, literally 'state-chairman') and CCP's General Secretary (总书记,) the two most important posts in China. The elections embody 民主集中制 (mínzhǔ jízhōng zhì, democratic centralism), which is superior to democracy, according to Chinese political theorists.
2 任 (rèn): It could have several related meanings, for example 'to appoint' as in 任命 (appoint,) 'appointment, post' as in 上任 (to assume post, office) and 'term' as in 任期 (term), which is usually five years for political posts.
3 聘 (pìn), 聘请 and 雇用 (gùyòng): In ancient China, 聘 means 'to betroth' or 'to recruit' with presents or rewards of high value. Now 聘请 and 雇用 both mean 'to hire,' but the post by 聘请 is high and formal, for example, a multinational company 聘请了一位CEO, and the post by 雇用 could be low and informal, for example, when you move, you can 雇用 two guys for help.

Exercises:

Part I: Use the given bound form as a guide to help you think of other words with the same character. Feel free to use your dictionary when needed. Then write down the English definition of each of the words you've written.

查 *(check)*: 查人数 *count the number of people*

____

____

____

____

审 *(try)*: 审犯人 *try a criminal*

____

____

____

____

招 *(recruit)*: 招新生 *recruit new students*

____

____

____

____

聘 *(engage, appoint): engage a professor*

____

____

____

____

选 *(choose):* 选组长 *choose a group leader*

____

____

____

____

评 *(judge, appraise):* 评奖 *discuss and determine the recipients of awards*

____

____

____

____

Part II: Read the following sentences and fill in each blank with the appropriate word or phrase from the options given.

1 检查、调查、查询、安检

a) 关于这个中国女孩被杀的案件, 警察正在进行__________.
b) 经过________, 医生确定他的身体没有问题.
c) 在机场登机以前要先通过_________.
e) 在中国拨打114就可以_________你想知道的地址或者电话号码.

2 监督、化验、考验

a) 有些疾病必须通过_________病人的血液 (xuèyè, blood) 才能检查出来.
b) 美国媒体有__________政府工作的作用, 所以媒体常常会报道政府的丑闻.
c) 小李不打算跟男朋友很快结婚, 她想再________男朋友一段时间, 看看他是不是真心爱自己.

3 考核、评论、评价、评选

a) 这家公司规定只有年底通过公司_______的员工才可以继续留在公司工作.
b) 美国中小学_________学生的标准跟中国不同.
c) 他被________为学校的最佳篮球运动员.

d) 有些美国人很喜欢_______政治.

4 竞选、招生、录取、选举

a) 他在一所大学的_______办公室工作.
b) 老李的孩子被哈佛大学_______了, 真是一件大喜事.
c) 这位总统的女儿将来也要参加美国总统的_______. 但是媒体 (méitǐ, media) 表示大部分美国人不会_______他的女儿当总统.

5 离任、提拔、聘用、撤换

a) 奥巴马_______总统以后, 全家人仍然住在华盛顿.
b) 这位总统就任不到半年就________了二十多位高级职位官员.
c) ________年轻有为的干部担任重要职务是中国共产党一项重要的工作.
d) 这个学校去年_______了二十位新老师.

6 解雇、裁员、上台、下台

a) 由于经济不景气, 这家公司不得不大规模________.
b) 小高最近被公司_________了, 所以着急找新工作.
c) 法国新_________的总统还不到四十岁.
d) 很多印度人对国家总理不满意, 希望他赶快________.

Theme 145: To approve, to establish 批准, 建立 (pīzhǔn, jiànlì)

1 创造 [創-] chuàngzào (initiate-make) <v.> create: ~文字 create written language || ~条件 create conditions || 新 ~ a new creation
2 建 [-] jiàn (build, establish) <v.> set up, build: ~校 found a school || ~市 set up a city || ~国 found a state/establish a state
3 建立 [-] jiànlì (establish-found) <v.> set up, build, found, establish: ~家庭 build a family || ~联系 (liánxì) establish contacts || ~新中国 establish a new China
4 成立 [-] chénglì (accomplish-establish) <v.> found, establish: 正式~ be officially established || 新公司~ a new company/business was founded/set up || ~小家庭 found a small family
5 重建 [-] chóngjiàn (renew-build) <v.> rebuild, reconstruct, reestablish: ~军队 reconstruct an army || ~王宫 rebuild a palace || ~家园 reconstruct homes
6 建设 [-設] jiànshè (build-establish) <v./n.> construct, construction: 城市~ urban construction || 经济/文化~ economic/cultural construction || 搞~ do construction
7 树立 [樹-] shùlì (build-up) <v.> establish, build: ~信心 build confidence || ~人生观 build up a life philosophy || ~新思想 establish a new idea
8 组建 [組-] zǔjiàn (organize-establish) <v.> form, build, organize, establish: ~大型集团 establishment of large enterprise groups || ~公司 set up a company || ~新政府 form a new government
9 开 [開] kāi (open, start) <v.> open, run: ~公司 run a company || ~银行 run a bank || ~饭店 open a restaurant
10 办 [辦] bàn (handle, do) <v.> do, run, manage: ~厂 run a factory || ~学 run a school || ~教育 manage education

11 设 [設] shè (display, create, establish) <v.> set up, establish, open: ~医院 establish a hospital || ~大学 open a university || ~在北京 be established in Beijing

12 创办 [創辦] chuàngbàn (create-run) <v.> found, establish: ~杂志 found a magazine || ~工厂 establish a factory || ~学校 found a school

13 创建 [創-] chuàngjiàn (create-establish) <v.> create, set up, establish, found: ~公司 found a business/company || ~实验室 create a laboratory || ~文明 create civilization

14 创立 [創-] chuànglì (create-set up) <v.> build, establish: ~国家 build a state || ~新学科 establish a new discipline || ~文字 invent characters

15 开创 [開創] kāichuàng (initiate-create) <v.> initiate, create: ~新局面 create a new situation || ~新世界 create a new world || ~新时代 initiate a new era

16 开设 [開設] kāishè (initiate-establish) <v.> open, set up, start: ~学校 open schools || ~商店 open a shop/store || ~外语课 start foreign language courses

17 设立 [設-] shèlì (establish-set up) <v.> set up, establish, found: ~医院 establish a hospital || ~银行 set up a bank || ~各级学校 establish schools at all levels

18 确立 [確-] quèlì (firm-establish) <v.> establish, set: ~关系 establish a relationship || ~目标 set a goal || ~地位 establish a status

19 举办 [舉辦] jǔbàn (hold-do) <v.> hold, sponsor: ~活动 hold an event || ~晚会 hold an evening party || ~比赛 hold a competition

20 设置 [設-] shèzhì (establish-establish) <v.> set, set up: ~密码 set a password || 警方在广场的入口处~了路障. The police barricaded the entrance to the square.

21 报警 [報-] bàojǐng (report-police) <v.> call the police, give an alarm: 自动~ automatic alarm || 电话~ telephone alarm/call the police || 及时~ call the police immediately/in time

22 报到 [報-] bàodào (report-arrival) <v.> register, check in: 新生~ new students enroll || ~时间 registering time || 准时 ~ register on time

23 注册 [-] zhùcè (enroll-notebook) <v.> enroll, register, login: 在大学~ enroll in a university || ~不同专业 register different majors || 正式 ~ register officially

24 登记 [-記] dēngjì (record-note down) <v.> register: ~结婚/离婚 register a marriage/register for divorce || ~信息 register information || 户口~ register hukou/household

25 挂号 [-號] guàhào (register-order) <v.> register at a hospital: ~ 费registration fee || ~ 处registration office || ~看病 register at a hospital and see a doctor

26 申请 [-請] shēnqǐng (express-request) <v.> apply for: ~奖学金 apply for scholarship || ~加入 apply for participation || ~贷款 apply for loan

27 反映 [-] fǎnyìng (reverse-reflect) <v./n.> report, response, reaction, reflect: ~强烈 a strong reaction || 得到~ receive a response || ~情况 report a situation

28 汇报 [匯/彙報] huìbào (assemble-report) <v.> report: 向领导~ report to a leader || ~情况 report a situation || ~成绩 (chéngjì) report results

29 批准 [-] pīzhǔn (approve-permit) <v.> approve, authorize, give permission: ~成立 authorize to establish. . . || ~加入 approve to join. . . || 得到~ receive an approval

30 批 [-] pī (slap, write instruction, comment) <v.> approve: ~资金 (zījīn) approve funds || ~项目 approve a project || ~地皮/车皮 approve a land for building/approve a railway carriage for transporting

31 许可 [許-] xǔkě (permit-allowed) <v.> permission, permit: 获得~ get the permission || 未经~ without permission || 条件~ conditions permit
32 签 [簽] qiān (sign) <v.> sign: ~字/名 sign a name || ~合同 sign a contract || ~协议 (xiéyì) sign an agreement
33 签证 [簽證] qiānzhèng (sign-certificate) <v./n.> visa: 出国~ a visa to leave a country || 旅游 (lǚyóu) ~ tourist visa || 拿到~ get a visa
34 签名 [簽-] qiānmíng (sign-name) <separable word> sign, signature: 签他的名 sign his name || 签一个名 sign a name || 亲笔~ autograph
35 签字 [簽-] qiānzì (sign-graph) <separable word> sign, signature: 签个字 sign || 正式 ~ sign officially || 本人/双方~ sign by himself/herself or by both parties
36 盖章 [蓋-] gàizhāng (to stamp-seal) <separable word> seal, stamp: 签字~ sign and seal || 盖一个章 to have a stamp

Tips:

1 签字 vs. 签名: 签字 and 签名 can both mean to sign (signature) for legal purposes, but 签名 can also mean to autograph for a souvenir or collection purposes.
2 盖章: 章 means 'a seal' which is a symbol of administrative power in China. At the beginning of Chinese economic reforms, one had to get more than 100 seals to be able to start a business. Now the process is much simpler.
3 建, 设, 立: All mean 'to establish' and their combinations, 建设, 建立, 设立 have nearly the same meaning.
4 批准, 准许, 许可: All mean 'to approve, to permit, to allow,' but 批准 is the most formal and probably the hardest to get. 许可 can be slightly informal and colloquial.

Exercises:

Part I: Use the given bound form as a guide to help you think of other words with the same character. Feel free to use your dictionary when needed. Then write down the English definition of each of the words you've written.

签 *(sign):* 签名 *sign a name*

____

____

____

____

创 *(create):* 创办 *found, establish*

____

____

____
____

建 *(set up, build)*: 建校 *found a school*

____
____
____
____

Part II: Read the following sentences and fill in each blank with the appropriate word or phrase from the options given.

1 开设、设置、举办

a) 给电脑___________密码以后就忘记是一个令人头疼的问题.
b) 这所学校最近要_________一个大型的艺术节, 邀请 (yāoqǐng, invite) 其他学校来参加.
c) 这所高中___________了300多门课程供学生选择.

2 报到、报警、注册

a) 如果家里有危险 (wēixiǎn, dangerous) 情况一定要及时__________.
b) 今天是开学第一天, 很多新生来这个学校__________.
c) 据说每年哈佛大学有三百多学生__________上中文课.

3 挂号、登记、申请

a) 这个学校要招聘 (zhāopìn, hire) 一个中文老师, 大概有一百多人__________这个职位.
b) 在中国去医院看病需要先__________.
c) 小李跟女朋友昨天在北京民政局 (mínzhèng jú, Bureau of Civil Affairs) __________, 领取了结婚证.

4 汇报、许可、批准

a) 老王现在为美国军方工作, 如果他想离开美国旅行, 必须提前向美国政府__________, 得到美国政府的__________以后才能够离开美国.
b) 在美国想经营餐馆必须要先向政府有关部门申请__________证.

Theme 146: To promote, to forbid 宣传, 禁止 (xuānchuán, jìnzhǐ)

1 普及 [-] pǔjí (widespread-arrive) <v./adj.> popularize, universal: ~教育 universal education || ~计算机 popularize computers || 广泛~ widely popularized
2 推广 [-廣] tuīguǎng (promote-expand) <v.> promote, popularize: ~经验 promote experience || ~新技术 promote new technologies || ~普通话 promote Mandarin Chinese
3 宣传 [-傳] xuānchuán (propagate-broadcast) <v./n.> propagate, promote: ~婚姻法 propagate the marriage law || ~佛教 (Fójiào) promote Buddhism || 广告~ advertising

4 炒作 [-] chǎozuò (hype-make) <v.> hype, promote in the media: ~新电影 hype for that new movie || 媒体喜欢~名人丑闻. The media likes to hype up celebrity scandals.

1 动员 [動員] dòngyuán (mobilize-member) <v.> mobilize: ~全家mobilize the whole family || ~参加 mobilize to join || 积极~ mobilize actively
2 发动 [發動] fādòng (initiate-mobilize) <v.> initiate, launch: ~群众 mobilize the masses || ~内战 launch a civil war || ~飞机 goose a craft
3 鼓动 [-動] gǔdòng (incite-mobilize) <v.> motivate, arouse, agitate: ~大家 arouse the masses || ~观众 motivate audience || ~人心 agitate the heart
4 发起 [發-] fāqǐ (initiate-rise) <v.> initiate, launch, start: ~运动 initiate a movement || ~活动 initiate an activity || ~人 initiator
5 倡导 [-導] chàngdǎo (advocate-lead) <v.> advocate: ~科学 advocate science || ~西学/中学 advocate Western learning/Eastern learning || 大力~ strongly advocate
6 倡议 [-議] chàngyì (advocate-propose) <v.> propose: ~召开国际会议 propose holding an international conference || ~开办新学校 propose opening a new school || 积极~ propose positively
7 提倡 [-] tíchàng (promote-advocate) <v.> advocate, promote: 大力~ vigorously advocate || ~竞争 (jìngzhēng) advocate competition || ~国货 promote national products
8 号召 [號-] hàozhào (call on-call) <v.> call up (on), call for: ~捐款 (juānkuǎn) call for donation || ~人人学科学 call on people to study science || 响应~ respond to an appeal
9 响应 [響應] xiǎngyìng (echo-respond) <v.> respond: ~号召 respond to an appeal || 热烈 (rèliè) ~ warmly respond to || ~他的建议 respond to his suggestions
10 取消 [-] qǔxiāo (take-eliminate) <v.> cancel, call off: ~婚礼 cancel a wedding || ~计划 cancel a plan || ~比赛 cancel a match
11 撤销 [-銷] chèxiāo (withdraw-annul) <v.> withdraw, repeal: ~命令 undo a command || ~职务 (zhíwù) annul sb. position || ~案件 withdraw a case
12 解除 [-] jiěchú (relieve-eliminate) <v.> terminate, relieve: ~关系 terminate a relationship || ~烦恼 relieve anxiety || ~合同 terminate a contract
13 禁止 [-] jìnzhǐ (prohibit-stop) <v.> forbid, ban, prohibit: ~结婚 prohibit marriages || ~抽烟 forbid smoking, no smoking || ~出口 ban export
14 收回 [-] shōuhuí (take-back) <v.> call in, take back: ~贷款 (dàikuǎn) call in a loan || ~资金 call in funds || ~我刚才说的话take back what I just said
15 回收 [-] huíshōu (back-collect) <v.> recycle, recover: ~垃圾 recycle garbage || ~瓶子 recycle bottles || ~卫星 recover satellites

Tips:

1 炒作 (chǎozuò): It means 'hype,' which has become a way of promotion, ranging from the entertainment industry to serious businesses all over China.
2 号召 (call on) and 口号 (slogan): The Chinese Communist Party's propaganda is successful. They are good at calling on (号召) the people to do something they want, usually with a slogan (口号) each time. According to an official website, the CCP has had 80 plus major slogans in her history of 90 plus years, one slogan each year on average.

Exercises:

Part I: Read the following sentences and fill in each blank with the appropriate word or phrase from the options given.

1 推广、普及、宣传

a) 目前, 智能 (zhìnéng, smart) 手机在中国已经________了, 几乎每个人都有一个智能手机.
b) 中国政府一直在大力________普通话, 现在机会所有学校都在使用普通话.
c) 中国政府的卫生部门一直在大力________吸烟的坏处.

2 炒作、发动、鼓动、动员

a) 1966年, 毛泽东________了中国的文化大革命.
b) 美国前总统奥巴马是一个出色的演讲者, 他可以________听他演讲的人支持他的政策.
c) 这个女明星不断在网上公布自己的私人生活, 目的就是________自己, 让大家关注她.
d) 1966年, 毛泽东________了成千上万的中国学生参加文化大革命, 打到在中国跟他有不同政见的群体.

3 发起、倡导

a) 穆斯林国家的一些对美国不满的人________了恐怖袭击 (xíjī, raid) 事件, 造成大量美国平民伤亡.
b) 有的学者认为美国一直是民主和自由的__________者.

4 号召、倡议、响应

a) 1968年毛泽东________中国成千上万的年轻人到农村去劳动. 结果, 城市的年轻人几乎都________毛主席的号召去了中国最偏远的农村去劳动.
b) 中国的一些私人企业________在西部地区进行公益 (gōngyì, public welfare) 事业, 帮助西部地区的贫困人口.

5 取消、撤销、解除

a) 由于天气不好, 这次比赛就________了.
b) 据说最近中国很多政府官员因为有腐败 (fŭbài, corruption) 问题, 被________了职务.
c) 暴风雨过后不到半个小时, 这个地区就________了警报 (jĭngbào, alarm), 一切恢复正常.

6 禁止、收回、回收

a) 在中国的公共场合, 常常可以看到________吸烟的标志.
b) 在________垃圾方面, 中国应该向日本学习.
c) 据说, 在美国开亚洲风味的餐馆是最容易__________的成本生意.

Theme 147: To praise, to punish, to reform 奖励, 惩罚, 改革 (jiǎnglì, chéngfá, gǎigé)

1 表扬 [-揚] biǎoyáng (commend-praise) <v.> praise, commend: 受到~ be praised || 得到~ receive praises || ~孩子 praise kids
2 奖 [獎] jiǎng (encourage, reward) <v.> reward: ~一台电脑 reward a computer || ~三千元钱 reward three thousand *yuan* || 重~ be amply rewarded
3 奖励 [獎勵] jiǎnglì (reward-award) <v./n.> reward, award: ~新人 reward newbies || 物质~ material reward || 受到/给予~ receive/give an award
4 罚 [罰] fá (punish, penalize) <v.> punish, penalize: ~钱/款 impose a fine || ~球 score a penalty shot || ~ (她) 做饭 punish her to cook
5 罚款 [罰-] fákuǎn (penalize-money) <v.> impose a fine, fine: ~五元 fines 5 yuan || 乱~ impose an unjustifiable fine || 予以~ impose a fine
6 开除 [開-] kāichú (expel-dismiss) <v.> expel, fire, dismiss: 被公司~了 be fired by a company
7 制裁 [-] zhìcái (restrict-reduce) <v./n.> sanction, punish: 经济~ economic sanctions || ~这个国家 sanctions against this country || 严厉~ tough sanctions
8 除名 [-] chúmíng (remove-name) <v.> remove sb's name from, strike off: 被公司~ be struck off by the company || 把他~ remove him from the list
9 记过 [記過] jìguò (record-demerit) <v.> record a demerit: ~处分 recording demerit punishment || ~一次 demerit recording once
10 体罚 [體罰] tǐfá (physical-punish) <v.> corporal punishment: ~学生 make corporal punishment on students || 受~ receive corporal punishment || 实施~ impose corporal punishment
11 扣发 [-發] kòufā (intercept-issue) <v.> garnish: ~奖金 garnish bonus || ~工资 garnish wages || ~生活费 garnish living costs
12 检讨 [檢討] jiǎntǎo (examine-condemn) <v.> self-criticism, review, examine: ~错误 examine mistakes || 生活 ~ life review || 作~ make a self-criticism

13 改革 [-] gǎigé (reform-change) <v./n.> reform, reformation, improvement: 深化~ deepen/intensify the reform || 课程~ curriculum reform || ~制度 reform institution/system
14 改造 [-] gǎizào (change-form) <v.> transform, remold: ~世界 remold the world || ~社会 transform a society
15 开放 [開-] kāifàng (open-free) <v.> open: ~市场 open the market || ~门户 open doors || 对外~ open to the outside world
16 革新 [-] géxīn (change-new) <v./n.> innovate, innovation: 技术~ technical innovation || ~观念 innovate ideas || 全面~ an overall innovation
17 变革 [變-] biàngé (transform-change) <v./n.> change, reform: ~文字 reform a writing system || 社会~ social change || ~现实 change reality
18 闭关锁国 [閉關鎖國] bìguānsuǒguó (close-frontier-lock-country) <idiom> seclude/isolate a country from the outside world: 长期~ a long-term isolation from the outside world
19 闭关自守 [閉關--] bìguānzìshǒu (close-frontier-self-guard) <idiom> isolation from the outside world: 经济上~, 不能使国家富强. A closed economy will not put a country on the way to prosperity.

Tips:

1 革 (gé): It means animal skin with fur or hair removed, i.e., leather or hide. Many characters with 革 are related to leather, for example, 鞋 (xié, shoe,) 靴 (xuē, boot,) 靶 (bǎ, arrow target,) and 鞘 (qiào, sheath) etc. 革 has another meaning 'to change,' for example, 改革 (reform) and 革命 (revolt, revolution.)

2 改革开放: There was not only economic reform from 1978 on, but also a profound reform in ideology.

3 闭关锁国 and 改革开放: The Ming and Qing dynasties cut off the country from the outside (闭关锁国) and weakened a powerful imperial China decade by decade. Suppose that China had begun to reform (改革开放) from the mid-Qing Dynasty, what would China be like now?

Exercises:

Part I: Read the following sentences and fill in each blank with the appropriate word or phrase from the options given.

1 开除、罚款

a) 这两名学生因为在学校吸毒被学校________了.
b) 小李因为开车超速被________.

2 奖励、表扬

a) 小李最近学习上进步很大, 老师_______了他.
b) 这儿学校设立了专门奖学金, __________学习上取得突出 (tūchū, outstanding) 进步的学生.

3 体罚、检讨、扣发

a) 这个孩子一个星期没有交作业了，老师让他写一份________，反思自己的错误.
b) 他这个月几乎每天上班都迟到, 所以被_______了当月的奖金.
c) 中国学校规定老师不能________学生.

4 除名、记过、制裁

a) 这个学生因为在学校抽烟受到学校的_______处分.
b) 小张因为盗取公司财物而被公司________.
c) 美国希望中国对朝鲜进行经济上的_______, 以限制 (xiànzhì, restrict) 朝鲜的核试验.

5 改革、改造、变革

a) 这所学校最近要进行课程________, 以便更好地为学生服务.
b) 为了能够应对夏季暴雨及洪水，这个城市今天要________城市排水系统.
c) 中国历史上每一次社会_______都对社会产生了巨大的影响.

6 开放、闭关锁国、革新

a) 目前中国政府还没有完全________中国市场, 一些领域 (lǐngyù, sector) 是禁止外国公司投资的.
b) 中国的制造业正在进行技术________, 有些产品已经达到了世界先进水平.
c) 中国明清两个朝代, 实行__________的对外政策.

Theme 148: Trade, deals 贸易 (màoyì)

1 交易 [-] jiāoyì (hand over and take over-exchange) <v.> trade, deal, transaction: 现金~ cash transaction || 黑市~ black market transaction
2 贸易 [貿-] màoyì (trade-exchange) <n.> trade: 中美 ~ Sino-U.S. trade || 对外~ foreign trade || 出口~ export trade
3 招商 [-] zhāoshāng (attract-business) <v.> attract investment: 中国地方政府积极采取措施~. The Chinese local government takes many measures to invite investment.
4 出口 [-] chūkǒu (out-port) <v.> export: ~衬衫 export shirts || ~玉米 export corn || ~到美国 export to the United States
5 进 [進] jìn (advance, enter) <v.> purchase, introduce: ~货 purchase goods || ~书 purchase books || ~蔬菜 purchase vegetables
6 进口 [進-] jìnkǒu (enter-port) <v./n.> import: ~牛奶 import milk || ~食品 import food || ~电视机 import TVs.
7 输入 [輸-] shūrù (convey-in) <v.> import, input: ~橘子 import oranges || ~中国 import to China || 大量~ greatly import
8 输出 [輸-] shūchū (convey-out) <v.> export, output: ~粮食 export grain || ~信号 output signals || 商品~ export commodities
9 买 [買] mǎi (buy) <v.> buy, purchase, go shopping: ~菜 buy vegetables || ~书 purchase books || ~车 buy a car
10 购 [購] gòu (purchase) <v.> buy, purchase: ~票 buy tickets
11 采购 [採購] cǎigòu (select-purchase) <v./n.> buy, purchase: ~鲜奶 purchase of fresh milk || ~年货 purchase of necessities for the Spring Festival holidays || ~粮食 purchase of grain
12 收购 [-購] shōugòu (take-purchase) <v.> purchase, buy: ~大米 purchase rice || ~鸡蛋 buy eggs || ~农产品 purchase agricultural products
13 购买 [購買] gòumǎi (purchase-buy) <v.> buy, purchase: ~土地 buy a land || ~商品 purchase commodities || 高价~ purchase at a high price
14 购物 [購-] gòuwù (purchase-thing) <v.> shopping: 上街~ go shopping || 网上~ shopping online || ~环境 shopping environment
15 预订 [預訂] yùdìng (advance-reserve) <v.> reserve, book, subscribe: ~房间 reserve a room || ~机票 book a flight ticket || ~报纸 subscribe a newspaper
16 网购 [網購] wǎnggòu (online-shop) <v.> shopping online: ~衣服 shopping clothes online || ~食品 shopping food online
17 邮购 [郵購] yóugòu (mail-order) <v.> mail order: ~奶粉 mail order milk powder || ~新娘 mail order a bride

18 秒杀 [-殺] miǎoshā (second-kill) <v.> sec-killing: 低价~ sec-killing in a low price || ~电视机 sec-killing TVs. || ~促销 sec-killing promotion

19 抢购 [搶購] qiǎnggòu (rush-purchase) <v.> rush to purchase, panic buying, snap up: ~报纸 snap up newspapers || ~粮食 snap up food || ~黄金 rush to buy gold

20 代购 [-購] dàigòu (behalf-purchase) <v.> buy on sb's behalf: ~火车票 buy train tickets on sb's behalf || ~奶粉 buy milk powder on sb's behalf

21 团购 [團購] tuángòu (group-purchase) <v.> group buying: ~ 电影票 a group buying of cinema tickets || 零风险 (fēngxiǎn) ~ a risk-free group buying

22 卖 [賣] mài (sell) <v.> sell: ~鸡蛋 sell eggs || ~水果 sell fruits || ~手机 sell cell phones

23 出售 [-] chūshòu (out-sell) <v.> sell, for sale: 降价~ on sale || 六折~ 40 percent discount sale || ~商品 sell commodities

24 销售 [銷-] xiāoshòu (sell-sell) <v.> sell: ~产品 sell products || ~药品 sell medicine || 图书 ~ sell books

25 甩卖 [-賣] shuǎimài (dispose-sell) <v.> clearance sale: 这家商店为了清理库存, 正在~. The shop is having a sale to clear old stock. || 清仓~ Slash prices for a clearance sale.

26 倾销 [傾銷] qīngxiāo (dump-sell) <v.> dumping: ~ 土豆 dumping potatoes || 低价~ dumping goods at a low price

27 抛售 [-] pāoshòu (undersell-sell) <v.> undersell, sell sth. at low prices: ~商品 undersell commodities || 他低价 ~了所有股票. He dumped all his shares in the stock market at a low price.

28 专卖 [專賣] zhuānmài (exclusive-sell) <v.> sell exclusively: ~首饰 sell jewelry exclusively || ~钱包 sell purses exclusively

29 畅销 [暢銷] chàngxiāo (smooth-sell) <v.> sell well, be in great demand: 在市场上~ sell well in market || 产品~ products are sold well || ~全国 be sold well all over the country

30 热卖 [熱賣] rèmài (hot-sale) <v.> hot sale: 商品~ commodities in hot sale || 玩具~ toys in hot sale

31 批发 [-發] pīfā (batch-sell) <v.> wholesale: ~商品 wholesale commodity || ~衣服 wholesale clothes

32 零售 [-] língshòu (odd-sell) <v.> retail: 少量~ a small amount of retail || 商品~ commodity retailing

33 拍卖 [-賣] pāimài (gavel-sell) <v.> auction: ~书画作品 the auction of calligraphy and painting works || ~文物 cultural relics auction

34 转让 [轉讓] zhuǎnràng (transfer-make over) <v.> transfer (technology, good etc): ~财产 transfer the property || 技术~ transfer technology

35 展销 [-銷] zhǎnxiāo (exhibit-sell) <v.> exhibit and sell, exhibition sales: 图书~ book exhibition sales || ~商品 exhibit and sell commodities || 首次~ the first exhibition sales

36 上市 [-] shàngshì (on-market) <separable word> be listed, listing: ~公司 a listed company || 境外~ be listed abroad/listing overseas || ~交易 be listed for transaction

37 停牌 [-] tíngpái (suspend-plate) <v.> suspension: 股票~ stock suspension || ~一天 suspend a day

38 开张 [開張] kāizhāng (open-opening of a new business) <v.> open a business: 新店~ open a new business
39 推销 [-銷] tuīxiāo (promote-sell) <v.> promote sales, the sale, market: ~产品 promote the sale of products || ~食物 promote the sale of food || 大力~ greatly promote the sale
40 营业 [營業] yíngyè (do-business) <v.> do business: 对外~ do business || 照常~ do business as usual || 停止 ~ go out of business
41 成交 [-] chéngjiāo (close-deal) <v.> close the deal, conclude the bargain, finish a transaction: 买卖~. The bargain is concluded. || 生意~ close the deal || ~价格 transaction value
42 挣钱 [掙錢] zhèngqián (make-money) <separable word> make money, earn money: 挣大钱 make lots of money || ~多/少 earn much/little money
43 赚 [賺] zhuàn (gain, earn) <v.> earn: ~钱 earn money || ~外汇 earn foreign currency || ~一笔 earn much money
44 赚钱 [賺錢] zhuànqián (earn-money) <separable word> make money, earn money: 赚大钱 earn much money || 赚一点钱 earn little money
45 保本 [-] bǎoběn (keep-capital) <v.> break even, retain the capital value: 一些中国人认为投资房地产最安全, 至少可以~. Some Chinese think investing in real estate is the safest, at least keeping your investments safe.
46 分成 [-] fēnchéng (divide-percentage) <v.> divide profit according to previously agreed percentage, divide into, separate into: 利润~ divide profit || 对半~ divided profit into half-and-half || 收入~ divide income
47 分红 [-紅] fēnhóng (divide-dividend) [profits] <v.> share out bonus, receive dividends, draw extra dividends: 第一次~ the first dividend || 按股~ share out bonus according to contributions || 土地 ~ dividend on land shares
48 提成 [-] tíchéng (draw-percentage) <v.> deduct a percentage from a sum of money, draw a percentage: 高额 (gāo'é) ~ deduct a percentage from a high sum of money || 利润 (lìrùn) ~ draw a percentage from the profit
49 创收 [創-] chuàngshōu (create-income) <v.> generate renenue, extra income: 一笔~ an extra income|| 校办工厂可以为学校~. School-run factories can generate income for schools.
50 炒股 [-] chǎogǔ (hype-stock) <v.> invest in stock, speculate in stock, stock: ~热 stock fever || 公款~ invest public funds in stock || 个人~ individuals invest in stock
51 要价 [-價] yàojià (ask-price) <v.> charge, ask a price: ~太高 charge highly
52 讲价 [講價] jiǎngjià (bargain-price) <v.> bargain: 跟卖家~ bargain with sellers
53 讨价还价 [討價還價] tǎojiàhuánjià (ask-price-offer-price) <idiom> bargain with sb.: 不要~ do not bargaining
54 打折 [-] dǎzhé (go-discount) <separable word> discount, on sale: 打六折 sixty percent discount, 40 percent off || (打) 对折 half price || 鞋子~ shoes on sale

Tips:

1 讨价还价: It means 'to bargain,' of which scenes are perhaps fun to watch for non-Chinese but, to the best of my belief, destroyed mutual trust between buyers and sellers in China.
2 挣钱 vs. 赚钱: Both mean 'to earn money,' but 赚钱 is used for larger amounts or in an easier way. Bill Gates 赚钱, not 挣钱.
3 拍卖 vs. 典当 (diǎndàng): In ancient China, auctions were rare, but there was a form of business, 典当 (to pawn.) A 当铺 (dàngpù, pawnshop) can be seen, usually along with a bank, very close to every casino in Macao.
4 甩卖: It means 'clearance sale.' When Chinese shops have 甩卖, their signs usually have other words preceding these two characters: 挥泪 (huīlèi, to wipe away tears,) 吐血 (tùxiě, to spit blood,) 赔本 (péiběn, to lose capital,) 清仓 (qīngcāng, warehouse clearing,) or 关门 (out of business) 大甩卖, all too sentimental and, of course, not true.

Exercises:

Part I: Use the given bound form here as a guide to help you think of other words with the same character. Feel free to use your dictionary when needed. Then write down the English definition of each of the words you've written.

购 *(buy, purchase):* 购票 *buy tickets*

____

____

____

____

____

____

卖 *(sell):* 卖房子 *sell a house*

____

____

____

售 *(sell):* 出售 *sell*

____

____

____

销 *(sell)*: 销售 *sell*

____

____

____

Part II: Read the following sentences and fill in each blank with the appropriate word or phrase from the options given.

1 代购、贸易、收购

a) 据说全世界的商品都可以通过私人__________者销售到中国.
b) 中国一直向美国出口商品, 使美国的制造业遭受 (zāoshòu, suffer) 了巨大损失 (sǔnshī, loss), 所以中美________问题成为两国的重要问题.
c) 这家中国公司__________了美国所有的AMC影院, 引起了美国政府的关注.

2 停牌、转让、上市、展销

a) 这家公司的股票将在美国纽约证券交易所__________ __, 预计会有很多投资者来竞争购买公司的股份.
b) 中国股市规定, 股票下跌超过10%的时候, 要________, 不能进行交易.
c) 小王把自己的食品公司__________给了小李. 现在小李是这家公司的主人.
d) 小李要在食品展销会上, ________自己公司的产品.

3 保本、营业、成交

a) 据说美国石油公司原油的_______价格是每桶六十美元. 如果________价格低于六十美元, 石油公司就要亏损.
b) 美国很多餐馆都会有一天不_______, 有的是星期一, 有的是星期二.

4 炒股、分红、创收

a) 朝鲜政府通过在中国开设餐馆、出口煤炭等方式为国家_______.
b) 在朝鲜老百姓是不能______的, 因为这是资本主义经济方式.
c) 在中国, 大多数大公司都会在年底给股东________.

5 要价、讨价还价、打折

a) 在美国, 圣诞节过后很多商品还会________, 一直持续到新年.
b) 在中国的小商品市场买东西可以_________, 不一定要按照卖家的________付钱.

6 畅销、专卖、甩卖

a) 苹果公司的新产品非常_______, 很多______店都卖得断货了.
b) 美国梅西百货公司即将关闭很多商店, 目前正在进行关门前的大_______.

Theme 149: Investment 投资 (tóuzī)

1 理财 [-財] lǐcái (manage-money) <v.> manage money matters: 善于 ~ be good at managing money matters || ~有方 manage money matters very well
2 投资 [-資] tóuzī (invest-capital/money) <v./n.> invest, investment: ~房地产 invest in real estate || ~银行 investment bank || 在教育上~ invest in education
3 合资 [-資] hézī (joint-venture) <v.> joint venture: ~经营 joint-venture || 中美~ Sino-Us joint venture || ~拍摄 joint venture shooting
4 集资 [-資] jízī (raise-capital) <v.> raise funds: ~办厂 raise funds to open a factory/business || ~十万元 raise funds of 10,000 yuan || 自愿~ voluntary fund-raising
5 融资 [-資] róngzī (fuse-capital) <v.> financing: 多渠道 (qúdào) ~ multi-channel financing || 横向 ~ transverse financing || 民间~ private financing
6 拨款 [撥-] bōkuǎn (allocate-money) <v.> appropriation, allocate, allocation: 按计划~ allocate as planned || 财政~ fiscal appropriation || 大量~ a great number of allocation
7 征收 [徵-] zhēngshōu (impose-collect) <v.> levy, collect, impose, expropriation: ~消费税 levy excise duties || 直接~ direct expropriation
8 交 [-] jiāo (cross, deliver, pay) <v.> submit, pay: ~作业submit one's homework || ~学费 pay tuition fee || ~税 pay taxes
9 交费 [-費] jiāofèi (pay-fee) <v.> pay: ~五十元 pay 50 yuan || ~窗口 paying windows || ~上学 pay to go to school
10 纳税 [納-] nàshuì (pay-tax) <separable word> pay taxes: 纳营业税 pay business tax || 纳个人所得税 pay individual income tax || 向国家~ pay tax to the state
11 漏税 [-] lòushuì (evade-tax) <v.> evade taxation, tax evasion: ~严重 serious tax evasion
12 逃税 [-] táoshuì (avoid-tax) <v.> tax avoidance: 长期~ a long-term tax avoidance

Tips:

1 偷税漏税 (tōushuì lòushuì): It means 'tax evasion' and is one of the most frequently used words when taxes are mentioned in Chinese.
2 交学费: Besides 'to pay tuition fee (to schools,)' it has the extended meaning of 'to pay the price for incompetence,' for example, 这笔投资完全失败了, 就算是我们叫学费吧 (this investment is a total failure, we have to pay the price.)

Exercises:

Part I: Translate the following phrases into English and then answer the questions.

善于理财 ________________

投资房地产 ________________

集资办公司 ________________

中央政府拨款 ________________

征收消费税 ________________

向国家纳税 ________________

偷税漏税 ________________

合理避税 ________________

1 你觉得自己是否善于理财? 为什么?

____

2 在你们国家投资房地产是否赚钱? 为什么?

____

3 你们国家的中央政府是否给学校拨款? 数量多不多?

____

4 你们国家征收消费税吗? 你觉得征收这种税合理吗?

____

5 在你们国家偷税漏税与合理避税是合法的还是违法的?

____

Theme 150: Accounting 会计 (kuàijì)

1 记账 [記賬] jìzhàng (record-account) <v.> keep accounts: 他没学过会计, 但是会~. He isn't a trained accountant, but he can manage to keep accounts.
2 做假账 [--賬] zuòjiǎzhàng (make-false-account) <v.> falsify accounts: 财会人员~ 是违法行为. It is illegal for accounting personnel to falsify accounts.
3 结账 [結賬] jiézhàng (settle-account) <v.> settle accounts: 按时~ settle accounts in time || 年底~ settle accounts in the end of year
4 报销 [報銷] bàoxiāo (report-reimburse) <v.> reimbursement, be reimbursed: ~医疗费 the reimbursement of medical expenses || ~路费 the reimbursement of traveling expenses || 全部~ be reimbursed one hundred percent

5 算账 [-賬] suànzhàng (calculate-account) <v.> do accounts, make out bills: ~算得很快be quick at accounts || 每个月算一次账 do one's accounts every month

6 转账 [轉賬] zhuǎnzhàng (transfer-account) <v.> transfer: 自动~ automated transfer || 通过银行~ transfer via bank accounts

7 换 [換] huàn (trade, exchange, change) <v.> exchange, convert: ~钱 exchange money || ~人民币 exchange renminbi || ~美元 exchange U.S. dollars

8 换汇 [換匯] huànhuì (exchange-currency) <v.> exchange: 出口~ currency exchange in export

9 兑换 [兌換] duìhuàn (convert-exchange) <v.> exchange, convert: ~美元 exchange U.S. dollar || ~现金 exchange for cash || 自由~ free convertibility

10 兑现 [兌現] duìxiàn (convert-to cash) <v.> cash: ~合同 performance/execution of contract || 全部~ fully cash

11 出租 [-] chūzū (out-to rent) <v.> for rent: ~房子 house for rent || ~工具 tool for rent

12 租 [-] zū (rent) <v.> rent: ~房子 rent a house || ~车 rent a car || ~小说 rent a fiction/novel

13 赔 [賠] péi (compensate, lose) <v.> lose, compensate for: ~钱 lose money || ~本 sustain losses in business || ~东西 compensate for sth.

14 赔偿 [賠償] péicháng (compensate-refund) <v.> compensate for, reimbursement: ~损失 compensate for loss || ~财产损失 compensate for damage to property || 经济~ financial reimbursement

15 欠 [-] qiàn (yawn, owe) <v.> owe: ~钱 owe money, be in debt || ~债 in debt

16 开 [開] kāi (open, make out, pay) <v.> pay, write: ~工资 pay wages || ~支票 write a check || ~发票 write a receipt

17 支出 [-] zhīchū (branch, pay) <v.> expend, disburse: ~资金 expend fund || ~费用 disburse costs || ~一万元 disburse 10,000 yuan

18 支付 [-] zhīfù (spend-pay) <v.> pay: 现金~ pay in cash || ~房租 pay rent || ~学费 pay tuition fee

19 花钱 [-錢] huāqián (spend-money) <v.> spend money: 少~, 多办事 spend less money, do more work

20 付 [-] fù (hand over to, spend, pay) <v.> pay: ~钱/款 pay money || ~费 pay fee

21 付出 [-] fùchū (spend-out) <v.> pay, devote, contribute: ~代价 pay the price || ~精力 put energy in, devote energy || ~劳动 contribute labor

22 买单 [買單] mǎidān (buy/pay-bill) <v.> pay the bill: 轮流~ take turn in paying the bill

23 首付 [-] shǒufù (initial-payment) <n./v.> down payment: 购房~ a house down payment || 交~ make a down payment

24 预付 [預-] yùfù (advance-payment) <v.> prepay: ~定金 prepay deposit || ~房租 prepay rent

Tips:

1 账 vs. 帐: Both are pronounced as zhàng. 账户 and 帐户 were often identical when referring to 'account' before 2002, but later on 帐户 was removed

from new dictionaries. Now 账 is used for things related to 'money, finance, account' and 帐 for 'tent' only.

2 买单: It means 'to pay the bill' and was borrowed from Cantonese into Mandarin in the 1990s. It also has the extended meaning of 'to undertake a responsibility,' for example, 你在外面惹事 (rěshì), 却让我买单 (you made trouble, but it is me who fixes it.)

Exercises:

Part I: Translate the following phrases into English and then answer the questions.

做假账 ________________

报销医疗费用 ________________

抢着买单 ________________

预付租金 ________________

赔偿损失 ________________

支付学费 ________________

出口高科技产品 ________________

进口汽车 ________________

购房首付款 ________________

1 做假账在你们国家违法吗?

____

2 在你们国家是不是每个人都可以报销医疗费用? 为什么?

____

3 中国人在饭馆吃饭会抢着买单, 你会这样做吗? 为什么?

____

4 在你们国家租房子要不要预付一个月租金? 为什么?

____

5 在你们国家父母是否给子女支付大学学费? 为什么?

____

6 你们国家出口什么商品? 进口什么商品?

____

Theme 151: To accumulate 积累 (jīlěi)

1 积累 [積纍] jīlěi (store up-accumulate) <v.> accumulate, build up: ~经验 build up experience || ~资料 accumulate data || ~知识 accumulate knowledge
2 节 [節] jié (joint, economize, save) <v.> save: ~水 save water || ~电 save electricity || ~能 save energy
3 省 [-] shěng (decrease, save) <v.> save: ~钱 save money || ~时间 save time || ~事儿 save trouble
4 节约 [節約] jiéyuē (economize-save) <v.> economize, save: ~水 save water || ~时间 save time || ~用电 save electricity
5 节能 [節-] jiénéng (save-energy) <v.> save energy: ~产品 energy saving products || ~设备 energy saving equipment || ~灯具 energy saving lamps
6 节省 [節-] jiéshěng (economize-frugal) <v.> economize, save: ~时间 save time || ~费用/开支 save money/costs || ~体力 save one's strength
7 浪费 [-費] làngfèi (freely-spend) <v.> waste, lavish: ~时间 waste time || ~钱 waste money || ~电 waste electricity

8 够 [-] gòu (many, enough) <adj.> be enough: 三十元就~了. Thirty yuan is enough. || 五个人就~. Five people are enough. || 一句话就~. One sentence is enough.
9 足够 [-] zúgòu (ample-enough) <adj.> enough: ~的钱 enough money || ~的人 enough people || 时间~ enough time
10 不足 [-] bùzú (not-enough) <v.> lack: 经验~ lack experience || 时间~ lack time || 人手~ lack people
11 缺 [-] quē (imperfect, lack) <v.> lack, miss: ~六页 miss six pages
12 少 [-] shǎo (few, little, lack) <v.> lack, miss: ~了三个 three people are missed
13 缺乏 [-] quēfá (lack-inadequate) <v.> lack (of), be short of: ~休息 lack of rest || ~关心 lack of concern/interest || ~人才 be short of talents
14 剩 [-] shèng (be left) <v.> remain, be left: ~最后一个 the last person left || ~四个人 remain four people || ~一半时间 the half of time left
15 剩下 [-] shèngxià (left-remain) <v.> remain, be left: ~三棵树 three trees left || ~五块钱 five yuan left || ~半个面包 half a loaf of bread left
16 过剩 [過-] guòshèng (excessive-surplus) <v.> excess, surplus, redundancy: 人才~ surplus talents || 精力 ~ surplus energy || 商品~ merchandise surplus
17 剩余 [-餘] shèngyú (surplus-remain) <v.> surplus: ~劳动力 surplus labor || ~资本 surplus capital || ~价值 surplus value
18 亏空 [虧-] kuīkōng (loss-deficit) <v.> deficit, go into the red: 经济~ economic deficit || 连年~ years of deficit || ~一百万元 one million yuan deficit
19 亏本 [虧-] kuīběn (loss-capital) <v.> loss money in business: 长期 ~ money loss in business in a long period || ~出售 short sale, sell at a loss || ~生产 produce at a loss

20 一共 [-] yīgòng (all-together) <adv> in all, in total: ~八个人 eight people in total || ~七个小时 seven hours in total || ~五十块钱 fifty yuan in total
21 总共 [總-] zǒnggòng (sum-together) <adv.> altogether, in total, a total of: ~花了三十块钱 spent a total of 30 yuan || ~去了九个月 stay in a place for a total of nine months || ~有八种颜色 a total of eight colors
22 合计 [-計] héjì (add up-calculate/count) <v.> amount to, add up to, total: ~一百人 total of 100 people

23 总计 [總計] zǒngjì (sum-count) <v.> amount to, in total: ~一万元 amount to 10,000 yuan

Tips:

1 缺少 vs. 缺乏: 缺乏 means 'far not enough,' for example, 非洲缺乏水 (Africa lacks water.) 缺少 can mean 'be short of,' for example, 来了十位客人, 可是只有九把椅子, 还缺少一把椅子 (Ten guests came, but we have only nine chairs. We are short one chair.)

2 小计 vs. 合计 vs. 总计: All means 'sum, total,' but in accounting, 小计 is the sum of a section, 合计 of a category, and 总计 of the whole.

3 剩, 余, 下: All mean 'remain, left' and their combinations, 剩余, 剩下 and 余下 have almost the same meaning.

Exercises:

Part I: Use the given bound form here as a guide to help you think of other words with the same character. Feel free to use your dictionary when needed. Then write down the English definition of each of the words you've written.

节 (save): 节水 save water

____

____

____

省 (save): 省钱 save money

____

____

____

缺 (lack, miss): 缺钱 lack of money

____

____

____

剩 (remain, be left): 剩下 remain, be left

____

____

____

总 (total, all): 总数 the total number

____

____

Part II: Read the following sentences and fill in each blank with the appropriate word or phrase from the options given.

1 亏空、亏本、不足

a) 这家公司由于经营不善, 到今年年底已经________了一百万美元.
b) 老李已经_______开商店一年了, 家里的钱都赔光了, 所以只好关了商店.
c) 老李第一次经商, 由于经验_______, 所以亏本了.

2 缺乏、缺、剩

a) 年轻人因为________工作经验, 很难在公司担任重要职位.
b) 小李_____钱的时候就会给父母打电话要钱.
c) 小李花钱大手大脚, 父母一个给他五千块钱, 他花得一分钱都不_________.

3 省、够、一共

a) 很多中国人认为________钱是一种美德.
b) 小王上大学的时候很省钱, 父母每月给他五百块钱生活费就________了.
c) 一个中国大学生四年大学_________要花费十万左右人民币.

Theme 152: To build, to make 建造, 加工 (jiànzào, jiāgōng)

1 建 [-] jiàn (draw up, build) <v.> set up, construct, establish, build, erect: ~房子 build a house || ~铁路 build a railway || ~大楼 construct a building
2 造 [-] zào (go to, make) <v.> build: ~房子 build a house || ~船 build a ship || ~飞机build an airplane
3 建造 [-] jiànzào (build-make) <v.> construct, build: ~住宅 build houses || ~楼房 construct buildings || ~大桥 build a bridge
4 建筑 [-築] jiànzhù (build-construct) <v.> build, construct: ~机场 build an airport || ~大楼 construct buildings || ~蜂房 build a hive complex
5 兴建 [興-] xīngjiàn (start-build) <v.> build, construct: ~新厂 construct new factories || ~饭店 construct hotels
6 修 [-] xiū (decorate, repair, build) <v.> build, construct: ~大房子 build a big house || ~游泳池 build a swimming pool || ~长城 build the Great Wall
7 修建 [-] xiūjiàn (build-construct) <v.> construct, build: ~铁路 build a railway || ~水库 construct a reservoir || ~住宅 build houses
8 兴修 [興-] xīngxiū (start-build) <v.> build, construct: ~水利 build water conservancy project || ~铁路 build a railway
9 盖 [蓋] gài (cover, build) <v.> build, construct: ~房 build houses || ~楼 construct a building || ~工厂 build factories
10 翻新 [-] fānxīn (refurbish-new) <v.> refurbishment, renovate: 花样~ various innovations || ~花色品种 renovate various assortments
11 施工 [-] shīgōng (execute-construction) <v.> construction, execution: ~精细 refinement construction || 水下~ underwater construction || 野外~ field construction
12 架 [-] jià (put up, erect) <v.> construct, put on: ~桥 construct bridges || ~在空中 put on across the sky

13 铺 [鋪] pū (spread, pave) <v.> pave, lay: ~路 pave the way || ~铁轨 lay the tracks || ~地 pave the floor

14 铺设 [鋪設] pūshè (lay-set up) <v.> lay, pave, build: ~管道 lay the pipeline || ~铁路 lay the tracks || ~草坪 pave the lawn

15 装配 [裝-] zhuāngpèi (assemble-equip) <v.> assemble, fit together: ~零件assemble parts || ~汽车 assemble vehicles || ~电视机 assemble televisions

16 组装 [組裝] zǔzhuāng (put together-assemble) <v.> assemble, package: 重新~ reassemble || ~电脑 assemble a computer

17 安 [-] ān (peaceful, stabilize, install, fix) <v.> install, assemble: ~灯 install lights || ~窗户 install window || ~车轮 assemble wheels

18 装 [裝] zhuāng (baggage, dress up, install, assemble) <v.> install, be equipped with: ~空调 install/be equipped with an air conditioner || ~暖气 install a heating system || ~门铃 install a doorbell

19 安装 [-裝] ānzhuāng (install-assemble) <v.> install: ~软件install software || ~机器install machine || ~空调install an air-conditioner

20 设置 [設-] shèzhì (set up-establish) <v.> set, set up: ~时间 set time || ~障碍 (zhàng'ài) set up obstacles || 重复~ setting repeatedly

21 做 [-] zuò (make, do) <v.> make, do, produce: ~家具 make furnitures || 自己~裙子 make a skirt by oneself

22 打造 [-] dǎzào (do-build) <v.> make, build, forge: ~品牌 build a brand || ~飞船 build a flying boat || 精心~ meticulously build

23 制造 [製-] zhìzào (make-build) <v.> make, produce, manufacture: ~武器 produce weapons || ~家具 make furniture || 国内~ manufacture/produce in home country

24 制作 [製-] zhìzuò (make-do) <v.> make, produce, manufacture: ~金器 make goldware || ~点心 make pastry || ~动画片 produce animated cartoons

25 定做 [-] dìngzuò (customize-make) <v.> custom-made: ~家具 custom-made furniture || ~衣服 custom-made clothes || ~鞋子 custom-made shoes

26 酿酒 [釀-] niàngjiǔ (brew-liquor) <v.> make wine, brew beer: 用大米~ make wine of rice

27 仿造 [-] fǎngzào (imitate-make) <v.> counterfeit, reproduce, imitate: ~宝石 imitation gemstone

28 复制 [複製] fùzhì (replicate-make) <v.> copy, duplicate, replicate: ~信息 copy information || ~基因 replicate gene || ~光盘 copy discs

29 克隆 [-] kèlóng (*transliteration* of 'clone') <v.> clone: ~一只羊 clone a sheep || ~经典电影 cloning of classic movies

30 加工 [-] jiāgōng (exert-work) <v.> process: ~木材 process timber || 信息~ data processing

31 榨油 [-] zhàyóu (squeeze-oil) <v.> oil expression, squeeze oil: 用花生~ squeeze oil from peanut

32 发酵 [發-] fājiào (rise-ferment) <v./n.> ferment, fermentation: 自然~ natural fermentation || 充分~ full fermentation || 容易~ easily fermented

33 发电 [發電] fādiàn (generate-electricity) <v-o.> electric power generation, generate electricity: 发一千万度电 generate 10 million KWH || 风力~ wind power generation || ~量 the amount of electric power generation

34 生产 [-產] shēngchǎn (make-produce) <v.> make, produce, manufacture: ~鞋子 produce shoes || ~石油 produce petroleum || 中国~ made in China

Tips:

1 中国制造 (Made in China): Products made in China filled low-price stores worldwide in the first few decades following the Chinese economic reform in 1978. It has become a synonym of 'cheap' and of 'low quality.'
2 组, 装, 配: All mean 'to assemble' and their combinations, 组装, 组配, 装配 have almost the same meaning.

Exercises:

Part I: Use the given bound form on the left as a guide to help you think of other words with the same character. Feel free to use your dictionary when needed. Then write down the English definition of each of the words you've written.

修 *(repair):* 修车 *repair cars*

____

____

____

____

____

____

____

建 *(set up, construct):* 建房子 *build a house*

____

____

____

制 *(make, produce):* 制定法律 *make a law*

____

____

____

装 *(install, be equipped with),* 装空调 *install/be equipped with an air conditioner*

____

____

____

Part II: Read the following sentences and fill in each blank with the appropriate word or phrase from the options given.

1 施工、铺设、翻新

a) 这栋房子太旧了, 需要________.

b) 这栋老房子地下________了很多管道.
c) 一般来说, 像修路这种工程都会在晚上________, 以便不影响交通.

2 生产、加工、发电

a) 为了减少污染, 中国现在正在积极使用风力和太阳能__________, 产生电能.
b) 目前中国是世界上________自行车最多的国家之一.
c) 最近台湾的食品________行业也暴露 (bàolù, expose) 出一些食品安全问题.

3 打造、仿造、克隆

a) 由于中国政府加大对淘宝网 (taobao.com) 的管理, 淘宝上的________产品正在减少.
b) 随着生物技术的发展, 很多人担心________人的出现.
c) 台湾富士康公司 (Foxconn) 将在美国________一个全新的手机生产工厂.

Theme 153: To repair, to maintain 修理, 维护 (xiūlǐ, wéihù)

1 修 [-] xiū (decorate, repair) <v.> repair, fix, mend: ~车 repair cars || ~门窗 repair doors and windows || ~洗衣机 repair washing machines
2 保修 [-] bǎoxiū (guarantee-repair) <v.> warranty: ~三年 three years warranty
3 维修 [維-] wéixiū (maintain-repair) <v.> maintain, repair: ~电器 repair the electrical appliances || ~设备 maintain equipment || 古建筑 (jiànzhù) ~ maintain/repair ancient architecture
4 修复 [-復] xiūfù (repair-recover) <v.> restore, renovate: ~铁路 renovate railways || ~历史建筑renovate historical buildings || ~长城repair the Great Wall
5 修理 [-] xiūlǐ (repair-mend) <v.> repair, fix, mend: ~电器 repair electrical appliances || ~自行车 repair bicycles || 汽车 ~ repair cars
6 检修 [檢-] jiǎnxiū (examine-repair) <v.> examine and repair, overhaul: ~发动机 examine and repair engines || 飞机 ~ overhaul aircrafts || 定期~ regular overhauling
7 收拾 [-] shōushí (collect-pick up) <v.> save, clear up: ~局面 save the situation || ~残局 (cánjú) clear up a messy situation || ~烂摊子 (làn tānzi) clear up the mess
8 抢修 [搶-] qiǎngxiū (rush-repair) <v.> rush to repair, do rush repairs, make urgent repair on: ~铁路 rush to repair railways || 紧急~ do rush repairs
9 返修 [-] fǎnxiū (return-repair) <v.> return to repair: ~一次 return to repair once || 进行~ make repair

10 染 [-] rǎn (dye, catch, influence) <v.> color, to dye: ~色 to dye || ~发 color hair
11 织 [織] zhī (weave, knit) <v.> knit, weave: ~毛衣 knit a sweater || ~手套 knit gloves || ~布 weave cotton cloth
12 纺织 [紡織] fǎngzhī (spin-weave) <v.> spin, weave: 手工~ hand weaving || ~棉布 weave cotton cloth || ~羊毛 wool-weaving

13 编 [編] biān (to knit) <v.> weave, knit: ~毛衣 knit a sweater || ~花环 weave flowers || ~草帽 weave a straw hat

14 漂 [-] piǎo (rinse, bleach) <v.> rinse, bleach: ~洗 rinse || ~白 bleach
15 装饰 [裝飾] zhuāngshì (decorate-ornament) <v.> decorate, set off, embellish: ~会场 decorate a conference venue || ~房间 decorate rooms || ~豪华 (háohuá) luxurious decoration
16 装修 [裝-] zhuāngxiū (decorate-renovate) <v.> decorate: ~房子 decorate a house || 室内~ interior/indoor decoration || 重新 ~ redecorate
17 粉刷 [-] fěnshuā (powder-paint) <v.> paint, white wash: ~房子 paint a house || ~得雪白 whitewashed
18 油漆 [-] yóuqī (oil-paint) <n.> paint: 一罐~ a can of paint
19 环保 [環-] huánbǎo (environment-protect) <n./ adj.> environmental: ~主义 environmentalism || (不) 利于~ be (not) beneficial to the environment || 重视 ~ pay attention to environment
20 护 [護] hù (defend, guard, protect) <v.> protect: ~山 protect mountains || ~林 protect forests || ~眼 protect one's eyes
21 测 [測] cè (to measure) <v.> measure, gauge: ~身高 measure sb.'s height || ~温度 gauge temperatures || ~距离 measure distance
22 测量 [測-] cèliáng (measure-gauge) <v.> measure, gauge: ~水位 measure the water level || ~长度 measure the length || ~深度depth measurement
23 探测 [-測] tàncè (explore-measure) <v.> detect, probe: ~太空 explore the space || ~温度 detect temperatures || 海底~ undersea detection
24 采 [採] cǎi (pick, collect) <v.> pick, gather: ~苹果 pick apples || ~蜜 gather honey || ~花 pick flowers
25 开采 [開採] kāicǎi (exploit-mine) <v.> exploit, mine: ~石油 exploit oil || 露天 ~ strip mining || 大量~ excessive mining

Tips:

1 收拾 (shōushi): It has many meanings, including (1) 收拾房间 (to tidy up the room,) (2) 收拾床铺 (to make the bed,) (3) 收拾行李 (to pack one's luggage,) (4) 收拾自行车 (to repair a bike,) (5) 收拾庄稼 (to take care of the crops,) (6) 把蟑螂都收拾了 (to eliminated/killed all the cockroaches,) (7) [他不听话,] 收拾收拾他 ([colloquial] to settle with him, to fix him, to teach him a lesson) and several other less common meanings.
2 粉饰太平 (fěnshì tàipíng): It means 'to present a false picture of peace and prosperity.' These types of reports, articles, books, movies and TV programs are not hard to find on the Chinese media.

Exercises:

Part I: Use the given bound form as a guide to help you think of other words with the same character. Feel free to use your dictionary when needed. Then write down the English definition of each of the words you've written.

修 (repair): 修车 repair cars

____

____

____

____

____

____

____

Part II: Read the following sentences and fill in each blank with the appropriate word or phrase from the options given.

1 粉刷、装修、油漆

a) 小王家正在__________房子, 很多工人在屋里工作.
b) 小王想把家里的墙________成蓝色, 他决定买比较环保的_________.

2 染色、编织、纺织、装饰

a) 小王家里有很多手工_________品. 大部分是用毛线_________的, 有的还进行了_________, 颜色非常鲜艳.
b) 小王的目前退休前在北京市第一_________厂工作.

2 测量、探测、开采

a) 中国大庆油田的石油已经快________完了.
b) 据说在中国的内蒙古境内又__________到一个新的油田.
c) 据专业人员说, 在海上__________距离是最难的.

Theme 154: To publish 出版 (chūbǎn)

1 印 [-] yìn (seal, print) <v.> print, impress: ~书 print books || ~画 print paintings || ~钞票 (chāopiào) print money
2 印刷 [-] yìnshuā (print-brush) <v.> print: ~书籍 (shūjí) print books || ~传单 print flyers || 彩色~ color printing
3 打印 [-] dǎyìn (print-print) <v.> print: ~文件 print files || ~三份 print three copies || 双面~ print both sides
4 复印 [複-] fùyìn (copy-print) <v.> copy: ~一本书 copy a book || ~五份 copy five copies
5 拷贝 [-貝] kǎobèi (*transliteration* of 'copy') <v.> copy: ~文件 copy files || 互相~ copy each other || 免费~ copy for free
6 备份 [備-] bèifèn (backup-copy) <v.> backup: 数据~ data backup || 双~ double backup || 定期~ periodic backup
7 扫描 [掃-] sǎomiáo (scan-copy) <v.> scan: 安全~ safe scanning || 电子 ~ electronic scanning || 自动~ automatic scanning
8 打字 [-] dǎzì (type-letter) <v.> type: 电脑 ~ type on computer
9 录入 [錄-] lùrù (copy-in) <v.> input, entry: 数据~ data entry || ~表格 an entry form || 手工 ~ manually input
10 装订 [裝訂] zhuāngdìng (decorate-bind) <v.> bind: 单独~ a separate binding || ~成册 bind together in a book || ~旧书 bind a old book
11 排版 [-] páibǎn (set-printing plate) <v.> typesetting: 自动~ automatic typesetting || 电脑~ computerized typesetting
12 发行 [發-] fāxíng (issue-distribute) <v.> release, publish, issue: ~报纸 release newspapers || ~股票 issue stock || ~货币 issue currency

13 出版 [-] chūbǎn (publish-printing plate) <v.> publish: ~著作 publish a monograph || ~小说 publish a novel || 即将~ be published immediately/soon

Tip:

1 印 (yìn): The left part of 印 is 爪 (zhuǎ, hand) and the right part is 卩 (卩, a kneeling person,) and in combination they mean 'a man uses his hand (to seal a document.)' In ancient China, using a signature was uncommon. People instead used their seals to legalize something. In fact, the seals of famous people are usually great works of art, making them very enjoyable to read.

Exercises:

Part I: Read the following sentences and fill in each blank with the appropriate word or phrase from the options given.

1 打字、录入、扫描

a) 小王喜欢用扫描仪 (scanner) 把书_________以后存到电脑里.
b) 小王________的速度非常快, 一分钟可以__________一百多个汉字.

2 排版、发行、印刷

a) ________厂的__________工人在这本书第一页漏掉 (miss) 了一行字, 所以这本会推迟出版的时间.
b) 这本书会在世界上26个国家出版_________.

3 拷贝、打印、备份、复印

a) 这个学期的课程安排老师已经写好了, 但是还没有________出来.
b) 这篇文章写得特别好, 我想_________一下, 留着慢慢看.
c) 以前人们喜欢把电脑里的文件_________到移动盘上, 但是现在一般会________到 Google Drive上.

Theme 155: Traditional agricultural industries, 传统农业 (chuántǒng nóngyè)

1 开垦 [開墾] kāikěn (open up-reclaim) <v.> reclaim, cultivate: ~土地 reclaim land || 大面积~ a large area of land reclamation || ~农田 reclaim farmlands
2 种植 [種-] zhòngzhí (sow-plant) <v.> plant, cultivate: ~玉米 plant corn || ~蔬菜 plant vegetables || ~水稻 plant rice
3 种 [種] zhòng (sow, plant) <v.> farm, plant: ~地 farm || ~树 plant trees || ~花 plant flowers
4 栽 [-] zāi (cultivate, plant) <v.> plant: ~树 plant trees || 移 ~ transplant || 轮~ rotating plant
5 嫁接 [-] jiàjiē (bud-graft) <v.> graft: ~成功 successful grafting || ~苹果 graft apples || 人工~ manual grafting
6 除草 [-] chúcǎo (weed-grass) <v.> weeding: 人工~ manual weeding || ~剂 weed killer || 科学 ~ scientific weeding
7 灌溉 [-] guàngài (pour-irrigate) <v.> irrigate: 人工~ manual irrigation || ~植物 irrigate plants || 节水~ water-saving irrigation

8 施肥 [-] shīféi (apply-fertilizer) <v.> fertilize: 盲目 (mángmù) ~ fertilize blindly || 科学 ~ scientific fertilization || 合理~ reasonable fertilization

9 收 [-] shōu (arrest, receive, harvest) <v.> harvest, reap: ~庄稼 harvest crops || ~麦子 harvest wheat

10 收割 [-] shōugē (harvest-cut) <v.> harvest, reap: ~庄稼 (zhuāngjia) harvest crops || ~水稻 harvest rice || 机器~ machine harvest

11 收获 [-穫] shōuhuò (harvest-gain) <v.> harvest, gain: ~庄稼 harvest crops || ~粮食 harvest grain || ~五百斤南瓜 harvest 550 catty of pumpkins

12 绿化 [-] lǜhuà (green-*suffix*) <v.> make green with plants, reforest: ~城市 plan trees in and around the city

13 放牧 [-] fàngmù (unpen-herd) <v.> graze, pasture, pasture: ~羊群 graze sheep || 轮流 (lúnliú) ~ rotational grazing || 过度~ overgrazing

14 饲养 [飼養] sìyǎng (feed-raise) <v.> feed, raise: ~ 鸽子 raise doves || 人工~ artificial feeding || 室内~ laboratory feeding

15 喂 [-] wèi (feed) <v.> feed: ~羊 feed goats || ~鱼 feed fish || ~牛 feed cows

16 阉割 [閹-] yāngē (castrate-cut) <v.> castrate: ~公牛 castrate a bull

17 宰 [-] zǎi (slave, slaughter) <v.> slaughter, kill: ~牛 slaughter cattle || ~一刀 rip off

18 杀 [殺] shā (kill, slaughter) <v.> slaughter: ~鸡 slaughter chickens

19 钓鱼 [釣魚] diàoyú (to fish-fish) <v.> fishing: 喜欢~ like fishing || 到海上~ go fishing on the sea

20 撒网 [-網] sāwǎng (cast-net) <v.> casting net: ~ 捕鱼 casting a net || 到处~ casting a net everywhere

21 打猎 [-獵] dǎliè (hunt-hunt) <v.> hunting: 非法~ illegal hunting

22 培育 [-] péiyù (cultivate-breed) <v.> cultivate, foster, breed: ~民族精神cultivate the national spirit || ~树木 breed trees || 人工~ artificial breed

23 开发 [開發] kāifā (open-develop) <v.> exploit, develop: 土地~ exploit land || ~资源 (zīyuán) develop resources || ~智力 develop intelligence

Tips:

1 种 (種): When pronounced as 'zhǒng,' it means 'seed,' when 'zhòng,' 'to sow, to plant.'

2 漏网之鱼 (lòuwǎngzhīyú): It literally means 'a fish slipped through the net,' with an extended meaning of 'a criminal at large.'

Exercises:

Part I: Read the following words and then answer the following questions in Chinese.

开垦、种植、除草、灌溉、施肥、收割、收获、绿化、放牧、饲养、钓鱼、撒网、打猎、培育、开发

---

1 美国中部主要种植什么农作物?

---

2 在美国自己开垦农田是不是合法的?

---

3 在你们国家农民的日常工作有哪些?

---

4 你觉得美国哪些地方需要绿化? 为什么?

---

5 在你们国家打猎是合法的吗? 钓鱼呢?

---

6 在你们培育和开发新的农产品由个人来做还是由公司来做?

Theme 156: To travel 出行 (chūxíng)

1 驾驶 [駕駛] jiàshǐ (drive-gallop/drive) <v.> drive, fly: ~ 汽车 drive a car || ~飞船 drive a spacecraft || ~飞机 fly an airplane
2 开 [開] kāi (open, drive) <v.> drive, fly: ~车 drive a car || ~船 drive a ship || ~飞机 fly an airplane
3 开车 [開車] kāichē (drive-vehicle) <v.> driving: 酒后~ driving after drunk || 无证~ driving without a license || 会~ can drive
4 行驶 [-駛] xíngshǐ (run-drive) <v.> travel, drive: 安全~ safe driving || ~一百公里 drive one hundred kilometers || 在大路上~ drive on the road
5 超 [-] chāo (jump, surpass) <v.> go beyond, exceed, surpass: ~速 overspeed || ~时代 transcend an era || ~现实 surreal
6 酒驾 [-駕] jiǔjià (drunk-drive) <v.> drunk driving: ~肇事 (zhàoshì) an accident for drunk driving || ~闯祸 get into trouble with drunk driving
7 航空 [-] hángkōng (navigate-sky) <n.> aviation: ~公司 airline || ~运输 (yùnshū) air transportation || ~表演 (biǎoyǎn) air show
8 航天 [-] hángtiān (navigate-heaven) <n.> spaceflight: ~表演 the spaceflight performance || ~活动 the spaceflight activity || ~技术 space technology
9 航海 [-] hánghǎi (navigate-sea) <n./v.> navigation, sailing: 长期~ sailing for a long time || ~时代 navigation times
10 飞行 [飛-] fēixíng (fly-travel) <v.> fly: 三次~ fly three times || 向南~ fly to the south || ~两小时 fly a total of two hours
11 转机 [轉機] zhuǎnjī (transfer-plane) <v-o.> transfer: 转两次机 transfer twice || 在国际机场~ transfer at an international airport
12 起飞 [-飛] qǐfēi (off-fly) <v.> take off: 准备~ ready for take off || 飞机~ take off
13 上车 [-車] shàngchē (get on-vehicle) <v.> get on: 在总站~ get on at the general station || 排队~ line up to get on
14 下车 [-車] xiàchē (get off-vehicle) <v.> get off: 跳/走~ jump/walk to get off || 下一站~ get off the next station || 一起~ get off together
15 旅行 [-] lǚxíng (travel-go) <v.> travel: 长途~ a long travel || 太空~ space travel || 环球~ travel around the world
16 旅游 [-遊] lǚyóu (travel-tour) <v.> tour, travel: 到香港~ tour to Hong Kong || 短线~ go a short-line touring || 观光~ sightseeing tour

17 导游 [導遊] dǎoyóu (guide-tour) <v./n.> tour guide: 当~ be a tour guide || 英语~ a tour guide speaking English || 为我们~ be a tour guide for us

18 向导 [嚮導] xiàngdǎo (lead-guide) <n.> guide: 当~ be a guide || ~带路 lead by a guide

19 带 [帶] dài (take) <v.> take: ~你去看看 take you to see || ~他们去山区 take them to a mountain area || ~学生去旅游 take the students to travel

20 乘 [-] chéng (ascend, ride) <v.> take, embark: ~火车 take a train || ~船 by ship || ~飞机 take a flight

21 坐 [-] zuò (sit, take) <v.> take: ~车 take a train || ~船 by ship || ~飞机 take a flight

22 搭乘 [-] dāchéng (travel by-ride) <v.> travel by: ~商船 travel by ship || ~巴士 travel by bus || ~卡车 travel by truck

23 乘车 [-車] chéngchē (ride-vehicle) <v.> by car, ride: ~上班 go work by bus || 免费~ free ride || ~路线 bus route

24 乘坐 [-] chéngzuò (ride-take) <v.> drive, ride: ~快艇 (kuàitǐng) take a fast boat || ~飞船 travel by spacecraft

25 搭 [-] dā (travel by) <v.> take: ~汽车 take a bus || ~火车 take a train || ~飞机 take a flight

26 打车 [-車] dǎchē (take-taxi) <v-o> take a taxi: ~ 回家 go home by taxi || ~软件 an app for taking a taxi || 打一次车 take a taxi

27 渡 [-] dù (ferry sb. through) <v.> cross: ~河 cross a river || 远~ take a sea voyage || 南/东~ take a sea voyage southward/eastward

28 划船 [-] huáchuán (row-boat) <v.> go boating: 在湖上~ go boating on a lake || ~比赛 a boat race || ~去上学 go to school by boat

29 出发 [-發] chūfā (out-start off) <v.> set out, start off, depart: 重新 ~ start off again || 从北京~ leave from Beijing || 马上~ leave soon

30 出行 [-] chūxíng (out-travel) <v.> travel: 打车~ travel by taxi || 乘车~ travel by bus || ~路线 travel route

31 出国 [-國] chūguó (leave-country) <v-n> go abroad, out of country: 出一次国 go for an oversea tour || ~旅游 travel out of country || 第一次~ the first time to go abroad

32 途经 [-經] tújīng (path-via) <v.> pass by, by way of: ~上海 pass by Shanghai || ~本地 pass by the local

33 过 [過] guò (pass) <v.> over, cross: ~天桥 over the bridge || ~马路 cross the street || ~江 cross the river

34 经过 [經過] jīngguò (via-pass) <v.> go through, pass by: 从旁边~ pass by || ~商店 pass by the store

35 路过 [-過] lùguò (path-pass) <v.> pass by: ~这里 pass by here || ~一个公园 pass by a park || 从附近~ pass by nearby

36 通过 [-過] tōngguò (through-pass) <v.> pass through: 火车~一个小城市 the train passed through a small city || ~检查 pass an examination || ~考试 pass an exam

37 转弯 [轉彎] zhuǎnwān (to turn-turn) <v.> turn: 在前面~ make a turn ahead || 车要~ the car will turn

38 停 [-] tíng (stop) <v.> stop, park: ~在哪里 where did you park the car? || ~在机场 park at the airport || ~在门前 park at the door

39 靠 [-] kào (depend on, lean on, near) <v.> get close to: ~岸 pull in to shore || ~码头 dock || ~旁边 pull over

40 到 [-] dào (arrive, go to) <v.> go, arrive: ~英国去留学 go to U.K. to study || ~了公园 arrived at the park
41 到达 [-達] dàodá (arrive-arrived) <v.> arrive, reach: ~机场 arrive at the airport || ~公司 arrive at the company || ~月球 reach the moon
42 抵达 [-達] dǐdá (arrive-arrived) <v.> arrive, reach: ~目的地 reach the destination || ~现场 arrive on the scene || ~灾区 arrive at the disaster area
43 赶到 [趕-] gǎndào (hurry-arrive) <v.> hurry to arrive, reach: ~ 车站 hurry to arrive at the station || ~医院 hurry to arrive at the hospital || 马上~ reach sb./sp. soon
44 回 [-] huí (circle, return) <v.> go back, return: ~家 go home || ~办公室 go back to the office || ~国go back to the homeland country
45 回来 [-來] huílái (come-back) <v.> get back, come back, turn back: 留学~ get back after finish studying abroad || 拿~ bring sth. back || 寄~ send back
46 回去 [-] huíqù (go-back) <v.> get back, go back, turn back: 收~ draw back || 走~ walk back || 带~ bring back
47 返回 [-] fǎnhuí (return-back) <v.> return: ~住所 return to home || ~城市 return to the city || ~北方 return to the North
48 衣锦还乡 [-錦還鄉] yìjǐnhuánxiāng (wear-brocade-return-home) <idiom> return home gloriously: 中国人一直有赚钱后~的观念. The Chinese always thought they were going to move back to their hometowns after earning their fortune elsewhere.

Tips:

1 衣锦还乡: It means 'to return home gloriously,' which was an ideal for the ancient Chinese to show their success to their fellow townsmen.
2 到达 vs. 抵达: All mean 'arrive' and function almost the same when the object is a place. 抵达 appears to be slightly more formal than 到达. The object of 抵达 is only a place, whereas the object of 到达 can fall into other categories, such as 程度 (degree), 状态 (condition, state).
3 航空 (aeronautics) and 航天 (astronautics): When they are used together, the order is 航空航天, not the reverse.
4 打的 (dī): It means 'take a taxi' in spoken Chinese since the 的 (dī) is from the Cantonese transliteration of taxi '的士.'

Exercises:

Part I: Use the given bound form on the left as a guide to help you think of other words with the same character. Feel free to use your dictionary when needed. Then write down the English definition of each of the words you've written.

航 *(sail, fly, ship, navigate):* 航行 *sail, fly, navigate*

____

____

____

____

回 *(go back)* 回家*go back home*

____

____

____

____

旅 *(travel, trip)* 旅行 *travel*

____

____

____

____

过 *(cross, pass)* 穿过 *pass through*

____

____

____

____

出 *(out)* 出去 *go out*

____

____

____

____

Part II: Read the following sentences and fill in each blank with the appropriate word or phrase from the options given.

1 行驶、超速、酒驾、出行

a) 美国人_______的主要方式是开车.
b) 中国法律规定________是违法行为, 因此, 跟朋友吃饭时要想一下这个问题.
c) 小王喜欢开快车, 因此他常常_________, 收到很多罚单 (fádān, ticket).
d) 虽然已经是深夜一点了, 北京高速公路上还是有很多_______的车辆.

2 赶到、乘坐、衣锦还乡、到达、抵达、

a) 小王父母________上海到北京的高铁来北京看他. 他们将在四小时以后________北京. 小王要在下午四点以前________火车站接父母.
b) 昨日, 中国国家国家主席习近平__________德国进行国事访问.
c) 一般来说, 中国父母都希望自己的孩子取得巨大成功以后回到家乡看望父母, 这就是中国人所说的“_________.”

Theme 157: Transportation 交通 (jiāotōng)

(See also Themes 33, 37)

1 运输 [運輸] yùnshū (transport-convey) <v.> transport: 交通~ communication and transportation || 铁路~ railway transportation || ~食物 transport food
2 运 [運] yùn (revolve, transport) <v.> carry, transport: ~货 transport the goods || ~煤 (méi) transport coal || ~东西 transport stuff
3 输 [輸] shū (transport, convey) <v.> transfuse, transmit, deliver: ~血 transfuse blood || ~电 transmit electricity || ~水 deliver water
4 运载 [運載] yùnzài (transport-carry) <v.> carry: ~旅客 carry passengers
5 海 [-運] hǎiyùn (sea-transportation) <n./v.> sea transportation: ~频繁 frequent sea transportation || ~繁忙 a busy sea transportation
6 空运 [-運] kōngyùn (air-transportation) <n./v.> air transportation: 非法~ illegal air transportation || 紧急~ urgent air transportation || ~到灾区 air transportation to the disaster area
7 客运 [-運] kèyùn (passenger-transit) <n.> passenger survey: 国际 ~ international passenger survey
8 货运 [貨運] huòyùn (freight-transportation) <n.> freight transportation: 远洋~ ocean freight transportation || 长途 ~ long-distance freight transportation
9 春运 [-運] chūnyùn (spring festival-transit) <n.> transportation during the Spring Festival: 铁路~ the railway transportation during the Spring Festival
10 装 [裝] zhuāng (baggage, carry) <v.> load: ~船 ship loading || ~车厢 (chēxiāng) load on the carriage || ~在卡车上 load on the truck
11 装卸 [裝-] zhuāngxiè (load-unload) <v.> load and unload: ~简单 load and unload easily || ~货物 load and unload freight || 整车~ the vehicle loading and unloading
12 卸载 [-載] xièzǎi (unload-loads) <v.> unload: ~货物 unload freight || ~燃油 unload oil
13 超载 [-載] chāozǎi (over-load) <v.> overload: ~行驶 overloading vehicle operation || 严重~ serious overloading

Tips:

1 春运: It refers to the transportation during the Spring Festival, which usually lasts 40 days. This usually begins 15 days before the Lunar New Year and ends 25 days after it. The passenger ridership in mainland China during the 2017 春运 reached 3 billion people.
2 卸 (xiè, unload): According to the oldest Chinese dictionary, 卸 is related to 午 (upper left of 卸, horse), 止 (lower left of 卸, to stop) and 卩 (right part of 卸, man) which in combination means 'a man stops a cart to unharness a horse,' i. e., 'to unload.'

Exercises:

Part I: Read the following sentences and fill in each blank with the appropriate word or phrase from the options given.

1 卸载、原料、运载

a) 中国的东部的交通_______非常发达.

b) 中国铁路的________能力很强, 大部分货物是通过铁路运输的.
c) 电脑上不经常使用的软件最好_______掉, 因为会影响电脑的运行速度.

2 春运、客运、空运、海运

a) ________一般来说说输量大, 价格也非常便宜.
b) _________速度非常快, 但是价格非常贵.
c) _________是中国铁路最忙的事情, 因为中国人都要回家过年. 由于旅客大量增加, 每年春节前后中国铁路的________量都是平时的十倍以上.

Theme 158: To teach 教学 (jiàoxué)

(See also Theme 77)

1 教学 [-學] jiàoxué (educate-learn) <n.> teaching: 课堂~ classroom teaching || ~方法 teaching method || 传统~ traditional teaching
2 教育 [-] jiàoyù (educate-nurture) <v./n.> educate: ~儿童 educate children || ~子女 educate someone's kids
3 传 [傳] chuán (pass on) <v.> transmit, pass on, hand down: ~给下一代 pass on to the next generation || 把经验~下去 hand experiences down || 父~子 transmit from the father to the son
4 培养 [-養] péiyǎng (cultivate-raise) <v.> train, cultivate, foster: ~学生 train students || ~能力 foster one's capability || ~人才 personnel training
5 培育 [-] péiyù (cultivate-nurture) <v.> cultivate, foster: ~人才 cultivate the talents || ~青年 cultivate young people || ~骨干 foster key employees

6 以身作则 [---則] yǐshēnzuòzé (use-oneself-as-example) <idiom> make oneself an example, give a lead: 父母必须~. The parents must make themselves an example.
7 为人师表 [爲-師-] wéirénshībiǎo (be-people's-teacher-model) <idiom> be a model for others, be a model of virtue for others: 处处~ be a model for others everywhere

8 教 [-] jiāo (teach) <v.> teach: ~钢琴 teach piano || ~留学生 teach foreign students || ~大家打乒乓球 teach people to play ping pong
9 上课 [-課] shàngkè (have-class) <v-o.> have a class: 上两个小时课 take a two-hour class || 晚上~ have a class in the evening || 在教室~ have a class in the classroom
10 讲课 [講課] jiǎngkè (teach-class) <v-o.> give a lesson, teach: 讲一次课 give one lesson || 在教室~ give a less in the classroom || 开始~ start to teach
11 备课 [備課] bèikè (prepare-class) <v.> prepare the instruction: 精心~ prepare the instruction carefully || 认真 ~ carefully prepared instruction || 集体~ collective preparation of instruction
12 操练 [-練] cāoliàn (drill-practice) <v.> practice, drill: 反复~ practice repeatedly || 认真~ serious practice || ~句子 practice sentences
13 补课 [補課] bǔkè (make up-class) <v-o.> make up missed lessons, tutor: 补两次课 tutoring twice || 给他~ make up missed lessons for him or tutor him || ~费 fees for tutoring
14 启发 [啓發] qǐfā (enlighten-inspire) <v./n.> inspire, enlighten: ~读者 inspire/enlighten readers || 有~ have inspiration/enlightenment || 得到/受到 ~ get inspiration/enlightenment

15 示范 [-範] shìfàn (demonstrate-model) <v.> demonstrate: 重点~ a key demonstration || 当面~ site demonstration || 做~ make a demonstration
16 指导 [-導] zhǐdǎo (direct-guide) <v.> instruct: ~学生 instruct students || ~设计 instruct designs || 在他的~下 under his instruction
17 提醒 [-] tíxǐng (remind-clear) <v./n.> remind, reminder: 提一个醒 give a reminder || 再三~她 remind her again and again || 互相~ remind each other
18 教训 [-訓] jiàoxùn (educate-instruct) <v.> lesson, teach sb. a lesson: ~儿子 give the son a lesson || ~一顿 read someone a lesson || 吸取~ learn a lesson
19 警告 [-] jǐnggào (warn-tell) <v./n.> warn, warning: ~两次 warning twice || 发出 ~ give a warning

20 考 [-] kǎo (aged, strike, examine) <v.> examine: ~外语 take an examination/test of foreign languages || ~大学 the university entrance exam || ~不上 fail exams
21 考试 [-試] kǎoshì (examine-test) <n./v.> exam, examination, test: 参加~ take an exam || 通过~ pass an exam || 公开~ public examination
22 测试 [測試] cèshì (check-test) <v.> test: 心理~ psychological test || 现场~ site test || ~视力 eyesight test
23 口试 [-試] kǒushì (oral-test) <v.> oral test/examination: 参加~ take an oral test/examination || 进行 ~ take an oral test/examination || 汉语 ~ an oral test for Mandarin Chinese
24 期中考试 [---試] qīzhōngkǎoshì (term-middle-exam) <n.> mid-term exam: 举行~ hold a mid-term exam || 参加~ take a mid-term exam
25 期末考试 [---試] qīmòkǎoshì (term-final-exam) <n.> final exam: 年终~ a final exam in the end of year
26 面试 [-試] miànshì (face to face-test) <v.> interview: 现场~ an on-site interview || 主持~ hold an interview || 参加 ~ go for an interview
27 补考 [補-] bǔkǎo (make up-exam) <v.> make-up examination: ~两次 make-up examination twice || ~成绩 grade for make-up examinations || 进行~ take a make-up examination
28 高考 [-] gāokǎo (advanced-exam) <n.> college entrance exam: 成人~ the adult college entrance exam || 准备~ prepare a college entrance exam || 参加~ take an adult college entrance exam
29 科举 [-舉] kējǔ (subject-increased) <n.> imperial competitive examination: ~考试 imperial competitive examination || 废~ abolish the imperial competitive examination
30 托福 [-] tuōfú (*transliteration* of TOEFL) <n.> TOEFL: ~考试 the TOEFL examination || 考 ~ take a TOEFL examination

Tips:

1 托福 (tuōfú): It means 'thanks to you' in Chinese. Now the Chinese people still say '托您的福' (thanks to you) etc. When the Test of English as a Foreign Language (TOEFL) was introduced to China, it was translated as 托福 which, needless to say, has an auspicious connotation to the Chinese.
2 科举 (kējǔ): It means '(Chinese) imperial examinations' which lasted from 605 in the Sui Dynasty to 1905, almost the end of the Qing Dynasty. 科举 greatly shaped the Chinese education system as well as Chinese culture. In the Sui Dynasty, the imperial examinations only had several categories (科),

but the categories were increased (举) to more than 50 in the Tang Dynasty, so it was called 科举 (literally 'category-increased.')

3 补习班: It means 'cram class' which is very common in mainland China and Taiwan. The popularity of these classes may stem from the competitiveness of education, but a widespread conspiracy states that teachers want to make extra income to supplement their low salary.

4 为人师表: It means '(a teacher should be good enough) to be (为) the people (人)'s teacher (师) and model (表).' This phrase is seen in almost every school in China and sometimes in traditional form '爲人師表.'

Exercises:

Part I: Answer the following questions in Chinese.

1 在美国一个老师的日常工作有哪些?

___

2 美国高中一般来说会有哪些考试?

___

3 美国有没有类似高考的考试? 什么时候考?

___

4 美国历史上有没有科举制度? 你觉得这种制度 (zhìdù, system) 合理吗? 为什么?

___

5 美国学校也提倡 (tíchàng, advocate) 老师"为人师表"吗? 为什么?

___

6 你觉得父母应该"以身作则"吗? 为什么?

___

Theme 159: To study, to read 学习, 阅读 (xuéxí, yuèdú)

1 学习 [學習] xuéxí (study-practise) <v.> study: ~技术 study technology || ~方法 study a method || 向他~ learn from him
2 学 [學] xué (study, learn) <v.> learn: ~画画 learn to paint || ~游泳 learn to swim || ~吉他 learn the guitar
3 上学 [-學] shàngxué (go to-school) <v.> go to school: 一块~ one school || 天天~ go to school every day || 开车~ drive to school
4 读 [讀] dú (read) <v.> read: ~报纸 read a newspaper || ~三遍 read three times || ~一本书 read one book
5 读书 [讀書] dúshū (read-book) <v-o> study: 努力~ study hard || 在学校~ study at school || 读五年书 study for five years
6 念 [-] niàn (miss, read aloud) <v.> read aloud, study: ~书 read a book aloud || ~大学 go to college || ~报纸 read a newspaper aloud
7 听讲 [聽講] tīngjiǎng (listen to-lecture) <v.> listen to a lecture: 认真~ listen carefully || 注意~ pay attention to || 上课 ~ go to a class lecture

8 阅读 [閱讀] yuèdú (read-read) <v.> read: ~小说 read a novel || ~文章 read an article || 独立~ read independently

9 看 [-] kàn (look, watch, read) <v.> look, read silently: ~书 read a book || ~报 read a newspaper || ~小说 read a novel

10 精读 [-讀] jīngdú (careful-read) <v.> carefully read, intensively read: ~经典著作 study classic works || ~原著 study the original work || ~这篇文章 carefully read this article

11 泛读 [汎讀] fàndú (extensive-read) <v.> extensively read: ~十本书 read ten books || 课外~ extracurricular reading

12 浏览 [瀏覽] liúlǎn (speedy-look at) <v.> skim: ~网页 skim the internet || ~景色 glance at the scenery || 随意~ randomly skim

13 朗读 [-讀] lǎngdú (aloud-read) <v.> read aloud: ~课文 read the text aloud || 诗歌~ poetry recitation || ~汉语 read Chinese aloud

14 背诵 [-誦] bèisòng (memorize-recite) <v.> recite: ~台词 recite lines || ~一首诗 recite a poem || ~课文 recite text

15 背 [-] bèi (back of the body, turn around, recite by memory) <v.> remember by rote, recite from memory: ~ 生词 recite vocabulary || ~课文 recite text || ~了三遍 recite three times

16 填 [-] tián (fill in) <v.> fill in: ~表 fill in a table || ~数字/名字 fill in a name || ~歌词 write lyrics

17 识字 [識-] shízì (learn-character) <v-o.> learn to read: 识很多字 can read many characters || ~不多 can't read a lot

18 抄 [-] chāo (copy) <v.> copy: ~作业 copy homework || ~文章 copy from an article || ~一百遍 copy 100 times

19 抄写 [-寫] chāoxiě (copy-write) <v.> transcribe/copy by hand: ~论文 copy a paper by hand || ~诗词 transcribe a poem || ~五遍 copy down five times

20 记 [記] jì (bear in mind, write down) <v.> write down: ~在纸上 write down on paper || ~日记 write in a diary || ~功/帐 record a merit

21 练 [練] liàn (practice) <v.> practice: 勤~ practice diligently || ~太极拳 practice tai qi || ~书法 practice calligraphy

22 练习 [練習] liànxí (practice-practice/exercise) <v.> practice: 坚持~ persevere in practicing || 反复~ repeated practice || ~钢琴 practice the piano

23 复习 [復習] fùxí (review-learn) <v.> review: ~生词 review vocabulary || ~课文 review the lesson text || 一起~ review together

24 模仿 [-] mófǎng (model-imitate) <v.> imitate, model on: ~欧洲 model on Europe || ~动作 copy movements || 机械地~ imitate mechanically

25 自学 [-學] zìxué (self-learn) study <v.> independently: ~日语 independently study Japanese || ~成才 self-taught || ~新知识 self-study new information

26 补习 [補習] bǔxí (make up for-learn) <v.> take extra lessons: ~一年 take extra lessons for a year || ~数学 do extra study in math || ~功课 tutor work

27 实习 [實習] shíxí (in reality-practice) <v./n.> practice a skill: 毕业~ graduation practice || ~半年 practice for half a year || ~医生 intern as a doctor

28 必修 [-] bìxiū (required-study) <adj.> required: ~课程 required course || ~科 required section

29 选修 [選-] xuǎnxiū (selective-study) <v.> choose to take: ~课程 take an elective || ~外语 choose to study a foreign language || ~课 elective class
30 主修 [-] zhǔxiū (major-study) <v.> major in: ~经济 major in economics || ~历史 major in history || ~三门课 major in three classes
31 辅修 [輔-] fǔxiū (secondly-study) <v.> minor: ~新闻专业 minor in news studies || ~英语 minor in English || ~两门课 minor in two classes
32 旷课 [曠課] kuàngkè (absent-class) <v.> skip class: 无故~ miss class for no reason || ~两次 skip class twice || 经常~ routinely skip class
33 逃课 [-課] táokè (skip-class) <v-o.> skip class: 中途~ skip half the class || 频繁~ frequently skip class
34 休学 [-學] xiūxué (suspend-study) <v.> take a break from school: ~一年 take a gap year || 因病~ take a year off because of illness || 申请~ apply to defer studies
35 转学 [轉學] zhuǎnxué (transfer-school) <v.> transfer schools: 中途~ part-way through transferring || ~两次 transfer twice
36 留学 [-學] liúxué (stay-study) <v.> study abroad: 在美国~ study abroad in America || 出国~ leave the country to study abroad || ~十年 study abroad for 10 years

37 作 [-] zuò (get up, do, write) <v.> compose, write: ~文章 write an article || ~曲 compose a song || ~评价 write an assessment
38 做 [-] zuò (do) <v.> do: ~作业 do homework || ~研究 do research || ~文章 write an article

Tips:

1 作 vs. 做: Both are pronounced as 'zuò' and mean 'to make/do,' but 做 is a later form of 作, starting from the Song dynasty. Generally speaking, if the object of 'zuò' is more concrete, such as '衣服,' '饭', it is '做,' if the object of 'zuò' is more abstract or the 'zuò' is used in an idiom, such as '作罢' (zuòbà, to give up) and '无恶不作' (wú'èbúzuò, to stop at nothing in doing evil,) it is '作.' 'Do homework' is written as 做作业. 作 has another pronunciation 'zuō,' which means 'workshop' and is used in only one word '作坊' (zuōfáng, workshop.)
2 阅 (yuè): When a Chinese official needs to acknowledge that he has read a (government) document, he usually writes '阅' (read, here 'have read') on the paper.
3 识字 and 忧患 (yōuhuàn): 忧患 means 'suffering, hardship.' There is a famous saying: "人生识字忧患始" by a great man of letters, Su Shi (1037–1101). It means 'one's whole miserable life started from the beginning to learn to read,' which does not mean 'Chinese characters are hard to learn,' but 'if you are able to read, you will be able to comprehend the rise and fall, glory and misfortune of Chinese history.'

Exercises:

Part I: Answer the following questions in Chinese.

1 请说出至少三种阅读的方法

____

2 你在大学的时候主修什么？辅修什么？

____

3 你上学的时候有没有逃过课? 为什么?

---

4 你有没有转学或者休学的经历? 为什么?

---

5 在你们国家实习经历对大学生重要不重要? 为什么?

Theme 160: Research 研究 (yánjiū)

1 研究 [-] yánjīu (study-explore) <v.> research: ~历史 research history || ~问题 research an issue || 科学~ research science
2 调研 [調-] diàoyán (investigate-research) <v.> investigate, research: 市场~ research the stock market || 网上/在线~ go online to do research || 内部~ internal investigation
3 研发 [-發] yánfā (research-develop) <v.> research and develop: ~新产品 develop a new product || 技术~ develop a new technology || 软件~ develop new software
4 研制 [-製] yánzhì (research-make) <v.> manufacture: ~新产品 manufacture new products || ~飞机 manufacture a plane || ~药物 develop a drug
5 探索 [-] tànsuǒ (explore-seek) <v.> explore: ~新道路 explore new paths || 勇于~ have the courage to explore || 值得~ worth exploring
6 探讨 [-討] tàntǎo (explore-discuss) <v.> probe into: ~问题 probe into a question || ~方法 investigate a method || ~原因 inquire into a reason
7 解释 [解釋] jiěshì (solve-explain) <v.> explain: ~清楚 explain clearly || ~问题 explain a question || 作~ compose an explanation
8 分析 [-] fēnxī (dissect-analyze) <v.> analyze: ~问题 analyze a question || 科学~ scientific analysis || ~句子 analyze a sentence
9 分解 [-] fēnjiě (dissect-split) <v.> break down: ~动作 break down an action || 下回~ next breakdown || ~问题 break down the question
10 分类 [-類] fēnlèi (divide-class) <v-o.> classify: 分大/小类 classify into a big/small class || 分三类 separate into three classes || 垃圾~ classify trash
11 概括 [-] gàikuò (generalize-summarize) <v.> summarize, generalize: 高度~ highly generalized || 加以~ be summarized || 进行~ summarize
12 归纳 [歸納] guīnà (put together-collect) <v.> sum up: ~大家的意见 sum up everyone's opinions || ~看法 sum up a view || ~为三种方法 sum up three methods
13 演绎 [-繹] yǎnyì (deduce-sort out) <v.> deduce: 理性~ reasonably deduce || 反复~ repeatedly deduce || ~一遍 deduce one time
14 类比 [類-] lèibǐ (class-compare) <v.> analogy: 简单~ simple analogy || ~论证 analogous augumentation
15 举一反三 [舉---] jǔyī-fǎnsān (cite-one-return-three) <idiom> learn through analogy: 老师应该善于~. A teacher should be good at drawing inferences about other cases from one instance.
16 引用 [-] yǐnyòng (quote-use) <v.> quote: 多次~ many quotations || ~这个例子 reference this example || ~她的话 quote what she said
17 参考 [參-] cānkǎo (refer to-check) <v.> refer to: 供你~ for your reference || ~他的意见 refer to his opinion || ~资料 refer to the data

18 综合 [綜-] zōnghé (synthesize-summarize) <v.> synthesize: ~两个文件内容 synthesize the contents of two papers || ~各种资料 summarize many kinds of information || ~两种方法 integrate two different method
19 总结 [總結] zǒngjié (sum up-conclude) <v.> sum up: ~经验 sum up an experience || 工作~ summarize one's work || ~教训 sum up the lesson

Tips:

1 举一反三: It means 'to learn through analogy.' This is the Confucian way of learning and teaching. He said 'When I have presented one corner of a subject to any one, and he cannot learn the other three from it, I do not repeat my lesson.' This method requires a learner's own active engagement in learning, not to depend solely on the teacher's fine-fed instruction.
2 演绎 (yǎnyì): It means 'to deduce.' Some people say that the Chinese are not good at deductive reasoning (演绎推理, yǎnyì tuīlǐ,), which was poorly reflected in most classics (经典, jīngdiǎn.)

Exercises:

Part I: Use the given bound form as a guide to help you think of other words with the same character. Feel free to use your dictionary when needed. Then write down the English definition of each of the words you've written.

研 *(research)*: 研究 *research*

____

____

____

____

探 *(explore)*: 探求 *explore and pursuit*

____

____

分 *(divide)*: 分手 *break up*

____

____

Part II: Answer the following questions in Chinese.

1 进行研究的方法有哪些?

____

2 "他在学习上举一反三"意思是:

a) 他很聪明 b) 他很浪费 c) 他数学很好

Theme 161: To write 写作 (xiězuò)

1 写 [寫] xiě (write) <v.> write: ~字 write a character || ~信 write a letter || ~小说 write a novel

2 写作 [寫-] xiězuò (write-compose) <v.> write, compose: ~小说 write a novel || 新闻~ write news || 认真~ serious writing

3 创作 [創-] chuàngzuò (initiate-make) <v.> create: ~ 电影音乐 create a movie soundtrack || 小说 ~ produce a novel || ~活动 creative activities

4 编写 [編寫] biānxiě (compile-write) <v.> compile, write: ~剧本write a play || ~课本compile a textbook || ~词典compile a dictionary

5 编辑 [編輯] biānjí (compile-edit) <v.> compile, edit: ~新闻 edit news || ~教材 compile teaching materials || ~刊物 (kānwù) edit a publication

6 编 [編] biān (put in order, compile, write) <v.> edit, compile: ~故事 compile a story || ~词典 edit a dictionary || ~一本书 edit a book

7 翻译 [-譯] fānyì (translate-translate) <v.> translate: 机器~ machine translation || ~成英语 translate into English || ~文章 translate an article

8 查 [-] chá (to check) <v.> look up, consult: ~字典 look up a word in the dictionary || ~地图 consult a map || ~资料 consult reference materials (on a subject)

9 查看 [-] chákàn (check-look) <v.> look over, examine: ~ 账目examine the accounts || ~ 证件 examine the identification

10 改 [-] gǎi (change, correct) <v.> change, correct: ~文章 alter an article || ~内容 alter the contents || ~图纸 change the blueprint

11 修改 [-] xiūgǎi (amend-change) <v.> amend: ~作文 change the essay || ~合同 amend the contract || 反复~ repeatedly change

12 校对 [-對] jiàoduì (proofread-check) <v.> proofread: ~ 答案 proofread answers || ~时间 calibration period || 仔细地~ carefully proofread

13 画龙点睛 [畫龍點-] huàlóngdiǎnjīng (draw-dragon-dot-eye) <idiom> add the finishing touches: 她的议论~. Her talk added the crucial finishing touches.

14 登录 [-錄] dēnglù (register-record) <v.> log in: ~网站 log in to a website || ~主机 log in to a host computer || 自动~ automatic login

15 上传 [-傳] shàngchuán (up-transfer) <v.> upload: ~音频 (yīnpín) upload audio || ~照片 upload a picture || ~文件 upload a file

16 下载 [-載] xiàzǎi (down-load) <v.> download: ~文件 download a file || ~音乐 download audio || 免费~ free download

17 保存 [-] bǎocún (keep-save) <v.> save, keep: ~文件 save a file || 慎重 (shènzhòng) ~ carefully preserved || ~完好 well-kept

Tips:

1 校对 (proofread): Although the standard pronunciation is 'jiàoduì,' many people say it 'xiàoduì.'

2 上传 (upload): It is sometimes called '上载' (shàngzǎi.)

Exercises:

Part II: Multiple Choice. Make sure to choose the most appropriate answer.

1 一个好结尾对一篇文章会起到___________的作用.

A. 画龙点睛 B. 修改 C. 校对

2 下面哪组词最有可能会在描述"使用电脑"的时候使用:
A. 编写、查看、修改、校对 B. 写作、创作、翻译、编辑
C. 登录、上传、下载、保存

3 小张现在是《中国文学》的______, 负责查看所有的投稿 (tóugǎo, submission).
A. 编辑 B. 翻译 C. 校对

4 谷歌现在使用人工智能_________多种语言.
A. 登录 B. 翻译 C. 上传

5 一般来说美国学生喜欢美国老师________的中文教材, 因为话题和练习都比较适合美国学生.
A. 查看 B. 编辑 C. 编写

Theme 162: Performance 演出 (yǎnchū)

1 演出 [-] yǎnchū (act-open) <v./n.> perform: 一场~ one performance || 看~ watch a performance || ~节目 the show's program

2 表演 [-] biǎoyǎn (show-act) <v./n.> perform, performance: ~一个节目 perform a show || 体育~ sport performance || 观看~ watch a show

3 上演 [-] shàngyǎn (show-performance) <v.> screen, stage: ~新戏 perform a new play || ~一个节目 stage a performance || 即将~ soon to be staged

4 演 [-] yǎn (act, perform) <v.> act, play: ~主角 act as the protagonist || ~老人 play an old person || ~戏 act in a play

5 巡演 [-] xúnyǎn (tour-perform) <v.> be on tour: 环球~ global tour || ~欧洲 European tour || 各地~ tour all over

6 首演 [-] shǒuyǎn (first-performance) <v.> opening performance, debut: ~成功 successful premiere || 在华~ debut in China || 举行~ hold an opening performance

7 彩排 [-] cǎipái (full dress-rehearsal) <v.> rehearsal: 晚会~ party rehearsal || 公开 ~ public rehearsal || 观看~ watch a rehearsal

8 唱 [-] chàng (sing) <v.> sing: ~一支歌 sing a song || ~得好 sing well || ~一遍 sing once

9 唱歌 [-] chànggē (sing-song) <v-o> sing a song: 喜欢~ like to sing songs || 听她 ~ listen to her sing || 一起~ sing together

10 歌唱 [-] gēchàng (song-sing) <v.> sing: ~比赛 singing competition || ~演员 singing actor || 放声~ sing loudly

11 演唱 [-] yǎnchàng (perform-sing) <v.> sing in a performance: ~一首歌 perform a song || 登台~ sing on stage || ~民歌 perform a folk song

12 合唱 [-] héchàng (together-sing) <v.> chorus: ~一个歌曲 sing a song in chorus || 多声部~ multi-part chorus

13 跑调 [-調] pǎodiào (off-tune) <v.> be off key: 唱歌~ sing off key

14 假唱 [-] jiǎchàng (fake-sing) <v.> lip-sync: 制止~ stop lip-syncing || 反对 ~ opposed to lip-syncing

15 跳舞 [-] tiàowǔ (to dance-dance) <v-o.> dance: 跟她~ dance with her || 跳一支舞 do a dance || 跳芭蕾舞 do ballet

16 吹 [-] chuī (to blow) <v.> blow: ~小号 play the trumpet || ~笛子 play the flute || ~一首歌 play a song

17 拉 [-] lā (pull, draw) <v.> play (pull/draw): ~提琴 play the violin || ~二胡 play the erhu || ~一首歌 play a song

18 弹 [彈] tán (eject, strike, pluck, play) <v.> play (pluck): ~钢琴 play the piano || ~吉他 play the guitar || ~风琴/琵琶 play the organ/lute

19 奏乐 [-樂] zòuyuè (play-music) <v.> play music: 乐队 ~ the band played music

20 演奏 [-] yǎnzòu (perform-play music) <v.> give a musical performance: ~乐器 musical performance || ~乐曲 perform a piece of music || ~小提琴 perform on the violin

21 调音 [調-] tiáoyīn (adjust-tune) <v.> tune: 给乐器~ tune an instrument || 重新~ retune

22 扮演 [-] bànyǎn (play the part of-perform) <v.> play the part of: ~角色 act as a character || ~好人 play the part of a good person || ~反面人物 play the opposite person

23 化妆 [-妝] huàzhuāng (change-dress up) <v.> put on makeup: 夜间~ night makeup || 眼部~ eye makeup || 给演员~ put on an actor's makeup

24 出场 [-場] chūchǎng (appear-stage) <v-o.> appear on stage: 出两次场 appear on stage twice || ~顺序 order of appearance || ~动作 act of appearing onstage

25 出台 [-臺] chūtái (appear-stage) <v.> make a public appearance: 演员~ actor appearance || 新戏~ a new play's appearance || 小丑~ clown's stage appearance

26 舞 [-] wǔ (dance) <v.> dance: ~狮子/龙 lion/dragon dance || ~绣球 dance with a silk ball || ~剑 wield a sword

Tips:

1 舞 (wǔ): The oracle form of 舞 depicts a man holding cow tails (無, wú) and dances (舛, chuǎn, two opposite feet,) therefore, 舞 means 'dance.' Actually 舞 (dance) and 無 (无, nothing) shared the same form '無' in the oracle and bronze eras.

2 出场 vs. 出台: Both mean 'to appear on the stage,' but 出场 is next to 'performance' and 出台 'known to the public.' You can say a new policy 出台 but not 出场. 出台 has another meaning, 'a sex worker agrees to provide sex service to a guest elsewhere other than the place s/he works.'

3 吹拉弹唱 (chuī, lā, tán, chàng): It is a cover term for musical talents that mean 'to blow,' 'to draw/pull,' 'to pluck' and 'to sing' respectively.

4 All the world's a stage: This is a famous quotation from William Shakespeare's *As You Like It*. It is translated into Chinese as '人生是个舞台' (literally 'life is a stage,') but the more native translation is '人生如戏' (life is like a drama,) especially because the following line of Shakespeare's quotation is 'and all the men and women merely players.'

5 演员 (yǎnyuán) vs. 戏子 (xìzi): The modern term for actor/actress is 演员 but the traditional one is 戏子, which had a strong negative connotation. The Chinese 演员 received their due respect starting from late 1980s, partially in the form of monetary rewards.

Exercises:

Part I: Use the given bound form as a guide to help you think of other words with the same character. Feel free to use your dictionary when needed. Then write down the English definition of each of the words you've written.

唱 *(sing)*: 唱歌 *sing a song*

____

____

____

____

演 *(show, play, perform)*: 表演 *show, performance*

____

____

____

____

Part II: Answer the following questions in Chinese.

1 你会演奏什么乐器?

2 你参加过学校的演出吗? 一般来说演出以前需要不需要彩排?

3 你唱歌跑调吗? 唱歌的时候你喜欢独唱还是合唱? 为什么?

4 你最欢美国好莱坞 (Hollywood) 的哪部大片? 它是什么时候上演的? 电影的男主角是谁扮演的? 女主角呢?

Theme 163: Photography, painting 摄影, 绘画 (shèyǐng, huìhuà)

1 拍摄 [攝-] pāishè (take-shoot) <v.> take, shoot: ~电影 shoot a movie || ~照片 take a picture || ~风景 film the scenery
2 拍照 [-] pāizhào (take-photo) <v-o.> take a picture: 拍两张照 take two pictures || 拍拍照 take a picture || 给她~ take a picture of her
3 照相 [-] zhàoxiàng (to photograph-photo) <v-o.> photograph: 照两张相 take two photographs || 喜欢~ like taking pictures

4 摄影 [攝-] shèyǐng (shoot-photograph) <v.> photograph: 黑白~ black and white photography || 高空~ aerial photography || 水下 ~ underwater photography

5 照 [-] zhào (bright, shine, reflect) <v./n.> take, reflect: ~相片 take a picture || ~生活照 take photos of life || ~艺术照 take artistic photos

6 抓拍 [-] zhuāpāi (capture-shoot) <v.> capture an image: ~镜头 take a shot || 现场~ capture the scene || ~人物 take a candid shot of a person

7 抢拍 [搶-] qiǎngpāi (grab-shoot) <v.> grab (a photo): ~照片 snatch a picture || ~镜头 grab a photo of the scene || ~现场新闻 grab a photo of the live scene

8 航拍 [-] hángpāi (aerial-photograph) <v.> aerial photography: 高空~ high-altitude photography || ~照片 aerial photograph

9 调焦 [調-] tiáojiāo (adjust-focus) <v.> focus: 自动~ automatic focus || 手动 ~ manual focus || 进行 ~ being focused

10 自拍 [-] zìpāi (self-photograph) <v.> take a selfie: 年轻人都喜欢~. Young people like taking selfies.

11 洗 [-] xǐ (wash the feet, wash, develop) <v.> develop: ~照片 develop a photo || ~五张 develop five photos

12 摄像 [攝-] shèxiàng (shoot-video) <v.> videotape: 电视 ~ TV recording || 给她~ record her || 自动~ automatic recording

13 录像 [錄-] lùxiàng (record-video) <v./n.> videotape: 给他~ videotape her || 实况~ live recording || 水下~ underwater recording

14 录 [錄] lù (record) <v.> record: ~音 audio recording || ~两首歌曲 record two songs || ~唱片 record a record (phonograph)

15 录音 [錄-] lùyīn (record-sound) <v./n.> record: 听/放~ listen to/play back a recording || 重新~ re-record || 同期~ record simultaneously

16 播出 [-] bōchū (broadcast-out) <v.> broadcast: ~新闻 broadcast the news || ~电视节目 broadcast a TV program || 卫星~ satellite broadcast

17 放映 [-] fàngyìng (play-show) <v.> show, project: ~电影 show a movie || ~两小时 show for two hours || 专场~ special showing

18 上映 [-] shàngyìng (open-show) <v.> release: 电视剧~ TV series release || 即将 (jíjiāng) ~ upcoming release

19 公映 [-] gōngyìng (public-show) <v.> public screening: 海内外~ screened at home and abroad || 首轮~ first round of screenings || 近期~ recent screening

20 画 [畫] huà (divide, draw, paint) <v.> draw, paint: ~人物 paint a person || ~马 draw a horse || ~漫画 draw a comic

21 写生 [寫-] xiěshēng (sketch-nature) <v.> draw a sketch: 现场~ live sketch || 实地~ sketch on the spot || 外出~ go outside to sketch

22 调色 [調-] tiáosè (blend-color) <v.> blend colors: 后期~ late stage of mixing || 照片~ photo palette

23 雕刻 [-] diāokè (carve-engrave) <v.> carve: ~精细 (jīngxì) carve meticulously || ~人像 engrave a portrait || ~花纹 carve a pattern

Tips:

1 照相 vs. 摄影: Both mean 'to photograph,' but摄影 is more professional, therefore a 'photographer' is called '摄影师' but not '照相师.'

2 上车睡觉, 下车拍照: Guided tourists from China as well as other Asian countries have a common characteristic, and that is '上车睡觉, 下车拍照'

which means 'they will save a lot of energy by taking naps on their bus, but as soon as they get off the bus, they will be actively taking pictures.' In other words, they care much more about the pictures, not the sceneries themselves.

Exercises:

Part I: Read the following sentences and fill in each blank with the appropriate word or phrase from the options given.

1 公映、放映、播出

a) 这部中国电影已经在全世界________了, 在有的国家很受欢fl, 在有的国家反映 (fǎnyìng, reflect) 一般.
b) 纽约大部分电影院今天晚上将________一部好莱坞 (Hǎoláiwū, Hollywood) 大片.
c) 这部流行电视剧将在北京电视台每晚八点________.

2 录音、录像、自拍

a) 上世纪八十年代的时候, 中国学生学英语主要靠听英文_______.
b) 现在的父母都喜欢给自己的孩子_______, 记录他们的成长.
c) 现在的年轻人很喜欢用手机________, 然后放在脸书上.

3 照相、抓拍、航拍

a) 二十年前, 人们主要用_______机拍照片.
b) 这个摄影师的_______技术非常好, 他拍的照片非常生动.
c) 人们把使用飞机拍照的技术叫做_______.

Theme 164: Sports, games 运动, 比赛 (yùndòng, bǐsài)

(See also Themes 44, 85)

1 运动 [運動] yùndòng (revolve-move) <v.> activity: 坚持~ stick to exercise || 户外~ outdoor activity || 水下~ underwater activity
2 锻炼 [鍛煉] duànliàn (forge-smelt) <v.> exercise: ~身体 work out || ~动手能力 develop exercise skills || ~自己 personal workout

3 打球 [-] dǎqiú (play-ball) <v-o> play ball: 打两小时球 play ball for two hours || 打过三次球 played three times || 打什么球? Play what game?
4 发球 [發-] fāqiú (serve-ball) <v-o> serve a ball: ~失误serving fault || ~得分 ace || 换~ service change
5 扣篮 [-籃] kòulán (dunk-basket) <v.> dunk: ~成功 dunk successfully || ~得分 score on a dunk || 大力~ vigorous dunk
6 出界 [-] chūjiè (be out of-boundary) <v.> out of bounds: 发球~ serve out of bounds || 传球~ pass out of bounds
7 罚球 [發-] fáqiú (penalize-ball) <v.> penalty shot: 两次~ two penalty shots || ~得分 score on a penalty shot

8 跳高 [-] tiàogāo (jump-high) <v.> high jump: ~比赛 high jump competition || 练习~ practice the high jump || ~运动 high jump motion
9 跳远 [-遠] tiàoyuǎn (jump-long) <v.> long jump: 三级~ triple jump || 立定~ standing long jump || ~比赛 long jump competition

10 游泳 [-] yóuyǒng (swim-swim) <v./n.> swim: 学~ study swimming || 游了半小时泳 swim for half an hour || 去~ go swimming
11 跳水 [-] tiàoshuǐ (jump-water) <v.> dive: ~比赛 diving competition || ~逃跑 running dive || ~运动 diving motion
12 冲浪 [衝-] chōnglàng (surf-wave) <v.> surf: 海上~ surf in the ocean || 上网 ~ surf the web

13 登山 [-] dēngshān (climb-mountain) <v-o.> mountain climbing: 登一次山 climb one mountain || 登高山 climb a tall mountain || 喜欢~ enjoy mountain climbing
14 攀岩 [-] pānyán (climb-rock) <v.> rock climbing: ~比赛 rock climbing competition || ~运动 the movement of rock climbing
15 远足 [遠-] yuǎnzú (far-walk) <v.> hike: ~探险 adventure hike || ~锻炼 hiking exercise || 两次~ two hikes

16 下棋 [-] xiàqí (play-chess) <v.> play chess: 跟朋友~ play chess with a friend || 一起~ play chess together
17 射箭 [-] shèjiàn (shoot-arrow) <v-o.> shoot an arrow, archery: ~比赛archery competition || ~场archery range
18 击剑 [擊劍] jījiàn (hit-sword) <v.> fencing: ~ 比赛 fencing competition
19 赛马 [賽馬] sàimǎ (race-horse) <v.> horse racing: 参加~ take part in horse racing

20 竞赛 [競賽] jìngsài (compete-match) <v.> competition: 体育~ sports competition || 参加 ~ take part in a competition
21 竞争 [競爭] jìngzhēng (compete-contend) <v.> compete: 同他们~ compete with them || 公开~ public competition || 互相 ~ compete with each other

Tips:

1 锻炼 (duànliàn): Suppose a blacksmith is making a sword, he needs to smelt (炼) and forge (锻) the iron, so 锻炼 derived a meaning 'to temper' from 'to smelt and forge.' 'Exercise' is an extended meaning of 'to temper.'
2 游泳: 游泳 means 'swim, swimming' and the styles of swimming are called '*泳,' for example, 蝶泳 (diéyǒng, butterfly,) 仰泳 (yǎngyǒng, backstroke,) 蛙泳 (wāyǒng, breaststroke,) 自由泳 (freestyle) and 个人混合泳 (hùnhéyǒng, individual medley.) Winter swimming is 冬泳.

Exercises:

Part I: Read the following words and then answer the following questions in Chinese.

赛马、击剑、射箭、下棋、远足、登山、攀岩、游泳、冲浪、跳水、跳高、跳远、打球

1 上面这些运动中你最喜欢哪个?

---

2 上面这些运动中哪个需要很多脑力劳动?

---

3 上面这些运动中哪些跟"水"关系比较大?

---

4 上面这些运动中哪些跟"山"关系比较大?

---

5 你觉得你们国家"赛马"、"击剑"和"射箭"哪个是世界一流水平? 为什么?

Theme 165: Medical treatment 医治 (yīzhì)

(See also Themes 86, 103)

1 看病 [-] kànbìng (diagnose-illness) <v.> see a patient: 给人~ see a sick person || 为老百姓~ see common patients || ~难. It is hard to see a doctor.
2 治 [-] zhì (administer, treat) <v.> treat: ~病 treat a sick person || ~感冒 cure a cold || ~眼睛 treat eyes
3 治病 [-] zhìbìng (treat-illness) <v.> treat, cure an illness: ~救人 save people by treating illnesses || 给人 ~ treat somebody's illness || 用植物~ use plants to treat a sickness
4 治疗 [-療] zhìliáo (treat-therapy) <v.> treat: ~皮肤病 treat a skin disease || 早期~ early treatment || 食物~ food therapy
5 诊断 [診斷] zhěnduàn (diagnose-judge) <v.> diagnose: ~病情 diagnose a condition || 早期~ early diagnosis || ~病人 diagnose a sick person
6 急救 [-] jíjiù (urgent-rescue) <v.> first aid: 进行~ be giving first aid || 需要~ require first aid || ~手术 emergency surgery
7 住院 [-] zhùyuàn (stay-hospital) <v-o.> be hospitalized: 住了三天院 be hospitalized for three days || ~治疗 be hospitalized for treatment || 生病~ be hospitalized for a sickness
8 打针 [-針] dǎzhēn (do-shot) <v-o.> get a shot: 打两针 have two shots || 打三次针 get a shot three times || 打完针 finish getting a shot
9 吃药 [-藥] chīyào (take-medicine) <v.> take medicine: 免费~ free medicine || 需要~ need to take medicine || 生病~ take medicine to cure an illness
10 消毒 [-] xiāodú (eliminate-poison) <v-o.> sterilize, disinfect: 消一下毒 quickly disinfect || 严格 ~ strict sterilization || 给餐具~ disinfect eating utensils
11 注射 [-] zhùshè (inject-shot) <v.> inject: 给病人~ give an injection to a patient || ~药物 inject a drug (medical) || ~疫苗 inject a vaccine
12 按摩 [-] ànmó (press-massage) <v.> massage: ~额头 massage the forehead || ~肩膀 massage the shoulders || 全身~ whole body massage
13 化疗 [-療] huàliáo (chemical-therapy) <v.> chemotherapy: ~三次 get chemotherapy three times || 进行~ be undergoing chemotherapy
14 输血 [輸-] shūxiě (transfuse-blood) <v.> transfuse blood: 及时~ timely blood transfusion || 体内~ internal blood transfusion || 大量~ a large blood transfusion
15 补牙 [補-] bǔyá (mend-tooth) <v.> fill a cavity: 无痛~ painless cavity filling || 免费~ free cavity filling || 第二次~ the second cavity filling
16 解剖 [-] jiěpōu (dissect-cut open) <v.> dissect: ~尸体 dissect a corpse || ~小白鼠 dissect a mouse || 人体~ dissect a body
17 手术 [-術] shǒushù (hand-technique/operation) <n./v.> operation: 外科~ surgical operation || 做~ do an operation || 动 ~ be operated on

18 医疗 [醫療] yīliáo (cure-treat) <v.> medical treatment: 公费/免费~ state-paid/free medical treatment || 农村~ rural medical treatment || ~费用 medical treatment for a fee

19 体检 [體檢] tǐjiǎn (physical-examination) <v./n.> checkup: ~合格 checkup met the standards || 健康~ health checkup || 参加~ undergo a health checkup

20 防治 [-] fángzhì (prevent-treat) <v./n.> prevent and treat: ~疾病 prevent and treat diseases || ~地方病 prevent and treat endemic diseases || ~艾滋病 (àizībìng) prevent and treat AIDS

21 流产 [-產] liúchǎn (mis – bear) <v./n.> miscarry, abortion: 人工~ artificial abortion || 药物~ drug-induced miscarriage

Tips:

1 ICU: Intensive care unit (ICU) is called 重症监护室 (zhòngzhèng jiānhùshì, literally 'severe-symptom-monitor-room.')

2 人工流产: Artificial or induced abortion is abbreviated as 人流, which also means 'a stream of people.'

3 按摩 (ànmó): It means 'massage,' which is a Chinese traditional medical treatment. However, for a long period of time following the Chinese economic reform, it has been used as a synonym for sex service.

Exercises:

Part I: Answer the following questions in Chinese.

1 在美国人工流产是不是合法的? 为什么?

---

2 你会不会每年体检? 为什么?

---

3 在美国一般大家怎么对待一般的感冒?

---

4 你觉得防治疾病重要还是治疗疾病重要? 为什么?

---

5 在你们国家有没有公费医疗? 你觉得一个国家是否应该有公费医疗? 为什么?

Theme 166: Struggle 斗争 (dòuzhēng)

1 备战 [備戰] bèizhàn (prepare for-war) <v.> prepare for war: 积极~ active preparation for war || 时刻~ constantly preparing for war || 紧张~ nervously preparing for war

2 征兵 [徵-] zhēngbīng (conscript-soldier) <v.> conscription: 大举~ large scale conscription || 冬季~ winter conscription
3 装备 [-備] zhuāngbèi (equip-equipment) <v.> equip: ~军队 equip the troops || ~空军 equip the air force || ~武器 equip with arms
4 阅兵 [閱兵] yuèbīng (review/parade-military) <v.> military parade: 国庆 ~ (Chinese) National Day military parade

5 斗争 [鬥爭] dòuzhēng (struggle-contend) <v.> struggle: 对敌~ struggle against the enemy || 地下~ secret struggle || 内部~ internal struggle
6 争夺 [爭奪] zhēngduó (fight-grab) <v.> fight against somebody for something: ~奖牌 fight for medals || ~市场 vie for the market || ~冠军 fight for the championship
7 反 [-] fǎn (turn over, violate) <v.> anti, opposed: ~战 anti-war || ~社会 anti-social || ~科学 anti-science
8 罢工 [罷-] bàgōng (stop-work) <v-o.> go on strike: 罢了两次工 go on strike twice || 开始~ start a strike || 举行~ hold a strike
9 抗议 [-議] kàngyì (protest-dispute) <v.> protest: 提出~ have a protest || 强烈 ~ intense protest || ~厂方 factory layoff protest (裁员)
10 游行 [遊-] yóuxíng (parade-march) <v.> march, demonstration: 上街~ march on the streets || 学生~ student protest || 参加~ take part in a demonstration
11 革命 [-] gémìng (to skin-life) <v./n.> revolution: 思想~ ideological revolution || 技术~ technological revolution || 参加~ take part in a revolution
12 起义 [-義] qǐyì (rise in rebellion-justice) <v./n.> uprising, revolt: 农民~ peasants' uprising || 武装~ armed revolts

Tips:

1 革命 vs. 起义: Although 革命 (gémìng, revolution) appears in one of the oldest books, 周易 (*I Ching*,) it was not in active use until after the Japanese Meiji Restoration when it was borrowed back to Chinese from Japanese. 辛亥革命 (Xīnhài Gémìng, Xinhai Revolution in 1911) is the first frequently mentioned 革命. 起义 (qǐyì, revolt, uprising) were common in the history of China. The first one is the Uprising of Chen Sheng and Wu Guang (陈胜吴广起义) in 209 BCE and the last one might be in the 1940s. 起义 focuses slightly on the nature of the beginning of a revolution, and is used only for political revolutions, but 革命 could be for science, technology, culture or even thoughts. For example, 工业革命 means 'Industrial Revolution' and 文化大革命 refers to 'Cultural Revolution.'

2 阅兵: It means 'military parade' or 'review troops.' It seems mostly the socialist countries such as North Korea, China and Russia, the former Soviet Union are active in holding military parades. Are they demonstrating strength to the domestic people to demonstrate national pride or to foreign countries for the purpose of intimidation?

3 兵制 (bīngzhì): It means '(type of) military service.' North Korea and South Korea have 征兵制 (zhēngbīngzhì, conscription military service,) but China and the United States have conscription that is unenforced.

Exercises:

Part II: Read the following sentences and fill in each blank with the appropriate word or phrase from the options given.

1 起义、革命、游行

a) 为了反对"白人至上," 波士顿人民进行了和平的________抗议活动.
b) 很多人认为中国现代________是从1927年毛泽东领导的秋收________开始的.

2 抗议、罢工、斗争

为了________政府的种族歧视 (qíshì, discrimination) 问题, 公共交通方面的黑人团体举行了大规模的________活动, 使这个城市的公共交通彻底瘫痪 (tānhuàn, halted) 了. 黑人团体相信只有通过________方式才能够获得应得的权利.

3 备战、征兵、阅兵、装备

a) 目前朝鲜正处在全民________状态, 每个人都觉得美帝国主义会很快侵略 (qīnlüè, invade) 他们的国家.
b) 为了加强国防, 朝鲜开始了大规模的________, 来保证军队的数量.
c) 2017年中国在天安门广场举行了一场________仪式, 目的是向全世界展示自己的现代化军事__________.

Theme 167: To attack, to defend 进攻, 防守 (jìngōng, fángshǒu)

1 进攻 [進-] jìngōng (forward-attack) <v.> attack: ~乡村/城市 rural/city assault || 发起~ initiate the attack || 正面~ direct attack
2 攻击 [-擊] gōngjī (attack-strike) <v.> attack: ~船队 attack the fleet || ~敌人 attack the enemy || 武力 ~ forceful attack
3 打击 [-擊] dǎjī (fight-strike) <v.> crack down on, strike: ~敌人 strike the enemy || 严重~ severe crackdown || 受到 ~ be struck
4 袭击 [襲擊] xíjī (raid-strike) <v.> make a surprise attack: ~敌人 attack the enemy by surprise || ~大城市 attack the city by surprise || 遭风暴/狼群~ be surprised by a storm/pack of wolves
5 驻 [駐] zhù (be stationed) <v.> be stationed: ~意大利 be stationed in Italy || ~新疆 be stationed in Xinjiang || ~在这里 be stationed here
6 侦察 [偵-] zhēnchá (detect-examine) <v.> scout, investigate: ~案情 investigate a case || ~敌情 scout the enemy || ~地形 scout the terrain
7 巡逻 [-邏] xúnluó (patrol-patrol) <v.> patrol: 空中~ air patrol || 海上~ sea patrol || 来回~ back and forth patrol
8 执勤 [執-] zhíqín (be on-duty) <v.> duty: 文明~ civilized duty || 认真~ serious duty
9 挑战 [-戰] tiǎozhàn (provoke-fight) <v./n.> challenge: 向他们~ challenge them || 充满~ full of challenge || ~难题 challenge the issue

10 战斗 [戰鬥] zhàndòu (battle-fight) <v.> fight: ~力fighting capacity || ~在一起 fight together || 并肩/团结 ~ fight side by side

11 作战 [-戰] zuòzhàn (do-battle) <v.> do battle: 与敌人~ do battle with the enemy || 英勇 ~ heroic battle || 山地~ mountain battle

12 抵抗 [-] dǐkàng (withstand-resist) <v.> resist: ~敌人 resist the enemy || ~疾病 resist a sickness || ~暴风雪 resist the snowstorm

13 对抗 [對-] duìkàng (oppose-resist) <v.> withstand, resist: ~外力 resist an external force || ~政府 resist the government || ~公司 confront a company

14 反抗 [-] fankàng (rebel-resist) <v.> resist, rebel: ~爸爸 rebel against father || 武装~ armed resistance || ~社会 rebel against society

15 防守 [-] fángshǒu (defend-defend/guard) <v.> defend: ~城墙 defend a wall || ~十号球员 protect the number ten player || 正面 ~ active defense

16 守 [-] shǒu (duty, abide by, guard) <v.> guard: ~城 defend a city || ~着她 guard her || ~在父母身边 keep watch on parents

17 保卫 [-衛] bǎowèi (protect-defend) <v.> safeguard: ~国家 defend your country || ~生命 safeguard your life || ~人民 defend the people

18 困 [-] kùn (surround, hinder) <v.> trap, surround: 被~在楼上 was trapped upstairs || 给~在一家旅馆里 be strapped in a hotel || 大风把他们~在船上 high wing kept them trapped on board (a ship)

19 包围 [-圍] bāowéi (enclose-encircle) <v.> encircle: 农村~城市. The countryside encircles the city. || 被敌人~ be encircled by the enemy

20 突破 [-] tūpò (break-broken) <v./n.> break through: ~困境 break through a dilemma || ~记录 break a record || 重大 ~ major breakthrough

21 撤退 [-] chètuì (withdraw-retreat) <v.> withdraw: 安全 ~ safe withdrawal || 全部~ complete withdrawal || 被迫~ forced to withdraw

22 逃走 [-] táozǒu (escape-flee) <v.> flee: 抱头~ flee with your head in your hands || 纷纷~ flee one by one || 中途~ halfway through running away

23 反击 [-擊] fǎnjī (counter-strike) <v.> strike back: 主动~ initiate a counter-attack || ~侵略 fight back against aggression || 自卫~ strike back in self defense

24 反恐 [-] fǎnkǒng (counter-terrorism) <v.> counterterrorism: ~行动 counter-terror actions || 国际~ international counterterrorism || 联合~ joint counterterrorism

25 声东击西 [聲東擊-] shēngdōngjīxī (feint-east-attack-west) feint to the east and attack to the west (create a diversion): ~是中国古代战争中经常使用的一种策略. Feinting to the east and attacking to the west is a common tactic used in ancient Chinese warfare.

Tips:

1 斗 (dòu, 鬥): The oracle form of 斗 (鬥) depicts 'two soldiers fighting, with weapons like spears on their backs,' therefore, 斗 means 'to fight.' Some say that Chinese people are 内斗内行 (háng), 外斗外行, which means 'be extremely good at internal strife, but an ignoramus at fighting external enemies.' Mao Zedong once said, "与天斗, 其乐无穷, 与地斗, 其乐无穷, 与人斗, 其乐无穷," which literally means 'struggle with the heaven, the joy is boundless, struggle with the Earth, the joy is boundless, struggle with somebody, the joy is boundless.'

2 三十六计 (Thirty-Six Stratagems): They are a series of stratagems used in war, politics and even the daily life of the Chinese people, therefore, it is very understandable that those stratagems are cherished not only by Chinese elites, but also by ordinary people. It is mind-opening to know those stratagems, whether in Chinese or in English.
3 声东击西: It is one of the Thirty-Six Stratagems mentioned above.

Exercises:

Part I: Use the given bound form as a guide to help you think of other words with the same character. Feel free to use your dictionary when needed. Then write down the English definition of each of the words you've written.

抗 *(resist, fight)* 抵抗 *resist, resistance*

____

____

____

击 *(beat, hit)* 打击 *attack, crack down on sth.*

____

____

____

____

____

____

Part II: Read the following sentences and fill in each blank with the appropriate word or phrase from the options given.

1 袭击、挑战、作战

a) 最近恐怖分子在西班牙突然进行了两次恐怖 (kǒngbù, terror) ________, 让西班牙老百姓感到十分危险. 看来世界和平问题正在面临新的_________.
b) 目前欧洲很多国家的军队都在进行训练, 以便提高军队的________能力.

2 防守、保卫、包围、撤退

a) 当敌人入侵时, 每个人都应该_________自己的国家.
b) 毛泽东用"农村________城市"的战略打败了蒋介石的军队, 取得了中国大陆的领导权.
c) 蒋介石在1949年的中国内战中战败, _______到台湾, 通过_______的方式延续 (yánxù, continue) 国民党在台湾的政权.

3 困、突破、声东击西

a) 这支军队被________在山里一个多月了，他们必须________敌人的包围才能活下来.
b) 据说毛泽东的军队就是因为运用______________的办法，才逃出了蒋介石军队的包围，最后发展壮大起来.

Theme 168: To capture, to surrender 攻占，投降 (gōngzhàn, tóuxiáng)

1 瞄准 [-準] miáozhǔn (take aim-front sight) <v.> take aim: ~目标 take aim at an objective || ~市场 target the market || ~时机 take aim at an opportunity
2 射击 [-擊] shèjī (shoot-strike) <v.> shoot: ~敌人 shoot at the enemy || 开枪~ fire a shot
3 发射 [發-] fāshè (launch-shoot) <v.> launch, shoot: ~炮弹 (pàodàn) shoot a shell || ~火箭 (huǒjiàn) launch a rocket || ~卫星 launch a satellite
4 炸 [-] zhà (explode) <v.> explode, bomb: ~敌人 bomb the enemy || ~平bomb flat || ~桥 blow up a bridge
5 爆炸 [-] bàozhà (burst-explode) <v.> explode: 发生~ an explosion occurred || 飞船~ airship explosion || 地雷~ landmine explosion
6 破 [-] pò (burst, break) <v.> break, destroy: ~坏destroy || ~纪录 break a record
7 退 [-] tuì (retreat) <v.> retreat: ~敌 retreat from the enemy
8 败 [敗] bài (ruin, fail, defeated) <v.> lose: 打~ be defeated || ~在他手下 lose at his hands || 不战而~ no war, but defeat
9 侵略 [-] qīnlüè (infringe-seize) <v.> invasion, invade: ~别的国家 invade other countries || ~别的民族 aggression against nationalities || 军事~ military invasion
10 入侵 [-] rùqīn (enter-invade) <v.> intrude, invade: 步步~ step by step invasion || 疯狂~ crazy invasion || ~大陆 invade the mainland
11 占据 [佔據] zhànjù (take-occupy) <v.> occupy: ~住所 occupy a residence || ~主导地位 hold the leading position || ~城市 occupy the city
12 占领 [佔領] zhànlǐng (occupy-administer) <v.> capture: ~市场 capture the market || ~农村 occupy the countryside || ~舞台 occupy the stage
13 夺取 [奪-] duóqǔ (seize-take) <v.> seize: ~天下 seize the world || ~城市 seize the city
14 征服 [-] zhēngfú (conquer-surrender) <v.> conquer: ~海洋 conquer the seas || ~听众 conquer an audience || ~邻国 subdue neighboring countries
15 解放 [-] jiěfàng (liberate-set free) <v.> liberate: ~思想 liberate the mind || ~自己 liberate oneself || 性~ sexual liberation
16 俘虏 [-虜] fúlǔ (capture-conquer) <v.> capture: ~三个士兵 capture three soldiers

Tips:

1 解放 (jiěfàng): 解放 means 'to liberate,' and the Chinese army, including marine and air force, are called (中国人民) 解放军 (People's Liberation Army, PLA.)
2 农村包围城市: It means 'encircle the cities from the rural areas,' which is one of the core theories of Mao Zedong Thought.

Exercises:

Part I: Read the following sentences and fill in each blank with the appropriate word or phrase from the options given.

1 瞄准、射击、发射

a) 为了更好地保护自己, 小张周末去学了__________ _. 对于初学者比较难的是怎么__________目标.
b) 中国已经独立________了很多人造卫星.

2 爆炸、破坏、不战而败

a) 恐怖主义分子制造了很多_________案件, ________了世界和平.
b) 中国古代的《孙子兵法》 (*The Art of War*) 这本书里有一个计策是通过心理战术让敌人__________, 如果拿到今天来说就应该是"最环保"的兵法.

3 侵略、占据、占领

a) 在人类历史上, 强国________弱国的事情经常发生.
b) 在图书馆小王经常坐的那个座位被一个陌生人________了.
c) 这家公司通过广告和打折的方式使他们的产品________了整个化妆品 (huàzhuāngpǐn, cosmetics) 市场.

4 夺取、征服、解放、俘虏

a) 这个足球队在今天的比赛中非常幸运, 连续进了三个球, 最后_______了冠军.
b) 纳尔逊·曼德拉 (Nelson Mandela) 一生都在为_________结束种族隔离 (jiéshù zhǒngzú gélí, end apartheid) 的事业而奋斗.
c) 古罗马帝国曾经________了欧洲的大部分地区.
d) 在日本文化里一般来说不赞成士兵做________, 如果战败士兵就要自杀.

Theme 169: Lawsuit 诉讼 (sùsòng)

(See also Theme 69)

1 打官司 [-] dǎguānsī (fight-lawsuit) <v.> go to court: 跟人~ file a lawsuit against sb.
2 诉讼 [訴訟] sùsòng (accuse-argue) <n.> lawsuit: 法律~ legal proceedings || 集体 (jítǐ) ~ class-action lawsuit || 提起~ file a lawsuit
3 起诉 [-訴] qǐsù (file-accusation) <v.> sue: 向法院~ sue in court || ~离婚 sue for divorce
4 撤诉 [-訴] chèsù (withdraw-lawsuit) <v.> drop a lawsuit: 依法~ legal withdrawal || 主动~ choose to drop a lawsuit || 申请~ apply to withdraw
5 胜诉 [勝訴] shèngsù (win-lawsuit) <v.> win a lawsuit: 很难~ a difficult to win case || 全面~ completely win the lawsuit
6 申诉 [-訴] shēnsù (appeal-accusation) <v./n.> appeal: 提出~ put forth an appeal || ~理由 reason for appealing || 到处~ many appeals

7 举报 [舉報] jǔbào (expose-report) <v.> report, inform: ~案件 report in a court case || 群众~ reported by the masses || 公开~ public informer

8 报案 [報-] bào'àn (report-case) <v.> report to the authorities: 主动~ choose to report to the authorities || 及时~ timely report || 紧急~ urgently report to the authorities

9 检举 [檢舉] jiǎnjǔ (select-report) <v.> inform against someone: 公开~ publicly inform || ~不法行为 report wrongdoing || ~贪官 inform on corrupt officials

10 揭发 [-發] jiēfā (expose-exposed) <v.> expose: ~黑暗 expose darkness || ~黑幕 (hēimù) expose shadiness || 大胆~ bold exposal

11 告状 [-狀] gàozhuàng (accuse-plaint) <v.> bring a lawsuit: 四处~ complain everywhere || 恶人先~ wicked people go to court first || 当面~ complain to someone's face

12 控告 [-] kònggào (appeal-accuse) <v.> accuse: 这个明星以诽谤罪~了这家报纸. This movie star sued this newspaper for libel.

13 上诉 [-訴] shàngsù (higher-appeal) <v.> appeal to a higher court: 提出~ lodge an appeal || 驳回 ~ reject an appeal || 如果你不服判决, 可以~. You can appeal if you do not accept the verdict.

14 投诉 [-訴] tóusù (file-complaint) (as a customer) <v.> complain: ~不法企业 complain about a shady business || ~自己的遭遇 complain about your bad experience || ~伪劣商品 complain about fake goods

15 交代 [-] jiāodài (confess-tell) <v.> confess, explain: ~罪行 confess to a crime || ~问题 explain a question || 坦白 ~ frank explanation

16 投案 [-] tóu'àn (surrender-case) <v.> surrender to the police: 他犯罪后打算到警察局去~. After his crime, he decided to turn himself into the police department.

17 自首 [-] zìshǒu (self-surrender) <v.> turn oneself in: 向警察~ surrender oneself to the police || 投案 ~ surrender oneself to the police or judicial department

18 认罪 [認-] rènzuì (admit-guilt) <v.> admit guilt: 低头~ plead guilty || ~悔过 plead guilty and repent

19 供 [-] gòng (confess) <v.> confess, admit: ~认 confess || 招~ confess crimes || ~出罪行 confess for the crime

20 串供 [-] chuàngòng (collude-confession) <v.> collude to make up a confession: 这些人相互~, 想否认原来的供词. They were in collusion and attempted to retract their testimony.

21 翻供 [-] fāngòng (overturn-confession) <v.> withdraw a confession: 他作了假供词, 后来又~. He made a false confession, which he later retracted.

Tips:

1 衙门口朝南开, 有理无钱莫进来: 衙门 (yámén) means 'government court,' and 莫 (mò) 'not.' The entry was a popular saying in ancient China. It means 'the gate of the government court is facing the south, do not go in if you have only justification but no money,' in other words, 'money talks at the court.'

2 吃了原告吃被告: 原告 means 'plaintiff' and 被告 'defendant.' This phrase means that judges openly or covertly demand bribes from both the plaintiff and the defendant. It was a common practice in the Chinese legal system.

Exercises:

Part I: Use the given bound form as a guide to help you think of other words with the same character. Feel free to use your dictionary when needed. Then write down the English definition of each of the words you've written.

诉 *(sue)* 起诉*sue*

____

____

____

____

____

____

供 *(confess, admit)* 供认 *confess*

____

____

____

____

Part II: Read the following words and phrases and the put the similar meaning words and phrases in the same table.

打官司、赢了官司、交代罪行、坦白罪行、自首、投案、供认罪行、揭发、举报

1.告状:
2.胜诉:
3.认罪
4.检举:

Theme 170: To arrest, trial 逮捕, 审判 (dàibǔ, shěnpàn)

1 抓 [-] zhuā (scratch, grasp, arrest) <v.> catch, arrest: ~坏人 arrest a bad guy || ~小偷 catch a thief
2 捕 [-] bǔ (catch, arrest) <v.> seize: 被~ be seized || 逮~ arrest || 抓 ~ catch
3 抓捕 [-] zhuābǔ (arrest-catch) <v.> catch: ~嫌疑 (xiányí) 人 catch a suspect || ~罪犯 (zuìfàn) catch a criminal || ~凶手 arrest a murderer
4 通缉 [-緝] tōngjī (order-seize) <v.> order the arrest of someone: ~逃犯 (táofàn) order the arrest of a fugitive || 公开~ publicly order an arrest || 正式~ formal arrest warrant
5 逮捕 [-] dàibǔ (arrest-chase) <v.> apprehend: ~三百人 arrest 300 people || ~嫌疑人 apprehend a suspect
6 捕获 [-獲] bǔhuò (catch-get) <v.> catch: ~猎物 (lièwù) catch prey || ~嫌疑人 catch a suspect || ~一条鲨鱼 (shāyú) catch a shark

7 查获 [-獲] cháhuò (inspect-get) <v.> track down (something illegal): ~毒品 track down drugs || ~假药 track down fake medicine || ~非法枪支 track down illegal firearms

8 破案 [-] pò'àn (crack-case) <v.> crack a case: 用指纹~ use fingerprints to crack a case || 全力~ all out effort to crack the case || 共同~ jointly crack a case

9 一网打尽 [-網-盡] yīwǎngdǎjìn (one-net-catch-all) <idiom> catch everything at once: 将犯罪团伙~ catch an entire criminal gang at once

10 押送 [-] yāsòng (escort-send) <v.> escort: ~俘虏 (fúlǔ) escort a prisoner || ~到东北 escort to the northeast || ~犯人 escort a criminal

11 搜 [-] sōu (hunt after, search) <v.> search: ~身 body search || ~了一夜 search for one night

12 搜查 [-] sōuchá (hunt after-search) <v.> search: ~公民住宅 search through citizen housing || ~他人身体 search his body || 非法~ illegal search

13 查抄 [-] cháchāo (search-confiscate) <v.> confiscate: ~家产 confiscate family belongings || ~假药 confiscate fake medicine || ~盗版图书 confiscate many pirated books || ~黑工厂 confiscate illegal factory

14 抄家 [-] chāojiā (confiscate-house) <v.> search a house and confiscate possessions: 到处~. Houses are being raided everywhere. || 抄了他的家. His house was searched, and his possessions were confiscated.

15 办案 [辦-] bàn'àn (handle-case) <v.> handle a legal case: 文明~ handle a case civilly || 独立~ handle a case independently || 依法 ~ handle a case according to law

16 审问 [審問] shěnwèn (try-inquire) <v.> interrogate, examine: ~犯人 interrogate a criminal || ~案件 examine a case || 反复~ repeatedly interrogate

17 逼供 [-] bīgōng (force-confession) <v.> force a confession: 刑讯~ use torture to force a confession

18 开庭 [開-] kāitíng (open-court session) <v.> open a court session: ~审理 open a hearing || 正式~ formally begin a court session

19 受审 [-審] shòushěn (stand-trial) <v.> stand trial: 出庭~ appear in court to be tried || 在监狱~ be tried in prison

20 审理 [審-] shěnlǐ (try-treat) <v.> try (legal): 专门~ special trial || ~案件 try a case || 依法~ legally try

21 审判 [審-] shěnpàn (try-sentence) <v.> bring to trial: 末日~ the Last Judgment || 公开~ try in open court || 重新~ re-try

22 公审 [-審] gōngshěn (public-try) <v.> public trial: ~主犯 publicly try a culprit || 开庭~ begin a public court trial

23 举证 [舉證] jǔzhèng (offer-evidence) <v.> offer evidence: 出庭~ appear in court to provide evidence || 公开~ publicly offer evidence || 充分~ fully prove

24 判 [-] pàn (to sentence) <v.> judge, sentence: ~死刑 sentence to the death penalty || ~三年 sentence to three years || ~得重 judge harshly

25 宣判 [-] xuānpàn (pronounce-judgment) <v.> pronounce judgment: ~死刑 sentence to the death penalty || 公开~ publicly sentence || 当庭~ pronounce judgment in court

26 判刑 [-] pànxíng (to sentence-punishment) <v.> sentence: ~十年 sentence to ten years || 判重刑 pass a heavy sentence || ~不当 improperly sentence
27 服刑 [-] fúxíng (serve-sentence) <v.> serve a sentence: 在监狱~ serve a sentence in jail || ~一年 serve a sentence of one year || 终身~ serve a life sentence
28 缓刑 [緩-] huǎnxíng (postpone-punishment) <v.> probation: ~三年 three years of probation
29 减刑 [減-] jiǎnxíng (reduce-sentence) <v.> reduce a sentence: 予以~ have a sentence reduced || 直接~ directly commuted || 再次~ another sentence reduction
30 刑满 [-滿] xíngmǎn (sentence-completed) <v.> complete a prison sentence: ~释放 serve a sentence and be freed || 到年底~ complete a prison sentence at the end of the year || ~出狱 get out of prison after completing a sentence
31 劳教 [勞-] láojiào (labor-education) <v.> reeducation through labor: ~两年 two years of re-education through labor

Tips:

1 抄家: It means 'to search a house and confiscate possessions,' which was common in ancient China and in the Cultural Revolution. Now it is very rare.
2 刑不上大夫 (xíng bú shàng dàfū): It means 'physical torture will not be applied to higher government officials,' which was a privilege of the officials in ancient China. For example, if an official committed a crime, which was punishable by beheading, the emperor would ask the official to hang himself. In the post-Mao Era, the common assumption that 刑不上常委 (members of Standing Committee of Political Bureau of CCP are exempt from penalties) was broken by Zhou Yongkang's conviction of corruption in 2015.

Exercises:

Part I: Use the given bound form as a guide to help you think of other words with the same character. Feel free to use your dictionary when needed. Then write down the English definition of each of the words you've written.

捕 *(catch, capture)* 被捕 *be captured*

____

____

____

审 *(examine, investigate)* 审问 *question the suspect*

____

____

____

判 *(judge, sentence)* 判死刑 *sentence to the death penalty*

____

____

____

刑 *(penalty)* 死刑 *the death penalty*

____

____

____

Part II: Answer the following questions in Chinese.

1 "一网打尽"的意思是:

a) 都抓到了 b) 渔网用完了 c) 用网把人打死了

2 你们国家有没有"死刑"? 你觉得"死刑"合理吗?

____

3 在你们国家能不能用暴力 (bàolì, violence) 审问犯人? 为什么?

____

4 你们国家有没有"劳教"? 你觉得"劳教"的惩罚 (chéngfá, punishment) 方法有用吗? 为什么?

____

Theme 171: To violate (a law), 违法 (wéifǎ)

1 犯罪 [-] fànzuì (commit-crime) <v-o.> commit a crime: 犯了什么罪 committed what crime? || 犯了大罪 commit a big crime || 犯了盗窃罪 be a thief
2 犯法 [-] fànfǎ (break-law) <v-o.> break the law: 犯了什么法? What law was broken? || 打人~ break the law by hitting someone
3 违法 [違-] wéifǎ (violate-law) <v-o.> illegal: 违了法 broke the law || ~行为 illegal behavior || ~活动 illegal activity
4 侵权 [-權] qīnquán (infringe-rights) <v.> violate rights: 当事人~ a legal party infringed on somebody's rights || 商标~ trademark infringement || 继续~ continuing violating rights
5 作案 [-] zuòàn (commit-crime) <v.> commit a crime: 共同 ~ jointly break a law || 多次~ repeatedly break laws || 连续~ serial law-breaking
6 绑架 [綁-] bǎngjià (bind-kidnap) <v.> kidnap: ~富商 kidnap a rich businessman || ~人质 abduct a hostage
7 撕票 [-] sīpiào (tear/kill-ticket/hostage) <v.> kill a hostage: 惨遭~ brutally kill a hostage || 被绑匪~ be killed by kidnappers
8 杀害 [殺-] shāhài (kill-murder) <v.> murder: ~动物 kill an animal || 残忍(cánrěn)地~了他的同事 murdered his colleague brutally

9 行凶 [-兇] xíngxiōng (do-violence) <v.> violent crime, commit a violent act: 企图~ attempt a violent crime || ~杀人 violently kill someone || 疯狂 (fēngkuáng) ~ crazy attack

10 投毒 [-] tóudú (apply-poison) <v.> poison: ~杀人 kill someone with poison || 蓄意 (xùyì) ~ deliberately poison

11 谋杀 [謀殺] móushā (scheme-kill) <v.> murder: ~游客 murder a tourist || 蓄意~ deliberately murder

12 枪杀 [槍殺] qiāngshā (gun-shoot) <v.> shoot dead: 惨遭~ be brutally shot dead || ~囚犯 (qiúfàn) shoot and kill a prisoner

13 滥杀 [濫殺] lànshā (arbitrarily-kill) <v.> massacre: ~无辜 (wúgū) massacre innocents || ~野生动物 massacre wild animals

14 捕杀 [-殺] bǔshā (catch-kill) <v.> catch and kill (an animal): ~稀有动物 kill a rare animal || 严禁~ forbid the killing of animals || 大量~ catch and kill many animals

15 暗杀 [-殺] ànshā (secretly-kill) <v.> assassinate: 惨遭~ be assassinated || ~总统 assassinate a president

16 屠杀 [-殺] túshā (slaughter-kill) <v.> butcher: 大肆~ wantonly butcher || ~百姓 slaughter commoners || 集体 (jítǐ) ~ collectively slaughter

17 血洗 [-] xuèxǐ (blood-flood) <v.> blood purge, massacre: 遭到~ suffered a massacre

18 洗钱 [-錢] xǐqián (launder-money) <v.> money laundering: 黑帮 ~ gangster laundering money || 越洋~ money laundering across the ocean || ~网络 launder money online

19 诈骗 [詐騙] zhàpiàn (swindle-deceive) <v.> defraud: 金融 (jīnróng) ~ financially swindle || 信用卡~ credit card fraud || 保险~ insurance fraud

20 敲诈 [-詐] qiāozhà (blackmail-cheat) <v.> extort: ~游客 rip off a tourist || ~一万元 extort 10,000 yuan || ~钱财 extort money

21 碰瓷 [-] pèngcí (crash-porcelain) <v.> a currently widespread fraud in PRC involving deliberately crashing cars then demanding compensation: ~骗钱 crash a car to get money

22 拐卖 [-賣] guǎimài (abduct-sell) <v.> buy and sell, traffic: ~儿童 traffic children || ~人口 traffic people

23 贪污 [貪-] tānwū (corrupt-embezzle) <v.> embezzle: ~公款 embezzle public funds || ~粮食 embezzle food

24 受贿 [-賄] shòuhuì (receive-bribe) <v.> take a bribe: ~三千元 take a 3,000 yuan bribe

25 作弊 [-] zuòbì (do-cheat) <v.> cheat: 考试~ cheat on a test || 严重~ serious cheating

26 抄袭 [-襲] chāoxí (copy-repeat) <v.> plagiarize, copy: ~别人 plagiarize from others || ~他人作品 copy others' works

27 剽窃 [-竊] piāoqiè (plagiarize-steal) <v.> plagiarize: ~别人文章 plagiarize from other people's essays || ~他人劳动成果 plagiarize from the fruits of other people's labor (their achievements)

28 侵吞 [-] qīntūn (infringe-swallow) <v.> take, embezzle: ~国家财产 embezzle national property || ~公款 take public funds

29 抢占 [搶佔] qiǎngzhàn (rob/forestall-take) <v.> seize: ~先机 seize an opportunity || ~地盘 control a site || ~土地 seize territory
30 侵占 [-佔] qīnzhàn (infringe-take) <v.> take, embezzle: ~教育经费 embezzle education funding || ~财产 seize property || 非法~ illegally seize
31 克扣 [剋-] kèkòu (embezzle-deduct) <v.> skim off (embezzle): ~工资 skim off of wages || ~生活费 embezzle from living expenses || 任意 (rènyì) ~ embezzle at will

32 贿赂 [賄賂] huìlù (to bribe-goods) <v.> bribe: ~政府官员 bribe a government official || 商业~ commercial bribery
33 行贿 [-賄] xínghuì (give-bribe) <v.> give a bribe: 向工作人员~ give a bribe to the staff || ~一万元 give a 10,000 yuan bribe
34 走后门 [-後門] zǒuhòumén (go-back-door) <v.> go in through the back door (use unofficial channels): 托关系~ use a relationship to get something done || ~上了重点中学use a relationship to go into a key school

35 走私 [-] zǒusī (traffic-illegal goods) <v-o.> smuggle: ~汽车 smuggle a car || ~货 smuggle goods || ~香烟 smuggle cigarettes
36 贩毒 [販-] fàndú (traffic-drugs) <v.> traffic drugs: 大肆~ wantonly traffic drugs
37 嫖娼 [-] piáochāng (patronize whorehouses-prostitute) <v.> visit prostitutes: 多次~ repeatedly visit prostitutes
38 卖淫 [賣-] màiyín (sell-prostitution) <v.> prostitution, prostitute oneself: 男性/女性~ male/female prostitution || 公开~ public prostitution
39 强奸 [強姦] qiángjiān (forcefully-rape) <v.> rape: ~妇女 rape a woman
40 抢 [搶] qiǎng (rob, grab) <v.> rob, take: ~钱 rob money || ~银行 rob a bank || ~东西 rob stuff
41 偷 [-] tōu (steal, pilfer) <v.> steal, pilfer: ~东西 steal stuff || ~钱 steal money || ~自行车 steal a bike
42 盗窃 [盜竊] dàoqiè (pilfer-steal) <v.> steal: ~珠宝 steal jewelry || ~商店物品 steal store merchandise

Tips:

1 窃钩者诛, 窃国者侯 (qiè gōu zhě zhū, qiè guó zhě hóu): This famous quotation is from 庄子 (Zhuangzi) and means 'He who steals a hook gets hanged as a crook, he who steals the kingdom makes himself a duke,' or 'Petty thieves are hanged, but usurpers are crowned.'
2 偷 (tōu), 盗 (dào), 窃 (qiè): All mean 'to steal,' but the object of 偷 is of less value and that of 盗, which is highly-valued. Therefore we have two words, 小偷 (pilferer) and 大盗 (usurper), but not 大偷 or 小盗. The combinations of these three words, 偷盗, 偷窃, 盗窃 have almost the same meaning.
3 碰瓷 (pèngcí): It means '(to pretend to be) hit/bumped and claim high compensation.' It derived from a practice in the late Qing Dynasty. Some people would hide 'famous fine China (瓷)' in their clothes and intentionally get bumped (碰) by others. The China would break and the owners would extort a high compensation. The contemporary way of 碰瓷 is to be hit by a car.

Exercises:

Part I: Use the given bound form as a guide to help you think of other words with the same character. Feel free to use your dictionary when needed. Then write down the English definition of each of the words you've written.

贿 *(bribe)*: 贿赂 *bribe*

____

____

____

____

杀 *(kill)* 自杀 *suicide*

____

____

____

____

Part II: Read the following words and then answer the questions.

作弊、抄袭、剽窃、走私、贩毒、拐卖人口、洗钱、敲诈、碰瓷、诈骗、盗窃、嫖娼、卖淫 贿赂、行贿、受贿、杀害、枪杀、投毒、暗杀、谋杀、侵吞国家财产

1 上面哪些犯罪基本上是在学术领域 (academia) 发生的?

____

2 上面哪些犯罪是在国际社会常见的?

____

3 上面哪些犯罪主要跟政府官员有关系?

____

4 上面那些犯罪跟"杀人"有关系?

____

5 上面哪些犯罪跟"偷"和"骗人"有关系?

____

6 上面哪些犯罪跟"性"有关系?

____

Theme 172: To punish, to pardon 惩罚, 赦免 (chéngfá, shèmiǎn)

1 查处 [-處] cháchǔ (investigate-prosecute) <v.> investigate and prosecute: ~非法行为 investigate and prosecute illegal behavior || ~不法分子 investigate and prosecute criminals || 依法~ legal investigation and prosecution

2 惩处 [懲處] chéngchǔ (punish-prosecute) <v.> punish (legal): 依法~ legal punishment || ~腐败 (fǔbài) 分子 punish corrupt people || ~毒品犯罪 punish drug criminals

3 扣 [-] kòu (deduct) <v.> deduct: ~工资 deduct from a wage || ~奖金 deduct from a bonus || ~钱 deduct money

4 没收 [-] mòshōu (confiscate-take) <v.> confiscate: ~财产 confiscate property || ~土地 seize land || ~他的书 confiscate his book

5 查封 [-] cháfēng (check-seal) <v.> close down: ~ 公司 close a company || ~厂子 close a factory || 非法~ illegal closure

6 剥夺 [剝奪] bōduó (exploit-deprive) <v.> deprive: ~政治权利 deprive of political rights || ~继承权 (jìchéngquán) deprive of an inheritance || ~生命 deprive of life

7 关押 [關-] guānyā (imprison-take into custody) <v.> imprison: ~ 犯人 imprison a criminal || ~五年 imprison for five years

8 拘留 [-] jūliú (arrest-keep) <v.> detain: ~人犯 detain a guilty person || ~十天 detain for ten days || 依法~ legally detain

9 入狱 [-獄] rùyù (be in-prison) <v.> be sent to jail: ~一年 imprison for one year || 三次 ~ jailed three times || 被捕~ arrested and sent to jail

10 坐牢 [-] zuòláo (stay in-jail) <v-o.> be in jail: 坐了两年牢 be in jail for two years

11 双规 [雙規] shuāngguī (double-designated) <v.> detain and interrogate (for political prisoners): 被~了 was detained and interrogated

12 处决 [處決] chǔjué (execute-put to death) <v.> execute: 立即~ immediately execute || ~逃兵 execute a deserter || ~犯人 execute a prisoner

13 偿命 [償-] chángmìng (pay-life) <v.> pay with your life: 以命~ a life for a life || 杀人~ kill someone and pay with your life

14 赦免 [-] shèmiǎn (pardon-release) <v.> pardon: ~凶手 pardon a murderer || ~他的死罪 pardon his crimes

15 大赦 [-] dàshè (great-pardon) <v.> amnesty: ~天下 amnesty for everything || ~囚犯 pardon a prisoner || 实行~ give amnesty

16 免刑 [-] miǎnxíng (release-punishment) <v.> exempt from punishment: 一人~ exempt someone from punishment

17 释放 [釋-] shìfàng (release-set free) <v.> release: 无罪~ find not guilty || 当场 ~ release on the spot || ~犯人 release a prisoner

18 出狱 [-獄] chūyù (go out of-prison) <v.> be released from prison: 刑满~ complete a sentence and be released || 提前~ early release from prison

19 保释 [-釋] bǎoshì (release on bail-release) <v.> bail: ~朋友出狱 bail a friend out of jail

Tips:

1 查封 (cháfēng): It means 'to close down a company or prevent people from entering a place by the authorities, usually the police.' Many decades ago, the doors or goods involved would be markedand glued with two crossed long strips of paper with two 封 (seal) and date on them.
2 双规 (shuāngguī): It is often found in Chinese political reports, meaning 'to confess one's crimes or wrongdoings to the Chinese Communist Party at a designated (规定的) place at a designated (规定的) time.'

Exercises:

Part I: Translate the following phrases into English and then answer the questions.

被捕入狱 ________________
关押犯人 ________________
刑满释放 ________________
大赦犯人 ________________
剥夺政治权利 ________________
惩处腐败分子 ________________
扣工资 ________________
没收财产 ________________
查封公司 ________________

1 在美国刑满释放的人会不会受到歧视? 为什么?

____

2 中国政府正在大力惩处 (chéngchǔ, penalize) 腐败分子, 你认为中国政府能够解决腐败问题吗? 为什么?

____

3 在美国老板是否可以随便扣工人工资? 为什么?

____

4 美国法律有没有剥夺公民的政治权利的规定? 你觉得合理吗? 为什么?

____

Theme 173: Religious activities 宗教活动 (zōngjiào huódòng)

(See also Theme 63)

1 祷告 [禱-] dǎogào (pray-tell) <v.> pray: 向上帝~ pray to god || 静静~ quietly pray || 集体~ pray in a group
2 祈祷 [-禱] qǐdǎo (pray-pray) <v.> pray: 向上帝~ pray to god || ~和平 pray for peace
3 许愿 [許願] xǔyuàn (make-wish) <v.> make a vow: 向上帝~ make a vow to god || ~给她加工资 vow to give her wages || 私下~ secret vow
4 做礼拜 [-禮-] zuòlǐbài (do-religious service) <v.> go to church: 在教堂~ be at a church service

5 做弥撒 [-彌-] zuòmísā (do-missa/mass) <v.> go to mass: 在教堂~ go to mass in a church

6 受戒 [-] shòujiè (receive-Buddhist monastic discipline) <v.> take oaths: 僧侣~ take oaths as a monk || 十六岁~ take oaths at 16 years old

7 受洗 [-] shòuxǐ (receive-baptism) <v.> be baptized: ~入教 be baptized and enter the church || 婴儿~ infant baptism || 无条件~ unconditional baptism

8 赐福 [賜-] cìfú (bestow/bless-fortune) <v.> bless: ~人类 bless mankind || ~给百姓 bless a commoner

9 朝拜 [-] cháobài (have an audience with-worship) <v.> worship, pilgrimage: ~圣地 make a pilgrimage to a holy land || 向天子~ worship the emperor

10 朝圣 [-聖] cháoshèng (have an audience with-sage) <v.> make a pilgrimage: 到西藏~ make a pilgrimage to Tibet

11 供奉 [-] gòngfèng (present with all respect-supply) <v.> consecration, offering: ~祖先 consecrate an ancestor || ~香火 incense offering

12 上供 [-] shànggòng (make-offer) <v.> make an offering: 烧香 ~ burn an incense offering || 给菩萨~ make an offering to the Buddha || 给领导~ give a gift to a leader

13 烧香拜佛 [燒---] shāoxiāngbàifó (burn-incense-worship-buddha) <idiom> burn incense and worship Buddha: 到寺庙~ go to the temple to burn incense and worship Buddha

14 算命 [-] suànmìng (tell-fortune) <v.> fortune telling: 给她~ tell her fortune || 看相 ~ read a fortune by appearance

15 看手相 [-] kànshǒuxiàng (read-palm) <v.> palm reading: 给他~ read his palm

16 算卦 [-] suànguà (tell-trigrams) <v-o.> use trigrams to tell fortunes: 抽签 ~ draw a fortune || 给她 ~ predict her fortune || 算一卦 count one trigram

17 占卜 [-] zhānbǔ (divine with milfoils-divine with tortoise shells) <v.> divine: ~吉凶 divine good and bad luck || ~胜负 divine an outcome || ~将来的职业 predict a future career

18 避邪 [-] bìxié (avoid-demon) <v.> avoid evil spirits: 以镜~ use a mirror to avoid evil spirits

19 冲喜 [沖-] chōngxǐ (counteract-wedding) <v.> marry to ward off a sickness: 娶媳妇~ marry a woman to cure a sickness

20 保佑 [-] bǎoyòu (protect-bless) <v.> blessing: ~平安 blessing of safety || 上帝~ god's blessing || ~父母长寿 blessing for parents' longevity

21 出家 [-] chūjiā (leave-home) <v.> leave home to be a monk: 半路~ become a monk part way through life || ~为僧 leave home to be a monk

22 修行 [-] xiūxíng (correct-behavior) <v.> practice Buddhism or Taoism: 带发~ bring the practice of Buddhism/Taoism || 刻苦~ strictly practice Buddhism/Taoism || 出家~ leave home to be a monk or nun

23 得道 [-] dédào (get-Tao/The Way) <v.> find The Way: ~成佛 find Buddhist enlightenment

24 一人得道, 鸡犬升天 [----, 雞---] yīréndédào, jīquǎnshēngtiān (one-person-get-The Way, chicken-dog-ascend-heaven) <v.> Once on person reaches enlightenment, his pets also go to heaven (one person's success benefits those around them).: 他当了大官以后，整个家族的人都得到了好处，真是~. When he

became a high-ranking officer, the whole family benefited. It's just like the saying that 'when a man attains the Tao, even his pets ascend to heaven.'

25 吃斋 [-齋] chīzhāi (eat-vegetarian diet) <v.> abstain from eating meat: 长期~ stop eating meat for a long time || ~念佛 abstain from meat and pray to Buddha || ~打坐 abstain from meat while meditating
26 念佛 [-] niànfó (pray-buddha) <v.> pray to Buddha: 专心 ~ concentrate on prayers || ~二十年 pray to Buddha for 20 years
27 念经 [-經] niànjīng (recite-scripture) <v.> recite scriptures: 高声~ loudly recite scripture
28 布道 [佈-] bùdào (preach-gospel) <v.> preach, give a sermon: 传经~ pass on doctrine in a sermon || 开坛~ preach at the altar
29 传道 [傳-] chuándào (spread-gospel) <v.> preach: 积极~ energetically preach
30 传教 [傳教] chuánjiào (spread-religion) <v.> do missionary work: 到非洲~ go to Africa to be a missionary
31 点化 [點-] diǎnhuà (enlighten-transform) <v.> enlightenment, transformation: ~众生 enlighten beings || ~凡人 transform a mortal
32 顿悟 [頓-] dùnwù (sudden-enlightenment) <v.> moment of enlightenment, satori: ~这个道理 a moment of realizing the Daoist truth || ~成佛 a moment of Buddhist enlightenment
33 布施 [佈-] bùshī (give-alms) <v.> practice of giving: ~钱财 give money || ~物品 donate money || ~给穷人 give to poor people
34 化缘 [-緣] huàyuán (beg-alms) <v.> monks' begging: 外出~ go out begging (as a monk) || 四处~ beg everywhere (as a monk)
35 化斋 [-齋] huàzhāi (beg-vegetarian food) <v.> beg for vegetarian food (as a monk): 沿路~ beg for food on the road || 和尚 ~ Buddhist monk begging for food

Tips:

1 儒释道 (rú shì dào): It is the Chinese literati's way to say Confucianism (儒家), Buddhism (佛教, fójiào, with the founder being 释迦牟尼, Shījiāmùní, Shakyamuni) and Taoism (道教.)
2 半路出家: Literally it means 'become a monk or nun late in life,' with a much more common extended meaning, 'adopt a profession rather late in one's life.' In this sense, the three authors of this dictionary are all 半路出家, since their Ph.D. dissertations are on experimental phonetics, syntax and history, respectively.

Exercises:

Part I: Read the following words and then answer the questions.

祷告、祈祷、许愿、做礼拜、做弥撒、受戒、受洗、朝拜、朝圣、烧香拜佛、看手相、算卦、算命、占卜、辟邪、冲喜、出家、得道、修行、吃斋、念佛、念经、传教、点化、顿悟、布施、化缘、化斋

1 上面哪些是佛教(Fójiào, Buddhism) 的宗教 (zōngjiào, religion) 活动?

____

2 上面哪些是基督教 (Jīdūjiào, Christianity) 的宗教活动?

3 上面哪些是伊斯兰教 (Yīsīlánjiào, Islam) 的宗教活动?

4 上面哪些是迷信 (míxìn, superstition) 活动?

Theme 174: To socialize 交际 (jiāojì)

(See also Themes 9, 65)

1 交际 [-際] jiāojì (associate-meet) <v./n.> communication: 互相~ mutual communication || 善于~ good at communicating || ~能力 ability to communicate
2 应酬 [應-] yìngchóu (deal with-reciprocate) <v.> social interaction: 出门~ go out for a social event || 无力 ~ socially inept || ~多 socialize a lot
3 交往 [-] jiāowǎng (associate-contact) <v.> associate with: 与人~ associate with someone || 友好~ friendly association || ~多/少 a lot/a little bit of interaction
4 来往 [來-] láiwǎng (come-go) <v.> contact, dealings: 跟他~ interact with him || 有/没有~ have/not have dealings with || 经济/信件~ economic/letter dealings
5 相处 [-處] xiāngchǔ (mutual-live) <v.> get along with, interact: 友好~ get along with in a friendly way || ~几天 interact with for a few days || 与人~ interact with someone
6 结交 [結-] jiéjiāo (get known-associate) <v.> make friends with: ~朋友 become friends with someone || ~网友 make an online friend || 跟农民~ become friends with a peasant
7 打交道 [-] dǎjiāodào (make-contact) <v.> come into contact with: 跟客户 ~ come into contact with a customer || 与市场~ deal with the market || 跟外国人~ come into contact with foreigners
8 拉关系 [-關係] lāguānxì (draw-ties) <v.> suck up to: 私下~ privately suck up to || 跟领导~ suck up to a leader
9 套近乎 [-] tàojìnhū (try to win-intimate) <v.> pal up with someone: 跟漂亮姑娘~ pal up with a pretty girl
10 约 [約] uē (cord, bind, arrange) <v.> invite, make an appointment: ~朋友去吃饭 invite a friend to dinner || 我~他星期天见面. I have an appointment to meet him on Sunday.
11 约定 [約-] yuēdìng (arrange-decide) <v./n.> arrange: ~见面时间 arrange a meeting time || 遵守~ keep an appointment
12 预约 [預約] yùyuē (forehand-arrange) <v.> make an appointment: ~服务 booking service || ~搬家 make an appointment to move || ~病人 make an appointment to see a patient
13 违约 [違約] wéiyuē (violate-agreement) <v.> breach a contract: 对方~ the other party breaches a contract || 背信~ breach of contract
14 失信 [-] shīxìn (lose-trustworthiness) <v.> break a promise: ~于人 break a promise to someone || 多次~ break many promises

15 看 [-] kàn (look) <v.> see, visit: ~朋友 see a friend || ~老师 see a teacher || ~长辈 (zhǎngbèi) see an elder

16 看望 [-] kànwàng (visit-visit) <v.> visit: ~病人 visit a sick person || ~朋友 visit a friend || ~奶奶 visit your grandmother

17 访问 [訪問] fǎngwèn (call on-visit) <v.> call on, visit: ~这位老人 call on this old person || 进行一次~ in the middle of a visit || ~一个国家 visit a country

18 作客 [-] zuòkè (be-guest) <v.> stay as a guest: 到家里~ come to this house as a guest || ~首都 be a visitor

19 出访 [-訪] chūfǎng (go-visit) <v.> go on an official visit: ~欧洲 go on an official visit to Europe || 多次~ many official visits || 先后~ successive official visits

20 上门 [-門] shàngmén (come to-door) <v-o.> drop in, visit: ~服务door-to-door service || ~费 house call fee

21 拜访 [-訪] bàifǎng (formally visit-visit) <v.> pay a visit: ~朋友 pay a visit to a friend || 上门~ come to visit

22 串门 [-門] chuànmén (walk in-door) <v.> drop in, visit sb.'s home: 互相~ visit each other || 去朋友家~ go visit a friend's house

23 等 [-] děng (class, equate, wait) <v.> wait for: ~车 wait for a car || ~船 wait for a boat || ~飞机 wait for a plane

24 等候 [-] děnghòu (wait-wait for) <v.> wait, wait for: ~ 结果 wait for results || ~消息 wait for news || 在门外~ wait outside

25 等待 [-] děngdài (wait-wait for) <v.> wait for, await: ~她的到来 wait for her to arrive || ~机会 await an opportunity || ~消息 wait for news

26 欢耳 [歡-] huānyíng (welcome-greet) <v.> welcome: ~客人 welcome a visitor || 热烈~ warmly welcome || 很受~ popular (receives lots of welcomes)

27 接 [-] jiē (meet) <v.> meet, pick up: ~人 meet someone || ~孩子 pick up a kid || 去机场~他 go to the airport to meet him

28 窃接 [-] yíngjiē (greet-meet) <v.> welcome: ~客人 welcome a visitor || ~新年 greet the new year || ~新生活 welcome a new lifestyle

29 会见 [會見] huìjiàn (meet-see) <v.> meet with a visitor: ~总统 meet with a president || ~外宾 meet with foreign guests || ~中国客人 meet with Chinese visitors

30 见面 [見-] jiànmiàn (see-meet) <v-o.> meet, see: 见一次面 meet once || 见过面 have met before || 跟朋友~ see a friend

31 陪 [-] péi (accompany) <v.> accompany: ~读 go with someone studying away from home || ~酒 drink with someone || ~聊 chat with someone

32 陪伴 [-] péibàn (accompany-accompany) <v.> keep company: ~客人 keep a visitor company || 轮流 (lúnliú) ~ keep company in turns

33 陪同 [-] péitóng (accompany-together) <v.> accompany (formal): ~代表团参观 accompany the visiting delegation || 全程~ accompanied the whole way

34 送 [-] sòng (see sb. off) <v.> see off: ~站 see sb. off at the station || ~客 see a visitor out || ~机 take somebody to the airport

35 送行 [-] sòngxíng (see sb. off-departure) <v.> see someone off: 给她~ send him off || 为他~ have a going-away party for him || 到机场~ go to the airport to see him off

36 告别 [-] gàobié (say-farewell) <v.> say goodbye to: ~家乡leave one's hometown || 和朋友~ say goodbye to friends || ~宴会farewell banquet

37 介绍 [-紹] jièshào (introduce-introduce) <v.> introduce: ~情况 introduce the situation || 自我~ self-introduction || ~一个朋友 introduce a friend

38 引见 [-見] yǐnjiàn (introduce-meet) <v.> present, introduce someone: 向总经理~ present to the general manager || 把约翰~给玛丽 introduce John to Mary

39 保送 [-] bǎosòng (recommend-send) <v.> recommend for admission to school: ~读博士 recommend to study for a Ph.D. || ~上大学recommend to go to college

40 推荐 [-薦] tuījiàn (recommend-recommend) <v.> recommend: ~ 一个学生 recommend a student || ~新书 recommend a new book

41 引进 [-進] yǐnjìn (introduce-from elsewhere) <v.> introduce: ~技术 introduce a technology || ~知识 introduce information || ~新东西 introduce something new

42 请 [請] qǐng (request, invite, ask) <v.> ask, invite: ~客人 invite a visitor || ~律师 request a lawyer || ~他去参观 invite him to visit

43 邀请 [-請] yāoqǐng (meet-invite) <v.> invite: ~她去我家 invite her to my home || 热情~ warmly invite || ~客人 invite a guest

44 对待 [對-] duìdài (deal with-treat) <v.> treat: 认真~ treat seriously || 分别~ treat separately || 平等~学生 treat students equally

45 看待 [-] kàndài (view-treat) <v.> regard, look upon: 如何~家庭 how to treat a family || 当母亲~ look on sb. as a mother || 同等~ regard as an equal

46 接待 [-] jiēdài (receive-treat) <v.> receive: ~客户 receive a client || 亲自~ personally receive || 热情~ warmly receive

47 虐待 [-] nüèdài (cruel-treat) <v.> mistreat: ~动物 mistreat an animal || ~儿童 mistreat a child

48 留 [-] liú (stay, ask sb. stay) <v.> remain, stay, ask sb. to stay, keep sb. where he is, detain: ~他吃饭 ask him to stay for dinner || ~他当老板detain him to serve as boss || ~她半年 ask her to stay here for half a year

49 赶 [趕] gǎn (catch up with, rush for, drive away) <v.> rush: ~出去 rush out || ~跑 drive away, expel || 别~她走 don't rush her out

50 收留 [-] shōuliú (take-stay) <v.> take in: ~三名病人 take in three patients

51 驱赶 [驅趕] qūgǎn (expel-drive away) <v.> drive away: ~出境 drive out of the country || ~人群 drive away a crowd || ~非法移民 drive out illegal immigrants

52 对付 [對-] duìfù (deal with-give) <v.> deal with: ~外人 deal with outsiders || ~危险 deal with danger || ~环境变化 deal with environmental change

53 应急 [應-] yìngjí (respond to-emergency) <v-o.> response to an emergency: 应应急 should respond to an emergency || ~办法 emergency responses || ~措施 emergency measures

54 敷衍 [-] fūyǎn (apply-disperse) <v.> be perfunctory, go through the motions: ~客人 be perfunctory towards guests || ~两句 two perfunctory remarks || 随便~ casually perfunctory, half-hearted

Tips:

1 见面: 见面 (to meet with) is a verb-object structure that does not require a direct object. You can say 跟朋友见面, or 见一个面, but not 见面他.

2 看望 vs. 访问: Both mean 'to visit,' but the object of 看望 are known people such as a friend(s) or a patient(s), whereas the object of 访问 could be a people or a place, known or unknown.

3 等 vs. 等待 vs. 等候: All mean 'to wait (for)' but the object of 等待 is abstract, such as 等待机会/消息. 等候 is more formal than 等. For example, 我会在门口等你 means 'I will wait for you at the door,' and 我会在门口等候你 means 'I will be right at the door waiting for you.'

Exercises:

Part I: Use the given bound form as a guide to help you think of other words with the same character. Feel free to use your dictionary when needed. Then write down the English definition of each of the words you've written.

约 *(invite)* 约朋友 *invite a friend*

____

____

____

____

访 *(visit)* 访问 *visit*

____

____

____

____

陪 *(accompany)* 陪伴*accompany*

____

____

____

____

待 *(entertain)* 接待 *receive a visitor*

____

____

____

____

Part II: Read the following sentences and fill in each blank with the appropriate word or phrase from the options given.

1 敷衍、应急、驱赶

a) 小王不喜欢现在的工作, 因此工作时常常随便________.
b) 小王父母常常劝小王要存一些钱, 以便_______使用.
c) 美国曾经 (céngjīng, once) 在19世纪的时候大规模_________亚洲移民.

2 收留、虐待、接待

a) 这位好心的老太太主动提出________那个无家可归的穷孩子.
b) 不管在美国还是中国, ________儿童都是违法行为.
c) 这个中国家庭20年前就开始__________来华学习的外国学生.

4 陪伴、陪同、送行

a) 在孩子成长的过程中, 父母的________非常重要.
b) 这个学校规定, 不准许在没有老师的________下进入化学实验室 (shíyànshì, lab).
c) 小王要去非洲工作了, 很多朋友来给他________.

5 会见、见面、迎接

a) 2017年3月, 美国总统特朗普________了中国国家主席习近平.
b) 特朗普总统在自己的私人俱乐部 (jùlèbù, club) __________习近平主席.
c) 小王跟客户约好早上十点在公司会议室________.

6 等候、拜访、串门

a) 小王在会议室________客户的到来.
b) 小王最近要去_________一位公司高层领导, 跟他谈谈公司发展的问题.
c) 小王没事的时候很喜欢到邻居家________.

7 拉关系、打交道

a) 有人说在中国做生意, __________、走后门非常重要.
b) 小王喜欢社交, 也善于跟各种人__________.

Theme 175: To speak 说话 (shuōhuà)

1 通信 [-] tōngxìn (communicate-letter) <v.> write a letter: 与朋友~ write a letter to a friend || 很少~ rarely write letters || 互相~ write letters to each other
2 拨打 [撥-] bōdǎ (dial-call) <v.> call: ~电话 call on the phone || ~手机 call with a cell phone || ~国际长途 make a long distance international call
3 邮 [郵] yóu (post, mail) <v.> mail: ~一本书 mail one book
4 邮寄 [郵-] yóujì (mail-send) <v.> send by mail: ~给学校 mail to the school || ~文件 mail a document || ~物品 mail goods
5 快递 [-遞] kuàidì (express-delivery) <v.> express delivery: ~到美国 express delivery to America || ~一个箱子 send a box with express delivery || 国际~ international express
6 寄 [-] jì (send, post) <v.> send by mail: ~信 send a letter || ~衣服 send clothes || ~钱 send money
7 汇 [匯] huì (remit) <v.> remit, send: ~钱 remit money || ~现金 remit cash
8 汇款 [匯-] huìkuǎn (remit-money) <v-o.> remit money: 汇一笔款 remit a sum of money || 到邮局~ go to the post office to send money || 直接~ directly remit money
9 说 [說] shuō (explain, speak, say) <v.> say, speak: ~清楚 speak clearly || 不停地~ constantly speak || 简单地~ speak simply

10 说话 [說話] shuōhuà (speak-word) <v.> talk: ~很慢 talk very slowly || 大声~ talk loudly || 爱~ love to talk
11 说明 [說-] shuōmíng (explain-clear) <v./n.> explain: 加以~ explain to someone || 详细地~ explain in detail || ~反复 explain repeatedly
12 讲 [講] jiǎng (say, speak, talk) <v.> speak, tell, say: ~ 汉语 speak Chinese || ~故事 tell a story || ~道理 speak reason
13 讲话 [講話] jiǎnghuà (talk-word) <v./n.> talk, present: 在大会上 ~ speak at a big meeting || 电视~ talk on TV || 会, 爱~ will, love to present
14 交流 [-] jiāoliú (mutual-communicate) <v./n.> communicate, exchange: 与他~ communicate with him || 互相~ mutual communication || ~思想, 感情, 经验 exchange ideas, feelings, experiences
15 谈 [談] tán (talk, discuss) <v.> discuss: ~体会 talk about experiences || ~看法 discuss a viewpoint || ~一个问题 discuss a question
16 谈话 [談話] tánhuà (talk-word) <v./n.> talk: 跟他~ talk to him || 谈两次话 talk twice || 个别~ individual tutorial/conversation
17 谈论 [談論] tánlùn (talk-discuss) <v.> talk about: ~一个问题talk about a question || ~别人talk about other people || ~这次展览talk about this exhibition
18 提 [-] tí (hold, raise, ask, suggest) <v.> mention: ~意见 mention an opinion || ~问题 mention a question || ~要求 bring up a requirement
19 提出 [-] tíchū (put-forward) <v.> put forward: ~看法 put forward an opinion || ~请求 put forward a request || ~建议 raise a protest
20 提问 [-問] tíwèn (raise-question) <v.> question: 自由~ freely question || 向她~ question her || 第二次~ the second question
21 问 [問] wèn (ask) <v.> ask: ~问题 ask questions || ~他们 ask them || ~消息 ask for news
22 问路 [問-] wènlù (ask-route) <v.> ask for directions: 向他~ ask him for directions || 投石~ throw a stone to find the way (test the waters)

23 演讲 [-講] yǎnjiǎng (explain-speak) <v.> give a speech: 公开 ~ give a public speech || 用英语~ give a speech in English || 在大会上~ make a speech at a convention
24 做报告 [-報-] zuòbàogào (make-report) <v.> make a report: 做两个报告 make two reports || 做书面报告 do a written report || 做口头报告 do an oral report
25 致辞 [-辭] zhìcí (extend-speech) <v.> make a speech: 即席 (jíxí) ~ make an off-the-cuff speech || 上台 ~ go onstage to make a speech || 分别~ speak separately

26 咬耳朵 [-] yǎo'ěrduǒ (articulate-ear) <v.> whisper in sb.'s ear: 对女儿~说 whisper in your daughter's ear || 跟同伴~ whisper in a companion's ear || 互相~ whisper in each other's ears
27 交头接耳 [-頭--] jiāotóujiē'ěr (cross-head-touch-ear) <idiom> whisper to each other: 纷纷~ whisper to each other in succession || 考生~ exam-takers whispering to each other || ~地议论着 whispered and talked
28 窃窃私语 [竊竊-語] qièqièsīyǔ (secretly-*reduplication*-privately-talk) <idiom> urgent, private whisper: 听众~ the audience whispers privately || 互相~ urgently whisper to each other
29 自言自语 [---語] zìyánzìyǔ (self-speak-self-talk) <idiom> think aloud: ~地说 talk to yourself out loud
30 吞吞吐吐 [-] tūntūntǔtǔ (swallow-*reduplication*-spit-*reduplication*) <idiom> speak hesitantly (hem and haw): ~不敢说 hesitate over something you are afraid to say

31 多嘴 [-] duōzuǐ (excessive-mouth) <v.> talkative: 嫌她~ talk too much to her || 有点~ a little bit talkative || 不敢~ afraid of talking too much

32 唠叨 [嘮-] láodāo (garrulous) <v.> chatter: ~两句 nagging || ~自己的事 prattle on about your own affairs || 爱~ love to chatter

33 耍嘴皮子 [-] shuǎzuǐpízi (show off-talk tricks) <v.> talk slickly: 跟警察~ talk slickly to the police

34 胡说 [-說] húshuō (recklessly-talk) <v.> talk nonsense: ~什么 talk nonsense about something || 别~ don't talk nonsense || 信口~ thoughtlessly talk nonsense

35 瞎扯 [-] xiāchě (blindly-gossip) <v.> talk randomly: 随意~ randomly talk about nothing || ~一大堆 talk a lot of nonsense

36 胡说八道 [-說--] húshuōbādào (northern people-talk-eight-scripture) <idiom> talk utter nonsense: 到处~ talk nonsense everywhere

37 倾诉 [傾訴] qīngsù (totally-tell) <v.> say everything on your mind: ~烦恼 pour out troubles || 互相~ tell each other everything || 向人~ tell someone everything on your mind

38 说实话 [說實話] shuōshíhuà (speak-true-word) <v.> speak the truth: ~, 我现在真高兴. to tell the truth, I am very happy || ~, 我真不知道他在哪儿. To tell the truth, I have no idea where he is || 决不~ not at all the truth

39 直说 [-說] zhíshuō (straight-speak) <v.> say directly: 直话~ speak frankly || 有话~ please speak frankly || 那我就~了. Then I'll speak very frankly.

40 实话实说 [實話實說] shíhuàshíshuō (true-word-truly-speak) <idiom> speak frankly: 跟家长~ speak frankly with parents || 向群众~ tell the truth to the masses

41 开门见山 [開門見-] kāiménjiànshān (open-door-saw-mountain) <idiom> get right to the point: ~地说明来意. Explain why you came right away. || ~地问. Get right to the point with the question. || ~地对记者说 get right to the point with a reporter

42 打开天窗说亮话 [-開--說-話] dǎkāi tiānchuāng shuō liàng huà (open-roof-window-speak-frank-word) <proverb> frankly speaking, let's not mince matters, not beat around the bush: 你~, 为什么不同意他们的婚事? Frankly speaking, why don't you agree with their marriage?

43 花言巧语 [---語] huāyánqiǎoyǔ (flowery-speech-deceitful-language) <idiom> flowery speech with no substance: 对女孩子~ speak prettily to a little girl || ~地想借钱 flatter someone to borrow money

44 能说会道 [-說會-] néngshuōhuìdào (able to-speak-good at-talk) <idiom> have the gift of the gab, be a glib talker: 个个~. They are all glib talkers.

45 唱高调 [--調] chànggāodiào (sing-high-tune) <v.> speak with fancy words: 少~, 多干事实. Be less vocal and more practical.

46 纸上谈兵 [紙-談-] zhǐshàngtánbīng (paper-on-talk-military) <idiom> military tactics on paper, armchair strategist: ~不能解决实际问题. Theoretical discussions won't fix real problems

47 夸大 [誇-] kuādà (flaut-big) <v.> exaggerate: ~难度 exaggerate the difficulty || ~损失 exaggerate a loss || ~病情 exaggerate a sickness

48 夸张 [誇張] kuāzhāng (flaut-enlarge) <v.> overstate: 语言~ hyperbolic language || 动作~ overstated actions

49 吹牛 [-] chuīniú (blow-cow) <v.> boast: 大声~ loudly boast || ~聊天 chat and brag

50 说大话 [說-話] shuōdàhuà (talk-big-word) <v.> talk big, brag, boast: 空口~ brag, boast || 喜欢~ like to talk big

51 吹捧 [-] chuīpěng (exaggerate-flatter) <v.> flatter: 相互~ flatter each other || 极力~ laud sb. to the skies

52 交谈 [-談] jiāotán (mutual-talk) <v.> talk with, have a conversation: 友好~ chat friendly || 用中文流利地~ talk fluently in Chinese || 跟朋友~ talk with friends

53 对话 [對話] duìhuà (bilateral-talk) <v./n.> dialogue: 师生~ teacher-student dialogue || 公开~ public dialogue || 第三次~ the third dialogue

54 插话 [-話] chāhuà (cut in-word) <v.> interrupt, chip in: 插一句话 interrupt for a sentence || 几次~ some interruptions || 不断~ constantly interrupting

55 抢话 [搶話] qiǎnghuà (grab-word) <v.> try to get the first word in: 抢她的话 try to get the first word in before her || 老~ always speak at once

56 打官腔 [-] dǎguānqiāng (talk-bureaucratic-accent) <v.> talk like a bureaucrat: 在下级面前 ~ talk officiously to a subordinate || 跟老百姓~ talk like a bureaucrat with a commoner

57 无话不说 [無話-說] wúhuàbùshu (no-word-can't-talk) <idiom> keep nothing from each other: 跟朋友~ keep nothing from a friend || 对媒体~ keep nothing from the media

58 聊 [-] liáo (chat) <v.> chat: ~工作 chat about work || ~家庭 chat about family || ~生活 chat about life

59 聊天儿 [--兒] liáotiānr (chat-aimlessly) <v-o.> chat: 聊一会儿天 chat for a little bit || 跟她~ chat with her || 网上~ online chat

60 侃大山 [-] kǎndàshān (piffle-big-mountain) <v.> chatter idly, boast or brag: 跟朋友~ chatter idly with a friend

61 拉家常 [-] lājiācháng (chat-domestic-trivia) <v.> talk or chat about ordinary daily life: 跟老人~ talk about ordinary life with an old person || 和大家 ~ chat about ordinary life with everybody

Tips:

1 言: The lower part of the oracle form of 言 is 舌 (shé, tongue) and the upper part is 一 which means 'something out of tongue,' therefore the whole character means 'to say, to speak.' When used as a radical, 言 is simplified as 讠. Most characters related to 'speak' have this radical, for example, 说, 话, 语, 讲, 谈, 论, 议. The simplified 夸 (kuā, to praise) does not have the radical, however, the traditional form 誇 does have it.

2 胡说八道: It means 'to talk nonsense.' There used to be a saying "胡人来说八道经" (the Chinese northern peoples preach eight scriptures), which means they are 'not reliable, talk nonsense' and was later shortened to 胡说八道.

3 吹牛: 吹牛 means 'to boast' and there are two variants. One is 吹牛皮, and the other 吹牛逼 (chuīniúbī) or 吹牛B. The 逼 and B are actually substituted forms of a colloquial taboo word meaning 'vagina.'

4 侃大山: 侃 (kǎn) means 'to talk nonsense' and 侃大山 means 'gossip.' It is said this phrase is the Beijing dialect 砍大山, which depicts 'a reckless man is brave enough to chop a big mountain.' Of course that is nonsense.

5 巧言令色鲜矣仁 (qiǎoyán lìngsè xiǎn yǐ rén): This is a quotation from Confucius and it significantly shaped the character of the Chinese people by making them despise people who are talkative. The maxim means 'fine words and an insinuating appearance are seldom associated with true virtue.' 仁 (rén, benevolent, benevolence) is one of the core values of the Confucianism.

Exercises:

Part I: Read the following words and then answer the questions.

聊天、侃大山、拉家常、插话、抢话、吹牛、说大话、花言巧语、耍嘴皮子、打开天窗说亮话、直说、开门见山、咬耳朵、交头接耳、窃窃私语、胡说、瞎扯、胡说八道

1.在上面表格的词中找出跟"聊天"意思相近的两个词:

______

2 在你们国家文化里大人们说话时小孩子来插话、抢话是不是礼貌行为?为什么?

______

3 "吹牛"跟上面哪个词的意思相近?

______

4 "耍嘴皮子"跟上面哪个词的意思相近?

______

5 "打开天窗说亮话"跟上面哪些词的意思相近?

______

6 "咬耳朵"跟上面哪些词的意思相近?

______

7 "胡说"跟上面哪些词的意思相近?

______

Part II: Read the following sentences and fill in each blank with the appropriate word or phrase from the options given.

1 无话不说、实话实说、纸上谈兵

a) 小张跟小王是好朋友, 他们__________.
b) 美国的政客基本都做不到__________ _.
c) 一般来说公司不愿意雇佣 (gùyōng, hire) 没有工作经验的工商管理硕士 (shuòshì, MBA), 他们认为这些人只会_________.

2 夸大、夸张、打官腔

a) 《纽约时报》 (*The New York Times*) 的记者很喜欢_________美国的种族冲突问题.
b) 有人说这位总统说话的时候表情太__________.
c) 中国的一些政府官员喜欢说话________, 老百姓非常不喜欢.

3 邮寄、快递、汇款

a) 使用美国邮局的服务________东西到中国又慢又贵.
b) 中国_________业发展非常迅速, 很多城市都可以实现24小时内到达.
c) 用软件________又快又方便, 所以在中国很少有人到邮局去寄钱.

Theme 176: To express 表达 (biǎodá)

1 告诉 [-訴] gàosù (report-tell) <v.> tell: ~他们一个消息 tell them a piece of news

2 通知 [-] tōngzhī (pass on-known) <v./n.> notify: ~开会 notify publicly || 重要~ important notification || 发~ send a notification

3 通报 [-報] tōngbào (pass on-notice) <v.> circulate a notice: ~情况 circulate a notice about the situation || ~表扬 circulate a notice of commendation || ~全校 notify the whole school

4 传达 [傳達] chuándá (pass-arrive) <v.> pass on: ~命令 pass on an order || ~感情 communicate a feeling || ~意义 pass on the meaning

5 报告 [報-] bàogào (report-announce) <v.> report: ~ 老板 report to a boss || ~工作 report on work || ~一个好消息 report on a good piece of news

6 发言 [發-] fāyán (deliver-speech) <v./n.> speak: 在大会上~ speak at the conference || 第一个 ~ the first speech || ~一分钟 speak for one minute

7 预报 [預報] yùbào (fore – cast) <v.> forecast: 地震 (dìzhèn) ~ earthquake forecast || 天气~ weather forecast || ~水温 forecast the water temperature

8 直播 [-] zhíbō (live-broadcast) <v.> live broadcast: 现场~ live on-site broadcast || ~比赛 live game || ~新闻 live news

9 暗示 [-] ànshì (indirect-show) <v./n.> hint, suggestion: 得到~ get a hint || ~要辞职 hint at resigning || 自我~ self-suggestion

10 叮嘱 [-囑] dīngzhǔ (exhort-enjoin) <v.> warn: ~孩子不要迟到 warn kids not to be late || 反复~ warn over and over again || 再三~ repeatedly warn

11 打听 [-聽] dǎtīng (to make-hear) <v.> ask about: ~消息 ask about the news || ~事情 ask about something || ~清楚 find out clearly

12 答 [-] dá (reply, answer) <v.> answer, reply: ~话 answer || ~错/对 answer right/wrong || ~不出/上 cannot answer

13 回答 [-] huídá (reply-answer) <v/ n.> answer: ~问题 answer a question || 大声~ loudly answer || 正确的~ correct answer

14 答复 [-覆] dáfù (answer-reply) <v./n.> answer, reply: 得到~ receive a reply || 书面~ written reply ||予以~ offer a (formal) reply

15 应对 [應對] yìngduì (respond-cope with) <v.> respond: ~国际竞争 respond to international competition || ~自如 respond freely || ~调查 respond to a survey

16 回复 [-復] huífù (reply-reply) <v.> reply to: ~ 邮件 reply by mail || ~来信 reply to a letter

17 回应 [-應] huíyìng (reply-respond) <v.> respond: ~观众的问题 respond to questions from the audience || 积极~ energetic response || 直接~ direct response

18 交代 [-] jiāodài (turn to-replace) <v.> explain, hand over: 把工作~清楚explain one's job clearly on handing it over || ~任务give information about a job

19 留言 [-] liúyán (leave-words) <v./n.> leave a message: 给他~ leave him a message || 电话~ phone message || 写~ write a message

20 表达 [-達] biǎodá (express-deliver) <v.> express: ~意思 express meaning || ~感情 express a feeling || 口头~ verbally express

21 表明 [-] biǎomíng (express-clear) <v.> make clear: ~态度 make clear an attitude || ~决心 clearly express determination || 事实~ make the facts clear

22 表示 [-] biǎoshì (express-show) <v.> show: ~感谢 show thanks || ~欢心 extend a welcome || ~关心 show concern

23 强调 [-調] qiángdiào (strong-tone) <v.> stress, emphasize: ~指出 stress a point || ~重点 emphasize a focus || 一再~ repeatedly emphasize

24 指出 [-] zhǐchū (point-out) <v.> point out: ~缺点 point out a shortcoming || ~错误 point out a mistake || ~一条路 point out a way (road)

25 打断 [-斷] dǎduàn (make-interrupt) <v.> interrupt: ~他的话 interrupt his speech || ~我的回忆 interrupt my recollection || ~她的介绍 interrupt her introduction

26 干涉 [-] gānshè (interfere-involve) <v.> interfere: ~别人 interfere with others || 进行~ in the process of interfering || ~婚姻 interfere with marriage

27 干预 [-預] gānyù (interfere-intervene) <v.> intervene: ~生产 intervene in production || ~市场 intervene in the market || 间接~ indirectly intervene

28 互动 [-動] hùdòng (mutual-act) <v.> interact: 跟他~ interact with him || 网上~ online interaction || ~游戏 interactive game

29 透露 [-] tòulù (leak-reveal) <v.> leak: ~消息 leak news || ~姓名 leak a name || ~秘密 leak a secret

30 承认 [-認] chéngrèn (receive-recognize) <v.> admit: ~事实 admit a fact || ~错误 acknowledge an error || 得到~ receive an admission

31 否定 [-] fǒudìng (deny-confirm) <v.> deny, reject: ~中医 reject Chinese medicine || ~别人 deny others || 完全 ~ complete denial

32 否认 [-認] fǒurèn (deny-admit) <v.> deny: ~个人的努力 deny someone's effort || ~这种说法 deny this type of statement || 公开~ publicly deny

33 论述 [論-] lùnshù (discuss-narrate) <v./n.> treatise, discourse, exposition: ~问题 discuss a question || 具体~ specific exposition || 多次~ many expositions

34 陈述 [陳-] chénshù (state-narrate) <v.> state, declare: ~ 事实 state a fact || ~意见 state a view || 简单~ simply declare

35 描述 [-] miáoshù (describe-narrate) <v.> describe: ~情况 describe the situation || ~感受 describe feelings || 详细~ detailed description

36 描写 [-寫] miáoxiě (describe-depict) <v.> depict, portray: ~生活 portray a lifestyle || ~故事 describe a story || ~生动 depict vividly

37 提起 [-] tíqǐ (mention-*suffix*) <v.> mention: ~这件事情 mention this thing || ~我的老板, . . . speaking of my boss, . . . || ~这个笑话 mention this joke

38 提示 [-] tíshì (mention-hint) <v.> prompt, point out: 他~她时间不早了. He hinted her that time is late. || ~他还书 prompt him to return a book || ~几点 point out a few things

39 形容 [-] xíngróng (describe-appearance) <v.> describe: 无法~ can't be described || ~不好 describe poorly || ~词 adjective

40 询问 [詢問] xúnwèn (inquire-ask) <v.> ask about: ~情况 ask about the situation || ~年龄 ask about an age || ~原因 inquire about the reason

41 咨询 [-詢] zīxún (consult-inquire) <v.> consult: ~问题 consult on an issue || 信息~ information consulting || 技术 ~ technical consulting || ~公司 consulting firm/company

Tips:

1 预*: 预 (yù) means 'in advance.' If it is followed by a verb in a compound word, it means 'pre-, fore-,' for example, 预报 and 预习 in this unit, and 预警 (yùjǐng, prewarn,) 预备 (yùbèi, prepare,) 预热 (yùrè, preheat,) 预售 (yùshòu,

pre-sale,) 预告 (yùgào, advance notice,) 预测 (yùcè, predict,) 预约 (yùyuē, make an appointment).

2 露: When functioning as a verb, 露 is pronounced as lù in standard Chinese, but has a colloquial pronunciation lòu. The Chinese are cautious not to 露白 (lòubái, reveal silver on you), which means 'not to let others know you have (a large amount of) cash with you.' When meaning 'dew,' 露 is pronounced as lù, not lòu.

3 否 (fǒu): The meaning of 否 is straightforward, 'say' (口) 'no' (不,) for example, 否定 (negate,) 否认 (deny.) 否则 means 'if not this way, then. . .' 是否 and 能否 mean 'is or not' and 'can or not,' respectively.

Exercises:

Use the given bound form as a guide to help you think of other words with the same character. Feel free to use your dictionary when needed. Then write down the English definition of each of the words you've written.

回 ***(reply, return):*** 回复 ***reply***

____

____

____

____

表 ***(express):*** 表现 ***show, display***

____

____

____

述 ***(state, narrate):*** 表述 ***explain sth. Precisely***

____

____

____

否 ***(no):*** 否定 ***deny, reject***

____

____

____

预 ***(in advance):*** 预习 ***preview***

____

____

____

Theme 177: To criticize 批评 (pīpíng)

(See also Theme 184)

1 批评 [-評] pīpíng (criticize-comment) <v.> criticize: ~学生 criticize a student || ~了一顿 criticized once || 公开~ public criticism
2 批判 [-] pīpàn (comment-judge) <v.> criticize: 彻底~ thoroughly criticize || 无情地~ ruthlessly criticize
3 提意见 [--見] tíyìjiàn (raise-opinion) <v.> make a comment on an issue, a proposal etc., make a complaint: 给领导~ give a leader suggestion || 我要见你们经理~. I want to see your manager to file a complaint.
4 驳斥 [駁-] bóchì (refute-rebuke) <v.> contradict: ~谎言 (huǎngyán) refute a lie || 进行~ be contradicting something || ~外方说法 contradict a foreign argument

5 怪 [-] guài (blame) <v.> blame: 都~他把事情搞砸 (zá)了. It's all his fault as he messed things up. || ~别人 blame others || ~父母 blame parents
6 骂 [罵] mà (abuse, scold) <v.> curse, scold: ~人 curse at someone || ~脏话 (zānghuà) swear || ~一顿 get a tongue-lashing
7 指责 [-責] zhǐzé (censure-reproach) <v.> criticize, blame: ~他自私 criticize him for being selfish || ~一顿 blame || 遭到/受到~ suffer/receive blame
8 责备 [責備] zébèi (blame-complete) <v.> blame: ~自己 blame oneself || 大声~ loudly blame
9 谴责 [譴責] qiǎnzé (condemn-reproach) <v.> condemn: 强烈~ strongly condemn || ~自己 condemn yourself || 加以~ be condemned

10 笑 [-] xiào (smile, laugh) <v.> laugh: 别~我！ don't laugh at me! || ~你傻 laugh at your silliness || ~他的发音 laugh at his pronunciation
11 笑话 [-話] xiàohuà (laugh-stock) <v.> joke, laugh at: 别~她! Don't laugh at her! || ~他笨 laugh at his stupidness
12 嘲笑 [-] cháoxiào (ridicule-laugh) <v.> ridicule: ~富二代 ridicule the rich second generation || ~现实 ridicule reality
13 讽刺 [諷-] fěngcì (satirize-mock) <v.> satirize, mock: ~别人 mock others || ~现实 mock reality
14 嘲讽 [-諷] cháofěng (deride-satirize) <v.> sneer at, ridicule: ~她的职业 sneer at her career || ~自己 ridicule yourself

15 诽谤 [誹謗] fěibàng (calumniate-defame) <v.> slander: 背后~ slander others behind their back || ~他人 slander others || 恶意~ malicious slander
16 贬低 [貶-] biǎndī (belittle-low) <v.> belittle: ~对手 belittle the opponent || ~妇女 belittle women || ~别人 belittle other people

Tips:

1 骂 (mà): 骂 is related to 吅 (xuān, loud noise) and 马 (mǎ,) meaning 'to abuse, curse, scold.' There is a popular tongue twister: 妈妈骑马, 马慢妈妈骂马 (māma qímǎ, mǎ màn māma mà mǎ. Mom rides a horse. The horse is slow and mom scolds the horse.)
2 批评 (pīpíng) vs. 批判 (pīpàn): Both mean 'to criticize' but 批判 is much more severe than 批评. A teacher or a parent can 批评 his student or child,

but does not 批判 him, because the receiver of 批判 must have done something seriously wrong and harmful to many people. The doer of 批判 usually has some authority and fame.

3 诽谤罪 (fěibàngzuì, crime of defamation): Defamation (诽谤) is condemned in ancient and modern societies, but in ancient China, there was a crime named '腹诽' (fùfěi), which means 'one criticizes the emperor in his heart (腹, belly.)'

4 责: The original meaning of 责 is 债 (zhài, debt), since it is related to 贝 (money.) Now the main meanings of 责 include 'blame' as in words such as 责备 and 'duty' as in words such as 责任.

5 责备: It means 'blame (责) others for not having done something perfectly (备, complete.)' There is an idiom 求全责备, which preserves the original meaning of 责备.

Exercises:

Part I: Multiple Choice. Make sure to choose the most appropriate answer.

1 小张因为家里有钱, 常常__________比他穷的孩子.
A. 笑话 B. 怪 C. 批

2 小张公司的员工不敢向老板_________, 因为他们怕老板解雇他们.
A. 驳斥 B. 提意见 C. 批评

3 小张管理公司的方法很差, 常常_________员工, 因此大家都在背地里_______他.
A. 批判、笑 B. 批评、骂 C. 批判、怪

4 很多人在网上写一些关于中国领导人的政治笑话来_________中国政治.
A. 讽刺 B. 提意见 C. 驳斥

5 这位总统对参加南方抗议活动的双方都进行了__________ __.
A. 谴责 B. 嘲笑 C. 诽谤

6 美国法律规定, 随意_________别人是违法的, 要受到法律制裁 (zhìcái, punish).
A. 笑 B. 诽谤 C. 嘲笑

7 最近美国总统__________ _中国政府在朝鲜问题上无所作为.
A. 指责 B. 骂 C. 笑

8 小张期末考试没有一门功课及格, 妈妈知道以后狠狠地_______了他.
A. 批判 B. 责备 C. 驳斥

Theme 178: To praise, to congratulate 赞扬, 祝贺 (zànyáng, zhùhè)

1 夸 [誇] kuā (praise) <v.> praise: ~学生 praise a student || ~自己 praise yourself || ~她聪明 praise her intelligence

2 夸奖 [誇獎] kuājiǎng (praise-encourage) <v.> praise: ~别人的孩子 praise other people's children || ~两句 say a few words of praise || 连连~ praise over and over

3 赞赏 [讚賞] zànshǎng (eulogize-appreciate) <v.> appreciate: 得到~ receive appreciation || ~他的话 appreciate his words || 大加~ greatly appreciated

4 称赞 [稱讚] chēngzàn (claim-eulogize) <v.> praise, commend: ~他中文说得很好 praise him for speaking Chinese very well || 受到~ receive praise || 值得~ worthy of praise

5 赞美 [讚-] zànměi (eulogize-praise) <v.> admire, praise: ~自然 admire nature || ~女性 admire women || 一致~ unanimously praise

6 叫好 [-] jiàohǎo (shout-good) <v.> applaud: 连声~ applaud repeatedly || 齐声~ applaud in unison || 为他~ applaud him

7 祝 [-] zhù (pray, wish) <v.> wish: ~全家身体健康 wish everyone good health || ~你生日快乐 wish you a happy birthday || ~你健康 wish you good health

8 庆祝 [慶-] qìngzhù (celebrate-congratulate) <v.> celebrate: ~生日 celebrate a birthday || ~大会 celebrate at a large meeting || ~胜利 celebrate a victory

9 祝贺 [-賀] zhùhè (congratulate-send a present with congratulation) <v.> congratulate: ~生日 congratulate someone on their birthday || ~他的喜事 congratulate him on his happy event || 表示 ~ show congratulations

10 祝福 [-] zhùfú (pray-bless) <v.> bless: ~刚出生的婴儿 (yīng'ér) bless a newborn baby || 为他们~ bless them || 互相~ bless each other

11 祝愿 [-願] zhùyuàn (pray-wish) <v.> wish: ~他幸福 wish him happiness || 美好的 ~ happy wishes || 衷心~ heartfelt wishes

12 拜年 [-] bàinián (worship-new year) <v.> wish a happy new year: 互相~ wish each other a happy new year || 给父母~ wish parents a happy new year

13 劝 [勸] quàn (encourage, persuade) <v.> encourage, recommend: ~他休息 encourage him to rest || ~爸爸 advise your father || ~几句 a few words of encouragement

14 奉劝 [-勸] fèngquàn (politely-advise) <v.> politely advise sb.: ~大家要注意自我保护 advise everyone to pay attention to self-protection || ~读者爱护图书 advise readers to love books

15 告诫 [-誡] gàojiè (advise-warn) <v.> warn, exhort: ~年轻人要多读书 exhort young people to read more books || 再三~ warn over and over || 反复~ warn repeatedly

16 忠告 [-] zhōnggào (sincerely-advise) <v.> advise sb.: 再三~ advise repeatedly || ~大家不要在长江里游泳 advise everyone not to swim in the Yangtze

17 劝阻 [勸-] quànzǔ (persuade-prevent) <v.> advise not to do: 极力~ strongly advise against doing sth. || ~别人不要赌博 (dǔbó) advise others not to gamble

18 鼓励 [-勵] gǔlì (encourage-inspire) <v.> encourage: ~学生 encourage a student || ~经商 encourage trade || ~自己 encourage yourself

19 激励 [-勵] jīlì (urge-inspire) <v.> encourage, urge: ~大家安心工作 encourage everyone to keep their mind on work || 互相~ mutually encourage

20 安慰 [-] ānwèi (comfort-comfort) <v./n.> comfort: 自我~ self-consolation || ~她的父母 comfort her parents || ~的话 comforting words

21 慰问 [-問] wèiwèn (comfort-extend regards) <v.> express sympathy: ~老人 express sympathy for the elderly || 表示~ show sympathy || 亲切~ kindly express sympathy

Tips:

1 庆 (慶, qìng): The components of 慶 include '鹿' (lù, deer), '心' (heart) and '夊' (suī, foot), and in combination they mean 'to sincerely (心) bring a precious gift like deer skin (鹿) to go to (夊) one's home,' in other words, 'to congratulate (a person.)'
2 Radical 礻: 礻 is the radical form of 示 (shì) which means 'tablet, god.' All Chinese characters with the radical 礻 are more or less related to god. For example, 祝, 福 in this unit and 神 (shén, god), 祖 (zǔ, ancestor) and 祸 (huò, disaster,) which was believed to be punishment from the god.
3 庆, 祝, 贺: All mean 'congratulate' and their combinations, 庆祝, 庆贺, 祝贺 have almost the same meaning.

Exercises:

Part I: Multiple Choice. Make sure to choose the most appropriate answer.

1 下面哪个词没有"夸奖"的意思:
A. 赞美　　B. 称赞　　C. 劝告

2 下面哪个词没有"劝告"的意思:
A. 奉劝　　B. 忠告　　C. 安慰

3 这家公司用发奖金的办法_______员工努力工作.
A. 激励　　B. 劝阻　　C. 告诫

4 中国政府一再_________印度政府要尊重 (zūnzhòng, respect) 中国的领土主权.
A. 祝愿　　B. 告诫　　C. 慰问

5 春节的时候中国人会互相__________, 祝愿彼此有好运气.
A. 劝　　B. 拜年　　C. 鼓励

6 小张请妈妈到一个豪华 (háohuá, luxurious) 餐厅吃饭, __________妈妈的生日.
A. 赞美　　B. 抬举　　C. 庆祝

7 中国乒乓球队赢了世界杯比赛, 台下的观众为他们________.
A. 忠告　　B. 祷告　　C. 叫好

Theme 179: To thank, to apologize 感謝, 道歉 (gǎnxiè, dàoqiàn), greet 问候 (wènhòu)

1 谢谢 [謝謝] xièxie (thank-*reduplication*) <v.> thank: ~你 thank you || ~他的帮助 thank him for his help || ~你的好主意 thank you for your good idea
2 感谢 [-謝] gǎnxiè (grateful-thank) <v.> be grateful: 非常~ be very grateful || ~我的老师 be grateful for my teacher || 表示~ express thanks
3 报答 [報-] bàodá (repay-reciprocate) <v.> repay, requite: ~父母 repay parents || ~他们的帮助 repay their help || ~他的好意 repay his kindness
4 回报 [-報] huíbào (return-repay) <v.> reciprocate, repay: ~父母 repay parents || 得到 ~ receive repayment || 感情的~ emotional reciprocation

5 感激 [-] gǎnjī (moved-inspired) <v.> be grateful: ~这位姑娘 feel indebted to this girl || 万分~ extremely grateful || ~生活 be thankful for life

6 别客气 [--氣] biékèqì (don't-guest-manner) <v.> don't mention it: 千万~ please don't mention it

7 不敢当 [--當] bùgǎndāng (not-dare-bear) <v.> you flatter me (polite): 实在~ you really flatter me || 叫我老师, 我可~. Calling me a teacher is really flattery.

8 道歉 [-] dàoqiàn (express-apology) <v.> apologize: 公开~ publicly apologize || 向顾客~ apologize to a customer || 赶忙~ quickly apologize

9 对不起 [對--] duìbuqǐ (match-not-able) <v.> sorry, feel sorry: ~朋友 feel sorry to a friend || ~大家 feel sorry to everyone || ~后代 feel sorry to future generations

10 赔礼 [賠禮] péilǐ (apologize-courtesy) <v.> make an apology: 向作者~ make an apology to the author || 公开~ make a public apology

11 赎罪 [贖-] shúzuì (atone for-crime) <v.> atone for a crime: 替前人~ atone for the crimes of predecessors

12 谢罪 [謝-] xièzuì (apologize-offense) <v.> apologize for an offense: 向老人~ apologize to an old person for doing something wrong || 正式~ formally apologize for an offense || 登门~ visit someone to apologize

13 问好 [問-] wènhǎo (ask about-good) <v.> say hello to: 互相~ say hello to each other || 向老师~ say hello to a teacher

14 问候 [問-] wènhòu (ask about-send respects to) <v.> extend a greeting: 互相~ greet each other || 请代我~你的父母. Please extend my greetings to your parents. || 节日的~ holiday greetings

15 再见 [-見] zàijiàn (again-see) <v.> goodbye, see you again: 挥手~ wave goodbye || 说声~ say goodbye || 十年后~ see each other ten years later

16 再会 [-會] zàihuì (again-meet) <v.> goodbye, until we meet again: 明天~ see you tomorrow

17 此致 [-] cǐzhì (here-extend) <v.> polite ending to a letter: ~敬礼 (jìnglǐ) salutations || ~谢意 with gratitude || ~良好的祝愿 with good wishes

18 请问 [請問] qǐngwèn (please-ask) <v.> excuse me: ~您贵姓? excuse me, what is your name? || ~你是谁? excuse me, who are you? || ~大家 please ask everyone

19 请教 [請-] qǐngjiào (please-instruct) <v.> ask for advice: ~医生 ask a doctor for advice || 向老人~ consult an old person || ~一个问题 ask for advice on a question

20 打扰 [-擾] dǎrǎo (interrupt-disturb) <v.> disturb: ~一下, . . . Excuse me, . . . || 别~他! Don't disturb him! || ~她的工作 interrupt her work || ~你休息 disturb your rest

21 打搅 [-攪] dǎjiǎo (interrupt-disturb) <v.> disturb, trouble: ~邻居 disturb a neighbor || ~别人 disturb others || ~他休息 disturb his rest

22 麻烦 [-煩] máfán (numerous-annoyed) <v.> bother: ~人 bother someone || ~您 trouble you

23 抱歉 [-] bàoqiàn (feel-apologetic) <adj.> be sorry: ~地说 apologetically say || ~的心情 an apologetic mood || 感到~ feel sorry

24 久闻 [-聞] jiǔwén (long-heard) <v.> heard about for a long time: ~大名. I've heard great things about you for a long time.

25 久仰 [-] jiǔyǎng (long-admire) <v.> I've been looking forward to meeting you: ~大名. I've been looking forward to meeting you for a long time.
26 久违 [-違] jiǔwéi (long-parted) <v.> haven't seen for a long time: ~的风光 haven't seen the scenery for a long time
27 怠慢 [-] dàimàn (treat coldly-cold shoulder) <v.> neglect: ~乘客 neglect a passenger || ~朋友 neglect a friend
28 失态 [-態] shītài (lose-manner) <v.> forget your manners: 过分~ misbehave excessively || 人前~ forget your manners in front of people || 酒后~ forget your manners while drunk
29 请便 [請-] qǐngbiàn (please-as you wish) <v.> please do as you wish!: 您要是想现在离开, 那就~吧. Well, if you want to leave now, go ahead.
30 您早 [-] nínzǎo (you-good morning) <v.> good morning (formal)
31 早上好 [-] zǎoshànghǎo (morning-good) <v.> good morning
32 早安 [-] zǎo'ān (morning-well) <v.> good morning (polite)
33 晚上好 [-] wǎnshànghǎo (evening-good) <v.> good evening: 大家~! Good evening, everybody!
34 晚安 [-] wǎn'ān (evening-well) <v.> good evening/ night (polite)

Tips:

1 对不起 vs. 抱歉 (bàoqiàn): Both mean 'I am sorry' but 抱歉 is closer to 'sorry about that,' which might not be very sincere. Both can be modified by 非常 (very), 实在 (really) or 万分 (awfully.)
2 死罪死罪 (death penalty and death penalty): From around the Western Han Dynasty to the Tang Dynasty, 死罪死罪 was widely-used to mean 'pardon me (if this is not appropriate)' in memos to the emperor or higher ranking officials or even between friends. In a short letter 劝进表 (quànjìnbiǎo) to the emperor on the lunar date March 18, 317, 刘琨 (Liú Kūn) used 11 死罪 (death penalty) and unsurprisingly 11 顿首 (dùnshǒu, kowtow.)
3 How to repay a favor? The Chinese maxim is "受人点水之恩, 当涌泉相报" (shòu rén diǎn shuǐ zhī ēn, dāng yǒngquán xiāngbào, if you received a drop of favor from others, you need to repay the favor like a gushing well.)
4 久: 久 is the ancient form of 灸 (jiǔ, cauterize.) How the meaning 'a long time' came into being is not clear. An explanation is that 久 refers to the gap between two legs.
5 麻烦: It has two basic meanings. One is 'troublesome, to bother' and the other 'please.' For example, 麻烦您给我一张纸 (please give me a sheet of paper.)
6 对不住 and 对不起: They can both mean 'let somebody down' or '(wrongly) do something bad to somebody' and are interchangeable when they are followed with an object, but 对不起 has more meanings such as 'pardon me,' which can be used alone.
7 打扰 (dǎrǎo) vs. 打搅 (dǎjiǎo): Both mean 'to disturb,' but 打搅 is more colloquial. The 'Do not disturb' sign in English is '请勿打扰' (qǐng wù dǎrǎo) in Chinese.

8 请安: 请安 was a custom in the Ming and Qing dynasties. One should ask for 'wellness' while kneeling to his parents in the morning and evening, and to other seniors when they meet.

Exercises:

Multiple Choice. Make sure to choose the most appropriate answer.

1 中国父母养孩子常常对孩子抱有很高的期望 (qīwàng, expectation), 期望孩子将来________他们.
A. 报答 B. 谢罪 C. 赎罪

2 这所农村小学收到了很多好心人的捐款 (juānkuǎn, donate money), 校长鼓励 (gǔlì, encourage) 学生好好学习, 将来_________社会.
A. 赔礼 B. 道歉 C. 回报

3 小张十分_______自己的小学老师, 每年教师节的时候都会去看望她.
A. 不敢当 B. 别客气 C. 感激

4 这位政治家由于说了不恰当的话而公开向人们_________.
A. 感激 B. 道歉 C. 感谢

5 日本政治家如果出现丑闻 (chǒuwén, scandal), 一般会公开向老百姓________.
A. 谢罪 B. 感谢 C. 赎罪

6 以前中国人见面________用"你吃了吗."
A. 问候 B. 再见 C. 再会

7 现在中国人见面________的时候已经不使用"你吃了吗," 而是用"你好."
A. 请问 B. 问好 C. 请教

8 一般中国人写信或者邮件的时候, 会在末尾写上"_________."
A. 对不住 B. 抱歉 C. 此致

9 中国人向别人请教问题的时候, 会先说: 对不起, __________了, ...
A. 打扰 B. 抱歉 C. 请便

10 中国人觉得在重要场合穿着不讲究是非常_______的表现.
A. 久仰 B. 失态 C. 请便

11 如果第一次见一个比较有名的人, 中国人一般会先说: 您好, ________大名 . . . .
A. 久违 B. 久仰 C. 请便

12 在酒桌上, 为了表示尊敬, 年轻人一般会对年纪大的人说: 我先干了, 您________.
A. 怠慢 B. 久闻 C. 请便

Theme 180: To request 请求 (qǐngqiú)

1 请 [請] qǐng (visit a person, request, invite) <v.> ask, invite: ~等一下 ask to wait a second || ~进来 invite in || ~看 please see. . .

2 求 [-] qiú (beg, request) <v.> request: ~别人帮忙 ask for help from others || ~医生救命 request help from a doctor

3 请求 [請-] qǐngqiú (request-beg) <v./n.> request: 再三~ repeatedly request || ~帮助 request help || 提出~ put forth a request

4 恳求 [懇-] kěnqiú (earnestly-request) <v.> implore: ~别人帮助 implore others to help || 苦苦~ strenuously implore || 反复~ repeatedly implore

5 呼吁 [-籲] hūyù (cry out-appeal) <v.> appeal: 公开~ public appeal || ~和平 appeal for peace || ~人们重视环境 call on people to value the environment

6 求助 [-] qiúzhù (seek-help) <v.> seek help: 向朋友~ seek help from a friend || ~于医生 turn to a doctor for help || 开口~ ask for help

7 求饶 [-饒] qiúráo (beg-forgive) <v.> beg for mercy: 跪地~ kneel and beg for mercy || 向对方~ beg for mercy from an opponent || 苦苦~ strenuously beg for mercy

8 乞求 [-] qǐqiú (plead-beg) <v.> beg for: ~保护 beg for protection || ~帮助 beg for help || 到处~ beg everywhere

9 征求 [徵-] zhēngqiú (solicit-seek) <v.> seek, ask for: ~意见 ask for an opinion || ~您的同意 seek your agreement || ~节目 ask for a program

10 求情 [-] qiúqíng (beg-mutual affection) <v.> plead: 向上级~ plead with a superior || 上门~ visit someone to plead with them || 再三~ plead over and over

11 托 [託] tuō (entrust, trust) <v.> entrust, ask: ~关系 use one's connections || ~我买东西 ask me to buy things

12 托付 [-] tuōfù (trust-entrust) <v.> entrust: 把孩子~给爷爷照顾 (zhàogù) entrust a grandfather with a child's care || ~终身 entrust for one's whole life || 把事情~给她 entrust her with a thing

13 委托 [-託] wěituō (entrust-trust) <v.> trust: ~加工 trust a process || ~他办事 trust him to resolve a thing || 受~ be trusted

14 寄托 [-] jìtuō (entrust-entrust) <v.> leave with, place: 把希望~在儿女身上 place your hopes in your children || ~思念 find sustenance in longing

Tips:

1 託 (托) and 托: Both are pronounced as tuō, and the convergence of these two forms is complicated. Basically, 托 means 'to entrust' and 託 'to trust.' 託 was simplified as 托, which made the differentiation of these two characters even harder.

2 求: 求 is the ancient form of 裘 (qiú, fur coat.) Because ancient people wore their fur coats with the fur side out, the lower four dots beside 亅 depicts fur. As a verb, 求 means 'to beg, request.'

Exercises:

Use the given bound form as a guide to help you think of other words with the same character. Feel free to use your dictionary when needed. Then write down the English definition of each of the words you've written.

求 ***(request)*** 请求 ***request***

____

____

____

____

____

____

____

____

____

托 ***(trust, rely on)*** 托关系 ***rely on relationships***

____

____

____

Theme 181: To give 送 (sòng)

1 送 [-] sòng (see sb. off, give) <v.> give as a gift: ~礼 give a present || ~东西 give something as a gift

2 赠 [贈] zèng (give as a present) <v.> give as a present: ~礼物 give a present || ~给我 given to me as a present

3 捐赠 [-贈] juānzèng (donate-give) <v.> contribute, donate: ~电子产品 donate electronics || ~食物 donate food || ~图书 donate books

4 赠送 [贈-] zèngsòng (present-gift) <v.> present as a gift: ~手表 gift a watch || 免费~ give a free gift || ~给她一件礼物 give her a gift

5 发 [發] fā (shoot an arrow, send, give) <v.> give: ~钱 give money || ~东西 give something || ~书 give a book

6 补发 [補發] bǔfā (make up for-give) <v.> reissue: ~工资 retroactively pay wages || ~奖金 (jiǎngjīn) reissue a bonus

7 转送 [轉-] zhuǎnsòng (divert-send) <v.> pass on: ~礼物 regift something || ~上级 pass on to a superior || ~给用户 pass on to the user

8 转赠 [轉贈] zhuǎnzèng (divert-present) <v.> regift: ~给别人 regift to someone else || ~一辆汽车 regift a car || ~他人 regift to another person

9 送礼 [-禮] sònglǐ (give-gift) <v-o.> give a gift: 送重礼 give a heavy gift || 送个礼 give one gift || 送大礼 give a big present || 送彩礼 send bridal gifts

10 捐 [-] juān (donate) <v.> donate: ~钱donate money || ~一百元 donate 100 yuan || ~衣服 donate clothes

11 献 [獻] xiàn (offer, present) <v.> offer, donate: ~血 donate blood || ~花 offer flowers || ~计, 酒, 礼 offer advice, alcohol, a gift

12 捐款 [-] juānkuǎn (donate-money) <v.> contribute money: ~五千元 contribute 5,000 yuan || 积极~ positive contribution || ~买飞机 contribute money to buy a plane

13 奉献 [-獻] fèngxiàn (offer-present) <v.> dedicate, devote: ~生命 dedicate life || ~爱心 devote one's love to || 无私~ unselfish devotion

14 贡献 [貢獻] gòngxiàn (offer tribute-present) <v.> contribute, dedicate: ~金钱 contribute money || ~时间 dedicate time || ~很多 contribute a lot

15 交换 [-] jiāohuàn (hand over and take over-exchange) <v.> exchange: ~商品 exchange goods || ~意见 exchange ideas || ~经验 (jīngyàn) exchange experiences
16 调换 [調換] diàohuàn (transfer-exchange) <v.> swap: ~大小 swap sizes || ~座位 swap seats
17 退换 [-換] tuìhuàn (return-exchange) <v.> return: ~商品 return merchandise || ~鞋子 return shoes

18 交 [-] jiāo (cross) <v.> hand in, give: ~作业 hand in homework || ~试卷 hand in a paper || ~货 deliver goods
19 交给 [-給] jiāogěi (hand over-to) <v.> give to: ~银行 give to the bank || ~老师 give to the teacher || ~自己 give to yourself
20 传递 [傳遞] chuándì (pass on-pass) <v.> transmit: ~信息 transmit news || ~小纸条 pass a note || ~信件 deliver a letter
21 传达 [傳達] chuándá (pass on-reach) <v.> pass on, relay: ~文件 pass on papers || ~消息 convey the information || ~指示convey instructions

22 借 [-] jiè (borrow, lend) <v.> borrow, lend: ~钱 borrow money || ~书 borrow a book || ~房子 borrow, use a room
23 还 [還] huán (return) <v.> give back, return: ~钱 pay back money || ~书 return a book || ~贷款 (dài kuǎn) pay back a loan
24 偿还 [償還] chánghuán (refund-repay) <v.> pay back: ~借款 pay back a loan || ~外债 (wàizhài) pay back a foreign debt || ~贷款 pay back a loan
25 赔 [賠] péi (compensate) <v.> lose, compensate: ~钱了 lost money || 我把你电脑丢了, 我~你吧. I lost your computer. I'll pay for it. || ~礼 make an apology
26 退款 [賠-] tuìkuǎn (return-money) <v.> refund: 如数~ full refund || ~一万元 refund 10,000 yuan
27 领 [領] lǐng (neck, to lead, receive) <v.> receive: ~钱 receive money || ~东西 receive something || ~养老金 receive a pension
28 领取 [領-] lǐngqǔ (receive-fetch) <v.> collect, receive: ~工资 collect a wage || ~结婚证 receive a marriage certificate || ~失物 collect lost property
29 取款 [-] qǔkuǎn (withdraw-money) <v.> withdraw money: 到银行~ go to the bank to withdraw money || ~自由 withdraw freely

30 供 [-] gōng (supply) <v.> supply: ~水 supply water || ~电 supply electricity || ~热 supply heating
31 供给 [-給] gōngjǐ (supply-provide) <v.> provide: 粮食~ provide food || ~热量 provide heating || 增加~ increase the supply
32 供应 [-應] gōngyìng (supply-pay) <v.> supply, provide: ~果汁 supply fruit juice || 货币~ provide with money || 产品~ provide with goods
33 提供 [-] tígōng (support-supply) <v.> furnish, provide: ~食宿 furnish with accommodations || ~经费 provide funding || ~帮助 provide help
34 提交 [-] tíjiāo (put forward-submit) <v.> submit: ~材料 submit materials || ~论文 submit a thesis || ~报告 submit a report

Tips:

1 取: The original meaning of 取 is to use one's hand (又) to cut off the left ear (耳) of a dead animal in hunting or a dead enemy in a war to count the number killed in ancient times.

2 献 (獻, xiàn): 献 means 'to offer a sacrifice (犬, dog) in a cauldron (鬳, yàn,)' in other words, 'to sacrifice.' Common words with this character include 贡献, 奉献 which are listed above, and 献出 (to sacrifice) and 献给 (to sacrifice to.)
3 给: As a verb, 给, when pronounced as gěi, means 'to give' as in words such as 送给 (to give,) when pronounced as jǐ, means 'to provide' as in words such as 供给 (to provide.)
4 捐, 赠, 送, 给: All mean 'to give' and their differences are: 捐 (donate) is associated with a special or a major event. 赠 (give as a present) is out of friendship. When Chinese people send a book or a gift to a person, they usually write '赠给***' on the book or a separate note. 送 is neutral, and 给 is neutral and slightly casual. Their combinations, 捐赠, 捐送, 捐给, 赠送, 赠给, 送给 have more or less the same meaning.

Exercises:

Part I: Use the given bound form as a guide to help you think of other words with the same character. Feel free to use your dictionary when needed. Then write down the English definition of each of the words you've written.

赠 *(give as a present)* 赠送 *present as a gift*

____

____

____

送 *(deliver, give)* 送礼 *give a gift*

____

____

____

取 *(fetch, take)* 取得 *acquire, get, obtain*

____

____

____

供 *(provide, supply)* 提供 *offer, supply, provide*

____

____

____

交 *(deliver, hand over)* 交换 *exchange, switch*

____

____

____

换 *(exchange)* 换手机 *change a cell phone*

____

____

____

Part II: Read the following sentences and fill in each blank with the appropriate word or phrase from the options given.

1 领取、提供、提交

a) 中国政府规定年满65周岁的农村老人也可以__________一定数量的养老金.
b) 据报道, 中国政府将为偏远 (piānyuǎn) 山区的中小学________了免费午餐.
c) 目前中国每年三月都会召开人民代表大会, 由代表向政府________议案 (yì'àn).

2 偿还、传达、传递

a) 小王在银行借了二百万人民币的购房贷款, 会用三十年的时间_________.
b) 据报道, 关于恐怖分子袭击 (xíjī) 的情报已经被__________到美国政府的安全部门.
c) 中国政府各级机关都有宣传(xuānchuán)办公室, 目的是__________中央政府的精神.

3 交换、调换、退换

a) 这两个大学每年_______五名学生, 到对方的学校学习.
b) 在美国顾客认为不合适的商品商店都会给__________或者退款.
c) 在美国顾客购买商品有90天内免费________的权利.

4 捐款、捐赠、贡献

a) 四川发生地震以后, 收到了来自全国各地的__________.
b) 很多志愿者给四川贫困山区的小学_________了书本和其他学习用品.
c) 很多美国学者认为邓小平为中国经济发展做出了巨大__________.

Theme 182: To consult 协商 (xiéshāng)

1 协调 [協-] xiétiáo (mediate-adjust) <v.> coordinate: ~意见 coordinate/bring together views || ~矛盾 solve/correct a contradiction || ~关系 coordinate relations
2 协议 [協議] xiéyì (mediate-discuss) <v./n.> agree: 达成~ reach an agreement || 签订 (qiāndìng) ~ sign an agreement || 共同 ~ joint agreement
3 商量 [-] shāngliang (consult-assess) <v.> consult: 跟他~ consult with him || ~一件事 discuss something || ~办法 discuss a method
4 协商 [協-] xiéshāng (mediate-consult) <v.> consult with: ~解决 solve through consultation || 内部~ internal consultation || 秘密~ secret consultation
5 商议 [-議] shāngyì (consult-discuss) <v.> discuss, negotiate: ~价格 negotiate a price || 紧急~ urgently discuss || ~对策 (duìcè) discuss a response

6 商讨 [-討] shāngtǎo (consult-inquire) <v.> discuss: ~对策 deliberate over a response || 共同~ joint discussions || ~国家大事 discuss national affairs
7 谈判 [談-] tánpàn (talk-decide) <v./n.> hold talks: 商业~ business talks || 正式~ official negotiations || 进行~ talks are underway
8 洽谈 [-談] qiàtán (consult-talk) <v.> discuss: ~生意 discuss business || ~合作项目discuss cooperative projects || ~工作 discuss work
9 和谈 [-談] hétán (peace-talk) <v.> peace talks: 对日~ hold peace talks with Japan || 两党~ two-party peace talks
10 会谈 [會談] huìtán (meet-talk) <v./n.> talks, hold a discussion: 电话~ phone conversations || 正式~ formal talks || 第二次 ~ the second set of talks

11 签订 [簽訂] qiāndìng (sign-conclude) <v.> agree and sign: ~条约 finalize and sign a treaty || ~合同 sign a contract || ~协议 sign an agreement
12 签约 [簽約] qiānyuē (sign-agreement) <v.> sign an agreement: 正式~ formally sign an agreement || 跟公司~ sign a contract with the company || 急于~ eager to sign a contract
13 协定 [協-] xiédìng (mediate-agree) <v.> reach an agreement: ~关税 agree on tariffs || ~价格 agree on a price

14 推托 [-託] tuītuō (refuse-pretext) <v.> make an excuse: ~责任 make an excuse for shirking responsibility || 互相~ dodge each other || 百般~ making all kinds of excuses
15 推卸 [-] tuīxiè (refuse-shirk) <v.> shirk: ~责任 shirk responsibility
16 承诺 [-諾] chéngnuò (undertake-promise) <v.> promise: ~帮助他 promise to help him || ~保密 promise to keep a secret || ~尽快完成 promise to do something as soon as possible
17 答应 [-應] dāyìng (replay-agree) <v.> agree: ~他的要求 agree to his requirements || ~这个条件 agree to this condition || 一口 ~ readily agree
18 许诺 [許諾] xǔnuò (promise-yes) <v.> promise: 公开 ~ publicly promise || 轻易~ lightly promise
19 允许 [-許] yǔnxǔ (allow-permit) <v.> permit: ~抽烟 permit smoking || ~离开 allow to leave || 得到~ receive permission
20 同意 [-] tóngyì (agree-idea) <v.> agree: ~结婚 agree to be married || ~参加 agree to participate || ~保守秘密 agree to keep a secret

21 接受 [-] jiēshòu (accept-receive) <v.> accept: ~意见 accept an opinion || ~批评 (pīpíng) accept criticism || ~任务 accept an assignment
22 受到 [-] shòudào (receive-*complement*) <v.> receive: ~奖励 receive a reward || ~赞扬 receive praise || ~邀请 receive an invitation
23 拒绝 [-絕] jùjué (refuse-reject) <v.> refuse, reject: ~他的要求 reject his requirement || ~这个建议 refuse this advice || ~帮助 refuse help
24 推辞 [-辭] tuīcí (refuse-decline) <v.> decline: 一再~ repeatedly decline || 借故~ make an excuse to decline || 反复~ repeatedly decline
25 让座 [讓-] ràngzuò (yield-seat) <v-o.> offer a seat: 让一个座 offer up one seat || 给你~ offer my seat to you || 马上~ immediately offer up a seat
26 劝说 [勸說] quànshuō (persuade-speak) <v.> persuade: ~别人 persuade others || 反复~ repeatedly persuade || 耐心~ patiently persuade
27 调解 [調-] tiáojiě (mediate-solve) <v.> mediate: ~纠纷 (jiūfēn) mediate a dispute || ~家庭问题 mediate a family issue || ~这件事help resolve this thing

28 疏通 [-] shūtōng (dredge-unblock) <v.> facilitate: ~关系 facilitate a relationship || ~意见 mediate between two opinions

29 守 [-] shǒu (observe, keep) <v.> abide by, guard: ~时 be on time || ~法abide by the law || ~纪律 (jìlǜ) abide by the discipline

30 遵守 [-] zūnshǒu (abide by-keep) <v.> comply with: ~纪律 comply with rules || ~约定 comply with the agreement || ~法律 comply with the law

31 遵循 [-] zūnxún (abide by-follow) <v.> follow: ~规律 follow the law || ~原则 follow a principle || ~正确的方向 follow the right path

32 遵照 [-] zūnzhào (abide by-according to) <v.> obey: ~命令 obey a command || ~指示 obey instructions || ~规定 obey a regulation

33 遵从 [-從] zūncóng (abide by-obey) <v.> follow (an order): ~医嘱 (yīzhǔ) follow doctor's advice || ~职业道德 (zhíyè dàodé) obey professional ethics || ~习俗 (xísú) follow customs

34 顺应 [順應] shùnyìng (obey-respond) <v.> adapt to: ~民意 adapt to public opinion || ~潮流 (cháoliú) adapt to trends

35 应 [應] yìng (respond) <v.> respond: ~他之约 respond to his appointment || ~她的邀请 respond to her invitation

36 服从 [-從] fúcóng (submit to-obey) <v.> obey, defer to: ~法律 obey the law || ~需要 obey a need || ~安排 defer to an arrangement

37 顺从 [順從] shùncóng (obey-obey) <v.> submit to: ~民意 submit to public opinion || ~自然 submit to nature || ~丈夫 submit to a husband

Tips:

1 答: The original meaning of 答 is to use bamboo (竹) to mend a fence. When it is pronounced as dá, it means 'to reply/answer' as in words such as 回答 (to answer) or 'to reciprocate (one's kindness)' as in words such as 答谢 (to express appreciation.) When it is pronounced as dā, it only means 'to reply/answer,' as in words such as 答应 (to reply, to agree.)

2 应 (應): When it is pronounced as yīng, it means 'should' or 'to promise' as in words such as 应该 and 应允 (yīngyǔn, to agree.) If it is pronounced as yìng, it means 'respond' or 'comply with' as in words such as 响应 (respond, echo) and 顺应 (comply with.)

3 How do you reject (拒绝, jùjué) a Chinese person in the Chinese way? It is an art, or more specifically, a convention/custom. Basically, you need to leave the rejected side 'face/dignity' (面子.) A straightforward 'no' is not considered to be polite.

Exercises:

Part I: Use the given bound form as a guide to help you think of other words with the same character. Feel free to use your dictionary when needed. Then write down the English definition of each of the words you've written.

协 *(assist, cooperate)* 协助 *to provide assistance, to aid*

____

____

____

____

商 *(discuss)* 商量 *to consult, to discuss*

____

____

____

____

谈 *(talk, discuss)* 谈判 *to negotiate, hold talks*

____

____

____

____

遵 *(abide by, obey, follow)* 遵守法律 *abide by the law*

____

____

____

____

Part II: Read the following sentences and fill in each blank with the appropriate word or phrase from the options given.

1 会谈、签订

美国总统与中国国家主席在2016年11月举行了__________. 两国_________了一系列关于中美贸易的协定.

2 达成协议、商量、协商解决、谈判

a) 中美这两家公司最近__________, 共同开发这种新产品.
b) 中国政府认为中美贸易 (màoyì, trade) 问题应该通过__________来____________.
c) 王先生最近正在跟妻子_________美国的问题.

3 推脱、承诺、答应

a) 王先生最近__________妻子给她买一辆新车.
b) 王先生的朋友请他去喝酒, 他不想去, 就_________说家里有事.
c) 美国民主党希望中美双方___________不打贸易战.

4 拒绝、服从、劝说

a) 王先生公司想派他到非洲工作, 王先生________了.
b) 这家公司_________王先生到非洲去工作, 理由是收入会增加三倍. 最后, 王先生_________了公司的安排.

5 调解、遵守、顺应
 a) 这家美国公司跟中国大客户发生了矛盾, 目前正在________之中.
 b) 在美国__________法律特别重要.
 c) 有人认为中国政府应该__________历史潮流进行经济和政治改革 (gǎigé, reform).

Theme 183: To help, care 帮助, 照顾 (bāngzhù, zhàogù)

1 帮 [幫] bāng (to aid) <v.> help: ~她一下 help her a little || ~不了 unable to help || ~ 儿子买个大房子 help your son buy a big house
2 帮忙 [幫-] bāngmáng (to aid-busy) <sep.> help out: 帮我一个大忙 help me with a big favor || 互相~ help each other out || ~看孩子 help out by watching someone's kids
3 帮助 [幫-] bāngzhù (to aid-to help) <v.> aid: ~老年人 aid the elderly || ~朋友找工作 help a friend look for a job || 大力 ~ energetic aid
4 出主意 [-] chūzhǔyì (give-idea) <sep.> give ideas: 给朋友~ give a friend an idea || 出个主意 give an idea
5 扶 [-] fú (support with the hand) <v.> support: ~贫 poverty support || ~困 help
6 辅助 [輔-] fǔzhù (assist-help) <v.> assist: ~教学 assist teachers teaching || ~工作 assist with work || ~治疗 supplementary treatment
7 协助 [協-] xiézhù (assist-help) <v.> provide help: ~工作 provide help with work || ~他 help him || 全力~ all-out assistance
8 支持 [-] zhīchí (support-hold) <v.> support: 积极~ actively support || 大力~ vigorously support || 得到~ receive support
9 追捧 [-] zhuīpěng (chase-hold with hands) <v.> follow: ~新星 follow a star || 热情~ enthusiastically follow || 值得~ worth following
10 援助 [-] yuánzhù (rescue-help) <v.> aid: 经济~ economic aid || 大力~ vigorously aid || 长期~ long-term aid
11 赞助 [贊-] zànzhù (sponsor-help) <v.> support, assist: ~这次活动 support this activity || 大力~ vigorously support || 独家~ exclusive supporter, sponsor
12 资助 [資-] zīzhù (provide-help) <v.> aid financially: ~这项活动 financially support this activity || ~贫困儿童 support poor children || ~衣物 subsidize clothing
13 支援 [-] zhīyuán (support-rescue) <v./n.> support: ~农业 support agriculture || 相互~ mutual support || ~灾民 aid disaster victims
14 增援 [-] zēngyuán (increase-assist) <v.> reinforce: 火速~ rush to reinforce || ~东路 reinforce the east road || 派人~ send people to reinforce
15 声援 [聲-] shēngyuán (express-support) <v.> express support: 互相~ express support for each other || ~工人 express support for workers || 有力~ forcefully support
16 扶持 [-] fúchí (support with the hand-hold) <v.> support: 重点~ focus on support || ~小企业 support a small business
17 救助 [-] jiùzhù (save-help) <v.> help someone in trouble: ~孤儿 help orphans || 及时~ timely assistance || 得到~ receive assistance
18 助人为乐 [--為樂] zhùrénwéilè (help-others-as-pleasure) <idiom> take pleasure in helping others: 她一直热心~. She has always been enthusiastic about helping others.

19 施舍 [-捨] shīshě (give-give alms) <v.> give to charity: ~药物 donate medicine || ~面包 donate bread || ~钱财 give money to charity

20 补助 [補-] bǔzhù (subsidize-help) <v.> subsidize: ~老年人 subsidize the elderly || ~三千元 3, 000 yuan subsidy || 互相~ mutual subsidy

21 雪中送炭 [-] xuězhōngsòngtàn (snow-period-send-charcoal) <idiom > send charcoal in a snow storm (provide timely help): 给老百姓~. give timely help to commoners

22 救 [-] jiù (save) <v.> rescue, save: ~人 rescue someone || ~命 save a life || ~国 save a country

23 救命 [-] jiùmìng (save-life) <v-o.> save someone's life: 救她的命 save her life || 救了一命 save a life || 救了他一命 save his life

24 救援 [-] jiùyuán (save-rescue) <v.> rescue: 紧急 ~ urgent rescue || ~灾区 support the disaster area || 全力~ all-out rescue

25 挽救 [-] wǎnjiù (reverse-save) <v.> remedy, save: ~危机 remedy a crisis || ~生命 save a life || ~森林 save a forest

26 抢救 [搶-] qiǎngjiù (rush-save) <v.> save, salvage: ~病人 save a sick person || ~伤员 save a wounded person || ~资料 (zīliào) salvage data

27 营救 [營-] yíngjiù (provide-save) <v.> rescue: ~遇难者 rescue victims || ~他出狱 rescue him from prison || ~失事飞机 rescue from a plane crash

28 拯救 [-] zhěngjiù (relieve-save) <v.> save: ~生命 save a life || ~企业 save a business || ~世界 save the world

29 救灾 [-災] jiùzāi (rescue-disaster) <v-o.> provide disaster relief: 救火灾 provide fire relief || 抢险~ emergency relief || ~现场 on the spot disaster relief

30 救火 [-] jiùhuǒ (rescue-fire) <v.> fight a fire: 全力~ all-out firefighting effort || 现场~ fight a fire at its site

31 消防 [-] xiāofáng (fight-prevent) <v.> fight a fire: ~车 fire engine || ~员 firefighter || ~队 fire department/brigade

32 抗洪 [-] kànghóng (fight-flood) <v.> fight a flood: ~救灾 flood relief || ~抢险 flood rescue

33 抗灾 [-災] kàngzāi (fight-disaster) <v.> fight natural disasters: 奋力~ struggle to fight natural disasters

34 抗震 [-] kàngzhèn (fight-Earthquake) <v.> Earthquake-resistance: 全力~ all-out Earthquake relief

35 抢险 [搶險] qiǎngxiǎn (rush-danger) <v.> react to an emergency: 全力 ~ all-out emergency relief

36 关爱 [關愛] guān'ài (care-love) <v.> care for: ~孩子 care for a child || ~地球 care for the Earth || 互相~ care for each other

37 关怀 [關懷] guānhuái (care-concern) <v.> show concern for: ~老人 show concern for the elderly || ~下一代 show concern for the next generation || 亲切~ kindly care for

38 照顾 [-顧] zhàogù (take care of-look after) <v.> look after: ~病人, 老人 look after sick people, old people || ~孩子 look after kids || 互相~ look after each other

39 照料 [-] zhàoliào (take care of-arrange) <v.> tend to: 细心~ carefully tend to || ~老人 tend to the elderly || 互相~ take care of each other

40 伺候 [-] cìhòu (serve-wait) <v.> serve, wait on: 小心~ carefully serve || ~病人 wait on a sick person || ~老人吃饭 serve an elderly person food

41 服侍 [-] fúshì (serve-wait upon) <v.> attend: ~病人 wait on a sick person || ~双亲 attend parents

42 看 [-] kān (look after) <v.> look: ~孩子 look after kids || ~家 take care of the house || ~着货物 look after cargo

43 看管 [-] kānguǎn (look after-in charge of) <v.> look after: ~ 小孩 look after little kids || 轮流 (lúnliú) ~ take turns looking after || ~房子 look after the house

44 照看 [-] zhàokàn (take care of-look) <v.> keep an eye on: ~这所房子 keep an eye on the house || ~孩子 keep an eye on a kid || 亲自~ personally keep an eye on

45 护理 [護-] hùlǐ (take good care of-handle) <v.> nurse: ~病人 nurse a sick person || ~伤员 nurse the wounded || ~皮肤 tend to skin

46 保护 [-護] bǎohù (guard-protect) <v.> protect: ~ 眼睛 guard your eyes || ~大熊猫 protect the giant panda || 环境~ environmental protection

47 保障 [-] bǎozhàng (guard-guarantee) <v.> guarantee, ensure: ~安全 guarantee safety || ~基本需求 ensure basic needs || ~稳定 ensure stability

48 护送 [護-] hùsòng (protect-send) <v.> escort: ~伤员 escort the wounded || ~到外地 escort outside || ~她回国 escort her to her home country

49 维护 [維護] wéihù (maintain-take good care of) <v.> defend: ~和平 defend peace || ~利益 defend interests || ~真理, 旧制度 uphold the truth, the old system

50 养 [養] yǎng (raise) <v.> raise: ~孩子 raise children || ~鱼 raise a fish || ~兔子 raise a rabbit

51 收养 [-養] shōuyǎng (receive-raise) <v.> take in and care for: ~孩子 take in a child || ~一个儿子 adopt a son

52 领养 [領養] lǐngyǎng (take-raise) <v.> adopt: ~孩子 adopt a child || ~小狗 adopt a little dog || ~孤儿 adopt an orphan

53 抚养 [撫養] fǔyǎng (foster-raise) <v.> foster, raise: ~孩子 foster a child || 无力~ unable to raise || ~子女 raise children

54 养育 [養-] yǎngyù (raise-bring up) <v.> bring up: ~子女 bring up children || ~幼儿 care for a baby || ~孩子 bring a child

55 赡养 [贍養] shànyǎng (provide for-raise) <v.> support: ~老人 support the elderly || ~父母 support parents

56 养老 [養-] yǎnglǎo (support-elder) <v.> provide for the elderly: 给你~ provide for your parents || 靠儿子~ rely on your son to provide for you in your old age || 回家~ return home to provide for your parents

Tips:

1 服: According to etymological dictionaries, 服 is related to 舟 (boat,) not 月 (flesh, body.) It originally means 'the cross support on a boat,' with an extended meaning of 'use.' But the meaning 'clothes' can be found in literature starting from a very early time period.

2 看: When pronounced as kān, 看 means 'to look after,' and when pronounced as kàn, it means 'to look, read.' For example, 妈妈让他看 (kān) 小弟弟, 可是他只想看 (kàn) 电视 means 'Mommy asked him look after his little brother, but he only wants to watch TV.'

3 Born into filial piety? Is filial piety a nature of the Chinese? Maybe, but in China, filial piety is required by law. Article 49 of the Constitution of the People's Republic of China (2004) stipulates: 成年子女有赡养扶助父母的

义务 (chéngnián zǐnǚ yǒu shànyǎng fúzhù fùmǔ de yìwù, Children who have come of age have the duty to support and assist their parents.)

Exercises:

Part I: Use the given bound form as a guide to help you think of other words with the same character. Feel free to use your dictionary when needed. Then write down the English definition of each of the words you've written.

救 *(rescue, save):* 救命 *save a life*

____

____

____

____

____

____

养 *(help)* 养孩子 *raise a child*

____

____

____

____

护 *(protect)* 爱护 *care for and protect*

____

____

____

____

援 *(help, aid, assist)* 救援 *rescue, come to sb's help*

____

____

____

____

助 *(help, aid)* 帮助 *help*

____

____

____

____

Part II: Read the following sentences and fill in each blank with the appropriate word or phrase from the options given.

1 领养、赡养、养老
  a) 一些美国人喜欢到中国_________孩子.
  b) 在中国_________老人是子女应尽的义务.
  c) 目前中国农村的社会保障 (Social Security) 制度还不是很完善, 很多老人还是靠子女__________.

2 保护、保障、维护
  a) 中国自2008年以来出台了很多法律________环境.
  b) 中国还需要进一步健全社会_________制度.
  c) 中国政府认为为了维护_________, 必须要有一支非常强大的军队.

3 援助、抢救、救灾
  a) 自然灾害发生后, 一般来说中国军队会积极参加地方政府的__________工作.
  b) 自然灾害发生后, 附近医院的医生尽全力_________受伤的灾民.
  c) 中国政府多年来给非洲国家提供了很多无偿的__________, 帮助他们发展经济.

4 助人为乐、雪中送炭、伺候
  a) 这家养老院急需一笔资金, 有家企业得知后立刻捐助了这笔钱, 真是__________ __.
  b) 这家养老院的护工__________老人非常周到, 受到了当地政府的表扬.
  c) 中国的很多小学教育孩子__________, 利用课余时间帮助需要帮助的人.

5 支持、追捧、伺候
  a) 中国政府现在_________文化产业的发展.
  b) 美国篮球明星在中国受到很多年轻人的__________.

Theme 184: To argue 争论 (zhēnglùn)

(See also Theme 177)

1 议论 [議論] yìlùn (discuss-comment) <v.> comment, discuss: 纷纷~ comment one by one || ~同学 talk about classmates || ~这件事 talk about this thing
2 辩论 [辯論] biànlùn (debate-comment) <v./n.> debate: 自由 ~ free debate || ~问题 debate a question || 参加~ participate in a debate
3 答辩 [-辯] dábiàn (answer-argue) <v.> reply (to a question or argument): 论文~ thesis defense || 就这个问题进行~ replying to this question
4 讲理 [講-] jiǎnglǐ (tell-reason) <v.> reason with: 跟大家~ reason with everybody
5 评理 [評-] pínglǐ (judge-truth) <v.> judge: 给咱们~ give us a decision/judgment
6 反驳 [-駁] fǎnbó (disprove-rebut) <v.> rebut: ~这种观点 refute this view || ~她爸爸 rebut her father || 无法~ unable to rebut
7 辩护 [辯護] biànhù (debate-defend) <v.> defend: 为自己~ defend yourself
8 分辨 [-] fēnbiàn (distinguish-differentiate) <v.> differentiate: ~是非 differentiate right and wrong || ~清楚 differentiate clearly || ~颜色 differentiate colors

9 争 [爭] zhēng (contend, vie) <v.> vie for: ~房子 vie for a house || ~地方 vie for land || ~钱 vie for money
10 争论 [爭論] zhēnglùn (contend-comment) <v.> controversy, debate: ~问题 controversial question || 热烈地 ~ hotly debate || 引起~ give rise to a debate
11 争辩 [爭辯] zhēngbiàn (contend-debate) <v.> argue: 进行~ be arguing || 跟经理 ~ argue with a manager
12 争议 [爭議] zhēngyì (contend-discuss) <v.> dispute: 发生~ a dispute occurs || 有/没有~ have/not have a dispute || 学术~ academic dispute
13 争执 [爭執] zhēngzhí (contend-stick to) <v.> disagree: 与经理~ disagree with a manager || ~这个问题 dispute this question

14 吵架 [-] chǎojià (argue-quarrel) <v-o.> quarrel, argue: 吵一架 have a quarrel || 吵过架 have argued before || 吵过一架 have argued once
15 吵嘴 [-] chǎozuǐ (argue-mouth) <v.> bicker: 跟哥哥~ bicker with your older brother
16 打闹 [-鬧] dǎnào (fight-quarrel) <v.> start trouble: 故意~ intentionally start trouble || 互相~ start trouble with each other
17 顶嘴 [頂-] dǐngzuǐ (go against-mouth) <v.> talk back: 跟妈妈~ talk back to your mother

18 诅咒 [詛-] zǔzhòu (curse-swear) <v.> curse: ~别人 curse someone || 愤怒地~ angrily curse
19 辱骂 [-罵] rǔmà (insult-scold) <v.> call names, insult: ~别人 call other people names
20 作对 [-對] zuòduì (do-opposite) <v.> oppose: 跟农民~ oppose peasants
21 唱反调 [--調] chàngfǎndiào (sing-opposite-tune) <v.> sing a different tune (express a different view): 跟领导~ sing a different tune than the leader
22 说服 [說-] shuìfú (try to persuade-convinced) <v.> persuade: ~他 persuade him || 把老师~ persuade the teacher || ~孩子学经济 persuade children to study economics

Tips:

1 争: The traditional form of 争 is 爭 which depicts a hand (爫) that is fighting with another hand (又, here the middle part of 争, like 彐) for something (亅, maybe a stick.) The meaning of 争 is clear, 'fight for something.'
2 辨, 辩, 辫: All are pronounced as biàn, which comes from 辡 (biàn, meaning 'two sides of a lawsuit argue.') 辨 means 'to differentiate' which is related to 刀 (the middle part of 辨.) 辩 means 'to debate' which is related to 讠 (言.) 辫 means 'pigtail, braid,' which is related to 纟 (sī, thread, silk.)
3 说服: The 说 in this word should be pronounced as 'shuì' although many Chinese pronounce it as 'shuō.' When pronounced as shuì, 说 means 'try to persuade,' and when pronounced as shuō, 说 means 'to speak.'

Exercises:

Part I: Translate the following phrases into English and then answer the questions.

a) 说服父母 ____________________
b) 跟父母唱反调 ________________

c) 跟父母顶嘴 ________________
d) 跟父母作对 ________________
e) 跟别人争辩是非 ________________
f) 辱骂学生 ________________
g) 跟别人争论是非 ________________
h) 跟别人发生争执 ________________
i) 为自己辩护 ________________
j) 这个人不讲理 ________________
k) 反驳这种说法 ________________

1 哪些短语的意思差不多?

____

2 你会不会跟父母争论是非?

____

3 你觉得自己是一个讲理的人吗?

____

4 如果老师的观点不对, 你会不会反驳他的观点? 为什么?

____

Theme 185: To violate, to cheat, to prevent 违背, 欺骗, 阻止 (wéibèi, qīpiàn, zǔzhǐ)

1 违反 [違-] wéifǎn (violate-opposite) <v.> violate: ~纪律 (jìlǜ) violate discipline || ~规定 (guiding) violate regulations || ~科学 run counter to science
2 违背 [違-] wéibèi (violate-against) <v.> violate, go against: ~历史事实 be contrary to the historical facts || ~意愿 (yìyuàn) go against the will || ~承诺 (chéngnuò) break one's promise
3 出轨 [-軌] chūguǐ (off-track) <v.> go off the rails: 火车~ train derailment || 感情~ emotionally derailed || 身体~ health derailment
4 毁约 [-約] huǐyuē (break-contract) <v.> break a promise: 公开~ publicly break a promise || 单方~ unilaterally break a promise || 随意 (suíyì) ~ arbitrarily break promises
5 违抗 [違-] wéikàng (violate-defy) <v.> disobey: ~命令 disobey a command || ~上级 disobey a superior || 公然~ openly disobey
6 抵制 [-] dǐzhì (withstand-restrict) <v.> boycott: ~日货 boycott Japanese goods || ~毒品 (dúpǐn) reject drugs || 坚决 (jiānjué) ~ resolutely boycott sth.
7 得罪 [-] dézuì (get-offend) <v.> offend: ~老板 offend the boss || ~人 offend someone
8 触犯 [觸-] chùfàn (offend-offend/commit) <v.> offend, violate: ~法律 violate the law || ~上司 offend a superior || ~纪律 violate discipline
9 亵渎 [褻瀆] xièdú (obscene-profane) <v.> profane: ~生命 profanity of life || ~上帝 profane an emperor || ~法律 profane the law
10 冲撞 [衝-] chōngzhuàng (assault-bump) <v.> collide, bump: ~父亲 bump into your father || 互相~ bump into each other || ~地球 collide with the ground
11 触动 [觸動] chùdòng (offend-move) <v.> touch, stir up: ~神经 (shénjīng) touch a nerve || ~旧伤 stir up an old injury || ~很大 touch greatly

12 冒犯 [-] màofàn (encroach-offend) <v.> offend: ~长辈 (zhǎngbèi) offend an elder || ~对方 offend the opposition

13 欺负 [-負] qīfù (bully-betray) <v.> bully: ~人 bully someone || 受/被~ be bullied || ~他老实 bully a nice person

14 欺压 [-壓] qīyā (bully-oppress) <v.> oppress: ~穷人 oppress the poor || ~百姓 oppress commoners

15 侮辱 [-] wǔrǔ (slight-insult) <v.> insult: ~妇女 insult a woman || ~人格 insult someone's personality

16 糟蹋 [-] zāotà (ruin-tread) <v.> waste, ruin: ~粮食 (liángshi) waste food || ~东西 ruin something || ~妇女 defile a woman

17 调侃 [調-] tiáokǎn (jeer-piffle) <v.> ridicule: ~自己 ridicule yourself || ~两句 ridicule briefly

18 捉弄 [-] zhuōnòng (tease-make fun of) <v.> tease: ~同学 tease a classmate || 相互~ tease each other

19 开玩笑 [開--] kāiwánxiào (make-joke) <v.> make a joke: 跟朋友~ joke around with friends || 爱/喜欢~ love, can, like to make jokes || 开一个玩笑 make one joke

20 挑逗 [-] tiǎodòu (incite-tease) <v.> provoke: 有意~ flirt on purpose || ~男性flirt males || ~的目光flirting glance

21 为难 [爲難] wéinán (make-difficult) <v.> make things difficult for: ~他 make things difficult for him || 与我~ make things difficult for me || 让他~ make me feel awkward

22 挑剔 [-] tiāotī (pick-scrape) <v.> nitpick: 百般~ nitpick everything || ~对方 nitpick the opponent || 无可~ cannot be nitpicked

23 挑刺儿 [--兒] tiāocìr (pick-thorn) <v.> nitpick: 挑挑刺儿 find fault, nitpick || 刻意 (kèyì) ~ nitpick on purpose

24 瞒 [瞞] mán (hide) <v.> hide the truth from: ~着家里 hide the truth from your family || ~不过我的眼睛 hide the truth from my eyes || ~着过去 conceal the past

25 隐瞒 [隱瞞] yǐnmán (conceal-hide) <v.> conceal: ~消息 conceal information || ~缺点 hide a flaw || ~收入 conceal income

26 背着 [-著] bèizhe (back-*suffix*) <v.> hide from: ~父母 hide something from your parents || ~中央 hide something from the central government || ~老师 hide something from your teacher

27 掩盖 [-蓋] yǎngài (cover-hide) <v.> cover up: ~矛盾 cover up a contradiction || ~缺点 cover up a flaw || 有意~ deliberately conceal

28 掩饰 [-飾] yǎnshì (cover-gloss) <v.> gloss over: ~不安 gloss over unease || ~痛苦 (tòngkǔ) cover up pain || ~错误 gloss over an error

29 遮掩 [-] zhēyǎn (hide from view-cover) <v.> cover up: ~错误 cover up an error || 互相~ mutual cover up

30 粉饰 [-飾] fěnshì (pink-gloss) <v.> whitewash: ~自己 whitewash yourself || ~现实 whitewash reality || ~太平 to pretend that everything's going well

31 匿名 [-] nìmíng (conceal-name) <v.> anonymous: ~ 投票 anonymous vote || ~信anonymous letter

32 保密 [-] bǎomì (keep-secrecy) <v-o..> maintain secrecy: 对我~ keep my secret || 绝对~ absolutely secret || 需要~ needs to be kept secret

33 撒谎 [-謊] sāhuǎng (throw off-lie) <v.> tell a lie: 有意~ deliberately lie || 对老师~ tell a lie to a teacher

34 造谣 [-謠] zàoyáo (fabricate-rumor) <v.> start a rumor: 故意 ~ intentionally start a rumor || ~生事 start a troublesome rumor

35 骗 [騙] piàn (cheat, deceive) <v.> cheat: ~人 cheat someone || ~钱 cheat somebody out of their money || ~贷款 (dàikuǎn) cheat a loan

36 欺骗 [-騙] qīpiàn (deceive-swindle) <v.> deceive: ~顾客 deceive a customer || ~对方 deceive the opposition

37 纠缠 [糾纏] jiūchán (wind-entangle) <v.> get entangled: ~不清 get into a murky situation || 反复~ repeatedly get entangled || ~一个姑娘 get entangled with a girl

38 干扰 [-擾] gānrǎo (interfere-disturb) <v.> interfere, disturb: ~别人 disturb other people || 受到~ be interfered with || 排除 (páichú) ~ rule out interference

39 惊动 [驚動] jīngdòng (alarm-alert) <v.> alarm, alert, disturb: ~路人alarm bypassers || ~亲友 alert friends and relatives || 别为这么点小事~他. Don't disturb him with such a trifling matter.

40 困扰 [-擾] kùnrǎo (trouble-disturb) <v.> perplex: 这个问题~了他十年. This problem troubled him for ten years. || 令人~ make you feel puzzled || 被这个问题~ puzzled by this question

41 扰乱 [擾亂] rǎoluàn (disturb-chaos) <v.> disturb: ~秩序 (zhìxù) disturb order || ~市场 disturb the market

42 烦 [煩] fán (annoyed) <v.> annoy: 别~我. Don't annoy me.

43 挡 [擋] dǎng (block) <v.> keep off, block: ~路 keep off the road || ~风 keep out of the wind || ~在面前 block in front of

44 阻拦 [-攔] zǔlán (obstruct-bar) <v.> stop: ~ 女儿养宠物 (chǒngwù) stop daughter from raising a pet || 拼命 (pīnmìng) ~ desperately stop

45 阻碍 [-礙] zǔ'ài (obstruct-prevent) <v.> hinder, block, impede: ~发展 obstruct development || ~交流 impede an exchange || ~新事物impede new things

46 阻止 [-] zǔzhǐ (obstruct-stop) <v.> prevent: ~他提升 prevent him from getting promoted || ~门关上 prevent the door from closing || 极力~ do your best to prevent

47 遏止 [-] èzhǐ (check-stop) <v.> hold back: ~人体老化 hold back aging || ~病情 curtail the illness spread || ~赌博 (dǔbó) stop gambling

48 封杀 [-殺] fēngshā (seal-kill) <v.> block: 彻底 (chèdǐ) ~ completely block || ~这部电影 block this movie

49 封锁 [-鎖] fēngsuǒ (block-lock) <v.> block off: ~消息 block the passage of information || 地区~ block off an area || ~水道 blockade a waterway

50 拖后腿 [-後-] tuōhòutuǐ (hold-back-leg) <v.> hold back: 给全班~ hold the whole class back

51 妨碍 [-礙] fáng'ài (hinder-prevent) <v.> hinder: ~进步 hinder progress || ~工作 hinder work || 严重~ severely hinder

52 碍手碍脚 [礙-礙-] ài'shǒu'ài'jiǎo (prevent-hand-prevent-foot) <idiom> be in the way: 站开点, 别在这儿~. Go away, don't be in the way. || 她的三个孩子老是~. Her three children are always under foot.

53 束缚 [-縛] shùfù (bind-bind) <v.> bind, fetter: ~人类 bind humanity || 受传统 (chuántǒng) ~ be fettered by tradition

54 限制 [-] xiànzhì (limit-restrict) <v.> restrict: ~人数 limit the number of people || 严格~ strictly limit || 受到~ receive restrictions

55 约束 [約-] yuēshù (restrain-bind) <v/n..> restrain, constraint: ~自己 restrain yourself || 受~ receive constraints || ~个人行为 restrain personal behavior

56 制约 [-約] zhìyuē (restrict-restrain) <v.> restrict: 受~ be restricted by || ~对方 restrict the opponent || ~经济发展 restrict economic development
57 牵制 [牽-] qiānzhì (check-restrict) <v.> pin down: 互相~ contain, tie up each other || ~敌人 pin down the enemy
58 遏制 [-] èzhì (stop-restrict) <v.> check, contain: ~想象力 check your imagination || ~错误 contain an error || ~犯罪 (fànzuì) contain an offense
59 压制 [壓-] yāzhì (suppress-restrict) <v.> suppress: ~对方 stifle the opposition || ~女性 suppress women || ~积极性 suppress enthusiasm
60 制止 [-] zhìzhǐ (restrict-stop) <v.> curb: ~不法行为 curb illegal behavior || ~暴力 (bàolì) curb violence
61 抑制 [-] yìzhì (restrain-restrict) <v.> inhibit: ~ 进口 inhibit imports || ~生长 inhibit growth
62 扼杀 [-殺] èshā (grip-kill) <v.> smother, snuff out: ~兴趣 (xìngqù) smother interest || ~个性 smother personality || ~爱情 smother love

63 恭维 [-維] gōngwéi (respect-obey) <v.> flatter: ~别人 flatter others || ~几句 say a few compliments
64 讨好 [討-] tǎohǎo (beg-favor) <v.> curry favor with: ~别人 curry favor with others
65 迎合 [-] yínghé (pander-conform) <v.> cater to: ~成人 cater to adults || ~现实 cater to reality || ~市场 pander to the market
66 拍马屁 [-馬-] pāimǎpì (pat-horse-butt) <v.> lick someone's boots: 爱~ love to suck up to || 拍上司的马屁 lick a superior's boots
67 拉拢 [-攏] lālǒng (draw in-gather) <v.> draw over to one's side: ~ 人 draw someone in || ~感情 win over someone's feelings || ~选民 draw over voters to his side
68 收买 [-買] shōumǎi (control-buy) <v.> bribe: ~ 人心 buy popular support || ~国家工作人员 bribe national staff || ~媒体 (méitǐ) bribe the media
69 包庇 [-] bāobì (wrap-shelter) <v.> cover up: ~ 犯罪 cover up a crime || ~黑社会 cover up evil society || 公开~ openly shield
70 偏袒 [-] piāntǎn (partial-shield) <v.> side with: ~对方 side with the other side || 公然~ openly side with
71 串通 [-] chuàntōng (conspire-exchange) <v.> collude: 跟他人~ collude with others || 互相~ mutual collusion || 恶意~ malicious collusion
72 勾结 [-結] gōujié (collude-knot) <v.> collude with, gang up with:互相~ mutual collusion || 暗中~ secretly collude
73 结拜 [結-] jiébài (knot-worship) <v.> swear, bind: ~为夫妇 swear the couple together || ~为兄弟 sworn as brothers
74 结盟 [結-] jiéméng (knot-alliance) <v.> form an alliance: 与贵族~ ally with the nobility || 友好~ friendly alliance

Tips:

1 保: From the current form of 保 it seems related to 呆 (dāi, dull,) however, the original form of 呆 was 子 (child,) therefore the character 保 indicates 'a child/baby on a man's back,' in other words, 'to carry on the back' with a further extended meaning 'to bring up.'
2 撒: When it is pronounced as sā, it means 'let go' as in 撒手, 'to cast' as in 撒网, or 'to throw off' as in 撒谎, when it is pronounced as sǎ, it means 'to spread, to scatter' as in 撒种 (to spread seeds.)

3 手 and 脚: When they are used in a word, the word carries a negative meaning, for example, 碍手碍脚 in this unit, 大手大脚 (to spend with a free hand,) 毛手毛脚 (clumsy or be flustered with movement,) 束手束脚 (timid and hesitant,) 动手动脚 (to get fresh with sb.) Aside from the four-character idioms, even phrases that are not fixed such as 做手脚 (to play a trick) and 动手脚 (to manipulate, fight) have negative meanings as well.

4 压 (yā), 抑 (yì), 制 (zhì): All mean 'to suppress, to restrict,' and their combinations 压抑, 压制, 抑制 have almost the same meaning.

Exercises:

Part I: Use the given bound form as a guide to help you think of other words with the same character. Feel free to use your dictionary when needed. Then write down the English definition of each of the words you've written.

制 *(make, manufacture):* 限制 *restrict*

____
____
____
____
____
____
____

阻 *(hinder, block, obstruct):* 阻挡 *stop, resist, obstruct*

____
____
____
____

Part II: Read the following words and then fill the appropriate words to the blank to explain the given word.

欺骗、撒谎、迎合、拍马匹、收买、偏袒、勾结、开玩笑、掩盖、掩饰、挑刺儿

瞒着: ____________________________
讨好: ____________________________
拉拢: ____________________________
包庇: ____________________________
串通: ____________________________
调侃: ____________________________
遮掩: ____________________________

挑剔: ______________________________

Part III: Read the following sentences and fill in each blank with the appropriate word or phrase from the options given.

1 欺负、造谣
   a) 他上小学的时候一些坏孩子经常________他, 弄坏他的东西.
   b) 上小学的时候, 有些坏孩子给他__________说他有女朋友了.

2 结拜、结盟
   a) 小张和小王在一次聚会 (jùhuì, gathering) 上认识了, 两个人关系特别好, 后来________成了兄弟.
   b) 美国希望中国跟它_________, 共同对付朝鲜 (Cháoxiǎn, North Korea).

3 限制、遏制
   a) 美国对每年的移民人数是有__________ _的.
   b) 中国近几十年发展得太快, 很多国家都想__________中国.

4 扰乱、困扰
   a) 大城市的高房价一直_________着年轻人.
   b) 中国政府正在打击"炒房"行为, 防止"炒房"__________中国房地产市场.

5 扼杀、恭维
   a) 有人认为中国古代的科举 (kējǔ, imperial examination) 制度 (zhìdù, system) __________ _了读书人的创造力.
   b) 如果一个人过分__________别人, 中国人就会说这个人是在拍马屁.

Theme 186: Harm, revenge 伤害, 报复 (shānghài, bàofù)

1 教唆 [-] jiàosuō (instruct-incite) <v.> instigate: ~犯罪 instigate a crime || ~儿子 instigate someone's son to do something || ~别人做坏事 instigate other people to do bad things
2 怂恿 [慫-] sǒngyǒng (instigate) <v.> egg on, incite: ~哥哥买游戏机 incite your older brother to buy a game console || 极力~ strongly egg on
3 挑 [-] tiǎo (incite) <v.> provoke: ~起矛盾 provoke a contradiction || ~起争端 provoke a dispute
4 指使 [-] zhǐshǐ (instruct-use) <v.> incite: ~别人 incite others || ~孩子干坏事 incite children to do bad things
5 煽动 [-動] shāndòng (flame-up) <v.> stir up: ~人心 stir up public feeling || 暗中~ surreptitiously stir up || ~工人闹事 incite the workers to make trouble
6 勾引 [-] gōuyǐn (seduce-lure) <v.> entice: ~异性 entice the opposite sex || ~女性 entice girls || 公开~ publicly entice
7 引诱 [-誘] yǐnyòu (lure-tempt) <v.> lure, seduce: 用钱~ use money to lure || ~人 lure someone || ~异性 seduce the opposite sex

8 吓 [嚇] xià (intimidate) <v.> scare: 我们~~她. Let's scare her. || ~了一跳 was scared || ~了一身汗 broke out in a sweat
9 吓唬 [嚇-] xiàhǔ (intimidate-bluff) <v.> frighten: ~别人 frighten others || ~小孩 frighten little children

10 要挟 [-挾] yāoxié (force-coerce) <v./n.> threaten, threat: 以死相~ use the threat of death || ~政府 blackmail the government

11 威胁 [-脅] wēixié (threaten-coerce) <v./n.> threaten, threat: 受到~ receive a threat || ~生命 threaten a life || 核 ~ nuclear threat

12 挟持 [挾-] xiéchí (coerce-control) <v.> seize: ~人质 seize a hostage || 被坏人~ seized by bad people

13 威慑 [-懾] wēishè (threaten-terrorize) <v./n.> deter, deterrent: 核~ nuclear deterrent || ~不法分子 deter criminals

14 破坏 [-壞] pòhuài (break-ruin) <v.> destroy: ~环境 destroy the environment || ~交通 disrupt traffic || 遭到~ was destroyed

15 做手脚 [-] (make-underhand method) <v.> defraud: 在合同上~ defraud a contract || 大~ large fraud

16 糟蹋 [-] zāotà (waste-tread) <v.> ruin: ~艺术 to ruin art || ~人才 spoil talent || ~东西 ruin something

17 侵犯 [-] qīnfàn (encroach-violate) <v.> encroach on: ~人权 encroach on human rights || ~领土 encroach on territory || ~自由 infringe upon freedom

18 侵害 [-] qīnhài (encroach-harm) <v.> encroach on: 非法~ illegal encroachment || ~他人利益 encroach on the interests of others

19 腐蚀 [-蝕] fǔshí (rot-erode) <v.> corrode, corrupt: ~人心 corrode public opinion || ~牙齿 corrosion teeth || ~干部 corrode a cadre

20 迫害 [-] pòhài (press-harm) <v.> persecute: ~科学 persecute science || 受到~ be persecuted || ~老干部 persecute the old cadre

21 剥削 [剝-] bōxuē (peel-pare) <v.> exploit: ~工人 exploit workers || 经济~ economic exploitation || 残酷 (cánkù) ~ cruel exploitation

22 搜刮 [-] sōuguā (search-scrape) <v.> plunder: ~钱财 plunder wealth || ~黄金 plunder gold || 肆意 (sìyì) ~ wantonly plunder

23 压榨 [壓-] yāzhà (press-squeeze) <v.> squeeze, extort: ~人 squeeze (something) out of someone || 野蛮 (yěmán) ~ brutally extort

24 逼 [-] bī (force) <v.> force: ~他们说话 force them to speak || ~她参加 force her to participate || ~得没办法 no way to force

25 逼迫 [-] bīpò (force-press) <v.> compel: ~儿子学习 make your son study || ~他做决定 compel him to make a decision || ~人说假话 compel people to lie

26 强迫 [-] qiángpò (forcefully-press) <v.> force: ~他走 force him to go || ~你听 force you to listen || ~劳动 force sb. to work

27 压迫 [壓-] yāpò (press-oppress) <v.> oppress: ~人民 oppress the people || 政治~ political oppression || 民族 (mínzú) ~ national oppression

28 勉强 [-] miǎnqiǎng (force-do with difficulty) <v.> do with difficulty, force sb to do sth, barely enough: ~女儿学钢琴 force his daughter to learn piano || ~自己 force yourself

29 遣返 [-] qiǎnfǎn (repatriate-back) <v./n.> repatriate, repatriation: 强制 (qiángzhì) ~ forced repatriation || ~难民 (nànmín) repatriate a refugee

30 诬陷 [誣-] wūxiàn (accuse falsely-frame) <v.> frame: ~她是第三者 frame her as a third party || ~好人 frame a good person

31 冤枉 [-] yuānwǎng (bend-crooked) <v.> treat unjustly, to accuse wrongly: ~好人 wrong a innocent people || ~官司unjust verdict

32 陷害 [-] xiànhài (frame-harm) <v.> frame: ~对手 frame an opponent || ~民族英雄 (yīngxióng) frame a national hero

33 暗算 [-] ànsuàn (secretly-plot) <v.> plot against: 遭人~ was plotted against || ~别人 plot against others

34 打架 [-] dǎjià (fight-quarrel) <v-o.> fight: 打一架 fight once || 跟人~ fight someone || 动手~ fist-fight

35 服 [-] fú (obey, convinced) <v.> serve, admit: ~输 admit a loss || ~兵役 serve in the military

36 收服 [-] shōufú (subdue-convinced) <v.> subdue: ~人心subdue popular feeling || ~小国 subdue a small country || ~一匹马 subdue a horse

37 驯服 [馴-] xùnfú (tame-convinced) <v.> tame: ~大自然 tame nature || ~一头狮子 tame a lion

38 屈服 [-] qūfú (yield-convinced) <v.> submit: ~于人 submit to someone || ~于压力 yield to pressure || 向强权 (qiángquán) ~ submit to power

39 让步 [讓-] ràngbù (give in-step) <v.> concede: 互相~ mutual concessions || 让一步 make a concession || 向中国~ concede to China

40 妥协 [-協] tuǒxié (stop-mediate) <v.> compromise: 对日~ compromise with Japan || 相互 ~ compromise with each other || 一再~ repeatedly compromise

41 退让 [-讓] tuìràng (back-give in) <v.> give in: 互相~ both parties back down || 一步步~ give in a bit

42 打压 [-壓] dǎyā (strike-press) <v.> suppress: 疯狂~ suppress insanity || ~对手 suppress the opponent || ~房价 suppress the price

43 排挤 [-擠] páijǐ (expel-push out) <v.> crowd, push out: ~对手 crowd out the opponent || ~移民 push out immigrants || ~出局 push out of office

44 排外 [-] páiwài (exclude-foreign) <v.> anti-foreign: 盲目~ blindly be exclusive to sth.

45 挑拨 [-撥] tiǎobō (incite-stir) <v.> instigate trouble: ~关系 instigate trouble in a relationship || ~是非 sow discord

46 搬弄是非 [-] bānnòngshìfēi (sow-discord) <idiom> make mischief: 喜欢~ like making mischief

47 决裂 [決-] juéliè (break-split) <v.> break with: 彻底 (chèdǐ) ~ completely break with || 公开 ~ publicly break off || 跟家庭~ break with family

48 绝交 [-] juéjiāo (break-association) <v.> break off relations: 两人~ two people break off relations || 跟朋友 ~ break off relations with a friend

49 一刀两断 [--兩斷] yīdāoliǎngduàn (one-cut-two-segment) <idiom> two segments with one cut (make a clean break): 跟过去~ make a clean break with the past || 正式~ formally break off

50 报仇 [報-] bàochóu (avenge-hatred) <v.> avenge: 为亲人~ revenge for one's close relatives

51 算账 [-賬] suànzhàng (calculate-account) <v.> get even with: 秋后~ wait until time is ripe to settle up || 算总账 get totally even with || 一笔一笔~ settle up with each other

52 报复 [報復] bàofù (avenge-retaliate) <v.> retaliate: ~社会 retaliate against society || ~他人 retaliate against others

53 以眼还眼, 以牙还牙 [--還-, --還-] yǐyǎnhuányǎn, yǐyáhuányá (with-eye-return-eye, with-tooth-return-tooth) <idiom> eye for an eye and tooth for a tooth: 一些人认为处理国家关系不应该~. Some people think dealings with international relations should not be treated as 'an eye for an eye and a tooth for a tooth.'

54 犯 [-] fàn (invade, violate) <v.> commit: ~错误 commit an error || ~法 commit a crime || ~上 offend superiors

Tips:

1 教: The upper left part of 教 is 爻 (yáo,) the sound part of this character. The lower left part is 子 (child), and the right part is 攵 (攴, pū), which depicts a hand holding a stick. Therefore, 教 means '(a grown-up) holds a stick to teach a child,' in other words, 'to teach' (jiāo) such as in words including 教学 or 'to educate' (jiào) such as in words including 教育 (jiàoyù, educate, education.)

2 挑: If it is pronounced as tiāo, it means 'to shoulder' (such as 挑水) or 'to choose' (such as 挑选,) if pronounced as tiǎo, it means 'to incite' (such as 挑拨 in this unit) or 'to raise' (such as 挑起灯笼, to raise a lantern.)

3 煽动 (shāndòng), 指使 (zhǐshǐ), 教唆 (jiàosuō), 怂恿 (sǒngyǒng): They all mean 'to make others do something bad,' but their meanings decrease in degree. 煽动 indicates that a (relatively) large population is stirred up. 指使 indicates its agent has (certain) authority or power over the patient of it. 教唆 indicates its agent is superior in intelligence to the patient of it. 怂恿 indicates its agent is unwilling to be exposed.

4 强, 逼/压, 迫: All mean 'to force sb to do sth,' and their combinations, 强逼, 强压 (not strong wordhood,) 强迫, 逼迫, 压迫 have the same meaning.

Exercises:

Part I: Read the following words and then fill the appropriate words to the blank to explain the given word.

以眼还眼，　以牙还牙、怂恿、挑拨、一刀两断、妥协、让步、冤枉、陷害、逼迫、压榨、侵害、威胁、吓唬、引诱

教唆: ______________________________
报复: ______________________________
绝交: ______________________________
退让: ______________________________
诬陷: ______________________________
强迫: ______________________________
剥削: ______________________________
侵犯: ______________________________
要挟: ______________________________
勾引: ______________________________

Part II: Read the following sentences and fill in each blank with the appropriate word or phrase from the options given.

1 排挤、排外
  a) 据美国《纽约时报》(*The New York Times*) 报道 (bàodào, report), 美国南部的有些地方比较__________, 不喜欢移民.
  b) 据美国《纽约时报》报道, 一些白宫官员由于受到他人__________, 将会在近期内辞职 (cízhí, resign).

2 收服、驯服
  a) 毛泽东时间曾经做过__________台湾的打算, 但是一直没有成功.
  b) 据说狗是一种最容易__________的动物.

3 破坏、做手脚
  a) 据说在中国有些病人非常不信任医生, 担心医生在治疗 (zhìliáo, treat) 时__________, 来增加自己的医疗费用.
  b) 医院的垃圾不经过特殊处理就扔对环境的__________非常大.

4 报仇、算账
  a) 小白在背地里说小李的坏话, 因此小李要找他_________, 问个清楚.
  b) 有的宗教国家认为西方国家侵犯 (qīnfàn, violate) 了他们的信仰, 侵占了他们的财物, 因为他们要_________, 让消灭西方国家.

5 遣返、闹事
  a) 在飞机上_________, 是违法行为, 会受到严厉处罚 (chǔfá, punishment).
  b) 美国共和党主张________非法移民, 但是民主党主张保护非法移民.

Theme 187: Weather 天气 (tiānqì)

1 晴 [-] qíng (clear) <adj.> clear: ~天 sunny day || ~空 clear sky || 天~ sunny
2 晴朗 [-] qínglǎng (clear-bright) <adj.> sunny: ~的天空 sunny sky || 天气~. The weather is sunny. || ~的夜晚 nice night
3 风和日丽 [風--麗] fēnghérìlì (wind-gentle-sun-fine) <idiom> bright sun and gentle breeze: ~的天气 warm and sunny weather || 上午~ warm and sunny morning
4 秋高气爽 [--氣-] qiūgāoqìshuǎng (autumn-high-air-freshening) <idiom> clear autumn sky and bracing air (good fall weather): ~的时候 the time of good fall weather

5 多云 [-雲] duōyún (much-cloud) <adj.> cloudy: 晴转~ sunny changes to cloudy || 终年 ~ cloudy year-round || ~天气 cloudy weather
6 雨过天晴 [-過--] yǔguòtiānqíng (rain-pass-sky-clear) <idiom> The sun shines after the rain passes.: ~的午后 rainy afternoon that changes to sun
7 阴 [陰] yīn (overcast) <adj.> overcast: 天~ the sky is overcast || ~天 cloudy day
8 阴沉沉 [陰--] yīnchénchén (overcast-low-*reduplication*) <adj.> dark: 天~的 a dark sky
9 乌云密布 [烏雲--] wūyúnmìbù (black-cloud-dense-spread) <idiom> black clouds covering the sky: 天空~. The sky was filled with dark clouds.

10 刮风 [颳風] guāfēng (blow-wind) <v.> be windy: 刮大风 be very windy || 刮狂风 be fiercely windy
11 狂风大作 [-風--] kuángfēngdàzuò (violent-wind-greatly-burst) <idiom> a gale broke out: 突然~. A gale unexpectedly began || 再次 ~. A gale began once again.
12 降水 [-] jiàngshuǐ (fall-water) <v./n.> precipitate, precipitation: ~不少 the precipitation was not small || 自然~ natural precipitation || 人工~ artificial precipitation
13 降雨 [-] jiàngyǔ (fall-rain) <v.> rainfall: 大范围~ large range of rainfall || 人工~ manmade rain
14 下雨 [-] xiàyǔ (fall-rain) <v-o.> rain: 下大雨 rain a lot || 常常~ rain often || 正在~ currently raining
15 倾盆大雨 [傾---] qīngpéndàyǔ (empty-basin-heavy-rain) <idiom> torrential downpour: 下着~ under a downpour || 冒着~ brave a downpour || ~下个不停 nonstop downpour

16 狂风暴雨 [-風--] kuángfēngbàoyǔ (violent-wind-sudden and violent-rain) <idiom> howling wind and torrential rain: 遇到~ suffer a violent storm

17 下雪 [-] xiàxuě (fall-snow) <v-o.> snow: 下大雪/小雪 snow a lot/little || 开始~ start to snow || 很少~ snow very little

18 大雪纷飞 [--紛飛] dàxuěfēnfēi (heavy-snow-disorderly-fly) <idiom> lots of snow swirling in the air: 一连几日~ heavy snow for a few days

19 闪电 [閃電] shǎndiàn (flash-lightning) <v.> lightning: 一道~ a lightning bolt

20 打雷 [-] dǎléi (strike-thunder) <v-o.> thunder: 打一个雷 a thunderclap || 打响雷 begin thundering || 打一次雷 one thunderstorm

21 电闪雷鸣 [電閃-鳴] diànshǎnléimíng (lightning-flash-thunder-roar) <idiom> a storm with lightning and thunder: 忽然~ a sudden thunderstorm || 一直~ constant lightning and thunder

22 天亮 [-] tiānliàng (sky-bright) <v.> daybreak: ~之前 before daybreak || ~以后 after daybreak || 大~ big/grand dawn

23 日出 [-] rìchū (sun-out) <v.> sunrise: ~前后 right before and after sunrise

24 日落 [-] rìluò (sun-set) <v.> sunset: ~ 时分 time of sunset || ~休息 rest at sunset

25 天黑 [-] tiānhēi (sky-dark) <v.> dusk: ~才回家 wait until dusk to go home

Tips:

1 降水, 降雨, 降雪 and 下雨, 下雪: The former three are meteorological terms and the latter two are for ordinary use.

2 风, 雨, 雷, 电: If they are mentioned together, they must be mentioned in this order.

3 风, 雨, 雪: When two of them are mentioned together, such as 风雨, 风雪, 雨雪, 风雨交加, 雨雪交加, 风 is always mentioned first and 雪 last.

Exercises:

Part I: Read the following words and then answer the questions.

下雨、下雪、刮风、打雷、闪电、晴、阴、多云、阴转晴、晴转阴、晴转多云

1 今天天气怎么样?

____

2 你喜欢下雨或者下雪吗? 为什么?

____

3 你怕不怕打雷和闪电?

____

Part II: Read the following words and then fill the appropriate 4 character words to the blank to modify the given word.

大雪纷飞、倾盆大雨、狂风暴雨、电闪雷鸣、风和日丽、秋高气爽、狂风大作、乌云密布

下雪: ______________________________

下雨: ______________________________

打雷: ______________________________

晴天: ______________________________

刮风: ______________________________

阴天: ______________________________

Theme 188: To freeze, to dissolve 冰冻, 溶解 (bīngdòng, róngjiě)

1 受潮 [-] shòucháo (suffer-damp) <v.> be damp: 花生~了. The peanuts are damp.
2 溶解 [-] róngjiě (dissolve-smelt) <v.> dissolve: 气体可以~在水里. Gas can dissolve in water. || 渐渐 ~ gradually dissolve
3 溶化 [-] rónghuà (dissolve-melt) <v.> melt, dissolve: 冰山~. The iceberg melted. || 积雪~. The snow melted.
4 融化 [-] rónghuà (thaw-melt) <v.> thaw: 冰雪~. The snow and ice thawed.
5 冷冻 [-凍] lěngdòng (cold-freeze) <v.> freeze: 低温~ cryogenic freezing || ~人体 freeze a body || ~治疗 cryotherapy
6 凝固 [-] nínggù (coagulate-solidify) <v.> solidify: 血液~ the blood congealed
7 速冻 [-凍] sùdòng (quick-freeze) <v.> quick freeze: ~食品 flash-frozen food || ~饺子 quick-frozen dumplings
8 冻 [凍] dòng (freeze) <v.> feel cold, freeze: ~病了 catch a cold || ~得发抖 shiver due to cold || ~硬了 freeze solid
9 冰镇 [-鎮] bīngzhèn (ice-cool) <v.> iced: ~汽水 iced soft drinks
10 冰冻 [-凍] bīngdòng (ice-freeze) <v.> freeze: ~小鱼 freeze little fish
11 上冻 [-凍] shàngdòng (became-freeze) <v.> freeze: 土地~ the ground froze
12 解冻 [-凍] jiědòng (smelt-freeze) <v.> unfreeze, thaw: 食品~ thawing food || 两国关系~ thawing of the relations between the two countries || ~资金unfreeze funds/assets
13 降温 [-] jiàngwēn (lower-temperature) <v-o.> lower the temperature: 降了温 the temperature dropped || 逐步~ gradually cool down || 迅速 (xùnsù) ~ rapidly cool

Tips:

1 冫 (liǎng): 冫 is the reduced form of 仌 (bīng,) which depicts the shape when the ice was just formed or broken. Characters with radical 冫 include 冰, 冷, 凝, 冻 in this unit and some other common characters such as 寒 (hán, bitterly cold,) and 冬 (dōng, winter.)
2 溶 and 融: Both are pronounced as 'róng' and their meanings are similar in some aspect. 溶 means 'dissolve' and 融化 'melt.'

3 溶/融, 化, 解: Their meanings are all close to 'dissolve, melt' and their combinations 溶化, 融化, 溶解, 融解, 化解 have similar meanings.

Exercises:

Part I: Use the given bound form as a guide to help you think of other words with the same character. Feel free to use your dictionary when needed. Then write down the English definition of each of the words you've written.

冻 (freeze, feel cold): 冷冻 freeze

____

____

____

____

Part II: Read the following sentences and fill in each blank with the appropriate word or phrase from the options given.

解冻、融化、降温、冰镇、速冻

1 夏天的时候, _______啤酒在这个城市特别畅销 (chàngxiāo, sell fast, very marketable).
2 这家公司的__________食品因为质优价廉特别受年轻人欢fl.
3 天气预报说这几天会大幅度_ (fúdù, range, scope) _______, 请市民做好防寒准备.
4 由于天气迅速升温, 冰雪开始_________了.
5 经过调查这家公司没有什么大问题, 于是银行_______了这家公司的全部资金.

Theme 189: Verbs of natural phenomena 自然现象动词 (zìrán xiànxiàng dòngcí)

1 刺耳 [-] cì'ěr (pierce-ear) <v.> ear piercing: 声音~ ear piercing sound || 音乐~ ear piercing music || ~的爆炸 (bàozhà) 声 ear piercing explosion
2 震耳欲聋 [---聾] zhèn'ěr yùlóng (shock-ear-will-deaf) <idiom> deafening: 响声~ deafening sound || ~的掌声 (zhǎngsheng) deafening applause
3 照 [-] zhào (bright, shine) <v.> look at, shine, photo: 阳光 ~在脸上. The sun shines on a face. || ~一张相 take a photo || ~镜子 (jìngzi) look in a mirror
4 照耀 [-] zhàoyào (shine-illuminate) <v.> shine, illuminate: 阳光~ bright sunshine || 红星~中国 *Red Star over China* (first account of Chinese Communism, by Edgar Snow)
5 照射 [-] zhàoshè (shine-shoot) <v.> light up: 灯光~ light illuminates ||用紫外线~消毒 irradiate with ultraviolet rays to disinfect

6 射 [-] zhàoshè (shoot) <v.> send out: 太阳光~在脸上 sun shone on a face || 眼光~到他身上 eyes saw his body
7 反光 [-] fǎnguāng (reflect-light) <v.> reflect light: 镜子~ the reflection of mirror || 雪地~ the reflection of snow
8 逆光 [-] nìguāng (back-light) <v.> against the light, backlighting: ~拍摄 (pāishè) take a backlighting photo
9 辐射 [輻-] fúshè (spoke-shoot) <v.> radiate: 太阳~ solar radiation || 核~ nuclear radiation

10 闪 [閃] shǎn (peek, flash) <v.> flash: ~红光 flashing red light || ~着光 flashing light || ~着灯 flashing light (manmade)
11 发光 [發-] fāguāng (send out-light) <v.> give off light: 闪闪~ sparkling with light || 眼睛~ shining eyes || 持续 (chíxù) ~ continue to give off light
12 闪光 [閃-] shǎnguāng (flash-light) <v.> gleam: 眼睛~. The eyes gleamed.
13 闪烁 [閃爍] shǎnshuò (flash-flicker) <v.> twinkle, glimmer: 灯光 ~. The lights twinkled. || 浪花~. The waves glistened. || ~着银光 glimmering silver
14 闪耀 [閃-] shǎnyào (flash-illuminate) <v.> glitter: 星光~ glittering starlight || ~着彩色的光芒 glittering with colorful light
15 晃眼 [-] huǎngyǎn (dazzle-eye) <v.> dazzle, twinkle: 灯光~ dazzling lights || 他刚才还在这儿, 一~就不见了. He was recently still here but was gone in the twinkling of an eye.
16 焚烧 [-燒] fénshāo (burn hill-burn) <v.> burn: 烈火~ set on fire || ~报纸 burn a newspaper || ~垃圾 burn trash/garbage
17 燃烧 [-燒] ránshāo (on flame-burn) <v.> burn, ignite: 充分~ fully ignite || 烈火~ burning fire || ~的火焰 (huǒyàn, flame) ignited flame
18 着火 [-] zháohuǒ (on-fire) <v.> be on fire: 房屋~ a house on fire
19 烧 [燒] shāo (burn) <v.> burn: ~火 fire || ~干草 burn hay || ~纸 burn paper
20 开 [開] kāi (open, boiled) <v.> boiled: 水~了 the water boiled || ~水 boiled water
21 沸腾 [-騰] fèiténg (gush-rise) <v.> boil: 开水 ~ the water is boiling || 人声~ vocally boiling over, to be impassioned || 球场(的观众)~了. The audience in the stadium is simmering with excitement.
22 蒸发 [-發] zhēngfā (evaporate-off) <v.> evaporate: 水分~ water evaporation || 大量~ a lot of evaporation || 液体 (yètǐ) ~ liquid evaporation
23 挥发 [揮發] huīfā (volatilize-off) <v.> volatile: 瓶子里的酒精都~ 光了. The alcohol inside the bottle has volatilized. || 容易~ easily made volatile || ~快 quickly made volatile

Tips:

1 火: 火 is a pictograph, meaning 'fire.' Characters with this radical in this unit include 烧, 燃, 照, 蒸, 焚 and 烁. A variant of 火 is 灬 as in 照 and 蒸.
2 光: The upper part of 光 is 火 (fire) and the lower part 人 which when combined mean 'light, shine.' Characters with this radical in this unit include 耀 (yào, illuminate) and 晃 (huǎng, dazzle.)

Exercises:

Part I: Use the given bound form as a guide to help you think of other words with the same character. Feel free to use your dictionary when needed. Then write down the English definition of each of the words you've written.

光 *(light):* 反光 *reflect light*

____

____

____

____

照 *(light up, shine, look at):* 照镜子 *look in a mirror*

____

____

____

____

烧 *(burn, fever):* 发烧 *get a fever*

____

____

____

____

闪 *(flash):* 闪红光 *flashing a red light*

____

____

____

____

Theme 190: Verbs of motion 状态动词 (zhuàngtài dòngcí)

1 翘 [翹] qiào (long feather, raise) <v.> raise: ~着二郎腿 (èrláng tuǐ) raise one's two legs || 不能有成绩就~尾巴. Don't get cocky when you've achieved something.
2 仰 [-] yǎng (face upward) <v.> raise up: ~头 raise one's head || ~脸 raise one's face || ~着身子 lift up one's body
3 突出 [-] tūchū (protrude-out) <v.> outstanding, prominent: 向前~ protruding outwards || ~主题 prominent theme || ~优势 (yōushì) highlight advantages
4 鼓出 [-] gǔchū (bulge-out) <v.> bulge out: 手上~一个大包 hold a big bulging bag in one's hand
5 耸立 [聳-] sǒnglì (lofty-stand) <v.> stand tall: 高楼~ towering high rise || 并肩~ stand tall side by side || ~在山坡上 stand tall on the hillside

6 挺 [-] tǐng (draw-straighten) <v.> straighten up: ~胸 puff out your chest || ~着大肚子 stick out one's stomach

7 挺立 [-] tǐng lì (straighten-stand) <v.> stand upright: ~在大地上 stand upright on the ground || 笔直地~ stand straight up || 傲然/昂首 (àorán/ángshǒu) ~ proudly, with one's head high, haughtily stand upright

8 拔地而起 [-] bádì'érqǐ (rise-ground-and-rise) <idiom> rise steeply: 高楼~ the building rises sharply || ~一座高楼 a sharply rising building

9 垂 [-] chuí (hang down) <v.> droop, let fall: ~泪 shed tears || 低~ droop low || ~着脑袋 hang one's head

10 陷 [-] xiàn (sink) <v.> sink into: 身体~在软绵绵的沙发里. The body sank into the soft sofa. || ~在绝望 (juéwàng) 里 sink into despair

11 凹进 [-進] āo jìn (sunken-inward) <v.> recess: 向内~ recess inwards || ~一大块 a large piece goes inwards

12 下沉 [-] xiàchén (down-sink) <v.> sink: 地面~ sink underground || 迅速~ rapidly sink || 太阳~ the sun sank (in the sky)

13 沉没 [-] chénmò (sink-submerge) <v.> sink: 船只~ a vessel sinks || ~在海里 sink at sea

14 蒙 [-] méng (cover) <v.> cover: ~着眼睛 cover your eyes || ~一块布 cover with a piece of cloth || ~着白雪 covered with snow

15 掩盖 [-蓋] yǎngài (hide-cover) <v.> conceal: ~矛盾 conceal a contradiction || ~缺点 conceal a shortcoming || ~真相 conceal the truth

16 遮挡 [-擋] zhēdǎng (conceal-block) <v.> keep out: ~视线 keep out of the line of sight || ~阳光 keep out of the sunlight || ~光线 keep out light

17 遮盖 [-蓋] zhēgài (conceal-cover) <v.> cover: ~得严严实实 cover securely || 甜味能~辣味 (làwèi, piquancy) sweet flavor can conceal the spice || 黑夜~了一切. The night concealed everything.

18 屏蔽 [-] píngbì (screen-shelter) <v.> screen, shield: ~风浪 shield the wind and waves || ~辐射 (fúshè) screen from radiation || ~信号 shielded signal

19 笼罩 [籠-] lóngzhào (envelop-cover) <v.> envelop: 黑云~ black clouds enveloped || ~在月光下 enveloped in moonlight || 夜色~大地. Night shrouded the land.

20 落 [-] luò (fall) <v.> fall, drop: (太阳) ~山. The sun falls behind a mountain. || ~地 fall to the ground

21 跌 [-] diē (tumble) <v.> fall: ~在地上 fall on the ground || ~在床下 fall under the bed || ~跟头 tumble

22 倒塌 [-] dǎotā (fall, collapse) <v.> collapse: 房屋~ the house collapsed || 楼房~ the building collapsed || 全部~ completely collapse

23 雪崩 [-] xuěbēng (snow-landslide) <v.> avalanche: ~严重 severe avalanche || 发生~. An avalanche occurred.

24 塌方 [-] tāfāng (collapse-earth) <v.> cave in: 出现~ currently caving in || 岩洞~ cave collapsed

25 伸 [-] shēn (stretch) <v.> stretch: ~手 stretch out one's hand || ~舌头 stick out one's tongue || ~脑袋 stick out one's head

26 伸缩 [-縮] shēnsuō (expand-contract) <v.> expand and contract: ~自如 smoothly expand and contract || 自由~ free to expand and contract || 灵活~ flexibly move back and forth

27 蔓延 [-] mànyán (creep-extend) <v.> spread: 大火~ the big fire spread || 害虫~ the pests spread || 四处~ spread everywhere

28 延长 [-長] yáncháng (extend-long) <v.> extend: ~时间 extend time || ~生命 prolong a life || ~寿命 (shòumìng) extend a lifespan
29 延伸 [-] yánshēn (extend-stretch) <v.> stretch: 向前~ stretches ahead || 铁路的~ the railway's extent || ~到远方 stretch into the distance
30 张 [張] shū zhāng (draw, open) <v.> open: ~嘴 open your mouth || ~大眼睛 open big eyes || ~开口 open one's mouth and start to talk
31 舒张 [-張] shūzhāng (stretch-open) <v.> expand, dilate: 心脏~ diastolic heart (relaxed) || 血管~ blood vessels expand
32 伸展 [-] shēnzhǎn (stretch-spread) <v.> extend, stretch: ~四肢 stretch one's arms and legs || 向前~ extends forward

33 缩 [縮] suō (contract, shrink) <v.> shrink, pull back: ~脖子 draw in one's neck || ~着头 pull in one's head || ~成一团 shrink into one group
34 缩短 [縮-] suōduǎn (contract-short) <v.> shorten: ~ 时间 shorten time || ~距离 (jùlí) shorten the distance || ~长度 shorten the length
35 缩小 [縮-] suōxiǎo (contract-small) <v.> reduce: ~范围 (fànwéi) reduce the scope || ~差别 reduce the difference || ~面积 narrow down the area
36 浓缩 [濃縮] nóngsuō (densely-contract) <v.> concentrate: ~劳动时间 concentrated working time || ~果汁 concentrated fruit juice || 高度~ highly concentrated
37 关上 [關-] guānshàng (close-up) <bf> close: ~门 close a door || ~电视 turn off the TV || ~灯 turn off the light
38 关闭 [關閉] guānbì (close-closed) <v.> close: ~窗口 close the window || ~大门 shut the door || 自动~ automatically turn off
39 紧闭 [緊閉] jǐnbì (tightly-closed) <v.> close tightly: 窗户~. The window is tightly closed. || ~眼睛 squeeze shut one's eyes || 城门 ~. Shut the city gate.

Tips:

1 遮, 掩, 盖: All mean 'hide, conceal' and their combinations, 遮掩, 遮盖, 掩盖 have the same meaning.
2 延, 伸, 展: All mean 'stretch, extend' and their combinations, 延伸, 延展, 伸展 have almost the same meaning.

Exercises:

Part I: Read the following sentences and fill in each blank with the appropriate word or phrase from the options given.

1 拔地而起、下沉
   a) 这座城市的现代化速度真快, 才短短几个月就有一座座高楼_______.
   b) 由于过度使用地下水资源, 城市的一些地方开始________.

2 倒塌、关闭
   a) 由于大暴雨, 一些村民的房子________.
   b) 由于天气恶劣 (èliè, bad), 机场不得不________.

3 缩短、屏蔽、蔓延
   a) 脸书等社交媒体的使用________了不同地区人们之间的距离.

b) 在中国无法使用脸书, 因为政府已经________了这个网站.
c) 最近中国互联网上________一种病毒, 使很多人的个人信息被盗.

4 延长、掩盖、耸立
a) 据说苹果公司推出的新手机可以________带电时间到一个星期.
b) 苹果公司总部________着一座座现代化建筑 (jiànzhù, building).
c) 这家公司的管理者一直尽力________公司出现的种种丑闻.

Theme 191: To store, to display 存放, 展示 (cúnfàng, zhǎnshì)

1 存 [-] cún (exist) <v.> store, hold: ~包 hold a bag || 这个车库能 ~八辆汽车. This garage can store eight cars. || ~钱deposit money
2 放 [-] fàng (banish, release, to place) <v.> place: ~在桌子上 put on the table || ~在哪里了? Where was it put? || ~在房间里 put in a room
3 放置 [-] fàngzhì (put-store aside) <v.> lay aside: ~在干净的地方 put aside in a clean place || 随意 (suíyì) ~ randomly lay aside ||乐器应该~在通风的地方. Musical instruments should be put in a ventilated place.
4 停放 [-] tíngfàng (park-to place) <v.> park: ~汽车 park a car || ~在操场上 park at the playground || ~两个月 park for two months
5 寄存 [-] jìcún (deposit-store) <v.> store: ~行李 store luggage || ~贵重物品 store expensive objects || 自动 ~ voluntarily store
6 列 [-] liè (break up, list) <v.> list: ~名单 make a name list || ~细节 list the details || ~人数list the number of people
7 列入 [-] lièrù (list-in) <v.> include in a list: ~计划 include the plan || ~比赛 include the game || ~正式项目 included in the project
8 列为 [-為] lièwéi (list-as) <v.> classified as: ~重点 classified as a focus || ~毒品 classified as a drug || ~保护对象 listed as a protected object
9 陈列 [陳-] chénliè (display-display) <v.> display: ~中国画 display a Chinese painting || ~在博物馆 display in a museum
10 罗列 [羅-] luóliè (spread-list) <v.> set out, explain: ~一堆数字 set out a pile of numbers || ~例子 set out an example || ~缺点 explain a disadvantage
11 排列 [-] páiliè (arrange-list) <v.> arrange: 按顺序~ arrange in order || ~卡片 arrange cards || ~整齐 arrange neatly
12 排 [-] pái (arrange) <v.> order, line up: ~第四名 ranked fourth || ~队买票 line up to buy tickets || ~着长龙 in a long line
13 分布 [-佈] fènbù (separate-scatter) <v.> scatter, distribute: ~不均 scatter unevenly || 对称~ symmetrically distributed || 城乡~ urban and rural distribution
14 布置 [佈-] bùzhì (arrange-put) <v.> arrange, lay out: ~房间 arrange a room || ~工作 decoration work || ~整齐 arrange neatly
15 悬挂 [懸掛] xuánguà (suspend-hang) <v.> hang, fly: ~国旗 fly the national flag || ~彩球 hang a colored silk ball || ~银牌 hang a silver medal
16 倒挂 [-] dàoguà (upside down-hang) (hang) <v.> upside down: 身体~ unnatural (topsy-turvy) health || ~金钩 (jīngōu) hang a gold hook upside down || ~在墙壁上 hang upside down on the wall
17 颠倒 [顛-] diān dǎo (top-upside down) <v.> put upside down, invert: ~是非 invert right and wrong || ~次序 reverse the order || ~主次 switch the primary and secondary

18 堆 [-] duī (heap, pile) <v.> pile up: ~满了书 pile full of books || ~成山 pile into a mountain

19 堆积 [-積] duī jī (heap-store up) <v.> pile, heap up: ~事实 pile up facts || 商品~ heap up merchandise || 杂乱地 ~ messily heap up

20 积压 [積壓] jīyā (stock up-held) <v.> overstock: 产品~ overstock goods || 大量~ large glut || ~严重 severely overstock

21 沉淀 [-澱] chéndiàn (sink-precipitate) <v.> settle, precipitate: ~杂质 settle out impurities || 防止~ prevent precipitate

Tips:

1 悬 (懸 xuán): The original form of 悬 is 县, which depicts 'a beheaded head hanging upside down.' A 系 (thread, rope) was later added 縣, which, however, was borrowed to mean 'county.' A 心 was added again 懸 so as to keep its original meaning 'hang.'

2 罒 (网): This radical 网 (wThis radica'net' which was used to catch birds and beasts in ancient times. Characters with this radical usually have negative meanings, such as 罗 (羅, luó, catch birds with a net,) 罢 (bà, dismiss from office,) 罪 (zuì, crime,) 罚 (罰, fá, punish,) 罹 (lí, suffering).

Exercises:

Part I: Use the given bound form as a guide to help you think of other words with the same beginning character. Feel free to use your dictionary when needed. Then write down the English definition of each of the words you've written.

列 *(list):* 列名单 *make a name list*

____

____

____

____

____

____

Part II: Read the following signs and then answer the questions.

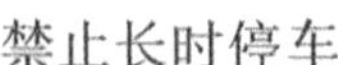

禁止长时停车

禁止停车

图1

1 图一很可能放在什么地方? 请从下面三那个选项中选一个
a) 学校门前 b) 教室里 c) 餐厅里

2 图一中"禁止长时停车"里面的"长时"是什么意思?

---

3 图一中"禁止停放车辆"是什么意思?

图2

4 图二告诉我们如果想存行李, 应该到哪里?

图3

5 图三告诉我们商家卖的东西多少钱一件? 为什么卖这么便宜?

Part III: Translate the following sentences into English.

1 请把会议室布置一下
2 请把这些人名按字母顺序排列

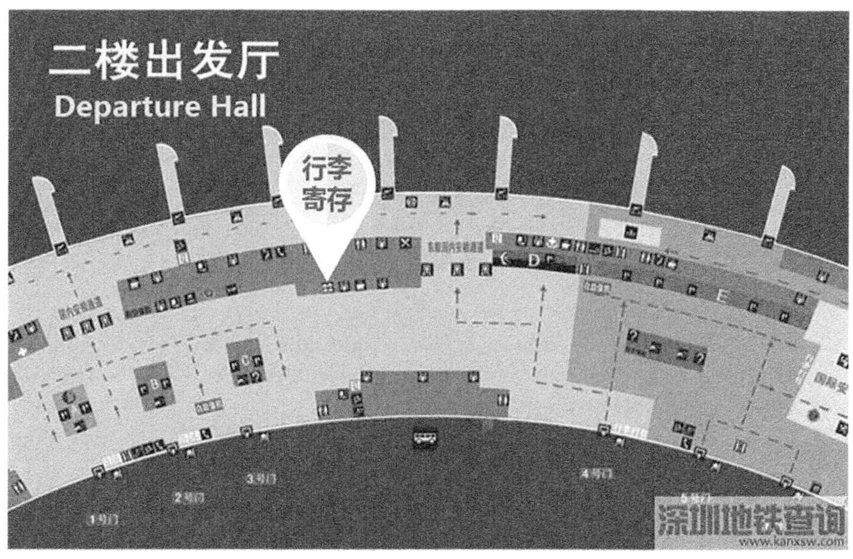

3 北京天安门上悬挂着毛泽东画像
4 做人应该诚实, 不要颠倒是非.
5 这家韩国公司积压了大量产品, 需要尽快销售 (xiāoshòu, sell) 出去.

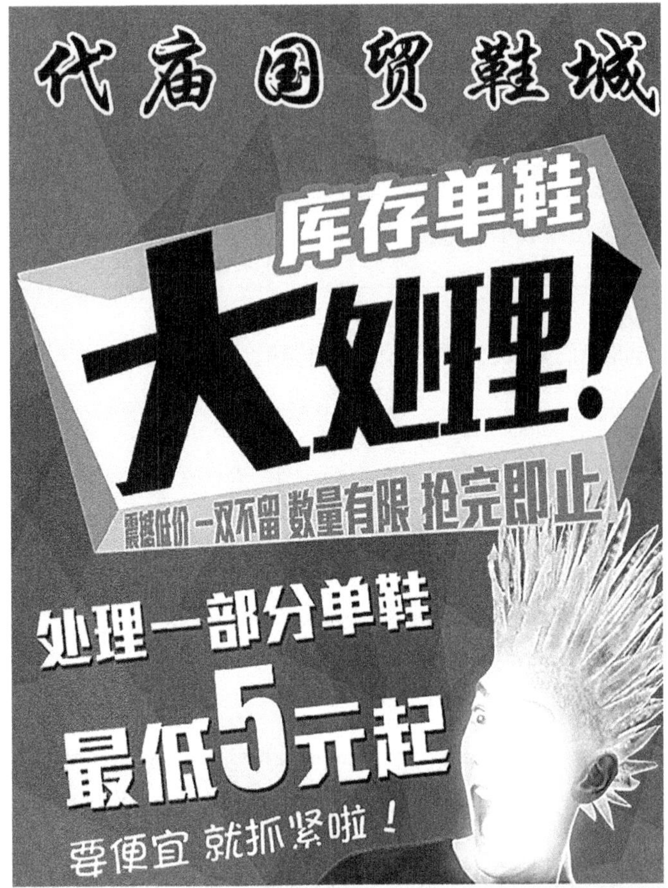

Theme 192: Close, separate, contact 靠近, 隔开, 接触 (kàojìn, gékāi, jiēchù)

1 交界 [-] jiāojiè (cross-boundary) <v.> come into contact: 中英 ~ Chinese-British associations || 两省~ where two provinces meet || 城乡~ where the city meets the countryside

2 相邻 [-鄰] xiānglín (mutual-adjacent) <v.> neighbor: 两个房间 ~ two rooms neighbor each other || 与法国~ neighbor France

3 接近 [-] jiējìn (connect-close) <v.> be close to: 和她~ be close to her || ~半夜 approach midnight || ~地面 be near the ground

4 靠近 [-] kàojìn (near-close) <v.> near: ~市区 near an urban area || ~地铁站的房子比较便宜. The houses near subway stations are inexpensive. || ~大厅 near the hall

5 接触 [-觸] jiēchù (connect-touch) <v.> contact: 同他~ come into contact with him || ~新事物 come into contact with new things || 广泛~ extensive contact

6 离 [離] lí (part, from) <v.> from (distance): ~得不远 not far from || ~银行八百米 800 meters from the bank || ~学校近 near the school

7 距离 [-離] jùlí (away-from) <v.> away from: ~地球很远 far away from the ground || ~学校很近 very near the school

8 相距 [-] xiàng jù (mutual-away) <v.> separated by a given distance, be apart, be away from: ~很远 be far apart || ~十万八千里thousands of miles apart

9 远离 [遠離] yuǎn lí (far-from) <v.> far from: ~故乡 far from home || ~家庭 far from family || ~城市 far from the city

10 离开 [離開] lí kāi (part-parted) <v.> leave: ~家乡 leave your hometown || ~办公室 leave the office || ~父母 depart from your parents

11 偏离 [-離] piānlí (deviate-from) <v.> deviate: ~目标 deviate from the objective || ~轨道 (guǐdào) drift off course || ~航线 deviate from the route

12 脱节 [-節] tuōjié (separate from-junction) <v.> come apart: 与社会~ part from society || 严重~ severely disjointed

13 脱钩 [-鈎] tuōgōu (escape-hook) <v.> cut ties, be out of touch: 大鱼~ the big fish got away || 人民币与美元~. The RMB and the dollar cut ties. || 收支~ income and expenses are out of touch

14 隔 [-] gé (block) <v.> be apart from: ~很远 be far away from || ~五年 be apart for five years || ~音 sound insulation

15 隔开 [-開] gékāi (block-separated) <v.> separate: 把他们~ make them separate || 与海洋~ separated from the sea || 用墙~ use a wall to separate

16 分隔 [-] fēngé (divide-separate) <v.> divide: ~房间 divide a room || 用木板~ use a board to divide || ~成两个部分 divide into two pieces

17 相隔 [-] xiānggé (mutual-separated) <v.> separate by: ~不远 separated by a long distance || ~两年 separated by two years || 与外界~ separated from the outside world

18 隔绝 [-絕] géjué (separate-off) <v.> isolated: 与外界~ isolated from the outside world || ~空气 isolated from the atmosphere || 完全~ completely isolated

19 隔离 [-離] gélí (separate-apart) <v.> keep apart: 互相~ keep apart from each other || ~病人 isolate a patient || 单独~ self-isolation

20 隔音 [-] géyīn (block-sound) <v.> soundproof: 窗户~ soundproof a window || 房间不~. The room is not soundproof.

21 与世隔绝 [與--絕] yǔ shì gé jué (with-world-separate-off) <idiom> be cut off from the rest of the world: ~的环境. The environment was shut off from the rest of the world.

22 滚 [-] gǔn (roll) <v.> get away: ~出厨房 get out of the kitchen || ~开 get out || ~蛋 get away

23 撤离 [-離] chèlí (withdraw-from) <v.> withdraw from: ~危险地带 withdraw from a dangerous area || ~现场 withdraw from a scene || 马上, 立刻~ immediately withdraw

24 滚蛋 [-] gǔndàn (roll-egg) <v.> scram: 请你~！ get lost || 给我~！ get away from me

25 围 [圍] wéi (enclose) <v.> surround: ~着她 surround her || ~上去 go up to surround || ~在一起 encircle together

26 围绕 [圍繞] wéirào (enclose-surround) <v.> center on: ~一个中心 revolve around a center || ~这个问题 center on this issue || ~生产 center on production

27 绕 [繞] rào (wind, coil) <v.> move around: ~圈子 circle around || ~弯儿 go for a stroll || ~地球飞 flying around the Earth

28 面向 [-] miànxiàng (face-toward) <v.> turn towards: ~东方 turn towards the east || ~未来 turn towards the future || ~大海 face the sea

29 撞 [-] zhuàng (bump, collide) <v.> run into: ~车 collide with car || ~在门上 bump into the door || 他在夜里~死了一头鹿. Last night he drove his car, and hit and killed a deer.

30 撞车 [-車] zhuàngchē (bump-vehicle) <v.> crash: 酒驾~ drunk driving collision || 他俩申请的项目~了. The topics they applied for clashed.

31 追尾 [-] zhuīwěi (caught-tail) <v.> tailgate: 连环~ chain of tailgaters || 我的车子被人~了. My car was tailgated by someone.

32 冲 [衝, 沖] chōng (charge, rush) <v.> charge, rush: 往里~ charge inside || ~在前面 rush in front of || ~下来 rush down

33 冲击 [衝擊] chōngjī (charge-strike) <v./n.> assault, charge: 受到~ be charged || 巨大~ huge assault || ~世界记录 chase the world record

34 闯 [闖] chuǎng (rush, break) <v.> rush: ~红灯 rush through a red light || ~祸(huò) get into trouble, bring disaster || 他身上装着二百美元就去~世界了. He ventured out into the world with only $200 in his pocket.

35 闯关 [闖関] chuǎng guān (charge-barrier) <v.> break through barriers, overcome a difficulty: ~成功successfully break through barriers || 连闯四关~ go through four ordeals in succession

36 触摸 [觸-] chùmō (touch-feel) <v.> touch: 互相~ touch each other || 轻轻~ lightly touch || ~屏幕touch the screen

37 碰到 [-] pèngdào (meet-*suffix*) <v.> come across: ~朋友 come across a friend || ~困难 run into difficulties || ~问题 run into an issue

38 碰见 [-見] pèngjiàn (meet-seen) <v.> run across: ~熟人 run across an acquaintance || ~一个老乡 run across someone from the same town as you

39 遇 [-] yù (encounter) <v.> encounter: ~水 come across water || ~火 catch fire || ~热 run into heat

40 遇到 [-] yùdào (encounter-*suffix*) <v.> run into: ~困难 run into difficulties || ~问题 meet with a question || ~朋友 run into a friend

41 遇见 [-見] yùjiàn (encounter-seen) <v.> meet, come across: ~警察 come across a policeman || ~熟人 meet an acquaintance || ~朋友 meet a friend

42 久别重逢 [-別--] jiǔbiéchóngféng (long-apart-again-meet) <idiom> meet after a long separation: 和亲人 ~ reunite with your father || 老同学~ reunite with an old classmate

43 错过 [錯過] cuòguò (miss-pass) <v.> miss: ~机会 miss an opportunity || ~时机 miss an opportune moment || ~关键期 let a critical period slip by

44 摩擦 [-] mócā (rub-scrub) <v.> chafe, rub: 来回 ~ rub back and forth || 相互~ chafe on each other || ~地面 rub the ground

45 磨损 [-損] mósǔn (rub-lose) <v.> wear and tear: 容易~ wears easily || ~设备 wear on equipment || ~严重 wear severely

46 蹭 [-] cèng (rub) <v.> rub, scrape, scratch: ~破一块皮 scrape a piece of skin || ~他的脸 rub his face

Tips:

1 离: The traditional form of 离 is 離, which was the original form of 鹂 (lí, Chinese oriole.) The current 离 (離) was borrowed from 剺 (lí), which means 'to part, to leave each other.'

2 Characters with a part 麻 (má): (1) 磨, 摩, 魔, 麽. Their pronunciations are all 'mó.' (2) 糜, 靡. Their pronunciations are both 'mí.'

Exercises:

Part I: Use the given bound form as a guide to help you think of other words with the same beginning character. Feel free to use your dictionary when needed. Then write down the English definition of each of the words you've written.

隔 *(be apart from):* 隔开 *seperate*

____

____

____

____

____

____

离 *(from):* 离开 *leave*

____

____

____

____

Part II: Read the following sentences and fill in each blank with the appropriate word or phrase from the options given.

1 面向、撞车、冲击
   a) 日本汽车的产品一向是________中产阶级消费者, 质优价廉.
   b) 韩国汽车公司的产品越来越好, ________给日本汽车公司带来一定的_________.
   c) 据报道, 很多交通事故是因为追尾以后________引起的.

2 遇见、久别重逢、错过
   a) 小张在美国________了自己的小学同学. __________, 两个人都觉得特别兴奋.
   b) 小张因为跟老同学一起唱卡拉ok, 忘了登机时间而_________了航班.

3 触摸、围绕、脱节
   a) 小张公司主要生产新型_______屏电脑.
   b) 小张昨天的公司会议主要是_________产品销售的问题开的.
   c) 一般来说知名大公司的技术研究不会跟实际应用_________.

4 撤离、交界、靠近、与世隔绝
   a) 据说中国跟印度在________两国_______的地方要发生战争.

b) 在国外一旦有战争发生，中国政府就会帮助当地华人__________该地区.

c) 在中国西藏地区还有一些藏民 (zàngmín, Tibetan) 在偏远地区过着_________的生活.

Theme 193: To combine, to cross, to gather 结合, 通过, 集中 (jiéhé, tōngguò, jízhōng)

1 复合 [複-] fùhé (compound-combine) <v.> get back together: 与前夫~ get back together with ex-husband || 分手后~ get back together after breaking up || ~材料 composite material

2 结合 [結-] jiéhé (knot-combine) <v.> link, combine: 中西~ link China and the West, combination of Chinese and western || 与实际~ link with reality || 紧密~ closely link

3 联系 [聯繫] liánxì (connected-tied) <v./n.> connect: ~实际 connect reality || 互相~ connect with each other || 内在~ internal connection

4 构成 [構-] gòuchéng (constitute-form) <v.> constitute, make up: ~矛盾 constitute a contradiction || ~一个整体 make up a whole || ~因素 (yīnsù) constitute a factor

5 组合 [組-] zǔhé (organize-form) <v.> make up: 动作~ action combinations || 不同的~ different compositions || 重新~ reassemble

6 融合 [-] rónghé (fuse-combine) <v.> mix together: 文化~ cultural fusion || 民族~ nationalities mixing together || 长期~ long-term fusion

7 融入 [-] róngrù (fuse-into) <v.> integrate: ~社会 integrate into society || ~新家庭 integrate into a new family || 积极~ actively integrate

8 融为一体 [-為-體] róngwéiyītǐ (fuse-into-one-body) <idiom> fuse into one: 两者~ two fusing into one || 东西方~ the East and West fusing || 紧密地~ closely fuse together

9 合成 [-] héchéng (combine-into) <v.> synthesize: 人工~ synthetic || ~食品 synthetic food || ~蔬菜 synthetic vegetables

10 并 [併] bìng (conjoin) <v.> merge: 两张床~在一起 two beds combined as one || 两张桌子 ~起来 two tables placed together || 小公司~进大公司 a little company merged into a big company

11 合并 [-併] hébìng (combine-conjoin) <v.> merge: 公司~ company merges || 两国~ two countries merge into one || ~计算 merge plans

12 汇 [匯] huì (converge) <v.> converge: ~成大河 flow together into a big river || ~在一起 converge together || ~向大海 converge into the ocean

13 统一 [統-] tǒngyī (unite-one) <v./ adj.> unify: ~国家 unify the country || ~认识 unified knowledge || ~看法 unified view

14 联合 [聯-] liánhé (join-combine) <v.> unite: ~各地学校 unite schools from different regions || 互相~ ally with each other || 经济~ economic unity

15 组成 [組-] zǔchéng (organize-into) <v.> form: ~合唱队 form a choir || ~代表团 form a delegation || ~一个大家庭 from a big family

16 连 [連] lián (link) <v.> connect, link: 心~心 heart to heart || ~在一起 connect together || 山~着山 mountain connected to a mountain

17 接 [-] jiē (connect) <v.> connect: ~天线 connect the antenna || 一个~一个 one-by-one || 上气不~下气 be out of breath

18 连接 [連-] liánjiē (link-connect) <v.> join: 互相 ~ join to each other || ~两个城市 join two cities || ~成句 link into a complete sentence

19 拼 [-] pīn (put together) <v.> join together: ~ 图 puzzle || ~贴 collage || ~装 assemble || ~车 car-pool

20 沟通 [溝-] gōutōng (ditch-link up) <v.> link up, communicate: 互相~ link up with each other || 信息~ communicate information || 电话~ communicate by phone

21 通 [-] tōng (unimpeded, through, pass) <v.> open, communicate: ~电话 talk on the phone || ~车 open to traffic || ~航 open to boats

22 不通 [-] bútōng (not-through) <adj.> be obstructed, illogical: 想~ can't figure it out || 道路~. The road is blocked. || 线路~. The route is blocked.

23 畅通 [暢-] chàngtōng (smooth-through) <adj.> unblocked: 道路~. The road is unblocked. || 水流~. The water flows unimpeded. || 信息~. Information is free-flowing.

24 通行 [-] tōngxíng (through-pass) <v.> pass through, general: 美国~西班牙语. Spanish is spoken in the Unites States. || 全国~ valid throughout the country || 禁止~ don't enter

25 联网 [聯網] liánwǎng (connect-net) <v.> network: 电脑/计算机~ computer network || 手机~ phone network || ~游戏 online game

26 承接 [-] chéngjiē (undertake-accept) <v.> undertake: ~工程 undertake a project || ~业务/任务 undertake a piece of business, a task || ~香火 continue the family line

27 挂钩 [-鈎] guàgōu (hang-hook) <v.> link: 与收入~ linked to income || 直接~ directly linked || 与美元~ linked to the dollar

28 交 [-] jiāo (crossed, associate) <v.> associate: ~朋友 make a friend || ~心 open your heart to || ~好口 good luck

29 交叉 [-] jiāochā (crossed-cross) <v.> intersect: 双腿~ legs crossed || 相互~ intersect with each other || ~路口 intersection

30 纠缠 [糾纏] jiūchán (wind-tangle) <v.> get entangled: ~不休 endless tangles || 跟坏人~ get entangled with a bad person || ~一个姑娘 entangled with a girl

31 混 [-] hùn (mix) <v.> mix: ~在一起 mix together || ~血 mix blood || ~进来 mix in

32 混合 [-] hùnhé (mix-together) <v.> blend: ~计算 blend plans || 水和土~ water and soil mixed || ~气味 mix odors

33 集合 [-] jíhé (assemble-together) <v.> gather: 到操场~ gather on the playground || 八点~ gather at 8: 00 || 紧急~ urgent assembly

34 拼凑 [-湊] pīncòu (join together-gather together) <v.> piece together: 任意~ randomly piece together || ~四百块钱 piece together $400

35 东拼西凑 [東--湊] dōngpīnxīcòu (east-join together-west-gather together) <idiom> scrape together: ~地写了一篇文章 scraped together an article || ~地弄了一点钱 scrape together a little bit of money

36 集中 [-] jízhōng (gather-together) <v.> concentrate: ~注意力 concentrate your attention || ~学习 concentrate on studies || ~大量现金 concentrate a lot of money

37 聚集 [-] jùjí (flock together-gather) <v.> gather: 群众~ a crowd gathered || ~资金 assemble funds || ~在一起 gather together

38 凝聚 [-] níngjù (agglutinate-together) <v.> condense, curdle: 高度 ~ quickly condense || ~着所有人的心血. Everybody's blood curdled. || ~着人民的感情. The feelings of the people curdled.

39 物以类聚 [--類-] wùyǐ lèi jù (thing-by-kind-gather) <idiom> similar things come together: ~, 人以群分 similar people group together

40 密集 [-] mìjí (dense-gather) <v.> concentrate: 知识~ concentrated knowledge || 人口~ densely populated || 高度~ highly concentrated

41 裂 [-] liè (cut, divide, split, crack) <v.> crack: 冻~ freeze and crack || ~一个口子. There is a crack. || 鞋子~了. The shoes split open.

42 裂开 [-開] lièkāi (split-open) <v.> split open: ~一道缝儿 split a seam || 伤口~ split open a wound || 蛋壳~. The egg shell cracked.

43 各奔东西 [--東-] gèbèndōngxī (each-rush to-east-west) <idiom> go separate ways: 毕业后同学们就~了. Classmates go their separate ways after graduating.

44 同床异梦 [--異夢] tóngchuángyìmèng (same-bed-different-dream) <idiom> share a bed but dream differently (strange partners): 这对夫妻早就~了, 总是吵嘴. This couple has always been a strange pair. They are always arguing.

45 割裂 [-] gēliè (cut-split) <v.> separate, sever: 把两者~开来 split the two apart || ~它们的内在联系 sever their internal connection

46 断 [斷] duàn (cut off, break) <v.> break: 剪~ cut off || 电话~了 the phone cut out || ~了一条腿 break a leg

47 分散 [-] fènsàn (separate-disperse) <v.> scatter: ~难点 scattered difficulties || 信息~ the information is dispersed || ~学习 scattered studies

48 扩散 [擴-] kuòsàn (expand-disperse) <v.> spread: 废气~ exhaust gas spreads || 向外 ~ spread out || ~消息 spread news

49 散 [-] sàn (disperse, distribute) <v.> distribute: 包裹~了. The package was distributed. || ~架 fall apart || ~传单 hand out leaflets

50 散落 [-] sànluò (disperse-fall) <v.> scatter: ~一地 scattered to the ground || ~在地上 scattered on the ground

51 畅通 [暢-] chàngtōng (unimpeded-through) <v.> unblocked: 信息~ information flows freely || 高速公路~. The highway is unblocked (no traffic). || 水流~. The water flow is unimpeded

52 通风 [-風] tōngfēng (pass-wind) <v.> ventilate: ~良好 well-ventilated || 经常~ often ventilated

53 透 [-] tòu (pass through) <v.> pass through, penetrate: ~光 translucent || ~气 breathable || ~风 let in air

54 漏 [-] lòu (leak) <v.> leak: ~水 leak water || ~气 leak gas || ~油 leak oil

55 渗漏 [滲-] shènlòu (ooze-leak) <v.> seepage: 严重~ serious seepage || 养分~ nutrient leakage

56 走光 [-] zǒuguāng (reveal-naked) <v.> flash: 明星~ celebrity flashings || 不慎~ inadvertently flash || 多次~ often flash

57 堵塞 [-] dǔsè (block-stop up) <v.> clog up: 交通~ traffic jam || 下水道~ sewer blockage || ~严重 seriously clogged up

58 闭塞 [閉-] bìsè (closed-stop up) <v.> stop up: 交通~ traffic jam || 消息~ ill-informed || 社会 ~. Society is closed-up.

59 密封 [-] mìfēng (closely-seal) <v.> seal up: ~得严严实实 seal up tightly || 真空~ vacuum sealed

60 堵车 [-車] dǔchē (block-vehicle) <v-o.> traffic jam: 堵了四小时车 a four-hour traffic jam || 老~ always jammed up || 路上~ traffic on the roads

61 隔热 [-熱] gérè (block-heat) <v.> insulate: 屋顶~ roof insulation || ~垫 heat insulating mattress

62 卡 [-] qiǎ (wedged, stuck) <v.> stuck, wedged: ~住了 be stuck || ~了一根鱼刺 (yúcì) a fish bone is stuck || 用价格~他们 use the price to block them

Tips:

1 交 and 叉: The bronze character of 交 depicts 'a man's two legs crossed,' from which evolved the meaning 'cross, meet'. The original form of 叉 indicates the direction (、, actually '一') of a hand (又,) together meaning 'cross.'
2 聚, 会/汇, 集: All mean 'gather,' and their combinations, 聚会, 聚汇, 聚集, 会集, 汇集 have almost the same meaning.
3 卡: 卡 is a syssemantograph character. If something is neither high (上) nor low (下,) it is 'wedged' or 'stuck.'
4 走光: 走 here means 'escape, reveal,' and 光 'a part of body not supposed to be seen in public.' It is almost exclusively used for entertainers, especially women. Shooting pictures of 走光 is the paparazzi's hobby.

Exercises:

Part I: Use the given bound form as a guide to help you think of other words with the same beginning character. Feel free to use your dictionary when needed. Then write down the English definition of each of the words you've written.

合 *(combine, conjunction):* 合并 *merge*

____

____

____

____

____

____

通 *(open, commute):* 通车 *open to traffic*

____

____

____

____

Part II: Multiple Choice. Make sure to choose the most appropriate answer.

1 小张的文章是在网上__________抄袭 (chāoxí, plagiarize) 的, 交上去以后立刻被老师发现了.
A. 东拼西凑 B. 聚集 C. 物以类聚

2 王教授坚持让学生上课的时候关手机, 以免学生注意力不够__________.
A. 密集 B. 集中 C. 凝聚

3 苹果手机在中国的工厂几乎都设在劳动力_________的地区.
A. 密集 B. 集合 C. 凝聚

4 有人说人工智能可以把世界所有的东西__________, 使整个世界__________.
A. 联网、融为一体 B. 联系、东拼西凑 C. 联网、物以类聚

5 关于婚姻, 在美国很多人赞成与其夫妻关系不好, __________, 不如分开, _________, 追求自己想要的生活.
A. 同床异梦、各奔东西 B. 各奔东西、同床异梦 C. 同床异梦、东拼西凑

6 不管是纽约还是北京都有一些"大城市病," 比如常常_________, 交通不够________.
A. 堵塞、畅通 B. 堵车、畅通 C. 畅通、堵车

7 在中国西部地区农村不存在交通__________的问题, 但是存在严重的文化_________问题.
A. 闭塞、堵塞 B. 堵塞、闭塞 C. 堵车、关闭

8 据说欧洲目前面临的问题是如何让移民尽快__________当地文化与生活, 否则就会使社会与文化__________.
A. 融合、融入 B. 割裂、融入 C. 融入、割裂

Theme 194: To move 移动 (yídòng)

1 动 [動] dòng (act, move) (of sth) <v.> move: 躺着别~ lay down and don't move || ~不了can't move

2 动动 [運動] yùndòng (revolve-move) <v.& n.> move, movement: 头部~ the head movement || 地球~ Earth movement || ~的物体 moving object

3 活动 [-動] huódòng (move-move) <v.> move about: 自由~ free activities || ~一下 warm up, limber up the joints || 人类~ mankind's activity

4 颤动 [-動] chàndòng (vibrate-move) <v.> vibrate, quiver, tremble: 全身~ one's whole body trembles || 上下~ tremble from top to bottom

5 振动 [-動] zhèndòng (shake-move) <v.> shake, vibrate: 空气~ air vibration || 强烈地~ fierce shaking

6 颠簸 [顛-] diānbǒ (bump-jolt) <v.> jolt, bump: 上下~ bump from top to bottom || 剧烈地~ to bump terribly || 汽车~. The bus bumped.

7 移动 [-動] yídòng (shift-move) <v.> move, shift: 冰山~ an iceberg moved || 快速~ move fast || 冷空气向南~. A cold air mass is moving southward.

8 滑行 [-] huáxíng (slide-move) <v.> slide, coast glide: ~一百米 slide a hundred meters || 在冰上~ slide on the ice || 飞机在跑道上~. The plane taxied along the runway.

9 反弹 [-彈] fǎntán (back-bounce) <v.> rebound, bounce back: 股市~ the stock market rebounded || 减肥~ bounced back after losing weight || 迅速~ quick rebound

10 跳动 [-動] tiàodòng (jump-move) <v.> move up and down, throb: 他的心脏在剧烈~. His heart is beating wildly. || 脉搏~ pulse || ~的火苗jumpy flame current

11 摇晃 [搖-] yáohuàng (shake-sway) <v.> rock, sway: ~着脑袋 rock one's head || 前后~ rock back and forth || 不断~ sway without stopping

12 摇动 [搖動] yáodòng (shake-move) <v.> sway: ~瓶子 shake the bottle || 前后~ sway forwards and backwards || ~身体sway one's body

13 摆动 [擺動] bǎidòng (swing-move) <v.> swing, sway: ~尾巴 wag one's tail || ~手臂/身子 sway one's arms/body

14 飘扬 [飄揚] piāoyáng (fly-fly high) <v.> wave, flutter, fly: 国旗~ A flag is flying. || 高高~ wave high/ fly high

15 旋转 [-轉] xuánzhuǎn (spin-rotate) <v.> rotate: ~一圈 rotate a circle || 向左~ rotate left || 顺时针~ rotate clockwise

16 运行 [運-] yùnxíng (revolve-move) <v.> move, be in motion: 火车~时, 请不要打开车门. Don't open the door while the train is in motion || 在轨道上~ move in orbit || 正点~ run on schedule

17 滑 [-] huá (slide) <v.> slide: ~雪 ski || ~冰 skate || ~滑梯 slide down the slide

18 滚 [滾] gǔn (roll) <v.> roll: ~下来 roll down || ~雪球 rolling snow ball || ~来~去 roll back and forth

19 转 [轉] zhuàn (rotate, turn) <v.> turn, revolve: ~圈 revolve in a circle || 绕着太阳~ revolve around the sun

20 转动 [轉動] zhuàndòng (rotate-move) <v.> turn, move: ~身体turn one's body || 快速~ turn quickly || 向左~ turn to the left

21 流 [-] liú (flow) <v.> flow: ~汗 flowing sweat || ~泪 flowing tears || 河水向东~ the river flowed to the east

22 流动 [-動] liúdòng (flow-move) <v.> (of water, air, etc.) flow, circulate: 资金~ flowing currency || 人才~ circulating talent || 来回~ continuously circulate

23 流通 [-] liútōng (flow-unimpeded) (of air, money, commodities) <v.> flow, circulate: 空气~ circulating air || 血液~ flowing blood || 商品~ circulating goods

24 溅 [濺] jiàn (splash) <v.> splash, spatter: ~了一身水splash all over one's body || 四处乱~ spatter in all directions

25 喷 [噴] pēn (spurt) <v.> spurt, spout: ~水 spurring water || ~火 spurting fire

26 射 [-] shè (shoot) <v.> shoot: ~箭 shoot an arrow || ~进一球 kick the ball into the goal

27 滴 [-] dī (drop) <v.> drop: ~水 a drop of water || ~血 a drop of blood || ~眼泪 a tear

28 泡 [-] pào (soak) <v.> bubble, soak: ~澡 soak in a bath || ~茶 make tea

29 淹 [-] yān (drown, flood) <v.> flood, submerge: ~水 submerge in water

30 浮 [-] fú (float) <v.> float: ~在水面 float on the water

Tips:

1 *动: 动 (動) is a general verbal term or hypernym for movements. Verbs with '动' in this unit include 运动, 活动, 移动, 跳动, 摇动, 摆动, 流动, 转动, 振动, 颤动.

2 Direction of Chinese rivers and revolutions: The majority of Chinese revolutions in history started in the northwest but succeeded in the southeast. This happens to be in accordance with the directions of most Chinese rivers.

Exercises:

Part I: Translate the following phrases into English.

中文	英文
滑倒在地上	
从楼梯上滚下来	

从这儿转过去	
脸上流着泪水	
溅了一身水	
喷泉向上喷水	
泡个热水澡	
掉在水里淹死了	
浮在水面上	

Part II: Answer the following questions in Chinese.

1 写出你知道的带"动"字的词 (至少写六个)

______

2 有人说节食减肥最容易反弹, 你觉得呢?

______

3 在你们国家人们可以自由流动吗, 想去住在哪儿就住在哪儿?

______

4 做哪些事情可以让房间里的空气流通得快一些?

______

Theme 195: To begin, to process, to end 开始, 进行, 结束 (kāishǐ, jìnxíng, jiéshù)

1 开始 [開-] kāishǐ (begin-start) <v./n.> start: ~出现 start to appear || 晚会~ start the evening party || 从四五岁~ started at four or five years of age
2 开业 [開業] kāiyè (open-business) <v.> start a business: 书店~ start a bookstore || 尽快~ start a business as soon as possible
3 开机 [開機] kāijī (start-machine) <v.> start a machine, start a phone: 自动~ start automatically || ~半小时 run a machine for a half an hour || ~时间 start-up time
4 开学 [開學] kāixué (start-school) <v.> start school: 即将~ be about to start || 正式~ formal start || ~典礼 start of a school ceremony
5 入学 [-學] rùxué (enter-school) <v.> enter school, enter a school: 新生九月~ the new students enter school in September. || ~考试entrance examination (school) || 免试~ enter school without taking the entrance exam
6 入门 [-門] rùmén (enter-door) <v.> cross the threshold, enter a door, primary: ~书 introductory book || ~课 introductory class || 音乐~ introduction to music
7 开幕 [開-] kāimù (open-curtain) <v.> open (a conference), inaugurate: 大会~ open a large conference || ~ 时间curtain time || 展览会明天~. The exhibition will open tomorrow.
8 召开 [-開] zhàokāi (call on-hold) <v.> convene: ~大会convene a conference || ~交流会 start an exchange || ~发布会 convene a news conference

9 动手 [動-] dòngshǒu (start-hand) <v.> set about a task, start work: ~早 start a task early || ~做 start doing || 马上~ quickly start doing

10 启动 [啓動] qǐdòng (start-move) (of a machine) <v.> start, switch on: ~电脑switch on a computer || 列车 ~ start a train || ~市场 open up a market

11 进行 [進-] jìnxíng (advance-march) <v.> in progress, carry on, carry out: ~交谈 carry on a conversation || ~调查carry out an investigation || 顺利~ be in smooth progress

12 举行 [舉-] jǔxíng (hold-go) <v.> hold: ~婚礼hold a wedding || ~大会 hold a large ceremony || ~宴会 hold a banquet

13 开展 [開-] kāizhǎn (launch-develop) <v.> develop, launch: ~工作 launch work || ~活动 launch an activity || ~竞赛 start a competition

14 展开 [-開] zhǎnkāi (spread-unfold) <v.> carry out, set off: ~讨论 set off an discussion || ~攻势carry out an offensive || 广泛~ carry out on a broad scale

15 进展 [進-] jìnzhǎn (progress-spread) <v.> make progress: 工作~很顺利The work is making good progress. || 毫无~ make no headway, have no any progress || 取得~ obtain progress

16 推动 [-動] tuīdòng (push-move) <v.> push forward, promote: ~工作 push the work forward || ~社会向前发展propel the society forward.

17 推行 [-] tuīxíng (push-implement) <v.> carry out, pursue: ~新方法 carry out a new method || ~新政策 carry out a new policy

18 落实 [-實] luòshí (land-solid) <v.> implement, fix in advance, work out: ~政策implement policy || ~责任work out one's responsibility || ~经费 implement funds

19 实行 [實-] shíxíng (actually-implement) <v.> put into practice, implement, carry out: ~优惠政策 implement preferential policy || ~这一办法 implement this solution || ~民主 practice democracy

20 实践 [實踐] shíjiàn (actually-fulfill) <v./n.> practice, put into practice: 亲身~ practice personally || 看重~ attach importance to practice || 知识起源于~. Knowledge comes from practice.

21 执行 [執-] zhíxíng (enforce-implement) <v.> carry out, execute, implement: ~规定enforce a rule || ~任务carry out a task || ~政策 enforce a policy

22 承前启后 [--啓後] chéngqián qǐhòu (succeed-past-herald-future) <idiom> follow the past and herald the future: 他是一位~的科学家. This scientist is a link between the future and past. || 这是一次~的大会. This meeting served as a link between past and future.

23 暂停 [暫-] zàntíng (temporarily-stop) <v.> suspend: 比赛~ suspend the competition || ~工作 suspend work || ~练习 suspend practice

24 继续 [繼續] jìxù (continue-resume) <v.> continue: ~工作continue work || ~找 continue to search || ~走 continue to walk

25 延续 [-續] yánxù (prolong-continue) <v.> extend: ~两千多年extend over 2000 years || ~到现在extend to the present || 长期~ extend over the long term

26 持续 [-續] chíxù (sustain-continue) <v.> continue, sustain: ~八年sustain for 8 years || ~上升 continue to rise || ~不断 unceasingly continue

27 重复 [-複] chóngfù (again-repeat) <v.> reappear, recur, repeat: ~使用repeatedly use || ~一次reappear once || ~她的话repeat her words

28 循环 [-環] xúnhuán (circulate-circle) <v.> circulate, cycle: 血液~ blood circulation || ~运动 a circular movement || 良性~ positive cycle

29 翻来覆去 [-來--] fānlái fùqù (flip-*this way*-flop-*that way*) <idiom> toss and turn, do over and again: 他~睡不着. He tossed and turned in bed, unable to sleep. || 她~老提过去的事. She talked about the past events over and over. || 我~地仔细检查这个地方. I struggled to review the details of this place.

30 新陈代谢 [-陳-謝] xīnchéndàixiè (new-old-replace-decline) <idiom> metabolism: 小孩子~快, 可是老人~慢. Children's metabolisms are fast, but old people have slow metabolisms.

Tips:

1 **入门: In college there are many introductory courses named 'Introduction to. . .,' which is usually translated as '**入门' in Chinese.

2 开展 vs. 展开: The focus of 开展 (launch) is on 开 (begin, start) while the focus of 展开 is on 展 (spread out.) For example, 开展宣传活动 means 'start publicizing activities' while 展开宣传活动 means 'expand the publicizing campaign.'

3 实践 (shíjiàn): Maybe the most famous sentence using 实践 is '实践是检验真理的唯一标准' (shíjiàn shì jiǎnyàn zhēnlǐ de wéiyī biāozhǔn), which means 'practice is the only test of truth.' This sentence paved the way for Deng Xiaoping to take the highest position of power in China in 1978 after the death of Mao Zedong in 1976.

4 持续 (chíxù) vs. 延续 (yánxù): 持续 means 'continue' and 延续 'be prolonged.'

Exercises:

Part I: Translate the following phrases into English.

中文	英文
开学典礼	
经济持续发展	
推动社会进步	
研究生入学考试	
这家新书店下个月开业	
会议早上八点开始	
今天奥运会正式开幕	
公司召开股东大会	
美国总统到中国进行访问	
中国实行九年义务教育	

Part II: Read the following sentences and fill in each blank with the appropriate word or phrase from the options given.

1 翻来覆去、新陈代谢、承前启后

a) 小王的奶奶总是喜欢_________讲一件很多年前的的事情，使他觉得很无聊.

b) 老人的_________相对比较慢, 所以要避免暴饮暴食.

c) 2001年是新世纪_________的第一年，　也是中国经济发展"十五计划"的第一年.

2 循环、重复、持续

a) 人体内的血液在全省_________流动.
b) 中国小学生学语文的时候一个字常常要_________写五遍.
c) 自1978年以来, 中国经济一直在_________发展.

3 继续、延续、暂停

a) 如果中国西部地区的环境问题_________恶化, 就会完全变成沙漠.
b) 这个地区结婚的风俗习惯是从汉朝_________下来的.
c) 这个机场因为特大暴风雪不得不_________使用.

4 实践、执行、实行

a) 马克思主义认为_________是检验真理的的唯一标准.
b) 中国是在1995年开始_________五天工作制的.
c) 在医院里, 护士一般要_________医生的命令.

5 启动、动手、开机

a) 这辆汽车坏了, 完全没办法_________.
b) 很多航空公司规定在飞机完全着陆的时候乘客才能_________，　使用手机.
c) 因为装修公司的价钱很高, 所有小王决定自己_________装修厨房.

31 结束 [結-] jiéshù (tie-bind) <v.> finish, conclude, end: 大会~了. The conference concluded. || ~讲话wind up a speech || 学期~. The semester is over.
32 放学 [-學] fàngxué (dismiss-school) <v.> classes are over: 下午三点~. Classes are over at 3 pm. || 学生们都~回家了. The students have all left school and gone home for the day.
33 下课 [-課] xiàkè (finish-class) <v-o.> finish class: ~后 after finishing class || ~休息 after class rest || 三点~ end class at three
34 下班 [-] xiàbān (get off-work) <v-o.> get off of work: ~后 after getting off work || ~回来return after getting off work || 五点~ get off work at 5
35 关机 [關機] guānjī (turn off-machine) <v.> turn off (a machine, computer or phone): 自动~ for a machine to automatically turn off || 定时~ turn off at a set time || ~时间off time, unused time
36 毕业 [畢業] bìyè (finish-study) <v-o.> graduate: 毕不了业/毕得了业 be unable graduate/ be able to graduate || 中学~ graduate from a middle school
37 散会 [-會] sànhuì (disperse-meeting) <v.> disperse a meeting, adjourn: 宣布~ declare the meeting over || 一直到晚上才~. The meeting didn't end until night,
38 闭幕 [閉-] bìmù (shut-curtain) <v-o.> lower the curtain, come to an end (of a meeting): 大会胜利~. The conference has come to a successful close.
39 关门 [關門] guānmén (close-door) <v-o.> close the door, close: 工厂~ the factory closed || 商店 ~ the store closed || ~停业 stop business
40 完 [-] wán (finish, complete) <v.> finish, complete: 写~ finish writing || 做~ finish doing || 听~ finish listening
41 完成 [-] wánchéng (complete-completion) <v.> complete: ~任务 finish a task || ~作业 finish homework || 完不成 cannot finish

42 竣工 [-] jùngōng (complete-project) t<v.> complete a project: 这栋大楼已经~. The building has been completed.

43 获 [獲] huò (capture, get) <v.> obtain, win: ~一等奖win the first prize || ~冠军 win the championship || ~诺贝尔奖 win the Nobel Prize

44 获得 [獲-] huòdé (obtain-get) <v.> obtain, win, gain, achieve: ~好评win acclaim || ~第一名win first place || ~独立 gain independence || ~巨大的成功achieve great success

45 赢得 [贏-] yíngdé (win-get) <v.> win: ~比赛 win a competition || ~好感 achieve a good feeling || ~了学生的尊重 won the students' respect

46 得到 [-] dé (get-*suffix*) <v.> get, obtain: ~帮助 get help || ~好成绩get good grades || ~好处get benefit

47 得出 [-] déchū (get-out) <v.> reach a conclusion, obtain results: ~结论 to reach a conclusion || ~答案 to reach an answer || ~结果 to achieve results

48 得分 [-] défēn (get-score) <v.> score: 连连~ continuously score || 发球~ shoot and score || ~最多 score the most points

49 达成 [達-] dáchéng (reach-*completion*) <v.> reach (agreement): ~协议 reach an agreement || ~共识reach a consensus on sth. || ~交易 strike a bargain

50 达到 [達-] dádào (reach-at) <v.> achieve, reach, attain: ~目的 achieve a goal || ~要求 reach one's requirements || ~世界先进水平 come up to advanced world standards

51 取得 [-] qǔdé (get-get) <v.> gain, get: ~好成绩 get good results || ~进步 make progress || ~胜利 gain a victory

52 实现 [實現] shíxiàn (reality-realize) <v.> realize: ~愿望realize one's desire || ~梦想realize one's dream || ~计划realize a plan

53 收 [-] shōu (arrest, receive, accept) <v.> collect, receive: ~费 collect a fee || ~礼物receive a gift || ~邮件receive a email

54 收到 [-] shōudào (receive-*suffix*) <v.> receive, get: ~来信 receive a letter || ~效果 get result || ~一个礼物receive a gift

55 收取 [-] shōuqǔ (collect-take) <v.> receive, collect: ~费用 collect a fee || ~手续费collect service charges || ~运费 collect transportation expenses

56 中断 [-斷] zhōngduàn (middle-break) <v.> suspend, break off: 交通~ break off traffic || ~活动suspend an activity || 谈判~ break off the negotiations

57 终止 [終-] zhōngzhǐ (terminate-stop) <v.> stop, end: ~合同 end a contract || ~生命 end a life || 任务~ end an assignment

58 停 [-] tíng (stop) <v.> stop: 雨~了. The rain stopped. || ~电 cut off electricity || ~工 stop work

59 停车 [-車] tíngchē (stop/park-car) <v.> stop the car: 马上~ immediately stop the car || ~休息stop the car to rest

60 停止 [-] tíngzhǐ (stop-stopped) <v.> stop: ~工作 stop working || ~呼吸 stop breathing || ~活动 stop an activity

61 为止 [爲] wéizhǐ (be-end) <bf.> up to, until: 到今天~ up until today || 到懂了~ up until they understood || 到目前~ up until the goal

62 找出 [-] zhǎochū (find-out) <v.> seek out, find: ~特点 find a characteristic || ~方法 seek out a method || ~根源 find the source

63 作出 [-] zuòchū (make-out) <v.> make: ~决定make a decision || ~判断make a judgment || ~结论make a conclusion

Tips:

1 All good things must come to an end: There are several equivalents in Chinese, for example, 天下没有不散 (sàn, disperse, over) 的筵席 (yánxí, banquet) and 花无百日红 etc.
2 算了 (suànle): It means 'forget (about) it.' One of the authors of this book, Liwei Jiao once came across a pun with 'suànle.' When his wife asked him to give her some scallions (葱, cōng) for cooking, he said '没葱了' (no scallions.) Then she said 'méi cōng jiù suàn le,' but Jiao was at a loss and had to ask her for clarification since it could mean two things. One is 没葱就算了 (if there are no scallions, then forget it) and the other 没葱就蒜了 (if there are no scallions, then use garlic.)

Exercises:

Part I: Translate the following phrases into English.

中文	英文
终止合同	
找出根源	
做出决定	
获得奖学金	
大桥顺利竣工	
顺利完成任务	
两国达成协议	
很多家工厂关门	
奥运会胜利闭幕	

Part II: Read the following sentences and fill in each blank with the appropriate word or phrase from the options given.

1 迎来、作出、忍住
   a) 虽然父母的话让小王非常生气, 但是小王________不发脾气.
   b) 最近小王父母________一个重要决定，卖掉自己的房子供小王到英国读硕士.
   c) 很多学生认为暑假总是很快, 不知不觉就________了新的学期.

2 收到、得到、达到
   a) 小王最近________了哈佛大学法学院的录取通知书.
   b) 小王最近也________了一个到中国免费留学的机会.
   c) 小王最讨厌为了________目的, 不择手段的人.

3 实现、赢得、完成
   a) 经过三年的法学院学习, 小王终于________自己的梦想, 成了一名律师.
   b) 小王对待工作认为, 为每一位客户着想, 在律师界________了良好的声誉.
   c) 小王________了今年的工作目标, 客户已经达到了五百多人.

Theme 196: In advance, to postpone 提前, 推迟 (tíqián, tuīchí)

1 提前 [-] tíqián (move-forward) <v.> move to an earlier date, do sth in advance: ~上班 start work early || ~到达 arrive in advance || ~五个月 5 months in advance
2 加快 [-] jiākuài (increase-fast) <v.> quicken, speed up: ~速度 quicken in speed || ~脚步 hasten one's steps || 心跳~. The heart beats faster.
3 加速 [-] jiāsù (increase-speed) <v.> quicken, speed up: ~前进 speed up || ~发展 quick development || ~增长 speed up growth
4 来得及 [來--] láidejí (do-*complement*-enough) <v.> there's still time: ~告诉他 there's still time to tell him || ~看 there is still time to see || 时间~ there's still time
5 赶上 [趕-] gǎnshàng (catch-up) <v.> catch up with, encounter: ~发达国家 catch up with developed countries || ~飞机 catch the flight

6 推迟 [-遲] tuīchí (postpone-late) <v.> put off, postpone: ~时间 postpone (a time) || ~婚礼 postpone a wedding || ~两三天 postpone for two or three days
7 放慢 [-] fàngmàn (release-slow) <v.> decrease: ~速度 decrease in speed || ~脚步 walk more slowly
8 缓解 [緩-] huǎnjiě (alleviate-relieve) <v.> relieve, alleviate: ~压力 relieve stress || ~病情 ease the patient's condition || ~疲劳 relieve fatigue
9 落 [-] là (leave out) <v.> leave out, be missing, fall behind: ~在后面 fall behind || 他~了一个星期的课. He missed a week's lessons.
10 拖 [-] tuō (drag, delay) <v.> pull, delay: 这件工作~得太久了. This work has been dragging on far too long.
11 拖延 [-] tuōyán (delay-postpone) <v.> delay, put off: ~时间play for time || ~付款要受到罚款. Late payment will be penalized.
12 延期 [-] yánqī (postpone-date) <v-o.> postpone, defer: 延一次期 postpone once || ~回来 postpone one's return || ~五天 postpone five days
13 来不及 [來--] láibují (do-not-enough) <v.> there's not enough time: 时间 ~. There's not enough time. || ~说话 no time to speak || ~穿衣服 no time to put on clothes
14 赶不上 [趕--] gǎnbushàng (catch-not-up) <v.> unable to catch up with, there's not enough time to do sth.: 计划~变化 can not keep up with the plan || ~约会 can not keep the appointment || ~火车 be unable to catch the train.

Tips:

1 Excuse for a change of time: The Chinese usually use 计划不如变化 (literally 'plan cannot follow with change,' changes always go beyond plans) to excuse themselves from being able to make a due date.
2 放*: If the character/word after 放 is an adjective, it is likely to be one denoting 'relaxation' such as 缓 (slow,) 慢 (slow) or 松 (loose.)

Exercises:

Part I: Read the following sentences and fill in each blank with the appropriate word or phrase from the options given.

1 加快、赶上、提前
   a) 小王工作非常积极, 总是_________半小时到办公室.
   b) 今天早上小王因为没有_________公共汽车, 所以上班迟到了.
   c) 太阳快下山了, 山上的游客_________脚步, 下山回家.

2 放慢、推迟、缓解
   a) 因为天气原因, 飞机不得不________起飞的时间.
   b) 在美国的居民区开车一定要________速度, 以免撞到行人.
   c) 目前世界上还没有彻底治愈癌症 (cancer) 的药物, 现有的药物只能________病人的病情.

3 误、落、推
   a) 老师为了不让这个孩子在学习上________在别人后面, 常常利用午饭时间辅导他.
   b) 小王妈妈不喜欢做家务, 常常找借口把所有家务________给丈夫.
   c) 小王打车去机场的时候堵车了, 结果________了飞机.

4 拖延、来不及、延期
   a) 由于总经理不能按时回来, 全公司大会________一周举行.
   b) 为了赶地铁, 小张常常早上________吃早饭.
   c) 小张同屋常常找各种借口________交房租.

Theme 197: To appear, to disappear 出现, 消失 (chūxiàn, xiāoshī)

1 出现 [-現] chūxiàn (out-appear) <v.> appear, arise: ~健康问题 have health problems || ~在东边儿 appear in the east || 经济~泡沫. The economy is in a bubble.

2 出面 [-] chūmiàn (show-face) <v.> act in an official or personal capacity: ~调停 act as a mediator || ~说明情况sb. personally appears to explain the matter

3 形成 [-] xíngchéng (form-finished) <v.> take shape, form: ~石油form oil || ~鲜明的对比 form a sharp contrast || ~ 独特的风格have evolved a style of its own

4 养成 [養-] yǎngchéng (cultivate-finished) <v.> develop, raise: ~良好的习惯 form the good habit || 让宠物~用马桶的习惯make pets develop the habit of using the toilet || 不要~ 抽烟的习惯. Don't get into the habit of smoking.

5 生成 [-] shēngchéng (borne-finished) <v.> come (or bring) into being, generate: 自然/天然 ~ natural generation || 地球的~ generation of the Earth || ~二维码generate a two-dimension code

6 层出不穷 [層--窮] céngchūbùqióng (layer-appear-not-end) <idiom> emerge in an endless stream: 新东西~. New things are created in an endless stream. || 新技术~. New technologies are always being created.

7 脱颖而出 [-穎--] tuōyǐng'érchū (off-wheat glume-and-out) <idiom> pale others by showing one's ability and talent: 我在小组面试中~. I stand out in a group interview.

8 发生 [發-] fāshēng (start-happen) <v.> happen, occur, take place: ~车祸 have a car accident || ~关系 have sexual relations with sb. || ~地震have an earthquake

9 产生 [產-] chǎnshēng (generate-happen) <v.> generate: ~想法 generate a new idea || ~问题 generate an issue || 同时 ~ generate at the same time

10 发 [發] fā (shoot an arrow, start off, happen, send) <v.> dispatch, send: ~消息 dispatch information || ~邮件send a letter || ~信 dispatch mail

11 发出 [發-] fāchū (send-out) <v.> send, emit: ~声音emit a sound || ~光 emit light || ~信号emit a signal

12 发送 [發-] fāsòng (send-deliver) <v.> transmit by radio, dispatch (letters, ect), send (an email): ~信号transmit signals || ~邮件 send emails || ~信件dispatch letters and mails

13 爆发 [-發] bàofā (burst-emit) <v.> erupt, burst out, break out: 火山~. The volcano erupted. || 战争~. War broke out. || 这一事件导致全球金融危机~. This incident led to the breakout of the global financial crisis.

14 显露 [顯-] xiǎnlù (appear-show) <v.> become visible, appear: ~才能 for one's talents to become visible || ~天性 show one's nature || ~缺点 show one's fault

15 光 [-] guāng (light, bright, bare) <v.> bare: ~身子 bare body || ~屁股 bare butt

16 呈现 [-現] chéngxiàn (appear-show) <v.> present (a certain appearance), appear: ~在眼前 appear in front of one's eyes || ~出繁荣的景象 present a vast scene of prosperity

17 凸显 [-顯] tūxiǎn (protruding-appear) <v.> show (or present) clearly (or distinctly): ~价值 clearly show one's value || ~个性 clearly show one's personality

18 表现 [-現] biǎoxiàn (out-appear) <v.> display, show, express: ~很好behave oneself well || ~出很大的兴趣 show great interest in sth. || 在这场演出中, 他充分~了自己的才能. He showed his talent fully in this performance.

19 发挥 [發揮] fāhuī (send-wield) <v.> bring into play, give free rein to: ~想象力give free rein to one's imagination || ~积极性 bring one's initiative into full play

20 展现 [-現] zhǎnxiàn (spread-appear) <v.> unfold before one's eyes, emerge: ~在眼前 present in front of one's eyes || ~美好的前景 present a wonderful front || ~聪明才智 show one's wisdom and creativity

21 揭露 [-] jiēlù (disclose-show) <v.> to expose: ~秘密 to expose a secret || ~真相 to expose a truth || ~黑暗 to expose truth

22 释放 [釋-] shìfàng (release-set free) <v.> release, set free: ~能量release energy || ~人质free a hostage

23 消失 [-] xiāoshī (vanish-disappear) <v.> eliminate: 完全~ completely eliminate || 渐渐~ gradually eliminate || ~在人群中be lost in a crowd

24 丧失 [喪-] sàngshī (lose-lose) <v.> lose: ~信心lose confidence || ~劳动能力 lose the ability to work || ~机会 lose the opportunity

25 化解 [-] huàjiě (dissolve-solve) <v.> dissolve, resolve: ~矛盾resolve a conflict || ~危机 resolve a crisis || ~困境 be resolved of a predicament

26 失去 [-] shīqù (lose-lost) <v.> lose: ~生命 lose life || ~信心 lose confidence || ~希望 lose hope

27 恢复 [-復] huīfù (restore-return) <v.> recover: ~经济 recover the economy || ~疲劳 recover from fatigue

Tips:

1 失 (shī): The original form of 失 shows 'a man dropping something,' which indicates 'to lose.'

2 现 (xiàn): 现 is related to 玉 (王, jade) and 见 (visible,) therefore means 'appear, show.' It is also a kind of jade and the meaning (money) is kept in words such as 现金 (cash,) 现款 (xiànkuǎn, cash) and 套现 (tàoxiàn, to cash out.)

Exercises:

Part I: Translate the following phrases into English and then answer the following questions in Chinese.

中文	英文
恢复经济	
失去信心	
化解矛盾	
丧失人性	
揭露真相	
出现问题	
揭露真相	
发挥作用	
爆发战争	
层出不穷	
脱颖而出	

1.你觉得美国经济已经完全恢复了吗? 为什么?

____

2 你会不会对美国失去信心, 为什么?

____

3 你觉得美国的民主党与共和党会不会化解他们之间的矛盾? 为什么?

____

4 你认为你们国家的领导人是否在社会发展中发挥重要作用? 为什么?

____

5 你觉得什么样的公司会在激烈的竞争中脱颖而出?

____

Theme 198: Verbs (yet, not yet) 已然, 未然 (yǐrán, wèirán)

1 已然 [-] yǐrán (already-formed) <adv.> already: 山上的树~全都红了. All the trees on the mountain have already turned red.
2 注定 [-] zhùdìng (predestine-destine) <v.> doomed, to be bound to: ~要失败 be bound to lose
3 生效 [-] shēngxiào (produce-effect) <v.> go into effect: 合同~ The contract has gone into effect. || 正式~ officially go into effect. || 立即~ immediately go into effect.
4 起作用 [-] qǐzuòyòng (happen-effect) <v.> take effect: 药水~了. Medicine has had an effect. || 随时~ effect at any time. || 短时间内~ effect for a short time.

5 防患于未然 [--於--] fánghuànwèirán (prevent-hazard-at-not-formed) <idiom> take preventive measures: 平时要多洗手以~. One should regularly wash their hands as a preventive measure.
6 相持 [-] xiāngchí (mutual-hold) <v.> locked in a stalemate: ~一个多小时 locked in a stalemate for over an hour || 双方~不下. Neither side could end the stalemate.
7 防 [-] fáng (dam, guard, prevent) <v.> guard against, prevent: ~火墙 firewall || ~水 water resistant
8 防止 [-] fángzhǐ (prevent-stop) <v.> prevent, guard against: ~危险 prevent danger. || ~错误再次发生 prevent mistakes from happening again || ~坏人 guard against evil people
9 防范 [-範] fángfàn (prevent-guard) <v.> be on guard, keep a lookout: ~风险 be on the lookout for danger || 加强~ increase one's guard
10 预防 [預-] yùfáng (beforehand-prevent) <v.> prevent, take precautions against: 事先~ take advanced precautions || ~万一 take precautions just in case || ~疾病 take precautions against illness
11 避 [-] bì (avoid) <v.> avoid, evade: ~而不答 avoid without answering || ~暑 prevent heatstroke || ~难 take refuge, seek asylum
12 避免 [-] bìmiǎn (avoid-from) <v.> avoid, refrain from: ~缺点 avoid one's flaws || ~浪费 avoid making waste || ~争吵 avoid quarrels
13 逃避 [-] táobì (escape-avoid) <v.> escape, evade: ~责任 escape one's responsibility || ~困难 escape one's hardship || 无法~ have no chance of escaping
14 回避 [-/迴-] huíbì (averse-avoid) <v.> evade, dodge: ~问题 avoid questioning || 有意~ willfully evade
15 免得 [-] miǎnde (avoid-*suffix*) <v.> so as not to, so as to avoid: ~闹笑话 avoid making a fool of oneself || ~着急 avoid being worried || ~不愉快 avoid being unhappy
16 以免 [-] yǐmiǎn (in order to-avoid) <v.> in order to avoid: ~发生危险 avoid danger || ~出错 avoid making a mistake || ~上当 avoid being taken advantage of
17 失效 [-] shīxiào <v.> (lose-function) lose efficacy, loose effectiveness: 证件~ credentials are expired || 药物~. The medicine has lost its effectiveness

Tips:

1 防 (fáng): The original meaning of 防 is a dam since it is related to 阝 (阜, mound.) Since dams are used to 'guard' the river and 'prevent' floods, 'to guard' and 'to prevent' evolved and are the now the primary meanings of this character.
2 免得 vs. 以免: Both mean 'so as not to' or 'in order not to' but 免得 is colloquial. For example, you can say 'The central bank raised the savings interest rate 以免出现经济危机 (in order to avoid economic crisis)' but you cannot say ' . . . 免得出现经济危机.'
3 回避 (迴避): In ancient China, when government officials travel in the street, two large signs would be held in front of the procession, and on one sign would say 迴避 to remind the masses to avoid blocking the way.

Exercises:

Part I: Read the following sentences and fill in each blank with the appropriate word or phrase from the options given.

1 以免、失效、避免

a) 小张的护照已经_________了, 所以航空公司不准许他登记.
b) 出国旅行前一定要仔细检查护照是否到期, _________不能合法登机.
c) 为了_________堵车, 小张每天早上六点起床坐公共汽车上班.

2 防患于未然、逃避、回避

a) 有些青少年沉迷于网络游戏当中, 是因为他们想_________现实, 生活在虚拟的世界中.
b) 她的儿子几年前死于车祸, 因此她常常_________谈论关于孩子的事情.
c) 为了_________, 这个学校常常进行火灾演习.

3 防范、防止、预防

a) 为了_________流感, 学校要求每个学生都要打流感疫苗 (vaccine).
b) 为了_________小孩子用电脑打游戏, 这对父母设置了电脑密码.
c) 为了_________股市风险, 巴菲特 (Warren Buffett) 建议投资者要分散投资.

4 注定、生效、起作用

a) 这份新的法律文件将在总统签字后才能_________.
b) 有人认为如果中国的政治制度不改革, 经济发展将_________要受到阻碍.
c) 一些西方人认为中药不科学, 很难对治疗疾病_________

Theme 199: To exceed, to spread 到期, 传播 (dàoqī, chuánbō)

1 到期 [-] dàoqī (arrive-due time) <v-o.> expire, due: 我的签证月底~. My visa will expire at the end of the month. || 我们这套公寓的租约下月~. Our apartment lease will expire next month.
2 过 [過] guò (pass) <v.> pass, go over: ~期 expired || ~去 go over, go across (away from the speaker) || 他去买东西了, ~了一个小时以后才回来. He went shopping, and brought something back an hour later.
3 晚点 [-點] wǎndiǎn (behind-time) <v.> (of a train, ship, flight etc.) late, behind schedule: 火车~ 二十分钟 The train is 20 minutes overdue.
4 迟到 [遲-] chídào (late-come) <v.> be late, come late: ~半小时 be late half hour || 不许 ~ don't be late || 差一点儿 ~ almost late
5 直到 [-] zhídào (untill-come) <v.> until: ~现在 until now || ~目前为止up until now || 她一直住在北京, ~念完大学. She has lived in Beijing until she finished her college.
6 播 [-] bō (broadcast) <v.> broadcast: ~节目 broadcast program || ~电视 broadcast TV || ~消息 broadcast news

7 传 [傳] chuán (pass along) <v.> spread news or rumor: 消息~开了The news spread

8 传播 [傳-] chuánbō (pass along-spread) <v.> spread, propagate, disseminate: 广泛~ wide spread || 到处~ spread everywhere || ~文化 disseminate culture

9 广播 [廣-] guǎngbō (broad-broadcast) <v./n.> broadcast: 新闻~ newscast || 英语~ English broadcast || 收听 ~ listen to a broadcast

10 传来 [傳來] chuánlái (pass along-come) <v.> (of a sound) to come through, to be heard, (of news) to arrive: ~好消息 a good news arrives || ~笑声 to hear laughter from somewhere

11 传说 [傳說] chuánshuō (pass on-speak) <v./n.> It is said, they say, legend: 民间~ folktale || ~这就是泰坦尼克号沉船的地方. They say this is the place where the Titanic sank.

12 传输 [傳輸] chuánshū (pass-transmit) <v.> transmit: ~信号transmit signals || 信息~ information transmission || ~文化transmit culture

13 遗传 [遺傳] yíchuán (inherit-pass) <v.> pass to the next generation, be hereditary: ~病hereditary disease || ~学genetics || ~基因 genetic genes

14 播放 [-] bōfàng (broadcast-play) <v.> broadcast (radio or TV programs): ~电影 play movie || ~半小时play (music, radio or TV programs) half hour || ~比赛实况broadcast the match live

15 流行 [-] liúxíng (flow-go) <v.> be fashionable, be popular: 今年~绿色. The green color is in fashion this year. || ~歌曲pop song || ~文化popular culture

16 流传 [-傳] liúchuán (flow-spread) <v.> spread, hand down, circulate: ~久远 hand down for a long time || ~一个故事handing down a story || 广为~ spread far and wide

17 盛行 [-] shèngxíng (extensive-go) <v.> be in vogue, be very popular: 冬季流感~. The flu is very prevalent in the winter. || 在一些中国大城市给宠物狗美发很~. Hairdressing for pet dogs is popular in some big Chinese cities. || ~一时 prevail for a time

Tips:

1 迟到 (chídào) vs. 晚点 (wǎndiǎn): 迟到 means 'be late for work, school or an appointment,' while 晚点 means 'be behind scheduled time,' for example, 公共汽车/火车/飞机/电视节目晚点了.

2 现在流行什么**? Chinese young people are reasonably concerned with popular culture, so '现在流行什么** (e.g. 衣服/电视剧)?' is a good topic to start a long dialogue or monologue.

Exercises:

Part I: Read the following sentences and fill in each blank with the appropriate word or phrase from the options given.

1 盛行、流行、播放
 a) 年轻人一般都很喜欢听_________歌曲.
 b) 很多人喜欢一边开车一边在车里_________流行音乐.
 c) 佛教在东南亚国家很_________, 因为到处都可以看到寺庙和上香的老百姓.

2 传说、传输、传来、遗传
  a) ________这个地方就是泰坦尼克号 (Titanic) 沉船的地方.
  b) 尽管现代医学很发达, 但是在________病治疗方面效果还不理想.
  c) 中国的电力________方式在世界上处于领先地位.
  d) 我听见从客厅里________笑声, 一定是爸爸和客人在开玩笑.

3 传播、广播、传染、播
  a) 流感也算是一种________病. 如果不加预防会_______得非常快.
  b) 小李每天早上都听《美国之音》的________. 它的_______出时间是北京时间早上七点.

4 迟到、直到、过期、到期
  a) 小李上班常常________, 他跟公司的劳动合同________以后就被公司辞退了.
  b) 半年来小李一直忙着找工作, ________上个星期他才收到谷歌公司的录用通知.
  c) 对于________的饮料一定不要喝, 否则会危害身体健康.

Theme 200: To change 变化 (biànhuà)

1 变化 [變-] biànhuà (transform-convert) <v./n.> change, variation: 不断~ constantly change || 气温 ~ variations of temperature || 我老家有了很大的~. Great changes have taken place in my home village.
2 变 [變] biàn (transform, change) <v.> transform, change: ~大 become large || ~好 become better || ~黑 turn black
3 改变 [-變] gǎibiàn (alter-change) <v./n.> change, alter: ~方向 change direction || ~颜色 change color || ~方法 change method
4 改 [-] gǎi (alter) <v.> change, alter: ~名字 change one's name || ~日期 change the date || ~主意 change one's attention
5 变成 [變-] biànchéng (transform-complete) <v.> turn into, transform into, become: ~蝴蝶 turn into a butterfly || ~蓝色 become blue || 从丑小鸭~白天鹅(é) transform from an ugly ducking into a white swan
6 成 [-] chéng (accomplish, succeed, become) <v.> accomplish, complete: ~了爸爸became a father || ~了好朋友 became good friends || ~了一个大花园 became a big garden
7 同化 [-] tónghuà (same-convert) <v./n.> assimilate, assimilation: 自然~ naturally assimilate || ~少数民族 assimilate minorities
8 变动 [變動] biàndòng (change-change) <v./n.> change, alter: 大~ big change || 不断~ unceasingly change || 剧烈的~ radical changes
9 波动 [-動] bōdòng (fluctuate-change) <v.> fluctuate, wave motion: 湖水~ the lake water fluctuated || 心理/情绪~ one's mentality/ emotions fluctuated || 经济/价格~ the economy/price fluctuated
10 变更 [變-] biàngēng (change-change) <v.> change, alter: ~计划 change plans || ~事实 alter the facts || ~姓名 change one's name
11 变换 [變換] biànhuàn (change-change) <v.> vary, alternate: ~颜色 change color || ~话题 change topics || ~工作change work
12 换 [換] huàn (trade, exchange, change) <v.> exchange, change: ~地点 change places || ~衣服 change/exchange clothes || ~外币exchange some foreign currency

13 更换 [-換] gēnghuàn (change-change) <v.> change, replace: ~旧电脑replace old computers || ~密码 change one's password || 展品经常~. The exhibits keep changing.

14 变形 [變-] biànxíng (change-form) <v.> change shape: 容易~ easy to change shape || 弯曲~ easy to bend || 骨头~. The bone is deformed.

15 进化 [進-] jìnhuà (progress-change) <v.> evolution: 人类~ human evolution || 社会~ societal evolution || 动物~ animal evolution

16 绿化 [綠-] lǜhuà (green-change) <v.> make green with plants: ~城市 plan trees in and around the city || ~地带 green belt || 庭院~ courtyard greening

17 改装 [-] gǎizhuāng (change-assemble) <v.> change one's costume, refit: ~汽车 refit a car || ~飞机 refurbish a plane || ~机器 refit machinery

18 过渡 [過-] guòdù (pass-cross) <v.> transit: 慢慢~ slowly cross over || 和平~ peaceful transition || ~阶段 a transition stage

19 转 [轉] zhuǎn (turn, change) <v.> turn, change direction: ~好/坏 change for the better/worse || ~专业/学校 change major/school

20 转变 [轉變] zhuǎnbiàn (turn-change) <v.> change, transform: ~观念 change one's views || ~思想 change one's thought || 地位~ change one's position

21 转化 [轉-] zhuǎn huà (turn-change) <v.> change, transform: ~矛盾transform a contradiction || ~为太阳能 convert into solar power || 把先进技术~为生产力turn advanced technology into a productive force

22 转换 [轉換] zhuǎnhuàn (turn-change) <v.> change, transform: ~话题 change topics || 图像~ change images || ~镜头 change lenses

23 转移 [轉-] zhuǎnyí (turn-shift) <v.> shift, change: ~工作重心 shift one's work focus || ~注意力 shift one's attention || ~资金 shift capital

24 倒车 [-車] dǎochē (reverse-vehicle) <v-o.> change trains or buses: 倒三次车 transfer trains three times

25 开倒车 [開-車] kāidàochē (drive-reverse-vehicle) <v-o.> put back the clock: 新法律是~, 要退回到50年前的水平. The new law will roll the clock back 50 years.

26 变为 [變爲] biànwéi (change-into) <v.> change into, turn into: ~气体 turn into gas || 把沙漠~绿洲 turn the wilderness into green fields

27 成为 [-為] chéngwéi (become-into) <v.> become, turn into: ~一家 become a family || ~老板 become a boss || 梦想~现实 one's dream turned into reality

Tips:

1 更, 改, 变, 动/换: All mean 'to change' and their combinations, 更改, 更变, 变更, 更动, 更换, 改变, 改动, 改换, 变动, 变换 have almost the same meaning.

2 *化: The oracle form of 化 depicts one man straight up and one man upside down, thus 化 got the meaning 'change.' For example, 化学 (chemistry) is a subject about change. Now 化 functions almost as a suffix of high productivity, for example, 绿化 (to green,) 美化 (beautify, to glorify,) 西方化 (to Westernize) and 机械化 (jīxièhuà, to mechanize). 化 and its compound words or phrases can serve as an indicator of your proficiency of Chinese. If you understand all of the above-mentioned words with 化, you are at the intermediate level. More advanced words or phrases and their levels are below: 去中国化 (De-sinicization) and 大事化小, 小事化了 (to reduce a big problem

into a small one, and a smaller one into nothing,) advanced level, 化悲痛为力量 (to turn sorrow into strength,) superior, 化干戈为玉帛 (huà gāngé wéi yùbó, to bury the hatchet,) near native, 化腐朽为神奇 (huà fǔxiǔ wéi shénqí, literally 'to turn decadent into miraculous,' a more free translation would be close to 'to wave a magic wand,') native.

Exercises:

Part I: Use the given bound form as a guide to help you think of other words with the same character. Feel free to use your dictionary when needed. Then write down the English definition of each of the words you've written.

转 *(to turn, to change direction):* 转变 *change, transform*

____

____

____

____

变 *(change):* 变化 *change*

____

____

____

____

Part II: Read the following sentences and fill in each blank with the appropriate word or phrase from the options given.

1 改变、变化、变成

a) 最近二十年, 很多美国城市根本没有什么_________.
b) 这个地方原来是一所学校, 但是现在_________了一个商业区.
c) 有人说青年人总是想着要_________世界， 但是中年人知道要想生活更好得先改变自己.

2 变形、更换、绿化

a) 美国银行建议用户每六个月_________一下个人网上银行的密码.
b) 隐形眼镜 (contact lenses) 要放在在远离高温的地方, 因为在高温下它会发生_________.
c) 经过十几年的_________， 北京的树木覆盖率 (coverage) 已经到了20%以上.

3 改装、过渡、转变

a) 这对兄弟一起把一辆汽车_________成了赛车.
b) 中国监狱希望通过劳动改造使罪犯_________成对社会有用的公民.
c) 毛泽东认为中国不能立刻建成共产主义， 应该先建设社会主义， 因为它是走向共产主义的_________阶段.

4 倒车、转移、转向

a) 很多中国富人正在向海外________个人资产， 因为他们担心中国经济会崩溃.
b) 历史像一个人的人生一样, 都是不能开________的, 经过了就无法再回去.
c) 由于抗癌 (anti-cancer) 药物的研究竞争非常激烈, 这家药品公司决定________研发其他新药.

Theme 201: Damage, to deteriorate 损坏, 变坏 (sǔnhuài, biànhuài)

1 损坏 [損壞] sǔnhuài (damage-broken) <v.> damage, impair: 严重 ~ serious damages || ~公物 damage public property || 房屋~. The house was ruined.
2 毁坏 [-壞] huǐhuài (destroy-broken) <v.> destroy, damage: ~机器 damage to the machine || 全部~. The whole thing was destroyed.
3 毁 [-] huǐ (ruin, destroy) <v.> destroy, ruin: 烧~ destroyed through burning || ~了前途 ruin one's prospects || ~了事业destroy one's career
4 分裂 [-] fènliè (divide-split) <v.> split, divide: 国家~. The nation is divided || 社会~ social divisions || 精神~ schizophrenia
5 崩溃 [-潰] bēngkuì (collapse-overflow) <v.> collapse, crumble: 经济~ an economic collapse || 精神~ mental breakdown || 完全~ a complete collapse
6 折断 [-斷] zhéduàn (break-broken) <v.> snap sth off, break off sth: ~翅膀 break one's wing || ~树枝 break a branch
7 腐烂 [-爛] fǔlàn (decay-rotten) <v.> decompose, rot: 容易~ easy to decompose || ~的食物 rotting food
8 发霉 [發-] fāméi (become-moldly) <v.> go moldy, mildew: ~的大米 for the rice to go moldy || 面粉 ~ for the flour to go moldy
9 生锈 [-銹] shēngxiù (emerge-rust) <v.> rust: 铁锅~ the iron cooking pot began to rust || 容易~ easy to rust || 防止~ prevent rust
10 褪色 [-] tuìsè (fade-color) <v.> fade (of colors): 衣服 ~ the color of the clothes faded
11 恶化 [惡-] è'huà (worse-change) <v.> worsen, deteriorate: 健康~ one's health is deteriorating || 经济~ the economy deteriorates || 逐渐~ gradually deteriorate
12 衰弱 [-] shuāiruò (decline-weak) <v.> weak, feeble: 身体~ a weak body || 神经~ weak nerves || 逐渐~ gradually weaken
13 破败 [-敗] pòbài (broken-ruined) <v.> ruined, dilapidated: ~ 不堪crushed || ~的街道run down streets

Tips:

1 崩溃 (bēngkuì): It means 'collapse.' 崩溃 has to come with power, and the formation of this word shows that. 崩 is related to '山, mountain,' meaning 'landslide' and 溃 is related to '氵, river,' meaning 'burst of a dam.'
2 毁 (huǐ): It is related to 土 (the original bottom left part, pottery) and 毇 (huǐ.) 毁 originally meant 'pottery/vessel is broken,' and now means 'to ruin, destroy.'

Exercises:

Part I: Multiple Choice. Make sure to choose the most appropriate answer.

1 虽然这个大学生通过简历造假的方法得了在大公司的实习机会, 但是学校决定不开除他, 以免________了他的前途.
A. 损坏 B. 毁 C. 坏

2 美国一些城市的年轻人以"反对种族主义"为名_________了一些历史雕像或者建筑.
A. 折断 B. 坏了 C. 毁坏

3 有人认为这位总统支持"白人至上" (white supremacy)的观点, 这种政治理念正在________美国.
A. 分裂 B. 分手 C. 裂了

4 有人认为如果朝鲜持续进行核武器实验, 中国和朝鲜的关系将会进一步_________.
A. 丑化 B. 恶劣 C. 恶化

5 委内瑞拉 (Venezuela) 的经济以石油为主, 由于近五年来石油价格持续下降使这个国家经济________了.
A. 破了 B. 破败 C. 崩溃

6 这栋老房子有很多问题, 房子里的木地板因为潮湿已经开始________, 房子外面的油漆已经完全________了, 完全看不出来颜色.
A. 生锈、腐烂 B. 腐烂、褪色 C. 褪色、腐烂

7 进到这所老房子里, 你会闻到一股________的味道, 另外房子里的水管、冰箱、烤炉等这些金属制成的东西因为长期没人使用已经_________了.
A. 发霉、生锈 B. 折断、生锈 C. 切断、生气

8 一场暴雨过后, 这个地区的很多房子都遭到了不同程度的__________.
A. 损失 B. 损坏 C. 有害

Theme 202: To improve 好转 (hǎozhuǎn)

1 滋润 [-潤] zīrùn (nourish-moisten) <v.> moisten, comfortable: ~心灵 comforting for the spirit || ~皮肤 moistening for the skin
2 柔顺 [-順] róushùn (soft-smooth) <adj.> gentle and agreeable: 丝绸衣服很~. Silk clothes are soft and smooth. || 性情~ of gentle disposition, meek and mild
3 刺激 [-] cìjī (pierce-stimulate) <v./n.> stimulate, stimulation: 受~ receive stimulation || ~皮肤 stimulate the skin || 外部~ stimulation from outside
4 晒 [曬] shài (sun dry) <v.> (of the sun) shine upon: ~干 dry in the sun || ~小麦 dry wheat || ~被子 dry a comforter
5 好转 [-轉] hǎozhuǎn (better-turn) <v.> take a turn for the better: 情况~ for matters to turn for the better || 身体~ for one's body to take a turn for the better || 生活~ for life to take a turn for the better
6 改善 [-] gǎishàn (change-good) <v.> improve, make better: ~条件 improve conditions || ~生活 improve life || ~关系 improve relations

7 改进 [-進] gǎijìn (change-progress) <v.> improve, make better: ~方法improve a method || ~工作 improve work || ~教学 improve one's teaching

8 创新 [創-] chuàngxīn (create-new) <v./n.> bring forth new ideas, innovate, innovation: ~能力 the ability in innovation || 医学~ a great innovation in medicine || 勇于~ be bold in making innovations

9 更新 [-] gēngxīn (change-new) <v.> renew: ~内容 renew contents || ~知识 renew knowledge || ~观念 renew one's opinion

10 复苏 [復蘇] fùsū (back-revive) <v.> come back to life (or consciousness): 经济~ economic recovery || 市场~ market recovery || 万物~ all living things to come back to life

11 再生 [-] zàishēng (again-live) <v./adj.> regenerate, renewable: 我们的皮肤有~能力. Our skin has the ability of regeneration. || ~资源 renewable resources

12 耳目一新 [-] ěr'mùyīxīn (ear-eye-complete-new) <idiom> a pleasant change of atmosphere or appearance: 令人~ make someone see things like new

13 兴起 [興-] xīngqǐ (prosper-rise) <v.> rise, spring up: 不断~ unceasingly spring up || ~经商热. The business fever is rising up. || 大战~ for a war to rise up

14 振兴 [-興] zhènxīng (inspirit-prosper) <v.> revive, revitalize: ~农业 revive agriculture || 民族~ revive the nation || ~经济 revive the economy

Tips:

1 改善 (gǎishàn) vs. 改进 (gǎijìn): Both mean 'to improve,' but 改善 has a connotation of 'from not good to good' and 改进 'from okay to better.' 改善 usually refers to condition, relation etc. and 改进 is used for a method.

2 振兴中华 (zhènxīng Zhōnghuá): It means 'to revitalize China.' Guangzhou Railway Station, presumably, has the last large public sign with this once very popular slogan.

Exercises:

Part I: Read the following sentences and fill in each blank with the appropriate word or phrase from the options given.

1 兴起、好起来、振兴

a) 从2000年开始中国政府一直致力于_________东北经济， 可是效果一直不显著.
b) 目前人工智能的研究正在_________, 并且已经应用到很多领域.
c) 2017年以来中国消费的市场开始_________， 居民消费总量明显增加.

2 起作用、再生、复苏

a) 1929年美国遭受了经济危机, 直到1935年才有了_________的迹象.
b) 中国政府决定积极推广风能、太阳能等_________能源的使用， 以减少空气污染.
c) 现在看来北京政府减少空气污染的措施_________了， 2017年北京的空气污染天数下降了很多.

3 耳目一新、好转、更新
   a) 苹果公司的销售情况不乐观, 因此公司决定继续推出新产品, 来使公司的销售状况________.
   b) 中国的《人民日报》 (*People's Daily*) 手机版, 每两个小时________一次内容.
   c) 《人民日报》手机版改变了以前严肃、枯燥的写作风格, 刊登了很多贴近人们实际生活的文章, 令人________.

4 刺激、改善、改进
   a) 中美关系从1972年尼克松 (Nixon) 访华以后开始渐渐________.
   b) 目前谷歌正在积极________语音翻译中文的技术.
   c) 谷歌决定增加员工的加班费, 来________员工的工作积极性.

5 滋润、晒、柔顺
   a) 好的文学作品可以________人的心灵, 给人生以智慧和动力.
   b) 很多中国女孩子喜欢日本的洗发产品,因为可以使头发________、闪亮.
   c) 很多中国人喜欢洗完衣服以后, 挂在太阳下面________干, 因为他们觉得阳光有杀菌的作用.

Theme 203: To increase, to decrease 增加, 减少 (zēngjiā, jiǎnshǎo)

1 增加 [-] zēngjiā (increase-add) <v.> increase, raise, add: ~人数 increase the number of people || ~收入 increase revenue || ~困难 add hardship
2 增长 [-長] zēngzhǎng (increase-grow) <v.> increase, rise, grow: 不断~ unceasingly increase || 迅速~ increasing speed || ~经验 grow the experience
3 增多 [-] zēngduō (increase-more) <v.> grow in numbers or quantity: 病人~ The number of patients is increasing || 我们的问题~了. Our problems have multiplied.
4 加 [-] jiā (slander, increase, add) <v.> add, plus: 二~一等于三. Two plus one equals three. || ~一个字 add a character || ~宽 add with || ~点盐 add some salt
5 添 [-] tiān (add) <v.> add, increase: ~负担 add a burden || ~麻烦 incommode
6 增产 [-產] zēngchǎn (increase-production) <v-o.> increase production: ~电视机 increase production of TVs || 珍珠~ increase production of pearls
7 增值 [-] zēngzhí (add-value) <v.> rise (or increase) in value: 房产~ real estate value added || 人民币~. The value of the Chinese yuan increased. || 土地~. The land increased in value.
8 升值 [-] shēngzhí (rise-value) <v.> rise in value: 货币~ for currency to increase in value || 房子~ for a house to rise in value || 股票~ for stocks to rise in value
9 放大 [-] fàngdà (go-large) <v.> enlarge, magnify: ~照片 make a picture larger || ~图像 make an image larger
10 增大 [-] zēngdà (increase-large) <v.> enlarge, expand: 过去十年美国贫富差距~了. The gap between the rich and the poor has widened in the past decade.
11 扩大 [擴-] kuòdà (expand-large) <v.> enlarge, expand: ~词汇量expand one's vocabulary || ~内需expend domestic demands || ~眼界widen one's outlook
12 上涨 [-漲] shàngzhǎng (up-rise) <v.> rise, go up: 物价~ rise in price || 河水~ for the water in the river to rise || 费用~ increase in cost

13 涨价 [漲價] zhǎng jià (rise-price) <v.> (of prices) rise: 乱~ wild increase in prices || 产品~ increase in price of a good || ~十元 increased by 10 yuan

14 上升 [-] shàngshēng (up-uprise) <v.> rise, go up: 逐步~ gradually rise || 慢慢~ slowly rise || 价格~ for price to rise

15 升 [-] shēng (uprise) <v.> rise, ascend: ~一级 rise a level || 往上~ rise in an upward direction || ~大学 enter into college

16 升高 [-] shēnggāo (uprise-high) <v.> raise, ascend: 太阳~ for the sun to rise || 温度 ~ for the temperature to rise || 血压~ for the pressure to rise

17 补偿 [補償] bǔcháng (make up-compensate) <v.> compensate, make up: 经济~ economic compensation || 得到~ receive compensation || 作为~ serve as compensation

18 补充 [補-] bǔchōng (replenish-supplement) <v.> replenish, supplement: ~水分 replenish moisture || ~一些意见 supplement some opinions || ~几句话add in a few lines

19 充电 [-電] chōngdiàn (charge-electricity) <v-o.> recharge batteries: 充一次电 recharge a battery || 充八小时电 recharge 8 hours of battery life || 自动~ automatically recharge

20 扩展 [擴-] kuòzhǎn (expand-spread) <v.> extend, expand: 向外 ~ expand outward || ~势力 expand power/influence

21 抓紧 [-緊] zhuājǐn (grasp-tight) <v.> grasp firmly, make the most of: ~时间make the best use of one's time || 你得~学习. You have to study hard. || ~机会. Seize the opportunity.

22 看好 [-] kànhǎo (view-promising) <v.> be optimistic (about the outcomes): ~大陆市场 be optimistic about the mainland market || ~电子行业 be optimistic about the electrical industry

23 提高 [-] tígāo (raise-high) <v.> raise: ~价格 raise in price || ~质量raise in quality || ~能力 raise one's ability

24 增进 [-進] zēngjìn (increase-closer) <v.> promote, enhance: ~友谊 promote friendship || ~了解 promote understanding || ~感情 promote feelings

25 增强 [-] zēngqiáng (increase-strong) <v.> increase, strength: ~信心 heighten confidence || ~免疫力 improve one's immunity || ~体力 build up one's strength

26 加强 [-] jiāqiáng (add-strong) <v.> reinforce, strengthen: ~营养 reinforce nutrition || ~ 力量 increase strength || ~合作 enhance one's cooperation

27 强化 [-] qiánghuà (intense-*suffix*) <v.> strengthen, intensify: ~管理 strengthen management || ~训练intensive training

28 深化 [-] shēnhuà (deep-*suffix*) <v.> deepen, intensify: ~改革deepen the reform || ~认识 deepen cognition || 矛盾的 ~ intensification of a contradiction

29 加深 [-] jiāshēn (add-deep) <v.> deepen: ~友谊 deepen one's friendship || 逐步 ~ gradually deepen || ~理解get a deeper understanding

30 减 [減] jiǎn (reduce) <v.> lower, decrease: ~人 decrease the number of people || ~价 decrease the price || ~工资 decrease wages

31 减少 [減-] jiǎnshǎo (reduce-lessen) <v.> decrease: ~人数 decrease the number of people || ~错误 decrease the errors || 收入~ decrease revenue

32 负增长 [負-長] fùzēngzhǎng (negative-grow) <v.> negative growth: 经济~ economic recession || 人口~ decrease in population growth

33 消费 [-費] xiāofèi (decrease-consume) <v.> consume: 高/低~ high consumption/low consumption || 个人~ individual consumption || 合理~ rational consumption

34 消耗 [-] xiāohào (decrease-use up) <v.> use up, consume: ~精力 consume one's energy || ~时间 use up time || ~金钱 use up money

35 裁军 [-軍] cáijūn (reduce-soldier) <v.> reduce armaments, disarm: ~一百万 make a million disarmaments (large scale disarmament) || 核 ~ nuclear disarmament

36 降 [-] jiàng (lower, fall, descend) <v.> descend, fall: ~温decrease in temperature || ~价 cut the price || ~ 职 reduce to a lower rank

37 下降 [-] xiàjiàng (down-drop) <v.> decline, drop: 地位~ decline in position || 速度~ decline in speed || 慢慢~ slowly decline

38 降落 [-] jiàngluò (descend-fall) <v.> descend, land: 飞机~ landing of an aircraft || 在机场~ landed at the airport || 安全 ~ land safely

39 降低 [-] jiàngdī (descend-low) v.> reduce, lower: ~标准 reduce the standard || ~生产成本 reduce production costs || 气温~了. The temperature dropped.

40 降价 [-價] jiàngjià (decrease-price) <v-o.> cut the price: 降一次价 cut the price once || ~出售 cut the price in order to sell || 大~ a large drop in price

41 减轻 [減輕] jiǎnqīng (reduce-lighten) <v.> lighten, ease: ~疼痛ease the pain || ~体重 ease the weight || ~病情 ease the patient's conditions

42 花费 [-費] huāfèi (spend-coast) <v.> money spent, expenditures: ~时间 spend time || ~金钱 spend money || ~精力/力气 spend energy/strength

43 暴跌 [-] bàodiē (rapidly-fall) <v.> fall steeply, (economics) slump: 股票价格~ There was a slump in share prices. || 油价~ drastic drop in oil prices

44 放松 [-鬆] fàngsōng (release-loosen) <v.> loosen, relax: ~手指relax one's fingers || ~心情 relax oneself || ~管理loosen administration

45 松 [鬆] sōng (loose, loosen) <v.> loose: ~一口气 release a breath || ~皮带 loosen a belt || ~手 loosen one's hand

46 退 [-] tuì (retreat) <v.> retreat, decline: 敌人~了. The enemy has retreated. || 高烧~了. The high fever has gone down.

Tips:

1 加: It means 'to add, increase,' however, the original meaning of 加 was to 'to add untrue words,' in other words, 'to slander.'

2 减 (jiǎn): It means 'to reduce.' 减 is a popular form of the orthodox form 減 which is related to 氵 (water,) not 冫 (ice.)

3 Spend time (with somebody): It is not 花时间, but 度过时间 or more naturally (跟他) 一起verb (during which time is spent.) For example, 'you should spend time with your children' is '你应该跟你的小孩儿玩儿.'

Exercises:

Part I: Use the given bound form as a guide to help you think of other words with the same character. Feel free to use your dictionary when needed. Then write down the English definition of each of the words you've written.

增 *(increase, gain, add):* 增加 *increase*

____

____

____

____

加 *(add, plus)*: 加强 *reinforce, strengthen*

____

____

____

____

减 *(reduce, subtract)*: 减少 *reduce, decrease*

____

____

____

____

降 *(fall)*: 降低 *cut down, lower*

____

____

____

____

Part II: Translate the following phrases into English and then answer the questions.

股市暴跌 ________________
社会矛盾加深 ________________
房地产增值 ________________
收入增加 ________________
得到补偿 ________________
人民币升值 ________________
扩大国际影响力 ________________
减轻企业负担 ________________
降低企业税率 ________________

1 经济危机的时候一般不会出现下面哪种情况

a) 股市暴跌 b) 社会矛盾加深 c) 房地产增值

2 最近十年, 你们国家的老百姓收入增加得快吗? 为什么?

____

3 最近十年, 你觉得哪个国家扩大了自己的国际影响力?

____

4 你赞成美国政府降低企业税率的主张吗? 为什么?

____

5 你觉得人民币会一直升值吗? 为什么?

Theme 204: To eliminate, need 消除, 需要 (xiāochú, xūyào)

1 杜绝 [-絕] dùjué (break off-stop) <v.> stop, put an end to: ~腐败 (fǔbài) put an end to corruption || ~浪费 stop waste || ~失误put an end to errors
2 根除 [-] gēnchú (root-eliminate) <v.> thoroughly do away with: ~恶习rid oneself of a bad habit || ~腐败现象 put an end to corrupt dealings || ~不正之风 do away with an unhealthy tendency
3 扫除 [掃-] sǎochú (sweep-get rid of) <v.> clean, clear away: ~障碍 (zhàng'ài) clear away a barrier || ~文盲do away with illiteracy || ~偏见 resolve bias
4 斩草除根 [斬---] zhǎncǎo chúgēn (cut-grass-root out-root) <idiom> cut the weeds and dig up the roots: 对待黑社会, 必须~. When dealing with the underworld (black market), one must cut the weeds and dig up the roots.
5 斩尽杀绝 [斬盡殺絕] zhǎnjìn shājué (decapitate-all-kill-extinct) <idiom> kill all, wipe out: 尽管我们公司非常强大, 但是没有强大到能把所有的对手~的程度, 所以还是要注意一下公众形象. Although our company is very powerful, it is not so powerful as to be able to wipe out all competitors, therefore we still need to pay some attention to our company's public image.
6 排除 [-] páichú (exclude-eliminate) <v.> get rid of, remove: ~困难 remove hardship || ~竞争remove competition || ~险情remove a dangerous state or situation
7 消除 [-] xiāochú (get rid of-eliminate) <v.> eliminate, dispel: ~危险 eliminate danger || ~疲劳 dispel fatigue || ~烦恼 dispel distress
8 消灭 [-滅] xiāomiè (get rid of-extinguish) <v.> eliminate, wipe out: ~城乡差别 eliminate the difference between urban and rural areas || ~敌人 eliminate enemies || ~老鼠 eliminate rodents
9 铲除 [鏟-] chǎnchú (eradicate-eliminate) <v.> root out, eradicate: ~杂草 root out weeds || ~恶势力wipe out evil forces || 彻底~ thoroughly eradicate
10 拆除 [-] chāi chú (tear-eliminate) <v.> dismantle, tear down: ~楼房tear down a building || ~路障 tear down road blocking || 强行~ tear down by force
11 打消 [-] dǎxiāo (*prefix*-get rid of) <v.> give up (an idea, etc), dispel (a doubt, etc.): ~顾虑 (gùlǜ) dispel concerns || ~疑问dispel sb.'s suspiction || ~ 养狗的想法give up the idea of raising a dog
12 免去 [-] miǎnqù (dismiss-remove) <v.> excuse from doing, remove from office: ~职务 remove from one's post || ~赔款remove compensation
13 清除 [-] qīngchú (clear-eliminate) <v.> clear away, eliminate: ~毒素 (dúsù) clear away toxins || ~垃圾clear away trash || ~灰尘 clear away dust
14 解脱 [-] jiětuō (untie-separate) <v.> free (or extricate) oneself, absolve: ~痛苦 free oneself from suffering || 从烦恼中~ 出来free yourself from worries || 精神 ~ mental/spiritual relief
15 辟谣 [闢謠] pìyáo (refute-rumor) <v.> refute a rumor, deny a rumor: 及时~ urgently deny a rumor || 官方~ officially denied the rumor
16 消灾 [-災] xiāozāi (get rid of-calamity) <v.> be rid of calamities: 祈福~ pray for luck and sacrifice to avoid disasters || ~免祸 avert calamities, avoid disasters

17 去火 [-] qùhuǒ (relieve-inflammation) <v.> reduce internal heat, relieve inflammation: 清热~ relieve internal heat || 喝绿豆汤~. Drink green bean soup to relieve internal heat. || 快速~ quickly remove internal heat

18 消火 [-] xiāohuǒ (extinguish-inflammation) <v.> extinguish body internal fire/heat: 吃水果~. Eat fruit to extinguish internal heat.

19 解毒 [-] jiědú (remove-toxic) <v.> detoxify, relieve internal heat: 清热~ relieve internal heat and detoxify

20 杀毒 [殺-] shādú (kill-toxic) <v.> kill virus, sterilize, disinfect: 给电脑~ kill virus for the computer || ~软件antivirus software || ~剂sterilizer

21 解乏 [-] jiěfá (relieve-fatigue) <v.> recover from fatigue: 茶能~. Tea can help you recover from fatigue. || 喝点酒可以~. Drinking a little bit of alcohol can help one recover from fatigue.

22 解馋 [-饞] jiěchán (relieve-ravenous) <v.> satisfy a food craving: 这种零食最~. This type of snack can help satisfy your craving.

23 解渴 [-] jiěkě (relieve-thirsty) <v.> quench the thirst: 夏天吃西瓜最~. Eating watermelon is the best way to quench one's thirst in summer.

24 消磁 [-] xiāocí (eliminate-magnetism) <v.> demagnetize: 自动~ automatically demagnetize. || 手机会使各种卡~. The cellphone can demagnetize all kinds of credit cards.

25 戒 [-] jiè (guard against, give up) <v.> give up or stop doing sth: ~ 烟 quit smoking || ~酒 quit drinking || ~毒. Stop doing drugs.

26 抛弃 [-棄] pāoqì (throw-discard) <v.> abandon, forsake: ~妻儿 abandon one's wife and kids || ~家庭 abandon one's family || 被社会~ be abandoned by the society

27 遗弃 [遺棄] yíqì (abandon-discard) <v.> abandon, forsake, desert: ~子女 forsake one's children || ~老人 forsake the elderly or parents

28 舍弃 [捨棄] shěqì (give up-discard) <v.> give up, abandon: ~生命 give up one's life || ~金钱 give up money || 他决定 ~工作, 在家照顾孩子. She decided to give up her job and take care of her children at home.

29 废除 [廢-] fèichú (abolish-eliminate) <v.> abolish, repeal: ~终身制 abolish tenure || ~死刑 abolish the death penalty

30 作废 [-廢] zuòfèi (become-abolished) <v.> become invalid: 宣布合同~ declare a contract null and void || 全部~ for the whole thing to become invalid || 声明~ declare invalid

31 丢开 [-開] diūkāi (cast-away) <v.> cast away, put aside: ~幻想 cast away illusions

32 放下 [-] fàngxià (put-down) <v.> lay down, put down: ~笔 put down one's pen || 轻轻地~ lightly put down || 把茶杯~ put down the teacup

33 抛开 [-開] pāokāi (throw-away) <v.> throw out, get rid of: ~事实 get rid of facts || ~烦恼, 放松自己get rid of worries and relax yourself || ~现实 get rid of the reality

34 放弃 [-棄] fàngqì (put-discard) <v.> abandon, give up: ~机会abandon an opportunity || ~工作 abandon work || ~兴趣 abandon one's interest

35 弃权 [棄權] qìquán (waive-right) <v.> abstain from voting, waive the right (to play): 这个提议五人赞成, 两人~. Five members voted for the proposal and two abstained. || 上次选举时他~了. At the last election, he abstained (from voting/the vote).

36 葬送 [-] zàngsòng (bury-end) <v.> ruin, spell an end to: ~友谊 ruin friendship || ~幸福 ruin happiness

37 断送 [斷-] duànsòng (stop-end) <v.> forfeit (one's life, future, etc), ruin: ~生命forfeit one's life || 性丑闻~了这位总统的前途. The sex scandal ruined the President's future.

38 埋没 [-] máimò (bury-drown) <v.> cover up (with Earth, snow, etc), neglect, stifle: ~人才stifle real talent

39 解 [-] jiě (dissect, split, separate, untie) <v.> untie, undo: ~开上衣undo a jacket || ~题 to solve a mathematical problem

40 解决 [-決] jiějué (solve-result) <v.> solve, resolve: ~问题 solve a problem || ~困难 overcome a difficulty || ~争端 settle a dispute

41 破解 [-] pòjiě (break-solve) <v.> analyze and explain, decode: ~密码decode a password

42 速战速决 [-戰-決] sùzhàn sùjué (quick-fight-quick-end) <idiom> fight a quick battle to force a quick decision, act promptly: 他们打算~, 上半场就打败对手. They were going to fight a quick battle and beat their opponents in the first half.

43 迎刃而解 [-] yíngrèn'ér jiě (meet-blade-and-solve) <idiom> (bamboo) splits as it meets the edge of a knife: 问题~. This issue is easily resolved with the right solution. || 困难~. This hardship is easily resolved with the right solution.

44 过关斩将 [過關斬將] guòguān zhǎnjiàng (to pass-pass-behead-general) <idiom> surmount all difficulties (on the way for success): 他们一路~, 终于进入了决赛. Along the way, they surmounted all difficulties, finally bursting into the finals.

45 需要 [-] xūyào (need-need) <v.> need: ~阳光need sunlight. || ~时间 need time. || ~水 need water

46 急需 [-] jíxū (urgent-need) <v.> be badly in need of, urgently need: ~药物 urgently need medicine. || ~解决 urgently need an issue solved. || ~改变 urgently need reform

47 必需 [-] bìxū (must-need) <v.> essential, indispensable: ~的知识 essential knowledge. || ~的资金 essential funds || 日常生活~品 daily necessities

48 无需 [無-] wúxū (no-need) <v.> needless: ~多说 It's needless to say more. || ~担心 It's needless to worry

49 不够 [-夠] búgòu (not-enough) <v./ adv.> insufficient, not enough: 钱~ insufficient funds. || ~好 not good enough. || 准备~ inadequately prepared

50 缺 [-] quē (incomplete, lack) <v.> be short of, lack: ~钱 be short of money || ~水lack water || ~人 be short of hands

51 缺少 [-] quēshǎo (lack-short of) <v.> lack, be short of: 不可~ cannot lack || ~朋友 lack friends || ~经验lack experience

52 欠火候 [-] qiànhuǒhòu (short of-heat control maturity) <v.> have not been cooked or heated long enough: 这部作品还~. These pieces of art have not been heated long enough. || 他的中文还~. His Chinese still needs more practice.

53 僧多粥少 [-] sēngduō zhōushǎo (monk-many-porridge-less) <idiom> little gruel but many monks (not enough to go round): 美国大学的教职~, 因此博士生毕业在大学很难找到工作. There are too many professors and few vacancies in American universities, so it is hard for Ph.D. students to get a job at a university.

Tips:

1 火: In traditional Chinese medical science, 火 is 'inflammation' or 'internal fire' that often appears in a corner of one's mouth, whereas Western doctors think it is a sign of a lack of vitamins. When someone 上火, the Chinese will usually eat bitter melon or green bean porridge, but Westerners will eat oranges, and both ways work. In this battle, Traditional Chinese Medicine (TCM) and Western medicine tie.

2 灭 (滅, miè): It means 'to extinguish.' The simplified form (灭) is a remnant of the traditional form '滅' but it also makes sense since the upper part 一 signifies 'cover.' When fire (火) is covered (一,) it will 'extinguish.'

3 埋没 (máimò): It means 'cover up, stifle.' The formation of this word is clever since 埋 means 'bury in Earth' and 没 'drown in water.'

4 谣言 (yáoyán) and 辟谣 (pìyáo): 谣言 means 'rumor' and 辟谣 'to refute/deny a rumor.' In this information era, some 'rumors' turn out to be the 'truth' so Chinese netizens call 谣言 '遥遥领先的预言' (yáoyáolǐngxiān de yùyán, far ahead prediction.) If a rumor occurs and someone immediately 辟谣, it can be said that '越辟谣越真实' (the more one denies a rumor, the more likely it is true.)

Exercises:

Part I: Use the given bound form as a guide to help you think of other words with the same character. Feel free to use your dictionary when needed. Then write down the English definition of each of the words you've written.

解 *(untie, undo):* 解开上衣*undo a jacket*

____

____

____

____

消 *(vanish):* 消灭 *wipe out*

____

____

____

____

除 *(get rid of):* 排除 *remove*

____

____

____

____

Part II: Read the following sentences and fill in each blank with the appropriate word or phrase from the options given.

1 迎刃而解、过关斩将、速战速决
  a) 邓小平认为中国的经济发展了, 很多社会问题就会__________ ___.
  b) 《孙子兵法》 (*The Art of War*) 中有一个战争策略 (cèlüè, strategy) 是__________, 意思就是打击敌人的时候动作要快, 快速出击, 快速消灭敌人, 结束战争.
  c) 小王经过一轮又一轮的面试, __________, 最后拿到了投资银行的录用通知.

2 斩草除根、欠火候、僧多粥少
  a) 制作北京烤鸭的时候至少要花费一个小时, 时间短, __________, 会使这道菜不地道.
  b) 在中国想当政府公务员的大学毕业生数量远远高于政府新增的工作岗位, 真是__________ _啊!
  c) 很多人认为各个国家应该团结起来, 打击恐怖主义, 最后要__________彻底解决这个问题.

3 打消、断送、埋没、解脱
  a) 尼克松总统的政治丑闻__________ __了他的政治生涯.
  b) 在中国文革时期, 很多有才能的青年都被_________了, 不得不到农村种地当农民.
  c) 有的国家认为安乐死 (euthanasia) 对于重病患者 (patient) 来说是一种_________, 所以他们支持安乐死.
  d) 心理医生会用很多办法来劝说患者________自杀的念头.

4 戒毒、缺少、急需、解乏
  a) 一般的中国人都认为洗热水澡和蒸桑拿能够__________.
  b) 染上毒瘾的人很难靠自己的力量来__________ _.
  c) 这家工厂_________一千名技术工人来生产新产品.
  d) 据有关研究表明, 长期__________家庭温暖的孩子性格上会有缺陷, 比如孤僻 (withdrawn) 、没有爱心等等.

Theme 205: Copula, connection 系词 (xìcí)

1 是 [-] shì (be) <v.> be, is: 狗~人类最好的朋友. Dogs are man's best friends.
2 系 [係] xì (be) <v.> to be, system, series: 死者~中毒死亡. The dead died of poisoning. || 玛丽~我校外语系老师. Mary is my school's foreign language teacher.
3 乃 [-] nǎi (be) <v.> be, so: 此~西方"天主教会"的由来. This is the origin of the West's 'Catholic Church.' || 李先生~我们旧上司. Mr. Li is our old boss. || 婚姻~终身大事. Marriage is a lifelong matter.
4 即 [-] jí (that is, namely) <v.> be, mean, namely: 春节~农历新年. The Spring Festival/Chinese New Year is called the Lunar New Year. || 非此~彼It must be either this or that
5 为 [為] wéi (female monkey, do, make, become, be) <v.> be, do, act: 少说~好. To speak less is for the better. || 门票的价格~一百五十元. The price of tickets at the door is 150 yuan.

6 正是 [-] zhèngshì (just-be) <v.> precisely: 事实~这样. These are precise facts. || 他~这样做的. He did it precisely this way. || 现在~忙的时候. Right now is our busy period.

7 指 [-] zhǐ (finger, point at, refer to) <v.> mean, refer to: 他说有些人很坏, 不知道是~谁. I don't know to whom he was referring when he said some people were very bad.

8 泛指 [-] fànzhǐ (generally-refer to) <v.> make a general reference: "昨天"~过去, "明天"~未来. Yesterday represents the past, tomorrow represents the future. || 汉语的"汤"原来~一切的热水. The Chinese character for "tang" originally represented all hot water.

9 特指 [-] tèzhǐ (particularly-refer to) <v.> refer in particular to: 传统的"中国画"~文人画. Traditional Chinese paintings refer particularly to 'literati' paintings. || "同志"~同一个政党的成员. The word comrade refers to members of the same party.

10 不外乎 [-] búwàihu (not-beyond-of) <v.> not be beyond the scope of: 原因~两个. The reason is not beyond two things. || 人类的目标~是与自然和谐共处. The goal of human beings is nothing more than living in harmony with nature.

11 不愧是 [-] búkuìshì (have no-qualms-to be) <v.> be worthy of, deserve to be called: 这本书~公认的高质量的课本. This book is worthy of being recognized as a high quality textbook.

12 绝非 [-] juéfēi (absolutely-not) <v.> absolutely not: ~巧合. This is absolutely not a coincidence. || ~偶然 absolutely; not occasionally || ~一件容易的事. This is absolutely not an easy matter.

13 是否 [-] shìfǒu (to be-not) <bf.> whether or not, whether: 你~依然爱她? Do you still love her?

14 与否 [與-] yǔfǒu (and-not) <bf.> whether or not: 我们应该先看质量, 再考虑外表的美观~. We should consider the quality, then consider whether the appearance is beautiful or not. || 工作的态度决定了我们的快乐~. Whether we are happy or not is decided by our working attitudes.

15 当 [當] dāng (equal, face, undertake, work as) <v.> work as, severe as: ~医生 serve as a doctor. || ~科学家 serve as a scientist.

16 当作 [當-] dāngzuò (regard-as) <v.> treat as, regard as: 把友谊~爱情 treat friendship as love || 把明星们~自己的偶像 treat stars as idols || 把石头~宝贝 treat a rock as a treasure

17 当成 [當-] dāngchéng (regard-be) <v.> regard as, treat as: 把好人~坏人 treat good people like bad guys || 把韩国人~日本人 treat Koreans the same as Japanese

18 堪称 [-稱] kānchēng (worth-call) <v.> worth being called as: ~一流 worthy of being called the same || ~奇迹 worth being called a miracle

19 看作 [-] kànzuò (view-as) <v.> look upon as: 他把练书法~运动. He saw practicing calligraphy as an activity. || 他把上网~自己的工作. He puts his own work online for people to see.

20 权当 [權當] quándāng (for the time being-as) <v.> to act as if: 死马~活马医. The dead horse was treated as if it were still living.

21 视为 [視爲] shìwéi (view-to be) <v-o.> view as, take as: 视她为好友 take her as a good friend || ~奇迹 take as a miracle || ~国宝 take as a national treasure

22 作为 [-為] zuòwéi (as-be) <v.> regard as, look on as, take as: 气功~古老东方文化的一部分, 对医学院的学生更有吸引力. Qigong, a system of deep breathing exercises, is regarded as a part of ancient Eastern culture, so it attracts the interest of many students in medicine.

23 算作 [-] suànzuò (count-as) <v.> be counted as, equate to: 怎样才能~"汉语好"? What conditions equate to good Chinese (language level)? || 能创造价值的人才能 ~人才. People who are able to create ethical value equate to talented people.

24 不失为 [--為] búshīwéi (not-miss-to be) <v.> may after all be accepted as, can be regarded as: ~一种好办法. This can be regarded as a good solution.

25 称得上 [稱--] chēngdéshàng (call-*complement*-able to) <v.> deserve to be called: ~画家 deserve to be called an artist. || ~英雄 deserve to be called a hero.

26 比作 [-] bǐzuò (liken-to) <v.> liken to: 把首都北京~心脏 liken the capital of Beijing to a heart. || 把果树~摇钱树 liken fruit trees to the cash cow

27 比喻 [-] bǐyù (compare-analogize) <v.> metaphor, analogy: 中国人用松树~革命者. The steadfast revolutionaries are often likened to pine trees. || 把国际市场~为大海 use the sea as a metaphor when talking about international markets

28 譬如 (比如) [-] pìrú (analogize-as) <v.> for example, for instance: 这所大学的学生有很好的实习机会, ~学经济的, 可到世界500强企业实习. Students in this university have a very good chance of interning. For example, students who major in Economics can go on to intern at global Fortune 500 companies.

29 打比方 [-] (make-analogy) <v.> make an analogy: 你可以先定一个能够达到的小目标, ~说, 一年之内当经理. You can set small targets for you to achieve. For example, becoming a manager a year from now.

30 称 [稱] (weigh, call) <v.> call, declare: 男同学~她为女神. The male classmates call her a goddess. || 孩子们~那人叔叔. The children call that person 'uncle.' || 他被 ~为球迷. He was declared as a sports fan.

31 称为 [稱爲] (call-as) <v.> declare as: 他被~乡下人. He is called a countryman. || 质量好才能~好的产品. Only when the quality is good can one call it a good product. ||她被~ "美女教授." She is known as the 'beauty professor.'

32 号称 [號稱] (title-call) <v.> be known as: 中国的四川 ~天府之国. Sichuan Province in China is known as a land of plenty. || 狮子~兽中之王. The lion is called the king of beasts.

33 称之为 [稱-爲] (call-its-as) <v.> call it, known as: 以前把那些说我们要登上月球的人都~空想家. In the past, those who said we will go on the moon were called visionaries.

34 简称 [簡稱] (abbreviated-name) <v./n.> be abbreviated as: 中国共产党党员~党员. Members of the Chinese Communist party are called 'party members' for short.

35 全称 [-稱] (full-name) <v./n.> full name full name (of a thing), unabbreviated form: 中国的~是中华人民共和国. China's full name is the People's Republic of China. || 英国的~是大不列颠及北爱尔兰联合王国. The full name of the U.K. is the United Kingdom of Great Britain and Northern Ireland.

36 自称 [-稱] (self-address) <v.> call oneself, claim to be: 小王~会给人算命. Little Wang claimed that he could tell people's fortunes. || 他~是孔子的后代. He claims to be a descendant of Confucius.

37 所谓 [-謂] (so-called) <bf.> what is called: 这种~的大减价不过是个骗局! This so-called bargain is just a con! || ~朋友, 就是紧要关头肯支持你的人. A friend is someone who will stand by you when it comes to the pinch.

38 所说的 [-說-] (what-said) <bf.> that which was said: 他们~是一件事. They were talking about the same thing. || 他 ~不一定是真的. What he says is not necessarily true.

39 可谓 [-謂] (can-say) <v.> one may well say: 这个学生的进步~神速. This student's progress can be described as marvelously quick. || 西安~是历史古城. Xi'an can be described as an ancient city of history.

40 可以说 [--說] (can-say) <v.> it can be said: ~, 十二岁以前是人类学习语言的最佳时间. It can be said that before the age of twelve is the best time for humans to learn a language.

41 代表 [-] (represent-express) <v./n.> deputy, represent, stand for, on behalf of: 这只是他个人看法, 不 ~公司的立场. This is only his personal opinion, which does not represent the view of the company. || ~大多数人利益 represent the interests of most people || 他~全体学生向老师表示感谢. On behalf of all the students, he expressed gratitude to the teacher.

42 象征 [-徵] (resemble-symbol) <v./n.> symbol, emblem: ~快乐 a symbol of happiness || ~自由 a symbol of freedom || 秃鹰是美国的~. The bald eagle represents the U.S.A.

43 意味 [-] (meaning-tone) <v./n.> meaning, significance: 美国即使有新闻自由, 也并不~ 着一切新闻都是真实的. Even if the United States has freedom of the press, it does not mean that all of the news is true.

44 代替 [-] (replace-substitute) <v.> replace, substitute for: 中国人用筷子~刀叉吃饭. Chinese people use chopsticks in the place of knives and forks at meals. || 一些科学家研究如何用海水~石油. Some scientists have studied how to replace oil with seawater.

45 取代 [-] (take over-replace) <v.> replace, substitute: 一些人认为机器人会~人力劳动. Some people think robots will someday supersede manual labor.

46 表现 [-現] (outside-show) <v./n.> show, expression, manifestation: ~了他的风格 showed his style || ~出男子气概 showing masculinity || ~在态度上. It is manifested in one's attitude.

47 体现 [體現] (body-show) <v./n.> embody, incarnate: 美国宪法~ 了自由和平等的理想. America's Constitution embodies the ideals of freedom and equality.

48 出示 [-] (out-show) <v.> show, produce: 警察让他~身份证. The police asked him to show his identity card. || 过海关以前要 ~护照和签证. You should show your passport and visa before you pass Customs.

49 显出 [顯-] (show-out) <v.> show, reveal: 她~几分忧虑. She showed her anxiety. || 跟其他国家比, 就可以~美国经济的优越性了. Compared to other countries, the American economy shows its superiority.

50 展示 [-] (open up-show) <v.> open up before one's eyes: 向公众~ exhibit to the public || ~内心世界 reveal one's inner world || ~才华 display one's talent

51 演示 [-] (play-show) <v.> demonstrate: 有人试图用电子计算机代替试管去~化学反应. Someone tried to demostrate the chemical reaction with a computer instead of test tubes. || 学生们向老师~了他们的发明创造. The students presented their innovation to their teacher.

52 预示 [預-] (forehand-indicate) <v.> indicate, foreshadow: 有的人认为梦~着将要发生的事情. Someone thinks their dreams indicate what will happen. || 革命 ~着一个新的时代即将来临. The revolution indicates a new era will come very soon. || 晚霞~好天气. The splendid evening glow means fine weather.

53 看淡 [-] (view-unpromising) <v.> show a tendency towards, decline be expected to fall: 老年人一般会~爱情. Older people tend to regard love lightly.

54 预兆 [預-] (forehand-foretell) <n.> omen, presage: 吉祥的~ auspicious omen || 下雨的 ~ sign of coming rain

55 见证 [見證] (witness-testify) <v./n.> witness, testimony: ~奇迹witness a miracle || 二十世纪九十年代~了中国经济的迅速发展. The 1990s saw the rapid development of the Chinese economy.

56 证明 [證-] (prove-demonstrate) <v./n.> certificate, identification: 出生 ~ birth certificate || 出具~ issue a certificate || 充分 ~ fully prove

57 论证 [論證] (expound-prove) <v./n.> demonstration, proof: 文章~了改革的必要性. The article proves the necessity of reform.

58 认证 [認證] (admit-prove) <v./n.> legalize, certify, authenticate: ~中心authentication center || 获得 ~ get a certificate

59 验证 [驗證] (test-prove) <v./n.> verify, prove: ~理论verify a theory || 经过 ~ 的遗嘱verified (copy of a) will

60 证实 [證實] (prove-true) <v.> confirm, verify: 大量的证据~了他的罪行. A large quantity of evidence confirms his crimes. || 得到~ obtain confirmation || 他说的话~了我的猜测. What he said confirmed my conjecture.

Tips:

1 譬如 (pìrú): It means 'for example,' which is supposed to be a common word, however, for northern Chinese, the sound of 譬 'pì' is the same as 屁 (pì, fart), which is unpleasant to hear, so the northern Chinese usually say 比如 (bǐrú) instead.

2 系 (係, xì): The upper part of the oracle form of 系 is a hand (爪) or a palm (一), and the lower part is 糸 (silk,) which combine to mean 'hang.' The meaning of 系 in this unit, 'to be' will be evolved later.

3 Typical written words in this unit: 系, 乃, 与否, 堪称.

Exercises:

Part I: Use the given bound form as a guide to help you think of other words with the same character. Feel free to use your dictionary when needed. Then write down the English definition of each of the words you've written.

当 *(work as, serve as):* 当医生 *to serve as a doctor*

____

____

____

____

作 *(be acted as sth.)*: 当作 *to treat as, to regard as*

____

____

____

____

称 *(declare)*: 被称为 *be declared as*

____

____

____

____

____

证 *(prove, confirm)*: 验证 *verify, prove*

____

____

____

____

____

Part II: Link two words with the same meaning together.

所谓　　所说的
譬如　　乃
可谓　　把......视为......
把......看作.....　　可以说
是　　比如
自称　　自己说是
把......比作.....　　把......比喻成......

Part III: Read the following sentences and fill in each blank with the appropriate word or phrase from the options given.

1 即、系、为
   a) 王朋, _________中华人民共和国公民, 于1992年赴美留学, 1998年获得哈佛大学哲学博士学位. 现_________耶鲁 (yélǔ, Yale) 大学化学教授.
   b) 有些大学生在大学期间既不努力学习也不参加社会实践, 结果几乎没有公司愿意录用他们. 对他们来说毕业_________失业

2 不愧是、不外乎、不失为
   a) 小王每个周末_________只是跟朋友们一起吃吃喝喝, 没有什么特别的事情.
   b) 小王_________宅男 (otaku, homeboy), 可以在家呆一个星期不出门.

c) 降低中小企业税收_________刺激 (stimulate) 中国经济发展的一种好办法.

3 显示、预兆、代表、象征
a) 中国和印度两国_________就两国边界冲突的问题进行了为期 (wéiqí, lasting) 三天的谈判.
b) 龙是中国的_________. 所以中国人总是说自己是龙的传人.
c) 小王在管理方面_________了非凡的才能, 因此公司提升他为副总经理.
d) 一些科学家认为一些动物非常反常, 可能是大地震发生以前的_________.

4 预示、证明、取代、表现
a) 这种药物经过临床实验 (clinical experiments) _________效果非常好.
b) 一般来说, 火红的晚霞 (sunset clouds) _________明天的天气会非常好.
c) 小王在实习的时候_________非常好, 因此那家公司决定正式录用他.
d) 现在很少有人寄信了, 电子邮件几乎__________ _了传统信件.

5 展示、比喻、验证
a) 中国人喜欢把老师_________成燃烧 (ránshāo, burning) 的蜡烛.
b) 中国政府喜欢邀请各国领导人来华访问, 以便_________中国改革开放的成就.
c) 爱因斯坦 (Einstein) 的量子力学 (quantum mechanics) 经过物理学者们几十年的_________证明是正确的.

Theme 206: To originate, to belong 起源, 归属 (qǐyuán, guīshǔ)

1 起源 [-] qǐyuán (begin-origin) <v.> originate, stem from: ~于中国 stems from China || 舞蹈~于劳动 dance stems from work || ~汉朝 originate from the Han Dynasty

2 发源 [發-] fāyuán (rise-origin) <v.> rise, originate: ~于欧洲originate from Europe || 长江~于青藏高原. The Yangtze River originates from the Qinghai Tibetan Plateau.

3 根源 [-] gēnyuán (root-origin) <n.> source, origin: 思想~ source of an idea || 内在 ~ internal origin

4 出于 [-於] chūyú (out-from) <v.> be out of, from: ~自愿 from one's own will || ~关心 from one's caring || ~好奇 from one's curiosity

5 出自 [-] chūzì (out-from) <v.> come from, originate from: 这个故事~《圣经》. This story originates from *The Bible*.

6 发自 [發-] fāzì (start-from) <v.> come from: ~内心 come from the heart || ~真情 come from one's true feelings

7 来自 [來-] láizì (come-from) <v.> come from, be from: ~地球 come from Earth || ~农村 come from a village || ~海底 come from the ocean floor

8 始于 [-於] shǐyú (begin-from) <v.> start from: 草莓的种植~十四世纪. The cultivation of strawberries commenced in the 14th-century.

9 源于 [-於] yuányú (origin-from) <v.> have its origins from: 英语~希腊语. English has origins in Greek language. || 佛教~印度. Buddhism originates from India.

10 源自 [-] yuánzì (origin-from) <v.> originate from: "芭蕾"一词~意大利. The word 'ballet' originates from Italian.

11 取决于 [-決於] qǔjuéyú (decide-by) <v.> be decided by: 孩子的幸福并不~家庭的贫富. A child's happiness is not decided by how wealthy or poor a family is.

12 在于 [-於] zàiyú (be-on) <v.> depend on, rest on: 问题的关键~没有足够的资金. The key of the problem rests on inadequate funding. || 他来留学的目的~学习先进的技术. The reason why he came to study abroad is to learn about advanced technology.

13 有赖于 [-賴於] yǒulàiyú (*prefix*-rely-on) <v.> rely on, depend on: 他们的成功~合作. Their success rely on cooperation. || 他的论文~老师的指导. His thesis relies on his teacher's guidance.

14 着落 [著落] zhúoluò (touch-fall) <v.> whereabouts, assured source: 工作还没~. Work does not have a settled place. || 费用没~. The payment has not yet been settled. || 厂房还没~. The factory building still does not have a confirmed location.

15 归入 [歸-] guīrù (include-into) <v.> classify, include: 云南是什么时候正式~中国的? When did Yunnan Province come under Chinese rule officially? || 这些书应该~戏剧类. All these books should be grouped under theater.

16 归结于 [歸結於] guī jiéyú (include-conclude-at) <v.> come to a conclusion, sum up: 所有的问题都可以~钱. All problems can be summarized by money.

17 归因于 [歸-於] guīyīnyú (include-reason-at) <v.> return to, be related to: 这些疾病的产生都应该~吸烟. These diseases all stem from smoking tobacco.

18 属 [屬] shǔ (join, belong to) <v.> be subordinate to, belong to, be born in the year of: 1997年以前, 香港~英国殖民地. Hong Kong was a colony of the U.K. before 1997. || 中国的公立大学都~教育部. All Chinese pubic universities belong to the education department. || 他~猴. He was born in the Year of the Monkey.

19 纯属 [純屬] chúnshǔ (purely-belong to) <v.> completely, absolutely: 这件事~意外. This has happened by sheer accident. || ~幻想 a complete illusion || ~虚构 out-and-out fabrication

20 实属 [實屬] shíshǔ (really-belong to) <v.> really be: ~不易 not be easy at all. || ~不该 should really not do || ~荒唐 be completely absurd

21 属于 [屬於] shǔyú (belong-to) <v.> belong to, be part of: 这种化石是~全世界的. This kind of fossil belongs to the whole world. || 鲸鱼~哺乳动物. Whales belong to mammals. || 土地~农民. The land belongs to peasants.

22 从属 [從屬] cóngshǔ (subordinate-belong to) <v.> subordinate: 在旧社会, 女人是 ~ 于男人的. In old times, women were subordinate to men. ||在任何时代, 艺术都是~于政治的. In any era, art is always subordinate to politics.

23 附属 [-屬] fùshǔ (adhere-belong to) <v.> subsidiary, auxiliary: ~小学affiliated primary school || 这个工厂~于大学. This factory is attached to the university.

24 所属 [-屬] suǒshǔ (what-belong to) <v.> what is subordinated to one or under one's command: ~单位 affiliated unit || ~部队 troops under one's command

Tips:

1 有*: When 有 is put before some verbs, the words have a 'polite' connotation, for example, 有请 (Welcome,) 有劳 (thanks for the trouble,) 有赖 (to depend on) and 有烦 (thanks for the trouble.)

2 归 (歸, guī): The original meaning of 歸 is '(of a woman) to get married or return to her parent's home after marriage.' The character is composed of three parts, the phonetic part 2¤, 止 (foot, walk) and 帚 (abbreviated signific of 婦, woman.)

3 属 (屬, shǔ): It was originally pronounced as zhǔ and meant 'join, connect.' Of 屬, the 蜀 is the phonetic part and the other part is 尾 (wěi, tail.) A tail (氺, actually '毛') is 'connected' to the body (尸), and from this association, evolved the first meaning 'to join, connect' and an extended meaning 'to belong to.'

Exercises:

Part I: Use the given bound form as a guide to help you think of other words with the same character. Feel free to use your dictionary when needed. Then write down the English definition of each of the words you've written.

源 *(source):* 起源 *originate, stem from*

____

____

____

____

自 *(from):* 来自 *come from*

____

____

____

归 *(be back to, return):* 归入*classify, include*

____

____

____

属 *(be subordinate to, belong to):* 属于*belong to, be part of*

____

____

____

____

于 *(to):* 取决于 *to be up to*

____

____

____

____

Theme 207: Existent, non-existent 有无 (yǒuwú)

1 在 [-] zài (exist) <v.> exist, be at: 我的书还~. My book is still there. || 他爷爷还~. His grandfather is still alive.
2 存在 [-] cúnzài (exist-exist) <v.> be present, exist: ~危险 danger is present || ~ 问题 a problem exists || ~缺点 a flaw exists
3 并存 [並-] bìngcún (side by side-exist) <v.> exist side by side: 同时~ both exist at the same time || 多党~. Multiple parties exist at the same time. || 新旧~. The new and the old exist at the same time.
4 共处 [-處] gòngchǔ (together-exist) <v.> coexist: 和平~ peacefully coexist || 长期~ coexist for a long time || 很难~ hard to coexist
5 永生 [-] yǒngshēng (forever-live) <v./ adv.> eternal life, all one's life: ~难忘never forget for a lifetime || 得到~ obtain immortality || ~不死 eternal life

6 有 [-] yǒu (have, possess) <v.> have, possess, there is: ~时间 have time || 俄罗斯~很多地方没人住. There are many uninhabited places in Russia. || ~危险. There is danger.
7 有着 [-著] yǒuzhe (have-*being*) <v.> possess, have, there is: ~根本的区别 there is a fundamental difference || ~密切的联系 have a close relationship || ~重要的作用 have an important role
8 现有 [現-] xiànyǒu (current-have) <v.> there is(or are), have on hand, in possession: ~人口 current population || 我们公司~五十辆车. Our company has 50 cars on hand. || 保持~水平remain at current levels
9 拥有 [擁-] yōngyǒu (own-have) <v.> possess, have: ~资源 have resources || ~地产 have property || ~知识 have knowledge
10 持有 [-] chíyǒu (hold-have) <v.> hold: ~护照 hold a passport || ~不同意见 have different opinions|| ~公司百分之五十的股份 have a 50 percent holding in the company
11 特有 [-] tèyǒu (specially-have) <v.> peculiar, characteristic: ~的产品 particular characteristic of the product || ~的现象 peculiar phenomenon || ~的东西 a peculiar thing
12 具有 [-] jùyǒu (possess-have) <v.> have (sth. immaterial): ~重要意义 possess important meaning || ~中国特点 possess Chinese characteristics || ~幽默感 have a sense of humor
13 共有 [-] gòngyǒu (commonly-have) <v.> have altogether: ~房屋 have a shared room || ~财产 have wealth || ~的优点 have a benefit
14 富有 [--] fùyǒu (rich-have) <v.> have plenty of, be rich in, be full of: ~想象力 be full of imagination || ~活力 be full of vitality || ~经验be rich in experience

15 占 [佔] zhàn (occupy) <v.> occupy, seize: ~世界第一位 rank first in the world || ~四分之三 occupy three-fourths || ~优势 be superior in
16 占有 [-] zhànyǒu (occupy-have) <v.> own, possess, occupy: ~土地 own land || 在议会中~ 多数席位hold a majority in the parliament || ~重要地位 have an important place

17 没有 [-] méiyǒu (not-have) <v.> not have, be without: ~车 to not have a car || ~钱 to not have money || ~理由 to not have a reason

18 无 [無] wú (not have) <v.> not have, there is not: ~意义 no meaning || ~理由 no reason || ~条件 no condition
19 毫无 [-無] háowú (at all-not) <bf.> none, nothing: ~意义 absolutely no meaning || ~兴趣 absolutely no interest || ~动静 absolutely no movement

20 留 [-] liú (stay, reserve) <v.> remain, stay: ~胡子 have a beard || ~着长发 have long hair || ~痕迹 leave a scar
21 留下 [-] liúxià (leave-behind) <v.> leave (behind), stay (for): ~很多问题 for many questions to remain || ~美好的回忆 leave beautiful memories || ~不好的印象 leave a bad impression
22 遗留 [遺-] yíliú (hand down-leave behind) <v.> leave over, hand down: 历史~的问题 a question handed down through history || 祖先~给我们的财富 wealth left by our ancestor || 酒店~物品 goods left at a hotel
23 残留 [殘-] cánliú (remnant-leave behind) <v.> remain, left over: ~农药 leftover pesticide || 低~ left over remains || 大面积~ a leftover large area

24 保持 [-] bǎochí (keep-hold) <v.> maintain, remain: ~不变maintain consistency || ~联系 maintain content || ~清洁 remain clean
25 保留 [-] bǎoliú (keep-reserve) <v.> continue to have, retain: ~邮件 retain mail || ~证据 retain proof || ~意见 retain an opinion
26 维持 [維-] wéichí (maintain-hold) <v.> keep, maintain, preserve: ~现状 maintain the current status || ~生活 maintain life || ~关系 maintain relations
27 支撑 [-撐] zhīchēng (support-sustain) <v.> prop up, sustain: ~身体 prop up one's body || 用木头~ use wood to prop up oneself || 独立 ~ sustain independently
28 顶住 [頂-] dǐngzhù (withstand-firm) <v.> withstand, stand up to: ~压力 withstand pressure || 使劲~ exert strength to withstand
29 保温 [-溫] bǎowēn (keep-warm) <v.> preserve heat, keep warm: 防寒~ protect against cold weather and preserve heat || 外墙~. The outer wall preserves heat.
30 水土保持 [-] shuǐtǔbǎochí (water-soil-maintain) <n./v.> water and soil conservation: 河流~ river water and soil conservation || 做~工作 do conservation work || 进行~ commence conservation efforts
31 自保 [-] zìbǎo (self-protect) <v.> defend oneself, self-defense: 养兵~ maintain an army to defend oneself || 为了~, 中国决定跟朝鲜断绝一切经济关系. In order to protect themselves, China decided to cut off all economic relations with North Korea.

Tips:

1 在: The bottom right part of 在 is 土 (soil, earth) and the upper left part is the phonetic and semantic part 才 (cái, sprout, newborn.) Thus, the whole character means 'a sprout just comes out of the soil,' in other words, 'be living, exist.'
2 有: The upper left part of 有 is 又 (手, hand) and the bottom right part is 月 (肉, meat.) Thus the whole character means 'to possess, have, rich.'

Exercises:

Part I: Use the given bound form as a guide to help you think of other words with the same character. Feel free to use your dictionary when needed. Then write down the English definition of each of the words you've written.

有 *(have)*: 拥有 *possess*

____

____

____

____

____

____

____

留 *(remain)*: 保留 *retain*

____

____

____

____

Part II: Read the following sentences and fill in each blank with the appropriate word or phrase from the options given.

1 留下、保持、维持

a) 国与国之间_______友好关系对世界和平非常重要.
b) 台湾的国民党主张两岸关系应该是"不独立、不统一," 只是_______现状.
c) 这场音乐会给观众________了深刻的印象.

2 并存、存在、自保

a) 这家公司________严重的管理问题.
b) 为了________, 中国决定跟朝鲜断绝 (duànjué, break off) 一切经济关系.
c) 几乎每个女人都希望自己能够美貌与智慧________.

3 特有、拥有、持有、有

a) 小张_______五个兄弟姐妹.
b) 小张________两个博士学位, 一个硕士学位.
c) 这所国际学校规定_______外国护照的学生才可以申请在这里就读 (study).
e) 沿着美国加州一号公路开车, 你会看到加州________的风景.

Theme 208: Same, different 相同, 不同 (xiāngtóng, bùtóng)

1 顶 [頂] dǐng (crown of the head, top, bear) <v.> match, equal to: 一个~俩 for one to take the place of two || 十个鸡蛋~一斤肉. Ten eggs take the place of half a kilogram of meat.

2 同 [-] tóng (converge, same) <v.> be the same as: ~一年same year || ~一个字same character || ~一个问题 same problem

3 同一 [-] tóngyī (same-one) <adj.> same, identical: ~影片 same film || ~商品 same product || ~时间 same time

4 相同 [-] xiāngtóng (each other-same) <adj.> identical, the same: 完全~ completely identical || ~条件 identical conditions || ~的看法 identical opinions

5 一样 [-樣] yíyàng (same-looking) <adj.> same, alike: 兴趣~ the same interests || ~的人 the same people || 时间 ~ the same time

6 一致 [-] yízhì (same-devote) <adj./adv.> showing no difference: ~的想法 no difference in ideas || ~的目标 no difference in goals || 完全~ completely no difference

7 一律 [-] yílǜ (same-law) <adv.> same, alike: 国家不论大小, 应该 ~平等. Whether it is a big country or a small country, it should be equal.

8 无异于 [無異於] wúyìyú (no-different-from) <v.> no different from: 有人认为炒股~赌博. Some people think that investing in stocks is a gamble.

9 一模一样 [---樣] yìmú yíyàng (same-model-same-looking) <idiom> exactly alike: 长得~ they grew to look exactly the same || ~的牙刷 same toothbrushes || ~照片 same picture

10 平等 [-] píngděng (level-equal) <adj.> equal: ~地位 equal position || 男女~ male-female quality || 机会~ equal opportunity

11 同班 [-] tóngbān (same-class) <v.> in the same class: ~同学classmate

12 同学 [-學] tóngxué (together-study) <v./n.> study at the same school, classmate: 老 ~ former schoolmate || ~会alumni association

13 同行 [-] tóngháng (same-profession) <n.> people of the same trade or occupation: 这位医生受到~的尊敬. The doctor is respected by his profession.

14 同乡 [-鄉] tóngxiāng (same-township) <n.> person from the same village, town or province: 他俩是~. The two are townsmen. || 小李是我的~. Xiao Li is my townsman.

15 同步 [-] tóngbù (same-pace) <adv.> synchronism, in pace with: ~卫星 synchronous satellite || ~增长grow in step with || 语言与文化~发展, ~变化. Languages and cultures develop and change simultaneously.

16 等于 [-於] děngyú (equal-to) <v.> equal to: 风速~每秒25米 The wind speed is equal to 25 meters per second || 一句不能~两句. A sentence is not equal to two sentences. || 二加二~五. Two plus two makes five. (from *1984*)

17 相当 [-當] xiāngdāng (each other-match) <v.> match, balance: 年龄~ well-matched in age || 身高~ well-matched in height || 两队实力~. The two teams are about equal in strength.

18 相当于 [-當於] xiāngdāngyú (equivalent-to) <v.> be equivalent to: 美国国会~ 英国议会. The American Congress corresponds to the British Parliament.

19 相等 [-] xiāngděng (each other-equal) <v.> be equal: 距离~ equal distance || 重量~ equal weight || 完全/几乎 ~ completely equal, almost equal

20 对等 [對-] duìděng (reciprocal-equal) <adj.> reciprocal, equal: 美国英语的一些用法在英国英语中没有~的词. Some words used in American English do not have an equivalent in British English.

21 抗衡 [-] kànghéng (contend-match) <v.> contend (or compete) with: 冷战时期, 苏联跟美国一直互相~. During the Cold War, the Soviet Union and the United States competed with each other. || 这家公司太小, 不能与国际性的公司~. The firm is too small to contend with large international companies.

22 抵得上 [-] dǐdéshàng (withstand-able to) <v.> be able to support: 这幅画的价钱~一栋房子. The price of this painting is almost the same as that house. || 一个好妈妈~十个好老师. A good mother is worth ten good schoolmasters.

23 不相上下 [-] bùxiāngshàngxià (not-each other-superiority-inferiority) <idiom> equally matched, almost on par: 能力~ of about the same ability, equally able || 水平~ nearly identical in quality (level)

24 平起平坐 [-] píngqǐ píngzuò (equal-stand-equal-sit) <idiom> sit as equals at the same table: 从1995年起, 东亚几乎与美国和欧盟~. Since 1995, East Asia has almost caught up with the United States and the European Union.

25 势均力敌 [勢--敵] shìjūn lìdí (power-equal-strength-match) <idiom> match each other in strength, evenly matched: 比赛双方~. The two teams are evenly matched. || 保持~ keep evenly matched

26 值 [-] zhí (place, hold, be worth) <v.> value, be worth: ~三千元 be worth 3000 yuan || 花得~ be worth the money || ~钱 valuable

27 差不多 [-] chàbùduō (difference-not-much) <adj./ adv.> about the same: 意思~ the meaning is about the same || 大小~ the size is about the same || ~写了两个小时 wrote for about two hours

28 大同小异 [---異] dàtóng xiǎoyì (majority-same-minority-different) <idiom> much the same but with minor differences: 所有的大城市都~. All big cities are quite similar.

29 相差无几 [--無幾] xiāngchàwújǐ (each other-difference-not-few) <idiom> almost the same: 价钱~. The prices are almost the same.

30 八九不离十 [---離-] bājiǔbùlíshí (8–9-not-far from-10) <proverb> about right: 猜个~ make a very close guess || 一个人的本质常常跟你看到他的第一印象~. A person's nature can be very close to their first impression.

31 五十步笑百步 [-] wǔshí bù xiào bǎi bù (50-step-mock-100-step) <idiom> One who retreats 50 paces mocks one who retreats 100, the pot calls the kettle black: 有人觉得奥巴马指责特朗普激化种族矛盾, 其实是~. Some people think that Obama accusing Trump of intensifying racial contradictions is the pot calling the kettle black.

32 相似 [-] xiāngsì (each other-similar) <adj.> resemble: 长得~ similar in appearance || ~的地方 similar place || 面积~ similar space

33 好像 [-] hǎoxiàng (just-like) <v.> seem, look like: ~要下雨. It looks like rain. || 天边的白云~一座雪山. The white cloud on the horizon looks like a snow mountain.

34 类似 [類-] lèisì (category-similar) <v./ adj.> similar (to), analogous (to): ~的礼物 a similar gift || ~的情况 a similar situation

35 犹如 [猶-] yóurú (just-like) <v.> just as, like: 在这座大城市里寻找一个人~大海捞针. Searching for one man in this big city is like looking for a needle in a haystack.

36 相近 [-] xiāngjìn (each other-close) <adj.> close, near, similar: 他跟弟弟性格~. He and his brother are similar in character. || 英语同德语很~. English has a close affinity to German.

37 诸如此类 [諸--類] zhūrúcǐlèi (many-like-this-sort) <idiom> things of that sort: 这家小商店卖各种水果、糖果、玩具、雪茄烟以及~的东西. This store sells fruits, candies, toys, cigars and all that.

38 像 [-] xiàng (resemble, alike) <v.> be like: ~狼 like a wolf || ~镜子一样 just like a mirror || ~根木头 to be just like a piece of wood

39 如 [-] rú (follow, like) <v.> be in compliance, like: 四季~春 (warm and pleasant) like spring all the year round || 骄阳~火. The blazing sun is like fire. || 并非~此 not like that

40 如同 [-] rútóng (like-same) <v.> like, as: 灯光把广场照得~白天一样. The lights illuminated the square like daytime. || 生命~玻璃一样脆弱. Life is as fragile as glass.

41 例如 [-] lìrú (example-like) <v.> for instance, for example: 有些汉字, ~日, 月, 火是从图画演变来的. Some Chinese characters, such as 日, 月, 火 are derived from pictures.

42 比如 [-] bǐrú (example-like) <v.> for example: 我喜欢吃中国菜, ~西红柿炒鸡蛋. I like to eat Chinese food, for example, tomatoes fried with egg.

43 如下 [-] rúxià (as-following) <v.> as follows: ~特点 the following characteristics || 原因~ the following reason || 内容~ the following content

44 不如 [-] bùrú (not-as good as) <v.> not as good as: 姐姐~妹妹. The little sister is not as good as the older sister. || 一次~一次. This time is not as good as another time. || 说得好~做得好. Saying you will do well doesn't mean you will do well.

45 不同 [-] bùtóng (not-alike) <v.> not alike, different: ~的地方 different places || 时间~ different times || 男人~于女人. Men are not like women.

46 差 [-] chà (mistake, difference) <v.> differ from, fall short of, be short of, be inferior to: ~远了 fall short of what is expected || ~得很大differ widely in || ~三本书be three books short

47 低 [-] dī (low) <adj.> low, droop hang: 价格~ low price || 工资~ low salary || ~要求 low requests

48 低于 [-於] dīyú (low-than) <v.> be lower than: ~市场价 be lower than market price || ~七岁 younger than seven || ~三百米 be less than 300 meters

49 赶不上 [趕--] gǎnbúshàng (catch up with-not-able) <v.> unable to catch up with: 我总是~她. I can't catch up with her. || 计划~变化. Plans always fall behind changes. || ~潮流 can't catch up with the trend, outdated

50 小于 [-於] xiǎoyú (smaller-than) <v.> less than: ~三厘米 shorter than 3 cm. || ~光速 slower than the speed of light || ~零 less than zero

51 超过 [-過] chāoguò (surpass-over) <v.> outstrip, surpass: ~两个小时 be longer than two hours || ~法国 surpass France || 女孩~男孩. Girls surpass boys.

52 超出 [-] chāochú (surpass-beyond) <v.> overstep, go beyond: ~常规 go beyond routine || ~能力 go beyond ability || ~传统 overstep tradition

53 超越 [-] chāoyuè (surpass-surmount) <v.> surmount, overstep: ~自身 surmount oneself || ~友谊 surmount friendship

54 不止 [-] bùzhǐ (nut-limited) <adv.> more than, not limited to: ~一次 more than once || 大笑~ can't stop laughing || 学校~同意他出国留学, 还给了他很多资助. The school not only approved his studying abroad but also sponsored him.

55 高于 [-於] gāoyú (higher-than) <v.> greater than, exceed: 前者~后者. The former is greater than the latter. || ~标准 greater than the standard || ~一切 greater than everything

56 相反 [-] xiāngfǎn (each other-opposite) <v./ adj.> contrary, opposite: 与别人~ different from others || 意见~ a different opinion || ~的方向 a different direction

57 保守 [-] bǎoshǒu (keep-guard) <v.> guard, keep: ~秘密 keep a secret || ~财产 guard wealth

58 依靠 [-] yīkào (rely-depend) <v./n.> fall back on, support: ~技术rely on technique || ~群众 rely on masses || ~农业rely on agriculture

59 具备 [-備] jùbèi (possess-complete) <v.> possess, have: ~ 条件 possess conditions || ~能力 possess ability || ~资格have qualifications

Tips:

1 如 (rú): It is related to 女 (woman) and 口 (mouth, instruction,) meaning '(a woman) follow (instruction)' from which evolved the meaning 'same, like.'

2 Idioms with markers of simile: Chinese idioms were coined roughly at the same pace that the Chinese language evolved in history. Main markers of simile in idioms include 犹 (yóu,) 若 (ruò,) 如 (rú) and 似 (sì.) There are no idioms with 像, the most common marker of simile in modern Chinese. If there are two markers in one idiom, the structure is very likely to be '如X似X,' for example, 如花似玉 (like-flower-as-jade, very beautiful) and 如饥似渴 (rújī sìkě, as-hungrily-as-thirstily, eagerly.)

Exercises:

Part I: Put the similar meaning words in the same table.

如同、犹如、相似、类似、诸如此类、好似、相同、一致、等于、相等、不相上下、平起平坐、势均力敌、大同小异、差不多、大同小异、八九不离十、相差无几

eg. 例如: 比如
好像:
差不多:
一模一样:
差不多一样:
双方力量差不多:
双方地位相同:

Part II: Use the given bound form as a guide to help you think of other words with the same character. Feel free to use your dictionary when needed. Then write down the English definition of each of the words you've written.

如 *(be in compliance, like)*: 如同 *like, as*

____

____

____

____

相 *(each other, mutually)*: 相近 *close, near, similar*

____

____

____

____

____

同 *(same)*: 同班*in the same class*

____

____

____

____

____

Part III: Read the following sentences and fill in each blank with the appropriate word or phrase from the options given.

1 一致、一律、无异于
   a) 美国宪法规定, 所有美国公民在法律面前_______平等.
   b) 在选大学的问题上, 父母跟我的看法________.
   c) 在寒冷的天气里到大海里游泳_________去自杀.

2 依靠、具备、保守
   a) 一般来说, 老年人在思想上比较_______, 不喜欢变革.
   b) 中国必须________科技创新来进一步发展经济.
   c) 这座小城市交通不便, 水资源贫乏, 因此不_______建立食品加工厂的条件.

3 不止、超过、八九不离十、五十步笑百步
   a) 欧洲的文艺复兴 (Renaissance)________是古代文化的复兴 (revival).
   b) 欧洲文艺复兴的深远影响______了人们的预期.

c) 有人觉得奥巴马指责 (criticize) 特朗普激化 (intensify) 种族矛盾 (racial tensions), 其实是______________, 因为奥巴马自己在这方面做得也不好.

d) 好莱坞大片的结尾几乎都是幸福、圆满的, 看了开头, 结尾就能猜个______________.

Theme 209: Match 匹配 (pǐpèi)

1 配 [-] pèi (match) <v.> join in marriage, match: 绿叶~红花. The green leaf matches the red flower. || 一个茶壶~四个杯子. A tea pot matches four cups. || 不~当老师 not fit to be a teacher

2 相配 [-] xiāngpèi (each other-match) <v.> well-matched, be a good match: 两两~ well matched pair || 他认为妻子与自己不~. He thought his wife was not matched to him. || 他们俩很~. They are well-matched.

3 般配 [-] bānpèi (same-match) <v.> well-matched (in marriage, etc): 长相~ be well-matched in appearance || 男女 ~ a good match for men and women || 跟他~ well-matched with him

4 匹配 [-] pǐpèi (company-match) <v.> mate, marry: 合理~ a rational match || ~不当 not well matched || 血型~ blood type matching

5 搭配 [-] dāpèi (coordinate-match) <v.> arrange in pairs or groups, fit: 合理~ a rational pairing || 颜色~ color pairing || 男女~ male-female pairing

6 配得上 [-] pèide'shàng (match-be able to) <v.> make a good match, deserve: 让你的努力~你的梦想. Let your hard work match your dreams. || 我们~这场胜利. We deserved this victory. || 找一段~这段舞蹈的音乐. Find a melody that can match this dance.

7 郎才女貌 [-] lángcái nǚmào (young man-talented-woman-beautiful) <idiom> a brilliant young scholar and a beautiful woman: 他们俩真是~啊! That pair is truly a great match – a brilliant young scholar and a beautiful woman !

8 门当户对 [門當戶對] méndān ghùduì (gate-equal-household-matched) <idiom> well matched in social and economic status (for marriage): 结婚~很重要. In marriage, it is important that a couple is well-matched in social and economic status. || 他俩门不当户不对. They are not well-matched in social and economic status.

9 顺风顺水 [順風順-] shùnfēng shùnshuǐ (favorable-wind-favorable-stream) <idiom> favorable wind and downstream: 过得~. Things have gone very favorably and smoothly. || 生意~. Business has been favorable and smooth.

10 合 [-] hé (close, conform to) <v.> suit, agree: ~要求 suit requirements || ~胃口 suit one's taste || 正~我意. It suits me fine.

11 符合 [-] fúhé (accord-conform) <v.> accord with, tally with: ~实际 be accord with reality, the situation || ~条件 be in accordance with conditions || ~国情be in accordance with national sentiment

12 合乎 [-] héhu (conform-with) <v.> conform with (or to), correspond to: ~逻辑 conform to logic || ~规律 to conform to standards || ~人性 conform with one's feelings.

13 适合 [適-] shìhé (suit-conform) <v.> suit, fit: ~人们的需要 fit people's needs || ~中国国情 fit Chinese basic conditions || 高度~ highly suitable

14 对劲儿 [對勁兒] duìjìnr (match-gusto) <v.> one's liking, suitable: 这支笔写起字来不~. The way this pen writes is not to my liking. || 他俩一向很~. Those two have been very suitable all along.

15 对头 [對頭] duìtóu (match-method) <v.> correct: 方法 ~. The method is correct. || 问得不~ ask in a wrong way

16 对路 [對-] duìlù (match-way) <v.> satisfy the need, fill a need: 方法不~. This approach does not satisfy the need. || 产品~. This product does fill a need.

17 投机 [-機] tóujī (agreeable-idea) <v.> congenial, agreeable, speculate: 谈得很~ have a congenial chat || 他们俩十分~. They are very congenial.

18 投缘 [-緣] tóuyuán (compatible-luck) <v.> hit it off: 聊天很~ they hit it off in conversation || 一见~ one look and they hit it off || 他俩很~. Those two really hit it off.

19 谈得来 [談-來] tán de lái (chat-*complement*-go) <v.> get along with: 跟老陈 ~ get along with Lao Chen || 他们非常~. They really get along quite well.

20 一见如故 [-見--] yījiànrúgù (once-meet-like-old friend) <idiom> feel like old friends at the first meeting: 两人~ two people who feel like old friends at the first meeting

21 巧合 [-] qiǎohé (coincidence-match) <v.> coincidence: 意外~ an unexpected coincidence || 偶然 ~ an occasional coincidence

22 衬托 [襯-] chèntuō (contrast-set off) <v.> set off, serve as a foil to: 互相~ mutually set off || 这件衣服将她~得更美. This dress sets off her beauty.

23 陪衬 [-襯] péichèn (accompany-contrast) <v.> foil, set off, serve as a contrast: 绿叶还得红花~. Red flowers stand out only when they are set off by green leaves.

24 点缀 [點綴] diǎnzhuì (embellish-ornament) <v.> embellish, ornament: ~着鲜花 embellish with fresh flowers || ~环境ornament the surrounding || ~得十分美好embellish beautifully

25 装点 [裝點] zhuāngdiǎn (decorate-embellish) <v.> decorate, dress: ~门面 act fake, decorate the outside || ~得分外美丽 decorate in an especially beautiful way || ~圣诞树 decorate a christmas tree

26 渲染 [-] xuànrǎn (properly dilute colorful paint on painting paper-apply colors to a painting paper) <v.> add washes of ink color to a drawing to emphasize it : 大肆~ exaggerate without warrant || ~气氛 play up the atmosphere

27 配套 [-] pèitào (match-set) <v.> complete a set, form a complete set or system: 窗帘和家具不~. The curtains do not match the furniture. || ~措施 supporting measure || 我们为顾客提供免费~服务. We provide customers free support services.

28 对立 [對-] duìlì (opposite-stand) <v.> oppose, set sth. against: 跟他~ be opposed to him || 完全~ be completely opposed || ~关系 have an opposing relationship

29 相对 [-對] xiāngduì (each other-opposite) <adv.> relatively, comparatively: ~来说 relatively speaking || ~论 the theory of relativity || ~比较安全的地方 a relatively safe place

30 针锋相对 [針鋒-對] zhēnfēngxiāngduì (pinpoint-sharp edge-each other-opposite) <idiom> oppose each other with equal harshness: 进行 ~的斗争wage a tit-for-tat, struggle against || 与他~ be harsh with words to him in return

31 矛盾 [-] máodùn (spear-shield) <n./v.> conflict, contradiction: 内部~ internal conflict || 主要 ~ primary conflict || 互相~ mutually contradictory
32 抵触 [-觸] dǐchù (withstand-butt) <v.> conflict, contradict: 互相~ be incompatible with each other || ~情绪 conflicting emotions || 发生~ for a conflict to occur
33 排斥 [-] páichì (repel-exclude) <v.> repel, exclude: 互相~ mutually exclude || ~美籍华人exclude American Chinese || ~外来者exclude outsiders
34 格格不入 [-] gégébúrù (hinder-*reduplication*-not-conform) <idiom> incompatible with: 跟时代~ incompatible with the times
35 自相矛盾 [-] zìxiāngmáodùn (self-each other-contradict) <idiom> contradict oneself: 逻辑上~ contradict oneself logically

36 对应 [對應] duìyìng (match-correspond) <v.> corresponding, homologous: 一一~ one-to-one correspondence || 互相~ mutually correspond || ~词 corresponding word
37 呼应 [-應] hūyìng (call-echo) <v.> echo, work in concert with: 互相~ echo each other || 写文章的时候上下文要~. When writing an article, the context should be coherent.
38 照应 [-應] zhàoyìng (compare-echo) <v.> look after, take care of, coordinate, correlate: ~老人 look after the elderly || 互相~ take after one another || 文章前后要~. A composition should be well-organized and coherent.

39 连贯 [連貫] liánguàn (connected-through) <v.> link up, piece together, coherent (narrative, argument): 前后~ link up from beginning to end ||说话~ speak coherently || 动作~make continuous movements
40 贯穿 [貫-] guànchuān (through-cross) <v.> run through, penetrate: ~始终 run through to the end || ~南北 penetrate through from north to south || ~全文 penetrate through the whole text
41 横穿 [橫-] héngchuān (across-cross) <v.> cross: ~马路 cross the road || ~南极 cross over the South Pole
42 跨 [-] kuà (stride, go beyond) <v.> stride: ~国公司transnational corporation || ~省 cross provinces || ~校 cross schools
43 横跨 [橫-] héngkuà (across-stretch) <v.> stretch over (or across): ~太平洋 stretch over the pacific || ~大河 stretch over the river || ~三大洲 stretch over the three major continents

Tips:

1 配 (pèi): 配 is related to 酉 (yǒu, fermentation) and means 'wine color,' which is the result of mixing unfiltered wine and clear wine. Now 配 means mainly as 'mix, match, marry,' all derived from its original meaning.
2 顺风: It means 'have a fair wind.' 'Fair wind and following sea' (顺风顺水) is a popular salutation in English, however, '顺风' is similar to a taboo in Chinese for mariners and passengers at sea or by air, since vessels and aircrafts do not operate well in the wind. Therefore, the once popular salutation '一路顺风' is almost replaced by '一路平安' (have a safe trip.) Since 顺风 was an auspicious word though, its sound has been borrowed by a Chinese courier 顺丰速运 (Shùnfēng Express, SF Express,) the largest private delivery service enterprise in China.
3 合适 (héshì) vs. 适合 (shìhé): 合适 is an adjective, meaning 'fit, suitable, appropriate,' while 适合 is a verb, meaning 'to agree with.'

4 Fundamentals of marriage: Young people say it is 'love' (爱情), but many Chinese parents say '门当户对' (well-matched in social and economic status.)

Exercises:

Multiple Choice. Make sure to choose the most appropriate answer.

1 "很多中国人认为男女结婚应该讲究门当户对"的意思是
A. 结婚双方的房子大小应该一样
B. 结婚双方的大门应该一样
C. 结婚双方的家庭背景应该差不多

2 小王父母认为小王女朋友没上过大学, 在学历上跟小王不_________, 另外家庭背景也不好, 所以_______小王.
A. 搭配、配不上 B. 相配、配不上 C. 匹配、配得上

3 "郎才女貌"的意思是
A. 男方很有才能, 女方相貌很美
B. 男方很有钱, 女方很有礼貌
C. 男方很有才能, 女方很有礼貌

4 "小王的事业顺风顺水," 这句话的意思是
A. 小王的事业是关于风水的
B. 小王的事业一直很顺利
C. 小王的事业跟顺风和顺水有关系

5 这位老人觉得自己跟所谓的现代生活_________.
A. 格格不入 B. 顺风顺水 C. 门当户对

6 这两个年轻人才见面几分钟, 就_________地聊个没完.
A. 针锋相对 B. 自相矛盾 C. 一见如故

7 很多中国家长希望自己的孩子能够上哈佛大学, 但是他们忘记了每个孩子的实际情况不同, 并不是所有的孩子都_________上哈佛大学.
A. 符合 B. 合乎 C. 适合

8 这家宠物公司的产品因为适销________, 受到了养狗爱好者的欢fl.
A. 对劲儿 B. 对路 C. 对头

9 "他们俩一见面就谈得很投机," 意思是
A. 他们俩一见面就很谈得来
B. 他们俩一见面就谈做生意的事情
C. 他们俩一见面就谈投资机场的事情

10 小王跟他老板的生日一模一样, 真是_________.
A. 巧合 B. 衬托 C. 相应

11 美国的新闻媒体有时候大肆 (dàsì, without any constraint) _______某个犯罪事件, 目的是增加收视率.
A. 点缀 B. 装点 C. 渲染

12. 这片建在郊区的别墅 (biéshù, villas) 因为交通便利, 各种_______设施齐全而受到买房者的欢迎.
A. 对立 B. 配套 C. 相对

13. 教育学家认为如果一味让孩子听从自己的安排, 很容易使孩子产生________情绪 (qíngxù, sentiment).
    A. 自相矛盾 B. 格格不入 C. 抵触

14. 有人既提倡保护动物, 又喜欢穿动物的皮毛衣服, 真是________.
    A. 前后连贯 B. 自相矛盾 C. 首尾照应

15 上世纪六十年代中国在武汉 (Wuhan) 修建了一座________长江的大桥, 这就是武汉长江大桥.
    A. 贯穿 B. 横着 C. 横跨

Theme 210: Relative relations 相对关系 (xiāngduì guānxì)

1 在 [-] zài (exist, at) <v.> exist, be at: 他~天津. He's in Tianjin. || 我~家里. I'm at home.
2 处在 [處-] chǔzài (stand-in) <v.> be situated at: ~初级阶段 be in the introductory stages. || ~变化之中 be in change || ~关键时刻be in a key moment.
3 立足于 [--於] lìzúyú (hold-foot-at) <v.> have a foothold somewhere: ~国内 have a foothold domestically || ~教育 have a foothold in education || ~现有条件 have a foothold in the existing conditions
4 居 [-] jū (dwell, reside) <v.> reside, hold a certain position, occupy a place: 身~海外 live abroad || ~世界之首be first in the world || 独~ live a solitary existence
5 位居 [-] wèijū (place-stay) <v.> be at, place: ~第一rank first || 这个城市~交通枢纽. This city was situated as the transportation hub. || ~中央 be at the center
6 高居 [-] gāojū (high-stand) <v.> stand above: ~首位 rank the top
7 居高不下 [-] jūgāobúxià (stay-high-not-drop) <idiom> (or prices, rates etc) to remain high (of prices, rates): 房价~. Housing prices have been consistently high. || 血压~ blood pressure has been consistently high
8 地处 [-處] dìchǔ (place-locate) <v.> be located at: ~市中心 be located at the city center || ~中国北部 be located in north China || ~山地 be located in a mountain area
9 屈居 [-] qūjū (unwillingly-stand) <v.> be forced to accept a place: ~下位 be forced into a lower position || ~亚军 be forced into second place || ~在工厂 be forced to accept work at a factory
10 身处 [-處] shēnchǔ (body-stand) <v.> in (some place), be in (adversity): ~逆境be in adverse circumstances || ~险境 be in a tight place || ~绝境 be in extremity
11 坐落于 [--於] zuòluòyú (sit-locate-at) <v.> (of a building) situated: ~西湖边 be located next to the west lake || ~山下 to be located at the foot of a mountain
12 置身于 [--於] zhìshēnyú (play-oneself-in) <v.> place oneself in the midst of: ~仙境be in fairyland || ~危险之中 be in danger
13 位于 [-於] wèiyú (locate-at) <v.> be located, be situated: ~西部 be located in the west || ~山脚 be located at the foot of the mountain || ~中心 be located at the center
14 沉浸 [-] chénjìn (immerse-steep) <v.> be immersed in, be steeped in: ~在音乐中 be immersed in music || ~在回忆里 be immersed in one's memory || ~在幸福里be immersed in happiness

15 陷于 [-於] xiànyú (fall-into) <v.> fall into (an unfavorable position): ~混乱fall into chaos || ~被动 fall into a passive position || ~困难fall into hardship
16 沉沦 [-淪] chénlún (sink-fall into) <v.> sink into (vice, degradation): ~在享受里sink into enjoyment || ~于日常生活sink into everyday life
17 沦落 [淪-] lúnluò (fall into-fall) <v.> wander, come down in the world, sink: ~街头 be driven onto the streets to become a tramp, beggar, etc. || ~风尘sink into prostitution || 家境 ~ decline of family fortunes
18 堕入 [墮-] duòrù (fall-into) <v.> sink (or lapse) into: ~情网fall in love || ~陷阱 fall in a trap
19 赶上 [趕-] gǎnshàng (catch-up, run-into) <v.> catch up with, run into (a situation), be in time for: ~时代的发展 keep abreast of the times || ~好时机 be in time for a good opportunity || ~了大雨run into a heavy rain

20 含 [-] hán (contain) <v.> contain: ~人工费 contain a labor cost || ~糖 contain sugar || ~铁contain steel
21 含有 [-] hányǒu (contain-have) <v.> contain, including: ~多种维生素 contain several kinds of vitamins || 桔子 ~维生素C. Oranges contain Vitamin C.
22 包含 [-] bāohán (include-contain) <v.> contain, embody: ~水份 contain moisture || ~两个问题 have a couple of questions || ~很多信息 to have a lot of information
23 包括 [-] bāokuò (include-include) <v.> include, consist of: ~所有人 include everyone || ~我自己 include oneself || ~两项内容 include two contents
24 孕育 [-] yùnyù (pregnant-give birth to) <v.> give birth to, be pregnant with: ~生命 be pregnant with new life || ~新思想be pregnant with a new idea || 黄河~了中国古代文明. The Yellow River gave birth to ancient Chinese civilization.

25 存 [-] cún (exist) <v.> exist/live: 不~希望 have no hope for || ~着疑问 for doubts to remain || ~着坏心 have a bad heart/bad intentions
26 容纳 [-納] róngnà (hold-collect) <v.> hold, have a capacity of, accommodate: ~四千人 have a capacity of 4000 people || 这座体育馆能~三万观众. This stadium has a seating capacity of 30,000.
27 包容 [-] bāoróng (include-hold) <v.> pardon, forgive: 互相~ mutually be magnanimous || ~别人 forgive others || ~错误 forgive one's mistakes
28 席卷 [-捲] xíjuǎn (mat-roll up) <v.> roll up like a mat, sweep across: 金融危机~全球. Financial crisis swept across the world. || 这场拒绝难民的运动~欧洲. The movement to refuse refugees swept across Europe. || 一场暴风雪~加州. A blizzard swept across California.

29 充满 [-滿] chōngmǎn (fill-full) <v.> fill, be filled with: ~泪水 be filled with tears || ~阳光 be filled with light || ~热情 be filled with warm emotions
30 布满 [佈滿] bùmǎn (disperse-full) <v.> be everywhere: 天空~星星. Stars are everywhere in the sky. || 房间里~了阳光. Light is everywhere in the room. || 脸上~了皱纹. The face was covered in wrinkles.
31 爆满 [-滿] bàomǎn (severely-full) (of theater, cinema, stadium) <v.> fill to capacity: 电影院~. The theater was filled to capacity. || 座位~. All the seats were filled.
32 无处不在 [無處--] wúchùbúzài (no-place-not-have) <idiom> be everywhere: 声音~ the voice was everywhere || 危险~ danger was everywhere
33 无孔不入 [無---] wúkǒngbúrù (no-hole-not-enter) <idiom> get in by every opening, seize every opportunity: 细菌~. Germs are everywhere || ~ 的宣传

all-pervasive propaganda ||在商业化的时代里, 广告~. In the age of commercialization, advertising is pervasive. || 在当今社会科技~. Technology is pervasive in today's society.

34 人满为患 [-滿爲-] rénmǎnwéihuàn (people-full-become-trouble) <idiom> be overcrowded with people: 医院~ the hospital to be overcrowded with people || 海滩上~ for the beach to be overcrowded with people

35 满怀 [滿懷] mǎnhuái (full-cherish) <v.> be filled with (or imbued) with: ~希望 be filled with hope || ~热情 be filled with positive energy || ~激动 be filled with excitement

36 胸怀 [-懷] xiōnghuái (heart-cherish) <v./n.> mind/heart: ~宽广/狭隘 (xiá'ài) broad-minded/narrow-minded || ~大志 cherish high ideals || 敞开~ for one's heart to be open wide

37 相关 [-關] xiāngguān (mutually-involved) <v.> mutually related: 密切~ be intimately involved || ~报道 related report || ~规定related regulations

38 关联 [關聯] guānlián (involve-connect) <v./n.> be connected, interrelation: 密切~ become intimately related || 互相~ be interconnected || 内部~ for internal affairs to be connected

39 涉及 [-] shèjí (involve-with) <v.> involve, relate to: ~一个问题 involve a issue || ~很多人 involve many people || ~各个方面 relate to many aspects

40 关系 [關係] guānxì (involve-relate) <n.> connections, relations: 搞好~ build good personal relations || 家庭~ family connections || 找~ seek for special connections

41 连锁 [連鎖] liánsuǒ (chain-lock) <n.> chain, linkage: ~反应 chain reaction || ~酒店 chain hotels || ~店chain store

42 有关 [-關] yǒuguān (have-involvement) <v.> have something to do with, relate to: 这件事跟他~. He has something to do with the matter. || 对这件事, ~的人都很为难. The people who are involved in this matter all feel embarrassed. || 与环境~ be related to the environment

43 打擦边球 [--邊-] dǎcābiānqiú (play-touch-border-ball) <v.> be on the border of legality: 通过钻法律空子来打~ circumventing the law by exploiting its loopholes

44 息息相关 [---關] xīxīxiāngguān (breath-breath-mutual-involve) <idiom> be closely linked: 个人与社会~ be closely linked to people and society || 彼此~ be closely linked to one another

45 凭借 [憑-/藉] píngjiè (base on-rely on) <v.> rely on, depend on: ~经验解决难题 rely on one's experience to resolve a question || ~想象力进行创作rely on one's imagination to create || ~才华找到工作 rely on one's literary talent to find a job

46 借助 [-] jièzhù (rely on-aid) <v.> have the aid of: ~外力 have the aid of outside resources || ~风力发电 rely on wind powered generation

47 依赖 [-賴] yīlài (rely on-depend on) <v.> rely on/dependent on: ~父母 rely on parents || 这些材料全部~进口. All these materials rely on imports. || 互相~ rely on others

48 无关 [無關] wúguān (not-involved) <v.> have nothing to do with: 与人~ have nothing to do with someone || 同他 ~ have nothing to do with him || 完全 ~ have completely nothing to do with

49 不相干 [-] bùxiānggān (not-mutual-relevant) <v.> irrelevant, have nothing to do with: 跟工作~ be irrelevant to one's work || 毫 ~ completely irrelevant

50 风马牛不相及 [風馬----] fēngmǎniú bù xiāng jí (wind/free-horse-cow-not-mutually-touch) <idiom> have nothing to do with each other: 两人的专业~ for two people's industries to have nothing to do with one another

51 牵连 [牽連] qiānlián (pull-connect) <v.> involve (in trouble), implicate: 这件事跟他有~. He is implicated in the affair. || 这个案子~到很多人. Many people were implicated in this case. || ~到邻居 involve one's neighbors in trouble

52 连累 [連-] liánlèi (connect-implicate) <v.> implicate, involve: 这件事~了很多人. This incident got many people into trouble.

53 拖累 [-] tuōlěi (drag-encumber) <v.> encumber, be a burden on: ~儿女 burden one's sons and daughters || 受到家务~ be tied down by household chores

54 卷入 [捲-] juǎnrù (involve-in) <v.> get drawn into, involved: ~贸易战 get drawn into a trade war || ~台风中心 get drawn into in the heart of a typhoon || ~一场纠纷 get drawn into a dispute

55 陷入 [-] xiànrù (fall-into) <v.> sink (or fall) into, lost in: ~一片汪洋 sink into the boundless ocean || ~思考 lost in thought || ~悲观 be in deep despair

56 牵涉 [牽-] qiānshè (pull-involve) <v.> involve, drag in: 这件事~到公司的利益. This thing involved the benefit of the corporation. || ~到许多问题 involve multiple problems || 改革~到家人 involve one's family

57 波及 [-] bōjí (spread-to) <v.> spread into, involve, affect: 经商的热潮也~到了大学. The business fervor has also spread to universities. || ~到青少年 affect the youth || 经济危机~全世界. The economic crisis has affected the entire world.

58 在内 [-] zàinèi (be-included) <v.> be included: 一切费用~ all fees included || 包括老人~ for old people to be included || 连他~ include him

Tips:

1 在: 在 is related to 土 (soil) and 才 (grass shoot,) meaning 'to exist' or 'be at.'

2 风马牛不相及: The 风 in this expression does not mean 'wind,' but 'to free, to lose.' The expression means 'even if you free cows or horses, they cannot reach that far,' and the extended meaning is 'two things not related at all, have nothing to do with each other.' China's first private satellite launched in February 2018 was named 风马牛.

3 关, 联, 系: All mean 'related,' and their combinations 关联, 关系, 联系 mean about the same thing.

Exercises:

Read the following sentences and fill in each blank with the appropriate word or phrase from the options given.

1 风马牛不相及、无处不在、人满为患

a) 一般来说冬季是流感季节, 病菌 (germs) __________.

b) 最近病人很多, 这家医院__________.

c) 小张从医学院毕业以后当了一名建筑工人, 听起来他现在的工作跟大学专业__________.

2 席卷、牵涉、在内
   a) 美国政府一直没有禁枪, 因为它________到很多大财团的利益.
   b) 上周一场暴风雪________了美国东部. 几乎全部学校都关门了, 包括一些大学________.

3 陷入、拖累、高居不下
   a) 小张的父亲得了癌症, 他不想________家人, 所以决定放弃治疗.
   b) 在中国一些家庭会因为子女或者父母的疾病而________贫穷, 再也无法使生活好转.
   c) 近几年中国的癌症发病率 (fābìnglǜ, incidence) 一直________.

4 充满、爆满、包容、容纳
   a) 不同文化的人相处应该讲究互相理解, 互相________.
   b) 每到周末这所大学的校园里就________了笑声、音乐声, 这是因为很多学生在开派对.
   c) 节日期间北京的各大电影院几乎天天________.
   d) 北京最大的电影院可以同时________五千人看电影.

5 包括、坐落于、置身于
   a) 看4D电影的时候, 你会觉得自己正________电影里的各个场景中.
   b) 这个村庄________长城脚下, 抬头就可以看到长城.
   c) 这个暑期中文班的全部费用是一万美金, ________飞机票、住宿费和文化旅游费用.

Theme 211: To cause 导致 (dǎozhì)

1 影响 [-響] yǐngxiǎng (shadow-echo) <v./n.> influence, effect: ~工作 influence one's work || 受~ receive influence || ~大 large influence
2 感染 [-] gǎnrǎn (move-catch) <v.> infect, affect, influence: 细菌 ~ be infected by bacteria || 受到病毒~ be infected by a virus || ~观众 affect audience
3 传染 [傳-] chuánrǎn (spread-catch) <v.> infect, be contagious: ~疾病 a contagious disease || 空气~. The air is contagious. || 互相~ mutually infect
4 染上 [-] rǎnshàng (catch-caught) <v.> catch (a disease): ~恶习 develop a bad habit || ~颜色stain with a color || ~疾病 catch a disease
5 沾染 [-] zhānrǎn (touch-catch) <v.> infected with, contaminated with: ~恶习 be contaminated with a bad habit || ~细菌 be infected by bacteria || ~花粉 be contaminated with pollen
6 熏陶 [-] xūntáo (smoke-mold, burn) <v.&n.> exert a graduate uplifting influence on: 受到~ receive a gradual and uplifting influence || 音乐~ uplifting music || ~孩子 exert a gradual positive pressure on a child
7 耳闻目染 [-] ěrwén mùrǎn (ear-immerse-eye-catch) <idiom> be unconsciously influenced by what one constantly hears or sees: 因为从小~, 所以他对色彩很敏感. He is sensitive to color because he has been exposed to the art of painting from a young age.
8 给 [給] gěi (ample, provide, give) <v.> give: ~她一台电脑当生日礼物 give her a computer as the birthday gift. || ~人一个好印象. Give people good influences.
9 予以 [-] yǔyǐ (bestow) <v.> give, render: ~表扬 give compliments || ~肯定 give a confirmation || ~重视give careful attention

10 给予 [給-] jǐyǔ (provide-bestow) <v.> give, render: ~方便 give convenience || ~表扬 give praise || ~机会 give an opportunity

11 加以 [-] jiāyǐ (impose-with) <v.> give, render: ~调整 make an adjustment || ~支持 give support || 有问题要及时~解决. Problems should be resolved in good time.

12 使得 [-] shǐdé (cause-that) <v.> make, cause, can be used: 这位歌唱家一开口就~听众如痴如醉. As soon as the singer opened his mouth, the audience were out of their minds. || 这些美食~客人不停地赞叹. These delicious foods drew unceasing praise from customers. || 这种情况~很多人都不满意. This situation made many people unhappy.

13 附上 [-] fùshàng (attach-up) <v.> attach, be enclosed here with: ~说明 attach a statement || ~自己的意见 enclose one's own opinion || ~卡片 attach a card

14 相加 [-] xiāngjiā (together-add) <v.> add together, plus: 金额~ add a sum together || 两个数~ add two numbers together

15 施加 [-] shījiā (exert-impose) <v.> exert, bring to bear on: ~影响 exert influence || ~压力 exert pressure

16 赋予 [賦-] fùyǔ (entrust-bestow) <v.> give, confer upon: ~生命 animate, vitalization || ~新的意义 give new meaning || ~权力/权利 confer power/rights on sb.

17 强加 [-] qiángjiā (forcefully-impose) <v.> impose, force: ~影响 impose force || ~给别人impose on others

18 触发 [觸發] chùfā (touch-off) <v.> trigger, touch off: ~危机 trigger a crisis || ~想象set off one's imagination || ~爆炸 set off an explosion

19 打动 [-動] dǎdòng (strike-move) <v.> move, touch: ~读者 move readers || ~人心 move one's heart || ~情感 emotionally move someone

20 撼动 [-動] hàndòng (shake-move) <v.> shake, vibrate: ~人心 shake one's heart || ~世界 shake the world || 轻易~ gently shake

21 轰动 [轟動] hōngdòng (rumble-move) <v.> cause a sensation, make a stir: ~全国 stir the whole nation || ~世界stir the whole world

22 震动 [-動] zhèndòng (vibrate-move) <v.> shake, shock, vibrate: ~世界 shake the world || 引起广泛的 ~ produce wide repercussions || ~中外 shake China and other countries

23 震撼 [-] zhènhàn (shock-shake) <v.> shake, shock: ~心灵 shake one's spirit || ~世界 shake the world

24 带动 [帶動] dàidòng (lead-move) <v.> drive, spur on: ~工作 drive on one's work || ~大家 drive everyone || ~经济 drive the economy

25 引起 [-] yǐnqǐ (give rise-to) <v.> give rise to, lead to: ~纠纷 lead to chaos || ~注意bring to sb's attention || ~不满 lead to dissatisfaction

26 诱发 [誘發] yòufā (induce-happen) <v.> induce, cause to happen: ~矛盾 spark conflict || ~犯罪 trigger off a crime || ~疾病 induce illness

27 造成 [-] zàochéng (cause-into) <v.> create, cause: ~损失 cause loss || ~困难 cause hardship || ~浪费 cause waste

28 逗 [-] dòu (tease) <v.> play with, tease, provoke laughter: ~妹妹玩 play with (one's) younger sister || 把大家都~笑了provoke everyone into laughter

29 惹 [-] rě (cause, provoke) <v.> provoke, invite or ask for (sth. undesirable): ~老师生气 make teacher angry || ~麻烦 provoke a trouble || ~事 provoke something

30 招 [-] zhāo (beckon, provoke) <v.> beckon, beckon: ~蚊子 attract mosquitoes || ~人喜爱 beckon one's love || ~人烦 make people annoyed

31 挑起 [-] tiǎoqǐ (stir-up) <v.> provoke, stir up: ~战争 stir up a war || ~边境冲突 provoke a border conflict || ~事端stir up incident

32 吸引 [-] xīyǐn (attract-draw) <v.> attract, draw: ~人 attract people || 受广告~ be attracted by an advertisement || ~注意力attract attention

33 诱惑 [誘-] yòuhuò (entice-puzzle) <v.> entice, tempt, seduce: 经不住~ let oneself be seduced || 抵制~ resist temptation

34 多管闲事 [--閒-] duōguǎnxiánshì<v.> (unnecessarily-care-others'-matter) meddling in other people's business: 从不~. Never meddle in other people's business.

35 致 [-] zhì (incur) <v.> cause: ~癌 cause cancer || ~病 cause illness || ~残cause disability

36 导致 [導-] dǎozhì (lead-result in) <v.> lead to, result in: ~失败result in failure || ~死亡 lead to death || ~严重后果 lead to serious results

37 以致 [-] yǐzhì (so as to-result in) <v.> (usu. referring to bad results so that, with the result that: ~延误病情 lead to result in a prolongment of a patient's illness || ~迷失方向 lead to losing one's way

38 致使 [-] zhìshǐ (cause-make) <v.> cause, result in: ~大批工人失业 result in a massive loss of jobs || ~房价升高 to cause an increase in housing prices

39 自找 [-] zìzhǎo (self-ask) <v.> suffer from one's own actions, ask for it: ~麻烦 look for trouble || ~苦吃 bring trouble on oneself

40 催产 [-產] cuīchǎn (expedite-delivery) <v.> expedite child delivery: 自然~ naturally expedite childbirth

Tips:

1 双: In the simplification of the traditional characters 轟 (轰, hōng) and 聶 (聂, niè), 双 was used to substitute the lower part, which is actually the doubling of the upper part, the source of the basic meaning of the character. But not all three-folded characters were simplified in this way, for example, 蟲 (虫,) 鱻 (鲜,) 麤 (粗,) 鑫 (鑫, xīn.)

2 影响: 影响 means 'influence,' which is derived from 影 (like a shadow to the object) and 响 (like echos to a sound.)

3 吸引, 引诱, 诱惑: These three words can represent the three phases of alluring. The first phase is A 吸引 B since A is attractive or alluring. The second phase is A 引诱 B, i. e., A is alluring B. The third phase is B was 诱惑 by A, i. e., B is allured by A.

Exercises:

Part I: Read the following sentences and fill in each blank with the appropriate word or phrase from the options given.

1 诱惑力、吸引、引诱

a) 婴儿常常用哭的办法来________父母的注意力.
b) 中国法律规定________未成年人犯罪要受到法律惩罚 (punishment).
c) 金钱对每个人来说都有巨大的________.

2 自找、致使、以致

a) 美国2017年拉斯维加斯枪击 (Las Vegas shooting) 事件________几百人伤亡.
b) 父母对孩子娇生惯养 (jiāoshēng guànyǎng, spoiled) 其实是_______苦吃, 因为惯坏的孩子长大后会给父母带来更多麻烦.
c) 这个学生平时除了喝酒就是打麻将, ________最后没有得到毕业证.

3 挑起、导致、多管闲事、招惹

a) 由于朝鲜一再进行核武器实验________它和美国以及中国的关系十分紧张.
b) 在朝鲜眼里美国是一个邪恶 (xié'è, evil) 国家, 总是到处________, 充当世界警察.
c) 为了避免 (bìmiǎn, avoid) 麻烦, 世界上很多国家都不愿意主动去_________像美国这样的军事大国.
d) 有人认为朝鲜首先会在世界上_________一场新的战争.

4 造成、赋予、给予、打动、轰动、逗

a) 酒后开车最容易_________车祸.
b) 这位中国女科学家获得了诺贝尔 (Nobel) 化学奖, 在中国引起了巨大的_______.
c) 这部关于亲情的电影非常感人, ________了每一位观众的心.
d) 这部电影里的男主人公非常______人, 常常做一些滑稽 (huájī, funny) 可笑的事情.
e) 美国宪法 (xiànfǎ, Constitution) 规定言论自由是宪法_______公民的权利.
f) 对于违反学校规定的学生, 学校应该_________一定的处罚.

Theme 212: Good, harmful 有利, 有害 (yǒulì, yǒuhài)

1 有利 [-] yǒulì (have-advantage) <adj.> advantageous, beneficial: 对大家~ benefit everyone || ~条件 advantageous conditions || ~的地位 advantageous position
2 给力 [給-] gěilì (give-strength) <adj.> amazing, cool: 折扣~ amazing discount || 网络很~ the internet is amazing || 快递很~. Express delivery is very fast.
3 有益 [-] yǒuyì (have-benefit) <v./adj.> beneficial, useful, be good for: ~的建议useful suggestion || ~的谈话useful conversation || 对健康~ be good for one's health
4 有利于 [--於] yǒulìyú (have-advantage-to) <v.> be good for: 运动~健康. Physical exercise is good for heath. || ~世界和平be in the interest of world peace || ~提高产量 be conductive to higher yields
5 有益于 [--於] yǒuyìyú (have-benefit-for) <v.> be beneficial to: ~保护环境 be beneficial for protecting environment || 新鲜空气~健康. Fresh air is beneficial for our health.
6 有助于 [--於] yǒuzhùyú (be-helpful-for) <v.> contribute to, be conducive to: ~世界和平 benefit world peace || ~身心健康 benefit one's physical and mental health || ~解决问题 help solve a question

7 占上风 [--風] zhànshàngfēng (hold-upper-wind) <v.> get the upper hand, win an advantage: 处处~ win an advantage in all respects || 在游戏中~ get the upperhand in a game

8 便于 [-於] biànyú (convenient-for) <v.> be easy to, be convenient for: ~管理 be easy to manage || ~操作 be easy to operate || ~使用 be easy to use

9 利己 [-] lìjǐ (benefit-oneself) <v.> be only concerned with one's own interest: 毫不~ not the least self-interested || ~主义 egoism

10 利国利民 [-國--] lìguó lìmín (benefit-country-benefit-people) <idiom> benefit both country and people: ~的政策 for a policy to benefit both country and people || 中国政府认为发展绿色能源~. The Chinese government believes that the development of green energy is beneficial to both the country and its people.

11 伤 [傷] shāng (wound, injure) <v./n.> wound, injury: 受~ be wounded || ~身体 wound one's body || 重/轻~ serious/not serious wound

12 有害 [-] yǒuhài (have-harm) <v.> harm: 对身体 ~ harm one's body || ~于健康 harm one's health || ~的污染 harmful pollution

13 伤害 [傷-] shānghài (injure-harm) <v.> injure, harm, hurt: ~身体 harm one's body || ~别人 hurt others || ~感情 hurt one's feelings

14 危害 [-] wēihài (endanger-harm) <v./n.> harm, endanger: ~健康 be detrimental to health || ~国家 endanger a nation || 严重的~ serious harm

15 损害 [損-] sǔnhài (damage-harm) <v.> do harm to, damage, impair: ~两国关系 impair bilateral relations || ~视力be bad for one's eyes || ~他人的名誉 impair another's reputation

16 妨害 [-] fánghài (hinder-harm) <v.> impair, jeopardize: ~消化impair digestion || ~公务 obstructing government administration || ~社会治安jeopardize public security

17 摧残 [-殘] cuīcán (destroy-injure) <v.> wreck, destroy: ~身体 destroy one's body || ~新生事物 destroy new things || 严重~ seriously destroy

18 挫伤 [-傷] cuòshāng (defeat-injure) <v.> contusion, bruise: ~积极性 bruise one's positivity || 严重~ a serious bruise, contusion || 受到~ receive a bruise, contusion

19 损伤 [損傷] sǔnshāng (damage-injure) <v.> damage, injury: ~健康 damage one's health || 脑~ injure one's brain || 受到~ be injured

20 误伤 [誤傷] wùshāng (mistakenly-injure) <v.> accidentally injure: ~顾客 accidentally injure a customer || 造成~ cause a accidental injure || ~他人accidentally injure others

21 危及 [-] wēijí (endanger-involving) <v.> endanger, jeopardize: ~安全 endanger safety || ~生命 endanger one's life || ~身体健康 endanger one's health

22 侵蚀 [-蝕] qīnshí (corrode-erode) <v.> corrode, erode: ~河岸 erode the river bank || 长期~ erode over time || 遭受~ suffer from corrosion

23 不利 [-] búlì (not-favorable) <adj.> unfavorable: 对我们~ not benefit us || ~的影响 unfavorable influence || ~的条件 unfavorable conditions

24 不利于 [--於] búlìyú (no-benefit-to) <v.> not be beneficial to: ~管理 be unfavorable to management || ~发展 not benefit development || ~团结 not benefit unity

25 祸国殃民 [禍國--] huòguó yāngmín (bring calamity to-country-bring disaster to-people) <idiom> bring calamity to the country and the people: 新中

国成立后, 中国政府认为鸦片~, 所以要禁止鸦片. After its establishment, the new Chinese government thought that opium would bring calamity to the country and the people, therefore it was necessary to prohibit opium.

Tips:

1 利, 害, 利害: The meaning of 利 is related to 刂 (刀, knife), 禾 (crops) and in combination 'use a sickle to reap crops,' in other words, 'sharp.' The extended meanings of 利 include 'quick,' 'lucky,' 'beneficial' and 'advantage'. The meaning of 害 is related to 宀 (house,) 口 (mouth) and 丯 (gài, dense weed grass.) The ancient Chinese believed that if a person spoke too much at home, it was harmful (to the family,) therefore, 害 means 'impair, harm.' 利害, when pronounced as lìhài, it means 'advantages and harm, gains and losses' or 'relation,' when pronounced as lìhai (with 害 being neutral tone,) means 'terrible, fierce.' For example, 这件事很复杂, 如果你能看清楚里面的利害关系, 那你就利害了 (This matter is quite complicated. If you can see clearly the gains and losses, then you are incredible.) The latter 利害 is usually written as 厉害 (厲害) nowadays.

2 利国利民: It means 'to benefit the country and benefit the people.' The wife of the lead author of this book is named 利国, and her elder sister is named 利民. This runs contrary to traditional Chinese culture, which puts the country (国) before the people (民,) however, the two sisters have an eldest sister who is named 利君 (benefit the monarch), which makes the logic of the naming clear: 君, 民, 国 (monarch, people, country.)

Exercises:

Part II: Read the following sentences and fill in each blank with the appropriate word or phrase from the options given.

1 利国利民、有助于、有益
   a) 据研究表明儿童学习外语_________大脑发育.
   b) 适当参加体育运动对孩子的健康成长________.
   c) 无论在哪个国家大力发展教育都是_________的好事.

2 便于、占上风、利己
   a) 美国运动队在历届奥运会比赛中都________.
   b) 中国的《共产党党章》 (*Constitution of the Communist Party of China*) 中写到: 共产党员应该毫不_______, 专门利人.
   c) 为了_______市民晚上购买生活必需品, 这家公司在居民区开了很多24小时营业的便利店.

3 有害、摧残、损害
   a) 中国政府规定禁止在公共场合吸烟, 因为吸烟对他人健康______.
   b) 韩国政府认为朝鲜的核武器实验________了韩国的国家安全利益.
   c) 第二次世界大战几乎_______了所有的欧洲大城市.

4 不利、危及、祸国殃民
   a) 美国有的州法律规定任何合法持枪 (possess a gun) 的公民都不能带枪到公共场合, 以免________他人生命安全.

b) 新中国政府认为毒品和妓女对社会发展________，因此就全面禁止这些东西.
c) 中国学校的历史教材上是这样评价慈禧太后 (Empress Dowager Cixi) 的: 阴险毒辣 (yīnxiǎn dúlà, insidious and spicy)、__________ _.

Theme 213: Big, small, long, short 大, 小, 长, 短 (dà, xiǎo, cháng, duǎn)

1 长 [長] cháng (long) <adj.> long, length: ~时间 long time || 三米 ~ three meters long || ~袖子 long sleeve
2 超长 [-長] chāocháng (super-long) <adj.> super long, exceeding length: ~时间的电影 super long movies
3 细长 [細長] xìcháng (thin-long) <adj.> long and thin: ~的身材 long and thin figure || ~的眼睛 long and thin eyes || ~的手指 long and thin fingers
4 狭长 [狹長] xiácháng (narrow-long) <adj.> long and narrow: ~地带 long and narrow belt || ~的睫毛 long and narrow eyebrows || 南北~ long and narrow on a north-south axis
5 短 [-] duǎn (short) <adj.> short, brief: 时间~ short time || ~外衣 short coat || 脖子~ short neck
6 短小 [-] duǎnxiǎo (short-small) <adj.> short and small: 四肢~ short legs || 身材~ short, stubby figure || 下巴~ short lower chin
7 长短 [長-] chángduǎn (long-short) <adj./n.> length: 假期~ short vacation || 时间~ short time || 比较~ especially short
8 大 [-] dà (big) <adj.> big: ~西瓜 large watermelon || 年纪~ old age || 数量~ large quantity
9 巨大 [-] jùdà (gigantic-big) <adj.> giant: ~变化 massive change || ~的力量 massive force || ~的影响 great influence
10 超大 [-] chāodà (super-big) <adj.> extra large: ~城市 an extremely large city || ~字体 an extra large font || ~尺寸 an extra large ruler
11 大小 [-] dàxiǎo (big-small) <adj./n.> size: ~不同 different size || ~事情 big or small events || 书本~ size of a book
12 大于 [-於] dàyú (big-than) <adj.> larger than: ~光速 larger than the velocity of light || 收入~支出. The revenue is larger than the expense. || 五~三. Five is bigger than three.
13 庞大 [龐-] pángdà (huge-big) <adj.> massive: 数量~ massive quantity || ~的怪物 massive monster || 无比~ comparatively large
14 大型 [-] dàxíng (large-scale) <非谓形容词> large-scale: ~画册 large-scale album || ~企业 large-scale business || ~城市 large-scale city
15 巨型 [-] jùxíng (gigantic-scale) <非谓形容词> giant, mammoth: ~飞船 giant airliner || ~公司 giant corporation || ~计算机 giant computer
16 特大 [-] tèdà (unusually-big) <adj.> especially large: ~城市 large city || ~新闻 big news || ~事故 big events
17 重型 [-] zhòngxíng (heavy-type) <非谓形容词> heavy-duty: ~卡车 heavy duty truck || ~武器 heavy weaponry || ~肝炎 serious Hepatitis
18 过大 [過-] guòdà (excessive-big) <adj.> especially large: 规模~ especially large scale || 希望~ large hopes || ~的差距large difference

19 中 [-] zhōng (center) <adj./n.> center, middle: 军队~ in the army || 运动 ~ in the process of exercising, in motion || 书~ in the book
20 半大 [-] bàndà (half-big) <adj.> medium-sized: ~孩子 teenagers || 这种~的包很方便. This kind of medium-sized bags are convenient.
21 中型 [-] zhōngxíng (medium-size) <adj.> medium-sized: ~企业 mid-sized business || ~城市 mid-sized city || ~词典 mid-sized dictionary
22 不大不小 [-] búdà búxiǎo (not-big-not-small) <adj.> neither too big nor too small: ~的玩笑 a joke that is not big or large || ~的问题 an issue that's not big or small || 房子~ a house that's not big or small

23 小 [-] xiǎo (small) <adj.> small: ~饭店 a small restaurant || ~朋友 a younger friend || ~问题 a small issue
24 微 [-] wēi (minute, tiny) <adj.> minute, little: ~辣 mildly spicy || ~形 small shape || ~低着头 slightly lower one's head
25 小于 [-於] xiǎoyú (small-than) <adj.> smaller than: ~三米 smaller than three meters || ~八岁 younger than eight || ~光速 smaller than the velocity of light
26 微小 [-] wēixiǎo (minute-small) <adj.> small, little: ~的数字 a small number || ~的信息 little information || ~的变化 a small change
27 细微 [細-] xìwēi (fine-tiny) <adj.> slight, fine: ~的区别 a slight difference || ~的声音 a slight voice || ~变化 a slight change
28 一丁点儿 [--點兒] yīdīngdiǎnr (a-tiny-bit) <adj.> a wee bit: 差~ a wee bit different || ~的事 a small matter || ~紧张a little bit tense
29 迷你 [-] mínǐ (*transliteration* of mini) <adj.> miniature: ~裙 a mini-skirt || ~小汽车 a mini-car || ~电脑 a micro-computer
30 微型 [-] wēixíng (minute-size) <非谓形容词> miniature: ~录音机 a miniature recorder || ~电脑 a miniature computer || ~电器 a miniature electrical device
31 小型 [-] xiǎoxíng (small-size) <非谓形容词> small size: ~飞机场 a small scale airport || ~动物 a small animal || ~会议 a small meeting
32 袖珍 [-] xiùzhēn (sleeve-treasure) <adj.> pocket-size: ~手电筒 a pocket-sized flashlight || ~录音机 a pocket-size recorder || ~笔记本 a pocket-sized notebook
33 微乎其微 [-] wēihūqíwēi (little-*particle*-very-little) <idiom> very little, next to nothing: 作用~ little use || ~的费用 little expense || 变化~ little change

Tips:

1 微: 微 is related to 彳 (walk,) originally meaning 'to walk in a clandestine way.'
2 Sizes from large to small: 巨, 大, 中, 小, 微 are sizes from large to small. Their adjacent combinations, 巨大, 大中, 中小, 小微 also refer to different sizes.
3 *型: 型 has two major meanings. One is 'size' or 'scale,' for example, 巨型 (gigantic size, scale,) and the other is 'type,' for example, 新型 (new style.)
4 细, 微, 小: All mean 'fine, small, little' and their combinations 细微, 微小, 细小 have almost the same meaning.

Exercises:

Part I: Use the given bound form as a guide to help you think of other words with the same character. Feel free to use your dictionary when needed. Then write down the English definition of each of the words you've written.

长 *(long)*: 超长 *exceed length*

____

____

____

____

大 *(big)*: 巨大 *giant*

____

____

____

____

____

小 *(small)*: 小型 *small size*

____

____

____

Part II: Read the following words and then answer the questions.

微乎其微、不大不小、巨型、大型、小型、中型、微型、迷你

1. "巨型、大型、小型、中型、微型," 请按照从小到大的顺序重新排列这些词

____

2 "小王认为他被提升 (tí shēng, promote) 为总经理的机会微乎其微," 这句话的意思是
   a) 小王当总经理的机会很大
   b) 小王几乎不可能当总经理
   c) 小王当总经理的机会过大

3 "小王家的客厅不大不小," 这句话的意思是
   a) 大小合适　　b) 过大　　c) 袖珍

4 日本有很多"迷你公寓," 里面各种生活设施 (shèshī, facility) 很齐全. 这里的"迷你"意思是
   a) 小于　　b) 小型　　c) 迷人

Theme 214: High, wide 高, 宽 (gāo, kuān)

1 高 [-] gāo (high, tall) <adj.> tall: 很~的地方 a very tall place || ~山 tall mountain || 两米~ two meters tall
2 高耸 [-聳] gāosǒng (high-lofty) <adj.> stand tall and erect: ~的烟囱 a tall chimney || ~的大楼 a tall building || 山峰 ~ a tall mountain peak
3 巍然 [-] wēirán (towering-*suffix*) <adj.> towering, lofty: ~不动 towering and unmoving || ~耸立 towering
4 高高大大 [-] gāogāo dàdà (*reduplication of* 'tall-big') <adj.> tall and big: 长得~ grow big and tall || ~的军人 a big and tall soldier

5 瘦长 [-長] shòucháng (skinny-long) <adj.> long and thin: 身材~ have a long and thin figure || ~脸 a long and thin face || ~的胳膊 long and thin arms
6 亭亭玉立 [-] tíngtíngyùlì (graceful-*prefix*-stand) <idiom> (of a beautiful woman) slim and graceful: 长得~ grow to be slim and graceful || ~的杨树 a slim and graceful tree || ~的姑娘 a slim and graceful woman
7 修长 [-長] xiūcháng (tall and thin-tall) <adj.> tall and thin: ~的手指 tall and thin finger || 身材~ a tall and thin figure || ~的腿 tall and thin legs
8 细高挑儿 [細--兒] xìgāotiǎor (thin-tall-slender) <adj.> tall and slender figure: ~女生 a tall and slender woman

9 矮 [-] ǎi (short) <adj.> short (of stature): 个子~ short stature || 长得~ grow to be short || ~桌子 a short desk
10 矮小 [-] ǎixiǎo (short-small) <adj.> short and small: 个子/身材~ for one's figure to be short and small || 显得~ look short and small
11 矮胖 [-] ǎipàng (short-stout) <adj.> short and stout: ~的男孩 a short and stout male || 身体~ a short and stout body

12 宽 [寬] kuān (spacious, wide) <adj.> wide, broad: 路很~. The road is wide. || ~边 a wide side || 四米~ width is four meters
13 宽广 [寬廣] kuānguǎng (wide-vast) <adj.> broad, extensive: ~ 的田野a broad expanse of country || 心胸~ broad-minded || ~的视野 broad vision
14 宽阔 [寬闊] kuānkuò (wide-broad) <adj.> broad, wide: ~的大路 a broad road || ~的院子 a wide garden || ~的舞台 a broad garden
15 广阔 [廣闊] guǎngkuò (vast-broad) <adj.> vast, wide: ~天地 a wide world || ~的前景 a broad foreground || ~的市场 a vast market
16 开阔 [開闊] kāikuò (open-broad) <adj.> open, wide, tolerant: 视野~ broaden one's horizon (view) || ~地带 to broaden a belt || 思路~ broaden one's thinking
17 宽敞 [寬-] kuānchǎng (wide-spacious) <adj.> spacious, roomy: ~的马路 a spacious road || ~的客厅 a spacious living room || 房间~ a spacious room
18 空荡荡 [-蕩蕩] kōngdàngdàng (empty-vast) <adj.> empty, deserted: ~的屋子 an empty room || 肚子里~的 an empty stomach || ~的操场 an empty playground
19 空旷 [-曠] kōngkuàng (empty-vast) <adj.> open and spacious: ~的校园 an open and spacious school || ~的地方 an open and spacious place
20 浩瀚 [-] hàohàn (grand-vast) <adj.> open and spacious: ~的大海 an open and spacious ocean || ~的星空 an open sky || ~的沙漠 an open and spacious dessert
21 无边无际 [無邊無際] wúbiān wújì (no-border-no edge) <idiom> boundless, limitless: ~的大海 a boundless ocean || ~的沙漠 a boundless desert || ~的森林 a boundless forest

22 一望无际 [--無際] yīwàngwújì (one-gaze-no-edge) <idiom> stretch as far as the eye can see: ~的大森林. The forest stretches as far as the eye can see. || ~的大海. The ocean stretches as far as the eye can see. || 草地~. The grassland stretches as far as the eye can see.
23 滔滔 [-] tāotāo (torrential) <adj.> torrential, surging: ~的江水 surging river water || ~的洪水 surging flood

24 肥 [-] féi (fat, loose) <adj.> loose, fat: 衣服很~ very loose clothes || 裤子~了 very loose pants
25 肥大 [-] féidà (loose-large) <adj.> loose, large: ~的脑袋 a large brain || ~的猎狗 a large hunting dog || 裤子~ loose, large pants
26 宽松 [寬鬆] kuānsōng (wide-loose) <adj.> loose and comfortable: ~衣裤 loose and comfortable clothes || ~环境 relaxed environment || 手头~ be in easy circumstances, be quite well-off at the moment
27 宽大 [寬-] kuāndà (wide-big) <adj.> spacious, roomy: ~的衬衣 spacious undergarments || ~的房间 spacious room || ~的政策 wide policy
28 巨幅 [-] jùfú (huge-width/size) <adj.> extremely large (painting, photographs): ~照片 large picture || ~屏幕 large screen || ~油画 large oil painting

29 窄 [-] zhǎi (narrow) <adj.> narrow: ~床 narrow bed || 路 ~ narrow road || 肩膀~ narrow road
30 狭窄 [狹-] xiázhǎi (narrow-narrow) <adj.> narrow, cramped: ~的胡同 narrow alley || ~的街道 narrow road || 心胸~ narrow-minded

Tips:

1 细高挑儿 (xìgāotiǎor): The segmentation of this word is 细-高挑儿. 高挑儿 means 'tall and slender.'
2 宽, 广, 阔: All mean 'broad' and their combinations, 宽广, 宽阔, 广阔 mean about the same thing.

Exercises:

Part I: Fill in each blank with the appropriate word from the options given.

浩瀚、狭窄、肥大、滔滔、空荡荡、一望无际、宽敞、修长、高耸

_______________的大海
_______________的街道
_______________的衣裤
_______________的江水
_______________的屋子
_______________的田野
_______________的客厅
_______________的身材
_______________的大楼

Part II: Read the following sentences and fill in each blank with the appropriate word or phrase from the options given.

1 高大、亭亭玉立、无边无际
   a) 在美国加州开车, 你可以看到高速公路两边是_________的沙漠.
   b) 几年没见到我小时候的朋友, 再次见到她时, 她已经长成了一个_________的少女.
   c) 小张是一个________帅气的男人.

2 宽松、空旷、巨幅
   a) 北京机场里有很多________电子屏幕 (electronic screen).
   b) 这座城市的南部原来是一片_________的原野, 可是最近被开发商买下, 建起了很多高楼大厦.
   c) 小张最近涨工资了, 手头开始比较_______, 于是就买了一辆新车.

3 矮小、细高挑儿、巍然
   a) 这座摩天大楼非常坚固, 在遭受多次地震后仍然________不动地耸立 (sǒnglì, stand tall) 在地面上.
   b) 这些偏远山区的孩子因为营养不良而身材_______.
   c) 一般来说身材________的女孩子穿紧身牛仔裤 (skinny jeans) 会比较好看.

Theme 215: Deep, thick 深, 厚 (shēn, hòu)

1 深 [-] shēn (deep) <adj.> deep: 水~五百米. The depth of the water is 500 meters. || 很~的洞 a deep hole/cave || ~水 deep water
2 深不可测 [---测] shēn búkě cè (deep-not-able to-measure) <idiom> unfathomable, bottomless: ~的内心an unfathomable heart || ~的大海 the ocean with unfathomable depths
3 幽深 [-] yōushēn (tranquil-deep) <adj.> deep and serene, deep and quiet: ~的森林 deep forest || ~的小巷a deep and quiet alley
4 深邃 [-] shēnsuì (deep-remote) <adj.> deep, profound: ~的山洞 a deep cave || 思想~ profound thought || ~的目光 deep in one's eyes
5 浅 [淺] qiǎn (shallow) <adj.> shallow: ~水 shallow water || ~溪 shallow brook || ~海滩 shallow beach
6 厚 [-] hòu (thick) <adj.> thick: ~衣服 thick clothes || ~被子a thick quilt || ~书a thick book
7 宽厚 [寬-] kuānhòu (generous-kind) <adj.> tolerant and generous: 心地~ a tolerant and generous mindedness || 待人~ be generous to people
8 薄 [-] báo (thin) <adj.> thin: ~裙子a thin dress || ~纸a thin paper || ~被子a thin quilt
9 超薄 [-] chāobáo (super-thin) <adj.> ultra-thin: ~笔记本 a ultra-thin laptop || ~手机a ultra-thin mobile phone
10 扁 [-] biǎn (flat) <adj.> flat: ~嘴/脸/鼻子a flat mouth/face/nose || ~盒子 a flat box
11 扁平 [-] biǎnpíng (flat-level) <adj.> flat: 身体~ a flat body || ~人物 a flat character || ~化 flattening

Tip:

1 人很浅 and 水很深: 人很浅 means a person is very shallow/superficial or naive. 水很深 means 'there is too much non-public information, which outsiders can hardly get (and if you are not cautious, you could suffer greatly.)'

Exercises:

Part I: Translate the following phrases into English and then answer the questions.

深洞: ________________________________
浅水: ________________________________
厚衣服: ________________________________
薄被子: ________________________________
目光深邃: ________________________________
待人宽厚: ________________________________
深不可测: ________________________________
扁平化: ________________________________
超薄电脑: ________________________________
幽深的小路: ________________________________

1 你觉得待人宽厚是优点还是缺点? 为什么?

____

2 你喜不喜欢跟深不可测的人做朋友?

____

3 你觉得世界是扁平化的吗? 为什么?

____

4 你觉得苹果公司的超薄电脑是否好用?

____

Theme 216: Thick, thin, fat 粗, 细, 胖 (cū, xì, pàng)

1 粗 [-] cū (coarse, thick, stout) <adj.> thick, burly, stout: 胳膊 (gēbo) ~ burly arms || ~树 a thick tree || ~绳子 a stout cord
2 粗壮 [-壯] cūzhuàng (thick-sturdy) <adj.> sturdy, stout: ~的胳膊 sturdy arms || 身材~ The body is stout. || 四肢~ stout limbs
3 五大三粗 [-] wǔdà sāncū (5-big-3-thick) <idiom> big and tall, stalwart: 长得~ someone looks stalwart || ~的小伙子 a stalwart man
4 细 [細] xì (fine, thin) <adj.> thin, slender: ~如牛毛 be fine as cow hairs || ~腰 a slender waist || ~腿 thin legs
5 纤细 [纖細] xiānxì (slender-slim) <adj.> thin, slim: ~的手 slim hands || 感情~ delicate affections || ~的线 a thin thread
6 臃肿 [-腫] yōngzhǒng (corpulent-swollen) <adj.> swollen, chunky: 机构 (jīgòu) ~ organizational overstaffing || 身材~ a chunky body

7 胖 [-] pàng (fat) <adj.> fat, stout, plump: ~姑娘a chunky girl || 长~ put on weight
8 胖乎乎 [-] pànghūhū (fat-*suffix-reduplication*) <adj.> chubby, pudgy: ~的脸 chubby cheeks || 长得 ~ sb. looks chubby || ~的阿姨 a chubby aunt
9 富态 [-態] fùtài (wealthy-looking) <adj.> stout, portly: ~的老太太 a stout old lady || 长得~ sb. is plump
10 瘦 [-] shòu (thin, slim) <adj.> thin: ~老头 a thin old man || 累~了 lose weight because of tiredness || ~了一圈 lost a lot of weight
11 骨感 [-] gǔgǎn (bone-feeling) <adj.> bony, skinny: ~美 skinny beauty || ~女生 a skinny girl || 现实很~. The reality is very skinny.
12 瘦小 [-] shòuxiǎo (thin-small) <adj.> thin and small: 身材~ a thin and small body || 长得~ short and skinny || ~的身子 a thin and small body
13 干瘦 [乾-] gānshòu (bony-thin) <adj.> bony, skinny: ~的手 bony hands || ~的老年人 skinny elders
14 骨瘦如柴 [-] gǔshòurúchái (bone-think-like-stick) <idiom> as thin as a lash, scrawny: ~的老人 a scrawny elder

Tips:

1 粗 (cū), 精 (jīng), 糙 (cāo): Their meanings, 'thick,' 'delicate' and 'rough' are all derived from the quality of rice, namely 'unpolished rice,' 'fine rice' and 'coarse rice.'
2 楚王好细腰, 宫中多饿死 (Chǔ wáng hào xì yāo, gōng zhōng duō è sǐ): It means '(Since) Duke Chu loves women with a slim waist, many women in the palace died of starvation.' This saying shows that Chinese women's figure did not even belong to them, not to mention their egos.

Exercises:

Part I: Read the following words and then answer the questions.

骨感、纤细、五大三粗、粗壮、瘦小、干瘦、骨瘦如柴、富态、胖乎乎、臃肿

1.上面哪些词可以用来形容一个人"很瘦"?

____

2 上面哪些词可以用来形容一个人"身材偏胖"?

____

3 哪两个词也是形容"瘦," 但是中国人认为这样的女性很美?

____

4 写出粗、细的反义词 (antonym)

____

Theme 217: Straight, upright 直, 正 (zhí, zhèng)

1 正 [-] zhèng (central, upright) <adj.> upright: 摆 ~ set right || 放得~ put right || 方向~ the direction is right

2 端正 [-] duānzhèng (straight-upright) <adj.> proper: 态度~ correct attitude || 五官~ have regular features || 品行~ having good conduct, well-behaved

3 周正 [-] zhōuzhèng (regular-straight) <adj.> regular: 这个人长得很~ this person has regular features || 把帽子戴~ put your hat on straight

4 方方正正 [-] fāngfāngzhèngzhèng (square-*reduplication*-straight-*reduplication*) <idiom> square: ~的脸盘 a square face || ~的石头 a square stone

5 对称 [對稱] duìchèn (opposing-match) <adj.> symmetrical: 动作~ symmetrical movement || 左右 ~ bilateral symmetry || ~的图形 symmetrical pattern

6 匀称 [-稱] yúnchèn (even-match) <adj.> symmetric, trim, well-proportioned: 身材~ a trim figure || 比例 (bǐlì) ~ well-proportioned || 排列~ a perfect symmetry

7 偏 [-] piān (leaning) <adj.> wide from the edge: 这张画挂~了. This painting is wide from the edge.

8 歪 [-] wāi (not straight, wry) <adj.> slanting, tilted: ~着头 tilt their heads || 身正不怕影子~. A straight foot is not afraid of a crooked shoe.

9 斜 [-] xié (tilted) <adj.> slanting, inclined: 西~ inclined toward the West || ~坡 slope || ~眼睛 slanting eyes

10 倾斜 [傾-] qīngxié (inclined-tilted) <adj.> slant, inclined: ~着身子 inclined someone's body || 向前~ inclined forward

11 东倒西歪 [東---] dōngdǎoxīwāi (eastern-fall-western-slant) <idiom> reel right and left, lying on all sides: 这个人喝醉了, 走路~. The drunkard staggered along the road || ~ 的房子 a tumbledown house

12 横七竖八 [橫-豎-] héngqīshùbā (horizontal-7-vertical-8) <idiom> in disorder: ~地倒在地上 falling down the floor in disorder || 写字写得 ~ write down characters in disorder

13 直 [-] (straight) <adj.> straight: ~路 a straight road || ~线 a straight line || 腿~ straight legs

14 笔直 [筆-] bǐzhí (pen-straight) <adj.> perfectly straight, upright: ~的街道 a perfectly straight street || 站得~ stay upright || ~地坐着 sit down upright

15 垂直 [-] chuízhí (perpendicular-straight) <adj.> vertical: ~下降 vertically downward || ~于地平线 from vertical to horizontal || 互相~ mutually perpendicular

16 弯 [彎] wān (bend) <adj.> bent, winding: ~路 winding course, crooked road, tortuous path || ~月亮 the curved moon || ~眉毛 curved eyebrows

17 弯曲 [彎-] wānqǔ (bend-curve) <adj.> curved, bending: ~的道路 winding roads || ~的头发 curved hair || ~的小河 a bending creek

18 曲折 [-] qǔzhé (crooked-zigzag) <adj.> zigzag, tortuous: 故事~ intricate plots || ~的道路 tortuous roads

19 蜿蜒 [-] wānyán (wriggling) <adj.> zigzag, creeping: ~的河流 creeping rivers || ~的小路 zigzag roads

20 迂回曲折 [-] yūhuíqǔzhé (roundabout-zigzag) <idiom> twists and turns: ~的道路 a winding road

21 卷曲 [捲-] juǎnqū (rolled-curved) <adj.> curved: 头发 ~ curved hair

22 皱巴巴 [皺--] zhòubābā (wrinkled-*suffix-reduplication*) <adj.> wrinkled, crumpled: ~的西服 a crumpled suit || ~的纸币 crumpled bills || 皮肤~ wrinkled skin

23 反 [-] fǎn (turn over, opposite) <adj.> opposite, reverse: ~着拿 hold upside down || 读~了 read in an opposite order || ~面 the reverse side

Tips:

1 歪 (wāi): 歪 is a syssemantograph character and its meaning comes directly from its two components, 不 (not) and 正 (straight.)

2 你想歪了: It means 'what's gotten into you?' or 'you are talking dirty.'

3 反: Its meaning comes from 厂 (hǎn, rock shelter) and 又 (hand,) i. e., 'to turn over (a hand.)' Its original meaning is still found in words such as 易如反掌 (yìrúfǎnzhǎng, easy-as-turn over-palm, as easy as pie.)

Exercises:

Part I: Read the following words and then answer the questions.

皱巴巴、卷、迂回曲折、蜿蜒、曲折、弯曲、笔直、横七竖八、匀称、对称、方方正正、周正、端正

1.你喜欢卷发还是直发?

____

2 他长得很"周正"跟他长得很"端庄," 意思差不多吗?

____

3 你觉得这个人长得"身材匀称"跟"身材对称," 哪个中文表达更准确?

____

4 如果衣服洗完以后皱巴巴的, 你穿不穿? 为什么?

____

5 你喜欢在笔直的高速上开车, 还是喜欢在弯曲的山路上开车? 为什么?

____

6 美国华盛顿有没有一个方方正正的广场?

____

7 在你们国家有没有一条非常有名的河, 在谷歌地图上的形状迂回曲折?

____

8 你觉得上面哪些词可以用来描写 (miáoxiě, describe) 长城?

____

Source: Wikimedia Commons. Photography by Ahazan.

Theme 218: Round, square, surface 圆, 方, 表面 (yuán, fāng, biǎomiàn)

1 凹 [-] āo (concave) <adj.> hollow, sunken: ~进去 concave, dent, cave in || 这张床中间~下去了. This bed sags in the middle.

2 低洼 [-窪] dīwā (low-deep pond) <adj.> low-lying: ~地带 low-lying areas || 地势~ low-lying

3 凸 [-] tū (convex, protruded) <adj.> protruded, raised: 上~下凹 a raised top and a concave bottom || ~凹不平full of bumps and holes

4 尖 [-] jiān (pointed) <adj.> pointed, sharp: ~下巴 a pointed chin || ~鼻子 a sharp nose || ~嘴巴 a sharp mouth

5 秃 [禿] tū (bald) <adj.> bald, bare: ~顶 a bald forehead || ~脑袋a bald head || ~树 bare trees

6 平 [-] píng (gentle, flat, level) <adj.> flat, even: 地面不~ uneven ground || ~地 flat ground

7 平坦 [-] píngtǎn (flat-level) <adj.> flat, plate: 地面~ flat floor || ~的道路 a flat road || ~的地方 a plate place

8 凹凸不平 [-] āotūbúpíng (concave-convex-not-flat) <idiom> uneven: ~的路 uneven roads

9 高低不平 [-] gāodībúpíng (high-low-not-flat) <idiom> uneven: ~的山路 uneven mountain roads

10 陡峭 [-] dǒuqiào (steep-rugged) <adj.> steep: ~的大山 steep mountains || 山路~ steep mountain path

11 起伏 [-] qǐfú (raise-fall) <adj.> rolling, waved: 波浪~ fluctuant wave || 情绪(qíngxù) ~ up-and-down emotion || 上下~ up-and-down

12 崎岖 [-嶇] qíqū (rough, uneven) <adj.> rugged, rough: 山路~ the rugged mountain road || ~的小路 a rough road

13 方 [-] fāng (parallel, square) <adj.> square: ~形 square || ~盒子a square box || ~桌子 a square table

14 四四方方 [-] sìsìfāngfāng (4-square-shape) <idiom> the shape of a true square, cube: ~的盒子 a box with the shape of real square || 叠 (dié) 得~ fold up sth. into cubes

15 圆 [圓] yuán (round) <adj.> round: ~形 round figure || ~脸 round face || ~眼睛 round eyes

16 圆滚滚 [圓滾滾] yuángǔngǔn (round-rolling) <adj.> chubby, plump: ~的身子 a chubby body || ~的西瓜 a round watermelon || 鸡蛋~的. Eggs are round.

17 椭圆 [橢圓] tuǒyuán (oval-round) <adj./n.> oval: ~轨道 (guǐdào) an oval track || ~形 an oval figure || 画~ draw an oval

18 扁圆 [-圓] biǎnyuán (flat-round) <adj.> oblate, oval: ~形 oblateness

19 拱形 [-] gǒngxíng (arch-shape) <非谓形容词> arched: ~屋顶 an arched roof || ~门 an arched door || ~长廊 an arched corridor

20 弧形 [-] húxíng (arc-shape) <非谓形容词> arc-shaped: ~桥 an arc-shaped bridge || 大/圆~ a big arc-shape/a circular arc

21 月牙形 [-] yuèyáxíng (moon-tooth-shape) <非谓形容词> crescent-shaped: ~的阳台 a crescent-shaped balcony

22 半月形 [-] bànyuèxíng (half-moon-shape) <非谓形容词> half-moon-shaped: ~的桌子 a half-moon-shaped table || ~的海湾 a half-moon-shaped gulf

Tips:

1 方 and 圆: The ancient Chinese thought the heaven (天) is round (圆) and the Earth (地) is square (方,) and therefore had a saying 天圆地方. There is another saying related to 方 and 圆, 没有规矩 (guījǔ, compasses and carpenter's square,) 不成方圆 which means 'if there is no rule, one cannot accomplish anything' or 'if one does not follow rules, he cannot accomplish anything.'

2 凹 and 凸: They are pictographic characters, meaning 'concave' and 'convex,' respectively.

Exercises:

Part I: Read the following words and use the appropriate words to describe the things given.

四四方方、圆滚滚、崎岖不平、上下起伏、凸凹不平、高低不平、平坦、低洼、陡峭

书桌: ____________________

西瓜: ____________________

山路: ____________________

群山: ____________________

质量很差的路面: ____________________

高速公路: ____________________

Part II: Translate the following phrases into English and then answer the questions.

椭圆、扁圆、拱形、半月形、月牙形、弧形

1 哪些词有圆形的意思?

---

2 哪些词有半圆形的意思?

---

3 下面这座桥是什么形状的? 在西方常见吗?

Source: https://commons.wikimedia.org/wiki/File:1400%E5%B9%B4%E5%8E%86%E5%8F%B2%E7%9A%84%E8%B5%B5%E5%B7%9E%E6%A1%A5_zhao_zhou_qiao_-_panoramio.jpg. Photography by wanghongliu.

Theme 219: Color 颜色 (yánsè)

1 红 [紅] hóng (red) <adj.> red: ~太阳 the red sun || ~灯 a red light || ~衣服 red clothes
2 粉红 [-紅] fěnhóng (pink-red) <adj.> pink: ~花 pink flowers || ~衬衫 (chènshān) a pink shirt
3 浅红 [淺紅] qiǎnhóng (light-red) <adj.> light red: ~色 a light red color || 颜色~ light red
4 枣红 [棗紅] zǎohóng (date-red) <adj.> purplish red: ~马 a purplish red horse || ~毛衣a purplish sweater
5 鲜红 [鮮紅] xiānhóng (bright-red) <adj.> bright red: ~的血 bright red blood || ~的大字 bright red characters || ~的嘴唇 bright red lips
6 紫红 [-紅] zǐhóng (purple-red) <adj.> purplish red: ~头发 purplish red hair || ~色 purplish red color || ~花 purplish red flowers

7 火红 [-紅] huǒhóng (fire-red) <adj.> fiery-red: ~的裙子a fiery-red skirt || ~太阳 a flaming sun || ~的青春 a fiery-red youth

8 通红 [-紅] tōnghóng (wholly-red) <adj.> very red: 满脸~ face reddens all over || 两眼 ~ red eyes || ~的太阳 the red sun

9 黄 [黃] huáng (yellow) <adj.> yellow: ~皮肤 yellow skin || ~头发 yellow hair || ~军装 the yellow uniform

10 枯黄 [-黃] kūhuáng (withered-yellow) <adj.> withered and yellow, brown: 脸色~ a withered and yellow face || ~的树叶 brown leaves

11 淡黄 [-黃] dànhuáng (light-yellow) <adj.> light yellow: ~颜色 a light yellow color || 面色 ~ a light yellow face || ~的夕阳 a light yellow sunset

12 米黄 [-黃] mǐhuáng (cream-yellow) <adj.> cream-colored: ~毛衣 a cream-colored sweater

13 嫩黄 [-黃] nènhuáng (tender-yellow) <adj.> bright yellow: ~的花朵 bright yellow flowers

14 鹅黄 [鵝黃] é'huáng (goose-yellow) <adj.> light/goose yellow: ~连衣裙a light/goose dress

15 土黄 [-黃] tǔhuáng (clay-yellow) <adj.> yellowish brown: ~大衣 a yellowish brown coat || 面色~ a yellowish brown face

16 深黄 [-黃] shēnhuáng (deep-yellow) <adj.> deep yellow: ~色 a deep yellow color

17 蓝 [藍] lán (blue) <adj.> blue: ~眼睛 blue eyes || ~裙子a blue skirt || ~猫a blue cat

18 海蓝 [-藍] hǎilán (sea-blue) <adj.> navy blue: ~裤子 navy blue pants

19 浅蓝 [淺藍] qiǎnlán (light-blue) <adj.> light blue: ~大衣a light blue coat

20 深蓝 [-藍] shēnlán (deep-blue) <adj.> dark blue: ~的天空 a dark blue sky

21 青 [-] qīng (cyan, turquoise) <adj.> cyan, green: ~草 green grass || ~衣 cyan clothing || ~苹果 green apples

22 淡青 [-] dànqīng (light-turquoise) <adj.> light greenish blue: ~色 a light greenish blue color

23 绿 [綠] lǜ (green) <adj.> green: ~草 green grass || ~灯green lights || ~衣服 a green coat

24 碧绿 [-綠] bìlǜ (bluish green-green) <adj.> azure green: ~的小草 green grass || ~的河水 green water

25 绿油油 [綠--] lǜyóuyóu (green-shiny-*reduplication*) <adj.> shiny green, glossy and green: ~的树叶 shiny green leaves || ~的蔬菜 shiny green vegetables

26 墨绿 [-綠] mòlǜ (ink-green) <adj.> blackish green: ~的叶子 blackish green leaves

27 草绿 [-綠] cǎolǜ (grass-green) <adj.> grass-green: ~色 a grass-green color

28 紫 [-] zǐ (purple) <adj.> purple: ~花 purple flowers || ~茄子 (qiézi) purple eggplants || ~衣a purple clothing

29 浅紫 [淺-] qiǎnzǐ (light-purple) <adj.> light purple: ~色 a light purple color

30 褐色 [-] hèsè (brown-color) <n.> brown: ~的眼睛 brown eyes || ~头发 brown hair

31 深褐 [-] shēnhè (dark-brown) <adj.> dark brown: ~色 a dark brown color

32 棕褐 [-] zōnghè (palm-brown) <adj.> medium brown: ~色 a medium brown color

33 浅棕 [淺-] qiǎnzōng (light-brown) <adj.> light brown: ~色a light brown

34 白 [-] bái (white) <adj.> white: ~ 色 a white color || ~纸a (white) paper || 黑 ~ black and white || ~天 daytime
35 白色 [-] báisè (white-color) <n.> white color: ~的鞋 white-colored shoes || ~衣服 a white-color coat || ~圣诞节a white Christmas
36 纯白 [純-] chúnbái (pure-white) <adj.> pure white: ~衣服 a pure white coat
37 雪白 [-] xuěbái (snow-white) <adj.> snowy white: ~的牙齿 snowy white teeth || ~的纸 snowy white paper || ~的头发 snowy white hair
38 银白 [銀-] yínbái (silver-white) <adj.> silvery white: ~的月光 silvery white moonlight || ~的世界 a silvery white world
39 乳白 [-] rǔbái (milk-white) <adj.> milky white: ~的牛奶 milky white milk

40 灰 [-] huī (gray) <adj.> gray white: ~眼睛 gray white eyes || ~衣服 a gray white clothing || ~兔 a gray white rabbit
41 浅灰 [淺-] qiǎnhuī (light-gray) <adj.> light gray: ~色 a light gray color
42 银灰 [銀-] yínhuī (silver-gray) <adj.> silvery gray: ~的头发 silvery gray hair || ~色a silvery gray color
43 深灰 [-] shēnhuī (dark-gray) <adj.> dark gray: ~大衣 a dark gray coat || ~T恤 a dark gray T-shirt

44 黑 [-] hēi (black) <adj.> black: ~眼睛 black eyes || ~鞋 black shoes || ~烟 black smoke
45 乌黑 [烏-] wūhēi (crow-black) <adj.> pitch black: ~的头发 pitch black || ~的眼睛 pitch black eyes || ~的皮鞋 pitch black shoes
46 黝黑 [-] yǒuhēi (light black-black) <adj.> dark: ~的皮肤 dark skin || ~的泥土 dark Earth || ~的脸 a dark face
47 黑乎乎 [-] hēihūhū (black-*suffix-reduplication*) <adj.> dark: ~的屋子 a dark room
48 黑暗 [-] hēi'àn (dark-black) <adj.> dark: ~的房间 a dark room || ~的世界 a dark world || ~的时代 a dark era
49 暗 [-] àn (dark, dull) <adj.> dark, dull: ~蓝色 dark blue || 灯光~ dim light

50 深 [-] shēn (deep) <adj.> deep, dark: 颜色~ a deep color || ~蓝 dark blue || ~棕色 dark brown
51 淡 [-] dàn (light) <adj.> light: ~颜色 a light color || ~黄色 light yellow || ~绿色 light green
52 浓 [濃] nóng (dense, thick) <adj.> thick, dense: ~烟 dense smoke || ~雾 heavy fog || ~云 dense cloud
53 嫩 [-] nèn (tender) <adj.> tender, bright: 颜色~ bright color || ~黄 bright yellow || ~绿 bright green
54 浅 [淺] qiǎn (shallow, light) <adj.> light: ~颜色 a light color || ~蓝色 light blue || ~绿色 light green
55 彩色 [-] cǎisè (colorful-color) <n.> colorful color: ~照片 color photos || ~电视机 color television set || 三种~ three kinds of color
56 迷彩 [-] mícǎi (deceiving-color) <adj.> camouflage: ~服 camouflage clothing || ~布 camouflage cloth
57 花 [-] huā (colorful) <adj.> colorful: 她穿的衣服太~了. She dressed too colorfully.

58 鲜艳 [鮮豔] xiānyàn (fresh-bright) <adj.> bright-colored: ~的花朵 bright-colored flowers || ~的裙子 a bright-colored dress || ~的玫瑰 bright-colored roses

59 大红大绿 [-紅-綠] dàhóngdàlǜ (deep-red-deep-green) <idiom> gaudy and showy: ~的衣服 gaudy and showy clothing || ~的颜色 a gaudy and showy color

60 五颜六色 [-顏--] wǔyánliùsè (5-color-6-color) <idiom> multicolored, colorful: ~的衣服 multicolored clothing || ~的花 multicolored flowers || 灯光~ colorful lights

61 花花绿绿 [--綠綠] huāhuālùlǜ (colorful-*reduplication*-green-*reduplication*) <idiom> colorful, multicolored: ~的衣服 colorful clothing || ~的世界a colorful world || 穿得~ be colorfully dressed

62 淡雅 [-] dànyǎ (light-elegant) <adj.> quietly elegant: ~的颜色 a quietly elegant color || ~的风格 a quietly color style

63 亮 [-] liàng (bright) <adj./v.> bright, on: 红灯~了. The red light is on. || 眼睛~ bright eyes || 天~了day breaks

64 明亮 [-] míngliàng (brilliant-bright) <adj.> bright: 眼睛~ bright eyes || ~的阳光 bright sunlight || ~的屋子 a bright room

65 灿烂 [燦爛] cànlàn (effulgent-radiant) <adj.> glorious, splendid: 阳光~ brightly shining sunlight || ~的笑脸 a bright smile || ~的文化 a splendid culture

66 昏暗 [-] hūn'àn (dim-dark) <adj.> dim, darky: ~的灯光 dim light || 光线~ dusky || ~的小巷 dark alleys

67 朦胧 [-朧] ménglóng (hazy, obscure) <adj.> misty, dim, hazy: ~的月光 misty moonlight || 夜色~ a hazy night || ~诗a dim poetry

68 清楚 [-] qīngchǔ (clear-distinct) <adj.> clear, distinct, obvious: 说得~ express clearly || 看~ see sth. clearly || 事实~ an obvious fact

69 清晰 [-] qīngxī (clear-legible) <adj.> clear, distinct: ~的脚印 clear footprints || ~的思路 clear mind || ~的声音 distinct sound

70 模糊 [-] móhú (blurry-opaque) <adj.> blurred, obscure: 视线~ a blurred vision || 图像~ image blurring || ~不清 obscure

Tips:

1 颜 and 色: 颜 originally means 'the area between eyebrows' since it is related to 页 (head, face.) The original meaning of 颜 still exists in some words such as 红颜 (red-face, beautiful woman) and a very popular contemporary word 颜值 (appearance, looking.) 色 originally means 'facial expression,' which is still kept in words such as 喜形于色 (happiness-expressed-by-facial expression.) In brief, both 颜 and 色 are originally related to (the color/expression of) face.

2 糸 (mì): Many colors are related to 糸 (mì, silk,) for example, 红 (紅, red,) 绿 (綠, green) 紫 (purple) and 纯 (純, pure.)

3 Chinese classification of colors: 赤, 橙, 黄, 绿, 青, 蓝, 紫 (chì, chéng, huáng, lǜ, qīng, lán, zǐ) are Chinese conventional colors, meaning 'red, orange, yellow, green, cyan/verdant, blue, purple.' Among all colors, 紫 (purple) and 红 (red) are noble or royal colors. For example, the Forbidden City is also called 紫禁城 (purple-forbidden-city) although technically speaking, the 紫 here refers to a star in the middle of the sky. 大红大紫 means '(of a person) very famous, in the limelight.'

Exercises:

Part I: Translate the following phrases into English and then answer the questions.

火红的太阳 ________________

灿烂的阳光 ________________

深蓝的天空 ________________

洁白的月亮 ________________

朦胧的月色 ________________

昏暗的灯光 ________________

绿油油的草地 ________________

五颜六色的花朵 ________________

清晰的思路 ________________

明亮的眼睛 ________________

乌黑的头发 ________________

两眼通红 ________________

脸色枯黄 ________________

1 上面哪些短语可以描写夜晚的自然景象 (natural scene)?

____

2 哪些短语可以用来描写一个春季白天的自然景象?

____

3 上面哪些短语可以描写人?

____

4 你觉得自己写文章的时候是不是常常思路清晰?

____

5 如果一个中国人"脸色枯黄," 表示他/她健康还是不健康?

____

6 一般来说什么情况下你会"两眼通红"?

____

Part II: Write Chinese words with their English translations.

1 写出四种你喜欢的 ________________________________

2 写出四种你喜欢的"绿"颜色: ________________________________

3 写出四种你喜欢的"黄"颜色: ________________________________

Theme 220: Clear, dull 清, 浊 (qīng, zhuó)

1 纯净 [純淨] chúnjìng (pure-clean) <adj.> pure: ~水 pure water || ~物 pure substance || ~的人 pure people
2 清澈 [-] qīngchè (clear-limpid) <adj.> limpid, clear: ~的湖水 limpid lake water || 音色~ clear sound || ~的眼睛 clear eyes
3 清亮 [-] qīngliàng (clear-bright) <adj.> clear, limpid: ~的嗓音 clear voice || ~的眼睛 clear eyes || ~的月光 clear moonlight
4 清 [-] qīng (clear) <adj.> clear: 看得~ visible || ~水 clear water
5 透明 [-] tòumíng (pass through-light) <adj.> transparent: ~的玻璃 (bōli) transparent glass || ~的墙壁 (qiángbì) a transparent wall || ~的人 transparent people
6 浑浊 [渾濁] húnzhuó (muddy-mucky) <adj.> muddy, turbid: ~的空气 foul air, stale air || ~的水 turbid water
7 响 [響] xiǎng (loud) <adj./ v.> loud, ring: 电话~了. The phone rang. || 铃~了. The bell rang. || 太~了 too loud
8 亮 [-] liàng (bright, clear) <adj.> bright: 房间里很~. The room is very bright. || 天~了. It's light already. || 她的嗓子 (sǎngzi) 真~. She has a resonant voice.
9 响亮 [響-] xiǎngliàng (loud-clear) <adj.> resounding: 提出~的口号 raise a clarion call || ~的回答a loud and clear reply || 声音~ a resounding voice

10 尖 [-] jiān (pointed) <adj.> sharp, high: 声音~ a sharp sound || ~嗓子 (sǎngzi) a high-pitched voice
11 尖声尖气 [-聲-氣] jiānshēngjiānqì (shrill-sound-shrill-voice) <idiom> in a shrill voice: ~地说话 speak in a shrill voice || ~的声音 a shrill voice || 说话~ talk in a shrill voice
12 细 [細] xì (little, small, fine) <adj.> high-pitched, gentle: 声音 ~ a high-pitched voice || ~声~语a very gentle voice
13 轻 [輕] qīng (light) <adj.> soft, quiet: 声音~ voice is soft || ~声 a soft voice || 脚步~ walk quietly
14 细声细气 [細聲細氣] xìshēngxìqì (gentle-sound-gentle-voice) <idiom> in a soft voice: ~地回答 speak in a soft voice || 说话~ talk in a soft voice
15 粗声粗气 [-聲-氣] cūshēngcūqì (coarse-sound-hoarse-voice) <idiom> in an injured voice: ~地说 speak in an injured voice || ~的声音 an injured voice || ~的大嗓门 an injured sound
16 低沉 [-] dīchén (low-deep) <adj.> deep: ~的声音 a deep voice || ~地说话 speak in a deep voice
17 沙哑 [-啞] shāyǎ (husky-hoarse) <adj.> hoarse, cracked: 声音~ voice is hoarse || 嗓子~ a hoarse voice || ~的声音a cracked voice

18 动听 [動聽] dòngtīng (attractive-to ear) <adj.> beautiful, sweet: ~的音乐 beautiful music || 说得~ speak beautifully
19 好听 [-聽] hǎotīng (pleasant-to ear) <adj.> pleasant: ~的声音 a pleasant voice || 唱歌~ good at singing || 说得~ sounds pleasant
20 悦耳 [-] yuè'ěr (pleasing-to ear) <adj.> sweet, wonderful: ~的歌声 wonderful songs || 音乐~ music is sweet
21 清脆 [-] qīngcuì (clear-crisp) <adj.> clear: ~的声音 a clear voice || ~的笑声 a clear laughter || ~的铃声 the clear bell

22 抑扬顿挫 [-揚頓-] yìyángdùncuò (fall-rise-pause-cadence) <idiom> speak in measured tone, cadence: ~的声音 a voice's cadence || ~的演讲 (yǎnjiǎng) the cadence of a speech
23 难听 [難聽] nántīng (unpleasant-to ear) <adj.> harsh, awful, unpleasant: 名字 ~ an awful name || 声音 ~ an unpleasant sound || ~的话 unpleasant words

Tip:

1 水至清则无鱼: It means 'if the water is too clear, there are no fish.' The true intent of this saying lies in the following words "人至察则无徒" (rén zhì chá zé wú tú, people-most-critical-then-no-peers), which means 'an overly critical man keeps no friends,' in other words, 'a man should not be too critical of his friends.' This is the Chinese golden rule on how to treat friends.

Exercises:

Part I: Read the following words and then answer the questions.

悦耳、清脆、低沉、沙哑、粗声粗气、清澈、透明、清亮、细声细气、尖声尖气、响亮、纯净、浑浊、抑扬顿挫

1 上面哪些词可以用来形容"水很干净"?

____

2 上面哪个词可以形容"水不干净"?

____

3 上面哪些词可以用来形容"女性声音"?

____

4 上面哪些词可以用来形容"男性声音"?

____

5 美国哪个总统喜欢抑扬顿挫地发表演讲?

____

Theme 221: Fragrant, smelly, taste 香, 臭, 味道 (xiāng, chòu, wèidào)

1 香 [-] xiāng (fragrant) <adj.> appetizing, fragrant: ~水 perfume || ~味 fragrance || ~气 fragrance
2 清香 [-] qīngxiāng (freshing-fragrant) <n.> faint and sweet scent: ~扑鼻 a sweet scent reaches the nostrils || 淡淡的~ light fragrance || 发出~ send forth a delightful fragrance
3 芳香 [-] fāngxiāng (fragrant grass-fragrant) <n./adj.> aroma, fragrance: 泥土的~ the fragrance of the Earth || 散发~ shed the fragrance || ~的气味 aroma, fragrance

4 香喷喷 [-噴噴] xiāngpēnpēn (fragrant-spurting-*reduplication*) <adj.> sweet-smelling, delicious-smelling: ~的味道 sweet-smelling fragrance || ~的饭菜 delicious-smelling food

5 香气扑鼻 [-氣撲-] xiāngqìpūbí (fragrant-smell-assail-nostril) <idiom> sweet-scented, a sweet smell greeted us: ~的甜瓜 sweet-scented melons || ~的花露水 sweet-scented floral water || 闻起来~ smells sweet

6 臭 [-] chòu (smell, stink) <adj.> smelly, rotten: ~味儿 odor, foul smell, stink || ~袜子 smelly socks || ~鸡蛋 rotten eggs

7 难闻 [難聞] nánwén (unpleasant-smell) <adj.> smell unpleasant: ~的气味 unpleasant smell

8 臭烘烘 [-] chòuhōnghōng (stinky-*suffix*) <adj.> foul-smelling: 全身~ the whole body stinks || ~的味道 a nasty smell

9 刺鼻 [-] cìbí (stimulate-nose) <adj.> pungent: ~的味道 a pungent smell

10 臭气熏天 [-氣燻-] chòuqìxūntiān (smelly-odor-stifle-heaven) <idiom> it smells to high heaven: ~的房间 a smelly room

11 腥 [-] xīng (fishy odor) <adj.> fishy smell: ~味 a fishy smell || ~气 a fishy smell

12 酸 [-] suān (sour) <adj.> sour: ~果子 sour fruits || ~奶 yogurt || 味道~ a sour taste

13 酸溜溜 [-] suānliūliū (sour-*suffix*) <adj.> sour, tart: ~的味道 a sour taste || ~地说 says sourly

14 甜 [-] tián (sweet) <adj.> sweet: ~菜 sweet food || ~点 dessert || ~食 dessert

15 香甜 [-] xiāngtián (fragrant-sweet) <adj.> fragrant and sweet: ~的食物 sweet food || 吃得~ a good appetite || 睡得~ sleep well

16 甜丝丝 [-絲絲] tiánsīsī (fragrant-*suffix*) <adj.> pleasantly sweet: ~的味道 sweet taste

17 苦 [-] kǔ (bitter) <adj.> bitter: ~瓜 bitter melon || 药 ~. Pills are bitter. || 味道~ a bitter taste

18 苦涩 [-澀] kǔsè (bitter-astringent) <adj.> bitter: ~的海水 the bitter sea || ~的心情 the bitter mood || ~的回忆 the bitter memory

19 辣 [-] là (spicy, hot) <adj.> spicy: ~萝卜 spicy radish || ~菜 spicy food || ~味 a spicy taste

20 麻辣 [-] málà (spicy-hot) <adj.> spicy and hot: ~牛肉丝 sauce beef with cayenne pepper || ~小零食 spicy and hot snacks

21 咸 [鹹] xián (salty) <adj.> salty: ~菜 salted vegetable || ~水 salty water || ~鸭蛋 salted duck eggs

22 清淡 [-] qīngdàn (light-bland) <adj.> light, slack: 吃得~ eat light || 饮食~ a light diet || 生意~ a slack business

23 好吃 [-] hǎochī (pleasant-eat) <adj.> delicious, tasty: ~的东西 delicious food || 十分 ~ very delicious || 大米~. Rice is delicious.

24 开胃 [開-] kāiwèi (stimulate-appetite) <adj.> appetizing: ~菜 appetizer || ~的食物 appetizing food

25 可口 [-] kěkǒu (agreeable-taste) <adj.> tasty, delicious: ~的饭菜 tasty food || 吃得~ Enjoy the tasty food.

26 爽口 [-] shuǎngkǒu (delight-taste) <adj.> tasty and refreshing: ~的蔬菜 (shūcài) tasty and refreshing vegetables

27 鲜美 [鮮-] xiānměi (fresh-delicious) <adj.> fresh and delicious: ~的水果 delicious fruits || 味道~ a delicious taste

28 鲜 [鮮] xiān (fresh) <adj.> fresh and delicious: 尝~ have a taste of what is in season || 味道~ a delicious taste || 汤很~. Soup is delicious.
29 难吃 [難-] nánchī (unpleasant-eat) <adj.> taste bad: 这个菜很~. This dish tastes bad.
30 油腻 [-膩] yóunì (oily-greasy) <adj.> oily: ~的菜 oily food

Tips:

1 香: It means 'fragrant' and has nothing to do with 日 (sun,) which should be 甘 (gān, sweet.)
2 香喷喷 and 喷香: They have almost the same meaning, 'delicious-smelling,' however, the 喷 is pronounced differently. In 香喷喷, the 喷 is pronounced 'pēn' while in 喷香 'pèn.'
3 臭: The meaning of 臭 (smell, stinky) comes from 自 (nose) and 犬 (dog) because dogs have the sharpest nose.
4 腥: It means 'fishy smelly.' 偷腥 (tōuxīng) means '(of a male) has extra marital affairs' and therefore comes a saying 哪个猫儿不吃腥/哪有不吃腥的猫 which means 'a leopard cannot change its spots' or 'all men lust.'
5 油腻: It means 'oily and greasy.' All say that Chinese cuisine is 油腻, however, the Chinese people even today are not fat. Why? Some say drinking tea helps to digest 油腻.

Exercises:

Part I: Read the following words and then answer the questions.

开胃、可口、爽口、鲜美、清淡、油腻、麻辣、咸、香甜、甜、香喷喷、酸、刺鼻、腥、臭烘烘、苦、清香、方向、香气扑鼻、甜丝丝

1 哪些词可以描写"香味"?

____

2 哪些词可以描写"臭味"?

____

3 哪些词可以描写"中国菜的味道"?

____

4 哪些词可以描写"一个菜好吃"?

____

5 哪些词可以描写"一个菜难吃"?

____

Theme 222: Hard, soft, heavy, light, sharp, dull 硬, 软, 重, 轻, 尖锐, 钝 (yìng, ruǎn, zhòng, qīng, jiānruì, dùn)

1 柔 [-] róu (supple) <adj.> soft, kind: ~发 soft hair || ~枝 soft limber || 性格 ~ a kind personality

2 软 [軟] ruǎn (soft) <adj.> soft: ~沙发a soft sofa || ~柿子 (shìzi) soft persimmon || ~泥巴 soft mud

3 柔软 [-軟] róuruǎn (supple-soft) <adj.> soft: ~的手 soft hands || ~的沙发 a soft sofa || 动作~ soft movements

4 软绵绵 [軟綿綿] ruǎnmiánmián (soft-cotton soft) <adj.> soft, downy: ~的身体 a soft body || ~的声音 a soft voice

5 松软 [鬆軟] sōngruǎn (loose-soft) <adj.> soft, spongy: ~的蛋糕 (dàngāo) fluffy cakes || ~的草地 the soft grass || ~的沙滩 (shātān) the soft beach

6 硬 [-] yìng (hard) <adj.> hard, stiff: 石头~ the stone is hard || 说话很~ express oneself in strong terms || ~的不行来软的. When hard tactics failed, soft methods were used.

7 坚硬 [堅-] jiānyìng (sharp-hard) <adj.> hard, stiff: ~的岩石 stiff stones || ~的骨头 hard bones

8 硬邦邦 [-] yìngbāngbāng (hard-*suffix-reduplication*) <adj.> hard, stiff: 这个馒头 (mántou) ~的, 像块石头. This steamed bun is as hard as rock.

9 烂 [爛] làn (thoroughly cooked) <adj.> well-cooked: 煮~ stew sth. until tender || 烧~ fried sth. until tender || 肉~了 well-cooked meat

10 稀烂 [-爛] xīlàn (mushy-mashed) <adj.> mashed, rotted: 踩得~ trample and crush || ~的衣服 rotted clothing

11 脆 [-] cuì (crisp) <adj.> crispy: ~萝卜 crispy radish || 苹果很~. Apples are crispy.

12 牢 [-] láo (pen for cows, firm) <adj.> firm, sturdy, solid: 关~ fasten sth. firmly || 记~ keep in mind || 根基 (gēnjī) ~ The foundation is solid.

13 耐穿 [-] nàichuān (endurable-wear) <adj.> durable: 这件衣服很~. These clothes are durable. || ~的球鞋 durable sneakers

14 耐热 [-熱] nài'rè (endurable-heat) <adj.> heat resisting, resistant: ~玻璃 heat-resistant glass || ~的花 heat-resistant flowers

15 耐用 [-] nàiyòng (endurable-use) <adj.> durable: ~的手机 a durable cellphone || ~的汽车 a durable car

16 轻 [輕] qīng (light) <adj.> light: ~箱子 a light box || 体重~ light weight || 重量~ in lightweight

17 轻飘飘 [輕飄飄] qīngpiāopiāo (light-flying-*reduplication*) <adj.> light: ~的身体 a light body || ~的气球 light balloons

18 重 [-] zhòng (heavy) <adj./v.> heavy, weight: ~箱子 a heavy box || 几斤~ weigh a few *jins* || ~五十斤 weigh 50 jins

19 沉 [-] chén (sink, heavy) <adj.> heavy: 睡得~ be in a deep sleep || 这个箱子很~. This trunk is very heavy. || 船~了. The boat sank.

20 沉重 [-] chénzhòng (heavy-weighty) <adj.> heavy: ~的脚步 heavy steps || ~的打击 a heavy blow || 心情~ with a heavy heart

21 沉甸甸 [-] chéndiàndiàn (heavy-*suffix*) <adj.> heavy: ~的包 a heavy bag || ~的脑袋 a heavy head

22 轻巧 [輕-] qīngqiǎo (light-easy) <adj.> light, easy: ~的身体 the light body || 说得~ say it easy

23 小巧 [-] xiǎoqiǎo (small-exquisite) <adj.> small and exquisite: ~的手 small and exquisite hands || 这个女孩子长得~. This girl looks small and cute.

24 轻快 [輕-] qīngkuài (light-fast) <adj.> brisk, light-footed: ~的步子 a brisk pace || ~的声音 a brisk voice || 动作~ the springy motion

25 快 [-] kuài (fast, sharp) <adj.> sharp: 这把刀不~ the knife is not very sharp || ~刀 a sharp knife
26 笨 [-] bèn (dull) <adj.> stupid, dull: ~方法 a stupid way || 脑子~ a stupid brain
27 笨重 [-] bènzhòng (cumbersome-heavy) <adj.> cumbersome, heavy: ~的家具 the heavy furniture || ~的体力劳动heavy manual labor
28 厚重 [-] hòuzhòng (thick-heavy) <adj.> dignified, thick and heavy, generous: ~的礼物 generous gifts || ~的历史 rich history
29 锋利 [鋒-] fēnglì (knife edge-sharp) <adj.> sharp: ~的刀子 a sharp knife || 说话~ talk sharply || ~的目光 sharp eyes
30 飞快 [飛-] fēikuài (fly-fast) <adj.> quick, fast: ~地跑 run quickly || 转得~ turn furiously
31 尖利 [-] jiānlì (pointed-sharp) <adj.> sharp, high-pitched: ~的钢刀 a sharp knife || 声音~ voice is high-pitched || ~的叫声 a shrill cry
32 尖 [-] jiān (pointed) <adj.> sharp: 声音~ a sharp voice || 眼~ have sharp eyes || ~叫scream
33 钝 [鈍] dùn (dull) <adj.> dull: ~刀 a dull knife || 声音~ sound is dull

Tips:

1 尖: The meaning of 尖 is 'pointed,' which can be easily guessed from the two components of 尖, namely 小 and 大. The rear is big and the front is small.
2 软绵绵, 硬邦邦, 沉甸甸, 轻飘飘: All are ABB adjectives. ABB adjectives indicate 'very A (adjective.)'
3 耐: The original form of 耐 is 耏, which is a punishment that involves shaving off one's whiskers, but the original meaning is lost in contemporary words. The current meaning of 耐 is mainly 'endure, endurable' as in words such as 忍耐 (endure,) 耐穿 and 耐用. Nike (耐克, Nàikè) shoes are 耐穿 and 耐用.
4 邦 (bāng): The meaning of 邦 is 'state,' for example '联邦' (liánbāng, federation.)
5 愚 (yú), 蠢 (chǔn), 笨 (bèn): They mean 'stupid,' 'foolish' and 'dull' respectively, and their combinations 愚蠢, 愚笨, 蠢笨 have almost the same meaning.

Exercises:

Part I: Match the following words by considering their opposite words.

1 轻________ a. 硬
2 软________ b. 重
3 尖________ c. 钝
4 轻快______ d. 笨重

Part II: Use the given bound form as a guide to help you think of other words with the same beginning character. Feel free to use your dictionary when needed. Then write down the English definition of each of the words you've written.

耐 *(patient, durable):* 耐心 *patient*

____

____

____

____

沉 *(heavy):* 深沉 *deep and heavy*

____

____

快 *(quick):* 快速 *quickly*

____

____

软 *(soft):* 柔软 *soft*

____

____

____

Part III: Translate the following Chinese into English.

1 这个蛋糕软绵绵的, 真好吃.
2 这个面包硬邦邦的, 太难吃了.
3 这双鞋穿起来轻飘飘的, 非常舒服.
4 中国小学生几乎每个人都背着一个沉甸甸的书包, 可见他们的学习压力很大.

Theme 223: Warm, cold, dry, wet, smooth 暖, 冷, 干, 湿, 滑 (nuǎn, lěng, gān, shī, huá)

1 冷 [-] lěng (cold) <adj.> cold: 天~. The weather is cold. || ~气 cold air || ~风 cold wind
2 寒冷 [-] hánlěng (chilly-cold) <adj.> cold, frigid: 天气~ a cold weather || ~的冬天 a cold winter || ~的地方 a cold place
3 冷冰冰 [-] lěngbīngbīng (cold-icy-*reduplication*) <adj.> frosty, icy: 她的手~的her hands are icy || ~的态度 an icy manner || ~的脸 a cold expression

4 严寒 [嚴-] yánhán (severe-cold) <adj./n.> severe coldness, freezing: 气候~ a harsh climate || ~的冬天 a freezing winter || 冒着~ brave a severe coldness

5 冰天雪地 [-] bīngtiānxuědì (icy-heaven-snowy-Earth) <idiom> a world of ice and snow: ~的季节 (jìjié). A season is all covered with ice and snow. || ~的世界 a world of ice and snow

6 热 [熱] rè (hot) <adj.> hot: 天气~ a hot weather || ~水 hot water || ~豆腐 hot tofu

7 热乎乎 [熱--] rèhūhū (hot-*suffix-reduplication*) <adj.> hot, warm: 心里感到~的 feel it heartwarming || ~的手 warm hands || ~的稀饭 warm porridge

8 滚烫 [滾燙] gǔntàng (boiling-hot) <adj.> boiling hot: 全身~. The whole body is scalding hot. || ~的水 the scalding hot water

9 炎热 [-熱] yánrè (scorching-hot) <adj.> burning hot: ~的夏天 a burning hot summer || 天气~ a burning hot weather || ~的沙漠 a burning hot desert

10 火辣辣 [-] huǒlàlà (fire-hot-*reduplication*) <adj.> burning: ~的太阳 the burning sun || ~的目光 hot eyes || ~地疼 a stinging pain

11 闷 [悶] mēn (gloomy, stuffy) <adj.> bored, stuffy: ~在家里 shut yourself indoors || 有什么事儿就说出来, 别~在心里 Speak out. Don't just brood over things || 打开窗户吧, 屋里太~了. Open the windows, It's too stuffy in here.

12 闷热 [悶熱] mēnrè (stuffy-hot) <adj.> stuffy: 天气~ a stuffy weather || ~的屋子 a stuffy room || ~的夜晚 a stuffy night

13 潮 [-] cháo (humid) <adj.> moist, humid: ~衣服 damp clothes || 家里~. Home is humid. || 天气~ a humid weather

14 潮湿 [-濕] cháoshī (humid-wet) <adj.> humid, moist: 空气~ the air is humid || ~的森林 the moist forests || ~的房间 a moist room

15 凉 [涼] liáng (cool) <adj.> cold, cool: ~水 cold water || 天~ cold days || 变~ cool off, cool down

16 凉快 [涼-] liángkuài (cool-pleasant) <adj.> cool: 觉得~ feel cool || 非常~ very cool || 天很~ It is quite cool.

17 阴 [陰] yīn (shady, dark) <adj.> cloudy, shady: ~天 a cloudy day || ~处 a shady place || 喜~ love shades

18 清凉 [-涼] qīngliáng (refreshing-cool) <adj.> cool and refreshing: ~的月光 the cool moonlight || ~的泉水 cool and refreshing spring water || ~的风 cool and refreshing wind

19 凉爽 [涼-] liángshuǎng (cool-happy) <adj.> nice and cool, pleasantly cool: ~的风 cool breeze || 气候 ~ a cool climate

20 暖 [-] nuǎn (warm) <adj.> warm: ~气 heating || ~水 warm water || 天~ It is warm

21 暖和 [-] nuǎnhuo (warm-mild) <adj.> warm: 车里~. It is warm in a car. || 天气~. The weather is warm. || ~的房间 a warm room

22 温暖 [溫-] wēnnuǎn (lukewarm-warm) <adj.> warm: 气候 (qìhòu) ~ a warm climate || ~的阳光 warm sunshine || 感到~ feel warm

23 暖洋洋 [-] nuǎnyángyáng (warm-*suffix-reduplication*) <adj.> warm: ~的阳光 warm sunshine || ~的房间 a warm room

24 春暖花开 [---開] chūnnuǎnhuākāi (spring-warm-flower-bloom) <idiom> Spring has come and the flowers are in bloom. It's a blooming spring: ~的季节 the blooming spring season || ~的时候 the time of blooming spring

25 温馨 [溫-] wēnxīn (warm-cozy) <adj.> warm and sweet: ~的家 a warm and sweet home || ~的话 warm and sweet words

26 干 [乾] gān (dry) <adj.> dry: 衣服~了. The clothes are dry. || ~的地方 a dry place || ~辣椒 (làjiāo) dry peppers

27 干燥 [乾-] gānzào (dry-torred) <adj.> dry: ~的地方 a dry place || 空气~ dry air || 皮肤~ dry skin

28 干巴巴 [乾--] gānbābā (dry-*suffix-reduplication*) <adj.> dull and dry: 文章写得~的 The article is dull || ~的土地 parched land

29 干旱 [乾-] gānhàn (dry-drought) <adj.> arid, dry: 天气~ the dry weather || ~地区 a drought area

30 干涸 [乾-] gānhé (dry-dried) <adj.> dry: ~的河流 a dry river || 血液~. Blood is drying up.

31 爽 [-] shuǎng (bright, happy) <adj.> bright, cheerful, very happy: 精神 ~ feel cheerful || 天气 ~ a bright weather || 玩得~ have a good time

32 枯竭 [-] kūjié (withered-exhausted) <adj.> exhausted, dried up: 资源 (zīyuán) ~ exhausted resource || 河水~. The river dried up.

33 湿 [濕] shī (wet) <adj.> wet: ~布 wet cloth || ~头发 wet hair || ~鞋子 wet shoes

34 湿润 [濕潤] shīrùn (wet-moist) <adj.> moist, wet: ~的眼睛 moist eyes || 空气~ moist air || 皮肤~ moist skin

35 湿淋淋 [濕--] shīlínlín (wet-dripping-*reduplication*) <adj.> dripping wet: ~的头发 wet hair

36 光滑 [-] guānghuá (smooth-slippery) <adj.> glossy, smooth: ~的地板 a slippery floor || ~的石头 glossy stones || ~的皮肤 smooth skin

37 光溜溜 [-] guāngliūliū (smooth-*suffix-reduplication*) <adj.> naked: ~的身子 a naked body || 脱得~的 strip off

38 滑 [-] huá (slippery) <adj.> smooth, crafty, slippery: 路~ the slippery road || 地~ the slippery floor || 鱼很~. The fish is very slippery.

39 细腻 [細膩] xìnì (delicate-velvety) <adj.> delicate, exquisite: 皮肤~ exquisite skin || ~的感情 delicate feelings

40 粗糙 [-] cūcāo (rough-coarse) <adj.> coarse, rough: ~的手 rough hands || 皮肤~ rough skin || 手工~ crudely made, of poor workmanship

Tips:

1 爽 (shuǎng): The 大 in the middle of 爽 indicates a man, and the 㸚 indicates 'fire under a man's armpits,' therefore the character 爽 means 'bright' and from which evolved the meaning 'happy.'

2 春暖花开: It means 'blooming spring.' This phrase, along with a proceeding 面朝大海 (miàn cháo dàhǎi, facing the blue sea) became well-known in the history of Chinese literature due to a poem with a title of the same verse in 1989 by the poet 海子 (1964–1989.)
3 冰冰: 冰 means 'ice.' When this book was being written, the names of two prominent Chinese actresses had these two characters, 范冰冰 and 李冰冰 whose relationship, according to many media, is 冷冰冰 (ice cold.)

Exercises:

Part I: Read the following words and then answer the questions.

湿润、凉爽、清凉、凉快、温暖、春暖花开、暖和、暖洋洋、炎热、闷热、潮湿、寒冷、严寒、寒冷、冰天雪地、光滑、细腻、粗糙、干巴巴、干旱、干燥

1 哪些词可以形容美国东北部的冬天?

____

2 哪些词可以形容美国东北部的春天?

____

3 哪些词可以形容上海的夏天?

____

4 哪些词可以形容你认为理想的夏天?

____

5 哪些词可以形容气候很干?

____

6 哪些词可以形容一个人的皮肤不好?

____

7 哪些词可以形容一个人的皮肤很好?

____

Theme 224: More, less 多, 少 (duō, shǎo)

1 多 [-] duō (many, much, more) <adj.> many, much: 很~人 many people || 钱~ have a lot of money || ~个朋友~条路. The more friends, the more ways/options.
2 许多 [許-] xǔduō (so-many) <adj.> a lot of: ~人 a lot of people || ~国家a lot of countries || ~大学a lot of universities
3 众多 [衆-] zhòngduō (masses-many) <adj.> numerous, large: 人口~ a large population || 数量~ in large quantities || ~国家 many nations

4 诸多 [諸-] zhūduō (various-many) <bf.> a lot of, a good deal: ~活动 a lot of activities || ~特点 a lot of characteristics || ~方面 a lot of aspects

5 有的是 [-] yǒudeshì (all have-is) <bf.> there is no lack of: ~时间. There is no lack of time. || ~钱. There is no lack of money. || ~人才. There is no lack of talents.

6 多如牛毛 [-] duōrúniúmáo (many-as-ox-hair) <idiom> as countless as hairs on a cow, countless: 温州的鞋厂~. The shoe factories in Wenzhou are countless.

7 大把 [-] dàbǎ (full-handful) <adj.> a lot of, a big bunches: ~的时间 a lot of time || ~的钞票 (chāopiào) a lot of money || 一~香蕉 the big bunches of banana

8 大量 [-] dàliàng (large-volume) <adj.> a large number of, much, a lot of: ~信息 (xìnxī) much information || ~照片 a lot of photos || ~使用 use sth. a lot

9 大批 [-] dàpī (large-batch) <adj.> large quantities/numbers, dozens of: ~工人 a large number of workers || ~飞机 a large number of aircrafts || ~逃跑 escape of dozens of people

10 大规模 [-規-] dàguīmó (large-scale) <n.> a large-scale: ~的比赛 large-scale events || ~的活动 a large-scale activity || ~使用 large-scale use

11 巨额 [-額] jù'é (huge-amount) <adj.> a huge sum, a big amount: ~资金 a huge sum of money || ~收入 a big amount of income || ~财富 (cáifù) an immense amount of treasure

12 成千上万 [---萬] chéngqiānshàngwàn (become-1, 000-surpass-10, 000) <idiom> tens of thousands of: ~的人 tens of thousands of people

13 一系列 [-] yīxìliè (a-series) <n.> a series of: ~的问题 a series of issues || ~的工作 a series of work || ~事情 a series of agendas

14 比比皆是 [-] bǐbǐjiēshì (everywhere-all-is) <idiom> can be found everywhere: 这样的商店 ~ such stores can be found everywhere

15 无数 [無數] wúshù (no-number) <adj.> countless: ~小鱼 countless small fish || ~青年 countless youth || ~的故事 countless stories

16 不计其数 [-計-數] bújìqíshù (unable-count-its-number) <idiom> countless, innumerable: ~的牛羊 countless cattle and sheep || ~的死者 countless dead people

17 绝大多数 [絕--數] juédàduōshù (overwhelming-majority) <n.> most, a majority of: 占~ take up a great majority of || ~学生a great majority of students|| ~情况in most cases

18 不少 [-] búshǎo (not-less) <adj.> quite a few/a little: ~人 quite a few people || ~书 quite a few books || ~东西 quite a little stuff

19 少 [-] shǎo (less, few) <adj.> little, few: ~说话 less talk || 活动~ few activities || 东西~ little stuff

20 少量 [-] shǎoliàng (less-volume) <n.> a few, a little, a small amount: ~水 a small amount of water || ~食用 only a little edible

21 有限 [-] yǒuxiàn (have-limited) <adj.> limited: ~的时间 limited time || ~的精力 limited energy || 长度~ a limited length

22 一点儿 [-點兒] yīdiǎnr (a-bit) <n.> a little: 差~ almost || 多~ a little more || ~不累 not tired at all

23 丝毫 [絲-] sīháo (1/100,000 Chinese foot-1/10,000 Chinese foot) <adj.> the slightest amount or degree, a bit: ~没想到 never realize || ~不累 not tired at all/never tired

24 一丝一毫 [-絲--] yīsīyīháo (a-tiny bit-a-tiny bit) <idiom> a tiny bit: 他没有~的怀疑. He had never any doubts. || ~的希望也没有. There is no hope at all.

25 一定 [-] yīdìng (all-certain) <adj.> certain, definite: ~的数量 definite quantity || ~程度 a certain extent || ~的市场 a certain market

26 紧张 [緊張] jǐnzhāng (tight-drawn) <adj.> tight, deficient, short: 油~ gas is deficient || 米~ rice is deficient || 资金 (zījīn) ~ a tight budget

27 多重 [-] duōchóng (multiple-fold) <adj.> multiple, multi: ~任务 (rènwù) multi task || ~世界 multiple worlds

28 多样 [-樣] duōyàng (multiple-type) <adj.> diverse, various: 方法~ various methods || 品种 ~ diverse varieties || 形式~ various forms

29 多元 [-] duōyuán (multiple-entity) <adj.> diverse, multi: ~文化 multiple cultures || ~标准 (biāozhǔn) multi-component standard

30 繁多 [-] fánduō (numerous-many) <adj.> massive, a wide range of: 人口~ a massive population || 种类~ a wide range of items || ~的商品 a wide range of goods

31 各种 [-種] gèzhǒng (various-kind) <bf> various kinds: ~食品 various kinds of food || ~笔 various kinds of pens || ~原 因 various kinds of reasons

32 各种各样 [-種-樣] gèzhǒnggèyàng (various-kind-various-type) <idiom> all kinds of: ~的水果 all kinds of fruit || ~的目的 all kinds of purpose || ~的颜色 all kinds of color

33 各式各样 [---樣] gèshìgèyàng (various-form-various-type) <idiom> all sorts of: ~的人物 all sorts of people || ~的问题 all sorts of issues || ~的花 all sorts of flower

34 丰富 [豐-] fēngfù (numerous-rich) <adj.> abundant, rich: ~的知识 rich knowledge || 想象力~ a rich imagination || 非常~ very rich

35 冗长 [-長] rǒngcháng (superfluous-long) <adj.> long, lengthy: ~的岁月 a long time || ~的句子 a long sentence || ~的内容 long contents

36 罕见 [-見] hǎnjiàn (rare-seen) <adj.> rare, unusual, infrequent: ~的事情 a rare thing || ~的病 a rare disease || ~的宝石 a rare gem

37 难得 [難-] nándé (hard-get) <adj.> hard to come by, rare: ~的机会 rare opportunities || ~休息 a rare rest || 她~看一本书. She seldom reads a book.

38 少见 [-見] shǎojiàn (less-seen) <adj.> rare, infrequent: ~的颜色 a rare color || ~的动物 a rare animal || ~的 a rare flower 花

39 稀少 [-] xīshǎo (rare-less) <adj.> rare, scarce, lack of: 人口~ sparsely populated || 动物~ animals are scarce || 雨水~ lack of rain

40 稀有 [-] xīyǒu (rare-have) <adj.> rare: ~的宝石 a rare gemstone || ~动物 a rare animal || ~品种 a rare species

41 百年不遇 [-] bǎiniánbúyù (100-year-not-encounter) <idiom> not occur even in a hundred years, once in a blue moon: ~的台风 a typhoon that did not occur even in a hundred years || ~的大旱 the worst drought in a century

42 千载难逢 [-載難-] qiānzǎinánféng (1, 000-year-hard-encounter) <idiom> very rare, occurring only once in a thousand years: ~的机会 a very rare opportunity || ~的考古发现 a once-in-a-lifetime archeological discovery

43 鲜为人知 [鮮爲--] xiǎnwéirénzhī (rarely-by-people-known) <idiom> little-known, rarely known: ~的景点 (jǐngdiǎn) a little-known scenery spot || ~的产品 a rarely known product

Tips:

1 众: The modern form of 众 displays the meaning of the character in a straightforward manner, 'three people' indicates 'many.' However, the traditional form of 众 is 衆, which might be harder to comprehend. If we trace the forms of 衆 back to the oracle form, we will find it is as simple as the modern form, only with an addition of a 日 (sun) on the top. The meaning of 衆 is 'three people working under the sun,' i.e., 'many.'

2 丝 and 毫: They are both length and weight units, and are both extremely short or light.

3 载: In 千载难逢 the 载 means 'year.' Other examples include 一年半载 (a year or so) and 三年五载 (a few years.)

Exercises:

Part I: Read the following words and then answer the questions.

稀少、稀有、百年不遇、罕见、鲜为人知、各种各样、各式各样、成千上万、不计其数、多如牛毛、比比皆是、千载难逢、许多、大量、大把、大批、大规模

1 上面哪些词可以用来形容"多样"?

____

2 上面哪些词可以用来形容"少见"?

____

3 上面哪些词可以用来形容"多"?

____

4 上面哪个词可以用来形容"机会难得"?

____

Theme 225: Adequate, exquisite 充足, 精美 (chōngzú, jīngměi)

1 足 [-] zú (foot, ample) <adj.> enough, adequate: 劲头~ energized || 经验~. The experience is enough. || 资金~ enough money, adequate finance

2 充足 [-] chōngzú (sufficient-abundant) <adj.> abundant, sufficient: ~的水 abundant water || ~的理由 sufficient reasons || 阳光~ sufficient sunlight

3 富足 [-] fùzú (rich-abundant) <adj.> rich, abundant: 人民~. People are well-off. || ~的生活 prosperous life, wealthy life, rich life, productive life || ~的家庭 rich families

4 充分 [-] chōngfèn (sufficient-component) <adj.> sufficient, adequate: ~的时间 sufficient time || ~的事实 the full facts || ~休息 have a full rest, have adequate rest

5 充实 [-實] chōngshí (sufficient-filled) <adj.> full, fulfilling: ~的生活 a fulfilling life || 内容~ full contents || 活得~ live full

6 旺盛 [-] wàngshèng (prosperous-flourishing) <adj.> exuberant, vigorous: ~的生命力 exuberant vitality || 精力 (jīnglì) ~ have energy || 长得~ growing strong

7 广博 [廣-] guǎngbó (wide-extensive) <adj.> extensive, wide: 见识~ wide in experience || ~的知识 extensive knowledge

8 渊博 [淵-] yuānbó (profound-extensive) <adj.> broad and profound: 学识 ~ have a large stock of information || ~的知识 broad and profound knowledge

9 地大物博 [-] dìdà wùbó (land-vast-product-abundant) <idiom> vast territory and abundant resources: ~的国家 a country of abundant resources || 中国~. China is a vast land with abundant resources.

10 博大精深 [-] bódà jīngshēn (extensive-big-profound-deep) <idiom> extensive/rich and profound: ~的思想 rich and profound thoughts

11 丰沛 [豐-] fēngpèi (numerous-copious) <adj.> plentiful, copious: ~的雨水 copious rain || 降水~ abundant rainfall

12 富饶 [-饒] fùráo (rich-plentiful) <adj.> rich, fertile, wealthy: ~的土地 a wealthy land || ~的海洋 a rich sea

13 精练 [-練] jīngliàn (refined-terse) <adj.> refined, terse: ~的新闻 terse news || ~的语言 refined words || 写得~ write tersely

14 贫乏 [貧-] pínfá (poor-lack) <adj.> poor, lacking: 生活~ poor life || 资源~ lacking resource || ~的山区 poor mountain areas

15 缺乏 [-] quēfá (short of-lack) <adj.> lack of, a shortage of: ~自信 lack of confidence || ~人才 a shortage of talent || ~兴趣lack of interest

16 紧缺 [緊-] jǐnquē (tight-short of) <adj.> be short of, sparse, scarce: 资金~ be short of money || ~商品 a sparse commodity || ~能源 (néngyuán) a scarce resource

17 精 [-] jīng (fine rice, fine) <adj.> refined, perfect, intensive: ~选 carefully selected || ~品 boutique || ~读 intensive reading

18 精美 [-] jīngměi (fine-beautiful) <adj.> exquisite, delicate: 制作~ exquisite production || ~的食品 delicacy || ~的图案 delicate patterns

19 精致 [-緻] jīngzhì (fine-close) <adj.> delicate: ~的房间 a delicate room || 做得~ be delicately made

20 精细 [-細] jīngxì (fine-delicate) <adj.> exquisite, delicate: ~的工作 delicate work || 做工~ exquisite workmanship || ~的图案 precise patterns

21 讲究 [講-] jiǎngjiū (strive for-until limit) <adj.> tasteful, fine: 衣着~ in smart clothes, well-dressed || 做得~ finely made || ~的包装 a tasteful packaging

22 豪华 [-華] háohuá (luxurious-grand) <adj.> luxurious, grand: ~生活 a luxurious life || ~别墅 (biéshù) a luxurious villa || 装饰 (zhuāngshì) ~ luxurious decoration

23 富丽堂皇 [-麗--] fùlì tánghuáng (grand-splendid-magnificent) <idiom> gorgeous, splendid: ~的大楼 a splendid building || 装饰得~ sumptuously decorated

24 阔 [闊] kuò (wide, wealthy) <adj.> very rich, wealthy: ~少爷 a very rich young man || ~太太 a very rich lady || 摆~ parade one's wealth

25 阔气 [闊氣] kuòqì (wealthy-style) <adj.> extravagant, luxurious: 穿得~ dressed luxuriously dressed || 生活~ live rich

26 财大气粗 [財-氣-] cáidà qìcū (wealth-much-manner-rude) <idiom> big budget, very rich: ~的公司 a deep-pocketed company || 老板 ~ the boss is very rich

27 珠光宝气 [--寶氣] zhūguāng bǎoqì (jewel-shining-treasure-spirit) <idiom> the splendor of jewels: ~的阔太太 a rich lady with the splendor of jewels || 浑身~ be resplendent with jewels

28 朴实 [樸實] pǔshí (simple-honest) <adj.> Earthy, simple: ~的性格 a simple character || ~的农民 simple farmers ||文风~simple style of writing

29 朴素 [樸-] pǔsù (simple-plain) <adj.> simple, frugal, plain: 生活~ live a thrifty life || 衣着~ simply dressed || ~的感情 simple feeling

30 质朴 [質樸] zhìpǔ (natural-simple) <adj.> plain, simple: 性格 ~ of simple and honest personality || ~ 的语言 a plain language || ~的姑娘 a plain girl

Tips:

1 地大物博: Before 1990s, the Chinese government used the following phrases to maintain people's patriotism: 中国历史悠久, 地大物博, 人口众多, China has a long history, a vast territory and a large population. Now the phrase has changed to 世界第二大经济体, the second largest economy (and forecasted to surpass the U.S.A. in some years.)

2 豪 (háo): It means 'luxurious, extravagant' and has been enjoyed by the Chinese people since the economic reform. People like to be connected with or marry 富豪 (the rich) who are of 豪门 (rich and powerful family,) live in 豪宅 (háozhái, mansion) and drive豪车 (luxury car.)

3 朴实: It means 'simple and honest' which used to be viewed as a compliment, but is now somewhat derogatory as if saying 'he is a bumpkin.'

Exercises:

Part I: Read the following sentences and fill in each blank with the appropriate word or phrase from the options given.

1 降雨丰沛、土地富饶、生活富足、地大物博、博大精深

a) 美国__________, 因此人均占有资源非常丰富.

b) 中国有五千年的历史, 因为文化__________.
c) 中国南方__________, 因此水资源丰富.
d) 中国东北部地区__________, 适合大面积种植 (grow) 农作物.
e) 一般来说中国东部沿海地区经济发达, 因此那里的老百姓__________.

2 精力旺盛、穿着朴素、语言精练、性格朴实、知识广博
a) 王教授的学术文章结构 (structure) 清楚 (clear) 、__________.
b) 王教授__________, 学生问什么问题他都能回答.
c) 王教授__________ _, 每天都工作到深夜.
d) 王教授__________, 常年穿一套深色西装.
e) 王教授__________, 平易近人, 见过他的人都喜欢他.

3 财大气粗、珠光宝气、富丽堂皇
a) 老王花钱非常阔气, 还可以说"老王__________ __."
b) 老王的家非常豪华, 还可以说"老王的家__________ _."

4 讲究、紧缺、缺乏、精美
a) 老王对喝茶很________, 家里有很多______的茶具.
b) 很多美国人对中国茶文化________了解, 这方面的人才目前在美国也比较________.

Theme 226: Complete 完整 (wánzhěng)

1 全部 [-] quánbù (all-part) <n.> whole, all: ~学生 all students || ~门票 all admission tickets || ~参加 all participate
2 全 [-] quán (whole) <adj.> whole: ~市 the whole city || ~国 the whole country || ~班 the whole class
3 全体 [-體] quántǐ (entire-body) <n.> entirety, all: ~代表 all delegates || ~师生 all teachers and students || ~坐下 all sit down
4 所有 [-] suǒyǒu (what-have) <adj.> all: ~的人 all people || ~的城市 all cities || ~的书 all books
5 完全 [-] wánquán (whole-complete) c <adj.> complete, entire, whole: ~的人 whole person || ~的信息 complete information || ~的自由 entire freedom
6 完整 [-] wánzhěng (whole-entire) <adj.> intact, complete, unbroken: ~的宝石 the unbroken gemstone || ~的家 an intact family || ~的国家 the complete state
7 整 [-] zhěng (whole, entire) <adj.> exact, whole: ~间教室 the whole classroom || ~八点 8:30 to be exact || 一年~ the whole year
8 整个 [-] zhěngge (entire-item) <adj.> whole: ~城市 the whole city || ~秋天 the whole autumn || ~人 the whole person
9 整整 [-] zhěngzhěng (full-*reduplication*) <adv.> full, entire: ~三个小时 the entire three hours || ~走了一天 walk for a full day || ~八十岁 eighty-year-old
10 齐全 [齊-] qíquán (complete-complete) <adj.> complete: 品种~ a complete range of articles || 资料~ complete material || 收集~ complete collection

11 齐 [齊] qí (complete) <adj.> complete: 开~课程 open a complete range of courses || 收~钱 collect money completely || 交~作业 submit homework completely
12 满 [滿] mǎn (full) <adj.> full, all over: ~山 all over the mountains || ~分 full score || ~两个月 two full months
13 百分之百 [-] bǎifēnzhībǎi (100-percent-'s-100) <n.> 100 percent: ~满意 100 percent satisfaction || ~正确 100 percent right || ~的信心 100 percent confidence
14 一切 [-] yīqiè (one-cut) <pron.> every, all: ~儿童 every child || ~困难 all difficulties || 他的~ his all
15 部分 [-] bùfèn (section-division) <n.> some, part: ~国家 part countries || ~职员 some employees || ~车辆 some vehicles
16 一部分 [-] yībùfèn (one-part) <n.> a part of, a portion of: ~人 some people || ~地区 part of the region || ~工作 part of work
17 大部分 [-] dàbùfèn (majority-part) <n.> most: ~地方 most area || ~时间 most of the time || ~国家 most countries
18 大多数 [--數] dàduōshù (vast-majority) <n.> majority, most: ~学生 a majority of students || ~词语 most of the words || ~人 the majority of people
19 少数 [-數] shǎoshù (minor-number) <n.> a small number of, a few: ~人 a small number of people || ~地区 a few regions || ~公司 a few companies
20 有的 [-] yǒude (have-it) <pron.> some: ~人 some people || ~地方 some regions || ~书店 some bookstores
21 有些 [-] yǒuxiē (have-some) <pron.> some: ~人 some people || ~学校 some schools || ~东西 some stuff
22 个别 [個別] gèbié (individual-exception) <adj.> individual: ~学生 individual students || ~公司 individual companies || ~差异 individual differences
23 单 [單] dān (big, single) <adj.> single: ~打 singles (in sports) || ~脚 single-foot || ~眼皮 single-fold eyelid
24 破 [-] pò (broken) <adj.> broken: ~瓶子 broken bottles || ~碗 a broken bowl || 打/抓~ break, scratch
25 烂 [爛] làn (soft, rotten) <adj.> messy, worn-out, lousy: 打~ batter down, || ~鞋 worn-out shoes || ~衣服 lousy clothes
26 破烂 [-爛] pòlàn (torn-tattered) <adj.> ragged, broken, shabby: ~的东西 broken items || 穿得~ dressed in tatters || 衣服~ shabby clothes
27 碎 [-] suì (smash, small) <adj.> fractured, fragmentized: ~玻璃 (bōli) fractured glass || 打~ break up || ~面包 bread crumbs
28 零碎 [-] língsuì (odd-small) <adj.> fragmentary, scrap: ~的东西 odds and ends || 材料~ fragmentary material
29 零散 [-] língsǎn (odd-scattered) <adj.> scattered: ~时间 scattered time || ~物品 scattered items

Tips:

1 整 (zhěng): This character seems quite complicated, but dissecting it will make it much easier to understand. First, the lower 正 (zhèng) is the sound part and means 'straight.' The upper left part is 束 (shù, to bind), which is actually

composed of a 木 (tree, branch) and a 口 (here a symbol of a band.) The upper right part is 攵 (pū, an action with a hand.) Therefore, the meaning of 整 is 'use a band to tie a bunch of branches to make them straight up,' in other words, 'to tidy.'

2 切: When it is pronounced as the first tone "qiē", it means 'to cut.' When pronounced as the fourth tone "qiè," it can be a verb 'be sure to' as in words such as '切记' (be sure to remember,) or an adjective 'anxious, deep' as in words such as '急切,' '心切' (both mean 'be eager to') and '深切' (deeply.)

3 百分之: It means 'percent.' Usually one only says '百分之X,' not '以百分之X.' Percentage is 百分数.

4 Percentage order in Chinese: 百分之百 or 全部 (100%,) 绝大多数 (overwhelming majority,) 大多数 (vast majority,) 多数 (majority,) 半数 (half,) 不足半数 (less than a half,) 少数 (minority,) 极少数 (a small/tiny percentage,) and 零 (líng, zero.)

Exercises:

Part I: Multiple Choice. Make sure to choose the most *inappropriate* ***answer.***

1 小张用____________的时间来自学中文.
A. 零碎 B. 零散 C. 碎

2 美国东北部的_________知名大学都开设了东亚研究专业.
A. 全体 B. 大部分 C. 大多数

3 美国只是_________城市对移民友好, 并不是每个城市都欢fl移民.
A. 有的 B. 完全 C. 有些

4 在中国只有__________国有企业有外籍员工工作.
A. 完整 B. 少数 C. 个别

5 小张对自己新工作__________满意.
A. 完全 B. 齐全 C. 百分之百

6 大学毕业后小张用了_________一年的时间找工作.
A. 整个 B. 一切 C. 整整

7 小张跟女朋友想登记 (dēngjì, register) 结婚, 但是因为证件不________, 没有办理成功.
A. 一切 B. 齐全 C. 齐

8 据说在美国性别歧视 (qíshì, discrimination) 的问题依然存在, 很多女性想打_________玻璃天花板 (glass ceiling), 担任领导 (leader) 职位 (zhíwèi, position) 是非常困难的.
A. 破 B. 烂 C. 碎

Theme 227: Tight, thick, dense, cooked 密, 紧, 稠, 熟 (jǐn, mì, chóu, shú)

1 密 [-] mì (dense) <adj.> dense, thick: 种得~ plant closely || ~林 a dense forest || 眉 毛很~ thick eyebrows

2 密密麻麻 [-] mìmìmámá (dense-*reduplication*-numerous-*reduplication*) <idiom> thickly, densely dotted: 写得~ write sth. closely and densely || ~的树叶 dense and thick leaves || ~地停满了汽车. The parking lot is densely packed with cars.
3 稠密 [-] chóumì (many and dense-dense) <adj.> dense: 人口~ densely populated || ~的铁路网 a dense network of railways
4 茂密 [-] màomì (lush-dense) <adj.> dense, lush: ~的森林 dense forest || 枝叶~ lush foliage
5 饱 [飽] bǎo (full) <adj.> full: 肚子~ a full stomach || 吃~ fill up
6 肥沃 [-] féiwò (fertilizer-fertile) <adj.> fertile, rich: 土地~ fertile/rich soil || ~的田野 the fertile fields

7 稀疏 [-] xīshū (scattered-sparse) <adj.> sparse, thin: 头发~ hair is thin || ~的树林 sparse woods || 人口~ sparsely populated
8 稀稀拉拉 [-] xīxīlālā (*reduplication* of scattered-*suffix*) <idiom> thinly scattered, sparse: ~的头发 sparse hair || ~走过来 walk over sparsely
9 空 [-] kōng (hollow) <adj.> empty: ~酒瓶 an empty wine bottle || ~信箱 an empty mailbox || ~房 an empty room
10 空白 [-] kòngbái (empty-blank) <adj.> blank, plain: ~支票 a blank check || ~的地方 a blank space || ~纸 a plain paper
11 荒凉 [-涼] huāngliáng (waste-bleak) <adj.> desolate, bleak: ~的地方 a desolate place || ~的景色 desolate scenes || ~的世界 a desolate world

12 紧 [緊] jǐn (tense) <adj.> tight: 裤子~ pants are tight || 抱~ hug tightly || ~身 skintight
13 严 [嚴] yán (urgent, stern, strict) <adj.> strict, tight: 关~ close tightly || 盖~ cover tightly || 包得~ wrap tightly
14 松 [鬆] sōng (loose) <adj.> loose: 裤子~ pants are loose || 抓得~ hold loosely || 外~里脆 crispy inside and loose outside
15 松散 [鬆-] sōngsǎn (loose-unfettered) <adj.> loose: 结构~ the structure is loose/loosely organized

16 生 [-] shēng (raw, uncooked) <adj.> raw: ~豆子 raw beans || ~土豆 raw potatoes || ~米 raw rice
17 半生不熟 [-] bànshēngbúshú (half-raw-not-cooked) <idiom> underdone, half-cooked: ~的牛排 a half-cooked steak || ~的朋友 friends who are not too familiar
18 嫩 [-] nèn (tender) <adj.> tender, young: ~黄瓜 young cucumber || ~叶 tender leaves
19 鲜嫩 [鮮-] xiānnèn (fresh-tender) <adj.> fresh and tender: ~的蔬菜 fresh and tender vegetables
20 熟 [-] shú (well-cooked) <adj.> ripe, cooked: 烧/煮~ well-cooked || ~鸡蛋 cooked eggs || ~菜 cooked food
21 老 [-] lǎo (overcooked) <adj.> over-cooked: 煮~了 be overcooked
22 糊 [-] hú (burned) <adj.> burned: 烧~了 be burned
23 焦 [-] jiāo (scorched) <adj.> burned, charred: 烧~了 be burned

Tips:

1 Steak doneness: The Chinese way of expressing steak doneness is 生 (raw,) 一分熟 (rare,) 三分熟 (medium-rare,) 五分熟 (medium,) 七分熟 (medium-well,) and 全熟 (well-done.)

2 焦 (jiāo): 焦 has two related meanings. One is 'burned' and the other 'anxious,' both of which are related to the two components of this character, 隹 (zhuī, bird) and 灬 (火, fire.) Imagine if you put something on a fire, it will definitely burn. If you are on the fire, you will be anxious spontaneously.
3 空: When it is pronounced as 'kōng,' it means 'hollow, empty, aero' as in "空洞" (hollow) and "空军" (air force.) If it is pronounced as 'kòng,' it means 'unoccupied, unfilled' as in "空闲" (leisure time) and "空地" (open ground.)
4 松: When it means 'pine,' it is written as 松 in both simplified forms and traditional forms. When it means 'loose,' the traditional form is 鬆.
5 稀稀拉拉: It might be a variant of 稀稀落落, which is a reduplication of 稀落 (sparse, scattered.)

Exercises:

Part I: Write an antonym for each word in the table and then answer the questions. Please refer to the given words.

管得松、松散、密密麻麻、空、很饿、人口稠密

管得严 v.s.	紧密v.s.	稀稀拉拉v.s.
满v.s.	很饱v.s.	人口稀少v.s.

1 中国东部人口稠密, 美国呢?

____

2 中国西部地区比较荒凉, 美国呢?

____

3 中国的东北部和西南部森林茂密, 美国呢?

____

Part II: Translate the following phrases into English and then answer the questions.

半生不熟的牛排 ______________
煮老的牛肉 ______________
烧糊的牛肉 ______________
烧焦的牛肉 ______________
生土豆 ______________
嫩黄瓜 ______________
鲜嫩的生菜 ______________
熟鸡蛋 ______________

1 以上这些食物哪些可以直接吃而不影响健康 (jiànkāng, health)?

____

2 以上这些食物哪些吃了对身体有害(harmful)?

____

Theme 228: Sex, gender 性别 (xìngbié)

(See also Theme 1)

1 性别 [-] xìngbié (gender-difference) <n.> gender, sex: 不分 ~ gender-neutral, unisex || ~差异 gender/sex difference || 人的~ gender, sex

2 两性 [兩-] liǎngxìng (two-gender) <n.> gender, sexuality: ~关系 sexual relations || ~平等equality between the sexes || ~问题 a gender issue

3 同性 [-] tóngxìng (homo-sex) <n.> homosex: ~交往 homosexual dating || ~恋 homosexuality || ~青年 homosexual youth

4 异性 [異-] yìxìng (hetero-sex) <n.> heterosex: ~交往 homosexual dating || ~朋友 homosexual friends

5 变性 [變-] biànxìng (change-gender) <v.> transsexual, transgender: ~人 transgender || ~手术 transsexual operation

6 男 [-] nán (man, male) <非谓形容词> male: ~同学 male students || ~青年 male youth || ~明星 a male star

7 女 [-] nǚ (woman, female) <非谓形容词> female: ~学生 female students || ~宿舍 female's dormitory || ~孩子 girls

8 不男不女 [-] bù'nánbùnǚ (not-man-not-woman) <adj.> androgynous: 不男不女 [----] bù'nán bùnǚ (not-man-not-woman) <bf.> neither a male nor a female, indeterminate: 打扮得~ dress neither like a woman nor a man || 这个人看起来~的。This person looks neither like a woman nor a man.

9 阴 [陰] yīn (yin, dark, nagative) <adj.> Yin, negative: 女为~, 男为阳 female is Yin, male is Yang || ~极 the negative pole || ~一套, 阳一套 act one way in public and another in private, be engaged in double-dealing

10 阳 [陽] yáng (yang, sun, positive) <adj.> yang, positive: ~极 the positive pole

11 阴盛阳衰 [陰-陽-] yīnshèngyángshuāi (women-flourishing-men-declining) <idiom> rise of Yin and fall of Yang, Women do better than men: ~的社会 the society of rise of yin and fall of yang

12 雌 [-] cí (female bird) <非谓形容词> female: ~花 female flowers || ~蜘蛛 female spiders || ~孔雀 female peacock

13 雄 [-] xióng (male bird) <非谓形容词> male: ~花 male flowers || ~猴 male monkeys || ~象 male elephants

14 一决雌雄 [-決--] yī juécíxióng (ultimately-decide-soft-strong) <idiom> fight a decisive battle, compete for championship: 与对手~ fight a decisive battle/compete for championship with rivals

15 公 [-] gōng (male) <非谓形容词> male: ~鸡 rooster || ~牛 bull, ox || ~鹿 male buck

16 母 [-] mǔ (female) <非谓形容词> female: ~鸡 hens || ~熊 female bears || ~兔 female rabbits

Tips:

1 性: The original meaning of 性 is 'nature, disposition' not 'sex/gender' because 性 is related to '忄 (心, heart).' Its original meaning is still widely kept in compound words such as 性格 (disposition,) 个性 (personality) and 性情 (temper) etc.

2 阴 (陰) and 阳 (陽): The original meaning of 阴 is the north side of a mountain and the south side of a river, and 阳 is just the opposite of 阴. This sentiment exists widely in Chinese place names, for example, there are 117 county-level-city names containing 阳 (i.e., 沈阳, 贵阳, 淮阳) and nine containing 阴 (i.e., 江阴, 山阴, 淮阴.)
3 阴盛阳衰: In Chinese place names, the phrase is 阳盛阴衰 ('yang 阳' prevails 'yin阴,') however, in many other societal fields, it is a prevailing 阴盛阳衰 (women do better than men.) A typical field is sports, and this will not be wrong until the Chinese national football team wins the second place in the FIFA World Cup.
4 雌 (cí) and 雄 (xióng): They originally mean 'female bird' and 'male bird' since both are related to 隹 (zhuī, bird with a short tail)

Exercises:

Part I: Multiple Choice. Make sure to choose the most appropriate one

1 一般来说, 人们用__________来表述 (describe) 人的性别.
A. 男女 B. 阴阳 C. 雌雄

2 一般来说, 人们用__________ _来表述动物的雌雄.
A. 男女 B. 阴阳 C. 雌雄

3 中国古代思想认为世界分为__________ _两极.
A. 男女 B. 阴阳 C. 雌雄

4 "一决雌雄"的意思就是
A. 比赛决定胜负 B. 看看谁是男谁是女 C. 看看谁是公谁是母

5 "两性关系"还可以说
A. 异性关系 B. 同性关系 C. 同性恋关系

6 "变性手术"用中文解释就是
A. 改变性格的手术 B. 改变生活的手术 C. 改变性别的手术

7 如果中国人说"小李不男不女的," 很可能他的态度是
A. 他夸奖小李 B. 他看不起小李 C. 他赞美小李

8 "小王这个人, 阴一套, 阳一套," 说明小王
A. 弱不禁风 B. 不诚实 C. 健康

Theme 229: Old, young, strong, weak 老, 小, 强壮, 弱 (lǎo, xiǎo, qiángzhuàng, ruò)

1 老 [-] lǎo (old) <adj.> old: ~人 old men || ~一代 an older generation || ~教授 (jiàoshòu) an old professor
2 长寿 [長壽] chángshòu (long-lifespan) <adj.> long life, longevity: 祝您健康~ wish you good health and a long life || ~老人longevous man || ~之道the course of a long life
3 年轻 [-輕] niánqīng (age-light) <adj.> young: ~的朋友 young friends || ~的医生 a young friend || 显得~ looks young

4 年青 [-] niánqīng (age-young) <adj.> young: ~人 young people || ~的生命a young life || ~一代 a young generation

5 幼小 [-] yòuxiǎo (little-small) <adj.> little, young: ~的生命 a little life || ~的儿女 young children || 年龄~ young age

6 健康 [-] jiànkāng (fit-health) <adj./ n.> healthy, health: ~成长 grow healthily || 身体~ be in a good health || 有益 (yǒuyì) ~ good for health

7 强壮 [-壯] qiángzhuàng (strong-robust) <adj.> strong, powerful: ~的身体 strong body || 长得~ look strong || 四肢~ powerful limbs

8 结实 [結實] jiéshí (stout-solid) <adj.> solid, firm, strong: 他身体很~. He has a robust body. || 长得~ looks strong || ~的孩子 a strong child

9 软 [軟] ruǎn (soft) <adj.> soft, weak: 他两腿发~. His legs felt weak or like jelly. || 心~ tender-hearted

10 虚弱 [-] xūruò (feeble-weak) <adj.> weak, poor: 身体~ be in a poor health || ~的声音 in a weak voice

11 疲软 [-軟] píruǎn (tired-soft) <adj.> fatigued and weak, bearish: 市场~ a bearish market

12 娇嫩 [嬌-] jiāonèn (delicate-tender) <adj.> delicate: ~的花朵 delicate flowers || 皮肤~ delicate skin

13 弱不禁风 [---風] ruòbùjīnfēng (weak-unable-withstand-wind) <idiom> too weak to withstand a gust of wind, extremely delicate, fragile: ~的身体 a vulnerable/fragile body

Tips:

1 弱不禁风: Ancient Chinese aesthetic judgment distorted many aspects of women. For example, they regarded women who were 弱不禁风 (too weak to withstand a gust of wind) as beautiful, not to mention the notorious practice of foot binding as a Chinese beauty standard.

2 长寿: The best way to please an old Chinese person is probably to wish him '健康长寿' (jiànkāng chángshòu, healthy and live a long life.)

Exercises:

Part I: Read the following sentences and fill in each blank with the appropriate word or phrase from the options given.

1 长寿、年轻、老

a) 中国很多________人热衷 (rèzhōng, crazy for) 于购买保健品 (bǎojiànpǐn, health product), 因为他们觉得保健品可以让他们____________.

b) 在中国一些中年女性觉得使用名牌化妆品可以让她们看起来更__________.

2 健康、强壮、结实

a) 小王喜欢购买名牌家具, 因为他觉得质量好, 很________.

b) 小王在美国留学时经常喜欢去有机食品超市购买_________食品. 他认为只有注重饮食, 身体才能_________.

3 虚弱、软、疲软

a) 小王只要在街上看到流浪汉 就会心__________, 掏 (tāo) 钱给他们.
b) 小王的朋友从小就身体__________, 经常生病.
c) 最近中国消费市场开始__________, 老百姓的消费能力明显下降.

4 娇嫩、弱不禁风、幼小

a) 王女士家里有三个__________的孩子需要照顾, 因此她周末不能加班.
b) 孩子的皮肤一般比较__________, 不适合使用成人化妆品.
c) 有人说其实中国经济现在已经__________, 出现一点点问题都会让它马上垮 (kuǎ, collapse) 下来.

Theme 230: New, old, beautiful, ugly 新, 旧, 美, 丑 (xīn, jiù, měi, chǒu)

1 新 [-] xīn (new) <adj.> new: ~鞋 new shoes || ~车 a new car || ~学生 new students
2 新型 [-] xīnxíng (new-style) <adj.> new, new-fashioned: ~产品 new-type products || ~电脑 new-fashioned computer || ~飞机 new-type airplanes
3 崭新 [嶄-] zhǎnxīn (brand-new) <adj.> brand new: ~的衣服 brand new clothes || ~的宿舍 brand new dorms || ~的车子 a brand new car
4 全新 [-] quánxīn (completely-new) <adj.> new, brand new: ~的生活 a brand new life || ~的变 化 new changes || ~的关系 a brand new relationship
5 鲜 [鮮] xiān (fresh) <adj.> fresh: ~蘑菇 (mógu) fresh mushrooms || ~鸡蛋 fresh eggs || ~牛肉 fresh beef
6 新鲜 [-鮮] xīnxiān (new-fresh) <adj.> fresh: ~蔬菜 fresh vegetables || ~空气 fresh air || ~虾子 fresh shrimp
7 新兴 [-興] xīnxīng (new-rise) <adj.> burgeoning, rising, newly-emerging: ~工业 newly-emerging industry || ~的学科 newly-emerging disciplines
8 文明 [-] wénmíng (colorful-bright) <adj.> civil, civilized: 高度~ highly civil || 不~的行为 uncivilized behavior || 讲~礼貌behave civilly
9 旧 [舊] jiù (old) <adj.> old: ~袜子 old socks || ~报纸 old newspaper || ~东西 new items
10 陈旧 [陳舊] chénjiù (antiquated-old) <adj.> outdated, old: 式样~ old-fashioned || ~的机器 old machines || ~的观念 outdated concept
11 二手 [-] èrshǒu (second-hand) <adj.> used, second-hand: ~车 a used car || ~房 a second-hand house || ~市场 secondary market
12 流行 [-] liúxíng (diffuse-go) <adj.> popular: ~歌曲 popular songs || ~服装 popular clothes || ~的看法 the popular view
13 洋气 [-氣] yángqì (foreign-style) <adj.> foreign flavor, Western style: 打扮 (dǎban) ~ dressed in style
14 潮 [-] cháo (tide, trendy) <adj.> new fashion: ~人 trendsetters || 新~ new trends || 穿得~ dressing in a trendy way
15 老 [-] lǎo (old) <adj.> old: ~ 房子 an old house || ~火车 an old train || ~船 an old boat
16 古老 [-] gǔlǎo (ancient-old) <adj.> old, ancient, antiquated: ~的文字 an ancient written language || ~的游戏 (yóuxì) ancient puzzles || ~的问题 an old question

17 古 [-] gǔ (ancient) <adj.> ancient: ~时候 ancient times || ~文字 an ancient written language || ~人 the ancients

18 土 [-] tǔ (soil, Earth, dirt) <adj.> rustic: 衣服~. The clothes are rustic. || 眼镜很 ~ glasses look rustic || 穿得~ rustic dressing

19 土里土气 [---氣] tǔlitǔqì (rustic-inflex-rustic-style) <idiom> rustic, countrified: ~的样子 a rustic look || ~的村子 a rustic village || ~的姑娘 a rustic girl

20 过时 [過時] guòshí (out of-date) <adj.> outmoded, out-dated: ~的衣服 out-dated clothes || ~的东西 out-dated stuff || ~的信息 out-dated information

21 美 [-] měi (beautiful) <adj.> beautiful: ~人 a beautiful people || ~极了 very beautiful || 真~ really beautiful

22 美丽 [-麗] měilì (beautiful-fine) <adj.> beautiful: ~的姑娘 a beautiful girl || ~的地方 a beautiful place || ~的花 beautiful flowers

23 靓丽 [靚麗] liànglì (pretty-beautiful) <adj.> beautiful, gorgeous: 打扮~ dressed up gorgeously || ~的姑娘 a gorgeous girl

24 华丽 [華麗] huálì (magnificent-beautiful) <adj.> magnificent, luxuriant: ~的王宫 the magnificent palace || 衣着~ gorgeously dressed

25 艳丽 [艷麗] yànlì (shining-beautiful) <adj.> gorgeous, beautiful: 打扮得非常~ be gorgeously dressed || ~的服装 gorgeous clothes

26 美好 [-] měihǎo (fine-good) <adj.> fine, beautiful, good: ~的爱情 beautiful love || ~的生活 a good life || ~的希望 a beautiful wish

27 古典 [-] gǔdiǎn (ancient-classic) <adj.> classical: ~音乐 classical music || ~文学 classical literature || ~哲学 (zhéxué) classical philosophy

28 优雅 [優-] yōuyǎ (graceful-elegant) <adj.> elegant, graceful: 环境 (huánjìng) ~ an elegant environment || ~的动作 graceful movement || ~的音乐 elegant music

29 优美 [優-] yōuměi (graceful-beautiful) <adj.> graceful, beautiful: ~的舞蹈 (wǔdǎo) a graceful dance || ~的文字 beautiful words || ~的景色 (jǐngsè) beautiful scenery

30 漂亮 [-] piàoliang (rinse-bright) <adj.> beautiful: ~的女孩 beautiful girls || 长得~ look beautiful || 做得~ beautifully done

31 好看 [-] hǎokàn (good-looking) <adj.> good-looking, nice, gorgeous: ~的脸 a nice face || 你穿这件衣服很~. This cloth looks nice on you.

32 英俊 [-] yīngjùn (outstanding-outstanding) <adj.> handsome: ~小伙 a handsome boy || ~青年 a handsome young man

33 帅 [帥] shuài (command, handsome) <adj.> handsome: 长得~ look handsome || ~小伙 a handsome young man || ~哥 a handsome man

34 难看 [難-] nánkàn (unpleasant-looking) <adj.> ugly, terrible-looking: 她脸色~ she looks pale || 显得 ~ look ugly || 长相~ a terrible-looking

35 丑 [醜] chǒu (hateful, ugly) <adj.> ugly: ~人 an ugly person || 变~ become ugly || 长得~ look ugly

Tips:

1 艳 (艷): 艳 means 'multi-colored and bright.' When it is used for women, it means a woman is '(fairly chubby and) beautiful.' This being said, the Tang Dynasty women were 艳丽, not the skinny women of modern society.

2 美: The upper part of 美 is 羊 which has an auspicious meaning. 美 means 'delicious, beautiful, good-looking.'
3 鲜: The meaning of 鲜 comes from its components, 鱼 and 羊, both meaning 'fresh.' In many Chinese neighborhoods, you can find on shop/store/restaurant signs 鱻 (xiān) or 羴 (shān), which indicates there is fresh fish or meat for sale or service.
4 英 and 俊: Both mean 'outstanding,' but 俊 is 'one in 100' and 英 'one in 1,000.' It is a shame that their combination "英俊" is used only for males (therefore meaning 'handsome.')
5 丑 (醜, chǒu): Ancient Chinese thought 鬼 (guǐ, ghost) were the ugliest creatures, therefore 丑 (醜) has a component 鬼.

Exercises:

Part I: Read the following words and then answer the questions.

新、新型、崭新、全新、新兴、旧、陈旧、二手、古老、老、古代、美丽、靓丽、华丽、艳丽、漂亮、英俊、帅、难看、丑、时尚、新潮、洋气、流行、很潮、很土、土里土气、过时、古典、美好、优雅、优美

1. 哪些词有"新"的意思?

____

2 哪些词有"旧"的意思?

____

3 哪些词有"时间非常久"的意思?

____

4 哪些词有"好看"的意思?

____

5 哪些词有"不好看"的意思?

____

6 哪些词可以形容一个相貌 (xiàngmào, looking) 很好的男性?

____

7 哪些词可以形容一个相貌很好的女性?

____

8 哪些词有"fashion"的意思?

____

9 哪些词有"out-dated"的意思?

____

10 你喜欢古典音乐还是现代音乐?

____

11 你觉得什么是最美好的事情? 是爱情吗?

12 你常去环境优雅的餐厅吃饭吗? 为什么?

13 你可以写出文字优美的现代诗吗? 为什么?

Theme 231: Early, late, fast, slow, long, short, far, near 早, 晚, 快, 慢, 长, 短, 远, 近 (zǎo, wǎn, kuài, màn, cháng, duǎn, yuǎn, jìn)

1 早 [-] zǎo (morning, early) <adj.> early: 来得~ come early || ~说 tell early || ~吃 eat early
2 晚 [-] wǎn (night, late) <adj.> late: 来~了come late || 太~了 too late || 睡得~ sleep late
3 迟 [遲] chí (slow, late) <adj.> late: 来得~ come late || 说~了 say it late || ~一天/一步 late for a day/too late
4 快 [-] kuài (pleasant, fast) <adj.> fast, quick: 跑得~ run fast, run quickly || 过得~ time goes fast || 时间~ Time is fast.
5 快速 [-] kuàisù (fast-speed) <adj.> fast, sudden: ~反应 fast reaction || ~前进 fast forward || ~通道 fast exit/lane; express entry
6 高速 [-] gāosù (high-speed) <adj.> high speed: ~公路 highway || ~电梯 high speed elevator || ~发展 high-speed development
7 特快 [-] tèkuài (super-fast) <adj.> express: ~火车 express train || ~专递 (zhuāndì) express mails || 跑得~ run too fast

8 急 [-] jí (urgent) <adj.> urgent, anxious: 很 ~ very urgent || ~事 urgent thing || ~着回家 be anxious to go home
9 急剧 [-劇] jíjù (rapidly-radically) <adj.> rapid, sharp: ~增加 (zēngjiā) a rapid increase || ~变化 a rapid change || ~下降 a rapid decrease
10 迅速 [-] xùnsù (quick-fast) <adj.> rapid, prompt, quick: ~爬上去 quickly climb up || 发展 (fāzhǎn) ~ develop rapidly || ~离开 leave rapidly
11 慢 [-] màn (slowly) <adj./adv.> slow: 写得~ write slowly || ~点说 speak slowly || 速度~ a slow speed
12 缓慢 [緩-] huǎnmàn (unhurried-slow) <adj./adv.> slow, slowly: 发展~ develop slowly || ~移动 a slow movement || 速度~ a slow speed
13 磨蹭 [-] móceng (dawdle-dillydally) <adj.> linger, dawdle, waste time : ~一个小时linger over an hour || 做事~ dawdle on doing sth. || 别~ 了! Stop dawdling!

14 久 [-] jiǔ (long) <adj.> long: 坐得~ sit down too long || 时间~ a long time || 这么/那么~ so long
15 长久 [長-] chángjiǔ (long-long) <adj.> permanent, long: ~的时间 a long time || ~的饥饿 (jī'è) the hunger for a long time || ~地站着 stand up for a long time
16 长远 [長遠] chángyuǎn (long-far) <adj.> a long-term, a long-range: ~利益 (lìyì) long-term interests || ~意义 long-term significance || ~眼光 a long-term vision

17 好久 [-] hǎojiǔ (quite-long) <adj.> for a long time: 走了~ walk for a long time || 谈了~ talk for a long time || ~不见. Long time; no see.

18 老 [-] lǎo (old) <adj.> old: ~朋友 old friends || ~会员an old member || ~习惯 (xíguàn) an old habit

19 漫长 [-長] màncháng endless <adj.> (endless-long): ~的冬天 an endless winter || 道路~ the road is long || ~的黑夜 endless night

20 永远 [-遠] yǒngyuǎn (forever-long) <adj.> always, forever: ~记着 remember forever || ~正确 (zhèngquè) always right || ~幸福 (xìngfú) be happy forever

21 永恒 [-] yǒnghéng (forever-eternal) <adj.> permanent, eternal: ~存在 a permanent existence || ~的美 eternal beauty || ~不变 invariability

22 世世代代 [-] shìshìdàidài (30 years-30 years-generation-generation) <idiom> from generation to generation: ~友好 live in friendship from generation to generation

23 暂时 [暫時] zànshí (temporary-time) <adj.> temporary: ~现象 (xiànxiàng) a temporary phenomenon || ~的失败 (shībài) a temporary failure || ~停止 temporarily discontinued

24 临时 [臨時] línshí (provisional-time) <adj.> temporary: ~工作 a temporary job || ~会议 a temporary meeting || ~住所 a temporary residence

25 不一会儿 [--會兒] bùyīhuìr (not really-a-moment) <adj.> only a while, in a moment: ~工夫 after only a while || 刚走~ leave just a moment

26 一下儿 [--兒] yīxiàr (a-moment) <n.> in a while, give it a go (used after a verb): 看了~took a look || 等~. Wait a minute. || 请来~. Please come over for a while.

27 一眨眼 [-] yīzhǎyǎn (a-twinkling-eye) <v.> in a wink: ~的功夫in the twinkling of an eye || ~就不见了disappear in the twinkling of an eye

28 远 [遠] yuǎn (distant) <adj.> distant, far: 五百米~ 500 meters away || 越走越~ go farther and farther || 看得~ see far

29 遥远 [遙遠] yáoyuǎn (remote-distant) <adj.> remote, distant, long: 路途 (lùtú) ~ a long journey/way || 相距~ a long distance || ~的地方 a remote place

30 长远 [長遠] chángyuǎn (long-distant) <adj.> long-term: ~打算 (dǎsuàn) a long-term plan || ~目标 a long-term goal || ~利益 long-term interests

31 长途 [長-] chángtú (long-distance) <adj.> long-distance: ~旅行 (lǚxíng) a long-distance journey || ~运输 (yùnshū) a long-distance transportation || ~汽车 a long-distance bus

32 近 [-] jìn (close) <adj.> close: 离得~ close up || 距离~ a close distance || ~地方 a close place

33 邻近 [鄰近] línjìn (vicinal-close) <adj.> adjacent, vicinal: ~国家 adjacent countries || ~地区 vicinity || ~学校 local schools

34 短途 [-] duǎntú (short-distance) <adj.> short-distance: ~运输 a short-distance transportation || ~旅游 (lǚyóu) a short-distance travel

35 近距离 [--離] jìnjùlí (close-distance) <n.> a close distance: ~观察 (guānchá) closely observe, a close observation

Tips:

1 快: The original meaning of 快 is not 'fast/quick' but 'pleasant' (痛快) since it is related to the 'heart' (忄, 心) as in a word '大快人心' (affording general satisfaction.)
2 永: Chinese calligraphy is a true art. If one wants to practice Chinese calligraphy, the very first character he should do is 永 because it contains the eight basic strokes of all Chinese characters. The term used to describe this is 永字八法.
3 世: One 世 is 30 years according to the original meaning of 世, but a 世纪 is 100 years.

Exercises:

Part I: Translate the following phrases into English and then answer the questions.

暂时现象 ______________________________
临时住所 ______________________________
高速铁路 ______________________________
迅速解决问题 ______________________________
做事儿磨蹭 ______________________________
发展速度缓慢 ______________________________
看了一下儿 ______________________________
一眨眼就到了 ______________________________
人应该长远打算 ______________________________
祝你永远幸福 ______________________________
两国世世代代友好 ______________________________
上帝永恒存在 ______________________________

1 哪些划线的词 (underlined word) 表示时间很短, 但是是口语?

____

2 哪些划线的词表示时间很短, 但是是书面语?

____

3 哪些划线的词表示时间很长?

____

4 哪些划线的词表示动作速度很快, 但是是口语?

____

5 哪些划线的词表示动作速度很快, 但是是书面语?

____

6 哪些划线的词表示动作速度很慢?

Theme 232: Real, fake, normal 真, 假, 正常 (zhēn, jiǎ, zhèngcháng)

(See also Theme 252)

1 真 [-] zhēn (real) <adj.> real, true, genuine: ~人true man || ~事real event || ~心sincere, heartfelt
2 真实 [-實] zhēnshí (real-true) <adj.> real, true, actual: ~情况 a real situation || ~的故事 true stories || ~原因 the real reason
3 真正 [-] zhēnzhèng (real-really) <adj.> real: ~的朋友 real friends || ~懂了 really understand || ~年轻 really young
4 实事求是 [實---] shíshìqiúshì (actual-situation-seek-original way) <idiom> seek truth from facts: ~的工作作风practical and realistic work style
5 货真价实 [貨-價實] huòzhēnjiàshí (goods-real-price-honest) <idiom> bang for the buck: 淘宝上的很多东西都不是~的. A lot of goods from Taobao are not genuine goods at fair prices.
6 名副其实 [---實] míngfùqíshí (fame-match-its-fact) <idiom> be worthy of the name, be true to one's name: ~的好老师 a good teacher in every sense of the word
7 属实 [屬實] shǔshí (be-true) <v.> verified: 情况~. It has been found to be true.
8 无疑 [無-] wúyí (no-doubt) <adv.> undoubtedly: 正确~ undoubtedly correct || 深信~ thoroughly convinced of || ~很重要 undoubtedly important
9 逼真 [-] bīzhēn (close to-real) <v.> lifelike, almost real: 效果 (xiàoguǒ) ~ the effect is very realistic ||这件仿冒品做得非常~. This imitation is very lifelike.

10 假 [-] jiǎ (false) <adj.> artificial, false, fake: ~结婚 fake marriage || ~名字 a false name || ~牙 false teeth
11 虚假 [-] xūjiǎ (void-false) <adj.> false: ~新闻fake news || ~广告 sham advertisement
12 荒诞 [-誕] huāngdàn (fantastic-absurd) <adj.> ridiculous: ~的谣言 (yáoyán) ridiculous rumor || ~的情节incredible plot || ~的故事 ridiculous story

13 普通 [-] pǔtōng (general-common) <adj.> common, general, ordinary: ~人 ordinary people || ~老百姓 common people || ~大学 ordinary universities
14 日常 [-] rìcháng (daily-normal) <adj.> daily, routine: ~工作 daily work, routine work || ~用品 daily supplies || ~生活 daily life
15 通常 [-] tōngcháng (common-normal) <adj.> usual, regular: ~情况下under normal conditions || 我~六点起床. I generally get up at six o'clock.
16 一般 [-] yībān (same-kind) <adj.> general, common, average: ~来说generally speaking || ~学校 an ordinary school || ~人 an average person
17 合格 [-] hégé (up to-standard) <adj.> qualified, certificated: ~的产品 a certificated product || 全部~ all qualified || 考试不~ fail the exam
18 及格 [-] jígé (reach-standard) <v-o.> pass: 及不了格 be not able to pass the exam || 考试~ pass the exam || ~分数 the passing grade

19 特别 [-別] tèbié (exceptional-especial) <adj.> extraordinary, especial, particular: ~的规定 a particular provision || ~情况 a special case || ~的人 a special person
20 特定 [-] tèdìng (specifically-designated) <adj.> specific, given, certain: ~社会 a specific society || ~条件 a given condition || ~时间 a certain time
21 特殊 [-] tèshū (exceptional-different) <adj.> special: ~意义 a special meaning || ~关系 a special relationship || 情况~ a special occasion
22 独特 [獨-] dútè (unique-exceptional) <adj.> unique: ~的味道 (wèidao) a unique taste || ~的东西 a unique item || ~的方法 a unique method
23 典型 [-] diǎnxíng (classic-type) <adj.> typical, representative: ~代表 typical representative || ~人物 the typical characters || ~的例子 a typical example
24 唯一 [-] wéiyī (only-one) <adj.> only, sole: ~原因 the only reason || ~的人 the only person || ~目的 the sole purpose
25 专门 [專門] zhuānmén (special-subject) <adj.> specialized: ~人才specialized talented person || ~为儿童写故事write a story especially for children

26 杰出 [傑-] jiéchū (distinguished-outstanding) <adj.> distinguished, outstanding: ~的代表 an outstanding representative || ~的贡献 (gòngxiàn) outstanding contributions || ~的诗人 a distinguished poet
27 突出 [-] tūchū (prominent-outstanding) <adj.> prominent, outstanding: 成绩 (chéngjì) ~ outstanding achievements || ~的地位 an outstanding status || ~的问题 a prominent problem
28 了不起 [-] liǎobuqǐ (wise-terrific) <adj.> extraordinary, amazing, terrific: ~的人 an extraordinary person || ~的大事a significant event || ~的成绩a tremendous achievement
29 奇妙 [-] qímiào (incredible-mysterious) <adj.> wonderful, fantastic, marvelous: ~的感觉 a fantastic feeling || ~的声音 a wonderful voice || ~的景色 fantastic sights
30 神奇 [-] shénqí (magic-incredible) <adj.> amazing magic: ~传说 amazing legends || ~的花 magic flowers || ~地出现 magically appear
31 十足 [-] shízú (fully-adequate) <adj./adv.> be full of, really: 干劲~ be full of energy || 孩子气~ really childish || ~的书呆子 a real nerd
32 正常 [-] zhèngcháng (just-normal) <adj.> normal, regular: ~的人 a normal person || ~温度 a normal temperature || ~工作 a normal work

33 常见 [-見] chángjiàn (common-seen) <adj.> common, familiar, usual: ~的词语 common words || 最~的软件 the most common software || 比较 ~的问题 very common problems
34 平凡 [-] píngfán (ordinary-mediocre) <adj.> commonplace, ordinary, mundane: ~的人 ordinary people || ~的事 mundane things || 出身~ born ordinary
35 不错 [-錯] búcuò (not-bad) <adj.> good, nice: 成绩~ good grades || 干得 ~ well done, good job, nice work || ~的电影 good movie
36 实在 [實-] shízài (really-is) <adj./adv.> honest, really: 他这个人很 ~. He is an honest and truly dependable man. || ~对不起. I'm really sorry.
37 实际 [實際] shíjì (real-situation) <adj./n.> practical, actual, reality: ~情况 a practical situation || ~问题 a practical issue/problem/question || 理论 (lǐlùn) 联系 (liánxì) ~ linking theory with practice, combine theory and practice, connection between theory and practice

38 反常 [-] fǎncháng (opposite to-normal) <adj.> unusual, abnormal: ~行为 anomalous/atypical behavior || 心理 ~ mental distortion || ~的地方 an unusual place

39 异常 [異-] yìcháng (different from-normal) <adj.> unusual, abnormal, aberrant: 情况 ~. The situation is unusual. || 性格~ an abnormal character || ~行为 an unusual behavior
40 敏感 [-] mǐngǎn (quick-sense) <adj.> sensitive, subtle, susceptive: ~话题 a sensitive topic || ~问题 a sensitive issue || 价格~. The price is sensitive.
41 奇怪 [-] qíguài (strange-weird) <adj.> strange, weird: 感到/觉得~ feel strange || ~的名字 a strange name || ~的帽子 a weird cap
42 怪 [-] guài (weird) <adj.> weird, strange: ~人 freak, wack, crackpot, screwball, kook || ~味道 a strange taste || ~地方 a strange place
43 古怪 [-] gǔguài (odd-weird) <adj.> weird, strange, odd: ~的问题 a weird question || 脾气 ~ an odd temper || ~的桌子an odd table
44 偶然 [-] ǒurán (by chance-*suffix*) <adj.> by accident: ~事件 accidents || ~机会 an accident opportunity || ~遇到 run into, come up against
45 突然 [-] tūrán (sudden-*suffix*) <adj.> sudden: ~的变化 a sudden change || ~的电话 ring suddenly || 太~ too sudden
46 意外 [-] yìwài (expectation-outside) <adj./n.> accident, unexpected, surprised: ~情况 an accident situation || ~消息 an unexpected message || 感到~ feel surprised

Tips:

1 实事求是 (shíshìqiúshì): According to *500 Common Chinese Idioms* by Liwei Jiao et al., 实事求是 is the most common Chinese idiom.
2 诞 (dàn): 诞 means 'birth' in words such as 圣诞节 (Shèngdànjié, saint-birthday, Christmas), 诞生 (birth) and 诞辰 (dànchén, anniverary of birthday) etc., however, the original meaning of 诞 is 'to boast,' from which the meaning of 'absurd' has evolved.
3 怪: Confucius is a sage, but he never discussed four subjects, 怪, 力, 乱, 神 (guài, lì, luàn, shén, extraordinary things, feats of strength, disorder and spiritual beings.)
4 典 (diǎn): The upper part of 典 is 册 (cè, book) and the lower part is 大 (here means 'hold with two hands,') therefore, the whole character means 'classic' as in words such as 经典 (classics) and 词典 (dictionary.)

Exercises:

Part I:

A: Use the given bound form as a guide to help you think of other words with the same beginning character. Feel free to use your dictionary when needed. Then write down the English definition of each of the words you've written.

真 *(real):* 真正 *real*

____

____

____

____

实 *(true)*: 诚实 *honest*

____

____

____

____

特 *(especial)*: 特别 *especially*

____

____

____

____

常 *(often)*: 常常 *often*

____

____

____

____

B: Translate the following phrases into English.

平凡而普通的人	__________________
日常生活	__________________
常见问题	__________________
真实情况	__________________
一切情况正常	__________________
表现反常	__________________
货真价实的商品	__________________
实事求是的工作作风	__________________
名副其实的好老师	__________________

Part III: Read the following sentences and fill in each blank with the appropriate word or phrase from the options given.

1 通常、普通

在美国__________大学毕业生的第一年收入_________低于五万美元.

2 逼真、虚假、荒诞、真正、属实

a) 据说"美丽中国"项目能够帮助美国大学生__________了解中国.

b) 办理中国签证的时候， 你的个人信息必须____________， 不能有__________信息.

c) 这部关于海底世界的电影虽然情节很__________ _, 但是画面拍得非常____________, 使人感觉到了真正的海底世界.

3 典型、唯一、特殊

a) 二战时期美国是世界上________研究出来核武器 (héwǔqì, nuclear weapon) 的国家.
b) 有人说美国是一个移民国家, 没有什么________的美国人.
c) 有人说中国经济发展没有什么________的方法, 无非是靠廉价 (liánjià, cheap) 劳动和消耗 (xiāohào, consume) 自然资源.

4 偶然、突然、意外

a) 据说住在加州的人最怕晚上________发生地震 (dìzhèn, earthquake), 因为他们会没有任何准备.
b) 一个________机会小张在美国遇到了他的中国小学同学, 他们都感到非常________.

5 敏感、杰出、专门

a) 种族 (zhǒngzú, race) 歧视 (qíshì, discrimination) 问题一直是美国的________话题.
b) 美国经济发展的一个重要原因是他们能够吸引世界各地的________人才来美国.
c) 美国政府__________有一个部门来处理 (chǔlǐ, deal with) 移民 (yímín, immigration) 问题.

Theme 233: Good, bad and worse 好, 坏, 差 (hǎo, huài, chà)

1 好 [-] hǎo (good) <adj.> good, nice: ~ 人 good people || ~天气 a nice weather || 说得~ well said
2 棒 [-] bàng (bravo) <adj.> excellent, wonderful, terrific: ~小伙 an excellent boy || 真~ really good || 太~了 great, wonderful, excellent
3 完美 [-] wánměi (impeccable-wonderful) <adj.> perfect: ~的人 a perfect person || ~的事 perfect things || ~的社会 a perfect world
4 十全十美 [-] shíquánshíměi (completely-complete-completely-wonderful) <idiom> be perfect in every way, leave nothing to be desired: 把工作做得~ finish the job perfectly || 天底下没有~的事. Nothing is perfect in every way.
5 一流 [-] yī liú (first-class) <adj.> first-rate, classic: ~的服务 the first-rate service || ~人才 the first-class talented person || ~城市 the first-class city
6 出色 [-] chūsè (outstand-spectrum) <adj.> excellent, outstanding, remarkable: 干得~ do a good job || 工作 ~ an excellent work || ~的人 an outstanding person
7 精彩 [-] jīngcǎi (vigorous-colorful) <adj.> wonderful, splendid: ~的节目 brilliant performance, wonderful program || ~的表演 (biǎoyǎn) wonderful performance || 唱得十分~. The singing was wonderful.
8 巧妙 [-] qiǎomiào (clever-ingenious) <adj.> ingenious, artful: ~地回答 answer deftly || ~的办法 an ingenious way || ~运用 an ingenious application
9 巧 [-] qiǎo (skillful, clever) <adj.> artful, cunning, skillful: 做得~ artfully made
10 高超 [-] gāochāo (high-superb) <adj.> superb, exquisite: 技术~ super-duper technology || ~的见解 superb view
11 惊人 [-] jīngrén (surprise-people) <adj.> amazing, horrendous: ~的速度 an alarming rate || 慢得~ surprisingly slow || 数字~ staggering numbers

12 最佳 [-] zuìjiā (most-good) <adj.> optimum, best: ~ 位置 the best position || ~方案 an optimum decision/option || ~时机 the best time

13 漂亮 [-] piàoliang (rinse-bright) <adj./adv.> beautiful, beautifully: 说得~ speak beautifully || 你汉字写得真~. Your Chinese characters are beautifully written. || 干得~ do something beautifully

14 可爱 [-愛] kě'ài (*prefix*-love) <adj.> cute, lovely: ~的孩子 cute kids || 可爱的小狗 a cute puppy || 长得~ look cute

15 迷人 [-] mírén (fascinate-people) <adj.> charming, attractive: ~的风景 enchanting scenery, beautiful scenery, charming scenery || ~的蓝眼睛 attractive blue eyes || ~姑娘 a charming girl

16 帅 [-] shuài (commander, model, handsome) <adj.> handsome: 长得~ looks handsome || ~哥 a handsome boy || ~小伙 a handsome guy

17 坏 [壞] huài (collapse, ruin, bad) <adj.> bad: ~消息 a bad new || ~习惯 a bad habit || 用~了 worn-out

18 差 [-] chà (mistake, bad) <adj.> bad, poor: 吃得~ eat poorly || 住得 ~ live poorly || 质量 (zhìliàng) ~ bad quality

19 破 [-] pò (broken) <adj.> broken, damaged: ~衣服 broken clothes || ~车 a broken car || ~房子 a damaged house

20 次 [-] cì (second) <adj.> inferior: ~品 inferior-quality products || ~货 inferior goods

21 不良 [-] búliáng (not-good) <adj.> bad, undesirable: ~后果 bad consequence || ~行为 bad behavior || 消化~ indigestion

22 糟 [-] zāo (draff, coarse, bad) <adj.> bad, terrible: 情况~ a bad situation || 考得~ did terribly in the exam || 影响 (yǐngxiǎng) ~ a worse effect

23 糟糕 [-] zāogāo (draff-cake) <adj.> bad, terrible: 心情~ a bad mood || ~的事 a terrible thing || ~的条件 a bad condition

24 赖 [賴] lài (bad) <adj.> poor, bad: ~脾气 a poor temper || ~年月 bad years || 这烟不~ this cigarette is not bad

25 烦人 [煩-] fánrén (annoy-people) <adj.> annoying: ~的亲戚annoying relatives || ~的雨 annoying rain

26 讨厌 [討厭] tǎoyàn (incur-loathe) <adj.> bothersome, disgusting, annoying, confounded, troublesome: ~的苍蝇 disgusting flies || ~的孩子 a bothersome child || ~的事儿 an annoying thing

27 该死 [該-] gāisǐ (ought to-die) <adj.> damn: ~的生活damnable life || ~的家伙damn guy || ~的天气 wretched weather

28 可怕 [-] kěpà (*prefix*-scare) <adj.> terrible, scare: ~的消息 the terrible news || ~的狼 a scare wolf || ~的病 a terrible disease

29 超级 [-級] chāojí (superb-level) <adj.> super: ~球迷 a superb football fan || ~大傻瓜 a super fool || ~大国 superpower

30 绝 [絕] jué (break, unique) <adj.> extinct, unique: ~招儿 a unique skill || ~法子 a unique method

31 妙 [-] miào (ingenious) <adj.> wonderful, good: 情况不 ~. The situation is not good. || ~主意 an excellent idea

32 优秀 [優-] yōuxiù (excellent-outstanding) <adj.> excellent: 成绩~ outstanding academic results, outstanding achievement || ~青年 outstanding young people || ~作品 excellent works

33 优良 [優-] yōuliáng (excellent-nice) <adj.> fine, good: ~传统 a fine tradition || ~品质 a fine quality || 成绩 ~ have good grades

34 优惠 [優-] yōuhuì (treat preferentially-benefit) <adj.> favorable, discount: ~的价格 a favorable price || ~条件 a favorable condition || ~门票 discount tickets

35 优质 [優質] yōuzhì (superb-quality) <adj.> superior, high-class: ~服务 superior service || ~产品 premium products || ~完成任务 finish the task of high quality

36 高级 [-級] gāojí (high-class) <adj.> high-class, superior, senior: ~饭店 a high-class restaurant || ~运动衣 superior sportswear || ~职员 senior staff

37 高档 [-檔] gāodàng (high-order) <adj.> fancy, high-grade/end: ~车 upscale cars || ~刀具 high-grade tool || ~商品 high-end commodity

38 高等 [-] gāoděng (high-grade) <adj.> high, advanced: ~教育 higher education || ~学校 high schools || ~动物 higher animal

39 高层 [-層] gāocéng (high-level) <adj./ n.> high-level, senior: ~人士/领导 high-level figures || ~管理者 senior managers || 公司~ the high-level personnel

40 良好 [-] liánghǎo (nice-good) <adj.> well, good: ~习惯 good habits || 表现 ~ behave well || 成绩~ have a good academic performance, get good grades

41 平常 [-] píngcháng (ordinary-common) <adj.> ordinary, usual, common: ~的事情 normal undertaking || ~人 an ordinary person || ~的生活 an ordinary life

42 中等 [-] zhōngděng (middle-grade) <adj.> medium, moderate: ~身材 medium-build || ~收入 middle income || ~城市 a middle city

43 中级 [-級] zhōngjí (middle-class) <adj.> secondary, middle-rank: ~学校 an intermediate school || ~干部 middle-rank cadres || ~人才 intermediate talents

44 低档 [-檔] dīdàng (low-order) <adj.> low-end, cheap: ~鞋 low-end shoes || ~衣服 cheap clothes

45 初等 [-] chūděng (beginning-grade) <adj.> elementary, primary, rudimentary: ~教育 the elementary education || ~水平 an elementary level || ~小学 elementary schools

46 初级 [-級] chūjí (beginning-class) <adj.> primary, elementary: ~班 the class for beginners || ~产品 primary commodities || ~小学 elementary schools

Tips:

1 厌 (厭): Now 厌 is used mostly in compounds such as 讨厌 (tǎoyàn) and 厌恶 (yànwù) both meaning 'dislike, annoying,' however, its original meaning is just the opposite, 'be well-fed, be content, satisfied.' The original meaning comes from the three components of 厭, 犬 (dog,) 月 (肉, meat) and 甘 (gān, sweet), i.e. 'one is well-fed with delicious (dog) meat.'

2 Chinese rating scales: English uses 'excellent, very good, good, fair, poor' to rate, and Chinese uses 优 (yōu, excellent,) 良 (liáng, very good,) 中 (good, fair) and 差 (chà, poor.)

Exercises:

Part I: Read the following words and then answer the questions.

漂亮、可爱、迷人、烦人、讨厌、该死、初级、中级、高级、抵挡、中档、高档、初等、中等、高等

1 上面哪些词可以形容一个漂亮的女孩儿?

____

2 上面哪些词可以用来骂人 (scold sb.)?

____

3 上面哪些词可以用来说明水平 (level)?

____

4 上面哪些词可以用来说明商品 (goods) 的档次?

____

5 上面哪些词可以用来说明教育层次 (education level)?

____

Part II: Read the following sentences and fill in each blank with the appropriate word or phrase from the options given.

1 完美、最佳、巧妙

a) 很多美国人认为她是一位__________的女性, 没有任何缺点 (quēdiǎn, weakness).
b) 她的情商很高, 总是会________地回答别人的问题.
c) 伊万卡·川普(Ivanka Trump)认为做生意成功的关键 (guānjiàn, key) 是把握 (bǎwò, grasp) ________时机.

2 出色、高超、十全十美

a) 一般来说美国总统的子女都很_________, 但不能说是_________.
b) 一般来说参加总统竞选 (jìngxuǎn, campaign) 需要__________ _的演讲技巧.

3 精彩、惊人

这部新电影太________了, 我看了很多遍. 里面的男主人公武打 (wǔdǎ, martial arts) 动作________.

4 一流、高档、高等

a) 美国______教育比较发达, 有很多世界_______大学.
b) 一般来说, 普通美国人出去旅行的时候不会选择住_______宾馆, 他们更喜欢使用Airbnb.

5 良好、优秀、平常

老李有三个孩子在上美国大学， 老大的成绩最好， 每门功课的成绩都是A+或者A, 也就是中国人所说的_________, 老二的成绩常常是A-或者B+, 也就是中国人所说的_________, 老三的成绩常常是B或者C+, 也就是中国人所说的_________.

6 优质、优惠、高层

a) 据报道, 美国优步 (Uber) 公司最近有很多法律纠纷 (jiūfēn, dispute), 为此公司_______领导紧急 (jǐnjí, urgent) 举行会议, 讨论应对危机的问题.
b) 美国优步公司决定将加强管理, 保证为乘客提供________服务.
c) 如果你是第一次使用优步打车, 你会得到二十美元的________.

Theme 234: Right or wrong 对, 错 (duì, cuò)

1 对 [對] duì (answer, correct) <adj.> right: 说得~ have spoken correctly || 做~了did right || 不 ~ not right
2 正确 [-確] zhèngquè (correct-true) <adj.> correct, proper: ~的意见correct suggestion || ~的方法correct method || 回答~ answer correctly
3 准确 [準確] zhǔnquè (accurate-true) <adj.> accurate, precise: ~地说明 explain in precise terms || ~的数字accurate figure || 回答~. The answer is accurate.
4 准 [準] zhǔn (accurate) <adj./adv.> accurate, exact: 发音~. The pronunciation is accurate. || 时间~. The time is accurate. || 真~ exactly
5 没错 [-錯] méicuò (not-wrong) <adj.> right: 都 ~ all is right || 回答~ answer correctly || 路~. The way is right.
6 科学 [-學] kēxué (borrowed from Japanese 'science') <adj.> scientific: ~的态度 scientific attitude || ~的方法scientific method || ~实验scientific experiment
7 可靠 [-] kěkào (can-rely) <adj.> reliable: ~消息reliable information || 这个人不 ~ this person is not reliable || 政治上~ politically reliable
8 合理 [-] hélǐ (conform to-reason) <adj.> reasonable, rational, equitable: 时间安排~ a well worked out timetable || ~的价格a reasonable price || ~利用资源 (zīyuán) put resources to rational use, make rational use of resources
9 合适 [-適] héshì (suitable-fitting) <adj.> suitable, fitting, appropriate: 小王做这个工作很~ the job is right for Little Wang || 大小~ just the right size || 在古建筑 (jiànzhù) 前, 建一个现代建筑不~. It is inappropriate to put up such a modern building in front of this ancient building.
10 适当 [適當] shìdàng (fitting-appropriate) <adj.> suitable, appropriate: 在~的时候 at an appropriate moment || ~的工作suitable work || ~调整 (tiáozhěng) appropriate readjustment
11 恰当 [-當] qiàdàng (just-appropriate) <adj.> proper, suitable, appropriate: ~的词 an appropriate word || 运用 ~ apply appropriately || ~处理take care of sth. properly
12 得体 [-體] détǐ (appropriate to-occasion) <adj.> appropriate to the occasion, fitting: 打扮 (dǎban) ~ be suitably dressed || 说话~ speak in appropriate terms

13 稳 [穩] wěn (stable) <adj.> steady, firm, stable: 等车停~了再下车. Do not get out of the car before it comes to a complete stop. || 坐~. Sit tight. || 把桌子放~. Make the table steady.

14 保险 [-險] bǎoxiǎn (to guard-danger) <adj.> safe: 坐飞机不~. Taking a flight is not very safe. || 网上买东西很~. It is very safe to go shopping online. || ~公司 insurance company

15 客观 [-觀] kèguān (object-view) <adj.> objective, impartial: 他看问题比较~. He looks at problems objectively. || ~事实objective reality || ~规律objective law

16 及时 [-時] jíshí (right-moment) <adj.> timely, in time, seasonable: ~发现 find in good time || 得到~治疗get timely medical treatment || ~解决 (jiějué) be resolved in good time

17 错 [錯] cuò (mistake) <adj.> wrong: 走~了 went the wrong way || 拿 ~东西take sth. by mistake || 方向~了wrong direction

18 错误 [錯誤] cuòwù (mistake-err) <adj./n.> wrong, mistake: ~的方向wrong direction || 犯~ make a mistake || 完全~ totally wrong

19 荒谬 [-謬] huāngmiù (unreasonable-err) <adj.> absurd, ridiculous: 观点~ absurd opinions || ~的历史a ridiculous history

20 悖论 [-論] bèilùn (contradicted-argument) <n.> paradox (logic): 一个~ a paradox || 明显的~ an apparent paradox

21 硬 [-] yìng (hard, obstinate) <adj.> hard, strong, obstinate: ~木家具hardwood furniture || ~不承认错误obstinately refuse to admit one's error || 牌子 ~ a trademark of high standing

22 不对 [-對] búduì (not-correct) <adj.> incorrect, wrong: 数字 ~ wrong number || 观点~ incorrect opinion || 这种说法是~的that's a false statement.

23 不当 [-當] bùdàng (not-proper) <adj.> improper, inappropriate: 方法~ inappropriate way || 处理~ not be handled properly || 用人~ not choose the right person for the job

24 不宜 [-] búyí (not-suitable) <adj.> not suitable, inadvisable, inappropriate: 儿童~ not suitable for children || 父母对孩子~要求过高. Parents shouldn't ask too much of a child. || ~居住unlivable

25 生搬硬套 [-] shēngbānyìngtào (raw-copy-stiff-apply) <idiom> apply or copy mechanically: ~地学习 study with the method of copying mechanically

Tips:

1 对 (對): The original meaning of 对 (對) is 'to answer/reply' as in 对答如流 (answer questions fluently) and 无言以对 (have nothing to say in response.) When you answer questions, you need to stand/sit face to face, therefore 对 (對) evolved into meanings such as 'to face,' then 'to match' and then 'correct.'

2 当 (當): The original meaning of 当 (當) is '(two pieces of land are) equal' and still exists in words such as 旗鼓相当 (qígǔxiāngdāng, flag-drum-mutual-equal, be well-matched) and 门当户对 (gate-equal-household-match, be well-matched in social and economic status for marriage.)

Exercises:

Part I: Write an antonym for each word in the table. You can refer to the given words.

荒谬、错误、不合理、不得体、不当、客观

科学 v.s.	正确v.s.	合理v.s.
得体v.s.	合适v.s.	主观v.s.

Part II: Read the following sentences and fill in each blank with the appropriate word or phrase from the options given.

1 荒谬、悖论、错误

a) 小李在工作中犯了很多________, 差点丢了饭碗 (lose one's job).
b) 小李建议公司到非洲去投资, 领导觉得他的建议很_________.
c) "节约是一种美德," 这种道德观点对一些经济学家来说是一种_________, 因为他们认为没有消费经济就会很差.

2 合适、适当、得体

a) 小李觉得现在的工作对他很_________.
b) 小李认为工作面试的时候穿着_________非常重要, 会给面试官留下好印象.
c) 小李会在________的时候向领导提出涨工资.

3 客观、不宜、保险、生搬硬套

a) 小李现在的工作很稳定 (wěndìng, stable), 很______.
b) ________地说, 贫困地区的学生________学习艺术专业, 因为花费太高.
c) 学习艺术不能__________, 应该具有创造性.

Theme 235: Advantage and disadvantage 利, 弊 (lì, bì)

1 利弊 [-] lìbì (advantage-disadvantage) <n.> advantages and disadvantages: 各有~ there are both advantages and disadvantages || 比较~ be compared with the advantages and disadvantages || 权衡 (quánhéng) ~ weigh the advantages and disadvantages
2 有利有弊 [-] yǒulì yǒubì (have-advantage-have-disadvantage) <idiom> there are both advantages and disadvantages: 任何事物都~. Everything has its own advantages and disadvantages. || 上网对孩子~. Surfing the Internet has pros and cons.
3 利大于弊 [--於-] lìdàyúbì (advantage-more-than-disadvantage) <idiom> advantages outweigh disadvantages: 网络~吗? Do advantages outweigh disadvantages when it comes to the Internet?
4 弊大于利 [--於-] bìdàyúlì (disadvantage-more-than-advantage) <idiom> disadvantages outweigh advantages: 玩电脑游戏~吗? Do the advantages of computer games outweigh the disadvantages?

5 有用 [-] yǒuyòng (have-use) <adj.> useful: ~的东西 useful staff || 我相信中文会越来越 ~. I believe the Chinese language will be increasingly useful.

6 适应 [適應] shìyìng (adapt-respond) <v.> adapt, fit: ~需要meet the needs of || ~时代的要求keep abreast of the times || ~新环境adapt to the new circumstances

7 可行 [-] kěxíng (*prefix*-practice) <adj.> feasible: ~的计划a feasible plan || ~的办法practical measure

8 灵验 [靈驗] língyàn (accurate-tested) <adj.> efficacious, effective, (of a prediction) accurate: 这种药非常~. This medicine is highly efficacious. || 天气预报 (yùbào) 果然~. The weather forecast turned out to be accurate.

9 有效 [-] yǒuxiào (have-effect) <v.> effective, valid: 方法~. The way is effective. || 感冒 (gǎnmào) 药~. This flu drug is effective. || 这张车票三日内~. This rain ticket is valid for three days.

10 方便 [-] fāngbiàn (compare-convenient) <adj.> convenient: 用起来很~ be easy to use || 这儿交通 ~ Transportation is convenient here. ||农村人口少, 生活不太~ The population in rural is scarce, and life is not so convenient.

11 便利 [-] biànlì (convenient-facilitate) <adj./v.> convenient, facilitate: ~的条件convenient conditions || 交通~ have convenient communications

12 实用 [實-] shíyòng (practical-use) <adj.> useful, practical: 这本词典很~ the dictionary is very useful || ~的知识practical knowledge || ~性practicability

13 实惠 [實-] shíhuì (real-benefit) <adj./n.> material benefit, substantial, solid: 这几年人民得到的~最多. In recent years the people have received greater material benefits than ever before. || 价格~ inexpensive price

14 没用 [-] méiyòng (no-use) <adj.> useless: 学了~. It won't help to study that. || 这本词典太旧, ~了. That dictionary is too old and is no longer useful. || ~的东西useless stuff

15 不便 [-] búbiàn (not-convenient) <adj./n.> inconvenient: 带来~ cause the inconvenience to someone || 行动~ have difficulty getting about || 交通~ have poor transport facilities

16 麻烦 [-煩] máfán (confusion-vexed) <adj./ n.> troublesome, inconvenient: 太~ too much trouble || ~事troubles || 对不起, 给您添 ~了. I'm sorry to have caused you so much trouble.

17 无效 [無-] wúxiào (no-effect) <adj.> invalid, ineffective, in vain: ~劳动labor in vain || ~合同invalid contract || 抢救~ fail to save the life

18 白 [-] bái (white, blank, in vain) <adv.> in vain, free of charge: ~来一趟make a fruitless trip || ~给give it free || 我的活儿~干了. All my work was wasted.

19 空 [-] kōng (empty) <adj./ adv.> for nothing, in vain: ~跑一趟make a journey for nothing || ~高兴一场have our happiness dashed to pieces

20 免费 [-費] miǎnfèi (free of-charge) <adj.> free of charge, free: ~医疗free medical care || ~入场admission free, be admitted gratis || ~午餐free lunch

21 无偿 [無償] wúcháng (no-repayment) <adv.> free, gratuitous: ~经济援助 (yuánzhù) free economic aid || ~服务free service || ~使用 free use

22 为难 [爲難] wéinán (feel-difficult) <adj.> feel awkward, make things difficult for sb.: ~的事an awkward matter || 感到~ be in an awkward situation || 老板故意~我. My boss deliberately makes things difficult for me.

Tips:

1 方便: 方便 has four meanings. The first and probably the original one is to take flexible means in order to achieve one's goal, in other words, convenient. The second is 'fit, suitable,' for example, 这儿说话不方便, 我们换个地方说吧 (It is not suitable to speak here, let's find another place.) The third is 'have money to spare or lend,' for example, 我手头不方便, 你能不能借我一点儿钱? (I am short of money. Could you lend me some?) The fourth is an euphemism of 'go to the bathroom/toilet,' for example, 不好意思, 我要去方便一下 (Excuse me for a moment.)

2 利 and 弊: They usually go in pairs, such as 有利有弊, 利大于弊, 弊大于利 as listed above in this unit, as well as 各有利弊 (each has its advantages and disadvantages) and 权衡利弊 (quánhéng lìbì, to weigh the pros and cons.)

Exercises:

Part I: Multiple Choice. Make sure to choose the most appropriate answer.

1 "中国给很多非洲国家无偿经济援助," 意思是

A. 中国给非洲国家经济援助是无效的
B. 中国给非洲国家经济援助是免费的
C. 中国给非洲国家经济援助是有用的

2 "那个老板故意为难我," 意思是

A. 那个老板有意让我感到困难
B. 那个老板故意为了我
C. 那个老板有意让我制造困难

3 有人说中国改革开放30多年, "大部分农村老百姓没有得到实惠," 意思是

A. 大部分农村老百姓不诚实
B. 对大部分农村老百姓没有优惠
C. 大部分农老百姓没有得到真正的好处

4 "任何事情都有利有弊," 意思是

A. 任何事情都有对有错
B. 任何事情都有好的一面和坏的一面
C. 任何事情都利大于弊

5 中国高铁非常__________, 但是在美国大规模建高铁却不_________.

A. 便利、可行
B. 方便、有效
C. 便利、利弊

Theme 236: Broad, mixed. 广泛, 杂 (guǎngfàn, zá)

1 广泛 [廣-] guǎngfàn (wide-extensive) <adj.> extensive, wide-ranging: 引起~关注cause widespread concern || ~使用电脑. Computers are extensively employed. || 内容~ a wide range of subjects

2 广 [廣] guǎng (wide) <adj.> wide, broad: 知识面~ a wide range of knowledge || 兴趣~ interests are wide || 流行~ be widely prevalent

3 广大 [廣-] guǎngdà (wide-large) (of people) <adj.> numerous, (of an area or space) vast: ~人民群众the broad masses of the people || ~地区vast areas || ~农村the vast countryside

4 普遍 [-] pǔbiàn (universal-everywhere) <adj./adv.> universal, general: ~意义universal significance || ~使用widely be used || ~现象general phenomenon

5 无边 [無邊] wúbiān (no-boundary) <adj.> without boundary, endless: ~的大海a boundless ocean || ~的沙漠a vast expanse of desert

6 无限 [無-] wúxiàn (no-limit) <adj.> unlimited, unbounded: ~的创造力unlimited creative power

7 狭隘 [狹-] xiá'ài (narrow-minded-narrow) <adj.> (of mind, views, etc.) narrow and limited: ~的看法a narrow view || 心地 ~ be narrow-minded

8 紧 [緊] jǐn (tense, tight) <adj.> tight, strict, urgent: 中国父母对孩子管得很~. Chinese parents are very strict on their children. || 日程安排得很~. The schedule is pretty tight. || 时间很~. The time is urgent.

9 紧密 [緊-] jǐnmì (firm-close) <adj.> close: ~联系 (liánxì) close contact || ~结合be closely integrated with || ~合作close cooperation

10 全面 [-] quánmiàn (all-side) <adj.> all-round, all-sidedly: ~地看问题look at problems all-sidedly || ~发展all-round development

11 宏观 [-觀] hóngguān (macro-view) <adj.> macro: ~角度macro perspective || ~经济macro economy || ~管理macro-control

12 健全 [-] jiànquán (healthy-complete) <adj.> sound, healthy: 身心~ sound in mind and body || ~的心灵 a sound mind || ~的制度 (zhìdù) a sound system

13 周全 [-] zhōuquán (well-considered-complete) <adj.> thorough, comprehensive: 想得~ be considerate || 考虑~ consider as comprehensive as possible

14 完善 [-] wánshàn (perfect-good) <adj./ v.> refine: 自我~ self-improvement || ~市场improve market || ~法律refine the law

15 圆满 [圓滿] yuánmǎn (complete-satisfactory) <adj.> satisfactory, perfect: ~解决solve it satisfactorily || ~完成complete successfully || ~的解释a satisfactory explanation

16 严谨 [嚴謹] yánjǐn (serious-strict) <adj.> rigorous, compact, well-knit: 态度~ rigorous attitude || ~的结构rigorous structure || 工作~ be meticulous and precise in work

17 片面 [-] piànmiàn (partial-side) <adj.> unilateral, one-sided: ~发展take a one-sided approach to problems || ~看法a one-side view || ~了解partial understanding

18 主观 [-觀] zhǔguān (subject-view) <adj.> subjective: ~看法 subjective opinion || ~感受subjective feeling

19 断章取义 [斷--義] duànzhāngqǔyì (break-text-get-meaning) <idiom> quote out of context: 有的美国媒体会对某位政治家的演讲~, 然后批评他是种族主义者. Some American media take a politician's speech out of context and criticize him as a racist.

20 坐井观天 [--觀-] zuòjǐng guāntiān (sit-well-watch-sky) <idiom> look at the sky from the bottom of a well-have a very narrow view: 人们用~来比喻一个人目光短浅. People use the word 'sitting in the well to watch the sky' to describe the ones who have a very narrow view.

21 单一 [單-] dānyī (single-one) <adj.> single, unitary: 内容~ the content is single || 功能~ the function is single || 方法~ The method is simplistic.

22 单纯 [單純] dānchún (single-pure) <adj.> simple, pure: 小王这个人很~. Little Wang is very simple. || 小孩子的想法常常很~. The kid's mind is very pure. || 环境~ simple environment

23 纯 [純] chún (pure) <adj./adv.> pure, purely: ~白pure white || 目的不~ impurity purpose

24 纯粹 [純-] chúncuì (pure-unadulterated) <adj.> pure, unadulterated, purely: ~的爱pure love || ~的音乐pure music || ~是浪费时间. It was a sheer waste of time. || 我帮她~是为了友谊. I helped her purely out of friendship.

25 杂 [雜] zá (mixed) <adj.> miscellaneous, mixed: ~草weeds || ~事miscellaneous affairs || 参加会议的人很~. A motley group of people attended the meeting.

26 复杂 [複雜] fùzá (complex-mixed) <adj.> complicated, complex: ~的心情mixed feelings || 使事情 ~ make things complicated || 情况很~. The situation is rather complicated.

27 琐碎 [瑣-] suǒsuì (petty-trivial) <adj.> trifling, trivial: ~的家务household chores || ~的日常生活trivial daily life || ~的事情 small things

28 烦琐 [煩瑣] fánsuǒ (numerous-petty) <adj.> loaded down with trivial details: ~的手续over-elaborate procedure || 这篇文章写得太~. This article is too long and wordy.

29 累赘 [纍贅] léizhuì (tied-burdensome) <adj.> a burden on sb., a nuisance to sb., superfluous: 家庭的~ the burden of family || 感到~ feel it is a burden to me.

Tips:

1 烦琐 and 繁琐: They are alternative forms of each other.

2 累: 累 has three pronunciations. One is lèi, meaning 'tired' as in 劳累. The second is lěi, meaning 'accumulate' as in 积累 (jīlěi, to accumulate, accumulation) and 累计 (lěijì, to add up.) The third is léi, meaning 'overlap, pile one on top of another' as in 累赘 in this unit.

3 杂: It seems 杂 (雜) is related to 'bird (隹),' however, the 隹 and the 木 (therefore 集) is the sound of 杂, and the upper left part (衣) is the radical. 杂 (雜) originally means '(of clothes) multi-colored.'

Exercises:

Part I: Write an antonym for each word in the table. You can refer to the given words.

复杂、片面、宏观、结构严谨、杂、无限

单一 v.s.	全面v.s.	微观v.s.
断章取义v.s.	纯v.s.	有限v.s.

Part II: Read the following sentences and fill in each blank with the appropriate word or phrase from the options given.

1 广泛、广大

a) 美国西部的________地区都十分干旱.

b) 美国的中部地区__________种植 (zhòngzhí) 玉米.

2 狭隘、纯粹、普遍

a) 美国人_______认为亚洲人的数学比较好. 其实这种看法比较_______.
b) 其实美国是一个移民国家, 没有什么_________的美国人.

3 健全、周全、完善

a) 一般来说, 美国的民主和法制是比较______和_________的, 能够基本保证人民的自由.
b) 一般来说, 美国学校对待残疾 (cánjí) 人会想得比较__________, 几乎所有的学校都有残疾人停车位和洗手间.

4 圆满、断章取义、严谨

a) 不管是哪一届美国政府都不能_______解决美国的种族歧视 (qíshì) 问题.
b) 有的美国媒体的新闻并不十分_________, 为了吸引人们注意力, 常常会__________.

5 繁琐、坐井观天、累赘

a) 中国人常常用__________来形容一个人思想狭隘.
b) 一般来说, 外国人觉得汉字写起来比较________.
c) 现在很多中国父母也会选择住养老院, 因为他们不想成为儿女的_________.

Theme 237: Detailed, fictional 详细, 虚拟 (xiángxì, xūnǐ)

1 详细 [詳細] xiángxì (detailed-meticulous) <adj.> detailed, minute: 内容很~ the content is detailed || ~地介绍了情况describe the situation in details || ~的地址 detailed address
2 详尽 [詳盡] xiángjìn (detailed-completely) <adj.> detailed: ~的计划 a detailed plan || 讲得很~ it is very detailed || 她对这个问题做了~的研究. She made a detailed study of this problem.
3 简单 [簡單] jiǎndān (brief-simple) <adj.> simple: ~地介绍introduce simply || ~的方法simple method || 问题很~. The question is simple.
4 简略 [簡-] jiǎnlüè (brief-short) <adj.> brief: 内容~ the content is brief || ~的语言brief language || ~地介绍introduce briefly
5 简练 [簡練] jiǎnliàn (brief-selected) <adj.> terse, succinct: 写得很~ be succinct in writing || 他的文章很~. His article is succinct in style.
6 大概 [-] dàgài (roughly-approximate) <adj.> general, rough: ~情况 general situation || ~意思general idea || ~数量rough numbers
7 切实 [-實] qièshí (correspond to-fact) <adj.> feasible, practical: ~的行动feasible action || ~解决问题solve the problem in real earnest || ~可行的计划 feasible plans
8 具体 [-體] jùtǐ (in detail-embody) <adj.> conceret, specific, particuar: ~时间specified time || ~情况specific situation || 你说得~一点儿! Please be more specific! || ~问题~分析 case by case; specific problem specific analysis
9 形象 [-] xíngxiàng (concrete-image) <adj./n.> image, vividly: 良好~ good image || 公众~ public image || ~地说明 explicate vividly

10 空洞 [-] kōngdòng (empty-hollow) <adj.> empty, hollow: ~的口号empty slogan || ~的理论hollow theory || 内容~ hollow contents
11 抽象 [-] chōuxiàng (abstract-image) <adj.> abstract: ~理论 abstract theories || ~知识abstract knowledge || 哲学家的话太~, 不容易懂. The philosopher's words are not easy to abstract.
12 概括 [-] gàikuò (cover-include) <adv.> briefly: ~地说sum up || 高度的~ high summarization || ~的了解understand briefly

Tips:

1 简 (jiǎn): 简 appears in three words 简单, 简略, 简练 in this unit. All the 简 in these three words mean 'brief, simple,' however, the original meaning of 简 is 'bamboo slips' which still exists in compound forms such as 竹简.
2 概 (gài): Now 概 means 'summarize' as in 概括 (gàikuò) or 'approximate' as in 大概 (approximate,) however, the originally meaning of 概 is a leveling scraper/beam.

Exercises:

Read the following sentences and fill in each blank with the appropriate word or phrase from the options given.

1 简单、抽象

爱因斯坦(Einstein) 的"相对论" (Theory of Relativity) 很______, 可是这位中学物理老师用了一个很______的实验就让中学生们明白了这个理论.

2 具体、空洞
一些美国学生认为最糟糕 (zāogāo) 的中文老师总是喜欢讲一些_______的语法或者单词, 没有生动、_______的例句和练习.
3 详细、简略
一些中国玩具的说明书非常________, 即使看了也不知道怎么玩这个玩具. 可是日本玩具的说明书却很_______, 非常有用.
4 简练、详尽、概括、大概
a) 中国政府_______在世界上设立了几百家孔子学院, 传播 (chuánbō) 中国文化.
b) ________地说, 文化传播跟经济发展的关系非常密切 (mìqiè).
c) 李教授讲课非常_________, 从来不说废话. 但其实他的教案 (lesson plan) 非常_______, 把教学中可能出现的情况都写了下来.

Theme 238: Flexible 灵活 (línghuó)

1 活 [-] huó (live) <adj.> live, vivid, flexible: 他脑子很~. He has a quick mind. || 语言是~的Language is vivid. || ~鱼live fish
2 活泼 [-潑] huópo (lively-vigorous) <adj.> lively, vivid: 性格 (xìnggé) ~ be vivacious by nature. || 这个孩子很~. The child is lively.
3 活跃 [-躍] huóyuè (lively-active) <adj.> brisk, active, dynamic: 年轻人的思想很~. Young people are full of questions and ideas. || 这两天股票 (gǔpiào)

市场很~. The share market is very brisk these days. || 在辩论赛 (biànlùnsài) 上她表现 (biǎoxiàn) 得很~. She was very active in the debate.

4 生动 [-動] shēngdòng (lively-vivid) <adj.> lively, vivid: ~的例子/故事lively examples/stories || 情节~ lively plots || ~有趣vivid and interesting

5 鲜活 [鮮-] xiānhuó (fresh-alive) <adj.> fresh and alive: ~商品fresh goods || ~的鱼虾fresh fish and shrimp || 卡通片里的人物很~. The characters in the cartoon are very vivid.

6 有神 [-] yǒushén (have-vigor) <adj.> full of vigor: 双目~ have a pair of piercing eyes

7 有声有色 [-聲--] yǒushēngyǒusè (have-sound-have-color) <idiom> vivid and dramatic: 说得~ speak dramatically || ~的故事vivid stories

8 活灵活现 [-靈-現] huólínghuóxiàn (alive-spirit-lively-appear) <idiom> vivid, lifelike: 画得~ give a vivid drawing || 说得~ give a vivid description

9 感人 [-] gǎnrén (move-people) <adj.> touching, moving: ~的电影a moving movie || ~的故事a moving story || 她的经历太~了. Her experience was so moving.

10 煽情 [-] shānqíng (instigate-emotion) <adj.> rouse emotion, sensational: ~的小说sensational novels || ~ sensational words || 这个电视节目太~, 让人忍不住落泪. This TV program is so sensational that you can't help crying.

11 催人泪下 [--淚-] cuīrénlèixià (move-people-tear-fall) <idiom> move sb. to tears, be extremely moving: ~的故事. the moving story || 这部电影~. The movie is weepy.

12 振奋人心 [-奮--] zhènfènrénxīn (inspire-people-heart) <idiom> fill people with enthusiasm, inspiring: ~的消息 inspiring news || 他的演讲 (yǎnjiǎng) ~. His speech is inspiring.

13 引人入胜 [---勝] yǐnrénrùshèng (attract-people-into-excitement) <idiom> fascinating, enchanting, thrilling: ~的风景fascinating scene || 侦探 (zhēntàn) 小说中的故事~. The story in the detective story is fascinating.

14 奔放 [-] bēnfàng (rush-unrestrained) <adj.> bold and unrestrained: ~的性格open nature || 现代舞很~. The modern dance is very bold || 思想~ the mind is unrestrained

15 龙飞凤舞 [龍飛鳳-] lóngfēifèngwǔ (dragon-fly-phoenix-dance) <idiom> (of mountains or calligraphy) like dragons flying and phoenixes dancing – lively and vigorous flourshes in calligraphy, of a flamboyant style: 写得~ writing characters lively and vigorously || ~的草书lively cursive writing

16 天马行空 [-馬--] tiānmǎ-xíngkōng (heavenly-horse-run-sky) <idiom> a heavenly steed soaring across the skies-a powerful and unconstrained style (of writing, calligraphy, etc.): ~的想象 the unconstrained imagination || 她的写作~, 让人难以理解. Her writing is so unconstrained that it is hard to understand.

17 有趣 [-] yǒuqù (full of-interest) <adj.> interesting, funny: ~的名字 an interesting name || ~的故事an interesting story || 他说话很~. He has a funny speech.

18 风趣 [風-] fēngqù (breezy-interesting) <adj.> witty, humorous: 她说话很~. She is a witty talker. || 他的演讲充满~. His speech was full of wit.

19 好玩儿 [--兒] hǎowánr (good-fun) <adj.> fun: 觉得~ feel fun || ~的地方fun places || ~的游戏fun games

20 有意思 [-] yǒuyìsī (full of-meaning) <adj.> interesting: ~的故事 a interesting story || 这个人很~. This person is very interesting

21 妙不可言 [-] miàobúkěyán (wonderful-not-able to-express) <idiom> wonderful: ~的书 a wonderful book || 坐一下过山车吧, 那种感觉简直~! Take a rollercoaster. It's a wonderful feeling!

22 来劲 [來-] láijìn (full of-enthusiasm) <v.> full of enthusiasm, in high spirits: 他越说越~. The more he talked, the more excited he became. || 那么无聊 (wúliáo) 的事他却做得挺~. It was so boring, but he did it with great vigor.

23 有劲儿 [--兒] yǒujìnr (have-strength) <v.> have strength: 干得~ have strength in doing sth. || 胳膊~ strong arms || 你瞎折腾什么啊? 是不是~没处使啦! What are you doing? Do you have limitless strength?

24 好笑 [-] hǎoxiào (very-funny) <adj.> funny: 感到~ feel funny || ~的事情funny things || 那个老头儿挺~的. That old man is so funny.

25 可笑 [-] kěxiào (*prefix*-laugh) <adj.> funny, ridiculous: 觉得~ feel funny || ~的人a ridiculous person || 这个故事太~了. This story is so ridiculous.

26 滑稽 [-] huájī (slippery-check) <adj.> funny: 长相~ funny looking || 他很~, 总是让周围的人大笑. He is funny and always makes people around him laugh

27 幽默 [-] yōumò (*transliteration of* humor) <adj.> humorous: ~地回答a humorous answer || ~的话humorous words || ~画humorous picture

28 笑掉大牙 [-] xiàodiàodàyá (laugh-off-molar tooth) <idiom> ridiculous, to laugh one's head off: 他连这个都不知道, 简直让人~. He doesn't even know this. It is ridiculous enough to make people laugh their heads off.

29 笑话百出 [-話--] xiàohuàbǎichū (joke-by hundred-appear) <idiom> make many stupid mistakes, make oneself ridiculous: 外国人到了中国, 因为文化的差异 (chāyì), 常常~. 当然, 中国人到了外国也是这样. Foreigners who come to China often make a lot of stupid mistakes because of cultural differences, and of course, the Chinese do the same things in the foreign countries.

30 木 [-] mù (wood, numb) <adj.> insensitive: 这个人太~了. This chap is rather insensitive.

31 呆板 [-] dāibǎn (dull-wooden) <adj.> rigid, dull: 表情 (biǎoqíng) ~ one's expression is rigid || 他的课教得太~, 学生上课都想睡觉. His lessons are so dull that the students want to sleep in class.

32 僵硬 [-] jiāngyìng (stark-stiff) <adj.> stiff, rigid: 态度~ rigid attitude || 觉得手脚~ feel stiff in the limbs || 工作方法~ work in a mechanical way

33 生硬 [-] shēngyìng (mechanical-stiff) <adj.> (of writing) not smooth, blunt, stiff: 他说话不柔和 (róuhé), 语调很~. He spoke in a rather blunt voice. || ~地拒绝 (jùjué) bluntly reject of others || 态度 ~ be stiff in manner

34 单调 [單調] dāndiào (simple-melody) <adj.> dull, monotonous, drab: 生活~ the life is dull || 色彩~ dull coloring || 节目~ dull program

35 乏味 [-] fáwèi (lack-taste) <adj.> dull, insipid, tedious: 高中生活很~. The high school life is dull and tedious || ~的事boring things || 感到~ feel dull

36 干瘪 [乾癟] gānbiě (dry-shrivelled) <adj.> dry, wizened, (of writing) dull and uninteresting: ~的脸/身体 a wizened face/body || 语言 ~ dull language, colorless language || 内容~. The content of the writing is very dull.

37 枯燥 [-] kūzào (withered-dry) <adj.> uninteresting, dry and dull: ~的课本 uninteresting textbooks || ~的数字dull numbers || 生活~ dull life

38 没趣 [-] méiqù (no-fun) <adj.> bored, idle, feel snubbed: 自讨~ court a rebuff, ask for a snub || 觉得~ feel put out

39 平淡 [-] píngdàn (flat-bland) <adj.> flat, dull: ~的日子a dull day || 故事 ~. The story falls flat. || 婚后的生活 (过得) 很~. Life after marriage is very flat.

40 干巴巴 [乾--] gānbābā (dry-*suffix-reduplication*) <adj.> boring, dull: 这个人~的, 很没趣. The person is really boring. || 讲得 ~ The speech is dull.
41 没意思 [-] méi yìsi (no-meaning) <adj.> boring, bored: ~的活动the boring activity || 觉得~ feel bored || 这个人太~. He is such a boring man.
42 千篇一律 [-] qiānpiān-yīlǜ (1, 000-article-same-tone) <idiom> stereotyped, following the same pattern: ~的内容stereotyped contents ||一些人认为中国《人民日报》上的文章几乎~. Some people think the articles on the *People's Daily* in China are monotonous.

Tips:

1 笑: The character 笑 appears in four words, 可笑, 好笑, 笑掉大牙, 笑话百出 in this unit. The origin of 笑 is unclear. There are three explanations. One is that 笑 is related to bamboo (竹, ⺮) and 夭 (yāo.) It depicts the motion of a man who is laughing like bending bamboo. The second explanation is 笑 is related to bamboo (竹, ⺮) and 犬 (dog) since 哭 (kū, to cry) is related to 犬 (dog.) The form of 夭 was 犬 before the Song Dynasty. The third explanation is 笑 is related to ⺮ (NOT bamboo 竹, but the shape of two curved eyebrows when a person laughs) and 夭 (yāo.)
2 笑掉大牙: It means 'laugh one's head off.' The 大牙 means 槽牙 (cáoyá, molar teeth,) not 门牙 (incisors.)
3 幽默 (humorous): A good sense of humor is greatly appreciated in the Western world, however, it was condemned in ancient China based on Confucius' teaching '巧言令色鲜矣仁' (qiǎoyán lìngsè xiǎnyǐ rén, Fine words and an insinuating appearance are seldom associated with true virtue.)" This mindset leads many Chinese people to speak in a very boring manner. But the situation is changing rapidly.
4 活灵活现: An alternative, or perhaps true form of 活灵活现 is 活龙活现.
5 滑稽 (huájī): 滑稽 is an old word that appeared in latest the *Records of the Grand Historian* (史记,) which has a volume named 滑稽列传 (*Biographies of Jesters*.) However, the 滑 was pronounced gǔ, not huá at that time.

Exercises:

Part I: Put the similar meaning words in the same table.

枯燥、干巴巴、没意思、千篇一律、好笑、滑稽、幽默、笑掉大牙、乏味、单调、平淡、有意思、好玩儿、僵硬、呆板、催人泪下、有声有色

没趣:
可笑:
干瘪:
有趣:
生硬:
感人:
活灵活现:

Part II: Read the following sentences and fill in each blank with the appropriate word or phrase from the options given.

1 有趣、风趣、笑话百出

a) 小张是一个非常__________的人，常常在午饭时间给大家讲________的笑话.

b) 小张非常粗心 (cūxīn, careless), 为此他在生活中常常_____________, 他的家人及亲戚 (qīnqi) 都知道他闹的笑话.

2 龙飞凤舞、天马行空、振奋人心

a) 中美两国关系有十分_____________的时期，也有令人担忧 (dānyōu) 的时期.

b) 这个美国学生的书法________________, 特别引人注目.

c) 这个美国学生的演讲______________, 没有任何逻辑 (luóji, logic) 关系, 让人很失望 (shīwàng, disappointed).

3 活灵活现、乏味、生硬、妙不可言

a) 很多人觉得住在美国农村比较___________，因为娱乐 (yúlè, entertainment) 活动太少了.

b) 有些人不喜欢这个美国总统, 因为他说话很______________, 不顾及 (gùjí, care) 别人的感受 (gǎnshòu, feeling).

c) 据说这位总统的女儿, 画画画得______________, 非常生动.

d) 总统女儿的文章写得太好了, 简直________________.

4 千篇一律、有神、笑话百出、有声有色

a) 美国总统华盛顿的肖像 (xiàoxiàng, portrait) 双目___________，给人留下了非常深刻的印象.

b) 这部电影_____________地讲述了美国总统华盛顿的故事.

c) 中国文革 时期的歌曲很单调 (dāndiào, dull), 基本上都是___________地赞美 (zànměi, praise) 毛主席.

d) 外国人到了中国, 因为文化的差异, 常常_____________. 当然, 中国人到了外国也是这样.

Theme 239: Easy or hard 容易, 困难 (róngyì, kùnnán)

1 难 [難] nán (difficult) <adj.> difficult: ~学It is difficult to learn || ~办It is hard to deal with || 骑自行车不~. It is not very hard to ride a bike.

2 不易 [-] búyì (not easy) <adj.> not easy, difficult: 学会围棋 (wéiqí) 很容易, 但是要学好很~. It is easy to learn how to play the game of Go, but it is difficult to learn it very well. || 相爱容易, 相处~. It's easy to fall in love with each other. But it's not easy to get along with each other. || ~理解. It is difficult to understand.

3 好 (不) 容易 [-] hǎo (bù) róng yì (very-not-easy) <adj.> not at all easy, very difficult: 孩子~才安静下来. The kids had a hard time calming down || ~才找到一个工作. It was very difficult to find a job. || 事情终于做完了, ~啊！Finally, it was done!

4 困难 [-難] kùnnan (stranded-difficult) <adj./n.> difficult, difficulty: 遇到~ have difficulties || 生活~ live in straightened circumstances || 克服 (kèfú) ~ overcome difficulties

5 疑难 [-難] yí'nán (doubt-difficulty) <adj.> difficult, knotty: ~问题 knotty problem || ~疾病 (jíbìng difficult and complicated illness || ~案件 (ànjiàn) difficult and complicated cases

6 难以 [難-] nányǐ (hard-to) <v.> be hard to, be difficult to: ~做到 be hard to do that || ~实现 (shíxiàn) be hard to realize it || 这个问题让他~回答. This question is difficult to answer for him.

7 来之不易 [來---] láizhībúyì (achieve-it-not-easy) <idiom> not easily come by, hard-earned: ~的胜利 (shènglì) hard-won victory || 老年人常说, 现在的幸福生活~. Old people often say that our current happy life was hard-earned.

8 难上加难 [難--難] nánshàngjiānán (difficult-above-add-difficult) <idiom> extremely difficult, all the more difficult: 找工作难, 女大学生找工作更是~. Finding a job is difficult, and female college students have an even more difficult time finding a job.

9 谈何容易 [談---] tánhéróngyì (talking-by no means-easy) <idiom> be difficult, by no means easy, not easy as you thought it to be: 他没读大学, 想当医生~. He didn't go to college, so it was very difficult for him to be a doctor. || 一个星期完成这项任务~！ It is not easy to finish the task in a week!

10 棘手 [-] jíshǒu (thorny-hand) <adj.> tough, tricky: ~的问题 though questions || 感到~ feel tricky || 令人~. It's tricky.

11 吃力 [-] chīlì (expend-strength) <adj.> strenuous, laborious: 在学习上感到~ encounter difficulties in their studies || 她以前没有工作经验, 现在工作起来有些~. She had no previous work experience, so it was difficult for her to get involved in her current job.

12 费劲 [費勁] fèijìn (cost-energy) <adj./v.> strenuous, need or exert great effort: 他看中文书一点儿不~. He can read Chinese books without any difficulty. || 学习~ exert great offort in studying || 求你做点儿事这么~, 算了, 不求你了. It is so hard to get your help. Forget it, I won't ask you again.

13 费力 [費-] fèilì (cost-strength) <adj.> strenuous, need or exert great effort: ~地往前走take the effort to move forward || 很~的事情hard work || ~不讨好 do a thankless job

14 费时 [費時] fèishí (cost-time) <adj.> take time, be time-consuming: 购物很~. Shopping takes lots of time. || ~三年take three years

15 伤脑筋 [傷腦-] shāng nǎojīn (hurt-brain) <adj.> naughty, cause sb. a headache: ~的事情 brainy problem || 选择好大学让人~. Choosing a good university gets on your nerves.

16 重 [-] zhòng (heavy) <adj.> heavy: 任务~ a heavy task || 负担~. The burden is heavy || ~活a heavy workload

17 繁重 [-] fánzhòng (tedious-heavy) <adj.> heavy, strenuous, onerous: ~的工作strenuous work || 任务 (rènwu) ~. The tasks are arduous.

18 艰巨 [艱-] jiānjù (hard-huge) <adj.> arduous, formidable: 任务~. The tasks are arduous || ~的工作arduous work

19 艰险 [艱險] jiānxiǎn (hard-dangerous) <adj./n.> hardships and dangers, perilous: 战地记者的工作环境很~. The working environment of the war correspondent is very difficult. || ~的道路 a perilous road

20 险恶 [險惡] xiǎn'è (dangerous-perilous) <adj.> dangerous, perilous, sinister: 病情~ dangerous ill || 他的用心很~. His intentions are sinister.

21 易 [-] yì (easy) <adv./adj.> easy: 十几岁的孩子的性格~变. A teenager's personality is fickle. || 由~到难from the easier to the advanced || 用儿歌教历史~学~记. It is easier to remember history with nursery rhymes.

22 容易 [-] róng'yì (unhurried-easy) <adj.> easy: ~接受easy to accept || ~理解 (lǐjiě) easy to understand || 学好日语并不~. It is not easy to learn Japanese very well.

23 轻易 [輕-] qīng'yì (rashly-easily) <adj./ adv.> easily, rashly: 别~相信陌生人. Don't trust strangers easily. || 别~辞掉 (cídiào) 工作. Don't quit your job rashly.

24 小儿科 [-兒-] xiǎo'ér kē (pediatrics-department) <n.> child's play, a piece of cake: 他计算机博士 (bóshì) 毕业, 玩这个游戏还不是~! He has a Ph.D. in computer science. It is a piece of cake for him to play this computer game!

25 举手之劳 [舉--勞] jǔshǒuzhīláo (raise-hand-'s-effort) <idiom> as easy as lifting one's finger-quite easy: 捡起地上的垃圾 (lājī) 只是~, 但是很多人不愿意做. It is just a piece of cake to pick up litter on the ground, but a lot of people don't want to do it.

26 轻而易举 [輕--舉] qīng'éryìjǔ (lightly-and-easily-do) <idiom> easy to do: ~的事情easy thing || ~地解决了solved the issue easily

27 易如反掌 [-] yìrúfǎnzhǎng (easy-as-turn-palm) <idiom> as easy as turning one's hand over: 做蛋糕对她来说~. It is very easy for her to make a cake.

28 深 [-] shēn (deep) <adj.> deep: 水~ deep water || 这个山洞很~. This cave is very deep. || 感情~ have a deep affection

29 深奥 [-奧] shēn'ào (deep-obscure) <adj.> abstruse, profound: ~的道理abstruse truth || ~的哲学 (zhéxué) abstruse philosophy || 这些话对小学生来说太~了. Such talk is too deep for school children.

30 高深 [-] gāoshēn (advanced-difficult) <adj.> advanced, profound: ~的理论 profound theory || 这个话题太~了, 一般人不懂. The topic is too deep for the common people to understand.

31 奥妙 [奧-] ào'miào (abstruse-wonderful) <adj./n.> secret, hidden, mystery: 宇宙 (yǔzhòu) 的~ the mystery of universe

32 晦涩 [-澀] huì'sè (dark-unsmooth) <adj.> obscure, unintelligible: ~的术语 (shùyǔ) unintelligible terms || 这篇文章~难懂. This article is full of obscurities.

33 别扭 [彆-] bièniu (discoordinated-twist) <adj.> uncomfortable and awkward: 闹~ being difficult || 感到 ~ feel uncomfortable and awkward || 我看这个人就~, 别理他. I think he is a weird guy. Leave him alone.

34 浅 [淺] qiǎn (shallow) <adj.> shallow: 内容~ The content is very shallow || 课文~ the text is very shallow

35 浅显 [淺顯] qiǎnxiǎn (easy-apparent) <adj.> plain, easy to read and understand: ~的道理plain truth || 文字~ the words are simple

36 粗浅 [-淺] cūqiǎn (coarse-superficial) <adj.> superficial, shallow: ~的意见 superficial opinions || ~的想法superficial thinking || 我的认识很~, 请多指正 (zhǐzhèng). My knowledge is very rough. Please correct me.

37 好懂 [-] hǎodǒng (easy-understand) <adj.> easy to understand: 南京话~. Nanjing dialects is easy to understand. || 经济学不~. Economics is not easy to understand.

38 通俗 [-] tōngsú (common-vulgar) <adj.> popular, common: ~歌曲 (gēqǔ) popular songs || ~的话simple words || 拿~的话来讲use a common expression

39 深入浅出 [--淺-] shēnrù qiǎnchū (deep-in-plain-out) <idiom> explain the profound in simple terms: 王教授 (jiàoshòu) 讲课~. Professor Wang had a useful simplification of his lecture.

40 平易近人 [-] píngyì jìnrén (amiable-easy-approachable-people) <idiom> amiable and easy to approach: ~的人a easy-going person || ~的态度kindly and approachable attitude || 虽然他地位很高, 但是~. Though he is a high-ranking official, he is so kind and approachable.

41 通畅 [-暢] tōngchàng (unimpeded-smooth) <adj./adv.> easy and smooth: 呼吸~ the breath is smooth || 交通~. Traffic is moving smoothly. || 高速公路~. The highway is very smooth.

42 流畅 [-暢] liúchàng (following-smooth) (of writing, speaking, etc.) <adj.> fluent, easy and smooth: ~的线条smooth lines || 文笔 ~ write with ease and grace || 表达很~ the expression is smooth

43 通顺 [-順] tōngshùn (smooth-coherent) (of writing) <adj.> clear and coherent, smooth: 这个句子不~. This sentence doesn't read smoothly || 逻辑 (luóji) ~. The logic is not clear and coherent.

44 流利 [-] liúlì (following-fluent) <adj./adv.> fluent, fluently: 说一口 ~的中文 speak fluent Chinese

45 朗朗上口 [-] lǎnglǎng shàngkǒu (loud and clear-*reduplication*-suitable-read aloud) <idiom> read aloud fluently, (of a tune, jingle etc.) be catchy: 简·奥斯汀的作品~. Jane Austen's work is catchy. || ~的歌曲a catchy song

Tips:

1 难 (難): 难 has two pronunciations. One is nán, meaning 'hard, difficult.' The other is nàn, meaning 'disaster.' For example, 难民 (nànmín) 的生活很困难 (kùnnán) means 'the life of refugees is hard.'

2 易: 易 has two basic meanings. One is 'easy' as in 容易, and the other 'exchange, change' as in 贸易 (trade) and 易经 (*I-Ching, the Book of Changes.*) The original meaning of 易 might be a lizard (蜴) or to spill (溢/益.)

3 难 or 易? How difficult/hard could a thing be? The Chinese say 难于上青天 (harder than climbing the blue sky). How easy could a thing be? 易如反掌. It means 'as easy as turning one's palm,' or 'as easy as pie.'

Exercises:

Part I: Use the given bound form as a guide to help you think of other words with the same beginning character. Feel free to use your dictionary when needed. Then write down the English definition of each of the words you've written.

深 *(deep):* 深奥 *profound*

____

____

____

____

浅 *(shallow):* 浅显 *plain*

____

____

____

____

易 *(easy):* 容易 *easy*

____

____

____

____

难 *(difficult):* 困难 *difficult*

____

____

____

____

费 *(cost, spend):* 费力 *strenuous*

____

____

____

____

Part II. Translate the following phrases into English and then answer the questions.

谈何容易 ________________
来之不易 ________________
难上加难 ________________
轻而易举 ________________
易如反掌 ________________
举手之劳 ________________
深入浅出 ________________
平易近人 ________________
朗朗上口 ________________

1 上面哪三个词可以形容非常难?

____

2 上面哪三个词可以形容非常容易?

____

3 你高中的物理老师讲课是不是深入浅出?

---

4 你的大学教授是否都很平易近人?

---

5 你觉得谁的诗读起来朗朗上口?

Theme 240: Primary and secondary 主要, 次要 (zhǔyào, cìyào)

1 基本 [-] jīběn (base-root) <adj.> fundamental, basic: ~问题basic questions || ~情况basic situation || ~概念 (gàiniàn) fundamental concept
2 起码 [-碼] qǐmǎ (rise-number) <adj./adv.> minimum, rudimentary: ~的要求minimum requirements || ~的知识rudimentary knowledge || 参加考试的人~有一百人. At least 100 people took this exam.
3 重大 [-] zhòngdà (important-big) <adj.> significant: ~问题vital problem || 取得~进展make significant progress || 意义 (yìyì) ~. The significance is great.
4 重要 [-] zhòngyào (important-key) <adj.> important: ~问题important problems || ~工作important work || ~事情important things
5 要紧 [-緊] yàojǐn (key-urgent) <adj.> important, essential: ~的事important things || 身体~. Health is very important. || 你忙吧, 我的事不~. Go on with your business. Don't worry about me.
6 紧要 [緊-] jǐnyào (urgent-key) <adj.> critical, vital: ~关头/时刻critical moment || ~的地方a vital place || 无关~ of no consequence
7 第一 [-] dìyī (number-one) <序数词> first: ~个 first || ~次for the first time || ~名number one
8 首要 [-] shǒuyào (primary-importance) <adj.> of the first importance, chief: ~问题most important issue || ~目标priority goal || ~任务the most important task
9 主打 [-] zhǔdǎ (main-promote) <adj.> leading, main: ~歌top song || ~产品main product || ~菜signature dishes
10 主要 [-] zhǔyào (main-key) <adj.> main: ~原因main reasons || ~缺点main shortcomings || ~特点main characters
11 要害 [-] yàohài (key-vital) <adj./n.> critical, vital: ~问题vital problem || ~地区vital area || 抓住~ get to the root of
12 根本 [-] gēnběn (root-primary root) <adj.> basic, fundamental, cardinal: ~原因basic reason || ~方向basic direction || ~问题basic problem
13 关键 [關鍵] guānjiàn (crux-key) <adj./n.> key, crux, critical: ~人物key figure || ~时刻critical moment || 抓住~ get to the key of || 这才是问题的~. This is the key to the problem.
14 举足轻重 [舉-輕-] jǔzúqīngzhòng (move-foot-light-heavy) <idiom> play a decisive role: ~的地位 a decisive position || ~的意义a decisive meaning || 出口对中国的经济来说~. Exports are important to China's economy.
15 至关重要 [-關--] zhìguānzhòngyào (most-crux-important) <idiom> most important, of the utmost importance: ~的问题 the crucial question || ~的

大事the most important thing || 自然资源 (zīyuán) 对经济发展~. Natural resources are vital to economic development.

16 人命关天 [--關-] rénmìng guāntiān (man's-life-relate-heaven) <idiom> a case involving human life is one of supreme importance: 安乐死和流产都是~的问题. Euthanasia and abortion are both involved in taking life of a human being.

17 核心 [-] héxīn (nucleus-center) <adj./n.> core: 问题的~ the core of the problem || ~问题 core issues || ~内容core content || ~力量core strength

18 为主 [為-] wéizhǔ (as-prime) <v.> give first place to: 这个团队以他~. He dominates the team. || 以制造业~. Manufacturing is the main industry. || 她的衣服以白色~. Her clothes are mostly white.

19 主导 [-導] zhǔdǎo (dominate-lead) <adj.> dominant, leading: ~作用leading role || ~地位dominant position || ~力量dominant force

20 中心 [-] zhōngxīn (center-heart) <adj./n.> center, central: 经济/文化~ economic/cultural center || ~地区central region || 以市场为~ focus on the market

21 副 [-] fù (secondary) <adj.> associate, vice: ~教授 associate professor || ~主任associate director || ~手deputy || ~总统the vice president

22 间接 [間-] jiànjiē (indirect-connect) <adj.> indirect: ~影响 (yǐngxiǎng) indirect effects || ~关系indirect relationship || ~方法indirect method

23 次要 [-] cìyào (secondary-important) <adj.> less important, secondary: ~问题secondary questions || ~地位a position of secondary importance || ~方面secondary aspect

24 其次 [-] qícì (its-second) <pron.> next, secondly: 这家店主要卖书, ~卖笔和各种文具. This store mainly sells books, and then sells pens and stationery. || 谈恋爱时性格是最主要的, ~才是相貌 (xiàngmào). When you're in a relationship with him or her, his or her personality is the most important, and the appearance is secondary.

25 区区 [區區] qūqū (trivial) <adj.> trifle: ~五毛钱a trifling 50 cents || ~小事, 何足挂齿. Such a trifle is not worth mentioning.

26 无所谓 [無-謂] wúsuǒwèi (no-so-called) <v.> not make much of, it doesn't matter: ~的态度uncaring attitude || ~真假. It makes no difference whether it's true or false. || 去不去~. It makes no difference whether you go or not. || 你怎么做都行, 我~. I don't care what you do.

27 不要紧 [--緊] bú yào jǐn (not-matter) <v.> it doesn't matter: 他的病~. His illness does not matter. || ~, 我会把事情处理好的. Don't worry. I'll take care of it.

28 没关系 [-關係] méi guānxi (no-significance) <v.> It doesn't matter: 一个人的外表跟他的能力~. A person's look has nothing to do with his abilities. || ~, 这次没成功, 下次一定会成功. It doesn't matter. It won't work this time. It will be successful next time.

29 没什么 [--麼] méi shénme (no-importance) <v.> nothing: ~特别nothing special || ~可怕. There is nothing to fear. || ~了不起. It is no big deal. || 我~可说的. I have nothing to say.

30 可有可无 [---無] kěyǒu-kěwú (may-have-may-not have) <idiom> not essential: 广播 (guǎngbō) 现在已经成为~的东西了. The radio is now a dispensable item.

31 微不足道 [-] wēibùzúdào (trivial-not-worth-say) <idiom> too trivial to mention, insignificant: ~的人物insignificant figure || 这点儿损失 (sǔnshī) 对他来说~. The loss was negligible to him.

32 无足轻重 [無-輕-] wúzúqīngzhòng (not-worth-significance) <idiom> if little importance, insignificant: ~的事情small things || 有一些人抗议 (kàngyì) 对总统的声誉 (shēngyù) 来说~. Those protesters are of no importance to the president's reputation.

33 无关大局 [無關--] wúguāndàjú (not-affect-overall-situation) <idiom> insignificant, of little account: ~的小事It is not about the big picture. || 尽管发生了一件意外的事, 但是已经~了. In spite of an accident, it has nothing to do with the big picture.

Tips:

1 要: This character has two pronunciations. One is yāo, which originally meant 'waist' (腰) from which evolved meanings such as 'invite, seek, request (要求)' etc. The other is yào which functions mainly as adjectives such as 'important (重要), essential, concise' and nouns such as 'important points (要点), scheme' etc.

2 次: The radical of 次 is 欠, not 冫 (ice). Actually the sound of 次 is related to 冫 (二.) Basically 次 has two clusters of meanings. One cluster means 'to stop' and the other 'the second, sequence.' The 次 in the words 次要, 其次 in this unit means 'second.'

Exercises:

Part I: Read the following words and put them in the column with the the similar words.

起码、关键、无关大局、可有可无、微不足道、无足轻重、不要紧、没关系、要紧、紧要、举足轻重、至关重要

基本:	
中心:	
无足轻重:	
无所谓:	
重要:	

Theme 241: Necessary, severeness 必要, 强烈 (bìyào, qiángliè)

1 必要 [-] bìyào (certainly-necessary) <adj.> necessary, essential: ~的一课 a necessary lesson || 空气、水和食物都是绝对 (juéduì) ~的东西. Air, water and food are absolutely indispensable. || ~的时候我会帮你. I will help when you need it.

2 少不了 [-] shǎobuliǎo (lack-not-able) <v.> cannot do without, be unavoidable: 我今天又没完成任务, 明天~挨老板的骂. I didn't finish the work today. So, I will be unavoidably scolded by my boss tomorrow. || 这次比赛~你. We can't do without you for this match. || ~哭鼻子be unavoidable to cry a lot

3 必不可少 [-] bìbukěshǎo (must-not-can-lack) <idiom> indispensable, essential: ~的内容necessary contents || ~的条件essential conditions

4 多余 [-餘] duōyú (extra-surplus) <adj.> unnecessary, superfluous: ~的人a unnecessary person || ~的担心 unnecessary worries || ~的话superfluous words

5 多此一举 [---舉] duōcǐyījǔ (unnecessary-this-one-act) <idiom> do something unnecessarily: 你这样做完全没必要, ~. It is absolutely unnecessary for you to do this.

6 毒 [-] dú (poison, fierce) <adj.> malicious, cruel, fierce: 太阳很~. The sun is fierce. || 他心肠真 ~! What a cruel man!

7 狠 [-] hěn (ruthless) <adj.> ruthless, relentless, firm: ~下功夫firmly work hard || 母亲安慰 (ānwèi) 孩子, 可是孩子哭得更~了. The mother tried to comfort her child, but the child cried harder. || 我把他~打了一顿. I gave him a good beating.

8 猛 [-] měng (violent, suddenly) <adj.> suddenly, fierce: ~回头turn around suddenly || 物价~涨a sharp rise in prices || 用力过~ use too much force

9 惨 [慘] cǎn (brutal, miserable) <adj.> miserable, tragic, cruel: 他们输得很~. They suffered a crushing defeat. || 他死得很~. He died a tragic death.

10 激烈 [-] jīliè (fierce-violent) <adj.> intense, heated: 竞争~ intense competition || ~的比赛closely fought game

11 猛烈 [-] měngliè (sudden-violent) <adj.> fierce, vigorous, violent: 心脏~地跳动rapid heartbeats || ~的风雨violent storm

12 剧烈 [劇-] jùliè (acute-violent) <adj.> strenuous, radical: ~变化radical changes || 饭后不要做~运动. Don't do strenuous exercises after meals. || ~的疼痛acute pain

13 强烈 [-] qiángliè (strong-violent) <adj.> strong: ~愿望strong desire || ~的感情strong feelings || ~反对strongly oppose

14 热烈 [熱-] rèliè (hot-roar) <adj.> warm, enthusiastic: ~欢迎warm welcome || ~鼓掌 (gǔzhǎng) warm applause || ~讨论have a lively discussion

15 霸道 [-] bàdào (tyrant-way) <adj.> unreasonable, bully: 他在学校里很~ he is a school bully. || 她这个人很~, 你没法儿跟她讲道理. She is very unreasonable, and there's no discussing it with her.

16 凶猛 [-] xiōngměng (ferocious-violent) <adj.> violent, ferocious: ~的老虎ferocious tiger || ~的大火a devastating fire || 来势~ come down with a devastating force

17 沉痛 [-] chéntòng (deep-grief) <adj.> with a deep feeling of grief: ~的教训painful lessons || 心情~. The mood is bitter. || . . . . . . ~宣告, ... 不幸于昨天去世, 享年84岁. An announcement of deep grief: unfortunately, he passed away yesterday at the age of 84.

18 严重 [嚴-] yánzhòng (urgent-serious) <adj.> severe: 病情~ be seriously ill || ~后果serious consequences || 日益~ more and more serious

19 致命 [-] zhìmìng (cause-life) <adj.> fatal, mortal, deadly: ~打击 a deadly blow || ~武器 (wǔqì) a deadly weapon || ~的缺点fatal weakness

20 重度 [-] zhòngdù (intensive-degree) <adj.> serious, severe: ~污染 (wūrǎn) heavy pollution || ~抑郁症 (yìyù zhèng) severe depression

21 不得了 [-] bùdéliǎo (not-right) <adj.> extremely: 高兴得~ extremely happy || 急得~ extremely anxious

22 了不得 [-] liǎobudé (terrific-terribly) <adj.> wonderful, terrific: 高兴得~ be extremely happy || ~的人物terrific figure || 他才12岁就取得了这样的成就, ~! He has had such accomplishments at only 12 years old. He is great.

23 水火无情 [--無-] shuǐhuǒ-wúqíng (flood-fire-no-mercy) <idiom> floods and fires know no mercy: ~, 因此, 防火防水很重要. Floods and fires know no mercy, so it is very important to prevent them.

24 翻天覆地 [-] fāntiān-fùdì (turn-heaven-cover-Earth) <idiom> Earth-shaking, world-shaking: ~的变化an Earth-shaking change

25 震天动地 [--動-] zhèntiān-dòngdì (shock-heaven-shake-Earth) <idiom> shake heaven and Earth-very loud, momentous: 欢呼声~. The cheers were deafening. || 外边是~的喊声. The din from the crowd outside was deafening.

Tips:

1 Idioms with 天/地: Among the 50,000 Chinese idioms, the pattern using "天/地" is the most productive one, yielding about 200 idioms. Since 天 and 地 have the largest difference in the Chinese perspective, the idioms with this pattern carry a connotation of 'extremely.' For example, the two idioms in this unit 翻天覆地 and 震天动地 mean 'huge change' and 'extremely shocking' respectively. Likewise, 天寒地冻 means 'extremely/bitterly cold.'

2 毒 (dú): The original meaning of 毒 is 'poisonous gas,' from which evolved meanings such as 'poisonous, poison, fierce, severe, malicious, cruel' etc.

Exercises:

Part I: Use the given bound form as a guide to help you think of other words with the same character. Feel free to use your dictionary when needed. Then write down the English definition of each of the words you've written.

烈 (fierce): 激烈 *intense*

____

____

____

____

____

多 (many): 很多 *many*

____

____

必 (necessary): 必须 *must*

____

____

Part II: Read the following sentences and fill in each blank with the appropriate word or phrase from the options given.

1 小张要到欧洲留学, __________到大使馆去排队办签证 (qiānzhèng).
A. 不得了 B. 了不得 C. 少不了

2 小张到使馆面签的时候, 人多得__________.
A. 不得了 B. 了不起 C. 少不了

3 小张去办签证那天北京出现了雾霾 (wùmái) 天气, 而且是 __________污染. 小张觉得北京的空气污染越来越__________了, 所以下决心一定离开北京.
A. 沉痛、重度 B. 致命、严重 C. 重度、严重

4 在去办签证的路上, 出租车司机对小张说: "自从出现了'嘀嘀打车' (Didi Chuxing), 传统出租车行业就遭到了__________打击."
A. 重度 B. 致命 C. 沉痛

5 改革开放30年以后, 中国发生了 __________的变化.
A. 水火无情 B. 翻天覆地 C. 震天动地

6 朝鲜在中国东北部边境进行了核试验 (hé shíyàn), 核导弹的响声__________.
A. 水火无情 B. 翻天覆地 C. 震天动地

7 有些人认为朝鲜能够进行核试验成功, 中国和俄罗斯对朝鲜的帮助__________.
A. 来势凶猛 B. 多此一举 C. 必不可少

8 有的环境学专家认为对抗 __________的自然灾害是不必要的, 甚至是__________.
A. 来势凶猛 B. 多此一举 C. 必不可少

Theme 242: Strong or weak 强, 弱 (qiáng, ruò)

1 强 [強] qiáng (strong) <adj.> strong, powerful: 能力 ~ strong ability || 她的化学很~, 物理就弱一些. His chemistry is strong and his physics is weak. || 记忆力 ~ good memory
2 强大 [-] qiángdà (strong-big) <adj.> big and powerful, formidable: ~的力量powerful force || ~的对手powerful opponents ||功能~ powerful function
3 强劲 [-勁] qiángjìng (strong-vibrant) <adj.> powerful, forceful: ~的风strong winds || 经济~增长stronger growth in economy || 涨势 (zhǎngshì) ~ a dynamic uptrend
4 强硬 [-] qiángyìng (strong-hard) <adj.> strong, tough, unyielding: 态度~ an uncompromising stand || ~的声明a strongly statement || 提出 ~的抗议 (kàngyì) lodge a strong protest
5 有力 [-] yǒulì (have-strength) <adj.> strong, powerful: ~支持strong support ||他的双手很~. His hands are very strong. || ~地推动公司的发展 vigorously promote the development of the company
6 强有力 [-] qiáng yǒulì (strong-powerful) <adj.> strong, forceful: ~的政府powerful government || ~的支持 powerful support

7 富强 [-] fùqiáng (rich-strong) <adj.> (of country) prosperous and strong: ~的国家prosperous and powerful country || 使祖国繁荣 (fánróng) ~ make our country more prosperous and powerful

8 强盛 [-] qiángshèng (strong-prosperous) <adj.> (of country) powerful and prosperous: ~的国家a strong country || 中国在十八世纪的时候很~. China was strong and prosperous in the 18th century.

9 威风 [-風] wēifēng (power-prestige) <adj./n.> awe-inspiring, power and prestige: 他开着一辆豪华 (háohuá) 车, 看起来很~. He was driving a fancy car and looked very imposing. || 我们得杀杀他的~. We should puncture his arrogance.

10 威武 [-] wēiwǔ (powerful-valiant) <adj.> powerful, mighty: ~的军官a mighty military officer || ~的样子the impressive looking || 相貌~ be impressive in appearance

11 雄伟 [-偉] xióngwěi (grand-great) <adj.> grand, tall and sturdy: 气势~的长城the imposing Great Wall || ~的建筑majestic architecture

12 宏伟 [-偉] hóngwěi (grandeur-great) <adj.> magnificent, grand: ~目标/蓝图grand goals/prospects || ~的大楼magnificent buildings || ~的事业magnificent undertaking

13 壮观 [壯觀] zhuàngguān (grand-sight) <adj.> magnificent, spectacular: ~ 的场面spectacular scene || ~的教堂a spectacular church || ~的瀑布 a spectacular waterfall

14 大张旗鼓 [-張--] dàzhāng qígǔ (greatly-show-flag-drum) <idiom> on a grand scale, in a big way: ~地庆祝celebrate with great fanfare || ~地宣传环保 give wide publicity to environmental protection

15 千军万马 [-軍萬馬] qiānjūn-wànmǎ (1000-soldier-10, 000-horse) <idiom> thousands upon thousands of men and horses – a powerful army, a mighty force: 中国的高考如同~过独木桥. The Chinese college entrance exam is so competitive that it seems like a 1,000 horses crossing in a canoe.

16 雄心勃勃 [-] xióngxīn-bóbó (ambitious-heart-exuberant-*reduplication*) <idiom> be puffed with ambitions: 这位总统制定了~的经济发展计划. This president has set ambitious economic development plans. || 他~要发财成名. He is filled with ambition to become rich and famous.

17 巩固 [鞏-] gǒnggù (consolidate-stabilize) <adj./v.> consolidate, strengthen, stable: ~成果consolidate results || ~知识strengthen your knowledge || ~地位consolidate position

18 坚固 [堅-] jiāngù (hard-solid) <adj.> firm, solid: ~的房子a sturdy house || 德国产品~耐用German products are sturdy and durable.

19 牢固 [-] láogù (firm-solid) <adj.> firm: ~的基础solid foundation || 他在公司的地位很~. He has a high status in the company. || 中国式教育要求高中生~地掌握 (zhǎngwò) 各门学科知识. Chinese education requires high school students to master the knowledge of each subject firmly.

20 稳固 [穩-] wěngù (stable-solid) <adj.> stable, solid: 地位~. The position is secure. || ~的婚姻a solid marriage

21 稳如泰山 [穩---] wěnrú-tàishān (stable-like-Tai-mountain) <idiom> as stable as Mount Tai, rock-firm: 别人急得不得了, 她却~. Other people are very anxious, but she is steady.

22 软 [軟] ruǎn (soft) <adj.> soft, mild: 心~ tender-hearted || 他明知自己错了, 可是嘴上还不服~. He knew perfectly well he was in the wrong, but stubbornly refused to admit it.

23 弱 [-] ruò (weak) <adj.> weak, inferior: 身体~ have a frail body || 能力~ lack ability || ~女子weak women
24 软弱 [軟-] ruǎnruò (soft-weak) <adj.> weak, feeble: ~的人 a weak person || 性格~ weak in character
25 薄弱 [-] bóruò (thin-weak) <adj.> weak, frail: 力量/能力~ lack power/ ability || 意志~ weak-willed || ~环节weak link, vulnerable spot
26 弱小 [-] ruòxiǎo (weak-small) <adj.> small and weak: ~的动物small and weak animal || ~民族small and weak nations || 身体~. The body is wimpy.
27 微弱 [-] wēiruò (tiny-weak) <adj.> faint, weak: ~的灯光weak light || ~的声音a faint sound || 力量~. The power is weak.
28 单薄 [單-] dānbó (slim-thin) <adj.> thin: 身体~ the body is thin || ~的衣服thin clothes || 力量~. The strength is lessening.
29 不堪一击 [---擊] bùkān-yījī (unable-withstand-single-blow) <idiom> cannot withstand a single blow, collapse at the first blow: 谎言总是 ~的. Lies are always flimsy. || 对手~. The opponent is vulnerable.

Tips:

1 弱: 弱 depicts a 'collection of bird feathers' and means 'weak.' Words with 弱 include 薄弱, 微弱, 软弱 in this unit as well as 瘦弱 (shòuruò, emaciated,) 懦弱 (nuòruò, coward) and 弱点 (weakness) etc.
2 劲: This character has two pronunciations. One is jìn and refers to the noun 'strength.' The other is jìng and signifies the adjective 'strong.'
3 雄 (xióng) and 雌 (cí): Both are originally related to bird (隹.) 雄 means 'male bird' and 雌 'female bird.' On April 1, 2017, the Chinese Central Government announced a state level new area 'Xiong'an New Area' (雄安新区), which includes three counties, 容城, 安新 and 雄县. According to the conventional way to name places, the new area should be called 容雄 since 容县 is on the left and 雄县 on the right, however, it was named 雄安 for its auspicious token like those of 天安 (门) and 地安 (门) in Beijing.

Exercises:

Part I: Use the given bound form as a guide to help you think of other words with the same character. Feel free to use your dictionary when needed. Then write down the English definition of each of the words you've written.

强 *(strong):* 强大 *strong and powerful*

____

____

____

____

____

固 *(firm)*: 巩固 *consolidate*

____

____

____

____

____

____

弱 *(weak)*: 软弱 *feeble*

____

____

____

____

____

Part II: Read the following sentences and fill in each blank with the appropriate word or phrase from the options given.

1 大张旗鼓、雄心勃勃、雄伟壮观

a) 中国制定了__________的经济发展计划.
b) 特朗普政府开始__________ __地吸引外商到美国投资 (tóuzī, invest), 美国多家媒体对此进行了报道.
c) 美国的科罗拉多 (Colorado) 大峡谷 (Grand Canyon)非常__________ _.

2 稳如泰山、不堪一击、千军万马

a) 中国人常常抱怨 (bàoyuàn, complain) 中国男子足球队太差了，简直__________ _.
b) 在中国考重点大学就像__________ ___过独木桥.
c) 中国政府认为不管世界经济形势如何不好， 中国经济都会_________.

3 强硬、强劲、强大

a) 目前印度 (India) 的经济发展比较_______.
b) 在领土问题上中国对印度的态度比较_________.
c) 印度觉得自己是亚洲最__________的国家.

4 微弱、单薄、薄弱

a) 小王不怕冷, 即使在冬天也穿得很________.
b) 小王在国际数学竞赛 (jìngsài, contest) 上以________的优势赢了美国学生.
c) 有人认为中国的基础教育还很________.

Theme 243: Honor and humiliation 光荣, 耻辱 (guāngróng, chǐrǔ)

1 荣幸 [榮-] róngxìng (honorable-lucky) <adj.> be honored: 感到~ feel honored || 不胜 ~ be greatly honored || 认识您很~. It is a great honor to know you.
2 体面 [體-] tǐmiàn (body-dignity) <adj.> decent, honorable: ~的家庭decent family || ~的工作decent jobs || 穿得~ be decently dressed || 有失/维持~ a loss of face/keep up appearances
3 要面子 [-] yàomiànzi (concern-dignity) <v.> be keen on face-saving: 她是个很~的人. She is touchy about her pride. || 死~活受罪. Gentility without ability is worse than plain beggary.
4 名垂青史 [-] míngchuí-qīngshǐ (name-pass down-history) <idiom> go down with history, be crowned with eternal glory: 乔治华盛顿在美国~. George Washington has earned his place in the American history books. || 很多政治家想~. Most politicians want to go down in history as great statesmen.
5 光宗耀祖 [-] guāngzōng-yàozǔ (honor-ancestry-glory-ancestor) <idiom> bring honor to one's ancestors: 一些中国家长认为孩子考上名牌大学就能~. Some Chinese parents believe that if their children are able to attend prestigious universities, they will bring honor to their ancestors.

6 可耻 [-恥] kěchǐ (*prefix*-shameful) <adj.> shameful, disgraceful: ~的第三者a shameful third party || ~的想法shameful thoughts || 浪费 ~. Waste is a disgrace.
7 无耻 [無恥] wúchǐ (no-shame) <adj.> shameless, brazen, impudent: ~的行为 shameful behavior || 他这个人太~了. He is such a shameless man.
8 羞耻 [-恥] xiūchǐ (shy-shame) <adj./n.> sense of shame, shameful: 感到~ feel shameful || ~心sense of shame || 不知~ lose all sense of shame
9 不要脸 [--臉] bú yào liǎn (not-concern-dignity) <v.> have no sense of shame, shameless: 只有~的人才能做出~的事. Only those who have no sense of shame can do such shameful things. || 他太~了, 竟然和已婚女人谈恋爱. He's so shameless that he's dating a married woman.
10 身败名裂 [-敗--] shēn bài míng liè (body-decay-reputation-broken) <idiom> lose all standing and reputation: 一夜~ lost one's reputation overnight || 那个名人有了婚外恋, 最后搞得~. The famous man had an extramarital affair and lost both fortune and honor.

11 伟大 [偉-] wěi dà (great-big) <adj.> great: ~的人great person || 林肯很~, 救了美国. Lincoln was great and saved the United States. || ~的胜利great victory
12 高大 [-] gāo dà (tall-big) <adj.> tall and big: 身材 ~ be of tall and sturdy stature || ~ 的建筑tall buildings
13 高大上 [-] gāo dà shàng (highend-elegant-classy) <adj.> (slang) high-end, elegant and classy: ~的职业 the high-end, elegant and classy occupation || 这家农村小饭馆有一个~的名字, "全球大饭店." This rural inn has a big name, 'The Global Hotel.'
14 远大 [遠-] yuǎndà (far-big) <adj.> broad, long-range: ~理想high ambitions || 前途 ~ great expectations || 目光~ have a broad vision
15 光辉 [-輝] guānghuī (shining-light) <adj.> brilliant, glorious: ~榜样 (bǎngyàng) shinging example || ~形象glorious image || 他在医学研究上取得了~的成绩. He achieved brilliant results in medical research.

16 光荣 [榮] guāngróng (glory-honor) <adj./n.> glorious, glory: 感到~ feel glorious || ~的任务glorious tasks || ~的历史glorious history

17 惊天动地 [驚-動-] jīngtiāndòngdì (shock-heaven-shake-Earth) <idiom> shake heaven and Earth, Earth-shaking: ~的大事业magnificent feat || ~的响声Earth-shaking sound || ~的消息world-shaking news

18 渺小 [-] miǎoxiǎo (tiny-small) <adj.> tiny, insignificant: 希望~ have slim hopes || 个人的力量是~的. One person's strength is small. || 在宇宙 (yǔzhòu) 面前, 人类是~的. Human beings are small in the face of the universe.

19 不起眼 [-] bùqǐyǎn (not-catch-eye) <adj.> not attract attention, not noticeable: 别看这人 ~, 人家可是一肚子学问. This guy seems to be insignificant. He is actually very knowledgeable. || 比尔·盖茨上大学的时候还很~. Bill Gates was still very common when he was at college.

Tips:

1 荣 (榮): The original meaning of 荣 is the Chinese parasol tree. The current meaning of 'splendid and flourishing' was derived from people's impression of flowers of parasol trees.

2 青史: In ancient times, books were written on green bamboo strips, therefore, 青史 became an alternative name for 'history.' Chinese intellectuals were particular about leaving names in history, i. e., '名垂青史' or '青史留名.' Be sure not to mix up 青史 (history) and 情史 (history of love affairs.) Now 青史 itself is an archaic term.

3 羞, 耻, 辱: 羞 means 'shy, ashamed.'耻 (恥) means 'disgrace, shame.' 辱 means 'to humiliate, humiliation.' The degree of shame of these three words increases. Additionally, their combinations have approximately the same meaning, for example, 羞耻, 羞辱 and 耻辱.

4 高大上: 高大上 is an abbreviated form of 高端, 大气, 上档次 which means 'high-end,' 'elegant' and 'classy.' The names of the three authors of this book are quite plain. If a person is named 'George W. Charles,' his name is really 高大上.

5 起眼: 起眼 (eye-catching) has to be used with a modifier such as 不, 太 or 有些 etc. The antonym of 不起眼 is 很惹眼 (hěn rěyǎn, very eye-catching.)

Exercises:

Part I: Translate the following phrases into English and then answer the questions.

名垂青史 ____________________

光宗耀祖 ____________________

身败名裂 ____________________

目光远大 ____________________

1 哪些词是褒义词 (commendatory term)?

____

2 哪些词是贬义词 (derogatory term)?

____

3 哪一位美国总统可以称得上是名垂青史?

---

4 如果美国总统有了婚外恋会不会身败名裂, 为什么?

Part II: Write an antonym for each word in the table. You can refer to the given words.

伟大、不要脸、惊天动地、不起眼

渺小 v.s.	默默无闻v.s.
要面子v.s.	高大上v.s.

Theme 244: Clean, corrupted 腐败 (fǔbài)

1 光明 [-] guāngmíng (light-bright) <adj./n.> bright, brightness: ~的前途a bright future || 事业无限~ his career is infinitely bright. || 热爱~ love brightness

2 美好 [-] měihǎo (fine-good) <adj.> fine, glorious: ~的理想a beautiful ideal || ~的回忆good memories || ~的日子happy days

3 前途无量 [--無-] qiántúwúliàng (future-no-limit) <idiom> boundless future: 这个人~. The man's future is boundless

4 前程似锦 [---錦] qiánchéngsìjǐn (future-like-brocade) <idiom> splendid prospects, glorious future: 她很会交际, 职场上会~. She is very sociable and has a promising career. || 祝你们毕业以后 ~. I wish you have a bright future after your graduation.

5 赏罚分明 [賞罰--] shǎngfáfēnmíng (reward-punish-distinctive) <idiom> be fair in meeting out rewards and punishments: ~的原则the principle of discriminating in one's rewards and punishments || 他很公正, 对员工~. He was fair to his employees in meeting out rewards and punishments.

6 黑暗 [-] hēi'àn (black-dark) <adj.> dark: 这个国家的政府真~. The government of this country is very corrupt.

7 昏乱 [-亂] hūnluàn (dazed-confused) <adj.> dazed and confused, benighted and disorderly: 头脑~ lost and puzzled

8 暗无天日 [-無--] ànwútiānrì (dark-no-sky-sun) <idiom> complete darkness, total absence of justice: ~的社会corrupt and unjust society || ~的生活the life on the dark

9 腐败 [-敗] fǔbài (corrupt-decay) <adj.> corrupt: 政治~ political corruption || 官员~ offical corruption || 反 ~ the anti-corruption

10 腐朽 [-] fǔxiǔ (decadent-rotten) <adj.> rotten: ~的思想rotten ideas || ~的生活a rotten life

11 权钱交易 [權錢--] quánqián jiāoyì (power-money-exchange) <n.> collusion between power and money, corruption: 搞~ do the collusion between power and money

Tips:

1 前途无量: It means 'has a bright/boundless (career) future' and can sometimes be used in a joking way by alternating the 前 (qián, future) with a homophone 钱 (qián, money).
2 腐 (fŭ): 腐 originally means '(of meat) spoil, spoiled' as in 腐烂 (fŭlàn, rotten) and 豆腐 (tofu.) The extended meaning 'corrupt, decay' as in 腐败 is apparent.
3 权钱交易 (quánqián jiāoyì): 权钱交易, or its close variant 钱权交易, means collusion between power and money. It is a form of corruption common in corrupt governments.

Exercises:

Part I: Translate the following phrases into English and then answer the questions.

权钱交易 ________________
政治腐败 ________________
老百姓生活暗无天日 ________________
政府黑暗 ________________
前途无量 ________________
前程似锦 ________________
赏罚分明 ________________

1 上面哪些短语可以用形容一个黑暗的政府?

____

2 上面哪些短语可以用来形容有美好前途的人?

____

3 你觉得美国是不是一个赏罚分明的社会, 为什么?

____

Theme 245: Noble or lowly 贵, 贱 (guì, jiàn)

(See also Theme 262)

1 贵 [貴] guì (expensive) <adj.> expensive: 很~ very expensive || 高~ noble || 宝~ precious
2 贵重 [貴-] guìzhòng (valuable-precious) <adj.> valuable, precious: ~的东西 valuables || ~物品 valuables || 礼物很~. The present is very expensive.
3 宝贵 [寶貴] băoguì (treasured-valuable) <adj.> valuable, precious: ~的时间 valuable time || ~的经验 valuable experience || ~文物 valuable cultural relics
4 珍贵 [-貴] zhēnguì (precious-valuable) <adj.> valuable, precious: ~的药材 valuable medicine || ~的照片 valuable picture || ~的资料 valuable resources
5 名贵 [-貴] míngguì (famous-valuable) <adj.> famous and valuable: ~的手表 rare and valuable watch || ~的字画 priceless calligraphy scrolls and paintings || ~的汽车 rare and valuable car

6 可贵 [-貴] kěguì (worth-cherish) <adj.> be treasured, praiseworthy: 难能~ rare and precious || ~的精神 treasured spirit, vigor || ~之处 treasured place
7 昂贵 [-貴] ángguì (highly-expensive) <adj.> expensive, costly: ~的钻石 expensive diamond || 价格~ expensive price || 收费~ expensive fees
8 珍稀 [-] zhēnxī (precious-rare) <adj.> treasure, value: ~动物 treasured animal || ~鸟类 treasured bird
9 值钱 [-錢] zhíqián (worth-money) <adj.> valuable, costly: ~的东西 valuable object || ~的家具 valuable furniture

10 高贵 [-貴] gāoguì (high-honorable) <adj.> grandeur, noble: ~的品质 noble character || ~的地位 noble positions || 举止~ have a noble carriage
11 贵贱 [貴賤] guìjiàn (expensive-cheap) <bf.> (of price) cheap and expensive, (of social status) high or low: ~分明 clearly cheap, low || 高低~ superiority and inferiority, lowliness and nobleness
12 上流 [-] shàngliú (upper-class) <adj.> upper class: ~社会 upper class society || ~人物 upper class character || ~的作品 upper class work (esp. of literature or art)
13 尊贵 [-貴] zūnguì (respectable-honorable) <adj.> honorable, respectable: ~的客人 honorable guest || ~的国王 honorable king || 显得~ seems respectable
14 高高在上 [-] gāogāo zàishàng (high-*reduplication*-at-above) <idiom> set up on high not in touch with reality (idiom): ~的样子 set up on high (manner) || ~的领导 admin who is not in touch with reality || ~地看着大家 look down on others

15 有名 [-] yǒumíng (have-name) <adj.> famous: ~的画家 famous artist || ~的地方 famous place || ~的人 famous person
16 知名 [-] (known-name) <adj.> well-known: ~人士 well-known person || ~画家 well-known artist || ~大学 well-known university
17 著名 [-] (famous-name) <adj.> famous, celebrated: ~画家 celebrated artist || ~人物 celebrated person || ~诗人 celebrated poet
18 闻名 [聞-] wénmíng (heard-name) <adj.> well-known, famous: 世界~ world famous || ~天下 famous everywhere || ~的公司famous company
19 资深 [資-] zīshēn (qualification-long) <adj.> senior: ~记者 senior reporter || ~教师 senior teacher
20 显赫 [顯-] xiǎnhè (prominent-illustrious) <adj.> prominent, illustrious: 声名~ great renown, well-known || ~的身份 a prominent identity || ~的地位 an illustrious position
21 老牌 [-] lǎopái (old-brand) <adj.> old or established brand: ~杂志 established magazine || ~商品 established good || ~的公司 established company
22 名牌 [-] míngpái (famous-brand) <adj.> famous brand: ~汽车 famous car brand || ~衣服 famous clothes || ~产品 famous good
23 大名鼎鼎 [-] dàmíng dǐngdǐng (big-name-great-*reduplication*) <idiom> famous, celebrated: ~的教练 a well-known coach || ~的钢琴家 a well-known pianist
24 举世闻名 [舉-聞-] jǔshì wénmíng (whole-world-heard-name) <idiom> world famous: ~的城市 world famous city || 中国菜~. Chinese food is world famous.
25 老少皆知 [-] lǎoshào jiēzhī (pld-young-all-know) <idiom> well-known: 这件事~. This matter is world famous.
26 得人心 [-] dé rénxīn (get-man's-heart) <v.> have the support of the people: 大~ have the support of the people || ~的好事. This positive event has the support of the people. || 这件事 ~. This item has the support of the people.

27 热 [熱] rè (hot) <adj.> hot,popular: 移民~ immigration craze || 经商~ intense popular interest in doing business || 英语~ popular enthusiasm for learning English
28 热门 [熱門] rèmén (hot-subject) <adj.> arousing popular interest: ~话题 popular topic || ~人物 popular character || ~新闻 popular news
29 香 [-] xiāng (fragrant, popular) <adj.> popular: 吃~ very popular || 他现在~得很. He is very popular right now.
30 叫座 [-] jiàozuò (draw-audience) <adj.> draw a large audience: ~的电影. That film has drawn a large audience. || ~的体育项目. A sporting event that draws a large audience.
31 紧俏 [緊-] jǐnqiào (short supply-sell well) <adj.> in great demand but short supply (using of consumer goods): ~商品 commodities in tight supply || 资金~ resources in tight supply
32 抢手 [搶-] qiǎngshǒu (seize-hand) <adj.> sought after: 门票十分~ tickets are very sought after || 这本书很~. This book is very sought after.
33 大红大紫 [-紅--] dàhóng dàzǐ (bright-red-bright-purple) <idiom> (of a person) very famous: ~的演员 a very famous actor

34 便宜 [-] piányi (small-advantage) <adj.> inexpensive, cheap: 价格~ inexpensive price || ~的水果 inexpensive fruit廉价 [-價] liánjià (low-price) low-priced, cheap: ~商品 low priced good || ~出售 low price sale
35 物美价廉 [--價-] wù měi jià lián (goods-good-price-cheap) <idiom> good quality and cheap: ~的商品 inexpensive and good quality goods

36 贱 [賤] jiàn (cheap, lowly) <adj.> lowly, inexpensive: ~卖sell at a lower price || ~人 slut, cheap person
37 卑微 [-] bēiwēi (humble-petty) <adj.> petty and low: 出身~ be of a lowly origin || ~的地位 low position
38 卑贱 [-賤] bēijiàn (humble-lowly) <adj.> lowly, humble: ~的行为 lowly actions || 地位~ lowly positions
39 下贱 [-賤] xiàjiàn (low-lowly) <adj.> low in social status, low, mean: ~行为 degraded behavior || ~的人 cheap person || 把劳动看作~ 的事情 look upon labor as degrading
40 低下 [-] dīxià (low-down) <adj.> low: 地位~ low status || 素质 (sùzhì) ~ low moral quality || 效率 (xiàolǜ) ~ low effect
41 低人一等 [-] dī rén yī děng (lower-others-one-level) <idiom> inferior to other: ~的工作 inferior work || ~的私生子 inferior child born out of wedlock
42 低三下四 [-] dīsān xiàsì (low-3-down-4) <idiom> lowly, humble, servile: ~地求人beg servilely for a favor || ~地讨好政府官员ingratiate oneself with a government officer
43 无名 [無-] wúmíng (no-name) <adj.> nameless: ~英雄 unnamed hero || ~作者 nameless author || ~火 indescribable anger
44 默默无闻 [--無聞] mòmò wúwén (silent-*reduplication*-not-known) <idiom> unknown to the public: ~的运动员 an unknown athlete || ~地过日子 move along without attracting the public eye
45 冷门 [-門] lěngmén (cold-subject) <adj., n.> not in demand, unexpected winner: ~专业 less popular major || 爆 ~ produce an upset (esp. in sports), unexpected turn of events

Tips:

1 贝 (bèi): Before gold, silver or copper money began to be used as currency, shells had the function of currency, therefore many Chinese characters with the radical 贝 are related to money. For example, 贵 (expensive,) 贱 (cheap, inexpensive,) 财 (wealth,) 货 (goods,) 贸 (trade) and 宝 (寶, treasure) etc.
2 物美 and 价廉: Chinese merchandise is famous for 物美价廉 (good quality and cheap) which suits Chinese consumers' mindset perfectly even today. The largest supermarket chain in Beijing is called 物美超市 (Wumart) and its slogan is '天天廉价, 永远物美' (literally 'every day the price is low, and the quality is good forever.')
3 珍, 宝, 贵, 重: All mean 'expensive, valuable, precious' but the degree of value decreases. Their combinations are usually adjectives or nouns meaning 'valuable' as well, for example, 珍宝, 珍贵, 宝贵, 贵重.
4 上流vs.下流: There is an upper class (上流社会) but not a 下流社会. 下流 means 'lewd, dirty.' 'Lower class' is 下层, 底层社会.
5 有名, 知名, 著名, 大名鼎鼎, 举世闻名: Their degree of famousness increases.
6 叫座 vs. 叫好: If a movie 叫座, it means the movie attracts audiences and the box office earnings is good. If a movie 叫好, it means it gets good reviews especially from movie critics.

Exercises:

Part I: Use the given bound form as a guide to help you think of other words with the same character. Feel free to use your dictionary when needed. Then write down the English definition of each of the words you've written.

贵 *(often):* 贵重 *expensive*

____

____

____

____

名 *(name):* 有名 *famous*

____

____

____

____

贱 *(inexpensive):* 贱人 *slut, cheap person*

____

____

____

____

低 *(low):* 地位低下 *low status*

____

____

____

Part II: Read the following sentences and fill in each blank with the appropriate word or phrase from the options given.

1 叫座、抢手

a) 苹果公司预计Iphone XV出来以后一定会非常__________.
b) 《狼战2》 (*Wolf Warrior 2*, 2017) 这部电影在中国很_________, 但是在美国却不受欢fl.

2 大名鼎鼎、默默无闻、高高在上、大红大紫

a) 《狼战2》的男主角很多年来一直在____________地拍电影, 但是这部影片让他开始__________, 火得不得了.
b) 《狼战2》的男主角因为这部影片变得_______________, 几乎所有的中国人都知道他.
c) 《狼战2》的男主角并不觉得出名了就可以______________, 自以为了不起, 他仍然跟没出名的时候一样.

3 物美价廉、热门、闻名

a) 很多中国大学生愿意选择__________专业, 因为毕业以后好找工作.
b) 美国的哈佛大学_____________世界.
c) 中国工厂能够生产______________的产品.

Theme 246: Intimate or distant 亲密, 疏远 (qīnmì, shūyuǎn)

1 熟 [-] shú (cooked, familiar) <adj.> familiar, well acquainted: 跟他很~ I am well acquainted with him. || 他俩很~ Those two are very well acquainted. || ~人 a familiar person
2 熟悉 [-] shúxī (familiar-known) <adj.> be familiar with: ~的声音 a familiar sound || 对西方文化很~ very familiar with Western culture || ~情况 familiar situation
3 耳熟 [-] ěrshú (ear-familiar) <adj.> familiar to the ear: 听着~ sounds familiar || 声音~ a familiar voice
4 面熟 [-] miànshú (face-familiar) <adj.> familiar face: 看着~ that face looks familiar || 那位老师很~. That teacher seems very familiar.
5 亲 [親] qīn (parents, close) <adj.> close, of blood relation: ~儿子/女儿biological son/biological daughter || 我跟大姐最 ~. I'm the closest with my eldest sister.
6 亲切 [親-] qīnqiè (close-earnest) <adj.> cordial, kind: 感到~ feel cordial || ~的声音 kind voice. || ~地说 said kindly

7 亲密 [親-] qīnmì (close-intimate) <adj.> close, intimate: ~关系 close relationship || ~的朋友 close friend || ~相处 get along (with one another)
8 密切 [-] mìqiè (intimate-earnest) <adj.> close, familiar: 关系 ~ close relationship || 来往~ have contact or dealings with || ~交往close interactions
9 亲热 [親熱] qīnrè (close-affectionate) <adj.> affectionate, intimate: 关系~ affection relations || ~地说 said affectionately || 显得~ appear affectionate
10 火热 [-熱] huǒrè (fire-hot) <adj.> intimate, fervent: ~的心 fervent heart, passionate || 谈得~ talk fervently || 打得~ be as thick as thieves

11 近 [-] jìn (near, close) <adj.> close: ~亲close relative || 关系~ close relationship
12 接近 [-] jiējìn (connect-close) <adj./v.> close to, near: ~完成 nearing completion || ~老百姓 close to the people || 那人不容易~. That person is rather standoffish.
13 贴近 [貼-] tiējìn (press-close) <v.> be close to: ~实际 stay close to reality || ~生活 stay close to life || ~人民stay close to people
14 贴身 [貼-] tiēshēn (press-body) <adj.> close fitting, next to the skin,personal: 这件新毛衣很~. The new sweater was a tight fit. || ~放着 to place close to one's body || ~仆人a personal servant
15 体贴 [體貼] tǐtiē (considerate-close) <adj.> show consideration for: ~父母 show consideration for one's parents || 互相~ show consideration for one another
16 贴心 [貼-] tiēxīn (press-heart) <adj.> intimate, close: ~的朋友 intimate friend || ~的话 intimate language
17 知心 [-] zhīxīn (understand-heart) <adj.> intimate, understanding: ~朋友 intimate friend
18 难舍难分 [難捨難-] nánshě nánfēn (hard-abandon-hard-part) <idiom> loath to part from each other: ~的关系 a relationship where people can't bear to be apart || 跟家人~ loathe to be a part from each other

19 和美 [-] héměi (harmonious-good) <adj.> harmonious: ~的家庭 harmonious household || ~的声音 harmonious voice
20 和谐 [-諧] héxié (coordinated-harmonious) <adj.> harmonious: 气氛 (qìfēn) ~ harmonious air || ~的关系 harmonious relationship || ~发展 harmonious expansion
21 融洽 [-] róngqià (melt-soak) <adj.> harmonious, friendly relationship: 感情~ feel friendly || 相处 ~ mutually friendly relationship || ~的关系 harmonious relations
22 要好 [-] yàohǎo (essentially-good) <adj.> be on good terms, be close friends: 跟她很~ on good terms with her || ~的朋友 close friends || 姐妹俩很~. The two sisters are very close.
23 友好 [-] yǒuhǎo (friendly-good) <adj.> close friend, friendly: ~关系 friendly relationship || ~往来 come and go in a friendly manner || ~相处 friendly interactions
24 友善 [-] yǒushàn (friendly-nice) <adj.> friendly, amicable: ~的态度 friendly bearing || ~地交流 friendly exchange

25 生 [-] shēng (unfamiliar) <adj.> unfamiliar, unacquainted: ~人 unfamiliar person || ~字 unfamiliar with a character || 我刚到这里, 对这里还很~. I've only just come here. I'm still not familiar with this area.

26 陌生 [-] mòshēng (strange-unfamiliar) <adj.> strange, unfamiliar: ~人 strange person || ~的地方 strange place || 感到~ feel strange
27 疏远 [-遠] shūyuǎn (distant-far) <adj.> drift apart, alienate: 关系~ estranged relationship || 跟她~ relationship with her is estranged

28 不和 [-] bùhé (not-coordinated) <adj.> discord: 夫妻~ husband and wife are not harmonious || 关系~ inharmonious relationship || 与姐姐~ be inharmonious with one's elder sister
29 别扭 [彆-] bièniu (disagreeable-twisted) <adj.> awkward, difficult: 闹~ provoke disagreement || 脾气~ unnatural temperament, temper || 感到~ feel awkward
30 势不两立 [勢-兩-] shìbùliǎnglì (situation-not-both-exist) <idiom> mutually exclusive, antagonistic, be irreconcilable: ~的敌人 completely incompatible enemy || 和他们~ be irreconcilable with them

31 土 [-] tǔ (Earth, native) <adj.> local, native: ~产品local products || ~办法indigenous methods || ~得掉渣 (diàozhā) extremely countrified || ~包子 country bumpkin
32 国产 [國產] guóchǎn (country-produced) <adj.> made in one's country, made in China: ~汽车 government produced car || ~电影 government produced movie || ~手机 government produced car
33 本土 [-] běntǔ (local-land) <adj.> one's native country, native: ~人 native || 美国~ American homeland || ~文化 native culture
34 土产 [-產] tǔchǎn (local-product) <n.> local products: 家乡~ local products of one's hometown || 收购~ purchase local products in bulk
35 洋 [-] yáng (ocean, foreign) <adj.> foreign, modern: ~博士foreign-educated doctor || ~快餐foreign fast food || ~办法modern methods
36 外来 [-來] wàilái (outside-come) <adj.> outside, external: ~事物 outsider character || ~力量 outside force || ~词 external world

37 兼职 [-職] jiānzhí (combine-job) <adj.> part-time: ~工作 part-time work || ~老师 part-time teacher || 业余~ part-time engagement
38 全职 [-職] quánzhí (full-job) <adj.> full time: ~工作 full time work || ~妈妈 full time mother
39 额外 [額-] éwài (allotment-addition) <adj.> extra, additional: ~工作 additional work || ~的好处 additional benefits || ~得些小费 get some additional tips
40 其他 [-] qítā (it-other) <adj.> other, else: ~人 other person || ~收入 additional income || ~国家 other nation
41 另外 [-] lìngwài (besides-addition) <adj.> in addition, besides: ~两个人 besides those two people || ~一面 additional aspect || ~的意义 another meaning

42 公共 [-] gōnggòng (public-common) <adj.> public, common: ~汽车 bus || ~交通 public transportation || ~图书馆 public library
43 集体 [-體] jítǐ (collective-body) <adj.> collective, group: ~利益 the interests of the collective || ~ 财产collective property || ~研究 team research
44 个人 [個-] gèrén (individual-person) <adj.> individual, single person: ~财产 individual wealth || ~意见 personal opinion || ~兴趣 personal interest
45 私人 [-] sīrén (private-person) <adj.> private, personal: ~交往 private interactions || ~秘书 private secretary || ~医院 private hospital

Tips:

1 别: 别 has two pronunciations. One is bié, and the other biè. When pronounced biè, 别 means 'disagreeable, insist on.' 别 (bié) means 'divide, distinguish, leave, another, other, special' etc.
2 洋*: When China was forced to open its doors to Western countries from the mid-1800s to the mid-1900s, foreign merchandise was introduced to China, usually with a 洋 (foreign) included in their names, such as 洋火 (火 means 火柴, match,) 洋胰子 (胰子 means 香皂, soap,) and 洋装 (foreign attire.)

Exercises:

Part I

A: Write an antonym for each word in the table. You can refer to the given words.

个人、私人、兼职、土、陌生、亲密

集体 v.s.	公共v.s.	全职v.s.
洋v.s.	熟悉v.s.	疏远v.s.

B: Use the given bound form as a guide to help you think of other words with the same character. Feel free to use your dictionary when needed. Then write down the English definition of each of the words you've written.

贴 *(close):* 贴心 *intimate*

____

____

____

____

亲 *(relative):* 亲兄弟 *blood brothers*

____

____

____

____

熟 *(familiar):* 熟悉 *be familiar with*

____

____

____

Part II: Multiple Choice. Make sure to choose the most appropriate answer.

1 "美国跟朝鲜势不两立," 意思是

A. 朝鲜跟美国是敌对关系
B. 朝鲜跟美国是友好关系
C. 朝鲜跟美国关系密切

2 "小王正在跟女朋友闹别扭," 意思是

A. 小王现在跟女朋友关系很和谐
B. 小王现在跟女朋友关系不太好
C. 小王现在跟女朋友很亲密

3 小王跟女朋友是在中国认识的, 认识以后他们相爱了, 互相__________.
A. 相处融洽 B. 难舍难分 C. 体贴

4 "小王最近跟保险公司一个女孩子打得火热," 意思是

A. 小王跟保险公司一个女孩子交往很多, 但是含有贬义 (negative) 的意思.
B. 小王跟保险公司一个女孩子打架了, 伤得很严重.
C. 小王跟保险公司一个女孩子关系很好, 但是含有褒义 (positive) 的意思.

Theme 247: Noticeable and unnoticeable 明显, 不明显 (míngxiǎn, bù míngxiǎn)

1 明显 [-顯] míngxiǎn (clear-apparent) <adj.> clear, obvious: ~的不同clear difference || ~的变化 clear change || ~的缺点 clear flaw
2 显然 [顯-] xiǎnrán (apparent-*suffix*) <adj.> obvious, evident: ~不可能 obviously not possible || ~不对 obviously incorrect || ~很满意 obviously pleased
3 显著 [顯-] xiǎnzhù (apparent-remarkable) <adj.> notable, marked: ~好转 notable difference, turning point (for the better) || ~的区别 notable difference || ~的效果 (xiàoguǒ) notable effect
4 鲜明 [鮮-] xiānmíng (bright-shining) <adj.> bright: 态度 ~ clear position (on a subject) || ~的色彩 brightly colored || ~的对比 clear contrast
5 黑白分明 [-] hēibái fēnmíng (black-white-distinguished) <idiom> sharp contrast, with black and white sharply contrasted: 斑马身上的条纹~. A zebra's stripes are in clear contrast to one another. || ~的眼睛 a contrast in one's eyes
6 显而易见 [顯--見] xiǎn'éryìjiàn (apparent-and-easy-seen) <idiom> obviously, evidently: ~的答案 obvious answer || 原因~ obvious reason || ~, 他还没有决定去哪儿. It's obvious he hasn't decided where to go.
7 一目了然 [--瞭-] yīmù liǎorán (one-eye-clear-*suffix*) <idiom> clear at a glance: 使人~ caused people to be immediately clear || ~地看清楚 to be able to see clearly || 他的优点和缺点都~. His flaws and strengths are clear at a glance.
8 家喻户晓 [--戶曉] jiāyù hùxiǎo (family-told-household-known) <idiom> known to every household: ~的民间故事. This story is clear to every household. || 新婚姻法~ The new marriage law is clear to every household.
9 众所周知 [衆---] zhòngsuǒzhōuzhī (everyone-*affix*-all-know) <idiom> as everyone knowns, as is known to all: ~的原因. The reason is known by all.

|| ~, 环太平洋地震 (dìzhèn) 特别多. Everyone knows, Pacific Ocean earthquakes frequently occur.

10 显眼 [顯-] xiǎnyǎn (apparent-to the eye) <adj.> conspicuous, eye-catching: ~的地方 showy place || ~的黄色 flashy yellow || 变化很~. The transformation is very eye-catching

11 引人注目 [-] yǐnrénzhùmù (attract-people-focus-attention) <idiom> noticeable, attracting attention: ~的颜色. The color really attracts one's eyes. || ~的发现 noticeable discovery

12 分明 [-] fēnmíng (distinguish-clear) <adj.> be clear, be distinct: ~不对 clearly incorrect || 是非~ clearly right or wrong, (of a person) righteous || 看得~ see clearly

13 肯定 [-] kěndìng (affirm-conclude) <adj.> affirm, be sure: ~的答案 clear answer || ~的语气 affirming voice || ~的态度 affirming bearing

14 明白 [-] míngbai (clear-plain) <adj.> understand, clear: 说得~ speak clearly || 写得~ write clearly || ~的答复 answer clearly

15 明确 [-確] míngquè (clear-definite) <adj./v.> make clear (or definite), clarify: ~规定 clear stipulation || ~的答复 clear answer || ~工作任务 clear work requirement

16 不言而喻 [-] bùyán'éryù (not-speak-but-understood) <idiom> it goes without saying: ~的结论 a summary that goes without saying || 其意义是~的. Its meaning goes without saying.

17 含糊 [-] hánhu (contained-blurred) <adj.> ambiguous, vague: 毫不~ not ambiguous at all. || 说得~ speak vaguely. || ~地回答 answer in a vague manner.

18 暧昧 [曖-] àimèi (dim-obscure) <adj.> ambiguous, shady: 态度~ shady manner. || ~的行为 shady behavior. || 关系~ shady relations

19 隐约 [隱約] yǐnyuē (dim-indistinct) <adj.> indistinct, faint: ~的声音 indistinct sound || ~听到一些 heard indistinctly || 我~感到她不高兴. I can faintly tell that she is unhappy.

20 公开 [-開] gōngkāi (public-open) <adj.> make public: ~演出 public performance || ~否认 repudiate publicly || ~反对 publicly oppose

21 当面 [當-] dāngmiàn (in the presence of-face) <adv.> face to face: ~拒绝 (jùjué) refuse to meet face to face || ~批评 criticize to one's face || ~说好话 speak positive words to one's face

22 当众 [當衆] dāngzhòng (in the presence of-public) <adv.> in the presence of all: ~宣布 promulgate to all || ~表扬 (biǎoyáng) praise in the presence of everyone || ~演讲 (yǎnjiǎng) lecture in front of everyone

23 公然 [-] gōngrán (open-*suffix*) <adj.> openly, publicly: ~反对 publicly oppose || ~拒绝 publicly refuse || ~抢东西publicly rob

24 光天化日 [-] guāngtiān huàrì (broad-heaven-bright-daylight) <idiom> broad daylight, light of day: ~之下打人 beat someone in broad daylight || 暴露 (bàolù) 在~之下 expose in broad daylight

25 法定 [-] fǎdìng (law-regulate) <adj.> legal, statutory: ~节假日 legal holiday || ~程序 (chéngxù) legal procedure || ~代表 legal representative

26 合法 [-] héfǎ (conforming with-law) <adj.> legal, lawful: ~ 地位 legal position || ~夫妻 lawfully husband and wife || ~使用 use in a legal manner

27 秘密 [-] mìmì (secret-secrecy) <adj.> secret: ~活动 secret activity || ~地点 secret location || ~约会 meet in secret

28 不可告人 [-] bùkě gàorén (not-able to-tell-others) <idiom> not to be divulged: ~的目的. The goal cannot be shared with others. || ~的事. This matter cannot be shared with others.
29 暗自 [-] ànzì (secretly-by oneself) <adv.> secretly: ~高兴 secretly happy || ~庆幸 (qìngxìng) secretly rejoice || ~议论 (yìlùn) secretly comment
30 暗中 [-] ànzhōng (dark-in) <adv.> in the dark, in secret: ~使劲 exert all of one's strength in secret || ~摸索 (mōsuǒ) search in the dark || ~观察 (guānchá) review in secret
31 私下 [-] sīxià (private-secretly) <adv.> in private: ~议论 discuss in private || ~交易 engage privately || ~商量 (shāngliang) privately discuss
32 私自 [-] sīzì (privately-by oneself) <adv.> privately, secretly: ~交往 be secretly in contact || ~约会 secretly date || ~出走 secretly leave
33 背地里 [--裏] bèidìli (back-place-*suffix*) <adv.> behind sb's back: ~议论 talk behind one's back || ~说坏话 speak badly behind one's back

34 偷 [-] tōu (steal, stealthily) <adv.> stealthily, secretly: ~看 secretly look || ~吃 steal a bite || ~跑 secretly run
35 偷偷 [-] tōutōu (stealthy-*reduplication*) <adv.> stealthily, covertly: ~哭 covertly cry || ~离开家 secretly leave one's home || ~打开门 secretly open the door
36 悄悄 [-] qiāoqiāo (quiet-*reduplication*) <adv.> quietly: ~地走了 quietly walk/depart || ~推开门 quietly open the door || ~告诉我 quietly told me
37 不动声色 [-動聲-] búdòng shēngsè (not-stir-voice-face) <idiom> maintain one's composure, stay calm: ~ 地听着 maintain one's composure while listening || ~地回答 maintain one's composure in answering
38 一声不响 [-聲-響] yīshēng bùxiǎng (one-sound-not-to ring) <idiom> not say a word, not utter a sound: ~地喝了三杯酒 drink three glasses of alcohol without saying a word || ~地坐在窗前 sit by the window silently

39 明明 [-] míngmíng (obvious-*reduplication*) <adv.> obviously, plainly: ~错了 obviously incorrect || ~去了 obviously have gone || ~没钱 obviously have no money
40 神秘 [-] shénmì (mysterious-secretly) <adj.> mysterious, mystical: ~色彩 mysterious color || ~的东西 mysterious object || ~地说 said mysteriously
41 非法 [-] fēifǎ (not-legal) <adj.> illegal, unlawful: ~出口 illegal export || ~买卖 illegal buying and selling || ~合同 illegal contract
42 地下 [-] dìxia (ground-under) <adj.> underground: ~工作 underground work || ~工厂 underground factory || ~斗争 underground struggle
43 灰色 [-] huīsè (grey-color) <adj.> gray (area): ~收入 gray income

Tips:

1 显 (顯): The original meaning of 显 (顯) is 'ornaments on the head' since the 頁 means 'head' and the lower left part refers to ornaments. Because the ornaments on the head appear to be seen, the character 显 (顯) got its extended meaning 'apparent, obvious.'
2 肯 (kěn): The original meaning of 肯 is 肎, flesh attached to bone. 肯 was later borrowed as the character intended to mean 可 (kě, agree, consent, allow) because their sounds are close.
3 明显 vs. 显然 vs. 显著: 显著 indicates the degree is remarkable. 明显 means 'apparently' and 显然 'obvious (ly).' For example, you haven't seen someone

for the last three months and saw him today. 他明显胖了, 显然, 他最近过得不错. (He apparently gained a lot of weight, and obviously, he has had a happy life recently. Note: This is based on the Chinese way of inference.) 显然 can be used singly, but 明显 cannot.

Exercises:

Part I: Read the following words in the table and fill them in the appropriate blank to explain that set phrase.

明显、鲜明、公然、显眼、悄悄

一目了然: ________________
黑白分明: ________________
光天化日: ________________
引人注目: ________________
一声不响: ________________

Part II: Multiple Choice. Make sure to choose the most appropriate answer.

1 "小高背地里说别人坏话," 意思不是下面哪一个

A. 小高偷偷说别人坏话.
B. 小高私下说别人坏话.
C. 小高在别人的后面说好的话.

2 "小高做了一些不可告人的事情," 意思不是下面哪一个

A. 小高秘密地做了些坏事.
B. 小高做了不能到法院(fǎyuàn, court) 告别人的事.
C. 小高暗地里做了坏事.

3 "小高最近有一笔灰色收入," 意思是

A. 小高最近拿到了一笔非法收入.
B. 小高最近拿到了一些灰颜色的钱.
C. 小高最近赚钱赚得很多.

4 "姚明在中国家喻户晓," 意思是

A. 姚明喜欢中国家庭.
B. 很多中国人都知道姚明.
C. 姚明在中国公开宣传(xuānchuán, publicize) 自己.

5 有人说总统应该情商 (IQ) 很高, 面对别人的批评要做到_________, 克制(kèzhì, restrain) 情绪.

A. 光天化日 B. 不动声色 C. 公开发对

6. _________, 美国总统特朗普上台以后美国经济正在好转, 失业率降到4.3%左右.

A. 是非分明 B. 总所周知 C. 当众宣布

Theme 248: Natural or man-made 自然, 人造 (zìrán, rénzào)

1 绿色 [綠-] lǜsè (green-color) <adj.> green, environmentally friendly: ~食品 green, environmentally friendly product || ~能源 (néngyuán) green energy

2 天生 [-] tiānshēng (natural-born) <adj.> nature, disposition: ~爱美 natural beauty || ~性格温和 naturally warm character || ~的领袖 (lǐngxiù) natural leader

3 先天 [-] xiāntiān (before-born) <adj.> congenital, inborn: ~不足 inborn weakness || ~条件 innate condition || ~疾病 inborn illness

4 原始 [-] yuánshǐ (original-beginning) <adj.> original, primitive: ~人 primitive man || ~的方法 primitive method || ~的舞蹈 primitive dance

5 天然 [-] tiānrán (nature-made) <adj.> natural: ~的环境 natural environment || ~食品 natural food || ~宝石 natural precious stone

6 自然 [-] zìrán (naturally-made) <n./adj.> natural world, nature: ~现象 natural phenomenon || ~的事 natural matter || ~形成 natural appearance

7 第一手 [-] dìyīshǒu (first-hand) <adj.> first hand: ~资料 first hand information

8 老 [-] lǎo (old) <adj.> old, former: ~样子old fashion || ~北京大学 former Beijing University || ~地址 former location

9 原 [-] yuán (original) <adj.> original, raw: ~版 original version || ~计划original plan || ~材料raw and processed material

10 原来 [-來] yuánlái (origin-incoming) <adj.> original, former: ~的公司 former company || ~的样子 original way || ~的地方 original place

11 原有 [-] yuányǒu (original-have) <adj.> original, former: ~的工人 original worker || ~的特色 original characteristic || ~的商店 original shop

12 本来 [-來] běnlái (root-incoming) <adj.> original: ~面貌 original face || ~的颜色 original color || ~的想法 original thought

13 固有 [-] gùyǒu (inherent-have) <adj.> intrinsic: ~的规律 intrinsic law || ~的观念 intrinsic perspective || ~的关系 intrinsic relationship

14 内在 [-] nèizài (inner-be) <adj.> inherent, intrinsic: ~矛盾 internal conflict || ~原因 internal reason || ~关系 internal relationship

15 土生土长 [---長] tǔshēng tǔzhǎng (local-born-local-grown) <idiom> locally born and bred: 在中国~ born and raised in China || ~的美国人 American, born and raised in America || ~的艺术家 natural born artist

16 人工 [-] réngōng (man-worked) <adj.> manual work, man power: ~湖 man-made lake || ~心脏 artificial heart || ~降雨 artificial rain

17 人为 [-為] rénwéi (man-made) <adj.> do by man, man-made: ~因素 human factors || ~地控制 (kòngzhì) 体重 artificial weight control || ~的错误 a human error

18 人造 [-] rénzào (man-built) <adj.> man-made, artificial: ~心脏 artificial heart || ~钻石 artificial diamond || ~太阳 artificial sunlight

19 电动 [電動] diàndòng (electricity-move) <adj.> electric motor: ~自行车 electric bike || ~汽车 electric car || ~门 electric door

20 机关 [機關] jīguān (machine-trigger) <n.> mechanism, government office: 起动密室的~ starting the mechanism of the secret room || 政府~ government agencies || 党政~ party and government organizations

21 自动 [-動] zìdòng (self-move) <adj./ adv.> automatic: ~开关 automatic open and close || ~停了 automatically stop || ~伞 automatic umbrella

22 半自动 [--動] bàn zìdòng (semi-automatic) <adj.> semi-automatic: ~长途电话 semi-automatic long distance phone call

23 全自动 [--動] quán zìdòng (fully-automatic) <adj.> fully automatic: ~相机 fully automatic camera || ~洗碗机 fully automatic dish washer

Tips:

1 天然 vs. 自然: 天然 emphasizes 'not altered by humans,' for example, the Victoria Harbor of Hong Kong is a natural harbor (天然港湾.) 天然气 is natural gas. 自然 emphasizes 'of nature,' for example, wind, rain, thunder are natural phenomena (自然现象). 自然 can modify abstract objects such as 自然选择 (natural selection) and 自然死亡 (natural death.)

2 人为 vs. 人造: 人为 emphasizes 'done by man (intentionally,)' for example, 人为灾难 is man-made disasters. 人造 means 'built, created by man,' for example, 人造纤维 (xiānwéi) is 'man-made fiber.' 人为 can modify abstract objects.

Exercises:

Part I: Translate the following phrases into English and then answer the questions.

人工降雨 ________________
人为灾难 ________________
人造太阳 ________________
土生土长 ________________
内在矛盾 ________________
自然现象 ________________
先天不足 ________________
绿色食品 ________________
天然食品 ________________

1 你觉得人造太阳可能成功吗? 为什么?

____

2 你是不是土生土长的纽约人? 为什么?

____

3 你们国家是不是经常使用人工降雨? 为什么?

____

4 一般来说, 美国或你所在的国家, 哪个超市买绿色食品最多?

____

Theme 249: Professional, amateur 专业, 业余 (zhuānyè, yèyú)

(See also Theme 7)

1 正规 [-規] zhèngguī (formal-regular) <adj.> regular, formal: ~教育formal education, regular education || ~学校regular school || ~途径regular procedures

2 标准 [標準] biāozhǔn (sign-water level) <adj./n.> standard, criterion: 公认的 ~ accepted standard || 合乎, 不够~ up to standard (or mark), below the standard (or mark) || 技术~ technical standards

3 规范 [規範] guīfàn (regular-model) <adj.> normal, standard: ~的操作standard operation || ~动作 the standard action || ~的论文normative paper
4 正式 [-] zhèngshì (formal-rule) <adj.> formal, official: ~开始start officially || ~成立formally established || ~代表formal representative
5 正统 [-統] zhèngtǒng (orthodox-system) <adj.> orthodox: ~观念orthodox ideas || ~语言orthodox language
6 专业 [專業] zhuānyè (special-profession) <adj.> professional: ~知识professional knowledge || ~精神professionalism || ~人才professionals
7 业余 [業餘] yèyú (profession-spare) <adj.> non professional, amateur: ~文艺工作者 amateur literary and art workers || ~音乐家amateur musician
8 山寨 [-] shānzhài (mountain-stockade) <adj.> bandit, copycatting: ~手机bandit phone || ~文化copycatting culture || ~产品copycat product
9 杂牌 [雜-] zápái (other than mainstream-brand) <adj.> less know and inferior brand: ~自行车miscellaneous bicycles || ~货goods of an inferior brand || ~军miscellaneous troops
10 编内 [編-] biānnèi (establishment-within) <adj.> on the permanent staff, on the regular payroll: ~人员personnel on the permanent staff
11 编外 [編-] biānwài (establishment-outside) (of personnel) <adj.> not on the permanent staff: ~人员temporary staff,employee not on the regular payroll || ~机构organization outside the authorized limit, extra organization

Tips:

1 准 (準): The radical of 準 is 氵 (水) and the sound (zhǔn) is from 隼 (sǔn.) Its original meaning is 'water level' from which evolved meanings such as 'rule, standard' etc.
2 山寨文化: 'Copycatting culture' has a strong base in China since many hold the opinion that the world owes a lot to China since the world has greatly benefitted from the Four Great Inventions of China throughout history but has not paid any patent fee to China. Many believe now it is time for China to even the score.
3 编内 and 编外: They mean 'permanent (staff)' and 'temporary (staff),' in other words, heaven or hell in terms of benefits.

Exercises:

Part I: Translate the following phrases into English and then answer the questions.

杂牌货 ____________________
业余画家 ____________________
专业画家 ____________________
编内人员 ____________________
编外人员 ____________________
山寨产品 ____________________
正规教育 ____________________
合乎标准 ____________________
正式成立 ____________________
正统思想 ____________________

1 你买过山寨产品吗? 是什么?

---

2 美国公司有没有编内人员和编外人员? 哪一种待遇 (dàiyù, benefit) 会高一些?

---

3 你觉得中国有没有正统思想? 是什么? 美国有正统思想吗?

---

4 美国是哪一年正式成立的, 中华人民共和国呢?

Theme 250: Relatives 亲戚 (qīnqi)

(See also Theme 3)

1 血亲 [-親] xuèqīn (blood-beloved) <n.> blood relations: 直系~ immediate blood relatives || 旁系~ side of blood relatives || ~关系blood relatives
2 亲生 [親-] qīnshēng (parent-born) <adj.> be sb's own child, biological (child, parents): ~儿子one's own son || ~子女one's own children || ~父母one's own parents, biological parents
3 嫡亲 [-親] díqīn (descent-relation) <n.> blood relations, close paternal relations: ~姐妹blood sisters || ~弟兄blood brothers, full brothers
4 同胞 [-] tóngbāo (same-womb) <n.> born of the same parents, fellow countryman, compatriot: ~兄弟full brothers || 港澳~ our compatriots in Hong Kong and Macao || 台湾~ our compatriots in Taiwan

5 旁支 [-] pángzhī (collateral-branch) <n.> collateral branch (of a family): 有人认为日本文化是中国文化的~. Some people think Japanese culture is related to Chinese culture. || 这位企业家没有后代, 只能从家族的~中挑选接班人. The entrepreneur has no descendants and can only pick up his successor from his family's branch.
6 表亲 [-親] biǎoqīn (of second generation kinship-relative) <n.> cousin, cousinship: ~关系cousinship

7 干爸 [乾-] gānbà (adopt-father) <n.> adoptive father, a man whose position is roughly equivalent to a foster father and godfather in Western countries without religious or legal complications: 认~ have an adoptive father
8 干妈 [乾媽] gānmā (adopt-mother) <n.> adoptive mother, a woman whose position is roughly equivalent to a foster mother and godmother in Western countries without religious or legal complications: 认~ have an adoptive mother
9 后爸 [後-] hòubà (step – father) <n.> stepfather
10 后妈 [後媽] hòumā (step-mother) <n.> stepmother
11 继父 [繼-] jìfù (step – father) <n.> stepfather
12 继母 [繼-] jìmǔ (step – mother) <n.> stepmother
13 养父 [養-] yǎngfù (raise-father) <n.> adopted father: ~对他比亲生父亲还要好. His adoptive father was better than his birth father.
14 养母 [養-] yǎngmǔ (raise-mother) <n.> adopted mother: ~不希望他找到自己的亲生父母. His adoptive mother didn't want him to find his birth parents.

15 拜把 [-] bàibǎ (sworn-brotherhood) <adj.> become sworn brothers: ~兄弟sworn brothers

16 结义 [結義] jiéyì (to knot-brotherhood) <v.> become sworn brothers or sisters: 桃园三~ the sworn brotherhood of the three Shu Han heroes in the Peach Garden (i.e. of Liu Bei, Guan Yu, and Zhang Fei) || ~兄弟sworn brothers

Tips:

1 生亲不如养亲: It means 'It is the real parents, not the blood parents that you should appreciate more.'

2 Various ways to refer to 'father': The following terms are used in contemporary Chinese, 爸, 爸爸, 父, 父亲, 家父, 令尊 (lìngzūn), 亲爹, 干爹, 干爸, 后爸, 继父, 养父. 爸: daddy, 爸爸: dad, 父: father (used in written language or in combination), 父亲: father, 家父: my father (addressing one's own father in a humble way), 令尊: your father (addressing the listener's father in a respective way), 亲爹: blood, birth father, 干爹: (nominal) adoptive father, 干爸: colloquial form of 干爹, 后爸: stepfather (colloquial), 继父: stepfather, 养父: adoptive (or foster) father.

3 亲爹 vs. 干爹 vs. 养父: 亲爹 is blood, birth father, but it can be used in a metaphorical way '你就是我亲爹' (you are like my blood, birth father) when one wants to express highest appreciation. However, many Chinese people would feel uncomfortable hearing this. 干爹 is the adoptive father, however, many 干爹 are nominal, without legal documentation. Also, 干爹 means 'sugar daddy' in certain circumstances. 养父 is an adoptive father and rarely means 'foster father' since foster care has not yet developed in China.

4 后妈养的: It means someone was raised by his stepmother, however, it has strong indications that the person involved was not given due care by his stepmother. Traditionally, 后妈 had a notorious reputation for treating stepchildren cruelly.

5 表亲: 表亲 refers to second generation kinship. Since Chinese families were populous throughout history, there is a saying 一表三千里, which means 'you can easily find a second generation relative in an area of thousands of square miles' or 'you can connect by a certain kinship with anyone in an area of thousands of square miles.' There is another saying 一代亲, 二代表, 三代就完了which means 'the first generation kinships are real, the second are not close and the third are gone.'

6 Typical colloquial words in this unit: 后爸, 后妈

Exercises:

Part I: Read the following words and then answer the questions.

亲爸、亲妈、后爸、后妈、干爸、干妈、养父、养母、拜把兄弟

1. 上面这些人哪些跟你有血亲关系?

____

2 上面这些人哪些跟你没有血亲关系?

____

Part I: Put the similar meaning words in the same table.

结义兄弟、亲爸亲妈、亲儿子亲女儿、表兄妹、同一父母

拜把兄弟: 亲生父母: 亲生子女: 表亲: 同胞:

Theme 251: Good or evil 善, 恶 (shàn, è)

1 好 [-] hǎo (good) <adj.> good, kind: ~人good person || ~事good things || 老板对我真~. The boss is really kind to me.

2 善 [-] shàn (lucky, good) <adj.> kind, virtuous: ~人 virtuous person || ~心 good heart, benevolent || ~举 benevolent actions

3 善良 [-] shànliáng (good-kindhearted) <adj.> good and honest: ~的人 good and honest person || ~的心 good and honest heart || ~的愿望 (yuànwàng) good intentions

4 贤惠 [賢-] xiánhuì (virtuous-favor) (of a woman) <adj.> kind, amiable: ~的妻子 amiable wife || ~媳妇 amiable daughter-in-law

5 慈 [-] cí (kindly love) <adj.> kind, loving: ~母 loving mother || ~眉善目 have a kindly face || 父~子孝 benevolent father, filial son

6 仁 [-] rén (benevolence) <adj./ n.> benevolence, kindness: ~爱 benevolence || ~心 benevolent heart || 麻木不~ apathetic, insensitive

7 慈爱 [-愛] cí'ài (kind-love) <adj.> love, affection (of an older person for a younger person): ~的父母 loving parents || ~地望着儿子 affectionately look at one's son || ~的目光 an affectionate gaze

8 仁慈 [-] réncí (benevolent-kind) <adj.> benevolent, merciful: ~的上帝 benevolent god || ~的心 benevolent heart

9 慈祥 [-] cíxiáng (kind-good) <adj.> kindly: ~的老人 kindly old person || ~地笑 kindly laugh || 目光~ kind eyes

10 手软 [-軟] shǒuruǎn (hand-soft) <adj.> irresolute, soft-hearted: 毫不~ be resolute, be ruthless || 无论干什么坏事都不会~. No matter the terrible actions, there was still no hesitation.

11 心软 [-軟] xīnruǎn (heart-soft) <adj.> be soft-hearted: 口硬~ hard mouth and soft heart

12 厚道 [-] hòudao (tolerant-moral) <adj.> honest and kind: 为人~ be honest and kind to others || ~人 honest and kind person

13 憨 [-] hān (foolish) <adj.> foolish, silly: ~儿子 foolish child || ~态 air of charming naivety || ~笑 foolishly laugh

14 憨厚 [-] hānhòu (foolish-tolerant) <adj.> straightforward and good-natured: ~的小伙子simple and honest young guy || ~地笑 laugh with good nature

15 忠厚 [-] zhōnghòu (sincere-tolerant) <adj.> honest and tolerant, sincere: 为人~ be honest to others || ~人 an honest person

16 老实 [-實] lǎoshi (*prefix*-honest) <adj.> honest, frank: ~孩子 honest child || 做人~ be honest || ~说 speak honestly

17 朴实 [樸實] pǔshí (plain-honest) <adj.> simple, plain: ~的姑娘 simple and honest young girl || 穿得~ dress plainly || ~的语言 plain words

18 纯朴 [純樸] chúnpǔ (pure-plain) <adj.> simple, pure: ~的生活 honest and simple life || ~的爱情 pure love || ~的农民 a simple farmer

19 尖刻 [-] jiānkè (acrimonious-caustic) <adj.> acrimonious, biting: 说话~ speak in a biting manner || ~的语言 biting language

20 刻薄 [-] kèbó (caustic-ungenerous) <adj.> sarcastic, unkind: ~话 sarcastic expression || 待人~ be unkind to others || 嘴巴~ have a cruel tongue

21 尖酸刻薄 [-] jiānsuān kèbó (tart-mean) <idiom> tart and mean, bitterly sarcastic: 说话~ speak in a bitter and mean manner || ~的话 bitter and mean talk

22 缺德 [-] quēdé (lack-virtue) <adj.> be mean (or wicked, rotten): ~的事 wicked and rotten matters || 做人很~ be a wicked and rotten person || 这个主意很~. This is a wicked and awful thought.

23 不仁不义 [---義] bùrén bùyì (not-benevolent-not-just) <idiom> cruel and unjust: ~的人 cruel and unjust person

24 毒 [-] dú (poison, malicious) <adj.> cruel, fierce: 心~ malicious heart || ~念 malicious idea || 狠~ vicious

25 狠 [-] hěn (vicious) <adj.> ruthless, relentless: 心~ ruthless heart || 下~心make a tough decision resolutely || ~主意 have ruthless intentions

26 辣 [-] là (peppery, ruthless) <adj.> vicious, spicy: ~妹子spicy girl, bold and vigorous girl || 手段~ viscous methods

27 凶 [-] xiōng (ominous, ferocious) <adj.> vicious: 狼很~ vicious wolf || 样子~ vicious manner || 对他~ be vicious to him

28 歹毒 [-] dǎidú (bad-cruel) <adj.> sinister and vicious: 心地~ sinister and vicious heart || 手段~ sinister and vicious methods

29 狠心 [-] hěnxīn (vicious-heart) <adj.> harden one's heart: ~的父母 harden one's heart to one's parents || 对自己的孩子很~ have a heart heart to one's children || ~作了决定 have a closed heart when making decisions

30 心狠手辣 [-] xīnhěn shǒulà (heart-vicious-hand-ruthless) <idiom> cruel and ruthless: 歹徒~ cruel and ruthless evildoers

31 无恶不作 [無惡--] wú'è bùzuò (no-evil-won't-do) <idiom> stop at nothing to do evil: ~的魔鬼. A demon will stop at nothing to do evil.

32 残暴 [殘-] cánbào (atrocious-brutal) <adj.> cruel and ferocious, brutal: ~统治 a cruel ruler || ~的军人 a cruel soldier || ~行为 cruel behavior

33 残酷 [殘-] cánkù (atrocious-cruel) <adj.> cruel, brutal: ~的环境 cruel environment || ~的事情 cruel affairs || ~的斗争 brutal struggle

34 奸诈 [姦詐] jiānzhà (treacherous-deceitful) <adj.> deceitful: 行为~ deceitful actions

35 阴险 [陰險] yīnxiǎn (sinister-dangerous) <adj.> sinister: ~目的 sinister goal || ~地笑 laugh in a sinister manner

36 两面三刀 [兩---] liǎngmiàn sāndāo (two-face-three-knife) <idiom> two faced, three knives (double cross): 对朋友不能~. Stop playing a double game with your friend.

Tips:

1 善 (shàn): The radical of 善 is 羊, which has an auspicious meaning. 善 means 'virtuous, kind.' There is a Chinese saying "百善孝为先," which means 'among all virtues, kindness is the best.'

2 老实 vs. 诚实: Both mean 'honest,' however, 诚实 means 'not lie' but 老实 has a connotation of 'foolish and timid,' which is not really a compliment to most Chinese people now.
3 仁 and 义: 仁 means 'benevolence' and 义 'justice.' 仁 is Confucius' teaching and 义 is from Mencius.' 仁义礼智信 (rén, yì, lǐ, zhì, xìn) are the five Confucian virtues, meaning 'benevolence, justice, courtesy, wisdom, sincerity' respectively. There is also a folk saying "你不仁, 我不义," which means 'since you are not sincere with me, don't blame me (for any improper behavior).'
4 歹 (dǎi): 歹 originally means 'cracked scapula' or 'remains of a person' neither of which is good, therefore, all characters with the radical 歹 have a negative meaning. For example, 残 (cruel,) 死 (die) and 殊 (shū, behead,) which however appears mainly in the compound word 特殊 (special.)

Exercises:

Part I: Read the following words and then answer the questions.

狠心、心狠手辣、无恶不作、残暴、奸诈、阴险、两面三刀、缺德、尖酸刻薄、朴实、老实
纯朴、厚道、忠厚、贤惠、善良、仁慈、慈爱、慈祥、歹毒

1 上面哪些词是褒义词 (commedatory term)?

____

2 下面哪些词是贬义词 (derogatory term)?

____

3 哪些词可以形容一个人非常坏?

____

4 哪些词可以形容一个人品质很好?

____

5 你希望自己的好朋友有哪些性格特征? (Choose the words from the above table)

____

Part II: Multiple Choice. Make sure to choose the most appropriate answer.

1 "小高为人两面三刀," 意思是
A. 小高不诚实 B. 小高功夫很厉害 C. 小高要面子
2 "这个人无恶不作," 意思是
A. 这个人不做坏事 B. 这个人做尽了坏事 C. 这个人不喜欢做坏事
3 "这个人不仁不义," 意思是
A. 这个人不知道仁义 B. 这个人没有意思 C. 这个人不讲道德, 没有仁义

4 "小高对种族歧视 (qíshì, discrimination) 的事情见得太多了, 已经麻木不仁 (mámù bùrén, unconcerned) 了," 意思是
 A. 小高很关注种族歧视
 B. 小高对种族歧视已经习惯了
 C. 小高因为种族歧视的问题得病了

Theme 252: Honest, hypercritical 诚实, 虚伪 (chéngshí, xūwěi)

(See also Theme 232)

1 诚恳 [誠懇] chéngkěn (honest-sincere) <adj.> sincere, heartfelt: 态度~ sincere manner || 做人~ be a sincere person || ~地批评 (pīpíng) sincerely criticize
2 纯真 [純-] chúnzhēn (pure-real) <adj.> pure, sincere: ~的感情 pure feelings || 心地~ pure heart
3 恳切 [懇-] kěnqiè (sincere-earnest) <adj.> earnest, sincere: 言词~ earnest words || ~希望 (xīwàng) earnest hopes || ~的目光 earnest vision
4 率真 [-] shuàizhēn (straightforward-real) <adj.> forthright and sincere: ~的情感 forthright and sincere feelings || 个性~ forthright and sincere manner
5 坦诚 [-誠] tǎnchéng (frank-honest) <adj.> frank and sincere: ~地对他说 speak in a frank and sincere manner || ~的目光 frank and sincere expression
6 虔诚 [-誠] qiánchéng (pious-honest) <adj.> pious, devout: ~的佛教徒 devout buddhist monk || 对上帝很~ be devout to god || 态度~ a pious manner
7 真诚 [-誠] zhēnchéng (real-honest) <adj.> sincere, genuine: ~的态度 sincere manner || ~地关怀 show genuine concern || ~的朋友 genuine friend
8 真挚 [-摯] zhēnzhì (real-cordial) <adj.> sincere, cordial: ~的友谊 (yǒuyì) sincere friendship || 感情 ~ sincere feelings || ~地相爱 to sincerely love one another
9 诚心 [誠-] chéngxīn (honest-heart) <n.> honest and trustworthy, sincerely: ~感谢 sincerely thank || ~道歉 (dàoqiàn) sincerely apologize
10 真心 [-] zhēnxīn (true-heart) <n.> wholeheartedly: ~相爱 wholeheartedly love one another || ~合作 wholeheartedly cooperate || ~愿意 (yuànyì) wholeheartedly be willing
11 诚心诚意 [誠-誠-] chéngxīn chéngyì (honest-heart-honest-faith) <idiom> genuine, sincere: ~地帮助别人 sincerely seek to help others || ~地相信 sincerely trust
12 真心实意 [--實-] zhēnxīn shíyì (true-heart-real-faith) <idiom> genuinely and sincerely: ~地合作 sincerely cooperate || ~地帮助他 genuinely try to help him
13 诚实 [誠實] chéngshí (honest-real) <adj.> honest: ~的人 honest person || ~的行为 honest behavior || ~劳动 honest work
14 表里如一 [-裏--] biǎolǐ rúyī (outside-inside-as-one) <idiom> consistent in thought and action: ~, 言行一致 for words and actions to be consistent
15 言行一致 [-] yán xíng yīzhì (speech-action-consistent) <idiom> the deeds match the words (or promises): 表里如一, ~ consistent in thought and action, the deeds match one's words
16 忠诚 [-誠] zhōngchéng (loyal-faithful) <adj.> loyal, faithful: 对朋友~ be loyal to one's friends || ~于自己的事业 be loyal to one's work || 为人~ be loyal to others

17 忠实 [-實] zhōngshí (loyal-true) <adj.> loyal, true: ~于现实生活 be loyal in life || 性格~ have a loyal personality || ~的伙伴 (huǒbàn) loyal partner

18 假 [-] jiǎ (false, fake) <adj.> artificial, fake: ~话 a lie || ~山 artificial hill || ~货fake goods || ~民主sham democracy

19 伪善 [僞-] wěishàn (pretend-kind) <adj.> hypocritical: ~的声音 a hypocritical voice || ~行为 hypocritical voice

20 虚伪 [-僞] xūwěi (feigned-false) <adj.> sham, false, hollow: ~的感情 hollow feelings || 性格~ hollow personality

21 假惺惺 [-] jiǎ xīngxīng (fake-hypercritic) <adj.> hypocritically, insincerely courteous: ~地哭 cry in an insincere way || ~地安慰 (ānwèi) insincerely comfort

22 虚荣 [-榮] xūróng (feigned-glory) <adj.> vanity, vainglory: 爱慕 (àimù) ~ vanity || 追求~ vainly chase glory

23 爱面子 [愛--] ài miànzi (concern-dignity) <v.> concerned with saving face: 文人~ scholars are very concerned about face || 极~ be obsessed with face, appearance

24 正 [-] zhèng (upright) <adj.> honest, upright: ~人君子man of honor, man of integrity || ~气healthy atmosphere (or tendency)

25 正直 [-] zhèngzhí (upright-honest) <adj.> honest, upright: 为人~ be honest to others || ~的行动 honest actions

26 坦白 [-] tǎnbái (frankly-speak) <adj.> confess, make a confession: ~承认 (chéngrèn) make honest confessions || ~真相 confess the facts

27 坦率 [-] tǎnshuài (frank-straightforward) <adj.> candid, frank: 态度~ candid manner || ~道歉 (dàoqiàn) candidly apologize || ~地回答 candidly reply

28 光明正大 [-] guāngmíng zhèngdà (openhearted-upright) <idiom> open and upright: 他~地做生意, 从来不偷税漏税. His business dealings were above board and never had tax evasion.

29 刁钻 [-鑽] diāozuān (tricky-crafty) <adj.> cunning, artful: 发球~ serve a ball in an artful manner || ~古怪 be artfully eccentric

30 刁蛮 [-蠻] diāomán (tricky-rude) <adj.> obstinate, unruly: ~的家伙 an unruly person

31 狡滑 [-] jiǎohuá (sly-slippery) <adj.> sly, crafty: ~的敌人 a sly enemy || 狐狸很~ the fox is very crafty

32 奸诈 [姦詐] jiānzhà (treacherous-sham) <adj.> fraudulent, crafty: 为人~ be fraudulent to others

33 口是心非 [-] kǒushì xīnfēi (mouth-yes-heart-no) <idiom> say yes and mean no: 政客们常常~. Politicians are often duplicity.

34 势利 [勢-] shìlì (influence-money) <adj.> snobbish: ~小人 be snobbish to others

Tips:

1 正: The upper part of 正 is 一, which means 'target' here, and the lower part is 止, which means 'foot,' therefore, the original meaning of 正 is 'central, not deviated.' This character is composed of five straight strokes, horizontal or vertical. It is widely used to note down small numbers, particularly for votes, because the distinction of parts is most clear.

2 惺惺 (xīngxīng): 惺惺 has two almost opposing meanings. One is 'smart,' for example, 惺惺惜 (xī) 惺惺 or 惺惺相惜 (smart people appreciate, admire each other.) The other meaning is to depreciate others for being hypercritical, for example, 假惺惺 and 惺惺作态 (xīngxīng zuòtài,) both meaning 'hypercritical.'

3 光明正大: An alternative form is 正大光明, which you can find above the throne of the Palace of Heavenly Purity (Qiánqīng Gōng) in the Forbidden City in Beijing. The script is written from right to left like most ancient Chinese scripts.

Exercises:

Part I: Read the following words and then answer the questions.

诚心诚意、真心实意、表里如一、言行一致

1 小王对人诚心诚意, 还可以这样说:

___

2 小王这个人表里如一, 还可以这样说:

___

虚伪、假惺惺、虚荣、爱面子、狡猾、奸诈

3 这个人假惺惺的, 还可以这样说:

___

4 这个人很爱面子, 还可以这样说:

___

5 这个人很狡猾, 还可以这样说:

___

Part II: Translate the following phrases into English and then answer the questions.

爱慕虚荣 ___
口是心非 ___
光明正大 ___
态度诚恳 ___
感情真挚 ___

1 哪些词是褒义词 (commendatory term)?

___

2 哪些词是贬义词 (derogatory term)?

___

3 你觉得自己有下面所说的哪些性格特点?

___

Theme 253: Strong, weak 刚强, 软弱 (gāngqiáng, ruǎnruò)

1 刚强 [剛-] gāngqiáng (firm-strong) <adj.> firm, unyielding: 意志 (yìzhì) ~ strong-willed || ~的性格firm character || ~地跑完了马拉松 to strongly finish running a marathon
2 坚强 [堅-] jiānqiáng (hard-strong) <adj.> strong, firm: ~的决心 strong determination || ~地站起来 to firmly stand || 性格~ strong character
3 顽强 [頑-] wánqiáng (stubborn-strong) <adj.> indomitable, tenacious: ~的性格 tenacious character || ~的生命力 tenacious life force || ~地活着 live tenaciously
4 快 [-] kuài (fast) <adj.> straightforward: ~人~语straight talk from a straight person || 心直口~ frank and outspoken
5 刚烈 [剛-] gāngliè (hard-staunch) <adj.> fiery and forthright: 性格~ fiery and forthright personality
6 坚毅 [堅-] jiānyì (hard-persistent) <adj.> firm and persistent: ~的目光 firm and persistent look || 性格~ persistent personality || ~地拒绝 firmly refuse
7 血性 [-] xuèxìng (blood-nature) <adj./n.> courage and uprightness: ~男儿courageous man || 有~ have courage
8 阳刚 [陽剛] yánggāng (manly-hard) <adj.> manly, virile: ~美 manly beauty || ~气质 manly temperament || ~之气manliness, virility
9 直 [-] zhí (straight) <adj.> frank, straightforward: 他喜欢有话~说. He likes to speak very frankly. || ~言 (不讳búhuì) speak bluntly
10 硬 [-] yìng (hard) <adj.> tough, firm: ~骨头hard bone-dauntless, unyielding person (opp.软骨头) ||口气~ a rough tone || 态度~ a tough manner

11 坚定 [堅-] jiāndìng (hard-fixed) <adj.> firm, staunch: ~的信念 firm beliefs || ~的立场 firm position || ~的语气 firm tone
12 坚决 [堅決] jiānjué (hard-resolute) <adj.> firm, resolute: ~反对 resolutely oppose || 态度~ determined attitude || ~支持 firmly support
13 果断 [-斷] guǒduàn (resolute-decisive) <adj.> resolute, decisive: ~决定 resolute decision || ~的回答 resolutely answer || 办事~ decisively handle affairs
14 干脆 [乾脆] gāncuì (dry-crisp) <adj.> clear cut, straightforward: 做事~ do things in a clear cut manner || 动作~ clear cut actions || ~地回答 clear answer
15 痛快 [-] tòngkuai (extremely-happy) <adj.> delighted, straightforward: 我们在海边玩得很~. We had a terrific time at the seaside || ~地答应了 readily agreed || ~人 a straightforward person
16 温和 [溫-] wēnhé (lukewarm-warm) <adj.> mild, gentle: 态度~ gentle temperament || 性格~ mild personality || ~地说 gently say

17 软 [軟] ruǎn (soft) <adj.> soft, mild, gentle: 嘴~ be afraid to speak out || 心肠~ gentle heart || 耳朵~ easily influenced
18 脆弱 [-] cuìruò (crisp-weak) <adj.> fragile, frail: 感情~ feel frail || ~的身体 frail body || 性格~ frail personality
19 娇气 [嬌氣] jiāoqì (delicate-style) <adj.> fragile, delicate: ~的女孩子 fragile girl || 这种花很~, 不容易养. This type of flower if very delicate. It is very hard to grow.
20 懦弱 [-] nuòruò (timid-weak) <adj./ n.> cowardly, weak, weakness: 性格~ cowardly personality || 我无法忍受他这种~. I could not stomach his weakness.

21 娇生惯养 [嬌-慣養] jiāoshēng guànyǎng (delicate-live-spoiled-raise) <idiom> pampered and spoiled since childhood: 对孩子~ be pampered and spoiled since childhood || ~的孩子 a pampered and spoiled child

22 勇敢 [-] yǒnggǎn (brave-dare) <adj.> brave, courageous: ~精神 brave and courageous spirit || ~地改正错误 bravely and courageously correct one's errors || 办事~ handle affairs in a brave and courageous manner

23 勇猛 [-] yǒngměng (brave-violent) <adj.> bold and powerful: ~杀敌 boldly and powerfully kill one's enemies || 打仗~ boldly fight || ~的大力士 powerful warrior

24 见义勇为 [見義-爲] jiànyì yǒngwéi (see-justice-brave-do) <idiom> see what is right and have the courage to do it: ~抓小偷 see a thief and have the courage to catch them

25 大胆 [-膽] dàdǎn (big-gallbladder) <adj.> bold, daring: ~地改革 (gǎigé) bold revolution || ~想法 bold thought || ~的推测 (tuīcè) bold principle

26 胆小 [膽-] dǎnxiǎo (gut-small) <adj.> timid, cowardly: 生性~ have a cowardly disposition || ~鬼 a coward

27 胆怯 [膽-] dǎnqiè (gut-afraid) <adj.> timid, cowardly: ~地说 timidly say || 心里~ be cowardly in one's heart

28 心虚 [-] xīnxū (mind-timid) <adj.> lacking in confidence, be afraid of being found out: 感到~ be lacking in confidence || ~地低下头 lower one's head in lack of confidence || ~得厉害 severely lack confidence

29 怯懦 [-] qiènuò (afraid-timid) <adj.> timid and overcautious: 生性~ have an over cautious nature || ~的办法 overcautious solution || ~地回答 timidly answer

30 胆小怕事 [膽---] dǎnxiǎo pàshì (gut-small-afraid-trouble) <idiom> lacking courage and confidence: 在工作中~ lack courage and confidence in work || 表现得~ show a lack of courage and confidence

Tips:

1 强 (強): The radical of 強 is 虫 (worm) and the sound component is 弘, which was similar to 强 in ancient Chinese. 强 means 'strong.' On the Internet, 小强 means 'cockroach' because it is strong and can survive in any environment.

2 痛快: It is not 痛 (painful) and 快 (happy), but 'extremely happy' since 痛 here is an adverb. Other examples of 痛 used in this way include 痛打 (to beat soundly,) 痛斥 (tòngchì, to bitterly attack, scold) and 痛改前非 (extremely-correct-previous-mistake, repent past mistakes) etc.

Exercises:

Part I: Read the following words and then answer the questions.

刚强、坚强、顽强、有血性、硬骨头、硬汉、勇敢
胆小、胆怯、怯懦、胆小怕事、懦弱、勇猛、见义勇为

1. 上面哪些词可以形容一个很坚强的人？

____

2 下面哪些词可以形容一个胆小的人?

---

3 上面哪些词可以形容一个勇敢的人?

Part II: Multiple Choice. Make sure to choose the most appropriate answer.

1 小王是一个非常诚实的人, 对公司出现的问题他会______________.
A. 态度硬 B. 直言不讳 C. 口气直

2 小王认为孩子不能______________, 否则会害了孩子.
A. 阳刚之气 B. 性格顽强 C. 娇生惯养

3 孩子做错事儿的时候一般都会______________, 不敢面对父母.
A. 脆弱 B. 心虚 C. 娇气

4 "小王快人快语"意思是
A. 小王心直口快 B. 小王心肠软 C. 小王喜欢动作快

5 这个女孩子虽然性格_______, 但是做事果断_______.
A. 温和、干脆 B. 干脆、坚定 C. 坚定、痛快

Theme 254: Solemn and humorous 庄重, 诙谐 (zhuāngzhòng, huīxié)

1 大方 [-] dàfang (generous-unrestrained) <adj.> generous, liberal: 说话~ speak liberally || 款式 (kuǎnshì) ~ elegant and in good taste || 打扮/穿着~ apply make-up or wear clothes liberally

2 庄重 [莊-] zhuāngzhòng (solemn-serious) <adj.> serious, grave: 态度~ grave manner || ~的服装 (fúzhuāng) solemn clothes || ~地行礼solemn act

3 端庄 [-莊] duānzhuāng (straight-solemn) <adj.> dignified, sedate: 举止~ dignified manner || 相貌~ dignified looking || ~地坐着sit in a dignified manner

4 得体 [-體] détǐ (appropriate to-occasion) <adj.> appropriate to the occasion: 说得~ spoke appropriately || 打扮 (dǎban) ~ apply make-up appropriately || ~的衣着 appropriate clothes

5 文雅 [-] wényǎ (civilized-elegant) <adj.> elegant, refined: 谈吐 ~ elegant manner of speech || 举止~ elegant actions || ~的气质 elegant temperament

6 风流 [風-] fēngliú (wind-flow) <adj.> distinguished and accomplished: ~人物 accomplished person

7 浪漫 [-] làngmàn (*transliteration of* Romance) <adj.> romantic: ~的生活 romantic life || ~诗人 romantic poet || ~色彩 romantic covers

8 潇洒 [瀟灑] xiāosǎ (fast-free) <adj.> confident and at ease, free and easy: 生活~ free and easy life || 动作~ free and easy motion || 过得~ going free and easy

9 落落大方 [-] luòluò dàfāng (poised-graceful) <idiom> natural and at ease: 教态~ natural and easy teaching style || ~地走上台 to naturally and easily walk on stage

10 自在 [-] zìzài (self-be) <adj.> comfortable and at ease: ~世界 carefree world || ~的生活 carefree life

11 豪放 [-] háofàng (forthright-unconstrained) <adj.> bold and unconstrained: 作风~ a bold and unconstrained style || ~的行为 bold and unconstrained actions || ~地大笑起来 laugh out loud in an unconstrained manner

12 洒脱 [灑脫] sǎtuō (free-easy) <adj.> free and easy, unrestrained: 个性~ free and easy personality || ~的姑娘 a free and easy young girl

13 不拘小节 [---節] bù jū xiǎo jié (not-restrained- (by) small-matter) <idiom> to not stress the small stuff: 行为~ act in way that does not stress the small stuff || ~的性格 a personality that does not stress the small stuff

14 自由自在 [-] zìyóu zìzài (free-unrestrained) <idiom> leisurely and carefree: ~的生活 live in a leisurely and carefree manner || ~地呼吸 breath carefree || ~地生长 grow in a carefree manner

15 自得其乐 [---樂] zìdéqílè (self-enjoy-its-pleasure) <idiom> derive pleasure from sth.: 叔叔每天看书, 画画, ~. Uncle derives pleasure from reading and drawing everyday.

16 悠然自得 [-] yōu rán zì dé (leisurely-*suffix*-self-enjoy) <idiom> be carefree and content: 心中~ one's heart is carefree and content || ~的生活 a carefree and content life || ~地玩耍 play in a carefree and content manner

17 厉害 [厲-] lìhai (severe-harm) <adj.> fierce, harsh, severe: 热得~ heated and harsh || ~的嘴 fierce mouth || 眼睛很~ fierce eyes

18 严肃 [嚴肅] yánsù (stern-solemn) <adj.> solemn, grave: 态度~ solemn manner || ~的问题 solemn question || ~地批评 to solemnly criticize

19 调皮 [調-] tiáopí (adjust-naughty) <adj.> naughty, mischievous: ~ 的孩子 a naughty child || ~捣蛋 mischievous || ~得很very naughty

20 顽皮 [頑-] wánpí (mischievous-naughty) <adj.> naughty, mischievous: ~小孩 mischievous child || ~地眨眼睛 mischievous eyes || ~的笑脸 a mischievous smile

21 活泼 [-潑] huópō (lively-rascal) <adj.> lively, vivacious: 个性~ lively personality || 她上课很~. She took classes in a lively manner.

22 好动 [-動] hàodòng (tend to-move) <adj.> be overactive: 天性~ naturally be overactive || ~的儿童 an overactive child

23 生龙活虎 [-龍--] shēnglóng huóhǔ (lively-dragon-lively-tiger) <idiom> doughty as a dragon and lively as a tiger, bursting with energy: ~地战斗to fight in a way that is bursting with energy || 小伙子一天到晚~的. The boy is vigorous from dawn to dusk.

24 本分 [-] běnfèn (duty-agendum) <adj.> one's duty, (to play) one's part: ~的渔民 a fisherman's duty || ~地过日子 to play one's parts in the passing days || 不安~ discontented with one's lot

25 狂 [-] kuáng (mad) <adj.> crazy, arrogant: 发~ go crazy || 那个人口气很~ that person is very arrogant

26 放肆 [-] fàngsì (loose-indulge) <adj.> unbridled, wanton: ~大笑 laugh in an unbridled way || 不敢~ not dare to be unbridled

27 猖獗 [-] chāngjué (ferocious-unruly) <adj.> rampant, raging: 虫害~ rampant pest || 走私~ rampantly smuggle

28 猖狂 [-] chāngkuáng (wild-arrogant) <adj.> savage, furious: ~进攻 savagely attack

Tips:

1 自由 and 自在: Everyone loves 自由自在 (leisurely and carefree), but a Song Dynasty proverb goes 成人不自在, 自在不成人 which means 'if you want to achieve something, you cannot live in a carefree style, and vice versa.'
2 狂, 猖狂 and 猖獗: All characters share the same radical '犭' (quǎn, dog.) It seems the animals were blamed for humanity's ill manners.
3 Typical colloquial words in this unit: 厉害, 狂

Exercises:

Part I: Translate the following phrases into English and then answer the questions.

举止文雅 ________________
谈吐大方 ________________
个性洒脱 ________________
相貌端庄 ________________
浪漫潇洒 ________________
仪态落落大方 ________________
不拘小节 ________________

1 哪些词是描写人的外表的?

____

2 哪些词是描写人的性格的?

____

Part II: Read the following sentences and fill in each blank with the appropriate word or phrase from the options given.

1 放肆、猖獗、发狂

a) 上课的时候几个学生在教室里________地大喊大叫.
b) 一些学生的恶作剧 (èzuòjù, mischief) 有时候让老师非常________.
c) 纽约少数公立学校的犯罪 (fànzuì, crime) 活动比较__________.

2 活泼、生龙活虎、本分、严肃、顽皮

a) 小白是一个很_________的学生, 非常听老师的话.
b) 小白养了一只小狗, 它非常_________, 一副________的样子.
c) 小白的弟弟好动, 也很_________, 经常会让爸爸妈妈生气.
d) 小白的弟弟犯了错误, 父母非常_________地批评了他.

3 自得其乐、自由自在

a) 小李是个自由职业者, 因为他喜欢没有老板约束 (yuēshù, restrain), _________地工作.
b) 小李每个周末都自己在家唱卡拉OK, _________.

Theme 255: Optimistic, pessimistic 乐观 and 悲观 (lèguān, bēiguān)

(See also Theme 107)

1 开朗 [開-] kāilǎng (open-bright) <adj.> cheerful: 性格 (xìnggé) ~ always cheerful || 他很 ~. He is very outgoing. || 心情~ be in a cheerful mind

2 乐观 [樂觀] lèguān (happy-view) <adj.> optimistic: ~精神optimism || 盲目 (mángmù) ~ blind optimism, pollyanna || 对前途 (qiántú) 很~ be optimistic about the future

3 明朗 [-] mínglǎng (bright-clear and bright) <adj.> clear, bright and cheerful: 态度~ the attitude is clear || 前景~. The prospects are clear. || 现在事情很~了, 那就是他一定会当选市长. Now it is clear that he will be elected mayor.

4 爽朗 [-] shuǎnglǎng (straightforward-bright) <adj.> frank and open, straightforward: ~的笑声hearty laughter || 性格~ the personality is frank and open

5 外向 [-] wàixiàng (out-bound) <adj.> extrovert: 她性格~, 可是她老公性格却很内向. She is outgoing, but her husband is introverted.

6 看得开 [--開] kàn de kāi (view-*auxiliary*-open) <v.> adopt a philosophical attitude towards: 他对人生看得很开. He is open to life. || 别那么悲观 (bēiguān), ~点儿, 事情会好起来的. Don't be so pessimistic. Take it easy. Things will get better.

7 想得开 [--開] xiǎng de kāi (think-*auxiliary*-open) <v.> not take to heart, try to look on the bright side of things: 凡事都要~. It is better to always look on the bright side.

8 无忧无虑 [無憂無慮] wúyōu wúlǜ (no-worry-no-anxiety) <idiom> free from care, free from all anxieties: ~地玩耍 (wánshuǎ) carefree playing || ~的童年 a carefree childhood

9 知足常乐 [---樂] zhīzú chánglè (know-content-always-happy) <idiom> contentment brings happiness: ~是一种乐观的人生态度. Contentment is an optimistic attitude in life.

10 积极 [積極] jījí (amass-utmost point) <adj.> positive, enthusiastic: ~工作work actively || ~参加慈善 (císhàn) 活动actively participate in charity || ~进取 (jìnqǔ) set high goals for oneself

11 肯干 [-幹] kěngàn (willing-do) <adj.> be willing to do hard work: 这些农村来的小伙子又老实又 ~. These country lads are honest and hardworking.

12 踊跃 [踴躍] yǒngyuè (jump-leap) <adj.> eagerly, enthusiastically: ~参加这个活动be eager to come to this activity || ~报名register enthusiastically || 大家在会上~发言. People took the floor one after another.

13 主动 [-動] zhǔdòng (initiative-move) <adj.> take the initiative: ~帮助别人 offer to help || 中国人认为在谈恋爱的时候, 一般是小伙子 ~一点儿. Chinese people think that normally young men take the initiative in a relationship. || ~打招呼greet others with the initiative and enthusiasm

14 悲观 [-觀] bēiguān (sad-view) <adj.> pessimistic: ~情绪 (qíngxù) pessimism || 态度~ be pessimistic || 别太~, 我们还有希望. Don't be too pessimistic. We still have hopes.

15 想不开 (看不开) [--開] xiǎng bu kāi (view/think-not-open) <v.> take things too hard, take a matter to heart: 他因为失恋~, 最后得了忧郁症 (yōuyùzhèng). He struggled with the breakup with his lover and ended up with depression.

16 万念俱灰 [萬---] wànniàn jùhuī (10, 000-thought-all-disheartened) <idiom> abandon oneself to despair, become totally disillusioned: 在全部财产被骗以后, 他~, 自杀了. After he was cheated out of his property, he was too despaired to kill himself.

17 低落 [-] dīluò (low-fall) <adj.> low, downcast: 情绪~ in low spirits || 遇到挫折 (cuòzhé) 以后, 大家的士气很~. After the setback, everyone's morale was low.

18 萎靡 [-] wěimí (listless-dejected) <adj.> listless, dispirited: 精神~ depressed || 出口~ exports slumped || 市场~ markets are flagging || ~不振dispirited and listless

19 被动 [-動] bèidòng (passive-move) <adj.> passive: ~接受passive acceptance || 处于~的地位in a passive position || 你做事怎么总是那么~, 能不能主动一点儿? How can you always be passive in your work? Can you take the initiative?

20 消极 [-極] xiāojí (disappear-utmost point) <adj.> negative, passive: ~情绪 negative mood || 态度~ take a passive attitude, remain inactive || ~等待just be in negative waiting

21 消沉 [-] xiāochén (dispirit-submerge) <adj.> downhearted, low-spirited: 她近来有些~. She's rather depressed these days. || 意志 (yìzhì) ~ demoralized, despondent

22 四大皆空 [-] sìdàjiēkōng (four-big-all-empty) <idiom> the sensuous world is illusory, all physical existence is vanity: ~是佛教的主要思想. 'The sensuous world is illusory,' which is the main idea of Buddhism.

Tips:

1 四大皆空: In Buddhism, the Four Great Elements (Mahābhūta) are earth, water, fire and air. The extended meaning of 四大皆空 is 'the physical world is illusory,' which resonates with the theme of the greatest Chinese novel, *Dream of the Red Chamber* (红楼梦).

2 知足常乐: 'Contentment brings happiness' is a phrase once highly cherished by the Chinese ordinary people.

3 积极 (positive) and 消极 (negative): It is hard to believe these two very basic words were borrowed from Japanese.

Exercises:

Part I: Match up the following expressions to the appropriate column. Make sure your words can describe the situation mentioned in the column.

性格外向、开朗、工作积极、情绪低落、常常想不开、性格外向、无忧无虑、意志消沉、精神萎靡、工作积极肯干、凡事看得开、知足常乐

小王是一个乐观的人	小李是一个悲观的人

Part II: Multiple Choice. Make sure to choose the most appropriate answer.

1 佛教提倡____________, 意思是世界上一切事物都是空的.
A. 无忧无虑 B. 知足常乐 C. 四大皆空

2 老高在财产全部被骗以后, _________, 跳楼自杀了.
A. 万念俱灰 B. 意志软弱 C. 盲目乐观

3 张小姐因为失恋而__________, 最后得了忧郁症 (depression).
A. 想得开 B. 想不开 C. 被动

4 自从2010年以来, 中国经济一直__________, 处于转型 (zhuǎnxíng) 时期.
A. 爽朗 B. 踊跃 C. 萎靡

5 ____________是一种乐观的人生态度.
A. 知足常乐 B. 情绪低落 C. 意志消沉

Theme 256: Cautious and careless 谨慎, 疏忽 (jǐnshèn, shūhū)

1 认真 [認-] rènzhēn (take to-conscience) <adj.> conscientious, serious: 小王是个很~的学生. Little Wang is a conscientious student. || 他是开玩笑, 你不要太~. He is joking. Don't take it too seriously. || 做得很~ do sth. with great care.
2 郑重 [鄭-] zhèngzhòng (solemn-serious) <adj.> serious, earnest: ~声明solemnly declare || ~地回答earnestly answer
3 一丝不苟 [-絲--] yīsī bùgǒu (a-bit-not-neglect) <idiom> not be the least bit negligent, be conscientious and meticulous: 对工作~. Be meticulous about your work. || ~的态度a meticulous attitude
4 郑重其事 [鄭---] zhèngzhòngqíshì (solemn-serious-its-matter) <idiom> seriously, in earnest: ~地宣布 (xuānbù) announce of the matter in earnest
5 正经八百 [-經--] zhèngjīng bābǎi (orthodox-classic-eight-hundred) <idiom> serious, earnest: 这是~的事. This is no joke. || ~的进口货authentic imports || 我没跟你开玩笑, 我是~地说呢. I am not joking with you. I am talking about this with you very seriously.
6 较真儿 [較-兒] jiào zhēnr (dispute-truth) <adj.> take sth. or sb. seriously: 别跟她~, 她是随便说的. Don't be serious with him. He said those casually. || 他特别喜欢~, 没法跟他开玩笑. He likes to be serious, and people can't make fun of him.
7 一是一, 二是二 [-] yī shì yī, èr shì èr (1-is-1, 2-is-2) <idiom> call a spade a spade, unequivocally: 他这个人非常诚实, 说话做事~. He is a very honest person who is incapable of pretending.
8 耐心 [-] nàixīn (patient-heart) <adj./n.> patient: 失去~ lose one's patience, be out of patience || ~等待wait patiently || 有/没/缺乏 ~ have/lack of patience in sth.

9 小心 [-] xiǎoxīn (caucious-mind) <adj.> mindful, careful: 她说话总是很~, 不乱说. He always speaks with care. || 这个街区不安全, 你得~. This block isn't safe. You have to be careful.

10 细致 [細緻] xìzhì (delicate-refined) <adj.> careful, meticulous, thorough: ~的工作 careful work || 观察~ the observation is meticulous

11 仔细 [-細] zǐxì (fine-careful) <adj.> careful, attentive: ~想think carefully || 看得很~ look at it carefully

12 密切 [-] mìqiè (close-earnest) <adj.> close: ~关注 pay close attention to || ~注视watch closely

13 客气 [-氣] kèqi (guest-manner) <adj./ v.> polite, courteous: 她说话很~. She is very polite. || 咱们是老朋友了, 不用太~. We are old friends. Let's not stand on ceremony.

14 热心 [熱-] rèxīn (warm-heart) <adj.> warm-hearted: ~人 a kind-hearted person || ~帮助别人warm-heartedly help others

15 热情 [熱-] rèqíng (warm-affection) <adj./n.> warm, warm-hearted: ~接待 (jiēdài) warm reception || 爱国~ patriotic passion || 她对人很~. She's warm-hearted towards others.

16 自豪 [-] zìháo (self-proud) <adj.> have a proper sense of pride (or dignity): ~地说speak proudly || 感到~ be proud of || 最让你父母~的事 things that make your parents the most proud of

17 谦虚 [-] qiānxū (humble-modest) <adj.> modest, self-effacing: 态度~ be modest || 他是大教授, 但是说话很~. He is a famous professor, but he is very modest. || ~使人进步, 骄傲使人落后. Modesty helps one to make progress, while conceit makes one lag behind.

18 虚心 [-] xūxīn (modest-heart) <adj.> open-minded, modest: ~请教 (qǐngjiào) be open to ask for advice || ~向别人学习be willing to learn from others || ~接受别人的意见accept other's opinions with an open mind

19 踏实 [-實] tāshi (trample-firm) <adj.> steady and sure, dependable: 工作~ be a steady worker || 心里~ feel peaceful || 办事不~ too frivolous to do solid work

20 沉稳 [-穩] chénwěn (calm-steady) <adj.> steady: 做人~ be steady || 她做事很~, 让人很放心. He is quite stable and reassuring.

21 低调 [-調] dīdiào (low-key) <adj.> low-keyed: ~做人keep a low profile || ~的人a low-keyed person || 一些美国人建议这位政治家~一点, 要不然联邦 (liánbāng) 调查局 (FBI) 该找他麻烦了. Some Americans advised this politician to keep a low profile, otherwise the FBI will investigate him.

22 冷静 [-靜] lěngjìng (cool-unhurried) <adj.> sober, calm: 保持~ keep calm, keep one's head || 请~些please calm down || 她的话使我~下来. Her words sobered me.

23 一步一个脚印 [-] yībù yīgè jiǎoyìn (one-step-one-MW-foot print) <proverb> every step leaves its print-work steadily and make solid progress: 做事不能太着急, 得~地去做. Don't be in a hurry when you do something, work steadily and make it solid.

24 文雅 [-] wényǎ (civilized-elegant) <adj.> elegant, refined: 她举止~, 说话非常斯文 (sīwén). She is refined and soft-spoken. || ~的姑娘 elegant girls

25 斯文 [-] sīwén (this-civilization) <adj.> refined, gentle: 说话~ soft-spoken || 他看起来很~, 不会做这种坏事吧? He looks every gentle. Will he do such a bad things?

26 文静 [-靜] wénjìng (gentle-quiet) <adj.> gentle and quiet: 他很~, 像个姑娘. He is quiet as a girl. || ~的姑娘gentle and quiet girls

27 文质彬彬 [-質--] wénzhì-bīnbīn (elegance-plainness-refined and courteous) <idiom> gentle: ~的知识分子an intellectual of good manners || 说话~ be gentle in speech

28 马虎 [馬-] mǎhu (horse-tiger) <adj.> careless, casual: 态度~ the attitude is sloppy || 工作~ work sloppiness || 你怎么这么~! 连生日都写错了! Why are you so sloppy? You even wrote your birthday wrong.

29 草率 [-] cǎoshuài (careless-rash) <adj.> sloppy, careless: ~决定hasty decision || ~结婚marry in haste

30 草草 [-] cǎocǎo (careless-*reduplication*) <adv.> carelessly, hastily: ~地洗个脸 a quick wash of the face || ~读了一遍a rough read

31 粗心 [-] cūxīn (careless-heart) <adj.> careless, thoughtless: ~的医生careless doctors || 他太~, 出门常常忘带钥匙 (yàoshi). He is so careless that he often forgets his keys when he goes out.

32 疏忽 [-] shūhū (neglect-overlook) <adj.> be careless, slip up: 工作~ the work is careless || ~大意carelessness || 对不起, 我一时~, 把您的名字写错了. Sorry, I just neglected to write your name correctly.

33 不慎 [-] búshèn (not-cautious) <adj.> careless: ~摔倒accidentally falls || 言语~ be careless in speaking || 本人~丢了钱包, 有拾到者请联系我, 必有重谢. I have lost a wallet carelessly. The person who picked it up contacted me. This is a great deal of thanks to you.

34 粗制滥造 [-製濫-] cūzhì lànzào (coarsely-manufactured-carelessly-made) <idiom> manufacture (or turn out) in rough and slipshod way: ~的产品shoddy products

35 偷工减料 [--減-] tōugōng jiǎnliào (pilfer-man hour-reduce-material) <idiom> do shoddy work and use inferior material: ~的工程the constructions of cutting corners. || 别找他们盖楼, 他们总是~. Don't hire them to build a building. They're always cutting corners.

Tips:

1 正经八百: It means 'seriously,' but its etymology is unclear today. 正经 can mean 'orthodox classics,' and 八百 is sometimes written as 八本 (8-volume.)

2 马虎: It means 'careless.' A folk story states that an artist painted a creature which looked like both a horse and a tiger. He was very proud of that and called the painting 马虎图 (horse-tiger-painting.) However, one day his eldest son saw a horse but he thought it was a tiger based on his impression of his father's painting, so he shot the horse. The other day his youngest son saw a tiger but he thought it was a horse, also based on his impression of his father's painting, so he tried to ride the animal but was eaten by the tiger. The tragedies made the word '马虎' unforgettable and passed down over the generations.

Exercises:

Part I: Match up the following expressions to the appropriate column. Make sure your words can describe the situation mentioned in the column.

a) 教书一丝 不苟　　b) 有耐心
c) 做事一步一个脚印　　d) 工作踏实
e) 办事沉稳　　f) 说话斯文
g) 文质彬彬　　h) 工作仔细
i) 热心帮助别人

描写一位工作认真的好老师

Part II: Multiple Choice. Make sure to choose the most appropriate answer.

1 中国有句老话: ________使人进步, ________使人落后.
A. 细心、粗心　　B. 谦虚、骄傲　　C. 认真、较真儿

2 "老王说话办事一是一, 二十二." 意思是
A. 老王很疏忽　　B. 老王很诚实　　C. 老王很小心

3 在中国有一些大桥因为__________ _、 __________ __, 质量不合格被称为"豆腐渣工程." (Jerry-built project, shabby project)
A. 偷工减料、粗制滥造　　B. 马虎草率、粗心草率　　C. 正经八百、较真儿

4 "老王做事一丝不苟," 意思是
A. 老王很踏实　　B. 老王很低调　　C. 老王很认真

5 下面哪组词可以描写人的性格
A. 郑重其事、正经八百　　B. 热心、对人热情　　C. 草草结束、耐心

Theme 257: Modest and rude 谦虚, 骄傲 (qiānxū, jiāo'ào)

1 鲁莽 [魯-] lǔmǎng (rude-reckless) <adj.> crude and rash, rash: ~的人reckless people || ~的举动reckless behavior || 言谈~ speak carelessly
2 冒昧 [-] màomèi (bold-ignorant) <adj.> make bold: ~地问问题take the liberty of asking queations || 恕我~, . . . with all due respect
3 冒然 [-] màorán (bold-*suffix*) <adj.> rashly, hastily: ~决定decide hastily || ~行动take action hastily || ~插手have a hand in it rashly
4 轻率 [輕-] qīngshuài (imprudent-rash) <adj.> rash, hasty: ~对待 take it lightly || 做事~ be rash in doing sth.
5 唐突 [-] tángtū (exaggerative-abruptly) <adj.> rude, blunt: ~地问 ask questions abruptly || 这句话说得太~了. This saying is too abrupt.

6 荒唐 [-] huāngtáng (absurd-abruptly) <adj.> absurd: ~透顶 (tòudǐng) very absurd || ~的梦absurd dreams || ~的行为absurd behavior

7 愣头愣脑 [-頭-腦] lèngtóu lèngnǎo (reckless-head-reckless-mind) <idiom> rash, reckless: 说话~ talk impetuously || ~的孩子the impetuous kid

8 冷 [-] lěng (cold) <adj.> cold in manner: ~笑sneer || ~言~语make sarcastic comments || ~着脸have a gloomy look

9 骄傲 [驕-] jiāo'ào (proud-arrogant) <adj.> arrogant, conceited: 他挺聪明的, 就是有点儿~. He's smart, but just a little bit proud. || 谦虚一点, 别太~. Be modest. Don't be too proud. || ~的小公主proud little princess

10 不耐烦 [--煩] bú nàifán (not-patient) <v.> impatient: 等得~ wait for long time, so one's impatience grows || ~地说said impatiently

11 轻浮 [輕-] qīngfú (imprudent-flippant) <adj.> frivolous, flighty: ~的女人a frivolous woman || 举止~ behave frivolously

12 张狂 [張-] zhāngkuáng (rampant-overbearing) <adj.> flippant and impudent, insolent: ~的人a flippant and impudent person || 个性~ insolent personality

13 性急 [-] xìngjí (temper-quick) <adj.> impatient, short-tempered: ~的人impatient person || 他很~, 一点儿都不能忍耐 (rěnnài). He is so impatient that he can't stand anythings with a slow pace.

14 粗鲁 [-魯] cūlǔ (rough-rude) <adj.> rough, rude: 言语~ speak rudely || ~的行为rude behavior

15 野蛮 [-蠻] yěmán (wild-barbarous) <adj.> uncivilized, barbarous: ~人barbarian || ~行为barbarous act, savage behavior

16 粗野 [-] cūyě (rough-wild) <adj.> rough, boorish: 动作/举止~ behave boorishly || 说话 ~ speak boorishly || ~的人rough person

17 眼高手低 [-] yǎngāo shǒudī (eye-high-hand-low) <idiom> have high standards but little ability: 他没什么真本事, ~. He has high aspirations but low abilities. || 年轻人找工作往往~. When young people look for work, they often have high expectations for job positions but little ability.

18 心浮气躁 [--氣-] xīnfú qìzào (heart-flippant-temper-impetuous) <idiom> flighty and impetuous: 做事~ do things with flighty and impetuous attitude || 现在社会上的人过于追求物质, ~. Nowadays, many people in our society are too materialistic and restless.

19 操之过急 [--過-] cāozhī-guòjí (act-it-too-hastily) <idiom> act with undue haste, be overhasty: 处理问题~ deal with problems in haste || 我们慢慢来, 不要~. Let's take our time. Don't be hasty.

20 欲速则不达 [--則-達] yù sù zé bú dá (want-haste-however-not able to-accomplish) <idiom> haste brings no success, more haste, less speed: 减肥要慢慢来, ~. Take your time to lose weight. More haste, less speed.

Tips:

1 冒: The upper part of this character is not 日 (sun,) or 曰 (yuē, to speak,) but 冃 (mào, hat.) Words with 冒 include 冒险 (take risk,) 感冒 (catch a cold,) and 冒犯 (màofàn, offend.)

2 欲速则不达: It means 'haste makes waste' and is very popular in both spoken and written Chinese.

Exercises:

Part I: Multiple Choice. Make sure to choose the most appropriate answer.

1 减肥要慢慢来, ________________.
A. 不能言语粗鲁 B. 不能动作粗野 C. 欲速则不达

2 现在一些年轻人__________, 能力不强, 却不愿做基础工作.
A. 骄傲自满 B. 眼高手低 C. 十分鲁莽

3 培养孩子的能力, 不能_________, 应该一步一个脚印慢慢来.
A. 严厉 B. 轻浮 C. 操之过急

4 一般来说中国人会觉得_______是缺点, 人应该尽量谦虚.
A. 愣头愣脑 B. 轻率 C. 冒昧

5 中国政府好像不会_______插手 (chāshǒu, intervene) 朝鲜 (Cháoxiǎn, N. Korea) 的事情.
A. 性急 B. 冷笑 C. 冒然

Theme 258: Selfish, unselfish 公, 私 (gōng, sī)

1 公 [-] gōng (public) <adj.> public, state-owned, fair: ~办学校public schools || ~用 for public use || ~认 general acknowledgment/public recognition
2 公正 [-] gōngzhèng (impartial-just) <adj./n.> just, fair: ~的待遇 (dàiyù) fair treatment || ~的态度 impartial attitude || 社会~ social justice
3 公平 [-] gōngpíng (impartial-fair) <adj.> fair, just: 买卖~ fair in buying and selling || ~竞争 (jìngzhēng) fair competition || ~比赛 a fair match
4 正义 [-義] zhèngyì (just-righteous) <adj.> just, righteous: ~行为 righteous action || ~立场 just stand || ~的事业 (a) just cause
5 公事公办 [---辦] gōngshì gōngbàn (official-thing-officially-do) <idiom> business is business, do official business according to official principles: ~的原则 accepted business principles || ~的人 a principled business person
6 一视同仁 [-視--] yī shì tóng rén (same-treat-equal-benevolence) <idiom> treat equally without discrimination: 对所有员工都~. All the employees are treated alike. || 老师对所有学生 ~. The teacher treated each student impartially.
7 一碗水端平 [-] yīwǎn shuǐ duānpíng (a-bowl-water-hold-level) <proverb> hold a bowl of water level – be impartial: 处理争执 (zhēngzhí) 应该~. When settling a dispute, one must be fair to both sides.
8 偏 [-] piān (leaning, inclined, partial) <adj.> inclined to one side, partial: ~左 leaning towards the left || ~低 on the lowside || ~心眼 leaning towards one's intuition儿
9 不公 [-] bùgōng (not-fair) <adj.> unjust, unfair: 分配 (fēnpèi) ~ unequal distribution || 命运 (mìngyùn) ~ starcrossed/unfair fate
10 偏心 [-] piānxīn (partial-heart) <adj.> partial, showing particular favor to: ~的父母 the parents are partial || 对儿子~ showing favor to one's son
11 偏见 [-見] piānjiàn (prejudiced-opinion) s<n.> prejudice, bia: 产生~ create prejudice || 种族 (zhǒngzú) ~ racial prejudice || 个人~ individual prejudice

12 偏听偏信 [-聽--] piāntīng piānxìn (partial-listen-partial-trust) <idiom> heed and trust only one side, listen only to one side, biased: ~别人的话 listen biasedly to the words of others/ having a closed mind
13 厚此薄彼 [-] hòucǐ báobǐ (favor-this-prejudice-that) <idiom> favor one and be prejudiced against the other: 对子女不能~. You should treat your daughters and sons equally. You cannot favor one over the other.

14 无私 [無-] wúsī (not-selfish) <adj.> selfless, disinterested: ~奉献 (fèngxiàn) selfless contribution || ~的精神selfless spirit || 给予~的帮助 selflessly provide help to others
15 廉洁 [-潔] liánjié (of integrity-honest) <adj.> honest and clean, incorruptible: 做官~ be an honest official || ~执政 (zhízhèng) uncorrupted by power || ~的干部 an honest official
16 清廉 [-] qīnglián (clear-of integrity) <adj.> honest and upright, free from corruption: 为官~ be an honest and incorruptible official || ~的官员 an honest and incorruptible official
17 舍己为人 [捨-爲-] shějǐ wèirén (sacrifice-oneself-for-others) <idiom> sacrifice oneself for the sake of others: ~的模范 (mófàn) an example of sacrificing for others || ~的精神 the spirit of sacrificing for others
18 自我牺牲 [--犧-] zìwǒ xīshēng (oneself-sacrifice) <idiom> self-sacrifice: 做出~ make a sacrifice (for others) || 勇于~ brave enough to make a sacrifice yourself || 不怕~ not afraid to sacrifice yourself
19 先人后己 [--後-] xiānrén hòujǐ (first-others-later-self) <idiom> put others before oneself: 在利益面前应该~. In times of benefit, you should put others before yourself.

20 自私 [-] zìsī (egotistic-selfish) <adj.> selfish, self-centered: ~的人 a selfish person || 想法~ selfish thinking
21 自我 [-] zìwǒ (egotistic-myself) <n.> self: ~介绍self-introduction || ~保护 self-defense || ~安慰 (ānwèi) self-consolation
22 损人利己 [損---] sǔnrén lìjǐ (harm-others-benefit-self) <idiom> harm others for one's personal gain: ~的思想 the thought of harming others for one's personal gain || 损人不利己 to harm others without benefiting oneself
23 自私自利 [-] zìsī zìlì (egotistic-selfish-self-benefit) <idiom> everything for self-benefit and personal profit: ~的人 a person who does everything for self-benefit and personal profit || ~的思想 the thought of doing everything for self-benefit and personal profit

24 贪 [貪] tān (greedy) <adj.> embezzle: ~小便宜 always on the lookout for petty advantages || ~钱/财 embezzle money/wealth || ~舒服 comfort through embezzlement
25 贪婪 [貪-] tānlán (greedy-covetous) <adj.> avaricious, greedy: ~的目光 greedy eyes || ~地呼吸着新鲜空气 to take in fresh air (as much as possible) || ~地阅读新书 to tear through a new book
26 贪心 [貪-] tānxīn (greedy-heart) <adj.> greedy, insatiable: ~的人 a greedy person || ~不足 insatiable greed
27 心黑 [-] xīnhēi (heart-evil) <adj.> be greedy, be evil: ~的老板 a black-hearted business person
28 贪便宜 [貪--] tān piányi (greedy for-cheap) <v.> eager to get a bargain: 企图~ always attempt to get a bargain/the better deal || 贪小便宜always on the

lookout for petty advantages || ~买低价大虾 eager to get a bargain, even to the extent of buying expired shrimp

29 惟利是图 [---圖] wéilì shìtú (only-profit-does-seek) <idiom> bent solely on profit: ~的商人 a business person concerned only about profit

30 贪财 [貪財] tāncái (greedy-money) <v.> greedy for money: ~的人 a person who has a lust for wealth

31 爱财如命 [愛財--] àicái rúmìng (love-money-like-life) <idiom> love money as one loves one's life: ~的人 a person who loves money as one loves one's life

32 见钱眼开 [見錢-開] jiànqián yǎnkāi (seen-money-eye-open) <idiom> be wide-eyed at the sight of money: ~的人 a person who becomes wide-eyed at the sight of money

Tips:

1 私 (sī) vs. 公 (gōng): Both 私 and 公 are related to '厶' which probably means 'self-centered' as well as 'private part of the body.' 私 is a later form of 厶, and 公 means 'impartial, just, opposite of 厶' since the upper part of 公, i. e., 八 means 'opposite.'

2 一视同仁: The original meaning of 一视同仁 is 'in the sage's eyes, everyone is equal' or 'the sage treats everyone with benevolence equally.'

3 惟利是图 (wéilì shìtú): It is an inverted structure, which is extremely rare in Chinese idioms. The normal word order should be 图惟利, meaning 'seek only (for) profit.'

4 人 vs. 己: 人 (others) and 己 (oneself) are often used in Chinese idioms for contrast, for example, 损人利己, 先人后己 and舍己为人 are annotated above. Others include 人不为己, 天诛地灭 (rénbúwèijǐ, tiānzhū dìmiè, every man for himself and the devil take the hindmost) etc.

Exercises:

Part I: Match up the following expressions to the appropriate column. Make sure your words can describe the situation mentioned in the column.

a) 对人一视同仁 b) 廉洁执政
c) 爱财如命 d) 见钱眼开
e) 惟利是图 f) 自私自利
g) 损人利己 h) 先人后己
i) 舍己为人 j) 必要的时候能够自我牺牲
k) 以自我为中心 l) 贪小便宜

描写一个自私的人	描写一个无私、公平的政府官员	描写一个贪婪的人

Part II: Multiple Choice. Make sure to choose the most appropriate answer.

1 老师对待学生应该"一碗水端平," 意思是
A. 老师对学生要偏心 B. 老师对学生要公平 C. 老师对学生要正义

2 老师对所有的学生都要公平, 不能__________.
A. 厚此薄彼 B. 公事公办 C. 先人后己

3 在美国应该看各种媒体关于总统报道, 不能只看CNN, 否则容易__________.
A. 见钱眼开 B. 自我牺牲 C. 偏听偏信

4 即使今天美国种族__________还是比较严重.
A. 偏心眼 B. 偏见 C. 偏心

5 "偏心眼儿"的意思是
A. 贪婪 B. 贪心 C. 不公平

Theme 259: Strict and tolerant 严, 宽 (yán, kuān)

1 严 [嚴] (strict) <adj.> strict, rigorous: 管得~ strict management || 要求~ strict demands || 管理 (guǎnlǐ) ~ the management is very strict
2 严格 [嚴-] yángé (strict-standard) <adj.> strict, rigid: ~管理 demanding management || ~的规定 demanding stipulations || ~地限制 (xiànzhì) demanding limitations
3 严厉 [嚴厲] yánlì (strict-severe) <adj.> severe, stern: ~批评 (pīpíng) severely criticize || ~的妈妈 (a) stern mother || ~的目光 (a) stern look

4 宽容 [寬-] kuānróng (lenient-tolerant) <adj.> broad-minded, tolerant: 态度~ an open minded manner || ~的宗教 (zōngjiào) a tolerant religion || ~的思想 open-minded/tolerant thoughts
5 网开一面 [網開--] wǎng kāi yī miàn (net-open-one-side) <idiom> leave one side of the net open-give the wrongdoer a way out, be lenient: 中国"只生一个孩子"的政策 (zhèngcè) 对少数民族~, 允许 (yǔnxǔ) 蒙古 (Ménggǔ) 人生两个孩子. The Chinese One Child Policy had a loophole, which allowed people of Mongolian minorities to have two children.
6 大方 [-] dàfāng (generous-poised) <adj.> generous, liberal: 花钱~ spend money liberally || 出手~ liberally purchase/spend money
7 大度 [-] dàdù (wide-magnanimity) <adj.> generous (in spirit), magnanimous: 胸怀 (xiōnghuái) ~ have a generous heart || ~的人 a generous person
8 大气 [-氣] dàqì (generous-manner) <adj.> distinguished, classy: 高端、~、上档次的品牌high-end atmospheric brand
9 仗义 [-義] zhàngyì (uphold-justice) <adj.> loyal, generous and ready to offer help: ~直言 speak out from a sense of justice || ~的朋友 a loyal friend
10 义气 [義氣] yìqì (brotherhood-code) <n.> loyal, brotherhood: 讲~ be loyal to friends, remain faithful to friends || 重~ strong loyalty || 江湖~ the code of the brotherhood
11 够朋友 [-] gòu péngyou (deserve to be-friend) <adj.> be a friend indeed: 老王~. Lao Wang is very loyal to friends.

12 小气 [-氣] xiǎoqi (miserly-manner) <adj.> stingy, narrow-minded, petty: ~的人 a narrow minded person || 她男朋友很~. Her boyfriend is very narrow-minded.

13 小心眼儿 [---兒] xiǎoxīnyǎnr (narrow-minded) <adj.> narrow-minded, petty: ~的人 a petty person || 她的~我一眼就看出来了. I read her petty mind at first sight.

14 吝啬 [-嗇] lìnsè (stingy-thrifty) <adj.> stingy, miserly, mean: ~的人 a miserly person || ~钱财 frugally spend money || 请别~你的微笑. Please don't hold back your smile to others.

15 抠门儿 [摳門兒] kōuménr (dig-door) <adj.> stingy, miserly: 她真 ~！ How stingy she is!

16 一毛不拔 [-] yīmáo bùbá (one-feather-not-pull) <idiom> unwilling to give up even a hair-very stingy: 铁公鸡~ a iron rooster (from which no feathers can be plucked) – a tightwad || ~的人a very stingy person/ a tightwad

Tips:

1 网开一面: When ancient Chinese people were catching birds or fish, they would cast only three sides and leave one side open. It showed their mercifulness.

2 一毛不拔: Historical stories go that when 杨朱 (Yáng Zhū), a philosopher in the Warring States period, was asked if he would pull a hair which could benefit the whole world, he answered 'No.'

3 抠门儿 (kōuménr): It means 'miserly' and is used in some northern Chinese dialects. A folk story says that when a miser went through the gate of a temple, he would scratch the thin layer of gold off the gate and take it home.

Exercises:

Part I: Match up the following expressions to the appropriate column. Make sure all similar meaning words in one column.

不大度、小心眼儿、吝啬、出手不大方、一毛不拔、仗义、讲义气、

小气	抠门儿	够朋友

Part II: Multiple Choice. Make sure to choose the most appropriate answer.

1 小张在工作中犯了严重的错误, 他恳请 (kěnqǐng, earnestly request) 领导对他__________.

A. 出手大方 B. 网开一面 C. 一毛不拔

2 胸怀__________的人一般不会和别人计较 (jìjiào, care about) 小事情.

A. 大方 B. 严格 C. 义气

3 "老李就是个铁公鸡, 大家一起吃饭的时候他一毛不拔." 这句话的意思是

A. 老李很严格 B. 老李很乐观 C. 老李很小气

Theme 260: Frugal and extravagant 简朴, 奢侈 (jiǎnpǔ shēchǐ)

1 省 [-] shěng (save) <v.> save, omit, leave out: ~钱 save money || ~时间save time
2 节俭 [節儉] jiéjiǎn (frugal-simple) <v.> thrifty, frugal: 生活~ be frugal || ~办婚事be frugal with one's wedding ceremony
3 精打细算 [--細-] jīngdǎ xìsuàn (careful-calculate-strict-budget) <idiom> careful calculation and strict budgeting: ~地使用use wisely || 他在生活上处处~. He was economical in all areas of his life.
4 省吃俭用 [--儉-] shěngchī jiǎnyòng (save-food-skimp-use) <idiom> skimp and save, live frugally: ~过日子lead one's life frugally

5 奢侈 [-] shēchǐ (extravagant-luxurious) <adj.> luxurious, extravagant, wasteful: ~品 luxury goods || ~的生活luxury life
6 挥霍 [揮-] huīhuò (spend-quickly) <v.> spend freely, squander: ~金钱 splurge on money || 大肆 (dàsì) ~ spend extravagantly || ~无度spend without restraint
7 奢华 [-華] shēhuá (extravagant-sumptuous) <adj.> lucurious, sumptuous, extravagant: ~生活luxury life || ~品牌luxury brands
8 大吃大喝 [-] dàchī dàhē (extravagantly-eat-extravagantly-drink) <idiom> eat and drink extravagantly: 我~ 了两个星期, 胖了20磅. I did extravagant eating and drinking for two weeks and gained 20 pounds. || 中国人喜欢过春节的时候~. Chinese people like to eat and drink extravagantly during the Spring Festival.
9 大手大脚 [-] dàshǒu dàjiǎo (lavish-hand-lavish-foot) <idiom> wasteful, extravagant: 花钱~ spend lavishly
10 灯红酒绿 [燈紅-綠] dēnghóng jiǔlǜ (lantern-red-wine-green) <idiom> red lanterns and green wine- feasting and revelry: ~的城市 the city that has a great nightlife || ~的娱乐 (yúlè) 场所the bright lights
11 挥金如土 [揮---] huījīn rútǔ (spend-money-like-dirt) <idiom> throw money about like dirt, spend money like water- prodigal, wasteful: 过着~的生活 live a befuddled life || ~的人 a spendthrift person
12 铺张浪费 [鋪張-費] pūzhāng làngfèi (extravagant-wasteful) <idiom> extravagant and wasteful: 反对~ oppose extravagance and waste
13 醉生梦死 [--夢-] zuìshēng mèngsǐ (drunk-live-dreaming-die) <idiom> live as if drunk or dreaming- lead a befuddled life: 过着~的生活living a life of intoxicating sleep

Tips:

1 Is being节俭 (frugal) still a virtue? 节俭 was a long-cherished virtue along with 勤劳 (qínláo, industrious) for the Chinese people throughout history. However, now, for some Chinese, it is not anymore.
2 省吃俭用 vs. 挥金如土: If you want to know what 省吃俭用 is, observe the lives of vendors in back lanes of large cities in China, if 挥金如土, go to (ideally a VIP room in) any casino worldwide.

Exercises:

Part I: Match up the following expressions to the appropriate column. Make sure your words can describe the situation mentioned in the column.

a) 花钱不大手大脚 b) 生活奢华 c) 精打细算
d) 挥霍无度 e) 省吃俭用 f) 大吃大喝
g) 挥金如土 h) 出入灯红酒绿的娱乐场所
i) 铺张浪费 j) 过着醉生梦死的生活

描写一个生活节俭的人	描写一个奢侈浪费的富人

Theme 261: Progressive and conservative 进步, 保守 (jìnbù, bǎoshǒu)

1 进步 [進-] jìnbù (advance-go) <adj.> progressive: ~力量 progressive force || ~书籍 (shūjí) progressive literature || ~歌曲 a progressive song
2 进取 [進-] jìnqǔ (advance-seek) <v./adj.> keep forging ahead, eager to make progress, enterprising: 不断~ continuous progress || 积极~ positive progress || ~精神 spirit of progress
3 先进 [-進] xiānjìn (ahead-advance) <adj./ n.> advanced, exceptional: ~技术 advanced technology || ~青年 ahead of their time (youth) || 表扬~ exceptional praise
4 好胜 [-勝] hàoshèng (eager-to win) <adj.> eager to outshine others, keen to out-do others: ~心 (a) competitive heart || ~的姑娘 a competitive girl || ~的性格 a competitive personality
5 要强 [-] yàoqiáng (anxious-to excel) <adj.> be eager to excel, ambitious: ~的人 an ambitious person || 性格~ an ambitious personality
6 争强好胜 [爭--勝] zhēngqiáng hǎoshèng (compete-powerhouse-eager-to win) <idiom> competitive, like to contest: ~的人 a competitive person with a strong desire to win || ~的性格 a competitive personality
7 左倾 [-傾] zuǒqīng (left-derivation) <adj.> left-leaning, progressive, inclined towards socialism: ~路线progressive path, method || ~主义 progressivist, socialist, support of the left || ~错误 a mistake associated with a left leaning ideology
8 激进 [-進] jījìn (radical-progressive) <adj.> radical: 态度~ radical attitude || ~的思想 radical ideology, ideas
9 反动 [-動] fǎndòng (counter-act) <adj.> reactionary, resistance: ~口号 reactionary slogan, slogan of the resistance || ~思想 reactionary thought || ~言论 reactionary speech
10 反革命 [-] fǎn gémìng (counter-revolution) <adj.> counterrevolutionary: ~活动 counterrevolutionary activities || ~势力 (shìlì) counterrevolutionary force || ~集团 (jítuán) counterrevolutionary group

11 落后 [-後] luòhòu (fall-behind) <adj./v.> backward, behind the times: ~国家underdeveloped country || ~地区underdeveloped area || 教育~ underdeveloped education

12 开明 [開-] kāimíng (open-enlightened) <adj.> enlightened, liberal-minded: 思想~ enlightened, liberal thought || ~的父母 enlightened, liberal parents

13 民主 [-] mínzhǔ (people-decide) <adj./ n.> democracy, democratic: 发扬~ bring forth democracy || 高度~ high level democracy || ~国家 a democratic nation

14 开通 [開-] kāitōng (open-liberal) <adj.> open-minded, liberal: 思想~ open-minded thought || ~的父母 open-minded parents

15 开放 [開-] kāifàng (open-unrestricted) <adj.> liberal, open-mindedl: 社会~ a liberal, open minded society || 思想~ open minded, liberal thought || ~政策 (zhèngcè) progressive policy

16 通情达理 [--達-] tōngqíng dálǐ (unimpeded-sense-reachable-reason) <adj./ n.> show good sense, understanding and reasonable: ~地解决 (jiějué) 问题solve a problem in a reasonable manner

17 右倾 [-傾] yòuqīng (right-deviation) <adj.> 'right' deviation, ideologically: ~观点 (guāndiǎn) right-leaning thought || ~错误 a right-leaning mistake || ~思想 right-leaning ideology, thought

18 封建 [-] fēngjiàn (subinfeudate-establish) <adj.> feudal, feudalistic: ~时代 feudal age || ~文化 feudal culture || ~国家 feudal nation

19 独裁 [獨-] dúcái (alone-judge) <adj./v.> dictatorial, dictatorship: ~国家 an autocratic, totalitarian nation || ~统治 (tǒngzhì) an autocratic government || 军事~ an autocratic army

20 专权 [專權] zhuānquán (monopolize-power) <adj.> arrogate all powers to oneself, monopolize power: 大臣~ A government office who consolidates power || 独断 (dúduàn) ~ exclusive rights, power

21 一言堂 [-] yīyántáng (single-speak-hall) <n.> single-word shop-no bargaining, uniform prices (a horizontal inscribed board hung over a shop): 搞~ engage in a sale with no bargaining || 领导干部~ the government official made a decision without further discussion

22 蛮横 [蠻橫] mánhèng (savage-perverse) <adj.> rude and unreasonable, arbitrary: 性情~ unreasonable and rude personality || ~拒绝 (jùjué) to to unreasonably refuse || ~的作风 an unreasonable working style

23 蛮不讲理 [蠻-講-] mán bù jiǎng lǐ (savage-not-listen to-reason) <idiom> be impervious to reason, unreasonable, obstinate: 这个人只在这家餐厅工作了一天, 但是~地让经理付他一个月的工资. The man worked for only one day at this restaurant, but unreasonably asked the manager to pay him a month salary.

24 不近人情 [-] bùjìn rénqíng (not-close-human-reason) <idiom> not normal human nature: 这家公司规定员工不能因为孩子生病而请假, 真是~! The company rules that employees can not ask for a leave when their children are sick, so it's inhumane! || ~的管理 inhumane management

25 不可理喻 [-] bùkě lǐyù (not-able to-with reason-understood) <idiom> impervious to reason, unreasonable: ~的行为 unreasonable behavior || 他自己做错了, 还怪别人, 简直~. He did himself wrong, but blamed others. That is really unreasonable.

26 强词夺理 [-詞奪-] qiǎngcí duólǐ (force-excuse-rob-reason) <idiom> use lame arguments, reason fallaciously: 他在人行道上开车撞了人, 还~地说,

人家没给他让路. He knocked down someone on the sidewalk and then complained about how that man should step aside.

27 一手遮天 [-] yīshǒu zhētiān (single-hand-hide-sky) <idiom> hide the truth from the masses: 大股东~. The major shareholder conceals the truth to controll this company. || 这个国家的领导人 ~, 进行独裁统治. The leader of this country hid the truth from the masses and ruled people by dictatorship.

28 安于现状 [-於現狀] ān yú xiàn zhuàng (content-with-current-situation) <idiom> be content with things as they ar: 这家手机公司在产品畅销以后并没有~, 而是继续开发新产品. After the product hit the market, the mobile phone company was not content with the present situation but continued to develop new products.

Tips:

1 左 and 右 in politics: In Chinese, 左 and 右 are exactly the opposite of what are in the Western countries. 左 indicates 'conservative' and 右 'liberal.'

2 封建 (fēngjiàn): 封 means 'to subinfeudate' and 建 'to establish a state.' The compound word 封建 means 'feudal.' Since the feudal society had such a long history in China, its influence will understandably last for a long time although the very last feudal dynasty, the Qing Dynasty ended in 1911, officially. There is a saying that reflects the feudal mindset. It is 强龙压不住地头蛇 (qiánglóng yābúzhù dìtóushé), which means 'the mighty dragon is no match for the native serpent.' 地头蛇 (native serpent), in other words, it is 土皇帝 (local emperor.)

3 反革命: 反革命 (counterrevolutionary) was a frequently used word before late 1970s, but now it is rarely heard.

Exercises:

Part I: Match up the following expressions to the appropriate column. Make sure your words can describe the situation mentioned in the column.

a) 蛮不讲理 b) 不近人情 c) 强词夺理 d) 一手遮天 e) 独断专权
f) 不可理喻 g) 思想开通 h) 封建独裁 i) 搞一言堂 j) 高度民主
k) 社会开放 l) 国家进步 m) 安于现状 n) 不断进取

形容一个性格蛮横的人	形容一个独裁的国家领导人	形容一个开明的国家领导人

Part II: Multiple Choice. Make sure to choose the most appropriate answer.

1 小王是一个喜欢__________的人, 凡事都想拿第一.
A. 通情达理 B. 安于现状 C. 争强好胜

2 美国是世界上军事技术最________的国家.
A. 先进 B. 进步 C. 进取

3 美国《纽约时报》(*The New York Times*) 曾经批评总统独裁, __________.
A. 反革命 B. 一手遮天 C. 右倾主义

4 一般来说, __________, 不开发新产品, 不追求创新的科技公司最后都会倒闭.
A. 不可理喻 B. 强词夺理 C. 安于现状

5 这家公司的管理特别________, 员工结婚、生子、伤病都不能请假.
A. 不近人情 B. 一手遮天 C. 一言堂

6 美国政治家常常批评中国的一党专政, 认为没有民主, 是搞________.
A. 不近人情 B. 不可理喻 C. 一言堂

7 无论父母怎么劝说, 这个孩子还是不愿意上学, 只喜欢在家打电脑游戏. 父母觉得他________, 只好求助于心理医生.
A. 无法无天 B. 不可理喻 C. 一言堂

8 他开车撞了行人, 还说行人没给他让路, 真是________!
A. 强词夺理 B. 开通 C. 开放

Theme 262: Noble, lowly 高, 下 (gāo, xià)

(See also Theme 245)

1 高尚 [-] gāoshàng (high-noble) <adj.> noble, lofty: ~的品格 noble quality || ~的行为 a noble act || ~的情趣 (qíngqù) a noble interest

2 高贵 [-貴] gāoguì (high-aristocratic) <adj.> noble, admirable, elitist: ~地位 an elite position || ~品质noble quality || 出身~ be born to an elite class, born with a silver spoon in one's mouth

3 崇高 [-] chónggāo (lofty-high) <adj.> lofty, sublime, high: ~的理想 a high ideal || ~的思想 a lofty thought || ~的行为 lofty action

4 神圣 [-聖] shénshèng (sacred-holy) <adj.> sacred, holy: ~的事业 sacred career || ~的土地 sacred ground || ~的感情 a sacred feeling

5 正当 [-當] zhèngdāng (fair-proper) <adj.> legitimate, proper, appropriate: ~要求 appropriate requirement || ~收入 appropriate (fair) income || ~关系appropriate relationship

6 正经 [-經] zhèngjing (orthodox-classic) <adj.> decent, proper, serious: ~八百儿 too serious || ~工作serious work || 假装 (jiǎzhuāng) ~ assume a mock-serious manner

7 正面 [-] zhèngmiàn (direct-manner) <adj.> positive, directly, openly: ~回答 direct response || ~引导 direct guidance || ~例子 a direct example

8 正派 [-] zhèngpài (upright-style) <adj.> upright, honest, decent: 作风~ have moral integrity || ~人decent person || 为人~ be honest and upright

9 自重 [-] zìzhòng (self-dignify) <v.> conduct oneself with dignity: 请~. Please watch how you conduct yourself. || 一个人想得到别人的尊重, 必须先学会~. To be respected by others, one must first learn to be self-respecting.

10 低俗 [-] dīsú (low-vulgar) (of remarks, manners, etc.) <adj.> vulgar, low, crude: ~小说 a crude novel (fiction) || 内容~ crude content || ~行为 crude behavior

11 色情 [-] sèqíng (erotic sexual desire-lust) <adj.> erotic, pornography: ~行业 sex and pornography business || ~电影 porn movie

12 黄色 [-] huángsè (yellow-color) <n.> pornographic, dirty: ~小说 pornographic novel || ~电影pornographic movie || ~网站pornographic website

13 天真 [-] tiānzhēn (natural-true) <adj.> innocent, native: ~的孩子innocent child (ren) || ~的想法 an innocent thought || 思想~ innocent/naive thinking

14 世俗 [-] shìsú (societal-custom) <adj.> secular, worldly: ~观念 a worldly perspective || ~生活 a worldly (common) life || ~社会 a worldly society

15 俗气 [-氣] súqì (vulgar-taste) <adj.> vulgar, in poor taste: 眼光~ tacky taste || 她穿得很~. The clothes she wears are in poor taste.

16 庸俗 [-] yōngsú (mediocre-vulgar) <adj.> vulgar, philistine, low: ~的商人 immoral business person || ~小报 vulgar newspaper

17 猥琐 [-瑣] wěisuǒ (wretched-base) <adj.> boorish, uncouth, rude: ~的男人 obscene man || 行为~ rude actions || 长得很 ~ of wretched appearance

18 俗不可耐 [-] súbùkěnài (vulgar-not-able to-bear) <idiom> unbearably vulgar: ~的行为 unbearable actions

19 风骚 [風騷] fēngsāo (licentious-coquettish) (of a woman) <adj.> coquettish, flirtatious: ~女郎 a flirtatious woman || 卖弄 (màinong) ~ flirt

20 肉麻 [-] ròumá (flesh-nauseating) <adj.> nauseating, sickening, disgusting: ~话. It's sickening to hear this kind of talk. || ~的举动. It's sickening to see such behavior. || 使人~ make one sick

21 轻佻 [輕-] qīngtiāo (light-frivolous) <adj.> frivolous, flippant, giddy: 动作~ flippant (or skittish) behavior || ~的歌声 a giddy (or skittish) voice

22 好色 [-] hàosè (fond of-woman) (usu. of a man) <adj.> lecherous, tend to pursue sexual pleasure: ~的男人 a lewd man/ a pervert

23 淫荡 [-蕩] yíndàng (loose-wanton) <adj.> loose in morals, lascivious, licentious: ~的生活 an immoral life || ~的笑话 a lascivious joke

24 伤风败俗 [傷風敗-] shāngfēng bàisú (harm-social custom-corrupt-social custom) <idiom> corrupt public morals: ~的行为 behaviors that corrupt public morals/decency

25 痴心 [癡-] chīxīn (besotted-heart) <adj.> be infatuated with: ~人 an infatuated person || ~地爱着 be infatuated with

26 多情 [-] duōqíng (excessive-affection) <adj.> full of tenderness or affection (for a person of the opposite sex): ~的姑娘 an over-affectionate young girl

27 多愁善感 [-] duōchóu shàn'gǎn (excessive-grieved-easy-sentimental) <idiom> sentimental and susceptible, weak and emotional: ~的少女 a sentimental teenager

28 无情 [-] wúqíng (no-affection) <adj.> heartless, merciless, ruthless: ~打击 a ruthless attack || ~的风暴unmerciful windstorm

29 喜新厌旧 [--厭舊] xǐxīn yànjiù (like-new-tired of-old) <idiom> like the new and tire of the old- fickle in love: ~的人 a fickle person || ~的行为 fickle behavior || 他太太~ his wife is very fickle

30 忘恩负义 [--負義] wàng'ēn fùyì (forget-favor-betray-morality) <idiom> devoid of gratitude, ungrateful, bite the hand that feeds one: ~的小人 a petty and unthankful person

31 翻脸不认人 [-臉-認-] fānliǎn bù rèn rén (turn-face-not-admit-people) <proverb> turn against a friend, to fall out with sb and become hostile: 有利可图的时候, 他立刻~. He turned his face away when he was profitable.

Tips:

1 色情 vs. 情色: 色情 is pornographic and therefore prohibited in most countries. 情色 is very mild 色情, without direct sexual content.
2 好色 (lecherous): 好色 might be human beings' nature and even Mencius admitted it. He said '食色性也' meaning 'the desire for food and sex is nature.'
3 正经: 正经 originally referred to the thirteen classics of Confucianism. 一本正经 means 'solemnly,' for example, '她一本正经地说, ...' 正经八百 means 'seriously, no kidding.'
4 多愁善感 and 喜新厌旧: When these two idioms are mentioned, the Chinese people will spontaneously think of 林黛玉 (Lín Dàiyù), a main character in *Dream of the Red Chamber* (红楼梦, Hónglóumèng, late 18th century), and 陈世美 (Chén Shìměi), a character in folk literature, respectively.

Exercises:

Part I: Match up the following expressions to the appropriate column. Make sure your words can describe the situation mentioned in the column.

a) 伤风败俗 b) 卖弄风骚 c) 轻佻淫荡 d) 俗不可耐 e) 忘恩负义
f) 对待感情喜新厌旧 g) 地位高贵 h) 情趣高尚 i) 作风正派
j) 低俗 k) 思想崇高 l) 色情 m) 黄色 n) 暴力

美国传统观点中的绅士	美国传统观点里的"坏女孩"	一般来说美国父母不会让孩子看这样的电影或者小说

Part II: Multiple Choice. Make sure to choose the most appropriate answer.

1 台湾女作家琼瑶 (Chiung Yao) 的小说里有很多这样的情节: ___________的少女________地爱着男主人公一直到老.
A. 多愁善感、痴心 B. 痴心、多愁善感 C. 低俗、庸俗

2 下面哪组词是贬义词 (biǎnyìcí, negative word)
A. 神圣、崇高 B. 无情、猥琐 C. 多情、正经

3 下面哪个词跟 "翻脸不认人"意思差不多
A. 无情无义 B. 俗不可耐 C. 多愁善感

4 一些中国父母认为在淘宝网上卖东西不是_________工作, 不够体面.
A. 正派 B. 正经 C. 自重

5 老王是一个________的人, 从来不去色情场所.
A. 崇高理想 B. 正当收入 C. 作风正派

Theme 263: Smart, stupid 智, 愚 (zhì, yú)

1 聪明 [聰-] cōngming (smart-wise) <adj.> intelligent, clever: ~人 smart people || ~的方法smart ways || ~的脑袋smart brain

2 高智商 [-] gāo zhìshāng (high-intelligence-quotient) <n.> high intelligence quotient (IQ): ~孩子a child with a high Intelligence Quotient

3 有头脑 [-頭腦] yǒu tóunǎo (have-brain) <v.> know better, have an excellent brain: 他做生意很~. He has an excellent brain for doing business.

4 耍小聪明 [-] shuǎ xiǎo cōngming (play-petty-smart) <v.> play clever tricks: 爱~ like to play petty tricks || 为了拿到好成绩, 她~, 抄一个好学生的作业, 结果被老师发现了. In order to get a good grade, she played a trick and copied the homework of a good student, which ended up being found out by the teacher.

5 自知之明 [-] zìzhīzhīmíng (oneself-know-*'s*-wise) <idiom> be able to have a proper appraisal off oneself: 有~ know yourself very well || 人贵有~. It is a good thing for one to be able to have a proper appraisal of oneself.

6 理智 [-] lǐzhì (rational-intelligent) <adj.> rational, sensible: ~地分析analyze rationally || ~的方法rational ways || ~的态度rational attitude

7 明智 [-] míngzhì (wise-intelligent) <adj.> sensible, wise: ~的选择wise choice || ~的建议wise suggestion

8 快 [-] kuài (quick, fast) <adj.> quick, fast: 脑子~ quick-witted || 手/眼~ deft of hand/quick of eye || 反应~ quick reaction

9 灵 [靈] líng (sharp, quick) <adj.> quick, sharp: 脑子~ quick mind || 鼻子~ quick nose || 这个办法~. This way works very well.

10 机灵 [機靈] jīlíng (swift-quick) <adj.> clever, smart: ~的猴子a clever monkey || ~的眼睛clever eyes

11 机智 [機-] jīzhì (swift-intelligent) <adj.> quick-witted, resourceful: ~ 的回答a witty rejoinder || ~的小伙子 ~ a resourceful young man

12 灵活 [靈-] línghuó (quick-flexible) <adj.> nimble, agile: 动作~ be quick in action || 反应~ be quick in reaction || ~的眼睛flexible eyes

13 敏感 [-] mǐngǎn (fast-sense) <adj.> sensitive, susceptible: ~的孩子sensitive children || 职业 (zhíyè) ~ career sensitivity || 对新事物~ be sensitive to new things

14 随机应变 [隨機應變] suí jī yìng biàn (along-condition-respond-change) <idiom> suit one's actions to changing conditions: 善于~ be good at rising to the occasion || ~地提问ask questions according to changing conditions

15 蠢 [-] chǔn (stupid) <adj.> stupid, clumsy: ~人a fool || ~办法a stupid way

16 傻 [-] shǎ (foolish) <adj.> stupid, foolish: ~小子 silly lad || ~念头cuckoo ideas || ~笑giggle

17 痴呆 [癡-] chīdāi (idiotic-dull) <adj./n.> dull-witted, stupid: ~症dementia || 老年~ senile dementia

18 愚蠢 [-] yúchǔn (silly-stupid) <adj.> stupid: ~的办法 stupid ways || ~的行为 stupid behaviors || ~的想法stupid ideas

19 弱智 [-] ruòzhì (weak-intelligence) <adj.> retarded, mentally deficient: ~儿童retarded children

20 傻里傻气 [---氣] shǎ li shǎ qì (foolish-*infix*-foolish-looking) <idiom> foolish-looking, muddleheaded: ~的孩子silly kids

21 笨手笨脚 [-] bènshǒu bènjiǎo (clumsy-hand-clumsy-foot) <idiom> clumsy, awkward: 做事~. It's clumsy to do things. || ~的人. He is clumsy.

22 呆头呆脑 [-頭-腦] dāitóu dāinǎo (dull-head-dull-mind) <idiom> stupid-looking: ~的样子 a stupid looking || ~的人 a person who has idiotic-looking

23 缺心眼儿 [---兒] quē xīnyǎnr (lack-heart-eye) <v.> inconsiderate: 他把一辆新车送给了一个刚认识三天的女孩子, 他妈妈骂他~. He gave his new car to a girl who had just known him for three days, and his mother scolded him, calling him stupid.

24 发晕 [發暈] fāyūn (feel-dizzy) <v.> feel giddy, lose one's head: 我觉得脑子~. I feel a bit giddy.

25 糊涂 [-塗] hútu (paste-mud) <adj.> muddled, confused: 装~ pretend not to know || ~话mush and molasses, drivel || 这位老人一时犯~, 让骗子 (piànzi) 骗走了三万块钱. The old man made a fool of himself and let the swindler take out $30,000.

26 盲目 [-] mángmù (blind-eye) <adj.> blind: ~崇拜 (chóngbài) worship blindly || ~乐观unrealistically optimistic || ~投资 (tóuzī) blindness in investment

27 糊里糊涂 [---塗] húlihútū (paste-*infix*-paste-mud) <idiom> muddle-headed, mixed up: ~过日子be foolish to live

28 聪明一世, 糊涂一时 [聰---, -塗-時] cōngming yī shì, hútu yī shí (smart-one-life, muddled-one-time) <idiom> clever all one's life but stupid this once: 他做了五十年的生意一直都很成功, 可是最近被一个年轻人骗了一大笔钱. 真是~! He has been doing successful business for 50 years, but recently he was cheated out of a lot of money by a young man. He was clever all his life but stupid this once!

Tips:

1 明 and 智: Today 明 (míng) and 智 (zhì) are said together as a compound, but the two adjectives are not identical. If you can comprehend others, you are 智, if you know yourself, you are 明 which is still preserved in an idiom '自知之明' (wisdom to know oneself).

2 大智若愚 (dàzhì ruòyú): The Chinese are quite dialectic, probably due to Lao-Tsu's wisdom. For example, 智 (wise) and 愚 (stupid) are completely different, but there is an idiom 大智若愚 (great-wisdom-like-stupidity), which means 'a man of great wisdom often appears slow-witted.'

3 蠢 (chǔn): 蠢 means 'stupid,' however, its original meaning is 'wiggle' depicting 'worms wiggling in the grass/spring.'

4 难得糊涂 (nándé hútu): 糊涂 means 'mud-headed' which is not desirable, however, a motto of Zheng Banqiao (1693–1765), '难得糊涂' has since been vastly cherished by the Chinese people. It means 'Where ignorance is bliss,'tis folly to be wise.' The calligraphy of this phrase is usually written in traditional characters and can be found almost on every stand selling Chinese calligraphy works.

5 *里**: Phrases in this pattern, such as 傻里傻气 and 糊里糊涂 (or 稀里糊涂) carry a connotation with a negative meaning.

Exercises:

Part I: Match up the following expressions to the appropriate column. Make sure your words can describe the situation mentioned in the column.

a) 对新事物敏感 b) 善于随机应变 c) 机智灵活 d) 盲目乐观
e) 呆头呆脑 f) 笨手笨脚 g) 傻里傻气 h) 有头脑、高智商
i) 有自知之明 j) 爱耍小聪明

形容一个人聪明	形容一个人愚笨

Part II: Word Classification

Which of the following are curse words, and which words are praise words?

机灵、明智、蠢、傻、弱智、痴呆、缺心眼儿、装糊涂、脑子快、反应快、动作快

curse words	praise words

Theme 264: Skillful, clumsy 巧, 拙 (qiǎo, zhuō)

1 巧 [-] qiǎo (skillful, coincidental) <adj.> skillful, (of hand, tongue) deft, glib: 他的手艺很~. His workmanship is excellent. || 花言~语sweet words || 太~了, 我一出门就来了一辆出租车. It was most opportune that a taxi arrived just as I was leaving the house.
2 乖巧 [-] guāiqiǎo (obedient-clever) <adj.> ingenious, agreeable: ~的孩子a sweet child || 做事~ do sth. agreeably
3 手巧 [-] shǒuqiǎo (hand-skillful) <adj.> handy: 他~. He is clever with his hands.
4 心灵手巧 [-靈--] xīnlíng shǒuqiǎo (mind-quick-hand-skillful) <idiom> clever and deft: ~的姑娘clever and deft girls
5 眼疾手快 [-] yǎnjí shǒukuài (eye-quick-hand-deft) <idiom> quick of eye and deft of hand, sharp-eyed and deft-handed: 打电脑游戏需要~. Playing computer games requires quick hands and eyes.
6 圆滑 [圓-] yuánhuá (round-slippery) <adj.> smooth and evasive, slick and sly: ~的手段 (shǒuduàn) diplomatic tact || ~的人a sly customer || 做人~ as slippery as an eel
7 世故 [-] shìgù (world-wise) <adj.> shrewd, canny: 这个人相当~. This chap is a very smooth character. || 不懂~ not know the ways of the world || 老于~ worldly-wise, experienced, knowing

8 善变 [-變] shànbiàn (apt-change) <adj.> be apt to change, be changeable: 性格 ~ one's personality is apt to change || ~的人a fickle person

9 滑头 [-頭] huátóu (slippery-*suffix*) <adj.&n.> slippery, shifty person: 耍~ act in a slippery way || 他是个老 ~. He is a sly old bird.

10 油嘴滑舌 [-] yóuzuǐ huáshé (oily-mouth-slippery tongue) <idiom> glib-tongued: 一个~的人 a glib talker || 小王喜欢在老板面前~. Little Wang likes to be glib in front of his boss.

11 八面玲珑 [---瓏] bāmiàn línglóng (8-direction-clever and nimble) <idiom> smooth and slick (in making social contacts): 他为人~. He is smooth and tactful.

12 呆 [-] dāi (dull-minded) <adj.> dull: 书~子nerd || 惊~了stunned

13 呆傻 [-] dāishǎ (dull-foolish) <adj.> slow-witted, muddle-headed: ~儿童 moron

14 死脑筋 [-腦-] sǐnǎojīn (stubborn-mind) <adj.> one-track mind, mule: 你真是个~. You're such a stubborn person.

15 木讷 [-訥] mùnè (wooden-slow of speech) <adj.> plain, slow-witted: ~的中年人a mid-age man with a dull heart || 性格~ one's character is dull

16 嘴笨 [-] zuǐbèn (mouth-clumsy) <adj.> clumsy of speech: 他~. He is clumsy of speech.

17 少言寡语 [---語] shǎoyán guǎyǔ (less-speech-few-language) <idiom> be reticent: ~的人a man of few words

18 死板 [-] sǐbǎn (stubborn-wooden) <adj.> rigid, stiff, inflexible: 脑子~ the brain is rigid || 画面~ the picture is rigid || ~的公式the rigid formula

19 呆板 [-] dāibǎn (dull-wooden) <adj.> stiff, rigid: 表情~ the expression is stiff || 面孔~ the face is stiff || ~的方法the mechanical method

20 刻板 [-] kèbǎn (carve-wood) <adj.> mechanical, inflexible: ~的工作rigid work || 动作~ rigid acts || ~印象stereotype

21 固执 [-執] gùzhí (obstinate-stubborn) <adj.> obstinate, stubborn: ~的人stubborn fish || 思想~ be stubborn || ~的性格stubborn character

22 顽固 [頑-] wángù (headstrong-obstinate) <adj.> stubborn: ~的家伙tough guy || ~坚持stick to it || ~的态度stubborn attitude

23 执着 [執著] zhízhuó (stick to-adhere) <adj.> persistent, persevering: ~追求 (zhuīqiú) persistent pursuit || ~的信念 (xìnniàn) persistent belief || ~的感情persistent feelings

24 死心眼儿 [---兒] sǐxīnyǎnr (stubborn-thoughtfulness) <adj.> stubborn, as obstinate as a mule: 他真~！ He is so stubborn.

25 不识时务 [-識時務] búshí shíwù (not-comprehend-current-affair) <idiom> show no understanding of the times, lack judgment: ~地提意见provide one's opinions without understanding of the times

Tips:

1 *头: If the suffix '头' means 'a person,' it usually carries a negative connotation. For example, 丫头 (yātou, girl, maiden), 姘头 (pìntou, paramour), 滑头 (slippery), 粉头 (fěntou, prostitute) and 对头 (foe) etc.

2 心眼儿: 心眼儿 (heart-hole) is hard to translate into English. Its meaning is close to '(being) clever enough not to be taken advantage of and in the meanwhile better to take some advantage of others.' According to a popular Chinese

historical novel, in the era of King Zhou (1105 B.C. to 1046 B.C.) the last king of the Shang Dynasty, Bi Gan, uncle of King Zhou, was said to have seven openings in his heart because he was like a sage. King Zhou ordered to have Bi Gan's heart extracted for testing. Usage of 心眼儿 is extensive, for example, 有心眼儿 (be able to outsmart), 没心眼儿 (candid), 没好心眼儿 (the fox preaches), 小心眼儿 (narrow-minded), 缺 (quē) 心眼儿 (lack common sense), 死心眼儿 (stubborn), 一个心眼儿 (single-minded), 斗心眼儿 (to compete to take the upper hand of the other), 耍 (shuǎ) 心眼儿 (to play tricks on sb).

3 Opposite of 不识时务: It is 识时务, and there is a saying '识时务者为俊杰' (shí shíwù zhě wéi jùnjié, understand-current-affair-'s person-is-hero), which usually carries a connotation of threatening, 'you had better do as you are advised, otherwise, prepare to reap the consequences of your stubbornness,' or simply 'a wise man submits to fate.'

4 Stereotype: It was once translated into Chinese as 成见 (existed-opinion) or 先入之见 (pre – formed-'s-opinion,) but now 刻板印象 is much more popular probably owing to its use in Taiwan. However, 成见 and 刻板印象 are not identical. 成见 can be used for a specific person or a type of people, but 刻板印象 is usually for a type of people.

Exercises:

Part I: Match up the following expressions to the appropriate column. Make sure your words can describe the situation mentioned in the column.

a) 喜欢耍滑头 b) 油嘴滑舌 c) 八面玲珑 d) 不识时务 e) 死心眼儿
f) 表情呆板 g) 性格木讷 h) 笨嘴笨舌 i) 少言寡语 j) 老于世故
k) 死心眼儿 l) 顽固不化 m) 性格固执 n) 工作刻板, 不灵活

你同学为人比较固执	这个公司员工死板、笨拙	一个特别圆滑、世故的人

Part II: Multiple Choice. Make sure to choose the most appropriate answer.

1 很多人批评美国前总统小布什______________.
A. 眼疾手快 B. 心灵手巧 C. 不识时务

2 小白在泰国旅游的时候遇到了自己的大学同学, 真是太巧了. 这里的"巧"意思是:
A. skillful B. clever C. coincidental

3 你真是个"死脑筋"!, 意思是:
A. 你脑子死了 B. 你真笨 C. 你是个滑头

4 这个姑娘不见长得漂亮, 而且____________.
A. 心灵手巧 B. 刻板印象 C. 油腔滑调

5 这个姑娘非常善变, 意思是:
A. 眼疾手快 B. 执着追求 C. 经常改变主意

Theme 265: Diligent, lazy 勤, 懒 (qín, lăn)

1 努力 [-] nǔlì (exert-strength) <adj.> make great efforts, try hard: ~学习study hard || ~工作work hard || ~完成任务try to get tasks done
2 卖力 [賣-] màilì (sell-labor) <v-o.> exert oneself to the utmost, spare no effort: 工作~ work hard || 他干活一向很~. He has always been hard-working.
3 勤奋 [-奮] qínfèn (industrious-strive) <adj.> diligent: 学习~ be diligent in one's studies || ~地工作bury oneself in one's work
4 勤快 [-] qínkuài (industrious-fast) <adj.> diligent, hard-working: 干活~ be diligent in work || 这个年轻人真 ~. This young man is very hardworking.
5 勤劳 [-勞] qínláo (industrious-labor) <adj.> diligent, industrious, hard-working: ~的中国人hardworking Chinese || ~的民族hardworking and brave people
6 好学 [-學] hàoxué (eager-learn) <adj.> being fond of learning: ~的人a studious person || 她很~, 所以进步很快. She is fond of learning, so she makes lots of progress quickly.
7 用功 [-] yònggōng (exert-effort) <adj.> study hard: ~学习be diligent in one's studies || 她读书很~. She studies hard. || ~的学生diligent students
8 用心 [-] yòngxīn (exert-attention) <adj.> diligently, attentively, with concentrated attention: ~听listen attentively to sth. || 学习很~ concentrate on one's studies. || ~思考think hard
9 笨鸟先飞 [-鳥-飛] bènniăo xiānfēi (clumsy-bird-first-fly) <idiom> clumsy birds have to start flying early-the slow need to start early (usu. said in self-deprecation): ~的办法 the way of clumsy birds || 他不聪明, 但是学习成绩很好. 因为他知道~, 总是比别人花更多时间学习. He is not smart, but his grades are always good. Because he knows the slow need to start early and always spends more time studying than others.
10 吃苦耐劳 [---勞] chīkŭ nàiláo (accept-hardship-endure-labor) <idiom> bear hardships and stand hard work, work hard and endure hardships: ~的民族(mínzú) a hardy nation || ~的精神the spirit of hard work || 他工作~, 从不抱怨. He works hard and never complains.
11 任劳任怨 [-勞--] rènláo rènyuàn (bear-work-bear-complait) <idiom> work hard regardless of criticism, willingly bear the burden of office, bear responsibility without grudge: ~地工作. Work hard without any complaint. || ~的人a man who bears responsibility without grudge || 对工作~ has/have grievance for one's work
12 事在人为 [---爲] shìzàirénwéi (thing-in-people-do) <idiom> It all depends on human effort: ~, 努力做下去就会成功. Nothing is impossible, and it all depends on human effort.

13 懒 [懶] lăn (lazy) <adj.> lazy: ~人a lazy person || ~于学习be lazy in learning || 她太~了, 早上十一点还不起床. She is too lazy to get up at 11 a.m. in the morning.
14 懒惰 [懶-] lănduò (lazy-slothful) <adj.> lazy, indolent, slothful: 小王特别~, 所以房间非常乱. Little Wang is so lazy so that his room is very disorderly. || ~成性be lazy by nature, be addicted to a lazy life

15 懒散 [懶-] lǎnsǎn (lazy-undisciplined) <adj.> sluggish: 作风~ the sluggish way of doing things || 他~惯了, 很难认真做点儿事. He has been sluggish, so it is hard for him to do anything seriously.

16 好吃懒做 [-喫懶-] hàochī lǎnzuò (like-eat-lazy-work) <idiom> piggish, be gluttonsous and lazy: ~的人a gluttonous and lazy guy || ~的恶习a bad habit of being gluttonous and lazy || 他是个富二代, ~. He is an affluent second generation and likes to be piggish.

17 游手好闲 [遊--閒] yóushǒu hàoxián (stroll-hand-enjoy-idle) <idiom> idle about: ~的生活 a life of idleness || ~的人a man of leisure

18 拖拉 [-] tuōlā (drag-pull) <adj.> sluggish: 办事~ be dilatory in doing things || 故意~ be sluggish in doing sth. intentionally.

19 拖泥带水 [--帶-] tuōní dàishuǐ (drag-mud-carry-water) <idiom> sloppy: 这篇文章写得~. This article is sloppily written. || 办事~ do things sloppily

20 虎头蛇尾 [-頭--] hǔtóu shéwěi (tiger-head-snake-tail) <idiom> with a tiger's head and a snake's tail- fine start and poor finish: 这个故事~ The story begins dramatically, but the plot peters out before the end. || 她做事总是~. She always starts off with a bang but ends with a whimper.

21 三天打鱼, 两天晒网 [---魚, 兩-曬網] sāntiān dǎyú liǎngtiān shàiwǎng (3-day-catch-fish, 2-day-dry-net) <idiom> go fishing for three days and dry the nets for two- work by fits and starts, lack perseverance: 她做事总是~. She always lacks perseverance.

22 纯熟 [純-] chúnshú (pure-skillful) <adj.> skillful, practised: ~的汉语 fluent Chinese || 手法~ skillful technique || ~地运用软件use software skillfully

23 内行 [-] nèiháng (inside-profession) <adj.&n.> expert, professional: ~话 comment or suggestion from a professional || 对医药产品, 她很~. She is an expert at medical products. || 冒充~ pretend an expert

24 在行 [-] zàiháng (in-profession) <adj.> expert at sth.: 样样~ expert at everything || 她对计算机很~. She knows a lot about computers. || 回答很~ answer questions very professionally

25 熟练 [-練] shúliàn (skillful-experienced) <adj.> skilled, practised, proficient: ~工人skilled worker || ~使用be skilled in doing sth. || 技术~ skilled in a technique

26 得心应手 [--應-] déxīn yìngshǒu (get-heart-echo-hand) <idiom> do things with great facility, with high proficiency: 工作~ work with great facility || ~地操作operate with high proficiency

27 熟能生巧 [-] shúnéngshēngqiǎo (practice-can-make-skillfull) <idiom> practice makes perfect: 学中文跟学钢琴 (gāngqín) 一样, 得多练习, ~. Learning Chinese is the same as learning piano. Practice makes perfect.

28 生 [-] shēng (grow, raw) <adj.> raw, unfamiliar: ~手new to a job || ~人stranger || ~米raw rice

29 手生 [-] shǒushēng (hand-unskillful) <adj.> lack practice and skill: 我三年没弹钢琴了, ~了. I haven't played piano for three years, and I'm a little bit out of practice now.

30 外行 [-] wàiháng (outside-profession) <adj.& n.> unprofessional, unspecialized: 我对股票 (gǔpiào) 很~. I know very little about stocks. || ~话lay language, mere dabbler's opinion || 内行看门道, ~看热闹. While the connoisseur recognizes the artistry, the layman simply enjoys the show.

31 半路出家 [-] bànlù chūjiā (half-way-became-monk) <idiom> become a monk or nun late in life-switch to a job one was not trained for, change professions completely: ~当医生switched professions to a doctor || ~的程序员 mid-career IT programmer

Tips:

1 内行 and 外行: Some say that the Chinese people '内斗内行, 外斗外行' (are experienced at internal strife, inexperienced/indifferent in fighting their real external enemies.) 内行 and 外行 people see differently. 内行看门道, 外行看热闹 means 'The dilettante watches the scene of bustle, the adept guard the entrance.'

2 勤劳 (industrious) and 吃苦耐劳 (bear hardships): These are two of the major virtues of the Chinese people.

Exercises:

Part I: Match up the following expressions to the appropriate column. Make sure your words can describe the situation mentioned in the column.

a) 工作勤奋 b) 好学上进 c) 吃苦耐劳 d) 做事拖拉
e) 做事拖泥带水 f) 做事虎头蛇尾 g) 工作三天打鱼, 两天晒网
h) 技术熟练 i) 工作得心应手 j) 任劳任怨 k) 工作卖力
l) 做事懒散

如果你是公司老板你会招聘这样的员工	如果你是公司老板你不会招聘这样的员工

Part II: Read the following sentences and fill in each blank with the appropriate word or phrase from the options given.

1 事在人为、外行、熟能生巧、半路出家、内行

a) 为了好找工作, 李小姐____________学起了计算机专业.
b) 虽然计算机专业很难, 但是李小姐觉得__________, 只要努力, 她一定可以从一个计算机_______变成一个__________.
c) 李小姐现在写软件还很吃力, 但是她相信_____________, 只要多花时间练习就行了.

2 生手、笨鸟先飞、手生

a) 王小姐是沃尔玛超市的新员工, 在业务上还是一个________, 因此工作起来有些________.
b) 王小姐每天很早就来超市工作, 她觉得__________ _, 只要她比别人勤奋努力, 就一定可以做好工作.

3 在行、纯熟、游手好闲

a) 王小姐的先生原来是一个电工 (electrician), 对修理 (xiūlǐ, repair) 电力设备 (electronics) 很_________, 技术也非常_________. 但是他后来吸毒 (xīdú, use drugs) 了, 变得_________, 好吃懒做.

Theme 266: Capable, incapable 能, 庸 (néng, yōng)

1 能 [-] néng (bear, capable) <adj.> able, capable: ~人able person || ~干able, capable, competent

2 行 [-] xíng (competent) <adj.> capable, competent: 你真~！这么难的事一天都能做完！ You are really great! You can get such a difficult thing done in a day.

3 牛 [-] niú (bull, super) <adj.> capable, arrogant: ~ 人top dog || 你有什么可~的, 你只不过是个富二代. You have nothing worth bragging about. You are just a rich second generation.

4 干练 [幹練] gànliàn (capable-experienced) <adj.> capable and experienced, keen-witted: 工作~ work efficiently || ~的经理 a professional manager || 她是一个很~的女强人. She is a very efficient career woman.

5 高明 [-] gāomíng (super-wise) <adj.> brilliant, wise: 想法~ brilliant ideas || 医术~ have superb medical skill || 这事儿恐怕 (kǒngpà) 我干不了, 你还是另请~吧. I'm afraid I'm not equal to the job. You'd better find someone better qualified.

6 能干 [-] nénggàn (good at-work) <adj.> able, capable: 这些工人真~. These workers really know their job. || 她是个~的女人. She is a woman of great ability.

7 全能 [-] quánnéng (all-capable) <adj.> almighty, all-powerful: ~运动员all-round athlete, all-rounder || 个人~冠军 (guànjūn) all-round champion

8 万能 [萬-] wànnéng (omni-capable) <adj.> omnipotent, all-powerful: ~胶水 (jiāoshuǐ) all-purpose adhesive || 金钱是~的. Money is everything. || ~的上帝all-powerful God

9 善于 [-於] shànyú (good-at) <v.> be good at, be adept in: ~研究be good at studying || ~交际be good at socializing || ~言词be good at expressing oneself

10 擅长 [-長] shàncháng (adept-good) <v.> be good at, be skilled in: ~唱歌/画画be good at singing/dancing

11 多才多艺 [---藝] duōcái duōyì (many-talent-many-skill) <idiom> versatile, gifted in many ways: ~的老师 a versatile teacher || 她~, 十六岁就被哈佛大学录取 (lùqǔ, admit to) 了. She was so versatile that she was admitted to Harvard at the age of 16.

12 能言善辩 [---辯] néngyán shànbiàn (capable-speak-good at-debate) <idiom> glib of tongue, eloquent, articulate: ~的人an eloquent person || 他~, 能把死人说活了. He is an eloquent man who could persuade the dead to live.

13 过目不忘 [過---] guòmù bùwàng (once-saw-never-forget) <idiom> to have a highly retentive memory, to have sth. imprinted in one's memory: 她读书~. Her memory retains everything she reads. || 这个广告让人 ~. This advertisement is unforgettable.

14 出口成章 [-] chūkǒu chéngzhāng (out of-mouth-become-article) <idiom> words flow from the mouth as from the pen of a master.- be an excellent speaker, quick

and clever talking, to speak like a printed book: 那个主持人 (zhīchírén) /大学教授 (jiàoshòu) ~. The host/university professor speaks like a printed book.

15 无能 [無-] wúnéng (no-capability) <adj.> incompetent, incapable: ~的政府incompetent government || ~的皇帝the incompetent emperor
16 低能 [-] dīnéng (dow-capability) <adj.> mentally deficient, incapable: 高分~ high in score but low in ability || ~儿童 (mentally) retarded child
17 平庸 [-] píngyōng (ordinary-mediocre) <adj.> mediocre, indifferent: 才能~ be of limited ability || ~的外表mediocre appearance || ~的官员a mediocre official || ~的看法the common level of observation
18 碌碌无为 [--無爲] lùlù wúwéi (ordinarily-no-achievement) <idiom> lead a vain and humdrum life, attempt nothing and accomplish nothing: ~地活着living a vain life || 他一生~. He was an unsuccessful man.

19 老练 [-練] lǎoliàn (shrewd-experienced) <adj.> seasoned, exprienced: ~的导游 (dǎoyóu) experienced tutor guide || 政治上~ be politically sophisticated || 他虽然很年轻, 但是做事很~. Though he is young, he is experienced and works with a sure hand.
20 少年老成 [-] shàonián lǎochéng (young-age-shrewd-mature) <idiom> accomplished though young, lacking youthful vigor: ~的人 a serious young man || 现在很多小孩都可以说是~. Now many children can be called young but experienced.
21 老谋深算 [-謀--] lǎomóu shēnsuàn (shrewd-plot-far-scheme) <idiom> circumspect and far-seeing, experienced and astute, cunning and crafty: ~的政客a canny politician || 他做事~, 很少失误. He is circumspect and farseeing and seldom fails.
22 见多识广 [見-識廣] jiànduō shíguǎng (saw-much-know-a lot) <idiom> experienced and knowledgeable: ~的记者 a well-informed journalist || 他去过很多地方, ~. He is well-travelled, and is a man of wide experience.

23 幼稚 [-] yòuzhì (young-childish) <adj.> childish, naive: 思想~ naive ideas || ~的问题childish questions || ~的孩子young and ignorant kids
24 不知天高地厚 [-] bù zhī tiāngāo dìhòu (not-know-heaven-high-Earth-deep) <idiom> not know the height of the heavens or the depth of the Earth- have an exaggerated opinion of one's abilities, ignorant, think one knows everything: 这个年轻人刚毕业, 还不知道~. This young man is fresh out of college but still wet behind the ears. || ~地吹牛a boast of ignorance
25 浅薄 [淺-] qiǎnbó (shallow-thin) <adj.> shallow, superficial: 他很~, 就认金钱和美女. He is very shallow and only knows money and beauty. || 作品~. The work is shallow. || 学识~ shallow knowledge
26 无知 [無-] wúzhī (no-knowledge) <adj.> ignorant: ~的问题an ignorant question || 出于~ be out of ignorance
27 才疏学浅 [--學淺] cáishū xuéqiǎn (talent-sparse-kowledge-shallow) <idiom> have little talent and less learning: 本人~, 如有不当之处, 请各位指正. I have little talent and less learning. If there is any mistake, please give me your valuable comments.
28 孤陋寡闻 [---聞] gūlòu guǎwén (isolated-limited-scant-information) <idiom> ignorant and ill-informed: 她~, 连"罗马"都没听说过. She is so ignorant that she doesn't even know 'Rome.'

29 不学无术 [-學無術] bùxué wúshù (not-study-no-skill) <idiom> have neither learning nor skill, ignorant and incompetent: ~的人a person without learning, ignoramus

30 一窍不通 [-竅--] yīqiào bùtōng (one-hole-not-through) <idiom> know nothing about (a subject), lack the slightest knowledge of, be utterly ignorant of: 对足球/数学~ know nothing about soccer/math

31 短浅 [-淺] duǎnqiǎn (short-shallow) <adj.> narrow and shallow: 目光~ lack vision, short-sighted, cannot see the wood for the trees || 见识~ lack knowledge and experience, shallow, green

32 有出息 [-] yǒu chūxī (have-prospect) <v.> show promise, promising: ~的孩子a promising child || 班里的每个孩子都希望自己~. Every kid in the class wants to be a successful person.

33 大有作为 [---為] dàyǒuzuòwéi (greatly-have-achievement) <idiom> have full scope for one's talents, be able to develop one's ability to the full, have great possibilities: 年轻人在这里会 ~. There are plenty of opportunities for young people. || 她又聪明又努力, 以后会~. She is smart and hardworking, and she'll make a big difference in the future.

34 不成材 [-] bùchéngcái (not-become-timber) <adj.> good-for-nothing, worthless: 中国古代人相信, 孩子不打~. The ancient Chinese believed that disciplining their children by physical punishment made them successful in the future.

35 不成器 [-] bùchéngqì (not-become-utensil) <adj.> good-for-nothing, never-do-well: ~的儿子the futile son || 玉不琢, ~. Jade cannot be made into anything without being cut and polished just as one cannot become useful without being educated.

36 没出息 [-] méichūxī (no-promise) <v.> worthless, useless: ~的家伙a loser || ~的专业a worthless major || ~的工作the dead-end job

37 无所作为 [無--爲] wúsuǒzuòwéi (no-what-do-achieve) <idiom> attempting nothing and accomplishing nothing (idiom), without any initiative or drive: 一辈子~ sb. has/have never done anything.

Tips:

1 能: The original meaning of 能 is 熊 (xióng, bear.) Because bears are mighty, powerful and capable, these meanings are naturally transferred to 能.

2 见识: 见识 means one's experience and knowledge. There is a saying that apparently discriminates against women, 头发长, 见识短, which means they have long hair but their knowledge and wits are less.

3 出息: 有出息 means 'have prospects,' and 没出息 'have no promise.' If one is very prospective, you can say he will '有大出息.' 出息 was originally a Buddhist term, meaning 'breath blown out.'

4 How to 成材/成才 (become successful in the future)? The Chinese traditional doctrine is 不打不成材 (spare the rod, spoil the child.)

5 有心机 (shrewd): The contemporary sayings for people who are very shrewd include 心机婊 (xīnjībiǎo, scheming bitch) and 心机男 (scheming man.) The old but still current expression is 老狐狸 (lǎohúli, old fox.)

6 Kindergarten: It is called 幼儿园 (yòu'éryuán) in mainland China, 幼稚园 (yòuzhìyuán) used in regions such as Taiwan and Hong Kong etc.

Exercises:

Part I: Match up the following expressions to the appropriate column. Make sure your words can describe the situation mentioned in the column.

a) 善于交际 b) 能言善辩 c) 多才多艺 d) 过目不忘 e) 出口成章
f) 成材、有出息 g) 大有作为 h) 见多识广 g) 才疏学浅
h) 无所作为 i) 孤陋寡闻 j) 目光短浅 k) 不学无术
l) 对艺术与科学一窍不通 m) 无知浅薄 n) 碌碌无为
o) 不成器、没出息 p) 全能冠军

你希望自己的孩子具有下面这些优点	你不希望自己的孩子有下面这些缺点

Part II: Read the following sentences and fill in each blank with the appropriate word or phrase from the options given.

1 干练、牛人、善于、平庸

a) 小王做事__________, ________社交, 刚工作不久就受到了老板的赏识 (shǎngshí).
b) 小王的同事其实非常__________ _, 工作十年也没特别突出的业绩 (yèjì).
c) 小王的老板据说是投资行业里的__________ ___.

2 老谋深算、少年老成、不知天高地厚

a) 小张__________ ___, 刚刚大学毕业就借了一百万人民币创业当老板, 结果不到一年就赔光了.
b) 生意场上有很多__________ _的人, 小张经验不足, 吃了很多亏.
c) 小张希望自己刚上大学时就能够在大公司实习, 这样经过锻炼 (duànliàn) 他可以__________ ___, 有能力处理创业中出现的问题.

3 万能、无能、低能、无知

a) 小张创业失败了, 他觉得自己很_________.
b) 小张的女朋友对艺术和科学一窍不通, 小张觉得她很_________.
c) 小张的女朋友热衷 (rèzhōng) 于公益事业, 她五年前就开始帮助_________儿童.
d) 小张的女朋友认为金钱不是_________的, 因为用钱买不到时间和真情.

Theme 267: Safe and dangerous 安, 危 (ān, wēi)

1 安全 [-] ānquán (safe-complete) <adj.&n.> safe, safety: 注意~ be mindful of the safety || 食品~ food safety || ~到达 safe arrival
2 平安 [-] píng'ān (safe-safe) <adj.> safe and sound: ~离开 safely away || ~回来 safely back || ~无事 all is well and safe || 一路~! Safe travels and a safe journey!

3 安定 [-] āndìng (safe-stable) <adj.> peaceful, stable: 社会~ social stability || ~的生活 peaceful/stable life || 情绪 (qíngxù) ~ emotionally stable

4 安宁 [-寧] ān'níng (peaceful-tranquil) <adj.> peaceful, calm: 心里不~ unpeaceful mind || 睡得~ sleep peacefully

5 和平 [-] hépíng (harmonious-peaceful) <n.&adj.> peace: ~年代 an age of peace || 世界~ world peace || 爱好 ~ love peace

6 平静 [-靜] píngjìng (calm-quiet) <adj.> peace, calm: ~的生活 a quiet life || 心情~ peace of mind || ~的水面 a calm water surface

7 平稳 [-穩] píngwěn (steady-stable) <adj.> stable, steady: ~发展 a steady development || 经济~ steady economic progress || 物价 ~ prices are stable

8 安居乐业 [--樂業] ānjū lèyè live (peaceful-live-enjoy-job) <idiom> and work in peace and contentment: 百姓/人民~ The people live and work in peace and contentment

9 安然无恙 [--無-] ānrán wúyàng (safe-*suffix*-no-ailment) <idiom> safe and sound, to come out unscathed (e.g. from an accident or illness): 他从楼梯上滚下来却~. He rolled down from the upstairs but was safe || 她被人绑架 (bǎngjià) 了一个星期, 最后~地回来了. She was kidnapped for a week and then came back safe and sound.

10 高枕无忧 [--無憂] gāozhěn wúyōu (high-pillow-no-worry) <idiom> rest easy: 别以为找到银行的工作就可以~了, 银行也可以倒闭 (dǎobì). Don't think that finding a job in a bank is secure, since banks can also fail.

11 一路平安 [-] yīlù píngān (all-trip-safe and sound) <idiom> to have a good journey, bon voyage: 祝大家~. I wish all of you a safe journey. || 我们到了北京了, ~, 你们放心吧. We arrived in Beijing, and it was a safe journey. No worries.

12 骚乱 [騷亂] sāoluàn (disturbance-chaos) <n.> rumpus, distemper: 引起~ raise a rumpus || 发生~ a rumpus took place || 政治~ political distempers

13 乱哄哄 [亂--] luànhōnghōng (chaos-noisy-*reduplication*) <adj.> noisy, tumultuous: ~的人群 tumultuous crowd || ~的教室 a noisy classroom

14 动荡 [動蕩] dòngdàng (turbulence-upheaval) <adj.> turmoil, turbulence, upheaval: ~的时代 an era of upheaval || 思想~ an ideological turbulence || 严重/剧烈 (jùliè) ~ a fierce/violent turbulence

15 不太平 [-] bú tàipíng (not-most-safe) <adj.> not peaceful: 世界/社会~ The world/the society is not peaceful.

16 动荡不安 [動蕩--] dòngdàng bú'ān (turbulence-upheaval-not-peaceful) <idiom> turbulent, troublous: ~的世界 a turbulent world || 股市~ a turbulent stock market

17 天下大乱 [---亂] tiānxià dàluàn (under-heaven-very-chaos) <idiom> wide-spread upheaval, great disorder under heaven: 如果没有强有力的领导, 必将~. There must be a widespread upheaval in this world without strong leadership.

18 险 [險] xiǎn (dangerous) <adj.> dangerous: ~情 a dangerous case || ~路 a dangerous road || 刚才很~, 两辆车差点撞上. It was very dangerous just now when two cars almost collided.

19 危险 [-險] wēixiǎn (perilous-dangerous) <adj.> dangerous: ~的地方 a dangerous place || ~情况 a dangerous situation || ~的人 a dangerous person || 高压~! Danger High Voltage!

20 惊险 [驚險] jīngxiǎn (frightening-dangerous) <adj.> breathtaking, adventurous: ~的经历 an adventurous experience || ~电影 an adventure film || 场面~ a breaktaking scene

21 高危 [-] gāowēi high risk <adj.> (high-danger): ~职业 a high-risk occupation || ~人群 a high-risk group || ~病人 a high-risk patient

22 虎口拔牙 [-] hǔkǒu báyá (tiger-mouth-pull-tooth) <idiom> pull out the tiger's teeth: 你要小心, 和他打交道 (dǎ jiāodào) 就像~. Be careful, dealing with him is like pulling out tigers' teeth.

23 人人自危 [-] rénrén-zìwēi (people-people-self-insecure) <idiom> feel insecure, self-danger: ~的时代 the age of self-danger || 弄得大家~. It made everyone feel insecure.

24 生死存亡 [-] shēngsǐ cúnwáng (life-death-survival-extinction) <idiom> survival or extinction, life and death: 国家~的关头 the survival or extinction of the nation || ~的问题 a matter of life and death

25 危机四伏 [-機--] wēijī sìfú (dangerous-crux-everywhere-hidden) <idiom> perilous, in crisis: ~的战场 a perilous battlefield || 房地产市场看起来好像很红火, 其实已经~了. The real estate market seemed to be booming, but it was already in crisis.

26 危在旦夕 [-] wēizài dànxī (dangerous-at-morning-evening) <idiom> on the verge of death or crisis: 生命~. Lives are on the verge of death or destruction. || 国家~ The state is on the verge of crisis.

27 引狼入室 [-] yǐnlángrùshì (lead-wolf-enter-home) <idiom> show the wolf into the house (idiom), to introduce a potential source of trouble: 这么做简直就是~. Doing such a thing is almost like opening the door to a dangerous person. || 他聘请 (pìnqǐng) 了一位CEO, 结果~, 把公司搞垮了. He hired this CEO in which he opened the door to a dangerous person because the CEO took the company down eventually.

28 朝不保夕 [-] zhāobùbǎoxī (morning-not able to-ensure-evening) <idiom> in precarious situation: 推销员是~的工作. Being a salesman is a precarious job. || 你还去求他呢, 连他自己都~了. You're begging him, but he is in a precarious situation as well.

Tips:

1 安: The upper part of 安 is 宀, which means 'home,' and the lower part, 女 means 'woman.' Therefore the meaning of the whole character is 'a woman in a house, peaceful' from which evolved meanings such as 'safe, secure'.

2 乱 and 治: 乱 means 'chaos' and 治 'peaceful and prosperous.' 天下大乱 is what we would not like to happen, and 天下大治 is our ultimate goal. However, Chairman Mao started the Cultural Revolution (1966–76) in high hopes that the country would progress from 天下大乱 to 天下大治, though he actually barely made it.

3 险: 险 originally means 'a narrow pass (in the mountain)' from which evolved the meaning 'dangerous.'

Exercises:

Part I: Match up the following expressions to the appropriate column. Make sure your words can describe the situation mentioned in the column.

老百姓生活安定 经济平稳发展 物价平稳 人们觉得高枕无忧 老百姓安居乐业 食品安全 和平安定 感觉朝不保夕 国家危在旦夕 国家危机四伏 社会动荡不安 老百姓人人自危、

描写瑞士 (Switzerland) 这个国家的情况	描写叙利亚 (Syria) 2016年的情况

Part II: Read the following sentences and fill in each blank with the appropriate word or phrase from the options given.

1 安然无恙、安居乐业、骚乱

a) 德国发生难民____________以后, 政府呼吁 (hūyù, appeal) 民众保持冷静.
b) 据报道, 遭遇 (zāoyù, encounter with) 难民骚乱 (sāoluàn, riot) 的市民大部分已经__________ _地回到家中.
c) 大部分德国人不喜欢移民到别的国家, 他们喜欢在故土__________.

2 高危、危险、惊险

a) 小李在德国留学的时候常常去看________电影. 有一次小李在看这种电影的时候因为害怕, 把手里的咖啡扔到了别人身上, 真是太_________了.
b) 小李打算大学毕业以后当消防员, 虽然属于________职业, 但是他不在乎.

3 虎口拔牙、生死存亡、引狼入室、天下大乱

a) 到叙利亚 (Xùlìyà, Syria) 去打击ISIS就像____________, 非常危险.
b) 有人批评奥巴马 (Obama) 对待叙利亚的政策, 说他是__________ __, 把灾难 (zāinàn, disaster) 引到了美国.
c) 有人说如果德国、法国继续 (jìxù, continue) 保持现在的难民政策, 30年后他们的国家就会处于____________的关头.
d) 一位历史学家说伊斯兰教国家和基督教国家之间的冲突将会导致______________, 发生第三次世界大战.

Theme 268: Prosperous, declining 盛, 衰 (shèng, shuāi)

1 火 [-] huǒ (fire) <adj.> booming, popular: 这首歌很~. This song is really popular. || 卖得~ sth. sells very well || 生意~. Business is booming.
2 红火 [紅-] hónghuǒ (red-fire) <adj.> booming, prosperous: 生意~ business is booming || 日子过得~ live a comfortable life

3 发达 [發達] fādá (rich-developed) <adj.> developed: ~国家developed country || 交通~ have a well-developed transportation || 经济~. The economy is flourishing.

4 昌盛 [-] chāngshèng (prosperous-flourishing) <adj.> prosperous, flourishing: 国家/民族~ a country/nation is thriving || 繁荣~ prosperous and flourishing

5 繁荣 [-榮] fánróng (grand-thriving) <adj.> prosperous, thriving: 经济~ economic boom || ~的社会a prosperous society

6 兴旺 [興-] xīngwàng (rising-vigorous) <adj.> prosperous, flourish: ~发达vigor and prosperity || 人口~. The population is thriving. || ~的市场prosperous market

7 繁华 [-華] fánhuá (grand-magnificent) <adj.> flourishing, busy: ~都市a busy city || ~的大街a busy street

8 蓬勃 [-] péngbó (flourishing-vigorous) <adj.> vigorous, full of vitality: ~发展vigorous development || ~兴起rising with full of vitality || 朝气~ full of youthful spirit, full of vigor and vitality

9 热火朝天 [熱---] rèhuǒ cháotiān (enthusiasm-fire-toward-sky) <idiom> surge with activity like a bolt of fire soaring heavenward: 干得~ be in full swing || ~的运动the movement bustling with activity

10 如日中天 [-] rúrìzhōngtiān (like-the sun-middle-day) <idiom> like the sun at midday, at the summit of one's power: 他的事业 (shìyè) ~. His career is moving into top gear. || 做了那件大事以后, 现在他的支持率 (zhīchí lǜ) ~. After doing that big thing, his approval ratings are now in full bloom.

11 欣欣向荣 [---榮] xīnxīn xiàngróng (flourishing-toward-prosperous) <idiom> flourishing, prosperous: ~地发展in the height of the development || ~的城市prospering cities || ~的事业prospering career

12 蒸蒸日上 [-] zhēngzhēng rìshàng (thriving-everyday-up) <idiom> becoming more prosperous with each passing day: 生产~. Production is flourishing. || 事业~ career is flourishing || 在新总统的领导下, 国家~. The country prospered under the new president.

13 淡 [-] dàn (weak, slack) <adj.> weak, slack: ~季off seasons || 生意~ business is slack

14 低迷 [-] dīmí (low-dispassionate) <adj.> low (spirits), in a slump (economy): 经济/股市~ economy/stock market in the doldrums || 持续~ the downturn continues || 心情~ depressed mood

15 不景气 [--氣] bù jǐngqì (not-prosperous) <adj.> depressing state: 经济~ economic recession || 生产~ production is slack || 生意~ business is slow

16 衰落 [-] shuāiluò (decline-drop) <adj.> decline: 日益~ be on the wane || ~的文明a civilization of decline || 经济~ economic decline

17 没落 [沒-] mòluò (sink-drop) <adj.> downfall, ruin: ~的家族 a falling family || 古代重男轻女 (zhòngnán qīngnǚ) 的思想现在~了. The idea of the ancient boy's preference is now in decline. || 日渐~ declining day by day

18 衰退 [-] shuāituì (decline-down) <adj.> decline: 经济~ economic recession || 人老了以后, 听力、视力和智力都会~. Hearing, vision and intelligence all decline when people are older. || 严重~ severe recession

19 千疮百孔 [-瘡--] qiānchuāng bǎikǒng (1,000-wound-100-hole) <idiom> riddled with gaping wounds, afflicted with many ills, in very bad condition: 经济~. The economy is riddled with gaping wounds. || ~的城市city in very

bad condition || 上一届政府留下一个~的烂摊子 (làn tānzi). The previous administration left a huge mess.

20 每况愈下 [-况--] měikuàng yùxià (each time-situation-even-worse) <idiom> go from bad to worse: 生活~ life is getting worse. || 身体~ sb. has/have been falling in health || 谈恋爱以后, 小王的学习成绩~. After falling in love, Little Wang's grades have been getting worse.

21 一落千丈 [-] yīluò qiānzhàng (one-fall-1, 000–10 feet) <idiom> a fall in a thousand feet, plummeted: 地位~ the position has plummeted || 实力~. The position has plummeted. || 心情~. The mood has plummeted.

22 强弩之末 [-] qiángnǔzhīmò (strong-crossbow-'s-end) <idiom> a spent force: 中国房地产行业 (hángyè) 可能已经是~. China's real estate market may be overblown.

Tips:

1 繁榮昌盛: 繁荣昌盛 (fánróng chāngshèng) means 'prosperous and flourishing,' which is supposed to be a very positive word, however, sometimes it is purposely used as 繁荣娼盛 with the third character 娼 being different from the original one, 昌. 娼 means 'prostitute, bitch.'

2 弓: 弓 (gōng) means 'longbow.' It needs strength to draw/pull a bow, therefore some characters with the radical 弓 are usually associated with strength. For example, 强 means 'strong,' and 弱 'weak.'

Exercises:

Part I: Match up the following expressions to the appropriate column. Make sure your words can describe the situation mentioned in the column.

a) 城市声誉 (shēngyù, reputation) 一落千丈
b) 老百姓生活水平每况愈下
c) 城市基础设施 (shèshī, facility) 千疮百孔
d) 经济衰退
e) 公共交通落后
f) 消费市场低迷, 商家不景气
g) 高新技术产业如日中天
h) 城市欣欣向荣
i) 经济蒸蒸日上
j) 街道繁华
k) 公共交通发达
l) 市场兴旺

描述中国城市深圳	描述美国城市底特律

Part II: Read the following sentences and fill in each blank with the appropriate word or phrase from the options given.

1 强弩之末、热火朝天

虽然有人认为中国的房地产行业已经是____________, 但是北京的房地产开发市场还是____________.

2 每况愈下、一落千丈

a) 最近美国底特律城市的房地产市场______________, 有些房子只卖一美元.
b) 底特律周边地区的房地产市场也是______________, 一天比一天差.

3 衰退、衰落、没落

a) 英国在19世纪是世界上最强大国家, 但是在二战后__________成为二流国家.
b) 历史学家认为每个世界大国都会有__________的过程, 没有永远的世界第一强国.
c) 英国经济在二战以后开始__________.

4 红火、发达、蓬勃

中国沿海地区的农村也属于 (shǔyú, belong to) 经济__________地区. 各种农村乡镇企业__________发展, 因此那里老百姓的日子一般都过得很__________.

Theme 269: Noisy, quiet, busy, leisure 闹, 静, 忙, 闲 (nào, jìng, máng, xián)

1 闹 [鬧] nào (noisy) <adj.> noisy: ~市downtown || ~心vexed, annoyed
2 吵 [-] chǎo (argue, noisy) <adj.> noisy: 图书馆不~ The library is quiet. || ~死了, 安静点儿! It's too noisy. Be quiet!
3 挤 [擠] jǐ (squeeze, crowded) <adj.> crowded: 房间很~ the room is very crowded. || 车上很~. The bus is very crowded.
4 热闹 [熱鬧] rènao (exciting-noisy) <adj.> noisy and exciting in a pleasant way (of a scene or occasion): ~的街道busy streets || ~的节日an exciting festival || 最 ~的地段the busiest areas
5 火爆 [-] huǒbào (fire-crack) <adj.> fiery (temper), popular: 脾气~ bad temper, be very fiery || 现在卖得最~的商品 the most popular item to sell now || 生意~. Business is very good.
6 吵闹 [-鬧] chǎonào (arguing-noisy) <adj.> noisy: ~声the noise || 大声~ make a loud noise || ~的环境a noisy environment
7 闹哄哄 [鬧--] nàohōnghōng (noisy-*suffix*) <adj.> noisy: ~的农贸 (nóngmào) 市场noisy farmers' markets || ~的场景 (chǎngjǐng) a noisy scene || 图书馆里的青少年阅读室总是~的. The youth reading room in the library is always noisy.
8 七嘴八舌 [-] qīzuǐ bāshé (7-mouth-8-tongue) <idiom> seven months and eight tongues- everybody trying to get a word in, all taking at once: ~地议论 (yìlùn) all discussing at once || ~地提问. Everyone is eager to get a question in.
9 满城风雨 [滿-風-] mǎnchéng fēngyǔ (whole-city-wind-rain) <idiom> wind and rain through the town (idiom), a big scandal: 这件丑闻 (chǒuwén) 闹得~. The scandal has created a sensation.
10 蜂拥而至 [-擁--] fēngyōng'érzhì (bee-crowd-marker of modifier-arrive) <idiom> flock, swarm: ~的人群people in flocks || 顾客~ customers flock in || 金融 (jīnróng) 市场开放以后, 国际投资者 (tóuzīzhě) ~. When financial markets opened up, international investors flocked to it.

11 人山人海 [-] rénshān rénhǎi (people-mountain-people-sea) <idiom> huge crowds of people: 到处~ there is sea of people everywhere || 新年的时候, 纽约时代广场~. During the New Year, New York's Times Square is a sea of people.

12 人来人往 [-來--] rénlái rénwǎng (people-come-people-go) <idiom> people come and go: 办公室里~, 非常忙碌 (mánglù). The office bustled with people and activity. || 大街上~. The street is bustling with people.

13 车水马龙 [車-馬龍] chēshuǐ mǎlóng (cart-stream-horse-dragon) <idiom> heavy traffic: ~的城市 a bustling city || 街道上~. The streets are full of traffic.

14 静 [靜] jìng (quiet) <adj./ v.> quiet: ~下心来the heart gets down || ~极了very quiet

15 安静 [-靜] ānjìng (peaceful-quiet) <adj. /v.> quiet: ~的房间 a quiet room || ~一点be quiet a little bit || ~下来quiet down

16 宁静 [寧靜] níngjìng (tranquil-quiet) <adj.> quiet, tranquil: ~的院子a quiet yard || 内心~ peace of mind || ~的大海the quiet sea

17 寂静 [-靜] jìjìng (silent-quiet) <adj./n.> silent, silence: ~的街道 the quiet street || 一片~ there was silence || ~无声silence

18 清静 [-靜] qīngjìng (desolate-quiet) <adj.> quiet: ~的地方a quiet place || 这座寺庙 (sìmiào) 在大山里, 很~. The temple is quiet in the mountains.

19 静悄悄 [靜--] jìngqiāoqiāo (quiet-quietly) <adj.> quiet: ~的房子 a quiet house || ~的夜晚a quiet night || 四周~. It was all quiet.

20 阴森森 [陰--] yīnsēnsēn (gloomy-ghastly) <adj.> gloomy: ~的目光 the gloomy gaze || ~的屋子a spooky room || 那个城堡 (chéngbǎo) 让人觉得~的. The castle was spooky.

21 偏僻 [-] piānpì (remote-secluded) <adj.> remote: ~ 的农村/山区a remote village/mountain area || 中国甘肃地处~, 除了敦煌 (Dūnhuáng) 以外, 游客很少. China's Gansu Province is remote, with few visitors except to see Dunhuang.

22 冷清 [-] lěngqīng (cold-desolate) <adj.> lonely, cold and cheerless: ~的道路The cold and cheerless road || 家里很~. The house was deserted.

23 荒无人烟 [-無--] huāngwú rényān (deserted-no-people-cooking smoke) <idiom> desolate and uninhabited: ~的地方a desolate place || 沙漠里~. The desert is desolate.

24 地广人稀 [-廣--] dìguǎng rénxī (land-vast-people-sparse) <idiom> the vast territory with a sparse population: 这个国家~. This vast country is sparsely populated.

25 孤独 [-獨] gūdú (lonely-solitary) <adj.> lonely, solitary: ~地生活living alone || ~的老人a lonely old man || 感到~ feel lonely

26 孤单 [-單] gūdān (lonely-isolated) <adj.> lonely: ~的孩子a lonely child || 感到~ feel lonely

27 孤立 [-] gūlì (lonely-exist) <adj.> isolated, without support or sympathy: ~发展develop in isolation || 她虽然学习好, 但是别的孩子都不喜欢她, 所以她很~. Her academic performance is a very good, but the other children don't like her. So she is so isolated. || ~的事实isolated facts

28 孤零零 [-] gūlīnglīng (lonely-high and dry) <adj.> solitary, alone: ~地坐着sitting alone || ~一个人alone

29 孤立无援 [--無-] gūlì wúyuán (isolated-no-help) <idiom> isolated and cut off from help: 那个国家在国际社会上~. The country was isolated in the international community.

30 无依无靠 [無-無-] wúyī wúkào (no-rely-no-support) <idiom> have nothing to rely upon: ~的孤儿a helpless orphan || 他刚到美国的时候, ~, 所以觉得压力 (yālì) 很大. When he first came to the United States, he had nothing to rely on, so he felt stressed.

31 单亲 [單親] dānqīn (single-parent) <adj.> single-parent: ~妈妈single mom || ~家庭one-parent family

32 单枪匹马 [單槍-馬] dānqiāng pǐmǎ (single-spear-single-horse) <idiom> single-handed, all by oneself, alone: 他偷渡 (tōudù) 到美国时只剩下二十美元了, 后来~打天下, 现在拥有几百家餐饮连锁店 (liánsuǒdiàn). When he came to America, he had only $20 left. Later he worked very hard on his own business. Now he has a chain of several hundred restaurants. || ~往前冲play a lone hand

33 忙 [-] máng (busy) <adj./ v.> busy, be busy in: ~生意be busy in business || 工作~ be busy in work || ~着赚钱be busy in making money || 最近~什么呢? What have you been up to lately?

34 繁忙 [-] fánmáng (numerous-busy) <adj.> busy: ~的工作busy work || 交通~ busy traffic || 家务~. The housework is busy.

35 急匆匆 [-] jícōngcōng (hurry-hurriedly) <adj.> in a hurry: ~地走了left in a hurry || ~的脚步hasty feet

36 四处奔波 [-處--] sìchù bēnbō (here and there-rush about) <idiom> rush about: 大学毕业以后, 他~找工作. After he graduated from college, he went around to looking for a job.

37 空 [-] kòng (empty, hollow) <adj./ v.> empty, unoccupied: ~房间a cacant room || ~行blank line || 你~着手, 怎么不帮我一把? Your hands are empty now. Why don't you do me a favor?

38 闲 [閒] xián (idle) <adj.> stay idle: ~功夫idle time || ~人idler || ~聊chat

39 空闲 [-閒] kòngxián (free-idle) <n. /adj.> free, idle: ~时间 free time || 我很少有~. I am seldom at leisure.

40 清闲 [-閒] qīngxián (desolate-idle) <adj.> leisurely, carefree: 工作~ the work is idle || ~的退休生活 the idle life of retirement || 新年是中国人最~的时候. New Year is the most idle time for the Chinese people.

41 闲散 [閒-] xiánsǎn (idle-unfettered) <adj.> free and at leisure, idle: ~资金idle capital || ~人员idle people

42 悠闲 [-閒] yōuxián (leisurely-idle) <adj.> ease, leisurely: 生活~ life is easy || 过得~ live with ease || ~的日子the idle days

43 无聊 [無-] wúliáo (no-depend) <adj.> bored, senseless: ~的日子boring days || 生活 ~ life is boring || 感到~ feel bored

44 默默 [-] mòmò (silent-*reduplication*) <adv.> silent: ~地坐着sit quietly || ~地看look silently || ~工作work in silence

45 无所事事 [無---] wúsuǒshìshì (no-what-do-thing) <idiom> have nothing to do: ~的日子idle days || 她每天~, 不是上网就是去购物. She has nothing to do everyday, so she's either surfing online or going shopping.

46 百无聊赖 [-無-賴] bǎiwúliáolài (very-no-depend-rely) <idiom> bored to death, bored stiff, overcome with boredom: ~地坐着a bored sitting || 他觉得生活~, 后来开始学佛. He felt life was boring and meaningless, so he began to study Buddhism.

Tips:

1 闹 and 静, 忙 and 闲: 闹 means 'noisy' and 静 'quiet.' There is a phrase 闹中取静 (nàozhōng qǔjìng) which means 'to seek peace and quiet in a noisy environment.' It is said that Mao Zedong liked to read at a noisy market when he was studying in Changsha, China from 1911 to 1918. 忙 means 'busy' and 闲 'leisurely.' There is a phrase 忙里偷闲 (mánglǐ tōuxián), which means 'to snatch a little leisure from a busy life.' Mao Zedong liked to practice calligraphy, and this was 忙里偷闲 for him.

2 地广人稀: When '地广人稀' (vast land with sparse population) is mentioned, a Chinese mind will naturally go to 澳大利亚 (Australia), 加拿大 (Canada) or 西伯利亚 (Siberia), but not 德州 (Texas).

3 ABB type adjectives: There are five ABB type adjectives in this unit, namely 闹哄哄, 静悄悄, 孤零零, 急匆匆 and 阴森森. The main meaning of each word comes from the first character (Character A), and what is left, i. e., Characters BB vividly describe the way of Character A.

Exercises:

Part I: Match up the following expressions to the appropriate column. Make sure your words can describe the situation mentioned in the column.

热闹的街道、闹哄哄的农贸市场、广场上人山人海、街道上车水马龙、商场里人来人往、交通繁忙、无所事事、百无聊赖、默默坐着、感到无聊、四周十分寂静、地广人稀、荒无人烟、一户孤零零的人家、一座阴森森的城堡、地处偏僻山区、冷清的道路

形容中国的一座大城市	形容英国一个极为偏远的农村	形容一个独居老人

Part II: Read the following sentences and fill in each blank with the appropriate word or phrase from the options given.

1 悠闲、闲散、空闲

a) 支付宝 (Chinese Paypal) 的一个作用是收集社会上的__________资金 (zījīn), 进行投资.
b) 中国女性一般55岁就可以退休, 过着____________的生活.
c) 中国年轻人一般工作繁忙, ____________时间很少.

2 孤单、单亲、孤立、四处奔波

a) 小张四岁的时候跟妈妈从老家来到北京, 从小在 ____________家庭长大. 他妈妈刚到北京时 ____________找工作, 很少有时间陪伴小张, 因此他觉得很__________.

b) 小张上小学的时候穿着破旧, 因此一些学生常常看不起他, ________他.

3 单枪匹马、急匆匆、孤立无援

a) 由于妈妈的劝说, 小张研究生毕业后 ____________地跟女朋友结了婚.
b) 婚后小张被公司派到非洲, ____________去开发非洲市场.
c) 小张在非洲感到 ____________的时候, 就会给妻子打电话.

4 满城风雨、无依无靠、七嘴八舌

a) 在非洲小张看到了很多____________的孤儿.
b) 小张召开公司会议跟大家讨论帮助非洲孤儿 (gū'ér, orphan) 的事情, 对此大家看法不同, 于是 ____________地发表个人意见.
c) 媒体报道 (bàodào, report) 了小张公司的产品质量问题, 结果弄得 ____________.

Theme 270: Greater or lesser urgency 缓急 (huǎnjí)

1 轻松 [輕鬆] qīngsōng (light-loose) <adj.> relaxed, light: ~的心情feel relaxed || 生活~ life is easy || ~地说talk with ease
2 缓和 [緩-] huǎnhé (slow-ease) <v./adj.> relax, ease up: ~矛盾mitigate a conflict || ~气氛defuse tension || 语气~ mild tone
3 舒缓 [-緩] shūhuǎn (slacken-slow) <adj.> slow and unhurried, relaxed, mild: 动作~ slow unhurried movements || ~的节奏soothing rhythm || ~的音乐soothing music
4 松弛 [鬆-] sōngchí (loose-unstring) <adj.> limp, flabby, loose: 肌肉~ flaccid muscles || 纪律~ lax in discipline || 管理~ lax in management
5 紧 [緊] jǐn (tense) <adj.> tight, tense: 时间~ be pressed for time || 工期~ time limited for a project || 学习~ be pressed for study
6 紧张 [緊張] jǐnzhāng (tense-draw) <adj.> nervous, tense: 神情~ look nervous || ~的比赛 a tense match || 日程安排得太~. It's rather a tight schedule. || 目前这里住房紧张 ~. Accommodation here is pretty tight at present.
7 紧急 [緊-] jǐnjí (tense-urgent) <adj.> urgent, critical: ~情况emergency || ~出口emergency exits || ~会议emergency meeting
8 紧迫 [緊-] jǐnpò (urgent-pressing) <adj.> urgent, imminent: 时间~ the time is urgent || 任务~ the task is urgent
9 迫切 [-] pòqiè (pressing-imminent) <adj.> urgent, pressing: ~需要urgent need || ~要求urgent request || ~任务urgent task
10 白热化 [-熱-] báirèhuà (white-hot – *nize*) <v.> turn white-hot: ~阶段the phase of incandescence || 比赛进入~ the game went into a white-hot
11 十万火急 [-萬--] shíwàn huǒjí (10–10, 000-fire-urgent) <idiom> most urgent (formerly on dispatches): 情况~. The situation is urgent.
12 火烧眉毛 [-燒--] huǒshāo méimao (fire-burn-eyebrow<idiom> the fire is singeing the eyebrows – a desperate sitution, at a crucial point: ~的事儿matter of the utmost urgency || 现在都~的时候了, 你还开玩笑! It is time to burn the eyebrows, you're still kidding me.
13 燃眉之急 [-] ránméizhījí (burn-eyebrow-*'s*-urgency) <idiom> as pressing as a fire singeing one's eyebrows- a matter of extreme urgency, extreme

urgency: 解决~ resolve the emergent issue|| 母亲寄来一万美金, 缓解了我的~. My mother sent me $10,000 to ease my urgent needs.

14 迫在眉睫 [-] pòzàiméijié (pressing-at-eyebrow-eyelash) <idiom> extremely urgent, imminent: 时间~. We are pressed for time. || 工作~. The work is imminent.

15 一触即发 [-觸-發] yīchù jífā (once-touch-will-break out) <idiom> may break out at any moment, on the verge of breaking out: 局势 (júshì) /战争~. It's an explosive situation/war.

16 惊心动魄 [驚-動-] jīngxīn dòngpò (stir-heart-shake-soul) <idiom> soul-stirring, profoundly affecting: ~的政治运动 stirring political movements || ~的事情soul-stirring things

Tips:

1 张: 'Zhāng' is a major surname in China and there are several written forms among which the two most common are 张 and 章. If someone said his surname is 'Zhāng' and you want to know which it is exactly, you can ask '哪个Zhāng? '弓长张'还是'立早章?' (Which Zhāng, 'gōng cháng zhāng' or 'lì zǎo zhāng?') From the etymological perspective, 章 should be explained as '音十' (music-end,) however, '立早章' is the common way to say.

2 张 and 弛: '张' means 'to draw a bow' and '弛' (chí) means 'to loosen a bow.' Now you can easily find that '弓' means 'bow.' The phrase '一张一弛' means 'to alternate tension with relaxation,' for example, '歇一会儿吧? 不能老工作啊? 一张一弛嘛.' (Please take a break. You can't work like a robot. It's good to relax for a while after working for quite a while.)

3 眉 and 'urgency': It might be that since 眉毛/眉 (eyebrows) are close to the eyes they can see immediate urgency, 眉毛/眉 is often involved in expressing 'urgency,' for example, 火烧眉毛, 燃眉之急 and 迫在眉睫, which are annotated in this chapter.

Exercises:

Part I: Match up the following expressions to the appropriate column. Make sure your words can describe the situation mentioned in the column.

心情轻松 语气缓和 动作舒缓 动作松弛 神情紧张 竞争处于白热化阶段 情况十万火急 情况火烧眉毛 问题迫在眉睫 战争一触即发 矛盾一触即发 时间紧迫 迫切需要

形容一个人很放松	形容某种情况非常紧张或紧迫

Part II: Read the following sentences and fill in each blank with the appropriate word or phrase from the options given.

1 惊心动魄、紧急

中国电影《战狼 2》(*Wolf Warrior 2*) 说的是一个中国军人在非洲____________救援的事情, 电影情节和场面________________, 受到观众好评.

2 迫在眉睫、火烧眉毛

a) 有人认为中国经济全面市场化已经____________.
b) 小王的心理素质非常好, 不管面对什么____________的事情, 他都会冷静处理.

3 紧迫、迫切、白热化

a) 目前手机的市场竞争已经到了____________阶段.
b) 三星 (Samsung) 手机公司______________需要开发新产品.
c) 创新是各大手机公司的____________任务.

4 松弛、缓和、紧张

a) 这家手机公司管理____________, 工作效率 (xiàolǜ, efficiency) 很低.
b) 经理跟小王的关系很____________, 因此想找时间跟经理谈一谈, __________他们之间的关系.

Theme 271: Clean, dirty 洁, 污 (jié, wū)

1 干净 [乾净] gānjìng (dry-clean) <adj.> neat and tidy: 洗~ wash it clean || ~的水clean water || 请把厨房打扫~. Please clean up the kitchen.
2 卫生 [衛-] wèishēng (safeguard-life) <adj./n.> hygiene, sanitary: 注意~ pay more attention to hygiene || 饮食~ food and drink hygiene || 个人~ personal hygiene
3 清洁 [-潔] qīngjié (clear-clean) <adj.> clean: 房间~. The room is clean. || ~工cleaner || 空气~. The air is clean.
4 整洁 [-潔] zhěngjié (tidy-clean) <adj.> clean and tidy: 道路~. The road is clean and neat. || 穿得~ neatly dressed
5 清爽 [-] qīngshuǎng (clear-pleasant) <adj.> fresh and cool: 空气~ the air is fresh and cool || 事情解决了, 我心里也~了. Now that the matter is settled, I feel relieved.
6 清新 [-] qīngxīn (clear-fresh) <adj.> pure and fresh: 空气~ the air is pure and fresh || ~的风fresh wind || 文笔~ written in a refreshingly lucid style
7 低碳 [-] dītàn (low-carbon) <adj.> low-carbon: ~生活low-carbon life || ~项目low-carbon projects || ~城市low-carbon cities
8 一尘不染 [-塵--] yīchén bùrǎn (one-dust-not-to soil) <idiom> spotless, not soiled by a speck of dust: ~的房间spotless rooms || 扫得~ clean it spotless || 家具~. The furniture is spotlessly clean.
9 脏 [臟] zāng (dirty) <adj.> dirty, filthy: ~衣服dirty clothes, dirty linen || ~东西dirty staff || ~水filthy water, slops, sewage

10 肮脏 [骯髒] āngzang (dirty) <adj.> dirty, filthy: ~的垃圾dirty trash || ~的想法dirty thinking || ~的政治交易dirty political deal

11 邋遢 [-] lāta (slovenly) <adj.> slovenly, sloppy: 外表~ sloppy appearance || 他工作总是~. His work is always sloppy.

12 污浊 [污-濁] wūzhuó (polluted-muddy) <adj.> dirty, muddy: ~的空气dirty air || ~的河流a foul river

13 脏乱 [髒亂] zāngluàn (dirty-messy) <adj.> dirty and disordered, in a mess: 环境~ the environment is dirty and disordered || ~的马路dirty and messy roads

14 脏兮兮 [髒--] zāngxīxī (dirty-*suffix*) <adj.> dirty, filthy: 全身~ get dirty from head to toe || ~的衣服dirty clothes

15 脏乱差 [髒亂-] zāng luàn chà (dirty-messy-rundown) <adj.> dirty, messy and rundown (of environment): 城市~. The city is dirty, messy and rundown.

16 灰头土脸 [-頭-臉] huī tóu tǔ liǎn (dust-head-dirt-face) <idiom> head and face covered with dust, dejected: ~的流浪汉 (liúlànghàn) a homeless person with dirty and sloppy appearance || ~的日子depressed days || 他被老板骂得~的. He was reviled by his boss.

Tips:

1 尘: The simplified character 尘 has a traditional form 塵, which depicts 'deer running and dust rising.' The simplified form 尘 (literally 'small dust') makes sense too.

2 一尘不染: This idiom originally came from Buddhism, meaning 'clear of six dusts that might pollute the ordinary people's six external sense bases, namely eye, ear, nose, tongue, body and mind.' Now it is used mainly as 'spotlessly clean (of rooms or other objects)' and 'maintain pure-hearted (in the bureaucratic environment etc.' For example, 他当了二十年省长却一尘不染, 从来没接受过别人的贿赂 (huìlù) means 'He has been governor for 20 years but is free of corruption. He has never taken bribery from others.'

3 脏 (髒): The simplified form is related to 月 (meat), but the traditional form is related to 骨 (bone.)

4 乱 (亂): The simplified form seems to be related to 舌 (shé, tongue,) however, the traditional form 亂 depicts 'to put silk in order' from which evolved the meaning of 'confused, disorderly.'

5 Typical colloquial words in this unit: 邋遢, 髒兮兮, 灰頭土臉

Exercises:

Part I: Match up the following expressions to the appropriate column. Make sure your words can describe the situation mentioned in the column.

衣着干净　衣着邋遢　家里一尘不染　家里脏乱不堪　空气清洁
家里整洁清爽　家里污浊肮脏　注意个人卫生　外表邋遢　家里脏兮兮的

形容小高是个干净整洁的人	形容小李生活习惯很差

Part II: Read the following sentences and fill in each blank with the appropriate word or phrase from the options given.

1 灰头土脸、脏乱、污浊

记者走访了纽约一个贫民区, 发现这里空气________, 环境_________, 一些___________的流浪汉睡在大街上.

2 低碳生活、清新、卫生

a) 据说青岛是中国有名的_________城, 空气_________, 街道整洁.
b) 青岛市政府提倡市民过_________, 减少环境污染与资源浪费.

Theme 272: Order and chaos 齐, 乱 (qí, luàn)

1 齐 [齊] qí (even, equal) <adj.> neat, even: 头发不~ untidy hair || 这些椅子放得不~. These chairs are arranged unevenly.
2 整齐 [-齊] zhěngqí (tidy-uniform) <adj.> in good order, tidy: ~的牙齿 straight teeth || ~的房子 an organized house || 书架上书摆得很~. The books are kept neatly in the shelves.
3 工整 [-] gōngzhěng (delicate-neat) <adj.> neat, fine work: ~的字 neat writing (penmanship)
4 利落 [-] lìluò (nimble-fall) <adj.> agile, nimble: ~的动作 a quick motion || 做事~ hastily work
5 井然有序 [-] jǐngrán yǒuxù (orderly-*suffix*-have-order) <idiom> everything clear and in good order, neat and tidy: ~地工作 orderly work || 安排得~ orderly arrangements
6 井井有条 [---條] jǐngjǐng yǒutiáo (orderly-*reduplication*-have-order) <idiom> everything clear and orderly, neat and tidy: 秩序~ in neat and tidy order || ~的房间 a neat and tidy room || 处理得~ managed carefully
7 有板有眼 [-] yǒubǎn yǒuyǎn (have-downbeat-have-weak beat) <idiom> (of speech or action) rhythmical, measured: 说话~ speak with in a orderly/rhythmic way
8 衣冠楚楚 [-] yīguān chǔchǔ (clothes-hat-immaculate) <idiom> immaculately dressed, well groomed: ~的记者 a well dressed reporter || 打扮得~ well put together (make-up and dress)
9 均匀 [-] jūnyún (even-equal) <adj.> even, well-distributed: 分布~ evenly distributed || 呼吸~ even/rhythmic breath || ~的速度 well paced speed/ even pace
10 平均 [-] píngjūn (equal-even) <adj.> average: ~工资 average salary || ~身高 average height || ~年龄average age
11 平衡 [-] pínghéng (equal-balanced) <adj.> balance, equilibrium: 发展~ equal expansion || 心理不~ be unbalanced (psychologically) || 生态~ in unbalanced environment || ~工作和生活 balance work and life
12 和谐 [-諧] héxié (harmonious-harmonious/accorded) <adj.> harmony: 色彩~ harmonious colors || ~的声音 harmonious sound || ~社会 harmonious society
13 调和 [調-] tiáohé (adjust-harmonious) <adj./v.> harmonious, meditate: ~矛盾 resolve a conflict || 色彩~ blend colors
14 协调 [協調] xiétiáo (coordinate-adjust) <adj.> coordinate, harmonize: 动作~ coordinated movements || ~发展 coordinated expansion || ~各部门的工作 coordinate the work of various departments

15 乱 [亂] luàn (disorder) <adj.> disorderly: 房间~ disorderly room || 把事情搞~了 put things into disorder || ~花钱 spend money recklessly

16 混乱 [-亂] hùnluàn (mixed-disorderly) <adj.> confused, disorderly: 思想~ disorderly thought || ~的市场 disorderly market || 管理~ manage in a disorderly fashion

17 杂乱 [雜亂] záluàn (medley-disorderly) <adj.> in a mess: 内容~ the content is disorderly || ~的脚步声 arrhythmic steps || ~地放着 leave/place sth. disorderly

18 零乱 [-亂] língluàn (odd-disorderly) <adj.> in a mess: ~的房间 the room is a mess

19 臃肿 [-腫] yōngzhǒng (corpulent-swollen) <adj.> obese, bloated: ~的身材 obese figure (body) || ~的肚皮 a bloated belly || 政府机构~ an oversized organization

20 乱七八糟 [亂---] luànqībāzāo (disorderly-7–8-messy) <idiom> everything in disorder: ~的事 disorderly affairs || 画得~ draw poorly || 大学生的宿舍~的. The undergraduate dorm is in disorder.

21 乱套 [亂-] luàntào (disorder-formula) <v.> in a mess,upside down: 事情~了. Things are in a great disorder. || 遭到突然批评之后他~了, 说话有些不得体. After unexpectedly receiving criticism, he was a little bit shaken up and was a little bit slow to collect his thoughts.

22 错乱 [錯亂] cuòluàn (mismatched-disorderly) <adj.> in disorder, deranged (mentally): 神经~ mental disorder || 言语~ speech disorder

23 忙乱 [-亂] mángluàn (hasty-disorderly) <adj.> hasty and disorderly: 工作~ work that is rushed and muddled || 各自~ each one was in a disorderly rush

24 紊乱 [-亂] wěnluàn (confused-disorderly) <adj.> disorder, chaos: 功能~ dysfunction || 市场~ a disorderly market || 因为在倒时差她的生物钟~. Because she is overcoming jet lag, her biological clock is off.

25 乱糟糟 [亂--] luànzāozāo (disorderly-messy-*reduplication*) <adj.> chaotic, in a mess: ~的房间 a messy room || ~的头发 hair is a mess || 心情~的. in a bad mood, in a bad state of mind

26 七手八脚 [-] qīshǒu bājiǎo (7-hand-8-foot) <idiom> even hands and eight feeds (with everyone lending a hand): ~地搬东西everyone lent a hand to move staff || 大家~地把房子打扫干净了. With everybody lending a hand, the house was soon swept clean.

27 乱成一团 [亂--團] luàn chéng yī tuán (disorderly-into-a-lump) <idiom> in a great mess, chaotic: 心里~ in a poor mental state ||东西~ everything was in a thorough muddle || 课堂上~ disorderly classroom

28 一团乱麻 [-團亂-] yī tuán luàn má (a-lump-messy-hemp) <idiom> a confused group, all over the place: 生活就像~. My life is all over the place. || 脑子~. My mind is all over the place.

Tips:

1 七*八*: When 七 and 八 are used in a four-character word, the word carries a connotation of 'messy, disorderly,' for example, 七上八下 (upset), 七嘴八舌 (7-mouth-8-tongue, all talking at once) as well as 乱七八糟 and 七手八脚 in this unit.

2 和谐: 和谐社会 (harmonious society) was a goal in Hu Jintao era (2002–2012), and all the high-speed trains were named 和谐号 (Héxiéhào).

Exercises:

Part I: Use correct vocabulary words and phrases to answer the questions.

A: Match up the following expressions to the appropriate column. Make sure your words can describe the situation mentioned in the column

整齐、工整、井井有条、井然有序、混乱、杂乱、零乱、乱七八糟、乱糟糟、乱成一团、利落

形容张老师家很干净	形容王老师家非常乱

B: Match the expression in the left column to the expressions in the right column to form sentences.

1	因为倒时差她生物钟	a)	紊乱
2	她现在的心情	b)	乱糟糟的
3	中国很多政府机构	c)	臃肿
4	中国经济应该	d)	井井有条
5	小王把工作安排得	e)	协调发展
6	看别人比自己有钱小王觉得	f)	心里不平衡

Part II: Read the following sentences and fill in each blank with the appropriate word or phrase from the options given.

1 七手八脚、有板有眼、衣冠楚楚

a) 小王平时做事__________, 非常认真.
b) 一些中国媒体说所谓的乐视总裁 (zǒngcái, President) 只不过是一个_________的骗子罢了.
c) 小王在办公室晕倒了, 大家____________把他送到医院.

2 乱套、错乱、忙乱

a) 小王公司的管理有问题, 所以每个人工作都很_____________.
b) 最近小王连续十天失眠 (shīmián), 好像神经都有点_____________了.
c) 小王工作和身体都出了问题, 他的生活完全_____________了.

3 均匀、平均、平衡

a) 在中国一些小城市老百姓的__________收入是两千元左右.
b) 中国大城市和小城市的经济发展非常不______________.
c) 中国各个省的自然资源分布非常不_____________.

Theme 273: Joy, sorrow 悲, 喜 (bēi, xǐ)

1 福 [-] fú (fortune) <n.> good fortune, happiness: 多子多~ the more sons/children, the more happiness || 享~ enjoy a happy life || 口/眼~ gourmet's luck/good fortune of seeing sth.

2 甜 [-] tián (sweet) <adj.> sweet: 笑得~ smile sweetly || 她的声音很~. Her voice is sweet. || 嘴~ ingratiating in speech, have a honey tongue

3 美满 [-滿] měimǎn (beautiful-fill) <adj.> happy, perfectly satisfactory: ~的生活 a happy life || 家庭~ a happy life || ~的婚姻 a happy marriage

4 甜美 [-] tiánměi (sweet-pleasant) <adj.> sweet, pleasant: ~的歌声 sweet and pleasant singing || ~的微笑 a sweet smile || 生活~ a pleasant life

5 甜蜜 [-] tiánmì (sweet-honey) <adj.> sweet (like honey), happy: 笑得很~ smile sweetly || ~的声音 a sweet voice || 感到~ feel happy/infatuated

6 幸福 [-] xìngfú (lucky-fortunate) <adj.> happy: ~的生活 happy life || 感觉 ~ feel happy || 家庭~ a happy family

7 喜庆 [-慶] xǐqìng (happy-celebration) <adj.> happy event or occasion, joyous: ~的日子 joyous days || ~的节日 a joyous holiday || 这幅画真~ this is a festive picture

8 双喜临门 [雙-臨門] shuāngxǐ línmén (double-happiness-arrive-gate) <idiom> two simultaneous happy events in the family: 春节结婚真是~啊 a spring festival wedding is truly two joyous events at once

9 舒服 [-] shūfu (stretched-clothes) <adj.> comfortable, feel well: 感到~ feel well || 心里不~ not feel good about this (feeling) || ~的衣服 comfortable clothes

10 舒适 [-適] shūshì (leisurely-comfortable) <adj.> cozy, snug: 住得~ live snugly || ~的房间 a cozy room || 飞机头等舱 (tóuděngcāng) 很~. The plane's first class is comfortable.

11 惬意 [愜-] qièyì (satisfied-will) <adj.> be pleased, be satisfied: ~地躺着 pleasantly lay || ~的样子 a pleasant way, demeanor || 他们高收入阶层日子过得很~. With a high salary, their days went very pleasantly.

12 滋润 [-潤] zīrùn (grow-moist) <adj./v.> moist, humid: 生活~ the life is comfortable || ~心灵 nourishing one's spirit || ~皮肤 moisten one's skin

13 惨 [慘] cǎn (brutal, miserable) <adj.> miserable, tragic: 死得~ a miserable death || 活得很~ a miserable life || 他过得很~, 连个稳定的工作都没有. He has such a miserable life that he doesn't have a stable job.

14 悲惨 [-慘] bēicǎn (sorrowful-miserable) <adj.> miserable: ~的生活 miserable life || ~世界 a miserable world || ~的故事 a story of misery

15 凄凉 [淒涼] qīliáng (miserable-desolate) <adj.> dreary, miserable: ~的声音 a dreary voice || 中国古人秋天看到树叶落下就感到~. In Chinese ancient times, seeing a leaf fall, would make one feel miserable. || ~地叫着 call out with a dreary voice

16 惨不忍睹 [慘---] cǎnbùrěndǔ (miserable-not-endure-seen) <idiom> a spectacle too horrible to endure, a tragic sight: ~的样子 a tragic sight/appearance || 车祸现场~. The site of the car accent was unbearable tragic.

17 倾家荡产 [傾-蕩產] qīngjiā dàngchǎn (empty-property-exhaust-property) <idiom> lose a family fortune, be reduced to poverty: 弄得~ cause the lose of a fortune || 他的工厂因为造假被罚得~. Because his factory made counterfeit goods, he was fined into poverty.

18 水深火热 [---熱] shuǐshēn huǒrè (water-deep-fire-hot) <idiom> the water is deep and fire is hot (harsh conditions): 生活在~之中 live in harsh conditions

19 可怜 [-憐] kělián (worth-pity) <adj.> pitiful, pathetic: ~的孩子 poor child || 那场演唱会的观众少得~. It was pitiful how few people attended the concert. || 她眼泪汪汪的让人~. Her eyes brimming with tears lead everyone to feel a sense of pity.

20 苦 [-] kǔ (bitter) <adj.> bitter, hardship, pain: 吃/受~ bear hardships || 生活~ a bitter life || 我们的~日子快要到头了. Our bitter days are almost over.

21 艰苦 [艱-] jiānkǔ (difficult-bitter) <adj.> arduous, difficult: ~的环境 a difficult environment || ~的劳动 arduous/taxing work || ~奋斗 to struggle to overcome difficulties

22 辛苦 [-] xīnkǔ (toil-bitter) <adj./ v.> work to the point of bitterness: 他早上六点就得离开家去上班很~. It's bitter that he has to leave at 6:00 am to go work. || 工作~ work is hard || ~的生活 a bitter life

Tips:

1 福: 福 was considered to be a fortune blessed by god, so it has a radical '礻' which means 'god.' In Chinese folk art, 福 is sometimes represented by a bat (蝙蝠, biānfú), which might be scary to many people but contains an identical sound 'fú.'

2 喜: 喜 means 'happy' which is sometimes associated with marriage. For example, 大喜 and 喜事 can both mean 'a happy thing' and 'a happy marriage.' When a marriage is celebrated, the character 喜 is written as 囍 since a marriage is about two people and two families. 有喜了means 'a woman is pregnant.'

3 双喜临门: 双喜临门 (two simultaneous happy events in the family) is auspicious, and understandably apt to produce similar phrases such as 三喜临门, 四喜临门 or even more, but one can never say 单喜临门

4 苦: 苦 (kǔ) originally means 'a bitter plant,' which is probably sow thistle (sonchus oleraceus). The lead author of this book had the experience of eating sow thistle as his staple in the 1970s when China was poor and many rural people did not have enough to eat.

5 同甘共苦: 同甘共苦 (tónggān gòngkǔ, to share weal and woe) should be a virtue, but many people think the Chinese can 共苦 but cannot 同甘 because they would support each other through hardships but will likely break up after they make their fortunes. However, the Americans can 同甘 but not 共苦 since they are likely to break up during hardships.

Exercises:

Part I: Match up the following expressions to the appropriate column. Make sure your words can describe the situation mentioned in the column.

a) 上班特别辛苦　b) 工资少得可怜　c) 做生意赔的倾家荡产
d) 日子过得很滋润　e) 最近双喜临门　f) 婚姻美满
g) 家庭幸福　h) 生活惬意舒适

形容小高生活很幸福	形容小李生活很不幸

Part II: Read the following sentences and fill in each blank with the appropriate word or phrase from the options given.

1 惨不忍睹、水深火热、可怜

a) 中东一些地区常年战争, 老百姓生活在________之中.
b) 遭受战争后的城市真是____________.
c) 战争过后, 最_________的是失去父母的孩子们.

2 艰苦、辛苦、受了很多苦

a) 小王童年时代母亲就去世了, 他_________.
b) ________的生活使小王的性格坚强, 非常独立.
c) 现在即使小王工作非常________, 但是他从来不抱怨 (bàoyuàn, complain).

3 享清福、舒服、喜庆

a) 小高父母都退休了, 目前在家_________.
b) 小高妈妈不喜欢生活得太________, 她觉得这样人容易老得很快.
c) 小高妈妈开了一个茶馆, 里面布置 (bùzhì, arrange) 得非常_____________.

Part III: Multiple Choice. Make sure to choose the most appropriate answer.

1 'Two simultaneous happy events in the family'最好的中文翻译是:
A. 两件好事 B. 单喜临门 C. 双喜临门

2 小王的太太"有喜了," 意思是
A. 小王的太太很高兴 B. 小王的太太怀孕了 C. 小王跟太太同甘共苦

Theme 274: Rich, poor 贫, 富 (pín, fù)

1 贫富 [貧-] pínfù (poor-rich) <bf.> wealthy and poverty: ~差距 wealth-poverty gap
2 富 [-] fù (abundant) <adj.> wealth: ~人 a wealth person || ~翁/婆 a wealthy old man/woman || ~爸爸 a wealthy father || ~二代 wealthy second generation (a spoiled child)
3 富有 [-] fùyǒu (abundant-rich) <adj.> rich, full of: ~的村庄a wealthy village || ~的家庭 a wealthy family || 人民~ people are wealthy
4 富裕 [-] fùyù (abundant-plentiful) <adj.> prosperous, well-to-do: ~的家庭 a well-to-do family || 生活~ a prosperous life
5 雄厚 [-] xiónghòu (powerful-rich) <adj.> rich, ample: 力量/实力~ ample strength || 资金~ ample resources || ~的基础 a solid foundation

6 有钱 [-錢] yǒuqián (have-money) <v.> have money: ~人 a rich person
7 宽裕 [寬-] kuānyù (spacious-plentiful) <adj.> well to do, comfortably off: 生活~ a comfortable life || 手头 ~ quite well off at the moment || 时间~ ample time
8 绰绰有余 [綽綽-餘] chuòchuò yǒuyú (ample-*reduplication*-have-surplus) <idiom> enough and to spare, more than sufficient: 时间~ more than enough time || 公司的科研费用~. The company has more than enough research funds.
9 温饱 [溫飽] wēnbǎo (warm-full) <adj.> have enough food and warm clothes, adequately provided: ~ 问题 problem of food and clothing, problem of feeding people || 维持~ maintain warmth and a full stomach
10 小康 [-] xiǎokāng (small-abundant) <adj.> well-off, moderately affluent: ~生活 no-frills life || ~社会society in which the material needs of most citizens are adequately met, a well-off society

11 穷 [窮] qióng (limited) <adj.> poor: ~人 a poor person || ~孩子a poor child || ~爸爸 a poor dad || ~光蛋 poor man
12 贫困 [貧-] pínkùn (impoverished-stranded) <adj.> impoverished, poverty: 生活~ an impoverished life || ~家庭 an impoverished household || ~地区 an impoverished area
13 寒酸 [-] hánsuān (cold-poor) <adj.> shabby and miserable: 穿得~ the clothes are shabby || 外表~ a shabby appearance || ~的生活 live shabbily
14 贫寒 [貧-] pínhán (impoverished-poor) <adj.> poor, poverty-stricken: 家境~ the family financial situation is in a poor state || 出身~ come from a poor family || ~人家 impoverished family
15 贫穷 [貧窮] pínqióng (impoverished-limited) <adj.> poor, impoverished: 生活~ an impoverished life || ~家庭 an impoverished family || 摆脱~ shake off poverty
16 穷苦 [窮-] qióngkǔ (poor-suffering) <adj.> impoverished, destitute: ~人家 a poverty -stricken family || 生活~ life is impoverished
17 艰苦 [艱-] jiānkǔ (arduous-suffering) <adj.> arduous, difficult: ~的生活 a hard life || ~的年代 a hard age || 条件~ harsh conditions
18 艰难 [艱難] jiānnán (arduous-hard) <adj.> difficult, hard: 生活~ a difficult life || 日子~ difficult days || 处境~ the situation is difficult. || 我们做这个决定很~. We have a tough time making this decision.

Tips:

1 有: The upper left part of 有 is 又, meaning 'hand.' The lower part is 月, meaning 'meat.' The whole character represents 'a hand with meat,' meaning 'rich.' In ancient times, if one could easily have meats to eat, he must be rich. 有 keeps its original meaning in 富.
2 贫, 穷, 困, 苦: All mean 'poor' but their ability to combine them is decreasing and the direction of combination is from left to right, without any exception. For example, 贫穷, 贫困, 贫苦, 穷困, 穷苦, 困苦.
3 *Rich Dad Poor Dad*: The 1997 book by Robert Kiyosaki and Sharon Lechter is translated into Chinese as 富爸爸穷爸爸, which impacted Chinese society just as much as it did American society.
4 艰苦奋斗: 艰苦奋斗 (jiānkǔ fèndòu, to struggle arduously) was, and hopefully still is one of the most cherished spirits and a strong work ethic of the Chinese.

5 从贫困到温饱到小康: It means 'proceed from being poor to adequately fed and clad then to fairly well-off) was one of the Chinese government's great achievements in the first 60 years since its establishment, as reported by the Chinese state news agency, Xinhua News Agency in September 2009.

Exercises:

Part I: Use correct vocabulary words and phrases to answer the questions.

A: Match up the following expressions to the appropriate column. Make sure your words can describe the situation mentioned in the column.

衣着寒酸　家境贫寒　生活贫穷　住在贫困山区　穷光蛋　生活艰苦
日子艰难　温饱绰绰有余　手头宽裕　有钱人 富二代

描述农民老张家很穷	描述农民老李家很富有

B: Match the expression in the left column to with the expressions in the right column to form sentences

1	中国发展高科技产业	a)	生活贫困
2	摆脱	b)	贫困的生活状态
3	公司的科研经费	c)	温饱水平
4	生活维持	d)	非常寒酸
5	山区人民	e)	资金雄厚
6	老张家里	f)	绰绰有余

Part II: Multiple Choice. Make sure to use the most appropriate answer.

1 下面哪一组字有相同的意思

A. 贫、富、困、苦　B. 贫、穷、困、苦　C. 贫、穷、困、难

2 Proceed from being poor to adequately fed and clad then to fairly well-off 的中文意思是

A. 从贫困到温饱到小康　B. 从贫困到富裕　C. 从贫困到温饱

3 下面哪一个说法是对的

A. 穷光蛋means 'a poor egg'
B. 绰绰有余means 'extra stuff'
C. 手头宽裕 means 'well off at the moment'

Theme 275: Fixed, flexible 定, 通 (dìng, tōng)

1 固定 [-] gùdìng (firm-fixed) <adj.> fixed, regular: ~的时间 fixed time || ~的地点 fixed place || ~的价格 fixed price

2 稳 [穩] wěn (stable) <adj.> settled, steady: 地位不~ an unstable position || 站得~ stand on stable ground || 价格不~. The price is not stable.
3 稳定 [穩-] wěndìng (stable-fixed) <adj.> stable, steady: ~的收入a steady income || 国家 ~ a stable nation || 家庭~ a stable home || 病情~. The patient's condition is stable.
4 稳步 [穩-] wěnbù (steady-step) <adj.> steadily, a steady pace: ~增长 increase at a steady pace (price) || ~发展 expand at a steady pace || ~前进 advance at a steady pace
5 静止 [靜-] jìngzhǐ (quiet-stop) <adj.> static, motionless: ~的物体 an unmovable option || ~不动 unmovable
6 一成不变 [---變] yīchéng bùbiàn (once-formed-never-change) <idiom> nothing much changes, always the same: ~的想法 a fixed idea || ~的模式 an unchangeable style || 事情不是~的, 所以我们得有发展的眼光. Things are not fixed, so we need to develop a vision for the future.
7 灵活 [靈-] línghuó (clever-alive) <adj.> flexible, nimble: 价格~ flexible pricing || ~的方法 flexible methods || ~运用 flexible application || 头脑~. His mind is very nimble.
8 变通 [變-] biàntong (change-pass through) <adj./v./ adv.> pragmatic, flexible: ~的办法accomodation/ adjustment || ~处理 dispose alternatively || 根据不同的情况~ make appropriate adjustments in the light of specific conditions
9 能屈能伸 [-] néngqū néngshēn (able to-bend-able to-stretch) <idiom> can bow and submit, or can stand tall, can lead or follow): 大丈夫~. A leader can submit or stand tall as required. || 他做人~. He is a person who can lead or follow when necessary.
10 能上能下 [-] néngshàng néngxià (able to-go up-able to-go down) <idiom> able to work either at the top or at the grassroots: 干部 (gànbù) 要~. The government officials should be able to work at a high administrative level or at the most basic position.

Tips:

1 变: It means 'transform, change.' Sun Wukong (孙悟空, the Monkey King) in the *Journey to the West* knows 72 transformations (七十二变) and is considered one of the mightiest warriors. There is a saying '女大十八变' (literally girl-grow up-18-changes), which means 'there is no telling what a girl will look like when she grows up' and is usually followed by 越变越好看 in the positive and 越变越难看 in the negative.
2 稳定: It means 'stable, stability,' which has been the Chinese government's priority since the Chinese economic reforms started in late 1978.

Exercises:

Part I: Match up the following expressions to the column. Make sure your words can express the situation mentioned in the column.

能屈能伸　能上能下　灵活变通　思维固定　事业上追求稳步发展
领导方式一成不变　家庭稳定

请用褒义 (postitive connotation) 词或者句子形容小王具有领导才能

Part II: Translate the following sentences into Chinese or English.

1 女大十八变, 越变越好看.
2 大丈夫能屈能伸.
3 'Stability' has been the Chinese government's priority since the Chinese economic reforms started in 1978.
4 The government official can work at a high administrative level or at the most basic position.

Theme 276: Adverbs, degree (mid-high and lower) 程度副词 (chéngdù fùcí)

1 稍 [-] shāo (tip, slightly) <adv> a little, a bit: ~大一点 make it a little bit larger || ~迟了些 be a little bit late || ~好一点 a little bit better
2 稍微 [-] shāowēi (slightly-tiny) <adv.> a little bit: ~暖和些 a little bit warm || 他~不注意就摔了一个跟头. He wasn't paying attention and fell. || ~慢点 a little bit slower
3 稍加 [-] shāojiā (slightly-impose) <adv.> a slight increase, Note: this word requires disyllabic words as the object.: ~注意 pay a little more attention || ~变化 a slight increase || ~练习 practice a little more
4 略 [-] luè (slightly, briefly) <adv.> slightly, a little bit: ~慢 a little slow || ~粗 a little blunt/careless || ~作改变 change slightly
5 不大 [-] búdà (not-very) <adv.> not very, not often: ~喜欢 not like very much || ~热 not very hot || ~关心 not be too concerned || ~去公园 not go to the park very often
6 不太 [-] bútài (not-too) <adv.> not very: ~远 not very far || ~长 not very long || ~想他 not really miss him
7 轻度 [輕-] qīngdù (light-degree) <n.> mild (symptoms etc.): ~发热 have a mild fever || ~污染 little pollution || ~失眠 have slight symptoms of insomnia
8 有一些 [-] yǒu yī xiē (have-some) <adv.> somewhat, rather: ~累 a little tired || ~渴 a little thirsty || ~不安 a little disturbed
9 不怎么 [--麼] bù zěnme (not-very) <adv.> not very, not particularly: ~好 not very good || ~重要 not very important || ~象 not very similar
10 有一点儿 [--點兒] yǒu yīdiǎnr (have-a-little) <adv.> a little: ~重 a little heavy || ~饿 a little hungry || ~着急 a little urgent
11 多多少少 [-] duōduō shǎoshǎo (*reduplication of* more-less) <adv.> to some extent, more or less: ~有一些联系. There is a connection to some extent. || ~有点不好意思 a little embarrassed || 请你~借我一点儿钱. I'm asking to you more or less lend me some money.
12 这么 [這麼] zhème (this-much) <adv.> so much, this much: ~高 so high || ~严重 so serious || ~冷 so cold

13 比较 [-較] bǐjiào (compare-to match) <adv.> relatively: ~高 comparatively high || ~认真 comparatively careful || ~贵 relatively expensive

14 更 [-] gèng (more) <adv.> more, even more: ~多 more || ~自由 more freedom || ~好 better

15 更加 [-] gèngjiā (even-more) <adv.> more, even more: ~迅速 even more fast || ~积极 be more positive || ~深刻 deeper (meaning)

16 越 [-] yuè (more and more) <adv.> more (often used to communicate gradual,progressive increases or decreases): ~看~清楚 see clearer || ~多~好 the more the better || ~走~远 walk further and further

17 进而 [進-] jìn'ér (proceed-and) <adv.> and then (what follows next): 邓小平说让一部分人先富起来, ~帮助其他人达到共同富裕. Deng Xiaoping said to allow a few people gain wealth first, and then let the wealthy help others accumulate wealth.

18 进一步 [進--] jìnyībù (further-one-step) <adv.> further, to move forward one step further.: ~说明 explain further || ~发展 expand further || ~学习 study further

19 较 [較] jiào (to match) <adv.> especially: ~重 especially heavy || ~强 especially strong || 病情~严重. The condition is especially serious.

20 挺 [-] tǐng (outstanding, very) <adv.> very, quite: ~贵 so expensive || ~舒服 so comfortable || ~喜欢 really like

21 多 [-] duō (many, much) <adv.> how (many), more: ~好how great it is || ~大 how big it is || ~漂亮 how beautiful it is

22 好 [-] hǎo (good, very) <adv.> good, very: ~高 very tall || ~大 very big || ~干净 very clean

Tips:

1 稍, 略, 较, 挺: These are words indicating a degree that is not very high. 稍 originally means 'tip of a standing grain' from which evolved meanings such as 'tip, small, a little, slightly.' 略 originally means 'to administer a territory (with boundaries)' from which evolved meanings such as 'outline, brief, slightly.' 稍 and 略 both indicate a very small degree, for example, '他比我稍/略高一点儿' means 'he is slightly higher than me.' 较 originally means 'a cart's axle' from which evolved meanings such as 'to match, to compare, comparatively.' 挺 originally means 'to straighten' from which evolved meanings such as 'to stick out, outstanding, rather.' 较 indicates a middle or middle-high degree, and 挺 a rather high degree.

2 一点儿 vs. 有一点儿: 一点儿 means 'a bit,' and it is usually used after an adjective to indicate a small degree. For example, '这件衣服大一点儿 (compared with the other piece of clothes)' means 'This piece of clothes is slightly bigger.' 有一点儿 means 'a bit' but in a negative sense. For example, '这件衣服有一点儿大' means 'This piece of clothes is slightly bigger (and I do not like it.)'

3 Typical written and typical colloquial words in this unit.

   a Written words: 略, 稍加, 进而

   b Colloquial words: 较, 挺, 多, 好, 不大, 这么, 不怎么, 多多少少

Exercises:

Part I: Match up the following expressions to the appropriate column. Make sure all words with similar meanings are in one column.

不算远　　不太远　　稍加注意　　有一些累　　挺好　　很好

1.不大远
2.稍微注意一下儿
3.有一点儿累
4.较好

Part II: Read the following sentences and fill in each blank with the appropriate word or phrase from the options given.

1 更加、进而、进一步

a) 最近中国电视因为物美价廉 (wùměi jiàlián, cheap and good) 在美国________畅销 (chàngxiāo, sell fast) 了.
b) 美国总统特朗普表示要__________改善美国的投资环境, 吸引中国商人来美投资.
c) 邓小平说让一部分人先富起来, __________帮助其他人达到共同富裕.

2 比较、轻度、多多少少

a) 刘老师在美国生活多年了, 但还是____________喜欢中国菜.
b) 刘老师平时____________也做一些美国菜.
c) 刘老师住在洛杉矶, 那儿的空气也有一些____________污染.

3 一点儿、有点儿、挺、稍

a) 刘老师__________喜欢她的学生们, 虽然他们还_________不成熟 (chéngshú, mature), 但是都聪明上进 (shàngjìn, upward).
b) 刘老师喜欢周末的时候写____________书法. 她练习书法很多年了, 只要_____________花一点儿时间就可以写得非常好.

Theme 277: Adverbs, degree (very high and up) 程度副词 (chéngdù fùcí)

1 很 [-] hěn (very) <adv.> very: ~深 very deep || ~轻 very light || ~重要 very important
2 太 [-] tài (way too) <adv.> too, so: ~快 so fast || ~深 so deep || ~自私 so selfish
3 非常 [-] fēicháng (un-normal) <adv.> very much: ~多 so many || ~麻烦 such a hassle || ~干净 so clean
4 十分 [-] shífēn (10–1/10) <adv.> to the greatest extent: ~冷 freezing (extremely cold) || ~聪明 genius (extremely smart) || ~好听 sounds amazing (sounds extremely good)
5 特别 [-别] tèbié (particular-different) <adv.> particular, especially: ~热 especially hot || ~忙 especially busy || ~喜欢 especially like

6 万分 [萬-] wànfēn (10, 000–1/10) <adv.> very much: 惊喜~ extremely shocked || 心疼~ extremely heart (emotionally) || ~危险 extremely dangerous
7 要命 [-] yàomìng (take-life) <v.> very: 疼得~ painful to death || 气得~ be angered to the point of wanting to claim a life || 臭得~ stench strong enough to take a life
8 要死 [-] yàosǐ (will-die) <v.> extremely, awfully: 怕得~ scared to death || 烦得~ annoyed to death || 口渴得~ thirsty (to death)
9 尤其 [-] yóuqí (outstanding-*suffix*) <adv.> especially, particularly: ~重要 especially important || ~需要 to especially need || ~热心especially warmhearted
10 大加 [-] dàjiā (greatly-impose) <bf.> to a large extent, extremely: ~夸奖 (kuājiǎng) extremely praise sb. || ~责备 (zébèi) blame to a large extent
11 大大 [-] dàdà (greatly-*reduplication*) <adv.> greatly, largely: ~减少 largely decrease || ~不同 large difference || ~提高了效率 (xiàolǜ) a large increase in efficiency
12 狠狠 [-] hěnhěn (fiercely-*reduplication*) <adv.> ruthlessly, furiously: ~地批评 (pīpíng) ruthlessly criticize || ~地打 ruthlessly hit || ~地踩了一脚 to ruthlessly stomp
13 紧紧 [緊緊] jǐnjǐn (tensely-*reduplication*) <adv.> closely, firmly: ~抓住 firmly grasp || ~拥抱 (yōngbào) firmly hug || ~贴在一起 stick together
14 深深 [-] shēnshēn (deep-*reduplication*) <adv.> deep: ~吸了一口气 take a deep breath || ~感谢他 deeply thank him || ~相信 deeply believe
15 远远 [遠遠] yuǎnyuǎn (distant-*reduplication*) <adv.> to a large extent: ~不够 far not enough || ~超过 far beyond || ~多于她 far more than her
16 完全 [-] wánquán (complete-whole) <adv.> completely: ~相同 completely similar || ~正确 completely correct || ~同意 completely agree
17 光 [-] guāng (bare) <adv.> only: ~靠父母 entirely rely on parents || 结婚的车队~宝马就有六十六辆. In the wedding procession, there were 66 BMWs (not counting any other types of cars).
18 全 [-] quán (whole) <adv.> whole: ~国/世界 whole nation/world || ~家 whole family || ~对 all correct
19 全然 [-] quánrán (whole-*suffix*) <adv.> entirely: ~无关 completely unconnected || ~不知 to know nothing (about) || ~一样 completely different
20 彻底 [徹-] chèdǐ (penetrate-bottom) <adj.> thorough, complete: ~失败 lose everything || ~解决 completely resolve || ~消灭 completely destroy
21 根本 [-] gēnběn (secondary root-primary root) <adv.> fundamentally, absolutely: ~不可能 absolutely not || ~没有去 absolutely didn't go || ~没想到 absolutely didn't think of
22 几乎 [幾-] jīhū (almost-*suffix*) <adv.> almost: ~完全相同 almost completely identical || ~都来了 almost all have come || ~天天练习 almost practice everyday
23 差一点儿 [--點兒] (off-a bit) chà yīdiǎnr <adv.> almost, nearly: ~哭了 nearly cried || ~忘了 nearly forgot || ~跳起来 nearly jumped
24 甚至 [-] shènzhì (even-arrive at) <adv.> to the extent that: 我以前犯过错误~是严重的错误. In the past, I took every mistake seriously.
25 极 [極] jí extremely (extreme) <adv.> extremely: ~好 extremely good || ~大 extremely big || 她对人~冷淡. She's extremely cold to others.

26 极其 [極其] jíqí (extreme-*intensifier*) <adv.> extremely, especially: ~复杂 extremely complicated || ~普遍 extremely wide-spread || ~认真extremely hardworking

27 极度 [極-] jídù (extreme-degree) <adv.> extremely: ~神秘 very mysterious || ~困难 extremely hard || ~紧张 extremely nervous

28 极了 [極-] jíle (extreme-*suffix*) <adv.> extremely: 累~ extremely tired || 高兴~ extremely happy || 安静~ extremely quiet

29 极为 [極爲] jíwéi (extreme-be) <adv.> most, extremely: ~关心 extremely care about || ~重要 extremely important || ~重视extremely emphasize

30 最 [-] zuì (most) <adv.> most: ~长 the longest || ~浅 the shallowest || 邮递员的工作~轻松. Post officers have the most relaxed work.

31 最好 [-] zuìhǎo (most-good) <adv.> the best: ~的画 the best drawing || ~的办法 the best solution || 你~问清楚. You'd better clarify.

32 无比 [無-] wúbǐ (no-comparison) <adv.> incomparable: ~丰富 incomparably rich/abundant || ~复杂 incomparable complicated || ~喜欢 like more than anything

33 过度 [過-] guòdù (over-limit) <adv.> excessively, over: ~学习 excessively study || ~疲劳 (píláo) feel excessively tired || ~使用use excessively

34 过分 [過-] guòfèn (over-propriety) <adv.> excessively, undue: 他~关心别人的隐私 (yǐnsī). He excessively considers the privacy of others. || ~要求demandingly, ask for too much || ~强调 excessively emphasizes

35 过于 [過於] guòyú (over-than) <adv.> too, excessively: ~安静 too quiet || ~直接too straightforward || ~严格too strict

36 够 [夠] gòu (enough) <adv./adj.> enough, sufficient: ~多了 more than enough || ~累的 adequately tired || ~忙的 adequately busy

37 再 [-] zài (again) <adv.> again, once more: 方法不对时间~多也没用. It will not work if the approach is wrong, no matter how much time you have. || 有你的信任工作~累我也不抱怨. I will not complain about the amount of work as long as you have confidence in me.

38 不得了 [-] bùdéliǎo (not-right) <adv.> extremely (used after an adjective and introduced by得): 急得~ be desperately urgent || 高兴得~ be extremely happy || ~了！ 市长被抓走了. It's a disaster! The mayor has been taken.

39 可 [-] kě (can) <adv.> very, can: 北京~玩的地方~不少. There are quite a few places worth visiting in Beijing. || ~难呢 very hard || ~研究的东西 be worth researching

Tips:

1 要命 vs. 要死: Both mean 'awfully' and are used after an adjective, for example, '冷得要命/要死.' Their differences include, 1) 要死 is slightly more awful than 要命, 2) you can say '真要命, . . .' which means 'it's too awful that. . .,' but you cannot say '真要死, . . .'

2 极了 and 不得了 appear after the adjective or adverb, for example '高兴极了' and '高兴得不得了.' There is a '得' between the preceding adjective and 不得了.

3 极为 vs. 极度: Both mean 'extremely' and require disyllabic words as the object. Their differences include, 1) 极为 can modify verbs but 极度 usually does not, 2) 极度 is closer to 'excessively' and 极为 'extremely.'

4 过度 vs. 过分: Both mean 'extremely,' but 过度 is more objective and measureable, but 过分 is more subjective.
5 Words which require a disyllabic word as the object: 大加, 极度, 极为.
6 Typical written and typical colloquial words in this unit.

a) Written words: 大加, 全然, 几乎, 极其, 极为, 无比, 过于
b) Colloquial words: 可, 光, 够, 要命, 要死, 极了, 不得了

Exercises:

Part I: Match up the following expressions to the appropriate column. Make sure all words with similar meanings are in one column.

极其 极为 无比 过于紧张 过分紧张 几乎 特别好
非常好 累得要死 累得不得了 全然相同

1. 极度
2. 过度紧张
3. 差一点儿
4. 十分好
5. 累得要命
6. 完全相同

Part II: Read the following sentences and fill in each blank with the appropriate word or phrase from the options given.

1 紧紧、狠狠、远远、深深

a) 40年前美国的经济实力______________超过中国.
b) 在发展高科技方面, 中国正在______________追赶美国.
c) 美国政府表示要_______________打击恐怖主义 (kǒngbù zhǔyì, terrorism).
d) 美国______________相信自由市场是经济发展的动力.

2 根本、几乎、彻底

a) 西欧国家的人__________都会说一点儿英语.
b) 西欧国家__________没有想到难民会对国家安全带来如此大的影响.
c) 有人认为一百年以后西欧国家会__________穆斯林 (Muslim) 化.

3 光、最、够、再、可

a) 北京__________去的地方非常多, _____________长城就___________你去一天的.
b) 北京故宫是北京______________大的建筑群, 有些人去过了还会_____________去.

Theme 278: Adverbs, scope 范围副词 (fànwéi fùcí)

1 光 [-] guāng (light, bare, only) <adv.> only: ~房租就得三千块钱. The price of rent alone is $3,000. || ~想不做 completely do not want to. . . || ~喝酒不吃菜 only drink beer and not eat food

2 仅 [僅] jǐn (only) <adv.> barely, only, merely: 年~十二岁 only 12 years old || 香蕉~三元一斤 bananas are only 3 yuan for a half kilogram. || ~两小时就做完了 It took just two hours to finish the work.

3 仅仅 [僅僅] jǐnjǐn (only-*reduplication*) <adv.> only, merely: ~见过四次 have only seen four times || ~三个月就分手了 only three months before breaking up || ~住了两天院 only stay in the hospital for two days

4 单单 [單單] dāndān (single-*reduplication*) <adv.> only, alone: ~留下他们两个人 only the two of them were left behind || 别人都不去为什么~让我一个人去? Other people aren't going, why would I be allowed to go on my own?

5 就 [-] jiù (near, just) <adv.> at once, just: ~五个人去了. Just five people went. || ~他通过了考试. He just (barely) passed the test.

6 只 [-] zhǐ (only) <adv.> only: ~买了两斤 only bought a kilogram (two half kilograms) || ~住了三晚 only staying three nights || ~看了一本小说 to have only read one fiction novel.

7 只有 [-] zhǐyǒu (only-have) <adv.> only have: ~ 一个目的 only have one goal || ~五家咖啡店 there are only five cafes || ~三个小时 only have three hours

8 唯独 [-獨] wéidú (alone-single) <adv.> only, all except: 他家别的没有~书多. His home had nothing except for a single book. || 兄弟几个~他没上大学. All of his brothers went to college except for him.

9 只是 [-] zhǐshì (only-be) <adv.> merely, only: ~随便看看 just freely look || ~笑笑 just a laugh || ~个别人 just one other person

10 只不过 [--過] zhǐbuguò (only-but) <adv.> not more than: ~用了三年 only use for three years || ~几分钟 not need more than a few minutes || ~随便说说. It's nothing more than idle talk.

11 起码 [-碼] qǐmǎ (lift-makeweight) <adv.> at the minimum, at the very least: ~两年 at least two years || ~八折 at least 20% off || ~得二十块 need at least 20 bucks

12 至少 [-] zhìshǎo (most-less) <adv.> at (the) least: ~要一天 at least one day || ~得五个人 at least need five people || ~对了一半 have at least one half correct

13 顶多 [頂-] dǐngduō (highest-more) <adv.> at the most, at best: ~十五六岁 no more than 15 or 16 years old || ~等半个小时 wait half an hour at most || ~一百米 a hundred meters at most

14 最多 [-] zuìduō (most-more) <adv.> the most: 在世界上中国人口~. Chinese people represent the largest population in the world. || 分布~ Dispersed the most widely || 吃得~ Eat the most

15 一半 [-] yībàn (one-half) <num.> one half: 占人口~ represent one half || ~员工都辞职 (cízhí) 了. Half of the employees resigned. || 便宜~ half price

16 大多 [-] dàduō (more than-majority) <adv.> for the most part: ~来自香港 the majority is from Hong Kong || ~是名牌. The majority are famous brands. || ~比较贵. Many are especially expensive.

17 大都 [-] dàdōu (majority-all) <adv.> for the most part: ~自己挣钱 for the most part to make one's own living || 朋友见面~在晚上吃饭的时候. Friends

see each other primarily in the evening for dinner. || ~是青年 majority of young people

18 基本上 [-] jīběnshang (basic – *wise*) <adv.> basically, on the whole: ~同意了 mostly agree || ~完成了 mostly completed || ~都忘记了 mostly forgotten

19 全都 [-] quándōu (complete-all) <adv.> all, completely: 同事~走了. The workers all left. || 头发~白了. The hair is completely white. || 衣服~洗了. The clothes were all washed.

20 统统 [統統] tǒngtǒng (all-all) <adv.> totally: ~忘了 totally forgot || ~带走 to take away completely || ~有问题 to have many questions

21 无不 [無-] wúbù (none-not) <adv.> all without exception: ~惊慌 (jīnghuāng) in complete panic || 听了这个故事, 在场的人~感动. After hearing this story, all people in attendance were moved. || ~同意 unanimously agree.

22 一律 [-] yīlǜ (same-rule) <adv.> same, uniformly: ~半价 all half price || ~免费 all free || ~欢迎 all are welcome

23 都 [-] dōu (all) <adv.> all: 他们~是医生. They are all doctors. || 两次~坐飞机 take an airplane both times

24 不光 [-] bùguāng (not-only) <adv.> not-only: ~她, 别的孩子也喜欢画画. Not only her, other children also like to draw. || ~年轻人, 老年人也喜欢玩手机. Not only young people, old people also like to use mobile devices. || ~小孩子, 大人也很好奇. Not only little children, old people were also curious.

25 不仅 [-僅] bùjǐn (not-just) <adv.> not only (this one), not just . . . but also: ~我知道, 别人也知道. Not only do I know, but others know as well. || 她学到的~是知识, 还有人生的经验. She has not only acquired knowledge through study, but also life experience.

26 也 [-] yě (also) <adv.> also: 他~来了. He also came. || 他昨天~来了. He also came yesterday. || 我~去. I'm also going.

Tips:

1 Reduplication and negation of some words which all mean 'only':

Word / grammar	仅	单	独	光	只
reduplication	仅仅	单单	独独	光光	*只只
negation	不仅	不单	不独	不光	不只

2 只 (simplified): 只, 隻, 衹 (all traditional). The simplified character 只 corresponds to three traditional characters, namely 只, 隻 and 衹. The traditional 只 is pronounced as zhǐ, meaning 'only, just,' 隻 as zhī, meaning 'measure word for birds, boats etc.,' and 衹 as zhǐ which is an ancient form of 只 but still used in some occasions.

3 Typical written and typical colloquial words in this unit.

a Written words: 无不
b Colloquial words: 光, 大都, 统统

Exercises:

Part I:

A: Match up the following expressions to the appropriate column. Make sure all words with similar meanings are in one column.

无不　统统　一律　不光　起码　顶多　大都　基本上　只有　只是

1. 全都	
2. 至少	
3. 不仅	
4. 最多	
5. 大多	
6. 单单	

Theme 279: Adverbs, manner 方式副词 (fāngshì fùcí)

1 共同 [-] gòngtóng (together-same) <adv./ adj.> common, joint, together: ~学习 study together || ~财产 (cáichǎn) common property || ~目标 common goals

2 联合 [聯-] liánhé (unite-combine) <adv.> combine, unite: ~举办 jointly organize or hold || ~调查 united investigation || ~声明 joint statement

3 双双 [雙雙] shuāngshuāng (pair-*reduplication*) <adv.> in pairs, both: ~离开 both left || ~失业 both lost their job || 夫妻~获奖. Husband and wife both won a prize.

4 一齐 [-齊] yīqí (all-same) <adv.> together: ~喊 call together || ~举起来 raise together || ~动手 take action together

5 同 [-] tóng (converge, same, together) <adv.> together: ~去 go together || ~走 walk together || ~生死live and die together

6 一同 [-] yītóng (all-together) <adv.> together, at the same time: ~吃饭 eat at the same time || ~出门 leave at the same time || ~起床 get up together

7 一起 [-] yīqǐ (all-start) <adv.> together: ~唱 sing together || ~吃 eat together || 坐在~ sit together

8 一块儿 [-塊兒] yīkuàir (one-piece) <adv.> together: ~走 go together || ~看电影 watch a movie together || ~旅游 travel together

9 互相 [-] hùxiāng (mutual-each other) <adv.> mutually: ~帮助 mutually help || ~照顾 (zhàogù) mutually take care of || ~了解 mutual understanding

10 分别 [-別] fēnbié (divide-differentiate) <adv.> part or leave each other: ~考试 test separately || ~谈话 discuss separately || ~离开 leave separately

11 各自 [-] gèzì (each-oneself) <adv.> each, respective: ~回家 each return home || ~练习 each practice || 夫妻两人~做饭 for husband and wife each to prepared a meal

12 各 [-] gè (each, every) <adv.> every, each: ~跑五百米 each ran 500 meters || ~有不同 each one is different || ~出二十块钱 each pay 20 bucks

13 单独 [單獨] dāndú (single-alone) <adv.> alone, by oneself: 我们需要~谈一谈. We need to discuss this separately. || ~坐在一边 sit separately on the side || 她喜欢~行动. She likes solo activities.

14 独自 [獨-] dúzì (alone-oneself) <adv.> alone, by oneself: ~出门 leave alone || ~去玩 go play alone || ~生活 live alone

15 亲耳 [親-] qīn'ěr (with one's own-ear) <adv.> with one's own ears: ~听见/到 heard with one's own ears

16 亲眼 [親-] qīnyǎn (with one's own-eye) <adv.> with one's own eyes: ~看见/到 see, saw it with one's own eyes

17 亲自 [親-] qīnzì (in person-oneself) <adv.> personally: ~动手 personally do || ~参加 participate in personally || ~做饭 personally make food

18 亲口 [親-] qīnkǒu (with one's own-mouth) <adv.> (say sth.) personally: ~答应 personally answer, reply || ~尝一尝 personally try || ~说出来 personally say

19 亲手 [親-] qīnshǒu (with one's own-hand) <adv.> with one's own hands, personally take care of: ~做饭 personally made food || ~检查 (jiǎnchá) personally inspect

20 另 [-] lìng (to separate, separately, other) <adv.> other, separate: ~买 buy an additional one || ~作打算 (dǎsuàn) think another way || ~想办法 think of another solution

21 混 [-] hùn (torrent, muddy, mix) <adv.> mix, mingle: ~在一起 mix things up || 双方~战 two sides engaged in chaotic warfare

22 直 [-] zhí (straight) <adv.> straight, direct: ~朝前开 drive directly forward || ~向大门冲去 rush directly to the door || 由两千人~增到三千人 from 2,000 people increase directly to 3,000 people

23 直接 [-] zhíjiē (direct-connect) <adj./adv.> direct, immediate: ~原因 direct reason || ~联系 direct connection || ~打电话 directly call

24 间接 [間-] jiànjiē (indirect-connect) <adj./adv.> indirect: ~提问 indirectly ask a question, || ~传染 indirectly infect, contaminate || ~关系 indirect relationship

25 面对面 [-對-] miànduìmiàn (face-to-face) <v.> fact to face: ~谈 talk face to face || ~坐下来 sit face to face

26 从中 [從-] cóngzhōng (from-within) <adv.> from within, out of them: ~学习 study within (a group or organization) || ~看到问题 saw an issue within || 一共有一百个候选人我们要~选择最好的五名进行面试. From 100 candidates, we want to select the top five to conduct an interview.

27 顺便 [順-] shùnbiàn (in passing-conveniently) <adv.> conveniently, in passing: ~说一句by the way || ~拜访 drop in (on sb.) || ~买东西 conveniently buy goods

28 就地 [-] jiùdì (at-spot) <adv.> on the spot: ~开会 to conduct a meeting on the spot || ~免职 (miǎnzhí) to immediately remove sb. of his post || 发现问题以后要~解决. After discovering the issue, it must immediately be resolved.

29 顺道, 顺路 [順-] shùndào, shùnlù (in passing-road) <adv.> on the way: ~去找他. We'll go find him on the way. || ~把钱交给她. Along the way, give her the money.

30 顺口 [順-] shùnkǒu (smooth-mouth) <adv.> read smoothly (of text), say without thinking: ~说了一句 say a line without thinking || 念起来很~ read out loud very smoothly || ~问问 ask smoothly

31 随机 [隨機] suíjī (according to-situation) <adv.> according to the situation, random: ~抽样 (chōuyàng) randomly sample || ~分布 randomly disperse || ~事件 a random event

32 随口 [隨-] suíkǒu (let-mouth) <adv.> (speak) without thinking the matter through: ~回答 answer without thinking || ~问 ask without thinking || ~答应 say 'yes' absent-mindedly

33 随手 [隨-] suíshǒu (let-hand) <adv.> conveniently, without extra trouble: ~扔了 toss in passing || ~关上门 close the door in passing || ~放在桌上 put on the desk in passing

34 信手 [-] xìnshǒu (randomly-hand) <adv.> do sth. spontaneously or without much thought or effort, casually: ~乱画 doodle || ~挑选两张照片 casually pick two pictures || ~举了一个例子 effortlessly give an example

35 瞎 [-] xiā (blind) <adv.> blind, groundlessly, foolish: ~说 speak unfoundedly || ~写 write foolishly || ~胡闹 act foolishly, mess about

36 胡乱 [-亂] húluàn (reckless-careless) <adv.> carelessly, reckless, absent mindedly: ~地洗洗脸 absent mindedly washed his face || ~吃了点饭 carelessly make a meal || ~解释 carelessly explain

37 分步 [-] fēnbù (by-step) <adv.> step by step: ~走 walk step by step || ~实施 (shíshī) do one step at a time || ~分析 (fēnxī) analyze one step at a time

38 分批 [-] fēnpī (by-batch) <v.> do something in batches or groups: ~出发 depart in groups || ~生产 produce in groups

39 分期 [-] fēnqī (by-period) <v.> do something by stages: ~付款 pay in installments || ~交货 deliver goods in stages

40 各个 [-個] gègè (each-one) <adv.> each, one by one: ~击破 (jīpò) destroy one by one || ~城市each city || ~方面 each aspect

41 相继 [-繼] xiāngjì (one another-succeed) <adv.> in succession, following closely: ~产生 produce in succession || ~关门 close doors in succession || ~成立 establish one after another

42 一一 [-] yīyī (one-one) <adv.> one by one, one after another: ~介绍 introduce one after another || ~列举 (lièjǔ) list off one by one || ~回答 answer one by one

43 依次 [-] (according to-order) <adv.> in order, in succession: ~介绍 introduce in order || ~进去 enter in order || ~离开 leave in order

44 挨个儿 [-個兒] āigèr (one by one-item) <adv.> by turns, one by one: ~拍照片 take turns taking pictures || ~检查身体have medical check-ups one by one || ~发言speak in turn

45 逐一 [-] zhúyī (in order-one) <adv.> one by one: ~分析 analyze one by one || ~加以研究 increase research one by one || ~讨论discuss one by one

46 轮流 [輪-] lúnliú (take turns-flow/go) <adv.> alternate, take turns: ~值班 (zhíbān) take turns being on duty || ~休息 take turns resting || ~使用 take turns using

47 边 [邊] biān (margin, edge) <adv.> simultaneously: ~吃~说talk while eating || ~听~想 think while lestening || ~工作~学习 work and study || ~开车~打电话很危险. To drive while talking on the phone is very dangerous.

48 一边 [-邊] yībiān (one-side) <adv.> one side, doing while: ~唱~跳 sing while dancing || ~工作~学习 work while studying || ~开车~聊天 talk while driving

49 一路 [-] yīlù (all-way) <adv./n.> all the way, throughout the journey: ~走好 enjoy the journey || ~辛苦 (xīnkǔ) continuously a struggle || ~领先 (lǐngxiān) be in the lead throughout

50 每 [-] měi (flourishly, every, each) <adv.> every: ~人 every person || ~天 every day || ~次 every time

51 定时 [-時] dìngshí (fixed-time) <v.> fix a time: ~吃饭/吃药 eat/take medicine at a fixed time || ~睡觉 sleep at a fixed time || ~给父母打电话 give parents a phone call at a fixed time

52 大幅 [-] dàfú (large-width/size) <n.> at a large scale, by a wide margin, substantial: ~照片 large scale picture || ~广告 large scale ad || ~下降 drop at a large scale
53 大肆 [-] dàsì (greatly-indulge) <adv.> without restraint, unbridled: ~宣传 (xuānchuán) advertise without restraint || ~活动 an unbridled event || ~攻击 attack without restraint
54 大幅度 [-] dàfúdù (large-width/breadth) <n.> by a wide margin, substantially: ~提高 raise substantially || ~下降 drop off substantially || ~上升 raise substantially
55 大踏步 [-] dàtàbù (big-step) <v.> in big strides, to take a big step: ~前进 stride along || ~走上去 make great strides forward
56 成倍 [-] chéngbèi (entire-time) <adv.> multiple: ~增加 multiply in number || ~上涨 (shàngzhǎng) grow to a large extent
57 成批 [-] chéngpī (entire-batch) <adv.> in batches, in bulk: ~生产 produce in bulk || ~地买 buy in bulk || ~的新车 a batch of new cars
58 超标准 [-標準] chāobiāozhǔn (exceed-standard) <v.> exceed quota (or standard): ~收费 collect a fee that exceeds the norms || 婴儿的食物和药品都是~的. The quality of infant foods and medicines is above the standard.

Tips:

1 每 (měi): The original meaning of 每 is related to 屮 (chè, sprout) and 母 (mǔ, mother,) e.g. '(grow) flourishly' from which 'each, every' was evolved.
2 另 (lìng): The original meaning of 另 is 'to live separately' from which 'part, single, alone, other' etc. were evolved.
3 直 (zhí): It is related to 十 (ten, many,) 目 (eye) and 曲 (the 乚 without the tip,) meaning 'with ten/many eyes it can not be 'crooked,'' in other words, 'straight.'
4 一一 vs. 各个: (1) 一一 is an adverb, but 各个 is an adverb and an adjective. So one can say 各个学校 (each school.) (2) When functioning as an adverb, 一一 is more like 'one after another' and 各个 'one by one.'
5 亲*: When 亲 is followed by an organ of the human body such as 眼 (eye,) 耳 (ear,) 口 (mouth,) 手 (hand,) 身 (body,) it means 'with one's own,' for example 亲眼看见 (saw with my own eyes.) A side note, owing to rapid development of internet, 亲 has become a term of address, meaning 'dear,' for example, 亲, 怎么不给我打电话? (Dear, why didn't you give me a call?)

Exercises:

Part I: Word and phrase composition

A: Match words in the left column with words in the right column to form phrases.

1 成倍 a) 前进
2 大踏步 b) 增加
3 大幅度 c) 提高工资水平

4	大肆	d	攻击
5	定时	e)	领先
6	一路	f)	给父母打电话
7	轮流	g)	值班
8	胡乱	h)	穿了一件衣服
9	面对面	j)	解释清楚
10	挨个	k)	问一遍

B: Use the given bound form as a guide to help you think of other words with the same beginning character. Feel free to use your dictionary when needed. Then write down the English definition of each of the words you've written.

亲(in person,oneself): 亲自 in person

____

____

____

____

顺(at one's convenience): 顺便 conveniently, in passing

____

____

分(divide, separate): 分步 step by step, one step at a time

____

____

Part II: Read the following sentences and fill in each blank with the appropriate word or phrase from the options given.

1 独自、联合、从中

a) 中国政府认为中国和日本应该搁置领土争议 (shelve territorial disputes), ____________开发公海资源.
b) 中国政府在上世纪六十年____________研究、制造出了核武器.
c) 历史上有过两次世界大战, 对人类造成了严重伤害, 我们应该____________吸取教训.

2 大肆、相继、轮流

a) 老王的父母最近生病, ____________住进了医院.
b) 老王跟兄弟姐妹____________到医院看望父母.
c) 其实美国医疗价格也是无人监管 (jiānguǎn, watch and control) 的, 一些医院漫天 (màntiān, wild) 要价, ____________对患者收费.

3 间接、顺便、就地、直接

a) 在美国很多老人死亡的__________ _原因是心脏病发作 (heart attack).

b) 很多医生提醒 (tíxǐng, remind) 心脏病人, 要注意天气变化, 有时候恶劣天气是心脏病人的__________ _杀手 (killer).

c) 王医生喜欢下班的时候__________ _到病房看一下, 发现问题时可以__________ _解决.

Theme 280: Generally, normally, probably, certainly, 一般来说 (yìbānláishuō), 应该 (yīnggāi), 可能 (kěnéng), 肯定 (kěndìng)

1 一般来说 [--來說] yī bān lái shuō (generally-to-speak) <adv.> generally speaking: ~年龄越小记忆力越好. Generally speaking, when one's age is younger, one's memory is better. || ~一天不能吃两次比萨饼. Generally speaking, one should not eat pizza twice in the same day.

2 原则上 [-則-] yuán zé shàng (principle – *wise*) <adv.> in principle, generally: ~的差异 difference of principles || ~的平等 on principle it is equality || ~通过 it passes in principle || ~同意agree the general principle

3 大体上 [-體-] dà tǐ shàng (overall – *wise*) <adv.> overall, in general terms: ~一致 overall the same || ~满意 all in all satisfied || ~同意 all in all agree

4 看样子 [-樣-] kàn yàngzi (look-appearance) <adv.> it seems, it looks like: ~二十多岁 appears to be at least 20 years old || ~你错了. It appears you are incorrect. || 这件事~很重要. It appears this matter is very important.

5 本该 [-該] běngāi (originally-should) <adv.> was originally expected to: 他~赢了比赛, 结果一紧张就输了. He was expected to win, but felt nervous and lost. || ~停下来 was originally expected to stop || ~早点结婚 was originally expected to wed early.

6 照理 [-] zhàolǐ (according to-norm) <adv.> according to reason, usually: ~他现在该来了. He usually arrives now.

7 或许 [-許] huòxǔ (perhaps-maybe) <adv.> perhaps, maybe: ~错了 perhaps incorrect || ~记得 perhaps I remember || ~有用处 perhaps be of use

8 恐怕 [-] kǒngpà (fear-afraid) <adv.> afraid: 他~迟到, 所以起得很早. He got up very early for fear of being late. || ~要下雨. It looks like rain. || ~很难. (I'm) afraid it's very hard.

9 怕 [-] pà (afraid, fear) <adv.> be afraid, to fear: 他~已经离开了吧. I am afraid he's gone. || ~很难有机会跟他再见面了. I'm afraid it will be very hard to find an opportunity to meet him again.

10 可能 [-] kěnéng (perhaps-maybe) <adv.> maybe, might: 他~走了. Maybe he left. || 游泳池里~有蛇. The pool may have snakes in it. || ~不对. Maybe it's incorrect.

11 也许 [-許] yěxǔ (also-perhaps) <adv.> perhaps, probably: ~有用. Perhaps it is useful. || 他~病了. Perhaps he's ill. || ~不贵. Perhaps it's not expensive.

12 大概 [-] dàgài (broad-probability) <adv.> roughly, approximately: ~都知道 to approximately know everything || ~是累了 tired (describing the general

situation) || ~没听到. I mostly didn't hear. || 他~三十岁. He's about 30 years old.

13 大致 [-] dàzhì (rough-extend) <adv./ adj.> more or less, roughly: ~相同 about the same || ~分四类roughly separated into four types || ~情况 general situation

14 并非 [-] bìng fēi (at all-not) <adv.> but not: ~天生的 not natural || ~偶然 (ǒurán) not by accident, not random

15 未必 [-] wèibì (not-necessarily) <adv.> not necessarily, maybe not: ~合适 not necessarily a fit || ~愿意 not necessarily agree || ~有用 may not be of use

16 不见得 [-見-] bújiànde (not-see-certainty) <adv.> not necessarily: ~小 not necessarily small || 中国人~都聪明. Chinese people are not necessarily all smart. || ~合适 not necessarily appropriate

17 不一定 [-] bù yīdìng (not-must) <adv.> not necessarily: ~对 not necessarily correct || ~好 not necessarily good || ~喜欢 to not necessarily like18
说不定 [說--] shuōbudìng (say-no-certainty) <adv.> unsure, not certain: ~是真的 not certainly true || ~赶不上飞机 not sure if (we'll) make the plane || ~会出事 not sure if there will be a problem

19 谁知道 [誰--] shuí zhī dào (who-know) <adv.> who knows? : ~对不对? Who knows if it is correct? || ~你去哪儿了? Who knows where you went?

20 想不到 [-] xiǎngbudào (think-not-arrive) <adv.> never considered: 万万~ absolutely never expected || ~的事 unexpected matters || 做梦也~. Even in my wildest dreams I didn't think.

21 必 [-] bì (must) <adv.> certainly, must: ~胜, 输 must win, lose || 这部电影是~看的. This is a must-see film. || 只要有免费的午餐他~到. If there is a free lunch, he certainly will come.

22 必然 [-] bìrán (must-this) <adv.> inevitably: ~会长高. You'll inevitably grow tall. || ~越学越好. If you study more, you're inevitably improve. || ~产生这样的结果. This kind of result is inevitable.

23 得 [-] děi (have to) <adv.> must: ~跑得更快才能进入决赛 (juésài) must run faster in order to make the finals || ~成绩好才能拿到奖学金 must have better results in order to receive a scholarship || ~减少支出 must decrease spending

24 总 [總] zǒng (bundle, all, always) <adv.> always, totally, completely: ~不高兴 always unhappy || ~迟到 always late

25 迟早 [遲-] chízǎo (later-sooner) <adv.> sooner or later: ~出事 sooner or later have an accident || ~会发生 sooner or later will happen || ~要来 sooner or later will come

26 肯定 [-] kěndìng (affirm-certainty) <adv.> be certain, be positive: ~会受欢fl definitely will be welcome || ~高兴 definitely happy || ~愿意 definitely willing

27 一定 [-] yīdìng (consistent-certainty) <adv.> surely, certainly: ~去 certainly go || ~买 certainly buy || ~给 certainly give

28 早晚 [-] zǎowǎn (sooner-later) <adv.> morning and evening, sooner or later: ~会变 sooner or later will change || ~你会知道 sooner or later will know || ~会见面 sooner or later will meet

29 毫无疑问 [-無-問] háowú yíwèn (at all-no-doubt) <idiom> no doubt: ~这是事实. No doubt this is true || ~是个玩笑 Not doubt this is a joke.

30 的确 [-確] díquè (indeed-really) <adv.> indeed, really: ~好 definitely good || ~贵 definitely expensive || ~喜欢 definitely like

31 确实 [確實] quèshí (really-actually) <adv.> indeed, in fact: ~好 indeed (it's) good || ~聪明 indeed smart || ~厉害 indeed talented
32 实在 [實-] shízài (actually-be) <adv.> really: ~没时间really no time || ~没办法 really no solution || ~太年轻了 really too young

Tips:

1 Modal verb serial: Modal verbs can sometimes be used together to express a complex mode. Remember two typical strings and you will get used to others. String one: 可能应该可以. For example: Daughter: 妈妈, 我能用一下爸爸的手机吗? (Mommy, may I use my daddy's cellphone for a while?) Mom: 可能应该可以. It literally means 'probably you are entitled to be allowed.' 可能 means 'probably, not 100% sure,' 应该 'ought to' (since daddy is not using it), and 可以 'allowed.' String 2: 可能会愿意. For example: A. 你觉得那位小姐会接受那个老头子的求婚吗? (Do you think that young lady will accept that old man's marriage proposal?) B: 可能会愿意 (因为那个老头子是个亿万富翁). Probably she will be willing to accept it (since that old man is a billionaire.) 可能 means 'probably,' 会 (will) and 愿意 (be willing.)
2 一定不 vs. 不一定: 一定不 means 'definitely not,' and 不一定 'not necessarily, not sure.'
3 一般来说 vs. e一般地说 vs. 一般说来: All means 'generally speaking,' but their frequency of use decreases. In other words, 一般来说 is the most common one and 一般说来 the least common.
4 Typical written and typical colloquial words in this unit.

   a) Written words: 并非, 必
   b) Colloquial words: 怕, 不见得, 谁知道, 得, 总

Exercises:

Part I: Match up the following expressions to the appropriate column. Make sure all words with similar meanings are in one column.

也许 可能 大概 不见得 说不定 的确没时间 确实没时间 迟早会成功 早晚会成功

1. 或许
2. 未必
3. 实在没时间
4. 最终会成功

Part II: Read the following sentences and fill in each blank with the appropriate word or phrase from the options given.

1 本该、照理、说不定、想不到

   a) ___________来说, 五岁的孩子___________上幼儿园. 可是老王非让自己五岁的儿子上小学.

b) 老王认为儿子五岁就能上小学，长大以后__________ _就可以考上清华大学了.

c) 老王跟太太商量让儿子上学事情， 可是__________ _被太太批评 (pīpíng, criticize) 了一顿.

2 必、得、总、一般来说

a) __________，孩子在成长中__________ _会遇到这样或者那样的问题.

b) 家长__________ _站在孩子的角度去帮助孩子.

c) 老王很喜欢看美国好莱坞 (Hollywood) 大片，只要电影院上映好莱坞大片，他__________看.

3 毫无疑问、必然、大致、谁知道

a) 中国的免费基础教育__________ _是在上世纪80年代开始实行的.

b) 发展教育__________ _对经济发展有促进 (cùjìn, promote) 作用.

c) 不让孩子上学__________ _是违反法律的. 可是在中国的一些非常偏远的农村__________有多少父母在违法 (wéifǎ, violate the law) 呢?

Theme 281: Originally, contrarily, purposely, eventually 本来 (běnlái), 相反 (xiāngfǎn), 故意 (gùyì), 最终 (zuìzhōng)

1 向来 [-來] xiànglái (always-was) <adv.> always (previously): ~重要 consistently important || ~温柔 (wēnróu) consistently warm, tender || ~脾气不好 always in bad temper

2 一贯 [-貫] yīguàn (all-constant) <adv.> consistent, constant: ~耐心 (nàixīn) consistent patience || ~重视 consistently emphasize || ~友好 consistently friendly

3 一向 [-] yīxiàng (all-was) <adv.> always (previously), a period of time in the recent past: 他们~有矛盾 (máodùn). They have consistently had problems. || ~认真 consistently hardworking || ~冷静 (lěngjìng) consistently calm

4 照样 [-樣] zhàoyàng (as-before) <adv.> as before, (same) as usual: ~生活 live a life as usual || ~完成任务 complete work as usual || ~吃喝 eat and drink as usual

5 原本 [-] yuánběn (origin-root) <adv./adj.> originally, original: ~不错 originally not bad || ~的样子 original form

6 原来 [-來] yuánlái (originally-was) <adv.> originally, formerly: ~是你 originally was you || ~打算早点出发 originally expected to depart || ~如此. So that's the way it is.

7 反而 [-] fǎn'ér (instead-but) <adv.> on the contrary, instead: ~容易. On the contrary, it's easy. || ~更难. On the contrary, it's more difficult. || ~看不清楚. On the contrary, I can't see clearly.

8 毕竟 [畢-] bìjìng (ultimately-after all) <adv.> after all: 对她耐心一点儿，她~还是个小孩. Please be more patient with her. She is, after all, still a child. || 中国~还是一个发展中国家. China is still a developing country, after all.

9 究竟 [-] jiūjìng (explore-end) <adv.> go to the bottom of a matter, after all: 问个~ ask a question that gets to the bottom of things || ~是什么? What exactly is there? || ~是什么意思? So whatever does this mean?

10 终究 [終-] zhōngjiū (eventually-explore) <adv.> eventually, in the end: ~无法实现. In the end, there was no way to realize. || ~还年轻. After all, (he's) still young.
11 总归 [總歸] zǒngguī (after all-return) <adv.> eventually, after all: 只要努力~会成功. You just need to be hardworking and eventually you'll succeed.
12 说到底 [說--] shuō dào dǐ (speak-to-end) <adv.> in the final analysis, boil it down: 公司直接的竞争 (jìngzhēng) ~是人才的竞争. All in all, the corporate competition is the competition in talents.
13 归根到底 [歸---] guī gēn dào dǐ (return-root-go-end) <idiom> after all in the final analysis: 历史~是人民群众创造的. History, after all, is created by the masses. || 她这样做~还是为了钱. She did it for money after all.

14 特意 [-] tèyì (specially-intended) <adv.> specially: ~来看你 specially came to see you || ~前去参观 specially went to visit || ~录了音 specially recorded
15 专程 [專-] zhuānchéng (special-trip) <adv.> specifically: ~拜访 (bàifǎng) specifically call on || ~前往 to leave on a specific trip || ~从北京来上海 specially went to Shanghai from Beijing
16 专门 [專門] zhuānmén (special-subject) <adv.> professionally: ~训练 (xùnliàn) professionally train || ~人才 professional talent || ~学科 propositional, specific subject
17 故意 [-] gùyì (deliberate-intention) <adv.> deliberately, on purpose: ~说错 deliberately said incorrectly || ~骗他 deliberately deceived him || ~捣乱 (dǎoluàn) deliberately make trouble
18 有意 [-] yǒuyì (have-intention) <adv.> intentionally: ~安排 to intentionally organize || ~培养 (péiyǎng) to intentionally train || ~回避这个话题 intentionally avoid this question
19 无意 [無-] wúyì (no-intention) <adv.> have no intention (of doing sth.), not inclined to: 我~为难你. I have no intention of making things difficult for you || ~地模仿 (mófǎng) imitate sth., sb. unintentionally || ~参加 have no intention of doing.
20 不知不觉 [---覺] bùzhī bùjué (not-know-not-feel) <idiom> unconsciously: ~睡着了 unconsciously slept || ~走到了车站 unconsciously walked to the station || ~加快脚步 increased pace without thinking about it.
21 下意识 [--識] xiàyìshí (sub – conscious) <adv.> subconscious mind, do sth. without thinking: ~地点点头 nodded without thinking || ~地抬起头 raised one's head without thinking || ~的动作 made a movement without thinking
22 悄悄 [-] qiāoqiāo (quiet-*reduplication*) <adv.> quietly: ~地说 quietly said || ~打开门 quietly opened the door || ~告诉我 quietly told me
23 硬是 [-] yìngshì (forcefully-be) <adv.> just, simply: ~不走 simply won't go || ~不信 simply won't believe || ~要去 simply want to go
24 任意 [-] rènyì (allow-will) <adv.> arbitrary, at will,willfully: ~欺负别人 bully people at will || ~摆布 (bǎibu) willfully decorate || ~挑选 freely select
25 擅自 [-] shànzì (arrogate-oneself) <adv.> without permission, of one's own initiative: ~改变 alter at one's one will || ~经商 do business without authorization || ~行动act presumptuously
26 自由 [-] zìyóu (oneself-follow) <adv.> freely: ~活动 free time (between organized activities), recess || ~选择be free to choose || ~讨论have a free exchange of views

Tips:

1 究, 竟: 究竟 means 'exactly, after all,' but where on Earth does this meaning come from? The upper part of 究 is 穴, meaning 'cave,' and the lower part 九 represents the sound 'jiu.' 究 originally means 'to explore (to the end of a cave).' It appears in 究竟 and 终究 in this unit. The upper part of 竟 is 音, meaning 'music,' and the lower part 儿 represents a man. 竟 originally means 'conclusion, end of music' from which evolved a meaning 'end.' It appears in 毕竟 and 竟然 in this unit.

2 意: 意 originally means 'idea, will' from which evolved the meaning 'intention.' Therefore all the following 意 have the meaning 'intention,' such as 有意 (have-intention, intentionally), 无意 (no intention, have no intention), 故意 (deliberate-intention, deliberately), and 特意 (special-intention, specially.) The 意 in 任意 keeps its original meaning 'will.'

3 Typical colloquial words in this unit: 总归, 硬是

Exercises:

Part I:

A: Use the given bound form as a guide to help you think of other words with the same character. Feel free to use your dictionary when needed. Then write down the English definition of each of the words you've written.

意(idea): 有意 intentionally

____

____

____

____

____

____

竟(after all) 竟然 unexpectedly

____

____

专(speacial): 专业 major

____

____

B: Match up the following expressions to the appropriate column. Make sure all similar meaning words in one column.

原本 向来 一贯 总归 说到底 归根到底 不知不觉

原来 (original)	一向 (always)	总归 (eventually)	下意识 (subconscious)

Part II: Read the following sentences and fill in each blank with the appropriate word or phrase from the options given.

1 擅自、任意、硬是

a) 老王生病了, 医生让他住院治疗, 可是他___________不听.
b) 老王觉得自己清楚得了什么病, 就___________买了些药吃了.
c) 医生批评老王: 你怎么可以___________乱来, 随便吃药呢?

2 归根到底、不知不觉、反而

a) 老王一边开车一边听音乐, ___________错过了高速出口.
b) 老王把车开到了河里, 他不但不觉得是自己的问题, ___________认为是他的GPS坏了.
c) 老王的故事告诉我们, 不愿意认错的人___________是情商 (qíngshāng) 太低 (low EQ).

Theme 282: Other modal adverbs 其他情态副词 (qítā qíngtài fùcí)

1 真 [-] zhēn (true, real) <adv.> really, truly: ~好 really good || ~热 really hot || ~高兴 really happy
2 真的 [-] zhēnde (true-*suffix*) <adv.> truly, it's really: ~飞起来了. It really flew. || ~下雪了 it really snowed || ~来了. It's really coming.
3 真正 [-] zhēnzhèng (true-genuine) <adv./adj.> genuine, real: ~的意义 genuine meaning || ~独立 (dúlì) genuine independence || ~平等 (píngděng) true equality
4 果然 [-] guǒrán (really-this) <adv.> really, sure enough: ~生气 angry as expected || ~不错 really not bad || ~严重 (yánzhòng) really serious
5 只好 [-] zhǐhǎo (only-option) <adv.> have to, without any better option: ~取消have to call off || ~承认 (chéngrèn) have to admit || ~服从 have to obey
6 只能 [-] zhǐnéng (only-can) <adv.> only able to: ~回去 only be able to return || ~在家呆着 have to stay at home || ~如此 the only way
7 只是 [-] zhǐshì (only-be) <adv.> only, merely: ~外行 (wàiháng) only (a) layman || ~暂时 (zànshí) 的 only temporary || 反对的人~少数. There are only a few who disagree.
8 只顾 [-顧] zhǐgù (only-concern) <adv.> be only concerned with: ~朝前走 to only be concerned about moving forward || ~赶路 only be concerned about

completing one's journey || 她~打电话忘了火上的锅了. She was so focused on talking on the phone that she forgot to turn off the stove.

9 总得 [總-] zǒngděi (after all-have to) <adv.> must, have to: ~想个办法 must think of a solution || ~休息一下 must take a rest || ~有个名字 must have a name

10 不得不 [-] bùdébù (not-able-not) <adv.> have no choice (or option) but to, cannot but, have to: ~去 have no choice but to go || ~休息 have to take a rest || ~说谎 (shuōhuǎng) have to lie

11 反正 [-] fǎnzhèng (reverse-obverse) <adv.> in any case, at any rate: 随你怎么说~我不在乎. In response to what you said, at any rate, I don't care. || ~差不多 at any rate, more or less

12 老实说 [-實説] lǎoshí shuō (honest-speak) <adv.> to be frank: ~我根本不相信她. To be frank, I don't trust her.

13 尽量 [盡-] jǐnliàng (to-full) <adv.> as much as possible: ~全面 as comprehensive as possible || ~多吃一点 try to have more || ~帮他一点. Please try to help him a little bit.

14 尽可能 [盡--] jǐnkěnéng (as far as-possible) <adv.> as far as possible: ~大 as large as possible || ~多 as much as possible || ~快地完成工作. Complete the task as fast as possible.

15 尽快 [盡-] jǐnkuài (as far as-fast) <adv.> as fast as possible: ~解决 (jiějué) resolve as quickly as possible || ~学会开车 study how to drive a car as quickly as possible || ~答复. Answer as quickly as possible.

16 从速 [從-] cóngsù (pursue-speed) <adv.> as soon as possible: ~准备 prepare as soon as possible || ~安排 arrange as soon as possible || ~回复. Reply as soon as possible.

17 赶快 [趕-] gǎnkuài (hurry-fast) <adv.> extremely fast: ~想办法 quickly think of a solution || ~回去 quickly return || ~喝点水 quickly drink some water

18 连忙 [連-] liánmáng (promptly-hurriedly) <adv.> hastily, hurriedly: ~告诉她 tell her at once || ~道歉 (dàoqiàn) hurriedly apology || ~穿上衣服 get dressed quickly

19 急忙 [-] jímáng (hastily-hurriedly) <adv.> hastily, hurriedly: ~问 hastily ask || ~回去 hastily return || ~打电话 hastily make a phone call

20 尽管 [儘管] jǐn'guǎn (only-care) <adv.> do not hesitate to, feel free to: ~放心 do not hesitate to relax || 有什么问题~问. If you have any questions, don't hesitate to ask.

21 大力 [-] dàlì (great-strength) <adv.> great strength, energetically: ~宣传 (xuānchuán) energetically disseminate || ~推广 (tuīguǎng) to energetically promote || ~发展 (fāzhǎn) to energetically expand

22 极力 [極-] jílì (utmost-strength) <adv.> do one's utmost, spare no effort: ~反对 do one's utmost to resist || ~阻止 (zǔzhǐ) do one's most to prevent || ~控制 (kòngzhì) 自己 do one's best to control oneself

23 全力 [-] quánlì (full-strength) <adv.> with all one's strength, full strength: ~支持 (zhīchí) support with all one's strength || ~投入工作 put all of one's efforts into work || ~应付 (yìngfu) try one's best to handle it

24 好好儿 [--兒] hǎohāor (good-*reduplication*) <adv.> in good condition, carefully: ~说 speak well || ~玩 play well || ~享受 (xiǎngshòu) 现在的生活 enjoy your current life

25 随便 [隨-] suíbiàn (follow-convenience) <adv.> as one wishes, as one pleases: ~骂人 scolding people as one wishes || ~看看 look around || ~坐 sit where you want || ~吃 eat as you want

26 随意 [隨-] suíyì (follow-will) <adv.> as one wishes: ~挑选 (tiāoxuǎn) select as one wishes || ~花钱 spend money as one wishes || ~改变 changes as one wishes

27 干脆 [乾-] gāncuì (direct-straightforward) <adv.> clear cut, straightforward, directly, bluntly: ~不说 just keep one's mouth shut || 这家公司对你不好, 你~辞职 (cízhí)算了. This company is not nice to you. You can just quit your job. || ~不用去 clearly no need to go

28 简直 [簡-] jiǎnzhí (simple-direct) <adv.> simply: ~不敢相信 simply can't believe || ~惊呆了. I'm simply stunned.

29 自然 [-] zìrán (self-that) <adv.> at ease, naturally: ~想到 naturally thought of || ~发生 naturally occurred || ~生长 naturally grow

30 最好 [-] zuìhǎo (most-good) <adv.> had better: ~不动. You'd better not move. || ~马上去. You better leave immediately. || ~别走. You'd better not go.

31 仿佛 [-] fǎngfú (seem) <adv.> like, just like: 二十年前的事, ~就发生在昨天. What happened 20 years ago seemed to have happened yesterday. || ~停止了呼吸 like stopping one's breath || ~变了一个人 like changing into a different person

32 纷纷 [紛紛] fēnfēn (tangled-*reduplication*) <adv.> (of comments, falling objects, etc) numerous and confused, one after another: ~发言 speak one after another || ~坐下 sit one after another || ~离开 leave one after another

33 似乎 [-] sìhū (seem-*suffix*) <adv.> it seems that: ~不太高兴seemed unhappy || ~感兴趣seem to be interested || ~满意了 (mǎnyì) seemed satisfied

34 算是 [-] suànshì (considerably-be) <adv.> considered to be, at last: ~工资高的. It's considered to be a high salary. || ~最好的. It's considered to be the best. || ~好人 considered to be a good person

35 为何 [爲-] wèihé (for-what) <adv.> why, what reason: 他~还不来? Why hasn't he come yet? || ~这么伤心? Why are you so hurt/sad? || ~这么难? Why is it this hard?

Tips:

1 尽: jǐn (儘) or jìn (盡)? 儘 (jǐn) and 盡 (jìn) are all traditional forms of the simplified character 尽, needless to say, their pronunciations are different as well. As for the differences in meaning and usage, we can single out a few simple rules among many.

a) jǐn (儘) is related to the subject and 盡 (jìn) to the object. For example, 'He is in trouble (huge debt,) and I am his good friend. 我会____帮他.' If the word is '儘 (jǐn) 量,' it means 'I will try my best (to help him).' If '盡 (jìn) 量' is used, it means 'I will offer whatever I can offer (to help him).' Similar words include 尽力 (儘力 or 盡力) and 尽快 (儘快 or 盡快.)

b) If 尽 appears in the last syllable of a usually disyllabic word, it is pronounced 'jìn.' For example, 用尽, 详尽, 无穷无尽 (endless), 筋疲力尽 (exhausted.)
c) A common word in which 尽 is pronounced jǐn is 尽管.
d) If you feel this is too complicated, pronounce all 尽 as jìn since this is a tendency in mainland China.

2 The pronunciations of 好好儿 and 好好:

a) The pronouncing of 好好儿 can easily tell if the speaker comes from a standard Chinese-speaking region or not. The standard pronunciation is 'hǎohāor.' For example, 好好儿玩儿! (Have fun!) should be pronounced 'hǎohāor wár.'
b) 好好: When two 好 are juxtaposed, they should be pronounced 'háohǎo' because of tone sandhi. For example, 'This game is great! (好好看!)' An exception is in 好好先生 (Mr. Goody-goody, Yes-man) which is pronounced 'hǎo hǎo (no tone sandhi).'
c) Chairman Mao Zedong had a famous call for young students to study hard, 好好学习, 天天向上 (literally 'good good study, day day up,' study hard and make progress everyday.) Three ways of pronunciation could be heard, 'hǎohāo,' 'háohǎo' and 'hǎohǎo.'

3 Typical written and typical colloquial words in this unit.

a. Written words: 从速, 仿佛, 似乎, 为何
b. Colloquial words: 总得, 好好儿, 干脆, 算是

Exercises:

Part I:

A: Match up the following expressions to the appropriate column. Put the formal expressions in the left column and informal ones in the right.

总得　好好儿　干脆　算是　从速　仿佛　似乎　为何　纷纷　从速

Formal expressions	Informal expressions

B: Put the following expressions with similar meanings in the same column.

只好、大力、全力、极力、尽可能、尽量、只能、尽快、从速、赶快

1.	2.	3.

Part II: Read the following sentences and fill in each blank with the appropriate word or phrase from the options given.

1 果然、反正、真

老王: 我昨天买了一套德国的炊具 (chuījù, cookware), 回家一用__________ _好用, __________名不虚传 (deserve the reputation one enjoys).
老白: 真的啊, 那我也去买一套吧, __________ _我新房子里还没有做饭的东西.

2 干脆、简直、纷纷

老王: 你今晚别做饭了, __________ _来我家一起做饭吧, 用一下我那些德国新锅 (guō, cooking-pot).
老白: 真的? 那__________ _太好了!
老王: 我把你做饭的照片发布在微信 (WeChat) 上了, 大家都_______点赞 (diǎnzàn, to like).

Theme 283: Adverbs, time (sequential or as planned) 时间副词 (shíjiān fùcí)

1 首先 [-] shǒuxiān (prime-first) <adv.> first (of all): ~到达 the first to arrive || ~发言speak first
2 初步 [-] chūbù (first-step) <adv.> beginning-stages, preliminary: ~决定 preliminary decisions || ~看到效果 (xiàoguǒ) to see results in the beginning stages || ~方案 (fāng'àn) a preliminary plan
3 首次 [-] shǒucì (first-time) <num.> for the first time: ~演出 first time acting || ~见面 first time meeting || ~合作 (hézuò) first time collaborating
4 率先 [-] shuàixiān (leading-first) <adv.> take the lead: ~跑起来 take the lead in a race || ~反对 be the first to oppose || ~赶到事故 (shìgù) 现场 (xiànchǎng) to be the first to the scene of the accident
5 先 [-] xiān (first, before) <adv.> first, primary: ~走 walk first || ~吃 eat first || 在快餐店应该~点饮料再点食物. At the fast food restaurant, you should first order drinks and then food.
6 预先 [預-] yùxiān (advance-before) <adv.> beforehand, in advance: ~练习 practice beforehand || ~安排 arrange beforehand || ~商量 (shāngliang) discuss beforehand
7 最初 [-] zuìchū (most-beginning) <adj./adv.> in the beginning: ~阶段 the beginning stages || ~印象 (yìnxiàng) first impression || ~很着急 panicked from the beginning
8 先后 [-後] xiānhòu (early-late) <adv.> successively, one after another: ~离开 leave one after another || 孩子们~长大了. Children are growing up gradually. || ~找到工作find a job one after another
9 随后 [隨後] suíhòu (soon-after) <adv.> soon after: ~进来 to enter soon after || ~再谈 discuss again soon after || ~追赶 to chase closely after
10 接下来 [-] jiē xià lái (follow-next) <adv.> next, following: 我们~讨论这个问题. Next we'll discuss this issue. || 他~还要去非洲旅游. Next he'll be travel to Africa.

11 下一步 [-] xià yī bù (next-step) <n.> the next step: ~的工作 work in the next step || ~的要求 requirements in the next stage || ~行动 actions for the next step

12 渐渐 [漸漸] jiànjiàn (gradually-*reduplication*) <adv.> gradually: ~长大了gradually grow || ~看得清楚了gradually see more clear || ~黑了gradually grow dark

13 逐步 [-] zhúbù (progressive-step) <adv.> step by step, progressively: ~提高 raise step by step || ~完成 complete step by step || ~发展develop step by step

14 逐渐 [-漸] zhújiàn (progressive-gradual) <adv.> gradually: ~了解gradually understand || ~增多 gradually increase || ~改变 gradually change

15 日益 [-] rìyì (day-more) <adv.> increasingly, more and more: ~增加 increase day by day || ~严重 be more serious day by day || ~强大 grow powerfully day by day

16 从此 [從-] cóngcǐ (from-this) <adv.> from now on, since then: ~开始 start from that point || ~消失 from now on will be revoked, eliminated || ~不理他 from now on pay no attention to him

17 从头 [從頭] cóngtóu (from-beginning) <adv.> from the beginning: ~说起 say from the beginning || 我们~开始. Let's start from the beginning. || ~来一遍. Let's start again from the beginning.

18 终于 [終-] zhōngyú (final-at) <adv.> finally: ~同意了finally agreed || ~离开了 finally left || ~回来了 finally returned

19 总算 [總-] zǒngsuàn (finally-regard) <adv.> at long last, finally: ~来了came at last || 他昏迷了好久, 现在~醒了. He has been in a coma for a long period of time and finally awoke. || ~明白了 finally understood

20 最后 [-後] zuìhòu (most-last) <adv.> finally, at last: ~赢了won at last || ~做好了finished at last || ~完成了 completed at last

21 最终 [-終] zuìzhōng (most-final) <adv.> finally: ~他赢了. He won in the end. || ~没去 did not go in the end || 他~当选法国总统. He was elected French President in the end.

22 按时 [-時] ànshí (according to-schedule) <adv.> timely, on time: ~完成任务 complete (an) assignment on time || ~吃饭 eat on time/in a timely manner || ~起床 get up on time

23 准时 [準時] zhǔnshí (punctual-time) <adv.> punctually, on time: ~到 arrive on time || ~出发 depart on time || ~上班 start work on time

Tips:

1 首先, 其次, 再次 . . ., 最后: If multiple steps are mentioned, the Chinese way to do so is 首先 (Firstly), 其次 (Secondly), 再次 (Thirdly), 再次 (Fourthly) . . ., 最后 (Lastly.)

2 先, 后 (後): 先 means 'early' and 后 'late.' The upper part of 先 is a foot and the lower part is a man. It represents 'a foot before a man' from which the meaning 'before' is derived. The left part of 後, i. e. 彳 means 'to walk.' The upper right part of 後, i. e. 幺 means 'small,' and the lower right part depicts a reverse foot, representing 'walk slowly.' Thus the whole character 後 means 'late.'

3 後 (后) vs. 后: In traditional Chinese, 後 (后) is related to time, such as 先后, 后来 etc. And 后 is related to queen, such as 王后, 皇后 etc.

4 渐渐, 逐渐, 逐步: Simply put it, their differences are similar to those of the English words or phrases 'slowly,' 'gradually' and 'step by step.'

Exercises:

Part I: Read the following sentences and fill in each blank with the appropriate word or phrase from the options given.

1 准时、预先

a) 最近中国各大航空公司收到很多投诉 (tóusù, complain), 说飞机不 ____________.

b) 很多乘客认为如果飞机不能按时起飞, 应该让乘客____________知道.

2 率先、日益、逐渐、随后

a) 据报道, 中国高铁____________使用买票实名 (real name) 制. ____________中国长途公共汽车也使用买票实名制.

b) 据报道美国乘客和航空公司之间的矛盾也____________增加. 为此美国各大航空公司都在_______________改善 (gǎishàn) 他们的服务.

3 首先、再次、其次、最后

a) 老王太太跟他离婚 (líhūn) 的原因____________是性格不合 (incompatibility of disposition), ____________是生活习惯不同, ____________是经济上有矛盾, ____________是老王有了第三者.

Theme 284: Adverbs, time (others) 其他时间副词 (qítā shíjiān fùcí)

1 正, 正在 [-] zhèngzài (right-in the middle of) <adv.> in the process of, in course of: ~吃饭 eating || ~下雨 raining

2 刚 [剛] gāng (just now) <adv.> just: ~坐下 just sat down || ~工作 just was at work || ~回来 just came back

3 刚才 [剛-] gāngcái (just-past) <n.> just now, a moment ago: ~听到的事 the things just heard. || ~的争吵 a quarrel that occurred just a moment ago || ~说的话 the words just said

4 才 [-] cái (just) <adv.> just now, a moment ago: 八点~起床 just get out of bed at 8 || 九岁~学钢琴 start playing piano at age 9 || 九点上班她中午~来. The work started at nine, and she just got off at noon.

5 事先 [-] shìxiān (think-ahead) <adv.> beforehand: ~写好 finish writing beforehand || ~规定 (guīdìng) stipulate beforehand || ~通知 (tōngzhī) message beforehand

6 先期 [-] xiānqī (ahead-time) <n.> in advance, beforehand: ~到达 arrive in advance || ~开工 go into operation in advance || ~行动 take action beforehand

7 曾, 曾经 [-經] céng, céngjīng (once-experience) <adv.> once, already: ~很喜欢 have liked once || ~来过美国 have already come to America once || ~当过老板 have already taken the role of a manager

8 不曾 [-] bùcéng (not-once) <adv.> hasn't yet: ~入睡 not yet have slept || ~离开 not have yet left || ~想到not yet have thought of

9 已 [-] yǐ (already) <adv.> already: ~退休 (tuìxiū) already retired || ~长大 already grown up || 账单 (zhàngdān) ~付 have already paid the bill

10 已经 [-經] yǐjīng (already-experience) <adv.> already: ~完成 have already completed || ~开始 have already started || 我~离开中国两个星期了. I have been away from China for two weeks.

11 早就 [-] zǎojiù (long before-already) <adv.> already at an earlier time: ~说过 have already said || ~忘了 have already forgotten || ~出去了already have gone out

12 早已 [-] zǎoyǐ (long before-already) <adv.> earlier: ~吃完have finished eaten earlier || ~看过 have seen earlier || 饭菜~凉了. The food is already cold.

13 忽然 [-] hūrán (suddenly-*suffix*) <adv.> suddenly, all of a sudden: ~想起 suddenly thought of || ~笑起来 suddenly laughed || ~下雨了 suddenly started to rain

14 突然 [-] tūrán (abruptly-*suffix*) <adv.> suddenly, unexpected: ~的变化 sudden change || ~生病 sudden illness || 电话~断了. The phone call was unexpectedly cut off.

15 偶尔 [-爾] ǒu'ěr (occasionally-this) <adv.> one in a while, occasionally: ~迟到occasionally be late || ~聊聊天 chat occasionally || 她在节食, ~吃点水果. On her diet, she only occasionally eats fruit.

16 有时候, 有时 [-時-] yǒu shí hou, yǒushí (be-time) <adv.> sometimes: ~很乐观 sometimes optimistic || ~看电视 occasionally watch tv || ~发脾气 (píqi) occasionally lose one's temper

17 临时 [臨時] línshí (just before-time) <adv.> at the last moment, temporary: ~决定 a last minute decision || ~工作 part-time job || ~找个人来帮忙 find someone to help at the last minute

18 慢慢 [-] mànmàn (slowly-*reduplication*) <adv.> slowly, leisurely: ~长大slowly grow || ~写 slowly write || ~安静下来 slowly grow more quiet

19 立即 [-] lìjí (immediately-instantly) <adv.> immediately: ~写 immediately write || ~出发immediately depart || ~告诉他 immediately tell him

20 马上 [馬-] mǎshàng (horse-on) <adv.> immediately: ~去 immediately go || ~停下immediately stop || ~离开immediately depart

21 眼看 [-] yǎnkàn (eye-see) <adv.> soon, in a moment: ~要开学了. School will start soon. || ~那家公司就要倒闭 (dǎobì) 了. The company will go bankrupt soon. || ~就要下雨了. Soon it will rain.

22 一下儿 [--兒] yīxiàr (one-stroke) <adv.> give it a go (used after a verb), once: ~就不见了 in a while someone will not be seen || ~就猜对了谜语 (míyǔ) guessed the answer to a riddle in the first try || 他的脸~就变红了. His face turned red immediately.

23 即将 [-將] jíjiāng (instantly-shall) <adv.> on the eve of, to be about to: ~出任公司首席执行官 (shǒuxí zhíxíngguān) be about to take the position of chief executive officer || ~开始 be about to start || 胜利~到来. The success is on the way.

24 将 [將] jiāng (shall) <adv.> will, shall: ~继续努力 will continue to work hard || 我们的团队~越来越大. Our team will be bigger and bigger. || ~变得更好 will become better and better

25 将要 [將-] jiāngyào (shall-will) <adv.> will, shall: ~出现 will emerge || ~到来 will arrive || ~开始 will start

26 就 [-] jiù (right away) <adv.> at once, right away: 我~来. I'll come at once. || 几天后~知道了. will know a few days later. || 一眨眼~过去了. It will pass in the blink of an eye.

27 就要 [-] jiùyào (right-will) <adv.> will, shall: ~下雨了. It will rain. || ~开始了. It will start. || ~走了 will leave
28 快要 [-] kuàiyào (soon-will) <adv.> be about to: ~开始了 be about to start || ~结婚了 be about to finish || ~到了about to arrive
29 正要 [-] zhèngyào (just-will) <adv.> be just about to: 你打电话的时候我~出去. When you called, I was just about to leave. || ~开口 to be just about to open one's mouth || ~回答 to be just about to answer

30 时时 [時時] shíshí (time-time) <adv.> often, constantly: ~变化 constantly change || ~注意constantly watch || ~微笑 constantly smile
31 始终 [-終] shǐzhōng (beginning-final) <adv.> from beginning to end, all along: ~没有答应 have not replied || ~不变 have not changed || 他~爱着初恋情人. He loved his first love all his life.
32 随时 [隨時] suíshí (whatever-time) <adv.> at any time: ~联系 to contact at any time || ~回去 to return at any time || ~可以给我打电话. You can give me a call anytime.
33 永远 [-遠] yǒngyuǎn (forever-everlasting) <adv.> always, forever: ~记着 always remember || ~不变 always remain unchanged || ~年轻 remain young forever

34 连 [連] lián (consecutive) <adv.> connect, in succession: ~写了三封邮件 wrote three emails in succession || ~看了四场电影 watched four movies in succession
35 连续 [連續] liánxù (consecutive-continuous) <adv.> continuously, in a row: ~打了四个电话 make four calls in a row || ~五天没下雨了 not rain for five days in a row. || ~工作了八个小时 work eight hours continuously.
36 陆续 [陸續] lùxù (land-continuous) <adv.> one after another, successively: ~回家 return home one after another. || 这件事的影响 (yǐngxiǎng) ~出现. The impact of this issue has appeared in multiple forms.
37 一连 [-連] yīlián (entire-connected) <adv.> in a row, in succession: ~几天 several days in a row || ~吃了三个苹果 eat three apples in a row || ~打了两个哈欠laugh in succession
38 一口气 [--氣] (one-MW-breath) yīkǒuqì <adv.> in one breath, without a break: 这封信她~看了九遍. She read the letter nine times without taking a break. || ~跑了五圈 run around the track five times at a stretch.
39 还 [還] hái (still) <adv.> still, still in progress: 她~在想爸爸. She is still thinking about her father. || ~在吃饭 still eating. || ~没睡觉 still not sleeping.
40 还是 [還-] háishi (still-be) <adv.> still, remain: ~想回去 still would like to go back || ~不努力 still is not working hard || ~没来 has not come yet
41 仍, 仍然 [-] réng, réngrán (still) <adv.> still: 那个课本是三十年前出版的现在~在使用. That textbook was published 30 years ago, but it's still in use. || ~有缺点 still have shortcomings || ~很新鲜 still very fresh.

Tips:

1 巳, 已, 己: Their forms are close but their meanings are poles apart.

a. 巳 (sì) is the sixth of the twelve Earthly Branches of the Chinese system for reckoning time. It associates with the year of the snake (蛇, shé) in the Chinese zodiac, and the time of 9 am to 11 am of the day.
b. 已 (yǐ) means 'to stop, cease' from which evolved the meaning 'already' as in 已经 and 早已.

c. 己 (jǐ) is the six of the ten Heavenly Stems of the Chinese system for reckoning time. But the most common meaning is 'oneself' as in, for example, 自己, 先人后己 (first-others-later-oneself, put others before oneself) etc.

2 要, 快要, 就要: All mean 'something is going to happen,' but 要 and 快要 are more quicker and 就要 the quickest. The quickness is quite relative and sometimes subjective. For example, 就要下雨了 could mean 'it will rain *in a few minutes*,' whereas 就要放假了 could mean 'the vacation will start *in one month*.'

Exercises:

Part I: Match up the following expressions to the appropriate column. Make sure all words with similar meanings are in one column.

将要 就要 快要 已经 正要 马上 立刻 仍然 还是
一口气 连续 一连 陆续

Eg.将 (will)	要 (will)	已 (already)
将要 即将		
还 (still)	连 (consecutive)	立即 (immediately)

Part II: Read the following sentences and fill in each blank with the appropriate word or phrase from the options given.

1 曾、刚、才、临时

a) 特朗普 (Trump) ___________当了一年总统就觉得非常累.
b) 特朗普___________是美国最成功的商人之一.
c) 他___________要坐飞机去德国开国际会议，结果就有人打来电话说德国遭到恐怖 (kǒngbù) 袭击 (xíjī), 机场___________关闭了.

2 随时、连续、刚才

学生: 你___________说的那个消息可靠吗?
老师: 不知道啊, 你还是__________上网看《纽约时报》(*The New York Times*) 的新闻吧.
学生: 《纽约时报》? 特朗普总统已经___________多次批评他们制造假新闻!

3 始终、偶尔、突然、永远

a) 他经常吃汉堡薯条, 喝可口乐乐. 但__________ _也吃一点新鲜蔬菜.
b) 他觉得如果朝鲜__________ _宣布拥有核武器 (héwǔqì, nuclear weapon), 将会令美国后悔莫及 (hòuhuǐ mòjí, too late for regrets).
c) 有人说在国际社会上没有永远的朋友, 只有__________ _的利益. 因此, 处理国际关系________是国家利益第一.

Theme 285: Adverbs, frequency 频度副词 (píndù fùcí)

1 重 [-] chóng (heavy, repeated) <adv.> repeatedly, duplicated: ~来一次 complete one more time || ~说一遍 say one more time
2 重新 [-] chóngxīn (again-anew) <adv.> again, once more: ~做一次 do once more || ~认识 meet once more || ~开始 to start again
3 再 [-] zài (second time) <adv.> again, once more: ~说一遍 say once more || ~看一次 see one more time || ~去一趟 to make one more trip、
4 一再 [-] yīzài (once-again) <adv.> repeatedly, time and time again: ~失败 repeatedly be defeated || ~强调 emphasize multiple times || ~请求request multiple times
5 再次 [-] zàicì (second-time) <adv.> one more time, again: ~道歉 apologize once more || ~举行会谈 enter into talks once more || 防止 (fángzhǐ) 类似的事~发生prevent stop similar events from happening once more
6 再度 [-] zàidù (second-time) <adv.> once more, a second time: ~当选 be elected again || ~出现appear again || 她跟子女~团聚. She was reunited with her children.
7 再三 [-] zàisān (second-third) <adv.> over and over again: ~考虑 think over and over again || ~检查investigate over and over again || ~强调 (qiángdiào) emphasize over and over again
8 再也 [-] zàiyě (again-no) <adv.> (not) any more: ~没有了 not have any more || ~听不到了not hear again || ~忍不住
9 多次 [-] duō cì (many-time) <n.> many times: ~出现emerge many times || ~检查 inspect many times || 重复~ repeat many times
10 频频 [頻頻] pínpín (frequently-*reduplication*) <adv.> again and again, repeatedly: ~换工作change one's job frequently || ~得分 get scores again and again || ~获胜win again and again
11 频繁 [頻-] pínfán (frequently-numerously) <adv.> frequently, often: 交往~ exchange frequently || ~发生occur frequently || ~停电 frequent power failures
12 屡次 [屢-] lǚcì (repeated-time) <adv.> repeatedly, time and time again: ~推辞 (tuīcí) turn down an appointment time and time again || ~提醒remind one repeatedly || ~出现appear repeatedly
13 屡屡 [屢屢] lǚlǚ (repeated-*reduplication*) <adv.> again and again, repeatedly: ~失败 the serial failures || ~想起 think of again and again
14 又 [-] yòu (again) (once) <adv.> again, also: ~来了return once again || ~去了一次go once again || ~说了一遍 repeat once again
15 反复 [-復] fǎnfù (over-again) <adv./ v.> repeatedly, over and over: ~读 read repeatedly || ~考虑 consider repeatedly || 多次~ repeat multiple times

16 三番五次 [-] sānfān wǔcì (3-time-5-time) <idiom> over and over again: 她~地找我的麻烦. She repeatedly caused trouble. || ~地邀请invite again and again.

17 常常 [-] chángcháng (often-*reduplication*) <adv.> frequently, usually: ~记不住 frequently not remember || ~一起玩 frequently hang out together || ~喝啤酒frequently drink together

18 经常 [經-] jīngcháng (regularly-often) <adv.> day-to-day, everyday: ~说 say everyday || ~见面 see everyday || ~迟到 be late everyday

19 时常 [時-] shícháng (time-again) <adv.> often, frequently: ~发生 frequently occur || ~下雨frequently rain || ~提到frequently mention

20 往往 [-] wǎngwǎng (formerly-always) <adv.> often, frequently: 最深刻的理论~很简单. The deepest theories are often very simple. || ~不重视 often not emphasize. || ~很复杂 (fùzá) often very complicated

21 老 [-] lǎo (old, always) <adv.> old, always: ~痛 always hurting || ~写不好 always write poorly || ~看电视 always watch TV

22 总 [總] zǒng (always) <adv.> always: ~想着孩子 always think of children || ~不相信 always not trust || ~迟到 always be tardy

23 老是 [-] lǎoshì (always-be) <adv.> always: ~哭 always cry || ~开会 always meet || ~下雨 always rain

24 总是 [總-] zǒngshì (always-be) <adv.> always: ~害怕 always be afraid || ~失败 always defeated || ~很忙 always be busy

25 一直 [-] yīzhí (continuously-straight) <adv.> consistently: ~不舒服 consistently not well || ~不满意 consistently not satisfied || ~唱下去 to always sing

26 一向 [-] yīxiàng (consistently-always) <adv.> always (previously), a period of time in the recent past: ~听话 have recently heard || ~老实 has always been honest || ~努力 has always been hardworking

27 常年 [-] chángnián (constant-year) <adv.> all year round: ~有病 be sick all year round || ~多雨rain all year round || ~洗冷水澡 have cold showers all year round

28 不断 [-斷] bùduàn (not-cease) <adv.> unceasingly: 物价~上涨. The price has unceasingly risen. || ~变化 constantly change || ~提高 constantly raise

29 不停 [-] bútíng (not-stop) <adv.> without stopping: ~地写 writing without stopping || ~地画 drawing without stopping || 电话响个~. The phone rang without stopping.

30 不时 [-時] bùshí (unexpected-time) <adv.> from time to time, now and then: ~地看手机上的信息 look at information on one's phone from time to time || ~地叹气 sigh from time to time || ~发出笑声 laugh from time to time

31 照常 [-] zhàocháng (as-usual) <adv.> as usual: ~营业 business as usual || ~上班 work as usual || 太阳~升起. sun rises as usual, *The Sun Also Rises* (a novel by Ernest Hemingway).

Tips:

1 一, 再, 三: They mean the first time, the second time and the third time, respectively. 一而再, 再而三 means 'again and again,' as do its short forms 一再 and 再三.

2 经: 经 (經) originally meant 'longitudinal threads (of a piece of cloth)' from which evolved meanings such as 'principle,' 'classics' and 'often.' Since 经 has a meaning 'often, periodical,' menstruation or menses is called 月经 (literally 'month-periodically') in Chinese. Many ancient classics are called 经,

among which are 诗经 (Shījīng, *Shih-ching*, the *Classic of Poetry*, or *Book of Songs*,) 易经 (Yìjīng, *I Ching*, the *Classic of Changes*) and 心经 (Xīnjīng, the *Heart Sutra*) etc. There is a common word 经济 (jīngjì, economy), which is derived from a phrase 经世济民 (jīngshì jìmín, literally 'govern-world-help-people') meaning 'govern and benefit the people.' Also in traditional Chinese medicine (TCM), the meridian system is called 经 (络).

3 常: 常 appears in many common words such as 经常, 常常, 反常, 失常, 常温, 常理, 常用 all of which have a meaning 'constant, normal,' which may be derived from 常, a length measurement of 16 inches in ancient China.

4 经常 vs. 常常: 常常 is taught much earlier than 经常 in the classes of Chinese as a Foreign Language (CFL), however, 经常 is much more frequent than 常常 from the mouths of native speakers.

5 老是 vs. 总是: 老是 is very colloquial.

Exercises:

Part I:

A: Use the given bound form as a guide to help you think of other words with the same character. Feel free to use your dictionary when needed. Then write down the English definition of each of the words you've written.

常 *(often)*: 常常 *often*

____

____

____

____

____

再*(again)*: 再次 *one more time*

____

____

____

____

____

经*(regularly)*: 经济 *economy*

____

____

____

____

B: Write at least two words which have similar meanings with the left column. Feel free to use your dictionary when you need it.

老是	
三番五次	
频频	
时常	

Part II: Read the following sentences and fill in each blank with the appropriate word or phrase from the options given.

1 一向、一直、常年

a) 老王是大学教授, 他对工作___________认真负责.
b) 昨天上午老王__________在办公室忙工作, 没时间给儿子打电话.
c) 老王的儿子在美国工作, ___________居住在国外.

2 常常、往往、不断

a) 老王__________通过邮件跟儿子交流学术 (academic) 上的看法.
b) 老王告诉儿子做研究要__________探索 (tànsuǒ), 这样才有可能成功. 真理___________掌握在少数人手里.

3 不时、照常、不停

a) 在北京很多餐馆春节期间__________营业.
b) 很多老人觉得他们小时候过春节最有意思, 因此会________跟别人讲起那时候的事情.
c) 大年三十的时候很多中国人会____________地用微信 (WeChat) 发红包.

4 频繁、重新、反复

a) 最近几年美国的水污染事件比较___________.
b) 美国新闻媒体__________报道一些州的水污染 (wūrǎn, pollution) 问题.
c) 有人认为美国应该__________制定保护环境的法律.

Theme 286: Adverbs, strong mood 强口气副词 (qiáng kǒuqì fùcí)

1 宁可 [寧-] nìngkě (rather-would) <adv.> would rather, prefer: 他~不休假 (xiūjià) 也要把工作做完. He would rather give up his holidays than not finish his work. || ~早点儿出发也不要迟到. I'd rather leave a little bit earlier than to be late. || 这些人~在城市失业 (shīyè) 也不愿回乡下工作. These people would rather lose their jobs in the city than return to their hometowns to work.

2 宁愿 [寧願] nìngyuàn (rather-want) <adv.> would rather, prefer: 她~自己租房住而不愿意跟父母一起住. She would rather rent her own place, than live with her parents. || 他~把钱存在银行也不买股票. He would rather keep

money in the bank than invest in stocks. || 我~走路也不愿意坐公交车去. I'd rather walk than take public transit to go there.

3 绝 [絕] jué (superb) <adv.> absolutely: ~不愿意 absolutely not be willing || ~没有说过 absolutely not have said || ~不能 absolutely not allowed

4 绝对 [絕對] juéduì (superbly-relative) <adv.> absolutely: ~完美 (wánměi) absolutely beautiful || ~办不到 absolutely can not run to it || ~不可能 absolutely impossible

5 千万 [-萬] qiānwàn (1, 000–10, 000) <adv.> one must by all means: ~记住. One must remember. || ~小心. One must be careful. || ~别干坏事. One must not do bad things.

6 万万 [萬萬] wànwàn (10,000–10, 000) <adv.> absolutely: ~没想到 absolutely not have thought about || ~动不得 be absolutely not allowed to remove

7 死活 [-] sǐhuó (die-live) <adv.> life or death, not matter what: ~不肯 refuse anyway || ~不同意 don't agree anyway || ~不让我做这件事. No matter what, don't let me do this.

8 竟然 [-] jìngrán (unexpectedly-this) <adv.> unexpectedly: ~忘了 unexpectedly forgot || 礼品盒里~是空的. Unexpectedly the gift box is empty. || 他在北京住了两年~没去过天安门广场. He lived in Beijing for two years, but unexpectedly, had never been to Tiananmen Square.

9 居然 [-] jūrán (unexpectedly-this) <adv.> unexpectedly, to one's surprise: 这本小说他~一天就读完了. He unexpectedly finished the novel in one day. || 我~不知道她. To my surprise I don't know her. || ~忘了爸爸的生日 unexpectedly forget father's birthday

10 偏 [-] piān (one-sided, leaning, stubbornly) <adv.> stubbornly: 你不让我去我~要去. If you don't let me go, I want to go more. || 不让吃~吃 not allow to eat, just want to eat more

11 偏偏 [-] piānpiān (specially-*reduplication*) <adv.> stubbornly (indicates that sth. turns out just the opposite of what one would expect or what would be normal), just: ~不知道 just don't know || ~如此 unfortunately it's this way || ~不听 just wouldn't listen

12 难道 [難-] nándào (can't-say) <adv.> don't tell me (a rhetorical question): ~你忘了? Don't tell me you forgot? || ~是真的 Don't tell me it's true. || ~你没有看见? Don't tell me you didn't see it?

13 岂不 [豈-] qǐbù (how-not) <adv.> how couldn't, wouldn't it: 两个人做~麻烦 (máfan)? When two people are involved, how couldn't it be troublesome? || 这样~更好? Would this way be better?

14 究竟 [-] jiūjìng (explore-end) <adv.> after all, on Earth: 你~去哪儿了? Where on Earth are you? || ~是什么意思? So whatever does this mean? || 你~想干什么? What on Earth are you trying to do?

15 何必 [-] hébì (why-must) <adv.> there is no need: ~告诉他 There is no need to tell him. || 有最好的医生在给他看病, 你~担心呢? The best doctor is helping him, there is no need to be nervous.

16 刚好 [剛-] gānghǎo (just-right) <adv.> just, exactly: ~相反 exact opposites || 来得~ came just in right time || ~四十岁 just 40 years old

17 恰好 [-] qiàhǎo (perfectly-right) <adv.> just right, as it turns out: ~看见 just caught sight of || ~一个月 just a month || ~相反be opposite just right

18 恰恰 [-] qiàqià (just-just) <adv.> jus, exactly: 我去找他他~不在. I went to find him, but he just wasn't there || 你的话~证明 (zhèngmíng) 了我的观点. Your words exactly proved my point. || ~相反 exactly opposite

19 碰巧 [-] pèngqiǎo (meet-by chance) <adv.> by chance, by coincidence: ~看到了 saw it by chance || ~见到一个朋友 saw a friend by chance

20 正 [-] zhèng (right) <adv.> exactly, right now: ~站在她旁边 standing next to her side. || ~相反 exactly opposite

21 正好 [-] zhènghǎo (just-right) <adv.> just (in time), just right: 来得~ came in good time

22 正巧 [-] zhèngqiǎo (just-by chance) <adv.> just in time: 你来得~我们正准备吃饭. You came just in time, we were just preparing to eat. || ~不在家 just left home. || ~出去了just went out.

23 反倒 [-] fǎndào (on the contrary-but) <adv.> but on the contrary: 雨不但没停~下得更大了. The rain didn't stop, on the contrary, it started raining harder.

Tips:

1 Characters, words to strengthen the mood: Words with the following characters likely coincide with a strong mood. All words except one are entries of this chapter.

   a. 宁: 宁可, 宁愿
   b. 竟: 竟然, 究竟
   c. 居: 居然
   d. 恰: 恰恰, 恰好
   e. 偏: 偏偏, 偏
   f. 正: 正, 正好, 正巧, 反正 (anyway)

2 Compounds with opposite constituents: They are also likely to carry a stong mood. For example,

   a. 反正 (fǎnzhèng, obverse-reverse): in any case, anyway. 反正这门课我过不了, 现在为什么不好好玩儿? I will fail this course anyway, why not have some fun now?
   b. 死活 (sǐhuó, die-live): no matter what. 无论我怎么求他, 他死活不答应. No matter how hard I begged him, he simply would not agree.
   c. 高低 (gāodī, high-low): on any account. 你不让我试, 我高低要试一下. You won't let me try? I will try it on any account.
   d. 好歹 (hǎodǎi, good-bad): in any case, anyhow. 我知道你也有难处, 但是我真的缺钱, 你好歹借我点儿吧? I know it is not easy for you either, but I really need money. Please lend me some money anyhow.

Exercises:

Part I:

A: Match the following words by considering their similar expressions.

1 反正我不同意	a. 这样难道不是更好
2 他死活不答应	b. 我绝不同意你去北京

3 我高低要试一试
4 你好歹也帮帮我
5 雨不但没停反倒越下越大
6 你何必帮他
7 难道你不知道
8 这样岂不更好
9 我恰好遇见她
10 我绝对不同意你去北京

c. 我碰巧遇到她
d. 你竟然不知道
e. 你为什么要帮他
f. 雨不但没停反而越下越大
g. 不管怎么样你都要帮帮我
h. 不管怎么样我都要试一试
i. 他无论怎么样都不答应
j. 无论怎么样我都不同意

B: Use the given bound form as a guide to help you think of other words with the same beginning character. Feel free to use your dictionary when needed. Then write down the English definition of each of the words you've written.

宁(rather): 宁可 would rather
宁 ________________
竟(unexpectedly): 竟然 unexpectedly
竟: ________________
恰(just): 恰恰 just, exactly
恰 ________________
正(exactly, right now): 正好 just in time, just right
正 ________________
正 ________________
正 ________________

Theme 287: Adverbs, soft mood 弱口气副词 (ruò kǒuqì fùcí)

1 不妨 [-] bùfáng (no-harm) <adv.> there is no harm in, might as well: ~试一试 might as well try || ~多住几天. Might as well stay a few more days. || 有话~直接说出来. If you have something to say, you might as well say it.

2 也好 [-] yěhǎo (also-ok) <adv.> it may not be a bad idea, no matter whether: 出去散散心~. Going out to drive away one's worries may not be a bad thing. || 当面~背面~, 大家都喜欢叫他"老好人." No matter whether it's to his face and behind his back, everyone says he's 'a nice guy.' || 工作~, 生活~, 都需要认真对待. Whether it's work or life affairs, they all must be taken care of appropriately.

3 还 [還] hái (fairly) <adv.> fairly, still: 我现在~好. I'm fine right now. || ~不敢面对她. I still don't dare to face her. || ~不太相信. I still don't really believe.

4 情愿 [-願] qíngyuàn (heartedly-want) <v.> be willing to,would rather: 心里~ the heart is willing || 不~认输 not willing to admit defeat || 两相~ both sides are willing || 心甘~ be most willing to

5 怎么 [-麼] zěnme (how-*suffix*) <adv.> how? what? anyhow: 他~也不肯休息. Anyhow, he would not like to rest.

6 当然 [當-] dāngrán (certainly-this) <adj./ adv.> of course: ~有困难 of course there will be hardship || 我~很开心. Of course I'm happy. || ~可以. Of course that's fine.

7 不用说 [--說] bú yòng shuō (not-need-say) <adv.> needless to say: ~一千块, 就是两千块他也付得起. Don't mention 1000, he could even afford to pay 2,000.
8 难怪 [難-] nánguài (hardly-blame) <adv.> no wonder: 他考了第一名, ~那么高兴. He got the top test score – no wonder he's so happy.
9 怪不得 [-] guàibudé (blame-not-able) <adv.> no wonder: ~他游得这么快, 原来他从小就开始练游泳. No wonder he swam so fast, he's been practicing swimming from childhood.
10 固然 [-] gùrán (truly-this) <adv.> firmly, definitely: 工作~重要, 但也得注意身体. Work is definitely important, but you need to monitor your health.

11 不至于 [--於] bùzhìyú (not-arriving-at) <adv.> cannot go so far, most unlikely: ~这么脏 It is not supposed to be so dirty || ~挨饿 (ái'è) be unlikely suffering from hunger || 虽然堵点儿车, 但是~用两个小时吧? Even though there is a little bit of traffic, it won't necessarily take two hours.
12 动不动 [動-動] dòngbudòng (easily-not-easily) <adv.> apt to happen (usually something unpleasant), frequently: ~发脾气 was apt to lose one's temper || ~就请假 apt to ask for leave || 她~就说她爸爸认识某某领导. It is habitual for her to say that her father knows a certain administrator.
13 其实 [-實] qíshí (its-fact) <adv.> in fact, in actuality, in reality: ~不难. In actuality, it's not very hard. || 他~很笨. In actuality he's really stupid. || ~不对. Actually, that's incorrect.
14 实际上 [實際-] shí jì shàng (fact – wise) <adv.> in reality, in fact, actually: ~她才二十岁. In reality, she's just 20. || ~这两兄弟很不一样. In reality, these two brothers are quite similar.
15 实质上 [實質-] shí zhì shàng (essence – wise) <adv.> virtually, in essence: ~的变化 virtual change || 这件事~两家大公司在竞争. This event is really about a competition between two corporations. || ~是一回事. This is actually one matter.
16 骨子里 [--裏] gǔzilǐ (bone-inside) <n.> beneath the bones, under the surface, at heart: 他表面上看很勇敢~却很懦弱 (nuòruò). On the surface, he seems very brave, but under the surface, he's very fragile. || 他~看不起穷人. He looks down upon the poor at heart.
17 不免 [-] bùmiǎn (not-avoidable) <adv.> unavoidably: ~伤心 unavoidably hurt || ~担心 unavoidably nervous || ~好奇 unavoidably curious
18 难免 [難-] nánmiǎn (hard-avoid) <adv.> hard to avoid: ~紧张 nervous feelings are hard to avoid || ~出错. Mistakes are hard to avoid. || ~失望 it's hard to avoid losing hope
19 未免 [-] wèimiǎn (un-avoidable) <adv.> truly, rather a bit too: 古典音乐~太无聊了. The classical music is rather too literal/boring. || ~太过分了. This is really going too far. || 这样做~太小气了. It's small of him to do so.
20 免不了 [-] miǎnbuliǎo (avoid-not-able) <adv.> cannot be avoided, unavoidably, inevitably: ~紧张. Nervousness cannot be avoided. || ~失败. Defeat cannot be avoided. || ~担心. Worry cannot be avoided.

21 相反 [-] xiāngfǎn (mutual-opposite) <v./adj.> contrary, opposite: 完全~ completly opposite || ~的作用 opposite effect || 她的想法常常与别人~. His thoughts are often different from others.
22 幸亏 [-虧] xìngkuī (fortunately-luckily) <adv.> fortunately: ~有朋友帮忙他的公司才没倒闭(dǎobì). Fortunately, with the help of friends, his company did not fail.

23 好在 [-] hǎozài (luck-lies) <adv.> fortunately, luckily: ~她是学医的, 知道怎么办. Fortunately, she's a medical student and knows what to do.
24 无故 [無-] wúgù (no-reason) <adv.> without cause: ~缺课 miss classes without cause || ~请假 ask for leave without reason || ~解除 (jiěchú) 合同 rescind the contract without reason
25 也 [-] yě (even) <adv.> also, at all: 一点儿~不错 not bad at all
26 莫非 [-] mòfēi (perhaps-not) <adv.> Can it be that: ~这位年轻的姑娘是这儿的领导? Can it be that this young girl is an administrator here? || ~她生病了? Can it be that she became ill? || ~他是坏人? Can it be that he's a bad person?

27 哪里 [-裏] nǎlǐ (what-place) <adv.> in rhetorical questions to express negation: 他~知道? How could he know? || 他说的是德文, 我~听得懂? He speaks German. How can I understand?

28 干嘛 [幹嘛] gàn ma (do-what) <adv.> Why? : 你~不去? Why are you not going? || 你~不说话? Why did you not speak? || 你~不穿衣服? Why are you not wearing clothes?
29 如何 [-] rúhé (like-what) <adv.> how, what way: 这个问题~解释? How to explain this question? || 她汉语说得~? How is her Chinese? || 你俩关系~? What is the relationship between the two of you?
30 为什么 [爲-麼] wèishénme (for-what) <pron.> Why? : 他~没来? Why is he not coming? || 草莓~这么贵? Why are strawberries so expensive?
31 能否 [-] néngfǒu (able-not) <aux. v.> whether or not: ~告诉我? Is it possible to tell me? || ~一起去? Is it possible to go together? ||一个人~成功关键 (guānjiàn) 在人际关系. The success of a person is dependent on his ability to build relationships.

Tips:

1 不免, 难免, 未免, 免不了: 免 originally means 'crown' (冕) from which evolved meanings such as 'take off,' 'set free' and 'avoid.' 不免 means 'unavoidably,' 难免 'inevitably,' 未免 'rather,' and 免不了 (cannot be avoided.) 未免 also carries a soft tone of criticizing or blaming.
2 难怪 vs. 怪不得: Both mean 'no wonder,' but 怪不得 (no wonder) is more colloquial than 难怪 (unsurprisingly.)
3 Words with a soft mood tend to be colloquial, but 能否, 如何, 莫非 and 固然 are more formal.

Exercises:

Part I:

A: Match the following words by considering their similar expressions.

1	能否成功	a.	实际上他才19岁
2	如何解释	b.	好在他朋友帮了他
3	无故请假	c.	免不了失败
4	难免失败	d.	很肤浅
5	心甘情愿	e.	可以试一试

6 不妨一试
7 未免太肤浅 (fūqiǎn)
8 幸亏他朋友帮了他
9 其实他才19岁

f. 心里很愿意
g. 没有原因就请假
h. 怎么解释
i. 能不能成功

B: Match the following phrases to the formal expression column and informal expression column.

Formal expressions	Informal expressions
1. 莫非他因病未来学校	难道他因为生病没来学校
2. 你为何不使用自己的电脑?	怪不得学习这么差
3. 本质上歧视 (qíshì) 穷人	动不动就不去上课
4. 经常旷课 (kuàngkè)	骨子里看不起穷人
5. 难怪成绩很差	你干嘛不用自己的电脑?

Theme 288: Adverbs, negation 否定副词 (fǒudìng fùcí)

1 不 [-] bù (not, no) <adv.> no, not: ~理想 (lǐxiǎng) not ideal || ~看 not see || ~红 not red
2 未 [-] wèi (future, not yet) <adv.> have not, not yet: 并~ not yet || ~成年 not yet an adult || 时机~成熟 (chéngshú). The time is not yet right.
3 无 [無] wú (no, nothing) <adv.> not to have, no: ~背景 (bèijǐng) no background || ~原则 no principles || 这个问题~解. This is an irresolvable problem.
4 非 [-] fēi (opposite, not) <adv.> to not be, not: ~去不可 must go there || ~正式 not formal || ~重点大学 non-key university
5 从不 [從-] cóngbù (ever-not) <adv.> never: ~喝牛奶 never drank milk || ~说假话 never told a lie || ~生气 never get angry
6 从没 [從沒] cóng méi (ever-never) <adv.> never (in the past): ~见过 have never seen each other in the past || ~来过. I've never come here. || ~去过. I've never been.
7 从未 [從-] cóng wèi (ever-not yet) <adv.> never: ~见面. I've never met. || ~想过 I've never thought of || ~请过假. I've never asked for vacation.
8 毫不 [-] háobù (least-not) <adv.> not in the least, not at all: ~复杂 not in the least complicated || ~在意. I've never cared at all. || ~怀疑. I've never suspected.
9 决不 [決-] juébù (for all the world-no) <adv.> on no account, never: ~低头 never given in || ~放弃 never give up || ~分开 to never publicize
10 决非 [決-] jué fēi (for all the world-not) <adv.> absolutely not: ~易事 absolutely not easy || ~偶然 absolutely not incidental || ~寻常 (xúncháng) absolutely not ordinary
11 绝不 [絕-] juébù (absolutely-no) <adv.> in no way, not in the least: 我说话~夸张 (kuāzhāng). My words are in no way exaggerated. || 他们的关系~正常. Their relationship is in no way normal.
12 不再 [-] búzài (not-again) <adv.> no more, no longer: ~看 no longer see || ~反对 no longer oppose || ~吃肉 no longer eat meat
13 未能 [-] wèi néng (not-able) <adv.> cannot, fail to: ~如愿 cannot have one's wishes fulfilled || ~赶到 cannot immediately arrive || ~恢复 (huīfù) cannot restore oneself

14 没 [沒] méi (disappear, none, not) <adv.> not: ~买 have not purchased || ~睡 have not slept || ~听说 have not heard
15 没有 [沒-] méiyǒu (not-have) <adv.> not have: ~参加 have not participated || ~看到 have not seen || ~下班 have not gotten off work
16 并未 [-] bìngwèi (at all-not) <adv.> and have not: ~消失 has not disappeared || ~改变 has not changed || ~实现 has not been fulfilled, realized
17 别 [別] bié (don't) <adv.> don't: ~说 don't speak || ~客气 don't be over polite, formal || ~回去 don't return
18 不要 [-] búyào (not-will) <adv.> don't: ~急 don't panic || ~吵架! Don't fight! || ~生气. Don't be angry.
19 不用 [-] búyòng (not-use) <adv.> not-use, don't need: ~工作就有钱花. You don't need to work, you have money to spend. || ~多说我都明白了. You don't need to say anything, I understand. || 你~来了. You don't need to come (here).
20 莫 [-] mò (dusk, not) <adv.> do not, there is none who: ~管他人. Do not mind other people. || 闲人~入. No admittance except on business, off limits to all unauthorized personnel.
21 请勿 [請-] qǐngwù (please-not) <v.> please don't: ~打扰 (dǎrǎo) Please don't disturb. || ~停车. Please don't stop, park your car. || ~随地吐痰 (tǔtán). Please don't spit on the ground.
22 休想 [-] xiūxiǎng (don't-imagine) <v.> don't imagine that it's possible: ~知道. I didn't know it was possible || ~逃跑 (táopǎo). Don't think escape is possible.

Tips:

1 Sound of the initials of negation words: Almost all of the negation words in ancient and middle Chinese have an initial of either [p-] or [m-].

2 不, 没, 未, 非, 别, 莫, 勿:

a. 不: 不 originally means 'a bird flew to the sky and would not come back' according to the oldest Chinese dictionary. The meaning 'not' is derived from the part 'would not come back' in the original meaning.

b. 没: 没 originally means 'submerged in water, disappear.' The meaning 'no' is derived from 'disappear.'

c. 未: 未might originally mean 'a tree with new branches' from which the meaning 'future, not yet' is derived.

d. 非: 非 depicts 'two opposite wings of a bird' from which evolved the meaning 'not the same.'

e. 别: 别 originally means 'to divide up' from which the meaning 'another' and later 'do not' are derived.

f. 莫: 莫 depicts 'the sun (sets) in the grass, dusk' from which derived meanings such as 'no one,' 'do not,' and 'not.'

g. 勿: 勿 means 'not, do not.'

不 can negate the past, the present and the future. 没 and 未 negate the past. 非, if used not in a compound word, usually functions as 'non-' and negates a noun, for example 非主流 (non-mainstream), and 非政府组织 (NGO.) 别, 莫 and 勿 are used in imperative sentences.

3 不用 and 甭: 甭 (béng) is a compressed form of 不用, and it is very colloquial, for example, 甭去了 (Don't go.)
4 Typical written words in this chapter: 未, 莫 and 勿.

Exercises:

Part I:

A: Match the following words by considering their similar expressions.

1 未成年	a. 一点儿也没改变
2 请勿打扰	b. 一定不是容易的事
3 休想知道	c. 别想知道
4 绝非易事	d. 请不要打扰
5 并未改变	e. 还没有成年

Theme 289: Prepositions, space and time 时空介词 (shíkōng jiècí)

1 从 [從] cóng (follow, from) <prep.> from, via, through: ~九点到十二点from nine o'clock to twelve o'clock || ~银行回来came back from the bank || ~她身边经过pass her by
2 由 [-] yóu (from) <prep.> from, via, through: ~内向外from inside to outside || ~北向南from north to south || ~外国进口 to import from foreign countries
3 于 [於] yú (at) <prep.> at, in,on: ~四月出生 Born in April || ~广州成立set up in Guangzhou || 生~1984年born in 1984
4 自 [-] zì (from) <prep.> from, since: ~南向北 from south to north || 产~意大利 made in Italy || ~六月以来since June
5 自从 [-從] zìcóng (start-from) (of time) <prep.> from, since: ~有了电脑, 我们的生活真的变了样. Our life has really changed since we used the computer. || ~吃素 (chīsù) 以后, 她的身体状况好多了. She feels much better since she became a vegetarian.
6 由此 [-] yóucǐ (from-this) <adv.> from this: ~不难看出. It is not hard to see from this. || ~可见thus it can be seen || ~可以知道. It can be seen, in light of this.
7 至 [-] zhì (arrive at) <prep.> to, until: 两点~四点半from two o'clock to four thirty || 八日~十日from the 8th to the 10th || 纽约~华盛顿from New York to Washington
8 直到 [-] zhídào (all the way-to) <v.> until: ~现在until now || ~九月底until the end of September || ~十八岁不能喝酒. You can't drink alcohol until you're 18.
9 等到 [-] děngdào (wait-to) <v.> by the time, when: ~九点以后, 你就可以唱歌了. By nine o'clock, you can sing. || ~你生日那天才能打开. You can't open it until your birthday.
10 当 [當] dāng (when) <prep.> when: ~他上小学的时候就对物理 (wùlǐ) 非常感兴趣. He was very interested in physics when he was in primary school. || ~你长大后才能明白这些道理. You cannot understand those truths until you grow up.

11 在 [-] zài (at) <prep.> be at, in, or on (a place): ~家里休息 rest at home || ~银行工作work in a bank || 远~天边, 近~眼前seemingly far away, actually close at hand (said playfully to call attention to sb. or sth. right in front of sb.'s eyes.)
12 经过 [經過] jīngguò (pass-through) <prep.> after, through: ~努力他终于成功了. After hard work, he finally succeeded. || ~调查, 事实清楚了. After an investigation, the facts are clear.
13 经 [經] jīng (pass) <prep.> after, through: ~他同意agreed by him || ~上级批准 (pīzhǔn) approved by a supervisor || ~朋友帮助through a friend's help

Tips:

1 自: It originally means 鼻 (bí, nose), and later obtained some meanings such as 'oneself,' and 'beginning, origin,' and ultimately 'from, since.'
2 自 vs. 自从: 自从 requires a specific, detailed time noun or event as its object, whereas a spatial or directional noun can be the object of 自.
3 至: It originally meant 'an arrow reached the ground,' and easily acquired the meaning '(arrive) at, to.'

Exercises:

I: Fill in the blanks with the Chinese characters of the given English words.

Since thus it can be seen

1 ________中国政府决定减少煤 (méi, coal) 产量 (chǎnliàng), 关闭火电厂以来, 山西省就停止了经济增长, __________, 保护环境对中国经济发展影响很大.

Approved by a supervisor In 2015

2 ________, 山西省政府决定____________开始经济转型 (zhuǎnxíng), 发展文化旅游产业.

Until the Ming Dynasty By the time of 1980s

3 山西历史上森林资源 (zīyuán) 非常丰富, _______________才开始慢慢减少. _______________山西的森林已经几乎没有了.

When he worked in Shanxi from North to South from East to West

4 ______________________, 他____________________, _________________走遍了整个山西.

Theme 290: Prepositions, directional 方位介词 (fāngwèi jiècí)

1 朝 [-] cháo (morning, facing) <prep.> facing, towards: ~东towards the east || ~前towards the front || ~阳towards the sun || ~远处走去head for a distant place
2 往 [-] wǎng (go, to) <prep.> in the direction of, towards, to: ~下go down || ~南边走 go southwards || ~左 go the left
3 向 [-] xiàng (face, toward) <prep.> in the direction of, towards, to: ~北to the north || ~你学习learn from you

4 朝着 [-著] cháozhe (facing-*suffix*) <prep.> facing, towards: ~出口的方向跑run in the direction of the exit || ~这个目标努力work towards that goal || ~新方向发展move in a new direction
5 面对 [-對] miànduì (face-to) <prep./v.> face, confront, be faced with: ~事实face the facts || ~挑战, 我们要团结一致. In the face of challenges, we must unite. || ~彼此face each other
6 顺着 [順著] shùnzhe (following-*ing*) <prep.> follow, following, along: ~河流往前走go along the river || ~这个思路做follow this line of thinking to do || ~一条小路走follow a path to go
7 向着 [-著] xiàngzhe (face-*ing*) <prep.> turn towards, face: ~这个目标努力work towards this goal || ~电影院走去go towards the cinema
8 背对 [-對] bèiduì (back-to) <prep./v.> be behind, be back to: ~大山back to the mountain || ~人群back to the crowd
9 背靠 [-] bèikào (back-against) <prep./v.> back on, back against, lean against: ~大树 leaning against a big tree || 把钢琴放在那儿, ~着墙. Put the piano there, with its back against the wall.

Tips:

1 朝, 向, 对: All have a meaning 'toward.' The original meaning of 朝 is early morning, derived from 'the sun (日) is visible in the grass (屮, 十) while the moon (月) is not yet set.' Therefore a meaning 'toward' was later added. 向 originally means 'a north-facing window,' but later it could be used in any direction. 对 (對) originally means 'to answer' and later acquired the meaning 'two people talk face to face.'
2 朝 vs. 朝着, and 向 vs. 向着: Neither 朝着 nor 向着 can have a monosyllabic direction, such as '东' as its object, whereas 朝 and 向 can.

Exercises:

Part I: Answer the following questions based on your own perspectives.

1 你家的门朝哪个方向?

____

2 你房间里的床背靠哪儿?

____

3 从你家开车一直往什么方向可以上高速公路?

____

4 你觉得房子朝着湖好还是背对着湖好?　　为什么?

____

5 一个人一定要有人生目标吗? 为什么?

____

6 你愿不愿意面对一些新挑战, 为什么?

____

Theme 291: Prepositions, disposal 处置介词 (chǔzhì jiècí)

1 把 [-] bǎ (hold, handle) <prep.> used to shift the object ahead of the verb, which must be reduplicated or accompanied by some other word or expression: ~门关上. Close the door. || ~水喝了. Drink up the water. || ~驾照给我看看. Show me your driver's license.

2 将 [將] jiāng (take, use) <prep.> same as "把," but only used in writing: ~糖放入牛奶中. Put the sugar in the milk. || ~衣服穿上. Put on your clothes. || ~座位让给老年人. Give up your seat to the senior.

3 被 [-] bèi (by) <prep.> used in a passive structure to introduce either the doer of the action, or the action alone: 他偷东西~看见了. He was seen stealing. || 他~狗咬了一口. He was bitten by the dog. || 他~打伤了. He was wounded.

4 叫 [-] jiào (by) <prep.> [in a passive sentence to introduce the doer of the action] make, let: ~人惊喜to surprise people || ~人难忘to make people unforgettable || 不要~他知道don't let him know

5 让 [讓] ràng (ask, let) <prep.> [in a passive sentence to introduce the doer of the action] make, let: ~蚊子咬了be bitten by a mosquito. || 我~他骗了. I was deceived by him. || ~小偷偷了. I was stolen from.

6 为 [為] wéi (do, by) <prep.> with 所in a passive sentence: ~我所用 be used by me || ~天下人所笑be laughed by everyone in the world || 他这样做也是~人所利用. He did this because he was taken advantaged of by someone.

Tips:

1 被: The original meaning of 被 is 'blanket, quilt,' from which evolved the meaning 'to cover,' and then 'to suffer.' Ultimately, it evolved into a grammatical marker of passive voice.

2 把, 将 and 让 introduce the object of the action verb, while 被, 让 and 为 introduce the subject of the action verb.

Exercises:

Part I: Use the given word or grammar to answer the following questions.

1 美国把哪一天定为国庆节? (将)
2 你觉得美国的哪个节日最让人难忘? (叫)
3 你觉得美国哪个总统最受大家喜爱吗? (为 . . . 所 . . .)

Part II: 填空 *Fill in the blanks*

Read the following passage and fill in each blank with the appropriate word or phrase from the given options.

把、让

1 小王的儿子虽然刚刚3岁, 但是小王已经在打算怎么可以______儿子上北京重点小学. 小王打算_____现在住的大房子卖了, 然后到一个北京重点小学附近买一个小房子. 他叫一个中介公司帮他办理这件事情, 于是于2017年9月和这个公司签了合同.

为、被、将

2 《北京晚报》新闻: 最近北京市民王先生______某中介公司所骗. 中介(zhōngjiè, agent) 公司______王某房产低价卖出后, 并没有积极帮助王某买到合适的学区房. 《北京晚报》提醒 (tíxǐng, remind) 市民, 买卖房屋时选择口碑 (kǒubēi, reputation) 较好的中介公司, 不要_______某些不良中介公司欺骗.

Theme 292: Prepositions, introducing objects 对象 (duìxiàng)

1 由 [-] yóu (cause, from) <prep.> be up to sb., rest with sb.: ~老板决定determined by the boss || ~大家选择choose from everyone || ~他们解决solved by them

2 跟 [-] gēn (heel, follow) <prep.> with, (expressing comparison) as: 她~我学中文. She studies Chinese with me. || 他的书~我的一样. His book is the same as mine. || 美国~以色列的关系一直很好. America and Israel's relationship has consistently been good.

3 和 [-] hé (with) <prep.> and, with: ~爸爸通话 have a conversation with father || ~姐姐一起走 go with one's older sister

4 同 [-] tóng (same) <prep.> with, and: ~他一起去 go with him || ~中国的关系 relationship with China

5 与 [與] yǔ (give, with) <prep.> with: ~她认识才两年have only known her for two years || ~他无关have nothing to do with him

6 随着 [隨著] suízhe (follow-ing) <prep.> along with, in the wake of: ~人口的增加with the increase of population || ~经济的发展with the development of economy || ~社会的进步with the progress of society

7 给 [給] gěi (give, for) <prep.> for, to: ~她讲故事tell her a story || ~他写信write him a letter || 卖~客人 sell to customers

8 替 [-] tì (take the place of) <prep.> substitute for: ~他做 to do it for him (replace him) || ~你拿着 hold it for you || ~她上课take her class

9 为 [為] wèi (for) <prep.> because of, in the interest of: ~了 in interest of || ~大家服务 do service for others || ~什么 what is it for

10 比 [-] bǐ (compare) <prep./v> compare, more: 弟弟~哥哥高. the little brother is taller than the older brother || 苹果~香蕉好吃. Apples are better tasting than bananas. || 飞机~火车快多了. A plane is much faster than a fire engine.

11 用于 [-於] yòngyú (use-for) <v.> use for: ~这个项目 (xiàngmù) use for the project || ~发展生产 use for the expansion of production || ~家庭建设 (jiànshè) use for family construction

12 为了 [爲-] wèile (for-*suffix*) <prep.> because of: ~吃上新鲜的食物她每天都去超市买菜. In order to buy fresh food, she will go to the market everyday. || ~维持 (wéichí) 社会稳定 (wěndìng) 政府限制 (xiànzhì) 老百姓访问外国网站. In order to preserve social harmony, the government limited the foreign websites that people can visit.

13 对 [對] duì (face, toward) <prep.> towards, to: ~她很关心 be very caring to her || ~动物的保护 be protective to animals || ~西方人的看法 view towards Western people
14 对于 [對於] duìyú (face-toward) <prep.> with regard to: ~我们来说这是很重要的. In our opinions, this is a very important matter. || ~孩子来说画画比写字更有意思. In the opinion of a child, drawing is more interesting than writing characters.
15 关于 [關於] guānyú (concern-with) <prep.> pertaining to, concerning: ~这个问题他们已经商量了很久. We've already had long discussions related to this question. || ~新老板的情况大家都不知道. In regards of the new management situation, we all know nothing. || ~这本书读过的人不多. In regards to this book, few people have read it.
16 至于 [-於] zhìyú (arrive-at) <prep.> as for, as to: 我不相信这件事, ~他信不信, 我就不知道了. I don't believe this thing. As to whether he believed it, I don't know. || ~生活习惯, 留学生的情况各不相同. As for living habits, international students are very different.
17 通过 [-過] tōngguò (pass-through) <prep.> by means of, through: ~朋友帮忙 through the help of friends || ~事实说话 let the facts speak
18 针对 [針對] zhēnduì (aim-at) <prep.> be direct at, aim at, be against: ~不法行为 directed towards illegal actions || ~这种情况我们调整了策略. In regards to this situation, we've already adjusted our strategy. || ~每个人的特点来安排工作 assign work to each person based on their own individualities

Tips:

1 于 (於): 于 (於) is one of the most frequently used characters in functional words. It could function as 'than, at, from, toward, with' etc. For example:

a. than: 大于 (greater than), 小于 (less than), 高于 (higher than), 好于 (better than)
b. at: 至于 (as for, as to)
c. from: 由于 (because of), 处于 (處於, be in a certain condition), 源于 (originate from)
d. toward: 对于 (with regard to)
e. with: 关于 (concerning)

All of the above-mentioned 于 (於) appear at the end of the words, but there is a word in which 于 (於) is at the beginning of the word, 于是 (於是, therefore.)

2 比, 从, 北, 化: These four characters look quite different, especially condisering their left parts. However, their meanings are all derived from the relative position of their parts, two people. 比 depicts two men standing side by side, thus getting its meaning 'to compare.' 从 depicts a man following the other, thus getting its meaning 'to follow, with.' 北 depicts two men back to back, thus getting its meaning 'opposite.' 化 depicts one man straight up and one man upside down, thus getting its meaning 'change.'

Exercises:

Part I: 填空 Fill in the blanks

A. Read the following sentences and fill in each blank with the appropriate word or phrase from the given options.

由、与、给、替、为、比、对

1 改革开放以后，美国______中国的交流越来越多了.
2 多吃蔬菜______身体是很有好处的.
3 你知道吸烟对身体不好，______什么还吸?
4 学生能不能上大学是______他们的考试成绩决定的.
5 要是你明天有事不能去开会, 我可以______你去.
6 城市里的工作机会______农村多得多.
7 上大学的时候, 小明常常______妈妈打电话.

B. Read the following passage and fill in each blank with the appropriate word or phrase from the given options.

用于、对于、关于、至于

小张是一位年轻的科学家，她______环境保护有非常大的兴趣. 这几年她在报纸上发表了好几篇______环境的文章. 她希望自己的研究 (research) 成果 (result) 能够______环境保护, 为国家做贡献 (contribution). 小张最希望以后能在研究所工作, ______是在北京还是在其他的地方, 她都觉得没关系.

为了、随着、通过、针对

______经济的发展，环境污染(pollution) 问题也越来越严重. 因此, ______解决各种各样的环境污染问题，政府采取了不同的措施 (measure). 比方说, "单双号"政策就是______汽车带来的污染而提出的办法. 政府也提倡 (advocate) 工厂______采用新设备 (equipment) 的方法来减少污染.

Theme 293: Prepositions, introducing tools 工具 (gōngjù)

1 按照 [-] ànzhào (according to-same) <prep.> according to, in accordance with: ~顺序 (shùnxù) according to the order || ~收入in the light to income || ~她说的办do as she says
2 按 [-] àn (to press down>> to control>> according to) <prep.> according to, in the light of: ~时on time, according to schedule || ~规定 (guīdìng) according to the regulations || ~比例 (bǐlì) in proportion to
3 照 [-] zhào (according to) <prep.> according to, in accordance with: ~道理来说according to common practice, by rights, normally || ~法律办事act in accordance with the law || ~老办法做 do it in accordance with the old way
4 依照 [-] yīzhào (follow-according to) <prep.> according to, in accordance with: ~计划adhere to a plan, on schedule || ~法律in accordance with the law || ~规定according to the regulations

5 根据 [-據] gēnjù (rooted-based on) <prep./ v.> according to: ~天气预报 (yùbào), 今天会下雨. According to the weather forecast, it will rain today. || ~学生的年龄分班 assign the class sections according to the students' ages

6 据 [據] jù (based on) <prep.> according to: ~他说according to what he said || ~统计 (tǒngjì) according to the statistics. || ~报道 (bàodào) according to reports, it is reported that

7 凭 [憑] píng (relying on) <prep.> go by, base on: ~兴趣找工作look for a job by interest || ~经验 (jīngyàn) 做事do things by experience || 你~什么批评我? Why do you criticize me?

8 顺 [順] shùn (following) <prep.> in the same direction as, along: ~路走follow this road to go || 汗~着脸往下流. Sweat streamed down his face.

9 沿 [-] yán (along) <prep.> along, to follow (a line, direction etc): ~海一带 coastal areas, coastland || ~公路一直走. Go straight ahead along the highway.

10 沿着 [-著] yánzhe (along-*particle*) <prep.> along, to follow (a line, direction etc): ~这个方向走. Go in this direction. || ~河边跑. Run along the river. || ~95号高速公路开. Drive down highway 95.

11 因 [-] yīn (because of) <prep.> because of, as a result of: 他~不舒服而没来上班. He didn't come to work because he was uncomfortable. || 他~营养 (yíngyǎng) 不良而身材矮小. Due to malnutrition, he is of small build. || ~雨取消 (qǔxiāo) 会议cancelled the meeting due to rain

12 正如 [-] zhèngrú (just-as) <prep.> just as: ~他所说as he said || ~六月的天气一样 just like the weather in June

Tip:

1 按, 照, 依, 据, 凭: All have the meaning 'according to,' 'in accordance with' or 'on the basis of.' 按 means 'to press down,' 'to control' which thus acquired the meaning 'according to.' 依 means 'lean on, rely on' which was derived from 'a man' (亻) in clothes (衣). 据 (據) means 'lean against (a walking cane)' which thus gained the meaning 'to rely on, depend on.' 凭 (凴/憑) means 'lean on, rely on,' which was derived from '(lean on) a table' (几). The above four characters are all related to a body action. 照 originally means 'shine' which was derived from 灬 (火, fire.) It then acquired several meanings such as 'sunshine, sunlight, reflect' and ultimately 'according to.' 照 has a variant form 曌 among many others. 曌 was coined as a given name by the only empress (Wu Zetian, Empress Wu) in the Chinese history. It means 'to shine in the sky (空) like the sun (日) and the moon (月),' which is not far from the original meaning of 照.

Exercises:

Part I:

A: Match the following words by considering their similar expressions.

1 凭什么	a. 因
2 沿着这条路走	b. 顺着这条路走

3 照理来说 c. 按照
4 因为 d. 按理来说
5 依照 e. 为什么

B: Provide the formal counterparts of the following informal expressions.

因为生病而迟到	
根据天气预报说	
照法律办事	
按规定办事	
像六月的天气一样	

Theme 294: Conjunctions, coordinating 并列连词 (bìngliè liáncí)

1 和 [-] hé (and) <conj.> and: 我~你 you and I, you and me || 火车~汽车trains and cars || 苹果~香蕉bananas and apples
2 跟 [-] gēn (follow, with) <conj./prep.> and, with: 我~你一起去. I will go with you. || 她买了肉~鱼. She bought meat and fish.
3 与 [與] yǔ (with, and) <conj./prep.> and, with: 他~我 He and I || 姐姐~弟弟sister and younger brother || 工作~生活work and life
4 同样 [-樣] tóngyàng (same-pattern) <conj.> as well as in, in the same way: 民主党反对共和党的移民政策, ~, 共和党也反对民主党的移民政策. The Democratic Party opposes the Republican immigration policy, and similarly, the Republican Party also opposes the Democratic Party's immigration policy. || 对中国古代的文化, 我们要吸取里面有益的东西, ~, 对外国的也应该这样. We should assimilate the good things in ancient Chinese culture, as well as in foreign cultures.
5 以及 [-] yǐjí (by means of-as well as) <conj.> as well as: 亲戚~朋友relatives and friends || 大陆、香港~台湾mainland, Hong Kong and Taiwan
6 并且 [並-] bìngqiě (side by side-moreover) <conj.> and, besides, moreover, furthermore: 我爸爸喜爱唱卡拉OK, ~唱得很好. My dad likes to sing karaoke, and he sings very well. || 这样想~说出来需要勇气. It takes courage to think this way and also say it. || 聪明~勇敢smart and brave
7 又 [-] yòu (again, and) <adv.> both. . . . . . and. . . . . ., also: ~干净~漂亮clean and beautiful || 小王没钱, 人~懒, 谁会嫁给他呢? Little Wang is poor, and what's more, he is lazy. Who will marry him?
8 而 [-] ér (and) <conj.> and, as well as: 巨大~深刻的变化huge and profound changes || 清晰~合理的规定clear and reasonable rules
9 而且 [-] érqiě (and-moreover) <conj.> and also: 她不但画得好, ~唱得好. He not only draws well but also sings well. || 中国城的菜不但种类多,~价格便宜. Not only are there many vegetables in Chinatown, but they are also inexpensive.
10 同时 [-時] tóngshí (same-time) <conj.> while, besides: 孩子在长大, ~他们的父母在变老. While the children are growing up, their parents are getting old. || 我们的收入在增加, ~生活费用也在增加. While our incomes

increase, the cost of living also increases. || 任务艰巨, ~时间又很紧. The task is arduous and besides, there's little time.

11 一方面 [-] yī fāngmiàn (one-side) <conj.> on the one hand: ~我们要发展经济, ~要保护环境. We should on the one hand develop the economy and on the other hand protect the environment. || 他们~鼓吹和平, ~准备战争. They preach peace while preparing for war.

12 另一方面 [-] lìng yī fāngmiàn (another-side) <conj.> on the other hand, for another: 一方面我是你的经理, ~我也是你的朋友. One the one hand, I am your manager, and on the other hand, I am also you friend. || 在大城市生活, 一方面工作压力很大, ~, 环境污染也很严重. Living in a big city is very stressful on your work, and the environmental pollution is severe.

13 或者 [-] huòzhě (other than-this) <conj.> or, either . . . or. . . : 去~不去 go or not go || 失败~成功failure or success || 自己~别人yourself or others

14 或 [-] huò (or) <conj.> or, either. . . . . . or. . . . . . : 东方 ~西方east or west || 农村~城市rural or urban || 早上~晚上morning or night

15 还是 [還-] háishi (or-be) <conj.> or, no matter what, whether. . . . . . or. . . . . . : 你去~我去? You go or I go? || 喝茶~咖啡? Tea or coffee? || 去银行~去超市? Go to the bank or go to the supermarket?

16 要么 [-麼] yàome (if-*particle*) <conj.> or, either. . . . . . or. . . . . . : ~现在去, ~下午去, 不能等到明天再去. Either go now or go in the afternoon. We can't wait until tomorrow.

17 相反 [-] xiāngfǎn (mutual-opposite) <conj.> on the contrary: 不是我在帮助她, ~, 是她在帮助我. It's not that I was helping him, on the contrary, he was helping me.

Tips:

1 并, 而, 且: The original meaning of 并 (並) is two people standing side by side, so an extended meaning 'and/both' has evolved. The original meaning of 而 is hairs on cheeks. Since cheeks are bilaterally symmetrical, 'both/also' has evolved as a meaning. 且 means 'also/moreover' and its original meaning is 'mat' according to the oldest Chinese dictionary, although some people think 且 depicts a penis since 祖 means 'grandfather, ancestor.' The connection between the original and current meanings is obscure.

2 'And' vs. 和: The English word 'and' has about 13 equivalents in Chinese. If you always translate 'and' into 和, the chance of error is not low, however, if you translate it into '还有,' the chance of error reduces significantly. Nevertheless, this is the last resort. You need to learn as many synonyms to make your language native-like.

Exercises:

Part I: Provide the informal counterparts of the following formal expressions.

工作与生活	
农村与城市	

成功或失败	
大陆、香港以及台湾	
聪明并且勇敢	

Part II: Read the following sentence and fill in each blank with the appropriate word or phrase from the options given.

1 又、要么、或者、相反

a) 中国人一般喜欢在方桌________圆桌上吃饭, 不用长桌吃饭.
b) 美国人认为在长桌上吃饭很好, _________方便又舒服.
c) 中国人喜欢先吃饭后喝汤, _________美国人喜欢先喝汤后吃饭.
d) 我们对待不同文化的态度应该是先理解, 而不是先判断: _______好要么坏.

2 还是、并且、同时、同样

a) 现在中国人的收入增加很快, 但__________生活费用增加得更快.
b) 美国的中产阶级生活压力比以前大多了, _________中国的中产阶级也有这样的问题.
c) 现在很多中国产品不但仅价格便宜, __________ _质量也很好.
d) 优先 (yōuxiān) 发展经济________优先保护环境, 这是中国政府目前面临的难题.

3 而、与、还是、一方面

a) 在大城市生活, _________工作压力很大, 另一方面也要交通堵塞 (dǔsè).
b) 不管是中国的大城市________美国的大城市都有交通问题.
c) 中国的"大城市病"________美国的"大城市病"很像.
d) 自2000年以来北京发生了巨大_________深刻 (shēnkè) 的变化.

Theme 295: Conjunctions, progressive 递进连词 (dìjìn liáncí)

1 不但 [-] bùdàn (not-only) <conj.> not only (. . . . . . but also. . . . . .): 这里的水果~种类多, 而且价格便宜. There are many kinds of fruit here, and the price is very cheap. || 她 ~写对了, 而且写得很漂亮. Not only did she write correctly, but she also wrote beautifully. || 今年夏天~热, 还很闷. This summer is not only hot but also stuffy. || 他~会做中国菜, 而且了解中国的饮食文化. He not only cooks Chinese food but also understands Chinese food culture.

2 不光 [-] bùguāng (not-barely) <conj.> not only: ~好看还有用not only look nice but also be useful || 在中国~年轻人用微信, 老年人也用微信. Not only young people use WeChat, but older people also use Wechat. || 手机~能打电话, 还能购物. Phones cannot only be used to make phone calls, but also to do shopping.

3 不仅 [-僅] bùjǐn (not-entirely) <conj.> not only, not just: 工作~多, 而且难. The work is not only a lot, but it's also difficult. || 这儿~热, 而且干. It is not only hot, but also dry. || 她~年轻, 而且漂亮. She is not only young, but also pretty.

4 何况 [-況] hékuàng (let alone-besides) <conj.> much less, let alone: 这个家具连小伙子都抬不动, ~老人呢. The furniture is too heavy even for a young fellow to lift, let alone an old man. || 别买了, 这些鞋太贵, ~也不好看. Those shoes are expensive- besides, they're not very pretty. || 我没租那个公寓, 因为太小, ~租金也太高. I didn't rent that apartment because it was too small, moreover the rent is too high.

5 加上 [-] jiā shàng (add-on) <conj.> moreover, in addition: 他从小聪明, ~学习又非常努力, 所以很轻松就考上了名牌大学. He had been smart since he was a child and also worked very hard, so he easily got into a famous university.

6 加以 [-] jiāyǐ (add-with) <conj.> in addition, moreover: 他努力上进, ~好的机遇, 很快就找到了好工作. He pushed for his improvement, in addition he got good opportunities, so he found a good job very quickly.

7 还有 [還-] háiyǒu (also-have) <conj.> furthermore, in addition: 大家喜欢他, 因为他工作努力, ~他很会说话. Everyone likes him because he works hard and also has good communication with people.

8 再说 [-說] zàishuō (more-speaking) <conj.> what's more: 时间太晚了, 现在不去找他了, ~他也不一定在家. It too late. Don't go looking for him now, and what's more, he might not be at home now.

9 甚至 [-] shènzhì (even-arriving at) <conj.> go so far as to: 他忙得~两天没睡觉. He was so busy that he didn't even go to bed for two days || 她到过中国很多地方, ~西藏也去过. She has been to many places in China, even to Tibet.

Tips:

1 不但, 不光, 不仅 are used in the first part of a sentence and there is usually corresponding word such as 而且 or 还 etc. in the second part of the sentence. 何况, 加上, 加以, 还有, 再说 etc. are used without fixed corresponding conjunctions.

2 何况 vs. 更不用说: Both mean 'let alone.' 何况 is more formal and 更不用说 more colloquial. There is usually a 了 at the end of a sentence to correspond to 更不用说.

Exercises:

Part I: Read the following sentences and fill in each blank with the appropriate word or phrase from the options given.

1 不但、再说

a) 小王________英文说得流利 (fluent), 广东话也说得很好.
b) 小王想到香港工作, 因为他了解香港文化, ________他女朋友也在香港.

2 不仅、更不用说、还有

a) 微信 (Wechat) 的使用方法特别简单, 连老人都会用, ________年轻人.
b) 其实微信________是一个软件, 它也代表中国人支付方式的变化.

c) 在中国除了城市可以使用微信支付, ________很多农村地区也可以用微信支付.

3 甚至、不光、加上、加以

a) 在中国________年轻人用微信, 老年人也用微信.
b) 微信不仅能用来发短信、打电话, ________还能用来购物、打车、买机票、交水电费等等.
c) 中国市场大, ________劳动力便宜, 因此推广 (promote) 任何一个新产品都会比美国快.
d) 看来在全球化的今天, 不仅仅是中国学习美国, 在某些方面美国也应该向中国________学习.

Theme 296: Conjunctions, concessive 让步连词 (ràngbù liáncí)

1 虽然 [雖-] suīrán (although-this) <conj.> though, although, even if: 他~睡得少, 但是一点不困. Although he slept little, he was not tired at all. || ~他年纪小, 但是很懂事. Although he is young, he is sensible.
2 虽 [雖] suī (although) <conj.> though, although, even if: 这家餐馆的饭菜~贵, 但很好吃. The food in this restaurant is expensive, but it is delicious. || 她妈妈~对她严厉, 但很爱她. Her mother is strict with her, but she loves her very much.
3 尽管 [儘-] jǐnguǎn (only-care) <conj.> though, even though, in spite of, despite: ~中文很难, 但他还是坚持 (jiānchí) 学中文. Although it is difficult to learn Chinese, he still persisted in learning it. || ~六十多岁了, 他还是显得 (xiǎnde) 很年轻. Although he is over 60, he still looks very young.
4 就是 [-] jiùshì (even-be) <conj.> [used correlatively with也] even if: 他每天想着赚钱, ~做梦梦见的也是钱. He was thinking about making money every day, even dreamed of money.
5 即使 [-] jíshǐ (even-if) <conj.> even, even if: ~报酬 (bàochou) 很高, 大家也不愿意干那份工作. Even if the pay is very high, people will not be willing to do that job. || ~今天记住了, 过两天又忘了. Even if you remember it today, you will forget it two days later.
6 哪怕 [-] nǎpà (whatsoever-maybe) <conj.> even, no matter how: 有了互联网, ~不出家门, 也能知道所有事情. With the internet, it is possible to know everything even if you don't go out. || ~不睡觉, 也要把事情做完. Get things done even if you don't sleep.
7 就算 [-] jiùsuàn (even-granted) <conj.> even if, granted that: ~做得很好, 你也不应该骄傲 (jiāo'ào) 吧. Granted, you have done well, but there is no reason to be conceited. || ~知道, 也不想告诉你. Even if I knew, I wouldn't tell you.
8 既 [-] jì (since) <conj.> since, as well as: 你~这么坚决要到中国工作, 我就不劝你了. Since you are so determined to work in China, I will not advise you anymore. || 这种手机~不实用, 又不美观 (měiguān). This kind of mobile phone is neither useful nor attractive.
9 既然 [-] jìrán (since-this) <conj.> since, as, now that: ~你已经感冒了, 吃这种药就没什么用了. Now that you've got a cold, it is useless to take this

medicine. || ~如此, 我们应该更爱护 (àihù) 环境. In this case, we should take better care of the environment.

10 要不然 [-] yàoburán (if-not-this) <conj.> otherwise: 等打折的时候再买苹果手机吧, ~太贵了. Buy an iPhone when it's on sale, otherwise it's too expensive. || 我起得太晚了, ~也不会上课迟到. I got up too late, but I won't be late for class. || 我们明天去游泳吧, ~就去钓鱼. Let's go swimming tomorrow, or we'll go fishing.

Tips:

1 虽: The original meaning of 虽 (雖) is a large lizard. The semantic part is 虫 and the phonetic part is 唯 (wéi) which is very close to 'suī.'

2 即 vs. 既: Both have the part 皀 (ancient form of the left part of both characters) which means 'a dish full of food.' 即 means a man comes close to eat food, while 既 means a man has eaten up the food and leaves. The 既 in 既然 still keeps a part of its original meaning, i.e., 'since,' which is derived from 'after (eating food).'

Exercises:

Part I: Make sentences of your own by following each of the examples given.

1 在西方国家中国菜虽________________, 但____________________.

(Example: 价格便宜, 味道非常好)

2 就算_________________, 很多西方人还是__________________.

(Example: 饭馆环境差一点儿, 喜欢到中国饭馆吃饭)

3 尽管__________ ___, 但是也应该_____________.

(Example: 中餐很流行, 注意质量

4 哪怕__________也要________________.

(Example: 花的时间多一些, 保证产品质量)

5 很多人认为日本产品既____________又_____________.

(Example: 美观 (be pleasing to the eye), 实用 (durable))

6 就算_________________大家也愿意_________________.

(Example: 日本产品贵一点, 买日本产品)

Part II: Use the given grammar to complete the dialogue.

1 儿子: 妈, 我手机坏了, 你再给我买个新的吧?

妈妈: 不行, 太浪费了. ______________________________________.
(要不然)

2 儿子: 听说iPhone 8 比iPhone 7要贵很多.

妈妈: 嗯, 听说了. 但是我不是"果粉" (iPhone fan),____. (即使……也……)

3 儿子: iPhone 8 非常酷, 有很多新功能!

妈妈: ____.
(尽管……还是……)

4 儿子: 妈, 我们中文老师长得不帅, 穿得也不好看, 所以我不喜欢学中文.

妈妈, 不行, ____.
(哪怕……也要……)

5 儿子: 我出生在美国, 是美国人, 为什么要学中文?

妈妈: ____.
(就算……也……)

Theme 297: Conjunctions, contrary 转折连词 (zhuǎnzhé liáncí)

1 但是 [-] dànshì (but-be) <conj.> but, yet, still: 这个公园有点远, ~很值得 (zhídé) 去. The park is a little bit far away, but it's worth it. || 虽然困难 (kùnnan) 很多, ~她一点也不怕. It was difficult, but he was not afraid at all.

2 但 [-] dàn (but) <conj.> but, yet, still: 她睡得很晚, ~一点也不困. He slept late, but he was not sleepy at all. || 已经四月了, ~天气还有点儿冷. It's April, but it's still a little bit cold.

3 不过 [-過] bùguò (not-exceeding) <conj.> but, however: 樱桃 (yīngtáo) 很好吃, ~有点贵. The cherries are delicious, but they are a little bit expensive. || 他去那儿了, ~没见到想见的人. He went there, but he didn't see the person he wanted to see.

4 可是 [-] kěshì (but-be) <conj.> but, however: 他努力工作, ~还是失败了. He worked hard, but he failed. || 她很饿, ~找不到饭店吃饭. He was very hungry, but he couldn't find a restaurant to eat.

5 可 [-] kě (but) <conj.> but, however: 她发出很多邀请 (yāoqǐng) 信, ~就是没人来. She sent out many invitation letters, but nobody came. || 到处是脏东西, ~谁也不在乎. There was dirt everywhere, but no one cared.

6 然而 [-] rán'ér (yet-but) <conj.> but, however: 他坚持健身 (jiànshēn) 两个月了, ~体重没有下降. He has been working out for two months, but he hasn't lost weight. || 听起来几内亚猪 (guinea pig) 是来自非洲几内亚的猪, ~, 它既不是猪, 也不来自几内亚. It sounds like guinea pigs are pigs from Guinea in Africa, but it is neither a pig nor from Guinea in Africa.

7 只是 [-] zhǐshì (only-be) <conj.> except that, only, but: 他不累, ~有点困. He's not tired, but just a little bit sleepy. || 他很爱这个女孩子, ~没有说出来. He loved this girl very much, but he didn't say it.

8 却是 [卻-] quèshì (however-be) <adv.> nevertheless, actually, the fact is: 虽然很累, 心情~愉快的. Although tired, he has a pleasant mood. || 我的公寓虽然很小, ~一个自由的天地. Although my apartment is small, it is a free world for me.

9 却 [卻] què (however) <adv.> but, yet, however: 他工作不认真, ~对领导的家庭私事极为关心. He is not serious about his work, but he takes great care of his leader's family affairs. || 演出都准备好了, ~被取消了. The show was ready, but it was cancelled.

10 不料 [-] búliào (not-expected) <conj.> unexpected, to one's surprise: 他计划三个月完成, ~一个月就完成了. He planned to finish the work in three months, but unexpectedly, it was done in a month. || 眼看她就赢了美国总统大选, ~电视上爆出了她的丑闻, 结果她输了. She was about to win the U.S. presidential election, but unexpectedly her scandal broke on TV, and she lost the election.

11 不然 [-] bùrán (not-this) <conj.> or else, otherwise, if not: 住手！~我报警了！ Stop it! Or I'll call the police. || 你得提前一个小时到机场, ~会赶不上飞机. You have to arrive at the airport one hour in advance, otherwise you'll miss the flight.

12 倒是 [-] dǎoshì (on the contrary-be) <adv.> on the contrary [indicating contrast, a turn in meaning, concession or modifying or toning down a preceding statement]：那个地方我~去过, 但是印象 (yìnxiàng) 不深. I've been there, but I'm not impressed with that place. || 他那些成绩好的大学同学现在都是普通白领, ~成绩最差的那个同学现在是中国首富. His college classmates with good grades are ordinary white collar workers, but the worst academic performer is China's richest man now.

Tips:

1 却: The place of 却 in a sentence is very different from that of other conjunctions. It is used after the subject while others are usually placed before the subject. Take the example in Entry 6 '他坚持健身两个月了, 然而体重没有下降' as an example, if 却 be added, it will be 他坚持健身两个月了, 然而体重却没有下降.

2 然: The original meaning of 然 is 'to burn, barbeque' and is derived from 月 (meat), 犬 (dog) and 灬 (fire). In the functional words 然而, 不然, the meaning of 然 is 'yet' and 'this.'

Exercises:

Part I: Choose the most appropriate word to fill in the blank.

1 中国大陆使用简体字 (simplified character), 台湾________使用繁体字 (traditional character). (却、可)

2 台湾的外省人喜欢说普通话, __________本省人一般只喜欢讲台语. (但、只要)

3 中国政府认为台湾是中国的一部分, _________当前的台湾政府反对这一看法. (然而、不然)

4 台湾民进党反对两岸统一, 台湾国民党_________认为在这个问题上两岸可以共同协商. (不过、倒是)

5 台湾一个大学教授在媒体 (media) 说: "大陆人太穷了吃不起茶叶蛋." _________他的说法遭到了很多台湾人的嘲笑 (mock), 笑他太无知. (不料、却是)

Part II: Translate the following sentences into Chinese. Make sure your translation includes the given grammar in each sentence.

1 Mr. Wang has been working out for two months, but he hasn't lost weight. (然而Subj.却 . . .)
2 Mr. Wang has been to Shanghai, but he is not impressed with Shanghai. (倒是)
3 It's Sunday today, but Mr. Wang got up earlier than on weekdays. (却)
4 Mr. Wang has to leave at once or he'll miss the train. (要不然)
5 She was about to win the U.S. presidential election, but unexpectedly her scandal broke on TV, and she lost the election. (不料)
6 Mr. Trump would like to learn Chinese history earnestly, it's just that he hasn't the time. (只是)

Theme 298: Conjunctions, conditional 条件 (tiáojiàn)

1 只要 [-] zhǐyào (only-if) [usu. with就or便] <conj.> if only, as long as, provided that: ~努力, 就会成功. You will succeed as long as you work hard. || 他是酒鬼 (jiǔguǐ), ~有酒, 就很高兴. He is a drunkard, so he will be very happy as long as he has alcohol.

2 只有 [-] zhǐyǒu (only-possessed) <conj.> only, alone: ~每天练习, 你才能学好中文. You can learn Chinese very well only by practicing every day. || ~上帝才能救他. Only God can save him.

3 除非 [-] chúfēi (except-otherwise) <conj.> [used correlatively with才] only if, only when: 这件事谁都处理不了, ~请她来. Nobody can handle this thing unless he is invited. || 我的工资根本不够花, ~再打一份工. My salary is not enough, unless I have another job.

4 除了 [-] chúle (except-*particle*) <conj.> except, [correlatively with还, 也, etc.] besides, in addition to, [correlatively with 就是] if not. . . (then. . .) : ~下雨, 我每天都坚持 (jiānchí) 长跑. I practice long-distance running every day except on rainy days. || 动物园~节日每天都开门. The zoo is open every day except holidays. || ~高薪 (gāoxīn) 以外, 公司还为他提供汽车和在纽约的住房. In addition to a high salary, the company offers him a car and an apartment in New York.

5 与其 . . . . . . 不如 . . . . . . [與---] yǔqí . . . . . . bùrú . . . . . . (rather-than) <conj.> would rather . . . than: ~说他是学者, ~说他是作家. He is a writer rather than a scholar. || ~说成功在于运气, ~说是努力. Success lies not so much in luck as in hard work.

6 不论 [-論] búlùn (not-discuss, speaking) <conj.> [often used correlatively with都or总] no matter (what, who, how etc.), whether . . . or. . ., regardless of: 中国人~走到哪里, 都爱问各种东西的价格. Chinese people love to ask prices of all kinds of things wherever they go. || ~我怎么问, 他都不说. No matter how I asked him, he said nothing. || ~贫穷还是富有, 我都永远爱你. Whether you are poor or rich, I will always love you.

7 无论 [無論] wúlùn (no matter what-is regarded) <conj.> no matter what, how etc., regardless of: 他~做什么工作, 都很认真. Whatever job he does, he takes them very seriously. || ~ 多忙, 她每天都要做一会儿瑜伽 (yújiā). No matter how busy she is, she has to do some yoga every day.

8 无论如何 [無論--] wúlùn rúhé (no matter-how) <conj.> in any case, whatever happens: 今天~别迟到. You can't be late today. || ~也要让她同意. Let her agree anyway.

9 不管 [-] bùguǎn (not-regard of) <conj.> regardless of, no matter (what, who etc.): ~天气怎样, 他每天都去公园锻炼 (duànliàn). He goes to the park to exercise every day, no matter what the weather. || 他~做什么都非常认真. Whatever he does, he takes it very seriously. || ~男女老少, 都喜欢吃这种小吃. Both men and women like to eat this snack.

10 任 [-] rèn (no matter) <conj.> no matter (how, what etc.): ~他怎么说, 老板都不同意. Whatever he says, the boss disagrees. || ~我怎么邀请, 她就是不跟我去吃饭. No matter how often I invite him, he won't go to dinner with me.

11 凡是 [-] fánshì (all-be) <conj.> every, any, all: 这种产品, ~用过的都说好. All people who have used this product say it's good. || 世界上~有中国人的地方, 都有中国饭馆. Wherever there are Chinese people in the world, there are Chinese restaurants.

12 只管 [-] zhǐguǎn (just-regard) <adv.> by all means, simply, just: 有什么问题你~问. If you have any questions, don't hesitate to ask. || 我能帮你什么忙, 你~说. Let me know how I can help you.

13 否则 [-則] fǒuzé (not-then) <conj.> otherwise, if not, or else: 快点儿走, ~要迟到了. go soon, otherwise you'll be late. || 你应该赶紧买房, ~就涨价 (zhǎngjià) 了. You should buy a property soon, otherwise the price will go up.

14 要不是 [-] yàobushì (if-not-be) <conj.> if it were not for, but for: ~为了孩子, 她早就跟丈夫离婚 (líhūn) 了. She would have divorced her husband if it was not for her children. || ~下雨, 我们早就去公园玩了. We would have gone to the park but for the rain.

15 此外 [-] cǐwài (this-besides) <conj.> besides, in addition, moreover: 我买了一个电脑, ~还买了一台空调 (kōngtiáo). I have just bought a laptop, and an air-conditioner as well. || 学生们 每个学期要交学费, ~还有住宿 (zhùsù) 费. Students pay tuition, meals and accommodation for each semester.

16 另外 [-] lìngwài (addition-besides) <adv.> in addition, besides: 她租的房子太远了, ~, 房子也很小. The house she rents is too far away. Besides, it is too small.

17 除 [-] chú (except) <conj.> except, beside, in addition: ~个别地方外, 大部分农村都有了网络. In addition to individual places, most rural areas have internet. || ~他外, 其他人都迟到了. Everyone else was late except him.

Tips:

1 Exceptional or all-inclusive: Conditions could refer to an exceptional one or all-inclusive. Exceptional ones include 只有, 除非, 除了, 除 etc., and all-inclusive ones include 不论, 无论, 无论如何, 不管, 任, 凡是 etc.

2 只要 vs. 只有: 只要 indicates a sufficient condition, besides all other possible ones. Take the above-mentioned example '他是酒鬼, 只要有酒, 就很高兴' for instance, to make him happy, '(he) has alcohol' is one sufficient condition, with others perhaps being 'he watches a soccer game' etc. 只要 is usually used in a pair with 就. 只有 indicates the one and only, or the sole condition, for example, '只有上帝才能救他' indicates only God and not anyone else can save him. 只有 is usually used in a pair with 才.

Exercises:

Part I: 填空 Fill in the blanks

Read the following passage and fill in each blank with the appropriate word or phrase from the given options.

1 除了、另外、还

喝茶在中国有很长的历史, 已经形成了一种文化. 中国人_______非常讲究茶的香味、颜色以外, _________讲究沏茶 (qīchá, make tea) 用的水, 喝茶用的茶杯等等. ________, 饭后饮茶也是中国茶文化的一部分. 这一点跟西方文化里的"下午茶"非常不同.

2 所以、此外、无论

_________在中国还是在美国, 现在大家都认识到饮茶对身体有很多好处. _________, 医生常常让大家少喝咖啡, 多喝茶. _________, 医生也会告诉大家绿茶比红茶更健康.

3 凡是、无论、要不是

在北京喜欢喝咖啡的年轻人越来越多. ________你什么时候去星巴克, 都会看到满满一屋子的年轻人. _________看到星巴克的中文菜单, 你会以为这是在美国. 另外, ________在美国星巴克有的产品, 在北京都可以买到.

Part II: Make sentences of your own by following each of the examples given.

1 除非________________, 要不然我不会__________________.

(Example: 有客人来, 到饭馆吃饭)

2 任________________怎么建议, 我就是__________________.

(Example: 餐馆服务员, 不点他们推荐 (recommend) 的茶)

3 小白非常喜欢喝茶. 只要______________, 他就_____________.

(Example: 商店有新茶, 去买)

4 在中国除__________外, _________________.

(Example: 少数农村, 大部分人都用智能手机)

5 凡是____________都____________________.

(Example: 用过小米手机的人, 说小米手机好)

6 小白认为与其________________不如________________.

(Example: 买苹果手机, 买小米手机)

Part III: Translate the following sentences into Chinese. Make sure your translation includes the given grammar in each sentence.

1 You should buy a property soon, otherwise the price will go up. (否则)
2 Chinese people love to invest in houses wherever they live. (无论 . . . . . . 都 . . . . . .)
3 Wherever there are Chinese people in the world, there are Chinese restaurants. (凡是 . . . . . . 就 . . . . . .)
4 Chinese people think success lies not so much in luck as in hard work. (与其 . . . . . . 不如 . . . . . .)

Theme 299: Conjunctions, expressing supposition 假设连词 (jiǎshè liáncí)

1 如果 [-] rúguǒ (as if-result) <conj.> if, supposing that: ~早一点出发, 就能见到他. If you had started earlier, you would have seen him. || 中国人觉得~喝凉牛奶, 就会肚子疼. Chinese people think you will have a stomachache if you drink cold milk.
2 假如 [-] jiǎrú (suppose-if) <conj.> if, supposing that: ~天气好, 我就会去公园跑步. If the weather is good, I will go jogging in the park. || ~你愿意的话, 我们就一起去吧. Let's go together, if you like.
3 要是 [-] yàoshi (if-be) <conj.> if, in case: ~下雨, 你就别回来了. If it rains, don't come back. || ~不舒服, 就别去上班了. If you don't feel well, don't go to work.
4 要 [-] yào (if) <conj.> if, in case: 他~不去, 我就去. If he doesn't go, I'll go. || 你~今天不去, 就明天去. If you don't go today, go tomorrow.
5 若 [-] ruò (if) <conj.> if: ~不是亲眼见到, 很难相信有这样的事情. If I hadn't seen it myself, it would be hard for me to believe that. || 你~见到她, 请告诉她这件事. If you see him, please tell him about this.
6 万一 [萬-] wànyī (10, 000–1) <conj.> just in case, if by any chance, what if: 晚上不要出去逛街, ~遇到抢劫 (qiǎngjié) 怎么办. Don't go shopping at night. What if you get robbed? || ~被妈妈发现了, 就要挨骂 (áimà) 了. If mom finds out, you will be scolded.
7 那么 [-麼] nàme (then, in that case) <conj.> [used to connect a clause expressing a logical consequence to a conditional clause] then, in that case: 如果有错误, ~请直接告诉我. If there is a mistake, please tell me directly. || 既然改变不了过去, ~就努力改变未来. If you can't change the past, try to change the future.
8 那 [-] nà (then) <conj.> then, in that case: 你如果现在不出发, ~就真的赶不上飞机了. If you don't start now, you'll really miss the plane.

Tips:

1 如, 若, 要: All mean 'if,' with 若 being more formal and 要 more colloquial. 如若 and 若要 both mean 'if' too, but they are more commonly used in written language.
2 一万 vs. 万一: 一万 means 10, 000, and 万一 means '1/10,000, just in case.' A common expression is 不怕一万, 就怕万一 which means 'prepare for the one risk in a million.'

Exercises:

Part I: Fill in the blanks

Read the following sentences and fill in each blank with the appropriate word from the given options.

1 一个中国电视广告这样说: “女人_______想漂亮就得变白一点儿！” (万一、若)
2 _______你对一个中国女人说“你变黑了,” 她一定会不高兴. _______, 虽然中国人喜欢女人白一点, 但是_______不喜欢男人长得白. (却、不过、如果)
3 _________一个中国男人长得白白净净 (fair and clear skin) 的, _______就会被人叫做“小白脸,” 认为他没有男子气. (那、假如、要)
4 在西方人们并不觉得女性皮肤白_________美. 为了有小麦色的皮肤, 很多西方女性去美容院 (beauty parlor) “美黑.” 但也有人不敢去, 她们觉得“不怕_______, 就怕________,” 如果“美黑”失败了, 会对身体健康造成严重的影响. (一万、就、万一)

Part II: Make a new sentence using the italicized expressions.

1 在北京坐地铁上班一定得早起. 要是你在早上七点以后坐地铁, 就一定非常拥挤 (yōngjǐ, crowd).
2 坐地铁的时候你得不怕挤. 假如你怕挤, 就一定坐不了地铁.
3 在北京你可以在晚上十点以后逛街 (window-shopping), 不会有安全问题. 但是若是在纽约, 你就不可以这样做了.
4 在美国上大学的时候父母常常提醒我不要坐陌生人的车. 因为万一遇到坏人就会有生命危险.

Theme 300: Conjunctions, causative 因果连词 (yīnguǒ liáncí)

1 因为 [-為] yīnwèi (because-for) <conj./prep.> because, as, because of, on account of, owing to: 年轻人~工作经验少, 所以不容易找到好工作. It's not easy for young people to find good jobs because they have less work experience. || 他~睡得晚, 觉得头很疼. He got a headache because he was sleeping late.
2 由于 [-於] yóuyú (from-for) <conj.> owing to, thanks to, because, since: ~粗心, 他常常做错事. Due to carelessness, he often did wrong. || ~离公司近, 她中午常常回家休息一下. As she lived close to the company, she often went home for a rest at noon.
3 因 [-] yīn (because of) <conj./prep.> because of, as a result of, because: ~病去世. He died of an illness. || ~害怕而报警call the police for fear || ~失业 (shīyè) 而心情不好. Someone was in bad mood because of losing his/her job.
4 所以 [-] suǒyǐ (that-for) <conj.> as a result, so, therefor: 因为我信任你, ~请你帮忙. I asked for your help because I trust you. || 你不看时尚 (shíshàng) 杂志, ~不知道现在流行什么服装. You don't know what clothes are in fashion now because you don't read fashion magazines.
5 结果 [結-] jiéguǒ (yield-fruit) <conj.> as a result: 我们看错了时间, ~没赶上飞机. We missed the flight as a result of misreading the time.. || 他没有好

好训练, ~输了这次比赛. He didn't train well for the match, so he lost the match.

6 因而 [-] yīn'ér (because of-therefore) <conj.> thus, as a result, therefore: 这家饭店服务周到 (zhōudào), 价格便宜, ~生意特别好. This restaurant is considerate and cheap, so their business is very good. || 他经常去中国谈生意, ~对中国特别了解. He often goes to China to do business, so he knows a lot about China.

7 因此 [-] yīncǐ (because of-this) <conj.> so, therefore, for this reason, consequently: 我们常常去同一家酒吧, 并~成为好朋友. We used to go to the same bar and became good friends. || 他的计划成功了, ~感到很高兴. He was very glad that his plan had succeeded.

8 为此 [爲-] wèicǐ (for-this) <conj.> to this end, for this reason (or purpose), in this connection: 老王的孩子考上了北京大学, ~他感到骄傲. The old Wang's child was admitted to Peking University, and he was proud of it. || 这个孩子的娃娃坏了, ~她哭了很久. This girl had a long cry when her doll broke.

9 可见 [-見] kějiàn (can-see) <conj.> it is thus clear (or evident, obvious) that, it shows that, that proves, so: 这家公司晚上十点召开会议, ~情况十分紧急. This company held a meeting at 10:00 pm. That proves that the situation was critical.

10 以至于 [--於] yǐ zhì yú (so-as to) <conj.> to such an extent as to. . ., so . . . that. . . : 我工作太忙了, ~好几个月没看过电影了. I was so busy working that I hadn't seen the film for months. || 前任总统的支持率太低, ~没有参加下届竞选 (jìngxuǎn). The former president's approval ratings were so low that he did not run for the next election.

11 之所以 [-] zhī suǒ yǐ (its-reason) <conj.> the reason why: 我~迟到, 是因为堵车 (dǔchē). I was late because of the traffic. || 他~没有告诉你真相 (zhēnxiàng), 是因为怕伤害你. He didn't tell you the truth because he was afraid to hurt you.

Tips:

1 因 originally means 'mat' from a man '大' on a mat '口.' 果 means 'fruit.' When put together '因果, ' it means 'cause and effect.'

2 The causative-result relationship is generally expressed in two related words, such as 因为 . . . 所以 . . . (because . . . therefore. . .), 由于 . . . 以至于 . . . (owing to . . . so as to. . .), 之所以 . . . 是因为 . . . (the reason why . . . is because. . .).

Exercises:

Part I: Fill in the blanks

Read the following sentences and fill in each blank with the appropriate word from the given options.

1 因而、由于、之所以、是因为

近几年来，中国人的饮食习惯也有了很大的变化. 以前________老百姓生活水平不高, 一般人都是自己买菜做饭, _______在一日三餐方面也要花很多时间. 现在越来越多的中国人选择在快餐店吃午饭, 他们_______这样做, ________快餐又方便又便宜.

2 所、只要、以至于

自2016年以来, 网上订餐 (dìngcān) 在中国的大城市越来越流行, 也就是大家_______说的"点外卖 (wàimài). " _______打开手机软件, 点击喜欢的食物, 然后在手机上付钱就可以了. "点外卖"实在太方便了, ________北京、上海等这些大城市的白领几乎不做饭, 天天吃"外卖."

Part II: Make a new sentence using the italicized expressions.

1 小王工作太忙了, 以至于好几个星期没约女朋友出去玩了.
2 小白的男朋友小王好几个星期没约她出去了, 为此她感到非常难过.
3 小白的好朋友说: 小白, 男朋友这么久没和你联系 (liánxì), 可见他并不是真心爱你.
4 小白的好朋友说: 小王之所以没有告诉你真相, 是因为怕伤害你.
5 小王因为工作忙没有时间交女朋友, 结果30岁了还单身.

Theme 301: Conjunctions, sequential 顺承连词 (shùnchéng liáncí)

1 于是 [於-] yúshì (from-that) <conj.> accordingly, so, then, thereupon, hence, as a result: 他觉得创业 (chuàngyè) 比上大学更重要, ~从哈佛大学辍学 (chuòxué) 了. He felt that starting a business was more important than going to college, so he dropped out of Harvard University. || 他喜欢喝拿铁 (nátiě, latte), 得了糖尿病 (tángniàobìng) 以后不能喝拿铁了, ~只好喝黑咖啡. He liked to drink lattes, but he couldn't drink lattes anymore when he got diabetes, so he had to drink black coffee.

2 然后 [-後] ránhòu (that-after) <conj.> then, after that, afterwards: 先学三年音乐, ~再学物理. study music for three years and then physics. || 他想了想, ~走了出去. He thought it over, after that, he walked out.

3 以便 [-] yǐbiàn (therefore-so as to) <conj.> so that, in order to, so as to, with the aim of, for the purpose of: 请大声点说, ~大家都能听到. Please speak up so that everyone can hear you. || 这部电影请了很多美国明星, ~吸引观众. The film invited lots of American movie stars to attract the audience.

4 就是说 [--說] jiùshì shuō (that-is-to say) <conj.> that is to say, in other words, namely: 他的名字不在最后一轮面试 (miànshì) 的名单上, ~, 他已经被淘汰 (táotài) 了. His name is not on the final interview list, which means he has been eliminated.

5 这就是说 [這--說] zhè jiùshì shuō (this-is-to say) <conj.> this is to say, which means: 成功需要勤奋和机遇 (jīyù), ~, 光勤奋是不够的. Getting success requires hard work and good opportunity, which means that only hard work is not enough.

6 具体地说 [-體-說] jùtǐ de shuō (specifically-speaking) <conj.> particularly, specifically: 我爸爸说要想成为优秀的中餐厨师 (chúshī), 至少需要三年的时间. ~, 第一年学习做菜的材料, 第二年学习切菜, 第三年学习做菜.

My dad said it will take at least three years to become a good Chinese cook. Particularly speaking, in the first year, I learn the ingredients of cooking, the next year I learn to cut vegetables, and the third year I learn to cook. || ~, 人工智能就是研究怎样让电脑模仿人脑去工作. Specifically, artificial intelligence is the study of how computers can mimic the work of the human brain.

7 如上所述 [-] rú shàng suǒ shù (as-above-what-mentioned) <conj.> as stated (or mentioned, described) above: ~, 我们坚信保护环境从长远看是有利于发展经济的. As we say above, we believe that protecting the environment will benefit the economy in the long run.

8 综上所述 [綜---] zōng shàng suǒ shù (comprehend-above-what-mentioned) <conj.> as above, in summary: ~, 不应该在中国鼓励使用私家车. As we say above, private cars should not be encouraged in China.

9 总之 [總-] zǒngzhī (all inclusive-it) <conj.> in a word, in short, in brief, anyway, anyhow: 到了国外以后, 你可以申请奖学金上学, 也可以打工, ~, 都会生活下去的. After arriving abroad, you can apply for a scholarship to go to school, and you can also work. In short, no matter what job you do, you will live. || ~, 她最后通过了考试. Anyway, he passed the exam at last.

10 总而言之 [總---] zǒng'éryánzhī (all inclusive-and-say-it) <conj.> in short, in a word, in brief, to make a long story short: ~, 我不想去. In a word, I don't want to go. || ~, 他的工作挺好的. In a word, his work is good.

11 总的来说 [總-來説] zǒng de lái shuō (all inclusive-to-say) <conj.> generally speaking, to sum up, in summary, in short: ~, 这家饭店的菜很好吃. Generally speaking, the food in this restaurant is delicious. || ~, 她的优点比缺点多. Generally speaking, she has more advantages than disadvantages.

Tips:

1 The key concept in this theme is how to express, either 'in another way' or 'comprehensively,' as shown in the words from #4 to #11, namely 就是说, 这就是说, 具体地说, 如上所述, 综上所述, 总之, 总而言之, and 总的来说.

2 言 means 'to speak,' and 述 means 'to narrate.' 总 means 'total, all,' and 综 means 'to sum up, comprehensively.' 总之 is the abbreviated form of 总而言之.

Exercises:

Part I: Match the following words by considering their similar expressions.

1 总而言之 a. 这就是说
2 综上所述 b. 如上所述
3 就是说 c. 总的来说
4 于是 d. 因此就
5 以便 e. 这样做是为了

Part II: Translate the italicized part of English into Chinese.

1 Because Al Baghdadi is within essentially five miles of one of the most active training locations we currently have in Iraq, there's no doubt that we have persistent surveillance – *that is to say*, 24/7 surveillance – on this location.
2 It was the best of times, it was the worst of times, it was the age of wisdom, it was the age of foolishness, ... – *in short*, the period was so far like the present period, that some of its noisiest authorities insisted on its being received, for good or for evil, in the superlative degree of comparison only.
3 It's a video that was posted on Twitter. And it calls on its followers to attack targets in the West. *It specifically mentioned* the United States, Canada, Great Britain and France.
4 Questions should be open-ended. Each question can aim at only one thing. Examples should be carefully made, *so as to* avoid misguidance. Avoid asking 'Why.' If necessary, it should be rewritten as 'What is the reason?'

Theme 302: Particles 结构助词, 时态助词 (jiégòu zhùcí, shítài zhùcí)

1 的 [-] de (target, *see below*) <structural particle> after an attribute, after a verb or between a verb and its object to stress an element of the sentence: 我~书 my books || 妈妈 ~衣服mother's clothes || 老师讲课~特点The characteristics of the teacher's lecture
2 地 [-/的] de (Earth, *see below*) <structural particle> used before a verb or adjective, linking it to preceding modifying adverbial adjunct: 高兴~说 speak happily || 认真 (rènzhēn) ~研究 (yánjiū) research it carefully || 慢慢~走 walk slowly
3 得 [-] de (get, *see below*) <structural particle> used after a verb (or adjective as main verb), linking it to following phrase indicating effect, degree, possibility etc.: 来~很早come early || 写~很好very well written || 唱~不好not sing well || 说~大家都笑起来talk in such a way that everybody starts laughing
4 之 [-] zhī (grow, go, of) <structural particle> possessive particle, literary equivalent of 的: 《美国~音》*Voice of America* || 三口~家a family of three people || 原因~一one of the reasons
5 所* [-] suǒ (sounds of logging, place, *prefix*) <prefix> particle introducing a relative clause or passive: ~见~闻what one sees and hears || 我~认识的人the person I know || 大家~提的意见the opinions that people put forward
6 *者 [-] zhě (this, *suffix*) <suffix> a nominal suffix denoting a person or people: 读~ reader (of book, newspaper, etc.) || 作~ author, writer || 记~ journalist, reporter || 无故 (wúgù) 迟到 (chídào) ~ people who are late for no reason
7 . . . . . . 等 [-] děng (bamboo slips, rank) <particle> and so on, and so forth, etc.: 医生、护士、病人~一千人 doctors, nurses, patients, etc., totally 1,000 people || 上海、北京 ~地Beijing, Shanghai and so on.
8 . . . . . . 似的 [-] shìde (particle) <particle> [after a noun, pronoun, or verb to indicate similarity] seems as if, rather like: 像乡巴佬 (xiāngbalǎo) ~ looks

like a country bumpkin || 没睡觉~ seems like not sleeping || 老朋友~ seems like old friends

9 . . . . . . 一样 [-樣] yīyàng (same-pattern) <particle> the same as, alike, as . . . as. . . : 像今天~ just like today || 跟大部分人~ like most people || 像花儿~漂亮beautiful as a flower

10 着 [著] zhe (write, *particle*) <particle> aspect particle indicating action in progress: 说~ saying || 下~雨raining || 工作~ working

11 了 [-] le (to wrap and bind an infant's arms, *particle*) <particle> modal particle intensifying preceding clause, completed action marker: 我买~一本书. I bought a book. || 我吃~晚饭就走. I'll leave after dinner. || 我刚打~电话. I just called.

12 过 [過] guò (pass through, *particle*) <particle> experience action marker: 我学~中文. I have learned Chinese. || 我去~中国. I've been to China. || 他研究~孔子 (Kǒngzǐ). He studied Confucius.

Exercises:

Part I: Match the English phrase in the left column with its Chinese translation in the right column.

1	a family of three people	a.	所见所闻
2	Voice of America	b.	无故迟到的人
3	the opinions that people put forward	c.	大家所提的意见
4	people who are late for no reason	d.	美国之音
5	what one sees and hears	e.	三口之家
6	like most people	f.	跟大多数人一样
7	looks like a country bumpkin	g.	看起来像个乡巴佬一样

Part II: Fill in each blank with the most appropriate word.

的 地 得 似的

1 小王是我最好________美国朋友. 他中文说________非常流利 (fluently).
2 小王收到了哈佛大学的录取 (admission) 邮件, 他高兴________跳到了桌子上又唱又跳, 好像喝醉了酒__________ _.
3 小王认真________研究了一下哈佛的录取邮件, 发现他只是在补录名单上 (waiting list). 于是失望 (disappointed) __________关上了电脑.
4 小王觉得人生中有些时候事情变化太快, 就像做梦 (dream) __________.

Part III: Translate the English sentences into Chinese. Make sure to use the given words.

1 Their dog died last week. (了)
2 He's put on weight, so his girl friend will be not happy for this. (了)
3 The TV program was interrupted by too many commercials. (了)

4 Crime has decreased since he took office as mayor. (自从, 了)
5 It is snowing outside. Please stay at home. (V.着)
6 He is wearing new clothes. (V.着)
7 I had learned Chinese before. But I totally forgot how to speak Chinese (V.过)
8 I had been to Beijing, Shanghai and so on. (V.过, A, B等地)

Appendix 1

English index of 302 themes

Appendix 2

Pinyin index of 302 themes

dòuzhēng 斗争 166
duǎn 短 213, 231
duì 对 234
dùliàng 度量 88
dùn 钝 222
duō 多 224
è 恶 251
fànchóu 范畴 55
fǎnduì 反对 115
fāng 方 218
fāngfǎ 方法 50
fángshǒu 防守 167
fāngwèi 方位 95
fàngxīn 放心 109
fāzhǎn 发展 139
fǎzhì 法制 69
fēngsú 风俗 66
fēnlí 分离 139
fènnù 愤怒 108
fù 富 274
fǔbài 腐败 244
fùcí, chéngdù 副词, 程度 276
fùcí, chéngdù gāo 副词, 程度高 277
fùcí, fāngshì 副词, 方式 279
fùcí, fànwéi 副词, 范围 278
fùcí, fǒudìng 副词, 否定 288
fùcí, píndù 副词, 频度 285
fùcí, qiáng kǒuqì 副词, 强口气 286
fùcí, qíngtài (qítā) 副词, 情态(其他) 282
fùcí, ruò kǒuqì 副词, 弱口气 287
fùcí, shíjiān 副词, 时间 283
fùcí, shíjiān (qítā) 副词, 时间(其他) 284
fúzhuāng 服装 42
gǎigé 改革 147
gān 干 223
gāngqiáng 刚强 253
gǎnjué 感觉 61
gǎnxiè 感谢 179
gāo 高 214, 262
gāoxìng 高兴 107
gékāi 隔开 192
gēwǔ 歌舞 82
gōng 公 258
gōngchǎng 工厂 75
gōngdiàn 宫殿 38
gōngjù (qítā) 工具(其他) 31
gōngzhàn 攻占 168
gōngzuò 工作 67
guǎngfàn 广泛 236
guāngróng 光荣 243
guānzhù 关注 112
guì 贵 245
guīlǜ 规律 50
guīshǔ 归属 206
gūjì 估计 116
guòchéng 过程 49
gùyì 故意 281
hàipà 害怕 109
hǎo 好 233
hǎozhuǎn 好转 202
hòu 厚 215
hòuhuǐ 后悔 111
huá 滑 223
huācǎo 花草 14
huāfèi 花费 74
huài 坏 233
huáiyí 怀疑 114
huǎnjí 缓急 270
huìhuà 绘画 163
huīxié 诙谐 254
hūnyīn 婚姻 131
huòbì 货币 72
huódòng 活动 67
hūshì 忽视 112
jiǎ 假 232
jiāchù 家畜 11
jiādiàn 家电 40
jiàgé 价格 72
jiāgōng 加工 152
jiājù 家具 40
jiàn 贱 245
jiǎnglì 奖励 147
jiànlì 建立 145
jiǎnpǔ 简朴 260
jiānruì 尖锐 222
jiǎnshǎo 减少 203
jiànzào 建造 152
jiànzhù 建筑 35

Appendix 3

English and pinyin index of 1,000 cultural and linguistic tips

Appendix 4

Stroke index of 1,000 cultural and linguistic tips